Geoffrey Payton

The Penguin Dictionary of

Proper Names

Revised by John Paxton

VIKING

VIKING

Published by the Penguin Group
Penguin Books Ltd, 27 Wrights Lane, London W8 5TZ, England
Viking Penguin, a division of Penguin Books USA Inc.
375 Hudson Street, New York, New York 10014, USA
Penguin Books Australia Ltd, Ringwood, Victoria, Australia
Penguin Books Canada Ltd, 2801 John Street, Markham, Ontario, Canada L3R 1B4
Penguin Books (NZ) Ltd, 182–190 Wairau Road, Auckland 10, New Zealand

Penguin Books Ltd, Registered Offices: Harmondsworth, Middlesex, England

First published as *Payton's Proper Names* by Frederick Warne & Co. Ltd 1969
First published in the USA in a revised edition as *Webster's Dictionary of Proper Names* by
G. & C. Merriam Co. 1970
Published in Viking 1991
10 9 8 7 6 5 4 3 2 1

Printed in England by Clays Ltd, St Ives plc
Typeset in 8/10 pt Lasercomp Photina

A CIP catalogue record for this book is available from the British Library

ISBN 0-670-825 735

Preface to the Viking Edition

The first edition of this dictionary was published in 1969 and received considerable acclaim. Geoffrey Payton died in 1985 but left notes and ideas for entries and some of this material has been incorporated in this edition. Extracts from his original foreword give the flavour of the book.

The purpose of this book, which is believed to be unique, is to help readers through the barrage of proper names with which we are daily bombarded by journalists, broadcasters, novelists and even the man next door. We are expected to know the difference, for instance, between BILLY BUDD, BILLY THE KID and BILLY LIAR; between BLUEBEARD, BLUEBIRD and BLUE STREAK.

Then again there are, alas, all those things which, unlike MACAULAY'S SCHOOLBOY, we *don't* know, although we ought to (1066 AND ALL THAT summed up the situation): the battle of ACTIUM, the CONGRESS OF VIENNA, the FIFTEEN and the FORTY-FIVE. Who dares admit to an Irishman that he cannot remember a thing about the Battle of the BOYNE?

The list is long; the dictionaries don't help; only a roomful of reference books can save us from embarrassment. Hence this book. It is aimed at all ages and all walks of life.

The critical will not fail to notice that the term 'proper names' has been stretched to its furthest limit (and indeed beyond). Others may ask: Why all the Greek mythology? (Answer: because it crops up in so many plays and operas, and even on the psychiatrist's couch.) Why the biblical names? (Because biblical allusions remain embedded in our language long after compulsory Bible-study has been abolished; and

there are, let's face it, quite a lot of people in the world who speak or read English but are not Christians.) Why the foreign names? (Because holidaying abroad has become so popular.)

The book is selective. It has to be; there is no reason why a book on these lines should not extend to several volumes. The author has therefore been forced to make a highly personal choice of names which he thinks are likely to be useful or interesting. It has to be stressed that this is in no way a dictionary of potted biographies, nor is it a gazetteer of place-names.

Dictionary-making is rather like gardening, because much weeding, planting and grafting takes place and for this edition over 1,000 new entries have been added. In the twenty years since the original publication there has been much political and social change and this is reflected in the variety of the entries. I would add that the titles of plays, poems and novels are often included because they are still used allusively, not because of any particular merit.

I did not know Geoffrey Payton, but working on this dictionary brought him to life for me and his own humour comes through. In his notes I found:

VIP Abbreviation for Very Important Person, which came into use in the Second World War to designate air passengers to be accorded special facilities and red-carpet treatment on arrival. This ensures that the only people who could put things right are never aware of the appalling conditions at some airports.

Should a conscientious editor delete the sentence after the word 'arrival'? I didn't.

Many people have helped me with the second edition, particularly Len Jones and also Dione Daffin, Marian and Nicholas Paxton and Penny White.

Geoffrey Payton dedicated the dictionary to his Mary 'without whose constant encouragement and advice this book would have been finished in half the time'. I too am very grateful to Mary, and to my Joan who seems to know everything without being a know-all.

To give the reader a general idea of what the contents are, a list of some of the main categories with a few examples appears below.

John Paxton
Bruton, Somerset
August 1990

A Selection of Entries by Subject Category

Aircraft: Concorde, Dakota, MiG, VG, V/STOL.

Animals: Cheshire Cat, Crufts, Lippizaner, 'Mad Cow' disease, Suffolk Punch.

Antiques and Antiquities: Chamberlain Worcester, Elgin Marbles, Empire style, Great Bed of Ware, Meissen, Portobello Road, T'ang dynasty.

Army: Desert Rats, Ever Readies, New Model Army, West Point.

Arts: Ashcan School, Bauhaus, By-pass Variegated, Grandma Moses, *Guernica*, *Rima*, *Rokeby Venus*, *Sistine Madonna*.

Astronomy: Betelgeuse, Big Bang theory, Jodrell Bank, Mt Palomar.

Awards: Betty Trask, Grammy.

Ballet: Ballet Rambert, Camargo Society, *Petrushka*.

Bible: Balaam's Ass, Dead Sea Scrolls, Septuagint, Susanna and the Elders, Tophet.

Big Business: AT & T, IBM, IG Farben, Shell-Mex.

Cars: De Dion Bouton, Genevieve, Tin Lizzie.

Cartoons and comic strips: Col. Blimp, Li'l Abner, Mr Chad.

Children's stories: Brer Rabbit, Struwwelpeter, Toad of Toad Hall, Winnie-the-Pooh.

Cinema: Battleship Potemkin, Birth of a Nation, Cannes Film Festival, Cinerama, Keystone Comedies.

Clubs: Boodles, Crockford's, Drones, Groucho, Hell Fire, In and Out, Leander, Monday, Royal and Ancient.

Code-names: Enigma, Former Naval Person, Mulberry, Overlord, Smersh.

Crime and punishment: Brides in the Bath, Guildford Four, Interpol, Jack the Ripper, Lemmy Caution, Moors Murders, Pinkerton's, The Maze, The Scrubs.

Economics: Black Monday, Community Charge, Dow-Jones averages, Eurodollar, Faceless Gnomes of Zurich, Footsie, Golden handshake, Guinness affair, Kennedy Round, Little Neddy, PEP.

Education: Butler Act, CAT, City and Guilds, Common Entrance, Dartington Hall, Denham College, Keele University, Millfield, Outward Bound, Pestalozzi village.

Farming: Bath and West, Charolais, Chillingham cattle, Dutch elm disease, Turnip Townshend.

Festivals: Aldeburgh, Edinburgh, Oberammergau.

Fiction: Animal Farm, Barchester novels, *Candida, Candide, Cold Comfort Farm, Dr Zhivago,* Leopold Bloom, Miss Matty, Raskolnikov, Sexton Blake, Walter Mitty, Widmerpool.

Food and Wine: Black Velvet, Bourbon, Calvados, Château-d'Yquem, Chicken Maryland, Coca-Cola, Daiquiri, Golden Delicious, Red Biddy, Slivovitz, Vinho Verde, VSOP, The Widow.

Games: Acol system, Blackwood convention, Monopoly.

Geography: Bessarabia, Buchan periods, Forties sea area, Meander, Roaring Forties, Silesia.

History: Bay of Pigs, Casket Letters, Comintern, Dachau, Defenestration, Diaspora, *Drang nach Osten*, Munich agreement, Rome Treaty, Tontons Macoute, Utrecht peace.

Homes and gardens: Capability Brown, Compton Wynyates, Fonthill Beckford, Fort Belvedere, Haworth, Hyde Park (Roosevelts).

Initials: CIA, DBS, PIN, U and non-U, UFO, Unicef, VIP.

Institutions: British Standards Institution, Burlington House, Chatham House, Cheshire Homes, Cinque Ports, KGB, Trinity House.

Legend: Daphnis and Chloe, Deirdre, Guinevere, Valkyries, Wandering Jew.

Lectures and professorships: Chichele Professor, Reith, Rede and Romanes lectures.

Libraries, museums, galleries: Bodleian, Fitzwilliam, Guggenheim, Prado, Uffizi.

Literary allusions: Admass, Bardell *v.* Pickwick, Big- and Little-Enders, *One Upmanship*, 007, Two Cultures, Yoknapatawpha County.

Local names: Carnaby Street, Boul' Mich', Great White Way, Ponte Vecchio, Sauchiehall Street, The Shambles, Street Called Straight, Trianon.

Medical: Aids, BUPA, Salk vaccine.

Music: Beatles, Blues, Brandenburg Concertos, The Choral Symphony, Dixieland jazz, Satchmo.

Nicknames: APH, Der Alte, FDR, Jersey Lily, LBJ, Praise-God Barebones, Stonewall Jackson, Swedish Nightingale, Teflon President, The Thunderer, Vinegar Joe, WG, Welsh Wizard.

Numbers: 47th Parallel, Four Freedoms, Fourth of July, Fourth of June, Fourteen Points, 19th Amendment, Sixth Commandment.

Opera: *The Bartered Bride, Carmen, Carmen Jones,* Duke of Plaza-Toro, Figaro, *Götterdämmerung,* La Scala, The Met.

Pen-names, etc.: Æ, Cicero (the spy), Elia, Gen. Leclerc.

Philosophy: Behaviourism, Existentialism, Hobbes's *Leviathan,* Logical Positivism.

Poetry and verse: archy and mehitabel, Barnacle Bill, Frankie and Johnny, Old Kaspar, Waste Land, Xanadu.

Political phrases: Bow Group, Brinkmanship, Cat and Mouse Act, Clause Four, Cliveden set, Doves, Hawks, New Deal, Politburo, Popular Front, Tammany Hall.

Politics: Bevanites, Christian Democrats, Colombey-les-deux-Églises, Coupon election, Duma, Élysée Palace, Fellow traveller, Glasnost, Lok Sabha, Plaid Cymru, Quai d'Orsay, Social Democrats, Storting, Two plus Four.

Prehistory: Abu Simbel, Altamira Caves, Beaker People, Carbon-14 dating, Cro-Magnon, Peking Man, Sumerians, Tutankhamen.

Press: Beachcomber, Beaverbrook Press, Peterborough, Tass.

Prizes and medals: Congressional Medal of Honour, Cornwell Badge, Fémina–Vie Heureuse, Hawthornden, Oscar, Pulitzer, Purple Heart.

Pub names: Goat and Compasses, Pig and Whistle.

Races and languages: Cape Coloureds, Franglais, Slav, Slovak and Slovenian, Tamil, Volapük.

Reference books: *Almanach de Gotha,* Cruden, DNB, Erskine May, Fowler, Keesings, *The Statesman's Year-Book.*

Religion: Christian Science, Cistercians, Exclusive Brethren, Pacem in terris, Papal Infallibility, Taizé.

Reports (Royal Commissions, etc.): Buchanan, Denning, Franks, Moloney.

Science: Appleton layer, Boyle's Law, CERN, Greenhouse effect, Lamarckism, Lysenkoism, Mendelism, Michelson-Morley experiment, Planck's constant.

Ships: Cutty Sark, Discovery, Dreadnought, Marie Celeste, Mary Rose.

Slang, etc.: The real McCoy, Mick, Micky Finn, Stockbroker Belt.

Societies, etc.: Apostles, Black Muslims, Cosa Nostra, Empire Loyalists, John Birch Society, Mensa.

Space age: Apollo space programme, Early Bird, Telstar.

Spooks, etc.: Borley Rectory, Cheiro, Cock Lane ghost, ESP, Mother Shipton, Tarot cards.

Sport: Arlberg-Kandahar, Bisley, British Lions, Brown Jack Stakes, Cowdray Park, Craven Cottage, Cresta, Dan, Doggett's Coat and Badge, Galway Blazers, Heysel Stadium, International 14s, Lonsdale Belt, Ryder Cup, VWH.

Theatre: Angry Young Man, Aunt Edna plays, *Chips with Everything, Chu Chin Chow,* Theatre of the Absurd.

Tourist spots: Baedeker, Bernese Oberland, Bondi Beach, Butlins, Costa Blanca.

Towns: Aldermaston, Little Rock.

TV and radio: Col. Chinstrap, *Coronation Street,* ITMA, TW 3, Voice of America.

Trade unions: AFL/CIO, ASLEF, Equity, Teamsters' Union.

University terms: The Backs, Bullingdon, Commem, Lady Margaret's, May Week.

USA: Beverly Hills, Bible Belt, Corn Belt, Daughters of the American Revolution, Lincoln Center, Volstead Act.

Notes on Conventions

Cross-references: Words in SMALL CAPITALS indicate references to main entries which appear in their appropriate alphabetical place.

Italics (or **bold italic** in the case of headings) are used for titles of books, plays, operas, paintings, etc., for example ***The Bartered Bride***.

Abbreviations: RSFSR, Russian Soviet Federal Socialist Republic, the largest republic in the USSR (Union of Soviet Socialist Republics, i.e. the Soviet Union). ASSR for Autonomous Soviet Socialist Republic.

Alphabetical order: Entry words are treated as if spelt out in full, e.g. VC-10 as vcten; 007 as ooseven; 18th Amendment as Eighteenth Amendment, etc.

Pronunciations

These are given only where they may prove useful; the system of indicating sounds has been kept as simple as possible; foreign vowel sounds are only rough equivalents:

a, e, i, o, u are ordinary short vowel sounds, as in fat etc.
ay as in fate
ah as in father
aw as in fall
ai as in air
ee as in seat
y as in kite
oh as in goat
oo as in food
ew as in cube
u as in good, bull
ow as in gout
oi as for boy

è for all indeterminate vowels such as mother
èr for French and German *eu* or *oe*, as in feu, Froebel, Goethe
awr as in Montessori
er as in sir

Consonants

th as in thin
dh as in thine
zh as in measure
n for French nasal n

AAA Amateur Athletic Association (1880). It controls all athletic events in England and Wales, including the AAA Championships in July; known as the 'Three A's'.

Aachen German town (French name Aix-la-Chapelle) in North Rhine-Westphalia.

Aaron Son of Levi and elder brother of Moses; he made the GOLDEN CALF (Exod. 32:4), and in some traditions is the founder of the Jewish priesthood.

Aaron's rod Name given to various garden plants, including golden rod and one of the verbascums (Num. 17:8).

Aase Mother of PEER GYNT, whose death is an important episode in Ibsen's play and in Grieg's incidental music.

Abbasids (750–1258). Dynasty of Caliphs who ruled at Baghdad after the massacre of the OMAYYADS.

Abbevillean culture Earliest of the PALAEOLITHIC cultures, lasting perhaps from 500,000 to 400,000 BC, during which early forms of ape-like creatures learnt to make crude flint hand-axes. (Abbeville, France; also called the Chellean culture.)

Abbeyfield Society (1959). Society which provides homes for the aged at minimum rents. It has over 1,000 houses, each accommodating 5–7 people, grouped as far as possible according to background and interests.

Abbey Theatre The Irish national theatre, Dublin, opened in 1904. It was burnt down in 1951 and reopened in 1966.

Abbots Bromley Horn Dance A festival held in September at Abbots Bromley, west of Burton-on-Trent, with an elaborate and sinister dance by 6 men in Tudor costume carrying reindeer antlers, accompanied by ROBIN HOOD and his men, and a hobby-horse.

Abbotsbury Swannery Situated near the coast between Weymouth and Bridport, Dorset, in the grounds of a 12th-century Benedictine abbey with subtropical gardens, open to the public.

Abbotsford Home of Sir Walter Scott, near Melrose, Roxburghshire (Borders Region), Scotland.

ABC American Broadcasting Company, one of the 3 coast-to-coast TV networks.

ABC teashops First of this chain was opened in 1884, 10 years before the first Joe Lyons; they were originally for women, who faced death (or a worse fate) if they went into a pub unescorted in those days. (Aerated Bread Co.)

Abd Arabic for 'slave of', 'servant of', as in Abdallah (Abdullah), 'servant of God'; Abdulkadir, 'servant of the great one' (i.e. God).

Abderite, The Democritus, Greek philosopher of the 5th and 4th centuries BC. (Born at Abdera, Thrace.)

Abdication Crisis (1936). Caused by the decision of King Edward VIII (later Duke of Windsor) to abdicate rather than renounce his intention to marry the twice-divorced Mrs Simpson.

Abdul the Damned Abdul Hamid II the Sultan of Turkey (1876–1909), a despotic ruler deposed by the YOUNG TURKS.

Abel Son of Adam and Eve, a shepherd killed by his elder brother, CAIN (Gen. 4:8).

Abélard See HÉLOÏSE.

Aberdeen Angus Breed of beef cattle, black and polled.

Aberfan disaster (1966). Death of nearly 150 persons, mostly children, caused when a slag-heap, which had been built up to a dangerous height, slipped and overwhelmed part of the village of Aberfan, Glamorgan, Wales, including the school. (Pronounced abèr-van'.)

Abernethy Hard biscuit, flavoured with caraway seed.

'Abide with Me' (1861). Hymn written by an English clergyman, H. F. Lyte; music by W. H. Monk.

Abigail (1) 'Handmaid' and wife of David (1 Sam. 25); (2) name given to maidservants in various plays and novels; (3) hence, a synonym for maidservant.

Abinger Harvest (1936). E. M. Forster's first collection of essays, on a variety of topics.

Abitur German equivalent of the GCE or French Baccalauréat. (Abbreviation of German *Abiturientenexamen*, 'examination of those about to depart', i.e. to the university; from Latin *abituri*, 'those about to go'.)

Abnaki Group of ALGONQUIAN tribes in Maine, who fought for the French against the English. About 2,000 survive in Quebec and New Brunswick.

Abo Australian abbreviation for 'Aboriginal'.

ABO blood groups Four groups, A, B, AB and O, to one of which everyone belongs. This is important (1) in blood transfusion, some groups being incompatible with others; (2) in ethnological research, as the incidence of the groups varies from race to race; (3) in eliminating suspects in criminal cases where bloodstains are present (see RHESUS).

A-bomb Atomic or nuclear-fission bomb. The Hiroshima A-bomb (1945) used uranium-235 and was 1/50th megaton, equivalent to 20,000 tons of TNT, 1,000 times as powerful as Grand Slam, the heaviest World War II bomb. The Nagasaki bomb, using plutonium-239, was even more powerful. See H-BOMB.

Abominable Snowman Unknown creature said to have been seen by Sherpas high up in the Himalayas; its presumed tracks have been described by several mountaineers. Also called Yeti.

Aboukir Bay Scene of the Battle of the NILE in 1798. (Pronounced ab-oo-keer'.)

Abracadabra Word possibly derived from *Abrasax*, a Gnostic deity, and said to be a powerful charm.

Abraham First Hebrew patriarch, who migrated with his wife Sarah and Lot from Ur of the Chaldees in Mesopotamia to the Promised Land of Canaan. Their son was ISAAC, through whom he was the ancestor of all Jews, and through ISHMAEL of all Arabs.

Abraham-men See TOM O' BEDLAM.

Abraham's bosom Resting place, in death, of the just (Luke 16:22).

Absalom Son of David, killed in a revolt against his father (2 Sam. 15–18). See AHITOPHEL

Absalom, Absalom! William Faulkner's chronicle (1936) of the rise and fall of the poor-white Sutpen family in Mississippi, as seen through the eyes of 3 of the characters. (Title from David's lament in 2 Sam. 18:33.)

'Absalom and Achitophel' Dryden's satire, in which Absalom is the Duke of Monmouth. (See MONMOUTH'S REBELLION, ACHITOPHEL.)

'Absent-minded Beggar, The' Kipling's ballad of the soldiers who fought in the Boer War.

Absinthe Drinkers, The (1876). Study by Degas of a man and woman in a bistro, a picture of deep despair. (Musée d'Orsay.)

Absolute, Sir Anthony in Sheridan's play *The Rivals*, the testy father of the young man who loves Lydia LANGUISH.

Absquatulate Humorous American term for leaving an illegal squat.

Abstract art Non-representational form of art which, reacting against naturalism, stresses the aesthetic values of form, colour and texture; leading exponents Kandinsky, Mondrian, Ben Nicholson.

Abstract Expressionism (Action Painting, Tachisme). Extreme form of ABSTRACT ART associated with the name of the American, Jackson Pollock, who covered vast canvases with splashes of paint in the 1950s.

Absurd, Theatre of the (1950). Movement born in Paris, numbering Ionesco, Beckett and Pinter among its chief exponents. They stress the ludicrous irrationality of human conduct and beliefs.

Abu Simbel Nile site in the Sudan north of Wadi Halfa of rock temples built by Rameses II (1250 BC); the temples were moved in the 1960s to prevent submersion by the lake formed behind the ASWAN HIGH DAM.

Abwehr Counter-espionage section of the German High Command (OKW), headed during World War II by Admiral Canaris.

Abydos (1) *See* SESTOS. (2) Ancient Upper Egyptian city north of Thebes, with temples dating back to 3000 BC, including the Great Temple of Osiris of the 14th century BC.

Abyssinia Older, and ethnographically more accurate, name for Ethiopia.

Academic Festival **Overture** (1881). Overture composed by Brahms after he had received an honorary doctorate at Breslau University; it makes use of student songs, including GAUDE-AMUS IGITUR.

Académie française (1635). French Academy, restricted to 40 members ('The Immortals') chosen from distinguished men of letters, formed to preserve the purity of the French language, in particular by the compilation of a dictionary.

Academy awards (USA) Awards (principally OSCARS) made by the Academy of Motion Picture Arts and Sciences.

Acadia Early name for Nova Scotia, still preserved in the form Acadian for Nova Scotian. (From name of local river.)

Acapulco Chief centre of the Mexican Riviera on the Pacific coast, a favourite winter resort for Americans.

Account Day (Stock Exchange). Date on which payment is due by customers, brokers and jobbers in respect of bargains made during the previous account (a 2- or 3-week period), on the 11th day after it ends. Also called Settlement Day.

Aceldama Name of the field of blood or potters' field bought with Judas' 30 pieces of silver, and used to bury strangers in (Matt. 27:3–8 and Acts 1:19). (Hebrew, 'field of blood'; pronounced a-sel'da-mah.)

Achaeans Bronze Age Greek race; the earliest references to them are in Hittite records from *c.* 1350 BC. They introduced chariots, bronze spears, helmets and armour. Homer used the name for Greeks in general.

Achaemenids (6th–4th centuries BC). Dynasty of Persian kings founded by Cyrus the Great, which extended Persian rule to the Indus and to Egypt; they included Darius and Xerxes. Defeated by Alexander the Great and succeeded by the SELEUCIDS.

Achates In Virgil's *Aeneid* the companion of AENEAS, always called *fidus Achates*, faithful Achates. (Pronounced a-kay'teez.)

Acheron In Greek legend the 'river of woe', one of the rivers of the Underworld. (Pronounced ak'ér-on.)

Acheulean culture Second of the main PALAEO-LITHIC cultures, perhaps lasting from 400,000 to 150,000 BC, during which PITHEC-ANTHROPINES in the Far East and in Africa learnt to use fire and to make improved flint hand-axes. (St Acheul, near Amiens, France; pronounced a-shool'e-an.)

Achillea Genus name of yarrow. (Supposed, like Achilles' spear, to have curative powers.)

Achilles Greek hero without whom Troy could not be taken. In the last year of the war his cousin Patroclus was killed by Hector, and this roused Achilles, who had retired sulking to his tent in a quarrel with Agamemnon about who should have the girl prisoner Briseis, to return to the fight and take his revenge on Hector, whose body he dragged round the walls of Troy. But Paris found his one vulnerable spot (see ACHILLES' HEEL) and killed him. (Pronounced a-kil'eez.)

Achilles and the tortoise Fourth-century BC Greek philosopher Zeno's paradox; if Achilles runs 10 times faster than a tortoise which has a 100-yd start, then while Achilles runs 100 yds the tortoise runs 10; while Achilles runs these 10 yd the tortoise adds another yard, and so on. Thus, theoretically, Achilles can never catch up with it.

Achilles Club (1920). Athletics club recruited by election from leading Oxford and Cambridge athletes.

Achilles' heel Phrase derived from the Greek myth that his mother dipped ACHILLES in the Styx to make him invulnerable, but the heel she held him by was not immersed and remained his one vulnerable spot. To it Apollo unsportingly guided an arrow shot by Paris.

Achilles statue Statue in Hyde Park, London, made from guns taken by the Duke of Wellington. It is in fact a copy of an Italian sculpture of some other hero.

Achilles tendon Tendon connecting the heel (see ACHILLES' HEEL) to the calf.

Achitophel Dryden's name, in 'ABSALOM AND ACHITOPHEL', for the Earl of Shaftesbury, leader of the Whig (Country Party) opposition to the succession of the Catholic James II. (See AHITOPHEL.)

Acid-house party Parties of up to 10,000 young people congregating to dance to music called House, which probably got its name from the Warehouse, a club in Chicago, where a style of pop music, with a repetitive bass beat, was originally played. The bands use considerable electronic equipment to produce sound effects. Drugs at these parties introduced the adjective acid.

Acis and Galatea In Greek mythology a Sicilian shepherd and his lass. POLYPHEMUS killed Acis as he wanted Galatea. The story is told by Ovid. (Pronounced ay'sis, gal-a-tee'a.)

Ackermann prints Hand-coloured aquatints and lithographs published by Rudolph Ackermann, a German inventor who came to London where he set up a print-shop (1795) and a press. He perfected the aquatint, employing an army of colourists to colour them, and was the first in England to establish lithography as a fine art.

Acol system Calling system at bridge, popular in Britain and developed from the old Culbertson and Lederer systems. The only opening bid forcing to game is 2 Clubs. Hand valuation is by both point counts and quick tricks, and additions are made for suit length.

Aconitum The genus name of monkshood.

Acrilan A man-made fibre used in making carpets, blankets and many other types of fabric.

Acropolis The fortified hill round which many ancient Greek cities were built; specifically, that at Athens; see PARTHENON. (Pronounced ak-rop'o-lis.)

Across the River and into the Trees (1950). Ernest Hemingway's novel in which, in the guise of a battered old warrior, Col. Cantwell, the author tried to sum up all he had learnt in life. Its failure to impress his public was a major shock in his career. (Last words of STONEWALL JACKSON, the Confederate general.)

Actaeon In Greek mythology a hunter who chanced upon the huntress-goddess ARTEMIS bathing in a pool. Being an untypically prudish goddess, she turned him into a stag and set her hounds upon him, who tore him to shreds. (Pronounced akt-ee'on.)

Action française (1899–1944). Journal of Charles Maurras's extreme right-wing monarchist movement (of the same name), edited under his direction at first by Léon Daudet.

Action Painting See ABSTRACT EXPRESSIONISM.

Actium (31 BC). Decisive naval battle in which Mark Antony, left in the lurch by CLEOPATRA, was defeated by OCTAVIAN (the future Augustus). Egypt became a Roman province and Antony and Cleopatra committed suicide. (A cape on the west coast of Greece.)

Act of Settlement (1701). Act vesting the succession to the English throne, after William and Anne, in the Protestant House of Hanover; it led to the accession of George I in 1714.

Act of Supremacy Act (1534). Appointing the King of England supreme head of the Church of England, repealed by Mary and re-enacted by Elizabeth (1559).

Act of Uniformity (1559). Act which made the Prayer Book the only legal form of worship in England; re-enacted in 1662 at the RESTORATION. See CLARENDON CODE.

Acton Former Middlesex borough, since 1965 part of the borough of EALING.

Acts of the Apostles Book of the New Testament ascribed to St Luke; it begins with Christ's Ascension, tells of the missions of Peter, Paul and Stephen, and ends with Peter's return to Rome, where he was placed under house arrest but still allowed to preach.

Acts of Union (1) In 1536, uniting England and Wales; (2) in 1707, uniting Scotland and England, thus creating Great Britain; (3) in 1800, uniting Ireland and Great Britain, thus creating the United Kingdom from 1 January 1801.

Adam Name of the first man, not mentioned until Genesis 2:19, although his creation is described in Genesis 1:27 and 2:7.

Adam Bede (1859). George Eliot's novel of Adam's love for Hetty Sorrel, who however sets her cap at the local squire, gets seduced by him, murders her child and is sentenced to transporta-

tion. Adam is said to have been based on the author's father.

Adam's apple Projection in the neck formed by the thyroid cartilage, which was supposed to have been caused by a piece of the apple that stuck in the throat of ADAM.

Adam style (1760). Neoclassical (see NEO-CLASSICISM) style introduced in England by Robert Adam, characterized by ornamentation with urns, festoons etc., applied especially to fireplaces, ceilings and doorways, and influencing HEPPLEWHITE and SHERATON. It yielded place to the more severe style of the REGENCY PERIOD. See ADELPHI.

Addenbrooke's Teaching hospital at Cambridge.

Addison's disease Condition caused by the malfunction of certain endocrine glands, resulting in undue loss of salt from the body, lassitude, and a bronze pigmentation of the skin. Formerly fatal, it is now treated by cortisone.

Addled Parliament (1614). Summoned by James I and lasted 2 months before he had the members arrested for refusing to grant him funds. (So called because it passed no laws.)

Adelphi, The (1768). Group of buildings between the Thames and the Strand in London, designed by the Adam brothers (see ADAM STYLE), and largely rebuilt in the 1930s. (Greek *adelphoi*, 'brothers', i.e. Robert Adam and 2 of his brothers, architects and interior decorators.)

Adieux, Les Beethoven piano sonata suggested by the Archduke Rudolph's departure from Vienna in the face of Napoleon's advance.

Adler school of psychology See INDIVIDUAL PSYCHOLOGY.

Admass J. B. Priestley's name for those who are over-susceptible to the pressures of mass advertising and modern publicity methods.

Admetus In Greek legend the king of Thessaly whom Apollo served for a year as shepherd. His wife was ALCESTIS. (Pronounced ad-mee'tus.)

Administrative Staff College (1946). College in a

country house near Henley which offers a 3-month course for business managers.

Admirable Crichton, The (1902). J. M. Barrie's play about a party of aristocrats shipwrecked on a desert island; the butler, Crichton, demonstrates his innate superiority to the rest, and takes command, only to revert to the previous social hierarchy after the party has been rescued and returned to England.

Admiral of the Red (Blue, White) Old titles of English officers commanding the vanguard (centre, rearguard) of the fleet in action; abolished 1864.

Admiral's Cup (1957). International trophy for teams of 3 boats from each country who compete in the FASTNET, BRITANNIA CUP and 2 other races; the unofficial championship of handicap offshore racing. (Presented by the Admiral and other members of the RORC.)

Admiralty Arch (1910). In London, a triple arch at the Trafalgar Square entrance to the MALL, designed by Sir Aston Webb as part of a memorial to Queen Victoria. It houses part of the library of the Admiralty, which adjoins it.

Admiralty House Apartments, in London, of the First Lord of the Admiralty until 1960. Residence of Harold Macmillan during Downing Street repairs 1960–63 and since 1965 of Secretary of State for Defence and other ministers.

Admission Day Date of admission in the USA of a state into the Union, kept in some states as a legal holiday; e.g. 9 September in California.

Adolf Beck case (1896 and 1904). Outstanding case of mistaken identity. Beck was twice arrested as having, under the name of Smith, defrauded several women; while serving his second sentence he learnt that the real culprit was known to be a Jew, whereas he was uncircumcised. He was released and compensated, and the real Smith was arrested. This mistake led to the establishment of the court of criminal appeal.

Adonai Another name for Jehovah, used by the Jews. (Hebrew plural of *adon*, 'lord'; pronounced a-doh'ny.)

Adonais (1821). Shelley's elegy on the death of Keats.

Adonis In Greek legend the beautiful youth whom APHRODITE loved, and who was gored to death by a boar; the anemone sprang from his blood. Another legend links him with TAMMUZ: Aphrodite gave him as an infant in charge to PERSEPHONE in the Underworld; the latter fell in love with him and refused to return him. Zeus then reconciled the two by arranging that Adonis (i.e. vegetation) should spend 8 months on earth with Aphrodite and 4 below with Persephone. (From a Semitic word meaning 'lord'; pronounced a-dohn'is.)

Adonis An aperitif of sherry, Italian vermouth and bitters.

Adoration of the Kings, The The visit of the MAGI, often depicted in art, notably by Mabuse (1500) and Pieter Brueghel (1525); both these paintings are in the London National Gallery. See next entry.

Adoration of the Magi Rubens picture painted in 11 days in 1634; now in King's College, Cambridge.

Adowa, Battle of (1896). Defeat of the Italians by the forces of Emperor Menelek of Abyssinia.

Adventists Generic term for various American sects who originally expected the Second Coming of Christ in 1843 (see SEVENTH DAY ADVENTISTS). In general, they hold that only members of their particular sect will be saved.

Advocaat Drink made of grape spirit, egg-yolk and sugar, of low alcoholic strength and not, strictly, a liqueur.

Advocates' Library, The (1689). Scottish National Library, at Edinburgh.

Æ Nom-de-plume of George William Russell (1867–1935), Irish poet and mystic, friend of W. B. Yeats.

Aëdes mosquito Generic name of a kind of mosquito, of which the species *Aëdes aegypti* is the only carrier of yellow fever; formerly known as *Stegomyia*. (Pronounced ah-eed'eez.)

Aegospotami (405 BC). Last battle of the PELOPON-NESIAN WAR, in which the Spartans destroyed the Athenian fleet in the HELLESPONT. (Pronounced ee-gos-pot'a-my.)

Aeneas Trojan hero of the AENEID, son of Anchises and Aphrodite, who set out after the fall of Troy to found a new race in Italy, from which the Romans claimed their origin. (Pronounced ee-nee'as.)

Aeneid (19 BC). Virgil's patriotic epic poem, left unfinished, in which he describes the adventures of AENEAS on his voyage from Troy to Italy, including his sojourn at Carthage (see DIDO) and his visit to the Underworld. (Pronounced een'i-id.)

Aeolus Greek god of winds. (Pronounced ee'o-lus.)

Aer Lingus Irish airline.

Aeroflot Soviet airline, run by the chief administrator of the Civil Air Fleet.

Aérospatiale (1970). French aircraft manufacturer formed by merger of Sud-Aviation, Nord-Aviation and Séreb.

Aesculapius Roman and better-known name of the Greek god of medicine, Asclepius. (Pronounced ee-skew-lay'pi-us.)

Aesop's Fables Collection of didactic tales in which talking animals illustrate human foibles; attributed to a slave who lived in Samos in the 6th century BC. In the form in which they are now known they date only from 15th-century Italy.

Affluent Society, The Phrase coined by Professor Galbraith, in his book (1958) of that name, for the social conditions resulting from the high average standard of living now prevailing in Western countries. He argues that economists need to recast their theories, born in an era of poverty, to fit the vast new opportunities of today.

Afghan hound Breed introduced into Europe from Afghanistan, where it had been used as a hunting dog for at least 4,000 years. It has a long silky coat and a long narrow head; colours vary.

Afghan rugs Rugs resembling coarse BOKHARA RUGS, normally red and characterized by large octagonal patterns, made by Afghan tribes.

AFL/CIO (1955). Initials used for the US federation of trade unions, the American Federation of Labor and Congress of Industrial Organizations.

African lily Agapanthus, a non-bulbous border plant with heads composed of many bright blue flowers.

African National Congress (1912). Formed in South Africa to fight for African rights, it denounced the pass laws as early as 1919. From 1952 until it was banned in 1960 it was led by the Nobel Peace prize-winner, Albert Luthuli. At this time the leaders were organizing guerrilla warfare and general sabotage. Nelson Mandela and his associates were given life sentences. In 1990 the movement was recognized by the South African government.

African Queen, The (1951). John Huston's film famous for its box-office success, based on C. S. Forester's novel (1935) in which a hard-drinking river trader rescues a female missionary during the German East African campaign of World War I and joins battle with a German gunboat.

African violet Popular house plant with violet, pink or white flowers and fleshy, hairy leaves; it is sensitive to draughts, temperature changes and overdoses of sunlight.

Afrikaans Simplified form of Dutch with borrowings from European and African languages, spoken by AFRIKANERS; became an official language in South Africa in 1925.

Afrika Korps Rommel's German army which arrived in North Africa in February 1941 to reinforce the Italians against the British.

Afrikanerbond (1880). Afrikaans party founded in Cape Colony which advocated an independent federal republic of South Africa.

Afrikaners Boers; the Afrikaans-speaking people in South Africa, of Dutch, German or Huguenot descent.

Afrit In Muslim mythology, a type of gigantic malicious devil.

Afternoon of a Faun, The (1912). English title of a ballet choreographed by Nijinsky to the music of *Prélude à l'*APRÈS-MIDI D'UN FAUNE.

Agadir Crisis (1911). Tension created in Europe when the German Kaiser sent the gunboat *Panther* to Agadir as a demonstration against French expansion in Morocco.

Agag King of the AMALEKITES, spared by Saul and slain by Samuel (1 Sam. 15:32–3). When summoned before Samuel he 'came unto him delicately', i.e. with tottering footsteps.

Aga Khan Title given by the British to the leader of the ISMAILI SECT when he settled in Bombay after his flight from Persia. (Turkish, 'master ruler'; pronounced ah'ga kahn.)

Aga Khan Cup Show jumping competition at the Royal Dublin Horse Show.

Agamemnon King of Argos, leader of the Greek army at Troy, and brother-in-law of the Helen who caused the Trojan War. On his return from Troy he was murdered by his wife, CLYTEMNESTRA and her lover Aegisthus. His murder was avenged by his son ORESTES. See ATREUS, HOUSE OF.

Agar's Plough Name of part of the playing fields of Eton, adjoining Dutchman's Farm.

Age of Innocence, The (1920). Edith Wharton's novel drawing on her childhood memories for a satirical picture of New York society in the 1870s, with a plot about a man's love for his wife's free-thinking cousin, frustrated by the conventions.

Age of Reason, The Another name for the EN-LIGHTENMENT.

Aggie Weston Naval nickname for a Sailors' Home or temperance bar, the first of which was built by Dame Agnes Weston.

Agincourt (1415). Battle in the HUNDRED YEARS WAR where Henry V's longbowmen defeated a superior French force on St Crispin's Day. (Village in the Pas-de-Calais.)

Agitprop Soviet organization for disseminating the views of the Communist Party to all parts of the country through a large staff of full-time workers, kept continually briefed with all changes in the Party line, and directed by the Central Committee from Moscow. (Abbreviation of Agitation and Propaganda.)

Agnus Dei (1) Part of the Mass beginning with these words. (2) Figure of a lamb bearing a banner with a cross, as emblem of Christ. (Latin, 'Lamb of God'; pronounced ag'nus day'ee.)

Aguecheek, Sir Andrew Silly man in Shakespeare's *Twelfth Night* who joins Sir Toby BELCH in playing tricks on MALVOLIO.

Ahab Ninth-century BC King of Israel who married JEZEBEL.

Ahab, Captain See MOBY-DICK.

Ahasuerus (1) Xerxes, see ESTHER. (2) One of the names of the WANDERING JEW.

Ahitophel David's trusted counsellor who deserted him to support ABSALOM'S rebellion.

Ahriman In the Zoroastrian religion the spirit of evil and enemy of man; see AHURA MAZDA.

Ahura Mazda (Ormuzd, Ormazd). In the Zoroastrian religion, the spirit of good, creator of all things, destined eventually to defeat AHRIMAN.

Aida (1871). Verdi's opera, written to celebrate the opening of the Suez Canal. Aida, the King of Ethiopia's daughter, is slave to the Pharaoh's daughter and in love with the latter's betrothed, the conquering hero Radames; accused of betraying his country, Radames is condemned to be buried alive, and Aida dies with him. (Pronounced ah-ee'da.)

Aids Acquired immunity deficiency syndrome, a disease first recognized 1979–80. See also HIV.

Ailanthus Genus of trees native to the Far East; the best-known is the Chinese Tree of Heaven, much planted in parks and gardens of Europe and America. It is tall and handsome and thrives in the smoky atmosphere of cities, but the small greenish flowers have an unpleasant smell.

Ailsa Craig Well-flavoured heavy-cropping variety of tomato; also the name of varieties of onion etc. (Scottish island.)

Aims for Freedom and Enterprise (1942). Founded (as Aims of Industry) as a pressure group to defend and promote capitalism. It regards itself as non-political.

Aintree Racecourse 5 miles north of Liverpool, famous as the scene of the chief steeplechase of the year, the GRAND NATIONAL.

Ainu Aborigines of Japan, who may have lived in the northern island of Hokkaido for 7,000 years. Tall, strong, hairy and comparatively fair in complexion, they are not Mongoloid in appearance; their language has no known affinities. Some 300 of pure blood and another 15,000 identifiable as Ainu are scattered about Hokkaido and include groups that once lived in Sakhalin and the Kurils; they are in process of complete absorption by the Japanese.

Air Canada (1964). Formerly TCA (Trans-Canada Airlines), established by government (1937) and operating to Europe. Canadian Pacific Airlines operate on the South American and Pacific routes.

Air Training Corps (1941). National voluntary youth organization for boys ages 14–18, sponsored by the Ministry of Defence to encourage a practical interest in aviation and provide preliminary training for entry into the RAF.

Aix-la-Chapelle French name of the German city of Aachen.

Ajanta caves Cave-temples near Bombay, richly carved and decorated by Buddhist monks who lived there from 200 BC to AD 600.

Ajax Greek hero of the Trojan War who went mad when the armour of Achilles was awarded to Ulysses instead of to him.

Akademgorodok 'Science City', site of the Academy of Sciences near Novosibirsk, Siberia.

Akela Adult leader of a pack of Cub Scouts after a character in the JUNGLE BOOK who is leader of a wolf pack.

Akhenaten The name taken by the Egyptian Pharaoh Amenhotep IV in the 14th century BC, when he introduced the monotheistic worship of the Solar Disc at AMARNA.

Akkadians Semitic race which under Sargon I conquered SUMER about 2370 BC and founded an empire stretching from Elam to the Mediterranean; it lasted for some 200 years. Their capital, Akkad, has not been identified.

Alabama **arbitration** (1871). Award of heavy damages against the British government by an international tribunal of arbitration for allowing the Confederate ship *Alabama* to sail in 1862 from Birkenhead, where she was built, to take part in the American Civil War.

Aladdin Poor Chinese boy of the *Arabian Nights* who comes into possession of a magic lamp which, when rubbed, calls up two Slaves of the Lamp to do his bidding; he acquires a palace and the King of China's daughter. British pantomime figure.

Alamein, Battles of (El) (1) 'First Alamein' (30 June to 25 July 1942), fought by Gen. Auchinleck, who took over direct command of the 8th Army and halted Rommel's advance on the Nile. (2) 'Second Alamein' (23 October to 4 November 1942), the more famous opening engagement of Gen. Montgomery's offensive in the Western Desert, after Gen. Alexander had replaced Auchinleck. (An Egyptian village 40 miles west of Alexandria.)

Alamo, The Fort in San Antonio, Texas, besieged in 1836 by Mexicans, who killed all its defenders. (Pronounced al'a-mo.)

Alaska Highway Road built in 1942, linking Fairbanks, Alaska, to the railhead at Dawson Creek, British Columbia.

Alastor In Greek legend an avenging deity who drives the sinner to fresh crimes. Shelley's Alastor is, however, the Spirit of Solitude.

Al-Azhar Ancient university of Cairo, founded

988, a centre of Muslim learning ever since; modernized in the 1960s. (Arabic, 'the brightest', one of Fatima's titles.)

Albany Ancient poetic name for the Scottish Highlands; also Alba, Albania, Albin etc. (Perhaps from Gaelic *alp*, 'cliff'.)

Albany London Georgian mansion on the north side of Piccadilly, built round a secluded central court; from 1802 converted into residential chambers, originally for bachelors only, and still one of the most fashionable London addresses. (Albany Chambers, once occupied by the Duke of York and Albany, son of George III.)

Albany Trust (UK) Charitable trust that deals with the problems of male and female homosexuals.

Alberich (1) In Scandinavian mythology the dwarf who guards the NIBELUNGS' gold. (2) In Wagner's RING OF THE NIBELUNG cycle, he steals the Rhine Gold from the RHINE MAIDENS and makes a magic ring from it which he is forced by the gods to yield up to them, but not before he has placed a curse on it.

Albert In Stanley Holloway's best-loved monologue, a little boy who inadvisedly prodded a lion at the Zoo with his stick (with a 'orse's 'ead 'andle). His parents' outrage at the carelessness of the Zoo officials is skilfully exploited.

Albert Hall, The Royal (1871). Domed circular hall opposite the Albert Memorial in Kensington Gardens, conceived by Prince Albert as a 'Hall of Arts of Sciences' but put to a multiplicity of uses, e.g. the PROMS, brass band and other concerts (despite a tremendous echo not cured until comparatively recently), recitals on one of the world's largest organs, the Chelsea Arts Ball, boxing, wrestling, karate, tennis, running, beauty contests, and meetings massed to hear Horatio Bottomley (see VICTORY BONDS), BILLY GRAHAM, Mosley (see BRITISH UNION OF FASCISTS) etc., the annual Festival of Remembrance and countless other events.

Albert Herring (1947). Benjamin Britten's comic opera in which the lady of the manor decides that as no village girl is morally qualified to be Queen of the May, there shall be a King

instead. The greengrocer's virtuous boy, Albert, is selected and succumbs to the temptation of spending his prize-money on his first binge.

Albertine (1909). Rambler rose, producing fragrant medium-sized orange-salmon flowers in abundance.

Albertine (Simonet) One of the chief characters in Proust's REMEMBRANCE OF THINGS PAST. The narrator meets her as a girl at Balbec and she eventually becomes his mistress. Tired of his jealousy of her lesbian relationships, she escapes from him, but is killed when thrown from a horse. Marcel (the narrator) is surprised to find how quickly he forgets her.

Albert the Good The Prince Consort, Queen Victoria's husband.

Albigensians Adherents of a form of MANICHAEISM widespread in southern Europe in the 11th–13th centuries and savagely suppressed by the Pope's Albigensian crusade under Simon de Montfort (father of the Simon de Montfort of English history) and by the Inquisition then set up to put down such heresies. The Albigensians were supported by the Counts of Toulouse, and in the crusade the aristocracy of Provence was virtually exterminated. (Albi, French town near Toulouse.)

Albion Ancient and poetical name for England. (Traditionally from Latin *albus*, 'white', in reference to the chalk cliffs of Dover.)

Alcalá The main street of Madrid.

Alcatraz US Federal prison on the island of that name in San Francisco Bay; closed in 1963. (Pronounced al'kė-traz.)

Alcázar Moorish palace in Spain; specifically that at Seville which became a royal palace famous for its architecture and gardens. The Alcázar at Toledo was famous for its prolonged and successful defence by the Nationalists against the Republicans in 1936 during the Spanish Civil War. (Arabic, 'castle'; pronounced al-kath'ar.)

Alcestis In Greek myth the wife of ADMETUS who, to save his life, surrendered herself to Hades, but was rescued from the Underworld by Heracles (HERCULES).

Alchemist, The (1610). One of Ben Jonson's best plays, in which a quack dupes various people who deserve no better.

Alcmene Mother of Heracles by Zeus; see AMPHITRYON. (Pronounced alk-mee'ni).

Alcock and Brown (1919). British aviators who made the first nonstop transatlantic flight.

Alcoholics Anonymous Organization which encourages alcoholics to meet others who have cured themselves, to obtain advice.

Aldebaran Orange-red star, the brightest in TAURUS, and one of the HYADES. (Arabic, 'the following', as following the PLEIADES; pronounced al-deb'a-ran.)

Aldeburgh Music Festival (1948). Annual festival of music and other arts founded by Benjamin Britten and the British tenor, Peter Pears. It presents Britten's own compositions, and other contemporary music. (Coastal town of Suffolk, north-east of Ipswich.)

Aldermaston Village near Reading, Berkshire, the site of the UK Atomic Energy Authority's atomic weapons research establishment. See next entry.

Aldermaston march CND's protest march from London to ALDERMASTON, first made on 4 April 1958 and thereafter each Easter in the reverse direction.

Aldershot Name associated since 1855 with the largest army camp in Britain. (Hampshire town near Farnham and Farnborough.)

Aldershot Tattoo See SEARCHLIGHT TATTOO. (See previous entry.)

Aldine Press (1490–1597). Venetian press which printed editions of the Greek and Latin classics, popularized the smaller octavo format which replaced the folio, and introduced italic type. (Aldus Manutius, Latinized name of the printer.)

Aldwych farce One of a series of farces at the Aldwych Theatre, London, in the 1920s and 1930s, starting with *Cuckoo in the Nest* (1925) and including *Tons of Money, Rookery Nook* etc. They were written by Ben Travers, produced by Tom Walls, and featured Robertson Hare and Ralph Lynn in various riotous roles.

Aleuts Eskimo people inhabiting the Aleutian Islands and speaking a language similar to Eskimo but not intelligible to mainland Eskimos.

A-level The GCE examination taken in Britain after 2 years in the sixth form, at age 18, and equivalent to the old Higher School Certificate; there are 5 grades, A to E. There used to be an A-S level of scholarship standard, later replaced by grades of Distinction and Merit for abler candidates taking supplementary (S) papers. (A for Advanced.)

Alex Short for Alexandria (Egypt).

'Alexander's Ragtime Band' (1911). Irving Berlin's slow march, one of TIN PAN ALLEY's earliest and most successful breaks with the tradition of sentimentality. Mistakenly regarded as a landmark in ragtime's history, it has almost no syncopation in it, despite the title.

Alexandra Palace Building on Muswell Hill, London, which was the first home of the BBC TV service and of experimental colour TV; there is also an adjacent recreation park with a racecourse.

Alexandra Rose Day (1912). Day in June when rose emblems are sold in aid of a fund to assist hospitals. (Inaugurated by Queen Alexandra.)

Alexandra Stakes, Queen Longest British flat-race, run at ROYAL ASCOT over a distance of 2 miles 6 furlongs 75 yds. See BROWN JACK STAKES.

Alexandria Quartet Novels (*Justine, Mountolive, Balthazar, Clea*) by Lawrence Durrell (1957–60) set against a background of sophisticated decadence in modern Alexandria.

Algeciras Conference (1906). Conference that ended the first MOROCCAN CRISIS by regulating international commercial relations in Morocco.

'Algérie française' (1960). Slogan of the French (*colon*) population of Algeria who opposed Algerian independence, chanted incessantly in the streets and represented also by 5 long notes on car-horns etc.

Algol Best-known of the eclipsing variable stars, in PERSEUS (beta-Persei), normally of 2nd magnitude but eclipsed by its companion star every 69 hours. (Arabic, 'destruction'.)

Algonquin Nomadic Indian race which once roamed over much of the eastern half of North America but was pushed westward in the 17th century by the Iroquois. There are now 1,000–2,000 survivors ('Ottawa Indians') in Quebec and Ontario. Their name is given to the Algonquian family of languages spoken by Arapaho, Blackfoot, Cree, Micmac, Narragansett, Ojibway, Sauk and Shawnee.

Alhambra Huge 13th-century fortified palace built by the Moors at Granada, Spain, with encircling walls of red sun-dried brick. (Arabic, 'the red'.)

'Ali Baba and the Forty Thieves' Traditionally, an *Arabian Nights* story, though not found in any manuscript edition of them. Overhearing the magic password 'Open Sesame' Ali Baba gains access to the thieves' cave and treasure; they swear vengeance, but his slave Morgiana pours boiling oil on them as they lie in wait for him.

Alice blue US name for a shade of greenish-blue admired by Alice, daughter of Theodore Roosevelt (President, 1901–9); rendered familiar in Britain by the song 'Alice Blue Gown'.

Alice in Wonderland (1865). Well-known book in English for children of all ages, by Lewis Carroll (Canon Dodgson), most of the characters of which have become household names; the keynote is sustained mad logic. It was illustrated by Sir John Tenniel.

Alids Descendants of Ali, husband of Fatima and thus Mohammed's son-in-law, and fourth Caliph (first according to the SHI'ITES). The FATIMITES and the sharifs of Morocco are among those who claimed descent from him.

Aligarh University (1920). Famous Muslim university in Uttar Pradesh, India, opened to non-Muslims in 1956.

Alitalia Chief Italian airline.

Alken prints Sporting prints by several members of the Alken family, of whom Henry (1784–1851) was the best, depicting foxhunting, steeplechasing and other English sports. Henry illustrated NIMROD and Surtees.

All-Africa Peoples' Conference (1958). First of a series of conferences, held at Accra, which led to the foundation of the ORGANIZATION OF AFRICAN UNITY.

Allan-a-Dale Minstrel of ROBIN HOOD's band.

All-Blacks New Zealand rugby team. On its first British tour (1905) it won all its games but one; on its second (1924) it was undefeated.

Allegro, L' and *Il Penseroso* Companion poems (1632), gay and grave, by Milton. (Italian, 'the gay', 'the thoughtful'.)

Allemande Savoury white sauce made with egg yolk and cream.

All England Lawn Tennis and Croquet Club Private club which owns the WIMBLEDON lawn-tennis courts, where the annual championships are held by joint arrangement with the Lawn Tennis Association.

All England Plate Lawn-tennis competition for men and women players defeated in the first 2 rounds of the Wimbledon singles championships.

All for Love (1678). Dryden's blank verse tragedy, with the subtitle *or the World Well Lost*, about the last days of Antony and Cleopatra.

All God's Chillun Got Wings (1924). Eugene O'Neill's tragedy about a mixed marriage.

All Hallows (Day). Older name for ALL SAINTS. (Old English *halig*, 'holy'.)

All Hallows Eve Another name for HALLOWE'EN.

Allium Genus name of garlic, onion, leek, etc.

Alloway Hamlet 2 miles south of Ayr, the birthplace of Robert Burns, where his cottage is preserved as a museum, with a memorial near by.

All Quiet on the Western Front (1927). One of the most famous novels about World War I, on the note 'war is hell'; written by a German, Erich Maria Remarque. (German title, *Im Westen nichts Neues.*)

All Saints (Day) 1 November, set aside in the Anglican and Roman Catholic calendars for a general celebration of the saints who have no day of their own; formerly called All Hallows.

All Souls (Day) 2 November, a day set aside in the Roman Catholic calendar for prayers to mitigate the sufferings of souls in purgatory ('all the faithful deceased').

All Souls, Oxford (1438). College with no undergraduates. Election to the 54 Fellowships of the college is an honour reserved for distinguished scholars. Some Honorary Fellowships for men distinguished in other fields and some Junior Research Fellowships are also given.

All's Well That Ends Well (about 1600) Shakespeare's late, disillusioned comedy recounting the wiles of Helena in forcing Bertrand to accept her as his wife; the happy ending is quite artificial.

All the Talents, Ministry of (1806–7). Coalition government formed by the Whig leader, Lord Grenville, after the death of his cousin, the Younger Pitt. Charles James Fox was Foreign Minister. It did nothing to justify its title except abolish the slave trade.

Allworthy, Squire Upright and benevolent foster-father and, as it transpires, uncle of the hero of Fielding's novel, TOM JONES.

Ally Pally Popular name for ALEXANDRA PALACE.

Almack's (1765–1890). Assembly rooms in St James's, London, started by the founder of Brooks's Club, used for gambling and society functions.

Alma Mater (1) Roman title for Cybele, Ceres and other goddesses. (2) (Britain) Used, with reference to its students, of a school or university. (3) In USA, a school or college song. (Latin, 'nourishing, bountiful, mother'.)

Almanach de Gotha (1763). Former German publication, in French and German, giving statistical and historical information regarding the countries of the world, but chiefly famous for its detailed genealogies of European royal and princely families. (Originally published in Gotha; pronounced goh'tha.)

Almansur Title given to various Muslim heroes, specifically to a 10th-century Moorish King of Andalusia. (Arabic, 'the victorious'.)

Almaviva, Count See BARBER OF SEVILLE; MARRIAGE OF FIGARO.

Almayer's Folly (1895). Conrad's first novel, about an ambitious trader in the Malayan Archipelago and his beloved halfcaste daughter; the 'folly' is the pretentious house he builds for himself.

Almoravids (11th–12th centuries). BERBER dynasty which conquered Morocco and OLD GHANA, and then took over Moorish Spain from the successors to the OMAYYADS.

Alnwick Castle Originally a 12th-century border fortress, in Northumberland, in Percy hands since Norman times and still the home of the Dukes of Northumberland. (Pronounced an'ik.)

Aloha State Nickname for Hawaii. (Hawaiian, 'greetings', also 'farewell'.)

Alouette Helicopters manufactured by AÉROSPATIALE of France.

Alph River of Coleridge's KUBLA KHAN at XANADU: 'Where Alph, the sacred river, ran / Through caverns measureless to man ...' A wicked man once printed this as: 'Where, Alf, the sacred river ran.'

Alpha and Omega First and last letters of the Greek alphabet (*a* and long *o*), used in Revelation 1:8: 'I am Alpha and Omega, the beginning and the ending, saith the Lord.' (Pronounced alf'a, oh'meg-a.)

Alsace–Lorraine Two French provinces (capitals, Strasbourg and Nancy respectively) seized by Germany after the FRANCO-PRUSSIAN WAR, regained in 1919 and once more lost to

Germany from 1940 to 1945; now comprising the *départements* of Haut-Rhin (Mulhouse) and Bas-Rhin (Strasbourg); that of Lorraine includes Metz, Épinal and Nancy.

Alsacienne (Cooking). With a garnish of sauerkraut, ham and Strasbourg sausage.

Alsatia Until the end of the 17th century a sanctuary for debtors and criminals at Whitefriars, London. (Named after Alsace.)

Alsatian See GERMAN SHEPHERD DOG.

Alstroemeria Half-hardy herbaceous plant (Peruvian lily) named in honour of Baron Alstroemer, a Swedish botanist.

Altaic languages Division of the URAL–ALTAIC LANGUAGES which includes MANCHU, Mongolian, Turkish and a Western Turkish group spoken in the southern republics of the USSR east of the Caspian, i.e. Kazakh, Turkmen, Uzbek, Kirghiz and Tadzhik. Japanese and Korean were once, but are no longer, considered to be distantly related. (From the Altaic mountains of west Mongolia.)

Altamira Site where the first examples of Old Stone Age cave art were discovered (1879) – strikingly naturalistic colour paintings of bison and other animals, perhaps 30,000 years old. (Village near Santander, Spain.)

Alter ego Latin: a second self. A double.

Altmark **incident** (February 1940). British destroyer's rescue of 300 prisoners of war from the German ship *Altmark* in neutral Norwegian territorial waters.

Alto Adige Name for the Italian province of Bolzano (German Bozen), called by the Austrians South Tirol; for many years an area disputed with Austria, which complained of the Italianization of the German-speaking inhabitants who form two-thirds of the population. (Italian, 'upper Adige', the river which drains it; pronounced ah'di-jè.)

Altona (1959). Sartre's play about a German family racked by guilt feelings regarding its Nazi past, and especially the use of torture; it refers obliquely to contemporary French conduct in Algeria. (French title, *Les Séquestrés d'Altona*.)

Amadis *de* *Gaul* 16th-century Spanish romance of chivalry, in which the knight Amadis de Gaul (Wales) falls in love with Oriana, the king of England's daughter. (Pronounced am'a-dis.)

Amalekites Nomadic Arab tribe to the south of Judah with whom the Israelites fought from the time of Joshua until David 'smote' them finally (1 Sam. 30:17); they are generally represented as notably treacherous.

Amalthea Nymph in Greek legend who fed the infant Zeus in a Cretan cave with the milk of a goat (also named Amalthea in some versions). Zeus gave her a horn of the goat, which he had magically transformed into a horn of plenty or cornucopia. (Pronounced a-mal-thee'a.)

Amaranthus Genus of plants that includes Lovelies-bleeding.

Amarna Ancient Egyptian city between Memphis and Thebes, founded by AKHENATEN as his capital; also called Tel el-Amarna.

Amaryllis Shepherdess in the pastoral poems of Theocritus; hence the name was widely used in later poetry for any rustic beauty.

Amaryllis belladonna Species name for the Belladonna lily.

Amazons In Greek legend, a race of female warriors of Scythia who burnt off their right breasts the better to shoot off their arrows. The River Amazon got its name from a local tale of a similar race. (The legend explains the (probably false) derivation from Greek *a-*, 'without'; *mazos*, 'breast'.)

Ambassadors, The (1903). Henry James's novel, which tells of a New England widow who sends an 'ambassador' to recall her son from Paris; her envoy is converted to the view that the young man is better where he is.

Amboina massacre (1623). Dutch massacre of English merchants in the Spice Islands (Moluccas), after which the EAST INDIA COMPANY turned its attention to India.

Amboise conspiracy (1560). Huguenot plot to seize the King of France and Catherine de Medici; it was discovered and foiled. Three years later, after the King's death, a reversal of policy brought the Huguenots considerable religious freedom. (Town on the Loire.)

Ambridge See THE ARCHERS.

Amerasian Person of mixed US and Asian parentage.

'America' (1831). National hymn with words (beginning 'My Country 'tis of Thee') by the Rev. Samuel Francis Smith of Boston, set to the tune of 'God Save the King' which was also used in 'God Bless Our Noble Land' (1844). This tune perhaps dates back to the 17th century and may have originally been a folk melody; it appears in several old European national anthems and in works by Beethoven and Weber.

American Civil War (1861–5). War between the CONFEDERATE STATES and the Union government, caused partly by the election of Abraham Lincoln as President after he had denounced slavery, and partly by a continued dispute on states' rights, i.e. the power to be delegated by the Union (or Federal) government to the individual states.

American Dream, The (1961). Edward Albee's Theatre of the ABSURD play in which a woman seeks happiness by adopting a son, who turns out to be an unscrupulous self-seeker; she symbolizes an American society divorced from reality by false ideals.

American Express Co. (1850). World-wide travel agency and banker, originally a carrying firm. As there was no US parcel post until 1913 and the railways did not like handling small consignments, private companies arose which ran express services from door to door, COD (the origin of the banking side of the modern firm).

American Federation of Labor See AFL/CIO.

American Field Service (1914). Privately sponsored non-political and non-sectarian organiza-

tion which operates an international scholarship programme (1946) for the exchange of high-school students between the USA and foreign countries. (Originally a volunteer ambulance service.)

American Indian languages A group distantly related to Mongolian languages. They include MAYAN LANGUAGE, KECHUAN, ARAUCANIAN and TUPÍ-GUARANÍ, among very many others.

'American in Paris, An' (1928). Orchestral tone poem written and orchestrated by George Gershwin, and inspired by his homesick boyhood in Paris. It also supplied the theme for a film (1951).

American Legion (1919). US veteran (ex-servicemen's) organization, now including veterans of both world wars and the Korean and Vietnam Wars.

American plan US term for *en pension* hotel rates, i.e. inclusive of meals. See EUROPEAN PLAN.

American Tragedy, An (1925). Theodore Dreiser's novel, based on a famous trial, of a young man from a poor home who, obsessed with dreams of luxury, causes the death of the girl he has made pregnant so that he can make a rich marriage. He is executed, but Dreiser indicts the materialist society into which he was born.

American War of Independence (1775–83). Revolt of the 13 American colonies on the issue of 'no taxation without representation' (i.e. at Westminster), ending in the recognition of their independence by the Treaty of Paris. See BOSTON TEA PARTY.

America's Cup International yacht race, held at the club of the previous winner. From the inauguration of the race, in 1851, to 1983, the yacht club at Newport, Rhode Island held off 24 challenges. (See SHAMROCK.)

'America the Beautiful' (1895). National hymn with words by Katherine Lee Bates, set to Samuel A. Ward's hymn-tune 'Materna' (1888); regarded by many as superior in words and music to 'The Star-Spangled Banner'.

Amerindian Ethnologists' term for American Indian.

Amer Picon French bitters, originally made as a tonic for French troops in Algeria in the 1830s, by a Dr Picon. (French *amer*, 'bitter'.)

Amethyst, HMS (1949). Gunboat which during the Chinese Civil War ran the gauntlet between Chinese shore batteries and made her escape down the Yangtse River by night with lights out, a remarkable feat of navigation.

Amharic Semitic language of the dominant minority, the Amharas, of Ethiopia. (Pronounced am-har'ik.)

Amiens, Peace of (1802). After the British and French had reached a stalemate in the Napoleonic wars, and Addington had replaced Pitt, a peace was made by which Britain restored French colonies but kept Ceylon (formerly Dutch) and Trinidad (formerly Spanish). War was resumed the following year.

Amish, Old Order Amish One of the strictest sects of MENNONITES; they settled in Pennsylvania and shun electricity, cars, and other subjects not mentioned in the Bible.

Amnesty International (1961). Organization founded by the British lawyer, Peter Benenson, which campaigns for the release of persons in any part of the world who have been detained in prison for their religious or political beliefs, provided they have not advocated nor been guilty of violence, racialism or espionage, and are serving a sentence of not less than 6 months.

Amoco Cadiz **disaster** (1978). Oil tanker forced on to rocks on the Brittany coast of France, following steering-gear failure, discharged 68 million US gallons of oil.

Amon (Ammon, Amun) Ancient Egyptian ram-headed god, originally local to Thebes, who became the state god of all Egypt under the 18th Dynasty (16th century BC) and was later linked with RA, the sun-god, as Amon-Ra. The Greeks identified him with Zeus (see JUPITER AMMON).

Amontillado A FINO sherry, darker, less dry and fuller-bodied than MANZANILLA.

Amor brujo, El (Ballet) See LOVE THE MAGICIAN.

Amoroso sherry See OLOROSO.

Ampelopsis veitchii Species name of Virginia creeper; also classified as *Vitis inconstans*.

Ampere Basic unit of electric current named after André Marie Ampère (1775–1836).

Amphion (Greek legend) The son of ZEUS, whose magic lyre caused the stones to leap into place in building the walls of Thebes. He married NIOBE. (Pronounced am-fy'on.)

Amphitrite (Greek legend) Wife of POSEIDON, mother of TRITON. (Pronounced am'fi-try-ti.)

Amphitryon (Greek legend) King of Thebes who married Alcmene; she became the mother of Heracles (Hercules) by Zeus when he invited himself to the house disguised as her husband, and gave a banquet, interrupted ineffectively by the arrival of the real Amphitryon. (Pronounced am-fit'ri-on.)

Amritsar massacre (1919). Killing of 379 rioters who had assembled in a square called the Jallianwala Bagh, during widespread disturbances in the Punjab. Gen. Dyer's action in ordering his troops to fire on the crowd was condemned by a committee of inquiry.

Amu Darya Modern name of the great Russian river which flows into the Aral Sea; formerly known as the OXUS.

Anabaptists (1) Extremists of the Reformation movement, so called because they rejected infant baptism; (2) at one time a derogatory term for English Baptists.

Anabasis (about 370 BC). Account by Xenophon, commanding a Greek mercenary force assisting Cyrus against his brother Artaxerxes in a Persian civil war, of his retreat from Mesopotamia to the Black Sea, which his soldiers greeted with the famous cry: *Thalassa! thalassa!*, 'the sea!'. (Greek, 'the walk up', i.e. 'the march to the north'; pronounced an-ab'a-sis.)

Anadyomene See APHRODITE ANADYOMENE.

Anagallis Genus name of the pimpernels.

Analects **(of Confucius)** Collection of random musings attributed to Confucius, which carried great authority in pre-Communist China. (From Greek, 'gleanings'.)

Ananias (1) Husband of Sapphira; both were struck dead for giving only part of what they had to the Apostles and pretending that it was the whole or, as Peter called it, 'lying to the Holy Ghost' (Acts 5:1–11). (2) High priest who ordered his men to smite St Paul on the mouth (Acts 23:2). (Pronounced an-an-*y*′as.)

Anastasia Title of a film and a play on the subject of Anna Anderson's claim to be the Russian Tsar's daughter and to have escaped from the EKATERINBURG massacre in 1918. She died in 1964.

Anatolia Another name for Asia Minor, virtually equivalent to modern Turkey in Asia.

Anatolian rugs Earliest oriental rugs to be imported into Europe, made from the 12th century in what is now Turkey, and showing strong Persian influence from the 15th century. Coarsely knotted and with bold colours, mostly red and blue, with the sacred green reserved for prayer rugs, their manufacture came to be largely monopolized by Greeks living in Turkey and ceased with their expulsion by Mustapha Kemal in the 1920s. See also GHIORDES RUGS.

Anatomist, The (1930). James Bridie's first successful play, based on the story of BURKE AND HARE.

Anatomy Lesson, The (1632). Rembrandt's first important work after he moved from Leyden to Amsterdam, commissioned by the Guild of Surgeons and portraying its members surrounding an opened cadaver. (Mauritshuis, The Hague.)

Anatomy of Melancholy, The (1621). Robert Burton's essay on mental maladies ranging from depression to extremes of insanity, enriched by copious quotations from classical sources on the afflictions of mankind; can also be read as a satire on the uselessness of learning

Anchises Trojan prince, father of AENEAS, who visits him in the Underworld. (Pronounced an-ky′seez.)

Ancien Régime Old order, especially in reference to pre-Revolution France, where absolute monarchy prevailed.

Ancient Mariner, The Rime of the (1798). Coleridge's hypnotic poem, written in his youth, of the spell cast on a sailor who broke an old taboo by killing an albatross. It contains many oft-quoted lines, such as: 'Alone, alone, all, all alone, /Alone on a wide wide sea.'

Ancient of Days, The God, a phrase used in Daniel 7:9. It merely means 'the old man'.

Ancona Light breed of domestic fowl kept as an egg-producer and used for crossing. (Italian port.)

Andalouse (1) Mayonnaise with tomatoes and pimento. (2) Of fish, meat or poultry, served with aubergines or rice pilaf, and tomato. (Andalusia, Spain.)

Anderson shelter Family air-raid shelter distributed at the beginning of World War II. (Sir John Anderson, Home Secretary.)

Andhra Pradesh (1956). State of India comprising the Telugu-speaking region (Andhra) of north-east Madras established as a separate unit in 1953, and the Telangana area of the former Hyderabad state; capital Hyderabad. (Pronounced ahn′dra prè-daysh′.)

Androcles Runaway Roman slave sent into the arena to fight a lion, which recognized him as the man who had once removed a thorn from its paw, and licked him affectionately. Bernard Shaw wrote a play on the theme, *Androcles and the Lion* (1912). (Pronounced an′dro-kleez.)

Andromache In Greek legend HECTOR's beautiful wife. In Euripides' play named after her she is carried off by Achilles' son and cruelly treated by the Spartans. Racine also wrote a play of that name (1667). (Pronounced an-drom′a-ki.)

Andromeda In Greek legend the daughter of CASSIOPEIA; she was chained to a rock exposed to a sea monster to placate Poseidon. PERSEUS rescued and married her. (Pronounced an-drom′e-da.)

Andromeda Northern constellation below CAS-SIOPEIA; it contains the Great Spiral Nebula, one of the 3 galaxies visible to the naked eye, about 2 million light-years away. (See preceding entry.)

Andy Capp Aggressively working-class creation of the *Daily Mirror* cartoonist, Reg Smythe, with built-in cigarette-butt and cap (or flat 'at).

Angel Investor, generally a backer of a theatrical production.

Angels of Mons Widely believed legend that angels had been seen at the Battle of MONS, started by a short story written by Arthur Machen for the *Evening News* in August 1914

Angevin Of ANJOU; see PLANTAGENETS.

Angiosperms Flowering plants, a division subdivided into the monocotyledons and dicotyledons.

Angkor Ancient KHMER capital in Cambodia (8th–15th centuries), the ruins of which were discovered in the jungle in 1860. See next 2 entries. (*Angkor*, 'ruins'.)

Angkor Thom Walled city of ANGKOR itself.

Angkor Vat Largest temple in the world, covered with Buddhist and Hindu carvings and sculpture; 1 mile south of ANGKOR THOM. (*Vat*, also spelt *wat*, 'temple'.)

Angles Teutonic invaders from Schleswig who, from the 5th century AD, settled in East Anglia, Mercia and Northumbria.

Anglican Church Communion of Protestant Churches, including the Church of England, Churches in Wales, Scotland, Ireland and the Commonwealth, and the Episcopal Church in the USA. The Archbishop of Canterbury presides over the LAMBETH CONFERENCE at which their representatives meet.

Anglo-American US citizen of English origin or descent; abbreviated to 'Anglo', especially in the south-west, with a shift of meaning to 'not of Mexican or Latin American descent'.

Anglo-American Corporation (1917). The late Sir Ernest Oppenheimer's mining group, with interests in South African gold, uranium, diamonds and coal, the Zambia Copperbelt and Zimbabwe.

Anglo-Catholicism Views and practice of the High Church party of the Church of England; see OXFORD MOVEMENT.

Anglo-Dutch Wars *First* (1652–4), the result of the NAVIGATION ACT passed by the RUMP PARLIAMENT. *Second* (1665–7), in which Charles II acquired New York and De Ruyter burnt British ships in the Medway. *Third* (1672–4), declared by Charles II under the Secret Treaty of DOVER.

Anglo-Irish War (1918–21). Name sometimes given to the period when Irish nationalists resisted suppression by the RIC (including the BLACK AND TANS) and troops; part of the period called the TROUBLES.

Anglo-Saxon Attitudes (1956). Angus Wilson's novel about a medievalist who starts to inquire into an apparent academic fraud, with surprising results.

Anglo-Saxon Chronicle Old English collection of sagas and annals covering English history to 1154, compiled by clergy from the time of King Alfred onwards.

Anglo-Saxon language See OLD ENGLISH.

Anglo-Saxons Name given to the Teutonic ANGLES, SAXONS and JUTES who invaded England in the 5th century AD.

Angora Older name of Ankara, now the Turkish capital. It survives in current use as the name of species of cat, goat and rabbit with long silky hair, and of a wool mixture made of Angora rabbit hair and sheep's wool.

Angostura A kind of bitters, formerly made at Angostura (Ciudad Bolívar) in Venezuela by a French doctor in 1825 as a tonic for Bolívar's army of liberation; now made in Trinidad for use in gin cocktails.

Angria and Gondal Settings of numerous melodramatic novels written by the Brontë family when they were young, Angria being an African and Gondal a northern country.

Angry Young Man A man who, like Jimmy PORTER, the chief character in LOOK BACK IN ANGER, impotently and indiscriminately lashes out at modern society as he sees it.

Angus Scottish county until 1928 known as Forfarshire.

Animal Farm George Orwell's satire (1946) on Stalinist Russia. Napoleon the boar is dictator of the farm animals; he keeps changing the party line as it suits him, even the basic slogan: 'All animals are equal,' which he then amended to end: 'but some animals are more equal than others.'

Anitra Arab girl whom PEER GYNT meets on his travels; her dance was set to music by Grieg.

Anjou Former French province (capital, Angers) west of Touraine, inherited by the Angevin (PLANTAGENET) kings of England but lost by King John. It occupied the modern *département* of Maine-et-Loire and adjacent districts.

'Annabel Lee' Poem by Edgar Allan Poe, containing among many other haunting lines: 'I was a child and she was a child, / In this kingdom by the sea; / And we loved with a love that was more than love – / I and my Annabel Lee.'

Anna Christie (1921). Eugene O'Neill's early play about an old barge captain and a woman redeemed by love.

Anna Karenina (1877). One of Leo Tolstoy's 2 greatest novels, in which the happy life of Squire Levin, married to Kitty and busy with schemes of improvement on his estate, is sharply contrasted with the miseries of Anna, who deserts her husband for the handsome young army officer, Vronsky, and commits suicide under a train when he abandons her. (Pronounced kar-ayn'in-a.)

Anna Livia Plurabelle Earwicker's wife in James Joyce's FINNEGANS WAKE, said to represent Eve, the River Liffey, etc.

Annapolis US Naval Academy (1845). (Seaport and capital of Maryland, near Chesapeake Bay.)

Ann Arbor Town of Michigan, USA, to which the University of Michigan (1817) was moved in 1841 from Detroit.

Anne Hathaway's Cottage Cottage at Shottery, near Stratford-upon-Avon, where Shakespeare's wife lived as a girl.

Annelids Phylum of segmented worms (including the common earthworm) and leeches.

Anne of Green Gables (1908). Story for girls by the Canadian novelist Lucy Maude Montgomery, who drew on memories of her youth in Prince Edward Island; it scored a world-wide success and was made into a play which had a long run in London. There were many sequels.

Annie Get Your Gun (1946). Rodgers and Hammerstein musical with music by Irving Berlin and based on the story of the American markswoman ANNIE OAKLEY, presented as a naïve backwoods girl. The hits included 'Doin' What Comes Natur'ly', 'Anything You Can Do (I Can Do Better)' and the eternal ensemble 'There's No Business Like Show Business'.

'Annie Laurie' Poem by Sir William Douglas (about 1700) concerning the daughter of Sir Robert Laurie of Maxwelton, who had jilted him; it was not set to music until 1855.

Anniversary, The Painting by Marc Chagall in the Museum of Modern Art, NYC.

Annual Register, The Record of the chief events of the year, published in England annually since 1758 and first edited by Edmund Burke.

Annunciation, The Gabriel's announcement to the Virgin Mary that she would bear a son, Jesus (Luke 1:26–38), a scene often depicted in art, notably by Fra Angelico, Fra Filippo Lippi and D. G. Rossetti.

Annus Mirabilis Name given by Dryden, in his poem, to the year (1666) of the Great Fire of London and the Dutch fleet's raid up the Medway. (Latin, 'year of wonders'.)

Anopheles mosquito Generic name of the type of mosquito of which many species carry malaria. (Pronounced an-oh'fel-eez.)

Another Country (1) (1961) Novel by the American Negro writer, James Baldwin, on the theme of race relations. (2) (1983) Play by Julian Mitchell, a fictional account of the schooldays of Guy Burgess (and later a film).

Ansafone Device to record telephone calls in the absence of the subscriber, e.g. after business hours; an automatic answering set plays a pre-recorded message telling the caller what action to take.

Anschluss (March 1938). The union with Nazi Germany imposed on Austria by Hitler, with considerable assistance from the Austrians. (German, 'union'.)

Anstey, F. Pen-name of Thomas Anstey Guthrie, author of VICE VERSA.

Antakya A Turkish city, formerly called Antioch.

Antarctic Treaty (1959). Thirty-year 12-nation treaty of agreement to suspend political claims to Antarctic territory and to co-operate in research.

Anthemis Genus name of the camomiles (also spelt chamomiles).

Anthony Adverse (1933). First of the mammoth best-selling historical novels, written by Hervey Allen and set in Napoleonic times.

Anthony Eden Black felt hat much in vogue in Whitehall before World War II, when Sir Anthony Eden (Lord Avon), Foreign Secretary (1935–8), set the trend.

Anthropophagi Name for cannibals, taken from the Greek by Shakespeare in the lines in *Othello*: 'The Anthropophagi, and men whose heads / Do grow beneath their shoulders.' (Greek, 'man-eaters'; pronounced an-thro-pof'a-gy.)

Anthroposophical Society (1913). Society founded by an Austrian former Theosophist, Rudolf Steiner, to propagate his eclectic mystical religion of which Goethe was the Messiah.

Antic Hay (1923). Aldous Huxley's early satirical novel about rootless aimless intellectuals in London. (*Hay* in sense 'country dance'; phrase from Marlowe's *Edward II*: 'shall with their goat feet dance the antic hay'.)

Antichrist (1) Christ's final adversary who was expected to appear before the Second Coming; identified with the Beast of the Apocalypse; the word is also used in the New Testament of an apostate. Later the name was applied to various obnoxious figures in history, from Caligula, who wanted to put a statue of himself in the Jewish Temple, to Napoleon. (2) Title of a book by Nietzsche.

Anti-Comintern Pact (November 1936). Agreement between Germany and Japan to co-operate in opposing Communism (see COMINTERN) made about the same time as the ROME-BERLIN AXIS came into being. It was joined by Italy a year later. In return Germany recognized Japan's puppet government of MANCHUKUO. See also TRIPARTITE PACT.

Anti-Corn-Law League (1839). Movement founded at Manchester, the home of Free Trade, which successfully campaigned under the leadership of Cobden and John Bright for the repeal of the CORN LAWS.

Antigone (Greek legend) Daughter of Oedipus who defies King Creon of Thebes by sprinkling earth on the corpse of her brother Polyneices. Creon condemns her to death but relents after a protest by TIRESIAS; too late, as Antigone and Creon's son, whom she was to marry, had both committed suicide. Sophocles' play was written in *c*. 440. Also the title of Anouilh's play (1942) on the same subject with contemporary implications. See OEDIPUS.(Pronounced an-tig'on-i.)

Antioch Older name of the city of Antakya, Turkey.

Antonines, Age of the (AD 96–180). The Golden Age of the Roman Empire, during which the dynasty founded by Nerva ruled, including Trajan, Hadrian, Antoninus Pius and Marcus Aurelius.

Antonine Wall The wall built by the Romans about AD 150, from Carriden on the Forth to Old Kilpatrick on the Clyde. (Antoninus Pius, Roman emperor.)

Antonio (1) The name of the Merchant of Venice in Shakespeare's play. (2) The character in Shakespeare's *The Tempest* who usurps the dukedom of his brother PROSPERO.

Antony and Cleopatra (1) (1606) One of Shakespeare's greatest plays, covering the relationship between Mark Antony and CLEOPATRA, the disaster of ACTIUM, and the suicide of the 2 protagonists. (2) Samuel Barber's opera (1966) written for the opening of the new Metropolitan Opera House in New York.

Anubis Ancient Egyptian jackal-headed god of the Underworld, local to ABYDOS, and later regarded as a son of OSIRIS. The Greeks identified him with HERMES. (Pronounced an-ew′bis.)

Anvil Code name for the Allied landings in the south of France, 1944 (later called Dragoon).

Anyang Chinese archaeological site in Henan Province, discovered in 1934. It revealed that the earliest (SHANG) Chinese Dynasty had already reached a high stage of civilization, with sculpture, bronzes, carved jade and pottery comparable with those of its successors.

Anzac Name formed from the initial letters of the Australian and New Zealand Army Corps in World War I, and applied to troops from those countries in both world wars.

Anzio bridgehead (January 1944). Formed by an Allied landing behind the German lines, south of Rome, hotly contested.

Apache (1) American Indian tribe of the southwestern states. (Pronounced a-pach′i.) (2) In France, the name given to Parisian gangsters. (Pronounced a-pahsh′.)

Apache State Nickname of Arizona. (Home of the APACHE Indians.)

Apalachin conclave (1957). Meeting of heads of MAFIA families from all parts of USA and from Cuba and Italy. It was convened at Apalachin, New York State, by the Neapolitan Vito Genovese to confirm himself in power. Raided by state police, 50 escaped, 60 were arrested, convicted and released on appeal. Vito was given 15 years in 1959.

Apartheid Racial policy, adopted (1948) by South Africa's AFRIKANER Nationalist Party, of segregating Africans, CAPE COLOUREDS, Asians and whites, in theory so that each community can develop separately, e.g. in BANTUSTANS such as TRANSKEI. It involves separate transport, schools, residential areas etc., and even the prohibition of mixed marriages. One of the most controversial of post-war policies, it led to South Africa's leaving the Commonwealth in 1961. (Afrikaans, literally 'apart-hood', officially called 'Separate Development'.)

A.P.H. Initials of (and used for) A. P. (Sir Alan) Herbert (1890–1971), humorous and controversial writer, novelist, librettist and sometime MP.

Aphrodite Greek goddess of love, who was born of the sea foam and stepped ashore on the isle of Cythera. She was the wife of HEPHAESTUS, who trapped her in bed with ARES by throwing a net over them, then calling the other gods to mock them. In later legend she is the mother of EROS. She derives from ISHTAR, and is the Roman Venus. See also ADONIS and PARIS. (Pronounced af-roh-dy′ti.)

Aphrodite Andyomene Painting of APHRODITE rising from the foam, painted by the 4th-century artist Apelles at the court of Alexander the Great; it was renowned in ancient times, but not even a copy has survived. See BIRTH OF VENUS. (Greek, 'rising up'; pronounced an-a-dy-om′en-ee.)

Apis Ancient Egyptian bull-god of Memphis, later identified with Osiris. Under the Ptolemies Osiris-Apis became the Serapis of SAKKARA, god of the Underworld.

Apocalypse Name given to any of several religious works (but applied specifically to the Book of Revelation in the New Testament) on the theme of the final triumph of God at the end of the world, after a period of extreme tribulation. Their purpose was to strengthen faith in times of distress. (Greek, 'revelation'; pronounced a-pok′a-lips.)

Apocrypha, The Ill-defined collection of books found in the SEPTUAGINT and VULGATE versions attached to the Old Testament, not accepted by the Jews (the Hebrew origins have been lost), and accepted only with reservations by Protestants and Catholics. They include The Wisdom of Solomon, Ecclesiasticus, Tobit, Judith, Maccabees, Esdras, Bel and the Dragon, The History of Susanna. (Greek, 'hidden things', i.e. withheld from general circulation as being of doubtful authenticity.)

Apollo Essentially Greek god; he has no Roman counterpart. The son of ZEUS and brother of ARTEMIS, he had very varied functions illustrated by numerous legends: he was god of prophecy (taking over the Delphic Oracle); of healing (father of AESCULAPIUS); of flocks (shepherd to ADMETUS); of light (as Phoebus – 'shining' – Apollo), the leader of the Muses. Statues depicted him as the ideal of male beauty, and to him are ascribed the famous counsels of moderation: Know thyself; Nothing too much.

Apollo Belvedere (4th century BC). Best-known Greek sculpture of a male figure, artist unknown. The bronze original is lost, but there is an inferior Roman copy in the Vatican Museum.

Apollonian Nietzsche's adjective for all he despised, the negative attitude to life which he saw in the 'slave religion' born of failure. resentment and vengefulness, as taught by St Paul, Roman Catholics and Protestants (but not by Jesus himself), haunted by guilt feelings inspired by a false belief in original sin. In a wider sense he applied it to all that individualizes and defines, to structure and form in art, to rational thought. See DIONYSIAN. (APOLLO as the god of light, which clarifies and defines.)

Apollo space program US project to land men on the moon, using a SATURN 5 rocket. *Apollo 4* (unmanned, 1967) tested a LEM module; *Apollo 7* (1968), first US 3-man flight, orbited the earth for 11 days; *8* (1968), first manned (3-man) flight to escape earth's gravity, to orbit the moon and send back live TV pictures; from *Apollo 10* (1969) the LEM *Snoopy* with a crew of 2 descended to within 9 miles of the moon. The historic *Apollo 11* put the first men on the moon, 20 July 1969 (Neil Armstrong and Edwin Aldrin, with Michael Collins as command pilot).

Apollyon (Abaddon) Devil, the 'king of the bottomless pit' of Revelation 9:11, and the 'foul Fiend' of Bunyan's PILGRIM'S PROGRESS. (From Greek, 'destroyer'.)

Apologia pro vita sua (1864). Cardinal Newman's remarkable autobiography, describing his transition from scepticism to acceptance of the Roman Catholic Church's authority. (Latin, 'defence of his life'.)

Apostles Cambridge University intellectual literary society founded in 1820. Membership has mainly been from Trinity and King's Colleges. Spy cases have brought the society into prominence; Anthony Blunt and Guy Burgess were members.

Apostles' Creed Oldest Christian creed, used only in Western Churches; attributed to the Apostles but in its present form it goes back only to AD 750; date of origin unknown.

Apostolic Fathers, The Those FATHERS OF THE CHURCH who were born in the 1st century AD and were thus approximately contemporaries of the Apostles, e.g. Clement of Rome, Ignatius of Antioch.

Apothecaries, Worshipful Society of (1617). LIVERY COMPANY with a fine hall (1670); it is an examining body which grants diplomas to dispensers and medical practitioners.

Appassionata, The Name given to a famous Beethoven piano sonata written in a mood of passionate despair. Op. 57.

Appian Way (4th century BC). First great Roman road, from Rome to Capua and Brindisi. (Named after Appius Claudius.)

Apple Cart, The (1929). Bernard Shaw's play in which he pillories Ramsay MacDonald for deserting the Labour Party. He represents him as Proteus, Prime Minister of a 'Socialist' government which is under the hidden control of industrialists. See King MAGNUS.

Appleton layer Two upper layers (F-1 and F-2) of the ionosphere which, being electrically charged by the sun's ultra-violet rays (ionized), reflect short-wave radio signals. F-1 lies at a height of about 100 miles, F-2 200 miles above the earth. See HEAVISIDE LAYER. (Sir Edward Appleton, Cambridge physicist.)

Appomattox Court House Place where the Confederate general, Robert E. Lee, surrendered to

Gen. Grant (April 1865), the virtual end of the American Civil War.

Apprentice Boys of Londonderry Ulster Protestant organization which holds a march each August to commemorate the occasion in 1689 when a boy closed the gates of the walled city, thereby preventing its capture by a Catholic army. See LONDONDERRY, SIEGE OF.

Après-midi d'un faune, Prélude à l' (1894). Debussy's sun-drenched symphonic poem based on a SYMBOLIST poem by Mallarmé.

April Fool's Day 1 April; by ancient tradition of unknown origin a day for playing practical jokes on the unsuspecting, particularly by sending them on a fool's errand. It is observed in English-speaking countries, France (where the joke is called *poisson d'avril*), Germany and elsewhere.

Apsley House 149 Piccadilly, Hyde Park Corner, bought by the 1st Duke of Wellington and now the Wellington Museum.

Aquae Sulis Roman name of the city of Bath, England.

Aquarius The Water-Bearer, 11th constellation of the Zodiac, between Pisces and Capricornus; the sun enters it about 21 January. Astrologers claim that those born under this sign may be strong-willed individualists, sincere and imaginative.

Aquila Northern constellation above CAPRICORNUS and AQUARIUS. (Latin, 'eagle'; pronounced ak'wi-la, ak-wil'a.)

Aquilegia Genus name of the columbine.

Aquitaine Province of Roman Gaul which became a duchy and, with GASCONY, was inherited by the PLANTAGENETS but lost by Henry VI. At one time it stretched from the Loire to the Pyrenees; the capital was Bordeaux. The modern development region includes the Dordogne, Bayonne and Pau.

Arabia Deserta, Travels in (1888). C. M. Doughty's classic of Arabian travel, a sensitive description of his sojourn with the Bedouin and of the antiquities he found in the desert.

Arabian Nights, The Short title for *The Arabian Nights' Entertainments or the Thousand and One Nights*, a collection of oriental (Indian, Persian, Arab) tales going back to the 9th century, supposed to have been told by SCHEHERAZADE. They include stories of Aladdin, Ali Baba, Sindbad, the Barmecide feast etc., many set in the time of HARUN AL-RASHID, 8th-century Caliph of Baghdad.

Arab League (1945). Properly, the League of Arab States, an association of Arab states for the promotion of common interests and opposition to Israel.

Arab Legion Elite camel corps built up in Jordan between the wars by 2 British officers, Peake Pasha and Glubb Pasha.

Arab Revolt (1916). Revolt that freed Arabia from Turkish rule, led by Hussein (Hashemite Sherif of Mecca and later King of Hejaz) and his son Feisal (later King of Iraq), with Allied support (including the secondment of Lawrence of Arabia). After their wartime successes, they were driven out of Arabia by the WAHABIS, implacable enemies of the HASHEMITES.

Arachne In Greek legend a girl who challenged Athene to a contest in weaving and defeated her. She was turned into a spider. (Greek, 'spider'; pronounced ar-ak'ni.)

Aragon Kingdom of north-east Spain, capital Saragossa, taken from the Moors (1131) and joined to CASTILE (1479) by the marriage of Isabella of Castile and Ferdinand of Aragon. See NAVARRE.

Aramaic Semitic language, once the lingua franca of the western Persian Empire. From about the 7th century BC it displaced Hebrew, which became a learned language; the Jews, including Jesus and the Apostles, conversed in Aramaic and the Gospels were probably originally written in it. Later, Greek replaced it in cities, but in the countryside a dialect of Aramaic, Syriac, was spoken over a wide area. (*Aram*, 'Syria'.)

Aramco Abbreviated name of the Arabian–American Oil Co. which exploits the petroleum of Saudi Arabia.

Ararat Traditionally the mountain on which Noah's Ark came to rest. It is in Turkey near the borders of the Armenian Republic of the USSR.

Araucanian American Indian language of Chile.

Arbela Alternative name for the battle of GAUGA-MELA, it was where Darius encamped before the battle. (Pronounced ar-bee'la.)

Arbor Day (USA) Annual date, varying from state to state, dedicated to the planting of trees; a custom which originated in Nebraska.

Arbor Low Neolithic stone circle and double-entrance tomb, near Bakewell, Derbyshire.

Arcadia Mountainous centre of the Greek Peloponnese, an Ancient Greek SHANGRI LA. *Et in Arcadia ego* is a tomb inscription, quoted now (probably incorrectly) as meaning 'I too (once lived) in Arcady', i.e knew perfect happiness, or even 'Even in Arcadia, there am I' (i.e. death). *Arcades ambo* ('Arcadians both') was used by Virgil of 2 shepherd-poets, but is now quoted with the meaning given it by Byron – 'blackguards both'.

Arc de Triomphe (Paris) Triumphal arch in the centre of the ÉTOILE, planned by Napoleon but not finished until 1836. It bears huge sculptures depicting the triumphs of Napoleon. The Tomb of the Unknown Warrior now lies under it. There is another Arc de Triomphe (1808) by the Louvre.

Archangels In the apocryphal Book of Enoch 21 there are 7, including Michael and Gabriel (who are also mentioned as chief angels in the Koran), and Raphael. See also PRINCIPALITIES.

Archduke **Trio, The** (1811). Beethoven's piano trio (No. 7), dedicated to Archduke Rudolph of Austria, his patron.

Archer-Shee case See WINSLOW BOY.

Archers, The (1951). BBC radio serial. The everyday story of a Midlands farming family living at 'Ambridge', it has twin functions: relaying up-to-the-minute information and instruction fed to it by the NFU, and reminding city-dwellers of what country life is like.

Archibald Bell-the-cat Archibald Douglas, a 16th-century Earl of Angus who, when his fellow nobles agreed that James III of Scotland's favourites should be put to death, undertook to do this, and in the presence of the King. (From an old fable of mice agreeing that a bell should be hung round a cat's neck to give them warning of its approach: a wise mouse asked: But *who* will bell the cat?)

Archimedean screw Spiral device for raising water through a tube. (See next entry.)

Archimedes, Principle of Loss of weight of a body immersed in water is equivalent to the weight of the water it displaces. (Archimedes, Greek mathematician of the 3rd century BC; pronounced ark-i-mee'deez.)

Archpoet Mythical leader of the Goliards of 12th–13th century Europe who wrote light satiric Latin verse. To him was attributed the famous medieval drinking song: 'Meum est propositium in taberna mori' ('It is my firm intention to die in a tavern').

archy and mehitabel (1927). Book of ingenious blank verse by the US journalist Don Marquis. It was allegedly composed at night on Marquis's typewriter by a cockroach (archy) who could not reach the shift-key (hence there are no capital letters). Archy recounts the adventures of mehitabel the cat, whose battle-cry was '*tourjours gai*, archy, *toujours gai*'. There were several sequels.

Arcos raid (1927). Police raid ordered by the British Home Secretary, Joynson-Hicks, on the Soviet trade mission in London thought to be engaged in subversive activities: Russia severed all relations with Britain.

Arctic Current Alternative name for the LABRADOR CURRENT.

Arcturus Brightest star in BOÖTES and the second brightest in the northern sky. (Greek, 'bearguard', as found at the tail of the Great Bear; in the Bible it is the Pole Star.)

Ardabil carpet (1540). One of the most famous antique rugs, now in the Victoria and Albert Museum, London. It was made for a mosque at Ardabil in northern Persia.

Ardagh Chalice Unique Celtic Christian silver chalice, possibly of the 9th century, decorated with enamel, mica, glass and amber; now in the National Museum, Dublin. (Village in Co. Limerick, Ireland, where found; pronounced ard'è.)

Arden, Forest of Forest covering the English Midlands long ago, the remnants of which account for the name 'leafy Warwickshire'; chiefly remembered as the setting of Shakespeare's AS YOU LIKE IT.

Ardennes Offensive (December 1944 to January 1945). Von Rundstedt's sudden counter-attack in the Ardennes, which took the Allies by surprise, creating a large salient and coming near to success. Also called the Battle of the Bulge.

Arden Shakespeare, The Standard annotated edition of Shakespeare's works, one volume for each play.

Areopagitica (1644). Milton's famous attack on a new law imposing censorship of books. (Pronounced ar-i-op-è-jit'i-ka.)

Areopagus Hill in Athens near the Acropolis, in ancient times the seat of a judicial council which also had administrative functions; called Mars' Hill in Acts 17:22. (Pronounced ar-i-op'a-gus.)

Ares Greek god of war (Roman Mars), a son of ZEUS and HERA. He was remarkably unsuccessful in his own wars and the Greeks liked to make fun of him (see APHRODITE). (Pronounced air'eez.)

Arethusa (Greek legend) A NEREID whom ARTEMIS changed into a spring in Sicily so that she could escape from the river-god Alpheus. (Pronounced ar-i-thew'za.)

Argenteuil (1) Finest French asparagus; (2) garnished with this.

Argive Of Argos, a town and kingdom of southern Greece. As Agamemnon, its king, was leader of the Greeks at Troy, Homer used the word as a synonym for Greek. (Pronounced ar'gyv.)

Argo Ship of the ARGONAUTS.

Argonauts (Greek legend) JASON and his companions, who included HERCULES, THESEUS, ORPHEUS and many other well-known heroes. They sailed in the *Argo* to capture the GOLDEN FLEECE, and MEDEA helped Jason to accomplish this task. (Pronounced ar'go-nawts.)

Argos See ARGIVE.

Argus (Greek legend) Hundred-eyed giant sent by HERA to watch IO, and slain by HERMES on behalf of ZEUS; hence *Argus-eyed*, vigilant.

Ariadne (Greek legend) The daughter of King MINOS who gave THESEUS a ball of thread to help him to find his way back out of the Labyrinth (see MINOTAUR). They escaped together but Theseus later deserted her and she married DIONYSUS.

Arian heresy that Jesus was of similar, but not of the same, substance as the Father, nor co-eternal with him; it was condemned by the Council of NICAEA. The UNITARIANS hold similar views. (Arius, Alexandrian priest, 256–336.)

Ariel (1) Angel, in Cabbalistic literature. (2) Rebel angel in *Paradise Lost*. (3) Fairy in Shakespeare's *Tempest* whom PROSPERO rescued from CALIBAN's victimization.

Ariel (1923). André Maurois's imaginative biography of Shelley.

Aries Ram, 1st of the constellations of the Zodiac, between Pisces and Taurus; the sun enters it at the spring equinox about 21 March. Astrologers claim that those born under this sign may be outspoken and aggressive. (Pronounced air'eez.)

Aristotelian method A priori reasoning, from general to particular; see NOVUM ORGANUM.

Arita ware Japanese ceramics; see IMARI PATTERN.

Ark of the Covenant Wooden chest carried by the Israelites in their wanderings (Num. 10:33), symbolizing Jehovah's presence and containing the tablets of the law.

Arlberg-Kandahar (1928). One of the events in Alpine (downhill and slalom racing) skiing, held

25

at various centres in the Alps. (First held at St Anton in Arlberg: named after Lord Roberts of Kandahar.)

Arles Ancient Roman town in Provence, associated particularly with the painter Van Gogh, who went there in 1888 and was joined there for a brief unhappy period by Gauguin.

Arlésienne (Cooking) With tomatoes, onion and, sometimes, aubergine. (Arles, in Provence.)

Arlésienne, L' (1872). Bizet's incidental music for Daudet's play of hopeless love and tragic death. (French, 'the woman of Arles'.)

Arlington National Cemetery (1864). Site in Virginia facing Washington across the river, on the estate which once belonged to Robert E. Lee and then to Washington's adopted son, where US soldiers from every war, including a few from the Revolution, lie buried. The chief features are vast rows of plain gravestones in the Fields of the Dead, the Tomb of the UNKNOWN SOLDIER.

Armada, The (1588). Spanish fleet which sailed to invade England and was defeated by Lord Howard of Effingham and his captains, Drake, Hawkins and Frobisher; the surviving ships were wrecked while trying to get home via the north of Scotland.

Armageddon Last battle of the kings of the earth before the end of the world; name often applied to World War I. (Rev. 16:16.)

Armagnac Darker, more pungent brandy than cognac, made in the Gers *département* of Gascony.

Armenia Originally a large region on the borders of Turkey, Persia and Russia, inhabited by Christian peoples of very mixed origin who nevertheless preserved a sense of racial solidarity akin to that of the Jews, and were persecuted for it (see next entry). The name Armenia is now only used of the small Armenian republic of the USSR.

Armenian massacres (1896). Worst of several massacres to which the Armenians have been subjected. They began in Constantinople after Armenian nationalists, as a demonstration to

world opinion, had seized the Ottoman Bank, and they spread to the provinces, lasting till the end of the year. There were other such massacres in Turkey in 1909 and 1915.

Armeria Genus name of the thrifts.

Armistice Day 11 November (1918), i.e. the last day of World War I; in the USA now called Veterans' Day.

Armorica Name of Brittany before the Celts from south-west England took refuge there in the 4th century AD. See BRETON.

Armoricaine (Cooking) With a white wine sauce, peppers, tomatoes and brandy. See previous entry.

Arms and the Man Bernard Shaw's play satirizing heroics about war. See also CHOCOLATE SOLDIER. (Title taken from the first words of Virgil's *Aeneid*: 'Arms and the man I sing . . .')

Army Cadet Force (1942). British Army's voluntary youth organization for boys aged 14–18 likely to be interested in an army career. Unlike the COMBINED CADET FORCE, it is organized on a local basis and not by schools.

Arnhem (September 1944). Dutch town on the Rhine where Gen. Montgomery tried unsuccessfully to establish a bridgehead across the river by a major parachute drop in World War II.

Arnolfini Marriage, The (1434). Jan Van Eyck's painting of a wedding ceremony, in which the artist is seen reflected in a mirror; now in the London National Gallery.

Arsenal Football team, formerly known as Woolwich Arsenal, who now play at the Arsenal Stadium in Highbury, north London. They are nicknamed the Gunners.

Art deco Name popularized by Bevis Hillier (1968) for the artistic styles of the 1920s and 1930s, evolved in reaction against ART NOUVEAU and inspired by the finds of TUTANKHAMEN'S TOMB and AZTEC art as well as by the Russian Ballet, the BAUHAUS and other sources of novelty; marked by strong colours, crisp lines, highly stylized flowers, etc.

Artemis Greek huntress-goddess, who became identified with the Asian mother-goddess (see DIANA OF THE EPHESIANS) and later with SELENE). (Pronounced art'em-is.)

Artful Dodger, The Young pickpocket trained by FAGIN in Dickens's OLIVER TWIST.

Arthropods Very large phylum of creatures with hard bodies and jointed limbs, including the Insecta, with 3 pairs of legs (HEMIPTERA, DIPTERA, LEPIDOPTERA, COLEOPTERA, HYMENOPTERA, ORTHOPTERA); the arachnids, with 4 pairs of legs (spiders, scorpions, mites); crustaceans, with many pairs of legs and mostly aquatic (crabs, lobsters, prawns, barnacles, wood-lice); centipedes and millipedes, among many others.

Arthur (1) Historically, perhaps a West Country chieftain and leader of the Romanized Britons in one of their last stands against Anglo-Saxon invaders in the 6th century; (2) in legend, the chivalrous king of all England, leader of the Knights of the ROUND TABLE. See next entry.

Arthurian legend Collection of stories about King ARTHUR and his knights, first mentioned some 300 years after his death; it absorbed other originally unconnected folk-tales and was transformed by medieval Church chroniclers and court bards in England and France, and by later poets.

Articles of Confederation (1781-9). Constitution of the 13 American colonies, replaced by the CONSTITUTION OF THE UNITED STATES.

Artiodactyla Order of 2-toed (cloven-hoofed) or 4-toed hoofed mammals, including sheep, goats, cattle, pigs, antelopes, camels, hippopotami, giraffes.

Artist's Mother, The Whistler's portrait of his aged mother; now in the Musée d' Orsay, Paris.

Artists' Rifles (1859). Territorial unit of which the painter Lord Leighton was the first Colonel.

Art nouveau (1890-1910). Style mainly of interior decoration, with long curves and writhing asymmetrical shapes inspired by vegetational forms, regarded with abhorrence until recently but now again being collected, ugly though most of it is, especially when rendered in cast iron. In Germany called Jugendstil after a magazine *Jugend*. (Named after a shop opened in Paris in 1895.)

Arts Club (1863). London club in Dover Street, originally founded for those interested in the arts, literature and science.

Arts Council of Great Britain (1946). Body partly subsidized by government which aims to develop a greater knowledge, understanding and practice of the fine arts (including drama, music and the visual arts), to increase their accessibility to the people as a whole, and to improve their standards.

Arum lily White lily especially associated with Easter; now classed in the genus Zantedeschia. *Arum maculatum* is the species name of lords and ladies or cuckoo-pint.

Arundel Castle Ancient Sussex castle rebuilt in the 18th century, the seat of the Dukes of Norfolk.

Aryan myth, The View, adopted by the German Nazis from Houston Stewart Chamberlain and others, that the Germans were the purest ('NORDIC') descendants of the ancient and noble ARYANS, and therefore entitled to massacre those who were not, such as Jews and Slavs, to preserve their racial purity. In Nazi jargon 'Aryan' was used of a German who (unlike Hitler) had no Jewish blood in his pedigree.

Aryans Term once used for the peoples who spoke INDO-EUROPEAN LANGUAGES'. It fell into disrepute, especially after Nazi misuse of it (see previous entry), but is still convenient in distinguishing between the pre-Aryan, Aryan and non-Aryan peoples of India. (Sanskrit *arya*, 'noble'.)

Arya Samaj (1875). Hindu religious reformist movement, founded in Gujarat, which renounces idol worship and endeavours to reconcile Hinduism with modern science.

Ascendancy, The Anglo-Irish Protestants who dominated Ireland, especially after the Protestant succession of William III.

Ascension Day Holy Thursday, the 40th day after the Resurrection, on which the Ascension of Christ is commemorated.

Ascent of F6, The (1936). W. H. Auden and Christopher Isherwood's verse play satirizing modern values.

Asclepius See AESCULAPIUS.

Ascot Gold Cup (1807). Chief event of GOLD CUP DAY at ROYAL ASCOT, a race over a distance of $2\frac{1}{2}$ miles. The original cup was stolen in 1907.

ASEAN (1968). Initials used for Association of South-East Asian Nations: Philippines, Indonesia, Thailand, Malaysia, Singapore. It is a regional organization and the main objectives are to accelerate economic growth, social progress and cultural development.

Asgard Scandinavian Olympus, at the centre of the universe; VALHALLA is one region of it.

Ashanti Wars (1807–1900). Four British expeditions against the Ashanti people of the northern Gold Coast (Ghana), which ended in the annexation of their country.

'A' shares Shares in a company that give the holder no voting rights; now in disfavour, they are often converted into ordinary voting shares.

Ashburton glass Glass fashioned in perhaps the earliest of general press-glass patterns, a form of moulding in large curvate thumbprint panels. This pattern, at the turn of the century, was often called Colonial.

Ashburton Shield (1861). Schools challenge shield for rifle-shooting held at BISLEY for teams of 8.

Ashcan School Nickname of an early-20th-century group of American Realist painters led by Robert Henri (1865–1929), sometimes called the Henri Group, and originally 'the Eight'. The nickname derived from their preoccupation with slum scenes, especially in the case of George Bellows, one of the best-known members. Another, George Luks, specialized in child studies. See SOCIAL REALISM.

Ashdown Traditional site, west of Lambourne, Berkshire, of the defeat of the Danes in 871 by King Ethelred and the future King Alfred.

Ashenden (1928). One of Somerset Maugham's novels, based on his experiences in the secret service in World War I. Ashenden reappears in CAKES AND ALE.

Ashes, The Symbol of victory in England *v.* Australia Test cricket series. When in 1882 Australia won, the *Sporting Chronicle* published an obituary on English cricket, adding 'the remains will be cremated and the ashes taken to Australia'. The ashes of a cricket stump in an urn were given to the English team when it won the next year.

Ashkenazim Jews of northern and central European descent, especially Germany and Poland. Until the second half of this century their common language was Yiddish. In Israel, although less numerous than the SEPHARDIM, they dominate politics and the economy. (Ashkenaz, Gen. 10:3 and Jer. 51:27; pronounced ash-kin-ahz'im.)

Ashmolean Oxford University museum and library of ancient history, the fine arts and archaeology, housed in separate buildings, the Old (1683) and New (1897). (Founded by Elias Ashmole; pronounced ash-mohl'yèn.)

Ashridge Country house in a beechwood park in the Chilterns, near Berkhamsted, now a residential college specializing in management training.

Ash Wednesday First day of Lent. (From the custom of sprinkling penitents with ashes on that day.)

Ash Wednesday (1930). T. S. Eliot's first poem after he became an Anglo-Catholic, and the first to speak of the consolation and joy to be found in Christianity.

Asian flu (1957–8). World epidemic of influenza, milder in type than the SPANISH FLU of 1918; it originated in China.

Asiento, The (1713). A 30-year contract made at the end of the War of the SPANISH SUCCESSION whereby Britain was to ship a specified number of slaves to Spanish America. (Spanish, 'contract'.)

Aslef Initials standing for the railway trade union, the Associated Society of Locomotive Engineers and Firemen, consisting mainly of drivers, a rival of the NUR.

Aslib (1924). Official name, abbreviated from Association of Special Libraries and Information Bureaux, of a London organization which helps to locate elusive documents and unpublished translations of technical papers, advises on planning libraries or information services, offers to do research on any subject in any depth, holds conferences and training courses, and publishes various directories and periodicals.

Asmodeus Devil in the Talmud and the Apocrypha, possibly derived from Persian mythology. His speciality was killing bridegrooms on their wedding day. (Pronounced as-moh'di-us; in *Paradise Lost* as-moh-dee'us.)

Aspasia Cultured mistress of the Athenian statesman Pericles; hence applied to any highly educated courtesan.

Asphalt jungle Colloquial term for a big city or a specified part of one.

Asquithian Liberals Those who remained loyal to Asquith after Lloyd George overthrew him in 1916 to form a coalition government with the Conservatives.

Assassins Persian Muslim secret sect of fanatics founded by the OLD MAN OF THE MOUNTAIN; its members, drugged with hashish, carried out widespread assassinations not only of Crusaders but of the leaders of rival Muslim sects. (Arabic, 'hashish-eaters'.)

Assassins Oxford University club of those who have fought for the university in 3 fencing matches.

Assizes Courts which, until 1972 (see COURTS ACT), were held in one town per county at least 3 times a year by High Court judges on circuit. The Assize towns were chosen in the 13th century; many are now unimportant but judges still had to visit them. The whole system was marked by pageantry, inefficiency and delay.

Associated Examining Board (AEB) One of the 8 boards setting papers for the GCE and GCSE examinations.

Assumption, The Bodily Dogma of the physical transfer to heaven of the Virgin Mary, proclaimed an article of Catholic faith (1950), and celebrated at the Feast of the Assumption on 15 August.

Assyria Originally a city-state of SUMER, became Babylon's chief rival; from the 9th century BC it came to dominate Mesopotamia, and conquered Syria, Palestine and Egypt. Assyrian rule ended when the Medes and Babylonians destroyed the capital, Nineveh, in 612 BC.

Astbury ware Label for a type of glazed earthenware made in Staffordshire from about 1730, some of it by John Astbury, of whom little is known. Typically it was a red (sometimes white or brown) clay covered with a yellowish transparent lead glaze, used to make quaintly naïve figures of pop-eyed musicians, horsemen and the delightful 'pew groups'. Models with coloured glazes are sometimes classified as Astbury-WHIELDON.

Astérix le Gaulois (1959). French cartoonist's creation, of international fame; a fiery little man with a drooping moustache who, with his pugnacious companion Obélix, lives in the village of Petitbonum, which alone of all 3 parts of Gaul has held out against the Roman conqueror.

Asti Spumante Sparkling Italian wine produced at Asti, Piedmont; there are also still wines of Asti, less famous.

Astrophel Name, based on an elaborate Greek pun, for the Elizabethan poet Sir Philip Sidney, used in poetry by him and about him.

Asturias, The Old province on the Biscayan coast of Spain; the heir to the throne is called the Prince of the Asturias. This region, the modern Oviedo, is noted for its coal and anthracite mines, and for unrest among the miners.

Aswan High Dam Dam a few miles upstream from the Aswan Dam, opened in 1902 at the First Cataract of the Nile near the Sudan border. The planned height is 350 ft to impound a lake 300 miles long, providing water for irrigation and hydro-electricity. Withdrawal in 1956 of an Anglo-American offer of finance led to the SUEZ CRISIS and the advent of Russian finance and technicians, who began the 10-year task of construction in 1960.

As You Like It (about 1600). Shakespeare's comedy of an exiled duke living in the Forest of ARDEN with his daughter Rosalind, who is disguised as a boy. Other characters are TOUCH-STONE and the 'melancholy' JAQUES.

At Colloquial abbreviation for a member of the ATS.

Atalanta In Greek legend a swift-footed girl of Arcadia who would only marry the man who could outrun her. Aphrodite gave one suitor, Melanion, 3 golden apples to drop on the course. Atalanta stopped to pick them up, and he won the race and her. See also CALYDONIAN BOAR.

Atalanta in Calydon (1865). Swinburne's dramatic poem in which he weds Romantic atheism to classical Greek tragedy in a version of the legend of Atalanta and the Calydonian boar-hunt. See previous entry.

Atalide, Princess See BAJAZET.

AT & T (1885). American Telephone & Telegraph Co., originally a subsidiary of the old American Bell Co., which it took over in 1900. It runs the Bell system; has many subsidiaries, e.g. Western Electric (which makes its equipment) and the Bell Telephone Laboratories; developed the GEMINI program, TELSTAR and early-warning systems; and is one of the 30 industrials that make up the DOW JONES Industrial Average.

Atatürk Name given to Mustapha Kemal in 1934 after he had become dictator of the new Turkey. (Turkish, 'father of the Turks'; pronounced at'a-térk.)

Ate Greek goddess of discord, retribution and hate. (Pronounced ah'tee.)

Aten Solar Disc god whom AKHENATEN tried unsuccessfully to establish as the sole god of ancient Egypt.

Athalie (1691). Racine's play about Athaliah, daughter of Ahab and Jezebel and wife of the King of Judah. She killed all the house of David except one, who survived to become king and take his revenge (2 Kgs 11).

Athanasian Creed Hymn on the Trinity incorporating the views of Athanasius (died 373) but not earlier than the 5th century, possibly much later. It stresses that the 3 Persons of the TRINITY are co-equal and co-eternal.

Athenaeum Club (1824). London club in Waterloo Place with a learned and distinguished membership of scientists, civil servants, bishops, vice-chancellors, professors, etc. Its particular cachet is summed up in the old story of its hall porter venturing the opinion that 2 of the 3 taxis which a departing member claimed to see were 'purely subjective phenomena'.

Athene Patron goddess of Athens, to whom the PARTHENON was dedicated. She sprang fully armed from the head of Zeus, and was the Greek goddess of war, wisdom, arts and crafts; frequently called PALLAS Athene. *Athene* is the Homeric spelling, Athena the later local Athenian form. The Roman equivalent is Minerva. (Pronounced a-thee'nee.)

Athens of the North, The Name for Edinburgh.

Athinganoi Byzantine name for Gypsies, from which are derived their names in German (Zigeuner), Italian (Zingari) and Spanish (Gitanos). (Greek, 'untouchables'.)

Athos, Porthos and Aramis The THREE MUSK-ETEERS.

Atlantic, Battle of the Campaign waged by the Royal Navy, Coastal Command and the Merchant Navy throughout World War II against German sea and air forces in the Atlantic.

Atlantic Charter (August 1941). Declaration of long-term aims issued by Churchill and Roosevelt (President of a still-neutral state) after their conference at sea off Newfoundland, affirming belief in self-determination, freer trade, freedom of the seas, and disarmament 'after the final destruction of the Nazi tyranny'.

Atlantic College (1962). Coeducational school at St Donat's Castle, near Cardiff, first of a projected series of international colleges giving a 2-year pre-university course. The ultimate aim is that anyone who passes out of an Atlantic College can enter any university of any country participating in the scheme, which was conceived by Kurt Hahn of GORDONSTOUN and the OUTWARD BOUND SCHOOLS.

Atlantic Community The states in membership of NATO.

Atlantic Monthly (1857). Distinguished US magazine published in Boston, Massachusetts, with articles on literature, politics, science and art, as well as short stories from new writers.

Atlantic Wall Coastal defence of France built by the Germans during their occupation (1940–45).

Atlantis Land submerged by the sea about 9500 BC according to a legend recorded by Plato, who attributed it to Solon (6th century BC) and ultimately to Egyptian sources; Plato assumed that it lay in the Atlantic beyond the Pillars of Hercules. See THIRA.

Atlas In Greek legend a Titan condemned to stand on the Atlas Mountains in North Africa and hold up the heavens; Atlantic and ATLANTIS are derived from his name. Mercator used the figure of Atlas with the world on his back as an emblem on his volumes of maps.

Atomic Energy Authority (1954). Body which controls nuclear research and development in Britain; see ALDERMASTON; CULHAM LABORATORY; HARWELL; RISLEY.

Atomic Energy Commission (1) UN body set up (1946–52) to consider measures for the international control of the production of nuclear energy. While the USSR wanted stockpiles destroyed before control was instituted, the USA wanted control first. It was replaced by the DISARMAMENT COMMISSION. (2) US body to supervise the nuclear energy programme in the USA. It also monitors nuclear tests abroad.

Atomic Weapons Research Establishment See ALDERMASTON.

Atoms for Peace Programme of international co-operation in the development of nuclear power for peaceful uses, launched by President Eisenhower (1953), implemented by the establishment of the INTERNATIONAL ATOMIC ENERGY AGENCY.

Atonement, Day of See YOM KIPPUR.

Atreus, House of Family (in Greek the Atreidae, sons of Atreus) that includes many of the most familiar figures of Greek tragedy. Thyestes placed an effective curse on it after his brother Atreus had induced him unwittingly to eat a stew made from his own sons' flesh; this crime was not expiated until the time of ORESTES, AGAMEMNON'S son. (Pronounced ay'trews.)

Atropos One of the 3 FATES. (Pronounced at'-rop-os.)

ATS (1938). Initials of the Auxiliary Territorial Service which replaced the WAAC (Women's Army Auxiliary Corps) of World War I and was replaced in 1949 by the WRAC (Women's Royal Army Corps).

At Swim-Two-Birds (1939). A novel by Flann O'Brien, strongly influenced by James Joyce. The less incomprehensible parts are uproariously funny.

Attic Greek Ancient Athenian dialect, used by most of the great Greek writers; on the analogy of 'Standard English', it might be called Standard Ancient Greek. (Athens was the capital of Attica.)

Attic salt Delicate wit characteristic of the Ancient Athenians. (In Latin, *sal* meant both 'salt' and 'wit'.)

Atticus Friend to whom Cicero wrote many letters, which were collected and published; also used by Pope as a pseudonym for Addison. (T. Pomponius, surnamed Atticus because of his long sojourn in Athens; see ATTIC GREEK.)

Attis Phrygian God of the spring, who was driven mad by the jealous CYBELE, and castrated himself.

Attorney-General See LAW OFFICERS OF THE CROWN.

Aubrey's Brief Lives Delightful short biographical notes on the leading figures of Tudor and Jacobean times, liberally spiced with gossip and anecdotes, written by John Aubrey (1690) but not published under his name until 1813.

Aubusson carpets French carpets of supreme quality in the 18th century, made at Aubusson where, traditionally, tapestry was made from the 8th century, and Savonnerie carpets and GOBELINS and Beauvais tapestries are woven on hand-looms to this day, also at Felletin near by. (Town in central France, east of Limoges.)

Auchinleck James Boswell's family estate in Ayrshire. (In his day pronounced af'lek.)

Audley End House Jacobean palace built near Saffron Walden, Essex, by the 1st Earl of Suffolk, and now owned by English Heritage.

Audubon prints Colour prints of American birds and animals made from excellent paintings by J. J. Audubon, American ornithologist and artist (1785–1851), who was born of French and Creole parents. (Pronounced awd'é-bon.)

Aufklärung ENLIGHTENMENT in Germany.

Augean stables In Greek legend the stables where Augeas, King of Elis, had kept 3,000 oxen for 30 years. It was one of Heracles' labours to cleanse them. (Pronounced aw-jee'an.)

Augsburg, League of (1685). Secret alliance of Holland, Spain, Sweden, the Empire and the Papacy, to prevent Louis XIV from gaining control of the Spanish Empire; joined by England in 1689. See next entry.

Augsburg, War of the League of (1689–97). War (see previous entry) which, after destroying French sea power, ended in the Treaty of Ryswick, by which France gave up its earlier conquests, and (temporarily) recognized William III as King of England.

Augsburg Confession (1530). Declaration of Protestant tenets drawn up by Luther and presented to the Emperor Charles V at the Diet of Augsburg. It is still accepted as authoritative by the LUTHERAN CHURCH.

Augustan Age (1) Golden age of Latin literature when Virgil, Horace and Ovid flourished, corresponding with the era of Augustus (27 BC to AD 14). (2) Golden age of English literature variously defined as that of Pope, Addison and Swift (and Queen Anne) or extended to include the earlier Dryden. (3) In France the era of Racine, Corneille and Molière.

Auguste Professional term for a circus clown of the silent, baggy-trousered buffoon type who gets in everyone's way. (The clown proper is a dignified white-faced figure in a conical hat.)

Augustinians Name covering various religious communities which followed the Rule of St Augustine of Hippo (not a formal Rule, but one compiled from his writings), such as the AUSTIN CANONS and AUSTIN FRIARS.

Augustus See OCTAVIAN.

Auk, The Nickname of Field Marshal Sir Claude Auchinleck, British Commander-in-Chief in India and in the Middle East during World War II.

Auld Alliance, The Name given to the traditional defensive alliance of Scotland and France against England, dating from the 13th century and still a force during the Jacobite rebellions. The royal families often intermarried, and French influences on Scottish language, law and customs still survive.

'Auld Lang Syne' Scottish song of uncertain origin, partly rewritten by Robert Burns, and beginning: 'Should auld acquaintance be forgot, / And never brought to mind?' (*Syne*, 'since'; auld lang syne, 'times of long ago'; pronounced syn, not zyn.)

Auld Reekie Scottish nickname for Edinburgh, meaning 'Old Smoky'.

Auld Robin Gray (1771). Scottish ballad written by Lady Anne Lindsay about her father's cowherd, set to a traditional air.

Aunt Edna plays Plays for people who go to the theatre to be entertained, to get away from the kitchen sink rather than to have their noses rubbed in it. (Phrase coined by Terence Rattigan.)

Aunt Sally Any person who is targeted for insults or criticism. She was a figure at fair grounds as a target for balls or other missiles.

Auriga Northern constellation between PERSEUS and GEMINI also called the Wagoner (as is BOÖTES). Alpha-Aurigae is Capella, the 5th brightest star. (Latin, 'charioteer'; pronounced awr-y'ga.)

Aurignacian culture Phase of the PALAEOLITHIC AGE, perhaps lasting from 70,000 to 18,000 BC, during which CRO-MAGNON MAN appeared in a comparatively warm interglacial period, and began to produce the remarkable cave paintings of ALTAMIRA and elsewhere. (Aurignac rock shelter in the Pyrenees, France.)

Aurora Latin name for the goddess of dawn (Greek EOS).

Aurora Borealis Vivid glow in the northern night sky, predominantly greenish yellow, often seen in high latitudes and sometimes much further south, particularly when sunspot activity is at its maximum. It is caused by charged solar particles attracted to the magnetic pole meeting the atmosphere at heights of 60–500 miles, but the process is not fully understood. The corresponding Antarctic phenomenon is called the Aurora Australis.

Aurora Leigh (1857). Elizabeth Browning's rather pedestrian blank-verse novel. When Mrs Browning died, Edward Fitzgerald commented 'No more Aurora Leighs, thank God!' and got trounced by Browning in a vituperative poem.

Aurora's Wedding A one-act ballet originally performed as the third act of *The Sleeping Beauty*, a ballet by Petipa.

Aurore (Cooking) With a thick tomato sauce. (Named from the resultant colour.)

Auschwitz (1939). Site near Katowice, Poland, of the first Nazi concentration camp to be equipped with gas chambers. (German form of Polish name Oświęcim.)

Ausgleich (1867). See DUAL MONARCHY.

Austerlitz (December 1805). Battle in which Napoleon defeated the Austrians and Russians and brought the HOLY ROMAN EMPIRE to an end. See THIRD COALITION. (Now Slavkov, Czechoslovakia, east of Brno.)

Austin Herbert Austin's car firm which made the famous Austin-20 and BABY AUSTIN, and under Len Lord took over MORRIS (1952). The name was retained in e.g. British Leyland's Austin Maxi and the Austin–Healey sports cars.

Austin Canons (12th century). Religious order of clergy following the Rule of St Augustine (see AUGUSTINIANS). They were not monks, but clergy living in communities though performing normal pastoral duties. Also called Augustinian Canons, Black Canons, and Canons Regular.

Austin Friars (13th century). Order of mendicant friars (originally hermits) who followed the Rule of St Augustine (see AUGUSTINIANS). Several communities still exist, especially in Ireland.

Australasia Australia, New Zealand and the islands of the south-west Pacific.

Australian over (Cricket) An 8-ball over.

Australopithecines ('southern apes') PLIOCENE apes living in South and East Africa from about 3 million years ago; the earliest to walk upright, and therefore classed as hominids (man-like). The earliest fossil specimen is thought to be an arm-bone found in Kenya by the US Professor Patterson of Harvard; it was announced in 1967 that this was $2\frac{1}{2}$ million years old.

Austrian Netherlands Southern NETHERLANDS (equivalent to modern Belgium) under the Austrian Hapsburgs from the Treaty of UTRECHT (1713) until Napoleon's time (1806).

Austrian Succession, War of the (1740–48). War precipitated by Frederick the Great's seizure of Austrian Silesia after Maria Theresa's succession under the PRAGMATIC SANCTION. France joined in the attack on Austria but was defeated at Dettingen by the Austrians, Hanoverians and English under George II; the position was reversed 2 years later at Fontenoy. Under the inconclusive Treaty of Aix-la-Chapelle Prussia retained Silesia.

Auteuil Paris racecourse adjoining the LONG-CHAMP course in the Bois de Boulogne.

Authentics Oxford University cricket club of the 60 best players in residence (elected for life); it has no ground of its own and mostly plays against schools.

Authorized Version (1611). English Bible published by command of King James I and still in general use; largely based on TYNDALE'S BIBLE.

Autobiography of a Super-Tramp (1908). Account by the Welsh poet W. H. Davies of his life as a hobo in America.

Autocrat of the Breakfast Table, The (1858). First of Oliver Wendell Holmes's series of 'Breakfast Table' collections of essays, in which he represents himself as expatiating on a wide range of themes to a largely silent company gathered at his table.

Autograss Speed event for saloon cars on a grass or unsealed surface.

Autolycus (1) In Greek legend a crafty thief, son of Mercury. (2) In Shakespeare's *Winter's Tale* the name of a thieving pedlar, 'a snapper-up of unconsidered trifles'. (Pronounced aw-tol′i-kus.)

Automobile Association (1905). One of the 2 chief British motoring associations. At first uniformed staff patrolled the roads on push-bikes; if they did not salute a car with an AA badge, the motorist would stop and be warned of a police trap ahead. Later, touring, legal aid, car inspection, free breakdown and many other services were developed.

Autostrada del Sole Motorway from Milan to Naples and on to the toe of Italy. (Italian, sunshine motorway.)

Autumn Double Bet on the CESAREWITCH and CAMBRIDGESHIRE horse races, both run in October.

Avalon (Arthurian legend) Island of the Blessed ruled by MORGAN LE FAY; mistakenly identified with GLASTONBURY. (Celtic, 'island of apples'.)

Avare, L' (1668). Molière's comedy of the rich miser Harpagon, whose children get their own way by impounding his money-box.

Avebury Site of one of the world's largest stone circles. There were originally 3 circles, with an outer diameter of a quarter of a mile, and a long avenue of stones leading to a neighbouring 'sanctuary'. (Village near Marlborough, Wiltshire.)

Ave Maria Salutation to the Virgin Mary, combined in the Roman Catholic Church with a prayer to her as Mother of God.

Avenue, Mittelharnis, The (1689). Hobbema's best-known painting, now in the London National Gallery.

Avernus Latin name for the Underworld, of which Virgil said: 'The descent to Avernus is easy, but the return journey – that is the difficulty', a passage applied to the picking-up of evil ways.

Avignonese Captivity (1305–78). Period during which 7 Popes reigned at Avignon, subservient to the King of France, while Italy was in a state of anarchy.

Avogadro's hypothesis (1811). That equal volumes of all gases contain the same conditions of pressure and temperature. (Italian physicist.)

Avro (1910). Aircraft firm founded by Sir A. V. Roe which produced many famous planes before it was absorbed by Hawker-Siddeley in 1936.

Axel Ice-skating jump; the single involves turning $1\frac{1}{2}$ times in the air; the double and treble are among the most difficult and spectacular manoeuvres in free skating. A quadruple has been performed (1988). (Axel Paulsen.)

Axel's Castle (1931). American Edmund Wilson's best-known work of literary criticism, a study of symbolism.

Axis See ROME–BERLIN AXIS.

Axis powers See TRIPARTITE PACT.

Axminster carpets (1) Carpets inspired by Persian models, made at Axminster (1755–1835) and thereafter at Wilton. (2) Trade term for a process of weaving carpets which economizes in materials as all the pile yarn is on the surface, with none hidden in the fabric. Multicoloured patterns are common, there is always a cut-pile surface, and the back is less smooth than in WILTON CARPETS.

Ayatollah Imam or spiritual leader of Moslems in Iran.

Ayers Rock World's largest monolithic outcrop in Northern Territory, Australia; it forms a red mass with a circumference of 10 km rising 335 metres above the plain. Its colours change with the position of the sun and according to atmospheric changes.

Ayesha (1) Favourite wife of Mohammed. (2) Title of a novel (1905) by Rider Haggard, a sequel to SHE (1887). Ayesha ('She') is here an African sorceress. (Pronounced y-yesh'a.)

Aylesbury duck Most popular breed of domestic duck for the table.

Ayot St Lawrence See SHAW'S CORNER. (Pronounced e'et or ay'ét.)

Ayrshire cattle Widespread dairy breed producing milk often used in cheese-making; coloured red, brown and white in varying proportions.

Azad Kashmir 'Free' Kashmir, the north-west part of Kashmir occupied by Pakistan. See KASHMIR DISPUTE.

Azania Preferred name for the Republic of South Africa by some black nationalists.

Azerbaijan Region bordering on the south-west shore of the Caspian Sea, now divided between the USSR constituent republic of that name (capital, Baku) and 2 adjoining Persian provinces: Eastern (capital, Tabriz) and Western Azerbaijan (capital, Rizayeh). (Pronounced az-ėr-by-jahn'.)

Aztecs American Indian race which flourished in Mexico in the 15th century and was conquered by the Spanish in the 16th. They had absorbed the Mayan culture passed on to them by their predecessors, the TOLTECS, exaggerating its feature of human sacrifice to insane extremes.

B

Baader-Meinhof gang (1969). Urban guerrillas, operating in the Federal Republic of Germany. They waged war on society by bank raids, gun battles, bombing police headquarters and US installations, calling themselves the 'Red Army Faction'.

Baalbek Site in Lebanon, 36 miles north-east of Beirut, of an ancient centre of Syrian Baal worship. The Greeks renamed it Heliopolis and the Romans built several temples there, that dedicated to Bacchus (2nd century AD) being one of the largest and best preserved of the Graeco-Roman temples.

Baathists Members of a radical pan-Arab movement, strong in Syria but less so in Iraq, Jordan and elsewhere; standing for democratic freedom. (Arabic, 'revival'.)

Babar the Elephant Chief character in a series of witty children's books written and illustrated by the Frenchman, Jean de Brunhoff (died 1937); they proved immensely popular and were translated into English.

Bab Ballads (1869). Collection of light verse by W. S. Gilbert, of which the best-known is 'The Yarn of the *Nancy Bell*'.

Babbitt (1922). Sinclair Lewis's novel of a parochial estate-agent who tries unsuccessfully to struggle free from the conformities of business life in the small Middle West town of Zenith.

Babel Probably Babylon, but Genesis 11:9 says, 'Babel; because the Lord did there confound the language of all the earth ...' The 'Tower of Babel' is probably a name given to the ziggurat at Babylon.

Babes in the Wood Story which originated from a 16th-century ballad of a man who hires 2 thugs to kill his infant nephew and niece in order to seize their inheritance. One of the thugs kills the other and abandons the children in a wood. They die, the birds cover them with leaves, and the uncle is suitably punished.

Babington's plot (1586). Last of a series of Roman Catholic plots against Elizabeth I, which led to the execution of Mary Queen of Scots.

Babi Yar (1941–3). Ravine outside Kiev where Nazis massacred 150,000 men, women and children, mainly Jews, lining them up on its edge and machine-gunning them; only one, a woman, escaped. This is the theme of a poem by Yevtushenko, a novel by Kuznetsov and Shostakovich's 13th Symphony.

Babu (1) Hindu equivalent of 'Mr'. (2) Used by the British of a Hindu, especially Bengali, clerk whose English had characteristic Indianisms (e.g. 'I am having' for 'I have'). (Pronounced bah'boo.)

Baby Austin (1921). AUSTIN Seven, a 7 h.p. car which was the first small mass-produced car to be made in Britain.

Babycham Perry (pear cider) made by Showerings of Somerset.

Babylonian Captivity (1) Period (586–538 BC) when leading Jewish families were in enforced exile at Babylon, deported there by Nebuchadnez-zar. When the Persian Cyrus took Babylon and freed them, most of them chose to stay (see DIASPORA). Also called the Exile. (2) Another name for the AVIGNONESE CAPTIVITY.

Babylonian Empire (1) First or Old Empire (1900–1600 BC), which flourished under Ham-murabi in the 18th century. (2) New or Chal-dean Empire (625–538 BC), which reached its height under Nebuchadnezzar II, who carried off the Palestinian Jews into captivity in Babylon. It fell to the Persian king, Cyrus the Great.

Bacardi rum (1862). White rum with the fla-vour of the raw spirit filtered out through char-coal and replaced by fruit flavours, wine, etc.

Baccalauréat French equivalent to the GCE or German ABITUR. (French, 'bachelor's degree' but not in the English sense; the equivalent to the English bachelor's degree is the *diplôme*.)

Bacchanalia Roman festival (Greek Dionysia) in honour of BACCHUS, orgiastic, licentious, and drunken.

Bacchants Followers (also called Maenads or Bac-chae) of DIONYSUS (Bacchus), who danced in the mountain forests, and tore animals and human beings to pieces.

Bacchus Roman name of DIONYSUS, taken from one of his Greek epithets (Bakchos).

Bacchus and Ariadne (1514). Titian's painting of Bacchus leaping from his chariot to console ARIADNE, whom Theseus had deserted; now in the London National Gallery.

Backbencher Member of Parliament who does not hold office in the government or opposition and who sits on the back benches of the House.

Backs, The Attractive grounds laid out on either side of the Cam at the backs of Trinity and neighbouring Cambridge colleges.

Back to Methuselah (1922). Cycle of 5 plays by Bernard Shaw in which he returns to the theme of Creative Evolution (see MAN AND SUPER-MAN) and adds the LAMARCKIAN theory of evo-lution through adaptation to environment.

The first play starts in the Garden of Eden and the last ends in the far future, by which time man has by will-power evolved himself into a being almost wholly intellectual and able to live for hundreds of years.

Baconian theory Theory that Francis Bacon wrote Shakespeare's plays; of 18th-century origin, it relied chiefly on the supposition that Shakespeare was too ignorant to have been their author. Ignatius Donnelly, in *The Great Crypto-gram* (1888), 'discovered' that the plays were one vast code message from Bacon to posterity; this he solved by making up a complicated code as he went along, and altering it as convenient.

Bactria Ancient name of a town and district of Persia, now in Afghanistan and named Balkh.

Bad Child's Book of Beasts, A (1896). Illustrated book of light verse by Hilaire Belloc, of which the following is typical: 'I shoot the Hip-popotamus / With bullets made of platinum, / Because if I use leaden ones / His hide is sure to flatten 'em.'

Badger State Nickname of Wisconsin.

Badlands Specifically, a region of western South Dakota and north-west Nebraska, arid, barren and eroded into deep gullies; similar regions else-where.

Badminton Horse Trials (1949). Three-day EVENT including dressage, a speed and endu-rance test over a varied and difficult course of 17 miles, and show-jumping; the rider with the highest total score is the winner. Held in the Duke of Beaufort's park at Badminton, Glou-cestershire, in April, and instituted by him to raise the standards of British horsemanship.

Badminton House Seventeenth-century home of the Dukes of Beaufort, near Chipping Sodbury, Gloucestershire.

Baedeker Name of a series of detailed and auth-oritative tourist guides, using the star system to distinguish points of particular interest, started in the early 19th century. For diligence in re-search, for accuracy and thoroughness in the recording of detail, these travel handbooks have never been equalled, let alone surpassed. (Name of German publishing firm of Leipzig, now moved to Hamburg; pronounced bay'dek.ër.)

Baedeker raids (April 1942). Series of air-raids on the historic towns of Canterbury, York, Bath and Exeter, in retaliation for the bombing of Lübeck, Rostock and Cologne. (Named after the BAEDEKER guides.)

Baha' i faith (1863). International eclectic mystical religion which tries to unite people of all religions and races in a crusade for universal peace; it won many converts among retired British officers. (Persian *baha-ullah*, 'splendour of God', title of the founder, pronounced ba-hah'ee.)

Bahasa Indonesia Modernized form of the Malay language, with Dutch and other loan-words, which has become the lingua franca of Indonesia since World War II.

Baignade, La (1884). Seurat's painting of youngsters bathing and resting on the banks of the Seine at Asnières, in which he tried to combine Impressionist technique with clarity of form in a method known as 'pointillisme'. Now in the Tate Gallery, London.

Baile Átha Cliath Official name of Dublin. (Erse, 'town of the ford of hurdles'; pronounced bay-la-klee'.)

Bailey bridge Type of temporary bridge much used in World War II, made of portable prefabricated interchangeable steel sections. (Sir Donald Bailey, inventor.)

Bailey Cup (1920). British amateur doubles championship at Real Tennis.

Bailey sea area That lying north of the ROCK-ALL, west of the Hebrides, and south-west of the south-east Iceland and Faeroes sea areas.

Baily's Hunting Directory (1897). Annual publication giving full details of hunts of all kinds in all parts of the world.

Bairam Name given to 2 major Muslim festivals: the Lesser Bairam (or Id al-Fitr) at the end of RAMADAN; and the Greater (or Id al-Kabir) 70 days later, when a ram or other animal is

sacrificed at the final ceremony of the pilgrimage at Mecca, and throughout Islam. (Persian and Turkish name, better known to the non-Muslim world than the Arabic forms.)

Bajazet, Bajazeth (1) Ottoman Turkish sultan conquered by TAMBURLAINE (1403), who was fabled to have carried him about in an iron cage; a character in Marlowe's play. (2) In Racine's play (1672) of the name, Bajazet is imprisoned in Constantinople in 1638; he pretends to fall in love with the Sultana Roxane, who plans to put him on her husband's throne until she finds out that his true love is Princess Atalide. The Sultan discovers the plot, executes both of them, and Atalide commits suicide.

Bakelite (1907). Synthetic resin created by Dr Leo Baekeland who succeeded in converting phenol formaldehyde into the first truly synthetic plastic.

Bakerian lecture (1775). Triennial lecture at the Royal Society on natural history or experimental philosophy.

Baker Street Irregulars (1) Gang of street arabs used by Sherlock HOLMES to glean intelligence from London's underworld. (2) Society of Holmes *aficionados* formed in 1934. (3) Also applied to the SOE, which had its headquarters in Baker Street. (In Conan Doyle's stories, the great Holmes had rooms at 22lb Baker Street.)

Bakers, Worshipful Company of (1486). LIVERY COMPANY.

Bakewell Tart Baked tart of breadcrumbs and almond lined with jam. (Bakewell, near Buxton, Derbyshire.)

Bakhtiari rugs Hard-wearing rugs in bold red, blue or cream, with floral decoration divided into small compartments; made by Persian nomads south of Isfahan.

Balaam's Ass Ass on which the prophet Balaam rode when sent by the Moabites to curse the Israelites; the ass stopped in her tracks, having seen the angel of the Lord barring the way (Num. 22:23) and, given the power of speech, reproached her master for beating her; then Balaam saw the angel, and changed his curse to a blessing. (Pronounced bay'lam.)

Balaclava (1854). Battle of the CRIMEAN WAR immortalized in Tennyson's 'CHARGE OF THE LIGHT BRIGADE'. (Town near Sebastopol.)

Balbec Fictitious French coastal resort on the shores of the English Channel, a setting for early scenes in Proust's REMEMBRANCE OF THINGS PAST.

Balcony, The (1957). Jean Genet's play about the habitués of a French brothel who amuse themselves by acting the parts of judge, general and bishop. When a revolution comes they find themselves playing these parts in real life.

Balder (Baldur) 'The beautiful', in Scandinavian mythology son of Odin and Frigg, the sun god whose death, contrived by Loki, led to the GÖTTER-DÄMMERUNG, or Twilight of the Gods.

Balenciaga Paris fashion house.

Balfour, David Hero of R. L. Stevenson's novel KIDNAPPED and its sequel CATRIONA.

Balfour declaration (1917). Promise of British support, provided Arab rights were safeguarded, for a Jewish National Home in Palestine, made by the Foreign Secretary, A. J. Balfour, to Lord Rothschild, a Zionist leader.

Balkan League (1912–13). Alliance of Bulgaria, Serbia, Greece and Montenegro, which declared war on Turkey; see BALKAN WAR, FIRST.

Balkan War, First (October 1912 to May 1913). War fought by the BALKAN LEAGUE to wrest MACEDONIA from Turkey. See next entry.

Balkan War, Second (June–August 1913). War in which Bulgaria turned against all her allies of the BALKAN LEAGUE, who were joined by Romania and even by Turkey. Turkey lost almost all its remaining European territory, Greece gained Salonica, Albania was created, and Serbia and Montenegro divided the rest of the spoils.

Balkh Modern name of BACTRIA.

Ballad of Peckham Rye, The (1960). Witty novel by Muriel Spark in which a mephistophelean Dougal Douglas upsets the lives of all he comes into contact with, against a background of London textile factories.

Ballad of Reading Gaol, The (1898). Oscar Wilde's poem, based on his own experiences in that gaol.

Ballet Rambert (1930). Founded in London by Polish-born (Dame) Marie Rambert and her husband Ashley Dukes, for the presentation of classical ballet; the company toured widely abroad and won a great reputation. It now performs as a modern-dance company.

Ball (Sidney) lecture (1919). Annual lecture at Oxford University on a modern social, economic or political question.

Ballsbridge Venue of the Royal Dublin Horse Show.

Balmain Paris fashion house.

Balmoral Royal castle near Braemar, Aberdeenshire; the estate was bought in 1852 by Queen Victoria, who built a Scottish-baronial type granite castle there among the lonely grouse moors.

Balthazar (1) One of the THREE KINGS, traditionally the King of Chaldea. (2) Measure, the equivalent of 16 bottles of champagne. ('Owner of treasure'; pronounced bal-thaz'ar.)

Baltic, Battle of the See COPENHAGEN.

Baltic, The London market for the chartering of cargo vessels of all nationalities; it also deals with marine insurance, etc. It is in St Mary Axe. (Abbreviation of the Baltic Mercantile and Shipping Exchange, named after the Baltic Coffee House in Threadneedle Street where they first met.)

Balts Letts (Latvians), Lithuanians and the Prussians (before they became Germanized), who for many centuries withstood the onslaughts of the Teutonic Knights (see TANNENBERG) but in the 18th century came mainly under Russian rule.

Baluba Tribe of the Kasai Province which tried to secede from the Congo (now Zaïre) after independence.

Baluchi Inhabitant, and Iranian language, of Baluchistan, formerly a province of India, now in Pakistan. (Pronounced bal-oo'chi.)

Baluchi rugs Attractively primitive Turkoman rugs in sombre red, brown and blue, with a sparing use of white lines on flower heads, and designs of stylized geometrical flowers. They are made by the Baluchi nomads of the Afghanistani-Persian borders and marketed for export at Meshed, north-east Persia. They were not exported until this century.

Balzan Foundation (1956). Italian fund which makes awards of up to £100,000 for work contributing to international progress of world peace, or in the fields of biology, mathematics, music, etc. Recipients include Pope John XXIII, the UN and the Nobel Foundation. The fund is administered by Father Zucca, Mussolini's reputed confessor, imprisoned in 1946 for hiding Mussolini's body and implicated in attempts in 1957 and 1967 to sell forged diaries attributed to Mussolini. Rumours that Father Zucca was connected with the 'treasure of DONGO' were denied (named after the founder, editor of the CORRIERE DELLA SERA; died 1953).

Bambi (1942). Walt Disney cartoon film of the life of a deer.

Bamboo Curtain Barrier between Communist and non-Communist countries in South-East Asia. (On the analogy of IRON CURTAIN.)

Bampton Fair October fair at which a major feature is the sale of Exmoor ponies. (Village north of Tiverton, Devon.)

Bampton lecture Lecture at Oxford University given every other year, alternating with the SARUM LECTURE, 'to confute heretics and schismatics', in the words of the founder.

Banana Republics Derisive name for the banana-producing republics of Central America, especially Honduras, Panama, Guatemala, Costa Rica and Nicaragua; connoting economic dependence on the US United and Standard Fruit Cos., which had a monopoly of the trade, and political dependence on the USA.

Banaras Alternative spelling of BENARES.

Banbury cake Slashed puff pastry filled with currants, spice, mixed peel, etc., oval in shape; made for at least 400 years at Banbury, Oxfordshire. See ECCLES CAKE.

Banbury Cross In the nursery rhyme, the cross destroyed in 1646 by the Puritan bigots for which Banbury was notorious.

B & K Newspaper headline shorthand for Bulganin (Soviet Prime Minister) and Khrushchev (Party Secretary), used during their visit to Britain in 1956.

Band of Hope Temperance society, now named the UK Band of Hope Union, with headquarters in London.

Bandung Conference (1955). Meeting of 29 Afro-Asian states convened by Indonesia; it was steered by the Indian Prime Minister, Nehru, into a policy of non-alignment, i.e. of neutrality as between the Western and Communist blocs, and condemned colonialism in terms that clearly included Russian interference in the term. Chou En-lai stated that China was ready to examine ways of easing tension with USA. (Town of Java.)

Banister Fletcher (1896). Author's name standing for his magnum opus, *A History of Architecture*, a standard work covering the architecture of many civilizations from ancient Egyptian to modern times, and notable for its copious illustrations.

Bank of England (1694). Britain's central bank, nationalized in 1946, which is the note-issuing authority and acts as bankers to government, the commercial banks and to overseas central banks; see THREADNEEDLE STREET.

Bank of International Settlement (1930). Established under the YOUNG PLAN as a means to facilitate German payments of reparations.

Bank Picquet Guard for the Bank of England, provided by the Guards Division.

Bank Rate Tribunal (1958). Tribunal under Lord Justice Parker which found that there was no basis for accusations that there had been improper disclosure about a proposed rise in Bank Rate.

Banksia Greenhouse shrubs named after Sir Joseph Banks (1743–1820), British botanist.

Bannockburn (1314). Battle in which Robert the Bruce decisively defeated Edward II and secured Scottish independence for another 300 years. (Village south of Stirling.)

Banqueting House (1622). Only surviving part of the old Whitehall Palace in London, designed by Inigo Jones; the site of Charles I's execution.

Banquo Fellow-general whose ghost haunts MACBETH in Shakespeare's play. Macbeth had had him murdered because the witches prophesied that his descendants would rule Scotland.

Bantu (1) Term applied to the numerous peoples and languages of Africa south of the Equator, including SWAHILI, the Kikuyu of Kenya, XHOSA, ZULU, the Basuto of LESOTHO and the Barotse. (2) In South Africa, applied by Afrikaners to Africans in distinction from 'Whites', 'Coloureds' and 'Asiatics'. But 'Blacks' is now more common. (Invented name of Bantu type, meaning 'people'.)

Bantustans In South Africa, areas set aside for Africans to run their own affairs in accordance with the apartheid policy of equal but separate opportunities for development for whites and blacks. TRANSKEI was the first. (Coined from Bantu + Pakistan, the latter an example of a state formed for a separate community – the Muslims of India.)

Baptists Protestants who believe in adult baptism (by total immersion) after confession of faith and sins.

Barabbas Rebel who had committed murder and whom the Jews asked Pilate to release in preference to Jesus (Luke 23:18).

Barataria, Isle of Imaginary island of which Sancho Panza is appointed governor in DON QUIXOTE.

Bar at the Folies-Bergères, A (1882). Manet's last major painting, a detailed study of a crowded bar, as seen reflected in a large mirror, in the famous Paris music-hall; the centre of the picture is dominated by a barmaid. Now in the Courtauld Institute Galleries, London.

Barbara Allen (1724). Ballad of a young man dying of love for the cruel Barbara, who taunted him but bitterly repented it when he died.

Barbarians (1890). A rugby football touring club with no ground of its own; players are drawn from the home countries (England, Scotland, Ireland, Wales), France and Commonwealth teams, and are noted for spectacular open football. By tradition they play certain home teams and, since 1948, overseas teams touring Britain, and now also tour abroad.

Barbarossa Nickname of the 12th-century Holy Roman Emperor, Frederick I. (Italian, 'red beard'.)

Barbarossa German code name for the invasion of Russia (1941).

Barbary Pirates Moorish CORSAIRS who plagued Mediterranean shipping from the 16th century until France occupied Algeria in 1830. (Barbary, old name for north-west Africa, inhabited by Berbers.)

Barber of Seville, The (1816). Rossini's opera dealing with the first of Beaumarchais's trilogy of plays, the second of which is the source of the MARRIAGE OF FIGARO. Count Almaviva, with the aid of the barber FIGARO, wins Rosina, ward of the sly Dr Bartolo.

Barber-shop Impromptu unaccompanied vocal harmonizing of popular songs by a male quartet (or any informal group) in the style traditionally associated with barber-shops of yore.

Barbers, Worshipful Company of (1461). LIVERY COMPANY which until 1745 controlled the crafts of barber, surgeon and dentist.

Barbican development (1959). Forty bombed-out acres of the City of London, rebuilt with skyscrapers not only for offices but for residential use, shops and schools. It also contains theatres, concert halls, library, art gallery and restaurants. (Name of a London street on the site of a watch-tower – 'barbican' – in the City walls.)

Barbizon School Colony of French painters who settled in the 1850s outside Paris in the village of Barbizon to paint unromanticized pictures of peasant life and rural landscapes; they included Corot, Millet and Théodore Rousseau.

Barbour Green waxed-cotton weather-proof jacket made by J. Barbour & Sons.

Barchester novels (or **Chronicles of Barsetshire**) Six novels (1855–67) by Anthony Trollope set in the imaginary town of Barchester (based on Salisbury and/or Wells) in 'Barsetshire', exploiting the humours of ecclesiastical intrigue and ambition. The most famous are THE WARDEN, *Barchester Towers* and *The Last Chronicle of Barset*. The many memorable characters are headed by Mrs PROUDIE.

Bar Council Committee of representatives of the Inns of Court, barristers elected by the profession, and the Law Officers of the Crown; nominally the governing body of the profession, it has failed to persuade the BENCHERS to emerge from their medieval fortresses and co-operate in dragging the Bar into the 20th century.

Bardell v. *Pickwick* Fictional breach of promise case in Dickens's *Pickwick Papers*, in which Mrs Bardell is awarded damages against her lodger, Mr Pickwick, who, since he will pay 'not one halfpenny', is consigned to the FLEET PRISON.

Bardolph With PISTOL, a swaggering follower of FALSTAFF in Shakespeare's *Merry Wives* and *Henry IV*, who also appears in *Henry V*; his face is 'all bubukles, knobs . . . and flames o'fire'.

Barebones Parliament (July–December 1653). Little Parliament, of 140 Puritan members elected by INDEPENDENTS, which at Cromwell's suggestion soon dissolved itself after proving its incompetence. (Named after PRAISE-GOD BAREBONES.)

Baring Bros (1763). London merchant bank and acceptance house, which played a major part in developing South America.

Barking London borough since 1965 consisting of the former borough of Barking and part of that of Dagenham; headquarters at Dagenham.

Barkis Carrier in Dickens's *David Copperfield* who conducted a long-range courtship of David's nurse, Clara PEGGOTTY, by sending messages that 'Barkis is willin'.'

Barlow report (1940). Royal Commission report on the geographical distribution of the industrial population. It made recommendations regarding remedial measures for the over-congested cities of London and the North which led to the NEW TOWNS Act of 1946.

Barmecide feast An imaginary feast such as in the *Arabian Nights* a jesting Barmecide prince of Baghdad serves to a beggar, who pretends to enjoy the non-existent food but draws the line at imaginary wine, pretends to get drunk and fells the prince; the latter takes the joke in good part and gives him a real meal.

Bar Mitzvah At age 13 a Jewish boy becomes a man after a synagogue ceremony in which he recites in Hebrew.

Barnaby Bright 11 June (OLD STYLE), St Barnabas's Day, the longest day of the year.

Barnaby Rudge (1841). Dickens's novel set in the times of the GORDON RIOTS, with a lurid plot about Barnaby, a half-wit, and his father, a murderer on the run.

Barnacle Bill the Sailor Polite form of the name of the virile hero in a 19th-century ballad.

Barnardo's (1866). Voluntary organization which runs homes for children in the UK. Founded by Dr Thomas John Barnardo (1845–1905).

Barnes Former borough of Surrey, since 1965 part of the borough of RICHMOND-UPON-THAMES.

Barnet London borough since 1965, consisting of the former boroughs of Finchley and Hendon and the urban districts of East Barnet and Friern Barnet; headquarters at Hendon.

Barnum & Bailey Show American travelling circus, the 'Greatest Show on Earth', developed from P. T. Barnum's circus (started in 1871) by James A. Bailey in the 1890s; notable for sensational sideshows and JUMBO the Elephant.

Barolo One of the best red table wines of PIED-MONT.

Baroque (1620–1720). Exaggeration of the trends in MANNERISM which flourished in the Roman Catholic countries of Italy, Spain, Bavaria and Austria, where it served the purpose of emotional religious propaganda reflecting the spirit of the Counter-Reformation. Painting (Rubens, Caravaggio, Murillo), sculpture (Bernini), architecture (Borromini) were all influenced. In France it took a more sober form. ROCOCO was its final phase. (Portuguese *bar- roco*, 'misshapen pearl'.)

Barotseland Region occupied by the Barotse, cattle-owners and fishermen, now a province of Zambia.

Barrack-room Ballads (1892). Collection of Kipling's verse about British soldiers serving overseas; it includes 'GUNGA DIN', 'Tommy Atkins', 'Mandalay' and 'When 'Omer smote 'is bloomin' lyre'.

Barretts of Wimpole Street, The (1930). Rudolf Besier's play on Robert Browning's struggle to rescue his future wife, Elizabeth Barrett, from the clutches of her possessive and formidable father.

Barsac Sweet white wine, sold under its own name but sometimes classed with the SAUTERNES wines.

Barsetshire See BARCHESTER NOVELS.

Bartered Bride, The (1866). Smetana's opera, based on Czech folk music and dance, about a village girl who rejects an arranged marriage and, in spite of the intrigues of a marriage-broker, is able in the end to marry the man of her choice.

Bartholomew Fair (1133). (1) England's chief cloth fair, held in the priory of St Bartholomew, Smithfield, London, at Bartholomew tide; later it developed into a riotous pleasure-fair, closed in 1840. (2) Title of a play by Ben Jonson (1614).

Bartholomew Massacre See ST BARTHOLOMEW MASSACRE.

Bartimaeus Blind beggar at Jericho whose sight Jesus restored, saying: 'Thy faith hath made thee whole.' (Mark 10:46–52.)

Bartlett pear Large yellow juicy pear widely used by the US canning industry. A variety of the European WILLIAM PEAR, grown also in Australia and South America. (Named after the first US distributor.)

Bartolozzi prints Coloured prints made from plates lightly etched in with dots (stipple engraving), all the colours being on one plate. The subjects included shepherdesses, dandies, children, sentimental mythological scenes, reproductions of paintings by Angelica Kauffmann, and some excellent portraits. Genuine Bartolozzis are rare, fakes plentiful. (Francesco Bartolozzi 1728–1813, Italian settled in London.)

Bart's (1132). Common abbreviation for St Bartholomew's Hospital at Smithfield, London, the oldest in Britain. (Founded by Rahere together with St Bartholomew's Priory, of which only the church remains, near by.)

Baruch (AD 70). Book of the Apocrypha, apparently meant to be used in religious services, containing a form of confession, a sermon on wisdom, and a song of consolation. (Attributed in the text to the Baruch mentioned in Jer. 36:4.)

Baruch plan (1946). Offer by USA to destroy its stock of atomic bombs and the fissionable material for them, provided that an international body was set up to see that no other nation produced such bombs (of which USA then had the monopoly) and to control all development of nuclear power for peaceful purposes. Russia rejected the plan, which was inspired by Dr Robert Oppenheimer (see OPPENHEIMER CASE.) (Bernard Baruch, member of the UN Atomic Energy Commission.)

Bashan (Basan), Bulls of Fat bulls of Bashan (a land beyond the Jordan) are mentioned in Psalms 22:12, and are thought to be the now extinct European wild oxen, or aurochs. (Pronounced bay'shan, bay'san.)

Basic Beginner's all-purpose symbolic instruction code, a computer language.

Basildon (1949). NEW TOWN in Essex, incorporating parts of the urban districts of Billericay and Thurrock, designed to take 106,000 inhabitants.

Baskerville (*c.* 1750). Early English typeface still in use today. (Designed by John Baskerville, University Printer at Cambridge.)

Basketmakers, Worshipful Company of (1569). LIVERY COMPANY.

Basques People of the western Pyrenees now found in a small coastal area facing the Bay of Biscay, from Bilbao in Spain to Bayonne in France. They are possibly the remnants of a Neolithic race displaced by the Indo-Europeans. Their language has no established affinity, and differs in every way from Indo-European languages.

Bassanio Character in Shakespeare's *Merchant of Venice* who wins PORTIA in the trial of the 3 caskets (with some help from Portia).

Bast Egyptian goddess; see BUBASTIS.

Bastille, Storming of the (14 July 1789). Event which marked the beginning of the French Revolution; the Paris mob regarded the fortress-prison of the Bastille as the symbol of despotic rule. Although all they found there were 6 common criminals and a lunatic nobleman, the anniversary of its capture is still kept as a national holiday commemorating the Revolution.

Basutoland Former British protectorate in South Africa, renamed LESOTHO when it became independent in 1966.

Batavia Former Dutch name of JAKARTA, capital of Indonesia.

Bateman cartoons Work of H. M. Bateman (1887–1970), who depicted extremes of rage, outrage or embarrassment arising from social gaffes, over captions such as 'The Man Who Lit His Cigar before the Royal Toast'. 'The Guest Who Called Pâté de Foie Gras "Potted Meat"', in which the forest of initial caps seemed to add to the enormity of the offence.

Bateman's Seventeenth-century house where Kipling lived, at Burwash, Sussex, preserved by the National Trust as a Kipling museum.

Bateman silverware Wares of Hester Bateman, who worked in London 1761–90 (by which time she was 81), 4 of her sons, and other members of the family (down to *c.* 1840). They produced great quantities of silverware, most of that bearing the mark *HB* being the work of the sons rather than the mother. The style is neoclassical; the smaller articles in particular, though attractive, are not outstanding and tend to be too light in weight.

Bates, Miss Kind-hearted chatterbox of Jane Austen's *Emma*; Emma gets into trouble for snubbing her.

Bath and West, Royal An annual agricultural show second only to the ROYAL and based at Shepton Mallet, Somerset.

Bath Oliver Delicately flavoured hard dry biscuit. (Named after a Dr Oliver of Bath in the 18th century.)

Bathsheba Wife of Uriah the Hittite, seduced by David, who brought about her husband's death in battle so that he could marry her (2 Sam. 11). (Pronounced bath'she-ba.)

Bathurst Cup Real Tennis contest between Britain and USA.

Batman (1939). Cartoon character created by Bob Kane, lacking the supernatural advantages of his rival, SUPERMAN, but endowed with immense strength, agility and scientific knowledge deliberately developed (after he had seen his parents killed in a hold-up) so that he could fight crime, adopting a bat disguise the better to frighten his adversaries. Batman has featured on television and a new film was released in 1989.

Bats Stock Exchange abbreviation for shares in the BRITISH–AMERICAN TOBACCO CO.

Battenberg Original name of the Mountbattens, the British branch of the family founded by Prince Alexander of Hesse and a Polish countess who, after her morganatic marriage, was created Princess of Battenberg (in Hesse); they changed their name in 1917 in deference to current popular prejudice against German names.

Battersea Former London metropolitan borough, since 1965 part of the borough of WANDSWORTH.

Battersea Dogs' Home Home for lost and starving dogs and cats, where unclaimed animals can be bought. It is in the Battersea Park Road, south of the Thames in London.

Battersea enamels (1) Snuff-boxes, watch-cases, plaques, wine labels, etc. of copper covered with opaque glass and hand-painted or transfer-printed with landscapes, lovers' messages, greetings from a spa, etc.; made at York House, Battersea, London, for the few years from about 1750 to 1756, and therefore extremely rare. (2) Similar articles made at Bilston, Staffordshire, and later in many other places, including countless deliberate fakes of (1).

Battery, The Park at the southern tip of Manhattan Island, New York City.

Battle Abbey Roll, The Fourteenth-century list, the earliest extant copy of which dates from the 16th century, of the families supposed to have come to England with William the Conqueror. It is spurious in part, if not altogether. (Found at Battle Abbey, Battle, near Hastings.)

'Battle Hymn of the Republic, The' (USA) Patriotic hymn, see 'JOHN BROWN'S BODY'.

Battle of Britain (1940). Hitler's daylight air attacks on Britain, intended as a prelude to invasion, defeated by 'the Few' (RAF Fighter Command). It opened on 10 July, the successive targets being Channel shipping and ports, the airfields of south-east England, and London; and ended (officially) on 31 October, overlapping the LONDON BLITZ.

Battle of Flowers Feature of the carnival festival, particularly associated with Nice, in the last days before Lent; see MARDI GRAS; ROSE BOWL.

Battle of the Books (1704). Jonathan Swift's pamphlet ridiculing contemporary scholarship in mock-heroic prose.

Battle of the Nations (1813). See LEIPZIG.

Battleship Potemkin (1925). Historic Russian film directed by Sergei Eisenstein, a realistic story of the naval mutiny of 1905.

Bauhaus School of architecture and industrial design founded by Walter Gropius at Weimar, Germany, after World War I to co-ordinate the skills of architects, artists and technologists.

Bauxite Hydroxide of alumina, one of the chief sources of aluminium, and originally found at Les Baux, near Arles, France.

Baxter prints (1836). Colour prints made by superimposing on an engraving (which combined aquatint, etching and stipple) up to 20–30 colour blocks in process invented by George Baxter (died 1867). The result was a 'poor man's oil painting', varying in quality from excellent to poor; many of the poorer ones were made by persons licensed by Baxter to use his process.

Bayard (1) Name of RINALDO's horse. (French, 'bay-coloured'.) (2) See CHEVALIER BAYARD.

Bayer letters Letters of the Greek alphabet used to identify the chief stars of a constellation, generally in approximate order of brightness, but sometimes in sequence of position. Although superseded by FLAMSTEED NUMBERS, the Bayer nomenclature is often used for the better-known stars, e.g. Alpha Centauri, the brightest star in Centaurus.

Bayeux Tapestry, The Piece of needlework made for Bayeux Cathedral, 230 ft long, depicting the life of Harold, including the Battle of Hastings. Traditionally it was supposed to be the work of William the Conqueror's wife, Matilda. The original is still at Bayeux, and a copy is in the Victoria and Albert Museum.

Bay of Pigs (April 1961). Landing on Cuba, with the support of the American CIA, of anti-Castro forces which were killed or captured within 3 days.

Bayreuth Festival (1876). Festival of Wagner's operas staged at the Wagner Theatre in July and August. (Town of Bavaria; pronounced by'roit.)

Bay State

Bay State Nickname of Massachusetts.

BBC-2 (1964). The alternative TV programme put out by the BBC with, on average, a higher artistic and intellectual standard than BBC-1; also used from 1967 as a vehicle for the first regular colour transmissions.

Beachcomber Zany column in the *Daily Express* started by D. W. Wyndham Lewis and continued from 1924 by J. B. Morton; it introduced a gallery of characters such as Dr STRABISMUS, Major Foulenough etc.

Beaconsfield, Earl of The title of Benjamin Disraeli from 1876. (Pronounced bee'kens-feeld, although the town is bek'ens-feeld.)

Beagle, HMS See VOYAGE OF THE BEAGLE.

Beaker People Early BRONZE AGE people who infiltrated north-west Europe and Britain from Spain about 1800 BC; they had gold ornaments, bows and arrows, and buried their dead under barrows (tumuli). They are named after the finely decorated beakers which they made.

Beale and Buss, The Misses Two 19th-century headmistresses (one of Cheltenham Ladies' College), the targets of an anonymous but famous little verse by their pupils: 'Miss Buss and Miss Beale / Cupid's darts do not feel. / How different from us, / Miss Beale and Miss Buss.'

Béarnaise sauce BÉCHAMEL-type sauce with egg yolk, vinegar and herbs, served with steaks.

Beast of Belsen Name for Josef Kramer, commandant at BELSEN.

Beat English version of RHYTHM AND BLUES, popularized by the BEATLES, who also borrowed from the ROCK 'N' ROLL tradition.

Beat generation (1950s). Those of the young generation who rejected the values of modern civilization and lived from day to day and from hand to mouth; they were characterized by contempt for the 'oldies' (i.e. anyone over about 26), who were all 'squares', and by sexual promiscuity, drug-taking and sartorial anarchy. The movement spread from Los Angeles, California, to Britain and elsewhere. Among their

spokesmen were Kerouac, Ginsberg and later Bob Dylan. (Term used by Jack Kerouac in the 1950s.)

Beatitudes, The Part of the SERMON ON THE MOUNT: blessed are the poor in spirit, the meek, the merciful, the pure in heart, the peacemakers; they that mourn, hunger after righteousness, are persecuted for righteousness' sake.

Beatles, The Extremely successful pop-music group which originated in the Cavern, Liverpool. The songs were mostly written by the bass guitarist Paul McCartney and by John Lennon (later joined by Yoko Ono), some by George Harrison; the quartet was completed by Ringo Starr (percussion). The group broke up in 1970. See 'A HARD DAY'S NIGHT'.

Beatniks Members of the BEAT GENERATION. ('Beat', variously interpreted as 'defeated by life' or referring to addiction to POP MUSIC with a strong rhythmic beat; plus a Russian or Yiddish suffix, nik perhaps after Sputnik.)

Beatrice (1) Dante's beloved, a historic person who also appears in the *Divine Comedy* as his guide in Paradise. (2) Heroine of Shakespeare's *Much Ado* who carries on a running battle of words with BENEDICK.

Beatties Naval lower-deck slang for 'officers'. (Admiral of the Fleet Lord Beatty, who commanded the Grand Fleet in World War I.)

Beau Brummell George Brummell, the arbiter of London fashion and friend of the Prince Regent, with whom he later quarrelled. He exiled himself to France, where he died in poverty, 1840.

Beauchamp's Career (1876). George Meredith's novel in which the gallant Nevil Beauchamp of the Royal Navy is frustrated in love and by his uncle's disapproval of his radical views and friends. All seems to have been brought to a happy ending, when he is drowned while rescuing a child.

Beaufort scale Scale of wind-strength on which Force 0 is calm; 1 light air (1–3 m.p.h.); 2 slight breeze (4–7 m.p.h); 3 gentle breeze (8–12); 4 moderate breeze (13–18); 5 fresh breeze (19–24); 6 strong breeze (25–31); 7 high wind (32–38); 8 gale (39–46); 9 strong gale (47–54); 10

46

whole gale (55–63); 11 storm (64–72); 12 hurricane (73–82) and so on up to Force 17 (120–136 m.p.h.). (Admiral Sir F. Beaufort; adopted 1838.)

Beau Geste (1924). P. C. Wren's best-selling novel of the rigours suffered by the high-minded expatriate Englishman who served under the name of Beau Geste in the French Foreign Legion in the Sahara.

Beaujolais Red, light, French wine, preferably drunk when it is young; grown in the hills between Lyons and Mâcon; the best bear the name of the village or origin, but most are blended.

Beaulieu Home near Lyndhurst, Hampshire, of Lord Montagu of Beaulieu and the Montagu Motor Museum. (Pronounced bew'li.)

Beaulieu Road Sales Sale of New Forest ponies held periodically at Beaulieu Road, near Lyndhurst. (Pronounced bew'li.)

Beau Nash Richard Nash, a gambler and at one time the arbiter of fashion at Bath. He outstayed his welcome and died poor in 1762.

Beaune See CÔTE DE BEAUNE.

Beauty and the Beast Fairy-tale dating back to at least the 16th century. Beauty, daughter of a merchant, goes to the palace of the Beast to save her father's life. She begins to feel quite sorry for the ugly monster and agrees to marry him, whereupon he is transformed into a handsome prince.

Beauty of Bath Early English apples.

Beaux' Stratagem, The (1707). Farquhar's comedy about 2 fortune-hunting friends (the beaux), Aimwell who pretends to be an invalid, and Archer who poses as his servant. They arrive at a Lichfield inn and get themselves invited to the home of Lady Bountiful, whose daughter and daughter-in-law they manage to win.

Beaver, The Nickname for the dynamic Lord Beaverbrook, newspaper proprietor and wartime Cabinet Minister. See next entry.

Beaverbrook Press The newspapers owned by Max Aitken, 1st Baron Beaverbrook (died 1964): the *Daily Express* (from 1919), *Sunday Express* (which he founded) and London *Evening Standard*. He used them to campaign for EMPIRE FREE TRADE and, in the last years of his life, against British entry into the Common Market.

Beaver State Nickname of Oregon.

Béchamel (Cooking) A basic sauce, nowadays made by pouring boiling milk on a white roux (butter and flour mixture). (Named after Louis XIV's steward; but in those days it was a rich cream sauce.)

Becher's Brook Most formidable fence in the GRAND NATIONAL; others are Valentine's and the Chair.

Bechuanaland Former British protectorate in South Africa, renamed BOTSWANA when it became independent in 1966.

Beckenham Former municipal borough of Kent, since 1965 part of the borough of BROMLEY.

Becky Sharp First 3-colour feature film (1935), in Technicolor; the story was based on Thackeray's VANITY FAIR.

Bedales (1893). First English coeducational boarding school, at Petersfield, Hampshire.

Bed Bug, The (1929). Vladimir Mayakovsky's social-realist play attacking vestigial bourgeois attitudes in Russia. (Russian title, *Klop*.)

Beddington and Wallington Former borough of Surrey, since 1965 part of the borough of SUTTON.

Bedford College for Women (1849). Now the Royal Holloway and Bedford New College, situated at Egham, Surrey.

Bedlam Corrupted abbreviation for the Hospital of St Mary of Bethlehem, Bishopsgate, London (now the site of Liverpool Street Station), which by the 15th century had become a lunatic asylum, moved to various sites later and now in Beckenham. It became notorious in the 17th century for the ignorant treatment of the inmates and as a public peep-show.

Bedlington Curly-haired terrier with a distinctive sheep-like head, bred in various colours. (Town in Northumberland.)

Beeb, The British Broadcasting Corporation (also Auntie, or the Corp).

Beecham Group Group of British firms which manufactures a wide variety of drugs, toilet requisites, soft drinks and foods under such well-known brand names as Eno's, Phensic, Phosphorine, Germolene, Scott's Emulsion, Maclean's, Yeast-Vite, Brylcreem, Lucozade, but first became famous for BEECHAM'S PILLS.

Beecham's pills (1847). Patent medicine first launched in Lancashire; 'worth a guinea a box', according to the advertisements, they were sold by Thomas Beecham (died 1907) at 1/1½d (cost of production, half a farthing); the ingredients were the same as for HOLLOWAY'S PILLS: aloes, ginger and soap.

Beeching report (1) Report (1963) which made recommendations intended to put British Railways on a sound financial footing by cancelling unprofitable passenger services, closing stations and branch lines, and concentrating on fast and efficient goods services. (2) The report of the Royal Commission on Assizes and Quarter Sessions (1969) which recommended extensive reorganization of the heavily overloaded assize system.

Beefeaters Popular name for: (1) YEOMEN OF THE GUARD; (2) YEOMAN WARDERS of the Tower of London. (Apparently referring to their well-fed look; no connection with French *buffetiers du roi*, a derivation once favoured.)

Beefsteak Club (1876). London club in Irving Street, Leicester Square, which makes a point of informality despite the distinction of its members, who eat at one long table, sitting where the waiters put them. There were several earlier clubs of the name.

Beehive State Nickname of Utah.

Beelzebub BAAL worshipped in Palestine, apparently as a healer (2 Kgs 1:2); in Matt. 12:24 he is the prince of devils; in *Paradise Lost* he is promoted next in rank to Satan. (Said to mean 'Lord of Flies', interpreted as 'preserver from fly-borne disease'; pronounced be-el'ze-bub.)

Beerage, The Collective nickname for the many brewers and distillers raised to the peerage (e.g. Viscount Younger and several of the Guinness family).

Beer-hall Putsch Another name for Hitler's MUNICH PUTSCH (1923).

Beetle Nickname, later adopted as a trade name, for the beetle-shaped VOLKSWAGEN car.

Beggar's Opera (1728). John Gay's opera, a parody of contemporary Italian opera, with a highwayman, Capt. Macheath, as hero. The plot was used in Brecht's THREEPENNY OPERA.

Begonia Tender perennial bedding and indoor plant named after Michael Begon, a French botanist.

Behaviourism (1913). School of psychology which restricts itself to the objective study of behaviour. The American, J. B. Watson, rejected Freudian introspection into the workings of the unconscious, minimized the importance of heredity and 'original sin', and borrowed the Russian Pavlov's theories of the conditioned reflex to explain all behaviour, the pattern of which derives ultimately from emotions of fear, anger (at restraint) and content (e.g. on being caressed).

Behistun inscription (5th century BC). Account of the reign of the Persian king, Darius the Great, inscribed on a mountainside in cuneiform writing in Persian, Babylonian and the language of Elam. (Site near Ardelan, between Kermanshah and Hamadan, Persia.)

Beit Professor Holder of the chair of History of the British Commonwealth at Oxford. (Pronounced byt.)

Bel Assyrian and Babylonian form of the Hebrew and Phoenician BAAL.

Bel Ami (1885). Maupassant's novel of a penniless Parisian journalist, Georges Duroy, who uses women (including his employer's wife and daughter) unscrupulously as stepping-stones to power and wealth.

Bel and the Dragon Book of the Apocrypha which tells how the prophet Daniel exposed the trickery of the priest of BEL in Babylon and convinced the king that Bel was only an image, not a living god.

Belch, Sir Toby Convivial uncle of Olivia in Shakespeare's *Twelfth Night*, who plays tricks on MALVOLIO.

Belém Brazilian seaport, now more usually called Pará.

Belfort gap Wide valley around Belfort between the Vosges and Jura mountains near the Franco-Swiss-German frontier, strategically a weak point in the natural defences of France, and from early times a main trade and communications route.

Belgrade Theatre (1958). First new British theatre to be opened after World War II, at Coventry; it produced Wesker's earlier successes.

Belial The Devil; the expression 'sons of Belial' appears in Deuteronomy 13:13 and elsewhere. He appears in *Paradise Lost* as a fallen angel who 'could make the worse appear the better reason'. (Hebrew, 'worthlessness'; pronounced bee'li-al.)

Belisha beacon Flashing amber light used in Britain to indicate a pedestrian crossing. Idea adopted by the Minister of Transport, Leslie Hore-Belisha, 1934–7. (Pronounced bel-eesh'a.)

Bell: Acton, Currer and Ellis Pen-names of the Brontë sisters, Anne, Charlotte and Emily.

Bellamy's veal pies It was the Younger Pitt whose last words (1806) were said to have been: 'I think I could eat one of Bellamy's veal pies.' A less unromantic tradition substitutes: 'My country! oh, my country!'

Bellarmine jugs Brown salt-glaze stoneware jugs with narrow neck and the mask of a bearded man.

Belle Dame sans Merci, La (1819). Keats's version of a medieval ballad of a 'knight-at-arms, alone and palely loitering' who has woken from a dream of meeting a 'faerie's child' to find himself on the cold hillside, where 'no birds sing'.

Belleck ware (1857). Form of PARIAN WARE with an imitation mother-of-pearl glaze, used in various marine fantasies involving mermaids, dolphins, shells, etc. made up into all kinds of tableware. (Village in Co. Fermanagh, Northern Ireland, where the factory still functions.)

Belle Époque, La Name given in France to the last 2 decades before World War I, during which it could be said that the rich and well-born 'never had it so good'.

Belle Hélène, La (1864). Offenbach's operetta in which the heroes of the Trojan War appear in comic roles.

Bellerophon In Greek legend a hero who spurned the advances of his queen and, unjustly accused by her, was set to do many hazardous tasks (e.g. killing the CHIMAERA). He tried to reach heaven on PEGASUS but was thrown. (Pronounced bel-ėr'o-fon.)

Bellerophon, HMS The ship where Napoleon made his formal surrender after defeat at Waterloo, and which took him to St Helena.

Belle Sauvage, The Famous 15th-century London inn on Ludgate Hill. (The original name may have been Savage's Bell Inn, romanticized into the French for 'the beautiful wild woman'.)

Bellis perennis Species name of the common daisy.

Bellman, The Captain of the crew in Lewis Carroll's *The Hunting of the* SNARK. His motto was: What I tell you three times is true.

Bellona Roman goddess of war, wife or sister of Mars.

Bell Rock (1844). Lighthouse and rock some 20 miles off the Firth of Tay, east Scotland. Also known as Inchcape.

Bells, The (1871). English melodrama adapted from a French story of a Polish burgomaster, Mathias, haunted by guilt for an undiscovered murder. It was in this play that Henry Irving had his first great popular success, at the Lyceum.

Belmont Park (USA) Oldest and largest US racecourse, in New York. It is the scene of the American Grand National and of the oldest of the 3 American classic flat-races, the Belmont Stakes for 3-year-olds run in June over a distance of $1\frac{1}{2}$ miles.

Beloe Committee (1960). In a report on the examination system in secondary schools, this committee recommended the establishment of the CERTIFICATE OF SECONDARY EDUCATION.

Bel Paese Mild semi-hard Italian cheese with, at its best, a delicate flavour. (Pronounced bel pah-ayz'é.)

Belsen Nazi concentration camp, north of Hanover, Germany, the second to be liberated, by the British in April 1945.

Belshazzar's feast (539 BC) (1) Feast given by the last King of Babylon, Belshazzar, son of Nebuchadnezzar, at which he saw the 'writing on the wall', interpreted by Daniel as meaning that his kingdom would be divided between the Medes and Persians, as happened the same night when Babylon fell to Cyrus (Dan. 5). (2) Choral work by Sir William Walton (1931).

Beltane Celtic feast on 1 May, celebrated by the lighting of bonfires and, possibly, maypole dancing.

Beluga caviare That taken from the great sturgeon of the Caspian, Azov and Black Seas, which grows to 24 ft in length, 1 ton in weight and is said to live up to 300 years. Despite its fame, the caviare of smaller species is better. (Russian name of the fish.)

Belvoir Fox-hunting pack with kennels at BELVOIR CASTLE, which hunts country in Leicestershire and Lincolnshire.

Belvoir Castle Seat, between Grantham and Melton Mowbray, of the Dukes of Rutland since Henry VIII's time, rebuilt by Wyatt in 1816. (Pronounced bee'ver.)

Benares (Banaras) Hindu holy city on the Ganges, now spelt Varanasi.

Benares ware Chased brassware in the form of trays, bowls, vases etc., brought to Europe in vast quantities by all who served in India. In the early years it was attractively decorated, but it deteriorated as the export trade grew.

Ben Barka case (1965–7). Disappearance in Paris of the Moroccan opposition leader, Ben Barka, last seen being driven away in a police car. Leading figures in France and Morocco were suspected of complicity, but the prolonged proceedings in a French court were stopped in 1967, the mystery remaining unsolved.

Bencher Master of the Bench, i.e. a senior member of an INN OF COURT, one of the governors responsible for its administration and for the discipline of its students and barristers. See BAR COUNCIL.

Bend Or Nickname of the second Duke of Westminster, from the name of the horse which won him the Derby in 1880.

Benedick Sworn bachelor, and sparring-partner of BEATRICE in Shakespeare's *Much Ado*, whom in the end he marries; hence any confirmed bachelor trapped into matrimony. (The spelling Benedict in the latter sense appears to arise from confusion with ideas of Benedictine celibacy.)

Benedictine Oldest liqueur, still made on the site of the Abbey of Fécamp, Normandy, where it originated *c.* 1510. The D.O.M on the label stands for Deo Optimo Maximo, 'to God, most good, most great'.

Benedictines (about AD 530). Oldest order of monks, founded by St Benedict in Italy, where MONTE CASSINO became the headquarters. It was supremely influential in Europe; in England it owned all the cathedral priories and most of the big abbeys, and founded several university colleges. Today it has abbeys at Downside, Ampleforth and elsewhere, as well as the rebuilt Buckfast Abbey in Devon. The CISTERCIANS and CLUNIACS were reformed Benedictine orders.

Benelux (1948). Customs union of Belgium, the

Netherlands and Luxembourg. (Name coined from the initial letters of those countries.)

Benesh notation (UK) System of recording the movements and position of a ballet (Rudolf and Joan Benesh, inventors).

Bengal Former Indian province, now divided between West Bengal in India, and Bangladesh.

Bengali Inhabitant, or the Indo-European language, of the Ganges delta area now divided between India and Bangladesh.

Ben Hur (1880). Novel by the American, Lew Wallace. Ben Hur is a Jewish aristocrat in the time of Christ, charged with trying to assassinate the Roman governor. Sent to the galleys he escapes, joins the Roman army, defeats in a famous chariot race the man who had betrayed him, and becomes a Christian.

Benin, Bight of Bay stretching westwards from the Niger delta. In the days before malaria and yellow fever had been conquered it was described as the place 'where few come out, though many go in'. See WHITE MAN'S GRAVE.

Benin bronzes Sculptures made at Benin in southern Nigeria, in the 17th century, by the *cire-perdue* process of bronze casting learnt from Ife (see IFE HEADS).

Benjamin Youngest and favourite son of Jacob (Gen. 35:18); hence any youngest (and favourite) son.

Benjamin, Tribe of Smallest of the 10 tribes of Israel, who claimed descent from Jacob's youngest son. King Saul and St Peter belonged to it.

Bennet family In Jane Austen's PRIDE AND PREJUDICE; consists of the sardonic Mr Bennet who keeps as far in the background as he can, and his hare-brained wife, distracted by the burden of 5 unmarried daughters. Her frantic efforts to marry them off do much to delay the marriage of Elizabeth to Darcy, and of Jane to Bingley, as well as to promote Lydia's foolish elopement with Wickham. See also Mr COLLINS; Lady Catherine DE BOURGH.

Benz (1885). The first petrol-driven car to be made on a commercial scale (first marketed in 1887); it was a 3-wheel horseless carriage with a single-cylinder engine. Benz continued to make horseless carriages while DAIMLER was inventing more modern types. (Carl Benz, German inventor.)

Beowulf Scandinavian hero of an Old English alliterative epic of that name which combines memories of real events with trivial tales of fabulous monsters; the earliest poem in a Teutonic language, probably 8th century. (Pronounced bee'o-wulf or bay'o-.)

Berbers Non-Semitic fair-skinned brown-eyed people of North Africa (see HAMITES), called by the Romans Numidians (Greek *nomades*, 'nomads'), Gaetuli or Mauri (Hebrew *mahur*, 'western', compare MAGHREB).

Berchtesgaden Village on the Austrian border, near Salzburg, where Hitler had his heavily fortified lair, the Berghof or Eagle's Nest, built into the mountainside 6,000 ft up, with another house at its foot.

Bercy sauce Sauce prepared with shallots and white wine, served with fish.

Berenice Name of several women and cities from the days of the PTOLEMIES onwards. (1) Bérénice of Racine's and Corneille's plays was the widowed Queen of Chalcis with whom the Emperor Titus fell in love but, in deference to Roman public opinion, did not marry. (2) Berenice who dedicated her hair to the gods for the safe return of her husband from a Syrian campaign was sister and wife of a 3rd-century BC Ptolemy king of Egypt. Her hair was wafted to heaven and became the constellation Coma Berenices. (Macedonian form of Greek *Pherenike*, 'victorious', Latin form *Veronica*; pronounced ber-e-ny'si.)

Bergère (Cooking). With mushrooms and parsley. (French, 'shepherdess'.)

Berghof Hitler's 'Eagle's Nest' at BERCHTESGADEN.

Bergsonian philosophy See CREATIVE EVOLUTION. (Henri Bergson. French philosopher, died 1941.)

Berkeleian philosophy Subjective Idealism; see

PRINCIPLES OF HUMAN KNOWLEDGE. (George Berkeley, Irish bishop, died 1753.)

Berkeley (1962). One of the earlier series of nuclear power stations; decommissioned 1989. (Village near the Severn, south of Sharpness, Gloucestershire.)

Berkeley (1873). University of CALIFORNIA at Berkeley (UCB), in Alameda County across the bay from San Francisco; in many ways the most important university west of Chicago. (Pronounced burk'li.)

Berkeley Castle Home of the Berkeley family for over 800 years, near Bristol; the oldest inhabited castle in England. (Pronounced bark'li.)

Berkeley Hunt Based on Berkeley Castle (see previous entry.) Hunt servants wear coats of yellow.

Berlin, Congress of (1878). Conference of the Great Powers under Bismarck's chairmanship which redrew the map of the Balkans. Romania, Serbia and Montenegro were finally freed from Turkish rule, Bosnia and Herzegovina were given to Austria, Cyprus to Britain, and many other changes were made, most of which lasted until World War I.

Berlin airlift (June 1948 to October 1949). The Anglo-US operation that kept West Berlin supplied by air during the BERLIN BLOCKADE.

Berlin–Baghdad railway (1899). German name for what was in fact a projected line from Constantinople to the Persian Gulf, opposed by Russia and Britain, and, though never constructed, a source of diplomatic tension up to World War I.

Berlin blockade (1948–9) Unsuccessful Russo-East German attempt to deter the West from recognizing a free West German state by cutting off ground access to Berlin from the west. It followed the merging of the 3 Western Allied zones of Berlin, and led directly to the establishment of NATO. See BERLIN AIRLIFT.

Berliner Ensemble (1949). Brecht's own theatrical company, in East Berlin; later a state theatre, run after his death by his widow. It confines itself to producing mainly Brecht's plays.

Berlin porcelain (1740). Products of the factory sponsored by Frederick the Great; it produced high-quality Meissen-inspired figures and other wares in its earlier years, and is still operating.

Berlin Wall (August 1961–November 1989). Wall built by the East Germans to separate East (Communist) and West Berlin. Unauthorized people trying to cross the wall were shot at sight by East Germans. It followed a serpentine course through the heart of the city, with the BRANDENBURGER TOR as the main feature. See also CHECKPOINT CHARLIE.

Bermondsey Former London metropolitan borough, since 1965 part of the borough of SOUTHWARK.

Bermuda race (1923). Race from New York to Bermuda jointly sponsored by the Cruising Club of America and the Royal Bermuda Yacht Club; held in alternation with the FASTNET, i.e. in even-numbered years.

Bermuda Triangle Sea zone off the south-east coast of the USA said to produce larger than normal number of accidents to ships and aircraft entering it.

Bermudian rig Rig for a sailing-boat characterized by a tall triangular mainsail tapering directly from the top of the mainmast, there being no gaff or topmast. Also spelt Bermudan.

Bernadotte dynasty Ruling house of Sweden since 1818, founded by one of Napoleon's Marshals.

Berne Convention (1886). The first international convention for copyright protection (not signed by USA), revised on several occasions, notably by a Universal Copyright Convention (1955), to which Russia did not adhere.

Bernese Oberland Alps overlooking Berne in Switzerland, of which the most famous peak is the Jungfrau, and the chief resorts Grindelwald, Mürren and Wengen. (Pronounced, in English, ber-neez'.)

Bertram family In Jane Austen's MANSFIELD PARK, Sir Thomas Bertram, his wife and 4 children; the heroine, Fanny Price, is Sir Bertram's niece and is brought up with the family; she eventually marries the youngest son, Edmund.

Bessarabia Former Romanian province, now part of the Moldavian and Ukrainian SSRs, Soviet Russia.

Bessemer process (1856). Cheap method of purifying pig-iron and converting it into molten steel; its invention revolutionized the steel industry. (Sir Henry Bessemer, died 1898.)

Bess of Hardwick Elizabeth Talbot, Countess of Shrewsbury, who died aged 90 in 1608 after a career which included 4 marriages, court intrigues and the building of HARDWICK HALL.

Beste-Chetwynde, Mrs Extremely wealthy, and odd, lady who appears in several of Evelyn Waugh's novels; she became Lady METROLAND.

Betelgeuse Red giant star in the east shoulder of ORION, of which it is the second brightest star; it is a cool irregular variable, and has a diameter of at least 200 million miles. (Pronounced bee-tl-zhèrz'.)

Bethel Name, meaning 'House of God', given by Jacob to the place where he had the vision of JACOB'S LADDER (Gen. 28:19); applied to a Nonconformist chapel.

Bethlehem Steel (1904). Large US group with interests in iron, steel, shipbuilding, coke and coke by-products, with headquarters at Bethlehem, Pennsylvania.

Bethnal Green Former London metropolitan borough, since 1965 part of the new borough of TOWER HAMLETS.

Betty Martin Unexplained name, occurring in the phrase, at least 200 years old, 'all my eye and Betty Martin' (i.e. humbug).

Betty Trask award (1983). Annual award given on the strength of a first novel for authors under 35. Total prize money £21,000, to be spent on travel.

Beulah Virtually a synonym for 'Promised Land'. Isaiah 52:4, prophesies a brighter future for Israel and says: 'Thou shalt be called Hephzibah ("my delight is in her") and thy land Beulah ("married").' In PILGRIM'S PROGRESS Beulah is the land where the pilgrims await their summons to the Celestial City.

Bevanites Name for Labour MPs in sympathy with Aneurin Bevan when he resigned office (1951) in protest against charges for NHS spectacles and false teeth imposed by Hugh Gaitskell; they also opposed their government's defence policy and its support for West German rearmament. They were never a united group, and Bevan rejoined the fold later.

Beveridge reports (1) 1942 report on which the WELFARE STATE legislation is based. (2) 1951 report on broadcasting which opposed the introduction of commercial broadcasting and supported the existing BBC monopoly.

Beverly Hills District of Los Angeles near Hollywood, California, famous for bizarre houses built by film stars.

Bevin Boys Name given in 1943 to young men directed to work in coal-mines as an alternative to service with the forces, under an Act sponsored by Ernest Bevin, then Minister of Labour and National Service.

Bewick wood engravings Accurate illustrations of animals, birds and rural scenes, produced by Thomas Bewick (1753–1828), using on wood a technique similar to that in engraving on copper.

Bexley London borough since 1965 consisting of the former boroughs of Bexley and Erith, and the urban districts of Crayford and part of Chislehurst-Sidcup; headquarters at Erith.

Bey Honorific in the Turkish Empire that survived in Egypt until 1952 and was retained by the Turk-descended Beys of Tunis until Tunisia became a republic in 1957. (Turkish *beg*, *bey*, 'lord'.)

Beyond the Fringe (1961). Revue with a cast of 4 talented young men who wittily satirized current attitudes to war, civil defence, religion, advertising etc.

Bezonian Beggar or rascal; used by PISTOL in Shakespeare's *Henry IV* Part II; 'Under which king, Bezonian? speak, or die!' (Italian *bisogno*, 'needy'.)

Bhagavad-Gita Section of the MAHABHARATA in

which KRISHNA preaches compassion and the duties of the caste system; also called the Gospel of Krishna. (Sanskrit, 'song of the blessed one'; pronounced bug-ė-vėd-gee'tah.)

Bhoodan campaign (1951). Campaign started by Gandhi's disciple, Vinobha Bhave, in Hyderabad. He travelled about on foot from village to village begging for land to give to the landless; these gifts totalled over 5 million acres.

Biafra Republic (1967). Name adopted by Eastern Nigeria when it decided to secede from the Federation of Nigeria. (Bight of Biafra, the bay between the Niger delta and Cape Lopez in Gabon.)

Bible Some Bibles are known by their errors, as the Wicked Bible (1632), which printed 'Thou shalt commit adultery', and the vinegar Bible (1717) which has the heading to Luke 20 as 'The parable of the vinegar' (instead of vineyard). The Authorized Version (1611) is that authorized by King James I, the Revised Version (1885) produced by 25 scholars.

Bible Belt (USA). Name for the states (Arkansas, Mississippi and, until 1967, Tennessee) which prohibited the teaching of the Darwinian theory of evolution, as it conflicts with the account of the Creation given in *Genesis*. See DAYTON ANTI-DARWINIST TRIAL.

Bible in Spain, The (1843). George Borrow's fictionalized account of his travels in Spain distributing Bibles for the British and Foreign Bible Society during the CARLIST WARS and against Catholic opposition.

Bickerstaff, Isaac Fictional astrologer in Jonathan Swift's attack (1708) on a contemporary publisher of almanacs.

Bicycle Thieves, The (1946). De Sica's charming Italian film about the adventures of a small boy and his father searching for the father's stolen bicycle in the streets of Rome.

Biedermeier style (1815–48). Austro-German version of the French EMPIRE and ADAM STYLES in furniture, using lighter wood (but ebony for pilasters and columns), dispensing with brass and ormolu, and adding painted pictures in the local cottage tradition. (Named after a magazine cartoon character, Papa Biedermeier, satirizing the unimaginative German middle class of the period, for whom such furniture was designed.)

Biennale, The (1895). Exhibition of modern painting and sculpture held in Venice from May to October in even-numbered years. (Pronounced bi-en-ah'le.)

Big Bang Deregulation of the City of London financial institutions in 1986.

Big Bang theory (1957). Prof. Martin Ryle's hypothesis that the universe is evolving from a gigantic explosion of super-dense matter about 5,000 million years ago, and will eventually die. Like the STEADY STATE THEORY with which it is contrasted, it was suggested by the EXPANDING UNIVERSE THEORY.

Big Ben Nickname of the $13\frac{1}{2}$-ton bell in the Clock Tower of the British Houses of Parliament which strikes the hours; it became particularly widely known during World War II when its sound continued to herald the 9 p.m. radio news nightly, despite the Blitz. (Named after Sir Benjamin Hall, Chief Commissioner of Works when it was installed in 1856.)

Big Berthas Nickname for the German long-range guns that shelled back areas of the Western Front in 1917 and Paris, at a range of 70 miles, in 1918. (German name, after Bertha KRUPP.)

Big Bill Thompson Nickname of William Hale Thompson, the pro-German Mayor of Chicago (1915–23 and 1927–31), during whose terms of office flourished the notorious gangsters led by SCARFACE AL CAPONE and others.

Big Brother The Head of State in Orwell's *1984*.

Big D Nickname for Dallas, Texas, as one of the world's oil centres.

Big-endian and Little-endian Lilliputian equivalents of Catholic and Protestant in *Gulliver's Travels*, to whom it was of supreme importance whether one broke one's egg at the big or the little end; hence used of any petty doctrinal disputation.

Biggles Air-ace hero of more than 80 boys' books written by an RAF pilot of World War I, Capt. William Johns (died 1968).

Bignonia Hardy climbing plant named after Abbé Bignon, librarian to Louis XIV.

Bikini Pacific atoll in the Marshall Islands, the scene (1946) of the first post-war tests of atomic bombs, which left it as bare as a bikini swimsuit leaves the body. (Pronounced bi-kee'ni.)

Billbergia Tropical herbaceous flowering plant named after J. G. Billberg, a Swedish botanist.

Billings, Josh Pen-name of the American humorist Henry Wheeler Shaw (1818–85), who wrote phonetically, like Artemus WARD.

Billingsgate Former fish market (1699) just below London Bridge, and earlier a coal and corn market; bargees and fishwives made it notorious for foul language. Now offices.

Billingsley flowers (1) Floral decorations on porcelain, much more naturalistic than those by his contemporaries, painted by William Billingsley (1760–1828) at Derby, NANTGARW, Coalport and other factories; his roses were especially famous. (2) Name applied indiscriminately to almost any cabbage rose painted on porcelain.

Bill of Divorcement, A (1921). Play by Clemence Dane on the hardship caused by the fact that insanity was not a ground for divorce; the law was subsequently changed.

Bill of Rights (1689). Act which embodied the provisions of the DECLARATION OF RIGHTS, barred Catholic succession to the British throne, and gave Scotland religious freedom.

Billy Budd (1951). Benjamin Britten's opera, based on a tale by Herman Melville. Billy, the innocent crew-hand, is falsely accused by the master-at-arms, Claggart, of incitement to mutiny (the action takes place in 1797, the year of the Mutiny of the Nore). He is goaded into hitting Claggart, who dies. The captain reluctantly condemns Billy to death.

Billy Bunter Owl of the remove in MAGNET

LIBRARY series. Fat and greedy and always waiting for a postal order from his godfather.

Billy Graham crusades US evangelist Billy Graham's campaigns in the USA, Britain (first in 1954) and elsewhere, held in large arenas with maximum publicity and theatrical display; the audience are invited to come forward and rededicate themselves publicly to their religion.

Billy Liar (1959). Novel by Keith Waterhouse of a Yorkshire working-class boy who gets into trouble with his lies and fantasies, which are especially about success with the girls; the plot was used by Willis Hall for a play (1960) and a film (1963).

Billy the Kid Nickname of William Bonney, a bandit and bank robber in the Wild West days of mid-19th-century USA.

Bingham's Dandies Nickname of the 17th (Duke of Cambridge's Own) Lancers.

Bingo Game in which numbers randomly selected are called out and those playing cover the numbers on their cards. The first to cover all of a series of numbers win. Other variants include Lotto and Housey-Housey.

Birds, The (414 BC). Aristophanes' fantastical comedy, satirizing Athenian politics, but notable for its poetic lyrics. See CLOUD-CUCKOO-LAND.

Birdseye (1925). A method of preserving fresh vegetables discovered by the American, Clarence Birdseye.

Bir Hacheim Outpost far south of Tobruk in Cyrenaica, where the Free French under General Koenig made a gallant stand in the North African campaign in May and June 1942.

Birkbeck College (1920). Unit of London University, originally the London Mechanics' Institution (1823), founded by a Yorkshire doctor, George Birkbeck. It is noted for part-time tuition given to mature working students.

Birkenhead, 1st Earl of F. E. Smith (known as 'F. E.'), Lord Chancellor 1919–22. Of him G. K. Chesterton wrote some famous lines of invective: 'Talk about . . . the souls of Christian peoples . . . / Chuck it, Smith!'

Birkin, Rupert Character in D. H. Lawrence's *Women in Love* who marries Ursula Brangwen, and is the mouthpiece of the author's views.

Birmingham, George A. Pseudonym of Canon J. O. Hannay, Irish author.

Birmingham Rep. (1913). Sir Barry Jackson's theatre, one of the most influential of provincial repertory companies, which had an early financial success with the IMMORTAL HOUR.

Birmingham Royal Ballet (1989). New name for SADLER'S WELLS Royal Ballet.

Birnam Wood An allusion to a line in Shakespeare's *Macbeth*. The witches prophesy that MACBETH will not be vanquished "till Birnam wood do come to Dunsinane'; Malcolm's army arrives under cover of branches felled from this wood, and overthrows him. (A former royal forest near Perth.)

Biro Proprietary name for a ball-point pen invented by Ladislao Biro.

Birthday Honours Awards and decorations given on the official birthday of the sovereign; these are also awarded at the new year.

Birth of a Nation, The (1915). One of the earliest and most famous spectacular films, produced by D. W. Griffith, and dealing with the American Civil War.

Birth of Venus, The (late 15th century). Botticelli's version of the theme of APHRODITE ANADYOMENE; now in the Uffizi, Florence.

Bishop Hot spiced wine drink, usually with port as a base.

Bishop Blougram's Apology (1855). Robert Browning's dramatic monologue in which the Bishop justifies his retention of office after he has lost faith in the doctrines he has to preach. Cardinal Wiseman is avowedly the model for Blougram. (Pronounced bloh'grèm.)

Bishop Rock (1858). Lighthouse and rock west of the Scilly Isles. Built of granite, the lighthouse is one of the most exposed in the world.

Bishops' Wars (1) Bloodless victory for the Scottish COVENANTERS who obtained Charles I's agreement to submit their disputes to a new Scottish Parliament and Church Assembly (1638). (2) Second victory for the Covenanters (1640), whom Charles I allowed to occupy the 6 northern counties of England and dictate their own terms.

Bisley (1890). Rifle-range near Woking, Surrey, the headquarters of the National Rifle Association, and the scene of the chief civil, military and schools championship matches.

Bismarck German battleship sunk in May 1941, 3 days after sinking the HOOD.

Bismarck hering Rolled or filleted pickled herring.

Bismarck Sea, Battle of the (March 1943). Action in which US carrier-borne aircraft sank the whole of a Japanese troop transport convoy bound for New Guinea, together with its escorts. (Bismarck Archipelago, north of New Guinea.)

Bitolj Town in Serbian Macedonia, Yugoslavia, formerly known by its Turkish name of Monastir. (Pronounced bit-ol'.)

Bitter Sweet (1929). Operetta by Noël Coward.

Black and Tan Mixed drink of beer and stout.

Black and Tans (1920). British recruits who filled vacancies in the Royal Irish Constabulary caused by the killing or intimidation of its Irish-born members during the TROUBLES. They gained a reputation for terrorist tactics. (From their khaki uniforms and black belts.)

Black and Tans (Scarteen) See SCARTEEN BLACK AND TANS.

Blackbeard Nickname of an English privateer, Captain Edward Teach, who turned pirate (*c.* 1714), converted a captured French merchantman into a 40-gun warship and terrorized the Spanish Main. He wintered in North Carolina, whose governor shared the loot, but with the help of the governor of Virginia the Royal Navy cornered Teach and shot him dead (1718).

Black Beauty (1877). Anna Sewell's 'autobiography' of a horse, a long-lasting favourite with the young.

Black Belt In judo, a member of one of the 5 lower DAN grades.

Black Bess Dick Turpin's mare on which, in Harrison Ainsworth's novel *Rookwood* (1834), he rides from London to York in a night, to establish an alibi.

Blackboard Jungle, The (1954). First novel (made into a film) of Evan Hunter (who also writes crime stories as Ed McBain). Written from personal experience, it is a sensational account of a city high school where the boys are ruffians, the headmaster a bully and the overworked teachers have additional problems in their private lives.

Black Country Industrial Midlands of England, including Birmingham and Wolverhampton, blackened by factory smoke.

Black Death (1349). Outbreak of bubonic plague which killed many millions of people in Europe, Asia and Africa. There was a further severe epidemic in London in 1665. Also see GREAT PLAGUE.

Black Dog Depression of spirits, originating as a term in the 18th century.

Black Douglas Nickname given to: (1) the Earls of Douglas, in distinction from the Earls of Angus (see RED DOUGLAS); (2) specifically, their earlier kinsman, Sir James Douglas, who ravaged northern England in the 14th century. (The name Douglas itself means 'black water', which may account for the origin of the nickname.)

Black Earth Belt of exceptionally fertile black or dark-brown soil, formed under natural grassland, which covers much of southern Russia (especially the Ukraine), Romania and Hungary. In Russia it is known as *chernozem*. A similar belt stretches from Saskatchewan in Canada to Texas.

Black-eyed Susan Name which occurs in song at least as early as the 18th century; given to a species of Rudbeckia (Coneflower) with striking dark-centred yellow flowers.

Blackfriars Thames-side section of London south of FLEET STREET, named after the DOMINICANS who moved there in 1276. The elder Burbage built the first roofed theatre there in 1596 (See also MERMAID THEATRE). Unilever House overlooks Blackfriars Bridge.

Black Friars See DOMINICANS.

Black Friday (15 April 1921) In the history of British trade unions, the day the railway and transport unions cancelled a strike in sympathy with the miners, thus breaking up the 'triple alliance' of these 3 major unions.

Black Hand (1911). Secret society which aimed at the unification of the southern Slavs, formed by 'Apis' (Col. Dimitriević), the man behind the SARAJEVO assassination.

Black Hole of Calcutta (1756). Cell at Fort William, Calcutta, where the Nawab of Bengal, Suraj ud Dowlah, placed 146 British East India Co. prisoners, of whom only 23 survived the night. Recently doubts have been cast on this tradition, apparently based on the account of one unreliable witness.

Black Hundreds (1905–9). Russian terrorists who carried out pogroms, murdering some 50,000 Jews.

Black (James Tait) Memorial Prize An annual prize awarded for the best novel and the best biography (or similar work), on the advice of the Professor of Literature, Edinburgh University. (In memory of a partner of the publishing firm, A. & C. Black.)

Black Knight First British rocket, built by Westlands to put a 300 lb payload into space; fired at Woomera in 1958, it was later used for research into re-entry problems during the development of BLUE STREAK.

Black Maria Nickname for the black-painted police van used for the transport of arrested persons and criminals.

Black Monday (Monday, 19 October 1987). When stocks and shares on world stock markets fell dramatically.

Black Muslims Black sect founded in USA in the 1930s by Elijah Muhammed, based on a corruption of Islamic beliefs and the view that the white man is the devil. See MALCOLM X.

Black Pope Name for the General of the Society of Jesus (i.e. the head of the Jesuits).

Black Power Slogan of Stokeley Carmichael (see STUDENT NON-VIOLENT CO-ORDINATING COMMITTEE). It summed up the views of those blacks who felt that integration with whites was no longer possible or even desirable and that the only practical course to attain black equality in positions of power was to oppose the evils of white authority by every means possible, including violence. Not clearly formulated, this policy appeared to verge on advocacy either of a black separatist movement in the USA or of a black-dictated form of APARTHEID.

Black Prince Edward Prince of Wales, son of Edward III; he died before his father, thus opening up the rivalry between descendants of his 2 younger brothers which led to the Wars of the Roses. (Traditionally so called because he wore black armour.)

Black Rod Gentleman Usher of the Black Rod, an official of the Lord Chamberlain's department who maintains order in the House of Lords and has the special duty of summoning the Commons thither to hear the Address from the Throne. (Carries an ebony wand of office.)

Blackshirts Another name for the Nazi ss.

Blacksmiths, Worshipful Company of (1571). LIVERY COMPANY, originally a guild which included gunsmiths, clockmakers and spurriers (makers of spurs).

Blackstone Short title of Blackstone's *Commentaries on the Laws of England* (1769), a standard popular, but not very accurate, exposition of the subject.

Black Tuesday (29 October 1929). Day of the WALL STREET CRASH.

Black Velvet Mixed drink of champagne and stout, known in Germany as a Bismarck.

Black Watch (Royal Highland Regiment), The A regiment of the HIGHLAND BRIGADE, an amalgamation of the 42nd and 73rd Foot. (So called from the dark colours of their tartan; 'watch' in the old sense 'guard'.)

Blackwood convention At Bridge, a bid of 4 No Trumps asking partner to indicate his Aces, and of 5 No Trumps to indicate Kings.

Blackwood's Magazine (1817). Edinburgh monthly (often called Maga) which began as a literary magazine, with contributors such as Walter Scott and De Quincey. Later it tended to specialize in stories written by Empire-builders.

Blades, The Nickname of the Sheffield United football team, Sheffield steel being famous.

Bladud Mythical king of England and father of King Lear, he built the city of Bath and dedicated the medicinal springs to Minerva.

Blair Castle Home of the Dukes of Atholl at Blair Atholl, near Pitlochry, dating back to the 13th century.

Blake case (1961). Trial *in camera* of George Blake, an MI-6 agent who betrayed his comrades to the East Germans. He was given the longest sentence in British history (42 years) but escaped in 1966. His father was an Egyptian-born Sephardic Jew named Behar who fought in the British Army in World War I. Blake was born in Holland and worked for the Dutch Resistance.

Blake, Nicholas Pen-name of C. Day Lewis.

Blake, Sexton Detective in a series of cheap novelettes published in Britain first in the *Marvel* and then as the Sexton Blake Library. He was invented by Hal Meredith in 1873, but when the copyright ran out Blake was taken over by numerous other writers, including Peter Cheyney. See Nick CARTER.

Blakeney, Sir Percy See SCARLET PIMPERNEL.

Blandings, Empress of Immense sow who is the centre of attention at Blandings Castle, seat of the P. G. Wodehouse character, the 9th Earl of Emsworth.

Blast Literary and artistic magazine produced by Wyndham Lewis and Ezra Pound to propagate their aggressive modernist views ('vorticism') and the ideology which landed them both eventually in the Fascist camp.

Blatant Beast, The In Spenser's FAERIE QUEENE, the spirit of slander, offspring of Envy and Detraction. It is chained up by a knight, but breaks loose again to plague the world.

Blaue Reiter, Der See BLUE RIDERS.

Bleak House (1853). Dickens's novel, notable for its attack on the old Court of Chancery in an account of the JARNDYCE V. JARNDYCE case. At Mr Jarndyce's home, Bleak House, live his 3 wards, one of whom is, unknown to all, the illegitimate daughter of Lady Dedlock. Tulkinghorne, lawyer to the latter's husband, discovers her guilty secret, and this leads to Lady Dedlock's death and his own.

Blenheim (1704). First major battle of the War of the SPANISH SUCCESSION, in which Marlborough in command of Anglo-German forces defeated a Franco-Bavarian army under Tallard which threatened Vienna. See KASPAR. (English corruption of Blindheim, north of Nuremberg; known on the Continent as the Battle of Höchstadt, a town near by; pronounced blen'im.)

Blenheim Orange (1818). Dual-purpose apple, with yellow and red fruit ripening in early October.

Blenheim Palace Vanbrugh's classical masterpiece in Woodstock, Oxfordshire, built for the 1st Duke of Marlborough; Sir Winston Churchill's birthplace.

'Blessed Damozel, The' (1850). D. G. Rossetti's poem in which a 'damozel' in heaven yearns for her lover on earth.

Blifil Malevolent and treacherous half-brother of TOM JONES in Fielding's novel.

Blimp, Colonel Cartoonist Low's choleric character whose *ex cathedra* pronouncements from a Turkish bath conveyed Low's left-wing sentiments under a die-hard cover ('Bayonets bring the best out of a man – and it stays out').

Blind Earl pattern Worcester porcelain pattern of which the main feature is a large sprig of leaves impressed on the plate; often copied by other factories. (Traditionally first made for a blind Earl of Coventry so that he could feel the pattern; actually made before his time.)

Blind Harry (15th century). Only known name of a Scottish poet who told the story of Wallace in heroic couplets.

Blithe Spirit (1941). Noël Coward comedy in which a man has to cohabit with his second wife and the ghost of his first, audible only to him.

Blitzkrieg German strategy of sudden all-out onslaught, using every available new device, such as reckless thrusts by small groups of tanks far ahead of the main force, STUKA dive-bombing, parachute drops on strong-points etc.; used successfully in overrunning Poland, the Low Countries and France in 1939–40. (German, 'lightning war'.)

Blondel French minstrel who, according to tradition, discovered where Richard I had been imprisoned (in Dürrenstein, Austria) by singing one of his favourite songs under his prison window.

Blondin Stage name of a French tightrope-walker who crossed the Niagara Falls on a rope in 1859 and subsequently repeated the feat blindfold.

Blood and Iron Basis of Prussian policy, according to Bismarck (1886). (Translation of German *Blut und Eisen*.)

Bloodless Revolution, The (1688). Another name for the GLORIOUS REVOLUTION.

Bloody Assize (1685). Name given to the trials by the brutal Judge Jeffreys of those implicated in MONMOUTH'S REBELLION.

Bloody Butcher, The Duke of Cumberland, son of George II, so named for his savage treatment of the Highlanders after the FORTY-FIVE and his victory at CULLODEN.

Bloody Mary Protestant name for Queen Mary I,

the Roman Catholic queen who intervened between Edward VI and Elizabeth I, and was responsible for the MARIAN PERSECUTION.

Bloody Mary (1940s). Mixed drink of vodka and tomato juice.

Bloody Sunday (22 January 1905). Day when troops fired on the St Petersburg workers at the beginning of the 1905 RUSSIAN REVOLUTION.

Bloom, Leopold Jewish advertising canvasser, chief character of Joyce's ULYSSES. He is humiliatingly aware of his wife's unfaithfulness (see next entry).

Bloom, Molly Unfaithful Penelope of Joyce's ULYSSES, wife of Leopold (see previous entry), remembered especially for her 40-page unpunctuated 'interior monologue' which ends the book.

Bloomsbury group Coterie of the British intelligentsia who met and worked in Bloomsbury, London (about 1904–39); they included Virginia and Leonard Woolf (of the Hogarth Press), Bertrand Russell, J. M. Keynes, E. M. Forster, Clive Bell, Roger Fry, David Garnett and Lytton Strachey.

Bloor Derby (1811–48). Products of the DERBY PORCELAIN factory after it was bought by Robert Bloor. In this period it lost its high reputation, wares being made for the cheaper markets, with gaudy IMARI PATTERNS and Rococo designs and, on the figures, elaborate gilding. The firm sold out to COPELAND & GARRETT.

Blue Angel, The Film in which the director Josef von Sternberg launched Marlene Dietrich as a star in the 1930s.

Bluebeard One of the MOTHER GOOSE'S TALES, with an eastern setting. Bluebeard's latest wife discovers a room full of the skeletons of her predecessors, and is rescued from his wrath by her brothers. See SISTER ANNE.

'**Bluebeard**' Nickname of Henri Landru, a Frenchman executed in 1922 for the murder of 10 women. (See previous entry.)

Bluebell line (1960). Branch railway line from

Sheffield Park to Horsted Keynes in Sussex, closed by British Railways, then bought up and run by a society interested in preserving this particularly picturesque line. (So called because in the old days the guard was alleged to stop trains to let passengers pick the bluebells en route.)

Bluebird (1935–67). Name of a series of racing cars, speedboats and hydroplanes used by Sir Malcolm Campbell and his son Donald in establishing various world speed records.

Blue Bird, The (1905). Maurice Maeterlinck's allegorical children's play, a theatrical fairy-tale first produced in Russia by Stanislavsky (see STANISLAVSKY SYSTEM). (French title, *L'Oiseau bleu*.)

Blue Book Parliamentary or Privy Council report, e.g. the yearly analysis of the nation's income and expenditure, or the Board of Trade return of world trade statistics.

Blue Boy, The Gainsborough's portrait, painted partly to confound Reynolds, who held that masses of blue spoilt a picture; now at San Marino, California.

Blue-coat School Christ's Hospital, so called because pupils wear a long blue coat with a leather belt at the waist; it was founded by Edward VI. There are several other blue-coat schools in England.

Blue Cross (1) London organization engaged in animal welfare, which provides veterinary treatment for the pets of those who cannot afford to pay fees. It has absorbed Our Dumb Friends League. (2) (USA; 1929) Non-profit-making health insurance scheme.

'**Blue Danube, The**' (1867). Most famous of the Strauss waltzes. The German title is 'An der schönen blauen Donau'; the 'blue' must be taken as poetic or patriotic licence.

Blue Devils Nickname of the Chasseurs Alpins, an élite corps of the French Army, originally raised and trained to guard the Alpine frontiers, skilled mountaineers and skiers.

Bluegrass, The Region of Kentucky around Lexington where there is a luxuriant growth of bluegrass especially suitable for pasturing horses; it thus became the centre of US racehorse breeding.

Bluegrass State Nickname of Kentucky. (See previous entry.)

Bluemantle Pursuivant of the COLLEGE OF ARMS.

Blue Point oyster Small oyster, esteemed by gourmets, farmed on the shores of Long Island, New York. (Name of a headland.)

Blue Ribbon of the Atlantic Title (later reinforced by a trophy) given to the liner which holds the speed record for trans-atlantic crossings in both directions.

Blue Riders School of German Expressionist art founded 1911 by Kandinsky and Marc, and joined by Klee. (Kandinsky explained: 'We both liked blue and Marc liked painting horses.')

Blues (1) Melancholy folk-songs originating in the early part of the 20th century among Black Americans. (2) Unhappiness or depression.

Blues and Greens, Factions of the Rival street gangs in Byzantium whose nightly brawlings rose to a climax in the 6th century. (Originally the colours of rival teams of charioteers from different quarters of the city.)

Blueshirts (1933). General O'Duffy's Fascist National Guard, formed in the Irish Free State.

Bluestockings (18th century). Literary coterie founded by Mrs Elizabeth Montagu, so named because the men attended its meetings in informal dress, typified by blue worsted stockings.

Bluff King Hal Name for Henry VIII.

Bluidie Clavers Scottish nickname of John Graham of Claverhouse, Viscount Dundee, notorious for his brutal persecution of COVENANTERS (1679–88); and also victor at KILLIECRANKIE.

Blundell's School at Tiverton, Devon; mentioned in *Lorna Doone*. (Founded in 1604 by Peter Blundell, a local man.)

BMA (1832). Initials used for the British Medical Association, the largest of various associations of medical practitioners. The profession is controlled by the GENERAL MEDICAL COUNCIL.

Boabdil Last Moorish King of Granada, died 1492. (Corruption of Abu Abdullah.)

Boanerges Sons of Thunder, Jesus' name for James and John, the sons of Zebedee (Mark 3:17); hence a mighty orator. (The name has come down in corrupt form; pronounced bohan-ėrj'eez.)

Boar's Head, The FALSTAFF'S favourite tavern, kept by Mistress QUICKLY in Eastcheap, London.

Boar's Hill Much favoured residential area near Oxford.

Boat people Escapees from Vietnam, many leaving in open boats.

Boat Race, The (1829). Annual race between Oxford and Cambridge University eights, rowed in March or April on the Thames, originally at Henley and later from Putney to Mortlake over a course of $4\frac{1}{4}$ miles.

Bobbety Nickname of the 5th Marquess of Salisbury.

'Bobby Shafto' 18th-century song about a man said to have lived in Co. Wicklow; given wider currency through application to a parliamentary candidate of that name.

Bobs Bahadur Field-Marshal Earl Roberts of Kandahar (1832–1914). (Hindi, 'gallant', used as a title of respect; pronounced bė-hah'dėr.)

Boche World War I name for a German.

Bodensee German name of Lake Constance, between Germany and Switzerland.

Bodhisattvas In MAHAYANA Buddhism, beings who attain Enlightenment in order to become Buddhas in future ages; they are worshipped as intercessors for mankind with the existing Buddha.

Bodiam Castle Well-preserved 14th-century moated castle near Hawkhurst, Sussex, owned by the National Trust.

Bodleian Oxford University Library founded by Duke Humphrey (1455), re-founded by Sir Thomas Bodley (1597) and extended (1940) with Rockefeller Foundation funds. (Pronounced bod-lee'an.)

Bodnant Gardens One of the finest gardens in Britain, at Tal-y-Cafn, near Conwy, Wales; given by Lord Aberconway to the National Trust.

Bodyline bowling controversy In the Australian Test series of 1932–3 the England fast bowler H. Larwood developed a style of aiming short-pitched balls at the batsman, which resulted in their being caught out by a packed field on the leg side. The Victoria Cricket Association authorized umpires to ban bowlers regarded as bowling to intimidate.

Boeing US aircraft and missile firm, with headquarters at Seattle.

Boeotian Boorish. (Boeotia, a comparatively isolated district of central Greece, capital Thebes, whose inhabitants in classical times were famed for stupidity; pronounced bee-oh'shan.)

Boers See AFRIKANERS.

Boer War (1899–1902). Name in common use for what historians call the Second SOUTH AFRICAN WAR, started by President Kruger of the Transvaal aided by the other Boer Republic, the Orange Free State, and supplied with German arms. The Boers besieged Mafeking, Kimberley and Ladysmith, all of which were relieved by Gen. Roberts in 1900. Kitchener then combated the guerrilla tactics of the Boer commandos by a system of blockhouses combined with concentration camps for civilian sympathizers. The war ended with the Treaty of Vereeniging.

Bofors Swedish light anti-aircraft gun firing 120 shells a minute, used in the Second World War. (Name of town where made; pronounced boh'-forz.)

Boghazköy Site in Turkey of the 17th-century BC Hittite capital, Hattusas, where tablets inscribed with cuneiform writing were found, which threw new light on Hittite history. (Village 90 miles east of Ankara.)

Bogomils Balkan religious community of MANICHAEIST views, which regarded the Orthodox Church as the work of Satan and was the source of many heresies in Russia. It was pacifist, egalitarian, and had no church or priest; it rejected most Christian dogma, but held that every individual could by intense effort and asceticism attain to the perfection of Christ. (Traditionally founded by Bogomil, a 10th-century Bulgarian Manichaean.)

Bog People, The Bodies of Iron Age Germanic peoples occasionally found by peat-cutters, especially in Denmark, almost perfectly preserved by bog-water after 1,500 years or more. They were sacrificial victims of a fertility cult, either strangled, hanged, beheaded or with their throats cut. TOLLUND MAN is a famous example.

Bohème, La (1896). Puccini's opera of Bohemian life in Paris. Rudolph, in one of the best-known love duets ('Your tiny hand is frozen'), falls in love with the frail consumptive Mimi; later they quarrel and part, but Mimi is brought back at the end of the last act for a famous death scene.

Bohn Name familiar to generations of schoolboys for literal translations of Greek and Latin classics, used as 'cribs'. (H. G. Bohn, 1796–1884, English publisher.)

Bokhara rugs Small rugs made by Turkoman nomads over a wide area of Central Asia and collected for export at Bokhara (where none were made). Predominantly rich red or brown, they have retained since the 18th century the same traditional motifs of complicated designs of octagonal shape. They are now mostly made in the USSR, but the design is also copied in Pakistan and Afghanistan.

Bolognese (Cooking) Garnished with meat sauce. (Bologna; pronounced bol-on-yayz'ay.)

Bolsheviks Name given to the opportunist majority group, led by Lenin, after the MENSHEVIKS had seceded from the Social Democrats in 1903.

The name was officially used as a synonym for Russian Communists until just before the end of the Stalin era. (Russian, 'majority group'.)

Bolshoi Theatre (1824). One of the principal theatres in Moscow, famous since 1939 as the home of the Bolshoi Ballet. (Russian *bolshoi*, 'big'.)

Bomba, King Name given to Ferdinand II, Bourbon King of the TWO SICILIES, on account of his ruthless bombardment of rebellious towns during the REVOLUTIONS OF 1848.

Bomb Alley Wry nickname for the parts of Kent and Sussex under the route taken by German flying-bombs in 1944; they suffered severe damage from the many which fell short of their London target.

Bombay duck Dried salted fish used as a relish with curried dishes; also called Bummalo and, deservedly, stink-fish. (Corruption of Mahratti *bombila*, a kind of small fish.)

Bomber Harris Nickname of Sir Arthur Harris, commander-in-chief of Bomber Command (1942–5), so called because he thought that the bombing of Germany should have the highest priority in the strategy of World War II.

Bond, James British secret agent, created by Ian Fleming, who as 007 battled with the dark forces of SMERSH. Gourmet, cad, womanizer and sadist, he became the *idéal laid* of the world.

Bondi Beach Australia's best-known surfing beach, at Waverley, a suburb of Sydney.

Boniface Jovial innkeeper of Farquhar's play *The Beaux' Stratagem* (1707); a generic term for innkeepers.

Bon Marché (1852). Prototype department store, opened in Paris in the rue de Sèvres, south of the river, where it still is.

Bonn Capital of the Federal Republic of Germany; the name is used as a synonym for the former West German government.

Bonneville salt flats Natural race track in Utah, USA, where world land-speed records were set up from 1937 onwards by racing motorists.

Bonnie Prince Charlie See YOUNG PRETENDER.

Bonny Dundee Kinder nickname for BLUIDIE CLAVERS.

Boodle's Club (1762). London club in St James's Street, with a membership drawn from country houses, banking families and the higher echelons of the Army and Navy; identifiable by its famous bow-window from which the masses (i.e. non-members) may be quizzed.

Boogie-woogie Chicago Negro style of (originally piano) BLUES featuring a passacaglia or continuous ground bass, as in 'Dardanella'. Cou-cou Davenport was an exponent.

Boojum A very special kind of SNARK; anyone sighting it will softly and suddenly vanish.

Booker Prize (1968) Annual British literary prize for British Commonwealth and South African fiction, established by Booker-McConnell and worth £20,000.

Book of Hours Roman Catholic breviary of psalms, lessons etc. for every day of the year (originally psalms for every hour of the day), used by priests rather than laymen.

Book of the Dead Ancient Egyptian guide for the dead in the next world, consisting of hymns, spells etc., placed in the tomb.

Boötes Constellation at the tail of the GREAT BEAR, also called the Wagoner (as is AURIGA). It contains the most distant galaxy known, perhaps 6,000 million light-years away; alpha-Boötis is ARCTURUS. (Greek, 'wagoner'; pronounced boh-oh'teez.)

Bór, General Underground name of Tadeusz Komorowski, leader of the Warsaw uprising (1944) crushed by the Germans; the Russians failed to come to his assistance as he was not a Communist.

Bordeaux mixture Fungicide of lime and copper sulphate, first used in the vineyards of Bordeaux.

Bordeaux wines Red (claret) and white wines from vineyards on either side of the River Garonne near Bordeaux, including MÉDOC, POMEROL, SAINT ÉMILION, SAUTERNES and GRAVES.

Bordelaise (Cooking). Rich brown sauce made with Bordeaux wine. (French, 'of Bordeaux'.)

Border Leicester Breed of long-wool sheep with a distinctive Roman nose; bred in the northern border counties and much used for crossing.

Boreas In Greek legend, the personification of the north wind; the adjectival form is Borealis. (Pronounced bor'i-as, bohr-i-ay'lis.)

Borgias, The Spanish family who settled in Italy and won a reputation as poisoners. They produced 2 Popes, the second of whom was Alexander VI (1492–1503). He had many illegitimate children, among them Cesare and Lucrezia, both patrons of art, the former guilty of many crimes which clouded the reputation of his sister, apparently unjustly.

Boris Godunov Title of Pushkin's blank verse play (1825), and of Mussorgsky's opera (1869), about a historical character of that name who usurped the Russian throne in 1598 after murdering the rightful heir Dmitri. In the play a false Dmitri raises a revolt, in quelling which Boris falls ill and dies. (Pronounced bor'is god'un-of.)

Borley Rectory Famous haunted house, investigated by the Society for Psychical Research, and burnt down in 1929. (Village near Sudbury, Essex.)

Boro, The Nickname of the Middlesbrough football team.

Borodino (1812). Battle during Napoleon's invasion of Russia in which the Russian commander Kutusov inflicted considerable loss on the French before continuing his withdrawal. (Village 70 miles west of Moscow.)

Borstal system (1902). System for the detention of criminals aged 15–23 in either closed or open prisons where the emphasis was on education, training and rehabilitation. (Named after the first such prison, at Borstal, Kent.)

Boscobel House Farm near Shifnal, Shropshire, famous as the place where Charles II hid in an oak (the Royal Oak) in September 1651 after his defeat at Worcester. See OAK-APPLE DAY.

Bosie Nickname of Lord Alfred Douglas. See WILDE (OSCAR) CASE.

Bosporus Bridge (1973). Six-lane suspension, box-girder bridge (1,075 metres) designed by the British consultants responsible for the Forth and Severn bridges, built by a multinational consortium to link European and Asian Turkey across the strait.

Boss (1969). (South Africa) Bureau of State Security, the official function of which is to gather information and intelligence concerned with security. As its exact role is unknown and as it is placed by law beyond the control of law, it is widely feared by the populace.

Bossa Nova Popular Brazilian rhythm in the 1960s, similar to the samba. (Portuguese, 'new voice'.)

Boston Strangler, The (USA) Man who murdered at least 11 women, and put Boston, Massachusetts, in a state of terror in 1962–4; he was later identified as Albert DeSalvo, who had been arrested for a separate series of several hundred sexual assaults from 1955 on. On the latter charges he was given a life sentence in 1967.

Boston Stump, The Tower of the very large parish church of Boston, Lincolnshire. Standing high above the flat countryside, it is a useful landmark for ships.

Boston Tea Party (1773). One of the incidents leading to the AMERICAN WAR OF INDEPENDENCE; disguised as Red Indians, American colonists threw a cargo of tea into Boston harbour as a protest against the new British tax on tea.

Bosworth Field (1485). Final battle in the Wars of the Roses, in which the Welsh Henry Tudor, Earl of Richmond, defeated and killed Richard III, and became the first Tudor king, Henry VII. (Market Bosworth, near Leicester.)

Botany Bay Traditional name of the first convict settlement in Australia (1788), although on arrival the leaders of the expedition preferred Port Jackson, a few miles to the north. The city of Sydney now lies between these 2 points.

Botany wool Fine grade of wool obtained chiefly from Australia. (See previous entry.)

Bo-tree Species of Indian fig-tree, under one of which, according to tradition, Gautama attained enlightenment and thus became the Buddha; hence it is sacred to Buddhists. Pilgrims visit a descendant of this tree at a village south of the holy city of Gaya, in Bihar, India. (From *bodhi*, 'enlightenment'.)

Bottom, Nick Weaver in Shakespeare's *Midsummer Night's Dream*. Even though Puck crowns him with an ass's head, Titania, under a spell, falls in love with him. In the play within the play, *Pyramus and Thisbe*, Bottom wants to play all the parts, and gets the lead.

Bottomley (Horatio) case See VICTORY BONDS.

Boudicca Pedantic spelling of the name of the Queen known to every schoolboy as Boadicea; see ICENI.

Bougainvillaea Greenhouse shrubby climbers named after Louis Antoine de Bougainville, French navigator and explorer.

Boulangist crisis (1889). Attempt by the popular French general and War Minister, Boulanger, to organize a right-wing coup d'état. His courage failed him, and he fled abroad, committing suicide 2 years later.

Boulder Dam See HOOVER DAM.

'Boule de Suif' (1880). Generally regarded as one of Maupassant's best short stories, about a group of respectable French citizens caught up in the Franco-Prussian War of 1870 and their changing attitudes to the little prostitute whom they had hoped to use to soften the hearts of their German captors.

Boul' Mich' Students' abbreviation for the Boulevard St-Michel which runs through the university quarter of Paris and where the cafés are thronged with students.

Boulter's Lock Thames lock near Maidenhead where, in Edwardian days, crowds gathered to quiz the fashionable as they passed through in their boats.

Bounty, HMS Captain Bligh's ship, the crew of which mutinied under Fletcher Christian (1789); they landed at Tahiti, and some went on to Pitcairn Island. Bligh survived a 4,000-mile voyage in an open boat to land at Timor.

Bourbon Ultra-Conservative who lives in the past, 'learning nothing, forgetting nothing', as was said of the BOURBONS; (US) 19th-century nickname for Southern Democrats.

Bourbons French dynasty, descended from the Capets, which reigned in France from the time of Henry IV of Navarre and, restored after the Revolution, till 1830 (and through a cadet branch till 1848); in Spain (1700–1931); in the TWO SICILIES, and elsewhere.

Bourbon whiskey (USA) Grain whiskey, named after Bourbon county, Kentucky. It must by law contain 51% maize. (Pronounced bér'bn.)

Bourgeois Gentilhomme, Le (1670). Molière's comedy of the nouveau riche M. Jourdain who, in his determination to make a gentleman of himself, tries to master dancing, fencing and philosophy, to the financial gain of his unscrupulous tutors.

Bourguignonne (Cooking) With onions, mushrooms and red wine sauce. (French, 'of Burgundy'.)

Bourse, La Specifically, Paris stock exchange.

Boursin French cheese, soft, white, speckled, usually slightly flavoured with garlic.

Boutique fantasque, La (1919). Fokine's ballet choreographed for Diaghilev using occasional music composed by Respighi (after Rossini). (French, 'the fantastic toyshop'.)

Bow (1748–75). Possibly the earliest English soft-paste porcelain factory, but products made before 1750 have not been identified. Characteristic are figures in garish colours with crude bocages, charming but far less skilful than contemporary works from Chelsea. Meissen and Chinese influences were strong. The factory was bought up by Derby.

Bow Bells Bells of St Mary-le-Bow, Cheapside, in

the centre of the City of London; hence 'born within the sound of Bow Bells' means 'a true cockney'. The bells and most of the church were destroyed in a 1941 air-raid, but the church has since been very well restored.

Bowen, Marjorie Chief pen-name of Margaret Campbell (later Mrs Long), the romantic historical novelist. She also used the names George R. Preedy, Joseph Shearing and many others.

Bowery, The Street running diagonally through the east side of lower Manhattan, New York City, now a disreputable slum. (Dutch *bouwerij*, farm.)

Bowes Museum Art collection housed in Barnard Castle, near Darlington. (Pronounced bohz.)

Bow Group (1951). Group of young Conservative intellectuals of the left and right, who produce carefully documented pamphlets from time to time.

Bowl games (US college football) Post-season matches, usually on 1 January, between winning teams of the major leagues. (Named after the ROSE BOWL where the first such match was played in 1916, between the champion teams of the eastern and western US universities; other university stadiums were subsequently named 'bowls' also.)

Bowling, Tom Roderick Random's uncle in Smollett's novel of that name, a naval lieutenant at home only on a ship's deck.

Bow Street Chief London Metropolitan police court, near Covent Garden.

Bow Street runners Court police established in the 18th century by Henry Fielding (the novelist) when JP for Westminster; predecessors of Peel's London police. (See preceding entry.)

Bowyers, Worshipful Company of (1621). LIVERY COMPANY, originally a guild which included the FLETCHERS. (Pronounced boh'-yẻrz.)

Box and Cox (1847). (1) J. M. Morton's farce, translated from the French and still played. A landlady lets the same room to 2 tenants, Box and Cox, one on day and one on night work, hoping that they will not get to know of each other. Hence the phrase is used of 2 people who do something turn and turn about. (2) Early comic opera, *Cox and Box*, by Sir Arthur Sullivan.

Boxer Movement Rebellion begun in China in the late 1890s by a peasant secret society and diverted by xenophobic Chinese officials against the imperialist powers, Christian missionaries and converts; see PEKING LEGATIONS, SIEGE OF. (From Chinese name, 'Society of Harmonious Fists'.)

Boycott (1880). English land agent in County Mayo. The captain was the first victim of the LAND LEAGUE'S campaign to shut him off from all social and commercial activities and the word boycott was coined from his name.

Boyhood of Raleigh, The (1870). Painting by Millais, in the Tate Gallery, London.

Boyle's Law (1662). That at constant temperature the volume of a gas varies inversely with its pressure. (Robert Boyle, son of the 1st Earl of Cork.)

Boyne, Battle of the (1 July 1690). Engagement in which James II's Catholic army of French and Irish fled before William III's Protestant army of 36,000 European mercenaries; see TWELFTH OF JULY. (Boyne, a river in Meath, Ireland.)

Boz Pen-name of Charles Dickens used, in particular, in writing *Pickwick Papers*. (Childhood corruption of Moses, nickname of his younger brother.)

Bozzy Nickname for James Boswell, Dr Johnson's biographer.

Brabançon Belgian breed of farm horse. ('Of Brabant'.)

'Brabançonne' (1830). Belgian national anthem. ('Woman of Brabant', the district in which Brussels lies.)

Brabazon airliner (1949). Aircraft built by the Bristol company to carry 120 passengers across the Atlantic. It was withdrawn in 1952 as un-economic.

Brabham Name of various racing cars made by the Australian Jack Brabham; in 1966 he designed, built and drove the car in which he became world champion, a unique perform-ance.

Bracknell, Lady See IMPORTANCE OF BEING EARN-EST.

Bracknell (1949). NEW TOWN in Berkshire, north and west of the old village of that name, 10 miles south of Windsor, designed for a popula-tion of 60,000.

Bradbury First £1 note issued by HM Treasury in 1914, to replace the gold sovereign. It was signed by John Bradbury as Secretary to the Treasury.

Bradshaw (1839–1961). Short title of *Brad-shaw's Railway Guide*, a timetable both com-prehensive and complex. (George Bradshaw, printer.)

Bradwell (1962). One of the earlier series of nuclear power stations. (Coastal village at the mouth of the River Blackwater, Essex.)

Braemar Castle 17th-century home of the Earls of Mar, in Aberdeenshire. (Pronounced bray-mahr'.)

Braemar Gathering, The Royal Highland Gather-ing held at Braemar in September, and usually attended by the Royal Family.

Brahamanas (700 BC). Second stage of Hindu religious literature in which, in contrast to the VEDAS and under contamination from the beliefs of the conquered Dravidians, prominence is given to ritual and sacrifices, caste and the sacred cow, and the BRAHMINS are exalted as the only repositories of true knowledge. The UPANISHADS were a reaction from these writ-ings.

Brahma (Originally the supreme god of the Hindu Trinity (the other members being VISHNU and SIVA), but now held in less veneration than they are.

Brahman Brahmahood, a complex concept of philosophical HINDUISM. It is the true reality, of which the visible universe is only a manifesta-tion; and also the Atman (breath, or the Self) in which all selves can merge through asceticism and meditation.

Brahmins (1) Hindu priesthood. (2) Highest Hindu caste, of priests and scholars. (3) (USA) Applied ironically, first by Oliver Wendell Holmes, to the pundits of New England, especi-ally of Boston. (4) Nickname for devotees of the music of Brahms.

Brahmo Samaj (1818). Hindu religious reformist movement, founded in Bengal, which preached belief in one God; it subsequently broke up into several sects. ('Church of God'.)

Braille (1837). Method of writing language by means of raised points, invented by Louis Braille (1809–52): although not in general use in his lifetime, it is now used all over the world by blind people.

Brains Trust (1941–56). BBC radio programme extremely popular during World War II; a panel of Sir Julian Huxley, Prof. C. E. M. Joad and Cmdr Campbell, under the chairmanship of Donald McCullough, answered questions put to them by the public. (Name originally given to the team of experts who advised Roosevelt on NEW DEAL measures.)

Bramall Lane Football home of Sheffield United.

Bramble, Col. Central figure of André Maurois's *The Silence of Colonel Bramble* (1918), an amus-ing study of the British officer at war as seen through French eyes by the author, who had served as a liaison officer with the British Expedi-tionary Force.

Bramley Seedling First-class cooking apple, ripen-ing in October and keeping well.

Brand (1865). Ibsen's symbolic verse play about a stern pastor who fights compromise in religion. In a distant town he sacrifices his wife and child to his ideals and is finally rejected by his parishioners. Ibsen felt strongly that un-reasoning sacrifice to ideals of goodness was pernicious.

Brandenburg Concertos J. S. Bach's 6 concertos for various combinations of instruments dedicated to the Margrave of Brandenburg.

Brandenburger Tor Eighteenth-century gateway in Berlin, built in imitation of the PROPYLAEA, at the end of UNTER DEN LINDEN. (German, Brandenburg Gate.)

Brand's Hatch Motor-racing circuit near Farningham, Kent, a favourite with Londoners.

Brandywine, Battle of (September 1777). Engagement in the American War of Independence in which Howe defeated Washington. (Brandywine Creek, a stream in Pennsylvania.)

Brangwen, Gudrun In D. H. Lawrence's *Women in Love*, a sculptor who falls in love with an industrialist; said to be based on the writer, Katherine Mansfield. She is a sister of Ursula (see next entry).

Brangwen, Ursula Rebellious daughter of a Nottinghamshire wood-carver, heroine of D. H. Lawrence's *The Rainbow* and *Women in Love*; in the latter said to represent the author's wife, Frieda.

Bratislava City of Czechoslovakia, once known by its German name, Pressburg.

Brave New World (1932). Aldous Huxley's preview of what is in store for the world. Human embryos are cultivated in laboratory bottles and there conditioned to perform the tasks to which they will be allotted. Any trace of individuality is a crime. In *Brave New World Revisited* (1958) Huxley commented that the world seemed to be approaching this state faster than he had expected. (Title from lines in *The Tempest*: 'O brave new world, / That has such people in't'.)

Brechtian An adjective with meanings as varied as Bertolt Brecht's plays and theories; it could refer to the A-effect, EPIC THEATRE, absence of stage props, Communist intensity, etc., and is in fact used with little discrimination.

Breck, Alan Young Jacobite of R. L. Stevenson's KIDNAPPED and its sequel *Catriona*.

Breda, Declaration of (1660). Issued by Charles, King in exile, promising religious toleration and amnesty, and resulting in the Restoration. (Town in North Brabant, Holland, where Charles had his headquarters.)

Bredon Hill Hill by the Worcestershire Avon north-east of Tewkesbury, especially remembered from A. E. Housman's poem in *A Shropshire Lad* beginning: 'In summertime on Bredon / The bells they sound so clear.' This was set to music by George Butterworth, Vaughan Williams and others.

Breeches Bible Nickname for the GENEVA BIBLE, so called because the word breeches is used instead of aprons in Genesis 3:7. See BIBLE.

Brehon law Tribal law of Gaelic Ireland, from the 3rd century BC, part of which has survived in manuscript copies. (English corruption of Gaelic *breiteamh*, 'judge'; pronounced bree'hon.)

Breitmann, Hans Character in Charles Leland's light verses; he is a German immigrant in the USA, remembered in the verse: 'Hans Breitmann gife a barty – / Vhere ish dat barty now? / All goned afay mit de lager-beer – / Afay in de ewigkeit.'

Bren gun Automatic rifle used in World War II. (Compounded from *Brno*, Czechoslovakia, where originally made, and *En*field, England, where the British version was made by BSA.)

Brensham Fictitious village which is the setting for John Moore's stories of Gloucestershire rural life. (The name seems to have been concocted from Bredon and Strensham, villages near Tewkesbury.)

Brent (1965). London borough consisting of the former boroughs of Wembley and Willesden; headquarters at Wembley.

Brentford and Chiswick Former Middlesex borough, since 1965 part of the borough of HOUNSLOW.

Brera, Pinacoteca di (1809). Important art gallery at Milan.

Brer Rabbit With Brer Fox, one of the chief characters of the UNCLE REMUS series of books. See also TAR BABY. (Brer, Negro corruption of 'brother'.)

Brest-Litovsk, Treaty of (March 1918). Treaty imposed by Germany on Bolshevist Russia, by which it lost the Ukraine, Poland, Finland and the Baltic provinces, representing a third of the population of Imperial Russia and much of its industry. (Town now called Brest, on the Polish frontier.)

Breton CELTIC LANGUAGE brought to Brittany by emigrants driven out of Cornwall by the Saxons (4th century AD) and still spoken there. See ARMORICA.

Bretonne (Cooking) With white haricot beans.

Bretton Woods Conference (1944). UN Monetary and Financial Conference which set up the INTERNATIONAL MONETARY FUND and the WORLD BANK. (Bretton Woods, New Hampshire, USA.)

Brewer (1870). Short title for *Brewer's Dictionary of Phrase and Fable* (and of words and phrases from archaeology, history, religion, the arts and science), first compiled by the Rev. Ebenezer Brewer, whose AMDG (*Ad majorem Dei gloriam*) still appears at the end of even the latest of the many revised editions.

Brewers, Worshipful Company of (1437). LIVERY COMPANY to which only those employed in the trade are admitted.

Briareus One of several hundred-handed giants born to Ge (Earth) and Uranus (Heaven). (Pronounced bry-air'i-ės.)

Bride of Lammermoor, The (1819). Walter Scott's historical novel of tragic love, on which is based Donizetti's opera, *Lucia di Lammermoor* (1835).

Bride of the Sea Venice. (Refers to an 11th-century ceremony in which the Doge drops a ring in the Adriatic to symbolize his city's marriage to the sea, i.e. its sea-power.)

Brideshead Revisited (1945). Evelyn Waugh's novel of a man billeted during the war in a country house he had known in peacetime; he recalls the alcoholic son and adulterous daughter who shattered the tranquillity of the aristocratic Roman Catholic family that had lived there. Television adaptation 1980.

Brides in the Bath case (1915). Trial of G. J. Smith, charged with murdering 3 'brides' whom he had bigamously married. He was brought to justice through evidence of systematic conduct – all his victims were found dead in their bath after an alleged fit.

Bridewell Successively a palace, hospital and 'house of correction' in Blackfriars, London; hence a generic name for other such institutions, where the unemployed, those who refused to work, and disobedient apprentices were herded under harsh discipline. The London Bridewell was closed in 1863.

Bridge Club, The Nickname for the 4 main participants in the KENNEDY ROUND – USA, UK, EEC, Japan.

Bridge of San Luis Rey, The (1927). Thornton Wilder's exploration of the theme whether chance or divine purpose brought together the 5 Peruvians who were killed when the bridge of the title collapsed.

Bridge of Sighs (1) Bridge at Venice connecting the Doge's Palace with the city's prison. (2) Bridge resembling it, at St John's College, Cambridge, over the Cam in the BACKS.

Bridge over the River Kwai, The (1952). French novel by Pierre Boulle about British prisoners of war in Japanese hands, made by David Lean into a film (1957). See BURMA RAILWAY.

Brie Soft white cheese similar to Camembert but saltier. (Originally made in the district so named, just east of Paris.)

Brief Encounter (1945). Film scripted by Noël Coward and produced by David Lean.

Brigade of Guards In order of rank: Grenadiers, Coldstreams, Scots, Irish and Welsh Guards. See GUARDS DIVISION.

Brighton Rock (1938). Graham Greene's sleazy novel of teenage criminals in unkempt bed-sitters, with a typically sadistic ending in which the gang-leader, Pinkie, shatters, from beyond the grave, the illusions of the girl he had used to further his crimes.

Brighton trunk murders (1934). Case in which the police found a body in a trunk deposited in a left luggage office at Brighton, and in the course of their investigations found a second trunk with a body in it at the lodgings of a man living under the alias of Tony Mancini. He was acquitted on the ground that although he admitted to concealing the corpse, the murders might have been committed by another. See also MANCINI CASE.

Bright Young Things (1926–9). London equivalent of the American JAZZ AGE generation. A revival of satirical interest in them led to a musical, *The Boy Friend* (1953), in which much play was made with their cloche hats, twirled knee-length necklaces and the spastic CHARLESTON. See also CHELSEA SET.

Brillat-Savarin Name of a French lawyer and gastronome, author *inter alia* of the classic book on the art of good eating: *La Physiologie du goût* (1825). (Pronounced, approximately, bree-yah′ sav-ar-an′.)

Brinkmanship Art of using world fear of a third world war as an instrument of policy, invented by the US Secretary of State John Foster Dulles.

Bristol Boy, The Thomas Chatterton, an 18th-century Bristol boy who at the age of 15 wrote poems he attributed to an imaginary 15th-century monk, Thomas Rowley. These 'Rowley poems' deceived many experts and showed that the boy had the makings of a genius, but he committed suicide at 17.

Bristol delft (1650–1770). Buff-coloured DELFT decorated with purple or blue spots.

Bristol fashion Shipshape and tidy. (Bristol was at one time the second greatest port of England.)

Bristol glass (1) Rare opaque glass which looks like porcelain, made at Bristol in the 18th century. (2) Coloured glass, made at Bristol and many other places from the 18th century. In particular 'Bristol blue' is a term used of almost any blue glass, wherever made.

Bristol milk (1640). Sherry, later adopted as a trade name by Bristol shippers; also Bristol cream, for a richer type. (Bristol, the port for Spanish trade.)

Bristol porcelain (1) Very rare soft-paste wares made 1748–52, after which the firm amalgamated with Worcester. (2) Hard-paste wares (1773–81) the making of which was taken over from Plymouth for a brief, brilliant period, influenced by LOUIS SEIZE Sèvres styles. After this the patents were sold to NEW HALL.

Britannia Gold coins of Britain, first issued in 1987, in four denominations, £100, £50, £25 and £10.

Britannia Cup (1951). International race for boats not less than 32 ft waterline length, held at Cowes in August. (Presented by King George VI to commemorate the centenary of the America's Cup.)

Britannia metal (1790). Alloy like pewter but without lead, which resembled silver when new and pewter when aged. From 1840 some of it was 'restored' by electroplating.

Britannia Royal Naval College (1905). College for officer cadets of the Royal Navy, at Dartmouth, Devon. Formerly known as the Royal Naval College, Dartmouth, and as HMS *Britannia*. See also OSBORNE HOUSE.

British Academy (1901). Learned society which promotes archaeological and oriental research and arranges numerous periodical lectures on literature, philosophy, art, history, law, etc.

British Antarctic Territory (1962). Land south of latitude 60° claimed by Britain; it includes Graham Land, the South Shetland Islands and the South Orkney Islands.

British Association (1831). Short title for the British Association for the Advancement of Science, founded to promote the dissemination of scientific knowledge. It holds a summer annual meeting at which papers are read on recent advances in all branches of science, addressed not only to fellow scientists but to the general public.

British Board of Film Certification Board financed entirely by the film industry, which licenses almost all the films shown in Britain.

British Boxing Board of Control The body which since 1929 has controlled professional boxing in Britain, having taken over some of the functions of the old NATIONAL SPORTING CLUB.

British Cameroons Now divided between Nigeria and Cameroon.

British Council (1934). A non-political government-sponsored organization for disseminating overseas an understanding of the British way of life, through libraries, lectures, etc.; it also provides educational and other facilities for overseas students in Britain.

British Empire, Order of the (1917). Order with civil and military divisions and 5 classes: Knight (Dame) Grand Cross (GBE), Knight (Dame) Commander (KBE, DBE), Commander (CBE), Officer (OBE), Member (MBE).

British Gazette, The Government newspaper published for a few days at the beginning of the GENERAL STRIKE (1926), edited by Winston Churchill, then Chancellor of the Exchequer.

British Indian Ocean Territory (1965). Various small islands in the western Indian Ocean, organized, after the transfer of the very sparse population, as 'stationary aircraft-carriers' for British and US long-range bombers.

British Israelites Members of the British Israel World Federation (1919), who believe that the British are descended from the LOST TRIBES OF ISRAEL.

British Legion, Royal (1920). An organization founded by Earl Haig for the welfare of men and women who served in World War I and subsequent wars; see EARL HAIG'S FUND.

British Lions Rugby team selected for overseas tours from the England, Wales, Scotland and Ireland teams.

British Oxygen Firm which manufactures gases for industrial and medical use, chemicals and precision engineering components.

British Standards Institution (1901). Body, given a Royal Charter in 1929, which in consultation with manufacturers and consumers sets standards of quality and encourages standardization in patterns and sizes. The results of its

work are published in a numbered series of *British Standards* (see KITEMARK). It is financed by government and by professional, industrial and trade organizations.

British Union of Fascists (1932). Oswald Mosley's blackshirted organization, founded after he had left the Labour Party and failed to form a NEW PARTY. From the original programme of setting the country to rights, they descended to rowdy marches in the East End of London, rabble-rousing and Jew-baiting. They spent World War II in an Isle of Man concentration camp.

Brixton Area of South London, scene of anti-police riots in April and July 1981.

Brixton prison Prison in south London mainly used for prisoners on remand and for those serving short-term sentences.

Broad Church (Anglican Church) 19th-century form taken by LATITUDINARIANISM – a similar movement away from rigid definition of dogma and strict rules of ritual, not to be confused with the Low Church (see EVANGELICALISM), but a stage towards the modernists.

Broadmoor (1863). Institution in Sandhurst Park, Berkshire, for persons accused of crime on whom has been passed the verdict of 'not guilty by reason of insanity'.

Broadway Street of New York City which runs 18 miles through Manhattan and the Bronx; the cinema, night-club and restaurant sector (the 'Great White Way') lies between 41st and 53rd Streets.

Brobdingnag Imaginary land in GULLIVER'S TRAVELS inhabited by highminded giants, whose king commented that, from Gulliver's description of them, his countrymen must be 'the most pernicious race of little odious vermin that nature ever suffered to crawl upon the surface of the earth'.

Brocken Highest peak of the Harz Mountains in Saxony, on the boundary between post-war East and West Germany; the most famous of the traditional sites of the Witches' Sabbaths held on WALPURGIS NIGHT.

Brocken, Spectre of the Magnified shadow of an observer on a mountain-top, thrown on to a bank of clouds or mist when the sun is low. (Observed on the BROCKEN.)

Brock's benefit A firework display; applied in both world wars to any spectacular display of Very lights, searchlights, flares, incendiary-bomb fires, etc. (From manufacturer of fireworks used in famous annual displays at Crystal Palace from 1865 onwards.)

Broderers, Worshipful Company of (1561). LIVERY COMPANY, originally a guild of embroiderers.

Brodick Castle Historic home, dating back to the 14th century, of the Dukes of Hamilton, on the Isle of Arran.

Bromley London borough since 1965 consisting of the former boroughs of Bromley and Beckenham, and the urban districts of Orpington, Penge and part of Chislehurst-Sidcup.

Brompton Oratory Common name for the Church of the London Oratory of St Philip Neri (1880) in Brompton Road, London, a fashionable Roman Catholic church with an Italian Renaissance interior, famed for its music.

Bronco Billy (1908–15). Hero of several hundred short Western films.

Bronx, The Only mainland borough of New York City, separated from Manhattan, to the south, by the Harlem River; it contains numerous parks, the Zoo, and university and college buildings; it is primarily residential. (After J. Bronck, who bought the area in 1639.)

Bronx cheer (US slang) 'Raspberry'.

Bronze Age Period following the NEOLITHIC AGE, when bronze (an alloy of copper and tin) replaced flint and stone in making tools and weapons. This culture began to spread from the Middle East about 4000 BC, reaching Western Europe via Troy and the Danube valley about 2000 BC; it was succeeded by the IRON AGE.

Brooke, Dorothea (Mrs Casaubon, Mrs Ladislaw) Heroine of George Eliot's MIDDLEMARCH, who longs to espouse some great cause but is disillusioned in turn by her pedant husband CASAUBON and by Dr LYDGATE.

Brook Kerith, The (1916). George Moore's story of a Jesus who did not die at the Crucifixion but lived on for 30 years with the ESSENES by the Brook Kerith, no longer believing in his own divinity. When he hears Paul preaching Christ Crucified, he wants to proclaim the true facts, but is persuaded that it is too late for him to be believed. (Name of the brook where the ravens fed Elijah, 1 Kgs 17:5, there spelt Cherith.)

Brooklands (1907–46). Formerly Britain's chief car-racing and testing circuit, with a banked track, near Weybridge, Surrey; now closed.

Brooklyn Borough of New York City at the west end of Long Island.

Brooks's Club (1764). London club, opposite BOODLE'S in St James's Street, originally a Whigs' gambling den, but now mainly Conservative, though retaining a faint flavour from the past.

Broomielaw, The Glasgow harbour.

Brother Jonathan Nickname for a US citizen, possibly deriving from the English colonists' penchant for Christian names taken from the Old Testament.

Brothers and Sisters (1929). Typical sample of Ivy Compton-Burnett's numerous witty *sui-generis* novels set in anonymous country-houses where everyone over the age of 3, whether above or below stairs, discourses endlessly in polite and polished English, and continues to do so even after the inevitable family skeleton has fallen noiselessly out of the cupboard.

Brothers Karamazov, The (1880). Dostoyevsky's greatest novel. Karamazov *père*, a wild old sensualist, is murdered. His impulsive son Mitya (Dmitri) is charged with the crime; the tortured sceptic, Ivan, feels guilty since he wished the old man dead; the saintly Alyosha is an onlooker; the degenerate bastard half-brother, Smerdyakov, is in fact the murderer. Most of the book is taken up with discussions of the problems of good and evil, of Russia's relationship to Western Europe, and above all with religious belief. See GRAND INQUISITOR. (Pronounced kar-a-ma'zof.)

Brougham (1838). Closed, four-wheeled one-horse carriage, built for and named after Lord Henry Brougham, one-time Lord Chancellor; the vehicle was designed for private use, but it soon went into public service. (Pronounced broo'am or broom.)

Brown (1764). US university at Providence, Rhode Island.

Brown Betty Pennsylvania Dutch baked pudding of sliced apples layered with breadcrumbs, flavoured with molasses, cinnamon, etc., and served with lemon sauce.

Brown Bomber Nickname of Joe Louis, world heavyweight champion 1937–48.

Brown Derby, The Hollywood restaurant once frequented by the élite of the motion-picture industry.

Brownian motion (1827). Apparently erratic movement of tiny particles suspended in a fluid. In 1905 Einstein showed that these movements satisfied a statistical law which confirmed finally that they were due to bombardment of the particles by the molecules of the fluid.

Browning automatic rifle The BAR, a shoulder-fired, 0.30, gas-operated rifle weighing 20 lb with the bipod support, used by the US army for 40 years after World War I. Designer, John Moses Browning.

Browning Version, The (1948). Terence Rattigan's notable one-act play about the decline of a well-meaning schoolmaster with a detestable wife, whose life had collapsed about him.

Brownists Sixteenth-century Nonconformist sect formed at Norwich and in Holland, and regarded as the parent of modern Congregationalism. See also INDEPENDENTS. (Founded by Robert Browne, who however came to terms with the Church later and held a benefice for 40 years.)

Brown Jack Stakes $2\frac{3}{4}$-mile flat-race at Ascot. (Instituted in memory of Sir Harold Wernher's horse, which won the ALEXANDRA STAKES in 6 successive years.)

Brown, Shipley (1810). London merchant bank and acceptance house.

Brownshirts Another name for the Nazi SA.

Brown's Hotel London hotel in Mayfair, once known as a favourite retreat for exiled kings.

Brücke, Die (1905–13). Group of German Expressionists who painted emotional protest pictures in bright colours. (German, 'the bridge'.)

Brumaire In the French Revolution calendar, the month from 22 October to 21 November; 19 Brumaire (1799) is the date of Napoleon's coup which destroyed the DIRECTORY and led to the CONSULATE. ('Fog-month'.)

Brummagem Adjective applied to cheap and nasty goods of the kind made in Birmingham in the early days of the Industrial Revolution. (Corruption of the old name of Birmingham; the abbreviation of this, Brum, is still used of the city itself.)

Brunel University Technological university, formerly a CAT at Acton, London, now moved to Hillingdon near Uxbridge.

Brunhild, Brünhilde In Scandinavian mythology a Valkyrie; in the Nibelungenlied the Queen of Iceland won by Siegfried for Gunther, and the instigator of Siegfried's death.

Brussels Treaty (1948). Mutual defence pact signed by Britain, France and the Benelux countries; it set up the BRUSSELS TREATY ORGANIZATION.

Brussels Treaty Organization (1948). Organization set up under the BRUSSELS TREATY, which in 1955 was renamed the WESTERN EUROPEAN UNION.

Bruxelloise (Cooking) Sauce of butter, asparagus and egg.

Bryn Celli Ddu Neolithic chambered tomb in Anglesey near the Menai Strait, Wales.

Bryophyta Division of plants comprising the mosses and liverworts.

Brythons Celts who invaded England in the Iron Age and became the ancestors of the Welsh, Cornish and Bretons; see CELTIC LANGUAGES. (Pronounced brith'ĕn; origin of the names Briton, Britain and Brittany.)

Bubastis Greek name for Bast or Pasht, the Ancient Egyptian cat-goddess of Love and femininity, daughter of Isis. The Greeks identified her with Artemis. (Name of the chief centre of her worship.)

Bubble and squeak Left-over boiled cabbage, potatoes and sometimes, cooked meat, fried together.

Bubbles (1886). Millais' sentimental portrait of a child blowing bubbles, which became famous through its use in advertising Pears soap. The child-model overcame this handicap to become Admiral Sir William James.

Bucephalus Alexander the Great's favourite charger.

Buchanan Medal (1897). Royal Society medal awarded 5-yearly for distinguished services to hygienic science or practice.

Buchanan report (1963). Report by Professor Colin Buchanan, entitled *Traffic in Towns*, which recommended that drastic action must be taken to deal with traffic jams in cities. It was received with official approbation, and then filed away.

Buchan periods (1867). Periods of relatively cold (6) or relatively warm (3) weather likely to occur at certain times of the year, as determined by Dr Alexander Buchan from meteorological records in Scotland.

Buchenwald (1937). First of the Nazi concentration camps to be liberated by the Allies (1945). It was near Weimar and the inmates were mostly men and boys, used for various medical experiments. Ilse Koch, wife of the commandant, was sentenced to life imprisonment (1951) for

her activities there, but committed suicide in 1967.

Buchmanism Early name for the movement for long misnamed the Oxford Group and later rechristened MORAL REARMAMENT. (From its founder, Dr Frank Buchman of USA.)

Buckeye State Nickname of Ohio. (Dominant tree.)

Buck House Once fashionable abbreviation for Buckingham Palace, originally named Buckingham House.

Buckingham Palace Since Victoria's accession, the British sovereign's London residence, at the western end of St James's Park and The Mall. Buckingham House was built for the Duke of Buckingham (1703), bought by George III, rebuilt (partly by Nash) for George IV, and refaced with Portland stone in 1913.

Buckinghamshire train robbery (1963). A mail train from Scotland to London was ambushed near Cheddington, Buckinghamshire, and over £2¼ million in paper money was stolen from it. For their part in this crime 12 men were sentenced to a total of 307 years' imprisonment.

Buckley's chance Australian expression for 'little or no chance'. (From a 19th-century convict who escaped from prison, and lived for 32 years among the aborigines of Victoria, where he was regarded as the reincarnation of a former chief.)

Buckmaster Divorce Act (1923). Matrimonial Causes Act which made adultery sufficient cause for divorce by either party; previously a wife had to prove cruelty or desertion in addition to adultery. (Lord Buckmaster, a former Lord Chancellor.)

Buck's Club (1919). London club in Clifford Street, originally founded, and named after, Capt. Buckmaster as a reunion club for officers of the Household Cavalry and their friends.

Buck's fizz Drink comprising equal parts of champagne and fresh orange juice. (Made at BUCK'S CLUB.)

Bucolics Alternative name for Virgil's ECLOGUES.

Buddenbrooks (1900). Thomas Mann's saga of a prosperous North German family whose fortunes decline with the decreasing interest in, and ability for, commerce of successive generations.

Buddha 'The Enlightened One', the name given to Gautama, a Hindu born in Nepal in the 6th century BC, after the revelation that came to him under the BO-TREE. See BUDDHISM.

Buddhism Religion founded by BUDDHA, at one time the religion of all India (under Asoka); it died out there but spread elsewhere in the MAHAYANA and HINAYANA forms. It took over the Hindu concepts of *karma* (that all acts are rewarded or punished in the present life or some future reincarnation) and transmigration of souls to a higher or lower form of life. The Four Truths and the Eightfold Way taught the means of attaining NIRVANA.

Buddleia Shrub named after Rev. Adam Buddle.

Budget leak tribunal (1936). Tribunal which found that J. H. Thomas, Colonial Secretary, had disclosed details of a forthcoming Budget to Sir Alfred Butt, who had used the information for private gain; the Minister resigned. See also DALTON BUDGET LEAK.

Budokwai (1918). Leading British judo club.

Buffalo Bill American cowboy, 'Colonel' William F. Cody, who founded a Wild West Show (1883) which he brought to Earls Court, London, in 1903.

Buggins's turn Phrase referring to promotion on long service rather than on merit.

Bukovina Part of Turkish Moldavia which became an Austrian duchy and was then ceded to Romania. In 1940 the northern half was seized by Russia and incorporated in the Ukraine. The capital was Czernowitz (now Russian Chernovtsy).

Bulgarian atrocities (1875). Brutal massacre of their subject Bulgarian men, women and children by the Turks under ABDUL THE DAMNED, after a nationalist agitation which had the support of Russia and the Orthodox Church.

Bulge, Battle of the See ARDENNES OFFENSIVE.

Bulldog Drummond Vintage English tough patriotic hero, little to modern taste, who manages to outwit the vintage Scandinavian villain, Carl Petersen, in SAPPER's novel of that name (1920) and its many sequels.

Bullingdon Club Oxford University exclusive club for the richer sporting section of the undergraduate community.

Bull Moose (1912) Member of the Progressive Party founded by ex-President Theodore Roosevelt to oppose his own former nominee. W. H. Taft. It split the Republican vote and let in the Democrats' presidential candidate, Woodrow Wilson, with a huge majority. (Roosevelt's own coinage.)

Bull Run Small river in north-east Virginia, near Washington, scene of the first major battle (July 1861) of the American Civil War, in which the Confederate general, Stonewall Jackson, won his nickname by keeping the Union forces at bay. Confederates won another victory there a year later, but on both occasions failed to press home an attack on the capital.

Bultitude, Mr See VICE VERSA.

Bumble Pompous workhouse beadle in Dickens's *Oliver Twist*, immortalized in the word 'Bumbledom' (petty officiousness). It was he who was so distressed when Oliver asked for more, and who said 'the law is a ass'. He becomes a henpecked husband, and himself ends up in the workhouse.

Bumppo, Natty See LEATHERSTOCKING TALES.

Bundestag Federal German Assembly.

Bundeswehr Federal German Army. (German, 'federal defence'.)

Bunker Hill, Battle of (June 1775). First battle of the American War of Independence. (Near Charlestown, now part of Boston, Massachusetts.)

Bunsen burner Used in chemistry laboratories, this consists of a metal tube with an adjustable air valve for burning a mixture of gas and air, giving a flame of great heat. Invented by Robert Wilhelm Bunsen (1811–99), a German chemist. Similar designs had been developed earlier by Faraday.

Bunthorne, Reginald 'Fleshly poet' of Gilbert and Sullivan's PATIENCE. He is supposed to be based on Oscar Wilde. 'Twenty love-sick maidens' pursue him through most of the opera.

BUPA (1947). Initials of the non-profit-making British United Provident Association, an extremely successful organization for insuring against the cost of private medical and surgical treatment by paying an annual fee.

Burge Character in G. B. Shaw's *Back to Methuselah* said to be based on Lloyd George.

Burger, Die (1915). Leading Afrikaans daily, published in Cape Town.

Bürgerbraükeller The Munich tavern where Hitler was wounded by a bomb. November 1939.

Burgess and Maclean case (1951). Two minor British diplomats. Guy Burgess and Donald Maclean, who had served in Washington and Cairo respectively, escaped from England to Russia just in time to avoid arrest by MI-5, having been warned by H. A. R. PHILBY, who joined them there in 1963.

Burghers of Calais, The (1895). Rodin's bronze group at Calais, of which there is a copy outside the Houses of Parliament in Victoria Tower Gardens. It depicts the 6 burghers who, with ropes round their necks and the keys of the town in their hands, pleaded with Edward III in 1347 to spare the town's inhabitants.

Burghley House Elizabethan mansion at Stamford, Lincolnshire, built by William Cecil, 1st Lord Burghley, and the home of the elder line of Cecils (Marquesses of Exeter) ever since.

Burgos government Rebel government set up by Gen. Franco in July 1936 at the beginning of the SPANISH CIVIL WAR. (Former capital of Castile, in northern Spain.)

Burgundy (1) Germanic 5th-century kingdom (capital, Lyons) of the Rhône valley and neighbouring district. (2) A smaller Frankish kingdom. (3) Independent duchy (capital, Dijon) united to France in 1477. (4) Today, the region of the Saône valley, including Dijon, Mâcon and Chalon-sur-Saône.

Burgundy wines (1) Red full-bodied wines made from the Pinot Noir grape grown in a defined area of the Côte-d'Or between Dijon and Chagny; see CÔTE DE BEAUNE, CÔTE DE NUITS. (2) White wines, usually dry, made from the Chardonnay grape grown in 3 separate districts: in the Côte-d'Or (notably Meursault and the Montrachets), Saône-et-Loire (Pouilly-Fuissé) and Yonne (Chablis).

'Burial of Sir John Moore, The' (1817). Only famous poem by Charles Wolfe, on Gen. Moore's death at Corunna in the Peninsular War: 'Not a drum was heard, not a funeral note, / As his corse to the rampart we hurried.'

Buridan's ass An ass placed between equidistant and equi-delicious bundles of hay, having no reason to eat one rather than the other first, would die of starvation, according to an ingenious suggestion attributed to the 14th-century French philosopher, Jean Buridan; hence used of an indecisive person. (Pronounced bewr'id-ahn.)

Burke and Hare Irish navvy, William Burke, and his accomplice William Hare, who smothered people to provide bodies to sell to the Edinburgh School of Anatomy; Burke was executed in 1829, Hare having turned King's evidence. See *The* ANATOMIST. Hence 'to burke' came to be used for 'to smother', 'hush up', an issue.

Burke's Landed Gentry (1837). Short title of *The Genealogical and Heraldic History of the Landed Gentry*, published by Burke's Peerage Ltd, who also publish *Burke's Peerage, Baronetage and Knightage* (1826).

Burlington Arcade (1819). London arcade of very exclusive shirtmakers and other shops, running from Piccadilly to Burlington Gardens (adjoining ALBANY and SAVILE ROW). In Edwardian times only a 'fast' woman would be seen in it. It still has beadles to ensure that no one whistles, plays a musical instrument or lingers there after an old brass bell tolls closing-time.

Burlington House Building in Piccadilly, London, which houses the Royal Academy, the Royal Academy Schools, the Royal Society (until 1967), the Society of Antiquaries and other learned societies. It is the scene of the Royal Academy's annual summer exhibition of contemporary works.

Burma Railway Railway (250 miles with 9 miles of bridges) through the jungle from Bangkok westwards into Burma which the Japanese made Allied prisoners of war build in atrocious conditions, thousands dying of brutal treatment, starvation or disease. It was abandoned after the war to return to jungle.

Burma road Road from Lashio, Burma railhead from Rangoon, to Kunming in south-west China, built just before World War II, which was the chief supply route to Chiang Kai-shek's forces after the Japanese had gained control of China's ports. Closed by Britain in 1940 as a gesture of appeasement to Japan, captured by the Japanese in 1941, reopened in 1945.

'Burma Road' Name given to the difficult West Course at Wentworth Golf Club, Virginia Water, Surrey.

Burney, Fanny Maiden name of Mme d'Arblay (1752–1840), diarist and novelist, author of EVELINA.

Burnham Beeches Stretch of woodland near Slough, Buckinghamshire, with heavily pollarded grotesque stunted beeches.

Burnham Week Chief East Coast regatta, catering particularly for Londoners, held at Burnham-on-Crouch, Essex, in August.

Burns's Cottage See ALLOWAY.

Burschenschaften German students' unions of the 19th century, at first high-minded patriotic societies advocating the unification of Germany, then centres of Liberal activities kept under control by the CARLSBAD DECREES, and finally non-political clubs. (German *Bursche*, 'youngster', 'student'.)

Burton, Gone for a Forces' expression for 'missing' or 'dead'. The Army, Navy and RAF supply differing derivations, but it is an old nautical phrase. A burton is a form of tackle and the phrase perhaps began life as a standard excuse for the absence of a shipmate from his post. The RAF undoubtedly assumed the word to refer to Burton ale; hence the capital initial usual today.

Burton Cup Championship for National Twelve dinghies, held at Weymouth in September. (Sir William Burton.)

Bush House Offices of the external (world) service of the BBC in London.

Bushido Code of honour and conduct of the Japanese SAMURAI, involving fanatical self-sacrifice in the service of the Emperor, and the practice of hara-kiri. (Japanese, 'way of the warrior'; pronounced boosh'e-doh.)

Bushmen African tribe of the Kalahari Desert in Botswana and neighbouring districts who, unlike the related HOTTENTOTS, have kept to a primitive hunting life. They are short in stature and the women often have a characteristic overdevelopment of the buttocks (steatopygia; also found in some Hottentots). Only some 26,000 now survive.

Bussy d'Ambois Sixteenth-century French courtier (a historical figure) who, given away by the King or the King's brother, is killed by the man he had cuckolded. The story is treated by George Chapman and Dumas.

Busy Lizzie See IMPATIENS.

Butchers, Worshipful Company of (1605). LIVERY COMPANY, with a membership still largely recruited from the meat trade.

Butler Act (1944). Important Act which reorganized state-aided education by instituting the 11 + division between primary and secondary schools; classifying secondary schools as grammar, secondary modern or technical, with the option to combine them in comprehensive schools; abolishing fees; raising school-leaving age to 15 (from 1947); and replacing the Board of Education by a Ministry. (R. A., later Lord, Butler, President of the Board.)

Butler's *Analogy* (1736). Short title of Bishop

Butler's *The Analogy of Religion*, in which he argued that if mankind with its known faults was created by God, then by analogy the Scriptures, with their imperfections, could well also be of God; faith is based on probability.

Butlins Colloquial abbreviation for a self-contained holiday camp, one of a series started by Sir Billy Butlin in 1936 at Skegness, designed so that the holiday-maker need not leave the camp to find amusement, and famous for organized mass merriment.

Butskellism Term coined by *The Economist* in the 1950s to express the feeling that there was not much to choose between the economic policies of the successive Chancellors of the Exchequer, Gaitskell (Labour) and R. A. Butler (Conservative).

Buzfuz, Serjeant Comic counsel who appears for the plaintiff in BARDELL V. PICKWICK; having no case he resorts to the traditional tactics of abusing the defendant ('a Being erect on two legs and bearing all the outward semblance of a man'). (Serjeant in the old sense of 'senior barrister'.)

Byelorussia Russian name of White Russia. (Pronounced bel'o-rush''ĕ.)

Byerly Turk One of the 3 sires imported into England about 1700 from which all racehorses are descended, the others being the Darley Arabian and the Godolphin Arabian.

By-pass Variegated Self-explanatory name, one of many coined by Osbert Lancaster for various 20th-century styles of 'architecture'.

Byronic Characteristic of Lord Byron's poetry, outlook, dress, appearance, or romantic heroes; defying the conventions or fate.

Byzantine architecture (5th century). Style based on Greek, oriental and, later, Islamic models. It is characterized by domes over square or polygonal plans, often in clusters; the round arch; rich mosaics, frescoes and icons, in which gold is prominently used. Santa Sophia, Istanbul (537), is typical of the early phase; St Mark's, Venice (1085), of the later. (See BYZANTINE EMPIRE.)

Byzantine Church Another name for the EASTERN ORTHODOX CHURCH.

Byzantine Empire (395–1453). Eastern part of the ROMAN EMPIRE, consisting approximately of the Balkans, Greece and western Anatolia, of which the capital Byzantium (Istanbul) was founded by Constantine in AD 330; the formal division did not take place until 395, when 2 sons of Emperor Theodosius (both minors) became emperors of east and west. The Byzantine (Eastern) Empire, Christian in religion, part Greek and part oriental in spirit, quickly gained ascendancy over the Western, which it ruled from 476 until Charlemagne's time. (Pronounce bi-zant'yn, or, increasingly, biz'an-tyn.)

C

Cabal (1667–73). Name given to the Committee of Foreign Affairs which replaced Clarendon as chief adviser to Charles II. Two members with Catholic sympathies alone knew of Charles's reversal of policy by the Secret Treaty of DOVER; another member, the Earl of Shaftesbury (Ashley Cooper), turned against Charles to lead the WHIG opposition. (Traditionally from the initials of Clifford, Arlington, Buckingham, Ashley Cooper, Lauderdale; also from CABBALA in the sense 'secret doctrine', hence 'intrigue'; pronounced ka-bal'.)

Cabbala (1) Traditions ascribed to Moses and transmitted orally by generations of rabbis. (2) In 9th–13th-century Spain and Provence, applied to mystical doctrines derived from the Old Testament.

Cabinet, Kabinett Name given to German wines of high quality.

Cabinet Office (1916). Cabinet secretariat, staffed by civil servants who prepare the agenda for Cabinet meetings, try to ensure that action is taken on Cabinet decisions, and co-ordinate the work of Cabinet committees.

Cable Street (1935–6). In Whitechapel, London, the scene of confrontations with the British Union of Fascists.

Cabots Aristocratic Boston, Massachusetts, family of whom it was written: 'The Lowells talk to the Cabots / And the Cabots talk only to God.'

Cadbury Castle Pre-Roman hill-fort south-east of Glastonbury, Somerset; pottery remains show that the site had been reoccupied by the 6th century AD by people of wealth.

Cadmus In Greek legend, brother of Europa, founder of Greek THEBES, legendary introducer of the alphabet from Phoenicia. He sowed the dragon's teeth from which sprang armed men who fought until only 5 were left – the ancestors of the Thebans.

Ca' d'Oro (1440). Old Gothic palace in Venice on the Grand Canal, housing the Franchetti collection of paintings by Titian, Tintoretto, Tiepolo, etc. (Italian, 'house of gold'.)

Caernarvon Castle (1284). Fortress built on the Menai Straits, North Wales, by Edward I, whose son was created the first Prince of Wales. One of the best-preserved British castles, it was the scene of the formal investiture as Prince of Wales of the future Edward VIII (1911) and of Prince Charles (1969).

Caerphilly Semi-hard Welsh cheese, white and mild. (Named after a town near Cardiff.)

Caesarian section Operation performed when normal birth would be dangerous, the child being removed through an incision in the abdomen. (Traditionally the way Julius Caesar was born.)

Caesar's wife Remark that 'Caesar's wife must be above suspicion' was, according to Plutarch, made by Julius Caesar to justify his decision to divorce his wife even though he did not believe accusations made against her.

Café de la Paix Large outdoor café in Paris, in the Place de l'Opéra.

Café Royal London restaurant in Regent Street, a meeting-place for artists in the earlier part of the century, and later for BBC staff, journalists, etc.

Cage Me a Peacock (1935). Noel Langley's lively, sophisticated version of the story of LUCRECE, later transferred to the stage.

Cagoulards (1935). French Fascists who, after various outrages, were suppressed in 1938. (French, 'hooded men'.)

Caillaux scandal (1914). Shooting in Paris of the editor of *Le Figaro*, Gaston Calmette, by the wife of Joseph Caillaux, Minister of Finance, who was forced to resign. The editor had threatened to publish incriminating personal letters; the wife was acquitted.

Cain Eldest son of Adam and Eve, the farmer who killed his brother ABEL; God made him a fugitive in the earth and set a mark on him lest any should kill him. (Gen. 4:8–15). The story may refer to the eternal quarrel between nomads and farmers, whose crops are damaged by the nomads' herds.

Cain, To raise To create a tremendous disturbance, make a great fuss. (From CAIN, the first recorded murderer.)

Caine Mutiny, The (1951). Novel by Herman Wouk about a mutiny in a US minesweeper, the *Caine*, during World War II.

'Ça ira' French revolutionary song with the refrain: 'Ah! ça ira, ça ira! / Les aristocrates, à la lanterne' ('Things are going to be OK! String up the aristocrats!').

Cairo Conference (November 1943). Meeting of Churchill, Roosevelt and Chiang Kai-shek, after which the Cairo Declaration of Allied war aims in the Far East was issued.

Caius, Cambridge Short title of Gonville and Caius College, founded by Edmund Gonville and enlarged by John Caius or Kay. (Pronounced keez.)

Cakes and Ale (1930). Somerset Maugham's novel which satirizes the novelists Hugh Walpole ('Alroy Kear') and Thomas Hardy ('Edward Driffield'); Edward's first wife, Rosie, an uninhibited barmaid, is said to be based on Maugham's great and only love, 'Nan', who has not been identified.

Calamity Jane (1) Nickname of Jane Burke, a famous frontierswoman, quick on the draw, who was buried at Deadwood (see DEADWOOD DICK) in 1903. (2) Heroine of a series of dime novels (1884) based on her career. (3) Synonym for a person who is always prophesying calamity, like Jane Burke.

Calcutta Cup (1878). Annual rugby contest between England and Scotland. (Cup presented by the old Calcutta Club when it wound up.)

Calcutta Sweep Sweepstake formerly run by the Royal Calcutta Turf Club on the result of the English Derby.

Calder Hall (1956). Atomic Energy Authority's nuclear-power station, the first in the world to produce electricity for commercial use, but principally engaged in the production of plutonium.

Caledonia Roman name for north Britain, used in poetical contexts for Scotland.

Caledonian Ball, Royal (1849). Charity ball, held since 1930 at Grosvenor House, Park Lane; the largest of the London season, attended by Scots from all over the world, and noted for its set reels and display of Highland dress.

Caledonian Market (New Caledonian Market) Friday street market in London for antique dealers, held since the last war in Bermondsey.

Calendula Genus name of some marigolds; others belong to the genus TAGETES, and the marsh marigold to *Caltha*.

Calgary Stampede Canada's most famous rodeo meeting, held in July at Calgary, Alberta.

Caliban Ill-disposed misshapen monster, son of the witch Sycorax, who appears in Shakespeare's *The Tempest* as PROSPERO's servant. He is a composite picture of the aborigines of then recently discovered lands drawn from travellers' tales.

Calicut Now Kozhikode, a city of Kerala, India.

California, University of (1869). State-supported university comprising 8 campuses, at BERKELEY, Los Angeles, San Francisco and elsewhere. The HQ is at Berkeley.

Caligula's horse Horse appointed Consul by the half-mad Roman Emperor Caligula (AD 37–41); a particularly unsuitable promotion is often derided with the words: 'There has been nothing like it since Caligula made his horse First Consul of Rome.'

Caliphate Rule of the Caliphs (see OMAYYADS, ABBASIDS, FATIMITES), the supreme civil and religious rulers of Islam; the Sultans of Ottoman Turkey and the Grand Sharifs of Morocco were also called Caliphs. (Arabic *khalifah*, 'successor', a title adopted by Abu Bakr on Mohammed's death; pronounced kal'if-ayt.)

Calliope In Greek legend, the muse of epic poetry. (Pronounced kal-*y*'o-pee.)

Callistephus Genus that includes the annual China aster.

Calluna Genus name of Scotch heather, in England called ling; most heathers belong to the ERICA genus.

Calvados Cider brandy made in the Calvados *département* of Normandy.

Calvary (1) Hill at Jerusalem which is the traditional site of the Crucifixion; Golgotha. (2) Representation of the Crucifixion. (Latin *calvaria*, 'skull', a translation of GOLGOTHA.)

Calvinists Extreme Protestant sect, strong in Switzerland and Holland, who believe that souls are predestined to salvation or to eternal hell-fire, and that human nature is totally depraved; a view recast by Karl Barth, since 1921 professor of theology in Germany and Switzerland. (John Calvin, 16th-century French theologian.)

Calydonian boar In Greek legend a ferocious boar sent by ARTEMIS to ravage the land of

Calydon (Aetolia). The Greek heroes hunted it down, ATALANTA wounded it, and Meleager killed it.

Calypso In the ODYSSEY, a nymph who falls in love with Ulysses, detaining him on her island of Ogygia for 7 years until Zeus orders her to release him.

Calypso coffee Coffee laced with TIA MARIA.

Camargo Society (1930). London ballet club formed to keep British interest in ballet alive after Diaghilev's death, by giving performances to members. Its work done, it handed over its properties to the Sadler's Wells Ballet. (Named after a celebrated 18th-century dancer.)

Camargue, La Desolate marshy area of the Rhône delta, southern France, famous for its flamingoes and other bird life, its white horses, and its small black bulls, used in a form of bullfight at Nîmes and Arles, in which the aim is to place a cockade (*cocarde*) on the bull's forehead.

Camberley Sometimes used as a synonym for the Army STAFF COLLEGE, situated at Camberley, Surrey.

Camberwell Former London metropolitan borough, since 1965 part of the borough of SOUTHWARK.

Camberwell Beauty Purely English name for a European and American butterfly, rare in Britain, which was occasionally found in the 19th century in what was then the village of Camberwell, now in London.

Cambrensis Latinism used in the signature of the Bishop of Monmouth, who is also Archbishop of Wales. It is used also in the Latinized name of Gerald Barry, the Welsh medieval historian, known as Giraldus Cambrensis.

Cambrian Period Earliest period of the PALAEOZOIC ERA, lasting from about 600 to 500 million years ago. In the later stages there are fossils of a great variety of marine creatures, but no vertebrates. (Latin *Cambria*, 'Wales', where rocks of this period were first studied, e.g. the Llanberis slates.)

Cambridge Complex, The (USA) Network of research establishments at Harvard (Cambridge, Massachusetts) and the Massachusetts Institute of Technology, forming one of the 'think-factories' which, like the RAND CORPORATION, advise the government on strategic policy.

Cambridge Platonists Group of 17th-century Cambridge men, led by Henry More and Ralph Cudworth, who, using the concepts of Plato and the Neoplatonists, tried to reconcile Christian beliefs with the new findings of science and to oppose with humanism the excesses of Calvinism on the one hand and the materialism of Hobbes and Descartes on the other.

Cambridgeshire, The Major flat-race, run over 9 furlongs at the Newmarket (Houghton) meeting in October.

Cambulic Marco Polo's name for Beijing. (From Mongol *Khanbalik*, 'Khan's city'.)

Camden (1965). Inner London borough consisting of the former metropolitan boroughs of Holborn, St Pancras and Hampstead; headquarters at Euston Road.

Camden Passage Site of a Saturday antique market, at Islington, north London.

Camden Professor Holder of a chair of Ancient History at Oxford.

Camden Town group (1911). Short-lived group of Post-Impressionist artists, led by Sickert. See LONDON GROUP.

Camellia Greenhouse evergreen flowering shrub named after George Joseph Kemel (Camellus), a Jesuit priest.

Camelot King Arthur's capital, identified in local tradition with the hill-fort of CADBURY CASTLE, near GLASTONBURY; also with Caerleon, Winchester, Camelford (Tintagel) etc.

Camembert Rich yellowish cheese with a thick rind; it turns almost liquid when ready to eat and has a flavour nearly as strong as Limburger. (Village of Normandy where originally made.)

Cameron of Lochiel Title of the chief of the Clan Cameron. (Pronounced lokh-eel', with the Scottish *ch* sound.)

Camford Alternative to OXBRIDGE as an abbreviation for Cambridge and Oxford universities.

Camorra Neapolitan secret society founded in the early 19th century and dissolved by Mussolini; originally a prisoners' protection society, it developed into a Mafia-type smuggling, blackmail and robbery club which gained political power by assisting in the expulsion of the Bourbons.

Campagna, The Mosquito-infested plains round Rome which, according to a historian nicknamed 'Malaria' Jones, contributed largely to the decline of the Roman Empire. They were drained by Mussolini.

Campaign for Nuclear Disarmament Better known by the initials CND.

Campanula Genus that includes the Canterbury bell and also the harebell of summer and autumn. In Scotland and northern England the latter is called the bluebell, which in the south is the name of the spring-flowering wild hyacinth.

Campari Italian aperitif, drunk by Italians with or without soda, garnished with slices of lemon.

'Campbells are Coming, The' Song of the 1715 Jacobite revolt, later the regimental march of the Argyll and Sutherland Highlanders. In 1857 Highland Jessie, wife of Corporal Brown, was the first to hear the pipers playing it as the regiment came to the relief of Lucknow; a favourite subject of popular art at the time.

Camp David US presidential retreat in Maryland, USA, best known for the meeting between President Sadat of Egypt and Prime Minister Begin of Israel in September 1978 when agreement on a peace treaty was discussed.

Camperdown (1797). Duncan's victory over the Dutch fleet. See FIRST COALITION. (Named after a village in north Holland off which it was fought.)

Campion Hall (1896). Private hall at Oxford University for Jesuits.

Campion House Roman Catholic theological training college at Osterley, London.

Campo Formio, Treaty of (1797). Treaty under which France and Austria divided up the ancient Venetian Republic, Napoleon securing possession of the Venetian fleet.

'Camptown Races' Well-known 19th-century song by the American, S. C. Foster, containing the words: 'I'll bet my money on de bob-tail nag.'

CAMRA (1971). Campaign for Real Ale, formed to promote the dispensing of beer by hand-pump or gravity rather than gas pressure, and to support the continued production of traditional ale.

Camulodunum Roman name for Colchester, capital of the Belgae.

Canaan Western Palestine, the PROMISED LAND of the children of Israel.

Canaanites Pre-Jewish inhabitants of CANAAN, i.e. the Phoenicians.

Canada Cup (1953). International professional golf tournament between teams of 2 from each country.

Canadian Shield Region of rocks of the PRE-CAMBRIAN ERA found over most of Canada east of the Rockies, characterized by low relief and numerous lakes; it is the source of most of Canada's minerals as well as much of its timber and hydroelectric power.

Canal du Rhône au Rhin, Le Grand Important link in the West European canal system, designed to enable barges of over 1,000 tons to navigate from Rotterdam to Marseille.

Cana marriage feast Scene of the first miracle performed by Jesus, who turned water into wine (John 2:1–11). Its best-known representation is a picture by Paolo Veronese in the Louvre. (A village said to have been near Nazareth; pronounced kay'na.)

Canard enchaîné, Le (1916). Paris satirical

weekly, famous for its witty cartoons and its bold stand against governmental interference.

Canaries, The Nickname of the Norwich City football team, from their yellow shirts.

Canasta Card game for 4, developed from Rummy. (Spanish, 'basket'; name in the original Uruguayan version for the highest-ranking combination of cards.)

Canberra RAF twin-jet bomber, in service since the early 1950s in the Far East, Nato and Cento theatres as a nuclear-strike aircraft; it was to have been replaced by the F-111, but the order was cancelled.

Cancer Crab, 4th constellation of the Zodiac, between Gemini and Leo; the sun enters it at the summer solstice about 21 June. Astrologers claim that those born under this sign may be home-loving, possessive, moody.

Candace (1) Title of Ethiopian queens in Roman times. (2) Legendary Queen of Tarsus who held Alexander the Great in thrall. (Pronounced kan'da-see.)

Candia Italian name for Crete and for its capital, Iráklion (Heraklion).

Candida (1903). Bernard Shaw's play in which Candida Morell, realizing that her sensible Christian Socialist parson husband needs her continued support, resists the temptation to leave him for an idealist, unpractical poet.

Candide (1759). Voltaire's satire on Leibniz; see Dr PANGLOSS. Its last words ('We must cultivate our garden', i.e. attend to our own affairs) are often quoted.

Candleford See LARK RISE TO CANDLEFORD.

Candlemas 2 February, the feast of the Purification of the Virgin Mary, and a Scottish quarter-day. (The year's supply of candles was consecrated on this day.)

Canebière, La Famous street of luxury shops and restaurants in Marseille, running from the Old Port.

Canis Major Southern constellation, below ORION, and called Orion's Dog; its chief star is SIRIUS (the Dog Star). (Latin 'great dog'.)

Canis Minor Southern constellation north of CANIS MAJOR; its chief star is Procyon. (Latin, 'small dog'.)

Cannae (216 BC). Crushing defeat of the Romans by Hannibal, see PUNIC WARS. (Village in Apulia.)

Cannes International Film Festival Most important of the film festivals, held in May.

Canopus Second brightest star in the sky (after SIRIUS), in the southern constellation Argo. (Name of Menelaus' helmsman; pronounced kan-oh'pus.)

Canossa Castle where in 1077 the Holy Roman Emperor Henry IV, who in a struggle over the right to appoint clergy had declared the pope deposed and had been himself excommunicated, made his submission to Pope Gregory VII, after being made to wait 3 days in the snow in a penitent's shirt; hence 'to go to Canossa' is a phrase meaning 'to climb down'. (Village near Modena, northern Italy.)

Canterbury lamb English name for lamb imported from the province of Canterbury, South Island, New Zealand.

Canterbury Tales Chaucer's poem (begun 1386, left unfinished), which gives a vivid picture of contemporary life through tales told by a group of pilgrims making their way from London to Becket's shrine at Canterbury.

Canterbury Week (1842). Oldest of the cricket week festivals, at which the Old Stagers (theatrical) club put on an entertainment; 'the Goodwood of cricket'.

Cantharides (1) Dried SPANISH FLY. (2) Also used of the live beetle of that name.

Canton Chinese city, officially Guangzhou (Kwangchow).

Canton china (1) Early 19th-century Chinese porcelain painted in enamel colours, typically with flowers and butterflies on a green ground. (2) US name, confusingly, for NANKING CHINA.

Cantor lecture Lecture delivered at the Royal Society of Arts on human problems in industry.

Cantos (1917–59). Ezra Pound's life work, an open-ended epic poem dealing with just about everything.

Cantuar Abbreviation for (Archbishop) of Canterbury.

Canuck Colloquial name for a Canadian, especially a French Canadian. (Pronounced ka-nuk'.)

Caodaist sect In Vietnam, the adherents of a synthetic religion with elements of Christianity, Buddhism, Taoism, Mormonism, etc.; its saints include the Duke of Wellington and Victor Hugo.

Caoimhghin Original Erse form of the Irish name Kevin.

Capability Brown Lancelot Brown (1715–83), a landscape gardener who laid out the grounds of Blenheim, Harewood and other great houses. (From his favourite comment: 'This land has capabilities.')

Cape Canaveral America's chief launching-site for satellites and space-probes in Florida.

Cape Coloureds In South Africa, a long-established community, mainly in western Cape Province, of mixed African or Asian and European descent, who are mainly Christians, and speak Afrikaans or English as their mother tongue; they are officially regarded as separate from the Africans.

Cape Kennedy Cape Canaveral, Florida. It was called Cape Kennedy 1963–73 and NASA still uses this name.

Capella (Astronomy) See AURIGA.

Capenhurst Site of one of the Atomic Energy Authority Production Group's factories for producing uranium and plutonium. (Cheshire village, north-west of Chester.)

Cape St Vincent (1797). Victory won by Admiral Jervis (later Lord St Vincent) and Capt. Nelson over the Spanish fleet. See FIRST COALITION. (In south-west Portugal.)

Capetians Dynasty which ruled France from the 10th century to the Revolution and for a short period thereafter, the VALOIS (1328) and BOURBON (1589) dynasties being branches of the Capet family. (From Hugh Capet, who seized the French throne from the CAROLINGIANS.)

Cape-to-Cairo railway Cecil Rhodes's dream of a railway spanning Africa from north to south, not destined to be realized.

Cape Triangle (1853–64). First non-rectangular postage stamp, issued in the Cape of Good Hope Colony, South Africa.

Capital Levy Levy on an individual's capital, suggested during World War I as a means to pay off the huge National Debt that was accumulating. The proposal received some support from all parties but was never implemented: the Labour Party continued to advocate it for many years.

Capitol, The (1) Ancient Roman national temple of Jupiter, on the CAPITOLINE, which contained the Sibylline Books. (2) (USA) Building in Washington DC where the US Congress meets; also applied to the state-house or building where a US state legislature meets.

Capitoline Roman hill on which the CAPITOL stood; earlier called the Tarpeian Hill.

Capitoline geese Sacred geese on the Capitoline Hill which, according to legend, 'saved Rome' in 390 BC by alerting the garrison when the Gauls tried to take the Capitol by stealth.

Capodimonte (1743–1821). Soft-paste porcelain made at Naples, extremely rare, but faked in hard paste in great quantity from an early date. Meissen and Chinese influences were strong, and mythological subjects treated in a lively flamboyant style were typical. Cups and saucers with coloured relief figures were for long erroneously thought to have been produced here.

Caporetto (October–November 1917). Disastrous defeat of the Italians in World War I by Austrian troops strengthened by German reinforcements. Allied forces had to be diverted to Italy to restore the situation. (Village north of Trieste on the ISONZO, then in Austria; now in Yugoslavia and renamed Kobarid.)

Capricornus Goat, 10th of the constellations of the Zodiac, between Sagittarius and Aquarius; the sun enters it at the winter solstice, about 21 December. Astrologers claim that those born under this sign may be conventional, single-minded and stubborn. (Latin *caper*, goat; *cornu*, horn.)

Caprivi appendix Long, narrow strip of territory giving Namibia access to the Zambezi: formerly part of German South-West Africa, incorporated in Bechuanaland (1922) and handed over to the Union of South Africa in 1939. (Named after a German Chancellor.)

Captain Kidd Almost a synonym for 'pirate'; Capt. William Kidd, Scottish sailor, was sent in 1696 to put down piracy in the Indian Ocean and there, it is alleged, turned pirate; he was hanged in 1701. Some think he was the innocent victim of political intrigue; nevertheless, the legend grew that he had left behind huge caches of loot.

Captains Courageous (1897). Kipling story about the pampered son of an American millionaire; he falls overboard and is rescued by a trawler skipper who makes him work, to his lasting benefit. (Title taken from an old ballad.)

Capuchins (1520). Reformed order of FRANCISCAN friars which returned to the strict observance of the Rule of St Francis. (French *capuche*, 'pointed hood', worn by them; pronounced kap'ew-shinz.)

Capulets In Shakespeare's *Romeo and Juliet*, the Verona family to which Juliet belonged, at feud with the Montagues, Romeo's family.

Caran d'Ache Pseudonym of Emmanuel Poiré (1858–1909), French inventor of the strip cartoon, who contributed to *La Vie Parisienne*, etc. (From Russian *karandash*, 'pencil'; he was born and educated in Moscow.)

Carbonari (1815). Secret society of Italian

republicans, numbering Louis Bonaparte among its members, which after an ineffective career was absorbed by Mazzini's Young Italy movement. (Italian, 'charcoal-burners'.)

Carbon-14 dating First of several new techniques for dating archaeological finds. Carbon-14 is a radioactive isotope which decays very slowly at a known rate; thus the age of certain organic remains (e.g. timber) can be deduced from the amount left.

Carboniferous Period Latest but one of the periods of the PALAEOZOIC ERA, lasting from about 350 to 275 million years ago. Fossils of the larger amphibians, and later of reptiles, appear, accompanied by many insects (dragonfly, mayfly, cockroach), and a rich flora of ferns and evergreen trees, fungi, etc. Rocks of great importance were formed, including the Coal Measures, Millstone Grits and Carboniferous Limestone. (Latin, 'coal-bearing'.)

CARD (1964). Initials used for the Campaigns Against Racial Discrimination, founded in London after the passing of the Commonwealth Immigrants Act. When it passed under the control of extremists in 1967, the moderates formed an 'Equal Rights' splinter group.

Card, The Nickname of Denery Machin, the slick and successful young businessman in Arnold Bennett's novel of that name (1911). (Slang = the 'character'.)

Cardiff Arms Park Cardiff home of Welsh rugby and of the Cardiff RUFC; cricket was also played there until 1966, and there used to be an athletics track.

Cardinal Virtues Defined by Plato as justice, prudence, temperance, fortitude; to these the SCHOOLMEN added the Christian theological virtues of faith, hope and charity.

CARE (1945). (USA) Initials standing for Cooperative for American Relief Everywhere Inc., an organization through which gift-parcels of food and clothing were sent to Europe after World War II (until 1952 its name was Cooperative for American Remittances to Europe) and later to any part of the world.

Caretaker, The (1959). Pinter's play of mutual incomprehension, in which Davies, a tramp, is too warped to be grateful for the accommodation given him by 2 brothers, and tries to play off one against the other until he is turned out.

Carey Street Site of, and used for, the London Bankruptcy Court, WC2, which deals only with cases arising in London.

Carfax Centre of Oxford. (Latin *quadrifurcus*, cross-roads.)

Caribs (1) Ferocious American Indians encountered by Columbus in the West Indies. They gave their name to the Caribbean Sea, and the word 'cannibal' is a corruption of the Spanish name for them. (2) Linguistic group of American Indians now scattered over the Guianas, Venezuela, Honduras and Nicaragua.

Carisbrooke Castle Medieval seat of government of the Isle of Wight, near Newport; it is still partly inhabited. Charles I was detained there for some time at the end of the Civil War.

Carley float Emergency raft of copper tubing, cork and canvas for survivors of shipwrecks at sea; it floats either side up and is provided with paddles, drinking water and a signal light. It was used in World War I.

Carliol: Abbreviation for (Bishop) of Carlisle.

Carlists Supporters of Don Carlos, pretender (1833) to the Spanish throne, of his grandson (also Don Carlos), and of their descendants; see next entry.

Carlist Wars (1834–96). Series of sporadic civil wars in Spain between CARLISTS, supported by the Church, and Royalists; the latter accepted the succession of a woman (Queen Isabella) to the throne, in spite of the SALIC LAW, which her father had declared invalid.

Carl Rosa Opera Company (1875). London and touring company formed to present opera in English; in 1958 it was absorbed by the SADLER'S WELLS Opera Company. (Name of a German musician who settled in England.)

Carlsbad German name of Karlovy Vary, the Czechoslovak spa.

Carlsbad decrees (1819). Imposed by the German-born Austrian Foreign Minister, Metternich, on the newly formed confederation of German states to suppress manifestations of Liberalism in the universities and professions; they inaugurated 30 years of police repression.

Carlton Club (1832). London club in St James's Street; it is the Tory club *par excellence* and absorbed the Junior Carlton Club in 1977.

Carlton Club meeting (19 October 1922). Crucial Conservative Party meeting which decided to withdraw from the coalition government formed in 1916; Lloyd George then resigned the premiership.

Carlton House Home of the Prince Regent (later George IV), which gave its name to CARLTON HOUSE TERRACE.

Carlton House Terrace London street overlooking St James's Park, formerly associated with the German embassy (no longer there), particularly during the Nazi Ribbentrop's inglorious tenure of office.

Carmelites (12th century). Roman Catholic order, originally of hermits, later mendicant friars (White Friars), founded in Palestine during the Crusades. In 1562 St Theresa formed a stricter sect of barefoot ('discalced') friars and nuns, which became dominant. They are active in missionary work. (Founded on Mt Carmel, traditionally in biblical times; they wear a white cloak over a brown tunic.)

Carmen (1875). Bizet's last opera, based on a short story by Mérimée. The gypsy Carmen flirts with Corporal Don José, who allows her to evade arrest for stabbing a girl and is persuaded to desert his regiment to join the smuggler's band. But Carmen is now interested in a toreador, Escamillo, and is stabbed dead by the jealous Don José.

Carmen, Worshipful Company of (1946). LIVERY COMPANY; a fraternity of carters was formed in 1517.

Carmen Jones (US) Successful modernized black film version of CARMEN in which the smugglers become soldiers, and the toreador Escamillo is renamed Husky Miller, the prize-fighter.

Carnaby Street Shopping street east of Regent Street, London, which leapt into fame in the 1960s as the fashion centre for modern youth.

Carnac Village in Brittany, site of tombs and a megalithic stone avenue dating back to about 2000 BC.

Carnatic, The Old European name for the part of Madras which lay between the Eastern Ghats and the Coromandel Coast; it was ruled by the Nawab of Arcot and acquired by the British in 1801 in their final struggle with the French for the domination of India.

Carnegiea Greenhouse cacti named after Andrew Carnegie (1835–1918) whose institute financed collectors of cacti in USA.

Carnegie Hall (1890). Famous New York concert hall, acoustically perfect and long the headquarters of the New York Philharmonic; it lies on Seventh Avenue and 57th Street, and has music studios, a smaller hall for chamber music, and other ancillary buildings.

Carnegie Medal An annual award by the Library Association for the best children's book written by a British subject.

Carnegie Trusts Series of trusts formed from 1896 onwards by Andrew Carnegie, the Scottish-born American millionaire steel-magnate; most of them are designed to further the cause of education in USA and Britain. He is particularly remembered for the public libraries he endowed.

Carnival (1912). Compton Mackenzie's novel of the theatre world into which he was born.

Carolingians (751–987). Frankish dynasty founded by Pepin and succeeded by the CAPETIANS. (Named after Pepin's son Charlemagne, or Carolus Magnus.)

Carpenters, Worshipful Company of (1477). LIVERY COMPANY which still finances instruction in all branches of the building trade through its foundation, the Building Crafts Training School, and by grants and scholarships.

Carrhae (53 BC). Scene of the Parthian defeat of the Roman army under Crassus, in the first of several unsuccessful attempts by Rome to gain control of Mesopotamia. (Town east of the upper Euphrates, near Urfa in southern Turkey; pronounced kar'ee.)

Carroll, Lewis Pen-name of the Rev. C. L. Dodgson, author of *Alice in Wonderland*.

Carter, Nick (1886–1920). US counterpart of the English Sexton BLAKE; he was portrayed as a shrewd, tough detective in a series of dime novels written by various hands and also adapted for the screen and radio.

Carter's Little Liver pills US patent medicine, the first to compete with BEECHAM'S PILLS in this lucrative trade.

Cartesian Adjective formed from Descartes. French mathematician and philosopher (1596–1650), who tried to argue from absolute certainties (*Cogito, ergo sum*, 'I think, therefore I must exist', was his starting point) reached by methodical doubt, arriving at the conclusion that mind and matter are quite separate entities which interact through the pineal gland; although his philosophy was purely materialistic, he placated the Church by saying that matter does not move of its own accord, the original impulse coming from God.

Carthaginian peace Very harsh terms imposed on the conquered, as by Rome on Carthage at the end of the 3rd PUNIC WAR.

Carthaginian Wars See PUNIC WARS.

'Carthago, Delenda est' 'Carthage must be destroyed', the phrase with which Cato the Censor ended every speech in the Roman Senate. He died just before his wish was fulfilled; see PUNIC WARS.

Carthusians (1084). (1) Roman Catholic order of monks founded on the Chartreuse plateau near Grenoble, France (La Grande CHARTREUSE); the original austere regime has lasted unaltered for 9 centuries, monks living in separate hermitages, vowed to silence, eating one (meatless) meal a day, growing their own food, meeting only for prayer and on designated occasions. A 'Chartreuse' (anglicized to 'Charterhouse') was first founded in England in the 14th century. (2)

Members of CHARTERHOUSE SCHOOL. (From Latinized form of *Chartreuse*.)

Carton, Sydney Dissolute character in Dickens's TALE OF TWO CITIES who during the French Revolution takes the place of Darnay, whom he closely resembles, at the guillotine, where he makes a famous last speech beginning: 'It is a far, far better thing that I do, than I have ever done . . .'

Casabianca The boy who stood on the burning deck in Mrs Hemans's poem, based on an incident aboard a French ship at the Battle of the Nile (1798).

Casablanca Conference (January 1943). Meeting of Churchill and Roosevelt (joined later by De Gaulle), which decided on invasion of Sicily, and at which Roosevelt first mentioned the 'unconditional surrender' policy.

Casanova Compulsive womanizer. (From the 18th-century Italian rake and rogue, Casanova, and his not always credible account of his amours, in 12 volumes.)

Casaubon, The Rev. Edward The uselessly pedantic but reputedly learned clergyman who disillusions his wife Dorothea Brooke in MIDDLEMARCH. (Pronounced kas-awb'en.)

Casbah, The Specifically, the old quarter dominating the modern city of Algiers. (Arabic for a fortress-village of Moorish feudal settlement, corresponding to a medieval European castle.)

Casement diaries Diaries of Sir Roger Casement, who was executed (1916) for treason after a farcical German-assisted gun-running escapade in Ireland during World War I. They included the Black Diary, which chronicled homosexual episodes, and were shown to the US government to forestall protests against his execution. In 1959 they were made available for public inspection to allay ill-founded suspicions that they were government forgeries.

Cash and Carry Act (November 1939). US Neutrality Act authorizing the export of arms to belligerents, but only on the basis that payment was to be made, and transport effected, by the purchaser.

Casket letters Love-letters to Bothwell allegedly in the handwriting of Mary Queen of Scots, produced after Darnley's murder at KIRK O'FIELD, and held to implicate her in it; she maintained that they were forgeries. Copies of them were discovered at HATFIELD HOUSE in the 19th century.

Cassal lecture (1959). Lecture on French art or literature, given at London University.

Cassandra Prophet of woe; strictly, a prophetess who is not believed but is nevertheless right. (Daughter of King Priam of Troy, brought home captive by Agamemnon. She correctly foretold the death of both of them.)

'Cassandra' Sir William Connor, who over a long period contributed a column under that name in the *Daily Mirror*. (See previous entry.)

Casse-Noisette (1892). Petipa's ballet, more commonly known as *The Nutcracker*, is now a Christmas staple. Tchaikovsky's music is familiar through the selections in the *Nutcracker Suite*, e.g. 'The Dance of the Sugar-Plum Fairy'.

Cassino (1944). See MONTE CASSINO.

Cassiopeia In Greek legend, a Queen of Ethiopia, mother of ANDROMEDA, who dared to say that her daughter was more beautiful than the NEREIDS. (Pronounced kas-i-o-pee′a.)

Cassiopeia Northern W-shaped constellation close to the North Pole and Cepheus. (See previous entry.)

Cassiterides The 'Tin Islands', a name first used by the Greek historian Herodotus: they are usually identified as the Isles of Scilly and Cornwall (or Britain as a whole), from which the Carthaginians had been the first to import tin to the Mediterranean countries. (Pronounced kas-i-ter′i-deez.)

Castel Gandolfo Ancient Roman castle overlooking Lake Albano, south of Rome; now the Pope's summer residence.

Casterbridge Town in Thomas Hardy's novels, said to represent Dorchester.

Castile Former kingdom of Spain, consisting in the 11th century of Old Castile, to the north and west of Madrid, to which Toledo, conquered from the Moors, was added in 1085. León in the 12th century, and Aragón in 1479. The capital was Toledo, with royal palace also at Valladolid.

Castle, The (1926). Kafka's novel in which 'K' (the novelist, or Everyman) continually struggles through mists and fantastic bureaucratic obstruction to gain admittance to the right department of an unexplained castle to obtain something unspecified; it is a moving allegory of man's struggle to comprehend the incomprehensible, and his search for Grace. (German title, *Das Schloss*.)

Castle Combe Motor racing track near Chippenham, Wiltshire.

Castleford ware (1790–1821). Best known for white stoneware teapots with 4 concave or convex corner panels, and decorated in relief; similar teapots were also made elsewhere. (Made at Castleford, Yorkshire, by Dunderdale & Co.)

Castle Howard Domed mansion near Malton. Yorkshire, which has been in the hands of the Howard family ever since Vanbrugh built it in the early 18th century. It contains fine art collections and from its earliest days has been open to the public.

Castle of Otranto (1764). The first major Gothic horror story, by Horace Walpole, in which various supernatural happenings lead to the destruction of the castle and its usurper, Manfred. See GOTHIC NOVELS.

Castle Rackrent (1800). Maria Edgeworth's novel of feckless Irish landlords and their equally feckless tenants.

Castor Double star, the brighter of the 2 stars in the heads of the GEMINI twins (the other being POLLUX). (See next entry.)

Castor and Pollux In Greek legend, the twin sons of Leda and a King of Lacedaemon (in later legend, of Zeus), brothers of Helen of Troy. Castor was the tamer of horses, Pollux (also called Polydeuces) the boxer. Together they were known as the DIOSCURI.

CAT (1962). Initials used for College of Advanced Technology, a state college, not under LEA control, for the education of technologists to university-degree standard. Several CATs have been given university status in recent years.

Catacombs, The Galleries dug in the underground quarries of ancient Rome, used by the early Christians as chapels and hiding-places; their dead were buried in the walls, which were decorated with symbolic scenes from biblical stories. (Name of unknown origin, originally given to the supposed burial place of Peter and Paul, under a church near Rome.)

Catalan Language of the people of CATALONIA, a dialect of Provençal, spoken also in Andorra, the Balearic Isles and in adjoining areas of France. It has its own literature, and there is also a distinctive type of Catalan music.

Catal Hüyük Important archaeological site in central Turkey, where evidence has been found of settled town life going back to at least 6800 BC. If this is confirmed, the beginning of the NEOLITHIC AGE must be much earlier than previously supposed.

Catalonia Old Mediterranean province of northeast Spain, capital Barcelona, which has continually sought independence or at least some measure of autonomy. See CATALAN.

Cat and Fiddle An inn sign, probably derived from the nursery rhyme 'Hey diddle diddle / The cat and the fiddle', and indicating that tip-cat could be played and that a fiddle was available for dances.

Cat and Mouse Act (1913). Popular name for the Prisoners (Temporary Discharge for Health) Act, passed to deal with hunger-striking suffragettes, who were released on parole but could be snatched back to prison as necessary.

Catch-as-Catch-Can (Wrestling) Lancashire style, in which tripping is allowed and both shoulders must be forced on to the ground for a win.

Catcher in the Rye, The (1951). J. D. Salinger's first novel, about a runaway prep-school boy, Holden Caulfield, who explores New York and the antics of grown-ups.

Catch-22 (1961). American novel about World War II by Joseph Heller which satirizes the ambitions and stupidities of senior air force officers through the story of a madly undisciplined member of a bomber crew stationed on a Mediterranean island.

Cateau-Cambrésis, Peace of (1559). Treaty which ended the Hapsburg-Valois wars; France abandoned hopes of conquest in northern Italy, which was surrendered to the dead hand of Spanish Hapsburg rule; the most serious result was the eclipse of the Italian Renaissance. (Town near Cambrai.)

Caterpillar Club Club formed in World War II for airmen who survived baling out in action and who could supply the number of the parachute that saved them to the founding firm, the US Irvin Parachute Co.

Cathal Irish name equivalent to Charles.

Cathari (10th century). Widespread community of MANICHAEISTS of southern Europe, sometimes identified with the ALBIGENSIANS and the BOGOMILS. (Greek, 'pure ones'.)

Cathay Poetical name for China; see for example, LOCKSLEY HALL. (Name possibly of Tartar origin; pronounced ka-thay'.)

Cathleen ni Houlihan Yeats's nationalist play (1904), in which an old beggar woman reveals herself as Cathleen ni Houlihan, the symbol of Ireland, struggling for freedom.

Catholic League (1587–98). League of Catholic powers led by Spain and supported in France by the powerful GUISE family, which tried to prevent the succession of the Protestant Henry of Navarre as King Henry IV of France. After a brief success they collapsed when Henry nonchalantly declared himself a Roman Catholic, saying, 'Paris is worth a mass'.

Catholic Revival Another name for the OXFORD MOVEMENT.

Cathy Come Home (1966). TV semi-documentary drama of the homeless, particularly families where the husband is compulsorily separated from his wife and children, written by

Jeremy Sandford, husband of Nell Dunn who wrote *Up the Junction*; both works shocked the nation's conscience.

Cato Manor riots (1960). Sudden African riot at Durban, South Africa, caused by a police campaign against illicit distilling in which much liquor had been confiscated; 9 police were killed. (Name of a squalid shanty-town on the outskirts of Durban.)

Cat on a Hot Tin Roof (1955). Tennessee Williams's play, set in Mississippi, in which 2 brothers and their wives manoeuvre for precedence in their dying father's will.

Cato Street conspiracy (1820). Plot to murder Lord Liverpool's Tory Cabinet at dinner. The plotters, led by Arthur Thistlewood, who was inspired by the French and American Revolutions and angered by PETERLOO and similar acts of repression, were caught and hanged. (Cato Street, Edgware Road, where the conspirators met.)

Catriona (1893). R. L. Stevenson's sequel to KIDNAPPED. (Gaelic, 'Catherine'; pronounced kat-reen'a.)

Cattle-raid of Cooley Best-known story of the Ulster cycle of legends, a 7th-century account of an event at the beginning of the Christian era.

Caucasian Chalk Circle (1954). Brecht's play, written 10 years before it was staged, based on an old Chinese play, in which Azdak, a rogue turned judge, decides the rival claims of 2 women to a baby by putting him in a chalked circle and telling them to pull him out. One hauls him out, the other is afraid of hurting him, and wins her case.

Caucasian languages Group including Georgian and CIRCASSIAN which, like Basque and Etruscan, may have been spoken in Europe long before the arrival of the Indo-Europeans. (Named after the mountain range between the Black Sea and the Caspian.)

Caucasian rugs Well-made long-lasting tribal rugs from north and south of the Caucasus, formerly exported through Persia, now through USSR. The primary colours predominate and the designs, including stylized animals and flowers, are geometrical.

Caucasians Obsolescent term for the dominant white races, more commonly heard in USA than Britain. It derived from a fivefold classification of mankind by J. Blumenbach into Caucasian, Mongolian, Ethiopian, Amerindian and Malayan. He chose the name because his collection of skulls from the Caucasus were most typical of the group; he also thought that the 'Indo-Europeans' might have originated there.

Caudillo, El The title assumed by General Franco as supreme head of the Spanish state. (Spanish equivalent of *Der Führer* and *Il Duce*.)

Caudine Forks (321 BC). Crushing defeat of the Romans by the Samnites; the Romans surrendered and were humiliated by being made to 'pass under the yoke'. Hence used of any crushing military defeat. (A mountain pass near Capua.)

Caudle, Mrs Nagging wife of a series of *Punch* articles by Douglas Jerrold, published in book form as *Mrs Caudle's Curtain Lectures* (1846). (The title refers to the curtains surrounding four-poster beds.)

Caughley (1775–1814). Factory making soft-paste porcelain, of which the best-known specimens are cabbage-leaf jugs with moulded mask spouts. The WILLOW PATTERN was invented here. The factory was bought by COALPORT in 1799. Also called Salopian. (Village in Shropshire; pronounced kahf'li.)

Cauldron, Battle of the Heavy tank engagements in May 1942 south of Tobruk in Cyrenaica, prelude to the final battle at 'KNIGHTSBRIDGE'.

Caution, Lemmy Peter Cheyney's detective, an English version of the American tough guy, who appears in *Dames Don't Care* (1937) and its successors.

Cautionary Tales (1907). Book of light verse in rhymed couplets by Hilaire Belloc, such as the poem about the untruthful Matilda who was burnt to death, since every time she shouted 'Fire!' her neighbours answered 'Little liar!'

Cavalcade (1931). Noël Coward's spectacular patriotic play dealing with the impact of historical events on an Edwardian family; the author later hinted that in writing it he 'came to scoff, remained to pray'.

Cavalier Parliament Strongly Royalist assembly summoned by Charles II at his restoration, which attempted to crush Puritanism by the CLARENDON CODE.

Cavaliers In the ENGLISH CIVIL WAR the name given to the royalists who fought for Charles I, or less specifically for the retention of the monarchy or of the bishops, or of both; strong in the north and west, and in cathedral towns.

Cavalleria Rusticana (1890). Mascagni's one-act opera of jealousy and revenge in a Sicilian peasant setting. See CAV. AND PAG.. (Italian, 'rustic chivalry'; pronounced kaval-èr-ee'a rusti-kah'na.)

Cavalry Club (1891). London club in Piccadilly for officers of the cavalry regiments.

Cav. and Pag. Opera-goers' shorthand for CAVALLERIA RUSTICANA and PAGLIACCI, which are always played together, the former being a one-act opera.

Cavell Memorial Memorial near Trafalgar Square, London, to Nurse Edith Cavell, who during World War I (1915) was executed at Brussels by the Germans for helping prisoners of war to escape.

Cavendish Laboratory (1874). Cambridge University physics laboratory, which Rutherford as director (1919–37) 'turned into the cradle of nuclear physics'. (Named after Henry Cavendish, the physicist.)

Cavendish Professor Holder of the chair of Experimental Physics at Cambridge.

Cawnpore Older English spelling of Kanpur, on the Ganges, Uttar Pradesh, India: scene of a massacre in the Indian Mutiny (1857).

Caxton Hall Former fashionable register office for marriage in Westminster, London. Originally opened in 1882 as Westminster town hall, it became a register office in 1933 and closed in 1977.

CBI (1965). The Confederation of British Industry, a merger of the Federation of British Industries (FBI), the British Employers' Confederation and the National Association of British Manufacturers, with associate members from the nationalized industries and other fields. It centralizes the guardianship of the interests of British industry, both in relation to government and internationally.

Cecil Sharp House Headquarters of the English Folk Dance and Song Society (1932), near Regent's Park. London. (Cecil Sharp, 1859–1924, collector of folk-songs.)

Ceefax Teletext system of the BBC.

Celebes Older name of Sulawesi, a group of islands in Indonesia.

Celestial City, The In PILGRIM'S PROGRESS, symbolizes Heaven.

Celestial Empire, The Chinese Empire. (Translation of a Chinese name.)

Celsius scale Name of a temperature scale. (Swedish astronomer, Anders Celsius (1701–44).)

Celtic Glasgow soccer team whose Roman Catholic supporters carry on a traditional feud with the Protestant supporters of RANGERS. (Celtic Park, home ground.)

Celtic fringe Celtic-speaking peoples inhabiting the fringes of Britain, i.e. the Scots, Welsh and Cornish, together with their Irish cousins.

Celtic languages Branch of Indo-European languages, subdivided into: (1) the Goidelic, Gaelic or Q-Celtic group, which includes Scottish Gaelic, Irish Gaelic (Erse) and Manx; (2) Brythonic or P-Celtic group, which includes Welsh, Cornish and Breton. The language of pre-Roman Gaul belongs to the latter, but survives only in place-names.

Celtic Twilight Mystic fairyland background to Irish literature, prominent in the works of such writers as W. B. Yeats. Æ and Lord Dunsany.

Celts Term commonly applied to the Celtic-speaking people of the British Isles (Scottish, Welsh,

Irish etc.), who are probably non-Celtic in origin but adopted CELTIC LANGUAGES and culture. (Originally used by the Greeks of fair-haired peoples living north of the Alps.)

Cenci, The (1819). Shelley's tragedy about the historical Beatrice Cenci, who had her father murdered; her lawyer's false plea that attempted incest had provoked the murder was rejected, and Beatrice was executed in 1599. (Pronounced chen'chi.)

Cenerentola, La See CINDERELLA.

Cenotaph (1920). Sir Edwin Lutyens's memorial in the middle of Whitehall to the memory of men and women of the 3 services and the mercantile marine who died in World War I; later it became a memorial to the dead of both world wars. The REMEMBRANCE SUNDAY service is held there each November. (Greek, 'empty tomb'.)

Cenozoic Era Most recent geological era, covering the last 70 million years down to the present, and divided into the TERTIARY *and* QUATERNARY PERIODS; sometimes called the Age of Mammals. During this era Man, mammals, trees and flowering shrubs evolved rapidly, but invertebrates changed little. The Alps, Himalayas, Andes and Rockies were formed. (Greek, 'modern life'.)

Centaurs Greek legendary lustful creatures of Thessaly, with men's heads and horses' bodies; see CHIRON. Their battle with another Thessalian race, the Lapithae, is depicted on the Parthenon frieze.

Centaurs Oxford University football club of the best 50 or so players in residence (elected for life).

Centaurus Southern constellation below VIRGO and LIBRA. Alpha Centauri is the 3rd brightest star in the skies and one of the pointers to the SOUTHERN CROSS; Proxima Centauri is the nearest known star, except the sun; Omega Centauri is a globular cluster. (Named after CHIRON.)

Centennial State Nickname of Colorado. (Joined the Union 100 years after the Declaration of Independence.)

Centipedes Oxford University athletics club of 50 members. (Named from the number of their feet.)

Central Committee, The (USSR) Theoretically the supreme executive organ of the Communist Party in the USSR, consisting of some 360 members elected by the Party Congress. In fact its actions are dictated by its POLITBURO and Secretariat, which have only about 10 members each and are led by the General Secretary of the Secretariat, who is also the senior member of the Politburo.

Central Criminal Court The Old Bailey.

Central Electricity Generating Board (1958). Government body which owns and operates the power stations and grid system in England and Wales. Similar bodies operate in the other parts of the UK.

Central Hall, Westminster (1912). Headquarters of the Methodist Church in Great Britain, opposite Westminster Abbey.

Central Intelligence Agency See CIA.

Central Office The headquarters of the Conservative Party in SMITH SQUARE.

Central Park Large park in central New York, containing the Metropolitan Museum of Art and CLEOPATRA'S NEEDLE.

Central Powers Coalition in World War I that included Germany, Austria–Hungary, the Ottoman Empire and Bulgaria.

Central Provinces (India) Older British name of Madhya Pradesh.

Central Standard Time (USA) Time in the east-central states, 6 hours earlier than GMT.

Centranthus ruber Species name of the Red Valerian or Pretty Betsy; the common valerian belongs to the genus *Valeriana*.

Centre Court Famous tennis-court at WIMBLEDON.

Century plant American aloe, a plant that after some 60 years flowers on stems up to 20 feet high, and then dies.

Cephalopods

Cephalopods See MOLLUSCS.

Cepheid variables Single stars which vary in light intensity over short periods (from a few hours to 50 days). (Pronounced see'fi-id.)

Cepheus Northern constellation between CASSIOPEIA, the GREAT BEAR and CYGNUS. (In Greek legend, husband of Cassiopeia; pronounced see'fews.)

Cerberus Three-headed dog that guarded the entrance to HADES. The Sibyl who took Aeneas to the Underworld threw him a drugged cake, the first 'sop to Cerberus'. (Pronounced sèr'bèr-us.)

Ceres Largest of the asteroids (or minor planets), about 400 miles across.

CERN (1954). An organization through which 13 Western European countries co-operate in maintaining a nuclear research station at Meyrin near Geneva, equipped with a proton synchrotron and a synchro-cyclotron, etc. (Initials of original name: Conseil – now Organisation – Européen pour la Recherche Nucléaire.)

Cerne Giant Figure of a man 180 ft high, with a club in his hand, cut in the downs above Cerne Abbas near Dorchester, Dorset. It may be a representation of Hercules and date from the 2nd century AD.

Certificate of Secondary Education (1965). Awarded after 5 years' secondary education on the results of a local examination, instituted as an alternative to GCE, mainly for secondary modern pupils but now replaced by GCSE.

Cesarewitch One of the last major races of the flat season, run at Newmarket over a distance of 2¼ miles (Pronounced sizar'é-wich.)

Cestodes See PLATYHELMINTHS.

Cestr: Abbreviation for (Bishop) of Chester.

Cetaceans An order of aquatic mammals; the whales, dolphins, porpoises.

Cetus Whale, a large southern constellation below ARIES and PISCES; it contains Mira, a long-period (330 days) variable. (Latin, 'whale'; it represented the sea-monster about to swallow ANDROMEDA; pronounced see'tus.)

Chablis Light wine, driest of the white Burgundies, traditionally drunk with oysters.

Chad, Mr Character who first appeared in a *Daily Mirror* cartoon in 1937, his head peering over a wall, with a caption such as 'Wot – no beer?' Adopted by the troops, he appeared in wall scribbling the world over during the ensuing war years. Compare KILROY WAS HERE. (Developed from an elementary electrical circuit diagram; e.g. one eye was a plus sign, the other a minus.)

Chadband, Rev. Mr Hypocritical and scarcely literate minister of an unspecified sect who, in Dickens's *Bleak House*, deploys the admired Chadband style of oratory, e.g.: What is peace? Is it war? No. Is it strife? No.

Chaenomeles Genus that includes the quince and 'japonica'; formerly classified under the genus *Cydonia*.

Chaeronea (338 BC). Defeat of the Athenians and their allies by Philip of Macedon, thus uniting Greece under Macedonian leadership. (Pronounced kair-on-ee'a.)

Chaffers Editor's name used for the standard reference book *Marks and Monograms on Pottery and Porcelain (European and Oriental)*, first pub. 1863, 15th edn 1965. (William Chaffers.)

Chairman Mao Usual Chinese designation for Mao Tse-tung, former Chairman of the People's Government of China and former Chairman of the Central Committee of the Chinese Communist party. (Pronounced mow.)

Chairman of Committees The SPEAKER's deputy and chairman of the WAYS AND MEANS COMMITTEE.

Chairman of the Council of Ministers Official designation of the Soviet Prime Minister.

Chairman of the Praesidium of the Supreme Soviet Official designation of the President of the USSR.

Chalcedon, Council of (451). Oecumenical Council which condemned the MONOPHYSITE HERESY, and defined the nature of Christ as true man and true God, having 2 natures, perfectly distinct, perfectly joined, partaking of one divine substance. (Town of Bithynia, Asia Minor; pronounced kals'ĕ-dn.)

Chaldea, Chaldaea (1) Province of Babylonia at the head of the Persian Gulf; see CHALDEANS. (2) In the Old Testament, 'the land of the Chaldees' is used of all Babylonia.

Chaldeans, Chaldaeans (1) Semitic race of unknown origin who settled at 'Ur of the Chaldees' (Gen. 11:28) and later came to dominate the second BABYLONIAN EMPIRE. Thereafter Chaldean and Babylonian became synonymous. (2) In Daniel (2:2 and elsewhere) and in Greek writings, the Chaldeans are represented as magicians, astrologers, astronomers and mathematicians.

Challenger US space shuttle programme. Highly successful until the disaster of January 1986 when 73 seconds after lift-off there was an explosion and 7 crew members were killed.

Challoner Club (1949–90). A London club for Roman Catholics, in Pont Street.

Chamberlain Worcester (1783–1840). Porcelain made by a firm at Worcester founded by Robert Chamberlain, formerly employed at the main WORCESTER PORCELAIN factory. It made both soft paste and bone china and was famous for services painted with old castles on apple-green grounds. It amalgamated with FLIGHT & BARR and then traded as Chamberlain & Co.; in 1862 this firm was again named the Royal Worcester Porcelain Co.

Chamber of Horrors Section of MADAME TUSSAUD'S, devoted to waxwork figures of famous criminals at their work.

Chambertin See CÔTE DE NUITS.

Champagne Former French province, capital Troyes, watered by the Marne. Rheims (Reims) is the centre of the sparkling-wine trade, famous from the 17th century onwards.

Champagne nature Non-sparkling wine from the Champagne country.

Champion Hurdle Major event under National Hunt rules, run over a distance of 2 miles at Cheltenham in March.

Chan, Charlie Chinese-American amateur detective, created by E. D. Biggers in *The House without a Key* (1925), who studied the characters of his criminal adversaries in order to predict their actions, and was much given to philosophical musings.

Chanak crisis (October 1922). Caused by Turkish entry into the Chanak neutral zone held by the British and French, just before the proclamation of the Turkish Republic by Mustapha Kemal; the Turks intended to wrest eastern Thrace from Greece. The Conservatives felt that Lloyd George acted rashly in sending reinforcements and withdrew from his coalition government (see CARLTON CLUB MEETING). (Chanak, the Asiatic side of the Dardanelles.)

Chance (1913). Joseph Conrad's sea story of Capt. Anthony's fidelity to Flora de Barral whose father, a fraudulent financier whom he had taken under his wing, tries to poison him.

Chancery Division Division of the High Court of Justice, nominally presided over by the Lord Chancellor, which deals, sometimes as a court of first instance, with such matters as wardship of infants, estates, real estate, partnerships and trusts. Most cases are taken in London by a judge sitting without jury. Until 1873 Chancery decisions constituted the law of equity, as distinct from common law.

Chanel Leading Paris fashion house started by Gabrielle (Coco) Chanel (died 1971, aged 87) which reached its peak in the 1920s, pioneering simple comfortable clothes (jersey, tweed, pearls), costume jewellery, and the famous perfume 'Chanel Numéro 5'. She opened in Deauville (1912) and waged war on the corset, retired in 1938 in face of the challenge of Schiaparelli, but made a successful come-back in 1954 with a shop opposite the Ritz.

Changing of the Guard (1) Changing of the Queen's Life Guard, provided by the HOUSE-

95

HOLD CAVALRY, at the HORSE GUARDS. (2) Changing of the Queen's Guard, normally provided by the GUARDS DIVISION, at Buckingham Palace.

Channel tunnel Plans for a tunnel between France and UK have existed since 1802. Britain abandoned one scheme in 1975 but in 1989 construction started.

Chanson de Roland (11th century). Troubadours' song of ROLAND's death at RONCESVALLES and Charlemagne's revenge on the Saracens and on Ganelon who betrayed him.

Chansons de Geste (11th–14th centuries). Epic poems of the troubadours of northern France, such as the CHANSON DE ROLAND, conforming to the traditions of courtly love and chivalry. (French, 'songs of heroic deeds'.)

'Chanticleer and Pertelote' Chaucer's version, in the *Nun's Priest's Tale*, of a theme from the REYNARD THE FOX cycle. (Pertelote, more familiar as Dame Partlet.)

Chantilly (Cooking) Served with rich cream. (French town noted for its cream.)

Chantilly porcelain (1725–1800). French soft-paste porcelain, at first covered with a tin-oxide glaze and decorated in KAKIEMON PATTERNS; from 1760 an orthodox glaze was used and Meissen-style decoration was introduced, in particular the 'Chantilly sprig' of cornflower and forget-me-nots (copied by Derby among others).

Chantrey Bequest Fund left to the Royal Academy to buy for the nation works by British artists, which are exhibited in the Tate Gallery. (Sir Francis Chantrey, sculptor, died 1841.)

Chanucah, Chanukah See HANUKKAH.

Chapeau de Poil, Le Rubens's charming portrait of the sister of his second wife (Hélène Fourment); now in the London National Gallery. (French, 'the beaver hat'.)

Chapelcross (1959). First Scottish nuclear power station and plutonium plant, a duplicate of CALDER HALL, run by the Atomic Energy Authority's Production Group. (Near Annan, on the coast of the Solway Firth, Dumfriesshire.)

Chapel Royal (1) Clergy, musicians (now an organist) and choir, in attendance on the monarch; the institution goes back to the 12th century. (2) Similar institution at Holyrood which attends on the monarch there and at Balmoral. (3) Chapel (1532) attached to the original St James's Palace. (4) A second chapel near by in Marlborough Gate, designed by Inigo Jones; also called the Queen's Chapel.

Chapman's *Homer* (1598–1615). Free translation into rhymed couplets of the *Iliad* and *Odyssey*, which inspired Keats's sonnet 'On First Looking into Chapman's Homer' (1816), where he compares the experience with that of 'stout Cortez' staring at the Pacific, 'silent, upon a peak in Darien'.

Chappaquiddick (1969). Place where Senator Edward Kennedy's car plunged off a bridge, drowning Mary Jo Kopechne. Kennedy was given a 2-month suspended sentence for leaving the scene of the accident but in April 1970 was finally cleared of any legal responsibility. (An island on Cape Cod, Mass.)

'Charge of the Light Brigade, The' Tennyson's poem on the British cavalry charge at BALACLAVA when – 'Into the valley of Death / Rode the six hundred.'

Charing Cross Road London street traditionally associated with second-hand books and music publishing.

Charlemagne prize (1949). Annual prize awarded by citizens of Aachen to those who have contributed most to European co-operation and understanding, e.g. Churchill, Hallstein, Spaak. (Aachen, formerly Aix-la-Chapelle, Charlemagne's capital.)

Charles de Gaulle International airport, also known as Roissy, to the north-east of Paris.

Charles's Wain Name for the PLOUGH. (For Charlemagne's wagon.)

Charleston Peculiarly ungraceful and energetic dance, with side-kicks from the knee as the chief feature, introduced in the Negro revue *Runnin' Wild* (1923).

Charley's Aunt (1892). Brandon Thomas's apparently immortal farce, in which the 'aunt' is impersonated by a male.

Charlie Brown (1950). Manic-depressive chief character of the comic strip PEANUTS, whose self-confidence, frequently pricked, springs eternal.

Charlus, Baron de In Proust's REMEMBRANCE OF THINGS PAST, a member of the GUERM-ANTES family, a secret homosexual who loses the violinist Morel to SAINT-LOUP.

Charmian Cleopatra's lively attendant in Shakespeare's *Antony and Cleopatra*, who follows her mistress to her death.

Charolais White breed of French cattle, imported from France in recent years to cross with British stock.

Charon In Greek legend, the man who ferried the dead across the Styx to Elysium, for the fee of one obol. (Pronounced kair'on.)

Charterhouse (1371). Originally a CARTHUSIAN monastery, near Smithfield, London; it then became a school (see CHARTERHOUSE SCHOOL). Now it is a home of rest for aged 'brethren', who must be members of the Church of England, bachelors or widowers over 60, and former officers, clergy or members of the professions.

Charterhouse School Public school, moved from London to Godalming, Surrey, in 1872.

Chartists (1838–49). Group of left-wing intellectuals and workers who issued a People's Charter demanding the extension of the vote to the working-classes, payment of MPs, and other reforms. There were riots at Birmingham, Newport and elsewhere, and a petition with over a million signatures was presented to the Commons.

Chartreuse Liqueur originally (and again, since 1940) made by monks at La Grande Chartreuse, the CARTHUSIAN headquarters near Grenoble; said to contain over 130 ingredients, of which angelica root is one. The green variety is much stronger than the yellow.

Chartreuse de Parme, La (1839). Stendhal's novel, a study of Italian life, which begins with a famous description of the Battle of Waterloo and ends in a Carthusian monastery.

Chartwell (1923–65). Home in Kent of Sir Winston Churchill.

Charybdis See SCYLLA AND CHARYBDIS.

Chateaubriand Thick slice of high-quality steak cut from the middle of the fillet and grilled; porterhouse steak.

Château du Prieuré Country house near Fontainebleau, where after the First World War GURDJIEFF set up his Institute for the Harmonious Development of Man, which Katherine Mansfield and other intellectuals attended. (French *prieuré*, 'priory'.)

Château-d'Yquem See SAUTERNES.

Château Gaillard (1196). Almost impregnable fortress built by Richard I high above the Seine, to defend Normandy against the French; now in ruins. (Near Les Andelys, between Rouen and Paris.)

Château la Pompe Jocular French name for water.

Château-Thierry French town associated with the first major action of US forces on the Western Front, in May 1918. (Town on the Marne, between Paris and Rheims.)

Chatham House Headquarters of, and standing for, the ROYAL INSTITUTE OF INTERNATIONAL AFFAIRS, in St James's Square, London. (Former residence of 1st Earl of Chatham.)

Chatsworth Seventeenth-century home of the Dukes of Devonshire, at Edensor, near Bakewell in Derbyshire, with many art treasures, fine gardens and parks.

Chattanooga (1863). Key point in Tennessee, won during the American Civil War by the Union generals, Grant and Sherman, after bitter fighting.

Chatterton lectures (1955). Annual lectures on English poets, sponsored by the British Academy.

Chauffeurs' Arms, The Nickname for the ROYAL AUTOMOBILE CLUB.

Chauvin, Nicolas French soldier of the Napoleonic Wars, an extremely bellicose patriot; he was lampooned in a number of French plays. Hence *chauvinism*, bellicose patriotism.

Chawton Village near Alton, Hampshire, where Jane Austen's home is preserved as a museum.

Cheapside London street in the CITY, running east from St Paul's Cathedral to Poultry; once the town's principal market-place (Anglo-Saxon *ceap*, 'barter' – which recurs in *Chip*ping Campden, etc.), with side streets called Bread, Milk, Wood, etc. Street. The MERMAID TAVERN was there, but no buildings of note survive.

Checkpoint Charlie Most notorious of the check-points between East and West Berlin, and the only crossing-point for foreigners. It was a barometer of East–West relations; when they deteriorated, the Russians would impose petty restrictions on through traffic, creating long queues of heavy lorries. Demolished 1990.

Cheddar cheese Smooth hard cheese, with an elastic consistency, traditionally made in Somerset but nowadays made across Britain and the cheddaring process is used throughout the world. It is even said that there is a French cheddar. Since about 1850 Cheddar has been made in factories or creameries.

Cheddar Gorge Limestone cliffs towering 400 ft over the road to Cheddar in the Somerset Mendips, with caves which were occupied by early man for tens of thousands of years.

Cheeryble brothers, The Two benevolent merchants in Dickens's *Nicholas Nickleby*.

Cheiranthus Genus name of the wallflowers.

Cheiro Pseudonym of Count Louis Hamon, a famous palmist who predicted the date of Edward VII's death; he was probably a clairvoyant rather than a palmist. (Name taken from cheiromancy, Greek word for palmistry, from *cheir*, 'hand'.)

Cheka (1917–22). Lenin's secret police, formed to check counter-revolutionary activities in Communist Russia. It had full powers to arrest, try, sentence and execute. It was replaced by the OGPU. (Name formed from the initial letters of the Russian for 'Extraordinary Commission': the full title added 'for Combating Counter-Revolution, Sabotage and Speculation'.)

Chellean culture Older name for ABBEVILLEAN CULTURE.

Chelsea Former metropolitan borough of London, now part of the borough of KENSINGTON AND CHELSEA.

Chelsea-Derby (1770–83). Porcelain of the period when the CHELSEA PORCELAIN factory was made subsidiary to Derby, as indicated by the usual mark, which was a D.

Chelsea Flower Show Britain's major flower show, held in May in the gardens of CHELSEA HOSPITAL.

Chelsea Hospital (1682). Properly, Chelsea Royal Hospital, London, founded by Charles II and begun by Wren, with additions by Robert Adam; it accommodates 500 old and invalid soldier pensioners, who wear a distinctive uniform.

Chelsea porcelain (1743–69). Soft-paste wares, at first showing strong Meissen and Chinese influences. The red-anchor period (1752–56) was the best, characterized by figures copied from Meissen, Watteau, Rubens, etc.; followed by the gold-anchor period (1758–69) with typical Sèvres-type tableware. It was in this period that the characteristic elaborate bocages (leafy 'arbour' background to figures) were introduced. Early Chelsea has been extensively faked ever since 1830. See CHELSEA-DERBY.

Chelsea set, The In some ways the 1960s revival of the BRIGHT YOUNG THINGS of the 1920s. They were mostly young socialites, less rich and less snobbish than their predecessors, the girls dressed by Mary Quant at her Bazaar (1956) in King's Road, Chelsea. Their only interest in life was to throw a good party. They were absorbed into SWINGING LONDON.

Cheltenham Gold Cup (1924). Major steeplechase event over a course of $3\frac{1}{4}$ miles, run at Cheltenham in March.

Chemnitz German city known for a time as Karl-Marx-Stadt.

Cheops, Great Pyramid of See GIZA.

Chequers (1921). Prime Minister's official country residence, presented to the state for that purpose by Lord Lee of Fareham. (Near Princes Risborough, Buckinghamshire.)

Chéri (1920). COLETTE'S novel of an ageing demi-mondaine, Léa, and her young lover, Chéri, who is torn between love for her and for his rich wife; in a sequel, *La Fin de Chéri* (1926), he kills himself.

Chernobyl Town in the Ukraine, scene of an immense nuclear disaster in April 1986 which left the town and much of the country surrounding uninhabitable; the cause of the disaster was said to be human error, the fall-out effect was felt world-wide.

Cherry Orchard, The (1904). Chekhov's play about an improvident landowning family who are forced to sell their estate and to hear at the end of the play the sound of their favourite orchard being cut down for a new housing estate; considering its early date, it is a remarkable preview of a major feature of life in the present century.

Cherry Ripe (1) One of Millais' most famous child portraits. (2) Title of a traditional song.

Cherubim First mentioned in Genesis 3:24 as guarding the tree of life; later regarded as the second order of angels, grouped with Thrones. (Plural of *Cherub*.)

Cherwell, The Tributary which joins the Thames at Oxford. (Pronounced char'wel.)

Cheshire Cat, The Duchess's grinning cat in ALICE IN WONDERLAND, who has the disconcerting habit of vanishing by degrees, starting at the tail and ending with the grin. (The phrase 'to grin like a Cheshire cat' is of unknown origin, but used long before Lewis Carroll's time.)

Cheshire Cheese, The Ancient inn (rebuilt in the 17th century) in Wine Office Court off Fleet Street, famous for old English fare, especially steak-and-kidney pudding, and for American tourists.

Cheshire Homes (1948). Homes for the permanently disabled and incurably ill, founded by Grp Capt G. L. Cheshire, VC. There are now nearly 50 such homes in Britain and abroad, managed by the Cheshire Foundation.

Cheshunt compound Fungicide containing copper sulphate, used to protect seedlings from damping-off disease.

Chessman case (USA). Extreme example of delayed execution: Caryl Chessman was sentenced to death on a kidnapping and murder charge in 1948, but was not executed until 1960.

Chesterbelloc Composite nickname for G. K. Chesterton and Hilaire Belloc, who often collaborated in the production of books humorously illustrated by Chesterton and written by Belloc.

Chesterfield's letters (1774). Letters written by Philip Stanhope, 4th Earl of Chesterfield, to his illegitimate son, giving (disregarded) instruction in good breeding for a man of the world or, as Dr Johnson less kindly put it, teaching him the morals of a whore and the manners of a dancing-master.

Chester Herald Officer of the COLLEGE OF ARMS.

Chestertonian Characterized by witty paradox, as were the writings of G. K. Chesterton.

Chetniks (1941). Guerrilla forces organized in Yugoslavia by Mihailović; the genuineness of their opposition to the German invaders became suspect, and Allied support was switched from them to Tito's PARTISANS.

Chevalier Bayard French hero of the 15th and early 16th century, known as the 'Chevalier sans peur et sans reproche'.

Cheviot (sheep). Breed of hill sheep, the wool of which is used in making tweeds.

'Chevy Chase' Ballad recounting an incident in the perennial border feud between the Percys and the Douglases.

Cheyenne American Indian tribe of the Great Plains, now found in Montana and Oklahoma. (Pronounced shy-en'.)

Cheynes-Stoke's respiration Rhythmical waxing and waning of breathing characteristic of deep coma.

Cheyne Walk Part of the Chelsea Embankment, London, associated with George Eliot, Rossetti, the artist Turner and many other famous people; in nearby Cheyne Row lived Thomas Carlyle. (Named after the former owner of the manor of Chelsea; pronounced chayn'i or chayn.)

Chianti Italian red wine produced in the mountainous area around Siena, Tuscany, and often bottled in distinctive straw-covered bottles.

Chichele Professor Holder of one of 5 Oxford University chairs: Economic History, History of War, Modern History, Public International Law, or Social and Political Theory. (Pronounced chich'il-i.)

Chichen Itza Eleventh-century Maya city in Yucatán, Mexico, with splendid ruins excavated from 1924 onwards. (Pronounced che-chen'eet-sah'.)

Chichester Theatre Festival (1962). Season of drama, old and new, staged annually from June to September at the Festival Theatre, Chichester, Sussex. The audience surrounds the stage on 3 sides.

Chichikov The 'hero' of Gogol's DEAD SOULS.

Chicken à la Derby Chicken served with rice and foie gras.

Chicken à la King Creamed diced chicken spiced with pimento or green pepper.

Chicken Maryland Chicken dipped in egg and breadcrumbs, fried, and served with banana and sweetcorn.

Chicot the Jester French court jester who appears in several novels by Dumas.

Chief Barker Title given to the President of the VARIETY CLUB OF GREAT BRITAIN. (From circus term for the man at a circus who entices the public into a sideshow.)

Chief Constable Head of a county, city or borough police force. The appointment is made by a standing joint committee of JPs and councillors.

Chieftain (1961). British medium tank (45 tons) with an exceptionally low silhouette.

Chief Whip MP responsible for the discipline of his party; his main task is, with his assistants, to secure the maximum necessary attendance of his party at a division (i.e. when a vote is taken) by written summons (also called a whip), on important occasions underlined 3 times ('3-line whip'). The government Chief Whip is salaried and holds the office of Parliamentary (Patronage) Secretary to the Treasury, responsible for recommending promotions and honours. (Abbreviation for 'whipper-in'.)

Chi'en Lung (Qian Lung) (1736–95). Emperor of the CH'ING DYNASTY during whose long reign artistic works became over-elaborate and thereafter deteriorated, never to recover.

Childe Harold Romantic hero of Byron's autobiographical poem, who turns from revelry to make a European pilgrimage. (*Childe*, a medieval title for a youth of noble birth.)

Childermas Archaic name of the Feast of HOLY INNOCENTS on 28 December.

Childe Roland Hero of a Scottish ballad ('Childe Roland to the dark tower came', *King Lear*, iii, 4) who rescued his sister from the fairies. Browning's poem of the name has no connection with the ballad. (For *Childe*, see CHILDE HAROLD.)

Children of Israel Collective name for the 12 Tribes of Israel; see JACOB.

Chillingham cattle Wild white cattle, reputed to be the survivors of the original wild ox of Britain, which still roam wild on Lord Tankerville's estate near Berwick, Northumberland.

Chiltern Hundreds Stewardship of the Chiltern Hundreds is a fictitious 'office of profit from the Crown', to which a member of Parliament is appointed if he wants to resign; this overcomes the difficulty that by law no MP may resign.

Chimaera In Greek legend a fire-breathing monster with a goat's body, dragon's tail and lion's head, killed by BELLEROPHON mounted on PEGASUS. (Pronounced ky-meer'a.)

Chimène Wife of El CID. (French spelling of Ximena.)

Chimonanthus Genus name of the Winter Sweet.

Chinaman (Cricket). Off-break bowled by a left-handed bowler to a right-handed batsman.

Chinatown (London). No longer in LIMEHOUSE but the area between Shaftesbury Avenue, Wardour Street and Gerrard Street with Chinese restaurants, gambling clubs, supermarkets, cinemas, bookshops, barbers, travel agents, etc.

Chindits Long-range penetration brigade which fought in Burma behind the Japanese lines under Brig. Orde Wingate, formed by Gen. Wavell in July 1942. (Burmese *Chinthay*, a mythical beast, the unit's badge.)

Ch'in dynasty (Jin dynasty) (221–207 BC). Short but brilliant period of Chinese history, which saw the building of the Great Wall, the institution of the Mandarin civil service system of orderly government, and the decline of the feudalism of the CHOU DYNASTY. The capital was near Sian (Shensi Province). The HAN DYNASTY followed.

Chinese Lowestoft Term used commonly, but mistakenly, for Chinese porcelain made for the European market which happened to resemble in decoration, though not in shape, contemporary Lowestoft wares.

Ch'ing dynasty (Qing dynasty) (1644–1912). Manchu dynasty, last of the Chinese imperial dynasties; their capital was Peking. The MANCHUS forced the Chinese to wear the pigtail as a token of loyalty to the new regime. In art

there were 2 main periods, the K'ANG HSI and the CHI'EN LUNG.

Chingford Former borough of Essex, since 1965 part of the new borough of WALTHAM FOREST.

Chinook (1) American Indians who once inhabited the Columbia valley from California to British Columbia. (2) Helicopters made by Boeing-Vertol of the USA.

Chinstrap, Colonel Bibulous character played by Jack Train in ITMA, with the signature-line 'I don't mind if I do'.

Chippendale Furniture made by a generation of fine cabinet-makers, of whom Thomas Chippendale (1718–79) was but one, his name having come to represent them solely because he published a book of designs (1754 with later revisions) which were widely copied. The characteristics were a restrained rococo style of flowing lines, plentiful carving, and strength combined with elegance. There were also Gothic and Chinese designs; and Chippendale himself in his later years produced furniture in the quite different ADAM STYLE. The furniture of later generations in these styles is also called 'Chippendale'.

Chips, Mr Schoolmaster of James Hilton's novel *Goodbye, Mr Chips* (1934).

Chips with Everything Wesker's play (1962) attacking the arrogance of the Establishment and the submissiveness to it of the sort of people who 'eat chips with everything'.

Chiron Most famous of the CENTAURS and, untypically, represented as wise and learned in medicine and music. He taught many of the greatest legendary heroes, notably Achilles, and was accidentally killed by Heracles. (Pronounced kair'on.)

Chislehurst and Sidcup Former urban district of Kent, now divided between the boroughs of BEXLEY and BROMLEY.

Chitty-Chitty Bang-Bang Maybach-Benz vintage car which raced at Brooklands in the 1920s and inspired Ian Fleming's children's book of that name, on which a film musical was based.

Chiuchuan (Jiuzhuan) Site in Tsinghai Province, China, of the missile-testing ground where China's first hydrogen bomb was tested in 1967. It lies in the Nan Shan mountain area 200 miles north of Lake KOKO NOR. (Also spelt Kiuchuan.)

Chloe See DAPHNIS AND CHLOE.

Chocolate Soldier, The (1908). Oskar Straus's comic opera based on Bernard Shaw's ARMS AND THE MAN.

Choral Symphony, The (1823). Beethoven's 9th Symphony, in which the climax of the last movement is, uniquely, vocal – Schiller's 'Ode to Joy': 'Freude, schöner Götterfunken, / Tochter aus Elysium' ('Joy, fair spark of God, daughter of Elysium'.)

Chosen Name given to Korea after it was annexed by Japan in 1910. (Pronounced choh-sen'.)

Chou dynasty (Zhou dynasty) (1050–256 BC). Early Chinese dynasty during which a type of feudalism evolved.

Christadelphians (1848). American sect of the ADVENTIST type, founded by an Englishman in New York.

Christian Hero of PILGRIM'S PROGRESS who makes the pilgrimage to the Celestial City.

Christian Action Movement founded (1946) by Canon Collins 'to put religion into politics'; it espoused post-war reconciliation with the Germans, opposition to apartheid, and the CND.

Christian Democrats Name widely adopted in Europe by political parties of the centre, which usually draw their support from both Protestants and Catholics and from all social classes.

Christian Science (1866). American religion founded by Mary Baker Eddy, who believed that, since God is good, sin, disease and death exist only for those who are blinded by error.

Christian Science Monitor (1908). Daily evening paper founded by Mrs Eddy (see previous entry) to fight the YELLOW PRESS; published at Boston, Mass., it still has an international reputation for its coverage of world news.

Christian Socialism (1848). Movement started by F. D. Maurice and the novelist Charles Kingsley, advocating active participation in social reform by the Church. One of its more recent intellectual leaders was the American theologian, Prof. Niebuhr. Protestant and Catholic clergy who take factory jobs and try to bring Christianity to the workshop are among the modern representatives of the movement.

Christie murder case See RILLINGTON PLACE MURDERS.

Christie's (1766). London auction rooms, a close rival of SOTHEBY'S in international reputation, situated in St James's.

Christmas Carol, A Dickens's novel; see SCROOGE, EBENEZER.

Christmas Club Savings account into which regular, usually weekly, deposits are made throughout the year to meet Christmas shopping needs.

Christmas Island Scene of the detonation in 1957 of the first British hydrogen bomb; a Pacific island half-way between Hawaii and Tahiti. (There is another Christmas Island in the Indian Ocean.)

Christopher Robin The hero of A. A. Milne's children's books and many of his verses; he is the author's son.

Christ Scientist, First Church of Mother church of CHRISTIAN SCIENCE, at Boston, Mass.

Christ's Hospital (1552). Originally a 'hospital' for foundlings established by Edward VI on a site now occupied by St Bartholomew's Hospital and the GPO; it soon became a school, which developed into the public school moved to Horsham, Sussex, in 1902; also called the Blue-Coat School (the boys wearing a uniform of blue coats and yellow stockings). A girls' school of the same foundation has also moved to join the boys at Horsham.

Christy Abbreviation for Christiania, a basic skiing turn with skis kept parallel.

Christy Minstrels One of the earliest black-faced minstrel shows, who played in New York and

London in the 1840s. (E. Christy, American impresario.)

Chronicles (4th century BC). Book of the Old Testament which repeats much of Samuel and Kings.

Chrysanthemum Genus that includes the marguerites and the Shasta or ox-eye daisy (*C. maximum*).

Chrysler (1925). A US car-manufacturing group based in Detroit.

Chu Chin Chow (1916). Spectacular musical based on the Ali Baba story in the *Arabian Nights*; starring Oscar Asche and Lily Brayton, it held the record for the longest London run until *The Mousetrap* surpassed it.

Chunnel Newspaper-headline name for the (English) CHANNEL TUNNEL.

Church Army (1882). Church of England mission which finds accommodation for those in need, and trains evangelists for work in remote parishes, prisons, among troops abroad, etc. It also runs youth clubs.

Church Assembly (1919). Body with 3 Houses, of bishops, clergy and (elected) laity, established by Parliament to legislate for the Church of England on non-theological matters; laws passed by it are subject to Parliamentary approval. Membership of the first 2 Houses is the same as that of the combined CONVOCATIONS of Canterbury and York. Officially known as the National Assembly of the Church of England.

Church Commissioners (1948). Body appointed by the Crown to administer the Church of England's finances. It was formed by merging the Ecclesiastical Commissioners and QUEEN ANNE'S BOUNTY.

Church House (1940). Headquarters of the Canterbury Houses of CONVOCATION and the CHURCH ASSEMBLY. (In Dean's Yard, Westminster.)

Churchill (1942). Standard British infantry tank of World War II: 40 tons, 340 h.p., 18 m.p.h.

Churchill College (1960). College of Cambridge University, named in honour of Sir Winston Churchill.

Churchill Downs Racecourse at Louisville, Kentucky, scene of the KENTUCKY DERBY.

Church Lads' Brigade (1891). Organization similar to the BOYS' BRIGADE, giving training in good citizenship; the boys drill in uniform.

Chuzzlewit, Martin See MARTIN CHUZZLEWIT.

CIA (1947). Initials used for the US Central Intelligence Agency, with headquarters at FOGGY BOTTOM, Washington; it gathers political and military intelligence, conducts psychological warfare, supports anti-Communist groups abroad, and was responsible for the BAY OF PIGS fiasco.

Ciba (1884). Swiss group with headquarters at Basle, which makes industrial chemicals, dyes, resins, adhesives and drugs.

Ciba Foundation (1947). International scientists' club established by Ciba Ltd (see previous entry) in Portland Place, London, to promote international co-operation in medical and chemical research, including biochemistry, endocrinology and geriatrics. Symposia, study groups, an annual foundation lecture, and publications of proceedings are features of its work.

'Cicero' *Nom de guerre* of a spy in World War II who was valet to a British ambassador; he was falsely credited with handing over the full details of OVERLORD to the Germans.

Cicestr: Abbreviation for (Bishop of) Chichester.

Cid, El Eleventh-century Castilian hero Don Rodrigo, whose story is told in many medieval ballads and by later authors, including Corneille (1637); he won fame by his campaigns against and (during a period of disgrace) for the Moors. (Corruption of Arabic *Al-Sidi* or *As-sayyid*, 'lord'.)

Cider with Rosie (1959). Poet Laurie Lee's delightful account of his childhood in a Cotswold village in the early 1920s, where he was brought up by his deserted, penniless but resourceful mother with 7 other children, 5 of them her stepchildren.

Cimmerians People who, according to Homer, lived in a land of eternal night; later applied to a coastal tribe of the Black Sea region, from whom the name Crimea is derived.

Cincinnatus Legendary Roman hero called 'from the plough' in the 5th century BC to save Rome from its enemies. Having succeeded in this, he declined office and honours, and returned to his plough 16 days later. (Pronounced sin-sin-ayt'us.)

Cinderella Heroine of a fairy tale, probably of oriental origin. The story of the family drudge whose fairy godmother sends her to a ball at which a prince falls in love with her is used in Rossini's opera *La Cenerentola* (1817).

CinemaScope (1953). First wide-screen cinema system, used for spectacular films in colour.

Cinerama (1952). Cinema system employing 3 cameras, 3 projectors, a wide curved screen and stereophonic sound, to produce an illusion of actuality.

Cinna Roman leader of a conspiracy against Augustus. In Corneille's play, *Cinna* (1640), he is betrayed by the rejected suitor of Amélie, the woman who loves him, but is pardoned by Augustus.

Cinquecento Italian for '16th century', used of the style of architecture and art that followed the Renaissance; see MANNERISM. See QUATTROCENTO. (Italian, '500' for '1500', i.e. the 1500s; pronounced ching'kwi-chen'to.)

Cinque Ports Ancient confederation of Channel ports reconstituted by William the Conqueror and given special privileges in return for supplying ships and men. The original five were Dover, Hastings, Sandwich, Romney and Hythe, later joined by Winchelsea and Rye; there are also associated town or 'limbs' (Folkestone, Deal, Margate, etc.). The Lord Warden is an honorary appointment, with an official residence at Walmer Castle, near Deal; there are also Barons of the Cinque Ports. (French *cinq*, 'five'; pronounced sink.)

CIO (1935). (USA) John L. Lewis's trade union organization, see AFL/CIO.

Circassian People, and CAUCASIAN LANGUAGE, of Georgia, USSR, whose womenfolk were from early times renowned for their beauty and highly prized as slaves and concubines. (Russian name.)

Circe In Greek legend, an enchantress who turns Ulysses' men into swine; Ulysses himself, protected from a like fate by the gods, compels her to restore them to human form. After that she becomes more friendly and gives Ulysses much useful advice, and also a son. (Pronounced sèr'si.)

Circumlocution Office Dickens's caricature of a government department in *Little Dorrit*, manned by such people as Barnacle Junior, author of the remark: 'Upon my soul, you mustn't come into the place saying you want to know, you know.'

Cirencester Park Polo ground reopened by Earl Bathurst in 1952, near Cirencester, Gloucestershire. (The 'county' pronunciation, sis'i-ta or siz'it-a, is dying out in favour of pronunciation as spelt; the locals simply call it Ciren.)

Cisalpine Gaul Ancient Roman province of northern Italy, consisting of the fertile Po valley region colonized by Gauls from over the Alps. (See next entry.)

Cisalpine Republic (1797). Union of the states of North Italy formed by Napoleon after his successful Italian campaign. (Latin, 'this side of the Alps'; pronounced sis-alp'yn.)

Cistercians (1098). Reformed order of BENEDICTINES, further reformed by St Bernard of Clairvaux (12th century), and revived by the TRAPPISTS. (*Cistercium*, Latin name of Cîteaux, near Dijon, France, where founded.)

Cistus Genus that includes the rock rose, a name also given to the hardier *Helianthemum*, which is better termed the sun rose.

Cities of the Plain Sodom and Gomorrah (Gen. 19:29).

Citizen Kane (1940). Film written and directed

by Orson Welles, who also starred in it, about a journalist who tries to find out the real facts about the recently deceased Kane, who bears a striking resemblance to William Randolph Hearst, the US newspaper proprietor.

Citizen King, The Another name for Louis Philippe, KING OF THE FRENCH.

Citizens, The Nickname of the Manchester City football team, to distinguish them from Manchester United.

City and Guilds Certificate Certificate awarded on the results of examinations in any of some 300 mainly technical subjects taken at Technical Colleges; organized by an independent body, the City and Guilds of London Institute, founded in 1878 by the London LIVERY COMPANIES and the City Corporation.

City and Guilds College (1885). Unit of the Imperial College of Science and Technology. See previous entry.

City Companies See LIVERY COMPANIES.

City Guilds See LIVERY COMPANIES.

City of Dreadful Night, The (1874). James Thomson's long pessimistic poem about an imaginary city, the product of the poet's nocturnal perambulations of London during bouts of insomnia.

City of London blitz (29 December 1940). Heavy incendiary raid which destroyed the Guildhall and several Wren churches.

City Remembrancer Legal official who represents the City of London Corporation at Parliamentary committees, etc.

City Technology College British secondary schools in inner-city areas giving science-based education. The first was established in 1988.

City, The SQUARE MILE that was the Roman town of Londinium, scene of the GREAT FIRE OF LONDON after which Wren rebuilt 52 of its churches (including St Paul's Cathedral), and, 3 centuries later, of the CITY OF LONDON BLITZ which destroyed many of them again. Long

since the financial and commercial centre of the UK, it contains the BANK OF ENGLAND (see OLD LADY OF THREADNEEDLE STREET).

City University, The (1966). University in Clerkenwell, London near St Paul's; formerly the Northampton CAT (named after the Marquess of Northampton).

Ciudad Trujillo (1936–61). Name of the capital of the Dominican Republic during the dictatorship of President Trujillo; on his assassination the old name of Santo Domingo was restored.

Civic Trust (1957). Voluntary body which encourages and co-ordinates efforts to preserve town and countryside against the encroachments of modern ugliness; for example, it promotes the 'face-lifting' of town streets, as at Norwich and Windsor, by removing clutter of all kinds and tidying up shop fronts.

Civil List Annual grant made by Parliament to the Monarch to cover the maintenance of the royal household, but not the upkeep of the palaces, grants to other members of the Royal Family, etc.

Civil Rights Commission (1964). (USA) Body set up under President Kennedy's Civil Rights Act to ensure the ending of segregation and of discrimination in voting qualifications between whites and blacks, as well as the provision of equal opportunity for employment, pay and promotion.

Civvy Street Return to civilian life after military service.

Clan-na-Gael (1881). Irish FENIAN organization founded in Philadelphia, USA; also known as the United Brotherhood.

Clapham Common murder (1911). Murder on Clapham Common, London, of Léon Béron. Steinie Morrison, a burglar and pimp, was sentenced to death; reprieved by Winston Churchill, then Home Secretary, he starved himself to death in prison (1921), vigorously protesting his innocence to the end.

Clapham omnibus, The man on the Term used by lawyers as typifying the ordinary reasonable man.

Clapham Sect Politically powerful 18th-century coterie of evangelical humanitarians, led by the abolitionists William Wilberforce and Thomas Clarkson. Most of them lived at Clapham (then a village near London). Also called The Saints. The sect is mentioned in Gosse's FATHER AND SON.

Clarence House (1825). House adjoining St James's Palace, London, which was the home of Princess Elizabeth and the Duke of Edinburgh, and later of the Queen Mother. (Built for William IV when Duke of Clarence.)

Clarenceux One of the Kings of Arms at the COLLEGE OF ARMS, responsible for England south of the Trent (compare NORROY AND ULSTER). (Pronounced clar'en-soo.)

Clarendon Code (1661–5). Four Statutes passed by the CAVALIER PARLIAMENT against the wishes of Charles II and, despite the name, of Lord Clarendon; they excluded Catholics and Puritans from office (Corporation Act), expelled non-conforming clergy from the Church (Act of Uniformity), banned non-conformist forms of worship (Conventicle Act) and teaching and preaching within 5 miles of a town (Five Mile Act).

Clarendon Laboratory Main physics laboratory at Oxford University.

Clarendon Press Another name for the Oxford University Press, more strictly applied to scholarly publications of that press published in Oxford itself. (From Clarendon House, Oxford, built with profits from the publication in 1704 of Clarendon's history of the English Civil War.)

Clarendon schools Eton, Harrow, Rugby, Winchester, Charterhouse, Shrewsbury, Westminster, Merchant Taylors' and St Paul's, the 9 public schools named by the Clarendon Commission (1864) as the leading schools at that time.

Clarkia Hardy annual named after Captain Clarke, an explorer of the Rocky Mountains.

Claudine Heroine of 4 of COLETTE's semi-autobiographical novels of adolescence (1900–1903).

Claudius In Shakespeare's play, the King of Denmark, uncle and stepfather of HAMLET, who murdered Hamlet's father and married Hamlet's mother so precipitately as a form of thrift.

Claudius the God See I, CLAUDIUS.

Clause Four Clause of the British Labour Party's constitution which pledges the Party to work for the common ownership of the means of production, distribution and exchange.

Clay, Cassius US black boxing champion who took the name of Muhammad Ali when he joined the BLACK MUSLIMS.

Clay Cross Urban District Council in Derbyshire which refused to implement the 1972 Housing Act.

Clayhanger Family, The (1925). Arnold Bennett's trilogy of novels of the FIVE TOWNS. *Clayhanger* (1910) tells of Edwin Clayhanger's difficult courtship of Hilda; *Hilda Lessways* (1911) retells the story from her point of view; *These Twain* (1916) describes their life together. The work is notable for its many references to contemporary events.

Clayton (Lucie) Diploma Diploma in fashion-designing.

Clearances, The Evictions of Scottish Highland crofters so that landowners could introduce sheep-farming. They continued from 1750 on into the 19th century; many of the crofters emigrated to Canada and the USA.

Cleon Athenian demagogue and general of the 5th century BC, son of a tanner and a favourite butt of Aristophanes.

Cleopatra Joint ruler of Egypt with her brother in the 1st century BC, deposed after his death; restored to her throne by Julius Caesar, by whom she had a son; aided against Augustus by Antony, by whom she had 3 children, but whom she deserted at ACTIUM. See next 2 entries.

Cleopatra's Needle Name given to 2 ancient Egyptian inscribed obelisks (1600 BC) erected at Heliopolis and later moved to Alexandria. One now stands on the Thames Embankment and the other in Central Park, New York. (No connection with Cleopatra.)

Cleopatra's nose Allusion to Pascal's famous note: 'Cleopatra's nose: had it been shorter, the whole face of the earth would have been changed'.

Clerihew Type of 4-line nonsense biography invented by E. Clerihew Bentley (author of TRENT'S LAST CASE), of which a typical example is: 'George the Third / Ought never to have occurred. / One can only wonder / At so grotesque a blunder'. They were published as *Biography for Beginners* (1905).

Clerk of the Peace County or borough officer (who is also usually Clerk to the Council); his main duties are connected with the courts of quarter sessions and he may act as deputy to the returning officer at elections. Usually a solicitor, he is not salaried but paid fees for duties performed.

'Clerk Saunders' Border ballad telling how a brother slew his sister's lover as she lay in his arms.

Clerk's Tale, The In the CANTERBURY TALES, the story of the patient GRISELDA.

Clink Sixteenth-century prison in Southwark, London, and a general slang word for prison.

Clio In Greek legend, the muse of history. (Pronounced kly'oh.)

Cliveden set Group of political notabilities who gathered at Cliveden, the Buckinghamshire home of the 2nd Viscount Astor and his wife Nancy, thought to have influenced British foreign policy in the 1930s, especially towards German appeasement. The Astors denied its existence. (Pronounced cliv'dn.)

Clochemerle (1934). Wickedly funny novel (also screened) by Gabriel Chevallier which centres round the erection of a public urinal opposite a Beaujolais village church by an anti-clerical group, led by a man whose halitosis kills all opposition to his scheme.

Clockmakers, Worshipful Company of (1631).

LIVERY COMPANY formed by secession from the Blacksmiths.

Cloister and the Hearth, The (1861). Charles Reade's 15th-century historical novel, which gives a romantic version of the birth of Erasmus.

Clostridium Genus of bacteria which do not need oxygen (are anaerobic); some of them attack the nervous system, as in lockjaw and botulism.

Closure, The (1882). (Parliament) Device to bring unfruitful debate to an end, taking the form of a motion 'That the question be now put'. If carried, the matter under debate is then put to the vote.

Clotho One of the 3 FATES. (Pronounced cloh'-tho.)

Clothworkers, Worshipful Company of (1528). Junior of the Great Twelve LIVERY COMPANIES. It assists the textile industries of northern England by grants for education and research.

Cloud-cuckoo-land Ideal city in the clouds, built in Aristophanes' *The* BIRDS by 2 young men, dissatisfied with Athenian political life, with the help of the birds. From this base they blackmail the gods into accepting their demands by intercepting the savoury smells of sacrifices on earth so that they do not reach up to heaven.

Cloud of Unknowing (14th century). Mystical work of unknown authorship.

Clouds, The (423 BC). Aristophanes' comedy which attacks Socrates by grossly distorting his methods and confusing him with the worst of the Sophists, as a man who can make the worse appear the better cause.

Club, The Mainly political club, in London; like the OTHER CLUB, it has no premises of its own.

Club Méditerranée (1950). French company that runs a chain of holiday camps in many countries, providing relatively cheap holidays with a near-Tahitian atmosphere (there is one in Tahiti). Started by a Belgian in the Balearics.

Club Row market London street market for animals, birds and aquarium fish, behind Bishopsgate station.

Clun Forest (sheep) Prolific breed of hardy short-wool sheep, producing excellent meat and fine wool. Originally from Radnor, and common in the Welsh border counties.

Cluniacs Order of monks which separated from the BENEDICTINES in the 11th century. It became very rich, with several opulent Romanesque daughter abbeys, and was frowned on by St Bernard and the CISTERCIANS. (Cluny Abbey, near Mâcon, France.)

Clyde Football team who play at Shawfield, south-east Glasgow, near Rutherglen.

Clyde Fortnight Scotland's premier regatta, held in June/July and catering particularly for keelboat classes, especially the DRAGON.

Clydesdale Farm horse bred in Lanarkshire, in colour dark brown or black with white markings.

Clydesiders Ginger group of left-wing members of the Independent Labour Party, all representing Clydeside constituencies, which formed in the 1920s round the leadership of John Wheatley, James Maxton and David Kirkwood.

Cmd, Cmnd Abbreviations of 'Command' used in the serial numbering of Command Papers (i.e. those laid before Parliament). Cd was used 1900–18, Cmd 1919–56 and Cmnd thereafter.

CND (1958). Initials used for the Campaign for Nuclear Disarmament, a movement launched by Bertrand Russell advocating the abolition of nuclear weapons. See ALDERMASTON MARCH: COMMITTEE OF 100.

Coaching Marathon (1909). Event first staged at the Royal International Horse Show (now also held at other shows) for four-in-hand coaches, which are driven over a distance to the Show. Points are awarded for the condition of the horses on arrival and for general turn-out but not for speed.

Coachmakers and Coach Harness-Makers, Worshipful Company of (1677). LIVERY COMPANY.

Coalbrookdale porcelain See COALPORT.

Coalport (1796). Porcelain factory founded by John Rose, who later bought up the Caughley, Swansea and Nantgarw factories; it made tableware in the style of Chelsea, Meissen, etc. and was fond of gaudy applied flowers. After changes of ownership it moved to the Potteries in 1926 and continued to make tablewares, with green and rose grounds. Sometimes called Coalbrookdale. (Village in Coalbrookdale, south of Wellington, Shropshire.)

Coastal Command Section of the RAF which during World War II operated with naval support against enemy submarines and surface craft, and was based on the British Isles, Gibraltar and Iceland.

Cobaea Half-hardy climbing tropical American plants named after Barnadez Cobo, a Spanish naturalist.

Cóbh Port for Cork, formerly known as Queenstown. (Pronounced kohv.)

Cobol Common business-orientated language, a high-level language for commercial and business data processing.

Coca-Cola (1885). Soft drink, first marketed in Atlanta, Georgia, as a brain tonic, by an American purveyor of patent medicines. It now contains 14 ingredients, including coca, kola-nut extract, caffeine and a secret substance called 7X. (Often abbreviated to 'Coke'.)

Cocacolaization Term coined in France for the infiltration of European culture by the American way of life as a result of World War II, symbolized by the phenomenal sales of the American soft drink, COCA-COLA, even in wine-drinking France.

Cockaigne, Land of In medieval legend, a land of luxury and idleness; the name has been applied, as a pun, to the land of the cockneys, i.e. London.

Cocker, According to Correct, accurate. (Edward Cocker, author of a 17th-century arithmetic book.)

Cock Lane Ghost (1762). Hoax at Smithfield, London. A man invented a story about rappings in his house by the ghost of a murdered woman, actually by his daughter.

'Cockles and Mussels' Traditional Irish song: 'In Dublin's fair city, where the girls are so pretty, / I first set my eyes on sweet Molly Malone ... / Crying, Cockles and mussels! alive, alive, oh!'

Cockney (1) 'Cockered' (i.e. pampered) child. (2) A soft townsman. (3) Londoner, later defined as one born within the sound of BOW BELLS. (4) Dialect spoken by (3).

Cockney School Derisive name given in *Blackwood's Magazine* to a group of writers living in London, including Keats, Shelley, Hazlitt and Leigh Hunt.

Cock of the North Bagpipe tune.

Cockpit of Europe, The Belgium, whose unhappy destiny it has been to provide the terrain for many a major battle between the Great Powers.

Cock Robin In the nursery rhymne 'Who killed Cock Robin?' perhaps BALDER or some other figure of Scandinavian myth; but the name gained wider currency when applied to Robert Walpole on his fall from power in 1742.

Cocktail Party, The (1949). T. S. Eliot's drama on the eternal Christian verities, written in conversational verse. At the party, a stranger (God, the psychiatrist) warns Edward that his decision to abandon his mistress Celia and return to his wife will have unforeseen consequences. Later the stranger lectures him on the 2 Christian ways of life – the acceptance of the humdrum obligations of everyday marriage, and the path of self-abnegation chosen by Celia, who goes as a missionary to the tropics, where she is murdered.

Coco Famous Russian clown, Nikolai Poliakov (1900–74), who came to Germany after World War I and to England in 1929.

Cocytus In Greek legend the river of wailing, one of the rivers of the Underworld. (Pronounced ko-sy'tus.)

COD Initials used for the *Concise Oxford Dictionary*.

Code Napoléon (1803–4). Codification of French civil law carried out under the direction of Napoleon as First Consul, the basis of the *Code Civil* today.

Codlin and Short Two characters in *The* OLD CURIOSITY SHOP, who run a travelling Punch and Judy show. Short is a nice little man, but the evil-minded Codlin, eager to make money out of little Nell's grandfather, assures her that Codlin's the friend, not Short.

Codrington Memorial Trophy Bisley grand aggregate championship, held under the auspices of the National Small-Bore Rifle Association.

Coelenterates Phylum of invertebrate, mostly marine animals, including jellyfish, sea-anemones, corals and the Portuguese man-of-war.

Cognac Brandy made from grapes grown in the immediate vicinity of the town of Cognac, on the Charente west of Angouleme.

Cohen inquiry (1955). An investigation into the COMET air disasters of 1954; it found that they were due to metal fatigue.

Cointreau White CURAÇAO liqueur.

Coke of Norfolk Thomas Coke, Earl of Leicester, of Holkham (1754–1842), who revolutionized English agriculture through his introduction of greatly improved methods, some taken over from TURNIP TOWNSHEND, at HOLKHAM HALL. (Pronounced kuk.)

Colbert (Cooking) Fish egged and crumbed before frying; tarragon-flavoured butter sauce served with it.

Colchicum Genus name of the meadow saffrons; *C. autumnale* is called the autumn crocus because the flower itself looks like a crocus, but the plant is entirely different in habit; the existence of autumn-flowering true crocuses adds to the confusion.

Cold Comfort Farm (1932). Riotous skit by Stella Gibbons on the gloomy rustic school of novelists (Hardy, PRECIOUS BANE etc.). Aunt Ada Doom when young had seen 'something nasty in the woodshed' which seemed to colour her whole life, though she never explained what it was. The purple passages were marked with asterisks for the greater convenience of the reader.

Coldstream Guards (1650). The second oldest regiment in the British Army (after the Royal Scots), originally Gen. Monk's regiment of the NEW MODEL ARMY. They wear their buttons in pairs, and a scarlet plume. (Village on the Scots border where they were stationed at the Restoration; see GUARDS DIVISION.)

Cold War Term popularized, perhaps coined, by the US columnist Walter Lippmann in 1947 to sum up the East–West IRON CURTAIN relationship.

Coleoptera Beetles, an insect order with horny forewings, the grubs of some of which do great damage, e.g. the boll-weevil to cotton, and the wireworm of click-beetles, a garden pest.

Colette Maiden name, also used as pen-name, of the French novelist, who wrote of CLAUDINE and CHÉRI She also used the pen-name Colette WILLY. (Died 1954.)

College of Advanced Technology See CAT.

College of Arms (1483). Royal corporation under the Earl Marshal (the Duke of Norfolk), authorized to grant armorial bearings, and responsible for all matters concerning the armorial bearings and pedigrees of English, Irish and Commonwealth families. Scottish families are dealt with by LYON KING OF ARMS.

Collegers Eton name for KING'S SCHOLARS.

Colles's fracture Fracture of the wrist, usually caused by falling on the outstretched hand.

Collins (1905). Editor's name used for the authoritative, selective *Authors' and Printers' Dictionary* giving the spelling (and, where necessary, pronunciation) of tricky words, names, foreign phrases, Americanisms, abbreviations, etc.; used by editors, typesetters, typists and (apparently decreasingly) by printers' proof-readers. Now metamorphosed into *The Oxford Dictionary for Writers and Editors*.

Collins, Mr Pompous snob of a country parson who has the effrontery to woo Elizabeth Bennet in Jane Austen's PRIDE AND PREJUDICE.

Collins Long iced drink of lemon juice with gin (JOHN COLLINS, TOM COLLINS), rum, whisky or Bourbon. (Said to be named after a New York barman.)

Colombey-les-deux-Églises Village, in Aube *département* south-east of Paris, famous as the home of President de Gaulle.

Colombo Plan (1950). British Commonwealth's counterpart to the US POINT-FOUR PROGRAM, which provides technical assistance to former British territories in South and South-East Asia, and to Indo-China, Indonesia, the Philippines and Siam. It also offers them facilities for technological training in Britain and the Dominions. (Proposed by a Commonwealth conference at Colombo, Ceylon.)

Colonel Warden One of the wartime code names for Winston Churchill.

Colonial Dames of America (1890). (USA) Patriotic organization resembling the DAUGHTERS OF THE AMERICAN REVOLUTION.

Colony Club Exclusive women's club in New York City.

Colorado beetle Serious menace to potato crops which first appeared in England in 1933; its native habitat is Colorado, USA. The grub is bright pink or red, and the beetle has longitudinal black and yellow stripes.

Colorado Springs Town in central Colorado, USA; the site of the Air Force Academy and the headquarters of NORAD are near by. See CHEYENNE MOUNTAIN.

Colosseum (AD 80). Huge amphitheatre in Rome, impressive even as a ruin, completed in the reign of Titus. It held over 100,000 spectators, and was used for gladiatorial combats or, flooded with water, for naval displays.

Colossi of Memnon Greek name for 2 seated figures at THEBES, 64 ft high, all that remains of the mortuary temple of Amenhotep III (14th century BC). One of these was reputed to sing when touched by the rays of the morning sun, a fanciful description of the soughing of the wind.

Colossus of Rhodes (3rd century BC). Statue of Helios, said to be over 100 ft high, one of the Seven Wonders of the World, destroyed by earthquake some 50 years after completion. The story that it bestrode the entrance to Rhodes harbour was a much later invention.

Colt (1830). First successful revolver, a 6-shooter designed by Samuel Colt of Connecticut, USA. His firm also produced the 0·45 automatic pistol (1911) used by US forces in both world wars; and the Colt Commander, a much lighter model with an aluminium frame.

Columbia University (1754). Oldest of the universities in New York City.

Columbine Daughter of PANTALOON and sweetheart of HARLEQUIN.

Combined Cadet Force (1948). School force intended to prepare boys for military or civil life by developing character and leadership. Each force consists of a general 'basic' section and one or more specific service sections (army, navy or air force). The CCF replaced the junior branch of the old OTC (Officers' Training Corps).

Combray Fictitious village, based on childhood memories of Illiers (near Chartres), the setting of the earlier books of Proust's REMEMBRANCE OF THINGS PAST.

Comecon (1949). Abbreviated name of the Council of Mutual Economic Assistance, established to further co-operation between socialist countries in the field of development, trade and other economic matters.

Comédie-Française (1680). French National Theatre, with a repertoire of tragedies and comedies that have won an established reputation. Recruitment to the company is an honour, but the rule which bound members to serve exclusively in it for long periods has now been abandoned. Choice of play and style of acting follow set traditions. The company has 2 theatres in Paris, the main one being known officially as the Salle Richelieu and colloquially as Le Français.

Comédie humaine (1829–50). Name Balzac gave to his works as a whole, indicating that he was trying to portray the whole French scene at all levels of society and in both Paris and the provinces. His chief characters mostly embody some single obsessive passion, and are set against a vividly detailed background.

Comet World's first jet airliner, built by De Havilland. Comet-1 opened a service from London to Johannesburg (1952) but later developed trouble with metal fatigue. Comet-4 opened the first transatlantic jet service in 1958 and was highly successful.

Comice pear Best of pears, but not easy to cultivate; the fruit is pale yellow and of medium size. The full name is Doyenne du Comice.

Cominform (1947–56). Abbreviated name for the Communist Information Bureau, an international organization formed, in succession to the COMINTERN, to co-ordinate, under Russian leadership, the policies of all Communist countries and the Communist parties of other countries. Its first objective was to ensure the rejection of MARSHALL AID.

Comintern (1919–43). Short name of the Third International, a Soviet-controlled world organization of Communist parties.

'Comin' thro' the Rye' Robert Burns's song, with the refrain: 'Gin a body meet a body / Comin' thro' the rye; / Gin a body kiss a body, / Need a body cry?'

Commedia dell'arte (16th century). Italian theatrical entertainment in which actors improvised on a skeleton plot, with such stock characters as the Doctor, SCARAMOUCHE and PANTALOON, HARLEQUIN and PULCINELLA were added later. Several of the best Meissen and other early porcelain figures are representations of these characters. (Italian, 'comedy of skill', as testing the actors' skill in improvisation.)

Commem., Commemoration June festival marking the end of the academic year at Oxford University: there is a ceremony commemorating benefactors and Commem. Balls are held.

Commission, The Body of 9 representatives of the supranational interests of the European Communities, which puts proposals to the COUNCIL OF MINISTERS.

Commission of the Peace (1) Collective term for JUSTICES OF THE PEACE. (2) Authority given to them.

Committee of 100 Executive of the CND, members of which, including Bertrand Russell, the founder, were sent to prison for their activities in 1961. It was formed of prominent people from show business, the arts and literature to take direct action against nuclear armament; it was the militant vanguard of the protest movement and the pioneer of the 'sit-down' protest, and joined in various other campaigns before its demise in 1968.

Committee of Public Safety (6 April 1793–5). Small cabinet of JACOBINS set up by Danton, only theoretically subordinate to the CONVENTION, to control army and foreign affairs. In July 1793 Robespierre was elected to it, pushed Danton into the background, and presided over the Reign of TERROR until his assassination by moderates in July 1794 (THERMIDOR). The Committee was later superseded by the DIRECTORY.

Common Agricultural Policy (CAP) Adoption of a common policy for agriculture by the member-states of the European Communities. See EUROPEAN COMMUNITIES.

Common Entrance (1903). Examination for entrance to public schools, taken at the age of 13.

Common Man, The Century of the Phrase coined by the US Vice-President, Henry Wallace, in 1942: 'The century on which we are entering can be and must be the Century of the Common Man.'

Common Market, The (1959). Name in general use for the European Economic Community set up by the Treaty of Rome (1957). Its main objectives were the abolition of customs tariffs within the area and the establishment of uniform tariffs for imports into it, and the working out of a common agricultural policy. See EUROPEAN COMMUNITIES.

Common Wealth (1942). Short-lived political party founded by Sir Richard Acland, who joined the Labour Party in 1945.

Commonwealth, The (1) Name given to the period (1649–53) of Cromwell's republican government from the time of Charles I's execution to the creation of the PROTECTORATE; or, loosely, up to the Restoration (1660). (2) (1931). A free association of 50 (1990) sovereign independent states whose head is the Queen. There is no charter, treaty or constitution: the association is expressed in co-operation, consultation and mutual assistance, for which the Commonwealth secretariat is the central co-ordinating body.

Commonwealth Centre See MARLBOROUGH HOUSE.

Commonwealth Day Originally Empire Day, set aside throughout the British Empire, to celebrate the birthday of Queen Victoria (24 May); it was renamed Commonwealth Day in 1958.

Commonwealth Development Corporation Established in 1948 as the Colonial Development Corporation to assist the economic development of dependent territories; in 1963 its scope was extended to cover those that had gained independence.

Commonwealth Fund (1918). Fund to provide scholarships for British students at US universities, founded by the mother of E. S. Harkness (see PILGRIM TRUST), who added his own bequest to it in 1930.

Commonwealth Institute Exhibition galleries illustrating the history and geography of the countries of the Commonwealth, housed since 1962 in a building in Kensington High Street, London. There is also a library and an art gallery, and a cinema showing documentary films. Formerly the Imperial Institute (1893).

Communist Manifesto (1848). Detailed programme for Communist revolution issued by Marx and Engels during the REVOLUTIONS OF 1848. It stated that history is a record of successive class struggles in which new classes replace the old; the final revolution would be of the proletariat against the capitalists, in which 'the workers have nothing to lose but their chains . . . Workers of the world, unite!'

Community charge New taxation system introduced in Scotland (1989) and the rest of the UK (1990) replacing rates paid by householders. Also called POLL TAX.

Companion of Honour (CH) Instituted in 1917, the Order is composed of the sovereign and not more than 65 members.

Companion of Literature Highest distinction conferred by the Royal Society of Literature; limited to 10 living writers.

Compiègne French town west of Soissons near which, in a forest clearing, the Germans signed the armistice of 11 November 1918; on the same spot, by Hitler's whim, the French had to sign the armistice of 22 June 1940.

Compleat Angler, The (1653). Izaak Walton's prose eclogue of English country life, in the form of a discursive dialogue between Piscator (the fisherman) and Venator (the hunter) on the joys of angling.

Compositae Largest plant family, the daisies, characterized by a flower head comprising many flowers clustered together. It includes dandelion, groundsel, thistle, aster, chrysanthemum, golden rod, dahlia, artichoke, lettuce.

Compostela One of the most famous pilgrimage places in medieval Europe, the shrine where the patron saint of Spain, St James the Elder, is supposed to be buried, in the cathedral of Santiago de Compostela. Galicia, north-west Spain.

Comprehensive school Large school which brings the grammar, secondary modern and technical streams under one roof, facilitates the move of children from one stream to another after the age of 11, and enables the clever and the dull to mix outside class.

Compton Wynyates Exceptionally beautiful Tudor house near Banbury. Warwickshire, with the interior largely unchanged; home of the Marquesses of Northampton.

Comstockery Misdirected zeal in censoring whatever is thought to be salacious. (Anthony Comstock, died 1915, a US crusader against 'vice'; word invented by Bernard Shaw when he heard that the New York Public Library had banned his *Man and Superman* under Comstock's influence.)

Comstock Lode, The (1873). Exceptionally rich silver deposits discovered at Virginia City, Nevada, USA. From 1882 the Comstock Mine declined in importance because of flooding and a slump in the price of silver.

Comte Ory, Le Rossini's opera in which young men disguised as nuns invade a castle in pursuit of a beautiful widow whose kinsmen are away at the Crusades.

Comus (1634). Milton's masque, composed for the 1st Earl of Bridgewater at Ludlow; a girl is wooed by the monster Comus, but is saved by Sabrina, nymph of the River Severn. (Comus, Roman god of sensual pleasure.)

Concert of Europe (1815). Agreement of the Quadruple Alliance (Austria, Prussia, Russia and Britain), made after the CONGRESS OF VIENNA, to meet periodically in order to concert diplomatic moves to preserve Europe from a repetition of the chaos caused by the French Revolution and Napoleonic Wars. Castlereagh, and his successor Canning, gradually withdrew British support (completely in 1822) when Metternich imposed his policy of suppressing Liberalism everywhere, even to the extent of interfering in the domestic affairs of other states. Also called the Congress System. See HOLY ALLIANCE.

Conchobar (Conor) Legendary King of Ulster at the beginning of the Christian era, who ruled at Emain Macha in Armagh (the ruins of which survive), with an army of RED BRANCH KNIGHTS. See CUCHULAIN; DEIRDRE; MAEVE.

Concorde First supersonic airliner, an Anglo-French project on which work began in 1963. Designed to carry 136 passengers at 1450 m.p.h.

Concordia Roman goddess of peace, represented in art as a veiled matron holding a horn of plenty in one hand and in the other a sceptre.

Condé, House of Branch of the BOURBON family founded by the first prince of Condé in the 16th century. He and his son were Huguenot enemies of the GUISES. The fourth in the line, called the Great Condé, was a general of Louis XIV's reign (see FRONDE).

Condition humaine, La (1933). André Malraux's novel based on the struggle between Chinese Communists and the Kuomintang forces in Shanghai in 1927. (English title, *Storm over Shanghai*.)

Coney Island Seaside resort and amusement centre, off the south-west point of Long Island, New York.

Confederate States of America The 11 States which seceded from the Union and set up (February 1861) a government at Richmond, Virginia, under Jefferson Davis as President. They were the original 7 – South Carolina, Alabama, Georgia, Florida, Louisiana, Mississippi and Texas – joined later by Arkansas, Tennessee, Virginia and North Carolina. See AMERICAN CIVIL WAR.

Confederation of British Industry See CBI.

Confederation of the Rhine (1806–13). Confederation of Bavaria, Baden, Württemberg and other German states, formed by Napoleon and subject to him.

Conference pear Excellently flavoured variety of pear, easy to grow, with a characteristic long tapering russet fruit which is picked during October.

Confessions of an English Opium-eater (1821). Thomas de Quincey's (1785–1859) autobiographical account of how he took to opium to ease pain and how after much suffering he managed to cure himself of the habit.

Confidential Clerk, The (1954). Verse drama by T. S. Eliot who disguises its classical origin and religious purpose by dressing it up as a conventional farce.

Confucianism (6th century BC). Down-to-earth conservative codes of personal morality, etiquette and statesmanship, taught by the Chinese magistrate and philosopher Confucius. His sayings, which had little influence during his lifetime, were recorded by his followers and, much later, under the HAN DYNASTY, became the basis of the official code of behaviour in China, continuing to guide the way of life of rulers and ruled until the coming of the Communists.

Congo Free State Private property of King Leopold II of the Belgians (1885–1908) until it was annexed by the Belgian government as a colony (Congo Belge), after disclosures from 1903 onwards by Roger Casement, E. D. Morel and others of scandalous maladministration; now Zaïre.

Congregationalists Nonconformist descendants of the BROWNISTS and INDEPENDENTS, who hold that the only head of the Church is Jesus Christ. Each of their churches is, therefore, completely self-governing and recognizes no outside ecclesiastical authority.

Congress House (1958). London headquarters of the Trades Union Congress, in Great Russell Street.

Congressional Medal of Honour US equivalent of the Victoria Cross, awarded by Congress.

Congress of Vienna (1814–15). Assembly of European powers after the Napoleonic Wars which (though interrupted by the HUNDRED DAYS) redrew the map of Europe; it was dominated by Metternich, Castlereagh, the Tsar Alexander and Talleyrand. A loose confederation of 39 German states was formed; the Austrian Netherlands (Belgium) and Holland were united; Russia took Poland (the Duchy of Warsaw); Austria took much of northern Italy and Dalmatia; and many other changes were made, bringing comparative peace for the next 40 years.

Congress Party (1885). A leading political party in India at Partition in 1947. Originally it was formed by Hindus and Muslims to improve relations between the 2 communities and with Britain. It developed into a Hindu nationalist party, with which the MUSLIM LEAGUE finally broke in 1935.

Congress System See CONCERT OF EUROPE.

Conibear style American rowing style with a short swing and fast recovery. (Hiram Conibear, Washington University coach.)

Coningsby (1844). Disraeli's contemporary political novel, which traces the career of Harry Coningsby through Eton and Cambridge, his love for the daughter of a Lancashire industrialist, Millbank (said to represent Gladstone), his disinheritance for such unaristocratic behaviour, and his rescue from drudgery at the Bar by Millbank, who gets him elected to the Commons. The story enabled the author to air his own views on TORY DEMOCRACY, and introduces SIDONIA and TADPOLE AND TAPER.

Connacht (Connaught) Western province of the Irish Republic, formerly a Celtic kingdom, now consisting of Galway, Leitrim, Mayo, Roscommon and Sligo.

Connaught The English spelling of CONNACHT.

Conscript Fathers (1) Roman Senate. (2) Medieval Venetian Senate. (Latin *patres (et) conscripti*, 'heads of families and the newly elected'.)

Consistory (1) In the Church of England, a diocesan court now mainly concerned with authorizing alterations to a church or parsonage, but also having power to try clergy accused of immorality. (2) In the Church of Rome, a senate of all the cardinals, presided over by the Pope.

Consolidated Fund (1787). The fund at the Bank of England of the British national exchequer, into which government revenues are paid and from which expenditure is met.

Consols (1751). The government securities of Britain consolidated into a single loan stock at 3% (from 1903 at 2½%), at one time forming a large part of the country's funded debt, but after 2 world wars accounting for only about 1% of the total national debt. (Abbreviation for 'consolidated annuities'; pronounced kon-solz' or, increasingly, kon'solz.)

Constable country Suffolk–Essex border country around the Stour where John Constable was born and which he loved to paint.

Constance, Lake See BODENSEE.

Constantia Best and most famous of South African wines. (Named after a vineyard near Cape Town.)

Constantinople Older name of Istanbul.

Constantinople, Fall of (1453). Ottoman Turk conquest which ended the Byzantine Empire, and scattered Greek scholars to Western Europe, there to reinforce the REVIVAL OF LEARNING.

Constant Nymph, The (1924). Margaret Kennedy's best-selling romantic novel about an eccentric Bohemian musician, Albert Sanger, and his large family; a long-running play was made from it.

Constellation See LOCKHEED AIRCRAFT.

Consulate (1799–1804). In French history, the triumvirate set up after Napoleon had overthrown the DIRECTORY in the BRUMAIRE coup. Napoleon was made First Consul and in 1802 First Consul for life; the other two Consuls were mere figureheads.

Consumer Council (1963). Body set up by the Board of Trade to protect shoppers from the industrial and advertising forces ranged against them.

Consumers' Association (1957). Private body to protect shoppers. It publishes a monthly periodical, *Which?*, where detailed reports are printed of tests on competing brands of goods or kinds of service, usually indicating which is best value for money.

Contemptible Little Army See OLD CONTEMPTIBLES.

Continental Congress (America) Name given to 3 meetings of representatives of the American colonies; the first (1774) met in Philadelphia to discuss the grievances which led to the AMERICAN WAR OF INDEPENDENCE; the third proclaimed the Declaration of Independence (1776) and thereafter carried on the government of the country.

Continental System (1806). Napoleon's attempt by various decrees (the Berlin Decree being the first) to close European ports to English trade; it was ineffective, as even France itself found it necessary to import British goods. It led to the PENINSULAR WAR and to Napoleon's invasion of Russia.

Contract bridge (1925). Form of Auction bridge invented by Harold S. Vanderbilt, introducing the factors of vulnerability, high slam bonuses and sacrifice bidding.

Contragate US scandal involving arms supply to Iran, the profits of which helped fund the Contras in Nicaragua. (Also known as Irangate, the Iran-*contra* affair.)

Contrat social, Le (1762). See SOCIAL CONTRACT.

Convallaria Genus name of the lily of the valley.

Conventicle Act (1664). See CLARENDON CODE.

Convention, National (21 September 1792 to 26 October 1795). Sovereign assembly of France, divided into the PLAIN and the MOUNTAIN. The latter gained complete control and was responsible for the execution of Louis XVI and the establishment of the TERROR.

Conventions, National (USA) Assemblies of party delegates from all the states, staged by Republicans and Democrats in the summer before the November presidential election to select their candidates for the presidency and vice-presidency, and to hammer out a 'platform' likely to win votes without splitting the party. This supreme exercise in 'wheeling and dealing' takes place in an atmosphere as hectic as an American football game.

Convocation Name of legislative bodies of various ministries.

Conway, HMS Merchant Navy Cadet School, Llanfair P.G., Anglesey, where officers were trained for the Royal and merchant navies.

Cook's tour Cheap excursion, a conducted tour, etc., from the business of Thos. Cook & Sons, which stemmed from the occasion in 1841 when Thomas Cook organized a 12-mile trip to a temperance meeting by special train from Leicester to Loughborough for 574 people, the great majority of whom had never been outside Leicester. Travel was still only for VIPs but by 1856 Cook was organizing a circular tour of Europe and, 10 years later, trips to the USA.

Cooks, Worshipful Company of (1482). LIVERY COMPANY.

Co-op, The Colloquial abbreviation for the cooperative store/society.

Coopers, Worshipful Company of (1501). LIVERY COMPANY, originally a guild of makers of hooped wooden casks, buckets, etc.

Co-optimists, The (1921–31). Highly successful London concert-party, starring Phyllis Monkman, Stanley Holloway and Davy Burnaby.

Copeland & Garrett (1847). Successors to SPODE, owned by the Copeland family, who first gained control of the older firm in 1829. The name was retained in many of their marks, e.g. 'Copeland late Spode'. They bought up the moulds and models of Derby, Bow, Chelsea and Longton Hall.

Copenhagen (Battle of the Baltic, 1801). Nelson's destruction of the Danish fleet at Copenhagen after Denmark and Sweden had closed the Kattegat to Britain.

Copernican theory (1543). That the sun, not the earth, is the centre of our universe; not generally accepted until the 17th century. (Copernicus, Polish astronomer.)

Cophetua Legendary African king of great wealth who married a beggar-maid; mentioned by Shakespeare, the story was also told in an old ballad, and a poem of Tennyson's; but is best known through a Pre-Raphaelite painting by Burne-Jones.

Copley Medal (1709). Royal Society medal awarded annually for philosophical research.

Coppélia (1870). Comedy ballet, music by Délibes (who introduced a Hungarian czardas), choreography by Arthur Saint-Léon (and others), and a story from E. T. A. Hoffmann about a young man who falls in love with a mechanical doll, Coppélia, made by the toymaker-magician Dr Coppélius.

Copperbelt, The Copper-mining area of central Zambia adjoining that of Shaba, Zaïre.

Copperhead Person in the Northern states who sympathized with the South in the American Civil War. (The name of a venomous snake.)

Coppins Former home of the Duke of Kent at Iver, Buckinghamshire.

Copts Christian heretical sect established from the 5th century in Egypt and Abyssinia. (Ultimately derived from Greek *Aiguptios*, 'Egyptian'.)

Coq d'or, Le (1909). Rimsky-Korsakov's fairy-tale opera. An astrologer presents the king with a golden cockerel which will give warning of danger. The king refuses the reward demanded by the astrologer and is killed by the bird.

Coral Sea, Battle of the (May 1942). First naval battle fought entirely by carrier-borne aircraft, with no contact beween ships; the Americans turned back a Japanese invasion fleet bound for New Guinea.

Corbillon Cup (1933). International table tennis championship for teams of women.

Corble Cup (1947). (Fencing) International individual sabre championship.

Cordelia Youngest and favourite daughter of KING LEAR who, misconstruing her words, disinherits her. She marries the King of France and brings an army to England to rescue her father from the clutches of her sisters GONERIL and REGAN, but is defeated and hanged.

Cordon Bleu (1) Blue ribbon of the highest Bourbon order of chivalry. (2) Applied to a first-class chef etc., in much the same spirit as BLUE RIBBON (of the Order of the Garter) is used in English.

Cordwainers, Worshipful Company of (1439). LIVERY COMPANY, originally a guild of boot-makers, which now fosters technical education

in the craft. (Originally Cordovaner, a worker in Córdova goatskin, from which the best boots were made.)

Corfu incident (1923). Mussolini's occupation of the Greek island of Corfu in retaliation for the murder by Greeks of Italian soldiers delimiting the Greek–Albanian frontier. The League of Nations managed to restore Corfu to Greece under Anglo-French pressure.

Corinthian In the 19th century, a man about town; a profligate. (From ancient Corinth, notorious in Greek literature for its licentiousness and luxury.)

Corinthian Order Most ornate of the 3 Greek orders of architecture, with slender columns of which the capitals were embellished with acanthus leaves. The order found more favour in Rome than in Greece.

Corinthians (New Testament) St Paul's 2 epistles to the Church at Corinth.

Coriolanus (1608). Shakespeare's play about a Roman general of the 5th century BC who, banished by the Romans after he had won them victory over the Volscians, joins the enemy in an attack on Rome, yields to his family's plea to make peace, and is killed by the Volscians for betraying their cause.

Corn Belt Midwestern region of USA, particularly Iowa, Illinois, Indiana and Nebraska, where the long summers and cool climate favour corn (US name for Indian corn or maize), which is the staple crop and used in feeding cattle.

Cornell (1865). US university at Ithaca, New York state.

Cornhusker State Nickname of Nebraska.

Cornish language CELTIC LANGUAGE, the basis of BRETON and itself preserved after the Norman Conquest by Breton overlords.

Cornish style (Wrestling) West Country style, in which contestants wear canvas jackets on which all holds must be placed. For a win, both shoulders and a hip (or both hips and a shoulder) must touch the ground.

Corn Laws, The (1804–28). Acts imposing restrictions and levies on the import of corn into Britain, passed by parliaments dominated by landowners. They caused much distress among the poor, especially during the HUNGRY FORTIES, and were repealed in 1846 by Sir Robert Peel. See ANTI-CORN-LAW LEAGUE.

Cornwell Badge Scouts' VC, awarded for an act of bravery or sustained brave conduct e.g. in overcoming a physical handicap. (Named in honour of J. T. Cornwell, a 'boy' in the Royal Navy, who won the VC at the Battle of Jutland at the age of 15, dying of wounds a year later.)

Coronation Cup Skiing competition held in April in the Cairngorms, Scotland.

Coronation Street (1960). TV serial created by Tony Warren, who drew on his memories of the back streets of Salford for the formidable female characters.

Coronel (November 1914). Naval engagement in World War I in which von Spee sank Cradock's cruisers *Monmouth* and *Good Hope*; see FALKLAND ISLANDS, BATTLE OF THE. (Chilean port.)

Corporation Act (1661). See CLARENDON CODE.

Corporative State State in which the electorate is organized not on a geographical basis but by trades and professions, delegates to the national assembly being elected by employers' and employees' federations. Originally a Syndicalist idea, it was adopted by Fascism, with support from the Roman Catholic Church. Deliberative bodies of this kind were set up in Italy, Spain and Portugal, but under dictatorial regimes have had no opportunity to demonstrate whether they could be effective.

Corpus Christi Thursday after TRINITY SUNDAY, falling in May or June, appointed for the commemoration of the Feast of the Blessed Sacrament or Body of Christ. In Roman Catholic countries it is a major festival, observed with processions and pageantry.

Corpus Professor holder of the chair of Latin at Oxford.

Corridors of Power, The See STRANGERS AND BROTHERS.

Corriere della sera (1876). Milan newspaper now, despite its name, a leading morning daily. (Italian, 'evening courier'.)

Corsairs Another name for BARBARY PIRATES. (Latin-French word for 'raider'.)

Corsican ogre, The Sobriquet for Napoleon I, who was born in Corsica.

Cortes Spanish legislative assembly. (Pronounced cor'tes.)

Cortez, Stout Phrase from Keats's sonnet; see CHAPMAN'S HOMER. In fact it was Balboa, not Cortéz, who first saw the Pacific.

Corunna (1809). Port in north-west Spain where Sir John Moore was killed in battle after his retreat before Napoleon's forces in the PENINSULAR WAR.

Corvo, Baron Pen-name of the British writer, Frederick Rolfe (1861–1913); see QUEST FOR CORVO.

Corydon Shepherd in the pastoral poems of Theocritus and Virgil, and thereafter in general poetic use for any rustic. (Pronounced kor'i-don.)

Cosa Nostra, La Name adopted by the Mafia in USA. There are said to be 24 groups under unified command (see JOE BANANAS): they have turned from bootlegging and prostitution to gambling, loans at astronomic rates of interest (e.g. 150% a week) and the wholesale import and retail trade in narcotics. (Italian, 'our business'.)

Così fan tutte (1790). Mozart's comic opera in which the cynical Don Alfonso bets that the sisters with whom 2 of his friends are in love will be flirting with others the moment their backs are turned. On his instructions they disguise themselves as foreigners and lay siege to the girls with such success that Alfonso wins his bet. (Italian, 'thus do all women'.)

Cosmonaut Russian term for astronaut.

Cosmos Club Washington DC social club.

Costa Blanca Coastal resorts of Valencia, in eastern Spain, lying between Alicante and Valencia.

Costa Brava Catalonian resorts of the Spanish Mediterranean coast from the French frontier to Barcelona.

Costa de la Luz Tourist industry's name for the Atlantic seaboard resorts of Spain around the Gulf of Cádiz, north-west of Gibraltar. (Spanish, 'coast of light'; pronounced looth.)

Costa del Sol Spanish coastal resorts of southern Andalusia, around Malaga and as far west as Estepona, near Gibraltar. (Spanish, 'sunny coast'.)

Costa Dorada Tourist industry's name for the Catalonian coast resorts from Barcelona to Valencia, south-west of the COSTA BRAVA (Spanish, 'golden coast'.)

Costa Smeralda Coastal resorts of north-eastern Sardinia. (Italian, 'emerald coast'.)

Côte d'Azur Better known in England as 'the South of France' or the Riviera, i.e. the coastal resorts from the Italian frontier to Marseille.

Côte de Beaune Southern part of the Côte d'Or, producing red (e.g. Beaune Pommard) and most of the best white BURGUNDY WINES.

Côte de Nuits Northern part of the Côte d'Or, producing the best red BURGUNDY WINES e.g. Chambertin, Vougeot, Nuits-Saint-Georges, Romanée-Conti.

Côte Vermeille Coastal tourist area in the south of France, adjoining the Spanish frontier.

Cottagers, The Nickname of the Fulham football team, which plays at Craven Cottage.

Cotter's Saturday Night, The (1786). Robert Burns's poem, famous for its description of the nobler side of Scottish rural life.

Cottesmore Fox-hunting pack with kennels at Oakham, which hunts country in Leicestershire, Rutland and Lincolnshire.

Cotton Bowl Sports stadium at Dallas, Texas.

Cotton State Nickname of Alabama.

Couéism Psychological panacea for the stresses of modern life which swept Europe in the 1920s; believers constantly assured themselves: 'Every day, in every way, I feel better and better.' (Professor Coué, French inventor.)

Council for Mutual Economic Assistance See COMECON.

Council for National Academic Awards (1964). Body that awards degrees to students taking approved (usually sandwich) courses at educational institutions other than universities, mainly in science and applied science, including higher degrees for postgraduate study and research, and all DIPLOMAS IN TECHNOLOGY. It was the result of the ROBBINS REPORT.

Council of Europe (1949). Organization of non-Communist countries of Western Europe (excluding Spain and Portugal) which Turkey and Cyprus, among others, joined later. There is a Committee of Foreign Ministers and a Consultative Assembly meeting at Strasbourg which makes recommendations to the Committee on matters other than defence.

Council of Foreign Relations (USA) See ROYAL INSTITUTE OF INTERNATIONAL AFFAIRS.

Council of Industrial Design (1944). Body established to provide courses of instruction to raise standards of industrial design. See DESIGN CENTRE: DESIGN INDEX.

Council of Ministers (EC) The European Communities' main decision-making body, consisting of the Foreign and other Ministers of member governments or their deputies, representing individual national interests. It votes on proposals put up by the Commission. The Council has a permanent committee in Brussels and a large secretariat.

Council of Ministers (USSR) State executive, elected by the SUPREME SOVIET. Its chairman is the equivalent of the premier in other countries.

Council of Trent (1545–63). Oecumenical council which, after the upheaval of the Reformation, laid down the main doctrines of the Roman

Catholic Church in their final form and checked various abuses attacked by the Protestants. See COUNTER-REFORMATION (Held at Trento, north Italy.)

Counterblast to Tobacco, A (1604). First attempt to stop people smoking, written by that very odd man, King James I.

Counter-Reformation (16th century). Catholic reaction to the Reformation, which began after the COUNCIL OF TRENT and, working through the newly formed Order of Jesuits and (chiefly in Spain) the Inquisition, tried to win back all Europe to the Mother Church, in the process all but extinguishing the Renaissance.

Countess of Huntingdon's Connection (1748). Calvinist Methodist sect, founded by a Countess of Huntingdon, at one time a follower of John Wesley, under the influence of her chaplain, George Whitefield (see METHODISM). Most of its chapels are affiliated with the Congregational Union, the consultative body of the CONGREGA-TIONALISTS.

Count of Luxembourg, The (1911). Franz Lehár's tuneful operetta set in the Paris of the 1890s, in which the Count falls in love with a woman he has married (but never seen) as part of a money-making bargain.

Count of Monte Cristo, The (1844). Alexandre Dumas's novel about Edmond Dantès who, framed on a political charge, escapes to the island of Monte Cristo (a real island, near Elba). There he finds buried treasure which enables him to wreak his revenge on his persecutors.

Country Party (1673). See WHIGS.

Country Wife, The (1673). William Wycherley's comedy of an uxorious husband whose suspicions drive his wife into the arms of a lover who has set it about that he is a eunuch. David Garrick wrote a less licentious version. *The Country Girl*, which replaced it from 1764 until modern times, when the old play was revived.

County Courts (1846). Civil courts held at least once a month by a County Court judge on circuit sitting alone or, exceptionally, with a jury. Jurisdiction is normally limited to cases in which the amount at issue is less than £5,000. There are some 500 such courts in England and Wales.

County Palatine In England, the title still applied to Lancashire, Cheshire and Durham, and formerly to all counties under an Earl PALA-TINE.

Coupon election (December 1918). Post-war election in which the Liberal Prime Minister Lloyd George and the Conservative leader Bonar Law arranged the uncontested election of coalition candidates – a device to ensure the return of at least 150 Liberals although public opinion was swinging overwhelmingly to the Conservatives. (Asquith's name for the joint sponsoring letter given to such candidates, which he contemptuously compared with wartime ration coupons.)

Coursers' Derby Alternative name for the WATERLOO CUP.

Court, The (Bank of England) Advisory body under the chairmanship of the Governor of the Bank of England, comprising representatives of banks, industry, commerce and the trade unions, which meets weekly to decide whether Bank Rate should be changed, and to give general advice to the Treasury on the financial outlook.

Courtauld Institute Galleries Art gallery in Somerset House, London with a fine collection of Impressionist and Post-Impressionist paintings as well as other important sections.

Courtauld Institute of Art Unit of the University of London in SOMERSET HOUSE, where the history and appreciation of art is taught.

Court of Justice The European Communities' supreme court, at Luxembourg, with 7 judges and 2 advocates-general.

Court of St James's Official name of the royal court of Britain.

Courts Act (1971). Act replacing ASSIZES and QUARTER SESSIONS in England and Wales by CROWN COURTS in an endeavour to remedy the delays caused by mounting arrears under a system dating back to the 12th century.

Cousine Bette, La (1846). One of the novels of Balzac's COMÉDIE HUMAINE, in which an ageing spinster eaten away by concealed jealousy ruins the romance of a young couple.

Cousin Pons, Le (1847). One of the novels of Balzac's COMÉDIE HUMAINE, of a musician who sacrifices everything to his obsessive collecting of works of art.

Covenant In the Bible, the name given to various pacts between Jehovah and the Israelites, e.g. those of the PROMISED LAND, the establishment of David on the throne (2 Sam. 7) and the giving of the priesthood to the tribe of Levi (Deut. 31:9); the New Covenant (later mistranslated as New Testament) is that of Jeremiah 31:31–4, which indicated the rebirth of Jewish religion (interpreted as referring to Christianity).

Covenanters (1) Scottish Presbyterians who in 1638 signed the National Covenant to defend their religion against Popery and tyranny; see BISHOPS' WARS. (2) Those who signed the Solemn League and Covenant (1643) and by promising military aid to the ROUNDHEADS in the Civil War obtained assurances from the English Church and Parliament that Presbyterianism would be established in both countries and in Ireland.

Covenant of the League of Nations Its constitution, which was incorporated in the Versailles Treaty.

Covent Garden (1638). (1) London residential area laid out by Inigo Jones. (2) Formerly Britain's largest market for fruit, flowers and vegetables, which occupied most of (1). (3) Royal Opera House, situated on the northern side of (1).

Coventry, To send to To ostracize, refuse to speak to. (Phrase of uncertain origin, perhaps dating from the English Civil War, when Coventry was held by the Parliamentarians.)

Coventry blitz (14–15 November 1940). Air-raid that destroyed Coventry Cathedral, made by German aircraft using X-apparatus, an improved beam-navigation system.

Coventry Stakes A 5-furlong flat-race for 2-year-olds, run at Ascot in June.

Coverdale's Bible (1535). First complete translation of the Bible into English, by Miles Coverdale. See GREAT BIBLE.

Covered Wagon, The (1923). American film about the conquest of the Wild West.

Coverley, Sir Roger de Typical old Worcestershire squire created by Addison in the *Spectator*. He was named after the country dance, which Addison said was invented by his character's ancestor. (Coverley is an older spelling of Cowley, near Oxford.)

Cowdray Park One of England's 2 main polo grounds, on the estate of Viscount Cowdray, near Midhurst, Sussex.

Cowes Week Annual regatta held at the end of July and beginning of August under the auspices of the Royal Yacht Squadron and other local yacht clubs; the BRITANNIA CUP is one of the major events. Cowes Week is a great social occasion marking the end of the London SEASON. (Cowes, yachting centre on the north coast of the Isle of Wight.)

Cox's Orange Pippin One of the best-flavoured dessert apples, but the tree is prone to disease and not easy to cultivate; the name is indiscriminately applied to inferior varieties.

Coyote State Nickname of South Dakota.

Crabbe incident (1956). Disappearance of the frogman, Commander Crabbe, who, apparently working independently, went exploring the underside of the Soviet cruiser in Portsmouth harbour which had brought Bulganin and Khrushchev to England; he was presumed drowned or killed, but occasionally rumours are revived that he is alive and behind the Iron Curtain.

Crab Nebula Bright nebula in TAURUS, the remains of the supernova observed by the Chinese in AD 1054; it is a strong source of radio noise.

Crack Highly addictive drug which is obtained by the separation of the adulterants from cocaine by mixing with water and ammonia hydroxide. US authorities claim that one use is enough to cause addiction. (Also called 'rock'.)

Cracker State Nickname of Georgia.

Crack Up, The (1936). Scott Fitzgerald's essays on his own sad downfall, induced by his wife's mental breakdown and by financial troubles.

'**Cradle Song**' See 'WIEGENLIED'.

Cranborne Chase School (1946). Girls' Public School, at Wardour Castle, Tisbury, Wiltshire, closed 1990.

Cranford Idyllic village of Mrs Gaskell's novel of that name, based on recollections of Knutsford, Cheshire, where she spent her childhood.

Cranwell RAF college near Lincoln.

Crataegus Genus name of the thorns, including hawthorn ('may').

Cratchit, Bob In Dickens, a clerk who has to keep a family of 9 on the pittance allowed him by his employer, SCROOGE; father of Tiny Tim.

Craven Cottage The football home of the Fulham club, in London.

Craven Meeting Earliest of the Newmarket flat-race meetings, held in April.

Crawfie Nickname of Marion Crawford, one-time governess to the Queen and Princess Margaret; the publication of her sentimentalized account of the home life of her charges (as *The Little Princesses* in *Woman's Own*) was regarded as a betrayal of trust. The phrase 'doing a Crawfie on' is used for similar indiscretions, especially if accompanied by cloying sentimentality.

Crawley, Rev. Josiah Perpetual curate of Hogglestock in Trollope's *Last Chronicles of Barset*, under suspicion of stealing a cheque though finally proved innocent, despite all Mrs PROUDIE's efforts, aided by his own, to provide evidence of his guilt.

Crawley, Rawdon In Thackeray's VANITY FAIR a spendthrift heavy dragoon, trapped into marriage by Becky SHARP.

Crazy Gang, The (1932–62). Music-hall show staged first at the London Palladium and then at the Victoria Palace; the cast consisted of Flanagan and Allen, Nervo and Knox, Naughton and Gold, and at one time Monsewer Eddie Gray. They are gratefully remembered for their cheerful coarseness and often inspired foolery during a particularly grim period in Britain's history.

Creative Evolution (1907). Bergson's theory stressing the creative element in evolution and explaining everything that exists in terms of the continual thrust of the LIFE FORCE. These ideas were popularized in MAN AND SUPERMAN and BACK TO METHUSELAH by Bernard Shaw as the religion of the 20th century; Man can will the acceleration of his development into SUPERMAN, instead of sitting back and waiting for the 'chapter of accidents' postulated by Darwin's theory of NATURAL SELECTION to do it for him.

Crécy (Cooking) Served with carrots.

Crécy, Battle of (1346). Victory, early in the Hundred Years War, of Edward III over Philip VI, in which, according to a disputed tradition, gunpowder was used for the first time. (Town near Abbeville.)

Credit-Anstalt Austrian bank whose collapse in 1931 marked the beginning of the DEPRESSION in Europe.

Creevey Papers (1903). Gossipy journals and letters of the Whig politician, Thomas Creevey (1768–1838); they are of considerable interest for the insight they afford into the political life of his day.

Creighton lecture (1907). Annual lecture on History, given at London University.

Crêpe Suzette Thin pancake with an orange sauce, served burning in a liqueur.

Cressida See TROILUS AND CRESSIDA.

Cresta, The (1884). (1) Run for one-man 'skeleton' bobs at St Moritz, Switzerland; it has an average gradient of 1 in 7.7 over 1,320 yd. (2) Used erroneously of a track parallel to (1) for 4- and 2-man bobs.

Cresta Run, The (1965). N. F. Simpson's Theatre of the Absurd play about spying, set in suburbia.

Cretaceous Period Most recent subdivision of the MESOZOIC ERA, lasting from about 150 to 70 million years ago. Mammals predominated, the primitive reptiles became extinct, marsupials appeared, flowering plants predominated over others. The climate was mild. (Latin *creta*, 'chalk', deposited in shallow seas covering most of north-west Europe.)

Creweian Oration (17th century). Public oration at Oxford University delivered in alternate years by the Public Orator and the Professor of Poetry. (Baron Crewe.)

Crichel Down case (1954). Case in which a man was prevented by bureaucrats from buying back land in Dorset which had been requisitioned from his wife during the war. It resulted in the resignation of the Minister of Agriculture.

Crime and Punishment (1866). Dostoyevsky's novel; see RASKOLNIKOV.

Crimean War (1853–6). War started by the Tsar's claim to be protector of the Balkan Christians against Turkey. Britain and Napoleon III, suspicious of Russian intentions, came to Turkey's assistance, landing in the Crimea and besieging Sebastopol (see BALACLAVA, INKERMAN). Russia was forced to withdraw its claims.

Crime de Sylvestre Bonnard, Le (1881). Anatole France's novel about an aged scholar who rescues from an unhappy school the daughter of his first love, now orphaned, whose guardian he eventually becomes.

Criminal Appeal, Court of See QUEEN'S BENCH DIVISION.

Criminal Investigation Department Headquarters at New Scotland Yard of the London Metropolitan detective force and of various branches which also serve the rest of the country, e.g. the SPECIAL BRANCH, CENTRAL OFFICE, Criminal Record Office, Fingerprint Department, Scientific Laboratory and FRAUD SQUAD.

Crimond Famous tune to which the metrical psalm 'The Lord is my shepherd' is sung.

Crimplene ICI's crimped version of TERYLENE used in women's and men's wear and claimed to be uncrushable, stretchable and washable though 'permanently waved'. It is made by several other firms ('the Crimplene Club') under licence. (Named after the Crimple beck that runs behind the ICI Fibres factory at Harrogate.)

Crippen murder case (1910). Murder of his wife by an American dentist and quack doctor living in London. He dissected the body and buried it in the cellar, then sailing for America with his lover, who was disguised as a boy. The ship's captain, suspicious of their conduct, sent a message to London by radio which resulted in their arrest – the first use of radio in crime detection. Crippen was executed; his mistress, defended by F. E. Smith (Lord Birkenhead) in his first big case, was acquitted.

Crippsian austerity Term referring to the period (1947–50) when the left-wing Socialist, Sir Stafford Cripps, was Chancellor of the Exchequer. Inflation and a serious balance of payments crisis (1949) led to the devaluation of the pound and to drastic economies.

Cripps mission (1942). Mission led by Sir Stafford Cripps, which offered India postwar Dominion status; the offer, described by Gandhi as a 'post-dated cheque', was rejected by the Indian Congress Party.

Crispin, Edmund Pen-name used by Robert Bruce Montgomery when writing his humorous detective stories.

Crispin, St Patron saint of shoemakers. He and his brother Crispian are said to have come from Rome to convert the Gauls in the 4th century, supporting themselves by shoemaking. Agincourt was fought on St Crispin's Day (Shakespeare's 'Crispin Crispian'), 25 October.

Criterion, The (1922–39). Literary quarterly edited by T. S. Eliot.

Croagh Patrick Pilgrimage Annual pilgrimage to the top of Ireland's Holy Mountain (Croagh Patrick 2,500 ft) near the coast of Co. Mayo; it starts on the eve of the last Sunday in July, from either Westport or Louisburgh. There is a small church on the summit, where mass is said.

Crockford (1857). Short title of Crockford's

Clerical Directory, an annual 'staff list' of the Church of England, famous for its anonymous prefaces on Church matters. These prefaces are now signed.

Crockford's (1827). London gambling club. (William Crockford, fishmonger, its founder.)

Crock of Gold, The (1912). James Stephens's best-known work, a collection of original fairy stories.

Croesus (6th century BC). Last King of Lydia (in south-west Anatolia), of legendary wealth, and the first to issue gold and silver coins. (Pronounced kree'sus.)

Croix de Feu (1935). Militant Fascist organization formed by Col. de la Rocque in Paris.

Cro-Magnon Man One of the earliest races of HOMO SAPIENS. He produced the ALTAMIRA cave paintings (see AURIGNACIAN CULTURE). (Name of cave in the Dordogne, France, where remains first found.)

Cromer prize Given by the British Academy for a Greek essay.

Cromwellian Settlement, The (1649–52). After the great Irish rebellion of 1641 in which thousands of Protestants were massacred, and after James Butler, Earl of Ormonde, had declared for Charles II in 1649, Cromwell quelled all revolt by massacring the garrisons at DROGHEDA and Wexford; he then left Ireton to complete the PLANTATIONS by evicting Catholic landowners east of the Shannon and replacing them by Protestants, including his own soldiers (who were soon absorbed into the native population).

Cronos In Greek mythology, a Titan who overthrew his father Uranus and was in turn overthrown by his son Zeus. He was also the father of Hera, Demeter, Poseidon and Hades. The Romans identified him with Saturn.

Croonian lecture (1684). Triennial lecture at the Royal Society on the structure and function of the brain.

Crop circles Circles and other shapes cut in standing corn, particularly in Wiltshire, England. They appear to take more complex shapes each year and the cause is unknown. Sightings were reported as early as 1678.

Crotchet Castle (1831). Thomas Love Peacock's 'novel', on much the same lines as NIGHTMARE ABBEY.

Crouchback, Guy Hero of Evelyn Waugh's SWORD OF HONOUR, the wondering, disillusioned observer of events and people.

Crown Agents, The (1833). Non-government non-profit organization in London that acts as financial and commercial agents to many governments and public authorities in, and outside, the Commonwealth, for whom it holds and invests about £1,000 million, places orders for supplies of every kind, engages technical staff, etc. It began as 'The Agents General for the Crown Colonies'.

Crown Courts (1972). Established under the COURTS ACT in England and Wales (which are divided into 6 circuits), operating at 24 first-tier centres with courts staffed by High Court judges and a newly created bench of full-time Circuit Judges to try both criminal and civil cases; 19 second-tier centres with courts similarly staffed but hearing only criminal cases; 46 third-tier centres with courts manned by Circuit Judges to try less important criminal cases. The professional judges are assisted by a newly created class of part-time RECORDERS.

Crown Derby (1786–1811). Name given to the products of the DERBY PORCELAIN factory in the period following its founder's death. Figures continued to predominate but, with the introduction of bone china, tablewares were made, often decorated with IMARI PATTERNS, figures and landscapes on pastel grounds in the Sèvres style, or (until 1796) BILLINGSLEY FLOWERS. The name was revived by the unconnected Royal Crown Derby Porcelain Co., not founded until 1876. See BLOOR DERBY.

Crown Estate Commissioners Administrators of revenue from the Crown Estates (formerly called Crown Lands), next to the Forestry Commission the largest landowners in Britain. The Crown Lands were those which George III surrendered to government in return for the CIVIL LIST; they do not include the Duchies of Cornwall and Lancaster.

Crowther report (1959). Entitled *15–18*, its recommendation that the school-leaving age should be raised to 16 by the late 1960s was rejected by the Conservative government in 1960. It strongly criticized the segregation of children at 11+ into the 3 types of school: grammar, secondary modern and technical.

Croydon London borough since 1965 consisting of the former county borough of Croydon and the urban district of Coulsdon-Purley.

Cruciferae Cabbage and wallflower family, characterized by the 4 petals arranged in the form of a cross. The chief group is the Brassicas (cabbage, turnip, watercress, etc.), but the family also includes nasturtium, aubretia, honesty, candytuft, etc. (Latin, 'cross-bearing'.)

Cruden Short title for the *Concordance to the Bible* (1737) compiled by Alexander Cruden, for long the standard concordance.

Cruel Sea, The (1951). Long and lusty best-selling novel by Nicholas Monsarrat about naval life during World War II.

Cruelty, Theatre of (1938). Type of play advocated by the French playwright Artaud, which should suppress reason and logic and use fantasies of torture, madness and perversion to act as a catharsis on actors and audience alike, bringing to the surface unavowable obsessions and desires. An outstanding example of the genre is MARAT/SADE.

Crufts (1886). Britain's premier dog show, held early in February at Olympia, London. (Founded by Charles Cruft, of Spillers, the dog-biscuit firm.)

Cruikshank cartoons Political cartoons, less coarse and a little less venomous than those of ROWLANDSON and GILLRAY, attacking in particular Napoleon and George IV; drawn by George Cruikshank (1792–1878), who later turned to attacks on the evils of gin, and then to illustrating the work of most of the great novelists of his time.

Cruise missile (1977). Subsonic missile with warhead which is air-breathing and is powered and guided throughout its flight. It can strike targets 2,500 miles away with an accuracy of less than 30 yards.

Crummles, Vincent Eccentric theatrical manager in Dickens's NICHOLAS NICKLEBY.

Cruncher, Jerry Minor character in Dickens's A TALE OF TWO CITIES; he works in a bank by day and at night is a body-snatcher. His wife spends her time 'flopping' (as he calls it), i.e. on her knees in prayer.

Crusaders Cambridge University cricket club of the best 75 players in residence (elected for life); the equivalent of the AUTHENTICS at Oxford.

Crusades (1095–1291). Series of campaigns to rescue the Holy Land from the Muslim Seljuk Turks. The first was carried out by an unorganized rabble which was massacred, and then by an army which took Jerusalem. In the third (1189) Richard I and the French king failed to recapture the city from Saladin. The fourth (1202) was diverted by the Venetians into sacking Byzantium. In the end the Crusaders lost all their Near Eastern territories except Acre, and that fell in 1291.

Crustacea See ARTHROPODS.

Cry, the Beloved Country (1948). Alan Paton's moving novel of the degrading effects of city (in this case Johannesburg) life on Africans who migrate there from the veld.

Crystal Palace (1851). Joseph Paxton's building, entirely of glass and iron, built to house the GREAT EXHIBITION in Hyde Park; it was then re-erected at Penge in South London, but was burnt down in 1936. The site, still named after it, is now used for the National Recreation Centre.

Crystal Palace Football team which plays at Selhurst Park, South Norwood, London.

CS gas Form of tear gas used in riot control and apprehending armed criminals. It is far less toxic than the traditional tear smoke (CN) and its effects are short-lived; nevertheless, it was held to be unsuitable for use in city areas during the Ulster riots of 1969 onwards.

Cuban crisis (October 1962). Tension resulting from the discovery by US reconnaissance planes that Russia was installing rockets in Cuba directed against the USA. President Kennedy's sharp reaction led to Khrushchev's agreeing to dismantle them at once. See PENKOVSKY SPY CASE.

Cubism (1907–14). Art movement started by Picasso and Braque; they brought out the 3-dimensional structure of an object by combining several views of it in cubic or other geometric patterns. Picasso described it as painting 'what he knew was there' rather than what he saw.

Cuchulain Achilles of Ulster legend, nephew of CONCHOBAR, the boy warrior who, single-handed, defended Ulster against MAEVE (Medb), Queen of Connacht. (Pronounced koo´ku-lin.)

Culbertson system (1930). Most famous of the calling systems at Bridge; in hand valuation points are counted instead of quick tricks as in the earlier versions; additions are made for long suits. A forcing two call indicates 23 points. (Ely Culbertson, USA, died 1955.)

Culham Laboratory Atomic Energy Authority's research centre for fusion (thermonuclear) power for use in generating electricity; see ZETA. (Village south of Oxford, near HARWELL.)

Cullinan diamond (1905). Large diamond found in the Premier mine, Transvaal, and presented to Edward VII.

Culloden (1746). Final defeat of the YOUNG PRETENDER, with great loss of life, by Cumberland (the 'BLOODY BUTCHER') in the FORTY-FIVE. (Moor east of Inverness; pronounced kĕ-lod´n.)

Cultural Revolution, Chinese (1966). Campaign launched by Chairman Mao Tse-tung against 'revisionists', i.e. opponents of his policies; its agents were the RED GUARDS.

Cumberland style (Wrestling) Style popular in north-west England and in Scotland; the initial hold is all-important and a win is scored simply by throwing an opponent to the ground.

Cumbernauld (1956). NEW TOWN in Dunbartonshire, designed to take Glasgow overspill population.

Cumbrians, The Nickname of the Carlisle United football team.

Cup Final Term used specifically of the final for the Football Association's Challenge Cup (1871), held at WEMBLEY, a competition open to any club in the country, although amateur sides rarely survive the first round. The original Cup was stolen in 1895. There is a separate Scottish Cup (1873).

Cupid Roman equivalent of EROS. See next entry.

Cupid and Psyche Story in the GOLDEN ASS, in which Cupid (Eros) falls in love with a king's daughter, PSYCHE, whom he visits nightly. She disobeys his command not to try to identify him, because he is one of the immortals, and he goes off in a huff; but in the end they are reunited and she too is made immortal.

Curaçao Liqueur, originally Dutch, made with the peel of bitter Curaçao oranges. (One of the Netherlands Antilles in the West Indies; pronounced kewr´a-soh.)

Curragh, The Extensive down east of the town of Kildare, from ancient times used as a racecourse, and now the scene of all the Irish classic races; also formerly used as a British military camp (see next entry). (Irish *cuirrech*, racecourse.)

Curragh 'mutiny' (March 1914). Occasion (not a mutiny) when British cavalry officers at the CURRAGH declared that they would resign rather than fight against Carson's ULSTER VOLUNTEERS.

Curriers, Worshipful Company of (1606). LIVERY COMPANY, originally a guild of leather-workers.

Curse of Scotland Name, since the 18th century, for the 9 of Diamonds; many explanations are suggested, e.g. the 9 lozenges in the arms of the Earl of Stair, blamed by some for the GLENCOE MASSACRE.

Curtis Cup (1930). Women's golf contest between USA and Britain, played annually in either country alternately.

Curzon Line Boundary between Poland and Russia first proposed by Lloyd George in 1920, when it was rejected, and imposed on Poland after the MOSCOW CONFERENCE ('Tolstoy') in 1944. It deprived Poland of areas where Russians, Ukrainians or Lithuanians are in the majority. (Lord Curzon, Foreign Secretary, who handled the negotiations in 1920.)

Cushites Non-Semitic people of north-east Africa. See HAMITES.

Custer's last stand (1876). Last fight of the American General Custer, when surrounded by Sioux in Dakota Territory; he and his troops were all killed.

Cutlers, Worshipful Company of (1416). LIVERY COMPANY, originally a guild of makers of swords, daggers and all kinds of knife.

Cutty Sark (1896). Last of the tea clippers, now lying in the Thames at Greenwich Pier, and open to the public. (Scottish, 'short shirt'; used in Robert Burns's *Tam O'Shanter* of a witch.)

Cwmbran (1949). NEW TOWN in Monmouthshire, 5 miles north of Newport, designed for a population of 55,000.

Cybele Phrygian mother goddess who loved ATTIS; worshipped with orgiastic rites by eunuch Corybants. Identified with RHEA by the Greeks, and worshipped in Rome as the Great Mother. (Pronounced sib'el-ee.)

Cyclopean masonry Ancient building works constructed without mortar of huge, perfectly fitting blocks of stone, examples of which can be seen at Tiryns and Mycenae in Greece, and in other parts of the world. (Traditionally built by the CYCLOPS giants; pronounced sy-klop-ee'an.)

Cyclops In Greek legend, any of several one-eyed giants who helped HEPHAESTUS to forge thunderbolts; POLYPHEMUS was a Cyclops. (Greek, 'round-eyed'; pronounced sy'klops.)

Cydonia See CHAENOMELES.

Cygnus The Swan, a northern constellation between Pegasus and Draco, with about 200 stars visible to the naked eye; it contains a dark nebula.

Cymbeline Shakespeare's name for Cunobelinus, a British king at the beginning of the Christian era, father of Caractacus. Shakespeare's play (1610) is about his daughter Imogen and her secret marriage. She is unjustly suspected of infidelity, but there is the final reconciliation scene characteristic of Shakespeare's last plays.

Cymric Welsh. (Welsh *Cymru*, 'Wales'.)

Cynthia Less common name for ARTEMIS. (Born on Mount Cynthus, on the island of Delos.)

Cypripedium Genus name of the Lady's Slipper orchids.

Cyrano de Bergerac (1897). Rostand's play about a 17th-century French soldier and dramatist, famous for his long nose, his duels and his accounts of visits to the moon and sun rather in the style of *Gulliver's Travels*. (Pronounced seer-ahn'o, bair-zhèr-ahk'.)

Cyriax Cup Rugby fives amateur doubles championship.

Cyrillic Slavonic alphabet, based on the Greek. Serbo-Croat is sometimes written in a modernized and simplified form of it, but a Latin alphabet is also used. (Traditionally introduced by St Cyril, a 9th-century Greek missionary to the Slavs.)

Cytisus Genus name of the common broom, thornless, deciduous, flowering in May–June; see also GENISTA; SPARTIUM JUNCEUM.

Czech crisis (1968). Invasion of Czechoslovakia by Russian, East German and Polish troops, allegedly to put down anti-Marxist elements, actually because, under the relatively liberal regime of the recently appointed Party secretary Dubček, fraternization with West Germans, especially by Czech academics, increased and was seen as a threat to Ulbricht's control of East Germany, Gomułka's of Poland, and to Soviet dominance in general. The Russians expelled Dubček and restored a regime subservient to Moscow.

Czestochowa Madonna See JASNA GÓRA.

D

Dachau (1933). Hitler's first concentration camp, near Munich.

Dacia Roman province which fell to the GOTHS in the 3rd century; corresponding to modern Romania and neighbouring districts.

Dacron American form of TERYLENE made by DU PONT.

Dadaism (1915). First of the really mad 'artistic' movements, started in unlikely Zürich. It took almost any form, from a lecture by 38 lecturers in unison to painting moustaches on Mona Lisa.

Daedalus In Greek legend a craftsman, symbolic of invention and creative activity, who built the Labyrinth at Knossos, was imprisoned in it with his son Icarus, but escaped. He fastened wings on their shoulders with wax and flew away. Icarus flew too near the sun, which melted the wax, and he fell into the Icarian Sea; Daedalus landed safely at Naples. (Greek, 'skilful', 'variegated'; pronounced dee'dal-us.)

DAF Series of ingenious Dutch cars with infinitely variable gears made possible by the (rubber) belt-driven transmission.

Dagenham Former Essex borough, since 1965 divided between the boroughs of REDBRIDGE and BARKING.

Dahlia Half-hardy tuberous herbaceous plant named after Andreas Dahl, a Swedish botanist, who was a pupil of Linnaeus (pronounced day-le-a in Britain but dahl-le-a in US).

Dáil Éireann Irish Republic's parliament. It was first formed (illegally) in 1919 by the Sinn Féin MPs who had refused to take their seats at Westminster; it set up a parallel administration to the British, with its own courts and raising its own taxes. In 1921, at the Partition, it became the legal government of the Irish Free State. (Erse, 'assembly of Ireland'; pronounced doil-yair'èn.)

Daily News (1846). London Liberal newspaper, of which Charles Dickens was the founder and first editor; absorbed by the *News Chronicle* in 1930.

Daimler (1885). One of the first petrol-driven cars to be marketed, a horseless carriage soon to be replaced by more modern types. A Daimler Co. was formed in 1891, and was later renamed MERCEDES. See BENZ. (Gottlieb Daimler, German inventor.)

Daiquiri Iced cocktail made with Cuban rum, lime juice and sugar. (A town near Santiago de Cuba; pronounced dy-keer'i.)

Dairen Chinese port built by Russia, also called Talien, and grouped with Port Arthur as the conurbation of Lü-ta.

Daisy-wheel printer Printer with a circular typehead with the characters attached round it.

Dakar expedition (September 1940). Gen. de Gaulle's expedition to Dakar, then the capital of French West Africa, in the expectation that Frenchmen there would rally to him; the Vichy elements were, however, in control and the expedition was repulsed.

Dakota British name for the US DC-3 aircraft, virtually the first modern airliner, a twin-engined all-metal plane which had an immense world-wide success.

Dalai Lama Chief priest of the Tibetan Buddhists; each is said to be a reincarnation of his predecessor, and is recognized as an infant by certain traditional signs. With the Chinese Communist invasion of Tibet, the last Dalai Lama took refuge in India. (Pronounced dal'*y* lah'ma.)

Dalcroze Institute of Eurhythmics (1910). Influential school founded in Bavaria and moved to Geneva, where children were taught to interpret the spirit of music in spontaneous dances. (Founded by Émile Jaques-Dalcroze, Swiss composer.)

Dale (Henry) Professorship Royal Society professorship of physiology or pharmacology.

Daleks (1963). DR WHO's most dangerous enemies whose war cry is 'ex-ter-mi-nate'.

Dallas (1980s). US television soap opera.

Dalmatian Medium-sized short-haired dog, white spotted with black or liver; it was originally trained to follow behind or under coaches, and kept in the stables. (Believed to have originated from Dalmatia.)

Dalriada (1) Ancient Gaelic kingdom of northern Antrim. (2) Kingdom of Argyll founded about AD 500 by emigrants from Irish Dalriada, the first Scots to arrive in Scotland. (Pronounced dal-r*y*'a-da.)

Dalton Budget leak (1947). Hugh Dalton, Chancellor of the Exchequer, resigned after it transpired that he had disclosed details of a forthcoming Budget to a journalist.

Dalton plan Helen Parkhurst's educational system in which children's initiative is developed by giving them monthly assignments to complete in their own way and with self-imposed discipline. (Dalton, Mass., where first tried out in 1920.)

Daltons Stock Exchange name for the issue (1946) of $2\frac{1}{2}\%$ Irredeemable Treasury Stock, made when Hugh Dalton was the Labour Chancellor of the Exchequer.

Damascus, The road to Allusion to the scene of St Paul's conversion after hearing a voice saying: 'Saul, why persecutest thou me?' (Acts 9.)

Dam Busters, The (1955). British film reconstruction of the MÖHNE AND EDER DAM-BUSTER RAIDS in which Guy Gibson won the VC and for which Sir Barnes Wallis devised 'bouncing' bombs to penetrate the dams' defences.

Dame aux camélias, La (1848). Novel by Alexandre Dumas *fils* on which he based a play, Verdi an opera (*La* TRAVIATA), and Hollywood a film (*Camille*, with Garbo). Marguerite Gautier, a fashionable courtesan, spurns a rich suitor, runs off with the penniless Armand Duval, gives him up at his father's request, and dies of consumption.

Dame Partlet Wife of Chanticleer; see 'CHANTICLEER AND PERTELOTE'.

Damocles Courtier who envied the wealth and happiness of Dionysius the Elder, tyrant of Syracuse in the 5th century BC. To teach him that 'uneasy lies the head that wears a crown' Dionysius gave him a banquet, during which he noticed a sword suspended over his head by a single hair. Hence *sword of Damocles*, ever-present danger, especially when all seems well. (Pronounced dam'o-kleez.)

Damon and Pythias Two Greeks of Syracuse in the 5th century BC, whose friendship was proverbial. When Pythias was condemned to death, Damon stood security for him at the risk of his own life; moved by this, the tyrant of Syracuse pardoned Pythias. (Pronounced day'mon, pith'i-as.)

Dan Grade of mastership of judo. Those placed in the 1st–5th Dan (the highest) wear black belts; 6th–8th Dan, red and white; 9th–10th, red belts. Pupils are graded as 1st–6th Kyu.

Danaë In Greek legend, the daughter of a King of Argos who locked her up because of a prophecy that her son would destroy him. Zeus visited her in the guise of a shower of gold, and fathered PERSEUS by her. (Pronounced dan'ay-ee.)

Dance of Death (1) Strindberg's realistic play (1901) about the love–hate of a tyrannical husband and his submissive wife. (2) See DANSE MACABRE.

Dane, Clemence Pen-name of Winifred Ashton (1888–1965), English novelist and playwright, best known for her play BILL OF DIVORCEMENT.

Danegeld Land-tax imposed in 10th-century England, and used by Ethelred the Unready to buy off the Danes.

Danelaw The area of England occupied by the Danes; Alfred the Great and Guthrum the Dane agreed on WATLING STREET as the boundary between it and Wessex in AD 878.

Dangerous Corner (1932). J. B. Priestley's play in which a chance remark leads a happy group into highly embarrassing mutual revelations; the play starts again, with the remark left unspoken, and all ends happily.

Daniel (6th century BC). Major prophet (see next entry). See BELSHAZZAR'S FEAST; SUSANNA AND THE ELDERS. The story of Daniel's being cast into the lions' den and escaping miraculously unharmed is told in Daniel 6:7–23.

Daniel (2nd century BC). Old Testament book which tells the story of Daniel (see previous entry), regarding whom there is no other source of information.

Daniel Deronda (1876). George Eliot's last novel. The eponymous hero, brought up as a Christian, discovers that he is a Jew, marries a Jewess and with her brother goes to Palestine fired with what would now be called Zionist ambitions (the Zionist movement started 20 years after the book was published).

Danilo See MERRY WIDOW.

Danish Blue Soft blue cheese, strictly that made from cow's milk and ripened in caves in Denmark; it has a much harsher flavour than the older-established blue cheeses.

D'Annunzio raid (September 1919). Seizure of Fiume from Yugoslavia by Italian irregular forces led by the swashbuckling poet Gabriele d'Annunzio. Defying the Allied Council of Foreign Ministers, he proclaimed a government there and was not ejected until January 1921.

Danse macabre Mimed dance of death of medieval German origin, in which Death seizes representatives of every age and condition of life one by one. It has often been depicted in art and music.

Dan to Beersheba Phrase from Judges 20:1, meaning from one end of Canaan (or by extension, any country) to another.

Danzig German name of the Polish port of Gdańsk.

Daphne In Greek legend a girl who escaped the advances of Apollo by being turned into a laurel.

Daphnis and Chloe Rustic lovers in a Greek pastoral romance of the 4th century AD.

D'Arblay, Frances See BURNEY, FANNY.

Darby and Joan Couple who have been long and happily married. (Name taken from a ballad, said to be based on a historical couple of London or, in another version, of Yorkshire.)

Darcy Character in Jane Austen's *Pride and Prejudice* whose snobbishness and pride eventually yield to admiration for Elizabeth Bennet (see BENNET FAMILY), whom he marries.

Dardanelles campaign (February 1915 to January 1916). Campaign sponsored in World War I by Winston Churchill as First Lord, designed both to outflank Germany via Turkey and to open up communications with Russia. It failed owing to hesitant support from the Cabinet and weak command on the spot. The Anglo-French fleet failed to penetrate the Dardanelles, and British and Anzac forces were landed on Gallipoli under Ian Hamilton at ANZAC COVE and later at Suvla Bay, under withering fire from the Turks who had had over-long notice of Allied intentions. The whole force was evacuated in December/January, having achieved nothing at heavy cost.

Darjeeling tea Best-known of Indian teas, grown in the extreme north of West Bengal, near the Sikkim border.

Dark Ages Term formerly used for the MIDDLE AGES, abandoned when historians discovered that they were not so dark; now sometimes applied to the first 4 centuries of that period, from the fall of Rome to Charlemagne.

Dark Lady of the Sonnets, The Woman to whom Shakespeare addressed *Sonnets* 127–52, and whom the poet loves despite her unfaithfulness. Described as 'as dark as night', 'black wires grow on her head', she has never been identified; she may have been Elizabeth's maid of honour, Mary Fitton.

Darkness at Noon (1940). Arthur Koestler's novel based on the Russian purges of the 1930s, a study of a Communist idealist forced to make a false confession of treason against the state.

Darley Arabian See BYERLY TURK.

Darling, Grace Daughter of a lighthouse keeper who with her father rescued survivors from a wreck off the Farne Islands (1838).

'Darling Daisy' letters Written by Edward VII to Frances, Countess of Warwick, who threatened at one time to publish them; auctioned in 1967.

Darracq Early French car. In 1906 a 200-h.p. V-8 model reached 122 m.p.h.

D'Artagnan See THREE MUSKETEERS.

Dartington Hall (1926). Imaginatively planned economic and cultural community near Totnes, Devon, now a trust with agricultural and commercial enterprises (including a sawmill, textile mill, cattle-breeding research centre), and a co-educational boarding school (now closed) where the children made their own rules and there were no compulsory lessons or games, no marks, punishments, prefects, bounds or religious services. (Founded by Leonard and Dorothy Elmhirst.)

Dartle, Miss Rosa Excitable spinster in Dickens's *David Copperfield* who falls inappropriately and violently in love with the cad Steerforth; her keynote line is: 'I only ask for information.'

Dartmouth College, USA (1769). University at Hanover, New Hampshire.

Dartmouth RNC Now named the BRITANNIA ROYAL NAVAL COLLEGE.

Darwin College (1963). First graduate college at Cambridge University, built on to an existing country house.

Darwinism See ORIGIN OF SPECIES; DAYTON ANTI-DARWINIST TRIAL.

Darwin Medal (1890). Royal Society silver medal awarded biennially for research connected with Darwin's theories, particularly in biology.

Darwin's finches Finches noted by Darwin on the Galapagos Islands during the VOYAGE OF THE BEAGLE. Isolated on the scattered islands of the archipelago, they had developed widely differing beaks to deal with the food locally available. He mentions this as among the main starting-points for his theory of the ORIGIN OF SPECIES.

Dashwood family Characters in Jane Austen's *Sense and Sensibility* (1811). Elinor, the heroine, represents 'sense' and her sister Marianne 'sensibility'; John, their stepbrother, is persuaded by his wife not to fulfil his obligations to them.

Daughters of the American Revolution (1890). Patriotic society of women descended from those who fought in the American War of Independence, dedicated to the preservation of the ideals of that war.

Dauphin, The Title of the French crown prince, from the 14th century until the ORLEANIST MONARCHY. His wife was the Dauphine.

Davallia Tropical and temperate ferns named after Edmund Davall, a Swiss botanist.

Davenport (1793–1876). (1) Pottery and china firm at Longport, Staffordshire, particularly noted for high-class bone china with fruit and flower decorations in brilliant colours, and for lustre-ware tea services. It also made earthenware and stoneware. (2) Small writing-table or desk.

David King of Israel who succeeded SAUL, slew the Philistine giant Goliath (1 Sam. 17:4–51), was the inseparable friend of Saul's son Jonathan (1 Sam. 18:1), fell in love with BATH-SHEBA, and whose son ABSALOM rose in revolt against him. He is the traditional author of Psalms.

David Copperfield (1850). One of the best-known of Dickens's novels, partly autobiographical. David, turned loose when young, leaves his nurse Clara PEGGOTTY, lodges with MICAWBER, is championed by his great-aunt Betsey TROTWOOD, works for a lawyer who is being blackmailed by Uriah HEEP, and marries the lawyer's daughter as his second wife.

Davidia Trees named after Armand David, a French missionary, who worked in China.

Daviot, Gordon Pen-name assumed by Elizabeth Mackintosh when she wrote the popular historical play *Richard of Bordeaux* (1933) and other plays. See also TEY, JOSEPHINE.

Davis apparatus Device to enable the crew to escape from a damaged submerged submarine.

Davis Cup (1900). Officially the International Lawn Tennis Championship, which began as a match between USA and Britain and grew into an international contest between teams playing 4 singles and 1 doubles matches; the winner in eliminating rounds (played in 3 zones: American, European and Eastern) challenges the holder. (Dwight Davis, US donor.)

Davy Crockett cap Racoon-skin cap, almost obligatory wear for small boys in the 1950s, in memory of an American hunter and trapper (died 1836) whose exploits against Red Indians and Mexicans are recorded in numerous books, including his own.

Davy Jones's locker Grave of those who are buried at sea. Eighteenth-century phrase; Davy Jones was the spirit of the sea, perhaps a name derived from Jonah.

Davy lamp (1815). Invented by Sir Humphry Davy to trace lethal, odorous methane gas in mines.

Davy Medal Royal Society medal awarded annually for the most important discovery in chemistry in Europe or Anglo-America. (Founded by Sir Humphry Davy's brother.)

Dawes Hicks lectures (1955). Annual lectures on philosophy sponsored by the British Academy.

Dawes Plan (1924). Scaling down of German reparations combined with a large German loan which produced a 5-year truce in the post-war wrangle over reparations. Superseded by the YOUNG PLAN. (C. G. Dawes, US statesman.)

Dawley (1963). A NEW TOWN in Shropshire, south-east of the Wrekin.

Daylight Saving Act (1916). Law which first introduced British Summertime, as a wartime economy measure.

Day of the Covenant (South Africa) See DIN-GAAN'S DAY.

Day of the Triffids, The (1951). John Wyndham's outstanding science-fiction novel, well known outside the circle of SF addicts, about the survivors of a world struck down with blindness and a plague, and menaced by huge ambulatory lethally-stinging vegetables evolved by man in the search for new sources of vegetable oil.

Daytona Beach US resort on the Atlantic coast of Florida with a 20-mile stretch of sandy beach on which many car speed records have been established from the 1920s onwards.

Dayton anti-Darwinist trial (1925). Deliberately sought test case in which a schoolmaster, J. T. Scopes, was accused of teaching Darwinism contrary to Tennessee law, and fined 100 dollars (later remitted). (Dayton, a small town of Tennessee, not Dayton, Ohio.)

D-Day (6 June 1944). First day of the Allied landings in Normandy.

Dead End Kids, The Young actors who appeared in Sidney Kingsley's play (1935) and movie (1937), *Dead End*, about New York slums during the Depression.

Dead March in Saul, The March from Handel's oratorio *Saul* (1739), often played at state funerals.

Dead Sea fruit 'Apple of Sodom', a legendary fruit of the desert which turned to ashes in the mouth; hence a symbol of frustrated hope. (Presumably a fanciful description of a desert fruit, still called by that name, which is quite uneatable.)

Dead Sea Scrolls Ancient manuscripts found (from 1947 onwards) in caves around Qumran, near the Dead Sea, possibly written by ESSENES (a Jewish sect) in the first century AD. They include the earliest extant manuscripts of the Old Testament, including the whole of ISAIAH, and the Apocrypha. Their age and other crucial points are still debated.

Dead Souls (1842). Gogol's great comic novel about a rogue, Chichikov, who travels round the country buying the ownership of dead serfs in a complex scheme to mortgage them for land. The fun lies in the landowners' reactions to this extraordinary proposition.

Deadwood Dick Hero of dime novels by Edward L. Wheeler about the 1876 Gold Rush. The character was based on an English-born frontiersman, Richard Clarke (1845–1930), who made his name as a guard of gold consignments. (Deadwood, town of South Dakota, USA.)

Deans, Jeanie Heroine of Walter Scott's *Heart of Midlothian*; she walks to London to obtain a pardon from the king for her half-sister Effie, who has been found guilty of murdering her illegitimate child (who however turns out to be alive).

Dear Brutus (1917). Play by James Barrie about lost opportunities and a second chance to seize them in Lob's magic Wood of the Second Chance.

Dear Octopus (1938). One of Dodie Smith's light comedies, the 'octopus' being family ties.

Death and the Maiden Quartet One of Schubert's string quartets, named after the song on which the variations in the second movement are based.

Death of a Hero (1929). Richard Aldington's disillusioned novel about World War I.

Death of a President (1967). William Manchester's detailed account of events on the day that President J. F. Kennedy was assassinated.

Death of a Salesman See LOMAN, WILLY.

Death Row US name for the 'death cells' where condemned prisoners await execution.

De Beers (1871). Group which, starting as a mining company near Kimberley, Cape Colony, South Africa, gained a virtual monopoly of African diamond mining and marketing.

Deborah Prophetess and judge of Israel (Judg. 4:4) whose song of triumph after Barak's defeat of SISERA (Judg. 5) is possibly one of the oldest parts of the Bible. (Pronounced deb'ĕr-a.)

De Bourgh, Lady Catherine Formidable female in PRIDE AND PREJUDICE who is outraged at the idea of Bingley and Darcy marrying into the despised BENNET FAMILY. (Pronounced de-berg'.)

Debrett Common abbreviation for Debrett's *Peerage, Baronetage, Knightage and Companionage* (1802), and 2 other derivative annuals, now published by KELLY'S DIRECTORIES. (John Debrett, London publisher.)

Decalogue, The Ten Commandments. (Greek, 'ten words'.)

Decameron (1353). Collection of tales supposed to have been told by a company of Florentines to while away their enforced confinement during an outbreak of plague, and compiled by Boccaccio. (Greek, 'ten days'.)

Decathlon Olympic Games or other contest in which individuals or teams compete in all of 10 events: long and high jump, pole vault, discus, putting the weight, javelin, hurdle race, 100, 400 and 1,500 metres. (Greek, '10 contests'.)

Deceased Wife's Sister Marriage Act (1907). Burning political issue in Britain over a long period, termed by W. S. Gilbert 'that eternal blister – /Marriage of deceased wife's sister'. The

Act authorized civil marriages of this kind but left it open to individual clergy to refuse to hold a church ceremony.

Decembrists (1825). In Russian history, revolutionaries, mostly Guards officers, who campaigned for the liberation of the serfs and the grant of a constitution. Their December revolt failed, and the ringleaders were hanged.

Declaration of Human Rights, Universal (1948). Declaration arising from the horrors of the German National-Socialist (Nazi) regime, passed by the General Assembly of the UN, with USSR, South Africa and Saudi Arabia among those abstaining. The rights are those individual freedoms normally associated with Western democracy.

Declaration of Independence (1776). Document declaring the independence of the 11 North American colonies, which contains the words: 'We hold these truths to be self-evident, that all men are created equal . . . with certain unalienable rights . . . among these are life, liberty, and the pursuit of happiness.' See FOURTH OF JULY.

Declaration of Indulgence (1672). Charles II's attempt to suspend discrimination against Nonconformists and Catholics under the CLARENDON CODE; he was forced by Parliament to rescind it a year later. Also similar declarations made by James II in 1687 and 1688.

Declaration of Rights (1688). Accepted by William and Mary at the GLORIOUS REVOLUTION; it established constitutional monarchy, with Parliament supreme; it was further strengthened by the ACT OF SETTLEMENT (1701). See BILL OF RIGHTS.

Declaration of the Rights of Man (1789). Drawn up by the French NATIONAL ASSEMBLY and reluctantly accepted by Louis XVI, it proclaimed the legal equality of men, their right to rule and make laws, and the freedom of the press; it condemned taxation without representation, and arbitrary imprisonment.

Decline and Fall (1928). Evelyn Waugh's first novel, famous for its opening chapters on the disreputable prep. school at Llanabba Castle in Wales, which has on its staff the ineffable Capt. GRIMES.

Decline and Fall of the Roman Empire, The (1776–88) Edward Gibbon's monumental history covering the period from the reign of Antoninus Pius to the fall of Constantinople, i.e. AD 138–1453.

Decline of the West See SPENGLER.

Decorated (1290–1375). Middle period of English GOTHIC ARCHITECTURE, characterized by ornate window tracery, elaborate external decoration of the spires, and complex vaulting, exemplified in Exeter Cathedral.

Dedalus, Stephen Hero of James Joyce's PORTRAIT OF THE ARTIST AS A YOUNG MAN (and thus clearly meant to be a self-portrait), and one of the chief characters in his ULYSSES. He is an artist, at war with Irish Catholicism and nationalism, but cannot completely free himself from the shackles of his Irish upbringing. (For the name, see DAEDALUS.)

De Dion–Bouton French firm that made a steam tractor articulated to a victoria carriage which won the Paris–Rouen race in 1894. Later they made the first practical high-speed petrol engine. (Count Albert de Dion and Georges Bouton.)

Deemsters Two justices of the Isle of Man, members of the TYNWALD. (From *deem*, 'to judge'.)

Deep South, The (USA) Southern, formerly slave and Confederate, states of America, traditionally anti-Civil Rights.

Defenestration, The (1618). The occasion at Prague when Protestants of the Bohemian National Council threw 2 Roman Catholic members out of the window of Hradčany Castle; this led to the THIRTY YEARS WAR. (Latin *de fenestra*, 'out of the window'.)

De Havilland (1920). The British aircraft firm which produced such famous types as the MOTH, MOSQUITO, VENOM and the first British plane to fly supersonic (1948). (Founded by Sir Geoffrey De Havilland, died 1965.)

Dehra Dun (1934). Site in Uttar Pradesh of the Indian Military Academy (the Indian Sandhurst). (Pronounced dair'a doon.)

Deianira See NESSUS. (Pronounced dee-i-an-yr'a.)

Deirdre In Irish legend, the daughter of King CONCHOBAR's harpist, the intended bride of the king, who was brought up in seclusion because of a prophecy that she would be the most beautiful woman in Ireland but would bring death to the RED BRANCH KNIGHTS. She fell in love with the king's nephew, Noisi, who carried her off to Scotland, but was persuaded to return and treacherously killed. Deirdre killed herself. The legend was treated by Synge (see next entry), Yeats and others.

Deirdre of the Sorrows (1910). J. M. Synge's unfinished verse drama on the DEIRDRE legend.

Deism Rejection of revelation, providence and miracles, coupled with the acceptance of God as a hypothesis required by reason; 'If God did not exist, it would be necessary to invent him' (Voltaire). God, having created the Universe, no longer intervenes (contrast THEISM); he is an 'absentee landlord'. Lord Herbert of Cherbury, brother of the poet, founder of English Deism (1624), held that the light of nature is an adequate guide. Spinoza said that miracles are impossible, Hume that they are impossible to prove.

Déjeuner sur l'herbe (1863). Manet's painting of a picnic, with one nude girl seated among dark-clad gentlemen; now in the Musée d'Orsay.

Delaunay (Henri) Cup See EUROPEAN NATIONS CUP.

Delectable Mountains Place in PILGRIM'S PROGRESS whence the Celestial City can be seen and where Christian and Hopeful talk with the shepherds Knowledge, Experience, Watchful and Sincere.

Delft Dutch and adopted English name for earthenware with a lead glaze made white and opaque by adding tin oxide; also called tin-enamelled ware. In France it is called faïence (from Italian town Faenza), and in Italy MAIOLICA. The chief English producers were LAMBETH, LIVERPOOL and BRISTOL; wares decorated in blue often lack interest, but the polychrome examples with yellow, purple etc. are highly regarded. Dutch Delft of the 17th and 18th centuries was decorated in imitation of Chinese styles. (Town in Holland.)

Delhi Pact (1950). Agreement signed by Nehru and Liaqat Ali Khan by which India and Pakistan undertook to protect each other's minorities and put an end to the communal massacres by Hindus and Muslims which had followed Partition.

Delilah Woman sent by the Philistines to worm out of SAMSON the secret of his strength; eventually he told her that it lay in his hair, for 'there hath not come a rasor upon mine head' (Judg. 16:4–20).

Delphi Ancient Greek site on the foothills of Mount Parnassus, overlooking the Gulf of Corinth, of the temple of Apollo whose priestess, Pythia, was his mouthpiece and oracle, consulted by the rulers of the ancient world before they made any important move. Her prophecies, couched in (deplorable) hexameters, were usually ambiguous enough to cover most eventualities, a lesson well learnt by newspaper astrologers today. (Pronounced del'fy.)

Demeter Greek goddess of corn (Roman Ceres), by Zeus the mother of PERSEPHONE. Her major festival was the ELEUSINIAN MYSTERIES.

Demidov (Cooking) Term applied to various elaborate dishes, especially chicken cooked with truffles and port or Madeira. (Name of a Russian epicure.)

Democratic Centre French political party.

Democratic Party (1828). (USA) Main body of the old Republican Democratic Party after the REPUBLICAN PARTY seceded. They supported low tariffs and, in the Civil War period, the maintenance of slavery. As 'trust-busters' and opponents of big business generally they swept into power under Woodrow Wilson, leading the country to abandon isolationism and to enter World War I; but Congress rejected their support of the League of Nations. They came back under F. D. Roosevelt to introduce the NEW DEAL and to enter World War II, and remained in power until the Eisenhower period

(1953–61). Since then there have been Democrat Administrations in 1961–9 (Kennedy/Johnson) and 1976–80 (Jimmy Carter).

Demoiselles d'Avignon, Les (1907). Picasso's semi-abstract painting in which the influence of African sculpture and the signs of transition to Cubism first appear. In the Museum of Modern Art, New York.

Denman College Adult-education college near Abingdon, Berks, run by the National Federation of WOMEN'S INSTITUTES. There are over 200 courses a year and husbands may take some courses.

Denning report (1963). The result of a judicial inquiry which found that there had been no disclosure of official secrets in the PROFUMO CASE; criticized in the SALMON REPORT because it was held in camera. (Lord Denning, Master of the Rolls.)

Department of Scientific and Industrial Research (1916–64). Government department which maintained numerous research stations, promoted research by industrial firms and awarded grants for research; now split into 3 departments.

Deposition, The Taking down of Christ from the Cross, a subject often treated by the old masters, e.g. Raphael and Memlinc.

Depression, The (1930s). Colloquial term for the world-wide effects of the WALL STREET CRASH.

De Profundis Letter written by Oscar Wilde from prison to Lord Alfred Douglas, not published in full until 1949. (Latin, 'from the depths'; taken from Psalms 130 and the Roman Catholic burial service.)

Deptford Former metropolitan borough of London, now part of the borough of LEWISHAM.

Der Alte Nickname of Dr Konrad Adenauer, who resigned the Chancellorship of Western Germany at the age of 87. (German, 'the Old Man'.)

Derby, Local Football match, or other sporting event, when two local teams play against each other.

Derby, The Premier classic flat-race, for 3-year-olds over $1\frac{1}{2}$ miles at Epsom in June.

Derby porcelain (1755–1848). Products of the firm founded at Derby by William Duesbury, who also bought the Chelsea factory in 1770 (see CHELSEA-DERBY) and Bow in 1775. In its earliest period Derby was famous for its figures based on Meissen models, with elaborate bocage backgrounds derived from Chelsea. For later periods see CROWN DERBY; BLOOR DERBY.

Derby Scheme System of voluntary registration for national service introduced by Lord Derby in 1915.

De rerum natura (1st century BC). Philosophical poem by Lucretius 'on the nature of things', in which he expounds the theory of Leucippus and his successors that the universe is composed of atoms come together fortuitously and not the creation of the gods. He wanted to rid men's minds of superstitious fear of the gods, for 'So great is the evil that superstition has persuaded man to do' (*Tantum religio potuit suadere malorum*).

Desdemona Wife of OTHELLO who, in Shakespeare's play, kills her when IAGO persuades him that she has been unfaithful.

Desert Fox, The Nickname of Field-Marshal Rommel, who commanded the German forces in North Africa during World War II.

Desert Rats British 7th Armoured Division, a famous unit of the Eighth Army in the North African and European campaigns of World War II. (Named after the divisional sign, a jerboa.)

Des Grieux, Le Chevalier See MANON LESCAUT.

Design Centre (London) Headquarters of the COUNCIL OF INDUSTRIAL DESIGN, with displays of the best-designed British goods. See next entry.

Design Index Photographic reference library of design, first formed for the Festival of Britain and now kept at the DESIGN CENTRE.

Desire under the Elms (1924). Eugene O'Neill's

Freudian tragedy set on a New England farm, in which a young wife seduces her stepson and, threatened with exposure, kills their child.

Deucalion and Pyrrha Sole survivors in a Greek version of the Flood legend. As instructed, they cast stones over their shoulders, from which men and women sprang. Zeus and Prometheus are fitted into the story, and the 'ark' grounded on Mount Parnassus. (Pronounced dew-kay'li-on, pir'a.)

Deuteronomy Last book of the PENTATEUCH, which repeats the Ten Commandments and other material from Exodus. (Greek, 'second law'.)

Deutsch Works of Schubert catalogued by Otto Erich Deutsch. (Abbreviated 'D'.)

Deutschemark (1948). Unit of currency (abbreviated DM) introduced in West Germany to replace the inflated Reichsmark (RM). This was regarded as the turning-point in post-war reconstruction which began the ECONOMIC MIRACLE.

Deutsches Kreuz One of the highest German military orders under the National-Socialist (Nazi) regime.

Deutschland (1931). German 'pocket battleship', small but fast, and well armed and armoured, the first of her kind.

'Deutschland, Deutschland über alles' (1841). German national anthem, sung to Haydn's tune for the old Austrian Imperial national anthem ('Gott erhalte unsern Kaiser'); as the words ('Germany over all') seemed inappropriate the West German government in 1950 adopted the third verse beginning 'Einigkeit und Recht und Freiheit' ('Unity, Right and Freedom') as the official anthem.

Deutzia Asiatic flowering shrubs named after J. van der Deutz.

Deuxième Bureau French military intelligence and security department of the Defence Ministry.

Deva Roman name of Chester.

Devil's Island Island off French Guiana, notorious as the place to which French convicts were transported and kept under harsh conditions; closed down 1953. Dreyfus (see DREYFUS CASE) spent 5 years there.

Devils of Loudun, The (1952). Aldous Huxley's novel about a historical event in 17th-century France. A convent of nuns succumb to mass hysteria, attributed to demonic possession induced by a priest, who is burnt at the stake. The story was used by John Whiting in his play *The Devils* (1961).

Devizes–Westminster race An annual canoe race over a course of 124 miles along the Kennet and Thames.

Devlin report (1) Outspoken report (1959) on the Nyasaland riots. (2) Report (1956) of a committee of inquiry into dock labour conditions. (3) Second report (1965) on dock labour which called for an end to daily employment and its attendant favouritism, sharply criticizing the whole industry and the lack of control over its members shown by the TGWU. (Lord Justice Devlin.)

Devonian period Fourth period of the PALAEOZOIC ERA, lasting from about 410 to 350 million years ago. There are fossils of spiders, insects, tree-ferns and the first land vertebrates (amphibians), while fishes are abundant. Northern Europe and America were inundated by a great flood. See OLD RED SANDSTONE.

De Wet rebellion (October–December 1914). Boer rebellion in South Africa at the beginning of World War I, suppressed by General Botha. (Led by Gen. de Wet; pronounced vet.)

Dewey decimal system System of classifying books used in most public libraries, with 10 main divisions (0–99, 100–199 etc.) and open-ended finer subdivisions by decimal points. (Introduced 1876 by Melvil Dewey, US librarian.)

Dewey educational system Based on theories advanced by the American, John Dewey (1859–1952), emphasizing that the primary purpose of education is not to impart knowledge for its own sake but to train children so that they will be able to make their maximum contribution to society according to their aptitudes and ability. Dewey held that too much weight was given to the arts, which were of interest mainly to the privileged few, and too little to the sciences which benefit all mankind.

Dexter Breed of small dual-purpose cattle derived from the KERRY and common in Ireland; black, sometimes red, in colour.

Dharma Bums, The (1959). One of Jack Kerouac's beatnik novels about Jack DULUOZ. (*Dharma*, a Buddhist and Hindu term, 'that which is made firm', 'doctrine', 'conformity to doctrine'; *bum*, US slang for 'tramp'.)

Diadochi, The Alexander the Great's generals, who divided up his empire at his death, and fought among themselves. From them sprang the dynasties of the PTOLEMIES and the SELEUCIDS. (Greek, 'successors'.)

Diaghilev Ballets Russes (1909–29). Ballet company promoted in Paris and London by the Russian impresario Serge Diaghilev, who had a genius for enrolling all the talents. His choreographers included Fokine, Massine, Balanchine and the dancers Lifar and Nijinsky and (occasionally) Pavlova; other dancers were Karsavina, Lopokova, Markova and Anton Dolin, de Valois; artists included Bakst, Utrillo, Braque, Matisse, Picasso; and he commissioned scores from Stravinsky, Milhaud, Poulenc, Ravel, Debussy and Falla.

Dialectical materialism Marx's explanation, using the logical method he adopted from HEGELIANISM (while discarding Hegel's philosophy), of historical development as arising solely from the conflict of social and economic forces generated by man's material needs, which operate in accordance with the dialectical laws of thesis, antithesis and synthesis. Thus to Marx the fall of capitalism, whether desirable or not, was simply an inevitable certain result of these laws, as was the end of slavery, feudalism, etc. before it.

Diamond Jubilee's Derby Derby of 1900, won by the horse of that name for the Prince of Wales (later Edward VII), which also won the Two Thousand Guineas and St Leger.

Diamond Sculls, The Diamonds (1884). Premier international sculling event, open to all amateurs and rowed at Henley.

Diamond State Nickname of Delaware.

Diana Ancient Latin nature and fertility goddess, worshipped by women; identified with the Greek Artemis.

Diana of the Crossways (1885). George Meredith's novel about political life, in which a high-spirited Irish girl, Diana Merion (said to be based on Sheridan's granddaughter), leaves her husband for a young politician.

Diana of the Ephesians Form of DIANA worshipped at Ephesus (south of modern Izmir) in Asia Minor; she had absorbed the characteristics of an earlier Asian multi-breasted fertility goddess. Acts 19:24–8 tells the story of the makers of silver images of Diana who, alarmed at the effect of Paul's preaching on their trade, staged a protest march, shouting 'Great is Diana of the Ephesians'.

Dianthus Plant genus that includes pinks, carnations and sweet williams.

Diary of Anne Frank, The Title of a play and a film (1949) based on the diary (published 1947) kept by a German-Jewish girl of that name who hid in Amsterdam (1942–4) until she, with her family, was betrayed to the Nazis and sent to die at BELSEN, aged 16.

Diary of a Nobody, The See POOTER.

Diaspora, The Dispersion of the Jews outside Palestine. When the BABYLONIAN CAPTIVITY ended, most of the Jews elected to remain in Babylon; they increased and multiplied until they far outnumbered those in Palestine, and gradually infiltrated into the main cities of the known world, although still regarding Jerusalem as their spiritual home. (Greek, 'scattering'; pronounced dy-asp'or-a.)

Dicentra spectabilis Species name of Bleeding Heart.

Dichterliebe Schumann's song-cycle composed for songs by Heine. At first the singer voices his happiness, which turns to despair when he is jilted. (German, 'a poet's love'.)

Dick, Mr Amiable idiot in DAVID COPPER-

FIELD who lodges with Betsey TROTWOOD; he has spent 10 years trying in vain to write a 'Memorial' without bringing King Charles's head, his pet obsession, into it; but the King 'had been constantly getting into it, and was there now'.

Diddle To cheat or swindle; the name of a character in a play by James Kenney, *Raising the Wind* (1803), Jeremy Diddler.

Dido Queen of the Phoenician colony of Carthage, where AENEAS and the Trojans were wrecked. She fell in love with Aeneas and, when he obeyed a divine command to continue his journey to Italy, she committed suicide.

Didymus Greek word for 'twin', applied to St Thomas (Thomas being derived from the Aramaic word for 'twin'); also used as a pen-name. (Pronounced did'i-mus.)

Die-Hards Name given to the 600 Conservatives who demonstrated (July 1911) at the Hotel Cecil against the readiness of their leader, A. J. Balfour, to acquiesce in the VETO BILL; hence any right-wing Tories.

Dieppe raid (August 1942). Commando raid on the French coast by Canadian and British troops and US RANGERS, which met with heavy losses but afforded valuable experience in commando tactics.

Dieppoise (Cooking) Term applied to seafood cooked in white wine and served with mussels.

Diervilla Flowering shrubs, synonym Weigela, named after a French surgeon, M. Dierville.

'Dies irae' Thirteenth-century hymn on the Last Judgement, sung in the Mass for the dead. (Latin, 'day of wrath', its first words; it continues, in translation, 'and doom impending, / Heaven and earth in ashes ending'; pronounced dee'ayz eer'y.)

Digger Colloquial term for an Australian. (Reference to the gold-digging era of 1857–60.)

Digitalis Genus name of the foxgloves.

Dignity and Impudence Popular Landseer painting of a dignified bloodhound and a Scotch terrier who has pushed his way into the picture; see MONARCH OF THE GLEN.

Diktat German word for 'dictation', 'arbitrary decree'; Hitler's favourite term for the Versailles Treaty, implying the startling doctrine that an aggressor state, after defeat, should not be dictated to by its intended victims.

Dillinger era (USA) See PUBLIC ENEMY NO. 1.

Dingaan's Day (16 December 1838). Day on which Boers defeated the Zulu chief, Dingaan, in Natal. A public holiday; also called the Day of the Covenant.

Dingley Dell In PICKWICK PAPERS, the place where Mr WARDLE lives at Manor Farm.

Dinmont, Dandie Farmer and dog breeder in Scott's *Guy Mannering*, whose name was given to a breed of hardy Border terriers. (Dandie for Andrew.)

Diocletian persecution, The (AD 303). General persecution of Christians ordered by the Emperor Diocletian, which continued in the west until 306, in the east until 313.

Dionysian Nietzsche's adjective for all he admired and advocated, the freedom of the strong put to wise and creative use; the passionate enjoyment of life freed from all the inhibitions imposed by Christian religion; enthusiasm and ecstasy instead of pallid virtues inspired by a sense of original sin. See APOLLONIAN. (DIONYSUS.)

Dionysus Thracian god of the vine and of fertility, adopted by the Greeks, who also called him Bakchos (see BACCHUS). Son of Zeus, husband of ARIADNE, he was worshipped as a vegetation god at the Dionysian festivals held in December and March. See ORPHEUS. (Pronounced dy-on-y'sus.)

Dior, Christian Paris fashion house.

Dioscuri See CASTOR AND POLLUX. (Greek, 'sons of Zeus'; pronounced dy-osk-ewr'y.)

Diploma in Technology Diploma with status

equal to a degree, obtainable after 4–5 years of sandwich courses taken at a CAT (or certain other colleges) in between periods of work in an industry related to the subject being studied.

Dipper, The US name for the PLOUGH; also *Big Dipper* for the GREAT BEAR and *Little Dipper* for the LITTLE BEAR. (A can used to ladle liquid.)

Diptera Order of insects with one pair of wings; the flies, including the housefly, mosquito and tsetse.

Directoire (1) Name given to a furniture style which during the DIRECTORY revived the NEO-CLASSICISM of Louis XIV's reign; a typical example is the couch on which Mme RÉCAMIER reclines in David's painting. (2) Women's dress style with very high waistline; the trend was set by the future Empress Josephine.

Directory (October 1795 to November 1799). First post-Revolution government of France, an executive body of 5 Directors set up after the VENDÉMIAIRE coup, opposed to Jacobins, Girondins and Royalists alike. They became increasingly dictatorial and corrupt, and were superseded by the CONSULATE after the BRUMAIRE coup.

Dirty Dick's Pub in Chinatown, Limehouse, in London's dockland famous in the 1920s when it was the smart thing to go 'slumming' there.

Dirty Half Hundred, The Alternative nickname to the BLIND HALF HUNDRED.

Dis Roman name for HADES. (Pronounced dis.)

Disarmament Commission (1952). UN organization which took over from the ATOMIC ENERGY COMMISSION and the Conventional Armaments Commission to prepare proposals for general disarmament. Its first success was the TEST-BAN TREATY.

Disarmament Conference (1932–4). See WORLD DISARMAMENT CONFERENCE.

Disasters Emergency Committee Body which coordinates the fund-raising activities of Oxfam, the Save the Children Fund, Christian Aid, War on Want and the Red Cross.

Discobolos, The (5th century BC). Discus-thrower, a sculpture by Myron. The original bronze is lost, but there is a marble copy in the National Museum, Rome. (Pronounced dis-kob'ol-os.)

Discoverer Name of a series of 36 US satellites used from 1959–61 to test the feasibility of manned space-craft.

Discovery, HMS (1901). Capt. Scott's ship, the first built for polar research; it contains relics of Scott's Antarctic expeditions (including the last, which was made in the *Terra Nova*). Now moored in Dundee dock, Scotland.

Dismal Science, The Thomas Carlyle's name for economics.

Disneyland, Disneyworld (1955). Large amusement parks in California and Florida, USA.

Disney Professor Holder of the chair of Archaeology at Cambridge.

Dispersion, The Another name for the DIASPORA.

Disraeli's Two Nations See TWO NATIONS.

Dissenters (1) Puritans. (2) Earlier name for NONCONFORMISTS.

Dissolution of the Monasteries (1536–9). Suppression of the monasteries and confiscation of their property by Henry VIII on the advice of Thomas Cromwell during the English Reformation.

Distillers (1877). Merger of whisky and gin distillers, with a near-monopoly in Scotch whisky, including Buchanans (Black & White), Dewars (White Horse), Johnnie Walker and Haig, together with Gordon's and Booth's gins.

Distillers, Worshipful Company of (1638). LIVERY COMPANY which is still in close association with the distilling trade.

Dives Latin word for 'rich', which has come to be used for the rich man 'clothed in purple and fine linen' of the parable in Luke 16:19–31. See LAZARUS. (Pronounced dy'veez.)

Divine Comedy, The (1320). Dante's major work, a poem in 3 parts: *Inferno*, in which Virgil guides the poet through the various circles of hell; *Purgatory*, describing the sufferings of the repentants as they await translation to Heaven; and *Paradise*, where the poet once more meets BEATRICE. (Italian title, *Divina Commedia*.)

Divine Sarah, The Sarah Bernhardt, the great French actress, who died in 1923.

Dixie, Dixieland Southern, formerly slave, states of the USA. (Said to be from early Louisiana 10-dollar notes, marked *dix* for the benefit of French Creoles, and popularized by a song 'Dixie' in 1859; apparently unconnected with the MASON AND DIXON LINE.)

Dixiecrats (1948). Southern US Democrats who seceded to form the States' Rights Party, which stood for white supremacy over the Negroes. They put up their own presidential candidate in 1948. (Formed from DIXIE and Democrats.)

Dixieland Jazz Name given to marches, foxtrots, etc. popularized by the 5-man white Original Dixieland Jazz Band of New Orleans (1910) and its successors.

Dizzy Nickname of Benjamin Disraeli (Earl of Beaconsfield), Conservative Prime Minister (1874–80) and novelist.

Djugashvili Family name of Stalin, the latter being a revolutionary name ('man of steel') of the kind affected by the early revolutionaries.

DNA Initials standing for deoxyribo-nucleic acid, an exceedingly complex molecule the structure of which was unravelled by Watson and Crick at Cambridge in 1944. It forms the basis of the gene found in the cell nucleus and plays a vital part, with RNA, in the transmission of hereditary factors from one generation to another.

DNB (1882). Initials used for the British *Dictionary of National Biography*, a standard work of reference in many volumes, with later supplements.

D-notice Formal letter sent confidentially by a government department to press and broadcasting editors, requesting them not to publish specified official secrets; the system works on a basis of mutual confidence. (D for 'defence'.)

Dobermann pinscher (1890). Medium-sized breed of terrier with long forelegs and short black-and-tan coat, developed as a watch-dog. There is also a miniature breed. (*Dobermann*, name of breeder in Thuringia, Germany; German *Pinscher*, 'terrier'.)

Dobruja Fertile borderland, including the Black Sea port of Constanţa, divided between Romania and Bulgaria. The latter lost southern Dobruja to Romania in the Balkan Wars but recovered it in World War II. (Pronounced do-broo'jah.)

Doctor, The (1936). Hybrid tea rose with a large and fragrant pure pink flower.

Dr Caligari, The Cabinet of One of the earliest horror films, produced in Germany in 1919.

Dr Faustus, The Tragical History of (1588). Christopher Marlowe's play on the FAUST legend.

Doctor Fell Target of the rhyme ('I do not like thee, Doctor Fell, / The reason why I cannot tell', etc.), a 17th-century Dean of Christ Church, Oxford; the verse is a free translation and adaptation of one of Martial's epigrams.

Dr Jekyll and Mr Hyde, The Strange Case of (1886). R. L. Stevenson's novel of the good Dr Jekyll who, as a research experiment into problems of good and evil, takes a drug which changes him into the evil Mr Hyde; although he has an antidote, the evil side takes increasing command and he, as Mr Hyde, commits murder. Unable to get back to his normal nature, he commits suicide.

Dr No (1959). First of Ian Fleming's James BOND stories to appear as a film (1962).

Doctor's Dilemma, The (1906). G. B. Shaw's satire on the medical profession; the dilemma is whether a distinguished surgeon should operate on the amoral artist Dubedat, or on an old colleague. The preface to the play suggested, 40 years before it was instituted, that what the country needed was a National Health Service.

Doctor's Mandate (October 1931). Term coined to describe the unformulated policy for which the British National Government, under Ramsay MacDonald, sought electoral approval during the crisis of the Great Depression. Each of the 3 party leaders (Labour, Conservative and Liberal) was left free to advocate his own policy during the elections, and the coalition government agreed to defer final decisions on their joint policy until after their return to power. They won 554 out of 610 seats.

Doctors' Plot (January 1953). Alleged plot by 9 Russian, mostly Jewish, doctors to poison the Soviet leaders they attended. Although completely baseless, Stalin chose to believe the story and had them arrested and 2 of them beaten to death; he was about to order the deportation of all Jews to Siberia when he died. According to one report, Stalin died of rage when rebuked by Marshal Voroshilov for his insane proposal.

Dr Strangelove (1963). Stanley Kubrick's film comedy about what happens when a madman acquires the final say in deciding whether to start a nuclear war.

Dr Syntax (1809–21). Ludicrous clergyman-schoolmaster whose tours on his nag Grizzle were depicted in a series of plates by Rowlandson (see ROWLANDSON CARTOONS), with verses written by William Combe.

Dr Wall period (1751–83). First period of WORCESTER PORCELAIN; also called First Period Worcester. Various styles of decoration were used, notably a fine underglaze blue, Meissen-style flower sprays, transfer printing, Sèvres-type grounds including the characteristic scale-blue, and 'Oriental Worcester' – a modification of the KAKIEMON PATTERNS. (Dr Wall was a founder member of the firm and took charge of it in 1772.)

Dr Who (1963). Successful TV series dealing with time and space in which aliens attack earth at any London underground station that is out of use (or available to TV) on Sundays.

Dr Zhivago (1957). Boris Pasternak's novel about a Russian Liberal doctor-poet's reaction to the Revolution; its implied criticism of Marxism as applied in Russia, its pervading religious tone, and the fact that Pasternak had it published abroad after the authorities had refused to publish it in Russia, all got the novelist into trouble, and he was forced to refuse the Nobel prize awarded him for it.

Dodgers, The Short for the Brooklyn Dodgers, a famous New York baseball team which moved to Los Angeles in 1957. (Said to derive from the general nickname of Brooklynites, as spending much of their time dodging the trams which were a major feature of Brooklyn streets.)

Dodson and Fogg The pettifogging attorneys who acted for Mrs Bardell in BARDELL V. PICKWICK.

Dogberry Comic constable of Shakespeare's *Much Ado*, whose approach to constabulary duties and the English language is eccentric.

Dogger Bank, Battle of the (January 1915). Naval engagement in which the German cruiser *Blücher* was sunk by Beatty's battle-cruiser squadron.

Dogger Bank incident (1904). Extraordinary incident of the Russo-Japanese War. The Russian Baltic fleet, ordered to sail to Japan, fired on some English fishing vessels off the Dogger Bank under the inexplicable delusion that they were Japanese torpedo-boats.

Doggett's Coat and Badge (1716). Prize for a sculling race, also called the Waterman's Derby, the oldest annual race in the British sporting calendar, rowed by 6 Thames watermen from London Bridge to Chelsea, on or about 1 August. (Endowed by Thomas Doggett, Drury Lane actor-manager.)

Dogra Warlike Hindu RAJPUT race of northwest India. (Pronounced doh'gra.)

Dog's Nose Mixed drink of gin and beer, a Yorkshire favourite.

Dogs of Fo Favourite Chinese porcelain figures made since Ming times, mythical guardian animals, with mouths drawn back in a horrific snarl, playing with a ball or a puppy, and usually green in colour; also called Lion Dogs of Fo.

Dolgelly older spelling of Dolgellau, a town in Wales.

Dolittle, Dr Whimsical character who appears in many children's books written and illustrated by the English-born American author, Hugh Lofting, from 1920 onwards.

Dollar Academy A coeducational boarding school in Clackmannan.

Dollar Diplomacy (1909–13). Name given to the foreign policy of the US Secretary of State, Philander C. Knox; it was based on finding outlets for American capital in China and Latin American countries.

Doll's House, The (1879). Ibsen's play about a spoilt daughter and wife who resorts to fraud to save her husband; his reaction opens her eyes to her status as a mere doll, and she leaves him to find her own personality.

Dom. Roman Catholic honorific prefix once given to the names of church dignitaries, now to certain Benedictine and Carthusian priests. (Abbreviation of Latin *dominus*, 'master'.)

Dombey and Son (1848). Dickens's novel about a proud businessman who concentrates his ambitions on fitting his only son to be a partner in his firm. When the son dies young, he vents his disappointment on his daughter, with whom he is reconciled only after the failure of his firm and of his second marriage.

Dome of the Rock Octagonal Great Mosque of Omar (7th century) in Jerusalem, built over a rock which is traditionally the site of Abraham's sacrifice, and of the temples of Solomon and Herod.

Domesday Book (1086). Detailed census of land, buildings and cattle covering most of England, made for taxation purposes in the reign of William I. It is now kept at the PUBLIC RECORD OFFICE. (Anglo-Saxon *dom*, 'judgement', as it was the final authority in disputes; pronounced doomz'day.)

Dominicans (1215). Order of mendicant friars (Black Friars), of whom St Thomas Aquinas (see THOMISM) was one; now widespread, with many mission stations. (Founded by the Spaniard, St Dominic, at Toulouse.)

Dominici murder case (1952). The murder of Sir Jack and Lady Drummond and child while on holiday at Digne in France. Gaston Dominici was found guilty and sentenced to death in 1954 but reprieved in 1957. Inconclusive investigations dragged on until Gaston's death.

Dominions and Powers Two orders of angels, grouped with Virtues; see also PRINCIPALITIES.

Dominion status (1926). Full political autonomy, equal status with Britain and common allegiance to the Crown; a status defined by the Balfour Commission and accepted by Canada, Australia, New Zealand and South Africa. It was redefined in the Statute of Westminster (1931).

Domini redemptoris (1937). Pope Pius XI's encyclical on Communist atheism.

Donald Duck Character, second in popularity only to Mickey Mouse, whose incoherent tantrums were long a feature of Walt Disney cartoon films.

Donbas Russian 'Ruhr', the coalfields and industrial area in the Donets Basin of the Ukraine. Donetsk (formerly Stalino) is the chief city, with iron, steel, chemical and engineering industries. The other major centre is Lugansk (formerly Voroshilovgrad), which makes diesel locomotives and textiles.

Don Camillo Parish priest who battles good-humouredly with the Communist mayor in *The Little World of Don Camillo* and other books of short stories by the Italian writer Giovanni Guareschi.

Don Giovanni (1787). Mozart's opera on the story of DON JUAN.

'Dongo, Treasure of' Hoard of gold supposed to have been in Mussolini's possession in April 1945 when he was captured by Italian partisans at Dongo, near Lake Como. See BALZAN FOUNDATION.

'Dong with a Luminous Nose, The' Nonsense poem by Edward Lear (1812–88), beginning: 'When awful darkness and silence reign / Over the great Gromboolian plain.'

Donington (1935–8) Car-racing track in a Derbyshire park; now closed.

Don Juan In Spanish legend, the devil-may-care womanizer of Seville, who invited to dinner the statue of a man he had murdered. The statue came, and dragged him down alive to hell. The legend has been treated by countless writers, artists and composers. See next entry; also DON GIOVANNI; MAN AND SUPERMAN. (Pronounced, in English, don-jew'an, not don-hwahn'.)

Don Juan Byron's satirical poem which, he said, was 'meant to be a little quietly facetious about everything'.

Donnithorne, Arthur Squire in George Eliot's ADAM BEDE who ruins Hetty Sorrel and rides up with her reprieve just as she is mounting the scaffold.

Donnybrook Fair Fair held near Dublin from the 13th century until banned in 1855, notorious for its rowdiness. (Former village, now a suburb of Dublin.)

Don Pasquale (1843). Donizetti's best comic opera, in which the old bachelor Don Pasquale is tricked into a bogus marriage with the girl his nephew loves, and loses her to him.

Don Quixote Scraggy old crackpot of La Mancha in Cervantes' romance (1605–15) who sallies forth in search of knightly adventure, mounted on ROSINANTE, accompanied by SANCHO PANZA, and having dedicated his deeds to the massive DULCINEA. He mistakes sheep for armies, windmills for giants, an inn for a castle. The book combines contemporary satire, a parody of chivalric romance, and an oblique statement of Christian values. (Pronounced, in English, don kwik'sot, not ki-hoh'tay.)

Doolittle, Eliza, and Alfred her father In Shaw's *Pygmalion*.

Doorn Village near Utrecht, The Netherlands, where the German ex-Kaiser, Wilhelm II, lived in exile (1918–41).

Doors of Perception, The (1954). Aldous Huxley's account of his experiences under the influence of mescalin; he followed it up with *Heaven and Hell* (1956).

Doppelgänger In German myth, a person's double, seen just before, and presaging, his death. (German, 'double-walker'; pronounced dop'el-geng-er.)

Doppler effect At very high speeds the colour of a luminous body appears bluer as it approaches and redder as it recedes; in the former case it is catching up with its own light waves, compressing them and shortening the wavelength; in the latter, the process is reversed. This phenomenon is used e.g. in estimating the speed at which distant galaxies are receding. A similar phenomenon obtains with radio and sound waves, e.g. a train whistle rises in pitch as it approaches an observer and falls after it has passed. (Christian Doppler, 19th-century Austrian scientist.)

DORA Initials commonly used for Defence of the Realm Act, under which numerous emergency, and unpopular, regulations were made during and after World War I.

Dorcas workers Women who make or supply clothing for charity, from the woman in Acts 9:36–41 who did this and who was restored to life by St Peter.

Dorian Gray, The Picture of (1891). Oscar Wilde's fantasy about a decadent dandy whose moral disintegration is symbolized by changes in a portrait of him painted when he was young and innocent. Finally he stabs the painter and the painting, and is found dead with a knife through his own heart at the foot of the picture, now restored to its original form, while his features have taken on the painting's decay.

Doric Of the Dorians (SPARTANS); rustic; (of accent) broad. (Pronounced dor'ik.)

Doric Order most austere of the 3 Greek orders of architecture; unlike the others, the columns have no base.

Dorking Breed of white domestic fowl with distinctive long full body and short legs, kept for meat production. (Dorking, Surrey.)

Dorneywood Country house with extensive grounds near Burnham Beeches, Slough, presented to the nation by Lord Courtauld-Thomson as an official residence for a Minister of the Crown selected by the Prime Minister.

Doronicum Genus name of Leopard's Bane.

Dorothy Perkins (1901). Popular old rambling rose, producing masses of small rose-pink flowers from mid-July on.

Dotheboys Hall The 'academy' in Dickens's *Nicholas Nickleby* where Nicholas serves as usher to the unspeakable SQUEERS. (Pronounced doo'thè-boiz.)

Douai Roman Catholic public school for boys, at Woolhampton, Berkshire.

Douai Bible English version of the Bible authorized by the Roman Catholic Church, translated from the VULGATE. The New Testament was published at Rheims (1582) and the old at Douai (1610).

Double zero See ZERO-ZERO.

Doubting-Castle Place in PILGRIM'S PROGRESS where Christian and Hopeful are imprisoned by the Giant Despair. Christian unlocks his cell with a key called Promise and escapes.

Doubting Thomas A sceptic. (When the other Apostles told St Thomas that they had seen Christ after the Resurrection, he said: 'Except I shall see in his hands the print of the nails . . . I will not believe.' See John 20:25.)

Douglas aircraft A range of US civil and military transport planes made by Douglas Aircraft of Santa Monica, California.

Douglasia Rock plants and the Douglas fir, named after David Douglas (1798–1834), a botanist who travelled in north America.

Doulton pottery (1815). Pottery made by Doultons at Lambeth, London. Apart from industrial and utilitarian wares, there were brown salt-glaze mugs with relief decoration, stoneware spirit flasks and, from 1871, art pottery made specifically for the collector and decorated by Hannah Barlow, George Tinworth, etc.

Dounreay Atomic Energy Authority's experimental nuclear research station in Caithness. (Coastal site west of Thurso in extreme north of Scotland.)

Dove Cottage The cottage at Grasmere in the Lake District where Wordsworth lived with his sister Dorothy (1799–1807). Now preserved as a museum.

Dover, Secret Treaty of (1670). Signed by Charles II and Louis XIV at a time when the CABAL's official policy was anti-French and pro-Dutch. Charles, in return for financial help, promised to support France against Holland and to make England Catholic.

Dover sole Name given to the true sole to distinguish it from the lemon sole, which is a kind of plaice.

Doves (USA) Supporters of a policy of caution and conciliation in foreign affairs, as opposed to the HAWKS.

Dow-Jones averages The best known of several US indices of movements in price on Wall Street of representative groups of stocks and shares; there are also indices of commodity prices, spot and future. (Dow-Jones & Co.)

Down and Out in Paris and London (1933). Old Etonian George Orwell's bug-ridden account of his voluntary period of utter poverty in these 2 cities.

Down breeds Generic name for lowland short-wool sheep, including the SOUTHDOWN, SUFFOLK, Hampshire, Dorset, Oxford and Shropshire breeds.

Downing Professor Holder of the chair of Laws of England at Cambridge.

Downing Street (1) A short cul-de-sac off Whitehall, London, containing the official residence of the Prime Minister (at No. 10), Chancellor of the Exchequer (No. 11) and Government Chief Whip (No. 12). (2) Used as a synonym for the British government, since the Cabinet meets at No. 10.

Downside Roman Catholic (Benedictine) public school for boys, near Bath.

Down's syndrome Chromosomal abnormality named after English physician John Langdon-Down (1826–96). See MONGOLISM.

Doxology, The Liturgical form of praise to God. The Greater Doxology, *Gloria in excelsis Deo* ('Glory be to God on high'), is used in the Communion service and mass; the Lesser, *Gloria patri* ('Glory be to the Father, and to the Son'), is used to conclude hymns, etc.; a metrical form begins: 'Praise God from whom all blessings flow.' (From Greek for 'praise'.)

D'Oyly Carte Opera Co. (1875). Company which produced the Gilbert and Sullivan operas at the Savoy, London. (Founded by Richard D'Oyly Carte; died 1901.)

Dracula (1897). Bram Stoker's bloodcurdling tale of vampires and werewolves from the one-time ruler of Wallachia, Vlad Dracula, died 1462.

Dragon (1929). Norwegian-designed keel-boat of 18 ft 11 in waterline length, originally intended as an expensive cruiser-racer class. Given international status in 1949, it developed into an expensive but popular purely racing class, for which there are world and European championships (see DRAGON GOLD CUP; EDINBURGH CUP).

Dragon Gold Cup (1937). International sailing championship for the DRAGON class, raced at the Clyde Regatta in June/July.

Drain, The Waterloo and City underground railway, London.

'Drake's Drum' (1897). Sir Henry Newbolt's poem included in *Admirals All and other Verses*.

Drambuie Scottish liqueur of whisky, honey and herbs. (Pronounced dram-bew'i.)

Drang nach Osten German urge, from the 12th century onwards, to expand eastwards, at the expense of the Slavs whom they despised. (German, 'drive towards the east'.)

Drapers, Worshipful Company of (1364). Third in precedence of the LIVERY COMPANIES; it now has little direct connection with the trade but makes large grants for technical and general education.

Drapers Professor Holder of the chair of Agriculture or of French at Cambridge.

Dravida Munetra Kazhagam (DMK) Political party of southern India, strong in Tamil Nadu, which opposes the use of Hindi as a national language and is antagonistic to the JAN SANGH party and to the north generally. (See DRAVIDIAN LANGUAGES.)

Dravidian languages Non-Indo-European languages spoken in South India, of uncertain origin. They include TAMIL, TELUGU, MALAYALAM and KANARESE. (Sanskrit *Dravida*, 'Tamil'.)

Dreadnought, HMS (1) First all-big-gun battleship, launched 1906. (2) Britain's first nuclear submarine, built in the UK but powered by a US reactor; commissioned 1963.

Dream of Gerontius (1865). Cardinal Newman's poem, inspired by Dante, on the experiences of the soul in Purgatory. Set to music by Elgar as an oratorio (1900). (Pronounced gẽr-ont'i-ẽs.)

Dreigroschenoper See THREEPENNY OPERA.

Dreikaiserbund (1872). German name for the league of the 3 emperors (Germany, Austria-Hungary, Russia); they agreed to co-ordinate their foreign policy and to unite in opposition to Socialist revolution.

Dresden porcelain (1) See MEISSEN. (2) Imitations of Meissen made by factories in and around Dresden and in many other parts of Europe. (3) Sometimes applied to 19th-century genuine Meissen to distinguish it from the superb products of the 18th century.

Dreyfusards Campaigners for the rehabilitation of Dreyfus (see next entry), led by Clemenceau and Zola. They included Liberal intellectuals and left-wing politicians, ranged against the High Command, the Church and the Right. The split went right through the nation, leaving a legacy of bitterness for decades.

Dreyfus case (1894–1906). Major French scandal. Capt. Dreyfus, a Jew, was sent to Devil's Island for selling military secrets to Germany. In 1896 it transpired that the real culprit was a Major Esterhazy, but the frightened High Command concealed this, even forging documents to bolster up their case. The DREYFUSARDS pressed home their attacks and Dreyfus was pardoned in 1899 and restored to his commission in 1906. He served with distinction in the First World War. (Pronounced dray'fès.)

Drogheda (1649). In the last phase of the ENGLISH CIVIL WAR Cromwell's army besieged the forces under the Earl of Ormonde, who had declared Charles II king, and annihilated them at Drogheda. (Seaport in Co. Louth, Ireland; pronounced droi'i-dè.)

Drones' Club, The Bertie WOOSTER's club in the P. G. Wodehouse books.

Drood, Edwin Chief character of *The Mystery of Edwin Drood*, Charles Dickens's only detective story, left unfinished; the orphan Edwin disappears and is presumed murdered; the author's intentions are unknown, and no satisfying solution to the mystery has been suggested.

'Dropping the Pilot' (1890). Most famous of Sir John Tenniel's political cartoons in *Punch*, depicting Kaiser Wilhelm II watching his dismissed Chancellor, Bismarck, leaving the ship of state.

Drosophila Genus of flies of which one species, the fruit-fly, is used in genetical research because of its rapid multiplication. (Pronounced drosof'i-la.)

Druckfehlerteufel Imp who supplies the misprints.

Druids Celtic priesthood of Gaul and Britain, described by Julius Caesar. Their religion was associated with veneration of the oak and mistletoe, belief in immortality and reincarnation, and, probably, human sacrifice. Stonehenge and other such monuments are much more ancient than the Druids, though coupled with them in popular belief.

Druids, The Order of Society which tries to keep alive the ancient Druid ceremonies at Stonehenge, etc. In 1963 there was a schism which resulted in there being 2 Chief Druids in England, heading respectively the British Circle of the Universal Bond and the Order of Bards, Ovates and Druids.

Druids, United Ancient Order of (1781). Friendly society founded in London, now with lodges, called 'groves', in USA and elsewhere; it has Masonic-type rites.

Drummond Professor Holder of the chair of Political Economy at Oxford.

Druses (11th century). Religious sect of Syria, of Muslim origin but rejecting Mohammed as Prophet; there is said to be an inner doctrine, kept strictly secret. Fanatically independent, they rebelled against Turkish, Egyptian and French (1925–7) rule. (Pronounced drooz'iz.)

DTs Delirium tremens.

Dual Alliance (1) Alliance of Germany and Austria-Hungary (1879); see TRIPLE ALLIANCE. (2) Alliance of France and Russia in the face of (1), consolidated in 1894.

Dual Monarchy, The (1867). Austria-Hungary as reorganized after SADOWA by the Ausgleich ('compromise') under which Hungary became self-governing in purely internal affairs.

Dubarry (Cooking) Served with cauliflower and mornay sauce.

Dublin Now officially known as BAILE ÁTHA CLIATH.

Dublin Bay prawns Rock lobsters about the size of prawns; the Italian scampi, French langoustes.

Dublin Castle Seat of British government in Ireland until the Irish Free State was established.

Dubliners (1914). Collection of short stories by James Joyce, written before he took to veiling his literary powers in linguistic obscurities.

Dubrovnik Medieval seaport, of which the Italian name was Ragusa; now in Yugoslavia.

Duce, Il Title taken by Mussolini; compare FÜHRER; CAUDILLO. (Italian, 'the leader'; pronounced doo'chay.)

Duchesse (Cooking, of potatoes) Creamed and blended with egg yolk, and baked in the oven.

Duchess of Malfi, The (about 1614). John Webster's grim tragedy of intrigue and crime, in which the widowed duchess marries her steward; they and her children are murdered by her outraged relations.

Duchy of Cornwall (1337). Estate established by Edward III for the Black Prince, inherited by his son and by the sovereign's eldest son ever since.

Duchy of Lancaster (1362). Estates and jurisdiction known as the Duchy and County Palatine of Lancaster, established by Edward III for his son John of Gaunt, and belonging to the Crown ever since. The Chancellorship of the Duchy is an honorary appointment held by a member of the government who has other, non-departmental, duties.

Duff Cooper Memorial Prize (1956). Annual prize for a literary work published in English or French. (In memory of Lord Norwich, formerly Sir Alfred Duff Cooper.)

Duffel Thick cloth coming from Duffel, near Antwerp in Belgium. Duffel coats were originally made from this cloth.

Duhallow, The An Irish fox-hunting pack with kennels at Blackrock, Mallow, in Co. Cork. It dates back to before 1745.

Duke Humphrey's Library Oldest part of the BODLEIAN, the library presented by the Duke of Gloucester (died 1447), son of Henry IV, who appears in Shakespeare's historical plays.

Duke of Beaufort's Fox-hunting pack with kennels at Badminton, which hunts country in Gloucestershire, Somerset and Wiltshire.

Duke of Edinburgh's Award (1956). Scheme to encourage enterprise in leisure activities among boys and girls aged 14–19, operated through schools, uniformed forces, firms, youth centres, etc., in Britain and the Commonwealth. Awards are made to those who show energy and perseverance in activities they select from each of 4 groups: service (e.g. first aid); expeditions; 'pursuits' (e.g. music, rock-climbing); and physical fitness for boys and 'design for living' (e.g. cooking) for girls.

Duke of Kent's Cup (1937). A ski competition restricted to competitors not domiciled in mountain resort areas.

Duke of York Grand old Duke of York of the nursery rhyme was Frederick Augustus, son of George III; the implied inefficiency in the rhyme has no basis in fact.

Dukeries, The District in north-west Nottinghamshire where the country seats of the dukes of Portland, Norfolk and Newcastle were once situated.

Duke University (1838). Methodist university at Durham, North Carolina, USA.

Dukhobors Russian religious sect, founded in the 18th century at Kharkov, which rejected the Orthodox Church. As a result of persecution, many emigrated (1899) to western Canada, where they caused much trouble by their resistance to taxation, education and conscription, their protests taking the form of arson, bombs and demonstrations in the nude. (Russian, 'wrestlers with the spirit'; pronounced dook'o-borz.)

Dulcinea Simple, though rather massive, country girl to whom, though she does not know it, DON QUIXOTE has decided to dedicate his deeds of chivalry; hence an idealized mistress. (Pronounced duls-in-ee'a.)

Duluoz, Jack Hero of a series of novels (1958 onwards) by Jack Kerouac, the French-Canadian-American beatnik leader of California.

Duma (1906–17). Russian Imperial Parliament, the establishment of which was announced in the OCTOBER MANIFESTO. The first two Dumas were too radical for the Tsar and lasted only a few months before being dissolved; the third (1907–12) was elected under a system which ensured the supremacy of the ruling classes; the fourth was swept away at the Revolution. (Pronounced doo'ma.)

Dumbarton Oaks Conference (1944). Meeting of delegates from Britain, USA, Soviet Russia and China at which proposals for UNO were discussed and arrangements made for the SAN FRANCISCO CONFERENCE. (Name of a country house near Washington, DC.)

Dun & Bradstreet Credit-rating agency, with offices in New York and London.

Dunbar, Battle of (1650). Engagement in the last phase of the ENGLISH CIVIL WAR in which Cromwell routed the Scots under Leslie, who had declared Charles II their king, and went on to take Edinburgh.

Dunciad, The (1728). Alexander Pope's 'dunce-epic', an astringent poem satirizing critics hostile to him.

Dundee University (1967). Formerly a unit of St Andrew's University, Aberdeen, and known as Queen's College, Dundee.

Dunedin Poetic name for Edinburgh. (Gaelic *dun*, 'fortress'; *Edin* for Edwin, King of Northumbria, who built it; pronounced dun-eed'in.)

Dunelm. Abbreviation of Latin for 'of Durham', used in the Bishop's signature and by Durham University.

Dungeness Site of a nuclear-power station with a MAGNOX REACTOR, and linked by power cable to France (1961); this site was also chosen in 1965 for the first of the AGR reactors. (Stretch of shingle in Kent, south of New Romney.)

Dungeness lighthouse The first fully automated lighthouse in Britain.

Dunkirk (May–June 1940). Miraculous evacuation of over 300,000 British and French troops from Dunkirk to Britain, using every available form of sea-craft, rendered possible by Rundstedt, with Hitler's consent, halting the German advance and by the Luftwaffe's abstention from attack.

Dún Laoghaire Port of Dublin, formerly known as Kingstown. (Pronounced dun-leer'i.)

Dunmow Flitch (1111). Flitch of bacon given to any married couple who, at the church door of Little Dunmow, Essex, swore that they had not quarrelled or wished themselves unmarried during the previous 12 months and a day. The custom has been revived many times, and persists today.

Dunne's theory of time See SERIALISM.

Dunster Force (1918). Detachment of the Mesopotamian Expeditionary Force under Major-General Dunsterville (the Stalky of STALKY AND CO.) which took Baku.

Dunvegan Castle Castle in the Isle of Skye inhabited continuously by the Chiefs of Macleod since the 13th century.

Dupin, Chevalier Auguste First fictional amateur detective, who appears in E. A. Poe's 'The Murders in the Rue Morgue' (1841) and subsequent tales.

Du Pont (1802). A US combine, in full, E. I. Du Pont de Nemours, which started as an explosives firm founded by a French refugee of that name, at Wilmington, Delaware. Its chemicals division first made nylon, DACRON and ORLON.

Dupree, J. M. W. G. Character in A. A. Milne's WHEN WE WERE VERY YOUNG: 'James James/ Morrison Morrison/Weatherby George Dupree/Took great/Care of his Mother/Though he was only three.' He insisted: 'You must never go down to the end of the town, if you don't go down with me.'

Durand Line (1892). The boundary between Pakistan and Afghanistan; see PAKHTUNISTAN.

Durham report (1839). Historic report, after disturbances in Canada, which first recommended responsible local self-government for a British possession. It also proposed the union of Upper and Lower Canada, which would put the French population in a minority; the encouragement of immigration; and the building of railways. (1st Earl of Durham, 'Radical Jack', previously Governor-General.)

Durovernum Cantiacorum Roman name of Canterbury.

Durrës Chief port of Albania, formerly known by its Italian name of Durazzo. (Pronounced door'ays.)

Dust Bowl Region where over-cultivation, drought, and dust-storms which carry off the top-soil combine to convert farmland into virtual desert; specifically, the area so created in 1932–7 around western Kansas and adjoining parts of Texas and Oklahoma.

Dutch auction Auction at which the asking price is gradually lowered until a buyer is found.

Dutch courage Evanescent courage inspired by drink.

Dutch elm disease Highly destructive fungus disease of elms, first identified in Holland (1921), reached North America in 1930 and England in 1970, transmitted by beetles. Leaves wilt and drop, and upper branches die; the disease spreads particularly rapidly on young trees.

Dutch Reformed Church Chief Protestant Church of the Netherlands and of the Boer population of South Africa; its government is presbyterian.

Dutch treat Meal or entertainment for which each pays his share; also called 'going Dutch'.

Dutch uncle To talk like a Dutch uncle is to administer a stern lecture.

Dutch William Name for William III of England, WILLIAM OF ORANGE.

Dyaks (Dayaks) Malayan name for a group of non-Muslim races of Borneo, including the Land Dyaks and the head-hunting Sea Dyaks, the latter so called because they used to raid the coastal areas, not because they are seafarers. (Pronounced dy'aks.)

Dyarchy (1919–37). Properly, government by two independent authorities; applied specifically to the system introduced in India as a result of the Montagu-Chelmsford Report, under which partial responsible government was granted to the provinces, the central government being retained under modified British control. (Greek, 'double rule'; more correctly spelt 'diarchy'.)

'D'Ye Ken John Peel' Hunting song written by a friend of Peel, the master of his own pack of hounds in the Cumberland fells who died in 1854. It was set to an older tune.

Dyers, Worshipful Company of (1470). LIVERY COMPANY which fosters research into dyeing, and shares with the Vintners the right to keep swans in the Thames and to participate in swan-upping.

Dying Gaul, The Hellenistic sculpture commemorating the victory of Attalus I of Pergamum over the Gauls (241 BC), artist unknown; now in the Capitoline Museum, Rome.

'Dying Swan, The' *Pas seul* choreographed by Fokine, to music by Saint-Saëns, rendered famous by Pavlova, among many.

Dynasts, The (1904–8). Thomas Hardy's ambitious verse drama (not intended for the stage) on Europe during the Napoleonic Wars.

E

Eagle, Solomon (1) Lunatic who, during the Great Plague (1665), ran naked through the streets of London with a pan of burning coals on his head, crying 'Repent!' (2) Pen-name used by (Sir) John Squire, the poet and critic, in the *New Statesman* (1913–19).

Eagle Day German name for their official date of the opening of the BATTLE OF BRITAIN (13 August).

Eagles, Fraternal Order of (1898). US fraternal organization with Masonic-type rites.

Eagle's Nest, The Hitler's Berghof at BERCH-TESGADEN.

Eagle Squadron Squadron (later 3 squadrons) of US volunteer pilots manning Spitfires of the RAF, which shot down 73 German planes before the time of Pearl Harbor; eventually transferred to the US 8th Air Force.

Ealing London borough, since 1965 consisting of the former boroughs of Ealing, Acton and Southall.

Ealing Studios comedies Sparkling series of films directed and produced by Sir Michael Balcon. The first was *Passport to Pimlico* (1948), which explored the situation arising when part of London was proclaimed French territory. Others were WHISKY GALORE (1948), KIND HEARTS AND CORONETS (1949), *The Ladykillers* (1955) – with its muscular crooks disguised as musicians pretending to rehearse Boccherini's String Quartet – and *The* LAVENDER HILL MOB (1952).

Éamon Irish name equivalent to Edmund. (Pronounced ay'mn.)

Earl Haig's Fund Earlier name of the Royal BRITISH LEGION, Haig's Fund for disabled ex-servicemen; one of its substantial sources of revenue is the collection made on POPPY DAY.

Earlham (1922). Percy Lubbock's nostalgic re-creation of Earlham Hall, the Norfolk mansion of an old Quaker family, the Gurneys, as he knew it when a child.

Earl Marshal Officer of state who is governor of the COLLEGE OF ARMS and supervises arrangements for all state ceremonies. The office has been held by the Dukes of Norfolk since 1672.

Earl's Court (1937). London exhibition hall at which are held the Royal Tournament, Royal Smithfield Show, and Motor Show; it can also be converted into a large swimming pool.

Early American Style of furniture made in the colonial and post-Revolution periods up to the 1820s, based on English styles but smaller, more informal and using local woods which offered better resistance to insects and heat.

Early Bird First commercial communications satellite, launched from USA in 1965. It is a 'stationary' (or synchronous) type, see SYNCOM.

Early English (1200–90). First period of English GOTHIC ARCHITECTURE, in which the pointed arch was introduced. It was also characterized by lancet windows with little or no decoration, and clusters of slender pillars (sometimes of PURBECK MARBLE round a stone centre) instead of the massive columns of NORMAN ARCHITECTURE. Salisbury Cathedral is an outstanding example.

Earnshaw family, The In WUTHERING HEIGHTS, Catherine, who marries Edgar Linton and dies giving birth to Cathy, and her brother Hindley, whose son Hareton is, at the end of the novel, free to marry his cousin Cathy and thus to unite the Earnshaw and Linton families which HEATHCLIFF had sought to destroy.

Earth (1930). Dovzhenko's documentary about farming which set new world standards in poetic cinematography, at a time when Russian films were at their zenith.

Earwicker, H. C. See FINNEGANS WAKE.

East African High Commission (1948–63). Joint council of the governors of Kenya, Uganda and Tanganyika, formed to co-ordinate the economic development of those colonies in anticipation, not realized, of the formation of an East African federation.

East African Protectorate Renamed Kenya Colony in 1920.

EastEnders Twice weekly BBC soap opera which holds top place in popularity ratings.

Easter Festival commemorating the Resurrection, celebrated on the Sunday following the first full moon after the spring equinox, i.e. between 22 March and 25 April. (Named after the Teutonic pagan festival held in honour of the dawn goddess Eostre at the spring equinox.)

Eastern Church Another name for the EASTERN ORTHODOX CHURCH.

Eastern Empire See BYZANTINE EMPIRE.

Eastern Orthodox Church Byzantine Church, which finally broke with the Western Church in 1054 (sometimes called the GREAT SCHISM) owing to the mutual antipathy of Greek and Roman cultures, but ostensibly on the minor theological point (the word *filioque* in the NICENE CREED) of whether the Holy Ghost 'proceeded' from the Father *and* the Son or *through* the Son (if the Son is one with the Father, the Holy Ghost must proceed from both). It is the Church of Russia, Greece, the Balkans and elsewhere; distinguished from the Roman Catholic Church by: married clergy, icons instead of 'graven images', no instrumental music, elaborate ritual, services held in Old Slavonic, Hellenistic Greek or other dead languages. The acknowledged head is the Oecumenical Patriarch, the chief bishop of Constantinople.

Eastern Question Historians' name for the problems created in the 19th century by Turkey's decline to the position of Sick Man of Europe. Manifestations included the Greek War of Independence, the Crimean War, Balkan rivalries, and disputes about the status of the Dardanelles; they usually involved clashes between Russian and European aims.

Eastern Schism (1054) Break between the (Greek) EASTERN ORTHODOX CHURCH of Byzantium and the Western Church of Rome.

Eastern Standard Time (USA) Time in the eastern states, 5 hours earlier than GMT.

Easter Parade Promenade by thousands of people on Fifth Avenue, New York City, on Easter Sunday, celebrated in a revue song (1933) and a Fred Astaire movie (1947) named after it.

Easter Rising (24–29 April 1916). Irish rebellion in Dublin, rendered abortive through the secret leadership (the IRB) keeping their fighting forces (the IRISH NATIONAL VOLUNTEERS and the CITIZENS' ARMY) in ignorance of their plans.

Easter term Legal term between Easter and Whitsun; at Cambridge, the term after Easter, equivalent to Oxford's TRINITY TERM.

East Germany See GERMAN DEMOCRATIC REPUBLIC.

East Grinstead (Queen Victoria Hospital) A plastic surgery hospital in Sussex where airmen were treated for burns during World War II. See GUINEA PIG CLUB.

East Ham Former Essex county borough, since 1965 part of the London borough of NEWHAM.

East India, Devonshire Sports' and Public Schools (1849). London social club in St James's Square, an amalgamation of 4 clubs.

East India Company (1600). English chartered company formed to trade with India and the East; it laid the foundations of British rule in India.

East Kilbride (1947). NEW TOWN in north Lanarkshire 7 miles south-east of Glasgow, designed to take 100,000 inhabitants.

East Lynne (1861). Romantic novel by Mrs Henry Wood, dramatized by various hands from 1864 on. Lady Isabel leaves her husband for another but, disguised as a nursemaid, returns to him after his re-marriage to look after their children. In the end the two are reconciled. The line 'Dead! . . . and never called me mother', inserted in one of the stage versions, released floods of tears from Victorian audiences, and then became a standard music-hall catch-phrase.

East Prussia Part of PRUSSIA which, while remaining under German rule, was in 1919 isolated from the rest of Germany by a tongue of territory transferred to Poland. East Prussia was divided between USSR and Poland after World War II.

Eatanswill Scene of a famous election visited by Mr Pickwick in Dickens's novel; it was on this occasion that he met the redoubtable Mrs Leo Hunter.

Eblis In Muslim legend, the Devil, also called Shaitan (Satan). See also VATHEK. (Traditional English spelling; also spelt Iblis; pronounced ee'blis.)

E-boat High-speed unarmoured motor-boat equipped with torpedoes and guns, used by the Germans and Italians in World War II. (For 'Enemy-boat'.)

Eboracum Roman name of York.

Ebor Handicap Flat-race run at York in August over a distance of 1¾ miles.

Ebury Street Street near Victoria Station, London, associated with George Moore (*Conversations in Ebury Street*) and with Noël Coward, both of whom lived there.

Ecce Homo (1) Pilate's words (Latin, 'behold the man!') as Jesus appeared, wearing the crown of thorns and the purple robe after he had been scourged (John 19:5). (2) Picture representing Jesus thus. (Pronounced ek'si hoh'moh.)

Ecclefechan Village where Carlyle was born, near Lockerbie, Dumfriesshire.

Eccles cake Lancashire version of the BANBURY CAKE, having the same ingredients but round in shape. (Eccles, a Lancashire town.)

Ecclesiastes (3rd century BC). Short book of the Old Testament, once attributed to Solomon, on the theme 'Vanity of Vanities . . . all is Vanity'. (Greek from Hebrew, 'preacher'.)

Ecclesiasticus (2nd century BC). Book of the Apocrypha which gives a disjointed but full account of the Jewish faith before the Christian era. It was written by a Sadducee, Jesus (i.e. Joshua) ben Sirach, and is also called *The Wisdom of Jesus the Son of Sirach* or simply *Sirach*. ('Church book', i.e. to be read in church though not part of the canon.)

ECG Initials used for electrocardiogram, a chart, produced by an electrocardiograph, showing the electrical impulses from the heart muscle. These, in health, have a characteristic pattern and abnormal rhythms are readily diagnosed.

Echinoderms Phylum of marine invertebrates, including sea-urchins and starfish. (Pronounced ek-yn'o-dėrmz or ek'in-o-dėrmz.)

Echinops Genus to which the Globe Thistle belongs; most of the common thistles belong to the genus *Carduus*.

Echo 1 First communications satellite, launched from the USA in August 1960. A metallized plastic balloon, some 1,000 miles up, it relayed radio and television signals without amplification (see SYNCOM).

Eclipse Eighteenth-century English racehorse, great-grandson of the DARLEY ARABIAN, never beaten; hence: 'Eclipse first, the rest nowhere'.

Eclipse Stakes Flat-race for 3- and 4-year-olds run at Sandown Park in July over a distance of $1\frac{1}{4}$ miles.

Eclogues (37 BC). Virgil's pastoral poems, also known as the *Bucolics*. The Fourth Eclogue, which refers to the birth of a child (probably to Augustus), was in early times taken to be a prophecy of Christ. (Greek, 'selections'.)

École Polytechnique See X, LES.

Economic and Social Committee European Community committee, representing employers, trade unions, consumers, etc., which has to be consulted on all major proposals.

Economic and Social Council One of the principal organs of the UN, dealing with economic, social, cultural, educational, health and related fields. It keeps in touch with the INTERNATIONAL AGENCIES and has established various specialist commissions (e.g. on narcotic drugs, human rights) and regional economic commissions.

Economic Commission for Europe (1947). UN agency set up by the ECONOMIC AND SOCIAL COUNCIL to assist in the post-war economic rehabilitation of Europe.

Economic Consequences of the Peace, The (1919). J. M. Keynes's unorthodox analysis of the likely consequences of trying to exact huge reparations from Germany after World War I, and of other major problems of international economics. See KEYNESIAN ECONOMICS.

Economic Co-operation Administration (1948–51). US body set up to administer the MARSHALL PLAN; it was replaced by the MUTUAL SECURITY AGENCY.

Economic Miracle, The Astonishing recovery of Western Germany after World War II, under the 'social free enterprise' policy of Ludwig Erhard, Economics Minister (1949–57) and later Vice-Chancellor and Chancellor. See DEUTSCHEMARK.

Economist, The (1843). Leading British weekly half of whose readership lives abroad. Despite its coverage of business matters, it is read especially for its outspoken non-party line on political, especially foreign, affairs.

ECT Initials used for electroconvulsive therapy. Electric shocks are applied to the head of a patient under anaesthesia. For reasons still unknown, this can alleviate the depressive phase of manic-depressive insanity and similar conditions.

Ecu European Currency Unit, a notional unit used within the European Communities. A former French coin was called the écu. See MONNET.

Ecumenical See OECUMENICAL.

Edam Hard-pressed yellow cheese, originally made of whole, now usually of skimmed, milk. The whole cheese is round with a red rind. (Dutch town; pronounced ee'dam.)

Edda Name given to two 13th-century Icelandic collections of Scandinavian poems and myths, known as the Prose Edda and Poetic Edda.

Eddystone (1882). Lighthouse on a rock 14 miles south of Plymouth, the fourth to be built there since 1698. The light is 133 ft above sea-level.

Eden, Garden of Garden planted by God as man's first home (Gen 2:8); i.e. the cradle of mankind; derived from Sumerian myths of a PARADISE where 'the lion killeth not, the wolf snatcheth not the lamb', and of a TREE OF LIFE. The Mormon leader, Joseph Smith, identified it with western Missouri (e.g. Kansas City?). (Eden from Sumerian for 'plain', i.e. the alluvial plains of Babylon, now Iraq; later confused with the Hebrew for 'luxury'.)

Edentates Order of New World mammals with no or only vestigial teeth, usually insect-eating; the sloths, armadilloes, ant-eaters, pangolins, etc.

Edgar award (1945). Prize for the best detective story of the year, awarded by the Mystery Writers of America Inc., a body of crime fiction writers who seek to raise standards in this field. (Named after Edgar Allan Poe.)

Edgbaston Warwickshire county cricket ground and, since 1902, a venue for Test matches. (Suburb of Birmingham.)

Edgehill (1642). First, and indecisive, battle of

the ENGLISH CIVIL WAR; Charles I marching on London was stopped by the ROUNDHEADS under the Earl of Essex but went on to take Oxford, which he made his headquarters. (A ridge north of Banbury.)

Edict of Nantes (1598). Grant by Henry IV of some degree of religious toleration to the HUGUE-NOTS of France; revoked by Louis XIV (1685).

Edinburgh Castle Located on a rock which dominates the centre of Edinburgh, the castle dates back at least to the 11th century, when a chapel was built named for Queen (Saint) Margaret, who died there.

Edinburgh Cup (1949). Sailing championship for the International DRAGON class, raced at the Clyde Regatta in June/July.

Edinburgh Festival (1947). Annual international festival of music (including opera), drama and ballet, held in August and September.

Edinburgh Festival Happening (1963). Parade of a naked woman on the stage at this august festival. (A 'Happening' is what used to be called a practical joke played on the public.)

Edinburgh Review, The (1802–1929). Whig political and literary quarterly, which savagely attacked Wordsworth and Southey, and was counter-attacked by Byron in *English Bards and Scotch Reviewers*. See QUARTERLY REVIEW.

Edison-Bell records Cylindrical records used on the earliest form of phonograph (gramophone). (Alexander Graham Bell and Thomas Edison, joint inventors, USA.)

Edjelé (1956). Scene of the first oil strike in the Sahara; it was followed by finds of more oil at Hassi-Messaoud, and of vast reserves of natural gas at Hassi R'Mel in the same year.

Edmonton Former Middlesex borough, since 1965 part of the borough of ENFIELD.

Edmund Ironside Edmund II, King of England for a few months in his last year (1016), defeated by Canute at Ashington in Essex, and possibly murdered by him. (A nickname alluding to his bravery.)

Edwardian cars Arbitrary name for cars which are neither Veteran nor Vintage, i.e. made between 1906 and 1918.

Edwards, Oliver Journalistic pen-name of Sir William (later Lord) Haley, Director-General of the BBC and afterwards editor of *The Times*.

Edwin Drood See DROOD, EDWIN.

Eeyore Old grey donkey of WINNIE-THE-POOH who lives by himself in a thistly corner of the Forest, gloomily mistrustful of all friendly advances.

Effluent Society, The Phrase, together with Gross National Pollution, used, but perhaps not coined, by Herman Kahn (see HUDSON INSTITUTE) to awaken the public to the dangers of environmental pollution. (Pun on AFFLUENT SOCIETY.)

Efik One of the main languages spoken in Eastern Nigeria. (Pronounced ef'ik.)

EFTA See EUROPEAN FREE TRADE ASSOCIATION.

Egdon Heath Stretch of heath described at the beginning of Thomas Hardy's *The Return of the Native* (1878) which plays a prominent part throughout the book. It is also mentioned in other novels and poems of Hardy's.

Egeria Woman who acts as guide and counsellor, especially to a statesman. (In Roman legend a nymph who advised the lawgiver Numa Pompilius, King of Rome; pronounced i-jeer'i-a.)

Egmont, Count Flemish leader of a 16th-century revolt against Spanish rule, who was executed by the Duke of Alva; the hero of a play by Goethe for which Beethoven wrote a famous overture.

Egoist, The See PATTERNE, SIR WILLOUGHBY.

Egypt P & O liner sunk off Ushant (1922) with a cargo of bullion which was salvaged 10 years later.

Egypt, Corn in Abundance, profits, available for the taking in a foreign country, a phrase taken from Genesis 42:2.

Egyptians, To spoil the To rob enemies or foreigners, a phrase taken from Exodus 3:22, and 12:36.

Eichmann trial (1961). Trial of Adolf Eichmann, Austrian Nazi head of the organization for the extermination of Jews; he was kidnapped in Argentina by Israeli agents, brought to trial at Tel Aviv, and hanged in 1962.

Eiffel Tower (1889). Tower designed by Gustave Eiffel (1832–1923), situated on the Champ de Mars, Paris; 300 metres high, and expected to have a life of only 20 years when erected, it is now also used for TV and radio communication.

'18' certificate (1982). Granted by British Board of Film Classification to films passed only for persons of 18 years and over.

18th Amendment (1919). Amendment to the US Constitution introducing Prohibition, which came into force in 1920 after the passing of the VOLSTEAD ACT.

18th Dynasty (1570–1370 BC). Period in the history of ancient Egypt, the first dynasty of the NEW KINGDOM, which included Thothmes III, Amenhotep III, AKHENATEN and TUTANKHAMEN. It saw conflicts with the Assyrians and Hittites and the building of the great temples of Amon at KARNAK and LUXOR.

1812 Overture (1880). Popular work by Tchaikovsky, with realistic gunfire effects and themes based on the French and Russian national anthems representing the opposing armies at BORODINO.

Eighth Commandment 'Thou shalt not steal' (Exod 20:15). To Roman Catholics this is the Seventh Commandment.

Eights, The Oxford University summer college boat-races.

Eights Week Celebration of the end of the academic year at Oxford University, with dances, tea-parties on college barges, etc. See previous entry.

Eilean Donan Castle Former Mackenzie stronghold, dating back to the 13th century, in the Kyle of Lochalsh, Wester Ross. (Pronounced ee'lan dohn'an.)

Einstein's theories Special Theory of Relativity (1905) which dealt with the physics of particles moving at near the speed of light, and showed that mass and energy are 2 aspects of the same concept; the General Theory (1915) which explained gravitation in terms of a 4-dimensional geometry of space-time in which space is curved, finite but expanding; and the Unified Field Theory (1950) which was a step towards linking gravitation and electromagnetism.

Eire (1) In common usage, the name of Southern Ireland from 1937 to 1949. (2) In official theory, the whole of Ireland, the six counties of Northern Ireland being only temporarily excluded from the operation of laws passed by the government in Dublin, pending reintegration of the whole country.

Eisenhower Doctrine (1957). US policy of giving aid to Middle Eastern countries to contain Communism. (President Eisenhower, during the Foster Dulles regime.)

Eisteddfod Annual meeting of Welsh bards at which there are contests in music and poetry. Compare FEIS CEOIL. (Welsh, 'assembly'; pronounced ys-tedh'vod.)

Ekaterinburg A town east of the Urals where the Russian Royal family were massacred in 1918; now renamed Sverdlovsk.

'El.', The New York City's elevated railway, closed down 1955.

Elaine In ARTHURIAN LEGEND, the LADY OF SHALOTT (or Fair Maid of Astalot) who died for love of LANCELOT.

El Al Name of the Israeli airline.

ELAS People's National Army of Liberation, the armed forces organized in Greece by EAM, the National Liberation Front. (Initials of the Greek name.)

E layer (ionosphere) See HEAVISIDE LAYER.

Elba Island between Corsica and Italy where

Napoleon was first exiled (1814–15); he was allowed to retain the title of Emperor and was nominally the ruler of the island. When he judged the time ripe, he embarked on the HUNDRED DAYS campaign.

Elder, The Character in Bernard Shaw's *Too True to be Good* said to be based on Dean Inge, the GLOOMY DEAN.

Elder Brethren Senior members of TRINITY HOUSE who, under a Master, administer the Corporation's affairs. They are divided into 'honorary' (members of the Royal family, Cabinet ministers, etc.) and 'active'; the latter sit as nautical assessors in the Admiralty Division of the High Court.

El Dorado Tribal chief in Colombia, smeared with gold-dust at an annual rite; rumours of this started the legend of El Dorado, a city paved with gold, sought by the Conquistadors, Ralegh and others. (Spanish, 'the gilded one'.)

Eleanor Crosses Nine crosses erected in the 13th century by Edward I to mark the places where the body of his Queen, Eleanor of Castile, rested *en route* from Nottinghamshire to Westminster Abbey. Three remain (Northampton, Geddington and Waltham Cross). That at Charing Cross (popularly derived from Chère Reine) is a modern replica.

Elector German prince entitled to vote in the appointment of the Holy Roman Emperor (911–1803).

Elector Palatine Count Palatine of the Rhine (PALATINATE).

Electra In Greek legend, the sister of ORESTES who conspires with him to murder their mother CLYTEMNESTRA. The story is treated by all 3 of the great Greek tragedians, and by numerous writers since, and in an opera by Richard Strauss; see also MOURNING BECOMES ELECTRA.

Electra complex Freud's term for the psychological effects of a girl's excessive attachment to her father and consequent (often unconscious) jealousy of and hostility to her mother. See OEDIPUS COMPLEX. (See ELECTRA.)

Elephant and Castle Road junction and railway station in Newington, south of the Thames, which took its name from a public house there. (Variously derived from the Infanta of Castile, and the arms of the Cutlers' Company, which included an elephant with howdah.)

Eleusinian Mysteries Festival held in honour of DEMETER and PERSEPHONE at Eleusis (near Athens), celebrating the return of vegetation each spring. Although the Mysteries were celebrated until well on in the Christian era, not much is known of their origin or nature.

11 Downing Street Official London residence of the Chancellor of the Exchequer, next door to the Prime Minister.

11-plus Examination taken at state schools at age 11 to determine whether a child should go to grammar, secondary modern, or technical school. The target of much criticism, as sealing a child's fate at too tender an age. Now mainly abandoned.

Eleventh Commandment Cynically said to be: 'Thou shalt not be caught out.'

El Fatah (1958). Arab guerrillas and the mainstream group in the PALESTINE LIBERATION MOVEMENT, dedicated to the liberation of Palestine.

Elginbrodde, Martin Subject of George Macdonald's epitaph: 'Here lie I, Martin Elginbrodde: /Hae mercy o' my soul, Lord God; / As I wad do, were I Lord God, / And ye were Martin Elginbrodde.'

Elgin Marbles Collection of Greek antiquities which includes parts of the frieze from the Parthenon and many other ancient sculptures, together with plaster casts of yet more, brought from Athens by the Earl of Elgin in 1803 and now in the British Museum. (Pronounced el'gin.)

Elia Pen-name under which Charles Lamb wrote his *Essays* (1820–25) for the *London Magazine*. He wrote on a wide range of topics, displaying a gentle, serene outlook which was not reflected in his personal life.

Elijah (9th century BC). Major prophet of Israel

in the reign of Ahab. He went up by a whirl-wind to Heaven (II Kgs 2:11) and Elisha took up his mantle as his successor. See also next entry.

Elijah and the ravens Biblical incident often treated in popular art, representing the prophet Elijah at the brook Cherith (Kerith) being brought 'flesh and bread' by the ravens. (I Kgs 17:3–6.)

Eliot, George Pen-name of Mary Ann Evans (1819–80), English novelist.

Eliot, Lewis See STRANGERS AND BROTHERS.

Eliot Memorial lectures (1967). Lectures on literature, endowed by the publishers, Faber & Faber, in memory of T. S. Eliot, given 4 times a year at Eliot College, Kent University.

Elisir d'amore, L' (1832). Donizetti's tuneful comic opera about lovesick rustics and a quack doctor with his love potions. (Italian, 'elixir of love'.)

Elizabeth Pen-name of Mary Annette Beauchamp, Countess Russell (1866–1941), author of *Elizabeth and her German Garden* (1898), an account of her life in Prussia with her first husband; her second was Bertrand Russell's brother.

Elks, Benevolent and Protective Order of (1868). A large US fraternal organization with Masonic-type rites.

Elliman's Proprietary name of an embrocation for bruises and sprains.

Ellis Island New York immigration station, notorious for the insolence and inhumanity of its staff; closed in 1954, reopened as a museum in 1990.

Elsinore Old English spelling of Helsingör, a seaport in Denmark, the scene of Shakespeare's *Hamlet*.

Elvas plums Crystallized plums, round and dark red, once a feature of Christmas fare. (Portuguese town whence imported.)

El Vino's Wine bar in FLEET STREET, London, frequented by journalists and lawyers.

Elvira Wife of DON JUAN, whom he abandons.

Elvis the Pelvis Nickname of Elvis Presley, the 1950s King of Rock (see ROCK 'N' ROLL).

Ely Professor Holder of a chair of Divinity at Cambridge.

Élysée Palace Official residence of the French President, situated just north of the Avenue des Champs-Élysées.

Elysium Abode of heroes and the virtuous dead, in Greek legend separate from the Underworld of HADES, and located somewhere in the far west in a land without cold or snow. See FORTUNATE ISLES.

Emanuel Quint (1910). Short title of Gerhart Hauptmann's novel *The Fool in Christ, Emanuel Quint*. The son of a village carpenter, Quint is Jesus in a modern setting; he is expelled by his outraged compatriots and is later found dead in the Alps.

Embarkation for the Island of Cythera (1717). Established title of a Watteau painting which in fact depicts the departure from Cythera, the island of Venus, of young couples preparing to leave it (i.e. love's young dream) for ever. There are versions in the Louvre and at Berlin.

Embarkation of the Queen of Sheba, The (1648). Claude Lorraine's combination of classical architecture and biblical story in a study of the play of sunlight on water; now in the London National Gallery.

Ember Days Three days in each season of the year appointed by the Christian Churches for prayer and fasting. (Derivation unknown.)

Emergent Evolution (1920). Philosophical theory put forward by an Australian, Samuel Alexander: matter emerged from space–time with an innate tendency to strive towards a higher state, life; life similarly to evolve into mind; and mind into deity.

EMI (1931). Initials of Electrical and Musical Industries, a leading British music-recording and electrical goods company, with headquarters at Hayes, London.

Éminence grise Grey or shadowy background figure exercising power and influence behind the scenes. (French, 'grey cardinal'; used of Père Joseph, Cardinal Richelieu's private secretary.)

Eminent Victorians (1917). Lytton Strachey's collection of revealing ironic biographical sketches of Cardinal Manning, Dr Arnold of Rugby, Florence Nightingale and Gen. Gordon.

Emma Colloquial abbreviation for Emmanuel College, Cambridge.

Emma (1816). Jane Austen's novel in which Emma Woodhouse, having little to do except run the house for her hypochondriac father, devotes her time to arranging other people's lives for them, with conspicuous non-success. Finally she marries the eligible Mr Knightley.

Emmanuel, Immanuel Son of a virgin birth mentioned in the Old Testament prophecy (Isa 7:14) referred to in Matt 1:23. (Hebrew, 'God with us'; spelt with *I* in OT, with *E* in NT.)

Emmaus Village not far from Jerusalem where Jesus appeared after his death to Cleophas and Simon Peter (Luke 24:15–31). (Pronounced em-ay′ès.)

Emmental Fairly mild hard-pressed cheese with a sweetish nutlike flavour, characterized by holes larger than those in GRUYÈRE. The whole cheese is very large, flat and round. (Originally made in the Emme valley, Switzerland.)

Emmy TV's OSCAR; a statuette awarded by the Academy of Television Arts and Sciences for the year's outstanding TV performance and programming. (Named after Faye Emerson, American entertainer.)

Emperor Concerto, The English name for Beethoven's last piano concerto, not used on the Continent.

Emperor Jones (1920). Eugene O'Neill's play about a black Pullman porter who sets himself up as emperor of an island in the West Indies.

'**Emperor's New Clothes, The**' One of Hans Andersen's original fairy-tales. Two rogues persuade the Emperor that they can weave him clothes which will be invisible only to those who are idiots or unfit for office. His courtiers are afraid to lay themselves open to either charge, and it is left to a child to cry out, when the Emperor parades through the streets in his 'new clothes': 'Why, he has nothing at all on!'

Empire, The (1804–15). Period in French history, also called the First Empire, from the time when Napoleon ended the CONSULATE by crowning himself Emperor, to the Battle of Waterloo.

Empire Day See COMMONWEALTH DAY.

Empire flying-boat (1936). Airliner built by Short Bros, for service with Imperial Airways on routes to Australia and South Africa. It carried 16 passengers, for whom comfortable sleeping quarters were provided, and took $9\frac{1}{2}$ days on the Southampton–Sydney trip.

Empire Free Trade Crusade launched by Lord Beaverbrook in 1929 for the conversion of the British Empire into a free trade area; unrealistic, since the Dominions had no intention of allowing free entry to British manufactures, it was killed by the OTTAWA AGREEMENTS. See UNITED EMPIRE PARTY.

Empire Loyalists Extreme right-wing political group, known to the public for the frequency with which they had to be thrown out of political meetings. They merged with the NATIONAL FRONT in 1966.

Empire Marketing Board (1926–33). British government body which promoted trade within the Empire by extensive advertising campaigns; it also had a scientific research branch.

Empire State Nickname of New York State.

Empire State Building Standing in midtown New York, 102 storeys and 1,250 ft high, the tallest building in the world when completed in 1931.

Empire style (1800–30). French style influenced by ancient Egyptian art (which became familiar through Napoleon's campaigns) and even more by ancient Greek and Roman models (e.g. Greek vases, the Parthenon), interest in which was stimulated by political sympathy with the revolutionary struggles of Greece and Italy. Furniture tended to be heavy and comfortless, embellished with brass and ormolu. The period corresponded with the reigns of Napoleon, Louis XVIII and Charles X, and with the English Regency.

Empiricism Philosophical view that knowledge is confined to what can be inferred by induction from observed facts; it rejects all that cannot be verified and the very concept of a priori knowledge. It is a typically English approach, shared by Berkeley, Hume, Locke and Mill, in constrast to the Cartesian RATIONALISM of Continental philosophers.

Empress of Canada Liner which caught fire and capsized in a Liverpool dock in 1953.

Empress of Ireland Liner which sank in the St Lawrence river in May 1914.

Ems telegram (1870). Telegram from the King of Prussia to the Chancellor of the new North German Confederation, Bismarck, reporting his acceptance of a French request not to support a Hohenzollern candidate for the Spanish throne; Bismarck altered it to convey a brusque refusal and published it, so causing France to declare war (see FRANCO-PRUSSIAN WAR).

Ena Harkness (1946). Hybrid tea rose with fragrant well-formed bright crimson flowers.

Encyclopédistes Group of contributors (including Voltaire and Rousseau) to the *Encyclopédie* (1751) in 34 volumes edited by Diderot and D'Alembert, in which all contemporary institutions, ideas and superstitions were challenged in the light of Reason; a major influence on the French Revolution.

Endgame (1957). Beckett's play about the sole survivors of some world disaster, the blind and paralysed Hamm, his legless parents who live in dustbins, and his would-be rebel servant, Clov. They all hate each other; Hamm has the only food, Clov alone can run away (as he wants to do); but since they are mutually dependent he never does.

Endor, The Witch of Witch who at SAUL's request calls up the ghost of SAMUEL; he pro-phesies the destruction of Saul's army by the Philistines (I Sam 28:7–20).

Endymion (1818). Keats's long, over-rich allegorical poem of a Greek shepherd's love for the Moon, apparently representing the poet's own search for ideal beauty. It begins: 'A thing of beauty is a joy for ever.'

Enemy of the People (1882). Ibsen's play in which Dr Stockman is regarded as an enemy by his fellow citizens when he tries to close down a spa because its waters are polluted.

Enfants du Paradis, Les One of the most famous of French films, directed by Marcel Carné. Set against the background of the Paris theatre of the 1830s, it concerns the lives, loves and careers of actors who are at the mercy of the gallery audiences.

Enfants terribles, Les (1930). Jean Cocteau's novel and play on the same kind of theme as HIGH WIND IN JAMAICA, i.e. the amorality of children.

Enfield London borough since 1965 consisting of the former boroughs of Enfield, Edmonton and Southgate.

Engadine Favourite tourist ground in south-east Switzerland, the valley of the Inn stretching from the Maloja Pass to the Austrian frontier.

English Bards and Scotch Reviewers See EDINBURGH REVIEW.

English Civil War (1642–51). War between the CAVALIERS and ROUNDHEADS, and its aftermath. After the battles of EDGEHILL, MARSTON MOOR and NASEBY, Charles I surrendered to the Scottish army at Newark, ending the first phase (1646). Cromwell then (1648) crushed royalist risings in Kent and Essex and a Scottish army at PRESTON, ending the second phase. Charles, Prince of Wales, then took the field and was defeated at DUNBAR and WORCESTER (1650–51), ending the third phase.

English disease, The (1) Name sometimes given to bronchitis on account of its particularly high incidence in England. (2) Name applied by foreigners to Britain's post-war problems in raising economic productivity.

English Heritage Popular name for the Historic Buildings and Monuments Commission for England.

English opium-eater, Confessions of an See CONFESSIONS OF AN ENGLISH OPIUM-EATER.

English Renaissance (16th century). Age of the Reformation; of Colet, More, Marlowe, Spenser, Shakespeare and Bacon; and of Tudor architecture. See RENAISSANCE.

English-Speaking Union (1918). Founded by (Sir) Evelyn Wrench to bring together Commonwealth and American people, and to help students and teachers of English throughout the world.

English Stage Company (1956). London repertory company which opened at the Royal Court Theatre, Sloane Square, Chelsea, and gained early fame from LOOK BACK IN ANGER. It stages the work of new British and established foreign playwrights, as well as occasional classical revivals. The associated English Stage Society gives experimental productions on Sundays.

Enigma Name the Germans gave to their electric machine which produced cipher messages; these vital secret signals were decoded by a brilliant team of cryptanalysts at Bletchley Park, Buckinghamshire, England. The Germans never realized that their most secret signals were being read in England. (See also ULTRA and SPY-CATCHER.)

Enigma Variations (1899). Elgar's Variations on an Original Theme, each a sound-portrait of one of his friends, who have since been identified. Elgar never disclosed the nature of the 'enigma'.

Eniwetok Pacific atoll, scene of the detonation of the first US hydrogen bomb on 1 November 1952 (Operation Ivy), not announced until 1954. (In the Marshall Islands, near Bikini.)

Enlightenment, The Eighteenth century as the period when political, moral, religious, social and other beliefs were put to the test of reason by such thinkers as Rousseau, Voltaire, Kant, Newton, Adam Smith; and enlightened despots such as Frederick the Great and Catherine the Great tried to put the new theories into practice.

Also called the Age of Reason. (Translation of German *Aufklärung*, used of this period in Germany.)

Ennui Sickert's vivid depiction of the deep boredom of a Sunday afternoon in a working-class home; now in the Tate Gallery, London.

Enoch Arden (1864). Tennyson's poem of a great renunciation. Enoch marries Annie but is shipwrecked and presumed dead. Annie marries another, Enoch returns and, watching their happiness from afar, decides not to ruin it by revealing himself.

Enosis Movement for the union of Cyprus with Greece which, with Church support, began in the 1930s and came to a violent head in 1954; see EOKA. (Greek, 'union'.)

Entente Cordiale (1904). Anglo-French agreement which formed the basis of the TRIPLE ENTENTE; it defined spheres of influence in Egypt and Morocco.

Enterprise National class of dinghy, 13 feet 3 inches long, cheap but exciting to sail, and raced regularly almost everywhere; designed by Jack Holt and built in many places.

Enterprise, USS (1961). First nuclear-powered aircraft carrier.

Enterprise Neptune Campaign sponsored by the National Trust to preserve those parts of Britain's coastline which have not yet been desecrated by uncontrolled modern development.

Enzian Incomparably foul liqueur made from gentian and drunk in Alpine regions presumably because of its bogus reputation as an aphrodisiac. (German, 'gentian'.)

Eocene Epoch Earliest subdivision of the TERTIARY PERIOD, lasting from about 70 to 50 million years ago. Carnivores, hoofed animals and the more primitive primates, e.g. the lemur, appeared. The London clay was deposited. (Greek, 'dawn of the modern', i.e. modern forms of life.)

Eoka Terrorist movement in Cyprus, led by a Greek, Grivas, which from 1954 conducted a campaign of callous brutality against British troops and the Turkish inhabitants of Cyprus, in the cause of ENOSIS.

Eonism Transvestism, the mania of men for wearing women's clothes. (Chevalier d'Éon, 18th-century French spy, who used to dress as a woman.)

Eos Greek dawn-goddess, sister of Selene and Helios; the Roman Aurora. (Pronounced ee'ohs.)

Eothen (1844). Kinglake's amiable description of the vicissitudes of travel in the Near East in the 19th century. (Greek, 'from the east'.)

Eozoic Period Earliest period of the PRE-CAMBRIAN ERA. (Greek *eos*, 'dawn', *zoé*, 'life'.)

Ephemeroptera Mayflies, an order of insects which, in their adult stage, live only a few minutes or hours.

Ephesus, Council of (431). Oecumenical Council which condemned the NESTORIAN HERESY.

Epic Theatre (1920s). Type of play advocated by Brecht and other Germans, appealing rather to reason than to the emotions, and using the A-effect (alienation) to put over political argument. The social and political background to a plot is presented by various devices, e.g. films and placards shown during the course of the play, which is itself broken up into many self-contained episodes (hence the name Epic). Piscator applied this idea in dramatizing Tolstoy's *War and Peace* (1955).

Epicureanism Greek philosophy which held that the highest good is happiness, to be sought through a virtuous life, avoidance of pain and the serenity that comes from the harmony of a healthy mind in a healthy body. The use of 'epicure' for one who is fond of luxury and comfort is due to a complete misunderstanding of this. (Epicurus, 341–270 BC.)

Epigoni (1) Sons of the SEVEN AGAINST THEBES who avenged their fathers by destroying Thebes, and, by extension, those of a succeeding and less distinguished generation. (2) Heirs to the DIADOCHI. (Greek, 'descendants'; pronounced ep-ig'on-y.)

Epiphany Manifestation of Christ to the Gentiles, in the persons of the MAGI, commemorated on 6th January. (Greek, 'an appearance'.)

Episcopalians Scottish name for Anglicans; the Presbyterians are the official Church of Scotland and the Anglicans are thus technically 'non-conformists' in Scotland. (Greek *episkopos*, bishop; the Presbyterians having no hierarchy of bishops.)

Epithalamion (1595). Spenser's bridal hymn, perhaps written for his own marriage. (Greek, 'at the door of the bridal chamber'; pronounced ep'i-thal-ay'mi-on.)

Epsom Downs Downs within the circle of Epsom racecourse in Surrey, where the gypsy caravans gather for the 4-day meeting in June and, since entry is free, particularly crowded on Derby day.

Epworth Old Rectory Lincolnshire home of John and Charles Wesley, where poltergeist phenomena were reported in 1716.

Equality State Nickname of Wyoming. (First state to give votes to women, 1869.)

Equity (1929). Shortened title of British Actors' Equity Association, the actors' trade union.

Erastian Adjective applied to the view that the Church should be subordinate to the state, then a shocking heresy, now Anglican orthodoxy. (Erastus, Greek translation of the German name of a 16th-century writer, Lieber.)

Erebus (Greek legend). Personification of darkness, and a dark cavern through which the dead passed on their way to Hades.

Erebus (1) Ship in which Ross sailed to Antarctica (1839–41), and which was abandoned by Franklin, with the *Terror*, north of Canada during his search for the North-west Passage (1848). (2) Antarctic volcano named after (1).

Erewhon (1872). Samuel Butler's Utopia in which Higgs, the narrator, comes upon an odd community in an unexplored part of New Zealand whose institutions provide the author with material for satirical attacks on English ways (e.g. criminals are sent to the doctor, the sick are punished). Higgs escapes by balloon (see next entry). (The title is 'nowhere' spelt, approximately, backwards; pronounced ėr'i-won.)

Erewhon Revisited (1901). In this sequel to EREWHON Higgs returns to find that, on account of his miraculous balloon ascent, he is worshipped as 'Sunchild'. He tries to explain, but is got quickly out of the country by the vested interests of the new religion.

Eric, or Little by Little (1858). Moralizing school story about a monumental little prig, by F. W. Farrar, later headmaster of Marlborough and Dean of Canterbury.

Erica Genus of most of the heathers; see CALLUNA.

Erigeron Genus name of the fleabanes.

Erin go bragh! Erse for 'Ireland for ever', quoted in a poem by Thomas Campbell.

Erinyes Older Greek name for the EUMENIDES. (Pronounced ėr-yn'i-eez.)

Erith Former municipal borough of Kent, since 1965 part of the borough of BEXLEY.

Eritrea Former Italian colony, now part of Ethiopia.

Erlking Black Forest elf who lures children to their doom; a legend used by Goethe in a poem made famous through Schubert's dramatic song based on it. A rider arrives at his destination to find that his child whom he was carrying lies dead in his arms, his spirit lured away by the soft-spoken elf. (German *Erlkönig*, 'king of the alders', a mis-translation of the Danish for 'king of the elves'.)

Ermine Street Pre-Roman road from London through Lincoln to York, extended by the Romans to Hadrian's Wall.

Ernie Initials by which the British Post Office's Electronic Random Number Indicator Equipment is known; it selects numbers in the draws for PREMIUM BOND prizes.

Eroica, The Beethoven's 3rd Symphony, which contains the Funeral March (there is another Funeral March in a piano sonata of his). Beethoven gave it its present name after deleting the original dedication to Napoleon when he betrayed the democratic cause by accepting the title of Emperor.

Eros (Greek legend). Son of Aphrodite, identified with the Roman Cupid, represented in art as a golden-winged child with bow and arrows, and sometimes as blindfold. Those pierced by his arrows fall hopelessly in love. See CUPID AND PSYCHE. (Greek, 'love'; pronounced eer'os.)

Eros (1893). Sir Alfred Gilbert's aluminium statue in the middle of Piccadilly Circus, London, part of a memorial to the 7th Lord Shaftesbury, philanthropist, and originally meant to represent the Angel of Christian Charity.

Erse Celtic (Gaelic) language spoken in Ireland, sometimes called Irish or Irish Gaelic. (Formerly used also of Scottish Gaelic.)

Erskine May Used as the short title of Sir Erskine May's *Treatise on the Law, Privileges, Proceedings and Usage of Parliament* (1844), still a standard work of reference.

Esau Son of Isaac and Rebecca and elder (twin) brother of JACOB, who cheated him of his birthright (which he sold for a mess of pottage (bowl of broth) (see Gen 25:29–34), and of his father's blessing (Gen 27:19–29). Esau was red and hairy at birth, symbolizing the sandstone mountains and black Bedouin tents of Edom (Negev) which he inherited.

Escallonia Shrubs named after the Spanish traveller Escallón.

Eschscholtzia Yellow-flowered Californian poppy, named after Dr J. F. von Eschscholtz, the German naturalist and physician.

Escorial (1584). Vast group of buildings 30 miles north-west of Madrid, comprising palaces, monastery, church, mausoleum, college and a famous library, built by Philip II in fulfilment of a vow. All subsequent kings (except Alfonso XIII, who died in exile) are buried there, and it has one of the finest art collections in the world. (From Spanish for 'refuse dump'.)

Esdras Two books of the Apocrypha, the first a compilation from old Hebrew texts of the Old Testament; the second an apocalyptic book written about AD 120 but using older material. (Esdras, Latin form of the name Ezra.)

Eskimo roll Method of righting a capsized canoe while remaining seated in it.

Eskimos Mongoloid people of the Arctic regions of Siberia, Alaska, Canada and Greenland. In Canada known as Inuits.

Esmond, Beatrix Beautiful and headstrong character in Thackeray's HENRY ESMOND who rejects Henry, flirts with the Old Pretender, marries her mother's chaplain (who becomes a bishop) and reappears in The VIRGINIANS as the sardonic old wife of Baron Bernstein.

ESN Abbreviation used for Educationally Sub-Normal, i.e. having an IQ of 60–80.

ESP Initials used for Extra-Sensory Perception, a term covering telepathy, precognition, clairvoyance and other forms of perception not apparently derived from the 5 senses; the phrase is particularly associated with J. B. Rhine of DUKE UNIVERSITY, who set up a parapsychological laboratory there for scientific statistical study of such phenomena.

Espagnole (Cooking) Basic rich brown sauce.

Esperanto (1887). Most successful of the synthetic universal languages, based mainly on the ROMANCE LANGUAGES and invented by Lazarus Ludwig Zamenhof (1859–1917). (Derived from Latin-type word for 'optimist'.)

Essay on Man (1734). Pope's attempt to justify the ways of God to man, best known in quotation, e.g.: 'Hope springs eternal in the human breast; / Man never is, but always to be blessed'; 'All are but parts of one stupendous whole, / Whose body nature is, and God the soul'; 'For forms of government let fools contest; / Whate'er is best administered is best.' Dr Johnson growled that it displayed vulgarity of sentiment and penury of knowledge, 'happily disguised'.

Essenes Ancient Jewish ascetic and mystical sect, founded about the 2nd century BC; the DEAD SEA SCROLLS have been attributed to them.

Essex rebellion (1601). Demonstration in London led by Robert Devereux, Earl of Essex, former favourite of Queen Elizabeth but by then in disgrace for mishandling the Ulster rebellion and for general insubordination. He was arrested, prosecuted by Lord Bacon among others, and executed for treason.

Esso Subsidiary of STANDARD OIL OF NEW JERSEY, now known as EXXON, Shell's chief competitor; it built the FAWLEY refinery. The group includes Esso Chemical, with headquarters in Brussels, and Esso Europe, an oil company with headquarters in London.

Establishment, The Term (originally derogatory) which came into use in 1954 to designate the guardians of traditional British institutions such as the Church, the Army, the public schools and the City, regarded as reactionary or out of date.

Esterházy family Ancient Hungarian family dating back to the 13th century which until recent years was always prominent in state affairs.

Esther In the Bible, a beautiful Jewess of the 5th century BC who keeps her nationality secret when chosen by the Persian king, Ahasuerus (Xerxes), as his queen. When his minister Haman plotted to exterminate the Jews of Persia, she and her uncle Mordecai foiled him and he was hanged. The story seems to have been invented to explain the Jewish festival of PURIM. God is never mentioned. (Pronounced est'ėr.)

Esther Waters (1894). George Moore's novel of the love of a housemaid for her illegitimate son, whose father later returns to marry her. He is now a publican and bookmaker, and the plot turns on his success on the racecourse.

Estragon One of the 2 tramps in GODOT.

Eternal City, The Rome; a name given to it from ancient times.

Etesian winds Strong dry northerly winds in the eastern Mediterranean which blow during the daytime from May to October, raising storms at sea and clouds of dust on land.

Ethiopia See ABYSSINIA.

Étoile, L' Huge roundabout in Paris at the top of the Champs-Élysées, site of the ARC DE TRIOMPHE and meeting-place of 12 avenues. Now called the Place Charles de Gaulle Étoile.

Eton fives Game which differs from RUGBY FIVES in having a 'pepper' (buttress) jutting out from the left-hand side and a step across the middle of the court to make the game more difficult. Only doubles are played.

Être et le Néant, L' (1943). Sartre's chief exposition of EXISTENTIALISM. (French, 'being and nothingness'.)

Etruscans Non-Indo-European predecessors of the Ancient Romans who left their name to modern Tuscany; they dominated north-west Italy (Etruria) from the 7th century BC and ruled Rome under the TARQUINS. Their numerous brief inscriptions are still largely undeciphered; their artistic remains, though impressive, indicate that they borrowed inspiration from all quarters. They bequeathed to the Romans the curious art of divination by inspection of entrails.

Ettrick Shepherd Name for James Hogg (1770–1835), the Scottish shepherd-poet born at Ettrick, Selkirkshire.

E-type Jaguar 150-m.p.h. 2-seater car (open or fixed-head coupé), esteemed as a status-symbol among young executives and the professional classes before shades of the prison-house of paternity begin to close / Upon the growing boy. Much mentioned in James Bond-type novels.

Eugene Onegin Title of a verse romance by Pushkin (1831) and an opera by Tchaikovsky (1879). The bored Byronic hero repulses the advances of the young Tatyana, who herself repulses Eugene's when, now married to a general, she meets him again years later. (Pronounced, in English, ew'jeen on-yay'gin.)

Eugénie Grandet (1833). One of the novels of Balzac's COMÉDIE HUMAINE, a study of a rich miser mewed up in his country house with his unfortunate daughter Eugénie.

Eumenides Greek name for 3 winged avenging goddesses (the Furies), who relentlessly pursued those who had failed in duty to their parents or who had otherwise contravened the accepted code of conduct. Also called ERINYES. (Literally, 'the kindly ones', a euphemism meant to placate them; pronounced ew-men'i-deez.)

Euphorbiaceae Spurge or milkweed family, characterized by an acrid milky juice, often poisonous; it includes poinsettia, cassava, castor-oil plant, rubber trees.

Euphues (1578). John Lyly's romantic picture of polite society, remembered not for its content but for its florid rhetorical style, full of antitheses and other literary quirks, which for a time set a fashion called euphuism. (Greek, 'well-cultivated'.)

EUR Initials of the Italian for 'Universal Exposition of Rome', still used as the sole name of a suburb of south-west Rome; originally the site for Mussolini's grandiose world fair planned for 1942 (which never took place). It has since been developed as a luxury suburb, with skyscrapers, government departments, and museums, all set in park-like surroundings.

Euratom (1958). European Atomic Energy Community, one of the European Communities, established to create a powerful joint industry to develop the peaceful uses of nuclear energy; the headquarters are at Brussels. See CERN.

Eurobonds Bonds issued in Europe by US companies, denominated, paid for and yielding interest in dollars. A by-product of the EURODOLLAR phenomenon.

Eurocrats Name given to the bureaucrats of the EUROPEAN COMMUNITIES.

Eurodollars Dollars put to use outside the US, not necessarily in Europe (despite the name). Not being governed by national currency restrictions, they become a freely convertible, almost a world, currency. Originating when Russia banked huge dollar reserves in Europe which were borrowed by other banks (thus acquiring, for obscure legal reasons, expatriate status), Eurodollars alarmed national banks as introducing an anarchic element into the gnomic calm of international banking.

Europa (1) Daughter of Agenor, King of Phoenicia, abducted to Crete by Zeus in the guise of a white bull. (2) Name suggested for a parallel European currency proposed in a report by the Federal Trust.

European plan System of hotel management in which a guest pays for room and service separately from payment for meals.

European Atomic Energy Community See EUR-ATOM.

European Coal and Steel Community (1952). One of the EUROPEAN COMMUNITIES, based on the SCHUMAN PLAN, which pooled its resources, abolished all internal trade restrictions, and more than doubled steel production in the first 13 years. The headquarters are at Luxembourg.

European Commission See COMMISSION.

European Communities (EC) Organization consisting of 12 member states established by the Treaty of Paris (1951) and Rome (1957) and subsequent treaties. The Communities consist of the European Coal and Steel Community (ECSC), the European Economic Community (EEC, sometimes called the Common Market) and the European Atomic Energy Community (Euratom). The aims are for a single European organization without frontiers by 1992 so that goods, capital and people can move freely between member states. Dreams of a political union are still unrealized.

European Cup (1955). Football tournament in which the champion (top of the league) club of each member of the European Union of Football Associations plays, and also the team which won the Cup in the previous year. Officially named the European Champion Clubs Cup.

European Cup-winners' Cup (1960). Football tournament run on much the same lines as the EUROPEAN CUP, but the entrants are the winners of the respective national knock-out cup competitions.

European Economic Community See COMMON MARKET.

European Free Trade Association (1960). Associ-

ation of Austria, Finland, Iceland, Norway, Sweden and Switzerland, with the objectives of achieving free trade in industrial goods between member countries, to help to create a single market for Western Europe and to expand world trade.

European Monetary Agreement (1955). Agreement by OEEC members to restore currency convertibility through a European Fund which provides short-term loans to facilitate monthly settlements between central banks. The Fund began work when the EPU ceased to operate in 1958.

European Nations Cup (1960). Football tournament run on the same elimination system as the World Cup, held every 4 years in between World Cup contests. The trophy is officially called the Henri Delaunay Cup.

European Parliament Parliament consisting of 518 directly elected members from the 12 member states of the EUROPEAN COMMUNITIES. The Parliament has a right to consultation on a wide range of legislative proposals and forms one arm of the Community's budgetary authority.

European Recovery Programme See MARSHALL PLAN.

Europe des patries, L' Phrase attributed to President de Gaulle to describe the ultimate objective of the FOUCHET PLAN. De Gaulle, however, claimed that his term was 'L'Europe des états' (i.e. a loose confederation of states), to distinguish it from the supranational European government envisaged by the COMMON MARKET organization.

Europoort (1961). International port at Rotterdam, opposite the Hook of Holland, able to take vessels up to 85,000 tonnes and, on completion of canals giving direct access to the sea, up to 100,000 tonnes. (In Dutch spelt Europoort.)

Eurospace A non-profit-making association of the aerospace equipment manufacturers of Western Europe, formed to co-operate in development and to co-ordinate policies.

Eurydice In Greek legend the wife of

ORPHEUS. When she died, Orpheus went to fetch her back from the Underworld, and so charmed HADES with his lyre that he was allowed to take her away provided he did not look at her until he had set foot on earth. He broke this condition and lost her for ever. (Pronounced ewr-id'i-see.)

Eustachian tube Tube connecting the middle ear with the back of the throat; it is the channel through which infections reach the parts of the ear lying on the inner side of the ear-drum.

Euxine Greek name for the Black Sea. (Greek, 'welcoming', a euphemism to propitiate it, as it was a stormy, treacherous sea; pronounced ewk'syn.)

Eva, Little In *Uncle Tom's Cabin*, the daughter of Tom's owner, to whom Tom is devoted.

Evangelical Church (1) American Church on Methodist lines, founded in 1800. (2) Name for the German Lutheran Church, now called the Evangelical United Brethren Church. (From Greek for 'bringing good tidings'.)

Evangelicalism Low Church doctrine, the opposite to ANGLO-CATHOLICISM: salvation is by faith in Christ as the redeemer of mankind through his sacrifice, and cannot be achieved through sacraments and good works; elaborate ritual is a distraction from true worship. (See previous entry.)

Evangelist (1) Any of the authors of the 4 Gospels. (2) Travelling missionary. (3) One who preaches the need for a 'new birth' (conversion) as an essential step to salvation. (See EVANGELICAL CHURCH.)

Evans of the Broke Admiral Evans (later Baron Mountevans), so called from a World War I incident when, as commander of the Dover patrol in HMS *Broke*, he sank 6 German destroyers. (Pronounced bruk.)

Evans the Leak Jocular name given to Harold Evans when he was public relations adviser to the Prime Minister, Harold Macmillan. (Portmanteau pun alluding to his Welsh name, the Welsh national symbol, and the Welsh habit of naming people after their occupations or characteristics.)

Eve Created from Adam's rib (Gen. 2:21–4), from a Semitic word possibly meaning 'life', as the 'mother of all living' (Gen. 3:20), and mother of Cain, Abel and Seth.

Evelina (1778). Delicate social comedy published anonymously by Fanny Burney (Mme D'Arblay), about 'a young lady's entrance into the world' of London Society.

Evelyn's *Diary* (1818). Interesting and amusing diary, covering the whole life from the age of 20, of John Evelyn (1620–1706), a Royalist who went into exile during the Civil War, returned to hold office under Charles II, and was one of the founders of the Royal Society.

Events Generic term for horse trials.

Eve of St Agnes, The (1819). Keats's narrative poem based on the superstition that girls dream of their future husbands on the night before St Agnes's Day (21 January). (St Agnes, child martyr in the DIOCLETIAN PERSECUTION, and patron saint of virgins.)

Everglades, The Wide area of swamp and subtropical forest in southern Florida, part of it a National Park, part reclaimed for agriculture.

Evergreen State Nickname of Washington State.

Ever Readies Territorial Army Emergency Reserve, now replaced by the T AND AVR 1. It provided units (mostly specialist) for peacetime emergencies overseas and for call-up on the outbreak of war.

Everyman Fifteenth-century Dutch morality play. Everyman, summoned by Death, is accompanied by Good Deeds alone of all his friends, among whom were Beauty, Strength, etc.

Évian agreement (1962). Agreement between France and the Algerian rebels which ended the Algerian revolt by the grant of independence. (French spa where secret talks were held from 1961; see next entry.)

Évian water An alkaline mineral water from Évian-les-Bains, a French spa on the south shore of the Lake of Geneva. (The spa took its name from the water, *évian* being formed from a local dialect word for 'water'.)

Excalibur Magic sword which ARTHUR alone was able to free from the stone or anvil in which it was embedded, thus proving his right to become king. (Pronounced eks-kal'i-bèr.)

Exclusion Bill (1679). Bill put forward by the Earl of Shaftesbury to exclude the Roman Catholic James, Duke of York, from succession to the throne. Charles II dissolved 3 Parliaments rather than let it pass.

Exclusive Brethren (1848). Sub-sect of PLYMOUTH BRETHREN, also called Darbyites, which itself split into several divisions. One, under 'Big Bill' Taylor in New York, attained notoriety by refusing to eat with members of other persuasions.

Exile, The In biblical history the BABYLONIAN CAPTIVITY; hence the adjectives *Exilic, post-Exilic.*

Existentialism Blanket-term for philosophies of lonely man, solely dependent on God (Kierkegaard), on Christian principles (Karl Jaspers), on himself in a meaningless godless world, with infinite potentialities for self-development (Sartre), or haunted by *Angst*, a general dread of nothingness (Heidegger).

Exocet French naval low-flight, ship-to-ship or air-to-ship missile.

Exodus Second book of the PENTATEUCH, telling the story of Moses, the Exodus of the Israelites from the Land of GOSHEN (at some time between the 15th and 13th centuries BC), their wanderings in the desert, and the giving of the Law.

Exon: Abbreviation for (Bishop) of Exeter.

Expanding Universe theory Hypothesis that all groups of galaxies are receding from all other groups at speeds proportionate to distance, which arose from Edwin Hubble's observations (1930) that distant spectra show 'red shifts' interpreted as Doppler shifts. It led to the BIG BANG THEORY and the STEADY STATE THEORY. See DOPPLER EFFECT; HUBBLE'S LAW.

Experiences of an Irish RM, Some (1899). A book by E. Oe. Somerville (1861–1949) and her cousin Martin ROSS which exploits the humours of Irish hunting and country life. They also wrote *Further Experiences* (1908). (RM, Resident Magistrate, title given in those days to a stipendiary magistrate in Ireland.)

Experiment with Time, An See SERIALISM.

Explorer Name given to a series of US research satellites. *Explorer 1*, launched 31 January. 1958, was America's first earth satellite, and sent back data which led to the discovery of the VAN ALLEN BELTS.

Exxon New name of Standard Oil of New Jersey.

Exxon Valdez **disaster** (1989). Oil tanker that ran aground in the Gulf of Alaska and discharged 11 million US gallons of crude oil.

Eyeless in Gaza (1936). First of Aldous Huxley's novels to show his growing preoccupation with oriental mysticism. A young profligate, Beavis, is converted in mid-life to the author's own views. (Title from Milton's *Samson Agonistes*.)

Ezekiel (6th century BC) Book of the Old Testament in which the major prophet, Ezekiel, an exile in Babylon, encourages his countrymen in Jerusalem not to despair.

F

Faber (Geoffrey) Memorial prize (1963). Annual award of £500 made alternately for a volume of verse and a novel, written by a British or Commonwealth author under 40 years of age.

Fabergé wares Products of the St Petersburg and Moscow workshops of the Russian-born jeweller and goldsmith, Carl Fabergé (1846–1920). He is especially famous for his Easter eggs made for the imperial family. His work was of great delicacy, sometimes exquisite, sometimes over-elaborate to suit the taste of his customers.

Fabian Society (1884). Founded by left-wing intellectuals such as Beatrice and Sidney Webb, Bernard Shaw, H. G. Wells and R. H. Tawney, who believed in 'the inevitability of gradualness' (Sidney Webb's phrase) in the spread of Socialist attitudes. It publishes pamphlets, advises the Labour Party, and stimulates fresh ideas. (See next entry.)

Fabian tactics Moving cautiously, as did Fabius Maximus Cunctator ('the delayer'), the Roman general who thwarted Hannibal by avoiding meeting him in pitched battle; of him it was written: *Unus homo nobis cunctando restituit rem* ('One man by delaying tactics restored our republic').

Faerie Queene, The (1590–95). National heroic poem by Edmund Spenser, chronicling the romantic adventures of medieval knights, each of whom portrays one of the cardinal virtues.

Fafnir In Scandinavian mythology the dragon who seized the Nibelungs' gold and was slain by Siegfried.

Fagin Head of a school for pickpockets in Dickens's *Oliver Twist*; the Artful Dodger was the most promising of his pupils, but Oliver himself was a backward learner.

Fahrenheit Temperature scale named after Gabriel Daniel Fahrenheit (1686–1736), instrument-maker. He used mercury instead of alcohol to register temperature, giving freezing point of water 32 degrees, body temperature 98·4 degrees, boiling point 212 degrees.

Fairbairn style Rowing style which put more emphasis on arm pull than body swing and sacrificed appearance to speed.

Fairchild family Family which appears in a children's book, Mrs Sherwood's *The History of the Fairchild Family* (1818–47), in 3 parts.

Fair Isle knitwear Wool knitted in gaudy patterns of yellow, red, green, etc, now made throughout Scotland, but originating in Fair Isle, a remote island of the Shetlands. The pattern may be local, or a Moorish tradition learnt from the crew of a Spanish Armada galleon wrecked there. Men's pullovers in these designs were made popular in the 1920s by the then Prince of Wales. (Gaelic *fair*, 'sheep'.)

Fair Isle sea area Area covering the Shetlands and Orkneys, west of the VIKING SEA AREA and south-east of the Faeroes sea area. (Named after the island midway between the Shetlands and Orkneys.)

Fair Maid of Perth (1828). Walter Scott's novel

of the 15th century; the maid is Katie Glover, who marries the armourer, Hal o' the Wynd.

Fair Rosamond One of the Clifford family, mistress of Henry II, who according to legend built her a house in a labyrinth so that no one could get to her; but his Queen, Eleanor, did so and poisoned her. She was buried in Godstow nunnery.

Faithful Shepherd **suite** Suite constructed by Sir Thomas Beecham from material in Handel's unsuccessful opera (1712) of that name.

Falaise Gap, Battle of the (13–20 August 1944). Crucial battle of World War II, in which large German forces were nearly encircled south of Caen, Normandy; a high proportion of them fought their way out before the gap was closed.

Falangists (1933). Spanish Fascist party founded by the dictator Primo de Rivera's son; although the only party permitted to exist, its relations with Franco were uneasy.

Falkland Islands, Battle of the (December 1914). Revenge for CORONEL in World War I, in which Sturdee's squadron sank von Spee's *Scharnhorst, Gneisenau* and other ships.

Falklands War (1982). On 2 April Argentine forces invaded the Falkland Islands and the Governor was expelled. Britain regained possession on 14–15 June after the Argentines surrendered.

Fall, The Fall of Man, the state of continuing sin in which mankind lives owing to the disobedience of Adam; a doctrine propounded by St Paul, and not mentioned by Jesus.

Fallen Angels (1925). Early Noël Coward comedy in which 2 wives get steadily drunk while awaiting an undesired visit from their former lover.

Fall Line (USA) Line formed by joining points marking the limit of river navigation east of the Appalachians; it runs approximately through Philadelphia, Baltimore and Richmond.

Fallodon Papers (1926). Literary papers of the first Viscount Grey of Fallodon, who as Sir Edward Grey was Foreign Secretary at the outbreak of World War I. (Name of his ancestral home near Alnwick, Northumberland; pronounced fal'ĕ-den.)

Fallopian tube Tube from ovary to womb, down which ova pass.

Falstaff, Sir John Fat knight who appears in Shakespeare's *Henry IV* and the *Merry Wives*, created as a foolish, sensual, lying glutton, but often played as a gay harmless old rogue, rather shabbily treated by Prince Hal.

Family Division Division of the High Court, dealing with such matters as matrimonial property, guardianship, custody and adoption.

Family Planning Association Voluntary body which advises on contraception, pregnancy diagnosis and marital problems.

Family Welfare Association Voluntary organization working in London through several branches, which deals with family sociological casework.

Fanmakers, Worshipful Company of (1709). LIVERY COMPANY which today encourages the development of all kinds of mechanical fan.

Fannie Farmer Short title of *The Fannie Merritt Farmer Boston Cooking-School Cookbook*, first published in the days of 12-course dinners (1896) and since continuously revised, like MRS BEETON, to suit the contracting stomachs of later generations.

Fanny's First Play (1911). Bernard Shaw's play about respectable parents whose son and daughter are sent to prison and make what their elders regard as unsuitable marriages.

Farewell to Arms, A (1929). Ernest Hemingway's novel of World War I; a young American is caught up in the CAPORETTO disaster in Italy in 1917, deserts, and eventually escapes with an English nurse into neutral Switzerland.

Far from the Madding Crowd (1874). Thomas Hardy's Wessex novel about Bathsheba Everdene, loved by 3 men. She marries one of them, who deserts her and is murdered by the second;

the murderer is sent to an asylum, and Bath-sheba eventually marries the third, the faithful Gabriel Oak.

Farmer George King George III, so named because of his bucolic tastes.

Farmers, Worshipful Company of (1952). LIVERY COMPANY formed to foster agriculture, improve marketing, develop farming machinery and encourage research into soil fertility and pest control.

Farm Street, Mayfair Name in common use for the Jesuit Church of the Immaculate Conception (1849), one of the best-known Roman Catholic Churches in London, and headquarters of the British Jesuits.

Farnborough Air Show Exhibition of military and civil aircraft staged biennially, alternating with the Paris show, by the Society of British Aerospace Companies at the Royal Aerospace Establishment, Farnborough, Hants.

Farne Islands Reserve (1925). National Trust property of 75 bare rocky islands off Northumberland which in May and June teem with sea-birds. (Also associated with St Cuthbert and Grace DARLING.)

Farriers, Worshipful Company of (1673). LIVERY COMPANY, originally a guild of shoe-smiths and horse-leeches. It now holds examinations for shoesmiths.

Farringford Home of Alfred Lord Tennyson near Freshwater, Isle of Wight, now a hotel.

Fasching German for 'Carnival', which in Bavaria takes the form of 6 days of masquerade balls and other uninhibited festivities, ending on Fastnacht (Shrove Tuesday, Mardi Gras).

Fashoda incident (1898). Encounter of British troops under Kitchener and a French force under Marchand in an area of the Sudan disputed by the two countries; the French yielded.

Fastnet, The (1925). Principal offshore race counting to the ADMIRAL'S CUP, but not confined to Cup teams. Sailed in August (in alternate years with the New York to Bermuda race) over a course of 605 miles from Cowes, Isle of Wight, to the Fastnet Rock (see next entry) and back to Plymouth.

Fastnet sea area That lying immediately south of Ireland. (Name of a rock and a lightship off Cape Clear, near Bantry Bay, south-west Ireland.)

Fat Boy, The Boy named Joe in Dickens's *Pickwick Papers* who spent in sleep any time he was not eating.

Fates, The In Greek legend the 3 daughters of Zeus who decide man's span on earth. Lachesis assigns the individual lot, Clotho spins the thread of life, and Atropos, the inflexible, cuts it. Called in Greek Moirai, in Latin Parcae.

Father Brown stories G. K. Chesterton's crime stories, in which the detective is a Roman Catholic priest with an unorthodox approach. The author and his creation regarded crime as a sin rather than as material for police investigation. The detective-priest first appeared in *The Innocence of Father Brown* (1911).

'Father O'Flynn' (1875). Irish dialect song written by Alfred Graves, in a familiar lilting metre exemplified by: 'Checkin' the crazy ones, coaxin' onaisy ones, / Liftin' the lazy ones on wid the stick.'

Father of the House Member of the House of Commons (or Lords) whose first entry into Parliament antedates that of all the other members of his House.

Fathers and Sons (1861). Turgenev's great novel on the rise of the Nihilists, represented by Bazarov.

Father's Day Third Sunday in June, founded in the spirit of sex equality to offset MOTHER'S DAY.

Fathers of the Church Influential among the orthodox Christian writers of the first 6 centuries AD, e.g. Augustine, Athanasius, Pope Gregory I, Chrysostom, Tertullian, Origen. See also APOSTOLIC FATHERS.

'Father William' A parody of a poem of Robert Southey's recited by Alice in ALICE IN WONDERLAND, beginning: '"You are old, Father William," the young man said . . ./ "And yet you persistently stand on your head; / Do you think at your age it is right?"'

Fatimites (908–1171). An independent dynasty of caliphs founded in North Africa when the ABBASID caliphate of Damascus became subservient to the Turks; they ruled Egypt, founding Cairo in 970. They were overthrown by Saladin. (The founder claimed descent from the Prophet's daughter, Fatima; pronounced fat'im-yts.)

Faubourg Saint-Germain Quarter where the élite of 18th-century Parisian society used to live, on the Left Bank opposite the Tuileries. The large houses are now foreign embassies or in government hands. (Originally a village built round the Abbey of Saint-Germain-des-Prés.)

Faust (German legend) An astrologer who sells his soul to the devil in return for enjoyment of all the pleasures of the world. This is the theme of Marlowe's *Dr Faustus*, Goethe's *Faust* (see next entry), and operas by Berlioz (*The Damnation of Faust*) and Gounod.

Faust Goethe's poem, in Part I of which (1808) Faust (see previous entry) is presented as having mastered all knowledge and yearning to taste all worldly experience. MEPHISTOPHELES grants his wish, and rejuvenates him; he seduces MARGARET (Gretchen) and the poem ends with the realization of the price he has to pay. Part II (1832) is a vehicle for Goethe's meditations on a very wide range of topics.

Fawcett Library London library devoted to the interests and achievements of women of all times in all countries.

Fawley refinery (1951). ESSO's petroleum refinery near Southampton.

Fax Machine resembling a photocopier which facilitates communication between offices (or other terminals) by its ability to reproduce letters, etc. – a document is fed into a slot and by electronic transmission a reproduction appears on the receiving machine. (From 'Facsimile transmission system'.)

FBI (USA) Federal Bureau of Investigation, established (1908) as an agency of the Department of Justice, with powers of arrest, to handle counter-espionage, treason cases and other internal security matters.

F.D.R. Initials used as nickname for Franklin Delano Roosevelt, 32nd President of the USA.

F.E. Initials used as nickname for F. E. Smith, later the 1st Earl of Birkenhead.

February Revolution (1917). (Russia) See OCTOBER REVOLUTION.

Fed., The (USA) Common abbreviation for the FEDERAL RESERVE SYSTEM.

Federal Reserve System (1914). (USA) System comprising a Federal Reserve Board and central banks in each of 12 districts, which controls and co-ordinates banking operations and policy throughout the country.

Federal States, The Northern states which fought the Confederates in the AMERICAN CIVIL WAR.

Feis Ceoil (1897). Competitive festival of traditional Irish music and folk dance held in Dublin and elsewhere in the Republic and in Northern Ireland; it resembles a Welsh Eisteddfod. Usually referred to as 'the Feis'. (Erse, 'festival of music'; see next entry.)

Feis of Tara (700 BC to AD 560). Assembly of the High Kings of Ireland, princes, priests and bards which met on TARA HILL every 3 years; after its political deliberations, it turned to festivity. (Erse, 'festival'; pronounced faysh.)

Felix Holt (1866). George Eliot's novel in which Felix, the radical hero, is the rival of Harold Transome in both love and politics.

Felix the Cat Cat with far more than 9 lives in Pat Sullivan's animated cartoon film series of the 1920s, who miraculously survived every kind of disaster and 'kept on walking'.

Fellow traveller Non-Communist who has sympathy with Communism.

Feltmakers, Worshipful Company of (1604). LIVERY COMPANY, originally a guild of hat and cap makers.

Fémina–Vie Heureuse **prize** (1904). Literary prize for the best work of imagination in French, founded by a group of French women writers and named after 2 French periodicals; also called the *Prix Fémina*.

Fenians (1860s). Members of a secret anti-British society formed in Ireland and the USA after the Potato Famine, pledged to expel the British and found a republic; their activities were confined to random dynamite outrages and the Phoenix Park murders. (Old Irish *Fene*, 'the Irish'; see FINN.)

Fenner's (1846). Cambridge University athletic ground until 1960, when it was superseded by a ground at Milton Road.

Ferdinand the Bull Bull created by Munro Leaf in a book for children, and popularized in a Walt Disney animated cartoon film (1939). Ferdinand loved to lie in the shade of a tree smelling the flowers, and did not care for bullfighting at all.

Fernet Branca An Italian bitters, drunk like CAMPARI.

Ferney, Château de Lakeside estate where Voltaire spent his last 30 years, near Geneva but in France (from which, officially, he was exiled); he could thus hop over the border should Louis XV try to arrest him.

Ferranti Electronics firm with headquarters in Manchester; it made the first commercial computer in Europe, and also makes missile guidance and control equipment.

Ferrari (1946). Italian car firm near Modena which specialized in sports and racing cars from 1947.

Fertile Crescent Name given to the fertile lands north of the deserts of Arabia, stretching from the Mediterranean (Syria and Palestine) to the Persian Gulf (Mesopotamia), settled from *c*. 9000 BC, united politically until the 2nd century BC and forming an economic unit which ever since has been divided politically; it now consists of Syria, Lebanon, Israel, Jordan and Iraq.

Feste Clown in Shakespeare's *Twelfth Night*; his song 'O mistress mine! where are you roaming?' is particularly remembered.

Festival Gardens Pleasure garden and Fun Fair established in Battersea Park, representing the lighter side of life at the FESTIVAL OF BRITAIN, and now a permanent feature of London.

Festival of Britain (1951–2). Imaginative and successful commemoration of the centenary of the Great Exhibition, centred on the South Bank site around Waterloo Bridge, London, where the ROYAL FESTIVAL HALL was built, and linked with exhibitions and festivals of music elsewhere in the country. At once a demonstration of British achievements in the previous 100 years, and a celebration of emergence from post-war austerities.

FHB For Family Hold Back, a traditional nursery warning to the children not to eat up all the best things before their guests have had a fair chance.

Fianna Fáil Middle party formed in Ireland by De Valera (1923) when he turned from armed to political opposition to the FREE STATERS; it first formed a government in 1932. (Erse, 'soldiers of destiny'; see FINN; pronounced fee′an-a foil.)

Fiat (1906). Italian motor manufacturers, with headquarters at Turin, who also make aircraft, steel, engineering equipment, etc.

Fidelio (1805). Beethoven's only opera, in which LEONORA, disguised as a youth called Fidelio, saves her husband Florestan from murder at the hands of the political rival who has imprisoned him.

Fidgety Phil See STRUWWELPETER.

Field of the Cloth of Gold (1520). Meeting near Calais at which the King of France, Francis I, unsuccessfully tried to get Henry VIII and Cardinal Wolsey to desert the Holy League (the Empire, Spain and the Papacy) and come to his aid. (From the magnificence of the pageantry provided.)

FIFA Governing body of international football. (Initials of the French title: Fédération Internationale de Football Association.)

Fifteen, The JACOBITE rebellion of 1715 led by

the OLD PRETENDER and the Earl of Mar in Scotland and northern England; after an inconclusive battle at Sheriffmuir, north of Stirling, Scotland, it eventually failed.

'15' certificate (1982). Granted by the British Board of Film Classification to films passed only for persons of 15 years and over.

5th Amendment (1791). Amendment to the US Constitution which enacted, *inter alia*, that no person should be compelled in a criminal case to be a witness against himself. It has been pleaded in self-defence by capitalists and Communists alike.

Fifth Avenue New York street, famous for luxury shops.

Fifth Commandment 'Honour thy father and thy mother' (Exod 20:12). To Roman Catholics this is the Fourth Commandment.

Fifth Estate Trade unions: see FOURTH ESTATE.

Fifth Monarchy men (1657–61). Fanatical English Puritans who decided that Christ was about to return and that they must therefore sever all allegiance to Cromwell, and later to the restored Charles II. (A reference to the fifth kingdom prophesied in Daniel 2:44, read with verse 40.)

Fifth Republic Period of French history from the time of de Gaulle's return to power in 1958.

Figaro Scheming barber, later valet, of Count Almaviva, in Beaumarchais's plays *The Barber of Seville* (1775) and *The Marriage of Figaro* (1784), and of Mozart's *Figaro*, Rossini's *Barber of Seville* and other operas. It says much for his skill in intrigue that he is able to outwit everyone, even his master.

Figaro, Le (1826). Right-wing Paris daily newspaper.

Fighting Téméraire, The (1839). One of J. M. W. Turner's masterpieces, now in the Clore Gallery at the TATE. It represents the veteran of Trafalgar being towed into port to be broken up. It commemorates the transition from sail to steam.

'Final Solution, The' Extermination of Jews, decreed by Hitler in April 1941. The term does not cover Hitler's extermination of millions of Slavs and half a million gypsies.

Financial Times (1888). London's financial daily, with a wide coverage of non-financial subjects (especially the arts).

Finchley Former Middlesex borough, since 1965 part of the borough of BARNET.

Fine Champagne Blend of COGNACS, usually of a single year, from the two best districts (named Grande Champagne and Petite Champagne; no connection with the wine of that name).

Fine Gael (1933). Irish political party founded by W. J. Cosgrave when De Valera was elected President, in opposition to the latter's FIANNA FÁIL. From 1948 to 1957 it formed a coalition government with MacBride's Clan na Poblachta, under a new leader, Costello, who declared a republic to forestall De Valera. (Erse, 'United Ireland'; pronounced fin'i gayl.)

Fingal See FINN.

Fingal's Cave (1) Large cave on the Isle of Staffa, in the Inner Hebrides of Scotland (see FINN). (2) Name given to Mendelssohn's *Hebridean Overture*, which was inspired by a Scottish tour.

Fings Ain't Wot They Used t'be (1961). Musical play about Soho produced by the THEATRE WORKSHOP from an outline by Frank Norman.

Finlandia (1901). Sibelius's symphonic poem, inspired by the natural beauties of his native land.

Finn (1) Chief hero of southern Irish legend (also called Fionn mac Cumhail), supposed to have lived in the 3rd century AD and to be the father of OSSIAN. He was leader of the Fianna, an army of muscular heroes whose name reappears in later history (see FENIANS; FIANNA FÁIL). In the OSSIANIC POEMS he becomes a Scotsman named Fingal. (2) An international class of centre-board dinghies designed for single-handed sailing, 14 feet 9 inches in length, with a large single sail on a flexible unstayed mast. There is a Gold Cup championship.

Finnegans Wake (1939). James Joyce's last novel, which carries to extremes the tendencies mentioned under ULYSSES. It takes the form of the dreams of a Dublin publican, H. C. Earwicker, representing Everyman, and his wife Anna Livia Plurabelle. Many books have had to be written to explain what it is all about; the main theme is said to be the recurring cycles of world history.

Finno-Ugrian languages One of the 2 main divisions of the URAL-ALTAIC LANGUAGES; it includes Finnish, MAGYAR, Lapp (Sami) and Estonian.

Fino One of the 2 main types of sherry (see OLOROSO), very dry and pale, drunk as an aperitif; includes AMONTILLADO and MANZANILLA.

Finsbury Former London metropolitan borough, since 1965 part of the borough of ISLINGTON.

Fir Bolg Legendary, perhaps Iberian, settlers in Ireland, driven later into the Western Isles of Scotland by CUCHULAIN and the TUATHA DÉ DANANN. In Irish legend they are said to have come from Greece via Norway.

Firebird, The (1910). First of Stravinsky's ballet scores written for Diaghilev, a fairy-tale based on Russian folk-stories choreographed by Fokine.

Firefly (1946). National one-design class of 12-foot dinghy, with moulded plywood hull and metal mast; designed by Uffa Fox, built only at Hamble, Hampshire, and raced in most parts of England.

Fireside Chats Name given to a series of informal radio talks to the nation, instituted by President Roosevelt on 12 April 1933, only 8 days after his inauguration, and continued during the critical period of the New Deal.

Fireworks Music (1749). Handel's 'Musick for the Royal Fireworks' written for a London celebration in Green Park of the Treaty of Aix (see AUSTRIAN SUCCESSION, WAR OF); the fireworks failed, but the music was a success.

First Aid Nursing Yeomanry (1907). FANYs, the élite of the women's corps, which provided amateur nursing, ambulance driving and other services in wartime, as well as being a source of recruitment for SOE. Now officially called the Women's Transport Service, but still better known as the FANYs.

First Coalition (1793–7). Alliance of Britain, Spain, Austria, Holland, Italian and German states, which drove the French out of the Netherlands but then began to disintegrate until finally Britain found itself fighting the Spanish and Dutch (CAPE ST VINCENT and CAMPERDOWN).

First Commandment 'Thou shalt have no other gods before me' (Exod. 20:3). Jews regard this as part of the Second Commandment.

First Consul (Napoleon). See CONSULATE.

First Empire (1804–15). See EMPIRE, THE.

First Gentleman of Europe Nickname for George IV.

First International (1864–76). Earliest attempt, sponsored by Karl Marx, to form a world organization of the working-classes.

First Lady, The Wife of the President of the US.

First Lord of the Admiralty (1673). Formerly the parliamentary chief of the Royal Navy, since 1964 styled Minister of Defence for the Royal Navy.

First Men in the Moon, The (1901). One of H. G. Wells's earliest novels, in the category now called science fiction.

First Reading (Parliament). Formal introduction of a Bill to the House, which does not debate it until the SECOND READING.

First Republic (1792–1804). Republic declared during the French Revolution and succeeded by the First Empire of Napoleon.

First Sea Lord Professional head of the Royal Navy, a post combined with that of Chief of the Naval Staff.

First State Nickname for Delaware as having been the first state to join the Union (1787).

Fisher Act

Fisher Act (1918). Education Act which provided for abolition of elementary school fees, compulsory attendance to age 14, nursery schools, special schools, and medical inspection; implementation was delayed by the war (H. A. L. Fisher, President of the Board of Education, and historian.)

Fisherman's Ring Signet ring placed on the Pope's finger at his election and broken up at his death. It bears the device of St Peter in a boat hauling in a fishing net.

Fisher sea area That lying between the Skagerrak and the Dogger sea area.

Fishmongers, Worshipful Company of (1363). LIVERY COMPANY with a fine hall, restored after wartime damage; it still has statutory duties in preventing the sale of fish under size or in a close season, and of unwholesome shellfish. It devotes large sums to charity and education.

Fitzbillies Colloquial abbreviation for Fitzwilliam College (formerly House), Cambridge.

Fitzwilliam Museum (1837). Important Cambridge museum of pictures, antiquities, and medieval and Renaissance exhibits, together with a library; it was enlarged by a Courtauld bequest. (Founded by the 1st Viscount Fitzwilliam.)

Five Members, The (1642). Pym (see GRAND REMONSTRANCE), HAMPDEN and 3 other MPs; Charles I went in person to the Commons 'to pull them out by the ears', but they had fled.

Five Mile Act (1665). See CLARENDON CODE.

Five-O-Five An international class of sailing boat, length 16 feet 6 inches. (For 5·05 metres = 16′ 6″ approx.)

Five Pillars of Islam Essential obligations of the true believer, given in the Koran as: belief in one God; prayer 5 times daily facing Mecca; the giving of alms; keeping the RAMADAN fast; pilgrimage to Mecca at least once in a lifetime.

Five-star General General of the army, the highest rank in the US army. (From the insignia worn.)

Five Towns Arnold Bennett's name for the (six) Potteries towns of Burslem, Hanley, Stoke-on-Trent, Longton, Fenton and Tunstall – all now merged (1910) in the borough of Stoke-on-Trent. He used the term in his novel *Anna of the Five Towns* (1902) and elsewhere.

Flamboyant architecture (15th–16th centuries). Last period of French GOTHIC ARCHITECTURE, corresponding to English PERPENDICULAR. It is marked by elaborate flame-like tracery in the windows and other features, as in Rouen Cathedral. (French 'flaming'.)

Flaminian Way (3rd century BC). The road from Rome to Rimini over the Apennines.

Flamsteed numbers Used to identify stars in a constellation; they increase from west to east and have largely superseded the BAYER LETTER system. (John Flamsteed, first Astronomer Royal.)

Flanders Name officially given only to 2 southwestern Belgian provinces (East Flanders, capital Ghent; West, capital Bruges); unofficially, the area where FLEMISH is spoken and Flemish architecture predominates; i.e. the Scheldt delta of Holland, most of north and west Belgium, and the adjoining Nord department of France. Brussels, Antwerp, Bruges, Ghent, Louvain and Tournai were the major towns of Flanders.

Flash Gordon (1936). Comic-strip character, well drawn by Alex Raymond and (from 1956) by John Prentice. He takes on all comers from Outer Space.

Flashman Cad in TOM BROWN'S SCHOOLDAYS, whose further career as Major-General Sir Harold Flashman, VC, was satirically sketched by George MacDonald Fraser in *Flashman* (1969), *Royal Flash* (1970) etc etc.

Flat-Earther Person whose views are so out of date or so untenable as not to merit rebuttal. Though Pythagoras suggested that the earth is round it was not until Magellan's expedition sailed round it (1519–22) that the idea began to gain general acceptance.

Flatford Mill Mill near East Bergholt, between Ipswich and Colchester, which figures in many of the paintings of John Constable, whose father owned it.

Flatiron Building (1902). New York's first sky-scraper, 20 storeys high, between Broadway, Fifth Avenue and 23rd Street. (Named for its odd shape.)

Flavian Emperors (AD 69–96). Emperors of Rome, Vespasian, Titus, and Domitian, all members of the Flavian family (*gens*).

Fléada Ceoil In Ireland, a festival of traditional music and dance, held each June at Thurles, Co. Tipperary; See FEIS CEOIL.

Flea Market Vast street markets on the northern outskirts of Paris between the Portes de Clignancourt and St-Ouen, where ready-made clothes, antiques and junk are sold from Saturday to Monday each week. (French, Marché aux puces.)

Fledermaus, Die (1874). Johann Strauss's pearl of comic operettas, set in an 18th-century European spa. It is loved for its delightful music rather than for the complicated plot, in which all is misrepresentation, misunderstanding and mischief. (German, 'the bat'.)

Fleet, The Former prison in Farringdon Street, London, dating back to Norman times; it became notorious as a debtors' prison and is often mentioned in Dickens's novels, etc. (See FLEET STREET, below.) etc.

Fleet Air Arm See RNAS.

Fleet Street Former world of London journalism, a short street running from the Strand to Ludgate Circus; associated with printing since Caxton's day. (Named from the River Fleet, which still flows through the sewers there, into the Thames.)

Fleming Report (1944). Report on public schools which recommended the reservation of 25% of the places in them for boys paying no or reduced fees, at the expense of the local education authorities; the response of parents was largely negative. (Lord Fleming.)

Flemings Flemish-speaking inhabitants of FLANDERS. They are less industrialized than

the WALLOONS, whom they are beginning to outnumber and dominate, and more loyal to the monarchy and to the Roman Catholic Church.

Flemish Dutch dialect spoken by the Flemings of FLANDERS; compare WALLOON.

Flemish School, The (1) Early School, which first perfected oil painting and, working in the 14th–16th centuries mainly at Bruges, painted religious pictures; the great names were the Van Eycks, Memlinc and Van der Weyden. (2) Unclassifiable painters of fantasies, Bosch and the Brueghels. (3) Seventeenth-century portrait painters of Antwerp (Rubens and Van Dyck), together with Teniers and others.

Fletchers, Worshipful Company of LIVERY COMPANY which has no charter of incorporation; originally a guild of arrowmakers.

Fleur (Forsyte). See MODERN COMEDY, A.

Fleurs du mal, Les (1857). Collection of poems by Charles Baudelaire, regarded by many critics and later poets as the greatest poet of the 19th century.

Flibbertigibbet (1) The foul fiend, Shakespeare's *King Lear*. (2) Light, frivolous, gossiping person.

Flight & Barr (1783–1840). Second period in the history of the WORCESTER PORCELAIN factory, during which it traded under this and similar names. It produced some very good wares, especially up to about 1800 when bone china was introduced. It amalgamated with the CHAMBERLAIN WORCESTER firm.

Floating voter Elector without permanent party allegiance.

Flodden (1513). Battle in which the English decisively defeated a Scottish army under James IV, Henry VIII's brother-in-law (who was killed), when they invaded Northumberland to help their French allies. France was under attack from the Holy League, to which England belonged. (Village near the Scots border.)

Florentine (Cooking) With spinach and mornay sauce.

Florizel (1) Character in Shakespeare's *A Winter's Tale*. (2) Nickname of the Prince Regent, see PERDITA AND FLORIZEL. (3) Prince Florizel, the chief character in R. L. Stevenson's *New Arabian Nights*.

Flowering Cherry (1958). Robert Bolt's tragicomedy of a man who spent his life dreaming about retirement to a country cottage; when the time came he did not want to go.

Flower People (1964). Proto-HIPPIES movement in HAIGHT-ASHBURY, San Francisco, led by those who had gone through the LSD experience, and referring to their use of flower motifs to symbolize the non-violence of their protest against materialism and governmental policies. Their slogan was 'Make love, not war'.

'Flowers of the Forest, The' Scottish lament for those who fell at FLODDEN; two 18th-century ballads have been set to it, with the refrain: 'The flowers of the forest are withered away.'

Fluellen The hot-tempered Welsh captain of Shakespeare's *Henry V*.

Flush Name of Elizabeth Barrett Browning's dog, which she took with her to Italy on her marriage; see *The* BARRETTS OF WIMPOLE STREET.

Flushing Meadow (USA) Headquarters of West Side Tennis Club since 1978; at Forest Hills 1923–78. Private club which stages the US Open (the American championship) by arrangement with the US Lawn Tennis Association.

Flying Dutchman International class of 2-man sailing boat, length 19 feet 10 inches, designed by a Dutchman.

Flying Dutchman, The Legendary ghost ship whose captain is doomed to haunt the seas south of the Cape of Good Hope eternally; she brings bad luck to all who sight her. In Wagner's opera (*Der fliegende Holländer*, 1843) her captain is freed from the curse laid on him when he finds a woman willing to sacrifice herself for him.

Flying Fortress (1935). BOEING B-17, a heavily armed US bomber used in raids on Germany from August 1942 onwards.

Flying Fox Duke of Westminster's horse which in 1899 won the 2000 Guineas, Derby and St Leger.

Flying Officer X Pen-name adopted by the novelist H. E. Bates when writing stories based on his experiences in the RAF during World War II.

Flying Saucers Name given in about 1947 to objects seen in the sky which some hoped were reconnaissance craft from outer space. Typically they are reported as round, illuminated, silent and flying erratically at high speed. Dignified with the official name of UFOs (Unidentified Flying Objects), they have usually been shown by expert investigation to be meteorological balloons or optical illusions, but some remain unexplained.

Flying Scotsman See LNER.

Flying Tigers Small air force manned by American volunteers, formed (August 1941) in Kunming to fight for China against Japan; the nucleus of an air task force established in China after USA entered the war.

Flymo Proprietary name for a hover mower for cutting lawns (flying mower).

Foch Professor Holder of the chair of French at Oxford.

Fogg, Phileas Hero of Jules Verne's *Round the World in 80 Days*, who performed this feat for a bet made in the Reform Club.

Foggy Bottom (USA) Former slum area of Washington, DC; now the site of the CIA headquarters and some offices of the State Department.

Föhn Warm dry south wind from the Alps, which may raise temperatures by 20°F in a few hours. In spring it causes avalanches and uncovers mountain pastures; in autumn it ripens grapes. (Pronounced férn.)

Fokker First aircraft to have a machine-gun firing through the propeller, which gave the German air force temporary ascendancy on the Western Front in 1915; name also given to other aircraft designed by Anton Fokker, Dutch-born naturalized German.

Folies-Bergères Paris music-hall famous for its opportunities for anatomical research, as also for its spectacular costume displays.

Folkboat BERMUDIAN 24-foot sloop designed by a group of Scandinavians as a people's cruiser, since become internationally popular; 5 tons (TM).

Folketing Danish Diet or Parliament.

F-111 (1968). US swing-wing (VG) fighter/bomber/reconnaissance aircraft, speed 1,600 m.p.h., range 2,000 miles; built by General Dynamics.

'Fonthill' Beckford William Beckford, author of VATHEK, so nicknamed for the extravagant fantasy he built – Fonthill 'Abbey' – at Fonthill Gifford, near Shaftesbury, Wiltshire, with a 260-foot tower which collapsed and destroyed the building.

Fontwell Park Racecourse 4 miles north of Bognor Regis.

Football League (1888). English League of 92 football clubs (in 4 divisions); it controls the principal professional matches, promotion, relegation, transfers, etc., and co-operates with the FA, which organizes an FA League Cup knockout competition (1960).

Footlights Club (1855). Cambridge University amateur dramatic society, which stages an annual revue.

Footsie Acronym derived from the initials FT–SE – Financial Times–Stock Exchange – 100 share index.

Forbidden City, The Lhasa, capital of Tibet, which foreigners were long forbidden to enter.

Ford Foundation (1936). Formed by Henry Ford I and his son Edsel, this fund is chiefly devoted to educational schemes and to technical assistance programmes in developing countries.

Ford Motor Co. (USA). One of the world's largest manufacturers of consumer goods, with headquarters at Dearborn, Michigan. It was built up on the basis of the MODEL T car, the Ford V8 (1932) and models designed for particular countries.

Ford Motors (UK). Financially the largest motor and tractor manufacturers in Britain, wholly owned by the US parent company; headquarters Dagenham, Essex. It became important with the marketing in 1932 of the first Ford Popular, designed specially for the British market.

Ford's Peace Ship (1915). Ship which sailed to Europe from USA with the pacifist car-manufacturer, Henry Ford, and a mission of like-minded Americans in an effort to end World War I by negotiation.

Ford's Theatre The scene of the LINCOLN ASSASSINATION in Washington, DC.

Fore and Aft Nickname of the Gloucestershire Regiment because of the second badge worn at the back of the cap.

Foreign Legion (1831). French regiment formerly stationed in North Africa and recruited from foreigners, who were not required to reveal their identity, serving under French officers. It was disbanded (1940–45) but re-formed, and took part in the Algerian crisis. It is now stationed in Corsica and near Marseille.

Foresters, Ancient Order of (1834). Large friendly society with lodges, called 'courts', in the UK and USA.

Forest Hills See Flushing Meadow.

Forestry Commission Body set up by Parliament; its programme is to double the forested area of Britain and to reafforest land felled and cleared during 2 world wars; it also gives grants to private landowners engaged in reafforestation. The Commission is the second largest landowner in Britain.

Forever Amber (1944). Long novel by the American Kathleen Winsor about a Restoration beauty whose amours raised it to best-selling status.

Forfarshire Scottish county now called Angus.

Former Naval Person Wartime code name used for himself by Winston Churchill in messages to President Roosevelt. (Reference to his having been First Lord of the Admiralty.)

Formosa European name for Taiwan, the Chinese island where Chiang Kai-shek set up a non-Communist republic in 1950.

Formula 1 cars Cars which compete in GRAND PRIX RACES. The formula (specification) is often changed in order to keep ever rising speeds within reasonably safe limits.

Formula 2 cars Class of racing car less costly than Formula 1 cars but like them raced by professional drivers in what are in effect prestige competitions between manufacturers. In 1957 a 'Junior' formula was introduced.

Formula 3 cars Comparatively inexpensive single-seater cars with production engines of limited capacity, raced by amateurs.

Forsyte Saga, The (1922). John Galsworthy's trilogy of novels, *The Man of Property* (1906), *In Chancery* (1920) and *To Let* (1921). Soames Forsyte is a stern Victorian lawyer with a strong sense of property, in which category he includes his wife Irene, whom he divorces and who marries YOUNG JOLYON. See also *A* MODERN COMEDY.

Forsythia Deciduous shrubs named after William Forsyth (1737–1805).

Fort Belvedere Prince of Wales's home near Sunningdale, Berkshire from 1929 until his abdication, as Edward VIII, in 1936.

Fort Hare (1916). Oldest black university college in South Africa, now the University College for the XHOSA group, TRANSKEI.

Forties (1970). Oilfield in the North Sea and the first to pipe oil into the UK, to the Grangemouth refinery on the Forth.

Forties sea area That lying between the Cromarty and Forth sea areas and the south-west tip of Norway, south of VIKING SEA AREA.

Fort Knox (1936). US Army camp where lie bomb-proof vaults containing US gold reserve. Ian Fleming's GOLDFINGER had an elaborate plan to raid it, foiled, of course, by James Bond. (Thirty-five miles south of Louisville, Kentucky.)

Fortnums Abbreviated name for London's leading grocers, Fortnum & Mason of Piccadilly.

Fortran Formula Translation, a high-level program language used for mathematical, scientific and engineering data processing.

Fort Sumter (12 April 1861). First incident of the AMERICAN CIVIL WAR, when Confederate troops fired on a Union garrison at Fort Sumter, South Carolina.

Fortunate Isles In Greek legend the Isles of the Blest beyond the Pillars of Hercules, another form of ELYSIUM; later the name was given to the Canaries and Madeira.

Fortunatus's purse Inexhaustible purse given by the goddess of Fortune to the hero of a medieval German legend; the gift proved the ruin of Fortunatus and his sons.

Fortune (1930). Influential business and financial monthly published by TIME Inc., aimed at an affluent readership, e.g. executives in multinational corporations, and noted for its annual lists of leading firms in USA (*Fortune 500*, May) and elsewhere (August).

Fortunes of Nigel, The (1822). Walter Scott's historical novel of young Nigel's efforts to recover money owed him by James I, in the face of the machinations of the Court and particularly of the villain, Lord Dalgarno.

Fortunes of Richard Mahoney, The (1930). Trilogy of novels by an Australian woman who used the pen-name Henry Handel Richardson, which give a brilliant picture of Ballarat, Victoria, during the gold rush of the 1850s. (Pronounced mah'ĕn-i.)

48, The Common name for Johann Sebastian Bach's 2 books of preludes and fugues for the clavier (now usually played on the piano); each book contains 12 in each major, and 12 in each minor key. See WELL-TEMPERED CLAVIER.

Forty-Five, The JACOBITE rebellion of 1745 in which the YOUNG PRETENDER, after a victory at Prestonpans near Edinburgh, led a Scottish invasion of England which reached Derby, but was defeated at CULLODEN by the BLOODY BUTCHER.

Forty-Niners Participants in the Californian gold rush of 1849, celebrated in the song 'O My Darling Clementine'.

49th Parallel Boundary between USA and Canada from the Pacific coast to a point south of Winnipeg.

'Forty Years On' Harrow's rousing school song, written by E. E. Bowen (died 1901), and beginning: 'Forty years on, when afar and asunder, / Parted are those who are singing today.'

For Whom the Bell Tolls (1939). Ernest Hemingway's novel of the Spanish Civil War, in which he took part as a war correspondent. It tells of the blowing up of a vital bridge by guerrillas, and echoes the accounts of members of the INTERNATIONAL BRIGADE in stressing the untrustworthiness of the Republicans, ever ready to subordinate military necessities to sordid internecine political squabbles. (Title from John Donne's 'Any man's death diminishes me . . . therefore never send to know for whom the bell tolls; it tolls for thee'.)

Fosco, Count Character in Wilkie Collins's WOMAN IN WHITE.

Fosse Way Roman road from Lincoln via Newark, Leicester, Moreton, Stow, Cirencester, Bath, Ilchester, Axminster and then possibly down to the coast at Mudbury or on to Exeter and Totnes.

Fotheringhay Castle Castle built by William I at a village in Northamptonshire near Peterborough, where Mary Queen of Scots was executed. Only a mound and a moat remain to mark the site.

Fouchet plan (1961). Plan for the first step towards the political unification of Europe, consisting of a high council and periodical meetings of heads of states.

Fougasse Pseudonym of Kenneth Bird, humorous artist and editor of *Punch*, who achieved fame during World War II for his posters warning against 'careless talk'. (French *fougasse*, a species of small landmine.)

Foulerton Professorship Royal Society professorship for independent research in medicine.

Founders, Worshipful Company of (1614). LIVERY COMPANY, originally a guild of those casting articles of brass and copper.

Foundling Hospital, London (1739). Institution for deserted children opened in Brunswick Square, Bloomsbury, but moved to Berkhamsted in 1929 as the Thomas Coram Foundation for Children; the site of the old building now houses an art gallery.

Fountains Abbey (1132). Ruined abbey near Ripon, Yorkshire, formerly the largest in northern England, a Cistercian foundation in a beautiful setting; the ruins today are roofless but extensive.

Four Courts, The (1796). Dublin's central courts of justice, blown up in June 1922 during the TROUBLES but restored from the original designs.

Four Feathers, The (1902). A. E. W. Mason's novel of the Sudan War, in which a man accused of cowardice vindicates himself.

Four Freedoms, The (1944). Proclaimed by President Roosevelt during World War II; they are: freedom from fear and want, freedom of religion and speech.

Four Horsemen of the Apocalypse Conquest, Slaughter, Famine, Death, who symbolize the horrors of war in Revelation 6:2–8.

Four Horsemen of the Apocalypse, The (1916). Blasco-Ibáñez's novel on World War I, from which a famous film was made (1921), starring Rudolf Valentino.

Four Hundred, The (USA). Expression used of the leading members of New York (later, US) society. (From a remark by the 'socialite', Ward McAllister, in the 1890s that there were only 400 people who really counted.)

Four Just Men, The (1906). Edgar Wallace's first novel, about a group of men who take it upon themselves to rid the world of various undesirables.

Four Last Things Theological term for death, judgement, heaven and hell. The doctrine of these is called eschatology.

4 May Movement (1919). Chinese student revolt led by Westernized left-wing intellectuals; regarded as marking the final rejection of traditional Chinese ways and beliefs.

Fourment, Hélène Rubens's second wife, whom he married in 1630 when she was 16, and of whom he painted many portraits.

Four Square Gospel (1915). Fundamentalist sect founded at Belfast by George Jeffreys, now part of the Elim Four Square Gospel Alliance. They believe in healing by anointment with holy oil, total immersion at baptism, and the Second Coming.

Fourteen Points (January 1918). President Wilson's formulation of the bases for a peace settlement with Germany. They included (omitting various qualifications): freedom of the seas, free trade, disarmament, respect for the interests of colonial peoples, aid to Communist Russia, Polish independence, self-determination for the peoples of the Turkish and Austro-Hungarian empires, restoration of Alsace-Lorraine, and an end to secret diplomacy.

14th Amendment (1868). The amendment of the US Constitution which enacted, *inter alia*, that no state shall make or enforce any law that shall abridge the privileges or immunities of citizens, nor deny to any person the equal protection of the law. Often quoted in disputes about racial segregation.

Fourteenth of July, The (France). Bastille Day, see BASTILLE, STORMING OF THE. (French *Quatorze juillet*.)

Fourth Commandment 'Remember the Sabbath' (Exod. 20:8–11). To Roman Catholics this is the Third Commandment.

Fourth Estate The Press; a phrase attributed to Burke (and later used by Macaulay) and applied originally to the Reporters' Gallery in the House of Commons, said to be more important than the 3 other Estates (see THIRD ESTATE).

Fourth of July; The Fourth US holiday commemorating the adoption of the Declaration of Independence; also called Independence Day.

Fourth of June; The Fourth Speech Day at Eton, celebrated by the procession of boats, cricket matches, etc. (Birthday of George III.)

Fourth Republic (1946–58). The period of French history from the resignation of de Gaulle as provisional head of the government until he was recalled to deal with the Algerian crisis. The constitution differed little from that of the THIRD REPUBLIC, and the constantly changing governments were quite as ineffectual.

Four Winds of Love, The (1937–45). Ambitious 8-volume novel by Compton Mackenzie.

Fowler Short title for Fowler's *Modern English Usage*.

Fox and Goose Inn name which used to indicate that the old game of Fox and Geese could be played there.

Foxe's Martyrs (1559). Common title of John Foxe's *History of the Acts and Monuments of the Church*, which gave an inaccurate and highly coloured account of the MARIAN PERSECUTION.

Foxhunter Famous show-jumper owned by Lt-Col. Llewellyn, which won the King George V Cup 3 times. His jumping career ended in 1956 and he died 3 years later.

Foyle's Literary Luncheons (1930). Form of entertainment invented by Christina Foyle as a girl, when working in her father's bookshop (W. & G. Foyle Ltd, founded 1903, in the Charing Cross Road); guests of honour have ranged from GBS and the Emperor Haile Selassie to the Beatles.

Fra Diavolo Nickname of an 18th-century Italian brigand who led a revolt against French rule in Naples, and was shot in 1806. He is the hero of Auber's comic opera (1830) of that name. (Italian, 'brother Devil'.)

Fra Lippo Lippi (1855). One of Robert Browning's dramatic monologues in which the painter-monk of the title (a historical character of 15th-century Florence) explains why he finds it necessary to break out of his monastery for a spree from time to time.

Fram (1893). Nansen's ship, specially designed for his Arctic explorations.

Framework Knitters, Worshipful Company of (1657). LIVERY COMPANY, originally a guild of makers of woollen and knit-silk stockings; its membership is still largely confined to those interested in the hosiery industry.

Framley Parsonage (1861). One of Trollope's BARCHESTER NOVELS.

Francesca da Rimini See PAOLO AND FRANCESCA.

Franchise Affair, The See TEY, JOSEPHINE.

Franciscans (1209). Order of friars founded by St Francis of Assisi, vowed to chastity, poverty and service; also called Grey Friars.

Francophone Africa French-speaking Africa, i.e. states where French is still the administrative lingua franca, e.g. those formerly included in FRENCH WEST AFRICA, FRENCH EQUATORIAL AFRICA.

Franco-Prussian War (1870–71). War caused by Napoleon III's fear of the new North German Confederation, brought to a head by the publication of the EMS TELEGRAM. After the French defeat at SEDAN, Paris withstood a 4-month siege; the war ended with its surrender. France lost Alsace-Lorraine and again became a republic; the King of Prussia became Emperor of a united Germany.

Franglais English terms freely used (more often misused) in smarter French circles and in advertising, e.g.: *le standing* ('status'), *le coming-man*, *un crack* ('crack shot', hence an 'ace' in any field), *les pulls fully-fashioned* ('pullovers'), *très snob, presque cad* (the latter probably apocryphal).

Frank, Anne See DIARY OF ANNE FRANK.

Frankenstein (1818). GOTHIC NOVEL by Mary Shelley, wife of the poet, in which Frankenstein, a student, creates out of corpses a monster whom he galvanizes into life, and by whom he is destroyed; sometimes regarded as the first science-fiction tale.

Frankfurt City of Frankfurt am Main, in Germany. Noted for trade fairs since the 13th century and especially for the autumn book fair.

'Frankie and Johnny' American folksong, with the refrain: 'He was her man / But he done her wrong'.

Franklin Institute (1824). US institute in Philadelphia, Pennsylvania, founded for the study of the mechanical arts and applied science.

Franks Group of Germanic tribes which came to rule France under the MEROVINGIANS.

Franks report (1966). Report on Oxford University, which recommended increasing its size by a third, doubling the number of postgraduate places, increased attention to applied science and technology, diminution of college autonomy through the setting up of a Council of Colleges, and the institution of a single entrance examination. (Lord Franks, chairman.)

Fraud Squad (1946). A branch at Scotland Yard which investigates company frauds.

Fraunhofer lines Dark lines in the solar spectrum caused by the absorption of specific wavelengths of radiation from the sun's inner core by the various gases making up its outer atmosphere, the chemical composition of which can thus be analysed. (Pronounced frown'hoh-fèr.)

Fred Karno Epithet applied, in particular, to Army or Navy units which were unfamiliar and thus proper targets for ridicule, as in World War I song 'We are Fred Karno's army, / No earthly use are we' (sung to the tune 'The Church's one foundation'). (Karno, 1866–1941, an acrobat who became a millionaire impresario, introducing circus slapstick to the music-hall and launching Robey, Chaplin, Laurel, Flanagan, Will Hay, Max Miller on their careers; he died poor, running a Dorset off-licence.)

Free Church Federal Council (1940). Co-ordinating body formed by the Free (i.e. unestablished) Churches of England and Wales: Presbyterian, Methodist, Baptist and Congregational.

Freedom March (1966). March of black

demonstrators under James Meredith to encourage the blacks of Mississippi to overcome their apprehensions about what would happen to them if they exercised their right to register as voters.

Freedom Riders (USA). Black demonstrators testing the desegregation of interstate bus terminals, as in the ride to Montgomery, Alabama, in May 1961.

Freedom 7 Name of the space-craft in which the first American in space, Cmdr Shepard, made one orbit of the earth, 5 May 1961.

Freefone Telephone service for subscribers who undertake in advance to pay for all incoming calls; these are connected on a reverse-charge basis without questioning caller or called.

Free Foresters (1856). Large touring cricket club, the members of which were originally drawn from Midland counties. (The 'forest' was the Forest of Arden.)

Free French, The (1940). Followers of Gen. de Gaulle, who opposed the Vichy government. They formed the French Council of National Liberation (1943), which in 1944 was proclaimed the provisional government of France.

Freeman, Hardy and Willis Naval nickname for the 3 medals of World War I; equivalent of PIP, SQUEAK AND WILFRED. (Name of a chain of shoe-shops.)

Freemasons (1) English medieval journeymen stonemasons who used secret signs to ensure that unqualified workmen were not employed in masonry; later they began to admit outsiders. (2) Fraternal society developed from (1), especially in the use of craft terms, secret signs and a 'history' of the craft going back to Solomon's Temple; it started with a London Lodge (1717), spread over the country and acquired great wealth, which enabled it to provide schools and hospitals for its members' families; it also spread to the Continent where it developed on quite different lines as a political anti-clerical movement, condemned by the Roman Catholic Church.

Freesia South African plants of the iris family. (Elias Fries, Swedish botanist 1794–1878.)

Free State, The Nickname of Maryland.

Free Staters Irish followers of Michael Collins who were engaged in civil war with the Republican IRA under De Valera, from Partition (1921) until 1923 when the latter called for a cease-fire.

Free Trade Doctrine that international trade should be freed from restrictions such as import duties or quotas, export subsidies, etc. It was held by the MANCHESTER SCHOOL and the Liberal Party, and was adopted as British policy from 1860 to 1932. See EMPIRE FREE TRADE; PROTECTION.

Free Will In philosophy, the view that man has freedom of choice in his actions; it was held by Socrates, Plato, Aristotle, Locke, Hume, Leibniz, Kant, Rousseau, Fichte, Schopenhauer and Hegel, among many others. Pascal, brushing aside the pros and cons of DETERMINISM versus Free Will, was content with being intuitively certain that man is free. EXISTENTIALISTS insist on man's full responsibility for his actions.

Freikorps German ex-officers' organization, used by the Ebert Socialist government to suppress the Communist SPARTACISTS in 1919, creating lasting bitterness between the 2 left-wing parties.

Freischütz, Der (German legend) A man to whom the Devil gives 7 bullets guaranteed to find their mark, retaining control of one of them. In Weber's opera (1821) of that name, a forester uses them to win a shooting contest in order to gain a bride. The Devil tries to kill her with the last bullet, but it ricochets off her bridal wreath. (German, 'the free-shooter'.)

Fremontia Shrubs named after the explorer Colonel John Charles Frémont (1813–90).

French, Inspector Conscientious CID detective created by Freeman Wills Crofts in *The Cask* (1920).

French dressing Salad dressing of which the basic ingredients are olive oil, wine-vinegar, salt and pepper; sugar and mustard may be added.

French fries French fried potatoes (English,

'chips'), i.e. triangular or rectangular strips of potato fried until brown in deep fat.

French leave Departure without permission or warning. (From the 18th-century French habit of leaving a party without saying thank you to the hostess; yet the French dare to call it *filer à l'anglaise*.)

French Revolution (1789–95). Caused by Louis XVI's arbitrary inefficient rule, new political theories, the influence of the American Revolution, antagonism to a wealthy Church and peasant unrest under feudal conditions. Major events were: BASTILLE (July 1789); the SEPTEMBER MASSACRES (1792); Louis's execution (January 1793); the setting up of the National CONVENTION and the COMMITTEE OF PUBLIC SAFETY (1792–3); the year of TERROR (1793–4) which ended after Robespierre's assassination in the THERMIDOR *coup*. See REPUBLICAN CALENDAR.

French Revolutionary Wars (1792–1802). Originally defensive war against Austria and Prussia as supporters of royalist refugees; soon transformed by Danton into aggressive wars, leading after VALMY to the FIRST COALITION, CAMPO FORMIO, the Battles of the PYRAMIDS and NILE, and the SECOND COALITION; ended by the brief Peace of AMIENS and followed by the NAPOLEONIC WARS.

French window Glazed door, single or double, usually opening inward; it serves as door and window.

French without Tears (1936). Terence Rattigan's farce, which had a long run owing to the high quality of its humour, a memorable example being the laboured translation of 'ideas above his station' into 'des idées au-dessus de sa gare'.

Frenglish French words borrowed by the English, e.g. Son et Lumière, expertise, ambiance, farouche, chi-chi. (An analogy of FRANGLAIS.)

Frensham (1946). Floribunda rose with large clusters of deep crimson semi-double flowers.

Freshfields Leading London firm of solicitors.

Freudian psychology Earliest form of psychoanalytic theory; it emphasized the role of the libido (sexual instinct in a wide sense, including all the appetites) as a prime motive force. Freud introduced the idea of the unruly unconscious id which the conscious ego tries to adjust to the requirements of social life, and of the super-ego which acts as a censor of the mind. Other features were stress on the part played by sublimation (as when the sadist turns surgeon) and repression, and on diagnosis through analysis of a patient's dreams. (Sigmund Freud, Austrian psychologist, 1856–1939.)

Freudian slip Generally a verbal mistake made because of mental preoccupation, as a result of which the subject ruling the mind comes unwittingly to the tongue.

Frey; Freyr In Scandinavian mythology, brother of Freya and god of agriculture, peace and plenty.

Freya; Freyja Scandinavian Venus, sister of FREY, and one of Odin's wives. Friday is named after her.

Friar Tuck The fat and jovial chaplain to Robin Hood's band.

Frick Collection Outstanding collection of 14th–19th century paintings, bronzes and enamels bequeathed to New York City by Henry Clay Frick, an industrialist who died in 1919, and since added to. They are displayed, together with appropriate antique furniture, panelling, etc. in the rooms of a large house on East 70th Street.

Friendly Islands Capt. Cook's original name, still used, for the Tonga Islands.

Friend of the People Nickname of Jean Paul Marat (1743–93), French revolutionary who edited *L'Ami du peuple*.

Friends, Society of See QUAKERS.

Friends' House Headquarters of the Society of Friends (Quakers), opposite Euston Station, London.

Frigg; Frigga In Scandinavian mythology, the Mother of the Gods and one of Odin's wives.

Frisco Abbreviation for San Francisco of which, it is said, its citizens do not approve.

Frisian (Friesian) Widespread breed of large black-and-white dairy cattle, yielding large quantities of milk of low butterfat content.

Froebel Institute Training college for teachers at Roehampton, with branches elsewhere, which pioneered the 3-year course on lines now generally accepted (e.g. emphasis on active instead of passive learning). See next entry.

Froebel system Theory of education developed from the PESTALOZZI SYSTEM, with emphasis on social adjustment; it resulted in the institution of kindergarten schools for infants aged 4–6. (Friedrich Froebel, German educationist, 1782–1852; pronounced frėr′bėl.)

Frogs, The (405 BC). Aristophanes' comedy in which Dionysus, made into a figure of fun, feels that dramatic talent on earth is running short, and goes to Hades to fetch back Euripides. After hearing a contest between Euripides and Aeschylus, he takes the latter instead. The plot enables Aristophanes to parody Euripides' style unmercifully.

From Here to Eternity (1951). James Jones's long novel about US Army life. (Title from Kipling's: 'Gentleman-rankers out on the spree, / Damned from here to Eternity.')

Fronde, The (1648–52). Revolt against absolute monarchy in France, first by the Paris *parlement* and then by the nobles led by the Great CONDÉ and directed against Cardinal Mazarin during Louis XIV's minority. (French, 'sling', as stones were flung through the Cardinal's windows.)

Fructidor In the French Revolution calendar, the month from 18 August to 21 September ('Fruit-month'). See REPUBLICAN CALENDAR.

Fruiterers, Worshipful Company of (1605). LIVERY COMPANY which still fosters the development of the trade through co-operation with horticultural organizations.

FT Indices *Financial Times* Industrial Ordinary Index of the movements of 30 major shares, and the Actuaries' Index of some 500 industrial shares. See FOOTSIE.

Fuchsia Shrubs named after Leonard Fuchs (1501–66), a German botanist.

Fuchs spy case Trial of Klaus Fuchs, Communist German-born British subject, who confessed to handing to Russian agents the plans of the first atomic bomb; sentenced to 14 years' imprisonment (1950), released (1959), and went to East Germany. See OTTAWA SPY RING; ROSENBERG SPY CASE.

Fudge Family, The Newly rich family invented by the Irish poet, Thomas Moore (1779–1852) in *The Fudges in England* and *The Fudge Family in Paris*.

Fugger family German family of rich bankers who gained political power in the 16th century through their loans to kings and emperors. The *Fugger Newsletters* (translated 1924–6) are an important source for the history of the period.

Führer, Der Title taken by Hitler; compare DUCE; CAUDILLO. (German, 'the leader'.)

Fujiwara period (7th–11th centuries). In Japanese history, the period when the country was virtually ruled by the pleasure-loving Fujiwara family, who were eventually swept from power by more militaristic dynasties.

Fulani Nomadic cattle-owning people who roamed over much of West Africa, many of whom since the early 19th century have settled to agriculture and even to urban life, forming the ruling caste over much of northern Nigeria. When pure-blooded they are fair-skinned and fine-featured. Their origin and the classification of their language are disputed.

Fulbright Committee inquiry (1966). Televised inquiry into the Vietnam War and other aspects of US foreign policy conducted by Senator Fulbright, Chairman of the Senate Foreign Relations Committee, and a leading critic of his government's conduct of the war. (See next entry.)

Fulbright scholarships (1948). Founded under the Fulbright Act of 1946 which provided for the interchange of U S and foreign students and the sending abroad of U S professors and other teachers to give assistance both in under-developed and developed countries. (William Fulbright, the Senator from Arkansas.)

Fulham Former London metropolitan borough, since 1965 part of the borough of HAM-MERSMITH.

Fulham Palace Official residence of the Bishop of London, on the north bank of the Thames at Putney Bridge.

Fulton report (1968). Committee report on the Home Civil Service. Government accepted its recommendations: for the transfer of management and recruitment from the Treasury and Civil Service Commission to a new Civil Service department; for a college giving courses in administration to reduce the amateurism which it said marked the administrative class traditionally drawn from Oxbridge classical and history scholars; for a classless unified service to break down barriers between administrative and executive grades; for the appointment of officials in each ministry to plan long-term policy; and for more temporary secondments from local government, nationalized industries, private in-

dustry and commerce. (Lord Fulton, Chairman of the British Council.)

Fulton speech (1946). Churchill's speech at Fulton, Missouri, in which he called for a drawing together of English-speaking peoples in face of growing Soviet imperialism, and first publicly referred to the Iron Curtain.

Fu Manchu, Dr Sinister Chinese doctor of Sax Rohmer's novels (from 1913 on), who keeps a varied collection of poisonous animals at his Wimbledon home and a gang of thugs in Lime-house.

Fünf German spy in ITMA, who made threatening phone calls to Tommy Handley in a baleful Teutonic voice.

Funk & Wagnall (1894). Leading American dictionary, of which a Standard College edition was published in 1963. (Dr Funk produced the first.)

Funkia Herbaceous perennial named after H. Funk, a German botanist, now renamed HOSTA.

Furies, The See EUMENIDES.

G

Gadarene swine Herd of swine which 'ran violently down a steep place into the sea' and were drowned, after Jesus had given permission for a legion of devils from a madman to pass into them. This man was then seen 'sitting, and clothed, and in his right mind' (Mark 5:1–20). The apparent indifference to the animals' fate is sometimes explained by Jewish abhorrence of pigs. (Of Gadara, a Greek settlement in Palestine; hence the presence of pigs.)

Gads Hill Place Dickens's home, 1858–70, for the last years of his life, at Gadshill, near Rochester, Kent. (Gadshill was also the scene of Prince Hal's plot to rob some travellers, in Shakespeare's *Henry IV*, Part 1.)

Gaelic football Type of football said to have been played in Ireland before the days of St Patrick, now, in a tamer form with established rules, played in Ireland and wherever the Irish have settled abroad. The ball is round and the goal a combination of rugby and football goals; a team has 15 players, and substitutes are allowed.

Gaelic coffee Coffee laced with Irish whiskey.

Gaelic language Term applied up to the 18th century to the CELTIC LANGUAGES spoken in Ireland and Scotland, now usually restricted to the latter, the former being called Erse.

Gaels Celtic-speaking people who reached Ireland from France and Spain about 300 BC and subsequently colonized Scotland (see DAL-RIADA).

Gaiety girls Chorus girls at the London Gaiety Theatre in the Aldwych when it was under the management of George Edwardes in late Victorian and Edwardian times; they were famous for their beauty and their infiltration into the peerage.

Gainsborough hat Large very wide-brimmed hat such as the women who sat for Gainsborough's portraits often wore.

Galahad In Arthurian legend the son of LANCE-LOT; a knight whose chastity was rewarded by the sight of the HOLY GRAIL and a seat at the ROUND TABLE.

Galeries Lafayette Large Paris department store near the Opéra.

Galicia (1) Former Austrian province north of the Carpathians; it was returned to Poland after World War I, and the eastern half (including Lvov, formerly LEMBERG) was absorbed into Soviet Ukraine after World War II. The chief town in the Polish section is Kraków (Cracow). (2) Former kingdom of north-west Spain.

Galilean Man of Galilee, i.e. Jesus. The last words of the Roman emperor, Julian the Apostate (AD 363), 'Thou hast conquered, Galilean', were echoed by Swinburne in his attack on Victorian religiosity in *Hymn to Proserpine*: 'Thou hast conquered, O pale Galilean; the world has grown grey from Thy breath.'

Gallipoli campaign See DARDANELLES CAMPAIGN (Pronounced gal-ip′o-li.)

Gallo-Romans The Romanized inhabitants of France before the FRANKS came.

Galloway Polled breed of beef cattle, bred chiefly in Scotland: it has a thick coat of curly black or dun hair.

Gallup Poll (1935). Method of testing public opinion, e.g. in election forecasts, by tabulating answers to key questions put to a cross-section of a community. See BRITISH INSTITUTE OF PUBLIC OPINION. (Dr G. H. Gallup, founder of the American Institute of Public Opinion.)

Galway Blazers, The Famous Irish foxhunting pack dating from the beginning of the 19th century, with kennels at Craughwell, near Loughrea, Co. Galway.

Gamaliel Doctor of law and president of the Sanhedrim who had taught Saul (Paul) – 'brought up at the feet of Gamaliel' (Acts 22:3) – and who persuaded the Jews not to kill the Apostles (Acts 5:34–41). (Pronounced ga-mayI-yel.)

Gamblers Anonymous (1957). Organization analogous to ALCOHOLICS ANONYMOUS which spread from California to the big cities of USA, the UK, Australia, etc.

Gamesmanship (1947). Stephen Potter's study of the art of winning games without actually cheating. To take an example from golf: excessive praise of an opponent's straight left arm just before he drives off, and asking him to demonstrate how he does it, should ruin his play for the rest of the game, and perhaps for life. The author applied similar principles to social situations in LIFEMANSHIP and ONE UP-MANSHIP.)

Gammer Gurton's Needle (about 1560). Vigorous comedy in doggerel verse by an unknown author: the plot is of sublime simplicity – the search for the needle; when Hodge sits down he literally jumps to the conclusion that it is in the seat of his breeches. (Gammer for 'godmother-grandmother', i.e. an old woman.)

Gamp, Sairey Bibulous monthly nurse in Dickens's MARTIN CHUZZLEWIT, whose baggy umbrella gave the word 'gamp' to the language she mishandled on so stupendous a scale. See also Mrs HARRIS.

Gandhism Policy pursued in India by followers of Mahatma Gandhi, who preached Hindu–Muslim unity, abolition of caste, pacifism, equality of women, and humane ideals in politics, as well as the attainment of independence by the whole subcontinent, through non-cooperation, non-violence, and the boycotting of British imports combined with the revival of cottage industries (including hand-spinning).

G and S Colloquial abbreviation for GILBERT AND SULLIVAN OPERAS.

Ganymede (Greek legend). Beautiful Phrygian youth who took Zeus' fancy and was carried off to Olympus to act as cupbearer to the gods.

Garbage in, garbage out In computer language garbage is 'incorrect input', which naturally produces garbled or 'corrupt' output.

Gardeners, Worshipful Company of (1605). LIVERY COMPANY which finances horticultural education and encourages window-boxes in the City of London.

Gardenia Evergreen fragrant shrub named after Dr Alexander Garden, a US botanist.

Garden State Nickname of New Jersey.

Garden Suburb (Lloyd George's) Nickname given to the private staff of expert advisers created by Lloyd George on becoming Prime Minister in December 1916, so called because it was housed in huts in St James's Park.

Gargantua and Pantagruel (1532–64). Rabelais's great work in 5 books about 2 giants, father and son, Rabelais embroiders their adventures with riotous buffoonery, wild panegyrics on food and drink, bawdy humour, satire and philosophic wit all intermingled with long lists of incongruous objects and fantastic coined names. Sir Thomas Urquhart's translation (1653) is a work of art in its own right. (The names mean 'gullet' and 'all-thirsty'; pronounced gar-gan'tew-a, pan-tag'ru-el.)

Garibaldi biscuit Biscuit better known as the squashed-fly biscuit, from the currants embedded in it. (Said to be a favourite of the Italian revolutionary; see next entry.)

Garibaldi's Thousand Redshirts Force made up of various nationalities, with which Garibaldi drove King BOMBA out of Sicily and Naples in 1860.

Garnett, Alf Epitome of loud-mouthed ignorant bigotry who was the chief character in Johnny Speight's delightful TV series *Till Death Us Do Part* (1966–9).

Garrick Club (1831). London club in Garrick Street, named after the actor, David Garrick.

Garter, Order of the (1348). Most ancient knightly order in Europe; Knights-Companions (KGs) are limited to 24; since 1946 this Order (like the THISTLE) has been in the gift of the Monarch and non-political. See next entry.

Garter ceremony Annual ceremonial gathering at Windsor Castle, usually on a Monday in June; the Queen and members of the Order of the GARTER walk in procession from the state apartments to St George's Chapel; new Knights may be installed on these occasions.

Garter King of Arms Principal King of Arms at the COLLEGE OF ARMS (see CLARENCEUX and NORROY AND ULSTER).

Gascony Originally a Basque province of France, later united with AQUITAINE. The Gascons were renowned for their pride, hot temper and boastfulness – hence, *gasconade*, 'a boastful tirade'.

Gaspar One of the THREE KINGS, traditionally the Ethiopian King of Tarshish (perhaps a Phoenician colony in Spain).

Gastropods See MOLLUSCS.

Gath Philistine city mentioned in David's lament for Saul and Jonathan (2 Sam. 1:19): 'How are the mighty fallen! Tell it not in Gath . . . lest the daughters of the Philistines rejoice.' 'Tell it not in Gath!' is properly used in the sense 'don't let our rivals hear of this setback'.

Gatling gun (1861). Early American machine gun used in the Civil War; it worked on the principle of the revolver, with up to 10 rifle barrels.

GATT (1947). General Agreement on Tariffs and Trade, an international treaty to promote freer trade through the phased elimination of tariffs, preferences and quotas by its 60 signatories. See KENNEDY ROUND, URUGUAY ROUND.

Gatton Notorious rotten borough near Reigate, Surrey, which elected 2 MPs up to 1832.

'Gaudeamus igitur' Rousing 13th-century student song adopted as a school song in many schools: 'Gaudeamus igitur, / Juvenes dum sumus. / Post jucundam juventutem, / Post molestam senectutem, / Nos habebit humus' ('Let us make merry therefore while still young; after happy youth and tiresome old age, the earth will claim us').

Gaugamela (331 BC). Battle in which Alexander the Great finally defeated the Persians under Darius; also called Arbela. (Town on the Tigris in Iraq; pronounced gaw-ga-mee'la.)

Gauleiter Supreme governor of a *Gau* ('district') in Germany and German-occupied territory under National-Socialism. ('*Gau*-leader'; pronounced gow'ly-ter.)

Gautama Family name of the Buddha. (Pronounced gou'ta-ma.)

Gautier, Marguerite See DAME AUX CAMÉLIAS

Gawain King Arthur's nephew, a knight renowned for courtesy.

Gay Liberation Movement US movement to end discrimination against homosexuals of both sexes; the Gay Liberation Front is its militant spearhead, the Gay Sisters its female branch, and the Gay Activists' Alliance pickets places which show such discrimination.

Gay Nineties, The The 1890s (also called the Naughty Nineties), the *fin de siècle* epoch when traditional Victorian religiosity and outward morality were flouted by such as Beardsley (see YELLOW BOOK) and Wilde (see WILDE, (OSCAR) CASE), while Society, led by the Prince of Wales (the future Edward VII), took to new habits such as race-going, and weekend country-house parties (see TRANBY CROFT SCANDAL).

Gaza Strip Small coastal desert area on the borders of, and disputed by, Egypt and Israel, awarded in 1947 to Arab Palestine and seized by Egypt in 1949. It became an Egyptian district under UN supervision to control border incidents. It contained 200,000 Arab refugees from Palestine, from whom Egyptians recruited forces to raid Israel. In 1967 the area was captured by Israeli forces.

GBS Initials commonly used for George Bernard Shaw, the playwright.

GCE (1950). Initials used for the General Certificate of Education which replaced the old School and Higher School Certificates. The O-LEVEL was taken at about age 16, but now replaced by GCSE, the A-LEVEL 2 years later. Papers are set and marked by various regional and national examining boards.

GCSE (1987). General Certificate of Secondary Education replacing General Certificate of Education (GCE) ordinary level, and the Certificate of Secondary Education (CSE) examinations. The purpose of the change was to improve the courses and raise the standards of all candidates.

Gdańsk See DANZIG.

Ge Greek legend, the Earth, personified as the wife of Uranus and mother of the Titans. (Pronounced gee.)

GEC (1900). Initials used for the General Electric Co., a British group making transformers, switchgear, nuclear plant and telephone, electronic and domestic equipment.

Geddes Axe (1922). Name for the drastic cuts in government, and especially defence expenditure carried out on the recommendations of a committee set up by Lloyd George under Sir Eric Geddes.

Geffrye Museum (1914). London museum at Shoreditch, with a series of rooms showing middle-class styles of furnishing for all periods after 1600; there are also photographs of period costumes and a library.

Gehenna Another name for TOPHET. i.e. Hell. (Pronounced gee-hen'a.)

Geiger counter (1928). Device for detecting and measuring radioactivity and other radiations. (Abbreviated from Geiger-Müller counter, named after its 2 German inventors; pronounced gy'ger.)

Geisha girls Highly trained girls hired out to amuse parties of tired Japanese businessmen with music and dance; they are mostly decorous and dull.

Gemini The Twins, third of the constellations of the Zodiac (also called CASTOR and POLLUX), between Taurus and Cancer: the sun enters it about 21 May. Astrologers claim that those born under this sign may be superficial and smooth. (Pronounced jem'in-y.)

Gemini US space program to work out techniques for orbital rendezvous as a step to establishing a permanently orbiting space station, and also to the inspection of hostile satellites.

Geminid meteors Shoal of meteors which orbit the sun and through which the earth passes each December, producing a display of shooting-stars emanating from the direction of GEMINI.

Gem State Nickname of Idaho. (Mistranslation of Indian name.)

General Agreement on Tariffs and Trade See GATT.

General Assembly (UN) The assembly of (up to 5) delegates from each member state. A two-thirds majority is required for any major decision, and each state has one vote, e.g. the Maldive Islands and USA carry equal weight.

General Certificate of Education See GCE.

General Electric (USA) Largest electrical group in the world. See also GEC.

General Medical Council (1858). Body set up by Act of Parliament to control the education, registration and discipline of members of the medical profession.

General Motors Corporation (1908). Largest US car manufacturer. Based on the Buick Company, it successively absorbed Oldsmobile, Pontiac, Cadillac and Chevrolet; in addition to motor vehicles it makes aero engines, locomotives, household appliances etc. Vauxhall Motors is a British and Opel a German subsidiary.

General Strike, The (1926). Nine-day strike, the only general strike that Britain has known. It began after government had abolished subsidies to the coal-mining industry, and mine owners had reduced wages. The miners, who continued on strike from 1 May to November, were supported by the TUC, which called out all the major unions in sympathy. Rail and road transport was paralysed except for lorries run by the Army and volunteers; and the only news-sheet was the BRITISH GAZETTE.

General Synod (1970). Replacing the Church Assembly it is responsible for government of the Church of England; membership is from the bishops, clergy and laity, and totals 574.

Genesis First book of the Old Testament, giving the stories of the Creation. Adam and Eve, the Flood, Abraham, Isaac, Jacob and Joseph. (Greek, 'creation'.)

Geneva (1) Used as a synonym, during its existence, for the League of Nations, which had its headquarters there. (2) Dutch gin (HOLLANDS). (French *genévrier*, 'juniper tree'; no connection with Geneva.)

Geneva Agreements (1954). Terms agreed for the ending of the French war in Indo-China, at a conference under joint UK and USSR chairmanship, attended by the parties concerned, together with China and the USA. The Dulles–Eisenhower administration failed to back up the settlement, substituted an ineffective SEATO, pushed their allies France and Britain out of Indo-China, and thus caused USA to become bogged down in Vietnam thereafter.

Geneva Bible (1560). English translation compiled by exiles from the MARIAN PERSECUTION living in Geneva; the first to be printed in roman (not black letter) type, and to be divided into verses. See BREECHES BIBLE.

Geneva Conventions (1864). International agreements under which the Red Cross was estab-lished and regulations laid down for the more humane treatment of prisoners of war and the wounded. A further agreement in 1906 strengthened these.

Geneva Summit Conference (1955). Four-power conference of heads of state (Eisenhower, Eden, Bulganin, Faure) called to discuss the reunification of Germany.

Genevieve (1953). Car which was the real hero of a film about the VETERAN CAR RUN, memorable also for Kay Kendall's heroic trumpet solo and Larry Adler's harmonica score. This typically English affair was scripted by an American.

Genevoise (Cooking) Term usually indicating the presence of anchovies.

Genista Genus of evergreen brooms, both spiny and spineless, many species of which resemble CYTISUS.

Genji, Prince Hero of a long Japanese psychological novel written in the 11th century by Lady Murasaki (translated by Arthur Waley as *The Tale of Genji*, 1933). In a realistic court setting, it tells of Prince Genji's many loves; scenes from it are often depicted in old scroll paintings.

Genoa Conference (1922). Abortive conference on world economic affairs attended by 29 nations; Soviet Russia made its first appearance at an international conference, and Germany its first post-war appearance.

Gentleman Jim Nickname of James Corbett, world heavyweight champion in the 1890s.

Gentleman's Relish (1828). Delectable anchovy paste, officially called 'Patum Peperium, the Gentleman's Relish'.

Gentlemen at Arms The Honourable Corps of Gentlemen at Arms is one of the 2 bodies forming the Queen's dismounted bodyguard (see YEOMEN OF THE GUARD); it consists of 40 retired officers of the Regular Army and the Marines. Their Captain is Chief Whip in the Lords.

Gentlemen Prefer Blondes (1925). Anita Loos'

study of the world of the gold-digging blonde, Lorelei, whose girl-friend, Dorothy, is the mouthpiece of the author's wit.

Gentlemen's Agreement Informal agreement between nations based on personal assurances only; specifically, that between Japan and USA (1908) restricting Japanese labour immigration.

Geordie Nickname for a Northumbrian, especially a Tynesider. (From the local pronunciation of 'Georgie'.)

George Cross (1940). Award instituted by George VI which takes precedence over all decorations except the VICTORIA CROSS. Primarily for civilians, it is made for the acts of the greatest heroism or the most conspicuous courage in circumstances of extreme danger. See MALTA, GC.

George Eliot Pen name of Mary Ann Evans (1829–80), English novelist; her *Middlemarch* was described by Virginia Woolf as '. . . one of the few English novels written for grown-up people'.

George Sand Pen name of Lucile-Aurore Dupin, baronne Dudevant (1804–76), French novelist who wrote many novels of which the first was *Indiana* – she had collaborated with Jules Sandeau under the pseudonym 'Jules Sand'. A prolific writer of novels, tales, essays and dramatic works, who had a colourful life with many lovers, notably Chopin, Alfred de Musset and Prosper Mérimée.

Georgetown (1789). US Roman Catholic university in Washington DC.

Georgette Thin silk crêpe fabric, named after a French dressmaker, Georgette de la Plante.

Georgian period (1714–1800). Term applied to styles of decoration prevalent in England up to the REGENCY PERIOD. The reign of George I (1714–27) was influenced by BAROQUE; mahogany and gesso came into vogue and William Kent began to revive PALLADIAN ARCHITECTURE. The reign of George II (1727–60) was influenced by LOUIS QUINZE ROCOCO and was the age of CHIPPENDALE. In George III's reign HEPPLEWHITE and SHERATON introduced simpler styles.

Georgian poetry (1912–33). Poetry of a series of anthologies produced (and so named) by Sir Edward Marsh for the POETRY BOOKSHOP, and continued later by Mrs Harold Monro. They were part of a successful movement to introduce poetry to a wider public, initiated by Rupert Brooke, Drinkwater, Harold Monro and others. Poets published included De La Mare, Masefield, Robert Graves, W. H. Davies, Housman, Blunden and Lascelles Abercrombie.

Georgics (30 BC). Virgil's 4 discursive poems on the delights of country life and the arts of agriculture. (Greek, 'farming topics'.)

Georgie Porgie (pudding and pie), of the nursery rhyme, variously and unconvincingly identified with Charles II, George I and George Villiers, Duke of Buckingham.

Geranium Genus of cranesbills; the pot or bedding plant called geranium is a Pelargonium.

German Democratic Republic (1949–90). Former official name of Eastern Germany. It now consists of the Länder of Thuringia, Brandenburg, Mecklenburg, Saxony Anhalt and Berlin. See GERMAN FEDERAL REPUBLIC.

German East Africa German colony which became British-mandated Tanganyika Territory in 1920, and is now part of Tanzania.

German shepherd dog Formerly known as Alsatian; used as a sheep-dog in Alsace.

German silver (1836). Alloy of copper, zinc and nickel, used in making British plate, a cheaper substitute for Sheffield plate which it replaced until the coming of electroplated nickel silver.

Germany, Federal Republic of (1949). The chief provinces (Länder) are: Baden-Württemberg, Bavaria, Berlin (West), Bremen, Hamburg, Hessen, Lower Saxony, North Rhine–Westphalia, Rhineland–Palatinate, Saarland, Schleswig–Holstein. Since 1990 it also includes Länder of the former GERMAN DEMOCRATIC REPUBLIC.

Germinal In the French Revolution calendar, the month from 21 March to 19 April ('Budding time.)'

'Gerontion'

'Gerontion' (1920). Pessimistic short poem by T. S. Eliot, a meditation on old age and decay.

Gestalt psychology Approach to psychology associated with the names of Koffka and Köhler, who held that analysis of psychological phenomena, especially perception, into separate elements is unrewarding; they must be studied as integrated wholes, which differ from the sum of the parts as a melody differs from a mere collection of the notes of which it is made up. This view has helped to a better understanding of the processes of learning and memory. (German, 'shape', 'pattern'; pronounced ge-shtaahlt'.)

Gestapo Hitler's Secret State Police, merged with the ss in 1936. (From Geheime Staats-Polizei; pronounced gě-stah'po.)

Gesta Romanorum (14th century). Collection of tales, each with a moral, about saints, knights and Roman emperors; though written in Latin, some of the tales are oriental. (Latin, 'deeds of the Romans'.)

Gethsemane, The Agony in Spiritual sufferings of Jesus in an olive grove of that name where he went to pray for his own death after the Last Supper (Mark 14:32–6), and where Judas betrayed him.

Gettysburg, Battle of (July 1836). Turning point of the AMERICAN CIVIL WAR; the Confederate army tried to invade northern territory across the Potomac, but were turned back. (Town in southern Pennsylvania.)

Gettysburg address (November 1863). President Lincoln's speech during the AMERICAN CIVIL WAR at the dedication of the cemetery of those killed in the Battle of GETTYSBURG; it ended with the words: '. . . that we here highly resolve . . . that government of the people, by the people, and for the people, shall not perish from the earth.'

Gezira (1925). An area in the Sudan of about 1¾ million acres, between the Blue and White Nile south of Khartoum, irrigated from the Sennar dam on the Blue Nile for the cultivation of the main export crop, cotton.

Ghiordes rugs Short-pile rugs made from the 17th century in north-west Anatolia, among the best of the Turkish family. They have a wine-coloured or puce ground, and columns as part of the multicoloured design.

Ghost Goes West, The (1935). First film made by René Clair after he went to Hollywood.

Ghosts (1881). Ibsen's play, in which Mrs Alving comes to realize that she had failed in love for her late husband from undue subservience to dead social conventions (the 'ghosts') which destroy happiness. The growing insanity of their son, who has inherited syphilis from his father, emphasizes the point.

Ghost Train, The Arnold Ridley's successful thriller play, of which there are several film versions.

Giant Despair See DOUBTING-CASTLE.

Gibraltar, Capture of (1704). Effected by Admiral Rooke a few days before BLENHEIM; Britain retained it under the Peace of UTRECHT.

Gibson Dry martini with an onion replacing the customary olive.

Gibson girls Perhaps the first 'pin-ups', drawings of girls with hour-glass figures by the American cartoonist, Charles Dana Gibson (1867–1944), which had a great vogue in their time.

Gideons Members of the Gideon Society (1899), an interdenominational laymen's evangelical association founded in USA as the Christian Commercial Men's Association, which distributes bibles to hotels, hospitals, schools, prisons, barracks, etc. (From the account in Judges 7 of how Gideon smote the Midianites.)

Gifford lectures (1885). Lectures at the 4 older Scottish Universities, in the words of the founder, to diffuse the study of Natural Theology, i.e. the knowledge of God; lecturers to be selected without reference to creed or sect. (Bequest of Adam Lord Gifford.)

GI Joe (US) A soldier. (From the initials GI – 'general issue' – on his equipment.)

Gilbert and Sullivan operas Comic operas composed by Sir Arthur Sullivan with witty lyrics by W. S. Gilbert (produced 1875–96); also called Savoy operas (see D'OYLY CARTE OPERA CO.).

Gilberte In Proust's REMEMBRANCE OF THINGS PAST, the daughter of SWANN by ODETTE DE CRÉCY; socially ambitious, she eventually marries SAINT-LOUP. The narrator has a great affection for her.

Gilbertian Ludicrously topsy-turvy. (From W. S. Gilbert, see GILBERT AND SULLIVAN OPERAS.)

Gil Blas (1715–35). First realistic picaresque novel, written by the Frenchman Lesage. The young Spaniard, Gil Blas, sets out to make his career and becomes pupil to the quack doctor, Sangrado. Although the setting is in Spain, the large gallery of characters are drawn, unsympathetically, from the author's own experiences in Paris.

Gilead, Balm in Phrase from Jeremiah 8:22: 'Is there no balm in Gilead; is there no physician there?' Jeremiah is bewailing the fate threatening Judah in troubled times, from which there seemed no escape. (Some now unknown medicinal herb for which Gilead was famous: the later antiseptic, balm of Gilead, was named after it.)

Giles cartoons (1943). Cartoons in the *Daily* and *Sunday Express* by C. R. Giles, usually peopled by diminutive mischievous infants of a working-class family ruled by the grim and determined Grandma.

Gilgamesh epic Collection of SUMERIAN legends, some at least 4,000 years old; the best-known is the story of the Flood, told to the hero Gilgamesh by Noah. The epic has survived, incomplete, on tablets written at Nineveh in the 7th century BC and now in the British Museum.

Gillette Cup (1962). County cricket knock-out competition, with one innings of 60 overs each, now known as the Nat West Trophy.

Gillray cartoons Venomous political caricatures executed by James Gillray from 1780 onwards. His main victims were George III, Pitt, Fox, Burke and the chief figures of the French Revolutionary period.

Gill Sans (1927). Abbreviation for Gill Sans-serif, a type in which strokes are of equal thickness and there are no serifs (the fine lines at the end of the terminal stroke of a letter). (Designed by the sculptor Eric Gill, 1882–1940.)

Gimcrack Club (1767). Committee which manages racing at York, originally the Anciente Fraternite of York Gimcracks. It holds a dinner in December at which the guest of honour is the winner of the GIMCRACK STAKES. (Named mysteriously after a non-Yorkshire horse which once ran at York only to lose.)

Gimcrack Stakes Six-furlong flat-race for 2-year-olds run at York in August: see previous entry.

Ginger Man, The Sprawling novel by J. P. Donleavy, notorious when published, about Sebastian Dangerfield, the manic-depressive anti-social hero who devotes his life to wine, women, stealing, lying and avoiding work.

Ginza Street in Tokyo of department stores and nightclubs.

Gioconda, La See MONA LISA.

'Giovinezza, La' (1921). Italian Fascist national anthem.

Gipsy Moth Name of yachts owned by Sir Francis Chichester. In No. III he won the first single-handed transatlantic race in 1960, taking 40 days. In No. IV he circumnavigated the world in 226 sailing days in 1966–7, again sailing alone. (Named after the Gipsy MOTH aircraft in which he made a solo flight to Australia.)

Girdlers, Worshipful Company of (1449). LIVERY COMPANY, originally a guild of makers of belts, including sword-belts.

Giro (1968). Girobank is the banking arm of the Post Office. Social-security payments are also made by this system and so 'Getting the Giro' has become part of the language.

Girondins (1791–93). Liberal middle-class republicans of the French Revolution who broke away from the JACOBINS; in their enthusiasm they rushed France into a war, for which it was quite unprepared, against Austria and Prussia after the Declaration of PILLNITZ: the consequent disasters swept them from power. (Named after the district of Gironde in south-west France, from which many of them came.)

Girton (1869). Oldest college for women at Cambridge. Now coeducational.

Giselle (1841). Ballet choreographed by Coralli and Perrot to music by Adam, about a village girl who falls in love with Albrecht, a nobleman disguised as a peasant. Her former lover betrays him and she goes mad and dies. Act II is set in a haunted dream world where Giselle and others who have been betrayed by their lovers lure to their doom all who come under their spell. However, through the intercession of Giselle Albrecht is saved as dawn breaks.

Gitanos Spanish name for Gypsies, see ATHINGANOI. (Pronounced git-ahn'os.)

Givenchy Paris fashion house.

Giverny Village north-west of Paris associated with Claude Monet, who lived and worked there for the last 43 years of his life, creating a famous garden and lily-pond which appear in many of his paintings.

Giza (Gizeh, etc.) Suburb of Cairo, north of SAKKARA; it is the site of 3 famous pyramids of the 4th Dynasty (26th century BC), including the Great Pyramid of Cheops (khufru), and of the largest and best-known of the many Sphinxes.

GKN Initials standing for Guest, Keen and Nettlefold, a large group of steel and engineering firms with a wide range of products.

Gladstone Professor Holder of the chair of Government and Public Administration at Oxford.

Gladstonian Liberalism Free Trade, retrenchment, political reform, a non-aggressive policy overseas, and Home Rule for Ireland. (W. E. Gladstone, Prime Minister 1868–74, 1880–85, 1886 and 1892–4.)

Glamis Castle Mainly 17th-century château-style home of the Earls of Strathmore, near Kirriemuir, Angus, scene of Duncan's murder in *Macbeth*. Birthplace of Queen Elizabeth the Queen Mother and her daughter Princess Margaret. (Pronounced glahmz.)

Glasnost Greater openness in Soviet society instituted by President Mikhail Gorbachev in the 1980s.

Glass-Sellers, Worshipful Company of (1664). LIVERY COMPANY.

Glass's Guide (1933). Monthly guide, strictly confidential to the trade, to the buying and selling prices of second-hand cars. (William Glass, founder.)

Glastonbury In Arthurian legend the place in Somerset where JOSEPH OF ARIMATHEA planted his staff (which flowers each Christmas) and hid the HOLY GRAIL. Said to have the tomb of King Arthur. See CAMELOT.

Glaziers, Worshipful Company of (1637). LIVERY COMPANY, originally a guild of those engaged in the glazing and leading of windows and the painting of glass; it still fosters the art of glass painting and has prominent artists among its members.

Gleaners, The Millet's painting of 3 sturdy peasant women in the sunlit fields, now in the Musée d'Orsay.

Gleditschia Trees named after Gottlieb Gleditsch, an 18th-century botanist.

Gleichschaltung 'Co-ordination', a Nazi euphemism for seizure of control by the Party of all the organs of government, including the armed forces.

Glencoe Massacre (1692). Massacre of 36 Roman Catholic Macdonalds in the pass above Loch Leven, Argyll, by soldiers (Campbells) of the Duke of Argyll's regiment who had accepted Macdonald hospitality for the previous 10 days.

Gleneagles agreement Agreement reached by the heads of COMMONWEALTH governments meeting at the Gleneagles Hotel, Scotland, on 11–12 June 1977 reaffirming their full support for the international campaign against APARTHEID and to continue to withhold support for, and by taking practical steps to discourage contact or competition by their nationals with sporting organizations, teams or sportsmen from South Africa or any other country where sports are organized on the basis of race, colour or ethnic origin.

Glenfinnan Site at the head of Loch Shiel, Inverness-shire, of a monument to the YOUNG PRETENDER, who raised his standard there in 1745.

Glenlivet A Scotch whisky made in Banffshire.

Glenrothes (1948). NEW TOWN in Fife. (Pronounced glen-roth'is.)

Glevum Roman name of Gloucester.

Globe Theatre (1599). One of the earliest London theatres, at Southwark, where many of Shakespeare's plays were produced.

Gloomy Dean, The Nickname for the Right Rev. W. R. Inge, Dean of St Paul's, a theologian and philosopher, and a prolific journalist who in the inter-war years contributed to the London *Evening Standard* many pessimistic articles on world affairs and the decay of Western civilization.

'Gloria in excelsis' (1) Hymn 'Glory be to God on high', sung in Communion and other services. (2) Musical setting of this.

Gloriana (1) Character in the FAERIE QUEENE, representing Queen Elizabeth. (2) Title of an opera by Benjamin Britten (1953).

Glorious First of June, The (1794). Lord Howe's defeat of the French fleet off Ushant during the French Revolutionary Wars.

Glorious Revolution (1688). Deposition of the Roman Catholic James II and his replacement by Protestant WILLIAM OF ORANGE and his wife Mary, 'to save the Protestant religion and the constitutional liberties of England'; William landed unopposed in Torbay, Devon, and James fled to Ireland (see BOYNE) and France.

Glorious 12th of July, The See TWELFTH OF JULY.

Glossina Generic name of the tsetse fly, carrier of the trypanosomes of human and animal sleeping sickness (trypanosomiasis).

Gloucester cheese Once a gourmet's delight, especially the double Gloucester (made from whole milk); it now seems to have suffered the same fate as WENSLEYDALE.

Glovers, Worshipful Company of (1639). LIVERY COMPANY which continues to encourage good craftsmanship in its trade.

Gloxinia Tuberous perennials named after P. B. Gloxin, a French botanist.

Glyndebourne Festival (1934). Festival of opera founded by John Christie (died 1962) and held each summer at his home near Lewes, Sussex. It is attended both by socialites and music-lovers. (Pronounced glynd'born.)

Glyptothek (Munich). Major museum of Greek and Roman art, rebuilt after World War II.

G-man (USA). 1950s slang for FBI detective. (For Government-man, i.e. Federal, not state, detective.)

Gnosticism Body of mystical beliefs derived from oriental religions, Pythagoras, Plato and Christianity; it flourished particularly in Egypt in the 2nd century AD. The main theme was the handing down of a body of esoteric knowledge attainable only from instruction by initiates, with strict self-discipine, contemplation and various physical drills, directed to individual salvation from the evil fate of the generality of mankind. The Muslim equivalent is SUFISM. (Greek *gnosis*, 'knowledge', specifically 'revelation'.)

Goat and Compasses Inn name corrupted from 'God encompasseth us', the usual sign in the Middle Ages for a pilgrims' hostel.

Gobbo, Lancelot Clown in Shakespeare's *Merchant of Venice* who deserts Shylock for easier working conditions under Bassanio.

Gobelins, Les (1440). French tapestry factory in Paris, bought by Louis XIV's minister, Colbert, and still run as a state factory, making carpets, upholstery and furniture; a large tapestry might take five people seven years to complete (the work is only undertaken in daylight). (Jean Gobelin, dyer, head of the family who founded it.)

'God Bless America' (1939). Patriotic march

chorus by Irving Berlin, written 22 years earlier but produced for Kate Smith to sing on the first Armistice (Veterans') Day after the outbreak of World War II. It is much easier to sing than the national anthem, which it has come near to displacing in popular esteem.

Godiva, Lady Wife of the 11th-century Earl of Mercia, Leofric, who kept his promise to cancel certain taxes if she rode naked through Coventry.

Godolphin Arabian See BYERLY TURK.

Godot Character in Samuel Becket's play *Waiting for Godot* (1955) whom 2 tramps await; he appears to symbolize a revelation of the meaning of life which, like Godot, never comes.

Gods, The The gallery (the cheapest seats) of a theatre.

God's Little Acre (1933). Erskine Caldwell's novel about the backward mountain-dwellers of Georgia, USA, which sold 9 million copies.

Godunov, Boris Fedorovich Tsar of Russia from 1598, who rose to importance under Ivan the Terrible; killed suppressing a revolt. His life is the theme of Mussorgsky's opera *Boris Godunov*.

Goetheanum See ANTHROPOSOPHICAL SOCIETY.

Gog and Magog (1) Ezekiel 38 and 39 Gog is the King of Magog, Israel's enemy. (2) In Revelation 20:8 they are both persons, enemies of the Kingdom of God. (3) In English legend they are 2 giant offspring of daughters of the Emperor Diocletian brought captive to London. Their 15th-century effigies, placed outside Guildhall, were destroyed in a 1940 air-raid; new figures have again been made. (Gog may have meant 'darkness', 'the north'; and Magog 'land of darkness'; pronounced gog, may'gog.)

Gogmagogs, The Hills near Cambridge, named after a legendary giant who fell in love with GRANTA. See GOG AND MAGOG; pronounced gog'mĕ-gogz.)

Goidelic languages See CELTIC LANGUAGES. (Goidels, old Irish name for GAELS.)

Gold and Silver Wyre Drawers, Worshipful Company of (1693). LIVERY COMPANY.

Gold Coast (1) Pre-Independence name of Ghana, West Africa. (2) Nickname for various parts of the world frequented by the rich, e.g. the Florida Lido at Miami Beach, USA; a residential area along Lake Shore Drive, Chicago; the Australian 'surfers' paradise' on the Pacific coast of Queensland.

Gold Cup Day, Ascot Thursday of ROYAL ASCOT and the climax of the meeting; see ASCOT GOLD CUP.

Golden Arrow, The The afternoon express train from London (Victoria) to Paris, which became La Flèche d'Or on the other side of the Channel. Discontinued in 1972.

Golden Ass, The (2nd century AD). Satiric fantasy by Apuleius in which Lucian, accidentally transformed into an ass, comments on his various owners and their ways. He is eventually restored to human form by Isis. The book, also called *The Metamorphoses*, includes the earliest version of the story of CUPID AND PSYCHE.

Golden Bough, The (1890–1915). Sir James Frazer's multi-volume comparative study of the beliefs and institutions of primitive man. (Title from the bough broken by Aeneas before going down to the Underworld, an echo of an ancient priest-slaying ritual.)

Golden Calf, The Idol made by Aaron (Exod. 32:4) and worshipped by the Israelites while Moses was on Mount Sinai receiving the Ten Commandments. Moses destroyed it. The phrase 'to worship the Golden Calf' came to mean 'to sacrifice principles in the pursuit of money'.

Golden Delicious Hard sweet dessert apple of American origin, now the world's most widely grown variety.

Goldenes Dachl (1500). High balcony at Innsbruck, Austria, roofed with gilded copper plates, built for spectators at city festivals by the Emperor Maximilian. (Austrian, 'golden little roof'.)

Golden Fleece In Greek legend the objective of the ARGONAUTS' expedition. It was the fleece of a ram hung on a tree in Colchis (the Black Sea coastal area of modern Georgia), guarded by a dragon. The legend may refer to a local method of collecting alluvial gold by putting sheepskins in rivers.

Golden Fleece, Knights of the (1429). Members of a chivalric order founded for the protection of the Church by Philip the Good, Duke of Burgundy and the Netherlands; later divided into 2 separate orders for Spain and Austria. (Name variously explained.)

Golden Gate, The One-mile-wide entrance to San Francisco Bay (California), since 1937 spanned by a single-span suspension bridge.

Golden Gloves US amateur boxing tournament, sponsored by the press.

Golden handshake Large lump sum to gild enforced premature retirement.

Golden Hind One-hundred-ton ship in which Drake circumnavigated the world in 1577–80.

Golden Horde, The (13th–15th centuries). Mongol forces established in south-east Russia by Genghis Khan's grandson, Batu (Bator) Khan, which dominated east Russia and west-central Asia until overthrown by Ivan the Great, the first Russian Tsar. (Turkish *orda*, 'camp'; translation of the Mongol name for Batu's luxurious field headquarters; the word *horde* subsequently passed into the English language with the meaning of 'troop', 'rabble'.)

Golden Horn, The An arm of the Bosporus separating Istanbul proper from its northern suburbs of Galata and Pera.

Golden Miller The Hon. Dorothy Paget's famous steeplechaser which won the Cheltenham Gold Cup in 5 successive years (1932–6) and the National in 1934.

Golden Rose, The (1961). Annual award at the Montreux International TV Light Entertainment Festival, held in April.

Golden Section The division of a line (or rect-angle) so that the whole line bears the same ratio to the larger section as the larger to the smaller section. This ideal proportion (equivalent approximately to 8:13) has been used extensively by artists and architects down the ages, consciously or unconsciously.

Golden State Nickname of California. (Gold-producing state.)

Golden Stool, The Sacred symbol of the Ashanti of the Gold Coast (Ghana), ornamented with gold. After the ASHANTI WARS it was hidden from the British, but again displayed openly, with official approval, from 1935.

Golden Temple Centre of Sikh religion, Amritsar (Punjab, India), stormed by Indian troops on 6 June 1984 (Operation Blue Star).

Golden Treasury, The (1861). Short title of Palgrave's anthology, *The Golden Treasury of the Best Songs and Lyrical Poems in the English Language*: many editions and reprints have since been made.

Golden West Name for USA and Canada given at the end of the 19th century when the limitless fields of (golden) corn there saved the Old World, which was suffering from an expansion of population unmatched by increase in food supplies.

Goldfinger, Auric A British-born SMERSH agent who, in Ian Fleming's *Goldfinger* (1959), organizes the leading US criminal gangs to loot FORT KNOX of all its gold.

Goldfish Club Club for RAF pilots of World War II who came down 'in the drink', i.e. the sea.

Gold Rush, The (1924). Sentimental Chaplin silent film, chiefly remembered for the scene in which the comedian is reduced to cooking and eating a boot, the laces of which serve as *ersatz* spaghetti.

Goldsmiths, Worshipful Company of (1327). LIVERY COMPANY with a fine hall where exhibitions of plate are held. It has statutory duties to assay and hallmark gold and silver plate, to assay new coin (see PYX), and to prosecute those guilty of illegal sale of plate.

Goldsmiths College (1891). Unit of London University with a teacher-training department of arts, sciences and education, a department of adult studies and a school of art.

Goldsmiths' Professor Holder of a chair of English Literature at Oxford or of metallurgy at Cambridge.

Gold Standard System in which the unit of currency is declared equivalent to a fixed weight of gold and the Central Bank has to exchange gold and currency at that rate. Invented by Britain (1821) and using Newton's calculation (1717) that 1 oz Troy of gold was worth £3 17s 10½d, it lasted there until 1914 and was reluctantly restored by Churchill at Montagu Norman's insistence in 1925, despite Keynes's fierce opposition, thus greatly overvaluing sterling and necessitating painful deflation until abandoned in 1931.

Gold Stick Honorary office of the Royal Household created by Charles II; also the gilt rod carried by its holders on state occasions. In England there are 2 Gold Sticks, who take it in turns to do monthly duty: the Colonels of the Life Guards and of the Blues and Royals. The Gold Stick for Scotland is the Captain General of the Royal Corps of Archers, the Queen's Bodyguard for Scotland.

Goldwynism Cross between an Irish bull and a Spoonerism, invented and exploited by the American film producer Sam Goldwyn (e.g. 'include me out'; 'stop messing about with the H-bomb . . . it's dynamite').

Golgotha CALVARY. (Aramaic word for 'skull'. Latin *calvaria*; pronounced gol'géth-a.)

Goliath See DAVID. (Pronounced gol-*ïj*ath.)

Gollancz (Sir Israel) Memorial lectures (1930). Lectures on Early English or Old English language and literature, sponsored by the British Academy.

Gollum Shapeless rubbery creature which trails the HOBBITS on their expeditions.

GOM Initials used for Grand Old Man, a name given by Lord Rosebery to Gladstone, who lived to be 89.

Gompelskirchner Austrian semi-sweet light wine of fine quality.

Goncourt, The See PRIX GONCOURT.

Gondoliers, The (1889). Gilbert and Sullivan opera. One of 2 gondoliers is thought to be the rightful heir to the throne of Barataria who was betrothed in infancy to the Duke of Plaza Toro's daughter. As she does not want either of them, and as they have just married, it is fortunate that a man she had already fallen in love with is finally identified as the true heir.

Gondwanaland Geologists' name for a hypothetical continent, now submerged beneath the ocean, which once linked South America, Africa, Australia and India. As this continent drifted northwards, it piled up the Himalaya, Atlas and Andes mountains. See LEMURIA. (Named after a region of central India.)

Goneril One of the 2 evil daughters of KING LEAR, who poisons the other (Regan) and has her youngest sister, CORDELIA, hanged.

Gone with the Wind (1936). Margaret Mitchell's only work, a long historical novel of life in the southern states during and after the American Civil War.

Goodbye to All That (1929). Poet Robert Graves's restrained autobiographical novel, generally regarded as the best British description of what life in the trenches during World War I was really like.

Good Companions, The (1929). J. B. Priestley's best-selling long novel in which Jess Oakroyd breaks away from the increasingly sombre world of mounting unemployment, tears up her National Insurance card and joins a travelling concert party called The Good Companions.

Good Friday Friday before Easter, commemorating the Crucifixion. ('Good' in the old sense of 'holy'.)

Goodison Park Football home of Everton, in Liverpool.

Good Samaritan, The Man of Samaria in the parable who succoured the victim of thieves left half dead by the wayside, after a priest and a Levite had 'passed by on the other side' (Luke 10:33).

Good Soldier Schweik, The (1923). Czech 4-volume (unfinished) satire by Jaroslav Hašek recounting the misadventures of a simple Czech soldier serving in the Austrian army during World War I. The author had himself deserted to the Russians and then to the Bolsheviks, so that Imperial Austria takes some hard knocks. See SCHWEIK IN THE SECOND WORLD WAR.

Good Templars See TEMPLARS.

Good Woman of Setzuan, The (1943). Brecht's play about the prostitute Shen Teh who opens a tobacco shop but is so generous that she soon fails. She then disguises herself as a man and, pretending to be a ruthless capitalist, does well.

Goodwood Racecourse near Chichester, Sussex, in Goodwood Park, the property of the Duke of Richmond and Gordon.

Goodwood Cup (1812). Flat-race over a distance of 2 miles 5 furlongs, run on Cup Day (a Thursday) at the end of July at GOODWOOD.

Goodwood House Home near Chichester of the Dukes of Richmond and Gordon designed by Wyatt in Sussex flint. See GOODWOOD.

'Goody Two-Shoes' (1765). Nursery story attributed to Oliver Goldsmith about a woman who had only one shoe; when given a pair she displayed them to one and all, delightedly exclaiming: 'Look *two* shoes!' (Goody for Goodwife (feminine of Goodman), applied to those who did not qualify as 'Mrs'.)

Goonhilly British Post Office's satellite ground terminal station in Cornwall for receiving and transmitting signals by communications satellites. A second station (1968) made Goonhilly the centre of Britain's TV and telephone traffic via satellites linking it to most parts of the world. (Goonhilly Downs, between Helston and the Lizard.)

Goon Show, The (1952–60). BBC radio series marked by zany satire, with Spike Milligan as the goofy Eccles, Harry Secombe as the swaggering Lord Hairy Seagoon, Major Bloodnok, etc. (*Goon*, a rubbery creature invented by Segar, who created POPEYE; became US slang for 'mindless thug'.)

Goop Ill-behaved or disagreeable person, an epitome of horrid naughtiness; from the fantastic creatures invented by Gelett Burgess (1866–1951) and featured in his *Goops and How to Be Them* (1900).

Goosestep Method of army marching in which the leg is swung without bending the knees, at an exaggerated height. Practised by several armies including the army of the German Third Reich.

GOP (1880). (USA) Initials used for Grand Old Party, i.e. the Republicans.

Gorbals, The Formerly notorious slum area of Glasgow, now rebuilt.

Gorboduc (1562). Tragedy, written in blank verse by Thomas Sackville (Earl of Dorset) and Thomas Norton, based on the legend of fratricide and murder in the family of a British king.

Gordian knot Intricate knot fastening yoke and pole of a wagon dedicated to Zeus by Gordius, father of MIDAS. The legend grew that whoever undid it would inherit Asia. Alexander the Great cut it with his sword. Thus, to cut the Gordian knot came to mean to take a violent, drastic or unorthodox short cut in resolving a problem or impasse.

Gordon Highlanders, The (1881). Regiment of the HIGHLAND BRIGADE, an amalgamation of the Stirlingshire (75th) and Gordon Highlanders (92nd).

Gordon Riots (1780). 'No Popery' riots in London fomented by a mad Protestant fanatic, Lord George Gordon, and suppressed by troops with considerable loss of life. Gordon was acquitted but other leaders were executed. The riots are described in Dickens's BARNABY RUDGE.

Gordonstoun (1934). Public school near Elgin, Morayshire, started by Kurt Hahn (see OUTWARD BOUND SCHOOLS), where the Duke of

Edinburgh and the Prince of Wales were educated. (Pronounced gord′enz-tèn.)

Goren system Calling system at Bridge, with a forcing two bid as in Culbertson. In hand valuation points are added for short suits and voids, instead of for length as in other systems.

Gorgons (Greek legend). Three sisters of horrific aspect, of whom the most famous was MEDUSA.

Gorgonzola Semi-hard blue Lombardy cheese made from ewe's or whole cow's milk; the name is used also of inferior types resembling Danish Blue. (Once made at Gorgonzola, near Milan.)

Gorki City of the RSFSR, which has now reverted to its traditional name of Nizhni Novgorod.

Goshen, Land of Biblical name for Egypt east of the Nile, where the Israelites were allowed to settle, driven there by hunger (Gen. 45:10); a land of plenty and of light (Exod. 10:23), i.e. of tolerance. (Pronounced goh′shen.)

Gosplan Soviet State Planning Commission, the supreme body for all industrial and economic planning.

Goss Small porcelain ornaments made at Stoke-on-Trent by W. H. Goss from about 1860. They bore the arms of towns and were sold in thousands to Victorian holiday-makers.

Gotham (1) Village near Nottingham proverbial in the Middle Ages for the stupidity of its inhabitants; hence the 'three wise men of Gotham' in the nursery rhyme. (Pronounced got′em.) (2) Washington Irving's name for New York, as a city of wiseacres. (Pronounced Goth′em.)

Gothic architecture (12th–16th centuries). Western European style which succeeded ROM-ANESQUE ARCHITECTURE, characterized by the pointed arch (of Persian origin), soaring lines, loftiness and light rendered possible by cross-ribbed vaulting and the flying buttress. In England the successive phases were EARLY ENG-LISH, DECORATED, and PERPENDICULAR; in France the final period was FLAMBOYANT. (Originally a term of disparagement, meaning non-classical.)

Gothic novels Horror stories set in haunted Gothic castles, for which there was a craze in the 18th century. The genre was invented by Horace Walpole (see CASTLE OF OTRANTO) and parodied by Jane Austen in *Northanger Abbey*.

Gothic Revival, The (1750). Revival of GOTHIC ARCHITECTURE in England, the fashion for which was started by STRAWBERRY HILL. Another example is the Houses of Parliament.

Goths Germanic race which, while in DACIA in the 4th century, split into OSTROGOTHS and VISI-GOTHS.

Götterdämmerung Twilight of the Gods, the Ragnarok of Scandinavian mythology, when a struggle between the powers of good and evil (led by ODIN and LOKI) ends in universal destruction and chaos. A younger generation of gods survive to create a new universe and a new race of men.

Götterdämmerung Title of the final opera in Wagner's *Ring of the Nibelungs*.

Gouda Mild semi-hard cheese with a yellow rind; the whole cheese is round and flat. (Originally made at Gouda, Holland; pronounced gow′da.)

'Go West, young man, go West!' Phrase first used by J. B. L. Soule in an article in the Terre Haute (Ind.) *Express* (1851) which was reprinted and given far wider currency by Horace Greeley in the *New York Tribune*. Greeley had travelled extensively in the West and well knew that it was a land of opportunity.

Grace, Princess (of Monaco) Formerly Grace Kelly, the film star, she died in a car accident in 1982.

Grace Abounding to the Chief of Sinners (1666). Bunyan's part fictional, part autobiographical confession, telling of a sinner's life and how he finds the 'miracle of precious Grace'.

Grace and Favour residences Houses and apartments in the gift of the Monarch, situated at Windsor Castle, the Hampton Court, Kensington and St James's Palaces, and elsewhere.

Graces, The In Greek legend, Euphrosyne, Aglaia and Thalia, daughters of Zeus, who lived with the Muses on Mount Olympus, and bestowed the gifts of happiness, kindness and charm on mankind. With the increase in world population it has perhaps proved too heavy a task for a staff of three.

Gradgrind, Thomas Industrialist in Dickens's novel HARD TIMES, who is solely interested in Facts, and the inadequacies of whose philosophy of life are pointed by the failure of his 2 children.

Graeco-Roman style (Wrestling) Style popular on the Continent, in which tripping and holds below the waist are barred.

Graf Spee German pocket battleship, blown up by her crew off Montevideo after the Battle of the RIVER PLATE.

Grafton Street Dublin's chief shopping street.

Graf Zeppelin (1) First airship to operate on a transatlantic passenger service (1928–37). (2) Second airship, tested in 1938 but never put to commercial use because of World War II. (Named after COUNT ZEPPELIN, German airship pioneer, died 1917.)

Grammy Gold-plated miniature replica of an early gramophone awarded by the National Academy of Recording Arts and Sciences for the best efforts of recording artists and the recording industry.

Gram-positive, Gram-negative Classification of bacteria which aids in their identification. Gram's stain will stain some, e.g. *Staphylococcus* and *Streptococcus*, but not others, e.g. *Gonococcus*, typhus bacillus.

Gran Chaco War (1932–5). War between Bolivia and Paraguay over a disputed boundary in the northern portion of the Gran Chaco region, settled by arbitration in 1938.

Gran Colombia (Greater Colombia). Short-lived union of Colombia, Venezuela and Ecuador formed by Simón Bolívar in 1819.

Grand Alliance (1701). Formed by William III from members of the former League of AUGSBURG on the eve of the War of the SPANISH SUCCESSION

and his own death. It included Britain, Austria, Holland, Denmark and Portugal, ranged against France, Spain and Bavaria.

Grand Banks CONTINENTAL SHELF extending 350 miles off south-east Newfoundland, and the meeting place of the LABRADOR CURRENT and GULF STREAM, which together produce constant fogs but, more important, ideal conditions for plankton and hence for fish. These waters are therefore extensively fished by the trawler fleets of many nations, especially for cod.

Grand Canal (1) Main canal in Venice. (2) Thousand-mile canal linking Hangchow to Tientsin and the Yangtse to the Yellow River, begun at least 2,500 years ago and much of it still in use, despite silting.

Grand Canyon Gorge of the Colorado River in north Arizona, up to more than a mile deep, 4–18 miles wide, with fantastically eroded and coloured rock masses giving a conspectus of geological time. Nearly half its length, which is well over 200 miles, lies in the Grand Canyon National-al Park (1919). Pueblo and Cliff Dweller ruins, motor-boat trips along the river and mule rides down to it are among the attractions which make it the mecca of tourists from all over the world.

Grand Challenge Cup (1839). (Henley) Original Henley Regatta trophy, the open 8-oar event.

Grande Armée, La Napoleon's army, particularly the force of some 400,000 with which he invaded Russia in 1812, two-thirds of them Germans, Austrians, Poles or Italians.

Grande Corniche Highest of the 3 mountain roads from Nice to Menton in the French Riviera. There are also a coastal Corniche and a Moyenne Corniche via Èze. (French, 'great cornice', which the mountain road resembles.)

Grand Guignol What in the modern idiom might be termed the Theatre of the Horror-comic: short eerie plays about ghosts, murder, etc. The term was made familiar in Britain in the 1920s by a series of such plays starring Sybil Thorndike. (Guignol, chief character in a French version of the Punch and Judy show.)

Grand Hotel, Brighton Scene of bombing in

October 1984 of Conservative conference head-quarters.

Grand Inquisitor, The Legend of the Most famous chapter of *The* BROTHERS KARAM-AZOV, reflecting Dostoyevsky's own religious doubts. Ivan Karamazov tells his brother Alyosha of how Christ returns during the Inquisition at Seville and is arrested. The Grand Inquisitor tells him that the Church no longer wants him, that mankind needs leadership, not freedom which it is too weak and foolish to put to proper use. He opens the prison door; Christ, silent throughout, kisses his cheek and departs.

Grandma Moses Mrs Moses (1860–1961). American painter of Irish and Scottish descent, who did not begin to paint until she was nearly 70 and then produced famous 'primitives' of rural life in New England, as she remembered it from her childhood days there.

Grand Marnier French version of CURAÇAO.

Grand Monarque, Le Louis XIV.

Grand National, The (1839). Chief event of the steeplechasing year, run in March/April over a $4\frac{1}{2}$ mile course with 30 fearsome fences, including BECHER'S BROOK, which have to be jumped twice. Held at Aintree, near Liverpool.

Grand Prix de Paris French equivalent of the Derby, run at LONGCHAMP in June over a course one furlong longer (i.e. 13 furlongs).

Grand Prix races (Car racing). Ten races for single-seater FORMULA 1 cars, held annually in 10 countries, in which points gained count towards the world championship for drivers and constructors.

Grand Remonstrance (1641). Resolution presented by John Pym condemning Charles I's policies and demanding Church reform, carried by a narrow majority in the LONG PARLIA-MENT. See FIVE MEMBERS.

Grand Siècle, Le Long reign of Louis XIV (1643–1715), during which France dominated Europe until 1685 (see Wars of the League of AUGSBURG: SPANISH SUCCESSION). It was the age of L'État c'est moi, Versailles, Corneille, Racine, Molière. (French, 'the great century'.)

Grandsire One of the principal methods of change-ringing church bells.

Grand Tour In the 18th century, part of the education of every young Englishman whose parents could afford it was a tour of the main artistic centres of Europe, especially France and Italy. Memorials to this custom remain in the names of hotels, e.g. Bristol, Carlton, etc.

Grand Trianon (1687). Palace built at Versailles for Louis XIV by Mansart, allowed to go to ruin in the middle of the 19th century. Now rebuilt as a great new show-place, where visiting heads of state can reside.

Grangerize Practice of adding to books, portraits, prints, etc., from James Granger, who published a *Biographical History of England* with blank leaves for additions.

Granicus (334 BC). First of the 3 battles in which Alexander the Great defeated the Persians. (River of north-west Anatolia, near the Dardanelles; pronounced gran-y'-kus.)

Granite State Nickname of New Hampshire.

Granny flat Addition to a house to accommodate an elderly parent.

Granny Smith Large, hard, green apple of excellent flavour imported into Britain from various parts of the world over much of the year. (Originated when Maria Ann Smith of New South Wales planted seeds from rotting apples found in a gin barrel in 1869.)

Granta (1889). Cambridge University undergraduate magazine. Since 1979 a mass-circulation literary magazine. (The name borne by the Cam south of the town.)

Grantchester Village near Cambridge especially remembered for Rupert Brooke's poem, 'The Old Vicarage, Grantchester' (1912), written with nostalgic playfulness in a Berlin café. Its most famous lines are: 'Stands the Church clock at ten to three? / And is there honey still for tea?'

Granth Sacred book of the SIKHS, the first part, Adi Granth ('original book'), dating from the 16th century and the rest compiled by the 10th and last Guru, Govind SINGH. After his death

(1708), the book came to symbolize the Guru and was called Granth Sahib ('holy book'). (Pronounced grunt.)

Grapes of Wrath, The (1939). John Steinbeck's saga of the Joad family, driven from the dustbowl of Oklahoma to California in search of work as fruit-pickers.

Grasmere Sports Lake District annual meeting held in a natural arena at the foot of Butter Crag; it includes wrestling, hound trails, and a fell race to the 900-ft summit of Butter Crag and back.

Grasshoppers (1) Cambridge University lawn tennis club. (2) Preston (Lancashire) rugby club.

Graves (1) Medium-sweet Bordeaux white wine, notably Château Carbonnieux. (2) Claret, notably Château Haut-Brion.

Gray's Anatomy Standard textbook on human anatomy, by Henry Gray, now in its 30th edition.

Gray's Elegy (1750). Thomas Gray's *Elegy Written in a Country Church Yard*, traditionally written in a tree (still standing) by the church door at Stoke Poges (near Slough). Deliberately using the simplest, shortest words, not one of them otiose, he managed to pack into a brief poem a wealth of meditative reflection on mortality and a moving evocation of English peasant life; almost every line is quotable, and quoted.

Gray's Inn Youngest of the INNS OF COURT, attended particularly by provincial barristers.

Great Assize Day of Judgement.

Great Bear English name of Ursa Major, the northern constellation in which the alpha and beta stars are the Pointers, pointing to the Pole Star. The 7 conspicuous stars are known as the PLOUGH.

Great Bible, The (1539). Revised edition of COVERDALE'S BIBLE commissioned by Thomas Cromwell, and reissued the following year with a preface by Archbishop Cranmer ('Cranmer's Bible').

Great Britain See ACTS OF UNION.

Great Britain SS *Great Britain* was launched in 1843. She was the first ocean-going, propeller-driven ironship and was designed by I. K. Brunel. After being abandoned in the Falkland Islands in 1886 she was towed back to Bristol in 1970, where she was built, and is being restored to her 1843 appearance.

Great Cham of Literature Nickname for Dr Samuel Johnson, coined by Smollett. (Cham, old French translation of *Khan*, i.e. ruler of the Tartars and Mongols, and emperor of China; pronounced kam.)

Great Commoner, The The Elder Pitt, Earl of Chatham.

Great Divide (1) Watershed of the Rocky Mountains in North America; (2) Death.

Great Eastern, The (1856). Largest steamship of its day, a 12,000-tonner designed by I. K. Brunel for the transatlantic run. It was a failure.

Great Elector Frederick William, Elector of Brandenburg (1620–88), who first made Brandenburg-Prussia a powerful state.

Great Exhibition, The (1851). First industrial exhibition, promoted by Prince Albert and held in Hyde Park in the CRYSTAL PALACE.

Great Expectations (1861). One of the best of Dickens's novels, in which the village boy Pip gets ideas above his station; cheated of his great expectations in London, he returns to his village friends and eventually marries the woman he loves.

Great Fear Panic that spread throughout France, with the exception of Alsace, Lorraine, Brittany and Lower Languedoc, from 20 July to 6 August 1789. It originated in a rumour that brigands in the pay of aristocrats were going to attack in order to restore the status quo. The peasants took up arms and barricaded their homes and property. Though no attack was forthcoming, once armed, the peasants made many attempts to destroy châteaux, and considerable destruction of manorial records resulted.

Great Fire of London (1666). Fire which destroyed more than half the City of London, including Old St Paul's.

Great Gatsby, The (1925). Scott Fitzgerald's only great novel, a fable of the American JAZZ AGE. Jay Gatsby dreams only of winning back his early love, Daisy, now married to another. He has made a fortune dishonestly, solely to dazzle her with riches, but fails. He shields Daisy who, driving his car, unknowingly kills her husband's mistress, Myrtle. Myrtle's husband, wrongly supposing that Gatsby has seduced and killed her, shoots him. Of the hordes of people he had so lavishly entertained at his luxury home, only one turns up for his funeral, together with Gatsby's humble father (Gatz) and the narrator, Daisy's cousin.

Great Harry (1540). First battleship, a 3-master of 1,000 tons re-equipped after a fire with 2 tiers of guns. (Her official name was *Henry Grâce à Dieu*, named after Henry VIII.)

Great-heart, Mr Character in Part II of PILGRIM'S PROGRESS who is appointed guide to Christian's wife and children on their pilgrimage.

Great Illusion, The (1910). Sir Norman Angell's book on the futility of war, for victor and vanquished.

Great Khan Title of the Mongol rulers of China.

Great Leap Forward (1958–9). Chinese name for Mao Tse-tung's programme for a national effort to double China's productivity in agriculture and industry, and for the introduction of the commune system of self-contained rural units in which workers are housed and fed by the state. Its complete failure was attributed to 2 bad harvests and the withdrawal of Soviet technical assistance.

Great Mogul, The The MOGUL Emperor.

Great Mother See CYBELE.

Great Patriotic War, The (1941–5). Russia's parochial name for World War II.

Great Plague (1665). Last serious outbreak of bubonic plague in Britain, said to have killed one-eighth of the population.

Great Plains Semi-arid region in Canada and USA east of the Rocky Mountains.

Great Powers Before 1914, Britain, France, Russia, Germany and Austria–Hungary. The USA held an isolationist policy until 1917 and so was not included.

Great Pyramid of Cheops See GIZA.

Great Rebellion, The Another name for the ENGLISH CIVIL WAR.

Great Rift Valley Deep valley, caused by faults in the earth's crust, running from Syria through the Dead Sea and Red Sea to Lake Rudolf and there dividing into two, one valley continuing through Lake Albert to Lake Tanganyika, the other extending to Lake Nyasa.

Greats Final BA examination at Oxford University, especially for honours in LIT. HUM.; see also MODERN GREATS.

Great Schism (1) Period 1378–1417 after the AVIGNONESE CAPTIVITY, when French efforts to maintain dominance over the Papacy led to a split in Western Christendom, with rival Popes ruling in Rome and in Avignon. (2) Less often used of the final break between the Western Church and the EASTERN ORTHODOX CHURCH (1054).

Great Society, The (1964). President Johnson's name for his proposed programme of social reform and racial toleration, which was hampered by Congressional opposition and preoccupation with Vietnam and the space-race with Russia. Compare NEW FRONTIER.

Great Tom The bell of Christ Church, Oxford; see TOM TOWER.

Great Train Robbery (1963). See BUCKINGHAMSHIRE TRAIN ROBBERY.

Great Train Robbery, The (1903). First successful one-reel narrative film, made by Edwin Porter, which marked the transformation of the cinema from a music-hall act to an entertainment in its own right.

Great Trek, The See VOORTREKKERS.

Great Wall of China Defensive wall along the old Chinese border with Manchuria and Mongolia;

the first section was completed in the 3rd century BC. but later greatly extended until it was 1,400 miles long. Restored under the Communist regime, it starts from the coast north of Tianjin, passes north of Beijing and reaches almost to the border of Xianjiang Uygur.

Great Wen, The William Cobbett's name for London.

Great White Way See BROADWAY.

Grecian Urn, Ode on a (1820). Keats's poem on the theme 'Beauty is truth, truth beauty' in which he contrasts, through the description of a Greek vase, the evanescence of mortal life and the timelessness of art.

Grecque (Cooking) Term usually indicating that the dish is fried in oil.

'Greek' Something not understandable, as in the phrase 'it's all Greek to me'. (From *Julius Caesar*, 1, ii, where Casca says: 'For mine own part, it was all Greek to me.')

Greek Anthology, The Collection of several thousand short poems covering about 17 centuries from the 7th century BC, which grew from earlier collections. The manuscript was not discovered until the 17th century.

Greek calends Phrase meaning 'never'. (Calends, first day of the month in the Roman calendar; there were no Greek calends.)

Greek Church Incorrect term for the EASTERN ORTHODOX CHURCH.

Greek fire An early form of flame-thrower used against the Arabs who attacked Byzantium in the 7th century AD.

Greek War of Independence (1821). Long struggle which began with revolts in the Peloponnese against the Turks, and in 1829 won the independence of mainland Greece south of Thessaly, thereafter ruled by a succession of foreign kings. The Ionian Islands, Thessaly, Crete, Macedonia and Thrace were all added by 1913.

Greenaway (Kate) Medal Library Association's annual award for the most distinguished work in illustrating children's books.

Green Belt Device to contain urban sprawl; a wide belt of countryside round a city is designated as an area in which all building development is under strict control, although permission is often granted for 'in-filling', i.e. putting up new buildings in among existing ones, a relaxation sometimes abused.

Green Bicycle case Murder case in the 1920s in which a schoolmaster named Light was charged with shooting a girl in a country lane. He had been seen with her pushing a green bicycle later found in a river. He pleaded that he had thrown it there in a panic, and was acquitted.

Greengage Green-gold plum from a tree imported from France by Sir William Gage.

Greenham Common (1983). Long-lasting demonstration by women against the siting of CRUISE MISSILES at this air base in Berkshire, and at Molesworth, Cambridgeshire.

Greenhouse effect Increase in global surface temperature due to increases of carbon dioxide and other gases, especially methane, nitrous oxide and chlorofluorocarbons. Some of the effects could be that sea-levels rise as a result and it could also lead to an alteration in agriculture because of rainfall patterns changing.

Greenmail Financial term for buying a significant stake in a company at one price and agreeing to be bought out by the directors at a large premium as an alternative to a takeover bid.

Green Mountain State Nickname of Vermont. (After the Green Mountains, clothed with evergreen forest.)

Green Paper Government publication outlining some project for radical reform on which it wants the views and suggestions of the electorate before deciding whether to commit itself to the proposal.

Green pound Represents the rate at which prices are fixed under the COMMON AGRICULTURAL POLICY designed to protect consumers of agricultural products against sudden movements of currency. These prices are fixed in European units of account (ECU) but the green pound was originally based on the US dollar.

Green Room Club (1877). London club in Adam Street for stage professionals. (The Green Room was formerly the name given to a rest-room for actors when not on stage; term now used for 'back-stage' as in 'green-room gossip'; the first such room, at Drury Lane, was decorated in green.)

Greens People and parties who favour and promote conservation of the earth and life in all its forms, opposing all kinds of pollution of the soil, the air, etc. This movement has grown in size and strength in many countries, and has become an increasingly powerful force in politics.

'Greensleeves' (1584). Elizabethan ballad and air, described as 'a new courtly sonnet of the Lady Greensleeves', which quickly became popular and is mentioned by Shakespeare.

Greenwell's Glory Successful fly for trout-fishing.

Greenwich Inner London borough since 1965 consisting of those parts of the former metropolitan boroughs of Greenwich and Woolwich that lie south of the Thames. See ROYAL OBSERVATORY.

Greenwich mean time Standard time in the UK and parts of Western Europe. See ROYAL OBSERVATORY.

Greenwich Village (The Village). Area of New York City west of Washington Square, once the haunt of artists and writers.

Gregorian Calendar See NEW STYLE. (Introduced by Pope Gregory XIII in 1582.)

Gregorian chant Form of plainsong dating from the 6th century and still used in Roman Catholic and Anglican High Church services. The music is sung in unison, unaccompanied, with the great freedom of rhythm also found in the Anglican chant used in singing psalms in English. (Named after Pope Gregory the Great.)

Grenadier Guards (1685). Ranks as the first regiment of the British Army, although the Royal Scots and the Coldstream Guards are older units. They wear their buttons set singly, and a white plume. See GUARDS DIVISION.

Gresham lectures Free public lecture courses on divinity, astronomy, music, geometry, law, 'physic' and rhetoric, given at Gresham College, now part of the City University, Finsbury. Lecturers are appointed by the MERCERS' COMPANY and the Corporation of London.

Gresham's Law (1558). That bad money tends to drive good out of circulation; e.g. if the gold content of the sovereign is reduced, the old coinage will be hoarded. (Attributed to Sir Thomas Gresham, but formulated first by Copernicus.)

Gretchen (In *Faust*) See MARGARET.

Gretna Green Village just over the Scottish border from Carlisle, favoured by English runaway couples since the 18th century, as parental consent to marriage is not required in Scotland for those aged 16 (18 in England, from 1970), and a simple declaration of intent before witnesses is sufficient. From 1856 21 days' residence in Scotland by one party was necessary. The village blacksmith used to augment his income by acting as witness, alleging a tradition that his predecessors of old used to perform such marriages themselves; in 1939 a court declared this tradition unfounded.

Gretna Green disaster (1915). One of the worst disasters in British railway history, involving 2 passenger trains and a troop train during World War I; 227 people were killed. (See previous entry.)

Greville Memoirs, The Three volumes of political memoirs covering the period 1817–60, written by Charles Greville and published posthumously at various dates but not in their complete form until 1938. They throw much light on the events and personalities of his times.

Grey Friars See FRANCISCANS.

Greyfriars School in the MAGNET LIBRARY series.

Greyhound buses (USA) Long-distance coaches providing swift cheap travel over much of the country.

Greyhound Derby (1927). Culminating event of the dog-track season, held towards the end of June at Wimbledon (1990).

Greyhounds Oxford University rugby club of the 60 best players in residence (elected for life).

Grimaldi, House of Ruling dynasty of the principality of Monaco since the Middle Ages; Prince Rainier III, who succeeded to the title in 1949, is the 30th of the line.

Grimalkin Old cat, especially a witch's familiar; a spiteful old woman. (From grey + Malkin, old diminutive of Matilda.)

Grimes, Capt Seedy prep-school master of Evelyn Waugh's DECLINE AND FALL who explains that he is always 'in the soup' but survives through the glamour conferred by a year or so at Harrow (before his expulsion), and his artificial leg (he was run over by a Stoke-on-Trent tram when drunk) which people assumed to be the reason for his brief war service (ended by court martial).

Grime's Graves Five-thousand-year-old flint mine, near Brandon, Norfolk.

Grimm's Law (1822). Law of regular consonantal changes from one INDO-EUROPEAN LANGUAGE to another. To take 2 examples: English brother (ten), in Sanskrit *bhratar* (*dasa*), Greek *phrater* (*deka*), Latin *frater* (*decem*), German *Bruder* (*zehn*). (Formulated by Jacob Grimm, one of the 2 brothers who wrote *Grimm's Fairy Tales*.)

Griselda (Grisel, Griseldis, etc.) Patient, faithful wife in a tale told by Boccaccio and by Chaucer in the Clerk's Tale, among others.

Grocers, Worshipful Company of (1428). LIVERY COMPANY, originally a guild of dealers in goods in 'gross', i.e. in bulk, including e.g. canvas, copper and iron in addition to groceries. Oundle School was founded by a Grocer who left funds in trust to the Company.

Grock Stage name of the famous Swiss clown Adrien Wettach, who died in 1959.

Grolier Club New York club named after Jean Grolier, a French bibliophile of the 18th century.

Groote Schuur Home of Cecil Rhodes outside Cape Town, later the official residence of the South African Prime Minister. (Afrikaans, 'great barn'.)

Gross National Product (GNP) Calculation of a country's income, being the market value of the total output of goods and services during the year.

Grosvenor Square See LITTLE AMERICA.

Grote Professor Holder of the chair of the Philosophy of Mind and Logic at London University.

Groucho (1985). London club, membership of which is mainly literary.

Groundnut Scheme (1948–53). British Labour government's scheme to start groundnut farming in East Africa, financed through the Overseas Food Corporation. It foundered through insufficient consultation with local experts, particularly on the cost of destumping virgin bush.

Group Areas Act (1950). South African Act which provided for the residential segregation of Whites, Indians, Coloureds and Bantu, a major apartheid measure.

Group of Ten USA, UK, Canada, France, West Germany, Holland, Belgium, Italy, Sweden and Japan who, after Britain's 1961 balance of payments crisis, agreed to pay extra quotas to the INTERNATIONAL MONETARY FUND as and when required, in order to increase its lending resources. Switzerland is an associate member.

Grove Short title for Sir George Grove's *Dictionary of Music and Musicians* (1878–89, with subsequent revisions). A standard work of reference on the subject. A completely new edition known as New Grove was published in 1980.

GRU Chief Soviet army intelligence organization, working under the KGB. It carries out subversion abroad, the breaking down of foreign ciphers, and frontier operations.

Grub Street Term of disparagement applied to literary hack-work of poor quality. (Former name of Milton Street, Moorfields, London, where such work was produced in the 17th century.)

Gruyère Mild hard-pressed cheese characterized by holes smaller than those in Emmentaler. (Originally made at Gruyères, Switzerland.)

GSB (1791). Usual abbreviation for the *General Stud Book* published periodically by Weatherby & Co. Only animals entered in this book may run on licensed racecourses.

G-string (1) String of a musical instrument tuned to G. (2) Garment, aptly termed *le minimum* by the French, which forms the strip-teaser's last defence.

G·suit Jet-pilot's tight-fitting inflatable suit designed to counteract the physical effects of acceleration due to gravity (G) in high-speed manoeuvres, thus preventing blackouts.

Guadalcanal, Battle of (November 1942). Series of naval actions ending in US victory over the Japanese fleet in the Solomon Islands.

Guantánamo US naval base in Cuba.

Guardian Fiction award An annual award of £1,000 for a novel written by a British or Commonwealth author.

Guardians, The (1834–1929). Colloquial term for the local elected Board of Guardians of the Poor, who administered the Poor Law (relief of the destitute) in a town or in a group ('union') of parishes (see UNION). This system was replaced by the Public Assistance Committees, and later by the National Assistance Board. 'On the Guardians' meant 'in receipt of Poor Law relief'.

Guards Chapel Chapel of the Brigade of Guards at Wellington Barracks, London, demolished by a flying-bomb during a Sunday service, June 1944; now rebuilt.

Guards Club (1810). London Club now amalgamated with the CAVALRY.

Guards Division, The (1968). One of the 6 infantry divisions, formed from the 8 battalions of the BRIGADE OF GUARDS.

Guelph Family name of the Elector of Hanover who became George I of England, and of his successors of the House of Hanover. See next entry; see WETTIN.

Guelphs and Ghibellines (1) in 12th-century Germany the supporters respectively of the Dukes of Bavaria and the HOHENSTAUFENS in their struggle for the imperial throne. (2) In medieval Italy the name was adopted by those who supported the Pope and the Emperor, respectively. (Guelph was a family name; Ghibelline derives from the name of a Hohenstaufen estate.)

Guermantes Representatives of the highest Parisian society in Proust's REMEMBRANCE OF THINGS PAST, the duchess being related to several European royal families. In the course of the novel both the despised Mme VERDURIN and GILBERTE marry into the family.

Guernica (April 1937). Ancient capital of the Basques in northern Spain, completely destroyed by German planes in the service of Franco during the SPANISH CIVIL WAR; a quarter of the population of this undefended little township were killed.

Guernica (1937). Picasso's famous painting, made immediately after the event, symbolizing the horrors of the purposeless destruction of Guernica (see previous entry).

Guernsey cattle Dairy breed, larger than the Jersey, producing high-quality yellow milk: particularly common in Cornwall; fawn, sometimes with white markings.

Guernsey Lily Most beautiful species of the Nerine lilies, a South African bulbous plant which can be cultivated out of doors in the Channel Islands but not in England.

Guest worker (1975). Foreign worker with limitations on the right to work and reside in a country.

Guggenheim Museum New York City's Museum of Non-Objective Art, designed by Frank Lloyd Wright on novel lines, access to exhibits being by a continuous spiral ramp.

Guildenstern See ROSENCRANTZ AND GUILDENSTERN.

Guildford Four (1974). Three Irish men and an English woman were given life imprisonment in 1975 for alleged IRA public-house bombings in Guildford and Woolwich in 1974, but on appeal in 1989 they were freed because of doubt about the honesty and integrity of a number of police officers.

Guildhall (1411). The 'town hall' of the City of London, off Cheapside. Badly damaged in World War II, the Great Hall where City banquets are held has been restored. There is also a large library and an art gallery.

Guild Socialism (1906). Form of Socialism in which industries would be run by their trade unions reorganized on the lines of medieval guilds; it rejected nationalization by the State.

Guillotin Though the instrument of execution was named after Joseph Guillotin (1738–1814), he did not actually design it.

Guillotine, The (1887). Parliamentary device to expedite consideration of a long, complicated or hotly disputed Bill; a time limit for debate on each clause is enforced.

Guinea Pig Club (1942). Club formed for Allied airmen who had wartime plastic surgery in the McIndoe Burns Unit at EAST GRINSTEAD.

Guineas, The Common abbreviation for the TWO THOUSAND GUINEAS.

Guinevere King Arthur's wife, who fell in love with LANCELOT.

Guinness affair (1986). Investigation by the UK government into the £2,700-million takeover by GUINNESS for the Distillers group which led to criminal charges being brought against the Guinness chief executive and his advisers.

Guinness (Arthur) (1799). Irish stout firm, which also produces Harp lager.

Guinness Book of Records (1955). Annual publication providing a means for peaceful settlement of record performances.

Guinness Mahon (1836). A London merchant bank and acceptance house.

Guise, House of French Catholic family prominent in the 16th-century religious wars and largely responsible for the ST BARTHOLOMEW MASSACRE. See HOLY LEAGUE.

Gujarati Indo-European language spoken by the majority of the inhabitants of GUJARAT.

Gulag Soviet penal system under Stalin; acronym for the chief administration of corrective labour camps.

Gulbenkian Foundation (1955). International foundation which provides funds for charity and to foster art, science and education. (Calouste Gulbenkian, Armenian financier; see MR FIVE PER CENT.)

Gulf Stream Warm ocean current which flows north from the Gulf of Mexico up the east coast of North America, meets the LABRADOR CURRENT off Newfoundland and then flows northeast to warm the climate of Western Europe and especially of the British Isles. See GRAND BANKS.

Gulliver's Travels (1726). Jonathan Swift's great satire on mankind, in the form of a journal kept by Lemuel Gulliver, a ship's doctor. See LILLIPUT; LAPUTA; BROBDINGNAG; HOUYHNHNMS; YAHOOS.

GUM Moscow's vast department store, state-owned.

Gummidge, Mrs Self-pitying widow who keeps house for Daniel Peggotty in DAVID COPPERFIELD; 'everything goes contrairy with me'.

Gunbatsu The military caste of Japan which led it into World War II.

'Gunga Din' Kipling's poem in BARRACK-ROOM BALLADS about an Indian water-carrier, ending with the often quoted line: 'You're a better man than I am, Gunga Din!'

Gunmakers, Worshipful Company of (1637). LIVERY COMPANY which still has the statutory duty of proving small arms and hand-guns.

Gunn, Martha Bathing attendant at Brighton

said to have given the infant Prince of Wales (George IV) his first dip in the sea; her name is perpetuated in 'female Toby' jugs.

Gunners, The (1) The Royal Artillery. (2) Nickname of the ARSENAL football team.

Gunpowder Plot (1605). Roman Catholic plot to kill James I at the state opening of Parliament on 5 November by exploding barrels of gunpowder in the vaults.

Gunther In the *Nibelungenlied*, King of Burgundy, husband of BRUNHILD and brother of KRIEMHILD.

Gupta dynasty (AD 320–647). Indian rulers who united northern India and revived Hinduism, which in time absorbed the Buddhist religion; literature and the arts flourished under their patronage. (Pronounced gup′ta.)

Gurdjieff's teachings Body of esoteric knowledge which, it is said, the Armenian Greek Gurdjieff was sent to the West by the SUFIS to impart as an experiment. Gurdjieff, a bizarre figure who wrote bizarre books, provided the mysticism, Ouspensky the brains, and intellectuals of Britain, France and USA the money. After his death the movement dissolved into dissentient sects. See CHÂTEAU DU PRIEURÉ.

Gurkhas Ruling race of Nepal, a Mongoloid mountain people of Hindu religion who since 1815 have provided the British Army with soldiers renowned for loyalty and courage. See next entry.

Gurkhas, The Brigade of Infantry brigade comprising: 2nd King Edward VII's Own Gurkha Rifles (The Sirmoor Rifles); 6th Queen Elizabeth's Own Gurkha Rifles; 7th Duke of Edinburgh's Own Gurkha Rifles; 10th Princess Mary's Own Gurkha Rifles. GHQ, Singapore.

Gussies Stock Exchange name for shares in Great Universal Stores.

Gustav Line German defence line across Italy, between Naples and Rome, with MONTE CASSINO as its central feature; breached May 1944.

Gutenberg Bible (1450s). First book printed in Europe from movable type, at Mainz, probably by Gutenberg, the inventor of modern printing; an edition of the VULGATE. Forty-six reasonably complete copies have survived, including the Mazarin Bible found in Paris (1760), and one in the HUNTINGTON LIBRARY.

Gutenberg Galaxy, The See MCLUHANISM.

Guy Fawkes plot See GUNPOWDER PLOT.

Guy Mannering (1815). Walter Scott's 18th-century novel about a child heir, Harry Bertram, smuggled out of the country by a lawyer who covets his estate. He joins the army in India, ignorant of his real name and parentage, but after many adventures returns to claim his inheritance. Meg MERRILIES and Dandy DINMONT appear in this book.

Guyot Flat-topped submarine mountain found in the Pacific named after A. H. Guyot (1808–84), a Swiss geographer.

Guy's (1721). Teaching hospital near London Bridge station. (Founded by Thomas Guy, bookseller and a governor of St Thomas's Hospital.)

GWR Initials of the Great Western Railway, with London headquarters at Paddington. It is now the Western Region of British Railways.

Gwynedd Welsh name for north-west Wales (Caernarvon, Merioneth and part of Denbigh).

Gymnast Early name for TORCH.

Gymnosperms Conifers, as opposed to the flowering ANGIOSPERMS.

Gypsies Nomadic people, probably from north-west India, who spread to Anatolia and North Africa (7th century BC) and from there into Europe; another stream went to Russia. Basically horse-copers, tinkers and fortune-tellers (a craft they claim to have learnt from the Chaldeans). (English name, derived from *Egypt*, one of the many lands where they dwelt.)

Gypsy Moth See GIPSY MOTH.

Gypsy Rose Lee Stage name of Rose Louise Hovick of Seattle (1914–70), erudite strip-teaser who took to the art (of which she disapproved) at 16, keeping to a colleague's advice, 'You gotta leave 'em hungry; you don't dump the whole roast on the platter', and enlivening her act by quotations from Spinoza or Aldous Huxley. On her retirement (at 23, a rival having dared to call her Lady Go-flops), she wrote a very funny autobiography, *Gypsy* (later staged and screened), and some best-selling thrillers, e.g. *The G-String Murder*.

H

Habakkuk Biblical prophet. His period is the time of the Babylonian conquests. A commentary on Habakkuk was one of the most valuable of the Dead Sea scrolls, found in 1947.

Habeas Corpus Act (1679). Shaftesbury's Act to abolish arbitrary imprisonment, which provided that every prisoner must be brought before a court within a specified time; passed in the reign of Charles II after the POPISH PLOT. (First words of the writ: (I hear) that you have the body.)

Haberdashers, Worshipful Company of (1448). LIVERY COMPANY, originally a guild of makers of fustian garments worn under armour. It gives largely to charity and education.

Haberdashers' Aske's Boys' Public School at Elstree, Hertfordshire, founded by Robert Aske, a Liveryman of the HABERDASHERS' COMPANY; there are 2 girls' and another boys' school of the same name.

Habsburg lip Protruding lower jaws which were a marked characteristic of the HABSBURGS for generations.

Habsburgs Family dynasty founded by Emperor Rudolf I (1273) which ruled over the HOLY ROMAN EMPIRE with occasional interregna until it ended in 1806, and then as Emperors of Austria–Hungary until 1918. In the 16th century, through Charles V, they inherited the Netherlands and the Spanish dominions of Ferdinand V (Spain, Naples, Sicily, Sardinia, and the Spanish American colonies), but the Spanish branch died out in 1700 and was succeeded by the BOURBONS. (Castle Habsburg, between Basle and Zürich, seat of the Counts of Habsburg.)

HAC See HONOURABLE ARTILLERY COMPANY.

Hackney Inner London borough since 1965 consisting of the former metropolitan boroughs of Hackney, Shoreditch and Stoke Newington.

Haddon Hall Best surviving example of a medieval manor house, situated near Bakewell, Derbyshire; it passed to the Earls (later Dukes) of Rutland through the elopement of Dorothy Vernon with Sir John Manners in the 16th century.

Hades (1) Greek god of the Underworld (Roman Pluto). (2) Underworld itself. (3) Hell (from its use to translate the Biblical Hebrew name *Sheol*, 'abode of the dead'). (Pronounced hay'deez.)

Hadith Oral traditions of the sayings and acts of the Prophet Muhammed, of varying authenticity, not committed to writing until 300 years after his death. Some of them are demonstrably spurious late additions. (Pronounced had'ith.)

Hadow report (1926). Report which recommended that children at English state schools should move at age 11 to separate post-primary schools instead of lingering on at elementary school until leaving-age of 14, learning little beyond the 3 Rs; and, secondly, that the leaving-age should be raised to 15. The leaving age was not implemented until after World War II.

Hadrian's Wall (AD 122–29). Roman wall in northern England, built from Bowness to Wallsend across the isthmus between the Tyne and Solway Firth.

Haganah Jewish underground force in Palestine which from Turkish times protected Jewish settlers. It offered only passive resistance to British mandatory rule, and condemned terrorist tactics. It later became the nucleus of the Israeli army. (Hebrew, 'defence'; pronounced hag-an-ah'.)

Hagar Sarah's servant, who bore ISHMAEL to Abraham; after Sarah had given birth to Isaac, she persuaded Abraham to drive out Ishmael and his mother into the wilderness (Gen. 21:14).

Hagen In the *Nibelungenlied* a henchman of Gunther who kills Siegfried, seizes KRIEMHILD'S gold and buries it in the Rhine. He refuses to reveal where it is hidden and is killed by Kriemhild.

Hague Conferences *First* (1899), called by the Tsar, originally to discuss limitation of armaments; it set up a Permanent Court of Arbitration at The Hague (the Hague Tribunal). *Second* (1907), made rules against the use in war of dum-dum (expanding) bullets, suffocating gases and missiles thrown from balloons.

Hague Court, The (1) Permanent Court of International Justice of the League of Nations (1922–45). (2) INTERNATIONAL COURT OF JUSTICE (1946), the principal judicial organ of the United Nations.

Hague Tribunal See HAGUE CONFERENCE (1899).

Haidée In Byron's DON JUAN, the lovely Greek girl who saves the hero from death. They are caught together by her pirate father, who sends him to slavery; she goes mad and dies. (Pronounced hy'dee.)

Haigh murder case (1949). Trial of J. G. Haigh, executed after being found guilty of murdering a woman and disposing of her body by rendering it down in an acid bath. In the period 1944–9 he treated 5 other women in the same way.

Hail and Farewell (1911–14). George Moore's 3-volume autobiography.

'Hail Columbia!' (1798). First national anthem of the USA, since superseded.

Haileybury Boy's public school near Hertford, established in 1806 by the East India Company to train cadets for service in the East.

Haj, Haji, Alhaji Title assumed by a Muslim who has made the pilgrimage to Mecca.

Hajji Baba Persian rogue in 2 novels (1824, 1828) by James Morier, who turns a satirical eye first on Persian and then on English ways.

Hakluyt Society (1846). Society with a high reputation for scholarly editions, carefully edited and annotated, of old books of travel. (Pronounced hak'loot.)

Hakluyt's *Voyages* In full *The Principal Navigations, Voyages and Discoveries of the English Nation* (1598–1600), compiled by an English clergyman, Richard Hakluyt, from English and foreign accounts of voyages made over the previous 1,500 years.

Half Ton Cup An international sailing contest similar to the ONE TON CUP, for boats rating not more than 18 ft.

Halifax (1941). Handley Page 4-engined heavy bomber used by the RAF in World War II.

Hall and Knight Authors (and short title) of a textbook on algebra which sold to countless generations of schoolchildren, and was published by Macmillan.

Hallé Orchestra Sir Charles Hallé, German-born British pianist and conductor (1819–95), founded the famous orchestra in Manchester.

Hallelujah Chorus By far the most widely known section of Handel's MESSIAH.

Halles, Les District in the 1st *arrondissement* of Paris where formerly the wholesale food trade was concentrated. The markets were transferred (1969–73) to Rungis, south of Paris. (Pronounced lay-zal'.)

Halley lecture (1910). Annual lecture at Oxford University on a subject connected with astronomy or terrestrial magnetism.

Halley's comet Comet observed in 1682, the return of which the astronomer Halley correctly predicted for 1759; last seen in 1985.

Hallowe'en 31 October, the 1st day of the old Celtic year, Christianized into the eve of All Hallows (see ALL SAINTS); celebrated particularly in Scotland and north England, and associated with witches, divination of future spouses, and various local customs.

Hallstatt Earliest IRON AGE culture of northern Europe, dating from the 7th century BC, and spread by Celts to LA TÈNE. (Named from a Celtic site in the Austrian Lake District.)

Hallstein doctrine (1955). That West Germany alone is competent to act on behalf of the whole German people (i.e. including East Germany), and that diplomatic recognition of Communist East Germany is an unfriendly act. (Dr Walter Hallstein, West German State Secretary.)

Halsbury report (1963). Report of a committee which recommended the adoption of decimal coinage, accepted in 1966 by the government, to come into force by February 1971.

Halsbury's *Laws of England* (1907–17). A 37-volume digest of English law in alphabetical order of subjects, edited by the first Earl of Halsbury, who had been Lord Chancellor.

Ham Son of Noah who offended by looking on his father when he was drunk and naked; according to the mutilated text of Genesis 9:22–3, Noah thereupon cursed not Ham but Ham's son Canaan, to be a 'servant of servants'. In Genesis 10:6 Ham is also the father of Cush (Ethiopia), Mizraim (Egypt) and Phut (Babylon). See HAMITES.

Ham, Son of (1) Person accursed (see previous entry). (2) A black man (according to one theory Ham was an ancient name for Egypt and meant 'black').

Hamadan rugs Hard-wearing Kurdish rugs (often in the form of long runners) with a heavy pile and bold designs in a limited range of good colours. They are named after the centre in north-west Persia where they were collected for export.

Hamamelis Genus name of the Witch Hazel.

Haman See ESTHER. (Pronounced hay'-man.).

Hambledon Club (1750). First cricket club, which ruled the game until the MCC took over control some 40 years later. It played on Windmill and Broadhalfpenny Downs in Hampshire. Its doings were chronicled by John Nyren (1764–1837), son of the founder.

Hambletonian Chief US trotting race for 3-year-olds, run at Goshen, New York. (Named after the ancestor of the best US trotting horses.)

Hambros (1839). Family merchant bank and acceptance house, founded by a Dane and still retaining its Scandinavian connections.

Ham House Jacobean house at Petersham, below Richmond Hill, Surrey, with a collection of Stuart furniture; administered by the Victoria and Albert Museum.

Hamilton Park Racecourse 9 miles south-east of Glasgow.

Hamites Inhabitants of North Africa and the Horn of Africa, brown, slender, with fine features; they include the BERBERS of North Africa (still distinguishable from the Semitic Arabs there), the ancient Egyptians and the Cushites (Ethiopians, Somali, Eritrean, etc.). See HAM; HAMITIC LANGUAGES.

Hamitic languages Those spoken by HAMITES, i.e. Berber (quite distinct from the Semitic languages, and most common in Morocco and the Sahara), Ancient Egyptian, and Cushitic (i.e. the non-Semitic languages of Ethiopia, Somalia, etc.). Roots of words tend to consist of 2 consonants instead of the 3 in Semitic languages.

Hamlet Introspective, vacillating Prince of Denmark of Shakespeare's play (1601), unable to steel himself to avenge the death of his father, whose ghost has accused Claudius, Hamlet's stepfather-uncle, of his murder; but the greatness of the play soars above the corpse-strewn plot.

Hamlet without the Prince A phrase used by Walter Scott (but of earlier origin) indicating that the most important person concerned has failed to appear or has not been mentioned etc. (See previous entry.)

Hamm See ENDGAME.

Hammer, Mike One-man police force and chief character in many of the novels of Mickey Spillane, America's Ian Fleming.

Hammer and sickle Symbol of the Soviet Union and the Communist Party, the hammer representing the industrial and the sickle the agricultural workers.

Hammer of the Scots Name of Edward I, earned by his attempts to subdue William Wallace and Robert the Bruce.

Hammers, The Nickname of the West Ham football team.

Hammersmith Inner London borough since 1965 consisting of the former metropolitan boroughs of Hammersmith and Fulham.

Hammond organ (1935). Electronic organ using not rotating magnetic generators but vibrating reeds and electrostatic conversion.

Hammurabi's code (1751 BC). Codification of existing harsh Babylonian law made by King Hammurabi. There are several copies inscribed on partially defaced stelae; the most complete, from Susa, is in the Louvre.

Hampden, Village Allusion to lines of GRAY'S ELEGY ('Some village-Hampden, that with dauntless breast / The little tyrant of his fields withstood'), referring to John Hampden, a Buckinghamshire squire who refused to pay ship money under Charles I in 1637, to force the issue of its legality. See also FIVE MEMBERS. (Pronounced ham'dn.)

Hampden Park International football ground at Glasgow, also the ground of the amateur club, QUEEN'S PARK. See next entry. (Pronounced ham'dn.)

Hampden roar, The Phenomenal noise which has become traditional at HAMPDEN PARK, generated by almost excessively partisan crowds, especially at the Scottish Cup Final.

Hampshire, HMS A cruiser, mined and sunk (June 1916) with all hands, while conveying Lord Kitchener, Secretary for War, to Russia.

Hampstead Former London metropolitan borough, since 1965 part of the borough of CAMDEN.

Hampstead Garden Suburb (1907). Privately developed estate on the edge of Hampstead Heath, London.

Hampton Court (1514). Palace built for Cardinal Wolsey but annexed by Henry VIII, now used in part for about 36 Grace and Favour apartments. Famous for its Great Vine, Maze and the Fountain Court by Wren. (Near Kingston upon Thames.)

Hampton Court Conference (1604). Summoned by James I in the first year of his reign, at which he rejected a petition by 1,000 Puritan clergy for greater religious freedom with the words 'No Bishop. No King'. It sanctioned the publication of the Authorized Version of the Bible (1611).

Handley Cross hunt Foxhounds of which JOR-ROCKS was appointed Master, as recorded in Surtees's *Handley Cross* (1843).

Handley Page British aircraft firm which made the first big twin-engine bomber (1917), many of the airliners used by Imperial Airways, and the HALIFAX bomber.

Handy Andy Nickname of Squire Egan's clumsy manservant in Samuel Lover's Irish novel of that name (1842); in the end he turns out to be an Irish peer.

Handy Man See 'HOMO HABILIS'.

Han Dynasty (206 BC to AD 221). Period during which all China came under one regime. Glazed pottery, lacquer work, silkweaving, calligraphy, portrait and other forms of painting were highly developed. The capital was Ch'ang-an, near Xian (Shensi Province). The next important dynasty was the T'ANG DYNASTY.

Hanging Gardens of Babylon One of the 7 Wonders of the World, a garden rising in terraces, said to have been built for his wife by Nebuchadnezzar.

Hankow See WUHAN.

Hannibalic War See PUNIC WARS.

Hanno's *Periplous* (5th century BC). Account of a Carthaginian coastal voyage down the west coast of Africa as far as Liberia or perhaps the Cameroons, during which trading stations were established. The account was inscribed on tablets in Phoenician, of which a Greek translation has survived. (Greek, 'sailing round'.)

Hanoi Capital of, and used as a synonym for the government of, North VIETNAM.

Hanover, House of (1714–1901). In Britain, the ruling house from the accession of George I (son of an ELECTOR of Hanover by James I's granddaughter) to the death of Queen Victoria. Hanover and Britain were united under one king until 1837, but on Queen Victoria's accession her uncle the Duke of Cumberland became King of Hanover.

Hanoverian Succession See ACT OF SETTLEMENT.

Hansard (1774). Official verbatim proceedings of the Houses of Parliament, since 1908 recorded by civil servants. (Luke Hansard, originator.)

Hanseatic League Thirteenth-century association of North German cities which once monopolized Baltic trade, but lost influence in the 17th century; leading members were Lübeck, Hamburg and Bremen. (Old High German *Hansa*, 'association'.)

Hänsel and Gretel Children of a broom-maker in Humperdinck's opera (1893) based on a fairy tale by the Grimm brothers. (Pronounced hans'l, gret'l.)

Hansom (1834). Cab, originally called 'Hansom's patent'; it was invented by Aloysius Hansom (1803–82).

Hanukkah, Chanukah Jewish festival of the Dedication of the Temple, on a date falling near Christmas Day. (Pronounced hah'nu-ka.)

Hanyang See WUHAN.

Hapsburg See HABSBURG.

Harappa One of the sites of the INDUS VALLEY CIVILIZATION.

Hard Day's Night, A (1964). The BEATLES' autobiographical film, script by Alun Owen, which depicted them as the exhausted victims of excessive fan-worship.

Harding, Rev. Septimus Character in Trollope's novels, see *The* WARDEN.

Hard Times (1845). Dickens's grim indictment of industrial England personified in Thomas GRADGRIND.

Hardwick Hall Country house near Chesterfield, Derbyshire, built by BESS OF HARDWICK, now owned by the National Trust.

Harewood House House near Leeds built by Robert Adam for the Lascelles family (Earls of Harewood), in a park laid out by CAPABILITY BROWN.

Haringey (1965). London borough consisting of the former boroughs of Wood Green, Hornsey and Tottenham; headquarters at Wood Green.

Harlem Black and Puerto Rican quarter in north Manhattan, New York City.

Harlem Globetrotters (1927). Team of highly skilled exhibition basketball players.

Harlequin Comic servant of the COMMEDIA DELL'ARTE, dressed in patchwork clothes of many colours, usually in love with Columbine. (Originally a jester in French mystery plays; Italian name Arlecchino.)

Harlequins (1) Leading rugby club, with headquarters at TWICKENHAM. (2) Oxford University cricket club, with membership limited to 20 men in residence, including Blues, elected for life.

Harley Street London street running north to Regent's Park, where some of the leading specialists have their consulting rooms, as also have psychiatrists, dentists, etc.

Harlots' Romp, The Nickname for QUEEN CHARLOTTE'S BALL.

Harmodius and Aristogeiton Two Athenian tyrannicides of the 6th century BC; they assassinated one of the joint tyrants of Athens, but the other had them put to death. There was a statue to them, of which a Roman copy survives in the National Museum, Naples.

'Harmonious Blacksmith, The' Name given, not by the composer, to one of Handel's compositions, said to have been suggested by the sound of a blacksmith's anvil.

Harmsworth Professor Holder of the chair of American History at Oxford.

Harpagon See AVARE, L'.

Harper's Bazaar (1867). US monthly magazine for women, published in New York.

Harper's Ferry (1859). Raid, 2 years before the AMERICAN CIVIL WAR, on an American government arsenal, led by the abolitionist John Brown (see 'JOHN BROWN'S BODY') to get weapons to arm a slave revolt in Virginia. No slaves joined him; he surrendered to Robert E. Lee (the future Confederate general) and was hanged. (Town in north-eastern West Virginia.)

Harper's Magazine (1850). An illustrated magazine published in New York, with general articles, short stories, etc.

Harrier (1967). Hawker-Siddeley V/STOL tactical strike-reconnaissance aircraft, a single-seat fighter able to fly close to Mach 1, developed from the KESTREL but more powerful.

Harris, Mrs Purely imaginary friend who is quoted in Sairey GAMP's anecdotes as corroborating her opinions. As Betsey Prig remarks: 'I don't believe there's no sich a person!'

Harris fire-raising case (1933). Burning down of several London warehouses in order to defraud insurance companies. Leopold Harris, who was charged with 13 others, was sentenced to 14 years for his leading part in the conspiracy.

Harris tweed Originally, tweed hand-spun, hand-woven and vegetable-dyed in the Outer Hebrides, soft in texture, coarse in appearance, usually made with wool from the SCOTTISH BLACKFACE. The craft developed in Harris in the 1860s and is now carried on in the Uists. Loosely applied also to hand-woven, aniline-dyed, machine-spun (with shorter fibre) tweed, mostly made in Lewis. See DONEGAL TWEED.

Harrison Cup (1947). Polo tournament played at Cowdray Park in July between teams with handicaps of 12–6 goals.

Harrods World-famous London department store, in Knightsbridge; it was founded by Henry and Charles Harrod in 1849, developing from a grocery store into the present grand emporium.

Harrow School founded and endowed by John Lyon (*c.* 1514–91) under Letters Patent and a Charter granted by Queen Elizabeth I; many great men were educated at Harrow, including Lord Byron and several prime ministers, notably Sir Winston Churchill.

Harry Price Library Collection of books on occultism, spiritualism and conjuring, now at London University.

Hartmannsweilerkopf German name in World War I for a Vosges mountain peak, fiercely contested between French and Germans, which plays in German war stories much the same role as HILL 60 in British.

Harun al-Rashid Caliph in the *Arabian Nights* who wandered through the streets of Baghdad at night seeking adventure; based on a historical person of that name, Caliph from AD 786.

Harvard (1636). Oldest US university, at Cambridge, Mass. The graduate school of business administration (the 'Harvard Business School') was established in 1908 and housed in Boston.

Harveian Oration (1657). Annual lecture given before the Royal College of Physicians in honour of William Harvey, on or about St Luke's Day,

18 October (St Luke is said to have been a physician.)

Harwell Atomic Energy Authority's centre for fundamental research into nuclear physics and nuclear energy. (Village in Berkshire, between Wantage and Didcot.)

Hashemites Arab family claiming descent from Mohammed's uncle Hashim, as did Abdullah, the first King of Jordan, and his brother Feisal, first King of Iraq, sons of Hussein, Sherif of Mecca. The WAHABIS drove them out of Arabia.

Haslemere Festival (1925). Annual festival of early music and instruments, held in July at Haslemere, Surrey, where the Swiss Dolmetsch family of musicians and makers of harpsichords, clavichords, recorders, etc. have long been established.

Hassan (1923). Melodramatic verse play by James Elroy Flecker about a fat confectioner of Baghdad and a pair of ill-starred lovers; spectacularly produced with ballets by Fokine and the music of Delius, it is remembered for its lyrics, notably the ode to Yasmin and 'The Golden Road to Samarkand'.

Hastings, Battle of (1066). Remarkably decisive battle, though probably fewer than 10,000 fought on either side, and only for a day. The bastard Duke William, with his Latinized ex-Viking Normans aided by Bretons, Angevins and Flemings, established himself at Hastings Castle while King Harold II was busy defeating Norway at Stamford Bridge. In the battle, on Senlac Hill (where Battle now stands and Battle Abbey, which William built in celebration), English infantry wielding the battleaxe were no match for William's mounted spear-cum-swordsmen and his archers.

Hatfield House Jacobean home in Hertfordshire of the junior line of Cecils (Marquesses of Salisbury) since it was built by Robert Cecil, 1st Earl of Salisbury; in the grounds is the Tudor palace where Queen Elizabeth I lived.

Hatha Yoga Form of YOGA best known in the West.

Hathor Ancient Egyptian goddess of the sky, daughter of Ra, whose symbol was a cow; she took many forms, and was associated with Isis, Osiris and Bast.

Hatry crash (1929). Major disaster in City history, when Clarence Hatry, who had financed UNITED STEEL, overreached himself and was sentenced to 14 years for fraud.

Hatters, The Nickname of the Luton Town football team, the town being once chiefly known for the manufacture of straw hats.

Hatter's Castle (1931). A. J. Cronin's first bestseller, about the career of an over-ambitious tradesman.

Hatton Garden Traditional centre in the City of London of British trade in diamonds and, to a lesser extent, in other precious stones.

Hauksbee, Mrs Character who appears in many of Kipling's stories of life in India. Lucy Hauksbee is a clever little flirt who loves to set the cat among the pigeons but is not bad at heart.

Haus der Kunst (Munich) Art gallery and museum in which are housed the best of the famous collections from the Alte and Neue Pinakothek, which were destroyed in World War II. (German, 'art-house'.)

Havana Declaration (1940). Made by the Pan-American Conference; in effect it prohibited the transfer of colonies in the western hemisphere to Axis powers.

Havering (1965). London borough consisting of the former borough of Romford and the urban district of Hornchurch; headquarters at Romford, Essex.

Havildar Sergeant in the (British) Indian Army. (Urdu, 'charge-holder'; pronounced hav'il-dar.)

Hawarden Market town of Flintshire, west of Chester, where Gladstone's home (Hawarden Castle, 1572) is situated. The house contains St Deniol's Library of theological and historical works. (Pronounced hard'n.)

Hawk US ground-to-air defence missile for use against low-flying aircraft; range 25 miles.

Hawker Siddeley Group Group of firms with factories in Britain, Canada, Australia, India and elsewhere, making aircraft.

Hawkeye State Nickname of Iowa.

Hawks (USA) Supporters of a militant foreign policy, in contrast to the DOVES.

Hawks Club Cambridge University social club for leading athletes.

Haworth Village near Keighley, Yorkshire, where the Brontës lived in the Parsonage, which is now preserved as a museum by the Brontë Society. (Pronounced haw'ĕrth.)

Hawthornden prize Annual award for the best imaginative work in prose or verse by a British author under 41.

Hawthorns, The Home of West Bromwich Albion football club.

Hay, Ian Pen-name of Maj. J. H. Beith, author of *The First Hundred Thousand* (1915) about the British Expeditionary Force, and of many light novels.

Haydn's Dictionary of Dates Standard work on the subject, first published in 1841, last revised in 1910. (Joseph Haydn, editor until 1855.)

Haydock Park Racecourse 5 miles south of Wigan.

Hay Fever (1925). Early Noël Coward comedy about a weekend party at the home of an ex-actress and her novelist husband.

Hays Office (1934). US censorship office set up by the film industry. (Established by Will Hays, president of the Motion Picture Producers and Distributors of North America, and former PMG.)

Hay Wain (1821). Most famous of Constable's paintings; now in the National Gallery, London.

H-bomb Hydrogen or thermonuclear fusion bomb, comprising an A-bomb as detonator surrounded by lithium deuteride. The detonation converts lithium to tritium which fuses with the

deuterium (both are hydrogen isotopes). The US exploded a thermonuclear device in 1952, said to be 5–7 megatons, i.e. 250 or more times the power of the Hiroshima A-bomb. In 1963 Russia claimed to have a 100-megaton bomb, equivalent to 5 million grand slams; or, put another way, to 14 years of nightly 1,000-bomber raids on one target, supposing each bomber dropped a Grand Slam.

H.C.E. Initials which recur throughout FIN-NEGANS WAKE, being the initials of the hero, H. C. Earwicker, and of key phrases such as Haveth Childer Everywhere, Here Comes Everybody, etc.

Head-hunter Person engaged in identifying and recruiting senior executives. In many cases, initially the hunted have had no thought or desire to change their place of employment.

Headingley Principal Yorkshire county cricket ground, at Leeds, and one of the Test match grounds.

Headlong Hall (1816). Thomas Love Peacock's 'novel' on much the same lines as NIGHTMARE ABBEY.

Headmasters' Conference (1896). Society of over 200 public schools and leading grammar schools for boys, admitted to membership on the bases of academic achievement, proportion of boys in the sixth form and going on to university, and degree of independence. The headmasters meet to discuss syllabuses, examinations and applications for membership.

Head of the River Race (1926). Timed race for eights over the University BOAT RACE course (but in the reverse direction), held at about the same date as that race; characterized by a very large entry. The name is also given to similar events elsewhere.

Hearst papers 'Yellow press' empire of sensational newspapers founded by the American Northcliffe, William Randolph Hearst (died 1951). He and his fantastic castle-home at San Simeon, California, were portrayed in the film CITIZEN KANE. The castle is now a museum.

Heartbreak House (1919). Bernard Shaw's

'fantasia in the Russian manner', an indictment of the cultured leisured classes of Western civilization who obstruct the LIFE FORCE with their apathy and muddle. Capt. Shotover says in the play: 'Every drunken skipper trusts to Providence – and Providence runs them on the rocks.'

Heartbreak Ridge Scene of bitter fighting in the KOREAN WAR, a strategic feature captured by US troops in September 1951.

Heart of Midlothian An Edinburgh football team which plays at Tynecastle Park. Usually abbreviated to 'Hearts'.

Heart of Midlothian (1818). Walter Scott's partly historical novel; see Jeanie DEANS. (Name of the prison or Tolbooth at Edinburgh, scene of a riot at the beginning of the book.)

Heart of the Matter (1948). Graham Greene's novel set in Freetown, Sierra Leone, it describes how a deputy commissioner of police, Scobie, is led to make various false moves. Finally he commits suicide; this is revealed by an intelligence agent who loves Scobie's wife. The novel has the overwhelming sense of sin which so often obtrudes in this Catholic convert's novels.

Hearts Nickname of the Heart of Midlothian football team.

Hearts of Oak Benefit Society (1834). Large Friendly Society.

Heath Clark lecture (1931). Annual lecture on a medical subject, given at London University.

Heathcliff Liverpool gypsy boy adopted and brought up by the EARNSHAW FAMILY in WUTHERING HEIGHTS. Humiliated by young Hindley Earnshaw and, as he feels, by his sister Catherine whom he passionately adores, he disappears, but returns later to dominate the household and wreak his revenge.

Heath murder case (1946). Trial of Neville Heath, executed for murdering 2 girls, within a fortnight.

Heath Robinson Name of a British cartoonist used adjectivally for anything resembling the whimsically intricate gadgetry to perform a simple operation which was the chief feature of his drawings for *Punch*. (W. Heath Robinson, 1892–1944.)

Heathrow (1946). Official name of London's main airport, commonly known as London Airport; used to distinguish it from London (Gatwick) Airport in Sussex. It lies east of Slough.

Heaven and Hell Book by Aldous Huxley; see DOORS OF PERCEPTION.

Heavenly Twins, The (Stars) CASTOR and POLLUX.

Heaviside layer Lower (E) layer of ionized gases in the ionosphere (see APPLETON LAYER) which reflects long-wave radio signals; sometimes used of the ionosphere as a whole. Also known as the Kennelly-Heaviside layer. (Oliver Heaviside. British physicist.)

Hebdomadal Council Governing body of Oxford University, so named because it meets weekly. (Greek *hebdomas*, 'week'.)

Hebe In Greek legend, a daughter of Zeus and Hera, and goddess of youth. She was cup-bearer to the gods until GANYMEDE took over the post; she then married Heracles (HERCULES). (Pronounced hee'bee.)

Hecate In early Greek legend the triple goddess of the sky, the earth and the Underworld; lately chiefly regarded as the patroness of witches, associated with cross-roads. (Pronounced hek'a-tee.)

Hector In Greek legend, the chief Trojan hero, son of Priam and Hecuba, husband of Andromache. He killed Patroclus (see ILIAD), and was himself killed by Achilles.

Hecuba In Greek legend, wife of King Priam of Troy. At the fall of Troy she was carried off by the Greeks and saw 2 of her children killed. She appears in Euripides' *The Trojan Women* and *Hecuba*. In Shakespeare's play, seeing an actor moved to tears by her tragedy, Hamlet muses: 'What's Hecuba to him, or he to Hecuba, / That he should weep for her?' (Pronounced hek'ewba.)

Hedda Gabler (1890). Ibsen's play in which Hedda, a self-centred woman who despises her husband, tries to experience life vicariously through Løvborg, who is in love with her. She steals and destroys his new manuscript, driving him to kill himself. Seeing no possible life for herself, she commits suicide.

Heep, Uriah The 'umble and greasy lawyer's clerk in DAVID COPPERFIELD, who blackmails his employer and is exposed by MICAWBER.

Hegelianism Philosophical view that everything in the universe (including thought and history) is a manifestation, striving towards perfection, of a cosmic spirit which operates through the dialectical process, i.e. every concept (thesis) implies and is in conflict with its opposite (antithesis), and their opposition is reconciled in a compromise (synthesis) between the two on a higher level; this synthesis in turn becomes the 'thesis' of the next stage of development. See DIALECTICAL MATERIALISM. (Hegel, German philosopher, 1770–1831; pronounced hay-geel'i-an-izm.)

Hegira Anglicized name for the flight of Mohammed from Mecca to Medina in AD 622, the year from which the Muslim era starts. (Arabic *hijrah*, 'separation, departure from home'; pronounced, in English, hejyr'a.)

Heidelberg Man Supposed early form of Man, reconstructed from a massive jaw, about 400,000 years old, found near Heidelberg in 1907.

'Heilige Nacht' A carol; see 'SILENT NIGHT'.

Heimwehr Illegal Austrian Fascist armed organization which fought against a similar Socialist body, the Schutzbund, in the 1920s and 1930s. (German, 'home guard'.)

Heinemann (W. H.) Bequest Fund, now administered by the Royal Society of Literature, from which awards are made primarily to authors of the less remunerative forms of literature; poetry, criticism, biography, history. There is also a Heinemann prize for French authors, reciprocal to the STOCK PRIZE.

Heinkel Name of manufacturer (abbreviated to He) given to a series of German aircraft, notably

the He-178 which was the first jet plane to fly, in August 1939 (but see MESSERSCHMITT); and the He-176, powered by a liquid-fuel rocket motor, also tested in 1939 (June).

Heisenberg's Uncertainty principle (1927). That the more accurately the position of an atomic particle is determined, the less accurately can its momentum be determined, and vice versa. Also called the principle of indeterminacy. (Werner Heisenberg, German originator of quantum mechanics.)

Helen of Troy In Greek legend, the daughter of Leda by Zeus and wife of King Menelaus of Sparta; her face 'launched a thousand ships', i.e. started the Trojan War, when PARIS carried her off to Troy. After the fall of Troy she returned to her husband.

Helianthemum See CISTUS.

Helianthus Genus that includes the sunflower and the Jerusalem artichoke.

Helicon, Mount See HIPPOCRENE.

Heligoland Bight (August 1914). First naval engagement of World War II, in which 3 German light cruisers were sunk and 3 crippled.

Heliopolis Centre, near modern Cairo, of the worship of the sun-god RA during the OLD KINGDOM. (Pronounced hee-li-op'o-lis.)

Helios Greek sun-god, brother of Selene and Eos; the Roman Sol. (Pronounced hee'lios.)

Hellas Ancient Greek name for Greece, still used today.

Hell Brueghel Nickname of Pieter II (1564–1638), son of PEASANT BRUEGHEL; so called because of his weird pictures of Hell.

Helleborus Genus that includes the Christmas Rose (*H. niger*) and the Lenten Rose (*H. orientalis*).

Hellenes Ancient Greek name for Greeks.

Hellenistic Age (323–30 BC). Period during which a cosmopolitan Greek civilization, centred on Alexandria in Egypt, dominated the Near and Middle East and North Africa, from the death of Alexander the Great until the Roman defeat of Cleopatra, last of the PTOLEMIES.

Hellespont Ancient Greek name for the Dardanelles. (Pronounced hel'es-pont.)

Hellfire Club (1745). Popular name for the Knights of St Francis, a club founded by Sir John Dashwood, Chancellor of the Exchequer. As its membership and activities were secret, sensational legends grew up about orgies at Medmenham Abbey on the Thames near Henley, and in the caves opposite Dashwood's home at West Wycombe Park, and their Rabelaisian motto *fay ce que voudras* ('do what you will'); but whether they have any basis in fact is not known.

Hello, Dolly! (1964). Highly popular musical adapted by Michael Stewart from *The* MATCH-MAKER; also a film directed by Gene Kelly.

Hell's Angels (1968). Under 25s, heirs to the ROCKERS. Their sole drug is speed, using powerful motorbikes (choppers) stripped of all inessential parts. The uniform is deliberately filthy Levis and denim tops, Nazi helmets and badges; qualification for entry into this close and highly organized fraternity is some outrageous, preferably revolting, act. Their females are either 'Old Ladies' attached to one Angel or Mammas, free for all. Unlike SKINHEADS, whom they loathe, they never take a steady job, but they have an odd symbiosis with HIPPIES, whose gatherings they sometimes police. (Name taken from more violent fraternities of California, recruited (1948) from middle-class dropouts.)

Hell's Corner (1940). Name given to the coast around Dover when it was being shelled by German guns from the coast opposite, as part of the Battle of Britain operation.

Helm Catalogue of the works of C. P. E. Bach compiled by Eugene E. Helm. (Abbreviation 'H'.)

Héloïse and Abélard Peter Abélard was a popular theological teacher in Paris in the early 12th century who advocated a rational approach to

religion, for which he was persecuted by the Cistercian, St Bernard. He fell in love with his pupil Héloïse, niece of Canon Fulbert, and married her secretly when she bore him a son. On learning this, Fulbert had him castrated. He became a monk, she a nun, exchanging letters of which 5 of his to her have been published. Their story has been treated by many writers, including George Moore in his novel *Heloise and Abelard* (1921), and Helen Waddell in *Peter Abelard* (1933).

Helsingfors Swedish name of Helsinki, capital of Finland.

Helsingör Site of Kronborg Castle, Denmark, the Elsinore of *Hamlet*.

Helsinki agreement (1975). 'Final Act' signed by 35 heads of state and heads of government (including USA, Canada, USSR, and all of Eastern and Western Europe countries) which agreed 'respect for human rights and fundamental freedoms'.

Helston Furry Dance Festival of pagan origin held on 8 May (Floral Day) at Helston, south-west Cornwall; the villagers dance through the streets to a traditional tune of great antiquity.

Helvetia Latin name for Switzerland.

Hemerocallis Genus name of the day lilies.

Hemiptera Parasitic bugs, an insect order which includes aphids (e.g. greenfly), bed-bugs, cochineal insects, leaf-hoppers and cicadas.

Hemlock and After (1952). Angus Wilson's satirical study of an ageing writer who has failed to live up to his ideals.

Hendon Former Middlesex borough, since 1965 part of the borough of BARNET.

Hendon Pageant (1920–37). Annual display by the RAF at Hendon aerodrome, London.

Hendon Police College (1934). London Metropolitan Police college founded by Lord Trenchard when he was the Metropolitan Commissioner.

Hengist and Horsa Traditional, perhaps historical, leaders of the Jutes who settled in Kent in the 5th century AD.

Henley (1839). Annual regatta in July, the major rowing events at which are regarded as the unofficial world championships. (Henley-on-Thames, in Oxfordshire.)

Henlow RAF Technical College, near Bedford; it provides training (including specialist training at postgraduate level) for officers of the RAF Technical Branch.

Henry, O. Pen-name of W. S. Porter (1862–1910), an American master of the short story with an unexpected twist in the last paragraphs.

Henry Esmond (1852). Thackeray's novel set in the time of Queen Anne, in which the hero, banished from the home in which he was brought up and to which he is the rightful heir, serves in Marlborough's campaigns and returns to marry his foster-father's widow, Lady Castlewood, and to claim his inheritance. Marlborough, Addison and Steele appear in the book. See ESMOND, BEATRIX; *The* VIRGINIANS.

Henry IV (1) Shakespeare's play (1598) in 2 parts, about the English King. (2) Pirandello's play (1922) about a man in modern times who takes on the personality of the 11th-century German Emperor Henry IV (see CANOSSA).

Henry VII's Chapel Tudor chapel added to Westminster Abbey in the early 16th century, famed for its perfect fan vaulting. It contains a memorial to those who fought in the Battle of Britain, and the banners of the Order of the Bath.

Hephaestus Greek god of fire, identified with the Roman Vulcan.

Hephzibah See BEULAH.

Hepplewhite Furniture inspired by the book of designs which George Hepplewhite published in 1788. Adapted from ADAM STYLE designs, mostly in mahogany, these were intended for the middle class; heart-, shield- and oval-shaped chair-backs are characteristic.

Heptameron, The (16th century). Collection of love stories written by Marguerite, Queen of Navarre. The title and setting of the tales were inspired by the DECAMERON.

Heptarchy, The Seven Anglo-Saxon kingdoms of England during the 5th–9th centuries: Northumbria, Mercia, East Anglia, Essex, Kent, Sussex and Wessex; they were not, however, permanent separate kingdoms throughout this period. (Greek, 'seven kingdoms'.)

Hera In Greek legend, sister and understandably jealous wife of Zeus, mother of Ares; identified with the Roman Juno.

Heracles Greek hero better known under his Latin name of HERCULES. (Pronounced heer'a-kleez.)

Herakleion Alternative spelling for Iráklion, capital of Crete.

Herald's College (or **Office**) Alternative names for the COLLEGE OF ARMS.

Herbert Divorce Act (1937). Act which extended the grounds for divorce to include desertion for 3 years, cruelty, or incurable insanity, but provided that no case could be brought in the first 3 years of marriage without special leave. (Private Member's Bill introduced by the novelist, A. P. Herbert.) See HOLY DEADLOCK.

Herculaneum Ancient Roman city overwhelmed by the eruption of Vesuvius which destroyed nearby Pompeii. Its existence was forgotten until the site was discovered by chance in the 18th century. (Pronounced hèr-kew-lay'ni-um.)

Hercules Latin and better-known name of the Greek Heracles, son of Zeus and Alcmena (the wife of AMPHITRYON), famous for his 'Twelve Labours'. He was killed by the shirt of NESSUS. (Pronounced hèrk'ew-leez.)

Hercules Lockheed turboprop transport plane (the US C-130) now in use by RAF Transport Command.

Here Comes Everybody (1965). Best attempt to

explain James Joyce, by Anthony Burgess; see H.C.E.

Hereford cattle Hardy beef breed, used in crossing with dairy breeds; red with white face and markings.

Hereford round In archery, a match in which 6 dozen arrows are shot at distances ranging from 50 to 80 yards.

Hereros Tribe of cattle people in South-West Africa who were almost exterminated (1903–7) in an early German exercise in genocide.

Hereward the Wake (1865). Charles Kingsley's semi-historical novel in which a Saxon outlaw, Hereward, defies the Normans from his hide-out in the marshes of the Isle of Ely.

Heriot-Watt University (1965). Formerly a central institution (advanced college administered by an independent board of governors) in Edinburgh.

Hermes Greek god of commerce, cunning and inventions, identified with the Roman Mercury. He was a son of Zeus, and invented the lyre, among other things. As messenger of the gods he wore a winged hat and winged sandals, and carried a herald's beribboned staff.

Hermes of Praxiteles, The (4th century BC). The only original statue by the Greek sculptor Praxiteles which has survived; Hermes is depicted with the infant Dionysus on his arm; it is in the museum at Olympia, where it was found. (Pronounced hèrmeeze, praks-it'è-leez.)

Hermes Trismegistus Name given by 3rd-century AD Neoplatonists to THOTH, identified with Hermes by the Greeks, as the author of the HERMETIC BOOKS. ('Hermes the thrice-greatest'.)

Hermetic books Books of unknown date and authorship attributed to HERMES TRISMEGISTUS but probably compiled in Greek at Alexandria in the first centuries of the Christian era. They dealt with alchemy, astrology and other occult subjects and have survived only through quotation (often extensive) in other authors. They show the influence of Jewish mysticism and Neo-platonism grafted on to Egyptian religious traditions.

Hermitage (1) Leningrad museum situated in the buildings of the Old Hermitage (1775–84), the New Hermitage (1839–50), and the Hermitage Theatre (1787). The Hermitage was originally constructed to house the art collection of Catherine I; under Catherine the Great it was a centre of musical and theatrical activity. It now houses one of the world's great art collections. (2) Famous wine, both red and white, of the Rhône valley.

Herne the Hunter Horned ghost in an English version of the widespread European legend of the Wild Hunter; he is a former keeper of Windsor Forest who walks at midnight in winter, destroying trees and cattle.

Hero and Leander (Greek legend) Hero was a priestess of Aphrodite at Sestos, visited nightly by Leander, who had to swim across the Hellespont from Abydos on the opposite shore. One stormy night he was drowned and Hero, in despair, threw herself into the sea. Marlowe retold the story in an unfinished poem (completed by Chapman), and Byron with a companion emulated the feat of swimming across the strait.

Herod, To out-Herod Surpass in wickedness even Herod the Great, who ordered the MASSACRE OF THE INNOCENTS. Originally, to rant louder than Herod in the old sacred plays (*Hamlet*, III, ii, 16).

Heroes and Hero-worship, On (1841). Collection of Thomas Carlyle's lectures on history viewed as the life stories of great men.

Herrenvolk Nazi name for Germans; corrupted by Churchill to 'Herring-folk'. ('Master race'.)

Herries Chronicle, The (1930–33). Quartet of novels by Hugh Walpole, forming a family saga set in the Lake District.

Herstmonceux Village in Sussex, near Eastbourne, to which the ROYAL (Greenwich) OBSERVATORY was moved in 1958. (Pronounced hèrst-mèn-sew'.)

Hertzian waves An earlier name for electromagnetic waves. (First demonstrated in 1888 by the German physicist H. R. Hertz.)

Hesperides (1) In Greek legend, 3 nymphs variously said to live in a western island paradise or on Mount Atlas, where they guarded some golden apples belonging to Hera, which Heracles (Hercules) wrested from them. (2) Collected poems (1648), mostly pastoral, of Robert Herrick. (So called because written in the West Country, i.e. Devonshire; see next entry; pronounced hes-per'i-deez.)

Hesperides, Islands of the Ancient Greek name for certain islands of the west, perhaps the Bissagos Archipelago south of the Gambia, West Africa; sometimes wrongly equated with the FORTUNATE ISLES. (Connected with the previous entry by common derivation from the Greek for 'western'.)

Hesperus Greek name for Venus when it is an evening star.

Hessen A *Land* of the Federal Republic of Germany, capital Wiesbaden, formed from the old states of Hesse, capital Darmstadt, and Hesse-Nassau, a Prussian province of which Frankfurt was the chief town.

Hess landing (May 1941). Unheralded landing by parachute in Scotland during World War II of Hitler's deputy, Rudolf Hess, as a self-appointed ambassador to negotiate peace terms with Britain; he was interned, and later imprisoned in SPANDAU Prison, West Berlin, where he died in 1987. Controversy arose over whether the man who died in Spandau actually was Hess.

Hestia See VESTA.

Heston and Isleworth Former Middlesex borough, since 1965 part of the borough of HOUNSLOW.

Hetty Pegler's Tump Neolithic chambered long barrow, at Uley, Gloucestershire.

Heuchera Rock and border perennials, named after Professor J. Heucher, a German botanist.

Heysel Stadium (1985). Scene of disaster in Brussels when riots took place between rival football 'fans' before the start of the European Cup Final; 39 died.

Heysham Site of the first nuclear power station (AGR reactor type) to be built near a centre of population, and fourth of the AGR or second-phase programme of stations. (Coastal site near Morecambe, Lancashire; pronounced hee'sh-ėm.)

Heythrop (1835). Fox-hunting pack with kennels at Chipping Norton, which hunts country in Oxfordshire and Gloucestershire. (Pronounced hee'throp.)

Heythrop College Leading Jesuit college near Chipping Norton, Oxfordshire. (Pronounced hee'throp.)

Hiawatha (1855). Longfellow's poem of a legendary Mohawk Indian chief and his Dakota wife, Minnehaha ('laughing water'). The simple metre and simple repetitive wording, though appropriate to the subject, cried aloud for parody – and got it, e.g. (on the subject of fur mittens): 'He, to get the warm side inside. / Put the inside skin side outside.'

Hibbert Journal (1902). Quarterly review of theology, philosophy, sociology and the arts, published at Oxford. (See next entry.)

Hibbert lectures (1878). Non-sectarian lectures intended to elucidate problems of Christian belief, organized by the Hibbert Trust which published the HIBBERT JOURNAL. (Endowed by Robert Hibbert, Jamaica merchant, died 1849.)

Hibernia Latin name of Ireland.

Hickstead (1961). All-England Jumping Course, owned by the British Show-Jumping Association, scene of the British Jumping Derby and many international championships.

Hidcote Manor National Trust property near Chipping Campden in the Cotswolds, particularly famous for its gardens, where rare exotic plants are grown.

Hidden Persuaders, The (1957). Vance Packard's entertaining attack on MADISON AVENUE's efforts to dragoon American consumers through 'motivational research' into buying what they neither need nor want.

Higgins, Professor Character in Shaw's PYGMALION, based on the phonetician Henry Sweet (died 1912).

High Church See ANGLO-CATHOLICISM.

High Court See LAW COURTS.

High German Hoch-Deutsch, modern standard German, which derives from the dialects of central and south Germany and was particularly influenced by Luther's translation of the Bible into the dialects of THURINGIA and SAXONY.

Highland Brigade Infantry brigade comprising: the Black Watch (Royal Highland Regiment); the Queen's Own Highlanders (Seaforth and Camerons); the Gordon Highlanders; the Argyll and Sutherland Highlanders (Princess Louise's), the disbandment of which was announced in 1968. Since 1968, part of the SCOTTISH DIVISION.

Highland Clearances See The CLEARANCES.

Highland Division 51st Division which surrendered when cut off at Saint-Valéry-en-Caux in June 1940 and, reconstituted and merged with the 9th Scottish Division, covered itself with glory in the Western Desert and in France.

Highland Jessie See 'CAMPBELLS ARE COMING'.

Highland Mary Girl invoked in several of Robert Burns's poems, perhaps a Campbell.

Highland (West Highland) cattle Shaggy hardy breed of high-quality beef cattle, with wide spreading horns and heavy dewlaps; bred in the Scottish Highlands.

High Renaissance (1500–27). Brief period when the Italian Renaissance reached its peak in the time of Michelangelo, Raphael, Leonardo and Titian.

High Sheriff Chief executive officer of a county, appointed annually at a 'Pricking of the Sheriffs' ceremony, when the Queen pricks a list of nominations with a bodkin, being careful to prick the first name under each county. His duties, apart from receiving judges at Assizes, are mostly delegated to an Under-Sheriff (a solicitor) or other officials.

High Wind in Jamaica, A (1929). Startling novel by Richard Hughes set in the early 19th century; a family of children who have survived a Jamaican hurricane are captured on their way to England by pirates, whose downfall they achieve by their utter absence of moral sense; one little girl commits murder.

Hi-Hi, The Nickname of the Third Lanark football team.

Hijra More correct spelling of HEGIRA.

Hilary term University or legal term beginning in January (called the Lent term at Cambridge). (St Hilary, commemorated on 17 January.)

Hill, The (1) In USA, the Capitol Hill which dominates Washington DC, and where the Congress buildings and Supreme Court stand. (2) In Britain, a name for Harrow School at Harrow-on-the-Hill, London.

Hillbilly music (1) Folk-style music of Appalachia, based on banjo, fiddle and guitar. (2) Commercialized form of this, often called Country-and-Western. (Hillbilly, name given to the impoverished, isolated mountain farmers of the southern US, e.g. of the Ozarks.)

Hillel Foundation lectures Given at various universities of Britain, USA and elsewhere to bring a knowledge of Judaism to students. (Founded in 1923 by the B'nai B'rith, 'Sons of the Covenant', an important Jewish organization.)

Hillingdon London borough since 1965 consisting of the former borough of Uxbridge and the urban districts of Hayes, Ruislip–Northwood and Yiewsley–West Drayton; headquarters at Hayes.

Hill Samuel (1965). London merchant bank and acceptance house, formed by the merger of M.

Samuel (1831) with Hill, Higginson, Erlanger (1907).

Hillsborough Site of Government House, Co. Down, Northern Ireland.

Hillsborough Home of Sheffield Wednesday football club and scene of a football disaster when 95 supporters were killed in April 1989.

Hill 60 Feature near Ypres, in the First World War the scene of fierce fighting, especially in April 1915 when it was captured by the British.

Hinayana Earlier of the 2 main forms of Buddhism, closer to Buddha's teaching; the 'Lesser Vehicle' (of Truth) or southern Buddhism of Sri Lanka, Burma, Siam, Indo-China and Indonesia. It is a pessimistic form of quietism, in contrast to MAHAYANA; more interested in morals than metaphysics, seeking the salvation not of all but of the individual. Buddha is venerated but not worshipped.

Hind and the Panther, The (1687). Dryden's poem written after he went over to Rome, in which the unspotted Hind is the Roman Catholic Church and the Panther the Anglican Church.

Hindenburg Last passenger airship on the transatlantic run; when it caught fire on landing in New Jersey, USA, its sister ship GRAF ZEPPELIN was withdrawn from service.

Hindenburg Line (Siegfried Line) In World War I, the Germans' defence line in Flanders to which they retreated in September 1918.

Hindi Form of HINDUSTANI which is the official language of India, spoken mainly by educated Hindus. Unlike URDU, it is written from left to right in the Devanagari script, and its vocabulary has been restocked with Sanskrit words in recent centuries.

Hindle Wakes (1912). Stanley Houghton's play about a Lancashire mill-girl who refuses marriage to a rich man whom she regards as unlikely to make a suitable husband, although she is quite happy to spend a weekend at Blackpool with him.

Hinds (Alfred) case Hinds was sentenced (1953) to 12 years' preventive detention for robbery at Maples furniture stores, London. He constantly appealed, and broke prison to draw attention to his case. In 1964 he was awarded damages in a libel suit against the police officer who had had him arrested.

Hind Trophy Skiing competition held in April in the Cairngorms, Scotland.

Hinduism Religion of most of India. BRAHMA was the chief god; BRAHMAN is the reality behind a world of illusion (*maya*), union with which is sought by release from *karma* and the chain of rebirth, through asceticism, meditation or yoga. As in other religions, there is every level of practice, from mysticism and philosophical speculation through ascetic extremes down to idol-worship.

Hindustani Lingua franca of northern India and West Pakistan, understood by Hindu and Muslim alike. It spread under the Moguls, who adopted Persian as their court language, and is thus rich in Persian borrowings. URDU and HINDI are closely allied to it. (*Hindustan*, Persian name for India.)

Hinkley Point (1963). Site of one of the earlier series of nuclear power-stations, designed also to produce plutonium. A second was planned and was opposed in 1989. (On the Somerset coast.)

Hippies (1967). Drop-outs, mostly young middle class, who reject the materialism of industrial society, preaching peace, love and freedom (i.e. anarchy). Deriving from the BEATNIKS and FLOWER PEOPLE of San Francisco.

Hippocleides Greek betrothed to the daughter of the local ruler who, according to Herodotus, started to dance at his wedding feast and finally stood on his head. Gravely displeased, the ruler said 'You have danced your marriage away'; to which the young man made the famous retort: 'Hippocleides doesn't care!' (Pronounced hip-o-kly'deez.)

Hippocratic oath Oath, still administered to doctors in some medical schools, to observe certain ethical standards, the chief point of interest to a layman being an undertaking not to divulge a patient's secrets. (Attributed to Hippocrates, Greek physician who died 357 BC.)

Hippocrene Greek legendary fountain on Mount Helicon, a part of the Parnassus range sacred to the Muses; hence used of poetic inspiration, as by Keats in his *Ode to a Nightingale:* 'O for a beaker full of the warm South. / Full of the true, the blushful Hippocrene.' (Greek, 'horse-fountain', as created by a blow from the hoof of Pegasus; pronounced hip'o-kreen.)

Hippolytus In Greek legend, the virtuous son of Theseus and an Amazon queen. He was falsely accused by his stepmother, PHAEDRA, of trying to seduce her, for which his father cursed him and brought about his death, learning the truth too late. This legend is the theme of Euripides' *Hippolytus* (428 BC) and of Racine's *Phèdre.* (Pronounced hip-ol'i-tus.)

Hippopotamus song, The Best known of the Michael Flanders and Donald Swann animal songs, with the refrain: 'Mud, mud, glorious mud, / Nothing quite like it for cooling the blood!'

Hiroshima bomb First atomic uranium bomb used in war, devastating the city on 6 August 1945. (City of Honshu, Japan; pronounced hirosh'im-a.)

Hiroshima, mon amour (1959). First of the NEW WAVE films directed by Alain Resnais, which deals with the impact of the heritage of World War II on a love affair between a Frenchwoman and a Japanese businessman.

Hispaniola Old name for the island where Columbus made his first landing in the New World; now divided between Haiti and the Dominican Republic.

Hispano-Suiza (1920s). Huge 8-litre, 200-h.p., 110-m.p.h. car designed in Spain by a Swiss (hence the name) and made in France in limited numbers for maharajas and such, but chiefly known to lesser fry as the choice of proto-Bond figures such as BULLDOG DRUMMOND and the

lady in the green hat – the DB-6 *d'antan.* (Pronounced, though never in England, is-pah'no sweeth'a.)

Hissarlik Turkish name of the site of TROY, 20 miles south-west of Çanakkale, opposite Gallipoli.

Hiss case (1950). Whittaker Chambers, an American Communist, stated that Alger Hiss, one of Roosevelt's aides, had in 1938 given him a secret, though unimportant, document. Hiss was imprisoned for perjury when he denied this (released 1954). It was widely believed that he had been 'framed'.

Hitachi (1920). Japanese group, with headquarters at Tokyo, which manufactures heavy electrical machinery, rolling stock, machine tools, computers, chemicals, atomic plant and electronic equipment.

Hitler–Stalin Pact (August 1939). Non-aggression pact unexpectedly signed in Moscow a few days before World War II, sealing a secret agreement to partition Poland between them and to award the Baltic states to Russia. Stalin thus bought 22 months in which to prepare for the inevitable German invasion. Sometimes called the Ribbentrop–Molotov Pact, from the names of the 2 signatories.

Hitler Youth German National-Socialist (Nazi) organization for the indoctrination of the young. (German, *Hitler Jugend.*)

Hittites Indo-European people from the Caucasus who settled in Anatolia about 2000 BC, and founded an empire whose capital was Hattuses (now BOGHAZKÖY, Turkey); they were absorbed into the Assyrian Empire in 709 BC.

HIV Human-immune-deficiency virus which leads to AIDS.

HMSO Her Majesty's Stationery Office, which prints and publishes Acts of Parliament, HANSARD, the LONDON GAZETTE, WHITE PAPERS, etc., is agent for the sale of UN publications, prints government forms (e.g. postal orders) and telephone directories, and supplies government departments at home and abroad with office requisites.

HMV Name of a gramophone and record company, from the initials of the words 'His Master's Voice', the caption to the early trademark, still used, of a dog listening to a gramophone. See EMI.

Hoare–Laval Pact (1935). Anglo-French proposal, made soon after Mussolini's invasion of Abyssinia, to give most of the country to Italy and leave a little for the Emperor. Instantly denounced by British public opinion, it had to be abandoned, and Hoare resigned. (The Foreign Ministers, Samuel Hoare, later Lord Templewood; Pierre Laval, later Vichy leader.)

Hobart House London headquarters in Victoria of the National Coal Board, established when the coal industry was nationalized in 1946.

Hobbits Benevolent furry-footed people, living in burrows in the SHIRE, of the weird world of Tolkien's The LORD OF THE RINGS.

Hobgoblin Alternative name for ROBIN GOOD-FELLOW.

Hobhouse Memorial lectures Annual lectures on sociology and history given at the London School of Economics. (L. T. Hobhouse. English sociologist, died 1929.)

Hoboken Hoboken catalogue of Haydn. (Abbreviation 'H' and Hob.)

Hobson-Jobson (1886). Title of a dictionary of Anglo-Indian words and phrases by Yule and Burnell. (Corruption of 'Ya Hasan! Ya Husain!', shouted at a Muslim festival, used by British soldiers in India as a name for the festival itself; chosen for the title as a typical example of what was in the book.)

Hobson's Choice (1) Phrase meaning 'no choice'. (Thomas Hobson, a 17th-century Cambridge man who hired out horses in strict rotation, giving his customers no choice of mount.) (2) Title of a play (1915) by Harold Brighouse (see MANCHESTER SCHOOL OF DRAMATISTS), a North Country dialect comedy about a Salford shoemaker.

Ho Chi Minh Trail US name for the network of roads and paths through the jungle and mountains of southern Laos and eastern Cambodia, used as a supply route by the North Vietnamese. (Named after the North Vietnamese leader.)

Hock White wine from the Rhine valley; the label sometimes gives the village of origin, vineyard, type of grape and quality, in that order. (From the town of Hochheim.)

Hodgkin's disease Malignant cancer of the lymph glands, which become enlarged; it is mainly confined to the young.

Hodson's Horse Regiment of irregulars formed during the Indian Mutiny, given the official name of the Corps of Guides, Punjab Irregular Force. (Raised by W. S. R. Hodson, 1821–58, killed at Lucknow.)

Hofburg (1275). Former Imperial Palace of the Habsburgs at Vienna: now a complex of buildings including the presidential offices, state apartments open to the public, museums, a national library and the SPANISH RIDING SCHOOL.

Hofkirche (1563). Royal church of the Holy Roman Emperors at Innsbruck, containing the tomb of the Emperor Maximilian.

Hogmanay Scottish name for New Year's Eve. (Derived through the French from Latin hoc in anno, 'in this year', part of the refrain of a song sung on that day.)

Hogsnorton Fictitious village where incredible events used to happen, recounted by the comedian Gillie Potter in a series of BBC radio sketches. (Name taken from a 17th-century proverb 'I think you were born at Hogs-Norton', i.e. 'your manners are atrocious'; from an Oxfordshire village now called Hook Norton.)

Hohenlinden (December 1800). Battle in which the French and Bavarians under Moreau defeated the Austrians, who were forced to accept the Peace of Lunéville which ended the SECOND COALITION and the French Revolutionary Wars. It was the theme of a poem by Thomas Campbell. (Village 20 miles east of Munich.)

Hohenstaufens German dynasty which provided kings and emperors in the 12th–13th centuries.

Hohenzollern candidacy, The (1869). See EMS TELEGRAM.

Hohenzollerns (1415–1918). Dynasty which provided the Electors of Brandenburg, Kings of Prussia (1701), and Emperors of Germany (1871); the main dynasty ended with Kaiser Wilhelm II's abdication, but the cadet branch of Hohenzollern-Sigmaringen ruled Romania until 1947. (Descended from Count Zollern of Swabia, one of Charlemagne's paladins; pronounced hoh'ent-sol-èrn.)

Holborn Former London metropolitan borough, since 1965 part of the borough of CAMDEN. (Pronounced hoh'bn.)

Holinshed's *Chronicles* (1578). Histories and descriptions of England, Scotland and Ireland by several writers (Holinshed wrote the history of England), chiefly remembered as the source of many of Shakespeare's plots, and used also by other Elizabethan dramatists.

Holkham Hall Palladian home of COKE OF NORFOLK, at Wells, Norfolk; still the property of the Coke family (the Earls of Leicester). (Pronounced hoh'kem.)

Holland See NETHERLANDS.

Holland House (1605). Kensington mansion which in the 18th and 19th centuries became famous as a salon of Whig politicians and writers. What remains of the house is now public property, used for open-air concerts, and as a hostel. (Earl of Holland – the Lincolnshire Holland – former owner.)

Hollands Dutch gin; also called Hollands GENEVA.

Holloway Largest British prison for women, in North London.

Holloway College, Royal (1883). Women's college, now a unit of London University, at Mount Lee, Egham, Surrey, and amalgamated as the Royal Holloway and Bedford New College.

Holloway's pills (1837). First of the patent medicines, claimed to cure rheumatism, gout, 'paralysis', bronchitis, wounds, scrofula, etc., etc.; made of aloes, ginger and soap (as were BEECHAM'S PILLS). Thomas Holloway (died 1883) used some of the profits to found the Royal HOLLOWAY COLLEGE, Egham, and the Holloway Sanatorium, Virginia Water.

Hollybush Summit (1967). Newspaper name for the meeting of President Johnson and Premier Kosygin, the first meeting for 6 years of the heads of state of USA and USSR. (Meeting held at Hollybush House, home of the president of Glassboro State College, New Jersey.)

Hollywood Used as a synonym for the American motion-picture industry, which made its headquarters there.

Hollywood Bowl (1919). Fifty-acre natural amphitheatre at Hollywood, California, where summer outdoor concerts are held, and an Easter sunrise church service.

Holmenkollen Hill Hill near Oslo, the Mecca of ski-jumpers, where an international Ski Week is held in March.

Holmes, Sherlock Violin-playing, cocaine-addicted gentleman detective of Baker Street, London, created by Conan Doyle and first appearing in *A Study in Scarlet* (1887). Tiring of him, the author had him killed off by MORIARTY in 1893, but popular demand forced his resurrection in 1903 in *The Empty House*. The author explained that Holmes had spent the intervening years in Tibet.

Holocaust Name given to the systematic slaughter of the Jews in concentration camps in Germany. One of the greatest crimes ever committed on a huge scale; the crime of genocide, performed with great cruelty.

Holy Alliance (1815). Agreement by the rulers of Russia, Austria and Prussia reached after Napoleon's downfall, ostensibly to be guided in their policies by Christian principles, but actually to suppress Liberal movements. The Pope and Britain refused to be parties to it. Also called the Metternich system. See CONCERT OF EUROPE; DREIKAISERBUND.

Holy Deadlock (1934). A. P. Herbert's satire on the divorce laws, which he was able to have amended 3 years later when, as an Independent MP, he introduced a Private Member's Bill (see HERBERT DIVORCE ACT).

Holy Ghost Third Person of the TRINITY, the Divine Spirit. Jesus promised the Apostles that his Spirit would remain with them, and this was manifested on the day of PENTECOST. Thereafter the Holy Ghost guided the Church in its life and teaching. This doctrine was defined at the Council of CONSTANTINOPLE, 381. In art the Holy Ghost is represented as a dove.

Holy Ghost, The Sin against the Mysterious conception, based on Matthew 12:1–2; its meaning is not there defined, but it is sometimes thought to refer to conscious thwarting of the good.

Holy Grail Chalice used by Christ at the Last Supper and brought by JOSEPH OF ARIMATHAEA (Matt. 27:57–60) to GLASTONBURY. In the versions of the legend by Chrétien de Troyes and Wolfram von Eschenbach, the Grail was located in the Hall of the Grail at Monsalvat, Spain.

Holy Innocents, Feast of The 28th of December, commemorating the MASSACRE OF THE INNOCENTS. Also known as Childermas.

Holy Joe (US slang) Forces chaplain.

Holy League (1) Name given to 2 16th-century alliances directed against France and Spain respectively. (2) Roman Catholic league against the Huguenots formed by the GUISE family, backed by Philip II of Spain, and defeated by Henry IV of France, who himself then turned Catholic. See RELIGIOUS WARS, FRENCH.

Holy Living and Holy Dying (1650–51). Devotional work by Jeremy Taylor.

Holy Loch Scottish loch in Argyll on the west of the Firth of Clyde, which from 1961 was used as a base for US Polaris submarines. Compare FASLANE.

Holy Office (1) Inquisition. (2) Modern successor to (1), which keeps a watch on heretical literature. Its official name is the Sacred Congregation for the Doctrine of the Faith.

Holy Rollers Derisive nickname for fringe religious sects whose members indulge in frenzied activity during services, running or dancing up and down the aisles, screaming, fainting and 'speaking in tongues' (see PENTECOSTALISM).

Holy Roman Empire In theory the unification of Europe with Papal blessing under a Christian Emperor, and a continuation of the Roman Empire. First founded by Charlemagne (800), it collapsed at his death; revived by Otto 1 (962), it fell (1273) into the hands of the HABSBURGS, who extended its boundaries. As a result of the THIRTY YEARS WAR the Protestant German states broke away in 1648, although the title and pageantry of the Holy Roman Empire lingered on until 1806, when Napoleon ended it (see AUSTERLITZ) and the last Holy Roman Emperor, Francis, became Emperor of Austria.

Holyroodhouse Ancient palace at the foot of Canongate, Edinburgh, reconstructed by Charles II; the British sovereign's official residence when in Scotland in early summer.

Holy See, The Papacy; the papal court; the authority and jurisdiction of the Pope.

Holy Sepulchre, Church of the In the old walled city of Jerusalem, the church built by Constantine (336) on what he decided was the site of the Crucifixion and Burial; rebuilt by the Crusaders (1099). The Church is now a collection of medieval buildings inharmoniously shared by Eastern Orthodox, Catholic, Armenian and other Christian denominations.

Holy Spirit Synonymous with HOLY GHOST.

Holy Week Week before Easter; also called PASSION WEEK.

Home Counties Those surrounding London, particularly those into which Greater London has encroached (Essex, Kent, Surrey and Hertfordshire); with the outward spread of the commuter belt, Buckinghamshire, Berkshire and Sussex have a claim to inclusion.

Home Guard (May 1940). Unpaid and at first voluntary force formed to repel German invasion of Britain, originally called Local Defence Volunteers. Men up to the age of 65 were eligible, and were armed with what miscellaneous weapons were available. Later it was possible to develop it into a fully trained and armed force, units of which manned anti-aircraft batteries. They stood down in November 1944.

Home Rule Term used from the 1870s for Irish internal self-government. An Act to establish it was passed in September 1914 but suspended for the duration of World War I. Another Act was passed in 1920 which, at the request of the 6 northern counties, provided separate parliaments for the Catholic South and the Protestant North.

Homo erectus Specific name first given to JAVA MAN, and now extended to cover all the PITHE-CANTHROPINES.

'Homo habilis' (Skilful Man) Professor Leakey's name for the creature of which he found remains, together with crude stone tools, at OLDUVAI GORGE in 1960–62. It is held by some to be a form of Man though anatomically an AUSTRALOPITHECINE, and thus possibly a link in the evolution of Man from ape. It has been dated to about 1,750,000 years ago.

Homo sapiens Modern Man, thought to have appeared about 30,000 BC.

Honest John US truck-launched artillery rocket, with range up to 15 miles, designed to take a nuclear warhead.

Hongroise Cooking term indicating the presence of paprika.

Honourable Artillery Company Oldest regiment in the British Army, originally a guild of archers and 'handgunmen'; now a Territorial unit reduced to one field regiment of artillery and one infantry battalion, it has reverted to its ancient function of training officers for other units.

Hons, The Family society formed by the children of Lord Redesdale. According to one of them, Jessica Mitford in *Hons and Rebels* (1960), the popular derivation from 'Honourables' is incorrect; the name is a childhood corruption of 'hens' (which were apparently a major feature in the Redesdale domestic economy), and is pronounced as spelt.

Hood, HMS The largest British battleship, sunk in May 1941 by the BISMARCK.

Hooray Henry (1980s). Term for upper-class young hedonist. See also LAGER LOUTS; SLOANE RANGERS.

Hoosier State Nickname of Indiana. (Derivation uncertain.)

Hoover Dam (1936). Huge dam on the Colorado River between Arizona and Nevada, temporarily renamed the Boulder Dam when President Hoover was out of favour: old name restored by President Truman in 1947.

Hoover moratorium (1931). Suspension of payment of intergovernmental debts and reparations proposed by President Hoover at the height of the DEPRESSION.

Hopalong Cassidy Romantic cowboy created by Clarence E. Mulford (1883–1956) in *Bar-20* (1907), a Western written 17 years before he ever set foot in the West. He reappeared in 28 other stories by Mulford and in countless scripts invented by others for cinema and TV from 1934, creating a juvenile cult of Davy Crockett proportions.

Hope, Anthony Pen-name of Anthony Hope Hawkins, author of novels about RURITANIA.

Hope G. F. Watts's painting of Hope sitting blindfold on the globe, trying to extract music from the last remaining string of her broken lyre; now in the Tate Gallery, London.

Hope diamond, The Forty-four-carat Indian diamond of a rare shade of blue, supposed to have been stolen from an idol and therefore to bring misfortune to its owners. It was sold to Louis XIV, bought by the Hope family, and after various changes of ownership came to rest in the Smithsonian Institution, Washington DC.

Hopetoun House William Adam mansion, residence of the Marquesses of Linlithgow, at South Queensferry, near Edinburgh.

Horatio In Shakespeare's play, Hamlet's only true friend.

Horatius, The brave Well-known hero who, 'facing fearful odds', held up LARS PORSENA at the gates of Rome.

Hornblower, Horatio Hero of a series of novels by C. S. Forester about the British Navy in Napoleonic times, the first of which was *The Happy Return* (1937). They cover Hornblower's career from midshipman to Admiral Lord Hornblower.

Horn Dance See ABBOTS BROMLEY HORN DANCE.

Horners, Worshipful Company of (1637). LIVERY COMPANY, originally a guild of those who made articles of horn. Its members include representatives of the plastics industry, in which it takes an interest.

Hornet National class of 16-foot dinghy, designed by Jack Holt; exciting to race and frequently capsizes.

Horniman Museum (1897). Museum and library in Forest Hill, London, devoted to the history of the development of man, with a collection of early tools, dance masks, musical instruments etc. Founded by the tea-merchant father of Annie Horniman who built the ABBEY THEATRE and ran the MANCHESTER GAIETY.

Hornsey Former London borough, since 1965 part of the borough of HARINGEY.

Horse Guards (1) used for the HOUSEHOLD CAVALRY or (2) specifically, the Royal Horse Guards (the Blues); (3) in London, an 18th-century building in Whitehall, on the site of a former guardhouse to the Palace of Westminster. See next entry.

Horse Guards Parade Parade ground adjoining the HORSE GUARDS (3), where the ceremony of Trooping the Colour is held on the Queen's official birthday.

Horse of the Year Show (1949). Show held at Wembley each October, chiefly to determine the leading show jumpers of the year.

Horserace Betting Levy Board (1961). Set up under an Act of Parliament, and financed by the HORSERACE TOTALIZATOR BOARD, it is responsible for modernizing racecourses, providing starting stalls, camera patrols and stable security, encouraging veterinary science and education, and augmenting prize money.

Horserace Totalizator Board (1961). Board set up by Act of Parliament to operate totalizators on racecourses; the profits are paid to the HORSERACE BETTING LEVY BOARD. It replaced the Racecourse Betting Control Board of 1928.

Horse's Mouth, The (1944). Joyce Cary's novel of the dedicated old artist, rogue and genius, Gulley Jimson.

'Horst Wessel Lied' (1933). German National-Socialist (Nazi) 'national anthem', written by Horst Wessel to an old music-hall tune; it began: 'Die Fahne hoch, die Reihen dicht geschlossen' ('Up with the flag and close the serried ranks').

Horus Ancient Egyptian hawk-headed god of the rising sun, opponent of the powers of darkness, son of Isis and Osiris; equivalent to the Greek Apollo.

Hosanna Cry, equivalent to 'God save Him', with which the 'multitudes' greeted Jesus on his entry into Jerusalem (Matt. 21:9); hence an exclamation of adoration.

Hosta Genus name of the Plantain Lily, also called *Funkia*.

Hot line Direct link by telephone or other electronic means to be used, in emergencies, by heads of governments.

Hotspur Nickname of Sir Henry Percy (1364–1403), eldest son of the 1st Earl of Northumberland, a gallant and hot-tempered warrior who was killed fighting for Owen Glendower against Henry IV. He appears in Shakespeare's *Henry IV*.

Hotspurs, The Short name, usually further shortened to 'The Spurs', of Tottenham Hotspur, the London football team which plays at White Hart Lane.

Hottentots South African community, now scattered, originally akin to the BUSHMEN, whose distinctive 'Kaffir click' they still retain. Unlike them they took to urban ways, and intermarried freely with Dutch and other races. (Perhaps an Afrikaans word for 'stammerers'.)

Houdini Generic term for an 'escapologist', a person who, however carefully he is trussed up, can free himself. (From Harry Houdini, died 1926, an American conjuror and illusionist, who excelled at the art; pronounced hoo-dee'ni.)

Houghton Meeting Last flat-race meeting of the season at Newmarket, in October, at which the Cambridgeshire is run.

'Hound of Heaven, The' (1893). Francis Thompson's devotional poem, in which he represents himself as in flight from God's love, pursued and overtaken. It begins: 'I fled Him, down the nights and down the days; / I fled Him, down the arches of the years.'

Hound of the Baskervilles, The (1902). Conan Doyle novel presented as an early exploit of Sherlock Holmes, whom the author had killed off in a previous story.

Hounslow London borough since 1965, consisting of the former boroughs of Heston–Isleworth–Hounslow and Brentford–Chiswick, and the urban district of Feltham.

House See ACID-HOUSE PARTY.

House, The (1) (Oxford University) Christ Church (College). (2) (City of London) The Stock Exchange. (3) (Politics) The House of Commons.

Household Cavalry Cavalry brigade of the HOUSEHOLD TROOPS, consisting of 2 regiments; the LIFE GUARDS and the ROYAL HORSE GUARDS (the BLUES).

Household Troops The sovereign's personal guard, consisting of the HOUSEHOLD CAVALRY and the 3 senior Guards regiments, the GRENADIER, COLDSTREAM and SCOTS GUARDS.

House of Keys Ancient elected assembly of the Isle of Man, with 24 members; part of the TYN-WALD. (*Keys*, possibly from a Norse word for 'chosen'.)

House of the Dead (1861). Dostoyevsky's novel based on his own experiences in a Siberian prison after his arrest as a revolutionary.

House of the Seven Gables, The (1851). Nathaniel Hawthorne's novel of a family under a curse; it is represented by an ageing spinster who lives in the ramshackle old family mansion of the title, joined by her brother back from a long prison sentence for a murder committed by his cousin. The innocent suffer, the wicked prosper, until the cousin's sudden death; then, the sin of their ancestor expiated, the curse broken, brother and sister spend their last few years in peace.

Houyhnhnms Race of horses which inhabited the last of the countries visited in GULLIVER'S TRAVELS, the embodiment of nobility, virtue and reason, who kept the YAHOOS in subjection. (Pronounced hwin'emz.)

Hovercraft Vehicle which floats a foot or two above ground or water on a cushion of air provided by a ring of air jets placed below it, all directed inwards. A British invention, by Christopher Cockerell. See SR-N.

Howard League for Penal Reform (1866). London society which works for improvement in prison conditions and in the treatment of delinquents and criminals. (Named after John Howard, 18th-century philanthropist, who was active in prison reform.)

Howards End (1910). E. M. Forster's novel on the theme of his key aphorism, 'only connect', i.e. about bringing together people, classes and nations through sympathetic insight and understanding. The Wilcoxes (wealth and business), Schlegels (culture) and Bast (the poor bank clerk) are brought together in the country house which gives the book its title.

How Green Was My Valley (1940). Richard Llewellyn's popular novel about a Welsh mining village.

'How They Brought the Good News from Ghent to Aix' (1845). Browning's dramatic poem, not based on historical fact, of 3 men galloping to save Aix: 'I galloped, Dirck galloped, we galloped all three.' (Pronounced gent, ayx.)

How to Win Friends and Influence People (1936). Sensationally successful book by Dale Carnegie of Missouri, USA, which was in effect a guide to salesmen on the techniques of persuasion, but apparently appealed to a much wider public.

Hoya Plant also known as the waxflower, named after Thomas Hoy, gardener at Sion House.

Hoylake Site of the Royal Liverpool Golf Club's Deeside championship course in The Wirral, Cheshire.

Hoyle, According to According to the rules of the game. (Edmund Hoyle, who wrote an authoritative treatise on Whist in 1742, later adding chapters on other card games; the name is perpetuated in *Hoyle's Games Modernised*, a standard work on all indoor games, including billiards, chess, roulette, etc.)

Hubble's Law (Astronomy). That the speed of recession of galaxies is proportional to their distance from an observer. See EXPANDING UNIVERSE THEORY.

Huckleberry Finn (1884). Mark Twain's masterpiece in which Huck, as he was called, a character from the earlier TOM SAWYER, escapes from his drunken father to float down the Mississippi on a raft with a runaway slave, Jim. The latter is captured, and Huck meets Tom Sawyer again.

Hudibras (1663–78). Samuel Butler's mock-heroic verse satire modelled on *Don Quixote*, in which Hudibras, a fat Presbyterian hunchback, sallies forth on an old nag with the Independent, Ralpho, as his Sancho Panza, to put the world to rights, and especially to stop people enjoying themselves. They spend much of their time quarrelling over trivial theological points. (Name taken from Spenser's *Faerie Queene*; pronounced hew'di-bras.)

Hudson Institute (1961). Organization in New York State founded by Dr Herman Kahn when he left the similar RAND CORPORATION. Dr Kahn (who coined the term 'megadeath' for a unit of 1 million dead in nuclear war) carried out research on the likely direction of scientific

progress in the far future, e.g. new methods of propulsion, sources of power and food, space travel and colonization, doubling man's allotted span – thus as a by-product providing SF writers with endless new material. The Hudson and Rand institutions are commonly called 'think-factories' or 'think-tanks'.

Hudson Memorial See RIMA.

Hudson's Bay Company (1670). Founded by Prince Rupert, chartered by Charles II and given the monopoly of the English fur trade with the Indians of North America in competition with the French. It is still the biggest fur trader in Canada, but derives most of its income from oil rights, department stores and other interests.

Hughenden Manor Disraeli's home near High Wycombe, Buckinghamshire, now owned by the National Trust.

Hughes Medal (1902). Royal Society medal awarded annually for original discovery in the physical sciences, especially electricity and magnetism.

Hugh the Drover (1924). Vaughan Williams's ballad-opera set in the Cotswolds, full of English folk music. Hugh is accused of being a spy for Napoleon, but his reputation is cleared by the arrival of a sergeant whose life he had once saved.

Huguenots French Protestants, mainly CALVINISTS; victims of the ST BARTHOLOMEW MASSACRE, tolerated under the EDICT OF NANTES, and again persecuted on its revocation, they scattered to England and other Protestant countries. (Corruption of German *Eidgenossen*, 'confederates'.)

Huis-clos (1944). Sartre's long one-act play about a man and 2 women who have died and are shut up in one room to torture each other endlessly ('hell is other people'). Finally offered freedom, they find they have become indispensable to one another. (English title, *In Camera*; US title, *No Exit*; French, 'closed door'.)

Hulot, Monsieur Clumsy, gangling, ever-so-apologetic character created and portrayed by the French cinema producer, Jacques Tati, in a series of near-silent comedies.

Humanae vitae (1968). Pope Paul VI's encyclical which reaffirmed the Church's previous condemnation of birth control; it aroused sharp controversy within the Church. (Latin, 'of human life'.)

Humanism. See REVIVAL OF LEARNING.

Humanité, L' (1904). French Socialist newspaper founded by Jean Jaurès, which in 1920 became Communist.

Humbert scandal (1903). Remarkable fraud when a very drab French widow, Thérèse Humbert, posing as beneficiary under an American millionaire's will, extracted 100 million gold francs over a period of 17 years from bankers, businessmen and lawyers. She got 5 years' solitary confinement.

Humble Petition and Advice (1657). Presented by the second PROTECTORATE Parliament, offering the title of king to Oliver Cromwell, which he refused, and suggesting the restoration of a Second Chamber in Parliament, which he accepted.

Humboldt current Cold current flowing from the Antarctic up the west coast of northern Chile and Peru, causing fogs and aridity in the coastal regions.

Humphry Clinker (1771). Smollett's comic novel in the form of letters written by the Bramble family, whose servant Humphry becomes; later it transpires that he is the illegitimate son of Mr Bramble. The book includes a picture of life at Bath ('Hot Wells').

Humpty Dumpty Egg of the rhyming riddle found, under various names, throughout Europe. In THROUGH THE LOOKING GLASS he becomes the scornful character for whom words meant just whatever he chose them to mean.

Humulus Genus name of the hop, of which there are garden varieties.

Hunchback of Notre Dame Quasimodo; see NOTRE DAME DE PARIS.

Hundred Days, The (1815). Period between Napoleon's escape from Elba in March and the Battle of Waterloo in June.

Hundred Flowers policy In China on 17 February 1957, Chairman Mao Tse-tung announced, 'Let 100 flowers blossom and 100 schools of thought contend', i.e. invited a flowering of public criticism of his regime. This turned out to be so virulent and widespread that the policy was abruptly reversed, and wholesale arrests followed.

Hundred Years War (1337–1453). Intermittent war waged by England, which claimed the French throne. Begun by Edward III, it ended in the reign of Henry VI, with England ejected from all its French possessions bar Calais. The main battles were Crécy, Poitiers, Agincourt, and the siege of Orleans, raised by Joan of Arc.

Hungarian rising (October 1956). Revolt against Russian domination, put down savagely by Russian troops. János Kádár was installed as premier to replace Imre Nagy, who was executed as ringleader. Nagy was rehabilitated in 1989.

Hung parliament Legislature with no political party having a working majority of representatives.

Hungry Forties, The The 1840s, when bad harvests and the Irish potato famine, combined with the CORN LAWS, caused great distress in Britain.

Huns Mongolian horsemen who swept into Europe to form a short-lived empire from the Urals to the Rhine, which collapsed when Romans and GOTHS defeated Attila at Châlons-sur-Marne (451).

Hunter Horse ridden in hunting, show-jumping and point-to-points; by a THOROUGHBRED out of a local mare, e.g. CLEVELAND BAY or Irish Draught, combining stamina, intelligence and quick reactions.

Hunter (1956). Hawker-Siddeley swept-wing ground-attack and short-range Army-support aircraft, replaced by the HARRIER. It was designed by the same man as was the Hurricane.

Hunterston (1964). One of the earlier series of nuclear power-stations, designed also to produce plutonium. A new AGR reactor is also projected. (Coastal site south of Largs, Ayrshire.)

Hunting Club Exclusive social club in Rome.

Huntington Library (1919). Library at San Marino near Los Angeles; among its treasures are a GUTENBERG BIBLE, Caxton's first book in English and a manuscript of the *Canterbury Tales*. With it are administered an art gallery (containing many valuable paintings, e.g. the BLUE BOY), and botanical gardens with 1,200 varieties of camellia and a collection of desert plants. (Collected and donated by Henry E. Huntington, a railway magnate.)

Huntington's chorea (1872). Hereditary incurable disease which appears in middle age, characterized by involuntary purposeless movements and mental deterioration. It is rare in black people. (George Huntington, a New York family doctor, discovered the disease.)

Hurlingham Club (1869). London club at Ranelagh Gardens, originally but no longer a polo club, now providing facilities for tennis, swimming, squash, croquet, etc. The Hurlingham Polo Association controls British polo.

Hurricane (1935). Hawker fighter plane which, with the Spitfire, won the battle of Britain.

Hush Puppies Proprietary name for shoes made of pigskin.

Husky Code name for the Allied assault on Sicily in 1943.

Hussites Bohemian followers of John Huss, who developed from a party of religious reform to a nationalist party opposed to German and papal domination. Successful in the Hussite War (1419–34), they won concessions from Sigismund, the Holy Roman Emperor. (John Huss, rector of Prague University, burnt at the stake in 1415 as an agitator for religious reform.)

Hutu Bantu people of Burundi and Rwanda in Central Africa, constantly at feud with the TUTSI. Also called Bahutu.

Hwang-ho (Huang ho) Chinese name of the Yellow River.

Hyades Open (or galactic) star cluster in TAURUS, which includes ALDEBARAN; when it rose with the sun it was thought to foretell rain. (Greek, 'the rainy ones', name of the daughters of Atlas; pronounced hya-deez.)

Hyde Park (1) Well-known London park. (2) Village in New York State overlooking the Hudson River, where the Roosevelt family house is now classed as a national historic site, with a Franklin D. Roosevelt library and museum.

Hydra In Greek legend, a many-headed monster slain by Heracles (HERCULES) as one of his Labours.

Hyksos Kings Rulers of Semitic nomads who invaded Egypt in the late 18th century BC, introducing new weapons and horse-chariots; they were expelled about 1570 BC by the founders of the NEW KINGDOM. (Egyptian, 'shepherd kings'.)

Hymen In Greek legend, the young god of marriage, son of Apollo. (Pronounced hy′men.)

Hymenoptera Order of insects with 4 membranous wings, the bees, wasps and ants (not including termites).

Hymettus Mountain overlooking Athens, famous in olden times for honey and marble.

Hymns, Ancient and Modern Collection, not specifically authorized for Church of England use, of only 130 hymns when first published as *Hymns* (1861), though expanded (1889 onwards) as it overtook earlier hymnals in popularity. See OLNEY HYMNS.

Hypatia Lecturer on Greek philosophy in 5th-century Alexandria, and the heroine of Charles Kingsley's historical novel of that name (1853). She was torn to pieces by a Christian mob who disapproved of pagan philosophy.

Hyperboreans In Greek legend, a people who lived in fertile land far to the north, where the sun always shone. (Pronounced hy-per-bor-eé anz.)

Hypericum Genus name of the St John's worts; *H. calycinum* is the Rose of Sharon.

Hyperion In Greek legend, a Titan, father of Helios (Sun), Selene (Moon) and Eos (Dawn), but later identified with the sun-god. (Pronounced hy-peer'i-on.)

Hyperion (1820). Keats's unfinished poem on the overthrow of the Titans by the new Greek gods (representing his own revolutionary ideas); see previous entry.

Hyperion Lord Derby's racehorse which in 1933 won the Derby (in record time) and the St Leger.

I

Iachimo Villain of Shakespeare's CYMBELINE who persuades Imogen's husband that she has been unfaithful. (Pronounced i-ak'im-o.)

Iago In Shakespeare's play Othello's ensign who, from malevolence and jealousy, persuades Othello that Desdemona has been unfaithful to him. (Pronounced i-ah'go.)

IAPS Initials used for the Incorporated Association of Preparatory Schools, the junior equivalent of the Headmasters' Conference.

IATA (1945). International Air Transport Association, the non-governmental organization of scheduled airlines to promote safe and efficient transport; successor to the International Air Traffic Association (1919); headquarters, Montreal.

Iberia The ancient name for the country of the River Ebro, hence the Spanish peninsula. (From *Iberus*, 'Ebro'.)

Iberia Name of the chief Spanish airline.

Iberians Dark-skinned race of small stature, not belonging to the Nordic or Alpine groups and speaking a language unrelated to any other known language, of whom the Basques are a remnant and traces survive in Wales, Ireland, Brittany, etc.: thought to have occupied most of Western Europe in neolithic times; also called Mediterranean or Eur-African.

Iberis Generic name for Candytuft.

IBM Initials normally used for the US firm of International Business Machines, with headquarters at Armonk, New York State.

Ibn Arabic, 'son of '.

Ibo Dominant people, and semi-Bantu language of eastern Nigeria. (Pronounced ee'bo.)

Ibrahim Arabic equivalent of Abraham. (Pronounced ib-ra-heem'.)

Ibrox Park Home of Glasgow Rangers football club. Scene of a disaster in 1971 when 66 died and 170 were injured. See CELTIC.

Icarus See DAEDALUS. (Pronounced ee'kar-us or ik'ar-us.)

Ice Age Period of about a million years, ending 20,000 BC, when northern Europe and America had a permanent ice cover; also, a previous period of this kind.

Iceman Cometh, The Eugene O'Neill's play (1946), the Iceman being Death.

Iceni The ancient Britons of East Anglia who, under Boadicea, revolted against Roman rule in AD 62. (Pronounced y-see'ni.)

Ichabod Son of Phinehas, born just after the deaths of his father and grandfather (1 Sam. 4:21): the name means 'the glory is departed (from Israel)'. (Pronounced ik'a-bod.)

I Chose Freedom (1946). Highly coloured autobiography of a Russian, Victor Kravchenko, who defected to the West in Washington DC (1944). It deals with the period of the Stalinist purges. The suggestion has been made that it is the work of a 'ghost'.

Ichthys

Ichthys Greek word for 'fish'; the early Christians noticed that the letters formed the initials of the Greek for 'Jesus Christ, Son of God, Saviour', and thus came to adopt the fish as a symbol of Christ.

ICI (1926). Firm which manufactures alkalis, dyestuffs, ammonia, Terylene and paints; among its other products are Perspex, Polythene and Paludrine. (Initials standing for Imperial Chemical Industries.)

Icknield Way Pre-Roman track running from near Marlborough through the Goring Gap on the Thames, to Letchworth and the Wash. (Possibly derived from ICENI, the tribe who lived in East Anglia.)

I, Claudius (1934). Robert Graves's novel in the form of Claudius' own story of the humiliations of his youth and, in the sequel *Claudius the God* (1943), his unwilling succession to Caligula as Roman Emperor.

Icon Image of Christ, the Virgin or of a saint or saints, painted to signify the presence of the subject, and used as an object of veneration and a channel for prayer.

Ida (1) Mountain near Troy. (2) Mountain in Crete in a cave of which Zeus was brought up. (3) Mother Ida, apostrophized in Tennyson's *Oenone*, is (1), where the nymph Oenone fell in love with PARIS. (4) Idaean Mother was CYBELE, associated with both (1) and (2).

Ida, Princess Heroine of Tennyson's fantasy, *The Princess*, and of the Gilbert and Sullivan opera, *Princess Ida*, based on it.

ID card Identity card; any card, preferably official, that helps to identify its bearer by name, address, etc.

Ides of March March the 15th in the Roman calendar; the fateful (or fatal) day, with reference to the day of Julius Caesar's assassination.

Idiot, The Prince Myshkin in Dostoyevsky's novel of that name; a Christ-like epileptic pauper prince, the type of the 'divine fool'.

Idler, The (1758–60). Dr Johnson's Addisonian essays, lighter in tone than those in the RAMBLER.

Idlewild Now Kennedy Airport, New York.

Idris Welsh legendary giant whose chair is the top of Cader Idris, a mountain in Merionethshire. He inspired poets and induced madness.

Idylls of the King (1857–85). Tennyson's version of Arthurian legend, based on Le MORTE D'ARTHUR; an allegory in which King Arthur represents the soul of man at war with the senses.

'If . . .' (1) Kipling's poem beginning 'If you can keep your head when all about you / Are losing theirs and blaming it on you' and ending 'Yours is the Earth and everything that's in it, / And, what is more, you'll be a Man, my son!' (2) British film that won the 1969 Grand Prix at CANNES FILM FESTIVAL, a melodramatic debunking of public schools.

Ife heads (13th century). Bronze and terracotta heads of great artistic merit made at Ife, the centre of Yoruba religion in Western Nigeria. The artistic tradition may have derived from the NOK CULTURE. (Pronounced eef'i.)

Iffley Road Oxford University sports ground.

If Winter Comes . . . (1920). Novel by A. S. M. Hutchinson which was immensely popular in its time. (A quotation from Shelley, which continues 'can Spring be far behind?')

IG Farben (1925). Huge German chemical group divided (1945) into 3 companies. (German *Interessen Gemeinschaften*, a vertical trust in which profits are shared; *Farbenindustrie*, 'dyes industry'.)

Ightham Near-perfect ancient moated manorhouse at Ivy Hatch, near Sevenoaks, Kent; still occupied. (Pronounced y'tèm.)

IHS The first 3 letters of the name Jesus in Greek, in which long *e* resembles *H*; variously taken to represent the Latin phrases *Iesus Hominum Salvator* (Jesus, Saviour of men), *In Hoc Signo (vinces)* (under this sign shalt thou conquer) or *In Hac (cruce) Salus* (in this Cross is salvation).

IJsselmeer Name given to the Dutch Zuider Zee when it was cut off from the sea by a barrage (1932). (Pronounced ee'sel-may-èr.)

Ike Nickname of General (later President) Dwight D. Eisenhower.

ILEA Initials standing for the INNER LONDON EDUCATION AUTHORITY. (Pronounced il'e-a.)

Île de France District round Paris bounded approximately by the Seine, Marne, Oise and Aisne; the French equivalent of the English Home Counties.

Ilford Former Essex borough, since 1965 part of the borough of REDBRIDGE.

Iliad, The Homer's epic poem about the events of a few days near the end of the TROJAN WAR. It begins with ACHILLES sulking in his tent and ends with a Trojan state funeral for HECTOR, whose corpse Achilles has been persuaded to return.

Ilium Another name for Troy. (Latin form of Greek name *Ilion*; pronounced *y*'li-um.)

'Ilkla Moor' Widely known song from Ilkley, Yorkshire, beginning: 'Wheer wer' ta bahn w'en Aw saw thee/ On Ilkla Moor baht 'at?'

Illustrated London News (1842). The pioneer in the sphere of illustrated journals.

Illyria Old name for the Adriatic coastal region of Yugoslavia, Albania and northern Greece, once a Roman province.

Ilyushin Name of a series of Russian civil and military aircraft.

Imaginary Conversations (1824–53). Series of dialogues between historical characters down the ages, on various subjects, by Walter Savage Landor; one of them is a conversation between Dante and Beatrice, for example.

Imagists (1910–18). Anglo-American group of poets led by T. E. Hulme, Ezra Pound. H. D. (Hilda Doolittle) and her husband Richard Aldington; they used images supercharged with intellectual and emotional significance to construct brief crystalline poems.

I'm All Right, Jack (1959). Best of the BOULTING BROTHERS' films, satirizing management and workers alike in a factory comedy of walk-outs, overmanning and time-and-motion study, with Peter Sellers as a henpecked shop steward.

Imam Arabic title applied to various religious leaders, from the earliest Caliphs and the leaders of the main Muslim sects down to the person who leads the prayers in a mosque. (Arabic, 'leader'; pronounced i-mahm'.)

Imari pattern Japanese style of decorating ceramics with intricate patterns of under-glaze blue, red and gold, made familiar to the West, where it was widely copied, by export wares in the late 17th and early 18th centuries. (Japanese port for the pottery district of Arita, where the KAKIEMON PATTERN also originated; these 2 together are sometimes called Arita ware.)

Imitation of Christ (1426). Mystical work on meditation thought to have been written by Thomas à Kempis or by a French preacher named Gerson. (Latin title. *De imitatione Christi*.)

Immaculate Conception Roman Catholic dogma (1854) that the Virgin Mary was conceived and born without original sin.

Immelmann turn Effective aerobatic manoeuvre developed in the First World War by the German air force, consisting of a half loop with a half roll at the top, the pilot thus gaining height and reversing direction. (Invented by Max Immelmann, shot down in 1916.)

Immortal Hour, The Rutland Boughton's CELTIC TWILIGHT opera (1914), which enjoyed an immense vogue as an escape from wartime realities.

Immortals, The Name given to the members (40) of the ACADÉMIE FRANÇAISE.

Imogen See CYMBELINE.

Impatiens Genus name of the balsams, which include Busy Lizzie, the cottage house-plant.

Imperial Airways (1924–40). Merger of 4 British airlines with governmental participation, from which BOAC and BEA were eventually formed, which in turn became British Airways.

Imperial College of Science and Technology Unit of London University, comprising the Royal School of Mines, City and Guilds (engineering), and the Royal College of Science (physics); established in South Kensington.

Imperial Defence College College where senior officers of the 3 services, civil servants and diplomats take courses in the handling of politico-strategic problems.

Imperial Institute See COMMONWEALTH INSTITUTE.

Imperial Preference Policy of encouraging trade within the British Empire either, when Britain was still a FREE TRADE country, by imposing tariffs on foreign imports into Britain and the Empire or, after Britain had begun imposing tariffs (the MCKENNA DUTIES and subsequent measures), by lowering them preferentially for Empire goods. Advocated by the TARIFF REFORM LEAGUE (1903) and introduced by the OTTAWA AGREEMENTS (1932).

Imperial War Museum (1917). Museum in Lambeth, London, devoted to all British military operations since 1914. In addition to exhibitions of military equipment, there are large libraries of books, films and photographs and a collection of paintings.

Importance of Being Earnest, The (1895). Oscar Wilde's last play, a brilliant, inconsequent fantasy about Jack Worthing who, since as a babe he was found in a handbag at Victoria Station, has difficulty in persuading Lady Bracknell that he is an eligible suitor for her daughter. He turns out to be an Ernest Moncrieff; hence the punning title.

Impressionism (1870s). Artistic movement, associated chiefly with Monet, Pissarro and Sisley, which aimed to capture fleeting impressions of colour and the play of light, by painting outdoors with swift strokes of bright colour what the painter's eye actually saw. The subjects were, necessarily, scenes of contemporary life, and did not tell a story. Whistler, Sickert and Wilson Steer, among many, were influenced by the movement. (Named after Monet's 'Impression: Sunrise' of 1872.)

In and Out See NAVAL AND MILITARY CLUB.

Inca (1) Title of the Emperor of Peru, whose capital was Cuzco. (2) Member of the KECHUA-speaking race dominant in Peru during the last 4 centuries before the Spanish Conquest (1532), by which time their rule extended to what are now Ecuador and northern Chile. See MACHU PICCHU.

In Camera Sartre's play; see HUIS-CLOS.

Incarvillea Herbaceous perennials, named after P. Incarville, a French Jesuit priest in China.

Incunabula Printed books produced before 1500. (Latin 'thing in the cradle', i.e. books produced in the infancy of printing.)

Independence Day (USA) The FOURTH OF JULY.

Independents Protestant sect who, at first called BROWNISTS, gradually from Tudor times took the position of rejecting both rule by bishops and rule by presbyters; they believed in complete religious toleration and that each congregation should manage its own affairs (hence the later name CONGREGATIONALISTS). Under Cromwell, who supported them, they elected the BAREBONES PARLIAMENT.

Index, The (1557). Short title of the Index Librorum Prohibitorum, a list of books prohibited to Roman Catholics because they might endanger faith or morals, compiled by the HOLY OFFICE. The works of Gibbon, Chaucer and Milton appeared in it, and at one time Dante's. It was abolished in 1966.

Indianapolis '500', The (1911). US Grand Prix 500-mile motor-car race, run in May at the Indianapolis motor speedway, Indiana.

Indian hemp One of the many names for *Cannabis* (marijuana, 'pot').

Indian mutiny (1857). Mutiny of about 35,000 Indian soldiers (sepoys) in the service of the British East India Company, which began on 10 May and lasted until July 1858. The chief result was that the rule of the British East India Company came to an end.

Indian rope trick Trick which apparently sober citizens claimed to have seen performed in India: a rope is thrown in the air and a boy climbs up it. This traveller's tale has had a remarkably long life but is now perhaps finally dead.

Indian summer Period of mild sunny weather in October; see ST LUKE'S SUMMER.

India paper (1875). Originally an import from China and used for proofs of engravings. Nowadays properly Oxford India Paper, a thin, tough, opaque printing paper.

Indienne (Cooking) Curried.

Individual Psychology Alfred Adler's system of psychoanalysis. Rejecting Freud's views, he stressed man's will to power and need to compensate for inferiorities, real or imagined, for which he invented the term 'inferiority complex'.

Indo-China War (1946–54). Nationalist war to drive the French from Indo-China, started by a sudden raid on the Tongking garrison and ended by DIEN BIEN PHU and the GENEVA AGREEMENTS.

Indo-European languages Group with 2 main divisions: (1) the eastern, including Sanskrit and the modern north Indian and Pakistani languages derived from it, Persian, and the SLAVONIC LANGUAGES; (2) the western, including Ancient Greek and Latin and their modern derivatives (see ROMANCE LANGUAGES), CELTIC LANGUAGES, and Germanic languages (e.g. German, English, Scandinvavian languages).

Industrial Christian Fellowship (1877). Society which works in industry in accordance with the principles of CHRISTIAN SOCIALISM.

Industrial Revolution Term used to described the long series of technological, economic, social and cultural changes which took place between c. 1760 and c. 1840, which changed Britain into an industrial nation. See IRONBRIDGE.

Industrial Workers of the World (1905–18). Militant organization of workers founded by US syndicalists to carry on class warfare through industrial sabotage.

Indus Valley civilization (2500–1500 BC). Pre-ARYAN civilization of India. The 2 chief sites excavated are MOHENJODARO and Harappa. Naturalistic figures of animals and stylized human figures, including dancers, are characteristic and interesting as foreshadowing many features of later (Aryan) Indian art.

Indus waters agreement (1960). Settlement of a long-standing dispute between India and Pakistan over the sharing for irrigation purposes of the waters of the Indus and its 5 tributaries.

'Inferno', Dante's See DIVINE COMEDY.

Ingoldsby Legends, The (1840). Collection of delightful and skilful light verse by the Rev. R. H. Barham, of which by far the best-known is The JACKDAW OF RHEIMS.

Inkerman (1854). Battle of the CRIMEAN WAR, 10 days after BALACLAVA, in which the Russians were thrown back by the British with heavy loss. (Ridge near Sebastopol.)

In Memoriam (1850). Tennyson's elegy on the death of his great friend Hallam and on the theme of personal immortality.

Inner City Arising from the tendency for the more prosperous elements of a city to move out to the suburbs, leaving the centre to degenerate into slums.

Inner London Education Authority (1965-90). Local education authority which served the City of London and 12 inner boroughs: Westminster, Camden, Greenwich, Hackney, Hammersmith. Islington, Kensington and Chelsea, Lambeth, Lewisham, Southwark, Tower Hamlets and Wandsworth.

Inner Mongolia Southern part of Mongolia, proclaimed an autonomous region of China by Chiang Kai-shek (1947); capital Huhehot (or Kweisui). See OUTER MONGOLIA.

Inner Temple Oldest and most richly endowed of the INNS OF COURT.

Inner Wheel clubs (1934). Clubs, formed by wives of ROTARY CLUB members, which are active in various kinds of social and charitable work.

245

Innes, Michael Pen-name assumed by J. I. M. Stewart when writing detective stories, e.g. *The Journeying Boy* (1949).

Innholders, Worshipful Company of (1514). LIVERY COMPANY, originally a guild of inn-keepers.

Innisfail Poetical name for Ireland.

Innisfree 'Lake Isle' of W. B. Yeats's best-known poem (1895), a nostalgic recollection of his homeland written in London; it begins: 'I will arise and go now, and go to Innisfree, / And a small cabin build there, of clay and wattles made.'

Innocents Abroad, The (1869). Mark Twain's novel exploiting the humours of provincial-minded American tourists travelling in Europe and the East.

Innocent X (1650). Velázquez's masterpiece of portraiture, in the Palazzo Doria, Rome.

Inns of Court Institutions founded in the reign of Edward I to train lawyers; 4 survive (INNER and MIDDLE TEMPLE, LINCOLN'S and GRAY'S INN), all in London, where law students keep 12 terms before being 'called to the Bar' (i.e. becoming barristers).

In Place of Strife (1969). Labour Party manifesto that outlined an industrial relations bill armed with penal clauses; this led to minor May Day demonstrations, in the face of which a revised version appeared (1970) innocuous enough to win TUC support. When the Conservatives published a similar bill, Labour leaders joined the unions in its denunciation.

Inquisition, The (13th century). HOLY OFFICE, a papal tribunal set up to stamp out heresy, starting with the ALBIGENSIANS; it earned damaging notoriety, especially in Spain where it lingered on until 1834, by its use of torture to extract confessions and by public burnings at the stake (*autos da fé*).

INRI Initials standing for the Latin for 'Jesus of Nazareth, King of the Jews', the inscription on the Cross. (Matt. 17:37; *Iesus Nazarenus Rex Iudaeorum*.)

Insectivora Order of small insect-eating, mostly nocturnal, mammals, including shrews, moles and hedgehogs.

Institutions, The City phrase for the insurance companies and pension funds which now dominate stock markets.

Interflora International flower-delivery service, with HQ in Detroit, a monopoly linking a worldwide network of flower shops numbered in tens of thousands.

International agencies UN's specialized agencies, such as the ILO, FAO, UNESCO, WHO, etc. A committee of the ECONOMIC AND SOCIAL COUNCIL acts as liaison between them and the General Assembly.

International Atomic Energy Agency UN agency, with headquarters in Vienna, which promotes the peaceful use of nuclear energy. See ATOMS FOR PEACE.

International Bank for Reconstruction and Development Better known as the WORLD BANK.

International Bible Students' Association Name for JEHOVAH'S WITNESSES.

International Brigade Body of volunteers who fought against Franco in the SPANISH CIVIL WAR; they defeated an Italian force at Guadalajara (1937) and were engaged in heavy fighting on the Ebro in 1938. Recruited from many countries, they included a contingent of British intellectuals who returned disillusioned by the ugly side of Spanish republicanism.

International Civil Aviation Organization UN agency, with headquarters at Montreal, which promotes uniformity of standards in civil aviation.

International Court of Justice (1946). UN body which took over the functions of the Permanent Court of International Justice (1921). Its 15 judges of 15 different nationalities represent the major legal systems of the world and are elected for 9-year renewable terms by the General Assembly and the Security Council.

International Date Line Line corresponding

to longitude of 180°, with deviations to keep all Siberia and Australia to the west of it. Time zones immediately to the west are 24 hours ahead of those to the east.

International Development Association (1960). International organization, affiliated to the WORLD BANK, which makes interest-free loans to developing countries, repayable over terms of 50 years; the headquarters are in Washington DC.

International Dragon etc. For classes of boat see under DRAGON, etc. See also INTERNATIONAL FOURTEEN.

'Internationale' Communist anthem written by Eugene Pottier and beginning: 'Debout, les damnés de la terre.' It was the Soviet national anthem until 1946, and then became the Communist Party song.

International Finance Corporation UN agency, with headquarters in Washington DC, which in association with the WORLD BANK invests funds in productive private enterprises in developing countries.

International Fourteen Oldest of the modern dinghy classes, given international status in 1927; the design varies greatly between the many boat-yards where it is built. They are meant to be tricky to handle and have no deck. The PRINCE OF WALES CUP (1927) is the leading championship.

International Geophysical Year (July 1957 to December 1958). Concerted world-wide meteorological investigation of the forces acting on the Earth.

International Horse Show, Royal (1907). Major show held at the National Exhibition Centre, Birmingham, in June. Events include the King George V, Queen Elizabeth and Prince of Wales Cups, a Coaching Marathon, hound show, costers' turn-out competition, and occasionally a display by the SPANISH RIDING SCHOOL.

International Hydrological Decade (1965). International effort on the lines of the INTERNATIONAL GEOPHYSICAL YEAR, in which 60 UNESCO countries cooperated in research on water supply, river control, etc.

International Institute for Strategic Studies (1958). Organization with international membership, which studies problems of defence strategy, disarmament and international security in this nuclear age. It publishes *Survival* (monthly), *Military Balance* (yearly), *Strategic Survey* (yearly) and other papers, and is consulted by British and US governments and NATO.

International Monetary Fund (1946). Fund set up after BRETTON WOODS to ease international payment difficulties, stabilize foreign-exchange rates and liberalize trade; of the total subscriptions, in gold and national currencies, half came from USA and Britain.

International Quiet Sun Years (1964–5). Cooperative study by scientists of 71 countries of the sun and earth during a period of minimum sunspot activity

International Refugee Organization (1947–51). International body which repatriated or resettled some 5 million refugees and displaced persons before it was replaced by the office of the UNITED NATIONS HIGH COMMISSIONER FOR REFUGEES.

Interpol International Criminal Police Commission, an organization for co-operation between the CIDs of member states; established in Vienna (1923) and re-established in Paris (1946).

Interstate Commerce Commission (1887) (USA) Powerful government body which exercises control over all forms of federal (as opposed to internal state) transport, by fixing rates, issuing licences, prohibiting racial discrimination, and supervising finance and planning.

In the Wet (1953). Nevil Shute's novel about the Queen's difficulties with a Socialist Britain in the 1980s.

Intimations of Immortality (1807). Shortened title of Wordsworth's *Ode: Intimations of Immortality from Recollections of Early Childhood*, on the theme that we are born 'trailing clouds of glory' but 'shades of the prison house begin to close / Upon the growing boy'.

Intourist Soviet state travel agency for foreigners.

Invalides, Les (1676). Founded in Paris by Louis XIV as a home for disabled soldiers and still housing about 100 of them. In the same group of buildings are an important military museum and the Church of the Dome, where Napoleon, Foch and other military leaders are buried. (On the South Bank, south of the Quai d'Orsay.)

Inveraray Castle Headquarters of the Campbell clan on Loch Fyne, Argyll, and home of the Dukes of Argyll since the 15th century.

Invergordon Mutiny (September 1931). Mutiny in the Royal Navy provoked by cuts in pay imposed by Ramsay MacDonald's National Government. (Naval base in Cromarty Firth.)

Invertebrates All animals which do not have backbones, e.g. snails, worms, flies, crabs, jellyfish, sponges and PROTOZOA.

Invincible, **HMS** (1908). First battle-cruiser, a type of capital ship in which armour was sacrificed to speed.

Invisible Man, The (1) Early SF novel (1897) by H. G. Wells. (2) Novel (1952) of the black American writer, Ralph Ellison, about a young black's growing disillusion not only with white people but with his own race.

Io (Greek legend) Daughter of a king of Argos whom Zeus turned into a heifer. The jealous Hera sent a gadfly to torment her, which made her run (or swim) all the way from Greece to Egypt, via the Bosporus ('cow-ford') and the Ionian Sea (named after her). There she regained human form and bore Zeus a son. (Pronounced *y'*o.)

Iolanthe (1882). Particularly tuneful Gilbert and Sullivan opera in which the Queen of the Fairies, who has banished Iolanthe for marrying a mortal (now Lord Chancellor) and has been slighted by the Peers, takes her revenge by ordering Iolanthe's half-fairy son into Parliament, where he has a high old time leading both parties and passing any measures he pleases, e.g. one throwing the peerage open to competitive examination. (Pronounced *y*-o-lanth'i.)

Iona monastery (563). Centre of Celtic Christianity founded by St Columba on an island of the Inner Hebrides; its ruins have been restored by the Iona Community.

Ionians First wave of Bronze Age Greek-speaking Aryan invaders from the north, who probably entered Greece soon after 2000 BC and were driven out of much of it (except Attica, in particular, where they were to become the ancestors of the Athenians) by the ACHAEANS around 1500 BC. Many (*c.* 1000 BC) crossed to the Aegean Islands and adjacent Asia Minor, where they founded Miletus, Ephesus, etc. There, and in Smyrna, in the 6th–5th centuries flourished the Ionian school of philosophers (Thales, Anaximander, Heraclitus, Anaxagoras and others). The Ionic dialect, used by Homer, resembled Attic Greek.

Ionic Order Order of Greek architecture intermediate between the Doric and the Corinthian in slenderness of columns and degree of embellishment and easily recognizable by the voluted capitals.

Iphigeneia In Greek legend, daughter of AGAMEMNON and CLYTEMNESTRA. When the start of the expedition to Troy was delayed by contrary winds, her father sacrificed her to placate the gods. In a later version, Artemis rescued her from the altar and spirited her away to the land of the Tauri (the Crimea) where she became a priestess and where her brother ORESTES found her. See next 2 entries. (Pronounced *y*-fijen-*y'*a, or if-i-.)

Iphigeneia in Aulis (406 BC). Euripides' unfinished play about the sacrifice of IPHIGENEIA at Aulis. Racine wrote a play (1674) and Gluck an opera (1772) based on this. See also next entry.

Iphigeneia in Tauris (414 BC). Euripides' play in which IPHIGENEIA is found in the land of the Tauri by her brother ORESTES, and they escape together. Goethe wrote a play (1787) and Gluck an opera (1779) based on this. ('In Tauris' is the Latin form of the title, and means 'among the Tauri', the people of the Crimea.)

Ipomoea Genus that includes Morning Glory.

IQ Intelligence Quotient, i.e. mental age divided by real age multiplied by 100, giving an average

IQ of 100 (10/10x100). A child of 8 who, in intelligence tests, shows the mental ability of the average 10-year-old has an IQ of 10/8x100 = 125. IQs range from below 20 for the feeble-minded (see also ESN) to 115 for an intelligent child and 180 for the exceptionally bright; they do not normally change very much after the age of 6. The degree to which intelligence is governed by heredity and/or environment has been hotly disputed for decades, being emotionally bound up with race and class discrimination.

IRA (1919) Irish Republican Army, dedicated to the establishment, by force if necessary, of an all-Ireland republic. First formed under Michael Collins, it fought for Irish independence until 1921; a hard core under De Valera then fought Collins's FREE STATERS until 1923; a still harder core have continued urban guerrilla war ever since, against the governments at Dublin, STORMONT and Westminster alike.

Iráklion (Herakleion) Capital of Crete, a Greek island formerly known by its Italian name, Candia.

IRB Initials of the Irish Republican Brotherhood, the revolutionary core of the 19th-century FENIAN movement; revived (1913) in USA and financed by Irish Americans, it formed the IRISH NATIONAL VOLUNTEERS. See EASTER RISING; IRA.

Ireland, Republic of Official designation of Southern Ireland from 1949, when it seceded from the Commonwealth. See EIRE

Irgun Zvai Leumi Zionist terrorist organization in Palestine, contemporary with the STERN GANG; its survivors now support the Israeli 'Liberal' party. (Pronounced eer'goon tsvah'ee lay-oom'i.)

Iris In Greek legend originally the rainbow; later she appears as the messenger of the gods.

Irish coffee Coffee laced with Irish whiskey and topped with whipped cream.

Irish Free State Official designation of Southern Ireland while it had Dominion status (1922–37).

Irish Guards (1900). Fourth regiment of the GUARDS DIVISION; they wear their buttons in fours, and a blue plume.

Irish Guinness Oaks Irish equivalent to the OAKS, run at the Curragh in July.

Irish RM, The See EXPERIENCES OF AN IRISH RM.

Irish stew Stew consisting of layers of mutton, onion and sliced potatoes, in thick gravy.

Irish Sweeps Derby Irish equivalent of the Derby, run at the Curragh in June. (Sponsored by the privately owned Hospitals Trust Ltd, which runs a world-famous sweepstake; one-fifth of the profits go to Irish hospitals.)

Iris kaempferi Species name of the Japanese iris.

Irlandaise (Cooking) With potatoes.

Iron Age Period which succeeded the BRONZE AGE, when iron replaced bronze in making tools and weapons, a skill which spread from the Middle East about 1200 BC to reach Europe (HALLSTATT) about 700 BC.

Ironbridge Scene of the remarkable breakthrough in iron smelting which led Britain to become the first industrial nation. The Iron Bridge, the first of its kind, was constructed in 1777–81.

Iron Chancellor Bismarck; see BLOOD AND IRON.

Iron Cross (1813). Best-known German military medal; the highest of its 4 classes, the Grand Cross, was awarded to a commanding officer who won an important victory.

Iron Curtain Phrase symbolizing the barrier against Western co-operation raised by Stalin, and later the whole Communist bloc; first used by Churchill in a telegram to Truman (May 1945) and, publicly, in his FULTON SPEECH.

Iron Duke (1) Nickname of the first Duke of Wellington. (2) Name of one of the earlier *Dreadnought*-type battleships.

Iron Gates Narrow 2-mile gorge of the Danube on the Romanian–Yugoslav border east of Belgrade; once a serious obstacle to navigation because of the rapids formed.

Iron Guard (1933). Fascist party in Romania.

Iron Lady Name originally coined by the Soviet magazine, *Red Star*, for Prime Minister Margaret Thatcher because of her determined and uncompromising stance at international meetings.

Iron Law of Wages That wages can never for long rise much above subsistence level, because that is the natural price of labour and any increase must be at the expense of profits (Ricardo); because if wages rise the working population increases and pushes them down again (Malthus); because workers are in no position to bargain, under capitalism (Marx). This basic assumption of the DISMAL SCIENCE proved unfounded almost as soon as it appeared in print, but the idea lived on until the end of the 19th century.

Iron Maiden of Nuremberg Seventeenth-century instrument of torture consisting of an iron box with spikes inside; when the door closed on a victim he was impaled on all sides. The original is now in Germany.

Ironmongers, Worshipful Company of (1463). One of the smallest of the LIVERY COMPANIES.

Ironsides Name given to Cromwell's army. (From a nickname given to Cromwell by the Royalists, alluding to that given to EDMUND IRONSIDE.)

Iroquois Member of the Five Nations, a confederation of American Indian tribes on the Canada–US border, which included the Mohawks and Oneidas. (Pronounced ir'ė-kwoi; plural spelt the same but pronounced ir'ė-kwoiz.)

Iroquois Cup English men's lacrosse club championship, played at Manchester between the winners of the Southern Flag and Northern Flag competitions.

Irredentists (1) Originally, from 1878, an Italian movement calling for the recovery of all Italian-speaking districts e.g. Tirol. (2) Applied to similar movements elsewhere, e.g. Hungarian claim-

ants to Transylvania after the First World War. (Italian *Italia irredenta*, 'unredeemed Italy'.)

Irvine (1966). NEW TOWN in Ayrshire, 7 miles west of Kilmarnock, designed to take 80,000 inhabitants.

Irvingites (1835). Religious sect founded in London by a former minister of the Church of Scotland; it combines Roman Catholic ritualism, a belief in contemporary miracles and primitive elements from early Christianity. Properly styled the Holy Catholic and Apostolic Church, it still survives. (Edward Irving, founder.)

Isaac Second Hebrew patriarch, only son of Abraham by Sarah, husband of Rebecca, and father of Esau and Jacob. In youth he was saved from sacrifice by his father by the substitution of a ram caught in a thicket (Gen. 22: 13).

Isabella colour Off-white or dirty white. (Traditionally derived from Isabella of Austria, daughter of Philip II of Spain, who vowed not to change her linen until her husband had taken Ostend. The siege lasted 3 years, until 1603; but in fact the term was used before her time.)

Isaiah (8th century BC). One of the major prophets, and traditionally the author of the first 39 chapters of *Isaiah*.

Isca Roman name of Caerleon, Monmouth.

Isca Dumniorum Roman name of Exeter.

Iseult (**Ysolde**, and many other spellings) In ARTHURIAN LEGEND daughter of a king of Ireland, who fell in love with TRISTRAM.

Isfahan carpets Beautifully designed multi-coloured carpets with rich red or beige grounds made from the 16th century to today at the old SAFAVID capital.

Ishmael Son of Abraham by HAGAR, whose 'hand will be against every man and every man's hand against him' (Gen. 16: 12). The Arabs are traditionally descended from his 12 sons.

Ishtar Babylonian goddess of love (derived from the Sumerian goddess Inanna), object of the most widespread cult of the Mesopotamian world, worshipped with orgies and ritual prostitution. She brought back TAMMUZ from the Underworld each year. Identified with the planet Venus, she is represented in the Greek pantheon by Aphrodite.

Isis Ancient Egyptian cow-goddess, sometimes regarded as a Moon goddess, represented in art as having a human head with horns. Mother by OSIRIS of HORUS, she avenged the death of Osiris by killing SET. She became the great nature goddess of the Mediterranean world, identified with various local deities.

Isis, The (1) Thames at Oxford, strictly only from its source to its junction with the Thame. (2) Oxford University undergraduate magazine. (From ancient error which assumed that the Latin *Thamesis* 'Thames', was a compound name formed from *Thame* and *Isis*.)

Isis crew Oxford University reserve crew for the Oxford and Cambridge Boat Race.

Iskenderun Turkish form of the name Alexandretta, a town and naval base in Hatay, Turkey.

Islam MUSLIM religion; the Muslim world, (Arabic, 'submission', i.e. to the will of Allah).

Isles of the Blest Another name for the FORTUNATE ISLES.

Islington Inner London borough, since 1965 consisting of the former metropolitan boroughs of Islington and Finsbury.

Ismaili sect SHI'ITE sect which considers that in the 8th century the elder son (Ismael) of the 6th Imam was wrongly disinherited by his father for drunkenness. The AGA KHAN is the spiritual leader of the sect, which has some 10 million adherents in India, Pakistan, the Middle East and East Africa.

Isonzo (June 1915 to September 1917). River then in Italy, the scenes in World War I of 11 battles between the Austrians and Italians. (Now the River Soca in Yugoslavia.)

Israel (1) Northern kingdom in Palestine, formed under Jeroboam, which seceded from the rule of King Solomon's son (see JUDAH) in the 10th

century BC; it was destroyed by the Assyrians in 722 BC. (2) Modern Jewish state, founded 1948.

Issus (333 BC). Battle in which Alexander the Great defeated the Persian Darius; see GAUGAMELA. (Town in south-east Cilicia, Asia Minor.)

Istanbul Turkish name of Constantinople. (Corruption of the Greek for 'into the city'; pronounced ist-an-bool'.)

Istiqlal (1943). Moroccan nationalist party. (Arabic, 'independence'.)

ITA Initials standing for: (1) Initial Teaching Alphabet, used with success in teaching infants to read; it consists of 43 phonetic characters. Once children have learnt to read fluently in it, they are switched to the orthodox, far from phonetic, alphabet, which they quickly assimilate. (2) Independent Television Authority, a body appointed by the PMG to operate a public service for disseminating information, education and entertainment, to erect transmitters, license programme contractors and to limit the proportion of advertising time in their programmes. See ITV.

Italia Nostra Society for the preservation of Italy's artistic and natural heritage; it did much, through a local branch, Venezia Nostra, to awaken the world to the dangers threatening Venice.

Italian Renaissance (14th–16th centuries). The first stage of the RENAISSANCE in art and literature, which began in the age of Giotto, Dante and Petrarch and culminated in the HIGH RENAISSANCE.

Italia prize Awarded at an annual international competition for documentaries, musical works and plays written specifically for broadcasting.

Ithaca Island kingdom of ODYSSEUS (Ulysses) off the west coast of Greece. (In modern Greek spelt Ithaki; pronounced ith'a-ka.)

ITMA (1939–49). Wartime radio show in which Tommy Handley made his name and which introduced characters such as Colonel Chinstrap. Mrs Mopp and Fünf the spy. (Initials taken from the signature tune, 'It's That Man Again'.)

ITN (1967). Initials standing for Independent TV News, a service which provides news bulletins for all the commercial TV services, given by a company owned jointly by the programme contractors.

ITV (1955). Initials standing for Independent Television, the commercial service operated by the ITA through various regional programme contractors, who pay rent to the Authority and part of their advertising revenue to government.

Ivanhoe (1819). Walter Scott's novel in which the hero Ivanhoe goes on crusade with Richard Cœur de Lion. The main features of the book are the tournament at Ashby de la Zouch, at which Richard fights incognito, and the depiction of Saxon hatred for their Norman masters. Robin Hood appears in this book.

Ivan the Terrible (1944). Title of an unfinished trilogy of films, and of the first of them, by Eisenstein; he completed the second, *The Boyars' Plot*, in 1946. They describe, in a stylized technique with mask-like make-up, the struggle of the young 16th-century Tsar to gain ascendancy over his boyars (feudal lords).

Iveagh Bequest Robert Adam house at Kenwood, north-west London, bought with its art treasures for London by public subscription and a gift from the 1st Earl of Iveagh. (Pronounced *y'vè*.)

Iveagh Professor Holder of the chair of Chemical Microbiology at Oxford.

Ivy League (1) US universities of the eastern seaboard who agreed to play football only against each other; they are: Harvard, Yale, Princeton, Cornell, Dartmouth, Columbia and Pennsylvania. (2) Students and graduates of these universities. (3) Applied also to their style of dress – quiet and neat.

Iwo Jima landing (February 1945). Particularly fierce engagement by US Marines against fanatical Japanese resistance, on an isolated volcanic island 700 miles south-east of Japan.

Ixion In Greek legend, a rascal who after being helped by Zeus tries to seduce Hera, his wife. As a punishment he was chained to a burning wheel which rolled eternally through the skies or, in a later version, in Hades. (Pronounced ik-*sy*'on.)

I Zingari (1845). Oldest of the touring cricket clubs. (See ZINGARI.)

Izmir Turkish name for Smyrna, ancient Greek port on the Aegean, now Turkish.

Izvestia (1917). Soviet Russian daily newspaper, representing the government view-point (see PRAVDA) and reproducing government documents at length. (Russian, 'news'.)

'Jabberwocky' Nonsense ballad which Alice finds in a book in THROUGH THE LOOKING-GLASS. It begins: ''Twas brillig and the slithy toves / Did gyre and gimble in the wabe.' There are many portmanteau words in it which have passed into common usage, e.g. 'burble', 'chortle', 'galumph' and 'uffish' (gruff + rough + huffy + -ish). See NONSENSE VERSE.

J'accuse (1898). Novelist Zola's trenchant attack on the handling of the DREYFUS CASE, in the form of an open letter to the French President published in a Paris newspaper.

Jack-a-Lantern Will-o'-the-wisp or ignis fatuus, the flickering light seen in marshes and due to the spontaneous combustion of methane (marsh gas). Thought to be the work of mischievous spirits trying to lure travellers into the marsh, ignis fatuus ('foolish fire') and its synonyms came to be used of delusive hopes.

Jack and Jill Characters in a nursery rhyme, and traditional names for any lad and lass. The rhyme has been unconvincingly linked with a Scandinavian myth about features visible on the Moon.

Jack and the Beanstalk World-wide folk story, usually interpreted as follows. Jack (mankind) climbs the heaven-high beanstalk (YGG-DRASIL), steals from a giant (God) a hen which lays golden eggs (the Sun), a harp (wind) and money (the fruit of rain, on which crops depend). He then shins down the stalk which he fells with an axe, bringing the pursuing giant crashing down to earth.

Jack Cade's rebellion (1450). Revolt of the men of Kent led by an Irish landowner who had settled there; it was put down by Henry VI.

'Jackdaw of Rheims, The' One of the IN-GOLDSBY LEGENDS. The Jackdaw steals the Cardinal's ring, and is cursed with bell, book and candle ('never was heard such a terrible curse!'). Reduced to a pitiable state, the unhappy bird returns the ring, reforms, and after his death is canonized as St Jim Crow.

Jackfield ware (1) Red earthenware covered with a jet black glaze and decorated with gilt, made in the mid 18th century at Jackfield, Shropshire; also copied by WHIELDON and others. (2) A revival of this by various Staffordshire potteries about 1855, chiefly in the form of cowcreamers, tea wares and figures, sometimes with multicoloured floral decorations, etc.

Jack Horner Character in a nursery rhyme, said to be a historical Jack Horner sent by the Abbot of Glastonbury to appease Henry VIII at the DISSOLUTION OF THE MONASTERIES with a pie in which were concealed the title deeds of some manors; he stole one of them.

Jack-in-the-Green Medieval May Day character, a boy chimney-sweep enclosed in a leaf-covered wicker cage; depicted in stained glass and carvings, and perhaps a relic of tree-worship.

Jack Robinson 'Before you could say Jack Robinson' (i.e. in a flash) is a phrase that goes back at least to the 18th century; origin unknown.

Jack Russell Small terrier bred to work with

guns or hounds; the Kennel Club does not recognize the breed, for which there is no accepted description; it is usually like a small fox terrier and should not be more than 12 inches high. (Named after the Rev. Jack Russell (died 1883), famous for his working terriers.)

Jacksonian democracy Further development of JEFFERSONIAN DEMOCRACY symbolized by the first self-made man to become US President – Andrew Jackson (1828–35); he believed that the good of the community as a whole would best be served by unrestricted majority rule, and went much further than Jefferson in appealing to the masses or 'common man'.

Jacksonian Professor Holder of the chair of Natural Philosophy at Cambridge.

Jack Straw Typical peasant name assumed by a leader in the Peasant Revolt of 1381.

Jack the Giant-killer Nursery story of a Cornishman who rid the country of giants, aided by a sword and other magic props.

Jack the Ripper (1888). The man who in the course of 4 months killed at least 4, possibly 7, prostitutes in a small area of Whitechapel, London. Never publicly identified, he is now thought to have been a deranged barrister, M. J. Druitt, who committed suicide.

Jacob Third Patriarch, son of Isaac, who cheated his twin, Esau, of his birthright (Gen. 25:29–34) and of his father's blessing (Gen. 27:19–29). His wives were Leah and Rachel. He became the father of 12 sons, founders of the 12 tribes of Israel. See JACOB'S LADDER.

Jacobean period (1603–42). Convenient if inaccurate term for the reigns of James I and Charles I. Furniture was still made in the Tudor style and in oak, but with lighter designs. Inigo Jones introduced PALLADIAN ARCHITECTURE to England.

Jacobins (1789–99). Extreme republicans of the French Revolution, from whom the GIRONDINS broke away early. They were, under Robespierre and Marat, responsible for the Reign of TERROR. (Members of a club which met in an old Jacobin convent.)

Jacobites Tories, led by Henry St John, Viscount Bolingbroke, who after the GLORIOUS REVOLUTION still wanted a restoration of the exiled STUARTS. See OLD PRETENDER; YOUNG PRETENDER; FIFTEEN; FORTY-FIVE. (Jacobus, Latin form of James, i.e. James II and James the OLD PRETENDER.)

Jacob's ladder Ladder reaching to heaven, with angels ascending and descending on it, seen in a dream by JACOB at BETHEL (Gen. 28:12–15).

Jacquard loom Loom invented by Joseph-Marie (1752–1834) Jacquard, French silk-weaver of Lyons. The mechanism is controlled by a chain of variously perforated cards.

Jacquard weave Intricate variegated weave made on a jacquard loom and used for brocade, tapestry and damask. (See previous entry.)

Jacquerie, The (1358). Desperate peasant rising in the north of France, marked by much bloodshed. (*Jacques Bonhomme*, French nickname for a peasant.)

Jacuzzi (1968). Whirlpool bath named after Candido Jacuzzi, who invented it to treat his son who had rheumatoid arthritis.

Jaffa Brand name of all varieties of orange from Israel.

Jags, The Nickname of the Partick Thistle football team.

Jaguar Cars made by a Coventry (originally a Blackpool side-car) firm, at first very good low-priced models, then highly successful racing cars, and GT saloons such as the E-TYPE and XJS (6-cylinder) version.

Jainism Indian religion founded by Mahavira in the same century as Buddhism (6th century BC), which it closely resembles, emphasizing compassion and non-violence. (Sanskrit *jaina*, 'one who has overcome', 'Buddha'; pronounced jyn'izm.)

Jallianwala Bagh Scene of, and sometimes used for, the AMRITSAR MASSACRE. (Name of open space at Amritsar.)

Jalna (1927). First of Mazo de la Roche's long series of novels (the last published in 1960) about 4 generations of the Whiteoak family, from their pioneering days on the Jalna estate in southern Ontario down to modern times.

Jamaica rum Original dark, heavy, highly flavoured (i.e. with a high esters content) rum; it must by law be matured for at least 3 years before sale. It is used in PLANTER'S PUNCH but has been overtaken in popularity by BACARDI RUM.

James, Jesse (1847–82). ROBIN HOOD of Missouri who, allegedly because Federal militia beat him and gaoled his mother (1863), joined the Confederate guerrillas (see QUANTRELL); then, according to a ballad, 'And with his brother Frank he robbed the Chicago bank, / And stopped the Glendale train.' A youngster in his gang shot him in the back in Kansas City for the $10,000 price on his head. A popular symbol of resistance to injustice, he is said to have paid off a widow's mortgage and stolen the money back from the mortgagee.

Jameson Raid (1895). Unofficial British armed raid on the Transvaal Republic, led by Dr Jameson and supported by Cecil Rhodes. The cause was irritation at President Kruger's refusal to grant political rights to the UITLANDERS, whom he taxed heavily. It united the Boers against the British and led to the BOER WAR.

James Sixth and First Scots name for James I of England, see STUARTS.

Jammu and Kashmir Official name in India of Indian-held Kashmir (see AZAD KASHMIR), Jammu being the south-western district of Kashmir where the Hindu minority live, forming one-fifth of the total population of Jammu and Kashmir, which is predominantly Muslim. See KASHMIR DISPUTE.

Jamshid Legendary king of Persia who reigned for 700 years, and under whom all the arts of civilization were developed. Because of his overweening arrogance, the gods reduced him to utter destitution and misery. The RUBAIYAT refers to 'the Courts where Jamshyd gloried and drank deep', which 'They say the Lion and the Lizard keep'.

Jane (1932–59). *Daily Mirror* comic strip (in both senses) by Norman Pett until 1949 (later by Mike Hubbard) remembered chiefly as a wartime pin-up and morale-booster. The innocent young heroine kept on losing items of her clothing in circumstances beyond her control.

Jane Eyre (1847). Name of Charlotte Brontë's study of selfless love surviving shocks, and of its shy heroine, governess to Mr ROCHESTER's ward.

Janissaries (14th century). Turkish bodyguard, at first recruited from Christian subjects; they waxed powerful and unruly, and were massacred at the instigation of the Sultan in 1826. (Turkish, 'new soldiers'.)

Jansenism (17th century). View that man is so depraved that there is no salvation except through divine grace. Recognizing its affinity with the predestination doctrine of CALVINISM, the Jesuits fiercely attacked this heresy, which was, however, supported by Pascal. The Jansenists had their headquarters at PORT-ROYAL. (Cornelius Jansen, Louvain professor, Bishop of Ypres.)

Jansky noise (1931). Radio signals from the Milky Way, first picked up by K. G. Jansky (USA) as a steady hiss on a short-wave band.

Janus Roman god who guarded doors, city gates and, in wartime, the city itself. He is represented with 2 faces, vigilantly facing past and future. January is named after him.

Jaques The 'melancholy' attendant on the Duke in AS YOU LIKE IT. (Pronounced jay'kwiz.)

Jarley, Mrs Owner of a travelling waxworks show who befriended Little Nell in *The* OLD CURIOSITY SHOP.

Jarndyce v. Jarndyce Fictional Chancery case which 'dragged its dreary length' interminably through Dickens's *Bleak House*.

Jarrow hunger march (1936). Best-known of

several marches to London organized by town councils to protest against unemployment.

Jarvie, Bailie Nicol Shrewd and cautious Glasgow magistrate who comes to Frank Osbaldistone's aid in Scott's ROB ROY.

Jasna Góra Place of pilgrimage of great national importance to Poles, an ancient monastery overlooking Częstochowa (between Warsaw and Cracow). Over the altar is an image of the Virgin (the Black Madonna) traditionally painted by St Luke. Pilgrimages to it have often been the occasion of demonstrations of unrest under Russian or Communist rule.

Jason Leader of the ARGONAUTS. The king of Colchis promised him the GOLDEN FLEECE if he ploughed a field with fire-breathing bulls and sowed it with dragons' teeth. The king's daughter, MEDEA, helped him to do this by giving him a fire-resistant lotion, but the king broke his promise. Medea then put to sleep the dragon who guarded the Fleece and, together with Jason, fled with it from Colchis.

Jasper ware (1775). Name given by Josiah Wedgwood to his fine stoneware stained blue and decorated with white figures in relief in the style of ancient Greek vases. Other colours were also used, and other potteries copied this ware, which is still made today by the Wedgwood firm.

Java Man First specimen of PITHECANTHROPINE to be found, in 1891 in Java.

Jaxartes Ancient name of the Syr Darya river, Kazakhstan, USSR.

Jazz Style of popular, mainly dance, music derived ultimately from the BLUES and the Negro brass bands of New Orleans in the 1880s, although the name dates from about 1917 (replacing RAGTIME), when jazz musicians began to migrate to Chicago after STORYVILLE was closed down. There the saxophone came to the fore and the characteristic syncopated improvisation ('hot' jazz) by soloists against a steady 4-4 rhythm set by the drums was developed, notably by Louis Armstrong (trumpet). Other features were blue notes (see BLUES), discords, wah-wah trumpets, hyena-laugh trombones, and noisy percussion. SWING, BEBOP, revivalist jazz

(a post-war revival of 1920s Negro jazz) and TRAD were later developments.

Jazz Age Term for the 1920s in USA, popularized by Scott Fitzgerald; it was characterized by the complete emancipation of women, general absence of moral restraint, and all the evils of the PROHIBITION period.

Jazz Singer, The Film which ushered in the era of 'talkies' (1927), with Al Jolson in the title role.

JCR Abbreviation for Junior Common (or Combination) Room, a room reserved for undergraduates (see SCR).

Jean-Christophe (1904–12). Romain Rolland's series of 10 novels in which France and Germany are seen through the eyes of the musician Jean-Christophe Kraft. The work explores the position of the artist in a corrupted modern society.

Jebusites (1) Pre-Israelite inhabitants of Jerusalem, later reduced to slavery. (2) Dryden's nickname for the Jesuits.

Jeeves Impeccable, imperturbable, sagacious gentleman's gentleman whose function in P. G. Wodehouse's books is to rescue WOOSTER from disaster and to restrain his sartorial extravagances. In *Much Obliged, Jeeves* (1971) published on the author's 90th birthday, it was revealed that Jeeves was called Reggie at the Junior Ganymede, *the* gentlemen's gentlemen's club; the Hon. Bertie heard this with his own startled ears when they were having a modishly democratic drink together.

Jeffersonian democracy Belief that people, who are born equal, free and with like potentialities, are well able to govern themselves through democratic institutions. The safeguarding of the rights of the individual, and of the individual state against a central federal government, was therefore of supreme importance. See JACKSONIAN DEMOCRACY. (Thomas Jefferson, 3rd US President, 1801–9.)

Jefferson Memorial (1943). On the Potomac shore, Washington DC, a large domed circular colonnade built in marble in the classical style which Thomas Jefferson himself introduced to

America; on the walls are inscriptions based on his writings.

Jehovah's Witnesses (1852). US sect founded by Pastor Russell. It teaches that Christ returned, invisibly, in 1874; Armageddon must occur before 1974; millions (i.e. Witnesses) now living will never die; all Churches and governments are of Satan; the Cross is a phallic symbol; vaccination and blood transfusion are evil. The luxury headquarters in California were built to house Abraham, Isaac and Jacob, due back on earth in 1925. The sale of Santonin (a cure for appendicitis and typhoid) and miracle wheat (60 dollars a bushel) helped finances.

Jehu (9th century BC). King of Israel who seized the throne from Ahab and slew all Ahab's descendants. He was a reckless chariot driver (2 Kgs 9:20); hence the name was applied to a cabby or coachman.

Jekyll and Hyde See DR JEKYLL AND MR HYDE.

Jellyby, Mrs Character in Dickens's *Bleak House*, whose preoccupation with the sorry state of the heathen of Borrioboola-Gha (on the left bank of the Niger) led her to overlook her own family's needs.

Jelly Roll Morton Nickname of Ferdinand Morton (1885–1941), a New Orleans Creole pianist and composer who claimed to have originated jazz, the blues and the stomp.

Jemadar Junior Indian officer in the (British) Indian Army; police officer; head servant; sweeper. (Urdu, 'leader of a crowd'; pronounced jem'a-dar.)

Jemima Puddle-duck (1908). Children's book written and illustrated by Beatrix Potter.

Jena, Battle of (October 1806). After the Prussians had joined the THIRD COALITION, Napoleon defeated and destroyed them at Jena and Auerstädt; see TILSIT, TREATY OF. (Former capital of Thuringia, Germany, pronounced yay'na.)

Jenkins, Nick Narrator in Anthony Powell's THE MUSIC OF TIME series.

Jenkins's Ear, War of (1739). War between Britain and Spain precipitated by a Capt. Jenkins, who alleged that Spanish customs officials had torn off his ear while searching his ship for contraband, and produced the ear in evidence in the House of Commons. In fact it had been cut off by a pirate (punished by the Spaniards). Robert Walpole half-heartedly declared a war which achieved nothing.

'Jennifer's Diary' Gossip column of the *Queen* and *Tatler*, unique for accuracy and discretion.

Jephthah Judge of Israel who swore that if he was victorious in battle he would sacrifice to Jehovah the first thing that met him on his return. This proved to be his only daughter (Judg. 11:30–40). The story was the theme of an oratorio by Handel (1752) and various other works.

Jeremiad Long tale of woe, from LAMENTATIONS, a book of the Old Testament once attributed to Jeremiah.

Jeremiah (6th century BC). Major prophet of Israel, who opposed his country's policy of playing off Egypt against Babylon and rebuked it for irreligion; he was therefore very unpopular and often imprisoned. With the fall of Jerusalem he fled to Egypt. See previous entry.

Jeremy Fisher, Mr (1906). Children's book written and illustrated by Beatrix Potter.

Jeroboam Large bowl or bottle, from Jeroboam, 'a mighty man of valour' (1 Kgs 11:28). Measure, the equivalent of 4 bottles of champagne.

Jersey cattle Smallest breed of dairy cattle, producing rich milk; widespread but particularly common in south-west England; fawn or cream-coloured.

Jersey Lily, The Nickname of a minor but beautiful British actress, Lillie Langtry. Edward VII's friend. (Born in Jersey.)

Jerusalem Bible, The (1966). New English translation of the Bible by 21 Roman Catholics, intended for use by all denominations; the notes and introduction are translated from the French

Jerusalem Bible (1956). (The French translation was edited by a member of the Dominican Institute, Jerusalem.)

Jesse window Stained-glass window depicting a genealogical tree of Jesus' descent from Jesse, father of King David. (Pronounced jes'i.)

Jesuitry Casuistry, equivocation, dissembling, speaking with mental reservations. (The Jesuits were thought to hold that the end justifies the means.)

Jesuits (1534). Members of the Society of Jesus founded in Paris by St Ignatius of Loyola, St Francis Xavier and others. A religious order entered after long and rigorous training, ruled autocratically by a General, and chiefly engaged in missionary and educational work, and the Spiritual Exercises laid down by Loyola. They were prominent in the Counter-Reformation.

Jesus, Society of See JESUITS.

Jesus Christ Superstar (1970). Title of a pop record, rock opera and film. Although the music and lyrics were by Englishmen, the opera was first produced on Broadway. The style may be gauged from the couplet: 'If you'd come today you'd have reached a whole nation. / Israel in 4 BC had no mass communication.'

Jesus Freaks Name adopted by what the Archbishop of Canterbury (1973) has described as a genuine religious movement of the young, from whose enthusiasm for Jesus the Church has something to learn. American in origin, it has had less fervent support in Britain.

Jesus style Development of the FAIRBAIRN STYLE of rowing, with a powerful catch at the beginning of the stroke. (Jesus College, Cambridge.)

JET Joint European Torus. Machine for undertaking research into fusion, the combination process occurring in the interior of the sun. Because of the great costs involved, the Council of the European Communities acting under the Euratom Treaty decided in 1973 to undertake a research programme using a Community-financed Joint European Torus. (Research carried out at Culham, Oxfordshire, England.)

Jet Set Envious name which conjures up a picture of exquisitely groomed creatures (the Beautiful People) taking endless jet flights from one luxury resort to another, only to discover that *coelum non animum mutant qui trans mare currunt* ('if it's a bore here it'll be a bore there').

Jeu de Paume Paris art gallery, see TUILERIES.

Jeunes filles, Les (1936–9) Four-volume work by the French novelist, Henri de Montherlant, giving scope to his view that the male is a noble virile creature beset by women bent upon his degradation.

Jewish Agency (1919). Zionist agency set up under the terms of the British mandate over Palestine, to advise on the establishment of a Jewish National Home there; now a world organization, with headquarters in Jerusalem and New York, acting as liaison between Israel and Jewish communities elsewhere.

Jew Süss (1925). Lion Feuchtwanger's long historical novel about a German Jewish community in the 18th century.

Jezebel (9th century BC). Wife of Ahab, King of Israel; she introduced Baal worship (1 Kgs 16: 31) to Israel. An unscrupulous woman of loose morals (see NABOTH'S VINEYARD), she was thrown, 'painted and tired', out of the window at JEHU's command and her carcase eaten by dogs (2 Kgs 9: 30–37).

Jim Crow Black or (adjectivally) for black Americans. (A runaway slave who composed the song and dance – 'Wheel about, turn about, jump Jim Crow' – which gained wide popularity when adopted by a white American comedian named Rice in 1828.)

Jimmy O'Goblins Rhyming slang for gold sovereigns, and still used of pound coins.

Jimmy's Nickname of the Army crammers, Carlisle & Gregson.

Jimmy the One The first lieutenant in the Royal and Merchant Navies; also called Number One.

Jimson, Gulley See *The* HORSE'S MOUTH.

Jingle, Alfred Impostor in PICKWICK PAPERS, famous for his tall stories, which have to be pieced together from staccato fragments, e.g.: 'Tall lady, eating sandwiches – forgot the arch – crash – mother's head off – sandwich in her hand – no mouth to put it in,' etc.

Jingoism Term said to have originated with those who supported sending a British fleet into Turkish waters in 1878 to resist the advance of Russia, it became a synonym for belligerent nationalism. 'We don't want to fight, but by Jingo, if we do,' is a line from a once-popular song.

Jitterbug Synonym for JIVE. (From US slang, jitters, 'nerves'.)

Jive Spastic form of dance in which young couples (then called hep cats), dancing apart, improvised their reactions to fast jazz or SWING. Originating in the USA at the end of the 1920s, it was spread to Europe by US troops during the Second World War; one offshoot was ROCK 'N' ROLL. Also called Jitterbug.

Job Rich patriarch in the Old Testament who is suddenly subjected to all the ills that flesh is heir to; he bears these with patience, staunch in his trust in God, and is rewarded (Job 43: 10–17). See next entry.

Job's comforter Friend to whom one turns in vain for consolation, getting a dusty answer. JOB'S 3 friends assure him that all his misfortunes are a punishment for sin (Job 2: 11).

Job-sharing System of dividing tasks between two or more people and so allowing part-time employment and helping to reduce unemployment.

Jocasta Mother and wife of OEDIPUS, by whom she became the mother of Antigone. When she discovered that she had married her son, she hanged herself.

Jockey Club (1750). Self-constituted body of 50 members, with headquarters at Newmarket, which has autocratic control of British flat-racing; it licenses and disciplines trainers, jockeys, handicappers, etc., makes and amends rules, and works through an executive arm consisting of 3 Stewards.

Jodrell Bank (1957). Giant steerable radio telescope, 250 ft in diameter, in Cheshire; directed by Sir Bernard Lovell, it belongs to Manchester University.

Joe Bananas (USA) Corruption of Joseph Bonanno, usually regarded as the head of La COSA NOSTRA.

Joey Professional nickname for a circus clown. (From Joseph Grimaldi, the Anglo-Italian clown, who died in 1837.)

'John Anderson, my Jo' Traditional song rewritten by Robert Burns, sung to her husband in old age by an affectionate wife. (*Jo* is dialect for 'sweetheart'.)

John Birch Society (1958). Extreme right-wing US group which held that the US government was threatened by a Communist takeover (in which Eisenhower and Foster Dulles were implicated) and urged the abandonment of the UN, NATO and foreign aid. Founded by Robert Welch and named after an American missionary turned intelligence officer, killed by Chinese Communists in 1954.

'John Brown's Body' Song celebrating the martyr (in the eyes of abolitionists) of HARPER'S FERRY. New words were written to an existing tune of 1862 by Julia Ward Howe, beginning: 'Mine eyes have seen the glory of the coming of the Lord.' This version was called 'The Battle Hymn of the Republic'.

John Bull Britain personified, a typical Britisher; from an anti-French satire by the Scot, John Arbuthnot, *The History of John Bull* (1721), in which he is represented as a bluff, good-natured farmer.

John Bull's Other Island (1904). Bernard Shaw's play about Irish Home Rule, commissioned by Yeats, in which Tom Broadbent, representing England, establishes complete ascendancy over Larry Doyle, representing Ireland.

John Collins COLLINS made with LONDON GIN.

John Doe and Richard Roe A legal phrase

standing for any plaintiff and defendant in a case (originally with a specialized meaning).

John Dory Edible marine fish with large head, a large dark spot on either flank and an extensible mouth which can be shot forward to take food.

John Gilpin (1782). William Cowper's poem about a Cheapside linen-draper whose horse bolted with him all the way to Ware and back again to Cheapside. Taught to many English children, perhaps because its thumping rhythm ('John Gilpin was a citizen/Of credit and renown') makes it easy to remember.

John Inglesant See LITTLE GIDDING.

John Innes Name of formulae for standardized seed and potting composts consisting of loam, peat, sand and fertilizers. There is no copyright in them and the John Innes Horticultural Institute (now associated with the University of East Anglia) has no control over the many firms marketing composts under this name. John Innes Nos. 1 and 2 are for seeds: JI No. 3 is for plants needing rich compost. The institute published the formulae in 1939.

Johnny-Come-Lately (1) New Zealand and Australian term for a recent and thus inexperienced immigrant. (2) Any newcomer, late or recent arrival.

Johnny Head-in-Air See STRUWWELPETER.

Johnny-on-the-spot Colloquialism signifying one who happens to be on hand for a job or to seize an opportunity, etc.

John of Gaunt Duke of Lancaster, fourth son of Edward III, ancestor of the LANCASTRIAN kings. (Born at Ghent, of which Gaunt is a corruption; died 1399.)

John o' Groats Traditionally (but not in fact) the northernmost point of mainland Britain. (Named after a Dutch immigrant, Jan Groot, whose house still stands.)

Johns Hopkins (1876). US university at Baltimore, Maryland.

John Sullivans Slang for long pants or combina-tions. (John L. Sullivan, famous 19th century prize-fighter who, as was then the custom, wore them when boxing.)

Joiners, Worshipful Company of (1571). LIVERY COMPANY, originally a guild restricted, after demarcation disputes to those whose work involved mortice and tenon and the use of chisel and plane.

Jolyon See YOUNG JOLYON.

Jonah (8th century BC). Prophet of Israel of whom the story is told in the 4th-century Old Testament book, *Jonah*, that when the ship in which he was travelling was struck by a mighty tempest the sailors cast lots to find out who was responsible for their plight. 'The lot fell on Jonah', who was thrown overboard and swallowed by a whale, which 'vomited out Jonah on the dry land'.

Jonathan See DAVID.

Jonathan American variety of red apple.

Joneses, The People next door, with whom it is necessary to keep up, according to ADMASS standards in the AFFLUENT SOCIETY. Thus, if the Joneses install central heating, the Smiths must, or lose caste. (Title of a US comic strip, 1913–31, by A. R. Momand.)

Jonkheer Dutch title, equivalent to baronet.

Jordan See TRANSJORDAN.

Jordan, Mrs Stage name of the actress who was for many years the mistress of the Duke of Clarence (later William IV).

Jordans Meeting House (1688). One of the first legitimate Quaker meeting-houses, the burial place of William Penn, and now preserved as a place of historic interest, with relics and manuscripts about Quaker history. (Hamlet near Beaconsfield, Buckinghamshire.)

Jorrocks Indomitable sportsman and Cockney grocer who first appears in *Jorrocks' Jaunts and Jollities* (1838) by R. S. Surtees, and in subsequent novels becomes MFH of the Handley Cross pack.

Joseph Jacob's son, whom his jealous brothers sold into slavery in Egypt, sending his coat of many colours dipped in blood to Jacob as proof of his death (Gen. 37). After the episode of POTIPHAR'S WIFE and his interpretation of Pharaoh's dreams, he rose to high office. In a time of famine Jacob, hearing that there was 'corn in Egypt', sent his sons to buy some; they were received kindly by Joseph, whom they failed to recognize, and who eventually persuaded the whole family to settle in Egypt (Gen. 43–7).

Joseph and his Brethren (1933–43). Thomas Mann's series of 4 novels, based on the biblical story of JOSEPH.

Joseph Andrews (1742). Henry Fielding's novel, part parody of Samuel Richardson's PAMELA, part plea that a kind heart is more important than a strict morality.

Josephine Butler Society (1870). Organization that campaigns for the rights of women, especially prostitutes. (Josephine Butler, 1828–1906, a leading English social reformer in these fields.)

Joseph of Arimathaea Jew who, according to English late medieval tradition, brought the HOLY GRAIL to GLASTONBURY, where he founded a church. (Pronounced ar-i-ma-thee'a.)

Joshua Book of the Old Testament which tells how Joshua, successor to Moses, led the Israelites into the Promised Land.

Joule Electrical unit, the amount of work achieved or heat generated by a current of one ampère acting for one second against a resistance of one ohm. Named after Dr J. P. Joule, English physicist (1818–89).

Jourdain, M. See *Le* BOURGEOIS GENTILHOMME.

Journal of a Disappointed Man (1919). Diary kept by Bruce Cummings and published in the year of his death under the pen-name of W. N. P. Barbellion. A scientist who knew he was dying (and died at the age of 30), he gave an objective analysis of his feelings about his predicament.

Journey's End (1928). R. C. Sherriff's play of the First World War, set in the trenches; though realistic in detail it is romantic in spirit.

Journey to the End of the Night (1932). Louis-Ferdinand Céline's vituperative and rambling novel attacking the sickness of the world during and after the First World War. (French title, *Voyage au bout de la nuit.*)

Juan in America (1931). Eric Linklater's amusing inter-war picaresque satire.

Judah (1) Fourth son of Jacob and Leah, ancestor of one of the 12 Tribes of Israel. (2) Southern portion of Palestine, including Jerusalem, which remained loyal to Solomon's son, Rehoboam, when the northern part, as ISRAEL, seceded in the 10th century BC. The kingdom was overrun by the Babylonians in 586 BC.

Judas hole Peep-hole, or spying hole, e.g. in a cell door to give sight of prisoner.

Judas Iscariot Disciple who betrayed Jesus with a kiss for 30 pieces of silver (Matt 26:14–15, 48–9), and then hanged himself (Matt 27:3–5). See ACELDAMA.

Jude the Obscure (1896). Thomas Hardy's Wessex novel of Jude Fawley and his cousin Sue Bridehead who, after unhappy marriages, live together. Under pressure of poverty they return to their spouses. Jude's son hangs Jude's 2 children and himself, 'because we are too menny'.

Judgement of Paris In Greek legend, the decision whether the Apple of Discord inscribed 'to the fairest' should be given to Hera, Athene or Aphrodite, entrusted by Zeus to Paris. He awarded the apple to Aphrodite, she having promised him the loveliest of women (Helen of Troy). The best of Rubens's paintings of this scene is in the Prado, Madrid.

Judges (mostly 7th century BC). Old Testament book describing how the Israelites conquered Canaan, their successive defeats by numerous enemies, their turning away from Jehovah to worship Baal and Ashtaroth, and their intermarrying with Philistines and Hittites. It includes the story of Samson. ('Judge', name given to various leaders of the Israelites, of whom Joshua was the first and SAMUEL the last, who rose to power in periods of crisis; they were military commanders rather than judges.)

Judges' Rules (1912). Rules laid down by High Court judges regarding the interrogation of accused persons by the police. They do not have the force of law, but evidence obtained by breaking them may be disallowed by the courts. The main feature is the caution given a person when charged or before he or she volunteers a statement while in custody. The rules about questioning have been further modified by the Police and Criminal Evidence Act 1984, backed up by a detailed Home Office Detention Code.

Judith (2nd century AD). Book of the Apocrypha, which tells the story of JUDITH AND HOLOFERNES.

Judith and Holofernes Romance told in JUDITH. When Nebuchadnezzar (here represented as King of Assyria) attacks Israel, Judith captivates the enemy general, Holofernes, gets invited to a feast at which, when he is in a drunken stupor, she cuts off his head, and carries it back to the Israelites; inspired by this act, they put the Assyrians to flight. The story has no basis in fact.

Judy O'Grady Name familiar from Kipling's lines in 'The Ladies': 'For the Colonel's lady an' Judy O'Grady/Are sisters under their skins!'

Juggernaut Title of KRISHNA, whose idol was drawn round Jagannath (in Orissa) in a huge wagon under which, Europeans once believed, fanatics used to throw themselves to their death; hence anything which demands or is given blind sacrifice. (Corruption of Jagannath, 'lord of the world'.)

Juilliard School of Music (1924). Graduate school, on Park Avenue, New York, for students of exceptional talent, established by the Juilliard Musical Foundation; in 1926 the Institute of Musical Art, the oldest US music school, became affiliated to it as its undergraduate school. The Foundation was set up under the will of August Juilliard (1840–1919).

Jules Rimet Trophy Official name of the Football WORLD CUP. (Rimet, president of FIFA, who did much to encourage international football.)

Julian calendar OLD STYLE calendar. (Introduced by Julius Caesar in 46 BC.)

Julienne (1) Clear vegetable soup. (2) Garnished with slow-cooked matchstick strips of vegetable.

Juliet See ROMEO AND JULIET.

July Monarchy Alternative name for the ORLEANIST MONARCHY. (Began in July 1830.)

July Plot, The Alternative name for the OFFICERS' PLOT (1944).

Jumbo Name of an exceptionally large elephant sold by the London Zoo to the BARNUM AND BAILEY SHOW in 1882; now applied to anything large, from cigarettes to airliners.

Jumbo jet (1970). Nickname of the BOEING-747 airliner.

Jungian psychology Psychoanalytic theory which, like Adler's INDIVIDUAL PSYCHOLOGY, rejects FREUDIAN emphasis on 'sex'. It classifies man as introvert or extrovert, and suggests the existence of a collective unconscious to which all have access, containing racial memories and ancient basic ideas (archetypes) on death, immortality, etc. Jung advocated the development of that part of the personality which is weakest, e.g. the intellectual should develop his emotional life. (Carl Jung, Austrian psychologist, 1875–1961.)

Jungle Books (1894–5). Kipling's 2 books of children's stories of animal life, of which the central figure is MOWGLI.

Junius, Letters of (1769–72). Series of anonymous letters that appeared in a London journal, violently attacking the Tories. The secret of their authorship was well kept, and speculation about it has tended to inflate interest in these unimportant writings. Sir Philip Francis is nowadays a favourite candidate for the authorship.

Junkers (1) Autocratic large landowners of East Prussia in the 19th century. (2) Typical jack-booted Prussian army officer-caste sired by (1), which later became the ruthless élite of the German imperial army.

Junkers aircraft German aircraft, including the Ju-52, one of the most successful civil and military transport planes; the Ju-88, a famous bomber of the Second World War; and the Ju-87, see STUKAS.

Juno Roman goddess equivalent to the Greek HERA.

Juno and the Paycock (1924). Sean O'Casey's tragi-comedy about the vain Paycock (Peacock) who solves all problems by having another drink, and his heroic wife Juno Boyle, battling not only with him but with the problems of slum poverty and the Irish TROUBLES, when the 'whole world is in a state of chassis' (chaos).

Jupiter Roman god equivalent to the Greek ZEUS.

Jupiter Ammon God combining the attributes of the Greek Zeus (Jupiter) and the Egyptian AMON; he is particularly associated with the famous oracle visited by Alexander the Great, situated in a Libyan oasis.

Jurassic Period Middle period of the MESOZOIC ERA, lasting from about 200 to 150 million years ago. Fossils appear of flowering plants, the brontosaurus, Archaeopteryx and the pterodactyl (the first flying, reptilian creatures), crocodiles, lizards, frogs, snakes. Portland limestone was formed. (Named after the Jura mountains.)

Jurgen (1919). James Branch Cabell's novel of a pawnbroker magically restored to youth who embarks on an odyssey which takes him to heaven and hell; after fantastic adventures he is glad to return to his normal henpecked life.

Justice (1910). Galsworthy's play criticizing prison administration, the process of the law, and society, which join in victimizing a solicitor's clerk sentenced for forging a cheque to help a woman in trouble.

Justices of the Peace Lay magistrates, unpaid and with limited powers, appointed by the Lord Chancellor. Originally local gentry appointed by the king to keep order in their districts. Judges, mayors, chairmen of county and district councils and other such office-holders are ex-officio JPs. (Term also used in USA.)

Justinian code (AD 529–34). Codification and simplification of Roman law by the Byzantine Emperor Justinian I, the basis of the CODE NAPOLÉON and other Continental systems, but described by Edward Gibbon as consisting of 'too often incoherent fragments'.

Just So Stories (1902). Kipling's illustrated book for children on such topics as How the Camel got his Hump; it contains many phrases which passed into common use, e.g. 'the great grey-green greasy Limpopo River', 'the Cat that Walked by Himself', 'a man of infinite-resource-and-sagacity'.

Just William (1922). One of the first of 37 books by Miss Richmal Crompton (who was still writing them when she died aged 79 in 1969) about a scruffy, freckled schoolboy rebel. English-language sales totalled 9 million, and the books were translated into many languages (e.g. Icelandic), films, plays, radio and TV series.

Jutes Teutonic invaders from the lower Rhine who, from the 5th century AD, settled in Kent and the Isle of Wight. They differed culturally from the Angles and Saxons.

Jutland, Battle of (May 1916). Naval engagement in the First World War in which the British Grand Fleet under Jellicoe, with a battle-cruiser squadron under Beatty, lost 6 major ships to 2 of the German High Seas Fleet, causing Beatty to remark: 'There's something wrong with our bloody ships today, Chatfield.' Despite its tactical success in the battle, the German fleet never again emerged, except to surrender in 1918.

Juvenile Courts Courts for the trial of those under 17; they consist of 3 magistrates, one of whom is usually a woman, and sit in private.

Juventas Roman name for Hebe, the goddess of youth.

K

K Narrator of Kafka's *The* CASTLE and, as Jozef K, of *The* TRIAL; a device supposedly indicating a certain autobiographical element in those novels.

K Abbreviation used for 'knighthood', as in 'he has at last got his K'.

Kaaba Islamic holy of holies at Mecca, a window-less cubic building said to have been built by Abraham; pilgrims circle it 7 times, kissing the Black Stone (a meteorite) in its walls which was traditionally given by Gabriel to Abra-ham. (Arabic, 'square house'; pronounced kah'é-ba.)

Kabaka Title of the former kings of Buganda, the province of Uganda inhabited by the Bagan-da. The last king became President of Uganda until he was exiled in 1966. (Pronounced ka-bah'ka.)

Kabuki Type of Japanese drama, deriving from the NOH-PLAY, but less elaborate and stylized.

Kabyle BERBER race of Algeria. (Pronounced ka-byl'.)

Kaffir click Indescribable suction sound used in some South African languages including those of the Hottentots and Bushmen, and of 2 minor tribes in East Africa.

Kaffirs (1) Old South African name for the Bantu peoples, formerly spelt Caffres. (2) On the Stock Exchange, colloquialism for South African mining shares. (Arabic, *kafir*, 'infidel', i.e. non-Muslim.)

Kafkaesque Resembling the world created by Kafka in *The* CASTLE, *The* TRIAL and other novels.

Kai Lung Urbanely witty Chinese character created by Ernest Bramah (pen-name of E. B. Smith) in his novels *The Wallet of Kai Lung* (1900) and *Kai Lung's Golden Hours* (1922).

Kailyard School Derogatory term for writers of sentimental dialect stories of Scottish peasant life, e.g. J. M. Barrie, S. R. Crockett. (Scottish, 'cabbage patch'.)

Kajar dynasty Family which, after an inter-regnum, succeeded the SAFAVIDS and ruled Persia from 1794 until Riza Khan Pahlavi seized power in 1921.

Kakiemon pattern Japanese style of decorating ceramics, with asymmetrical designs of flowers, birds (e.g. quails and pheasants), trees, children, etc., enamel-painted with a wider palette of colours than IMARI PATTERN, including yellow, blue, green and orange. It was made familiar to the West through exports in the late 17th and early 18th centuries, and extensively copied by Meissen, Chantilly, Chelsea, etc. (Name of a family of potters.)

Kalevala Finnish epic poem probably embodying legends of very great antiquity but not commit-ted to writing until the early 19th century. ('Land of Heroes'; pronounced kah'li-vah-la.)

Kali In Hinduism, the bloodthirsty consort of SIVA, represented with matted hair, blood-stained arms and hideous fangs; also the object of a fertility cult, especially at Calcutta. (Pronounced kahl'ee.)

Kalashnikov Automatic rifle named after its inventor, Mikhail Kalashnikov.

Kama Hindu god of love.

Kamakura period (1185–1392). Militaristic period of early Japanese history which succeeded the peaceful FUJIWARA PERIOD.

Kamikaze Group of Japanese pilots who performed suicidal missions in World War II, crashing their planes loaded with explosives on enemy targets.

Kanaka South Sea Islander, applied particularly to forced labour formerly employed on the sugar plantations of Queensland, Australia. (Hawaiian, 'man'; pronounced kan'a-ka.)

Kanarese DRAVIDIAN LANGUAGE spoken in Mysore and neighbouring areas of Hyderabad and Madras, having some affinity with TELUGU. Also called Kannada. (Pronounced kan-ar-eez'.)

Kangaroo (1923). Novel by D. H. Lawrence which vividly evokes the feeling that the infinitely ancient continent of Australia is under only temporary human occupation. There is also a plot of sex-war and politics.

Kangaroos (Stock Exchange) Colloquialism for Australian mining shares.

K'ang Hsi (Kangxi) (1662–1722). Emperor of the CH'ING DYNASTY, whose reign is associated with the *famille verte* colour scheme in decorating porcelain, and the beginnings of mass export of NANKING CHINA.

Kannada Indian language; see KANARESE.

Kano School (16th-19th centuries) School of Japanese artists who, under Chinese influence, evolved a vigorous new style, painting large bold designs, typically against a gold background. They worked mainly on decorating the houses of the Shoguns.

Kant's *Critique of Pure Reason* (1781). Most famous of Kant's philosophical works, which advances the view that the mind can record the appearance of a thing (phenomenon), which it fits into its own preconceptions; but it can never get at its cause, the thing-in-itself (*Ding-an-sich*), i.e. never know what the outside world is really like.

Kapital, Das Famous work of Karl Marx in which he develops his theories about the capitalist system; the first volume appeared in 1867, the second and third volumes were published posthumously in 1885–86, edited by Engels.

K*a*p*l*a*n, H*y*m*a*n Character created by the Polish-born American humorist Leo Rosten (under the pen-name Leonard Q. Ross) in a book (1937) based on his own struggle to teach immigrants English.

Kapp Putsch (1920). German armed rising under an American journalist, Wolfgang Kapp, which seized Berlin but was foiled by the declaration of a general strike. Some of the rebels wore swastikas, and their political views also foreshadowed the rise of the Nazis.

Karamazov, Mitya, Ivan and Alyosha See *The* BROTHERS KARAMAZOV.

Kariba dam (1960). Hydroelectric station run jointly by Zambia and Zimbabwe, situated on the Zambezi which divides the 2 countries.

Karl-Marx-Stadt German city, once again called CHEMNITZ.

Karnak Upper Egyptian village on the site of ancient THEBES, with many temples of the MIDDLE KINGDOM and the NEW KINGDOM; once joined to LUXOR by an avenue of ram-headed Sphinxes.

Kärntnerstrasse Fashionable shopping street of Vienna, running from the city's centre to the RINGSTRASSE, at the junction with which stands the Opera.

Kashan carpets Exceptionally dense multi-coloured carpets of graceful (especially medallion) design, typically on ivory grounds embellished with rich reds and blues; made from the 16th century south of Teheran. (Pronounced ka-shahn'.)

Kashmir dispute Struggle between India and Pakistan for possession of Kashmir, which broke into war in 1947–9 and 1965–6. At Partition, the Hindu Maharaja of Kashmir declared the accession of his state to India; Pakistan has never accepted this because Kashmir is predominantly Muslim and controls the main rivers of Pakistan (see INDUS WATERS AGREEMENT). See also AZAD KASHMIR; JAMMU AND KASHMIR.

Kaspar Old Kaspar, in Southey's poem, was unable to tell his grandchildren what good came of the Battle of Blenheim, 'but 'twas a famous victory'.

Katharina Shrew of Shakespeare's *Taming of the Shrew*, married and tamed by Petruchio after a long slanging-match.

'Kathleen Mavourneen' 'Irish' song (composed by an Englishman in 1835) with the opening words: 'Kathleen Mavourneen! the grey dawn is breaking, / The horn of the hunter is heard on the hill.'

Katyn massacre (April–May 1940). Massacre of thousands of Polish officers, generally attributed to the NKVD. The Russians have now accepted responsibility for the crime. (A wood near Smolensk in Russia, where their mass graves were found in 1943.)

Kay, Sir One of King ARTHUR's knights, a braggart and a boor.

Kechuan American Indian language spoken by the ancient Incas and still spoken in Peru. Also spelt Quechuan. (Pronounced kech'wan.)

Kedar Son of ISHMAEL (Gen. 25: 13) and traditional ancestor of the Bedouin. The black tents of Kedar (i.e. of the nomadic Arabs) are mentioned in the Psalms and in the Song of Solomon: 'I am black but comely . . . as the tents of Kedar.' (Pronounced kee'dar.)

Kedleston Hall Home near Derby of the Curzon family through 8 centuries, rebuilt by Robert Adam, now owned by the NATIONAL TRUST.

Keele University (1962). Formerly the University College of North Staffordshire (1951), at Keele, near Newcastle under Lyme.

Keep the Aspidistra Flying (1936). George Orwell's comic novel about working-class life.

Keesing's Short title of *Keesing's Contemporary Archives*, a weekly summary of world news, with a cumulative index; published since 1931. Now called *Keesing's Record of World Events*.

Kellogg Pact (1928). Pact for the renunciation of war as an instrument of policy, except in self-defence, signed by all the Great Powers (including USA and Russia which were not members of the League of Nations) and many others; also called the Kellogg–Briand Pact. (Suggested by the French Foreign Minister, Briand, to the US Secretary of State, Kellogg.)

Kells, Book of Illuminated Latin manuscript of part of the Gospels dating to about the 8th century, an outstanding example of Celtic Christian art, from the monastery of Kells, Co. Meath; now at Trinity College, Dublin.

Kelly's Directories (1799). Series of London, county and town directories published by Kelly's Directories Ltd, who also produce an annual *Handbook to the Titled, Landed and Official Classes* (1875).

Kelly's eye (Bingo) No. 1.

Kelmscott Press (1890). Private press established by William Morris.

Kelvin scale Scale of absolute temperature in which 0°K is the lowest attainable temperature (-273°C). Conversion of °K to °C is made by adding 273 (or more precisely 273.16) to the latter.

Kelvinside North-western area of Glasgow around the University and Kelvingrove Park, where the upper-middle-class residents were supposed to speak with a mincing ('Kelvinside') English accent, much despised by the true Scot.

Kemal Atatürk See ATATÜRK.

Kempe Short title for *Kempe's Engineers' Yearbook* (1895), a comprehensive annually revised reference book, indispensable to all types of engineer.

Kempton Park Racecourse near the Thames at Hampton, west of London.

Kendo An ancient Japanese form of quarterstaff (fighting with a long pole), highly stylized and ceremonious.

Kenilworth (1821). Walter Scott's historical novel of the fate of Amy Robsart, married to Queen Elizabeth's favourite, the Earl of Leicester, and victimized by the evil Richard Varney, his protégé. The turning-point of the plot takes place during the Queen's visit to Kenilworth Castle.

Kennedy Professor Holder of the chair of Latin at Cambridge.

Kennedy Round, The (1964–7). Round of negotiations under the auspices of GATT, which ended in 1967 and aimed originally at the abolition of industrial tariffs on goods in which USA + Common Market + EFTA control 80% of world trade, and a 50% cut in all others. Further aims were limitation of subsidies to agriculture and a food aid scheme for needy countries. After hard bargaining, especially by France, and a failure to persuade the USA that some of its tariffs were so high that even a 50% cut had little practical value, a package deal of untidy compromises was belatedly reached. (Suggested in 1961 by President J. F. Kennedy, who assumed an imminent merger of the Common Market and EFTA.)

Kennedy's *Latin Primer* Standard school textbook on the subject still, after nearly a century, a best-seller. (Benjamin Hall Kennedy, Cambridge professor.)

Kennel Club (1873). London club in Clarges Street, devoted to the improvement of dog-breeds.

Kennelly–Heaviside layer Alternative name for the HEAVISIDE LAYER.

Kenny polio treatment System of treating poliomyelitis cases by sustained exercises rather than vaccine injections; it gradually won approval against professional opposition. (Introduced by Sister Kenny, an Australian nurse.)

Kensal Green Large Roman Catholic cemetery in Willesden, West London, referred to in G. K. Chesterton's 'The Rolling English Road': 'For there is good news yet to hear and fine things to be seen, / Before we go to Paradise by way of Kensal Green.'

Kensington and Chelsea (Royal Borough) Inner London borough formed in 1965 from the royal borough of Kensington and the metropolitan borough of Chelsea.

Kensington Palace Palace on the west side of Kensington Gardens, bought by William III and altered by Wren; the birthplace of Queen Victoria and Queen Mary.

Kent (sheep) Breed of long-wool sheep which produce a heavy fleece used in making blankets, knitting yarns, etc. Also called Romney Marsh.

Kentish man Man born in Kent west of the Medway (which flows through Tonbridge, Maidstone and Chatham); those born east of it are called 'men of Kent'.

Kentucky Derby (1875). Most famous of the American classic flat-races, run over a distance of 1¼ miles on the first Saturday in May at CHURCHILL DOWNS.

Kenwood See IVEAGH BEQUEST.

Kenyapithecus africanus Name proposed (1967) by Dr Leakey for a species of very small hominid (man-like) creatures of which he found jaw and tooth fragments in Kenya. He considers them to be MIOCENE and 20 million years old, and in the ancestry of man but not of apes, thus pushing back the division in ancestry by some 15 million years. In 1960 he also found remains of what he called *Kenyapithecus wickeri*, 10 million years old.

Kepler's laws (1609). Three laws governing the orbit of planets round the Sun, announced by the German astronomer Kepler and later shown by Newton to arise from the law of gravitation.

Kepler's Star One of the 3 supernovae observed in the Milky Way, seen by Kepler and Galileo in the constellation Ophiucus in 1604.

Kerala The MALAYALAM-speaking Indian

state formed from Travancore-Cochin and Malabar. (Pronounced ker'ėl-ė.)

Kerensky government See OCTOBER REVOLUTION.

Kermess In the Low Countries, a boisterous celebration of the anniversary of a church's foundation; a scene often painted by the Dutch and Flemish Masters. (Equivalent to 'kirk-mass'; pronounced ker-mes'.)

Kerria Flowering shrubby climber, named after a Kew plant collector, William Kerr.

Kerry Breed of dual-purpose black cattle, found mainly in south-west Ireland.

Kerry blue (early 1800s). Irish terrier with silky blue or blue-grey coat. (Co. Kerry.)

Kerry Hill (sheep) Breed of short-wool sheep bred mainly in Wales and the Midlands. It produces a soft wool, and has distinctive black and white markings on face and legs.

Ketch, Jack (1) Public executioner who executed Monmouth (1685) and other famous people. (2) Generic nickname for a public hangman.

Kettle, Capt. Forceful mariner of many novels (1898–1938) by C. J. Cutcliffe Hyne.

Kew (1761). Royal Botanic Gardens in Surrey.

Keynesian economics Doctrines of J. M. (1st Baron) Keynes, particularly his recommendation that governments should 'spend their way out of a slump', i.e. greatly increase public expenditure to provide employment and stimulate markets; an essential corollary was that governments should cut back expenditure in a boom period, but this has never been tried. See ECONOMIC CONSEQUENCES OF THE PEACE. (Pronounced kayn'zi-an.)

Keys, Ceremony of the Nightly ceremony at the Tower of London, when the Chief Warder, with a Guards escort, locks the gates. There is also a ceremony by this name in Gibraltar.

Keystone comedies (1916–26). Films made at Hollywood by the Keystone Corporation under Mack Sennett, in some of which Charlie Chaplin appeared, together with the Keystone Cops.

Keystone State Nickname of Pennsylvania. (Centre of the original 13 states.)

KGB Soviet State Security Committee (i.e. secret police) which succeeded the MGB in 1954, with the same duties; it supervises the GRU and propagates Communism abroad.

Khadijah Rich widow who became the first wife of the Prophet Muhammad, and by him the mother of Fatima (see FATIMITES).

Khaki Campbell Popular breed of dual-purpose domestic duck.

Khaki election (1) Liberals' name for the 1900 election forced by Lord Salisbury, in which the Conservatives increased their majority at a time when the Boer War appeared to be all but over. (2) Name also sometimes given to the COUPON ELECTION (1918).

Khartoum, Fall of (1885). Capture of Khartoum, and the massacre of its defenders under Gen. Gordon, by the Mahdists after a 9-month siege; a relief force under Wolseley arrived 2 days too late. Gordon had been sent to withdraw the European and Egyptian population from the Anglo-Egyptian Sudan, after 10,000 men under Col. Hicks had been massacred in 1883.

Khedive Title of the Turkish governor of Egypt (1867–1914). (Persian, 'ruler'; pronounced kid-eev'.)

Khmer rouge Communists fighting in Cambodia supported by North Vietnam and China. From 1975 they instituted a harsh and highly regimented regime. All cities and towns were forcefully evacuated and the population was set to work in the field. By 1982 the Khmer Rouge claimed to have abandoned their Communist ideology.

Kibbutz Israeli collective farm.

Kid, The (1920). Charlie Chaplin's first full-scale film, in which he appeared with the boy actor, Jackie Coogan, in a comedy of slum life.

Kidbrooke (1954). One of the first British COM-PREHENSIVE SCHOOLS, accommodating over 2,000 girls, at Blackheath, London.

Kidnapped (1886). R. L. Stevenson's novel about David Balfour, defrauded of his inheritance by an uncle who has him kidnapped and sent to sea. With a Jacobite friend, Alan Breck, he is wrecked off the coast of Scotland, returns home and gets back his property. The sequel, CATRIONA, relates their further adventures.

Kikuyu Bantu race dominant in Kenya; their language. (Pronounced ki-koo'yoo.)

Kilauea Crater 'Pit of eternal fire', lying at 4,090 ft on the side of Mauna Loa, Hawaii. It is the largest and most spectacular of all active craters, 2 miles across with walls 500 ft deep. The last eruption was in 1955.

Kilkenny cats Expression 'to fight like Kilkenny cats' said to have originated from German mercenaries stationed at Kilkenny at the turn of the 18th century, who tied cats together so that they fought to the death.

Killiecrankie (1689). Battle between Highland JACOBITES led by John Graham of Claverhouse ('BLUIDIE CLAVERS') and Scottish troops under Mackay loyal to William III. Claverhouse won, but was fatally wounded. (Pass between Perth and Inverness.)

Kilroy Was Here Phrase scribbled everywhere by US troops in World War II. (Name of World War II US inspector of Liberty ships, who chalked his approval on them with this phrase.)

Kilvert's Diary (1870–79). Diary of a young clergyman living in Radnorshire, Wales, which gives a vivid picture of rural life of the period.

Kim (1901). Kipling's story of Kimball O'Hara, an orphan who travels through India with an old Tibetan lama, absorbing an intimate knowledge of Indian life which, while still a boy, enables him to give valuable help to the British Secret Service.

Kimberley Town in Cape Province, South Africa, west of Bloemfontein, famous for (1) its diamond mines, controlled by DE BEERS; (2) its relief by Gen. Sir John French in February 1900, after a long siege.

Kinder, Kirche, Küche Children, Church, Kitchen, a Nazi slogan delimiting women's sphere of activity.

Kind Hearts and Coronets (1949). Boulting Brothers film based on a story by Roy Horniman (1907), in which the hero successfully murders the 8 people who stand between him and the succession to a dukedom, only to give himself away at his moment of triumph. All the victims of this riotous farce were played by Alec Guinness. (Title taken from a Tennyson poem.)

King and I, The (1951). Rodgers and Hammerstein musical based on Margaret Landon's novel *Anna and the King of Siam* about an English governess who went to Siam in the mid 19th century to teach the king's children, and the resultant clash between eastern and western standards. Attractive songs such as 'Getting to Know You', 'A Puzzlement' and 'Shall We Dance?' helped to make both stage and screen versions highly successful.

King Charles's head Obsessive idea which a person cannot keep out of his writings or conversation; see Mr DICK.

King Edwards Best-known of the maincrop potatoes, kidney-shaped with a white skin splashed red. (Named after Edward VII.)

King Edward VII Professor Holder of the chair of English Literature at Cambridge.

King George V Cup (show-jumping; 1911). Chief competition at the Royal INTERNATIONAL HORSE SHOW, for individual men.

King George VI and Queen Elizabeth Stakes International flat-race run over $1\frac{1}{2}$ miles in July at Ascot Heath.

King George VI Steeplechase Race held on Boxing Day at Kempton Park.

Kingis quair (1453). Allegorical poem attributed to King James I of Scotland, telling of his first glimpse of his future wife from his prison window in the Tower of London. (Quair = quire, 'a short literary work'.)

King James's Bible Another name for the Authorized Version.

King Kong (1932). Giant ape who appeared in one of the earliest science-fiction sound films, written by Merian C. Cooper, and in many sequels.

King Lear (1605). Shakespeare's tragedy in which the English king, misconstruing the character of his 3 daughters, leaves his kingdom to GONERIL and REGAN, whose monstrous ingratitude sends him mad; too late he learns that CORDELIA was the one who loved him.

King Log and King Stork In Aesop's fable, 'The Frogs Desiring a King', Jupiter sent them a log; when they complained of its inertia he sent them a stork, which gobbled them up. Thus, a choice between lax and tyrannical rule, etc.

King of Jazz Nickname of Paul Whiteman, whose band (started 1919) became the most famous of the fashionable dance orchestras of its day. He did much to develop the commercialization of jazz, and also commissioned the RHAPSODY IN BLUE. The nickname is the title of a screen tribute to him (1930).

King of Rome Title Napoleon gave to his infant son by Marie Louise; later he became the Duke of Reichstadt, and was called Napoleon II by Bonapartists.

King of Swing Title awarded to Benny Goodman, Jewish clarinettist from Chicago, who gave new life to jazz in the 1930s.

King of the French (1830). Title given to Louis Philippe to stress the fact that he had been elected king by the Chamber of Deputies; see ORLEANIST MONARCHY.

King Philip's War (1675–6). First war to break the 54-year peace between the earliest New England colonists and the Indians, waged (with mutual savagery) against the son (known as King Philip) of the chief of the WAMPANOAGS who had made the original treaty (1621). Encroachment on their hunting grounds and suspicion of missionary activities were the chief causes. Some 500 colonists were killed or captured and the war ended only when Philip was taken and executed.

Kings (6th century BC). Name of 2 books of the Old Testament, completed at Babylon, during the Exile. 1 Kings tells of Solomon's reign and the stories of Elijah and Ahab; 2 Kings deals with events leading to the BABYLONIAN CAPTIVITY.

King's College (London) Unit, founded 1829, of the University of London and housed in a wing of SOMERSET HOUSE; it makes special provision for Anglican ordinands. In 1990 it included Chelsea College and Queen Elizabeth College.

King's County Old English name of the Irish county of Offaly.

King's Cup (1922). Annual air race held in July, originally intended to stimulate British aircraft design, and later thrown open to international competition. (Presented by King George V.)

King's Cup (tennis) Cup presented by the King of Sweden as the trophy for a men's team championship of the world at lawn tennis.

King's evil Early name for scrofula, from a 14th-century belief that it could be cured by a touch from the king.

Kingsmen Graduates of King's College, Cambridge.

King's Scholars At Eton, the 70 foundation scholars, who live in college (and thus are known as 'Collegers'), in distinction from the rest of the school (OPPIDANS), who call them 'tugs'.

Kingston Lacy House near Wimborne Minster, Dorset, occupied by the Bankes family of Corfe Castle for 300 years but now owned by the NATIONAL TRUST.

Kingston upon Hull Official designation of the town commonly known as Hull.

Kingston upon Thames London borough since 1965 consisting of the former boroughs of Kingston, Surbiton and Malden–Coombe.

Kingstown English name of Dún Laoghaire, the port of Dublin.

King Willow Personification and presiding

genius of cricket. (Bats are made of willow-wood.)

Kinsey reports Two studies, of the sexual behaviour of the human male (1948) and female (1951), compiled with a wealth of statistical detail by Alfred C. Kinsey and his colleagues at Indiana University, USA.

Kiplincotes Derby (1519). Claimed to be the oldest horse-race in the world, run in March over a 5-mile course through several parishes starting from South Dalton near Beverley, Yorkshire, and ending at Kiplincotes Farm. The stake money all goes to the runner-up, and usually exceeds the first prize in value.

Kipps, Arty Hero of H. G. Wells's semi-autobiographical novel *Kipps* (1905), the Folkestone draper's assistant who inherits a fortune, gets engaged to a superior girl who sets about grooming him, escapes to marry his boyhood love and, having lost his money to a fraudulent solicitor, is relieved to return to the quiet life of a shopkeeper.

Kirchner girls Favourite pin-ups of World War I.

Kirk, The Colloquial name for the Church of Scotland.

Kirk o' Field House outside Edinburgh where Lord Darnley was found strangled in 1567, possibly at the instigation of his wife, Mary Queen of Scots, and her future husband, the Earl of Bothwell. See CASKET LETTERS.

Kirkpatrick Ralph Kirkpatrick, who catalogued the sonatas of Domenico Scarlatti. Sometimes abbreviated to K or Kk.

Kirman carpets Extremely fine carpets with naturalistic floral (especially rose), tree and animal designs on grounds of pastel shades, made in the remote desert city of Kirman in south-central Persia, for many centuries. The name is also given to inferior Yezd products of similar design. (Also spelt Kerman; pronounced ker-mahn'.)

Kirov murder (1934). Assassination of a leading Communist, the Party boss of Leningrad. He was supposed to be a close friend of Stalin, but the circumstances of his death were sufficiently mysterious to start rumours that Stalin or those close to him were responsible for it. It was the pretext for beginning the STALINIST PURGES.

Kirsch, Kirschwasser Liqueur brandy made from wild black cherries, chiefly in Germany.

Kiss the dust To die, or to be killed. Psalm 72:9 says '. . . and his enemies shall lick the dust'.

Kit-Cat Club Founded in the 17th century by prominent Whigs. It met at the house of Christopher Cat, a pastry-cook, whose mutton pies were called Kit-Cats, hence the club's name. Membership was reputedly limited to 39, with replacements when vacancies occurred.

Kitchener's Army Army of volunteers raised by Lord Kitchener as Minister of War at the outset of World War I. They totalled 3 million before conscription was introduced in 1916.

Kitemark Trademark of the BRITISH STANDARDS INSTITUTION, which manufacturers are permitted under licence to use on goods conforming to a British Standard.

Kitty Hawk Scene of the first flight of a heavier-than-air machine (1903), made by Orville Wright. (Village in north-east North Carolina.)

Kiwis (1) New Zealanders. (2) Rugby team drawn from the New Zealand Expeditionary Force, which toured Europe in 1945–46.

KLM (1919). Chief Dutch airline, almost wholly owned by government.

Klondike District (and river) in Yukon Territory, Canada, on the Alaskan border, where the discovery of gold in 1896 led to the gold rush of 1897–8.

Knack, The (1961). Ann Jellicoe's comedy and film about the impact of an innocent girl on 3 men, one of whom is an expert at seduction, another most inexpert.

Knesset The Israeli Parliament.

Knickerbocker Club (1871). New York social club. (Knickerbocker, a descendant of the early Dutch settlers in New York, and hence any New Yorker; also a pen-name of Washington Irving, who mocked their pretensions.)

Knickerbocker Glory The crowning achievement of the US soda-fountain industry, a concoction of ice-cream, syrups and fruit served in a tall glass; still with us. (See previous entry.)

Knightley, Mr See EMMA.

Knight of the Burning Pestle, The (about 1607). Beaumont and Fletcher comedy, with a grocer's apprentice cast as a caricature of Don Quixote in a play within the play.

Knight of the Rueful Countenance Name for Don Quixote.

Knights, The (424 BC). Aristophanes' comedy in which he attacks the powerful demagogue Cleon without mercy – striking testimony to the freedom of speech then prevailing in Athens.

'Knightsbridge' Name given by the British to an area south of Tobruk in Cyrenaica, the scene of heavy tank fighting in May–June 1942, after which Rommel took Tobruk and advanced to ALAMEIN.

Knights Hospitallers See KNIGHTS OF ST JOHN.

Knights of Columbus (1882). US Roman Catholic fraternal organization.

Knights of Malta (1530–1798). Name given to the KNIGHTS OF RHODES after they left Rhodes and were given Malta by the Emperor Charles V.

Knights of Pythias (1864). US fraternal organization founded in Washington DC.

Knights of Rhodes (1310–1525). The name given to the KNIGHTS OF ST JOHN during their stay in Rhodes after the loss of the Holy Land.

Knights of St John (11th century). Religious nursing order, the Knights Hospitallers of St John of Jerusalem, which very soon became a military crusading order and acquired extensive possessions in Palestine and Europe; later they became the KNIGHTS OF RHODES and KNIGHTS OF MALTA. The original order survives in Europe but was suppressed in England, to be revived in the 19th century as a benevolent association, which now runs the ST JOHN AMBULANCE BRIGADE and the Ophthalmic Hospital in Jerusalem.

Knight's Tale, The In the CANTERBURY TALES, the story of PALAMON AND ARCITE.

Knights Templars (1) Religious order founded (1118) by French knights to protect pilgrims in the Holy Land. They then became a military crusading order, wealthy, corrupt and insolent, and were suppressed by the Pope in 1312, some of their property passing to the KNIGHTS OF ST JOHN. (Named after quarters given them at Jerusalem on the site of Solomon's Temple.) (2) Order of Freemasons.

Kniphofia Genus name of red-hot poker, named after Johann Hieronymus Kniphof, a German professor of medicine.

Knole One of the largest private houses in England, at Sevenoaks, Kent, mostly dating from the 15th century; home of the Sackvilles, and now the property of the NATIONAL TRUST.

Knossos Ancient city of Crete, excavated by Sir Arthur Evans; see MINOAN CIVILIZATION.

Köchel numbers Numbers given to Mozart's 626 compositions in the standard catalogue of them compiled in chronological order by the Austrian musicologist, Ludwig Ritter von Köchel (1800–77). (Pronounced kerk'l.)

Kodokan (1882). Judo school founded by Dr Kano in Tokyo; now the world headquarters of judo.

K of K Nickname for Earl Kitchener of Khartoum, who gained his title by recapturing Khartoum from the Mahdi (1898); he was Minister of War in World War I until his death in 1916 (see HAMPSHIRE, HMS).

Koh-i-noor diamond One of the Crown jewels, a huge diamond dating back to at least the 14th century but of unknown origin, presented to Queen Victoria after the annexation of the Punjab. (Persian, 'mountain of light'; pronounced koh-i-noor'.)

Ko-Ko See MIKADO.

Kolyma (1930). The site in far eastern Siberia of a Soviet forced-labour camp where some 2 million people are said to have died in the Stalin era; it has been called 'the frozen Auschwitz of Siberia'.

Komitaji (1895–1903). Guerrilla bands of the Supreme Committee for Macedonia, who fought for the incorporation of MACEDONIA in Bulgaria. Their activities were later merged with those of IMRO. ('Committeemen'.)

Komsomols (1918). Russian name for members of the All-Union Leninist Young Communist League.

Kon-Tiki Name of the balsa-log raft on which Thor Heyerdahl and 5 others sailed from Lima to the Tuamotu group (east of Tahiti) to demonstrate that people from Peru could have colonized the Pacific islands in ancient times, and could account for the fair-skinned element in Polynesia. (Name of the pre-Inca sun-god or king of Peru who, according to legend, sailed off into the Pacific with his white, bearded subjects.)

Köpenick hoax (1906). A Berlin ex-convict in search of a passport put on a Guards officer's uniform and, in the days when the officer class were all-powerful, was able to arrest the burgomaster and rifle his office; not finding a passport, he gave himself up. The incident was used in Zuckmayer's comedy *Der Hauptmann von Köpenick* (1931). (Name of a Berlin suburb.)

Koran Sacred book of the Muhammadans, the oral revelations of Muhammad collected in writing after his death, in Arabic.

Korean War (1950–53). War due to the joint occupation of Japanese Korea in 1945 by Russian and US troops, respectively north and south of the 38th parallel. When they went, the North Koreans, by then communized, invaded South Korea. The UN condemned the invaders, US troops returned and drove them back, but retreated when Chinese 'volunteers' joined in, despite reinforcement from other UN countries, including Britain. After great devastation and long negotiation a truce was signed, leaving the country divided as before.

Kosovo (1389). Decisive battle which began over 300 years of Balkan subjection to the Ottoman Turks. A confederation of Christian Slavs under Serbian leadership met with a crushing defeat; the Byzantines, unconscious of their own impending doom, gave no assistance to their fellow Christians. (Plain in southern Serbia.)

Krakatoa Island of Indonesia almost completely destroyed by a violent volcanic explosion in 1883, causing a tidal wave which killed 35,000 people in Java and Sumatra and reached as far as Cape Horn; dust affected the atmosphere all round the world. (Island between Java and Sumatra.)

Kraken Wakes, The (1957). Science fiction novel by John Wyndham, based on an old Norse legend (about which Tennyson wrote a poem) of a huge sea-monster. In the novel a radio script-writer and his wife describe how the Kraken came to menace mankind.

Krapp's Last Tape (1958). Beckett's short play in which Krapp listens to a tape-recording he made 30 years earlier and finds that it has lost all significance for him in old age.

K-ration (US army) Emergency ration.

Kremlin Generic term for a Russian citadel; specifically the huge walled enclosure in Moscow containing buildings dating back to the 15th century; the seat of, and a synonym for, the Soviet government.

Kremlinology 'Science' generated by the secretiveness of the Soviet government, especially in Stalin's day. Its practitioners study Russian newspapers, broadcasts, press photographs, etc. for individual Soviet leaders, and for signs of shifts of emphasis in the Party line. (Jocular formation from 'Kremlin'.)

Kretschmer's types (1925). Classification which tried to relate personality to types of physique, based on skeletal build (ignoring soft tissue). The 3 main types were (1) tall, slim men, tending to be introverted and serious (e.g. Don Quixote and the 'lean and hungry Cassius'); (2) short, thick-set (pycnic) men, tending to be extrovert and amiable (e.g. Sancho Panza), but liable to be manic-depressive in mental breakdowns; (3) the well-proportioned athletic type, rather negative in his reactions to life. (Ernst Kretschmer, German psychiatrist.)

Kreuger crash, The (1932). Downfall of the Swedish 'Match King', Ivar Kreuger, whose financial operations were on a huge scale, particularly in Sweden, USA and France. Detected in fraud and forgery, he committed suicide, leaving behind a trail of company failures.

Kreutzer Sonata (1) Beethoven's violin sonata, dedicated to a French musician of that name. (2) One of the Tolstoy's later novels (1890), based on his own sex life. (Pronounced kroit'sèr.)

Kriemhild In the *Nibelungenlied*, Gunther's sister who unwittingly betrays her husband Siegfried to Hagen. Her death symbolizes the fall of the Burgundians.

Krim Tartars TARTARS of the Crimea.

Krishna In Hinduism, the eighth and most popular incarnation of VISHNU, god of fire, storms and the sun, the Indian Apollo, particularly worshipped by women. Some sects worship him as the god of love in all its forms. He appears in the BHAGAVAD-GITA.

Kriss Kringle German–American name for Santa Claus. (From German *Christkindl*, 'Christchild', 'Christmas present'.)

Kristallnacht (1938). November night of broken glass when mobs looted and burned Jewish homes, shops and synagogues throughout Germany. Thousands of Jews were rounded up for the concentration camps.

Kristin Lavransdatter (1920–22). Sigrid Undset's trilogy of historical novels set in 13th/14th century Norway.

Kroger spy case (1961). Arrest of Morris and Lona Cohen (alias 'Peter and Helen Kroger'); both sentenced to 20 years' imprisonment in the PORTLAND SECRETS CASE. They were also involved in the earlier ROSENBERG SPY CASE.

Krokodil Soviet Russian humorous periodical.

Kronstadt mutiny (1) Russian mutiny against the Lvov government in July 1917. (2) Mutiny in 1921 put down by the Bolshevists with violence; one of the factors that led to the NEW ECONOMIC POLICY. (Russian island naval base in the Gulf of Finland, with a reputation for mutinies, e.g. also in 1825, 1905, 1906.)

Kruger telegram (1896). Kaiser's telegram congratulating President Kruger on the failure of the JAMESON RAID.

Krupps (1811). Huge German family firm with steel and engineering works at Essen; it armed Germany (1857–1945) and now makes locomotives, ships, transport aircraft, atomic plant, chemicals, etc. The Allies failed to break up the group in 1945 as no buyers would come forward. In 1967 the last Krupp died and the firm became a public company.

Kshatriyas Hindu military caste, second only to the Brahmins in rank. (Sanskrit, 'Rulers'; pronounced kshah'tree-ahz.)

K2 Himalayan mountain peak now known as Mt Godwin-Austen, or Chobrum.

Kubla Khan (1797, published 1816). Coleridge's poem, which came to him in a dream after reading about Kubla in PURCHAS HIS PILGRIMES. He jotted down as much as he could before he was interrupted by 'a person from Porlock', and was unable to remember the rest of it. See XANADU.

Ku Klux Klan (1866). Obscurantist secret society formed after the American Civil War to maintain white supremacy in southern USA; suppressed in 1871, it was revived in 1915 to persecute not only blacks, but Jews, Catholics, Darwinists, pacifists, etc. Bespectacled businessmen in city suits disguise themselves in white nightgowns and hoods, and burn 'fiery crosses', one of the saddest sights in Christendom. (Illiterate misspelt derivation from Greek *kuklos*, 'Circle'.)

Kulturkampf (1870s). German for 'cultural struggle', the name given to Bismarck's campaign to subordinate the Church to the state. He expelled the Jesuits, made civil marriage legal, and imposed restrictions on the Catholic Church, which he regarded as a threat to national unity.

Kümmel Old-established liqueur, now made in the Netherlands, Denmark and Latvia from grain or potato spirit flavoured with caraway or cumin seeds.

Kunsthistorisches Museum Vienna museum containing an exceptionally fine art collection.

Kuomintang (1912). Chinese nationalist party founded by Sun Yat-sen which under his successor Chiang Kai-shek formed the Nanking government in 1927. It included people of every shade of political opinion (short of Communism), united only in determination to free the country from Japanese and Western dominance, but was weakened by internal corruption and inefficiency, and its continual struggle against the Communists, to whom it succumbed in 1949. Chiang Kai-shek then set up a government in Formosa. (Chinese, 'nation-people-party'; pronounced kwo-min-tang'.)

Kurds Nomadic Iranian mountain race of KURDISTAN, speaking an Indo-European language and preserving its racial integrity despite being divided between Turkey, Persia and Iraq. Russians in 1954 tried to set up a separatist Kurdish state in Iran, with a capital at Mahabad, and encouraged the Kurds of the rich Mosul oilfield area in Iraq, who had similar ambitions and are still in conflict with the Iraqi government.

Kut, Siege of (December 1915 to April 1916). Turkish siege of Gen. Townshend's forces in a town on the Tigris in Mesopotamia, which ended in British surrender. (Also called Kut el-Amara.)

KVD (1960). Soviet Committee for Internal Affairs, the successor to MVD.

Kwangchow (Kuang-chou) Official name of Canton Guangzhou in Pinyin.

Kylsant case (1931). Sentencing of Lord Kylsant to one year's imprisonment for issuing a false prospectus of the RMSP (Royal Mail Steam Packet Co.), of which he was chairman.

Kyrie eleison (1) Short supplication 'Lord have mercy' used in various Church services. (2) Musical setting of this. (Greek words; pronounced kir'i-i e-lay'i-son.)

L

'L', The (USA). An alternative spelling of 'the El.', i.e. the New York elevated railway, closed in 1955.

Labanotation (USA). System of recording the positions and movements of a ballet. (Rudolf Laban, inventor.)

Labor Day In Canada and USA, a legal holiday on the first Monday in September, the equivalent of May Day.

Labrador Current Cold current which flows south along the Labrador coast from Baffin Bay and, fed by water from Greenland and Hudson Strait, often carries icebergs and even field-ice to its confluence with the GULF STREAM off Newfoundland, causing local fogs there in spring and early summer. Also called the Arctic Current. See GRAND BANKS.

Laburnum Grove (1933). J. B. Priestley's comedy about a criminal who, when 'resting', lives the life of a highly respectable suburban householder.

Lachesis One of the 3 FATES. (Pronounced lak'es-is.)

Ladakh crisis (1962). Chinese incursion into the Ladakh enclave of Indian-held Kashmir which juts into Tibet following the MCMAHON LINE (which the Chinese have never accepted), in order to safeguard communications between Sinkiang and western Tibet. Having gained their objective the main Chinese forces withdrew.

Ladbroke's Biggest UK betting firm, often men-tioned in the press as quoting odds about such semi-sporting events as the General Election; they have diversified into bingo halls, casinos, holiday villages, hotels, etc.

Ladies-in-Waiting The Queen has 11 Ladies-in-Waiting, of whom the senior is the MISTRESS OF THE ROBES; 4 are Ladies of the Bedchamber, usually peeresses, who attend on important occasions; 3 are Women of the Bedchamber, usually daughters of peeresses, who deal with correspondence and attend the Queen on most occasions; 3 are Extra Women of the Bedchamber.

Ladino Until the mid-20th century the common language of SEPHARDIM.

'La donna è mobile' Famous aria from RIGOLETTO (Italian, 'Woman is capricious') which plays a key part in the denouncement of the plot.

Lady Chapel Chapel in a cathedral or large church dedicated to the Virgin Mary, and normally situated behind the altar.

Lady Chatterley's Lover (1928). D. H. Lawrence's novel on the nature of sexual relationship, in which the aristocratic Connie runs away with her impotent husband's gamekeeper, Mellors. Its frankness was too much for the English courts until 1960 when Penguin, who had published it in cheap paperback form, forced the issue and were acquitted on the charge of publishing an obscene article.

Lady into Fox (1922). David Garnett's fantasy

of a woman who turned into a fox and her subsequent relationship with her husband.

Lady Margaret Boating Club of St John's, Cambridge; abbreviated to Maggie's. (College founded by Lady Margaret Beaufort, mother of Henry VII.)

Lady Margaret Hall (1878). Oldest women's college at Oxford University. (See previous entry.)

Lady Margaret Professor (1502). Holder of a chair of Divinity, the oldest chair at Oxford. (See LADY MARGARET.)

Lady Margaret's Professor Holder of a chair of Divinity at Cambridge. (See LADY MARGARET.)

Lady of Shalott In Arthurian legend, the girl who died from unrequited love for LANCELOT; in Tennyson she appears as Elaine, the lily maid of Astolat (said to be Guildford).

Lady of the Lake (1) In Arthurian legend, the enchantress Vivien, mistress of MERLIN; she made EXCALIBUR, stole the infant LANCELOT from his parents, and imprisoned Merlin in a tower or thorn-bush, there to remain ready to conjure up King Arthur when Britain again has need of him. (2) Title of Walter Scott's poem about another lady who lived by Loch Katrine.

Lady of the Lamp Florence Nightingale, who worked tirelessly and successfully at a hospital in Scutari (Üsküdar, opposite Istanbul) to raise the appallingly low standards of nursing of the sick and wounded in the Crimean War. (Name referred to her night rounds of the hospital, lamp in hand.)

Ladysmith, Relief of (28 February 1900). Episode of the Boer War; Ladysmith, a township in Natal, was besieged for 4 months before it was relieved by Gen. Buller.

Lady's Not for Burning, The (1949). Verse comedy by Christopher Fry about a young witch in Elizabethan times.

Lady Windermere's Fan (1892). Oscar Wilde's comedy of manners in which a trivial plot about the runaway Lady Windermere's restoration to her husband by her (unknown) mother is a vehicle for the witty dialogue for which Wilde was later to become so famous.

Laertes (1) In Greek legend, the father of Odysseus. (2) In Shakespeare's *Hamlet*, the man who, to avenge the death of his father Polonius and his sister Ophelia, fights a duel with Hamlet in which both die. (Pronounced lay-ért'eez.)

Lafayette Squadron (April 1916). Squadron of American volunteers which served with the French air force before USA joined in World War I.

Lager louts (1980s). Ill-behaved young drinkers of light continental beer. Down-market version of HOORAY HENRY.

La Guardia Airport Airport on Long Island, in the Queens borough of New York City, previously known as Idlewild.

Lake Poets Wordsworth, Coleridge and Southey, who lived in the Lake District for varying periods; the name was originally meant to be derisive but has long ceased to carry any such implication.

Lake Success Village in New York State, temporary headquarters of the United Nations before its move to Manhattan in 1952.

Lalique glass Glassware in ART NOUVEAU designs, produced on a factory scale from the early years of the 20th century. (Réné Lalique, 1860–1945.)

Lalla Rookh (1817). Thomas Moore's oriental tale in verse and prose of a daughter of the Mogul Emperor and the legends told her by a Persian poet.

Lamaism Degenerate form of Buddhism which was the religion of Tibet until Communist China took over the country. See DALAI LAMA.

Lamarckism View that habits (or, loosely, characteristics) acquired through adjustment to environment can be inherited. (Chevalier de Lamarck, French zoologist, 1744–1829.)

Lambaréné (1913). The site of the hospital-village in Gabon, West Africa, founded by Dr Albert Schweitzer.

Lambeth Conference (1867). Assembly of bishops of the ANGLICAN CHURCH from all over the world, held at Lambeth Palace, London, normally every 10 years. The Archbishop of Canterbury presides over its deliberations as the spiritual head of the Church.

Lambeth Delft (1) Blue and white DELFT made at Lambeth from the early 17th century to 1790. (2) Revival of MAIOLICA by Doultons of Lambeth, also called Lambeth faience (1873–1914).

Lambeth Palace London residence since the 12th century of the Archbishops of Canterbury, by Lambeth Bridge.

Lambeth Walk, The (1937). English dance excellently characterizing the Cockney 'image' of nonchalant jaunty good humour, in the form of a strutting march cum square dance; a similarly characteristic song, 'Doin' the Lambeth Walk', went with it. (A London borough south of the Thames.)

Lambs Club Distinguished social club in New York City.

'Lame Duck' Amendment In the USA the 20th Amendment to the Constitution. Previously, after the November national elections there was a final session of the old legislature lasting normally from December to 3 March, during which a President, Vice-President and all members who had failed to win re-election were necessarily ineffective 'lame ducks'.

Lamentations (6th century BC). Book of the Old Testament formerly attributed to JEREMIAH. It laments the fall of Jerusalem in 586 BC (see BABYLONIAN CAPTIVITY).

Lamellibranchs See MOLLUSCS.

Lamia (1820). Keats's narrative poem about a bridegroom who discovers on his wedding night that his bride is a lamia (a half-serpent monster who preys on human beings); a version of an old Greek legend, but taken by Keats from Burton's ANATOMY OF MELANCHOLY. (Pronounced lay'mi-a.)

Lammas 1 August, the Anglo-Saxon harvest festival; Scottish quarter-day. (From Old English for 'loaf-mass'.)

Lancashire style (Wrestling) Another name for CATCH-AS-CATCH-CAN.

Lancaster (1941). British Avro fast 4-engined long-range bomber, used in the first British-based raid on Italy (Milan) in October 1942.

Lancaster, Duke of In Lancashire, a title of the Queen. Queen Victoria decided to keep the title masculine.

Lancaster Herald Officer of the COLLEGE OF ARMS.

Lancaster House Late Georgian mansion in Stable Yard, St James's, now owned by the Department of the Environment; often used for conferences on Commonwealth affairs.

Lancastrians Descendants of JOHN OF GAUNT, Duke of Lancaster: Henry IV, V and VI (1399–1461), and Henry VII, who married a daughter of the YORKIST Edward IV; see WARS OF THE ROSES.

Lancelot One of King Arthur's knights, the lover of Queen GUINEVERE, loved by ELAINE.

Lanchester (1896). First British petrol-driven car to have most of the essentials of a modern car. For many years a distinguishing feature was the use of a horizontal bar instead of a steering-wheel.

Landau Four-wheeled carriage named from Landau in Germany, where it was first made.

Land League (1879–81). Organization of Irish farming tenants directed against their landlords and using the BOYCOTT in protest against evictions and high rents. One of the founders, Parnell, was arrested, but in 1880 Gladstone's Land Act was passed restricting rents and safeguarding security of tenure.

Ländler Austrian country dance to slow waltz-time, the forerunner of the true waltz. See SCHUHPLATTLER.

Land o' Cakes Scotland, a term used by Burns, referring to Scottish oatmeal cakes.

'Land of Hope and Glory' Song written by the novelist A. C. Benson to music by Elgar, part of the *Pomp and Circumstance* suite. At one time considered as a possible alternative national anthem, it was felt that the words 'Wider still and wider shall thy bounds be set; / God who made thee mighty, make thee mightier yet' had become inappropriate when successive governments were doing the exact opposite.

'Land of my Fathers' Welshman's national anthem, written in Welsh.

Land of Nod To go to this land is to go to bed, the reference is to Genesis 4:16, 'Cain went . . . and dwelt in the land of Nod.'

Land of the Midnight Sun (1) Norway, as the phenomenon is most easily observed there. (2) Nickname for Alaska.

Land o' the Leal Heaven; title of a poem by Baroness Nairne, died 1845. (*Leal*, Scottish word for 'loyal', 'faithful', hence 'blessed'.)

Landrace Leading Scandinavian breed of bacon pig, in Britain usually crossed with the LARGE WHITE or other breeds.

Land-Rover Light 4-wheel-drive vehicle designed by Maurice Wilks, first seen by the public in 1948. In 1970 the Range Rover, which has many more built-in facilities and great towing ability, was launched.

Landseer's Lions (1868). Bronze lions at the base of Nelson's monument, Trafalgar Square, London, the work of Sir Edwin Landseer.

Lanes, The Maze of alleys in Brighton noted for their antique shops.

Languedoc Once-powerful province (capital Toulouse), annexed by France (1271) after the ALBI-GENSIANS were crushed; the name is now confined to the eastern coastal area betwen Spain and the Rhône (capital Montpellier), a sleepy region content to live on the meagre proceeds of growing half France's *vin ordinaire*. (*Langue d'oc*, 'the language which uses *oc*' for yes, instead of the *oïl* of the *langue d'oïl* spoken in medieval north and central France.)

Languish, Lydia In Sheridan's play *The Rivals*, a niece of Mrs MALAPROP who prefers romantic elopement with a penniless ensign rather than a humdrum marriage to the rich baronet's heir chosen for her. As these turn out to be one and the same person, no great harm is done.

Langworthy Professor Holder of the chair of Physics at Manchester University.

Lansbury's Lido (1930). Open-air bathing-place on the Serpentine in Hyde Park, London. See LIDO. (Established by George Lansbury, Labour Commissioner of Works.)

Lansdowne letter (1917). Letter published in the press during World War I by the 5th Marquess of Lansdowne, a former Foreign Secretary (1900–06); it advocated a compromise peace with Germany lest Europe destroy itself.

Lansdowne Trophy Squash rackets 5-a-side knock-out competition for London West End social clubs.

Laocoön (1) In Greek legend the Trojan priest who offended Apollo and was punished by being crushed to death by 2 huge snakes, together with his 2 sons. (2) The 2nd-century sculpture depicting this, discovered in 1506 in Rome, and now in the Vatican. (3) Title of Lessing's essay 'on the limits of painting and poetry' (1776). (Pronounced lay-ok'oh-on.)

Laodicean Lukewarm in religion (or politics), like the Laodicean Church rebuked in Revelation 3:15–16, for being 'neither cold nor hot'. (Pronounced lay-o-dis-ee'an.)

Laoighis County of the Irish Republic, formerly Queen's County. (Pronounced leesh.)

Laputa Imaginary flying island in GULLIVER'S TRAVELS inhabited by unpractical scientists and philosophers who have attendants to flap them in the face with bladders to bring them down to consideration of mundane matters.

Large White (1) Yorkshire breed of bacon pig, from which the Middle White pork and bacon pig was evolved. (2) Another name for the Cabbage White butterfly.

Lari massacre (1953). Murder by Mau Mau in Kenya of nearly 100 fellow Kikuyu.

Lark Rise to Candleford (1939–43). Flora Thompson's trilogy (*Lark Rise, Over to Candleford,*

Candleford Green), in which Laura (representing the author) gives a delightful description of 19th-century village life in the south-east Midlands.

Larousse French encyclopaedia-dictionary, first published over 100 years ago, and still a leading French reference book. (Pierre Larousse, 1817–75, lexicographer.)

Lars Porsena Etruscan king, who appears to have conquered Rome in the 6th century BC; the story in *Horatius*, one of Macaulay's *Lays of Ancient Rome*, follows the Roman legend which conceals this humiliation.

Lascaux caves Caves near Montignac in the French Dordogne, discovered in 1940, with extremely impressive coloured animal paintings on the walls, probably belonging to the MAGDALENIAN CULTURE. Opened to the public in 1948, they had to be closed in 1960 owing to deterioration of the paintings.

Lassie Collie dog which became a star of the screen, in movies and TV.

Last Days of Pompeii, The (1834). Bulwer-Lytton's famous historical novel set in the time when Pompeii was destroyed by an eruption of Vesuvius in AD 79. (Pronounced pom-pee′y, pom′pi-y or pom-pay′ee.)

Last Enemy, The (1942). Richard Hillary's account of his wartime experiences in the RAF, published the year before his death.

Last Judgement Michelangelo's fresco behind the altar of the SISTINE CHAPEL, Rome.

Last of England, The (1855). Madox Brown's Pre-Raphaelite painting of 2 emigrants taking their last look at England; now in the Birmingham Art Gallery.

Last of the Mohicans, The See LEATHERSTOCKING TALES.

Last of the Romans Title given to the 14th-century Roman patriot RIENZI, and later to Horace Walpole, Charles James Fox and others.

Last Supper (1497). Leonardo da Vinci's painting in oil on the refectory wall of the Dominican convent church of Sta Maria delle Grazie at Milan. It deteriorated even in his lifetime and had to be much restored. It depicted the moment when the Apostles are saying 'Lord, is it I?' (Matt 26:22).

Las Vegas Town in Nevada, USA, which since 1945 has become notorious for its mushrooming gambling casinos and night-clubs. Situated in the south-east corner of the state, it is only a few hours from Los Angeles. (Pronounced lahs vay′gas.)

La Tène Improved IRON AGE culture developed from the HALLSTATT about 400 BC. (Named after a Celtic lake-side settlement in Switzerland.)

Lateran, The Former palace of the popes in eastern Rome, now a museum. (On the site of the house of the ancient Laterani family, confiscated by Nero and later given to the Popes.)

Lateran Treaty (1929). Concordat and treaty between Mussolini and Pope Pius XI establishing the VATICAN CITY as a sovereign power, and ending the self-imposed imprisonment of the Popes in the Vatican begun in 1870.

Lathyrus Genus of edible and sweet peas.

Latin Language spoken by the Romans; the Hebrews adopted very few Latin words, but the inscription on the cross was in Latin, the language of government, as well as in Hebrew and Greek, see John 19:20.

Latin America Central and South America. (Countries speaking Latin languages, i.e. Spanish, Portuguese, French.)

Latin Quarter LEFT BANK district of Paris where the Sorbonne University is situated; once the centre of the city's artistic life. (For French *Quartier Latin*, as the medieval students used Latin as a lingua franca.)

Latitudinarianism Acceptance of wide differences in doctrine and ceremonies in the Anglican Church; a term first used of the CAMBRIDGE PLATONISTS in the 17th century. This movement developed in the 19th century into the BROAD CHURCH.

Latter-Day Saints Members of the Church of Jesus Christ of the Latter-Day Saints, an American sect founded (1830) by Joseph Smith, with beliefs based on the Book of MORMON, and widely known as 'Mormons'. Their practice of 'plural marriage' caused public scandal and was abandoned in 1890 under governmental pressure. They are particularly numerous in and around Utah.

Latymer Upper (1624). Large grammar school for day-boys, in Hammersmith, London.

Laughing Buddha Familiar Chinese porcelain figure of an excessively fat man displaying his navel; he is a BODHISATTVA and represents riches and contentment.

Laughing Cavalier (1624). Famous portrait by the Dutch painter, Frans Hals, of a swashbuckling officer; now in the Wallace Collection, London.

Laurel and Hardy Stan Laurel (real name Arthur Stanley Jefferson, 1890–1965) and Oliver Hardy (1892–1957) formed a comedy partnership in 1929. The contrasting personalities and physical differences contributed to their genius. They made many films together.

Laurence Professor Holder of the chair of Ancient Philosophy or of Classical Archaeology at Cambridge.

Lausanne Treaty (1923). Post-war treaty with Turkey which replaced the SÈVRES TREATY. Turkey regained Smyrna and a little territory in Europe, but lost all the non-Turkish lands (Arabia, Palestine, Syria, Iraq and most of the Aegean Islands). The Dardanelles forts were demolished.

Lava-Tory, The Pun-name of the BATH CLUB since it amalgamated with the Conservative Club.

Lavender Hill Mob, The (1951). One of the best of the EALING STUDIOS COMEDIES, in which a timid bank clerk (Alec Guinness) and his sculptor friend (Stanley Holloway) recruit 2 inept crooks to stage a big bullion robbery.

Lavengro (1851). George Borrow's partly autobiographical novel in which the gypsy, Jasper Petulengro, appears; it also deals with the hero's life of struggling poverty in London. See ROMANY RYE. (Name given to the author by the original of Petulengro, meaning 'student of language'.)

Law Commission (1965). Permanent body given the Sisyphean task of bringing some order to the chaos of English law, e.g. by making it ascertainable and comprehensible.

Law Courts, The (London) Colloquial name for the Royal Courts of Justice, the building in the Strand which houses the Supreme Court (of Judicature); this comprises the Court of Appeal and the High Court (of Justice).

Law Lords Term covering past and present Lord Chancellors, the LORDS OF APPEAL IN ORDINARY and other peers who have held high judicial office.

Law Officers of the Crown Attorney-General and Solicitor-General who appear in the courts for the Crown and for government departments. They are political appointments.

Law Society Solicitors' trade union, lunch-club, library and information service, in Chancery Lane, London. Membership is usual but not compulsory. It is armed with extensive powers to call any member to account, examine his books, suspend him, strike him off the rolls, or authorize compensation to a defrauded client.

Laxton's Superb Very prolific apple, picked from late September, crisp and juicy.

Lay of the Last Minstrel, The (1805). Walter Scott's long narrative poem of how Baron Henry wooed Lady Margaret of Branksome Hall, despite the feud between their 2 families.

Lays of Ancient Rome (1842). Macaulay's ballads based on early Roman legends e.g. that of LARS PORSENA.

Lazarus (1) Beggar full of sores, of the parable in Luke 16:19–31, who when he died went to Abraham's bosom while DIVES lay in torment in hell. (2) Brother of Mary and Martha whom Jesus raised from the dead (John 11:43–4).

LBJ Initials used as nickname for Lyndon B. Johnson, US President 1963–9.

LDCs Abbreviation used in the financial press for Less Developed Countries, i.e. those which have been successively called undeveloped, underdeveloped and developing.

Leadenhall Market Six-hundred-year-old London market in Gracechurch Street, now dealing mainly in poultry, but also in greengroceries and groceries.

Leader of the House Cabinet Minister who arranges the order of business in the House of Commons in consultation with the Speaker, Clerk, Whips and the Leader of the Opposition.

League Covenant (1919). Constitution of the LEAGUE OF NATIONS, which was incorporated in the VERSAILLES TREATY and all subsequent treaties made with ex-enemy powers.

League of Nations (1920–46). Established under the LEAGUE COVENANT as a world organization for peace, but weakened at the outset by US refusal to join, and later by the defection of Germany, Japan and Italy (1933–7); Russia was a member for only 5 years. The League's only means of enforcing good behaviour was by 'sanctions', and these failed completely against Japan (Manchurian crisis, 1931) and Italy (Abyssinian War, 1935). The League's main achievements were the ILO and the MANDATES COMMISSION. The headquarters were at Geneva.

League of Nations Union British society which tried to stimulate public interest in, and active support for, the League of Nations. Its main achievement was the PEACE BALLOT.

Leander Greek legendary figure; see HERO AND LEANDER.

Leander Oldest English rowing club (founded early in the 19th century), recruited from the Oxford and Cambridge University crews, the 3 top eights at EIGHTS WEEK and the MAYS, and winners at Henley; the club house is at Henley.

Lease–Lend (1) US loan to Britain (1940) of 50 destroyers in exchange for bases in the West Indies; (2) US loans of arms and supplies (March 1941 to 1945) to countries fighting Axis powers; repayment was partly by 'reverse lease–lend', mostly waived.

Leathernecks Nickname for US Marines.

Leathersellers, Worshipful Company of (1444). LIVERY COMPANY which still fosters training in and development of its trade, particularly through the Leathersellers' College, Bermondsey.

Leatherstocking Tales, The (1823–41). Fenimore Cooper's 5 famous novels (including *The Last of the Mohicans*), of 18th-century frontier life and the Redskins. The hero is Natty Bumppo, who prefers Indians to most whites and excels them as a hunter. One of his nicknames is Leatherstocking, meaning tough backwoodsman.

Leaves of Grass (1855). Walt Whitman's chief volume of verse, frequently revised and augmented. His poems sing ecstatic praises of America and advocate a breaking loose from cultural ties with Europe to form a distinctively American democratic way of life.

Lebensraum German for 'living-space', used in connection with Hitler's thesis that Germany was overpopulated and had a divine right as HERRENVOLK to conquer its neighbours so as to provide room for the surplus. (Pronounced lay'benz-rowm.)

Le Bourget International airport north of Paris.

Leclerc *Nom de guerre* of the French general, Vicomte de Hautecloque, who led some 2,500 Free French 1,500 miles across the Sahara from Lake Chad to join Gen. Montgomery's army in North Africa in February 1943.

Le Corbusier Pseudonym of the imaginative Swiss architect Charles Jeanneret (1887–1965); see UNITÉS D'HABITATION.

Leda In Greek legend, wife of a King of Sparta whom Zeus, disguised as a swan, seduced while she was bathing. The result was CASTOR AND POLLUX, and HELEN OF TROY.

Leeds creamware Most famous of the cream-coloured earthenwares, made at the Leeds Pottery (1760–1821) and characterized by pierced decoration, a deep buttery glaze, and very light weight. The products were usually left undecorated.

Lees Knowles lectures Lectures on science and military affairs, given at Trinity College, Cambridge.

Lee's Professor Holder of one of 3 chairs at Oxford: Anatomy, Chemistry, Experimental Philosophy.

Leeuwenhoek lecture (1948). Royal Society lecture on microbiology. (Seventeenth-century microscope-maker; pronounced lay'ven-hook.)

Left Bank South bank of the Seine in Paris and the adjoining districts – the student world of the LATIN QUARTER and the Luxembourg, the Boulevard Saint-Germain (libraries, publishers, printers), etc.

Left Book Club (1936). Founded by the publisher, Victor Gollancz, to produce cheap books on all aspects of Socialism. It was so successful that any politically minded person who did not wish to be labelled Fascist had to have a few on his shelves in the years before the Second World War.

Left Hand! Right Hand! (1945–50). General title of Sir Osbert Sitwell's outstanding 5-volume autobiography, with its close-up of the author's eccentric father, Sir George, of Renishaw Hall, near Sheffield.

Leghorn Hardy breed of domestic fowl, a prolific layer of white eggs. (Originally imported from Italy via Leghorn or Livorno; pronounced lè-gorn'.)

Legionnaire's disease Infection of the lungs; symptoms include muscle pain, fever, and general respiratory disorder. It is spread by airborne droplets and there appears to be a link with water systems used for air-conditioning. The disease can be fatal.

Legion of Honour (1802). French order founded by Napoleon. It now has 5 classes: Grande Croix (restricted to 80 holders), Grand Officier (200), Commandeur (1,000), Officier (4,000), Chevalier (unlimited).

Legree, Simon Plantation overseer, the villain of UNCLE TOM'S CABIN.

Leguminosae Family of plants characterized by legume-fruits, i.e. pods. All the British examples belong to the subfamily PAPILIONACEAE. Mimosas and acacias form another main group.

Lehigh (1865). US university at Bethlehem, Pennsylvania.

Leicester (1) Large heavy-fleeced breed of sheep from which most of the lowland long-wool breeds have been evolved (e.g. the BORDER LEICESTER). (2) Hard, red medium-strong cheese.

Leinster Eastern province of the Irish Republic, formerly the 2 Celtic kingdoms of North and South Leinster, now consisting of Carlow, Dublin, Kildare, Kilkenny, Laoighis, Longford, Louth, Meath, Offaly, Westmeath, Wexford and Wicklow.

Leipzig, Battle of (October 1813). Defeat of the French by the combined German, Austrian and Russian armies in the War of Liberation, which, while crushing and bloody, did not prevent Napoleon from gaining further victories against them in 1814. Also called the Battle of the Nations.

Leix Spelling of LAOIGHIS used by the Irish up to 1935. (Pronounced leesh.)

Lélia (1952). André Maurois's biography of George Sand. (Title taken from a novel by George Sand.)

Le Mans Town south-west of Paris, the venue each summer of a 24-hour endurance race (1923) for GT (grand touring) and sports cars on public roads closed for the occasion. (Pronounced le-mon'.)

Lemberg Old German name of Lvov, now a city of the Ukrainian SSR; the Polish spelling is Lwow.

Lemuria Zoologists' name for a hypothetical continent now sunk beneath the Indian Ocean, which might once have linked Madagascar to Malaysia; this would account for the strange distribution of the lemur, a primate found only in those 2 regions. See also GONDWANALAND. Theosophists eagerly seized on these 'lost continents' (including ATLANTIS) and described their inhabitants who, they say, were far in advance of us, having not only jet planes but all the virtues too.

Lend–Lease See LEASE–LEND.

Lenin Vladimir Ilyich (1870–1924), Russian revolutionary, leader of the Bolsheviks and chief theoretician of Russian Marxism. His embalmed body lies in a mausoleum in Red Square, Moscow. (Formerly Ulyanov.)

Lenin (1959). Russian ice-breaker, the world's first nuclear-powered surface vessel.

Lenin, Order of (1930). High Soviet award made to individuals or associations for special services to the regime.

Lenin Canal (1952). Sixty-three-mile ship canal linking the Volga and the Don south of Volgograd (Stalingrad), USSR.

Leningrad Formerly St Petersburg and, briefly, Petrograd.

Leningrad, Siege of Germans besieged the city from September 1941 to January 1944.

Leningrad case (1949). Execution without trial of important followers of Zhdanov, the Party leader of Leningrad and possible successor to Stalin. Zhdanov himself died an apparently natural death in 1948. In 1954 Khrushchev said that Stalin, on false accusations supplied to him by Beria, had personally supervised the liquidation of these men.

Leninism See MARXISM–LENINISM.

Lenin Mausoleum Mausoleum in the Kremlin wall facing Red Square, Moscow. Stalin's body was placed by his side but removed in 1960.

Lenin Prize (1925). Russia's supreme award for achievements in science, technology, literature and the arts; called Stalin prize, 1940–54.

Lenin Stadium Moscow's arena for all sports.

Lenin's testament (1922). Letter written by Lenin to the Party Congress warning delegates against Stalin and suggesting his replacement as secretary-general of the Party.

Lents Cambridge University spring college boat-races. (Held in the Lent term.)

Leo Lion, 5th of the constellations of the Zodiac, between Cancer and Virgo; the sun enters it about 21 July. Astrologers claim that those born under this sign may be lazy, uncritical, romantic.

Leofric See GODIVA, LADY.

Leonora Overtures Beethoven's 4 versions of the overture to his opera FIDELIO, all of them still performed.

Leopard, The (1956). Prince of Lampedusa's novel of the attempts of an old Sicilian family to adapt itself to the social changes which followed the Garibaldi era.

Leopardstown A racecourse at Dublin.

Leotard One-piece suit worn by ballet dancers and acrobats, named after Jules Léotard, a 19th-century trapeze artist.

Lepanto (1571). Decisive naval victory over the Turks won by the combined forces of the Christian League (Spain, Venice, Genoa and the Papal States) under Don John of Austria. It was the last major engagement between fleets of oared galleys. (Italian name of the Greek port of Naupaktos, in the Gulf of Corinth.)

Lepidoptera Butterflies and moths, an order of insects with 2 pairs of large, scaly, coloured wings; the caterpillars feed on plants, the adults on nectar.

Lesbian Female homosexual, so named from the Aegean island of Lesbos, where in the 7th century BC 'burning Sappho loved and sung' (Byron's *Don Juan*).

Lesbia's sparrow Pet cage-bird of his beloved Lesbia, on whose death Catullus (1st century BC) wrote a famous little elegy beginning: 'Mourn, ye Loves and Cupids'.

Lestrade of Scotland Yard Inspector whom Sherlock HOLMES continually forestalled and outwitted.

Lethe In Greek legend the river of forgetfulness, one of the rivers of the Underworld, where the dead drank and forgot the past. (Pronounced lee'thee.)

Lettish Language spoken by the Letts of Latvia, closely related to LITHUANIAN.

Levant, The Obsolete term for the eastern parts of the Mediterranean, with its islands and coastal regions; but the pre-1914 (British) Levant Consular Service included Morocco, Persia, Arabia and the ex-Turkish Balkans. 'Levantine' was used of people of these areas, especially traders with Greek, Jewish, Italian or other European blood in them. See NEAR EAST. The Levanter is the east wind which blows strongly from the eastern Mediterranean in summer. (French, '(sun)rising', i.e. the east; pronounced lev-ant'.)

Levant Company (1581). English chartered company formed to trade with Asia via the Mediterranean, with depots at Aleppo, Damascus and Alexandria, thus weakening the MUSCOVY COMPANY.

Levellers Section of Cromwell's army, supported by many civilians, who (1648) advocated republican government, manhood suffrage, religious toleration and social reform. They mutinied and were suppressed by Fairfax.

Leverhulme Medal (1960). Royal Society gold medal awarded every 3 years for research in pure or applied chemistry or engineering.

Leviathan (1651). Thomas Hobbes's work on the nature of government; he believed that as man is guided by pride and egotism it is essential for the individual to surrender his rights completely to a strong central government, to which he gives the name Leviathan, taken from Job 41:34, where that unidentified monster is described as 'a king over all the children of pride'.

Levin See ANNA KARENINA.

Levis Blue jeans introduced in Gold Rush days in the USA, with copper rivets inserted to strengthen the pockets, in which miners were wont to put samples of ore. (Invented by Levi Strauss, who had a clothing shop in San Francisco; pronounced lee'vyz.)

Levites Priestly caste in Israel, traditionally descendants of the tribe of Levi.

Leviticus Third book of the PENTATEUCH, like Deuteronomy occupied with the law and priestly rules. ('The Levitical book', i.e. a manual for priests.)

Lewis and Short (1879). Name of compilers used for their (still) standard Latin–English dictionary.

Lewisham Inner London borough since 1965 consisting of the former metropolitan boroughs of Lewisham and Deptford; headquarters at Catford.

Lexington (April 1775). First skirmish of the American War of Independence. British forces set out from Boston to seize a stock of arms at Concord, but MINUTEMEN, warned by PAUL REVERE, repulsed them. (Town near Boston, Mass.)

Leycesteria Himalayan honeysuckle or flowering nutmeg, named after a former chief justice of Bengal, W. Leycester.

Leyte Gulf, Battle of the (October 1944). Biggest naval battle of World War II, in which the US fleet inflicted heavy losses on the Japanese. On this occasion the Japanese first used KAMIKAZE (suicide bombers). (A gulf in the east Philippines.)

Leyton Former municipal borough of Essex, since 1965 part of the borough of WALTHAM FOREST.

Liberator, The Simón Bolívar, who liberated Venezuela, Colombia, Ecuador, Peru and Bolivia from Spanish rule (1821–25).

Libermanism Views which Prof. E. Liberman of Kharkov University was allowed to put forward in 1962, advocating the reintroduction of the profit motive in USSR in order to raise quality and production, and decentralization to improve efficiency.

Liberty, Statue of Statue 300 ft high (with its pedestal) which stands on an island in the entrance to New York harbour.

Liberty Bell Bell in Independence Hall, Philadelphia, rung when the Declaration of Independence was adopted in 1776.

Liberty Hall Place where one is free to do what one likes. (From SHE STOOPS TO CONQUER, where Squire Hardcastle, puzzled by the extraordinary conduct of 2 young men, says: 'This is Liberty Hall, gentlemen.')

Liberty ships Mass-produced cargo-boats built at an immense rate in Kaiser's shipyards in USA during World War II to replace losses to German submarines.

Lib–Lab MP supporting one of various alliances of Liberal and Labour members, especially that which defeated Baldwin in January 1924 and brought in the first Ramsay MacDonald ministry.

Libra Scales, 7th constellation of the Zodiac, between Virgo and Scorpio, which the sun enters at the autumnal equinox about 21 September. Astrologers claim that those born under this sign may be weak, pacific and changeable. (Pronounced ly'bra.)

Library of Congress (1800). US national library, in Washington DC, the nucleus of which was Thomas Jefferson's library; it is now one of the world's largest and includes collections of manuscripts, music and maps, besides being entitled to a copy of any book copyrighted in the US. Its Catalogue Card Number system is internationally used.

Liddell and Scott (1843). Compilers' names used as the short title of the Greek lexicon which has been the standard Greek–English dictionary since it was first published.

Lidice (1942). Czech mining village razed to the ground by the Germans. The men were all shot, the women taken to concentration camps, in reprisal for the assassination of the infamous Heydrich, German 'Protector' of Bohemia, in which the village was accused of being involved. (Pronounced lid'i-tsi.)

Lido Elongated sandy island covering the entrance to the Venice Lagoon; a popular and fashionable bathing place for at least 150 years. See also LANSBURY'S LIDO. (Pronounced lee'do.)

'Liebestraum' Beautiful Liszt piano piece. (German, 'dream of love'.)

Liebfraumilch Name which can be given to any German Rhine wine of any quality. (Named after the Liebfrauenkirche, 'Church of Our Lady', at Worms.)

Life Force Translation of Bergson's *élan vital*, the spirit of energy and life by virtue of which all living things evolve and progress in a CREATIVE EVOLUTION. In Shaw's plays it becomes increasingly synonymous with the Will of God, or a sort of depersonalized Holy Ghost, which will not permit Man through apathy to obstruct its plans so that he may enjoy free will; rather would it be forced to replace Man by some more effective instrument – SUPERMAN.

Life Guards, The (1661). One of the 2 regiments of the HOUSEHOLD CAVALRY, originally formed from Cavaliers who were with Charles II before the Restoration. They take precedence over all other regiments, wear scarlet tunics and white plumes.

Lifemanship (1950). Stephen Potter's application of the principles of GAMESMANSHIP to the problems of gaining and keeping social ascendancy over one's fellows – problems further studied in ONE UPMANSHIP.

Light of Asia, The (1879). Sir Edwin Arnold's life of Buddha in blank verse.

Light Sussex Light breed of domestic fowl much used for crossing.

Liguria Italian coastal region around Genoa, briefly a Napoleonic republic. (*Ligures*, ancient tribe inhabiting this region and adjoining parts of France and Switzerland.)

Li'l Abner Hero of Al Capp's strip cartoon, introduced to Britain from USA in 1966. He lives at Dogpatch, an innocent American boy forever at odds with a corrupt world.

Liliaceae Very large family of mainly bulbous plants and a few shrubs; it includes lilies, tulips, bluebells, onions, aloe, yucca and asparagus.

Lilith (1) Babylonian demoness of the night. (2) In Isaiah 34:14, a marginal note identifies her with the screech owl or night monster there mentioned. (3) In Jewish folklore, Adam's first wife, who left him to become the 'devil's dam'. (Hebrew *lilatu*, 'night'.)

'Lilli Marlene' (1938). German song revived by Radio Belgrade in 1941, adopted by Rommel's Afrika Korps and borrowed by the British 8th Army opposing them. The English version began: 'Underneath the lantern / By the barrack gate, / Darling I remember / The way you used to wait.'

Lilliput Most famous of the 4 imaginary countries of GULLIVER'S TRAVELS. The inhabitants are as small-minded as they are small-bodied, divided into furious factions such as the BIG-ENDIANS and LITTLE-ENDIANS (Catholics and Protestants), and the High Heels (Tories) and Low Heels (Whigs) – just like England.

Limburger Soft white cheese resembling Camembert but with a stronger smell and its own characteristic taste. (Originally made at Limbourg, Belgium.)

Lime, Harry See THIRD MAN.

Lime Grove Site of, and used for, the original BBC TV studios. (Street just west of Shepherds Bush Common, West London.)

Limehouse (1) Generic name for political vituperation following speech by Lloyd George in 1901. (2) Home of David Owen and from that address came the 'Limehouse Declaration' which began the Social Democratic Party.

Limeswold Soft British cheese.

Limoges Hard-paste porcelain made at the French town of Limoges (near a large source of kaolin), by numerous factories from 1783 onward.

Linacre (1962). College of Oxford University. (Pronounced lin'ĕk-ĕ.)

Linacre Professor Holder of the chair of Zoology at Oxford. (Pronounced lin'ĕk-ĕ.)

Linaria The genus name of toadflax.

Lincoln (sheep). Long-wool breed of sheep, the largest and heaviest in Britain.

Lincoln, The (1849). Short name of the Lincolnshire Handicap, a flat-race over a mile, formerly the first important race of the season and run at Lincoln, since 1965 run at Doncaster and declining in prestige.

Lincoln assassination (April 1865). Shooting of the US President by John Wilkes Booth in a Washington theatre, a few days after Robert E. Lee had surrendered at APPOMATTOX COURT HOUSE.

Lincoln Center (New York City). In full, the Lincoln Center for the Performing Arts, a complex of buildings on the upper west side of Manhattan; it was virtually completed in 1966 with the opening of the new METROPOLITAN OPERA HOUSE; it also contains the new Philharmonic Hall, the New York State Theater and the Vivian Beaumont Theater.

Lincoln Memorial (1922). Classical building in Potomac Park, Washington, with 36 columns representing the 36 states existing at Lincoln's death, and a 20-ft statue of him by the American sculptor Daniel Chester French.

Lincoln Professor Holder of the chair of Archaeology at Oxford.

'Lincolnshire Poacher, The' Old English song with the refrain: 'Oh, 'tis my delight on a shining night, in the season of the year.'

Lincoln's Inn One of the INNS OF COURT, attended particularly by Chancery lawyers.

Lindbergh baby case (1932). Trial in USA of Bruno Hauptmann, who was found guilty of stealing and murdering the infant son of Charles Lindbergh, the transatlantic solo flyer; Hauptmann was executed in 1936.

Lindisfarne Gospels Illuminated manuscripts of the 7th century, the work of Irish monks on Lindisfarne (Holy Island) off Northumberland; now in the British Museum.

Lindum Roman name of Lincoln, and of Ardoch, north of Stirling.

Linear B script That used for inventories and trading accounts inscribed on tablets found at

KNOSSOS and elsewhere; Michael Ventris deciphered them in 1953 and found them to be in archaic Greek.

Lingard, Capt. Character who appears in 3 of Joseph Conrad's novels: *Almayer's Folly, An Outcast of the Islands*, and *The Rescue*.

Links Club A New York social club, a WASP stronghold.

Linlithgowshire Scottish county later known as West Lothian and now in Lothian Region.

Linnean Society (1788). Leading natural history society, publishing journals and papers on botany and zoology. The headquarters are at BURLINGTON HOUSE. (Named after the Swedish naturalist, Linnaeus; pronounced lin-ee′an.)

Linotype Printing machine which composes type in solid lines (slugs), which used to be used in newspaper work.

Linum Genus name of flax.

Lion and the Unicorn, The Supporting figures in the royal arms of England and Scotland respectively; represented in the nursery rhyme as 'fighting for the crown'.

Lion of the North, The Name for Gustavus Adolphus, King of Sweden; see THIRTY YEARS WAR.

Lions clubs (1917). Clubs primarily for businessmen under 50, who give practical help to less fortunate people, mainly the aged, the blind and the infirm, and also interest themselves in international relations and welfare.

Lipizzaners (1580). Famous breed of ceremonial horses, 16 hands, with small heads and silky coats; the dark brown colts turn pure white as they grow. They are controlled by 'seat, leg and hands' with no vocal commands. Originally bred from Roman and Moorish stock for Spanish cavalry fighting the Moors, the strain was kept pure at a Jerez monastery, whence Maria Theresa was presented with some stallions (see SPANISH RIDING SCHOOL). (Named from an earlier stud farm, founded 1580, at Lipizza near Trieste, now moved to Styria.)

Lisbon earthquake (1755). Earthquake virtually destroying the city and killing nearly 40,000. It was laid out in rectangular patterns and fully reconstructed by the Marques de Pombal.

Lithuanian Language closely related to LETTISH. These 2 languages are closer to SANSKRIT, and more archaic in structure, than any other living INDO-EUROPEAN LANGUAGE.

Lit. Hum. Abbreviation of Literae Humaniores, the honours school in classical studies and philosophy at Oxford University; GREATS. (Latin, 'the more humane letters'.)

Little America (London) Grosvenor Square and its environs, used as General Eisenhower's headquarters in World War II, and the site of the American Embassy (1962), President Roosevelt's statue, etc.

Little America's Cup (1961). International catamaran challenge trophy, the chief world multi-hull match race, usually held off Thorpe Bay, Essex. The participants have been Britain, USA and Australia.

Little Bear Ursa Minor, a small northern constellation that contains the NORTH STAR. Called the Little Dipper in the USA.

Little Boy Blue, of the nursery rhyme, has been doubtfully identified with Cardinal Wolsey who, as a butcher's son, may well have tended his father's livestock.

Little Buttercup See PINAFORE, HMS.

Little Chef Wayside cafes on major roads in UK providing simple and standard food in pleasant surroundings for travellers.

Little Church Around the Corner, The Church near the Battery, Manhattan, New York City, so called because it was favoured by young couples who wanted to get married in a hurry. Officially it is the (Episcopal) Church of the Transfiguration.

Little Corporal Nickname for Napoleon.

Little Dorrit (1858). Dickens's novel much concerned with the MARSHALSEA PRISON, where

Little (Amy) Dorrit's father and her future husband spend some of their time, and she herself was born. See CIRCUMLOCUTION OFFICE.

Little Eva In *Uncle Tom's Cabin*, the daughter of Tom's owner, to whom Tom is devoted.

Little Flowers of St Francis, The (14th century). Collection of folk-tales and anecdotes about St Francis of Assisi, made about a century after his death, and including his sermons, e.g. his sermon to the birds. One story tells how the saint persuaded a wolf to leave people alone in return for a promise of regular meals.

Little Gidding Seventeenth-century Anglican lay religious community formed near Huntingdon by the family of Nicholas Ferrar and frequented by the poets George Herbert and Richard Crashaw. It is the setting for J. H. Short-house's novel *John Inglesant* (1881) and T. S. Eliot's poem 'Little Gidding' (1942) in *Four Quartets*.

Little-go Colloquial name for the Cambridge PRE-VIOUS examinations, the equivalent of RES-PONSIONS.

Littlehampton, Lady (Maudie) Famous creation of the cartoonist Osbert Lancaster, a frantic and feather-brained commentator on current affairs.

Little John Robin Hood's companion, a large man originally called John Little.

Little Lord Fauntleroy (1886). Children's book written by a Manchester-born American, Frances Hodgson Burnett, about a horrible little mother's darling in black velvet and lace collar, who wins everybody's heart except the reader's.

Little Moreton Hall Sixteenth-century moated house near Congleton, Cheshire, owned by the NATIONAL TRUST.

Little Neddy Nickname given to any of a series of committees set up by the NATIONAL ECONOMIC DEVELOPMENT COUNCIL ('Neddy') to study conditions in individual industries and produce plans for increased efficiency and productivity.

Little Nell See *The* OLD CURIOSITY SHOP.

Little Orphan Annie (1) James Whitcomb Riley's poem, originally called 'The Elf Child' (1885), in the Hoosier dialect. It is a cautionary tale for children; if they don't behave 'the Gobbleuns'll git you / Ef you don't watch out!' – and they git Annie. (2) Comic strip by Harold Gray (1924) in which the pathetic orphan gradually developed a certain bossiness and a right-wing outlook.

Little Red Book Thoughts of Mao Tse-tung (1893–1976). Obligatory reading for Chinese during the cultural revolution.

'Little Red Riding-hood' Fairy tale of a little girl eaten by a wolf disguised as her grandmother, to whom she was bringing a present. Common to the countries of Western Europe, it was printed in Perrault's MOTHER GOOSE'S TALES. The Grimms added a happy ending in which child and granny are restored to life.

Little Rock Capital of Arkansas, USA, with a public image of extreme opposition to racial integration. In 1957 Federal airborne troops had to be brought in to force Governor Faubus to allow black children to register at the high school.

Little Tich Stage name of a diminutive music-hall comedian, Harry Relph (1868–1928), who always appeared in enormous long boots.

Little Women (1868). Children's book by the American writer, Louisa M. Alcott, based on her memories of childhood in New England.

Little Wonder, The Nickname of Tom Sayers, an English boxer who fought the first international heavyweight championship (1860) against an American, the Benicia Boy, in a match stopped by police after 37 rounds.

Liu Slave girl in TURANDOT who sacrifices herself to save the Unknown Prince and his father.

Liver bird Mythical bird invented in the 17th century solely to explain the name Liverpool, and now adopted as the city's emblem. (Pronounced ly'vėr.)

Liverpool Delft (1710–85). DELFT made at Liverpool; it had a bluish tinge, and some of it was transfer printed.

Liverpool pottery and porcelain (1756–1841). Wares made by several factories at Liverpool, including the Herculaneum factory (1793–1840) which made pottery jugs, printed pottery, stoneware and, from 1800, bone china. Soft-paste porcelain was made by a firm founded in 1756. See LIVERPOOL DELFT.

Livery Companies (City Companies) Corporations mostly descended from medieval guilds of the City of London which imposed standards of quality and honesty in crafts and trades. Many Companies make large grants to education, charity and technical research, and maintain associations with their trade or its modern counterpart.

Liverymen Members of the LIVERY COMPANIES who are Freemen of London, and virtually elect the Lord Mayor. (From the distinctive ceremonial dress worn.)

Livingston (1962). NEW TOWN in Lothian Region, designed to take 100,000 inhabitants.

Liza of Lambeth (1897). Somerset Maugham's first novel, written from insights gained during his brief career as a doctor in the London slums.

Llanfair P.G. Merciful abbreviation of Llanfairpwllgwyngyllgogerychwyrndrobwllllantysiliogogogoch, an Anglesey village on the Menai Strait. ('Church of St Mary by the hollow of white aspen over the whirlpool and St Tysilio's Church close to the red cave.')

Llangollen, Ladies of (1778–1831). Two eccentric and autocratic Irish bluestockings who lived in a house they named Plas Newydd at Llangollen, Denbighshire, where they were visited by Wellington, Wordsworth and other notabilities. (Pronounced thla-goth'len.)

Llareggub See UNDER MILK WOOD.

Lloyd-Baker estate Property in North London which was kept intact in the Lloyd-Baker family for 400 years until 1976; almost all profits were ploughed back, enabling rents to be steadily reduced. Tenants were personally selected by Miss Lloyd-Baker from a very long waiting list.

Lloyd George Fund Political fund derived from the sale of honours and formed 'to promote any political purpose approved by Lloyd George'. The Conservative Party, while in coalition with Lloyd George's Liberals (1918–22), was given its share; nevertheless the existence of the fund was used in propaganda to break up that coalition. See MAUNDY GREGORY CASE.

Lloyd's (1689). London's international market for 'non-Life' insurance (i.e. accident, etc.) and centre for marine and airline intelligence, now in Lime Street, off Leadenhall Street. (Named after the coffee-house where it began life.)

Lloyd's Register of Shipping (1760). Society formed to survey and classify ships, managed by a committee of over 100 shipowners, shipbuilders, underwriters, etc. It publishes *Lloyd's Register Book*, giving details of all seagoing vessels, and also *Lloyd's Register of Yachts*. (Named after the coffee-house; see previous entry.)

LMS Initials of the London, Midland and Scottish Railway, which had London termini at Euston and St Pancras and ran the *Royal Scot* service from London to Glasgow. It is now divided mainly between the London Midland and the Scottish Regions of British Railways.

LNER Initials of the London and North-Eastern Railway, which had London termini at King's Cross, Marylebone and Liverpool Street. It ran the *Flying Scotsman* service from King's Cross to Edinburgh, the record for the journey being 5 minutes under 6 hours. It is now mainly divided between the Eastern and Scottish Regions of British Railways.

Lobelia Herbaceous perennials and annuals, named after Matthias de Lobel, physician and botanical author.

Lobster à l'Américaine Raw lobster sautéd in oil with tomatoes. (Possibly a corruption of ARMORICAINE; not connected with America.)

Lobster Newberg Lobster cooked in sherry or madeira, served with rice, mushrooms and cream sauce, and finished with cognac.

Lobster Thermidor Lobster cooked in butter and white wine, served in the shell and covered with cheese and mustard sauce, crusted.

Local Defence Volunteers The force that was renamed HOME GUARD soon after its formation in 1940.

Locarno Pacts (1925) Group of treaties, suggested by Stresemann, the German Foreign Minister, by which France, Belgium and Germany, with Britain and Italy, jointly guaranteed the existing Franco-German frontier and also the demilitarization of the Rhineland. They were denounced by Hitler in 1936.

Lochiel See CAMERON OF LOCHIEL.

Lochinvar Hero of a song in Scott's MARMION who carries off the fair Ellen at her wedding feast; 'They'll have fleet steeds that follow' quoth young Lochinvar.

Loch Ness monster Prehistoric aquatic animal which has been reported on numerous occasions since 1934 as having been seen swimming in Loch Ness, Highland Region.

Lockerbie Aviation disaster on 21 December 1988 when a Pan Am Boeing 747 aircraft crashed on the town of Lockerbie, Scotland. All 259 passengers and 11 residents of the town were killed. The cause was an explosion in the forward hold caused by a plastic explosive.

Lockheed aircraft (1927). US civil and military planes made by the Lockheed Co. of Burbank, California. Their Constellations pioneered the regular transatlantic service in 1946.

Lockit, Lucy In the BEGGAR'S OPERA, the daughter of the cruel governor of Newgate prison, who falls in love with Macheath, incarcerated there, and helps him escape.

Lock-out Closing of factories or other places of employment to bring pressure on employees to agree terms.

Locksley Hall (1832). Tennyson's poem in which a man revisits his childhood home and meditates on the girl who rejected him for a richer suitor, feeling 'That a sorrow's crowning sorrow is remembering happier things'. Turning to wider issues, he is fortified by the thought: 'Yet I doubt not thro' the ages one increasing purpose runs' and, later, 'Better fifty years in Europe than a cycle of Cathay'.

Loeb editions (1912). Anglo-American standard series of the Greek and Latin Classics, with an English translation on the facing page. (Founded by James Loeb, US banker; pronounced lèrb in Britain, lohb in USA.)

Loganberry Named after the American laywer and amateur horticulturist James H. Logan (1841–1928).

Logan Gardens Gardens at Port Logan, Stranraer, Dumfries and Galloway, famous for the profusion and variety of their subtropical plants.

Log-cabin to White House (1910). Title of W. M. Thayer's biography of James Garfield, 20th US President, who was born in an Ohio log-cabin; he was assassinated shortly after assuming office in 1881.

Logical Positivism View that philosophical statements are of value only if they can be tested by the experience of the senses. Thus, arguments on metaphysical problems (the existence of God, for example) are meaningless. This school owes its inspiration to Wittgenstein's TRACTATUS LOGICO-PHILOSOPHICUS; its chief British exponent was Sir A. J. Ayer of Oxford.

Lohans Buddhist hermit-saints, of whom many vigorous statues and statuettes were made in China from the 10th century onwards.

Lohengrin (1850). Wagner's opera in which Lohengrin, the son of Parsifal (PERCIVAL), comes to Antwerp in his swan-drawn boat to rescue a princess of Brabant. He marries her on condition that she does not ask him who he is because, as a Knight of the Grail, his name must not be divulged; when she does, he is forced to tell the truth and departs in his boat. (Pronounced le'en-grin.)

Loi-cadre (1956). French 'outline law' which empowered the government to grant political concessions to overseas territories (except Algeria), including universal suffrage and a single electoral college for elections both to local legislatures and to the French parliament.

Loki In Scandinavian mythology the god of mischief and evil who caused BALDER'S death. See GÖTTERDÄMMERUNG.

Lok Sabha House of the People, the Lower House of the Indian Parliament.

Lola Montez Stage name of an Irish dancer who captured the heart of Ludwig I, running Bavaria for him in 1847–8, until both of them were driven out.

Lolita (1958). Novel by the Russian-American writer Vladimir Nabokov, about Humbert Humbert's love affair with a 12-year-old 'nymphet'; made into a film (1962) by Stanley Kubrick.

Lollards Pre-Lutheran Reformers, followers of John Wyclif (1320–84). (From old Dutch word, meaning 'mutterers'.)

Loman, Willy Commercial traveller in Arthur Miller's *Death of a Salesman* (1949) who gradually comes to realize that his life has been a complete failure, and commits suicide.

Lombards (Longobardi). Germanic race which ruled LOMBARDY from the 6th century until Charlemagne drove them out in 713.

Lombard Street Street in the City of London traditionally associated with banking; hence the London money market; financiers. (Street of the medieval LOMBARDY bankers.)

Lombardy Italian Lake district between the Alps and the Po, bounded east and west by Piedmont and Venice respectively; under French, Spanish and Austrian rule before incorporation in the Kingdom of Italy. The capital was Milan.

Lomé Conventions Four Conventions, or trade accords, signed by 66 members of African, Caribbean and Pacific nations (ACP states) and the European Community (EC). They grant to THIRD WORLD states quantity-free access to EC markets.

London Dr Johnson thought that '. . . when a man is tired of London, he is tired of life, for there is in London all that life can afford'; but he also wrote in his poem 'London': 'Prepare for death if here at night you roam / And sign your will before you sup from home.'

London, Secret Treaty of (1915). Allies' bribe to Italy to enter World War I. They offered South Tirol, Adriatic ports, the Dodecanese and freedom to expand its African colonies. Published in 1918 by the Bolshevists, it caused considerable trouble at the Peace Conference.

London, The Abbreviation commonly used for the London Hospital, Whitechapel, E1.

London blitz (7 September 1940 to May 1941). Series of night raids on London which developed from, and overlapped, the BATTLE OF BRITAIN. (Blitz, short for BLITZKRIEG.)

London Bridge (1) Until 1750 the only Thames bridge in London, built in the 12th century and carrying houses, shops and a chapel. (2) Its replacement (1831), which has been reconstructed and widened. The old facing stones, parapets, etc. were bought by a California oil tycoon (1969) for transportation to Arizona.

London Clinic Fashionable private hospital at the top of Harley Street, run by a group of Harley Street consultants.

Londonderry, Siege of (1689). Three-month siege by Irish Catholic supporters of James II of Protestant-held Londonderry, lifted after much hardship and 10,000 deaths by the English Navy. Commemorated each August by the Relief of Derry celebrations.

'Londonderry Air' Irish traditional folk-song from Co. Derry, first published in 1885 as 'Farewell to CUCHULAIN'. Since then the air has been arranged by various hands for all kinds of instruments.

London Gazette (1665). Twice-weekly government publication, listing official appointments and announcements, bankruptcies and, in wartime, casualties.

London gin Generic term for any dry gin.

London Group (1913). School of British artists who broke away from the NEW ENGLISH ART CLUB and, under the influence of Cézanne, Gauguin and Van Gogh, endeavoured to paint realistic interpretations of modern life. Sickert, Epstein, Wyndham Lewis and most of the CAMDEN TOWN GROUP belonged to it.

London Library (1841). Subscription library housed in St James's Square. Founded by Thomas Carlyle.

London Mercury (1919–34). Influential literary magazine founded and edited by Sir John Squire.

London, Museum of Museum with exhibits covering the history of London from the earliest times to the present. Formerly housed in Kensington Palace, it is now at the Barbican.

London Naval Conference (1) Meeting of the Great Powers (1930) which tried to apply the principles of the WASHINGTON NAVAL AGREEMENT to cruisers, destroyers and submarines, and to extend the naval holiday by 6 years. The resulting agreement was not ratified by France and Italy, and was denounced by Japan in 1934. (2) Further attempt (1936) to limit naval armament by fixing maxima for gun calibres in capital ships, tonnage of aircraft carriers etc. Italy and Japan rejected the agreement.

London School of Economics (1895). Branch of London University, near the Aldwych, founded by Sidney and Beatrice Webb and associated with Harold Laski and R. H. Tawney.

London Stone Stone believed to have marked the point in the Roman forum of London from which distances along the Roman roads were measured. It is now set in the wall of the Bank of China, opposite Cannon Street Station.

London University Federation of colleges and institutes and a dozen medical schools scattered over London and the Home Counties, with headquarters at Malet Street, Bloomsbury.

London Weekend TV (1968). Programme contracting company providing TV service for London from 7 p.m. on Friday until Sunday night.

Loneliness of the Long-Distance Runner, The (1962). Film made from the title story of a collection of short stories by Alan Sillitoe (1959); a Borstal governor (see BORSTAL SYSTEM) tries to use the athletic potentialities of one of his charges to turn him into a reformed character.

Lone Star State Nickname of Texas.

Longchamp Paris racecourse near the Seine in the Bois de Boulogne, where the GRAND PRIX DE L'ARC DE TRIOMPHE is run.

Long Day's Journey into Night (1956). Eugene O'Neill's semi-autobiographical play, written in 1941 but not performed until after his death.

Long Elizas Tall ladies painted on early Chinese export porcelain; copied on Dutch DELFT and later by most English factories, e.g. Worcester. (Corruption of Dutch for 'tall maidens'.)

Longest Bar in the World Once-famous 100-ft bar in what was the ultra-exclusive Shanghai Club, a meeting-place for bankers, diplomats and other Westerners. It still survives, in what is now a social club for Chinese and foreign seamen; ping-pong is the chief entertainment there today.

Long John Silver Smooth-tongued one-legged villain of Stevenson's TREASURE ISLAND who, having packed the crew with his own men, plans to stage a mutiny and take over command of the expedition.

Longleat House Tudor home near Warminster. Wiltshire, of the Marquess of Bath; to the attractions of pictures, furniture and books have now been added free-range lions.

Long March (October 1934 to October 1935). Strategic retreat out of reach of Chiang Kai-shek of Mao Tse-tung's 1st Front Red Army of 100,000 men, from Juichin (their headquarters in Kiangsi) through Kweichow and Szechwan to Yenan (Wuch'ichen) in Shensi, which became their headquarters for the next 10 years; the distance covered was 6,000 miles, and 70,000 men were lost on the way.

Longo Scarlatti's sonatas catalogued by Alessandro Longo. (Abbreviation 'L'.)

Long Parliament (1640–60). Parliament which released the victims of Charles I's personal rule, had Strafford executed and Archbishop Laud imprisoned, abolished the STAR CHAMBER and ship-money, and became the RUMP PARLIAMENT in 1649. Surviving members were recalled by General Monk in 1660, and voted for the RESTORATION.

Long-Range Desert Groups British units which in the North African campaign (1940–43) carried out sabotage behind the enemy's lines, on one occasion raiding Rommel's headquarters.

Longton Hall (1749–60). Earliest Staffordshire porcelain factory; most of its pieces were not particularly well made or decorated, but some now fetch high prices.

Lonicera Honeysuckle, named after Adam Lonicer, a 16th-century German naturalist.

Lonsdale belt (1911). Ornamented belt given to the winner of a British boxing title, and retained if won 3 times at the same weight. (Earl of Lonsdale, 1857–1944.)

Lonsdale Puissance championship (1947). Show-jumping contest at the Royal INTERNATIONAL HORSE SHOW over high or difficult jumps.

Lonsdale spy case (1961). Trial of 'Gordon Lonsdale' (alias of a Russian GRU commander, Conon Molody), sentenced in the PORTLAND SECRETS CASE to 25 years imprisonment; he was exchanged for Greville WYNNE (1964).

Look Back in Anger (1956). John Osborne's play which, set in a Midland bed-sitter, opened a new era of realism in the English theatre, and featured Jimmy PORTER as the first ANGRY YOUNG MAN.

Looking-Glass World World in which everything is back to front, as in THROUGH THE LOOKING-GLASS; a mad, illusory world.

Loom of Youth, The (1917). Frank account of public-school life by Alec, brother of Evelyn, Waugh, then 18; it was based on his own experiences at Sherborne.

Loop, The Main shopping centre of Chicago, occupying 7 blocks on State Street; a notorious slum area lies behind it. (In a loop of elevated railway tracks.)

Loran towers Navigational aids for ships and aircraft in the form of towers up to 1,400 ft high transmitting radio signals. By measuring the time displacement between signals from any 2 towers, a 'fix' is obtained. (Formed from initial letters of 'Long Range Navigation'.)

Lord Advocate Scottish equivalent of the Attorney-General.

Lord Chamberlain Chief officer of the Royal Household. He is responsible for the appointment of royal tradesmen and until 1968 censored plays. Not to be confused with the Lord Great Chamberlain.

Lord Chancellor Short title of the Lord High Chancellor of England, Keeper of the Great Seal, who is the senior judge and head of the legal profession, Speaker of the House of Lords and the government's chief legal adviser in the Cabinet; he presides over the Judicial Committee of the Privy Council and the House of Lords sitting as the supreme court of appeal. He appoints judges, JPs and QCs. As a member of the Cabinet he vacates office with his government. He controls the nationally unified CROWN COURTS system.

Lord Chief Justice Senior permanent member of the judiciary, ranking next to the LORD CHANCELLOR (a party appointment). He is president of the Queen's Bench Division and may also sit on the Courts of Appeal and of Criminal Appeal.

Lord Haw-Haw Journalists' nickname originally applied to the OFFICER IN THE TOWER (who *did* have an Oxford accent) who from Germany broadcast attacks on British morale early in World War II. It was most inappropriately transferred to William Joyce, who took over from him. The latter, an Irish–American member of the British Union of Fascists, had an accent all his own in which Germany, e.g., was pronounced Jairmany. He was hanged in 1946.

Lord Jim (1900). Joseph Conrad's novel about a ship's officer who tried to live down an early act of cowardice (jumping off an apparently sinking pilgrim ship in the Red Sea), and atoned for it by the vicarious sacrifice of his life; as in other Conrad novels, the story is told indirectly, through Capt. MARLOW.

Lord-Lieutenant Sovereign's local representative in a county, largely an honorific appointment usually held by a peer or large landowner. As head of the county magistracy he submits nominations of Justices of the Peace to the Lord Chancellor.

Lord Mayor's Show Annual procession on the second Saturday in November of the newly elected Lord Mayor of London to the Law Courts to be presented to the Lord Chief Justice.

Lord of the Flies (1955). William Golding's novel about a group of boys stranded on a desert island after an air crash, and their reversion to primitive savagery.

Lord of the Rings, The (1954–6). Trilogy in which J. R. R. Tolkien, a Professor of Anglo-Saxon, created a uniquely weird self-contained world of his own, inhabited by HOBBITS and situated in 'Middle Earth'. The main theme is a Hobbit expedition to break the power of the Dark Lord of Mordor.

Lord Protector Title sometimes given to a Regent, specifically to: (1) PROTECTOR SOMERSET; (2) Oliver and, briefly, Richard Cromwell during the PROTECTORATE.

Lord Randal Ancient ballad which spread throughout Europe, perhaps from Scotland, about a hunter poisoned by his stepmother who comes home to his mother to die; Lord Randal has been variously identified.

Lord's (1814). Headquarters of the MCC and of the Middlesex County Cricket Club in St John's Wood, London. (Thomas Lord bought the ground for the MCC.)

Lord's Day, The Sunday, the Christian equivalent of the Jewish Sabbath (Saturday), and often itself called the Sabbath. Traditionally, it commemorates the Resurrection.

Lord's Day Observance Society (1831). Body devoted to ensuring, under 17th-century Puritan laws which politicians shirk repealing, that the traditional English Sunday shall remain.

Lords of Appeal in Ordinary Members of the House of Lords who receive a salary specifically for their services in hearing appeals when the House is sitting as a court of appeal, and also as members of the Judicial Committee of the Privy Council. They are eminent lawyers who, if not already peers, are made life peers on appointment.

Lord's Taverners, The (1950). Cricket team of stage personalities, originally formed to raise money for the National Playing Fields Association. (Named after the Tavern at Lord's, where the idea was conceived.)

Lord Ullin's Daughter (1809). Thomas Campbell's ballad of a girl who elopes and is drowned before the eyes of her father who has come in pursuit.

Lord Warden See CINQUE PORTS.

Lorelei (1) Rock on the Rhine near Bingen, a danger to river traffic. (2) Legendary siren who lured boatmen to their doom there. (3) The gold-digging blonde of GENTLEMEN PREFER BLONDES. (Pronounced lawr'e-ly.)

Lorenzo the Magnificent Lorenzo de' MEDICI (1449–92), ruler of Florence, poet and patron of the arts and learning.

Loriners, Worshipful Company of (1711). LIVERY COMPANY, originally a guild of makers of bridle-bits and other metal horse-trappings.

Lorna Doone (1869). R. D. Blackmore's novel about the Doone family, outlaws of Exmoor in the West Country at the time of the MONMOUTH REBELLION. John Ridd marries Lorna, who had shielded him from the Doones, his father's murderers, and who turns out to be not a Doone but the kidnapped daughter of a Scottish nobleman.

Lorraine See ALSACE-LORRAINE.

Lorraine, Cross of Red cross with 2 horizontal cross-pieces on a blue ground, the emblem used by Joan of Arc and adopted (1940) by de Gaulle for the Free French.

Los In William Blake's private mythology, a protean figure who appears to personify imagination, energy and creative genius, and has a regenerating influence on URIZEN.

Lost deposit Parliamentary candidates deposit

£500 in cash with the returning officer. This is forfeited if the candidate fails to receive 5 per cent of the valid votes cast.

Lost Generation, The Young generation in Britain which was decimated by the heavy losses of World War I. Since the British forces were entirely composed of regulars and volunteers until well on into 1916, it was the most public-spirited elements which suffered the highest casualties, with lasting and ineradicable effect on the nation. (From Gertrude Stein's remark to Ernest Hemingway, 'You are all a lost generation.')

Lost Horizon See SHANGRI LA.

'Lost Leader, The' Robert Browning's poem beginning 'Just for a handful of silver he left us, / Just for a riband to stick in his coat', attacking someone (perhaps Wordsworth) he regarded as a turncoat.

Lost Tribes of Israel Tribes taken as slaves to Assyria from northern Palestine in 721 BC (2 Kgs 15:29), of whom nothing further is known, although the fate of the victims of the later BABYLONIAN CAPTIVITY is on record. See BRITISH ISRAELITES.

Lot Nephew of Abraham who was allowed to escape from the destruction of Sodom and Gomorrah with his family, but whose wife was turned to a pillar of salt for disobeying Jehovah's command 'look not behind thee' (Gen. 19:17, 26).

Lothair (1870). Benjamin Disraeli's political novel, in which many characters were thinly disguised contemporaries, about the competition between the Anglican and Roman Churches and Italian revolutionaries for the financial support of the wealthy young Lothair.

Lothario, The Gay 'Haughty, gallant, gay' and heartless rake of Nicholas Rowe's tragedy, *The Fair Penitent* (1703).

Lotus-eaters, The In Greek legend, the drowsy inhabitants of a land where, in Tennyson's words, 'it seemed always afternoon'; those who ate the lotus fruit forgot their homes and families and sank into luxurious apathy. ODYSSEUS and

his men found this ancient Costa Brava a great temptation; those who succumbed had to be forcibly carried aboard.

Louisiana Purchase (1803). Treaty by which the USA doubled its size through buying from Napoleon for $15 million an undefined area of the old French province of Louisiana lying between the Rockies and the Mississippi, which later became the states of Louisiana, Arkansas, Missouri, Iowa, South Dakota, Nebraska, Colorado, Kansas, etc.

Louis Quatorze Age of BAROQUE, in vogue in the reign of Louis XIV (1643–1715), during which Versailles was finished. It was characterized by elaborate and costly furniture (some of it made in silver), Boulle's tortoiseshell and brass marquetry work (generally known as buhl), and Gobelins tapestries.

Louis Quinze Age of ROCOCO, in vogue during the reign of Louis XV (1715–74); rooms were smaller, furniture lighter and more colourful, with wood marquetry, lacquer work and ormolu mounts.

Louis Seize Neoclassical (see NEOCLASSICISM) reaction to the LOUIS QUINZE style, in vogue during the reign of Louis XVI (1774–93), inspired by the Latin styles discovered during the excavations at Pompeii and Herculaneum begun 20 years before Louis XV died. Buhl (see LOUIS QUATORZE) came back into favour, ormolu ornamentation was refined and perfected, and furniture was veneered with mahogany, some of it decorated with porcelain.

Lourdes Town on the French side of the Pyrenees, a major place of pilgrimage for the sick since (1858) a shepherd girl (St Bernadette) saw visions of the Virgin Mary who told her of the healing powers of the local waters.

Louvain City of Brabant, Belgium, which at the beginning of World War I became a symbol of German 'frightfulness' when the fine old medieval buildings were deliberately razed in retaliation for civilian attacks on the occupation troops. The university library was rebuilt and restocked, only to be destroyed again by the Germans in 1940.

Louvre, The Huge museum and art gallery in Paris, on the site of a 12th-century castle and 16th-century royal palace, containing one of the finest collections of paintings, sculpture and antiquities in the world.

Lovat Scouts, The Regiment raised in the Boer War by Lord Lovat, head of the Clan Fraser. After many changes it is now the 540th Light Air Defence Regiment (The Lovat Scouts), Royal Artillery.

Love and Mr Lewisham (1900). H. G. Wells's partly autobiographical novel of a young science master in a Sussex school who sacrifices his high ambitions when he marries a very ordinary servant-girl.

Loved One, The (1948). Evelyn Waugh's witty exposure of the extent to which the people of Hollywood were at that time in the clutches of the morticians, i.e. undertakers, to whom vast sums were paid for elaborate funerals and para-disal burial grounds.

Love for Love (1695). Typically witty Restoration comedy by Congreve, in which a young man renounces his inheritance in favour of a younger brother in return for his father's settling his debts. He is rescued from the consequences of this act by the wiles of the girl who loves him.

Love's Labour's Lost (1594) Shakespeare's comedy in which a King of Navarre and his friends unsuccessfully endeavour to resist the charms of a visiting French princess and her entourage. A famous minor character is the tedious schoolmaster, Holofernes.

Love the Magician (1915). Falla's Andalusian gypsy ballet. (Spanish, *El amor brujo*.)

Low Church See EVANGELICALISM.

Low Countries Region around the deltas of the Rhine, Meuse (Maas) and Scheldt, i.e. Holland, Belgium and adjacent districts. (Translation of *Nederland*, 'Netherlands'.)

Lower Egypt Nile delta between Cairo and the Mediterranean; see UPPER EGYPT.

Lowestoft porcelain (1757–1803). Porcelain decorated in oriental or French styles, in under-glaze blue (resembling BOW) or polychrome, and made for use rather than for show. Genuine pieces are rare. See CHINESE LOWESTOFT.

Low German Platt-Deutsch, the dialects of North Germany from which Dutch and Flemish derive, closer in sound to English than is HIGH GERMAN.

Lowndean Professor Holder of the chair of Astronomy and Geometry at Cambridge.

Low Sunday Sunday after Easter.

Loyalties (1922). Galsworthy's play about an old solicitor, Jacob Twisden.

LSD Initials used for lysergic acid diethylamide, a drug producing hallucinations which appear to vary in content with the preoccupations of the individual concerned, from bliss to extremes of terror.

Lubin Character in Bernard Shaw's BACK TO METHUSELAH, said to be based on H. H. Asquith.

Lublin Committee Polish Communist Committee of National Liberation, first established in Moscow (July 1944), and at the end of the year proclaimed at Lublin, Poland, as the Polish provisional government, under Russian aegis.

Lubyanka Prison Moscow prison used by the GPU and still by the KGB, whose headquarters it adjoins in Lubyanka Street.

Lucasian Professor Holder of the chair of Mathematics at Cambridge.

Lucia di Lammermoor See BRIDE OF LAMMERMOOR.

Lucifer (1) Latin name for Venus as a morning star (Greek Phosphorus). (2) Fallen star in Isaiah 14:12, 'How art thou fallen from heaven, O Lucifer, star of the morning', which referred to the downfall of Nebuchadnezzar. (3) In Dante, the ruler of hell; in Milton, the name of the archangel expelled from heaven who became Satan.

Lucky Jim (1954). Jim Dixon, the REDBRICK

hero of Kingsley Amis's novel, who shambles hilariously through an understandably brief career as lecturer in history at a Welsh university.

Lucrece In Roman legend, a married woman raped by the son of the Etruscan King of Rome. She committed suicide and the TARQUINS were driven out of Rome, which became a republic. The story is told in Shakespeare's *The Rape of Lucrece* (1594). (Anglicized form of Lucretia.)

Lucullus (Cooking) Name that may be added to any especially elaborate dish. (Roman epicure of 1st century BC.)

Lucy Cavendish College (1965). Cambridge University's first graduate college for women.

Luddites (1811–16). Machine-wreckers of the Midlands and industrial north who protested against unemployment caused by new machinery brought in by the Industrial Revolution and against the enforcement of low wages and long hours; as there was no police force, the movement was suppressed by troops, and many rioters were hanged or transported. (Named after the leader called General Ludd, never identified, or a mad boy called Ned Lud.)

Lufthansa Chief German airline. (German *Luft*, 'air' + *Hansa*, see HANSEATIC LEAGUE.)

Luftwaffe German Air Force. (Pronounced luft'vaf-ė.)

Lüger German automatic pistol used in both world wars, and also in use in the USA.

Luguvallium Roman name of Carlisle.

Lukiko Parliament of the former kingdom of Buganda, Uganda.

Lullingstone silk farm Silk farm housed in the cottage where Charles II's mistress, Nell Gwyn, lived, at Salisbury Hall, London Colney, Hertfordshire.

Lumleian lecture (1584). Public lecture on surgery given each March at the Royal College of Physicians. (Endowed by Lord Lumley and Richard Caldwell.)

'Lump, The' Builders' term for the subcontracting of labour supply to self-employed men who are able to evade tax and social service payments.

Lumpen proletariat Common people; a term coined by Karl Marx.

Lumpkin, Tony Mischievous character who causes all the trouble in Goldsmith's SHE STOOPS TO CONQUER.

Luna Roman moon-goddess, equivalent to the Greek SELENE.

Lunaria Plant genus name of Honesty.

Lunar Orbiter The US programme for putting TV cameras into orbit round the moon in order to pinpoint suitable landing sites for the APOLLO SPACE PROGRAM. In November 1966 *Lunar Orbiter 2* relayed the first landscape photograph of the moon's surface.

Lupercalia Roman spring festival of expiation, later of fertility. (Latin *lupus*, 'wolf', identified with the wolf that suckled Romulus and Remus.)

Lupin, Arsène Master criminal created by the French journalist Maurice Leblanc in the early years of this century.

Lusitania Latin name for Portugal and western Spain.

Lusitania **sinking** (1915). Torpedoing without warning by a German submarine of a Cunard liner, with the loss of 1,200 lives, including 124 Americans; this event influenced US opinion towards joining in the war against Germany.

Lutetia Parisiorum Roman name of Paris.

Luther (1961). John Osborne's historical play, which shocked some by its literal rendering of that coarse monk's talk.

Lutheran Church Protestant Church which, in contrast to the REFORMED CHURCH, accepts the AUGSBURG CONFESSION as the basis of its beliefs. In Germany it is now called the Evangelical United Brethren Church; it is the established episcopal Church of the Scandinavian countries, and is powerful in the American Middle West.

Lutine Bell Bell which hangs in 'The ROOM' at LLOYD'S; one stroke is sounded for bad, 2 for good news. (Salvaged from the frigate *Lutine*, sunk in 1799 at a cost to Lloyd's of some half a million pounds; pronounced loo-teen'.)

Luton Hoo Eighteenth-century country house at Luton which contains the WERNHER COLLECTION.

Luxor Egyptian tourist centre on the site of ancient THEBES (south of KARNAK) where Amenhotep III built the Great Temple of Amon, to which Tutankhamen and Rameses II made additions. See also VALLEY OF THE KINGS.

LX Club Cambridge University rugby club of the best 60 players in residence (elected for life). (LX, Roman numerals for 60.)

Lyceum melodrama Plays such as *The* BELLS, in which Henry Irving made his name at the Lyceum Theatre; he then took over the theatre as manager, continuing to stage, and act in, both melodramas and Shakespeare.

Lychnis Genus name of the campions.

Lycidas (1637). Milton's elegy on the death of his young friend Edward King. (Name of a shepherd in Virgil's ECLOGUES; pronounced lis'i-das.)

Lydgate, Dr In George Eliot's MIDDLEMARCH, a young doctor with ideals who sinks to becoming a fashionable consultant.

Lynch law Summary execution, generally by a mob, without proper trial or hearing. There are many differing versions of its derivation.

Lynskey Tribunal (1949). Tribunal set up to investigate the alleged bribery of junior Ministers, by or through one Sydney Stanley; some resignations followed. (Justice Lynskey.)

Lyonesse In Arthurian legend a country, now submerged near the Scilly Isles, particularly associated with TRISTRAM and Iseult.

Lyon King of Arms Scottish equivalent of GARTER KING OF ARMS, with his own separate office.

Lyonnaise Cooking term indicating fried shredded onions.

Lyra The Harp, a northern constellation, which contains the Ring Nebula, the brightest of the planetary nebulae; alpha-Lyrae is VEGA. (The lyre of Orpheus or of Hermes.)

Lyrical Ballads (1798). Book of poems written in collaboration by Wordsworth and Coleridge, in which they deliberately restricted themselves to the language and incidents of common life.

Lysenkoism Prostitution of science to political ends. In 1948 the Russian Academician T. D. Lysenko attacked colleagues who held the generally accepted view that acquired characteristics are not inherited, because this clashed with the current Stalinist version of Marxist–Leninist theory.

Lysimachia Genus name of the loosestrifes; the purple loosestrife is *Lythrum*.

Lysistrata (415 BC). Aristophanes' comedy in which women on both sides of the Peloponnesian war terminate it by the simple procedure of refusing their husbands their 'marital rights' until they stop fighting. (Pronounced ly-sis'trat-a.)

Lytton report (1932). Report to the League of Nations which condemned the Japanese invasion of Manchuria (see MUKDEN INCIDENT) and recommended that they should be ordered to withdraw. The League Assembly approved the report but took no action on it – a failure sometimes regarded as the first sign of the disintegration of the League's morale.

M

'**M**' In Ian Fleming's novels, James BOND's service chief, modelled on the actual head of Britain's wartime Secret Service.

Mabinogion, The Collection of Welsh stories. Four 'Mabinogi' (instructions for young bards) are contained in the *Red Book of Hergest*, compiled in the 14th and 15th centuries; they deal with Celtic legends and mythology. Lady Charlotte Guest in 1838–49 published a collection of 11 Welsh tales with translation and notes.

Macadamized roads Originated by John Loudon McAdam (1756–1836), as surveyor to the Bristol Turnpike Trust he used his road-making system to remake roads there; his method has been used extensively in the world.

Macaulay's New Zealander Reference to Lord Macaulay's glimpse of the distant future – when some traveller from New Zealand shall, in the midst of a vast solitude, take his stand on a broken arch of London Bridge to sketch the ruins of St Paul's.

Macaulay's schoolboy Omniscient boy implied in Lord Macaulay's phrase: 'Every schoolboy knows who imprisoned Montezuma and who strangled Atahualpa.'

Macavity Mystery Cat of whom T. S. Eliot wrote, in a mood of relaxation: 'There never was a Cat of such deceitfulness and suavity' and 'He's the bafflement of Scotland Yard, the Flying Squad's despair: / For when they reach the scene of crime – Macavity's not there!' The poem appeared in *Old Possum's Book of Practical Cats* (1939).

Macbeth Historical 11th-century king who murdered King Duncan, seized the throne of Scotland, and was killed by Duncan's son Malcolm. In Shakespeare's play Macbeth also had BANQUO, Lady MACDUFF and her children murdered.

Macbeth, Lady Wife who urges on MACBETH in his crimes but in the sleep-walking scene goes mad and commits suicide.

Maccabaean lectures (1956). Lectures in jurisprudence, sponsored by the British Academy.

Maccabees Jewish family who led a successful revolt in the 2nd century BC against the Syrian SELEUCID king, Antiochus IV Epiphanes, who tried to Hellenize Palestine. They formed a priest-monarchy which was overthrown by Rome in 63 BC.

Maccabees Two books of the Apocrypha, telling the story of the revolt of the Maccabees (see previous entry).

Mac Cailein Mhor Gaelic title of the Chief of the Campbell clan, the Duke of Argyll. ('Son of Colin the Great', the 13th-century Sir Colin Campbell.)

McCarthyism Indiscriminate witch-hunting zeal against 'Communist' (i.e. left-wing) officials, as displayed by Senator Joseph McCarthy when chairman of a US committee investigating subversive influences in government, from 1951 until his policy was condemned by fellow Senators in 1954.

Macclesfield Type of silk originally produced in Macclesfield, England, having a variety of small patterns and used for men's neckties.

McCoy, The real Colloquialism for 'best of its kind'. (Probably originally McKay, referring to a Scotch whisky exported to North America in the 1880s, confused with the name of an American boxer, McCoy.)

Macdonald's (1950s). World's largest restaurant chain started in San Bernardino, California. By 1988 they had sold 70 billion hamburgers and served 20 million customers a day. They arrived in the UK in 1974 with one site in Woolwich and in 1989 had 340 outlets.

Macduff Former friend of MACBETH who joins Malcolm. When he hears this, Macbeth has Lady Macduff and their children murdered, and Macduff avenges them.

Macédoine (Cooking) Mixture of fruits or of vegetables. (Reference to the mixture of races in MACEDONIA.)

Macedonia Balkan region which after the breakup of the Turkish Empire was partitioned between Greece, Serbia (later Yugoslavia) and Bulgaria. The population is a mixture of at least 8 races, hence MACÉDOINE. See IMRO.

McGill Leading Canadian university, at Montreal.

McGonagall verse Relentless doggerel such as that which William McGonagall (1830–c. 1902), a Scottish weaver, wrote on topical catastrophes and recited in pubs. His main concerns were to get all the details in (e.g. year, date, exact dimensions) and to achieve a rhyme, *coûte que coûte*, as in: 'But he resolves to save the oncoming train, / So every nerve and muscle he does strain, / And he trudges along dauntlessly on his crutches, / And tenaciously to them he clutches.'

Macheath, Capt. Highwayman hero of the BEGGAR'S OPERA.

Machiavellianism, Machiavellism (The practice of) the policy, deliberately and exclusively founded on self-interest, recommended in Machiavelli's *The* PRINCE. (Pronounced mak-i-a-vel'i-an-izm, mak-i-a-vel'-izm.)

Machu Picchu INCA mountain city discovered in 1911 north-west of Cuzco, Peru, with well-preserved buildings and terraces skilfully constructed of huge stones. (Pronounced mah'choo peek'choo.)

McKenna duties (1915). Customs duties imposed temporarily in World War I to restrict luxury imports (cars, watches, etc.), and not intended to be Protectionist; abolished 1924. (Reginald McKenna, Liberal Chancellor of the Exchequer.)

Mackinnon Cup (1891). Rifle-shooting competition for teams of 12 from Great Britain, Ireland and the Dominions.

'Mack the Knife' One of the big song-hits of the THREEPENNY OPERA; Mack the Knife is a crook.

Maclean Mission (September 1943). British mission led by Brig. Fitzroy Maclean, parachuted into German-occupied Yugoslavia to assist Tito and his PARTISANS. (Pronounced mèklayn'.)

Macleod, Fiona Pen-name under which William Sharp wrote THE IMMORTAL HOUR and other CELTIC TWILIGHT works. It was not until after his death in 1905 that it became known that these were written by Sharp, who had also published various biographies and poems under his real name. (Pronounced mèklowd'.)

Macleod of MacLeod Chief of the clan MacLeod, members of which come from all over the world to Skye to see the present chief.

McLuhanism Vision of the world transformed by the electronic revolution (broadcasting, telephones, talkies) into a 'global village' where war and racialism will be unthinkable, and books no longer read. It is offered by Marshall McLuhan, the Canadian author of *The Gutenberg Galaxy* (1962) and *Understanding Media* (1964).

McMahon letters (1915–16). Letters (published in 1938) between the HASHEMITE Sherif Hussein of Mecca and the British High Commissioner in Egypt, McMahon. Hussein demanded independence after the war for the Arab lands which now comprise Iraq, Syria, Lebanon, Israel,

Jordan and Saudi Arabia. McMahon promised UK support except for an area corresponding to Lebanon and coastal Syria. The BALFOUR DEC-LARATION contradicted this, and moreover the League of Nations put the whole area under mandate except Saudi Arabi.

McMahon Line (1914). Boundary between Tibet and India which mainly follows the crest of the Himalayas. No Chinese government has ever accepted it, claiming that a Buddhist population having close ties with Tibet has been left on the wrong side of it in northern Kashmir. See LADAKH CRISIS.

M'Naghten Rules (1843). Rules laying down criteria for a successful plea of insanity in a criminal case; the chief rule was that the accused must either not have known what he was doing, or not have known that it was wrong. (Named after the accused in such a case; neither he nor anyone else knew for certain how his name should be spelt; some times given as M'Naughten or MacNaughten.)

Macy's (1858). Retail department store in Herald Square, New York City; also stores chain which, in contrast to its larger rival SEARS ROEBUCK, concentrates on midtown outlets; said to be the world's largest.

Madame As a title in pre-revolutionary France, see MONSIEUR.

Madame Bovary (1857). Flaubert's masterpiece, a realistic novel about the bored wife of a village doctor and her squalid love affair, written with the meticulous attention to details of style for which Flaubert was so renowned.

Madame Butterfly (1904). Puccini's opera about Lt F. B. Pinkerton, USN, who marries the Japanese geisha girl of the title, deserts her, and returns years later with his American wife to find her still waiting faithfully for him. Heartbroken, Butterfly takes her life.

Madame Tussaud's (1802). World-famous waxworks exhibition founded by Madame Anne Marie Tussaud (1761–1850), she was a gifted sculptress and exhibited works in Paris from where she brought the exhibition. She knew many of the personalities of the French Revolu-tion and modelled some from the guillotined heads. Among her acquaintances were Louis XVI, Marie Antoinette and Marat. The chamber of horrors is a notable feature of the waxworks.

'Mad Cow' disease (1985). Bovine spongiform encephalopathy (BSE), a fatal virus, causes brain damage in cows making them walk un-steadily and act aggressively. It was discovered in Britain and from 1986 to May 1990 13,000 head of cattle had died from the disease. It was believed that they had become infected because their feed included the remains of sheep infected with a similar disease, scrapie.

Maddermarket (1919). Theatre at Norwich, home of the Norwich Players, an amateur dramatic society.

Madeira Amber or brownish fortified wine vary-ing from sweet to dry, resembling sherry. It is heated for weeks in concrete tanks and then matured for years in casks. A favourite in Re-gency days. See MALMSEY.

Madeleine, The (1842). In Paris, the Church of St Mary Magdalen, near the Opéra, in external form a Greek temple.

Madeleine Smith case (1857). Trial in Glasgow of a Scots girl for the murder by arsenic of her lover, L'Angelier, a rather disreputable French-man who was possibly blackmailing her; a ver-dict of not proven was returned, and the mystery was never solved.

Mad Hatter's Tea Party Perpetual tea party in ALICE IN WONDERLAND, at which the Hatter, March Hare and Dormouse sit at a long table so that they can 'move round when things get used up'.

Madison Avenue New York centre since the 1940s for advertising and publicity firms, a street running between Fifth and Park Avenues, to both of which some of the leading firms have begun to move to escape the not entirely flatter-ing Madison Avenue 'image'. (James Madison, 4th President.)

Madison Square Garden New York indoor sta-dium famous primarily for boxing contests, but accommodating most sports; the 4th stadium of this name has been built over the Pennsylvania railway station, a long way away from Madison Square.

Mad Mullah Nickname of the Somali rebel leader, Mohammad Abdullah Hasan, who kept up an intermittent campaign against the British administration in Somaliland from 1900 to 1920. A year later he died in his bed, having escaped to Abyssinia.

Madonna lily White *Lilium candidum*, associated in medieval art with the Madonna.

Maeander River in Asia Minor, proverbial for its many windings – hence our word meander.

Maecenas Roman statesman and adviser of Octavian (Augustus), who was the patron of Virgil and Horace; hence any generous patron of literature. (Pronounced my-see'nas.)

Maenads See BACCHANTS. (Pronounced mee'n-adz.)

Maeve (Medb) Legendary Queen of Connacht who attacked Ulster (see CUCHULAIN). Disgusted with CONCHOBAR's treachery to DEIRDRE, many of his RED BRANCH KNIGHTS deserted to Maeve.

Mae West RAF slang for an inflatable life-jacket, named after a particularly buxom film star.

Mafeking, Relief of (May 1900). In the Boer War, the relief of a small British force under Baden-Powell after a siege of 7 months. London's riotous celebration of this event gave the word 'mafficking' to the language. (Town in northeast Cape Province. Now Mafikeng.)

Mafia (1282). Originally a secret society founded at the SICILIAN VESPERS to free Sicily from Angevin, later from other alien regimes. In the 19th century it sank to becoming a reserve of thugs who could be hired by landowners to bully and extort from the peasantry, and who specialized in blackmail, 'protection', vendetta and murder. Efforts to suppress it have failed and emigrants from 1889 spread the virus to the USA, where Sicilians replaced Jewish and Irish gangsters (by then rich enough to go straight) and are now, for similar reasons, yield-

ing place to the CRIME SYNDICATE, Blacks, Puerto Ricans and Latin Americans. Cover names such as COSA NOSTRA were preferred from the 1930s.

Maga, The Abbreviated nickname of BLACK-WOOD'S MAGAZINE. (Derived from the tradition that its founder used to refer to it, in his broad Scots, as 'ma maga-zine'.)

Magdalen See MARY MAGDALENE.

Magdalen College (1458). College of Oxford University. (Pronounced mawd'lin.)

Magdalenean culture Last of the PALAEOLITHIC cultures, perhaps lasting from 15,000 BC to about 8000 BC. Bone and antler carving was perfected, and cave painting brought to its highest level at LASCAUX by people who disappeared without trace at the end of the period. (La Madeleine, a rock shelter in the Dordogne, France.)

Magdalene College (1542). College of Cambridge University. (Pronounced mawd'lin.)

Magdalen Tower Tower of Magdalen College, Oxford, on the roof of which the college choir sings at dawn on 1 May.

Magee University College See QUEEN'S UNIVERSITY.

Magellanic Clouds Two nearest galaxies (extra-galactic nebulae), visible to the naked eye in the southern hemisphere. They are some 160,000 light-years away. (Named after Magellan, the first European to sail round South America.)

Magenta (1859). Napoleon III's costly defeat of the Austrians in Italy, where he had come to the aid of Cavour and the Piedmontese in the RISORGIMENTO. See SOLFERINO.

Maghreb, The Algeria, Morocco and Tunisia.

Magi, The Wise men from the east (i.e. Chaldean astrologers) who are described in Matthew 2 as coming guided by a star to Bethlehem to worship the infant Jesus. Later legend confused them with the THREE KINGS. See EPIPHANY. (Latin, 'wise men'; pronounced may'jy.)

Magic Circle, The Professional organization of British illusionists and conjurors, with its own club, theatre, library and museum.

Magic Flute, The (1791). Mozart's last opera, on a theme compounded of fairy-tale magic, broad comedy and hints of Masonic ideals (at a time when Freemasonry was banned). (German title, *Die Zauberflöte*.)

Maginot Line Defences on the German frontier built between the wars, behind which the French felt secure until the Germans easily out-flanked them in 1940. (André Maginot, Minister of War.)

Magna Graecia Cities of southern Italy colonized by the ancient Greeks, e.g. Tarentum (Taranto). Sybaris, Locri, Rhegium (Reggio). (Latin, 'Great Greece'.)

Magnet Library Name of the series of weekly instalments of the story of Billy Bunter, Hurree Jamset Singh and other fellow pupils at Grey-friars, written by 'Frank Richards', without break from 1908 to 1961.

Magnificat Virgin Mary's song of praise after the Annunciation, given in Luke 1:46–55, and sung in church services. Of its many musical settings, the most famous is Bach's *Magnificat in D* (1723) for orchestra, chorus and soloists. (First word of the Latin for 'My soul doth magnify the Lord'.)

Magnificent Ambersons, The (1918). Booth Tarkington's novel of snobbery in the American Midwest, on which Orson Welles based a famous film (1942).

Magnolia Shrubs and trees, named by Linnaeus after Pierre Magnol, a 16th-century professor of botany and medicine.

Magnolia State Nickname of Mississippi State.

Magnox reactor First generation of nuclear power-stations (also called 'Mark I gas-cooled'), used in the early nuclear power-stations at BERKELEY (being decommissioned in 1989), BRADWELL (both began to operate in 1962), HUNTERSTON A, TRAWSFYNYDD, HINKLEY POINT A, DUNGENESS A, SIZEWELL A, OLDBURY-ON-SEVERN and WYLFA.

Magnus, King Character in G. B. Shaw's play *The* APPLE CART, a King of England of the last quarter of the 20th century. He upsets the Social-ist government by his open criticisms of it and then threatens to abdicate in order to stand as candidate for the Royal Borough of Windsor. See PROTEUS.

Magpies, The Nickname of 2 football teams which play in black-and-white shirts – Notts County and Newcastle.

Magyar Language of Hungary, belonging to the FINNO-UGRIAN LANGUAGES. (Pronounced mag'yar or mod'yar.)

Mahabharata (500 BC). One of the 2 great Hindu epic poems (see also RAMAYANA), tell-ing of the deeds of the gods, including the Trinity of Brahma, Siva and Vishnu. It contains the BHAGAVAD-GITA. (Pronounced mah-hah-bah'ra-ta.)

Mahagonny (1929). Abbreviated title of *The Rise and Fall of the City of Mahagonny*, Brecht's opera on the Marxian but not very operatic theme of the inevitable collapse of capitalism, represented here by the US town of Mahagonny.

Mahatma (1) In Buddhism, a sage or adept who by asceticism and meditation has attained to exceptional wisdom and powers. (2) Honorific title bestowed on Gandhi. (Sanskrit, 'great-souled'.)

Mahayana The later of the 2 main forms of Buddhism, which appeared about the beginning of the Christian era; the 'Greater Vehicle' (of Truth) or northern Buddhism of Tibet, China, Japan, Korea. It is optimistic and positive, in contrast to HINAYANA; believers must try to train themselves to become BODHISATTVAS and so save all mankind. Mahayana Buddhists tend to take an active part in politics.

Mahdi Muslim Messiah, a title several times assumed, notably by the leader of the anti-foreign movement which swept the Sudan in 1883. (Arabic, 'the guided one'.)

Mahrattas Hindu Marathi-speaking race; they formed a strong military confederacy in west and central India which weakened MOGUL power. They founded states such as Indore and Gwalior, and now predominate in the state of MAHARASHTRA.

Maid Marian Character of the morris dance, who figures in the Robin Hood legend as his sweetheart. See SHERWOOD FOREST.

Maid of Orleans Name for St Joan of Arc, who raised the British siege of Orleans in 1429.

Maid of the Mountains, The (1917). Popular musical comedy which starred José Collins.

Maids of Honour, The Painting by Velázquez; see *Las* MENINAS.

Maigret, Inspector Strong-willed detective who first appeared in *The Crime of Inspector Maigret* (published in France 1930), by the Belgian-born writer Georges Simenon.

Main Sequence stars Type to which most stars, including the sun, belong; in them hydrogen is being converted into helium, and the end product is the RED GIANT. See also OBAFGKM.

Main Street (1920). Sinclair Lewis's novel recording the hopeless efforts of a doctor's wife to bring culture to the Midwest town of Gopher Prairie (based on the Minnesota birthplace of the author). (Main Street is the US equivalent of High Street.)

Maiolica (14th–17th centuries). Italian DELFT, decorated from the 16th century with elaborate historical, mythological and biblical scenes in brilliant colours; now rarely seen outside museums. See MAJOLICA. (Named after Spanish wares imported into Italy via Majorca.)

'Maison Tellier, Le' Short story of Maupassant's, a delightful account of an innocent Sunday outing in the country by the whole staff, including Madame, of a provincial brothel.

Maître d'hôtel (Cooking) Garnished with parsley, and perhaps with butter sauce and lemon juice.

Maja desnuda (1805). Goya's painting of the Duchess of Alba in the nude; there is a companion picture of her fully clothed, but the popular story that this was done to allay her husband's suspicions of their relationship does not stand up to examination – he had died several years earlier. Many authorities think the Duchess is not the person represented in the pictures. (Pronounced mah'ha dez-noo'da.)

Majlis Iranian National Assembly.

Majolica (1850). Confusing name (see MAIOLICA) given by Minton and other potteries to stoneware with opaque coloured glazes, used in making display and utilitarian wares, tiles, etc.

Major Barbara (1905). Bernard Shaw's play in which Major Barbara Undershaft of the Salvation Army conducts a verbal battle with her father (see UNDERSHAFT, ANDREW). She resigns from the Army rather than accept his donation of 'tainted money', but finds much truth in some of his views. 'I stood on the rock I thought eternal; and . . . it crumbled under me.'

Major-Generals, Rule of the (1654–5). Period during Cromwell's PROTECTORATE when the country was divided into 11 districts, each under a major-general, who enforced the strictest Puritan standards of conduct; the origin of English mistrust of standing armies.

Majuba, Battle of (1881). See SOUTH AFRICAN WARS.

Malachi Name of the last book of the Old Testament. (Malachi means messenger.)

Malade imaginaire, Le (1673). Molière's comedy in which 2 doctors batten on the hypochondriac Argon.

Málaga Strong sweet white wine from the Spanish province of that name, adjoining Gibraltar. (Pronounced mal'a-ga.)

Malaprop, Mrs Aunt and guardian of Lydia LANGUISH in Sheridan's *The* RIVALS, famous for her repeated and amusing misuse of the English language, as in 'Why, thou barbarous Vandyke!' Hence *malapropism*, a confusion of similar sounding words of very different meanings. (Name itself from French *mal à propos*, 'little to the point'.)

'Malaria' Jones See CAMPAGNA.

Malay Language of Malaysia, one of the chief MALAY–POLYNESIAN LANGUAGES. It has borrowed heavily from Sanskrit, Persian, Arabic and Tamil, and is an exceptionally easy language for a foreigner to learn. See also BAHASA INDONESIA; TAGALOG.

Malayalam DRAVIDIAN LANGUAGE, closely allied to TAMIL, spoken in Kerala. (Pronounced mal-a-yah'lam.)

Malay–Polynesian languages Widespread group of languages spoken from Madagascar to Hawaii and Easter Island. See MALAY; POLYNESIANS.

Malaysia, Federation of (1963). Formed from Malaya, Sarawak, Sabah and (until 1965 when it seceded) Singapore.

'Malbrouk s'en va-t-en guerre' Old French song about the wife of the warrior Malbrouk (not certainly Marlborough) awaiting his return from a war, in which he is killed. The tune resembles 'We won't go home till morning'. (French, 'Malbrouk goes off to war'.)

Malcolm See MACBETH.

Malcolm X Black American, born Malcolm Little, who was recruited in prison to the BLACK MUSLIMS, quarrelled with their leader, visited Africa and Mecca and became Malik el-Shabazz, a Muslim 'prophet', doubtfully converted to the view that all races form one great family. For this apostasy he was murdered in Harlem (1965) by Black Muslims.

Malden and Coombe Former municipal borough of Surrey, since 1965 part of the borough of KINGSTON UPON THAMES.

Maldon Scene of a 10th-century defeat of the men of Essex by Danish invaders, recounted in a contemporary poem, 'The Battle of Maldon'.

Malin sea area That lying between Northern Ireland and the Hebrides. (Malin Head, Northern Ireland.)

Malleus Maleficarum (1484). The Hammer of the Witches, a book published at Cologne by 2 professors of theology appointed by Pope Innocent VIII as Inquisitors into the practice of witchcraft (i.e. pre-Christian ritual). It constituted a guide for Inquisitors engaged in the wholesale persecution of 'witches' carried out by this Pope.

Mallory Park Motor-car and motor-cycle racing circuit near Hinckley, Leicestershire, at which international motor-cycle races are held in June and September.

Malmaison Château west of Paris where the Empress Josephine often stayed with Napoleon, and where she lived after their divorce. It now has a Napoleonic museum.

Malmsey Strong, sweet type of MADEIRA, much improved by age. Made from the Malvoisie grape originally grown in Greece and Crete, whence Henry the Navigator brought it to Madeira. 'False, fleeting, perjur'd Clarence' was, traditionally, drowned in a butt of it, 1478.

Malplaquet, Battle of (1709). Final defeat of the French in the War of the SPANISH SUCCESSION, by Marlborough and Prince Eugène of Savoy, won at heavy cost and while Anglo-French peace talks were in progress. (Village near Mons, in France; pronounced mal-plak-ay'.)

Malta dog Virulent Mediterranean stomach upset that can attack visitors to the island.

Malta, GC The island was awarded the George Cross (1942) for the bravery of its people under continual air attacks, a unique award to a community.

Malthusianism (1798). Theory that population increases in geometrical, food production only in arithmetical proportion, and that it is thus essential to keep down the rate of population increase by 'moral restraint', i.e. abstention from intercourse. (View put forward by the Rev. T. R. Malthus, economist.)

Malvern Festival (1929). Dramatic festival founded by Sir Barry Jackson in honour of Bernard Shaw, held annually until 1939 and revived occasionally since. Plays performed included not only the contemporary works of Shaw, Bridie, Priestley, etc. but revivals of 16th- and 17th-century classics.

Malvolio Pompous steward of Olivia in Shakespeare's TWELFTH NIGHT; BELCH and AGUECHEEK send him a forged letter which fools him into wearing cross-gartered yellow stockings ('a colour she abhors') to win his mistress's heart.

Mamelukes Originally the Sultan of Egypt's bodyguard, formed of Circassian slaves. They rapidly seized power, and ruled Egypt from 1254 to 1517; thereafter they held subordinate high office under the Turkish viceroys. In 1811 the KHEDIVE Mehemet Ali lured them to Cairo and had them massacred. (Arabic, 'slaves'; pronounced mam'i-looks.)

Mammon (1) Aramaic word for 'riches' used in Matthew 6:24 ('Ye cannot serve God and mammon') and Luke 16:9 ('mammon of unrighteousness'). (2) Mistakenly used by medieval Christians as the personification of greed and avarice, the god of the worldly.

Man and Superman (1905). Play in which Bernard Shaw introduced to the British public the ideas of CREATIVE EVOLUTION and the LIFE FORCE, and of the SUPERMAN, put into the mouth of John Tanner, who in the dream of Act III becomes Don Juan, representing the Superman he can never himself be.

Manassa Mauler, The Nickname of Jack Dempsey, world heavyweight boxing champion, 1919–26. (Born at Manassa, Colorado.)

Manchester Gaiety, The (1908–20). Theatre where Miss HORNIMAN set up the first modern repertory company in Britain, and where the MANCHESTER SCHOOL OF DRAMATISTS was launched.

Manchester Guardian (1821). Daily newspaper, renamed The *Guardian* in 1959.

Manchester School Advocates of FREE TRADE and *laissez-faire* led by John Bright and Richard Cobden, who in the 1840s were MPs respectively for Manchester and Stockport.

Manchester school of dramatists Playwrights launched into fame by Miss Horniman at the MANCHESTER GAIETY; they included Stanley Houghton (*Hindle Wakes*), Harold Brighouse (*Hobson's Choice*) and Alan Monkhouse.

Manchu Dynasty (Manzhu dynasty) Another name for the CH'ING DYNASTY.

Manchukuo (1932–45). Puppet state set up in MANCHURIA by the Japanese, under the ex-Emperor Pu-yi, and turned by them into a major industrial area which supplied them with armaments.

Manchu language One of the ALTAIC LANGUAGES, under the CH'ING DYNASTY the official language of China, now spoken only in parts of northern Mongolia. See MANCHUS.

Manchuria Industrial area of China, in the north-east now broken up into the provinces of Heilongjiang (capital Harbin), Liaoning (capital Shenyang) and Jilin; other parts were incorporated into the Chinese province of Hebei and the autonomous republic of Inner Mongolia.

Manchus TARTAR people first mentioned in Chinese records of the 10th century. They conquered MANCHURIA and then all China; see CH'ING DYNASTY.

Mancini case (1941). The trial of Tony Mancini, who killed a man in self-defence at a London club. His counsel failed to plead that the death was the unpremeditated result of sudden affray, and Mancini was hanged. Another Tony Mancini was involved in the BRIGHTON TRUNK MURDERS.

Mancun: Abbreviation for (Bishop) of Manchester. See next entry.

Mancunian Of Manchester. (From *Mancunium*, Latin name of the city.)

Mandarins, The (1954). Simone de Beauvoir's account, in fictional form, of her life among the Paris Existentialists, including Sartre, Camus and Koestler.

Mandates Commission (1919–45). Organization set up by the League of Nations to supervise the administration of ex-German colonies (Tanganyika, South-West Africa, Cameroons, Togoland, New Guinea) and ex-Turkish possessions (Iraq, Syria, Palestine, Transjordan). It was succeeded by the UN TRUSTEESHIP COUNCIL.

M. & B. 693 Sulphapyridine, one of the earliest sulpha drugs, discovered at May & Baker's pharmaceutical laboratories in 1938, and used as a cure for pneumonia, gonorrhoea, etc.

Mandelbaum Gate Until 1967 the control point for traffic between the Jordanian and Israeli sections of the then divided city of Jerusalem.

Mandingo Group of languages which predominate throughout most of the region formerly known as FRENCH WEST AFRICA.

Man for All Seasons, A Robert Bolt's radio play (1954), stage play (1961) and film (1966) in which an ironic Sir Thomas More tries warily to keep the overpowering Henry VIII at a distance but refuses to compromise his religious principles to save himself from the executioner's block.

Man Friday (1) 'Savage' whom ROBINSON CRUSOE rescues from death at the hands of cannibals and who becomes his general factotum. (2) Any faithful, versatile right-hand man. (So named because Crusoe found him on a Friday.)

Manhattan Island and borough which forms the central core of New York City; among its better-known features are Central Park, Greenwich Village, Harlem, Wall Street, Broadway, Fifth and Park Avenues, Washington Square and Times Square.

Manichaeism Dualist religion founded by the Persian Mani, derived from Zoroastrianism and with Buddhist elements. Mani claimed to be the latest of a succession of teachers (Abraham, Zoroaster, Jesus); he was crucified by orthodox Zoroastrians (AD 275). The Perfect or Elect lived a secluded life of extreme asceticism, while those who lived in the world were called Hearers or Believers. The religion spread to India and China, and survived at Samarkand until the 14th century; it was the inspiration of the ALBIGENSIANS. CATHARI and BOGOMILS. (*Manichaeus*, Latinized form of Mani.)

Man in the Iron Mask Man imprisoned by Louis XIV for 40 years at various places, including the Île Sainte-Marguerite off Cannes. When transferred to a new prison he wore a black velvet (not iron) mask. In Dumas's novel he is said to be the son of Cardinal Mazzini and the king's mother, but there are many other theories as to his identity.

Mannerheim Line (1939). Finnish defence system on the Russian border. (Field Marshal Mannerheim, later President of Finland.)

Mannerism (1530–1600). Period in Italian art following the HIGH RENAISSANCE which, under the impact of the Reformation and Counter-Reformation, abandoned the serenity of Raphael for the distorted, elongated human figures of, e.g. El Greco, and deliberately broke the rules established by the Renaissance.

Man of Aran (1934). Robert Flaherty's documentary film about the small fishing community on the Isles of Aran off the Galway coast, Ireland.

Man of Destiny Name for Napoleon Bonaparte.

Manon Lescaut (1731). (1) Title of Abbé Prévost's novel, in which the faithless luxury-loving Manon ruins the career of the Chevalier des Grieux, a brilliant student who is infatuated by her. On her being transported to America, des Grieux follows her, fights a duel with the governor of Louisiana's son and then escapes to the desert, where Manon dies in his arms. (2) Puccini's opera (1893) based on (1); the story was also used in Massenet's opera *Manon* (1884).

'Man on the Flying Trapeze, The' Song, of which there are many modern versions, derived from 'The Flying Trapeze' (1868) by the English singer and comedian, George Leybourne, music by Alfred Lee. It became a favourite with circus clowns and also inspired William Saroyan's fantasy story, 'The Daring Young Man on the Flying Trapeze' (1934).

Mansfield, Katherine Pen-name of Kathleen Beauchamp (1888–1923), later Mrs Middleton Murry, a New Zealand writer of highly polished short stories of great sensitivity.

Mansfield judgement (1774). The court ruling in the case of the slave, Somerset, by which an English lawyer, Granville Sharp, succeeded in establishing his contention that slavery was illegal in England.

Mansfield Park (1814). Jane Austen's novel on the theme of the differing values prevailing in London and the country, as revealed to the heroine, Fanny Price, by the BERTRAM FAMILY, the Crawfords and Aunt NORRIS.

Mansion House (18th century). Official residence of the Lord Mayor of London, at the Bank; it contains a banqueting room called the Egyptian Hall.

Mantoux test Test for tuberculosis.

Man Who Never Was, The (1955). Film based on Ewen Montagu's account of a real event during the war. In April 1943, MI6 used a submarine to deposit the corpse of a Marine officer on the Spanish coast; on him were documents indicating that the Allies were to invade not Sicily but Sardinia. German reinforcements were accordingly rushed to Sardinia. Before the story was declassified, Duff Cooper incorporated it in his novel, *Operation Heartbreak* (1950).

Man Who Was Thursday, The (1908). G. K. Chesterton's fantasy about anarchists and spies, with a Catholic moral.

Manx People, and the CELTIC LANGUAGE, of the Isle of Man.

Manzanilla FINO sherry, paler, drier and lighter in body than AMONTILLADO.

Mapai Israeli Labour Party, based on the rural agricultural worker, and moderate in outlook. See next entry.

Mapam Israeli United Workers' Party, a left-wing Socialist party of urban workers. See previous entry.

Maple-leaf flag, The Canada's national flag which replaced the Canadian red ensign in 1965; the design is a red maple leaf on a broad white ground between 2 vertical red borders.

'Maple Leaf Forever, The' (1867). Canadian song, beginning:'In days of yore / From Britain's shore.'

Maraschino Sweet liqueur, originally Dalmatian, distilled from bitter black cherries. (Italian *amaro* 'bitter'.)

Marathas Alternative spelling of MAHRATIAS.

Marathi Indo-European language of the MAHRATTAS, and the principal language of MAHARASHTRA.

Marathon (490 BC). (1) Decisive battle in which the Greeks under Miltiades defeated the much larger Persian army sent by Darius the Great. (2) Twenty-six-mile race, so named because the news of (1) was brought to Athens from the field of battle by a messenger who ran this distance and dropped dead on arrival. (A coastal plain north of Athens.)

Marat/Sade (1964). Convenient abbreviation for *The Persecution and Assassination of Marat as Performed by the Inmates of Charenton under the Direction of the Marquis de Sade*, by Peter Weiss.

Marble Arch London arch, designed by John Nash for Buckingham Palace (1820), removed to the north-east corner of Hyde Park (1851) and now marooned there on a traffic island, inconspicuously housing a police post with, near by, SPEAKERS' CORNER to keep them busy and the site of TYBURN TREE to remind them of times when capital punishment was a popular entertainment.

Marchand de vin (Cooking) Flavoured with claret.

March brown Large ephemerid fly of rocky rivers, taken by trout. (Appears in March; brown in colour.)

Marcher Lords Feudal lords who held the troubled Scottish and Welsh border areas; in the 13th century called Earls of March (the Mortimers on the Welsh, and the Dunbars on the Scottish border). (Germanic word *marko*, boundary; whence margrave, marquess, etc.)

'Marchioness, The' See SWIVELLER, DICK.

March on Rome (1922). Fanciful name given in Italian Fascist mythology to Mussolini's journey to Rome (by train) at the King's invitation, and the subsequent arrival of thousands of Fascisti by bus, lorry and cart; the birth of Fascist Italy.

March through Georgia (1864). March of the

Marconi affair, The

Federal troops under Gen. William T. Sherman through Georgia to capture the Confederate arsenal at Atlanta, and on to the sea, ruthlessly burning down towns on their way. See AMERICAN CIVIL WAR.

Marconi affair, The (1912). Purchase by the Chancellor of the Exchequer, David Lloyd George, on the advice of the Attorney-General, Rufus Isaacs (Lord Reading), of shares worth £2,000 in the Marconi Co. at a time when the Post Office were negotiating a contract with it. The Liberal majority of a committee of inquiry acquitted both men of indiscretion, the Conservative members dissenting.

Marco Polo Bridge incident (July 1937). The Japanese-fabricated incident which provided their pretext for the renewal of the Sino-Japanese War that had begun with the MUKDEN INCIDENT. Also called the Peking incident.

Mardi Gras French name for Shrove Tuesday, the last day of the Carnival which precedes Lent in France and other Catholic countries. (French, 'fat Tuesday'.)

Marengo (1800). Victory of Napoleon (as First Consul) over the Austrians. (Italian village in Piedmont near Alessandria.)

Mareth Line Rommel's defence line on the southern frontier of Tunisia, originally built by the French to keep the Italians out; breached by Montgomery's 8th Army in March 1943.

Margaret In Goethe's poem, the ignorant young girl seduced by FAUST; she drowns their child and, in the dungeon scene at the end of Part 1, though awaiting execution, refuses Faust's offer to rescue her, preferring to be saved through suffering. Also called Gretchen, the German diminutive of Margaret.

Margot Familiar name of Mrs H. H. Asquith (later Lady Oxford and Asquith).

Maria Marten of the Red Barn Name of several Victorian melodramas based on a sensational murder at Polstead, near Ipswich, which caught the popular imagination in 1827.

Mariana of the Moated Grange (1) Girl who is

rejected by Angelo in Shakespeare's *Measure for Measure*. (2) Subject of 2 poems of Tennyson's suggested by (1). (3) The title of a famous painting by Millais (1851).

Marianne Young woman, dressed in red, white and blue, who symbolizes the French Republic. (Named after a secret society formed during the SECOND EMPIRE to restore the Republic.)

Marian Persecution Wholesale burning of Protestants (including Cranmer, Ridley and Latimer) as heretics, under Queen Mary I (1553–8).

Maria Theresa dollar Coin (the Austrian thaler), originally 90% silver and weighing an ounce, which became the chief unit of currency in Abyssinia until banned in 1946. Still minted today (dated 1780), it is widely used from Saudi Arabia to West Africa, as raw material for jewellery, as a unit of weight, or strung on necklaces. 'Thaler' became 'dollar' in pronunciation.

Mariolatry Undue preference to the worship of the Virgin MARY over that of Christ. (Pronounced mair-i-ol'a-tri.)

Marius the Epicurean (1885). Walter Pater's mannered novel about the development of a Roman of the 2nd century AD who, after sampling the various philosophies of his time, is finally attracted to Christianity.

Mark, King In Arthurian legend, a King of Cornwall who loses his wife ISEULT to TRISTRAM. In some versions he is a tragic and sympathetic figure, in others a poltroon.

Markham, Mrs Pen-name of a Mrs Penrose who produced a celebrated period-flavoured history of England for children in 1823.

Marlborough House (1710). Wren house built for the 1st Duchess of Marlborough, later the home of Queen Mary, and since 1962 a Commonwealth Centre where conferences are held. It is open to the public.

Marlow, Capt. Narrator in several of Joseph Conrad's novels and stories, including LORD JIM and *Chance*, who assembles the evidence about the events recorded and tries to analyse the motives of the participants: this forms the basis of Conrad's oblique impressionistic approach, with the author aloof and sceptical in the background.

Marlow, Philip Detective in Raymond Chandler's studies of American decadence, one of the earliest of the new-style hard-boiled private eyes of the 1930s.

Marly Château, of which nothing survives, designed by Mansart for Louis XIV and built in a park west of Paris.

Marly horses Famous pair of Numidian horses made in bronze by W. Coustou (1677–1746) for the Marly Palace at Versailles; now at the Place de la Concorde entrance to the Champs-Élysées, Paris.

Marmion (1808). Walter Scott's poem of Flodden Field and the manifold love intrigues of Marmion. But ' "Charge, Chester, charge! On, Stanley, on!" Were the last words of Marmion.'

Marne, Battles of the (1) *First Marne* (September 1914), a decisive battle in which Anglo-French forces saved Paris by driving the Germans back to the Aisne. (2) *Second Marne* (July 1918). In which French and US troops again drove the Germans back on the Aisne; together with Haig's attack at Amiens in August, it formed the final decisive counter-offensive of World War I.

Marriage à la Mode (1745). Hogarth's masterpiece, a series of satirical oil-paintings (from which engravings were made) in which the canvas is crowded with detailed figures whose gestures enact a drama in dumb-show (as he explained).

Marriage at Cana, The Painting by Veronese ostensibly of the CANA MARRIAGE FEAST but, apart from the figure of Christ, a 16th-century Venetian banqueting scene; now in the Dresden gallery.

Marriage of Figaro, The (1786). Mozart's opera based on the second part of Beaumarchais's play (see BARBER OF SEVILLE). Count Almaviva, now tiring of his wife Rosina, foolishly tries to seduce her maid Susanna. Since the latter is engaged to FIGARO he is, of course, outwitted.

Mars Roman god equivalent to the Greek ARES.

Marsala Sicilian light-coloured wine resembling sherry. (Port from which shipped; pronounced mar-sah'la.)

'Marseillaise, The' (1792). French national anthem, sung by a Marseille volunteer unit as they marched into Paris shortly before the Republic was proclaimed. It begins: 'Allons, enfants de la patrie. / Le jour de gloire est arrivé.'

Marshall Aid US aid given under ERP (the European Recovery Programme or Marshall Plan). (Proposed in 1947 by the US Secretary of State, General Marshall.)

Marshall Fields (1865). American department store founded in Chicago by Marshall Field; see FIELD ENTERPRISES.

Marshalsea Debtors' prison in Southwark, London, which was as notorious as the FLEET, and is described in Dickens's *Little Dorrit*. Closed in 1887.

Marston Moor (1644). Biggest battle of the ENGLISH CIVIL WAR, in which Cromwell's newly raised cavalry decisively defeated Prince Rupert; it led to the loss of the north of England to Charles I's cause. (Moor near York.)

Marsupialia One of the 3 subclasses of mammals; the young are born in an undeveloped state and usually complete their development in a pouch (*marsupium*). The subclass includes the kangaroos, wallabies, wombats, koalas and Tasmanian devils of Australia, and the opossums of America.

Martello towers Small round watch-towers built at various points on the coasts of south-east England when Napoleon threatened invasion. Many still survive, thanks to massive construction. (Inaccurately named after a similar tower captured at Cape Mortella, Corsica.)

Martha and Mary Two sisters of LAZARUS; when they were entertaining Jesus. Mary was intent on getting spiritual instruction from him, Martha was fussing about getting him a proper meal.

Martian invasion panic (1938). (USA) Result of Orson Welles's little joke, when he broadcast the gist of H. G. Wells's *War of the Worlds* as a news bulletin. People are said to have died of shock as he described the landing in America of men from Mars.

Martin Chuzzlewit (1844). Dickens's novel in which Martin is sent out into the world by his rich grandfather more or less penniless in the hope that hard experience might cure his self-ishness. He goes to America (of which Dickens paints a highly unflattering and unconvincing picture) with Mark TAPLEY, and comes back a sadder and wiser man. See also PECKSNIFF; Sairey GAMP.

Martinmas 11 November, the feast of St Martin, in the Middle Ages the day when livestock were slaughtered and salted for the winter supply of meat. See ST MARTIN'S SUMMER.

Martinware (1873–1915). Individual pieces of salt-glaze stoneware grotesqueries in a wide range of subdued colours, made by the 4 Martin brothers of Southall, London; each piece is signed and dated. The most usual form is an owl-like bird with a detachable head; mask jugs and many kinds of vase decorated with strange fish, birds or dragons were also made.

Marxism Main thesis was that humankind developed politically through three stages, leading to the dictatorship of the proletariat and the withering away of the state and the emergence of a classless society. Karl Heinrich Marx's (1818–83) best-known work is *Das Kapital*. He is buried in Highgate Cemetery, north London.

Marxism–Leninism Theories arising from the adaptation of 19th-century MARXISM to 20th-century facts, and in particular to the problems of governing Russia; it includes belief in 'SOCIALISM IN ONE COUNTRY' and peaceful coexistence with countries under different social systems, in contrast to TROTSKYISM. (Lenin, leader of the OCTOBER REVOLUTION.)

Mary, The Virgin Mother of Jesus (Matt. 1:18), present at the Crucifixion, and last mentioned in Acts 1:14; venerated particularly in the Roman Catholic Church, as the Blessed Virgin Mary, the Madonna, the Mother of God, Our Lady,

Mater Dolorosa and under many other names. The title 'Mother of God' originated at the Council of EPHESUS. She was represented in art as wearing a blue robe. See also MARIOLATRY; IMMACULATE CONCEPTION.

Mary Barton (1848). Mrs Gaskell's novel depicting the hard lot of workers in the Manchester cotton-mills.

Mary Celeste (1892) US ship found abandoned in North Atlantic with evidence of very recent occupation and no indication of a reason for her abandonment. The mystery was never solved.

Marylebone Former London metropolitan borough, since 1965 part of the borough of WESTMINSTER (City of). (Usual abbreviation of St Marylebone; pronounced mar'ė-lė-bėn, or mar'ė-bėn.)

Mary Magdalene Woman of Magdala from whom Jesus cast 7 devils (Luke 8:2); identified in Christian tradition with the prostitute of Luke 7:37, who anointed Jesus' feet; also mentioned as present at the Crucifixion and as the person to whom Christ first appeared after it (John 20:1–18); the patron saint of penitents. (Pronounced mag-da-lee'ni; also spelt Magdalen, pronounced mag'dal-en.)

Mary Poppins Children's book by P. L. Travers about an unusual nannie who is blown through the door of No. 17 Cherry Tree Lane before the post has even been advertised. She promises to stay to look after the children '. . . till the wind changes'. Also made into a successful film.

Mary Rose Remains of a warship of the time of Henry VIII which sank off Portsmouth in 1545. They were raised in 1982 and are displayed at Portsmouth. The artefacts recovered are of considerable interest.

Mary Rose (1920). J. M. Barrie's play about Mary's 'Island that Likes to be Visited'.

Masai African race of mixed Hamitic stock living in south Kenya and north Tanzania. Originally a nomadic cattle people, they are now settling to agriculture. (Pronounced ma-sy'.)

Maskelyne & Devant shows Conjuring and illusionist shows started in London by Maskelyne (1873), partnered from 1905 by Devant. He built St George's Hall (near Broadcasting House), where shows were held from 1904 to 1933.

Mason, Perry Lawyer-detective who first appeared (1933) in a novel by the American writer E. S. Gardner, and who became more widely known to the world through a TV series.

Mason–Dixon Line (1767). Originally the settlement of a boundary dispute between Pennsylvania and Maryland, which came to be regarded as the boundary between free and slave (or northern and southern) states. (Names of 2 British surveyors who demarcated it.)

Masonic Societies See FREEMASONS.

Masons, Worshipful Company of (1677). LIVERY COMPANY.

Mason's Ironstone (1813). Tough highly decorated earthenware, of which octagonal jugs with snake handles are the commonest examples.

Masorah (6th–9th centuries AD). Jewish commentary on the Old Testament text meticulously compiled by the Masoretes (biblical scholars) from oral traditions. (Pronounced ma-sawr'a.)

Masquerade (1950). Floribunda rose producing semi-double flowers which change from yellow to pink and then to red.

Massachusetts Institute of Technology See MIT.

Massacre of St Bartholomew See ST BARTHOLOMEW MASSACRE.

Massacre of the Innocents When Herod the Great, King of the Jews, heard that a child had been born in Bethlehem destined also to be King of the Jews, he ordered the massacre of all male children born there at that time; but Jesus escaped (Matt 2:16). See HOLY INNOCENTS.

Massacre of the Innocents, The Painting (see previous entry) by PEASANT BRUEGHEL, thought by some to be a veiled reference to Spanish oppression of the Netherlands, although the painter appears to have been on good terms with the regime.

Masséna (Cooking) With artichoke hearts and bone-marrow.

Massilia Roman name of Marseilles.

Mass Observation (1937). London society founded by the sociologists Tom Harrisson and Charles Madge to gather through teams of observers objective facts about the British way of life and thought; these were then as far as possible reduced to statistical form. It was the first of a flood of surveys and opinion polls to be let loose on Britain.

Master Builder, The (1892). Ibsen's play about the architect Solness who kills himself in his attempt to achieve the impossible. The symbolism of the new house he has built tends to overburden the play.

Master Mariners, Honourable Company of (1930). LIVERY COMPANY whose membership is confined to master mariners; it promotes education and research in matters related to their profession.

Master of Ballantrae, The (1889). R. L. Stevenson's study of brotherly hate in the days of the FORTY-FIVE. The unscrupulous Master, James Durrie, fights for the Young Pretender, flees abroad and is presumed dead. His younger brother, who fought on the other side, succeeds to the title and marries the unloving Alison, who had been intended for James. James returns to plague both of them for the rest of the novel.

Master of the Rolls One of the ex-officio judges of the Court of Appeal, and in practice its president; he ranks next below the Lord Chief Justice.

Masters, The (1934). Leading US international golf tournament; entry is restricted to those invited by the Augusta National Golf Club, Georgia, who ask the leading golfers of the year. The tournament is played on Bobby Jones's course at Augusta. See also DUNLOP MASTERS.

Mastersingers, The (1868). Wagner's only comic opera, about a song-contest in which the prize is a girl who, since this is comedy, is won by the right man after various machinations. (German title, *Die Meistersinger von Nürnberg*.)

Masurian Lakes, Battle of the (February 1915). 'Winter battle' in World War I in which Hindenburg and Mackensen drove the Russians out of Galicia, Lithuania and Courland, and went on to take Warsaw.

Mata Hari Alias of Margaret Zelle, a Dutch-born woman who posed as a Javanese and spied for Germany from 1905 until her execution in France in 1917.

Matapan, Battle of Cape (March 1941). British naval victory over an Italian force off southern Greece.

Match King, The See KREUGER CRASH.

Mater et Magistra (1961). Pope John XXIII's encyclical on social questions which, in contrast to RERUM NOVARUM, gave qualified approval to some forms of Socialism. (Latin, 'Mother and Teacher'.)

Mathias See BELLS, THE.

Mathis der Maler (1934). Hindemith's opera based on the life of the 16th-century German painter Mathias Grünewald, who was caught up in a peasants' revolt in the days of Luther. (German, 'Mathias the painter'.)

Matteotti murder (1924). Murder of a Socialist opponent by Fascists. Mussolini was forced by public reaction to have them arrested in 1926, but they were given only light sentences.

Matthiola Generic name for stocks, named after Piero Antonio Matthioli, an Italian physician and botanist.

Matty, Miss Best-loved of the innocent but indomitable spinsters in CRANFORD.

Maud (1855). Tennyson's poem in which a man describes how he wooed the daughter of the squire who had ruined his family, killed his brother in a duel, and fled the country. It contains the familiar lyric 'Come into the garden, Maud'.

Maud Committee (1940–41). Code name of a UK committee under Sir George Thomson which finally recommended the development of a uranium bomb.

Mau Mau Kikuyu nationalist secret society, formed in Kenya possibly in 1944, not known to the authorities until 1950, or to the world till 1952, when it murdered its first European victim. Members were bound by oaths of degrading bestiality and freely murdered white settlers and Kikuyu opponents alike, in a terrorist campaign that lasted till 1960. (Kikuyu, 'get out! get out!'.)

Maundy Gregory case (1933). Trial of J. Maundy Gregory, charged with trafficking in honours.

Maundy money Specially minted coins, distributed in white leather purses by the Royal Almoner at Westminster Abbey and at cathedrals around Britain, as a substitute for the ceremony described under MAUNDY THURSDAY.

Maundy Thursday Day before Good Friday, on which popes and kings washed the feet of the poor in commemoration of Christ's washing the feet of the Apostles (John 13:14); see previous entry. (Corruption of French and Latin words for 'command', i.e. Christ's command to love one another. (John 13:34.)

Maurice debate (May 1918). Commons debate on whether Lloyd George had misled the House as to the army's strength in France. The official opposition under Asquith divided the House against the government, and lost the debate together with what prestige they had left. (Sir Frederick Maurice, director of military operations, who made the accusation.)

Mauritshuis (1644). Dutch Royal Museum of Painting at The Hague.

Maurya dynasty (320–184 BC). Indian military dynasty which, under the enlightened Asoka, united most of India and Afghanistan, adopting Buddhism as the national religion.

Mauser Name of the Prussian army rifle of 1871 and subsequent models which were sold to the armies of the world; also from 1898 of automatic pistols. (German firm at Oberndorf am Neckar; pronounced mow'-zėr.)

Mausoleum, The (352 BC). One of the seven wonders of the world, the tomb of Mausolus, King of Caria, built at the capital, Halicarnassus (now Budrum, in Turkey) by his widow.

Max Gate Name of a house near Dorchester built in 1883 by the writer Thomas Hardy, who lived there for most of the latter half of his long life.

Maxim's Paris restaurant and night-club which became a household name through a song in the MERRY WIDOW, 'Da geh' ich zu Maxim'. It is still going strong.

Mayan civilization That which flourished in Guatemala from the 3rd century AD and later in Yucatán, where the Mayans were joined by the TOLTECS. They invented a pictorial script in the 4th century, and had an accurate calendar reflecting a deep knowledge of astronomy. They were in an advanced state of decline by the time of the Spanish conquest. The AZTECS inherited their culture. (Pronounced mah'yan.)

Mayan language American Indian language of the Mayan and AZTEC civilizations (see previous entry).

Mayday English name of the international radio-telephone SOS signal used by ships and aircraft. (Anglicized form of French *m'aidez*, 'help me'.)

May Economy Committee (1931). Government committee which recommended drastic pay cuts for civil servants and the forces, and in the dole (unemployment pay), implemented by Philip Snowden. This led to the INVERGORDON MUTINY and the collapse of the second Labour ministry of Ramsay MacDonald.

Mayerling affair (1889). Austrian Crown Prince Rudolf, only son of Emperor Franz Josef, together with his mistress were found dead at the prince's hunting lodge at Mayerling, near Vienna, after the Emperor had ordered him to break off the liaison. Finding the lodge surrounded by police, Rudolf shot her and committed suicide. (This is the most generally accepted version of what happened; but it has been questioned by some.)

Mayflower Ship, of 180 tons, in which the PILGRIM FATHERS sailed.

Mayflower Compact, The Agreement to set up a government, made by the Pilgrim Fathers at a meeting in the *Mayflower*'s cabin on 11 November 1620.

Mayflower II (1957). Replica of the *Mayflower*, which sailed from Plymouth, Devon to Plymouth, Mass.

Mayhew Author's name used for his major work, *London Labour and the London Poor* (1851–62), humane and methodical sociological surveys among the street vendors and vagrants of London, many of whom emerge as vividly portrayed 'characters'.

Maynooth (1795). Theological training college in Co. Kildare, near Dublin, which provides a 7-year course for Roman Catholic priests.

Mayo Clinic (1889). Large clinic at Rochester, Minnesota, USA, attended by patients from all over the world; it is staffed by a voluntary association of doctors, surgeons and others engaged in medical research. The clinic comprises several hospitals, and hotels for out-patients. See also MAYO FOUNDATION. (Founded by W. W. Mayo and his 2 sons.)

Mayo Foundation In full, the Mayo Foundation for Medical Education and Research, a very large graduate medical school at Rochester, Minnesota, USA, and part of the University of Minnesota. (See MAYO CLINIC.)

Mayor of Casterbridge, The (1886). Wessex novel by Thomas Hardy about Michael Henchard who, when drunk at a fair, sells his wife and baby to a sailor. He becomes Mayor of CASTERBRIDGE; his wife, and later the sailor, return, the story of his wife's sale comes out, and he dies after experiencing every kind of misfortune and frustration.

May-week At Cambridge University a period (now a fortnight in June) when the end of the academic year is celebrated with boat races, college balls, etc.

Maze, The Prison in County Antrim, Northern Ireland, where many terrorists were confined from 1968 and the scene of a hunger strike in 1981.

MCC (18th century). Initials used for the Marylebone Cricket Club, London, the controlling body of English cricket, which made its headquarters at LORD's from 1814.

Meals-on-Wheels Service, usually organized by the WRVS, which brings hot meals to the home of aged and bedridden people who live by themselves.

Means Test Inquiry into a person's private income to determine eligibility for a state or local authority benefit – a political issue ever since the MacDonald government proposed (1933) that unemployment benefit should be graded according to need. The issue has been revived whenever it is suggested that such benefits should not be granted irrespective of need.

Measure for Measure (1604). Late comedy of Shakespeare's, showing signs of disillusion; the happy ending, in which the 6 main characters are paired off in marriage after many frustrations, is contrived and artificial.

Meccano Trade name of an ingenious toy construction set introduced early in the century, consisting of perforated metal strips, nuts and bolts, wheels, pulleys, etc. enabling children to build up an infinite variety of trucks, cranes, etc. to their own design. (Pronounced me-kahn'o.)

Mecklenburg Old German province on the Baltic, capital Schwerin, reinstated as a province in 1990.

Medea Legendary sorceress, daughter of the king of Colchis who helped JASON win the Golden Fleece on his promising to marry her. To effect their escape she killed her brother, and on arrival at Jason's home she arranged the murder of Pelias. When Jason deserted her she sent his new bride a robe which burnt her to death, and also killed Jason's children. She then tried to poison Theseus; and someone who disliked Medea added that she retired finally to Asia, to become the ancestress of the Medes. (Pronounced me-dee'a.)

Medes Ancient people of the Persian–Mesopotamian borders, whose capital was Ecbatana. In 550 BC their Persian subjects revolted and the Persian Cyrus the Great founded the kingdom of the Medes and Persians. The 'law of the Medes and Persians' is one which 'altereth not' (Dan. 6:8).

Medical Research Council (1913). Body, formerly the Medical Research Committee, set up by Act of Parliament, financed by government and from private sources. It has under it numerous specialized research units working in various hospitals, universities and medical institutions.

Medicare (1966). (USA) First cautious approach to an American national health service, restricted by strong professional lobbying to those over 65. The same name is used in Canada for a scheme introduced in 1968.

Medici, The Italian family, originally bankers, which ruled Florence and Tuscany (1434–1737), provided 2 Popes, and the wives of Henry II (Catherine) and Henry IV (Marie) of France. The first to rule Florence, Cosimo, and his grandson Lorenzo the Magnificent (1449–92) were great patrons of literature and the arts. (Pronounced med'i-chi.)

Medici 'Mercury', The (1580). Remarkable sculpture by the Fleming, Giovanni da Bologna, who settled in Florence; now in the Bargello Museum, Florence.

Medici prints Coloured prints of Old Masters and modern paintings, produced by the Medici Galleries, London.

Mediterranean climate Technical term in geography for a type of climate characterized by dry sunny summers and mild wet winters, usually found between latitudes 30° and 40° north or south of the equator, especially on the western side of a continent. Examples are central coastal California, central Chile, southern Australia, Cape Town, and the Mediterranean itself.

Mediterranean race See IBERIANS.

Medmenham, Monks of See HELLFIRE CLUB.

Médoc Claret from the communes of Pauillac (notably from the Châteaux Latour, Lafite and Mouton-Rothschild), Margaux, St Julien and St Estèphe.

Medusa (Greek legend) One of the Gorgons, whose gaze turned the beholder to stone, even after PERSEUS had cut off her head, thus providing him with a secret weapon of which he made great use. (Pronounced me-dew'za.)

Meech Lake accord Series of constitutional amendments designed to persuade the province of Quebec to sign the Canadian Constitution. These were to be ratified by 23 June 1990 but three provinces, Manitoba, Newfoundland and New Brunswick, opposed the accord.

Meek, Private Character in G. B. Shaw's *Too True to be Good* said to be modelled on Lawrence of Arabia.

Mehitabel See ARCHY AND MEHITABEL.

Meiji Restoration (1868). Restoration of the power of the Japanese Emperor, in abeyance during the TOKUGAWA SHOGUNATE. The Meiji period is the name given to the reign of Mutsuhito (1868–1912), during which Japan became a world power, absorbing the knowledge and techniques of the West.

Mein Kampf (1924). Hitler's political testament, written while he was in prison; in it he gave clear warning of his plans, but as he was then an obscure agitator few took notice of it at the time. (German, 'my struggle'.)

Meissen (1710). Porcelain of the first European firm to make true hard-paste porcelain. The early pieces are among the most highly prized (and priced) of all European porcelain, especially the COMMEDIA DELL' ARTE figures modelled by Kändler (1737–44); but in the 19th century quality declined as production rose. (Village near Dresden, Saxony; see DRESDEN PORCELAIN.)

Meistersinger See MASTERSINGERS.

Melanesians Negroid races of the Western Pacific, including the people of Papua New Guinea, Fiji, the Solomons, New Hebrides and New Caledonia. (Greek, 'black islanders'.)

Melba toast Narrow slices of very thin toast. (Named after Dame Nellie Melba, Australian soprano.)

Melbourne Cup (1860). Australia's classic weight-for-age flat-race, run at Flemington, Melbourne, in November, over a course of 2 miles.

Melchior One of the THREE KINGS, traditionally a King of Nubia. (Pronounced mel'ki-or.)

Mellors See LADY CHATTERLEY'S LOVER.

Melpomene The Greek muse of tragedy. (Pronounced mel-pom'en-i.)

Melton Mowbray Town north-east of Leicester famous for (1) pork pies, (2) Stilton cheese, (3) its countryside hunted by 3 leading packs, the Quorn, Belvoir and Cottesmore.

Melungeons Small dark-skinned community living on a mountain ridge (Newman's Ridge) in Hancock County, north Tennessee, USA, whose origin has long puzzled anthropologists. It has been suggested that they descend from the ROANOKE ADVENTURE settlers, or from marooned Portuguese sailors (*melungo* is said to be Afro-Portuguese for 'shipmate'). Also called Ridgemanites.

Memel Now Klaipéda, city of Lithuanian SSR.

Memento mori Object or picture to remind the onlooker of death, for example, a skull often included by artists in their paintings, or seen on tombs or memorials.

Memoirs of a Fox-Hunting Man See SHERSTON'S PROGRESS.

Memoirs of a Midget (1921). Walter De La Mare's delicate and poetic fantasy of a world seen through the eyes of a midget heroine.

Memphis Capital of Ancient Egypt during the OLD KINGDOM, situated at the apex of the Nile Delta on the opposite (right) bank of the river to GIZA and SAKKARA. To its north lay HELIOPOLIS.

Menai Bridge (1826). Thomas Telford's 1,000-ft suspension road bridge between Anglesey and mainland Gwynedd. Near by is Robert Stephenson's tubular iron Britannia Railway Bridge (1850), badly damaged by fire 1970, reopened 1972 for single-line traffic.

Mendelism (1860s). A theory of heredity which attracted no attention when published but was accidentally rediscovered in 1900 and is now the accepted basis of genetics. The idea of dominant and recessive characteristics played a part in it. (Gregor Mendel, Abbot of Brünn, who derived his theory from breeding experiments with sweet peas.)

Menelaus in Greek legend, a King of Sparta, brother of AGAMEMNON, husband of HELEN OF TROY.

Meninas, Las (1656). One of the most famous of paintings by Velázquez, depicting the young Infanta of Spain with her maids of honour and her dwarfs, the painter at his easel, the King and Queen reflected in a mirror, and other figures; now in the Prado, Madrid. (English title, 'The Maids of Honour'.)

Menin Gate (1927). Memorial at Ypres to the nearly 55,000 British soldiers gazetted as missing in the 3 battles of Ypres in World War I.

Mennonites Dutch and Swiss ANABAPTISTS, who founded communities in Russia and North America.

Men of Good Will (1932–47). Name given by Jules Romains to a continuous novel in 27 volumes, depicting many aspects of life in France in the period 1908–33. (French title, *Les Hommes de bonne volonté*.)

'Men of Harlech' Welsh war-song about fighting the Saxons; there are several differing versions of the words in English.

Men of the Trees (1922). Society formed to encourage the protection, preservation and planting of trees throughout the world, and to educate the public regarding the advantages of afforestation.

Mensa (1946). International organization to 'gather together people who share similar views and understandings' now with 60,000 members world-wide. All members have an IQ of at least 148. (Latin for mind, *mens*.)

Mensheviks Minority group of the Social Democrats who in 1903 split into the Mensheviks and Bolsheviks. Led by Martov, they held that the Russian Revolution should be directed not by the workers but by the bourgeois. They were permanently split in 1914 between those who wanted to rally to the fatherland and those who opposed any participation in the war. (Russian, 'minority'.)

Mentor Wise old friend of ODYSSEUS; in the *Odyssey*, when TELEMACHUS is searching for his father, Athene goes with him in the guise of Mentor as counsellor and guide.

Men, Women and Dogs (1943). Collection of James Thurber's drawings on his favourite themes of domineering wives driving their menfolk to the bottle and to the placid company of conspicuously non-pedigree dogs.

Mephistopheles Cynical, malicious Devil to whom FAUST sells his soul. (Traditionally a corruption of Greek words standing for 'hating the light'; sometimes abbreviated to Mephisto; pronounced mef-i-stof'e-leez.)

Mercantile System Doctrine that government should regulate overseas trade, boosting exports and limiting imports, in order to amass gold and silver reserves, regarded as the only true wealth. Colonies, such as North America, should be used as sources of raw materials and as markets for British products, local industry being discouraged. Adam Smith first demonstrated the fallacies in this then generally accepted theory, and the advantages of a *laissez-faire* policy.

Mercator projection Gerhardus Mercator, the Latinized form of Gerhard Kremer (1512–94), a Flemish mathematician, cartographer and geographer; the projection which bears his name was used in his map of 1568.

Mercedes (1901). Name given to German DAIMLER cars to overcome French sales-resistance to German products. Mercedes introduced the pressed steel chassis and honeycomb radiator. A 1905 model reached 109 m.p.h. (Christian name of Daimler's daughter.)

Mercers, Worshipful Company of (1393). First in precedence of the LIVERY COMPANIES, originally a guild of clothes-hawkers, later of silk merchants; among the beneficiaries of its great wealth are St Paul's School and Gresham College.

Merchant of Venice, The (1596). Shakespeare's comedy; see PORTIA; SHYLOCK.

Merchant Taylors' Public school which moved to Moor Park, near Northwood, Middlesex, in 1932. The northern branch of the school is at Great Crosby, near Liverpool.

Merchant Taylors, Worshipful Company of (1327). One of the oldest of the LIVERY COMPANIES, originally a guild of makers of armour lining and men's clothing, later of general merchants. Large sums are devoted to education, particularly to MERCHANT TAYLORS' School.

Mercia Kingdom of central England, founded by the Angles in the 6th century.

Mercury Roman god equivalent to the Greek HERMES.

Mercutio Romeo's mettlesome friend in Shakespeare's *Romeo and Juliet*, a man of sharp wit, killed by Tybalt in a duel.

Meredith, We're in Edwardian catch-phrase derived from one of FRED KARNO'S music-hall sketches about bailiffs trying to get into a debtor's house.

Merion, Diana Heroine of DIANA OF THE CROSSWAYS.

Merit, Order of Order instituted in 1902 by King Edward VII, limited in number to 24 men and women of eminence; membership is designated by the letters OM. Florence Nightingale was the first woman member, 1907.

Merlin (1) Historically, possibly a bard at Arthur's court; (2) in Arthurian legend, a magician and seer sired by a fiend but baptised; see LADY OF THE LAKE.

Mermaid Tavern Famous 17-century tavern in Cheapside, London, frequented by Ralegh, Beaumont, Fletcher, Donne, Ben Jonson and possibly Shakespeare.

Mermaid Theatre (1959). City of London's first theatre for 300 years, built at Puddle Dock, Blackfriars, on the site of a bombed-out warehouse by the actor-producer Bernard Miles to revive Elizabethan traditions.

Merovingians Dynasty founded by Clovis which ruled the Frankish kingdom (France) 481–752; succeeded by the CAROLINGIANS. (Named after Clovis's grandfather.)

Merrilies, Meg Queen of the gypsies and a seer in Scott's GUY MANNERING, who recognizes Harry Bertram on his return from India and helps him to defeat his enemies.

Merrill's Marauders US equivalent of the CHINDITS, operating in Burma in 1944. (Brig.-Gen. F. D. Merrill.)

Merrimac and *Monitor* Two American ships which during the AMERICAN CIVIL WAR fought at Hampton Roads (1862) in the first action between ironclads. The Federal *Monitor* was the first ship to have a revolving armoured gun-turret (with two 11-in guns). The action was indecisive, and no one was killed.

Merry Andrew A clown. (Origin unknown.)

Merry Millers, The Nickname of the Rotherham football team, which plays at Millmoor Ground.

Merry Monarch Name for Charles II.

Merry Widow, The (1905). Franz Lehár's ever-popular operetta about the dashing young diplomat, Danilo.

Merry Wives of Windsor, The (1601). Shakespeare's comedy of the penurious FALSTAFF's efforts to court both Mrs Ford and Mrs Page, who put him in a dirty-linen basket and throw him in a ditch. Meanwhile Page's daughter Anne foils the advances of Dr Caius and Slender and runs off with Fenton.

Mers el-Kebir (July 1940). French naval base at Oran, Algeria, where the British were forced to put the French fleet out of action to prevent its passing into German hands.

Mersey Sound, The (1961–4). POP MUSIC popularized by the BEATLES at the Cavern, Liverpool, and by subsequent Pop groups brought to London from Liverpool. Also called the Liverpool sound.

Merton London borough since 1965 consisting

of the former boroughs of Wimbledon and Mitcham and the urban district of Merton–Morden; headquarters at Wimbledon.

Merton Professor Holder of one of 2 chairs at Oxford: English Literature, English Language and Literature.

Mesembryanthemum Genus of succulent plants including the Livingstone daisy (*M. criniflorum*) and the ice plant (*M. crystallinum*).

Mesolithic Age (Middle Stone Age) Transitional period between the Palaeolithic and Neolithic Ages when with the end of the Ice Age the steppe and tundra developed into forest and man turned from dependence on herds of reindeer, etc. to fishing and collecting shellfish.

Mesopotamia Ancient name of the area now occupied by Iraq, and formerly by Akkad, Sumer, Assyria and Babylonia; generally regarded as the cradle of Western civilization. (Greek, 'between rivers', i.e. the Tigris and Euphrates.)

Mesozoic Era Geological era lasting from about 240 to 70 million years ago, divided into the TRIASSIC, JURASSIC and CRETACEOUS PERIODS. The characteristic fossil is the ammonite (a marine cephalopod, ancestor of Nautilus). The climate was mild; it was the age of the great reptiles (dinosaurs, etc.) which finally yielded place to mammals, and of ferns and evergreens which yielded to flowering plants. (Greek, 'middle life', i.e. middle era between Palaeozoic and Cenozoic.)

Messerschmitt Name of manufacturer (abbreviated to Me) given to a series of German aircraft, including the Me-262, the first jet fighter to go into action (1944) and the Me-109, the mainstay of the Luftwaffe in World War II.

Messiah (1) Saviour and king who, according to Jewish belief from the 2nd century BC onwards, would appear when God had gathered his Chosen People into a new kingdom; the dead would rise again to share in its glories, and God would judge their oppressors. The Muslim equivalent is the MAHDI. (2) Jesus who, in Christian belief, was the promised Messiah of (1). (3) Hence, any liberator from oppression. (Hebrew, 'anointed', of which the Greek translation was *Christos*, 'the Christ'.)

Messiah, The (1742). Handel's oratorio on the life of Christ, using words from the Bible, mainly from Old Testament prophecy, and containing such famous airs as 'He shall feed his flock', 'I know that my Redeemer liveth', and the Hallelujah chorus. It has become almost an institution in Britain, sung wherever enough people can be found to sing it.

Met., The (USA) Used as an abbreviation for the New York METROPOLITAN OPERA HOUSE.

Metamorphoses (1st century BC). Ovid's version in hexameter verse of Greek and Roman myths involving magical changes of form.

Metaphysical poets Group of 17th-century poets, led by John Donne and including Vaughan, Marvell and George Herbert; criticized by Dr Johnson for using complex imagery, above the heads of the common reader, drawn from science, philosophy, the arts and theology, and for their innovations in metre. (The name was first used by Dryden.)

Method acting System taught at the New York Actors' Studio and developed from the STANISLAVSKY SYSTEM.

Methodism (1739). Revivalist movement within the Church of England started by John and Charles Wesley; it broke away from the Church in 1795 and subsequently split into various sects (Wesleyan, Primitive, United, Calvinist, Independent), some of which later reunited (see next entry). George Whitefield, an original co-founder, seceded to form the COUNTESS OF HUNTINGDON'S CONNECTION. (Originally 'Methodists' was the name given to the Wesleys' religious club at Oxford University, so named for its methodical rules of fasting and prayer.)

Methodist Church (in Britain) Formed by the re-union of the Wesleyan, Primitive and United Methodist Churches in 1932. See previous entry.

Methuselah (1) Son of Enoch and grandfather of Noah; he died aged 969 according to Genesis 5:27. (2) Measure, the equivalent of 8 bottles of champagne.

Metric system There was no uniformity in French

weights and measures before the Revolution of 1789, but in 1790 the Constituent Assembly ordered the preparation of a single system of weights and measures.

Metroland Area served by the London Metropolitan District Railway, a nickname given added currency by Evelyn Waugh's fictional Lady Metroland, formerly Mrs Beste-Chetwynde.

Metropolitan Opera House (New York City) Premier opera house of USA, reopened (1966) in a new building in LINCOLN CENTER, replacing the 'Old Met.' at Broadway and 39th Street.

Metro-Vic Moscow trial (1933). Trial of 6 British engineers of the Metropolitan-Vickers Electrical Co., charged by Soviet Russia with espionage and sabotage.

Metternich System See HOLY ALLIANCE.

Meudon, The Curate of Name for Rabelais.

Meursault See BURGUNDY.

Mexican War (1846–8). War which arose from a frontier incident on the US border. As a result, Mexico ceded New Mexico and California to USA and relinquished claims to Utah and Texas.

Meynell Fox-hunting pack with kennels at Sudbury, which hunts country in Derbyshire and Staffordshire. (Pronounced men'l.)

Mezzogiorno, Il Italian name for Italy south of Naples, until recently neglected and impoverished. ('Noon', 'south'.)

MGB (1945–54). Soviet Ministry of State Security, the secret plain-clothes police employed in internal security, counter-intelligence, and espionage throughout the world; renamed KGB.

MGM Initials used for Metro-Goldwyn-Mayer, a US cinema company formed from Metro Pictures and Goldwyn Pictures by Marcus Loew, managed by L. B. Mayer. Sam Goldwyn resigned before it was formed.

Micawber, Mr Wilkins DAVID COPPERFIELD'S penurious landlord, who lives in eternal hope that 'something will turn up', as indeed it does.

Michaelmas 29 September, the feast of the archangel Michael, an English quarter-day, formerly celebrated by eating Michaelmas goose.

Michaelmas term University and legal autumn term beginning after MICHAELMAS.

Michaelson–Morley experiment (1887). A demonstration that the velocity of light was a universal constant for all observers irrespective of their motion; it was the starting-point for EINSTEIN'S THEORIES.

Michael X Pseudonym of Michael Abdul Malik, a West Indian BLACK POWER leader in Britain, sentenced to 12 months' imprisonment in 1967 for stirring up racial hatred. The *Sunday Times* was fined £5,000 for its version of his earlier career.

Mick (1) In Ulster, an Irish Roman Catholic. (2) Person of Irish descent.

Mickey Finn (Slang, originally US) Any doctored drink intended to make the victim unconscious. (Originally used of 'knock-out drops' composed of liquid chloral and alcohol.)

Mickey Mouse Hero of the first animated sound cartoon, made by Walt Disney (1928); his squeaky voice soon became known throughout the world.

Micks, The Nickname of The IRISH GUARDS.

Micronesians Mixed Polynesian races inhabiting the groups of small islands north of Melanesia in the Pacific, including the Marianas, Marshalls, Carolines and Gilberts. (Greek, 'small-island people'.)

Midas In Greek legend, a King of Phrygia to whom Dionysus granted his request that everything he touched might turn to gold; but as 'everything' covered food and drink, he had cause speedily to regret his request. (Pronounced my'das.)

Middle Ages Period from the deposition of the last Western Roman Emperor, Romulus Augustulus, in AD 476, to the RENAISSANCE of the 14th century.

Middle Earth The world of the HOBBITS, where the SHIRE is.

Middle East Eurocentric term increasingly used after 1921 to include what had been called the NEAR EAST (except the Balkans), plus Iraq, Persia, North and North-East Africa, etc.

Middle English Form of English spoken from the 11th to the 14th centuries; by the end of this period the south-east Midlands and London dialect used by Chaucer had displaced the Wessex dialect of OLD ENGLISH; it is the basis of the spoken and written form now called Received Standard (or the Queen's) English.

Middle Kingdom (Ancient Egypt) Period of some 400 years from about 2100 BC, the second period of Egyptian greatness, when the pharaohs of the 11th–13th Dynasties ruled at THEBES.

Middlemarch (1872). George Eliot's masterly, partly autobiographical, study of the Midlands society of her time, and the impact of new values brought by the Industrial Revolution on 2 young idealists, Dorothea BROOKE and Dr LYDGATE.

Middlesex County west and north of London, abolished in 1965 and absorbed into Greater London.

Middle Temple See INNS OF COURT.

Middleton Cup (1922). Inter-county bowls championship (originally the John Bull Cup, 1911).

Midgard In Scandinavian mythology the abode of man, joined to ASGARD by a rainbow bridge.

Midlothian campaigns (1879 and 1880). Gladstone's electoral campaigns which brought him back to Parliament and to his second term as Prime Minister.

Midnight Steeplechase, The Legendary cross-country steeplechase allegedly ridden in nightshirts from the cavalry barracks, Ipswich, to Nacton Church, in 1803. The only evidence for it is a famous painting by Henry Alken (1839). Also called the Moonlight Steeplechase. (Cross-country races with a church steeple as objective are recorded in Ireland as early as 1752.)

Midnight Sun, Land of the Scandinavia north of the Arctic Circle, where the sun is visible night and day from mid-May to late July.

Midsummer Night's Dream, A (1596). (1) Shakespeare's gentle comedy of 2 pairs of lovers in the woods near Athens, much bemused by PUCK's magic spells, as is TITANIA, who falls in love with the ass-headed BOTTOM, leading actor in the 'tedious-brief scene' of PYRAMUS AND THISBE. (2) Mendelssohn's famous overture (1826) on these themes.

Midway Island, Battle of (June 1942). Naval engagement fought mainly by carrier-borne aircraft, which ended in US victory over the Japanese, a decisive turning-point in the war in the Pacific.

Midwich Cuckoos, The (1957). One of John Wyndham's science-fiction novels, from which the film *The Village of the Damned* was made. The matrons of Midwich find that they have mysteriously produced a generation of yellow-eyed children, human in looks but utterly alien and terrifying.

Mif Abbreviation for 'Milk In First'. According to the Mitford family, arbiters of U AND NON-U, putting milk in the cup before the tea is a terrible thing to do, and the sort of people who did it were dubbed Mif.

MI-5 (1909). British Security Service, engaged in detecting, watching and foiling spies, saboteurs and subversive elements in Britain (see MI-6). When an arrest is necessary the case is transferred to the SPECIAL BRANCH of Scotland Yard. MI-5 is responsible to the Home Secretary but also has direct access to the Prime Minister.

MiG Name of a series of Russian fighter aircraft, including the outstanding MiG-15 (1948) jet plane used in the Korean War against US SABREJETS; the supersonic MiG-19 (1955), and the highly specialized MiG-21 fighter (1959). (Initials of Mikoyan-Gurevich.)

Mighty Atom, The (1896). Best-selling novel by Marie Corelli.

Mikado, The (1885). Gilbert and Sullivan opera. The Mikado orders his Lord High Executioner,

Ko-Ko, to execute somebody – anybody – or forfeit office and life; Pooh-Bah, Lord High Everything Else, is reluctant to volunteer, although assured that 'criminals who are cut in two can scarcely feel the fatal steel'; the Mikado's son, Nanki-Poo, offers himself, but Ko-Ko has to confess that he cannot bring himself to kill anyone, and bursts into tears. All, however, is eventually settled to the Mikado's satisfaction.

Mildenhall Treasure (1942). Hoard of 4th-century Roman silver tableware of great beauty and in excellent condition, found buried at West Row, near Mildenhall, Suffolk.

Milestones (1912). Comedy by Arnold Bennett and Edward Knoblock about resistance to new ideas through 3 generations. The pioneer of iron ships who is frustrated in Act 1 himself opposes steel ships in Act 2.

Milk Race Round Britain Bicycle Race, called the Tour of Britain until the Milk Marketing Board took over sponsorship (1957). An international amateur, 1,100-mile race held in May/June. See TOUR DE FRANCE.

Milk round Employers, particularly large companies, tour universities to explain job prospects and recruit those about to graduate.

Milky Way, The Luminous band of stars and nebulae which encircles the sky; it is a cross-section of the flattened plane in which are concentrated most of the stars of the spiral galaxy to which our solar system belongs. The diameter of this incomprehensibly vast galaxy is 100,000 light-years (600,000 million million miles); yet it is only one of perhaps 1,000 million such galaxies ('extra-galactic nebulae'), of which the MAGELLANIC CLOUDS and the galaxy in ANDROMEDA are visible examples. ('Galactic' comes from a Greek word meaning milky.)

Millamant Elegant witty flirt of Congreve's *The* WAY OF THE WORLD.

Mille Miglia (1927–57). Italian road race for sports cars, run from Brescia to Cremona and back. (Italian, 'thousand miles'; pronounced mil′li meel′ya.)

Miller, The Affectionate name for the horse GOLDEN MILLER.

Miller's Tale, The In the CANTERBURY TALES, a typical medieval story of cuckoldry, in which a young lodger persuades his landlord to prepare for a second Flood, while he makes free with the wife.

Millfield (1935). Coeducational school founded at Street, Somerset, by R. J. O. Meyer who believed that everybody has some gift and it was up to the teaching profession to find and develop it. He did not believe in rigid age grouping and many pupils took GCE O-levels before joining the senior school. Noted for training many sports personalities but inability at sports was no handicap. It has a teacher–pupil ratio of one to five or six.

Million, Le (1931). One of René Clair's early comedy films.

Millionaires' Row Nickname for Kensington Palace Gardens, especially the part overlooking Palace Green, on the west boundary of Kensington Gardens. Formerly noted as the sanctuary of the very rich, it is now largely occupied by embassies.

Mill on the Floss, The (1860). George Eliot's novel about Maggie and her beloved brother Tom Tulliver who disapproves of the men she loves. The two are reconciled only at the moment of final disaster, when both are drowned in a flood at the mill. See TULLIVER AUNTS.

Mills & Boon (1908). Publishers identified with romantic fiction since the 1920s and publishing over 500 titles a year.

Milner kindergarten Nickname for the band of brilliant young men who worked under Viscount Milner when he was Governor of the Transvaal and Orange Free State after the Boer War; they included the future editor of *The Times* (Geoffrey Dawson), John Buchan, Lord Lothian and Lionel Curtis.

Milner report (1921). Report which recommended the grant of full independence to Egypt. (Alfred, 1st Viscount Milner; see previous entry.)

Milton Keynes (1967). NEW TOWN, in north

Buckinghamshire, between Wolverton, Stony Stratford and Bletchley.

Milton Road Cambridge University sports ground; see FENNER'S.

Milton's Cottage House at Chalfont St Giles, Buckinghamshire, where Milton finished *Paradise Lost* during the Great Plague; now preserved as a museum.

Milton Work point count Method of valuing the hand used in most Bridge systems: A, K, Q, J Count 4, 3, 2, 1, respectively.

Mimi See *La* BOHÈME.

Mimulus Genus name of the musks, including common musk and monkey musk.

Mincing Lane Street in the City of London long associated with the tea trade, and later also with other commodities.

Minerva Roman goddess equivalent to the Greek ATHENE.

Ming dynasty (1368–1644). Chinese dynasty which ended the Mongol rule of the YÜAN DYNASTY. In art the main features were blue and white porcelain, tall vases with brightly coloured floral designs, and lacquer ware; in the 17th century porcelain specifically designed for the European market was first exported. The capital was moved from Nanking back to Peking in 1421. The CH'ING DYNASTY followed.

Mini (1) (1959) Car designed by Issigonis and manufactured by Austin/Morris with a transverse engine and front-wheel drive. (2) Short skirt.

Miniver, Mrs Fictional compiler of a diary showing the reactions of an upper-middle-class English housewife to events of the period from Munich to the opening weeks of World War II; published as *Mrs Miniver* (1939) and written by Jan Struther, pen-name of Joyce Anstruther.

Minnehaha See HIAWATHA.

Minoan civilization Bronze Age civilization of Crete from 2500 BC until the destruction of the capital, Knossos, by fire, or possibly by MYCENAEANS, in 1400 BC. The Minoans may have originally come from the Anatolian mainland. (Named after MINOS.)

Minorca Medium-sized breed of domestic fowl, kept as an egg-producer.

Minos In Greek legend, a King of Crete; see MINOTAUR; PASIPHAË. After his death he became the judge of the dead.

Minotaur In Greek legend the offspring of PASIPHAË, half man half bull, hidden by MINOS in the Labyrinth built by DAEDALUS at KNOSSOS; it was fed by the sacrifice of Athenian youths and maidens. THESEUS slew it. The legend was based on bull-sports at Knossos, where paintings have been found of young men somersaulting over the horns of charging bulls. (Minos + Greek *tauros*, 'bull'.)

Mint, The Royal Mint, formerly on Tower Hill, London, now at Llantrisant, Wales, where coins of the realm and medals are made.

Mint, The (1955). T. E. Lawrence's diary of his life as Aircraftman Ross of the RAF. It failed to live up to advance publicity about its revelations of character and motives.

Minton (1793). Firm making earthenware and bone china, much influenced by Sèvres in early years. It produced PARIAN WARE in the 1840s, Solon's extravagantly elaborate *pâte-sur-pâte* pieces from 1870 (they now fetch high prices), and a wide range of other products, e.g. MAJOLICA.

Minutemen Name given in the American War of Independence to the militia, as holding themselves ready at a minute's notice; especially applied to those who fought at LEXINGTON.

'Minute Waltz, The' Piece by Chopin (which cannot be played in a minute) that attained a wider popularity in the movie *A Song to Remember* (1945) about the composer's life, and was also the basis of 'Castle of Dreams', a fox-trot.

Miocene Epoch Third subdivision of the TERTIARY PERIOD, lasting from about 25 to 10 million years ago. PROCONSUL belongs to this epoch. The Alps were formed. See also KENYA-PITHECUS AFRICANUS. (Greek, 'less of the modern', i.e. fewer of the modern forms of life are found.)

Mirabeau (Cooking). With anchovies and olives.

Mirabell See *The* WAY OF THE WORLD.

Mirage Name of a wide range of French military aircraft, including the Mirage strategic bomber, which carries atomic bombs.

Miranda In Shakespeare's *The Tempest*, PROS-PERO's daughter.

Misanthrope, Le (1666). Molière's comedy in which Alceste, disgusted with social convention and hypocrisy, resolves to act with complete honesty, with disastrous results.

Misérables, Les (1862). Victor Hugo's story of Valjean, who steals a loaf of bread and goes to the galleys for 19 years. He then begins a new life, succeeds in business, becomes mayor, but is recognized by the police and again arrested. There are famous chapters on the Battle of Waterloo and Valjean's flight through the sewers of Paris.

Miserere (1) 51st Psalm, beginning 'Have mercy upon me, O God', one of the Penitential Psalms. (2) Shelving projection on the underside of a hinged seat in a choir stall, which when turned up gave support to one standing, frequently curiously carved (sometimes called a misericord).

Mishnah Oral instruction in the Jewish law, dating from the 2nd or 3rd centuries AD, later included in the TALMUD. (Hebrew, 'oral instruction'.)

MI-6 (1911). British Secret Intelligence Service (SIS), engaged in spying abroad, often through disaffected nationals. The Foreign Secretary deals with Parliamentary questions about its work. Its US equivalent is the CIA. See MI-5.

Missa Solemnis (1823). Beethoven's Mass in D, written for choir and full orchestra, primarily for performance in church. (Latin, 'Solemn Mass', i.e. High Mass in which the celebrant is assisted by a deacon and sub-deacon.)

Mission of Charity (1950). Founded in Calcutta by an Albanian, Mother Teresa; the 600 nuns, of various nationalities, live in poverty and, with tens of thousands of co-workers (not predominantly Catholic or even Christian), now work among the poor, drug addicts and alcoholics in Sri Lanka, Africa, Venezuela, Rome, Melbourne, London, etc.

Miss Lonelyhearts (1933). American novel by Nathanael West about a man who writes a newspaper 'lonely hearts' column. He becomes involved with a troubled couple and is accidentally killed.

Miss Muffet Character in the nursery rhyme, said to be Patience Muffet, daughter of a 16th-century entomologist who studied spiders.

Missolonghi Site on the west coast of Greece of a monument to Lord Byron, who died there while working for Greek independence. (Traditional spelling of modern Mesolongion.)

'Miss Otis' Cole Porter's song written for *Bricktop*: 'Miss Otis regrets she's unable to lunch today . . . / She's sorry to be delayed, / But last evening down lovers' lane she strayed . . .'

Missouri Compromise (1820). Attempt to solve the controversy about whether slavery should be permitted in newly admitted states of USA; it fixed latitude 36°30′ as the line between free and slave states, but Southern states resented this as an interference with states' rights.

Mr Bolfry (1943). James Bridie's witty play in which the Devil (in the guise of the Rev. Mr Bolfry) descends on a Scottish manse and gives everyone a lot to think about, especially after the umbrella he had left behind makes its own way after him.

Mr Britling Sees it Through (1916). H. G. Wells's novel of how the coming of the war affected the life of a secluded Essex village, and especially of Mr Britling, whose son is killed in it.

Mr Deeds Goes to Town (1936). Frank Capra's film of the unsophisticated hero of the back-woods (played by Gary Cooper), who out-manoeuvres the city slickers trying to cheat him of a large legacy.

Mr Five Per Cent Nickname for Calouste Gulbenkian (see GULBENKIAN FOUNDATION), who retained a 5% interest in the Iraq Petroleum Co, which he founded.

Mr F.'s aunt In Dickens's *Little Dorrit*, an elderly dotty widow supported by Mrs F. (Finching), and given to remarking apropos of nothing: 'There's milestones on the Dover Road.'

Mister Johnson (1939). Joyce Cary's novel about an African clerk whose imagination outruns his education. Believing his own lies, he finishes up on the scaffold. The story is set in Nigeria, where the author briefly served in the administrative service.

Mr Midshipman Easy (1836). One of the best-known of Capt. Marryat's novels of British naval life.

Mr Norris Changes Trains (1935). Christopher Isherwood's novel of a corrupt, amoral Berlin between the wars. Mr Norris, pretending to be a Communist, is selling secrets to Nazis and foreign-ers.

Mr Perrin and Mr Traill (1911). Hugh Wal-pole's study of rivalry and hate in a public-school senior common room.

Mr Polly H. G. Wells's novel; see POLLY, ALFRED.

'**Mr Sludge the Medium**' (1864). Poem in Robert Browning's *Dramatis Personae*, in which the fraudulent medium (representing an Ameri-can, Daniel Dunglas Home, whose seances Browning had attended) makes his defence, putting some of the blame on the public's cre-dulity.

Mrs Beeton Abbreviated title for *Mrs Beeton's Cookery Book* (1861), a standard work on the subject, constantly revised and still published today, when the recipes no longer tend to start with 'Take a dozen eggs'.

Mrs Dale's Diary Radio serial; at times 5 million housewives dropped everything at 4.30 to listen to the latest domestic triumphs and tribulations of Dr and Mrs Dale, her mother (Mrs Freeman) and her daughter (Gwen).

Mrs Grundy Personification of the fear of what the neighbours will say, who developed into a symbol of English prudery. (A character in an 18th-century play, who never appears but is often invoked, in terms of 'What will Mrs Grundy say, or think?')

Mrs Mopp Office-cleaner in ITMA, with the signa-ture line, 'Can I do you naow, sir?'

Mrs Tiggy-Winkle (1905). Washerwoman-hedgehog complete with apron, heroine of *The Tale of Mrs Tiggy-Winkle* by Beatrix Potter.

Mrs Warren's Profession (1898). Bernard Shaw's play in which Mrs Warren confesses to her daughter Vivie that her education has been paid for by her mother's takings as a prostitute; the girl's sympathetic understanding lasts only until she realizes that her mother has not ceased to ply her profession.

Mistinguett Stage name of a star of the Paris music-halls, whose legs were insured for a fabu-lous sum. Her real name was Jeanne Bourgeois (1873–1956).

Mistress of the Robes Senior of the Ladies-in-Waiting, who attends the Queen on all state occasions.

MIT (1861). Initials commonly used for the Massachusetts Institute of Technology, which moved from Boston to Cambridge, Massa-chusetts, in 1916. It gives higher education in all branches of engineering, architecture, the humanities and social science, but it is chiefly famed for its many research laboratories, uniquely well equipped with a nuclear reactor, supersonic wind-tunnel, servo-mechanisms and electronic devices of all kinds. It has built up a world reputation as a research centre.

Mit brennender Sorge Pope Pius XI's encyclical, written in German and addressed to the German nation, condemning anti-Semitism under Nazi rule. (German, 'with bitter sorrow'.)

Mitcham Former municipal borough of Surrey, since 1965 part of the borough of MERTON.

Mithraism Worship of the Persian bull-god (later sun-god) Mithras; this mystery religion became popular among the Roman legionaries who spread it over Europe, where it became a powerful rival to Christianity, to which it bore some resemblance. Remains of a temple of Mithras were unearthed in the City of London in 1954.

Mitre, The (1) Fleet Street inn near Fetter Lane, London, frequented by Dr Johnson. (2) Fleet Street inn west of (1), frequented by Ben Jonson and Pepys.

Mitsubishi Group of Japanese firms ranking second to the MITSUI GROUP in its share of foreign trade. Its main interests are aircraft, cars, shipbuilding, machinery and metal mining.

Mitsui group (1947). Group of Japanese firms, re-formed after the war, which accounts for over 10% of the country's overseas trade; they build power-stations and dams in various parts of the world, and are also engaged in mining and shipping.

Mitteleuropa See PAN-GERMANISM. (Pronounced mit-el-oir-ohp'a.)

Mitty, Walter Character in one of James Thurber's short stories who retreats from the realities of henpecked domesticity into daydreams of heroic deeds.

Mizpah Place where Jacob and Laban came to an agreement; the name meant 'watch-tower' and Laban explains it in Genesis 31:49, as symbolizing 'The Lord watch between me and thee, when we are absent one from another', i.e. 'may he guard my daughters from your ill-treatment'. But taken literally, and out of context, the name is engraved on rings by lovesick spouses.

M-number In astronomy, the Messier number given in a short list of star clusters, often used instead of the NGC number.

Moabite Stone, The (9th century BC). A monument put up by a King of Moab, bearing the earliest-known Phoenician inscription; now in the Louvre.

Möbius loop Model used in topology (the branch of mathematics which studies such subjects as the geometry of knots). A strip of paper is twisted and the ends glued together. If it is twisted through 180° there is only one edge; if through 360°, and cut down the middle, 2 interlocked loops result. It has other unexpected properties to delight mathematicians.

Moby-Dick (1851). Novel by Herman Melville which combines a detailed description of every aspect of whaling with an allegorical story of Captain Ahab's obsessive hunt for the white whale, Moby-Dick.

Mocha ware (1784–1914). Pottery mugs and jugs for domestic and public-house use, with bright coloured bands on a brown ground. All have feathery tree-like designs, automatically traced out by the spreading of a drop of a preparation called mocha tea applied to the slip while still wet. (Pronounced mok'a).

Mock Turtle, The Lachrymose character in ALICE IN WONDERLAND who teaches Alice the Lobster Quadrille to a song with the chorus: 'Will you, won't you, will you, won't you, will you join the dance?'

Model T First mass-produced car, made by Henry Ford from 1908.

Moderations See MODS.

Moderator See PRESBYTERIANISM.

Modern Comedy, A (1929). Second trilogy of the FORSYTE SAGA, consisting of *The White Monkey*, *The Silver Spoon* and *Swan Song*. They tell the story of Fleur, daughter of Soames Forsyte and his second wife. There was also a third trilogy, *End of the Chapter* (1933).

Modern Greats Final BA examination at Oxford University in philosophy, politics and economics (PPE). See GREATS.

Modern Love (1862). George Meredith's irregular sonnet sequence on the tragic decline of a married couple's love, based on his own experiences during his first marriage.

Modern Pentathlon Annual world championship

in which individuals and teams compete in all of 5 events: cross-country riding and running, épée fencing, pistol shooting and swimming. See MODERN TETRATHLON; PENTATHLON. (Greek, '5 contests'.)

Modern Tetrathlon MODERN PENTATHLON without the riding contest. (Greek, '4 contests'.)

Modern Times (1936). Charlie Chaplin comic film satire on the horrors of a mechanical age.

Modern Woodmen of America (1883). US fraternal organization.

Modred (Mordred) King Arthur's treacherous nephew. According to Geoffrey of Monmouth, he seduced GUINEVERE; according to Malory and his French originals, she repulsed his advances. Subsequently, Modred mortally wounded Arthur and was himself killed in the last battle in LYONESSE.

Modulor, Le Original system of architectural measurement, invented by Le Corbusier and used in his UNITÉS D'HABITATION; it is related to the proportions of the human body.

Moffat Bible Translation of the Bible into colloquial English by a Scotsman, the Rev. James Moffat. He completed the Old Testament in 1899 (revised edition 1924) and the New in 1925.

Moguls (1526–1857). Indian Muslim dynasty founded at Delhi by Babur, who claimed descent from TAMBURLAINE (hence the name, a corruption of 'Mongol'). Under Akbar (died 1605) and the last great emperor, Aurungzebe (died 1707), the Mogul Empire extended over almost all India. Thereafter their power was broken by the MAHRATTAS, although they ruled at Delhi until the last nominal emperor was deposed by the British. (Pronounced moh-gulz'.)

Mohacs Scene of 2 battles with the Ottoman Turks: (1) In 1526 Suleiman the Magnificent defeated Hungary, which was under Turkish rule for the next 150 years. This led to the revival of the Holy Roman Empire under the Habsburgs as the champion of Europe in succession to Hungary. (2) In 1687 the Austrians defeated the Turks and drove them out of Western Europe. (Hungarian town on the Danube, near the Yugoslav border south of Budapest.)

Mohammed (also **Mahomet**) Traditional English spellings of the Prophet's name, more correctly spelt Muhammad.

Mohawk Indians One of the FIVE NATIONS.

Mohenjodaro Chief centre of the INDUS VALLEY CIVILIZATION, in Pakistan on the Indus north of Hyderabad; it is remarkable for its planned streets, water supply system and covered drains.

Mohicans Confederacy of Algonquin American Indians who formerly occupied the region of the upper Hudson. (Pronounced, in England, moh'i-kanz; in USA, correctly, mo-hee'kanz.)

Möhne and Eder dam-buster raids (May 1943). Low-level attacks aimed at cutting off water supplies to the German steel industry in the Ruhr and flooding the area; only partially successful.

Moho, The Abbreviation used for the Mohorovičić Discontinuity, the sharply defined boundary between the earth's crust and the mantle which envelops the inner core, at a depth varying from 30 miles below land to 5 miles under the ocean floor. (Named after a Czech scientist.)

Mohocks Well-born ruffians who infested London streets in the early 18th century. (Corruption of Mohawks.)

Mohs scale Scale of hardness (H) in minerals, in which talc has H1, gypsum H2, fluorspar H4, felspar H6, quartz H7, topaz H8, sapphire H9, and diamond H10. Each can be scratched by all those below it in the scale. A penknife has H6·5.

Mole Spy who brings to light hitherto unknown information. John Le Carré uses the expression in his novels.

Molesworth Air base in Cambridgeshire, scene of demonstrations against CRUISE missiles.

Moll Flanders (1722). Daniel Defoe's picaresque novel of a lady of easy virtue who becomes an accomplished thief and, after transportation to Virginia, 'at last grew rich, liv'd Honest, and died a Penitent'.

Molluscs Phylum of mostly aquatic creatures with non-segmented bodies, including Gastropods (snails, slugs, limpets), Lamellibranchs or bivalves (mussels, oysters) and Cephalopods (octopuses, squids, cuttlefish).

Moloch (1) Canaanite god mentioned in Leviticus 18:21, and 2 Kings 23:10, to whom the Israelites sacrificed children as burnt offerings at TOPHET. (2) Anything calling for terrible sacrifice, e.g. war. (From *melek*, 'king'; also spelt Molech; pronounced moh'lok.)

Molony report (1962). Report on consumer protection which led to the setting up of the CONSUMER COUNCIL.

Molotov cocktail Home-made anti-tank bomb, first used by the Finns against the Russians in 1940. (Named ironically after the Soviet Foreign Minister.)

Momus Greek god of savage mockery.

Mona Island mentioned by Tacitus as being associated with the Druids; it may have been the Isle of Man or Anglesey.

Monaco Grand Prix (1929). Motor-racing contest run in May over the Monaco circuit of about 2 miles round the streets of Monte Carlo. (Pronounced mon'a-ko.)

Mona Lisa (about 1500). Leonardo da Vinci's portrait of the wife of a Florentine official, Francesco del Giocondo (hence the alternative name, *La Gioconda*), famous for her enigmatic smile. It is in the Louvre at Paris, whence it was stolen in 1911 (recovered 1913). (Pronounced moh'na lee'za.)

Mona Lot Chronic grouser in ITMA, with the signature-line 'It's being so cheerful as keeps me going'.

Monarch of the Glen, The One of numerous stag paintings by Sir Edwin Landseer, Queen Victoria's favourite painter. His animal studies are well observed and well painted, and possibly this picture should not have been singled out, as it has been, for scorn as typical of the philistine, sentimental taste of the Victorian age.

Monarda Genus name of bergamot.

Mona's scale (Angling) Scale for assessing the weight of landed fish from their length, assuming average condition.

Monday Club (1961). Conservative society founded by Lord Salisbury and Julian Amery. Right-wing and opposed to Harold Macmillan's middle way.

Monde, Le (1944). Serious independent French newspaper published in the afternoon but has next day's date. Founded, on the suggestion of Charles de Gaulle, by Hubert Beuve-Méry after the liberation of France.

Monégasque Of Monaco, the principality at Monte Carlo.

Monetarism Control by a government of balance of payments, employment or other economic activity, growth, inflation, by means of the regulation of the supply of money.

Moneymaker Ubiquitous and prolific variety of tomato, not notable for flavour.

Mongolia See INNER MONGOLIA; OUTER MONGOLIA.

Mongolism Type of disorder of unknown cause, marked by MONGOLOID facial characteristics. Now called DOWN'S SYNDROME.

Mongoloid Term applied to races with MONGOL characteristics – yellow skin, straight hair, slant eyes, high cheekbones and flat noses – found in Asia and Europe east of a line from Lapland to Thailand.

Mongols Asian nomadic race of obscure origin, first mentioned by the Chinese in the 6th century AD. They emerged suddenly into history in the 12th century, and under Genghiz Khan (1206–27) conquered Manchuria, northern India and south Russia. In the same century they overran eastern Europe, established the GOLDEN HORDE and founded the YÜAN DYNASTY in China. In the 14th century TAMBURLAINE created a second empire which collapsed at his death (1405); the Mongols then reverted to nomadic life. See MOGULS; MONGOLOID; TARTARS.

Monk Lewis Name given to M. G. Lewis, author of *Ambrosio or the Monk* (1795), a psychological development of the GOTHIC NOVEL. A demon in the form of a monk turns into a woman and tempts the Abbot Ambrosio, who is condemned by the Inquisition; the Devil rescues Ambrosio but later destroys him.

Monmouth's rebellion (1685). Rising against James II by the Protestant Duke of Monmouth, illegitimate son of Charles II, who landed at Lyme Regis from Holland and was defeated at SEDGEMOOR. See BLOODY ASSIZE.

Monnet Suggested European currency to be named after Jean Monnet (1888–1979) one of the founders of the European Communities – it also has overtones of 'money'. See ECU.

Monomark Anonymous registered address, in the form BM/XYZ, London WC1, obtainable by annual subscription to British Monomarks, who redirect letters from it.

Monophysite heresy (5th century onwards). View that Christ's human and divine nature were one and the same; condemned by the Council of CHALCEDON, but still held by the Coptic Church of Egypt and Abyssinia.

Monopolies Commission (1948). Permanent government body which reports on matters referred to it by the Department of Trade, including monopolies, mergers, collective boycotts, etc.

Monopoly Table game belonging to the snakes-and-ladders family, in which rewards and hazards are such as might occur in the course of large-scale financial operations.

Monotremata Sub-class of primitive egg-laying mammals, represented now only by the duck-billed platypus and spiny ant-eaters of Australia.

Monroe Doctrine (1823). Declaration by the American President Monroe that, as USA would not intervene in European affairs, so it expected European countries not to intervene in any country of the western hemisphere, other than existing colonies.

Mons (23 August to 5 September 1914). First major engagement of the British Expeditionary Force in World War I, in which the British delayed the German advance to good effect, but were then forced to retreat.

Monsieur Under the *ancien régime* this form of address designated the first brother of the king of France. In its general sense it was accepted by all classes in the country, but by the end of 1792 'Monsieur' was replaced by 'Citoyen', 'Madame' by 'Citoyenne'. The title was attached to one's job-description or title – 'Citoyen-Boucher', 'Citoyen-Général'.

Monsieur Beaucaire (1900). Novel by the American Booth Tarkington, about the adventures in 18th-century Bath of a cousin of Louis XV's, disguised as a barber. A play (1901) and an operetta (1919) were based on it.

Mons Meg A 15th-century big gun at Edinburgh Castle. (Perhaps made at Mons.)

Mons Star See 1914 STAR.

Monstrous Regiment of Women, First Blast of the Trumpet against the (1558). Calvinist John Knox's attack on the rule of Catholic Queen Mary in England and of the Scottish Regent, Mary of Lorraine; of no importance save for the magnificent title, which has passed into everyday use in the incorrect sense of 'monstrous tribe of women'. ('Regiment' meant 'Rule'.)

Montacute House E-shaped Elizabethan house near Yeovil, Somerset, now owned by the NATIONAL TRUST.

Montague Burton Professor Holder of the chair of International Relations at Oxford and the London School of Economics, or of Industrial Relations at Cambridge.

Montagues (Romeo's family) See CAPULETS.

Montagu Motor Museum Collection of veteran and vintage cars and motor-cycles at BEAULIEU.

Montaigne's *Essays* (1580, 1588). Great work of the French inventor of the modern essay, published in 3 volumes 17 years before Bacon's

Essays. Theological dogma and academic preconceptions were discarded in an unprejudiced survey of the main topics affecting man in his daily life. An English translation by John Florio was published in 1603.

Montbretia Hardy perennials, named after the French botanist, Montbret.

Monte Bello Islands Scene of the detonation (1952) of the first British atomic bomb, in a ship in the Indian Ocean about 100 miles from North-West Cape, Western Australia.

Monte Carlo Rally Car event held in January; individual competitors and teams entered by car manufacturers, from a choice of starting-points in Europe and Britain race through mud, snow and mountains to Monte Carlo, where they are assessed for condition on arrival, punctuality at check-points, etc.

Monte Cassino (February 1944). Hill between Naples and Rome, crowned by a 6th-century Benedictine monastery, destroyed by Allied bombing and rebuilt in 1956. The hill and town of Cassino were the scene of fierce fighting lasting until May, in which Polish forces greatly distinguished themselves.

Montessori system Further development of the PESTALOZZI and FROEBEL SYSTEMS, emphasizing self-education by the children themselves through play, minimum teacher-control, and the training of hand and eye. (Maria Montessori, Italian educationist, 1870–1952; pronounced mon-tès-awr'i.)

Montgomery bus boycott (1955–6). Black boycott of bus services, in protest against racial segregation at bus terminals, organized by Martin Luther King at Montgomery, Alabama, where he was a Baptist pastor. See SOUTHERN CHRISTIAN LEADERSHIP.

Montgomery Ward (1872). Large Chicago mail-order firm, with a chain of retail stores.

Montlhéry Banked motor-racing track south of Paris.

Montmartre Hill and a quarter of Paris dominated by the SACRÉ COEUR. Throughout the 19th century it was the artists' and writers' quarter, and a few still live there, though most have moved to MONTPARNASSE. It is now chiefly associated with night life.

Montparnasse Area of Paris (south-west of the Latin Quarter) to which most artists and writers moved from MONTMARTRE during the present century, others going to Montsouris further south. Like Montmartre, Montparnasse is also famous for its night life, and the great outdoor cafés such as the Dôme and Coupole.

Montrachet See BURGUNDY.

Montreux Convention (1936). International agreement to permit Turkish refortification of the Dardanelles, and to prohibit the passage of specified types of warship in peacetime; it modified the STRAITS CONVENTION (1841).

Montreux Festival See GOLDEN ROSE.

Monty Field Marshal Viscount Montgomery of Alamein.

Monty Python's Flying Circus (1969–74). Zany television variety show written and performed by 5 former students of Cambridge University. Completely incomprehensible to many viewers.

Monument, The (1677). Column 202 ft high designed by Wren and erected at Fish Street Hill, Billingsgate, London, to commemorate the Great Fire of 1666. The energetic can climb the 311 steps to the top for a view of London.

Monza (Park) Banked motor-racing track near Milan, built in 1921; the home of the Italian Grand Prix.

Moodie cards (Stock Exchange) Summaries of significant data about firms whose shares are quoted on the Exchange, provided by Moodies Services Ltd of London.

Moon and Sixpence, The (1919). Somerset Maugham's novel, suggested by the life of Gauguin, here represented by Charles Strickland, who abandons his career as a London stockbroker to take up painting, and dies in Tahiti of leprosy.

Moonies Religious movement, founded by Sun Myung Moon, whose name is the Unification Church.

Moonlight **Sonata, The** (1801). Misleading name given by a critic to the most popular of the piano sonatas by Beethoven, who intended it to reflect melancholy rather than romantic sentiment.

Moonlight Steeplechase See MIDNIGHT STEEPLE-CHASE.

Moonstone, The (1868). First English detective novel, by Wilkie Collins, in which the first fictional detective, Sergeant Cuff, solves the mystery of the loss of a huge diamond taken from an Indian idol.

Moor, The Colloquialism for Dartmoor prison, Devon.

Moor Park Golf club near Rickmansworth, Hertfordshire.

Moors (1) Berbers of north-west Africa (Morocco, Algeria and Tunis) who were conquered by the Arabs in the 7th century and converted to Islam. (2) Arabs and Moors who dominated Spain from AD 711 to 1238, and Granada until 1492. See MORISCOS. (From Spanish *Moros* from Latin *Mauri*, 'BERBERS'.)

Moors Murders case (1966). Murder of at least 3 young people by Ian Brady and Myra Hindley as pointless exercises in sadism directly inspired by Sade. The bodies were buried on the moors near Manchester; Brady and Hindley were given life sentences.

Moose, Loyal Order of (1888). US fraternal organization with Masonic-type rites.

Moral Re-Armament (MRA; 1921). US revivalist movement founded by Dr Frank Buchman which spread to many countries, as buchmanism or the Oxford Group. Its members, committed to absolute purity and honesty, practise group confession and meditation ('quiet times').

Moravians (18th century). HUSSITE sect founded by Moravians settled in Saxony. It made converts in Britain and America, and is still active in mission work.

Mordred See MODRED.

Morgan Grenfell (1838). A London merchant bank and acceptance house founded by the American George Peabody (see PEABODY'S BUILDINGS).

Morgan le Fay King Arthur's fairy sister, who revealed to him LANCELOT's amour with Guinevere, and carried the dead king to AVALON.

Morgenthau Plan Proposal to 'pastoralize' Germany after World War II (i.e. to destroy its industrial potential), accepted at the OCTAGON (second Quebec) Conference (September 1944) but later rejected. (Put forward by Henry Morgenthau, US Secretary of the Treasury; pronounced mawr'gen-thaw.)

Moriarty, Professor Napoleon of crime, locked in whose arms Sherlock HOLMES fell to his (apparent) death in 1891.

Moriscos MOORS who stayed on in Spain after the Spaniards had regained control of the country. The Moriscos were expelled in 1609.

Morland, Catherine chief figure in Jane Austen's NORTHANGER ABBEY, her mind empty except for romantic fancies derived from too much reading of novels, especially GOTHIC NOVELS.

Morley–Minto reforms (1909). First step towards self-government in India, introducing a majority of elected members in the provincial legislatures, which were given increased powers, and a separate Muslim electoral roll. (Lord Morley, Secretary of State for India; Lord Minto, Viceroy.)

Mormon, Book of Supplementary bible of the MORMONS, a history of America from the time of Babel, predicting the Millennium and the foundation of a New Zion in America; it was written on gold plates in 'reformed Egyptian' and revealed to Joseph Smith. The plates are not available to students as he handed them back to an angel after he had translated them. (Coined name.)

Mormons (1830). Name given by non-members of the Church of Jesus Christ of Latter-Day Saints, an American sect formed by Joseph Smith, with beliefs based on the Book of

MORMON: they became notorious for their practice of polygamy (abandoned under government pressure in 1890), and are strong in and around Utah, with a few adherents in Britain.

Mornay sauce Béchamel-type sauce prepared with cheese.

Morning Post (1772). High Tory daily, absorbed by the *Daily Telegraph* in 1937.

Moroccan Crisis (*First*) Created when in 1905 Kaiser Wilhelm landed at Tangier and made a speech supporting Moroccan independence and, by implication, against France. (*Second*) An alternative name for the AGADIR CRISIS.

Morpheus In classical mythology, the god of dreams, son of Hypnus, the god of sleep. (Pronounced mor'fews.)

Morris Motors Ltd Car firm founded by a cycle repairer, William Morris (later Lord Nuffield), which made the bull-nosed Morris-Oxford (1912); the Morris-Cowley (1925; named after the Cowley works at Oxford), sold at £200 with 'balloon tyres'; and the Morris Minor (1948), the first British £100 car, which reached the millionth sale in 1961 and was designed by Issigonis, who also designed the Mini (1959) and 1100/1300 (1962–7). From 1922 to 1938 Morris bought up Hotchkiss, SU Carburettor, Wolseley, MG and Riley. It then merged with AUSTIN in the British Motor Corporation (1952).

Morris, William (1834–96). Artist, poet, decorator, printer and socialist. He founded a manufacturing company which made furniture, prints, textiles, wallpapers, and stained glass. He founded in 1880 the Kelmscott Press at Hammersmith, West London; his house Kelmscott Manor, Lechlade, Gloucestershire, is open to the public. The Kelmscott *Chaucer*, called Morris's most splendid achievement, was edited by F. S. Ellis and decorated with 87 illustrations by Sir Edward Burne-Jones, highly prized by bibliophiles.

Morse Code Telegraphic code used internationally for transmitting messages. Letters and numbers are represented by groups of dots and dashes. Invented by Samuel Morse (1791–

1872) who also invented the magnetic telegraph. The best-known signal is SOS, but by 1992 distress signals will be sent by pushing a single button when the Global Maritime Distress and Safety System is adopted internationally.

Morte d'Arthur Fifteenth-century version of AR-THURIAN LEGEND written by Sir Thomas Malory, using English and French sources. The original MS, discovered in the Winchester College library and first published in 1947, differs substantially from the version prepared by Caxton, and is now accepted as the authentic text.

Morton's Fork View that the rich can well afford to pay taxes, and those who appear poor must have saved enough to do so, used by Bishop Morton to extort more revenue for Henry VII.

Moscovite (Cooking) Served with caviare.

Moscow, Retreat from (1812). Napoleon's winter retreat from a burnt-out Moscow, begun on 18 October, during which the GRANDE ARMÉE was virtually annihilated, more by indiscipline than by winter conditions.

Moscow Art Theatre Founded in 1898 by Konstantin Stanislavsky and Vladimir Nemirovich-Danchenko, it achieved world-wide acclaim for its theatrical naturalism. The theatre performed plays by Gorky, Andreyev, Maeterlinck, and Hauptmann, and especially by Chekhov. The theatre's influence has been universal.

Moscow Conference (October 1944). Known by the code name Tolstoy, a meeting at which Churchill and Stalin decided to impose the CURZON LINE on Poland.

Moselle German light wines from the Moselle valley, including Berncasteler; they are less potent than HOCK.

Moslem, Mohammedan, etc. See MUSLIM.

Mosleyites Name given to the BRITISH UNION OF FASCISTS.

Mosquito (1940). De Havilland twin-engined fast fighter-reconnaissance-bomber, built of plywood for speedy mass production and used with success by the RAF in World War II.

Moss Bros London firm which built up a reputation by hiring out men's attire for formal occasions. (Pronounced, colloquially, mos'bros.)

Most-favoured nation Clause in international trade agreements by which each party to the treaty agrees to grant to the others any tariff reduction or trading advantage it might offer to third parties. This prevents preferential treatment of any particular country.

Moth (1925). A famous light aircraft made by De Havilland, from which were developed the Gipsy Moth (1928) and the Tiger Moth.

Mother Carey's chickens Sailors' name for stormy petrels and, formerly, for snow. (Perhaps from Italian *madre cara*, dear mother, i.e. the Virgin Mary.)

Mother Courage (1938). Brecht's play about a camp-following mother whose children one by one meet violent death, in the THIRTY YEARS WAR.

Mother Goose rhymes Name used in the USA for 'nursery rhymes' and derived from a legend invented, with much circumstantial detail, in 1860 by a man who claimed to be descended from a Boston printer named Fleet, who married the daughter of a real Mrs Goose. Fleet was said to have printed *Songs for the Nursery or Tales from Mother Goose* in 1719, but no 18th-century copy was ever traced. See next entry.

Mother Goose's Tales (1697). Subtitle of a collection of fairy-tales made by the Frenchman Charles Perrault, including such famous tales as CINDERELLA, BLUEBEARD, etc. (French title, *Contes de ma mère l'oye*.)

Mother Hubbard (1) Folk-lore character, accompanied by a dog, known long before the nursery rhyme was composed in 1804. (2) Long shapeless dress, as depicted in illustrations of the rhyme; much favoured by missionaries in clothing Pacific islanders in the 19th century.

Mothering Sunday Fourth Sunday in Lent, the day when apprentices were allowed to go home for the day in medieval times. See MOTHER'S DAY.

Mother of the Gracchi (2nd century BC). Cornelia, mother of 2 famous Roman tribunes, Tiberius and Gaius Gracchus; hence a mother of brilliant children. (Pronounced grak'y.)

Mother's Day (1913). US custom of recent invention enshrined in an Act of Congress setting aside the second Sunday in May for remembering mothers. Brought to Britain by US troops in World War II, and inextricably confused with MOTHERING SUNDAY, it has been propagated by all the weapons of modern commercialism.

Mother Shipton (1488–1561). Yorkshire prophetess, whose prophecies were not published until long after her death. Successive editions were 100% accurate on the past but not on the future; the famous line 'Carriages without horses will go' was inserted by the 1862 editor, being by that time a safe bet.

Moulin Rouge Paris dance-hall, with a show which traditionally begins and ends with a spirited cancan; it became famous when Toulouse-Lautrec designed posters for it.

Mountain, The In the French Revolution, the extreme republican minority, mostly JACOBINS, which, led by Danton and Robespierre, dominated the PLAIN and won complete control of the CONVENTION. (So called because they occupied the highest seats in the assembly hall; in French, *La Montagne, Les Montagnards*.)

Mountains of the Moon Legendary source of the Nile, so named from at least the 2nd century AD. Eventually they were identified by H. M. Stanley as the Ruwenzori Mountains just north of the equator on the Uganda–Congo border.

Mount Athos Peninsula in Macedonia, Greece, occupied by numerous long-established monasteries of the Greek Orthodox Church. It is said that no woman or female domestic animal is allowed entry.

Mount Badon Site of King ARTHUR's last battle against the West Saxons at the turn of the 6th century. (Possibly Liddington Camp, Badbury, near Swindon.)

Mountbatten Family name of the Duke of Edinburgh, the Marquesses of Milford Haven and

Earl Mountbatten of Burma. See BATTENBERG.

Mounties Abbreviated name of the Royal Canadian Mounted Police, before 1920 the Royal North-West Mounted Police.

Mount Palomar Observatory (1948). California Institute of Technology's observatory on Mount Palomar, California, with a 200-in Hale reflector telescope, for long the largest in the world. It is about 100 miles from MOUNT WILSON OBSERVATORY, with which it is administered.

Mount Vernon George Washington's home, on the Potomac near Alexandria, Virginia. He was buried there and it is now a national monument. (Named after the British Admiral Vernon.)

Mount Wilson Observatory (1917). Carnegie Institution's observatory on Mount Wilson, near Pasadena, California, with a 100-in reflector telescope; administered in conjunction with the MOUNT PALOMAR OBSERVATORY.

Mourning Becomes Electra (1931). Eugene O'Neill's trilogy of plays in which he refashions the story of the ORESTEIA in the 19th-century setting of Puritan New England.

Mousetrap, The (1952). Agatha Christie's thriller, which has enjoyed by far the longest run in theatre history, kept going by coachloads of pensioners from all parts.

Mousterian culture Main culture of the middle PALAEOLITHIC period, perhaps lasting from 150,000 to 70,000 BC, when NEANDERTAL MAN appeared, living in caves, making implements of mammoth and reindeer bones, and burying the dead. (Le Moustier, a rock shelter in the Dordogne, France.)

Mowgli Indian boy in Kipling's JUNGLE BOOKS who is brought up in the jungle by wolves and is taught the Law of the Jungle by Baloo (a bear) and Bagheera (a panther). (Pronounced mow'gli.)

Much Ado about Nothing (1598). One of the 3 comedies of Shakespeare's later years, mainly in blank verse; see BEATRICE; BENEDICK.

Much Hoole Site of Lancashire's second AGR-reactor nuclear power-station, scheduled for construction after the completion of HEYSHAM. (Village south-west of Preston.)

Mufti of Jerusalem Haj Amin el-Huseini, a pro-German Arab rebel in Palestine who was a thorn in the flesh of the British administration throughout and after World War II.

Muggletonians (1651). Sect founded by Muggleton and Reeve, who claimed to be the 2 witnesses of Revelation 11:3. It survived for 200 years, although their subsequent careers must have been difficult to reconcile with the succeeding verses.

Mugwump (1884). (USA) Voter who does not support his party's candidate; one who is too detached to satisfy US standards of party fanaticism. (Algonquin American Indian word, 'great man'.)

Muhammad Ali See CLAY, CASSIUS.

Muirfield Golf links near Gullane and North Berwick, East Lothian, Scotland.

Mukden Old name of the former capital of Manchuria, now called SHENYANG.

Mukden incident, The (September 1931). Explosion used by the Japanese as an excuse for the seizure of MUKDEN, which began their conquest of Manchuria and the undeclared Sino-Japanese War destined to last until 1945. See MARCO POLO BRIDGE INCIDENT.

Mulberry Code name for the artificial harbours used in the Normandy landings, 1944.

Muldergate scandal (1979). Multi-million-dollar propaganda and influence-buying scheme whereby the foreign media were bribed to support the actions of the government of the Republic of South Africa. The discovery led to the resignation of the State President, B. J. Vorster, the heads of the secret service, and the information minister.

Müllerliede See SCHÖNE MÜLLERIN.

Mulliner, Mr P. G. Wodehouse character, always ready to cap anyone's story with a quite incredible 'true' story of his own.

Mummerset Stage name for any pseudo-rustic dialect with a thick burr. (Mummer + Somerset.)

Munchausen, Baron Historical person who served in the Russian army and had a weakness for telling the tallest of tall stories, e.g. of snow so deep that he tethered his horse to what he took for a fence and found him next morning dangling from the top of a church steeple. R. E. Raspe compiled an English version of these tales in 1785. (German Münchhausen.)

Munich (30 September 1938). Name symbolizing the agreement signed by Neville Chamberlain, Daladier, Mussolini and Hitler, under which Hitler occupied Czech SUDETENLAND, and described by Chamberlain as bringing 'peace in our time'; hence any shameful act of appeasement and betrayal.

Munich Putsch (November 1923). Premature and ill-prepared rising staged by Hitler to overthrow the Bavarian government with the help of Gen. Ludendorff. Hitler was arrested and given a 5-year sentence, during which he wrote MEIN KAMPF. (Plotted in a Munich beer-hall; hence its alternative name, the Beer-hall Putsch.)

Munro Scottish summits of 3,000 ft or more are called Munros; they are named after Sir Hugh Munro, who published a list of all such peaks in the *Journal* of the Scottish Mountaineering Club for 1891.

Munster South-western province of Ireland, formerly a Celtic kingdom, now consisting of Clare, Cork, Kerry, Limerick, Tipperary and Waterford.

Murano glass Venetian glass; the 11th-century factories were transferred in 1291, for fear of fire, from Venice to the nearby island of Murano, and have remained there ever since. The best was the clear crystal glass made in the period from the 16th to the 18th centuries, which was followed by a decline and a revival in the 1850s. Characteristics are light weight, attractive colours, lacelike designs of opaque white threads (*latticinio*) and other ingenious innovations.

Murder in the Cathedral, (1935). T. S. Eliot's first verse play, on the Thomas à Becket story. There is a chorus of Canterbury Women, and 4 knights offer him temptations in modern guise and language, which Becket rejects. They then become his executioners, addressing their comments on the event directly to the audience.

'Murders in the Rue Morgue, The' (1841). Story by Edgar Allan Poe, published in a Philadelphia magazine, in which the murder of a mother and daughter is solved by the Chevalier Dupin in what is generally regarded as the first detective story.

Murder Squad Small branch of the CID at Scotland Yard to whom murder cases of particular difficulty are referred.

Murphy's Law That law which, traditionally, says that if it is possible for anything to go wrong with a project, scheme, or plan it certainly will.

Murrayfield Edinburgh headquarters of Scottish rugby; the ground is also used for the Highland Games.

Musae Muses, daughters of Jupiter and Mnemosyne; nine in number, they presided over the different kinds of poetry, the arts and sciences. Their names and attributes were: (1) Calliope, the muse of epic poetry; (2) Clio, of history; (3) Erato, of erotic poetry and mime; (4) Euterpe, of lyric poetry; (5) Melpomene, of tragedy; (6) Polyhymnia, of the sublime hymn; (7) Terpsichore, of choral song, and dance; (8) Thalia, of comedy; (9) Urania, of astronomy. Mount Helicon was their favourite place, in Boeotia, where the sacred fountains of Aganippe and Hippocrene were. Mount Parnassus was also sacred to them.

Muscari Genus name of the grape-hyacinth.

Muscat of Alexandria Sweetest variety of grape, provided it is grown in a well-heated greenhouse.

Muscovy Company (1555). English chartered company formed to trade with Russia; it opened up trade with Asia via Russia and Persia.

Musicians, Worshipful Company of (1469). LIVERY COMPANY still active in the cause of music and musicians.

Music of Time, (A Dance to) The Series of novels by Anthony Powell (started in 1951), forming a witty study of upper-class attitudes as they have developed since the First World War, exemplified by a host of characters who drift in and out of each novel; Nick Jenkins, the narrator, Lady Molly, Stringham, the composer Moreland and the revolting, unaccountably successful Widmerpool.

Muslim Follower of the religion of ISLAM; also, as an adjective, 'of Islam'. The more usual Western name, 'Mohammedan' is not liked by Muslims as it implies that they worship Muhammad rather than the one God, Allah. Also spelt Moslem.

Muslim Brotherhood (1929). In Egypt, a politico-religious party even more fanatically anti-West than the WAFD; it was banned in 1954, the year Nasser came to power, and moved its headquarters to Damascus.

Muslim League (1906). Originally an All-Indian religious movement to protect Muslim interests in British India; under Jinnah it broke with the Hindu CONGRESS PARTY (1935) and became a political party in opposition to it, demanding Partition (1941). The League continues to function both in Pakistan (where its influence has waned) and in India.

Mustapha Kemal See ATATÜRK.

Mut Egyptian mother-goddess, wife of AMON, usually depicted with the head of a vulture.

Mutt and Jeff (1) Characters in the first strip cartoon, Bud Fisher's 'Mr Mutt', published in USA 1907. (2) Nickname for the British War and Victory medals given to most of those who served in World War I.

MVD (1945–60). Soviet Ministry for Internal Affairs which succeeded the NKVD. Its uniformed personnel carried out police, licensing and registration duties and also supervised frontier troops; it issued passports to Russians and visas to foreigners. It was succeeded by the KVD.

Mycenaean civilization That brought to southern Greece by the ACHAEANS about 1500 BC; based on Mycenae and neighbouring Tiryns, it had close ties with the MINOAN CIVILIZATION, but the exact nature of these is still a matter for dispute. (Pronounced my-seen-ee'an.)

'My Country, 'tis of Thee' (1832). Second of USA's national anthems, since superseded, sung to the tune of 'God Save the King'.

My Fair Lady See PYGMALION.

My Lai massacre (1968). Massacre of a large number of civilians including many women and children in a south Vietnam hamlet by US troops. Lt William Calley, the commander of the platoon responsible, was convicted by court martial in 1971 of the premeditated murder of at least 22 people and was sentenced to life imprisonment, later reduced to 20 years.

'My Old Dutch' Old Cockney music-hall song sung by Albert Chevalier. ('Dutch' for Duchess = wife.)

Myosotis Genus name of the forget-me-not.

Myres Memorial lecture (1959). Lecture at Oxford University on archaeology in Mediterranean countries.

Myrmidons In Greek legend, ants (Greek *murmekes*) turned into human beings by Zeus; later, the warlike, brutal race of Thessaly led by Achilles at Troy. Hence used of a swarm of people, especially underlings or hired ruffians. (Pronounced mèr'mid-onz.)

Myshkin, Prince See *The* IDIOT.

Mysteries of Udolpho, The (1794). GOTHIC NOVEL by Mrs Ann Radcliffe, of a heroine kept in durance vile in an Apennine castle by a villainous step-uncle.

Mysterious Universe, The (1930). Masterly popular exposition of cosmogony by Sir James Jeans, now rendered rather out of date by subsequent discoveries.

N

Nabataeans People who came from south Arabia to Palestine and, before the Christian era, were able to make the Negev desert flower by an ingenious system of irrigation, and to found an advanced civilization centred on PETRA. They traded widely, learning to speak Greek and Aramaic.

Naboth's vineyard Object so coveted that one will commit any crime to get it. (In 1 Kings 21 Naboth is stoned to death at JEZEBEL's instigation so that her husband, King Ahab, can confiscate his vineyard; pronounced nay'both.)

Naffy Colloquial synonym for the NAAFI, the Navy, Army and Air Force Institutes, an organization which provides canteens for the forces, at home and abroad.

Naffy medal Nickname of 2 World War II medals: (1) the 1939–45 Star; (2) the Africa Star for the North African campaign.

Nagas Mongoloid people of eastern Assam; although numbering only a million, they began in 1956 an armed revolt for independence of India. Nagaland was formed as a separate Indian State in 1963.

Nagasaki bomb Second and final atomic (plutonium) bomb of World War II, dropped on 9 August 1945. (City of Kyushu, Japan; pronounced nag-a-sah'ki.)

Nailsea glass (1788–1873). Glassware with brightly coloured stripes, made into walking-sticks, rolling pins, flasks, etc., originally at the village of Nailsea near Bristol, but much copied elsewhere.

Naked and the Dead, The (1948). Norman Mailer's novel of World War II, about a US attack on a Japanese-held Pacific island.

Nalgo Initials used for the National and Local Government Officers' Association, a fast-growing trade union.

Name In insurance, an underwriting member of Lloyd's of London.

Naming (House of Commons) SPEAKER's last resource in dealing with a recalcitrant member; he calls him by his surname (instead of his constituency) and the Leader of the House then moves the suspension of the offender.

Nanking china European name for the Chinese underglaze blue-and-white ware made in great quantity in the 18th and 19th centuries for European markets. (In USA called CANTON CHINA.)

Nanki-Poo See MIKADO.

Nanook of the North (1922). Robert Flaherty's documentary film about the Eskimos in Baffin Land.

Nansen bottle Oceanographer's instrument devised by Fridtjof Nansen (1861–1930) in the late 19th century for obtaining samples of sea water at various depths.

Nansen passport League of Nation's passport for stateless persons.

Nantes, Edict of See EDICT OF NANTES.

Nantgarw (1813–23). Porcelain factory founded at Nantgarw in the Taff Vale, South Wales, by Billingsley (see BILLINGSLEY FLOWERS); it produced much work resembling Sèvres. See SWANSEA PORCELAIN. (Pronounced nant-gar'oo.)

Napier Early British car which won the GORDON BENNETT CUP in 1902 and put up a 24-hour record at Brooklands in 1907 which remained unbeaten until after World War I.

Napoleon The boar who is the Stalin of Orwell's ANIMAL FARM.

Napoleon brandy Term given by some firms to indicate age and high quality; having no defined meaning it can be used indiscriminately.

Napoleonic Wars (1805–15). Wars waged from the time Bonaparte became Emperor Napoleon, comprising campaigns against Austria (1805, Austerlitz); Prussia (1806, Jena); the Peninsular War (1808–14); Austria (1809, Wagram); the invasion of Russia (1812); the German War of Liberation (1813, Leipzig); and Waterloo (1815). More loosely, the term is extended to cover the wars waged from the time Bonaparte became First Consul in 1799.

Napoleon of Notting Hill, The (1904). G. K. Chesterton's fantasy novel about a future kingdom of London which, from boredom, had reverted to medieval customs. The borough of Notting Hill under 'Napoleon' fights the rest of London over the building of a road.

'Napoleon II' See KING OF ROME.

Narcissus In Greek legend, a beautiful youth who pines away from hopeless love for his own reflection seen in pools, and is turned into the narcissus flower.

NASA (USA) See NATIONAL AERONAUTICS AND SPACE ADMINISTRATION.

Naseby (1645). First battle fought by the NEW MODEL ARMY, which decisively defeated the CAVALIERS. (Village near Northampton.)

Nash terraces Terraced stucco houses round Regent's Park, London, designed by John Nash and Decimus Burton in the 1820s. Internally, the lofty rooms and long climbs to upper floors make them inconvenient and uneconomic in modern conditions, but a move to replace them was strongly opposed on aesthetic grounds.

Nasmyth's steam hammer (1838). Power-driven hammer, similar in operation to the modern pile-driver, used in making heavy forgings, the manufacture of which it revolutionized. (Pronounced nayz'mith.)

Nassau Former German duchy incorporated in Prussia, see HESSEN.

Nassau Conference (1962). Meeting between President J. F. Kennedy and Harold Macmillan at which Britain accepted the offer of POLARIS instead of the cancelled Skybolt missiles, having just rejected de Gaulle's offer of co-operation in developing an Anglo-French substitute. This convinced de Gaulle that Britain was submitting to a US dominance which he himself was almost obsessively resisting.

Natasha (Rostova) See WAR AND PEACE.

National, The Common abbreviation for the GRAND NATIONAL.

National Aeronautics and Space Administration (1958). US government body which controls research and development in the non-military aspects of these fields.

National Assembly Name adopted by the THIRD ESTATE of the STATES–GENERAL (10 June 1789) when it broke away from it. Banned by Louis XVI, it took the TENNIS COURT OATH but dissolved itself when Louis accepted a constitution in 1791. The name was revived in 1946 for the reconstituted Chamber of Deputies.

National Book League (1944). Society of publishers, booksellers, librarians, authors and readers, which tries to raise the standard of books and to encourage reading; formerly the National Book Council (1925). Now called the Book Trust.

National Certificate (Higher and Ordinary) Awarded after part-time study, in other respects resembling the NATIONAL DIPLOMA.

National Coal Board Public but semi-independent body which took over the coal-mining industry in 1947.

National Debt Total debt owed by a state, in Britain managed by the Bank of England. It comprises all government stocks, National Savings securities and the floating debt of short-term loans (e.g. Treasury Bills.)

National Diploma Awarded after full-time courses for 2 years (3 for the Higher grade) at a College of Technology in subjects related to the student's career.

National Economic Development Council (1961). Known familiarly as Neddy, a committee composed of representatives of employers, unions and government, to plan ways of increasing the productivity of British industry. See also LITTLE NEDDY.

National Enterprise, etc. For classes of boat see under ENTERPRISE, etc. See also NATIONAL TWELVE.

National Film Theatre British Film Institute's experimental and research cinema which was developed from the Telekinema built for the Festival of Britain, and occupies the same site under Waterloo Bridge on the South Bank of the Thames.

National Front (1967). Amalgamation of the League of EMPIRE LOYALISTS and the British National Party, pledged to extreme right-wing, racialist and anti-Semitic views.

National Guard (USA) Civilian armed force recruited and controlled by each individual state (and the District of Columbia), but equipped and paid by the Federal government; they are also liable for service in the Federal army.

National Health Service (1948). Welfare service set up by the Labour government and established under Aneurin Bevan as Minister of Health, financed partly by compulsory contributions but mainly from general taxation, providing medical, dental and allied services for all.

National Hunt Committee Body which controlled British steeplechases and hurdle races, i.e. those 'over the sticks' as opposed to flat-races. Now incorporated in the JOCKEY CLUB.

National Incomes Commission (1962–5). Body set up to watch and comment on the level of profits and dividends, and to consider pay claims referred to them either by the parties to a dispute or by government in the national interest. The objective was to keep the rate of increase of incomes of all kinds to a level justified by growth in national productivity. It was replaced by the Prices and Incomes Board.

National Labour Party (1931). Party formed by Ramsay MacDonald with Snowden and J. H. Thomas, which joined a National Coalition with Conservatives and Liberals; the rest of the Labour Party regarded this as a great betrayal.

National Maritime Museum See QUEEN'S HOUSE.

National Physical Laboratory (1900). Government institution at Teddington, London, under the Ministry of Technology, engaged in research on industrial applications of the physical sciences, with divisions specializing in molecular science, autonomics, aerodynamics, metallurgy, etc. It works in close association with the Royal Society.

National Plan (1965). The British government's first 5-year plan, sponsored by the NATIONAL ECONOMIC DEVELOPMENT COUNCIL under George Brown. It provided for a 25% increase in national output by 1970 – given expansion of productive capacity, improvement in managerial and labour efficiency, and achievement of more competitive prices on world markets. The provisos were not satisfied.

National Recovery Administration (1933). (USA) One of the NEW DEAL organizations, intended to stimulate industry, reduce unemployment and control industrial competition; declared unconstitutional in 1935.

National Recreation Centre See CRYSTAL PALACE.

National Schools (1811–1902). Village primary

schools founded by the (Anglican) National Society. They formed the vast majority of the voluntary schools which provided primary education. Expenses were paid for by private subscription, with a very small government grant in 1833 that was doubled in 1870.

National Science Foundation (USA) Government body formed after World War II to stimulate, co-ordinate and assess fundamental scientific research and, with the National Academy of Sciences and the President's Science Advisory Committee, to advise the government on such matters.

National Security Agency (1952). US government agency, under the Defense Department, responsible for code-making and breaking, radio monitoring, reconnaissance by satellite and u-2, and other forms of 'electronic intelligence' (see ECM). Its heavily guarded headquarters are at Fort Meade, Maryland.

National Socialist Movement English society of the few who followed the lead of a Coventry teacher, Colin Jordan, and modelled themselves on the teachings of Hitler.

National Sporting Club (1891). London club which, at its premises at King Street, Covent Garden, held important boxing contests for its members and guests until 1937, when it turned to public promotions, becoming defunct in 1940. Another club of the same name was formed in 1947; see SPORTSMAN OF THE YEAR.

National Theatre (1976). Theatre on the South Bank of the Thames; it contains three separate theatres, the Lyttelton, Cottesloe and Olivier. A driving force behind the scheme was the late Lord Olivier.

National Trust (1895). Organization incorporated by Act of Parliament but financed by voluntary gifts, which promotes the preservation of land and buildings of historic interest or natural beauty for the benefit and access of the people. It owns many famous country houses, gardens, homes of great men, ancient monuments, and whole stretches of coastline, countryside and parks.

National Twelve The most popular restricted class of dinghy, for use in inland and coastal waters. 'Twelve' refers to the overall length of 12 feet.

Nato (1949). North Atlantic Treaty Organization, set up by the ATLANTIC PACT as a defensive measure against the Communist bloc. After the virtual withdrawal of France in 1966, the headquarters were moved from Paris to Evere, near Brussels airport, pending the completion of permanent quarters at Heysel. The organization is directed by a Council of Foreign Ministers; the military headquarters is known as Shape.

Nats Abbreviation commonly used by English-speaking South Africans for members of the predominantly Afrikaner Nationalist Party.

Natural Environment Research Council (1965). A government body which promotes research in the earth sciences and ecology, and the establishment of nature reserves.

Natural History and Antiquities of Selborne (1789). Most charming of naturalists' notebooks, in the form of correspondence with friends, written by Gilbert White, whose home was at Selborne, Hampshire.

Natural Selection In the Darwinian theory, the method by which evolution proceeds; only those individuals best adapted to their environment survive to breed, so that certain characteristics become established; if the environment changes, so may the characteristics. Darwin also called it the SURVIVAL OF THE FITTEST. See ORIGIN OF SPECIES.

Nausicaa In Homer's *Odyssey*, the delightful young princess whom Ulysses found playing ball on the island of Phaeacia where he was shipwrecked. (Pronounced naws-ik-ay', naws-ik'e-a.)

Nautilus, USS (1955). World's first nuclear-powered submarine with a range of 40,000 miles. (Named after the submarine in Jules Verne's *Twenty Thousand Leagues under the Sea*.)

Naval and Military Club (1862). London club in Lord Palmerston's old home in Piccadilly; known as the 'In and Out' from the conspicuous signs in the forecourt.

Navarino (1827). Naval battle in the GREEK WAR OF INDEPENDENCE, in which the British, French and Russian fleets defeated the Turkish and Egyptian fleets. (A bay in south-west Greece.)

Navarre Old Spanish Biscayan kingdom, inherited by the King of France in 1284 and divided between ARAGON and France in 1479, the French part being given to the grandmother of the Henry of Navarre, who later became Henry IV of France.

Navicert British licensing system for neutral ships, used in both world wars; the British consul at the ship's port of origin issued a certificate (Navicert) that it was not carrying cargo likely to help a blockaded enemy country.

Navigation Acts Series of Acts from the Middle Ages to the 19th century, partially restricting trade with England or English colonies to goods carried in English ships; they led to the ANGLO-DUTCH WARS of the 17th century and contributed to the revolt of the American colonies.

Navy List Official List of all Royal Navy command officers in service and of those on the reserve.

Neandertal Man Cave-dwelling form of early Man, first discovered in the Neander valley near Düsseldorf in 1856; he probably lived 70,000 years ago and became extinct before HOMO SAPIENS appeared. (The old spelling was Neanderthal.)

Neapolitan Club Complicated Italian calling system at Bridge, with numerous artificial bids. An opening 1 Club shows strength, and the partner responds by indicating the number of Aces and Kings he holds.

Near East Obsolete term for the area comprising Turkey and regions formerly part of the Turkish Empire, e.g. parts of the Balkans, Egypt, Palestine. From 1921 this area tended to be grouped under the MIDDLE EAST.

Nebuchadnezzar Measure, the equivalent of 20 bottles of champagne.

Neddy Nickname for the NATIONAL ECONOMIC DEVELOPMENT COUNCIL.

Needlemakers, Worshipful Company of (1656). A LIVERY COMPANY, still associated with the trade.

Nefertiti Egyptian Queen, wife of AKHENATEN. (Pronounced nef-èr-tee'ti.)

Negritos (1) Ancient pygmy people of South-East Asia, forced into widely scattered pockets of mountain and forest country by subsequent waves of migration. The Andaman Islanders are typical examples. (2) Pygmies of the Ituri forests of the former Belgian Congo; also called Negrillos.

Negus Title of the former supreme ruler of Abyssinia. (Amharic *n'gus*, 'crowned'; pronounced nee'gus.)

Neighbours (1985). Highly successful Australian soap opera set in Melbourne. Seems to end with at least two cliff-hangers nightly.

Nemesis Greek goddess of retribution; she punished those who prospered unduly (e.g. POLYCRATES) and also, in later legend, criminals.

Nemo, Capt. See TWENTY THOUSAND LEAGUES UNDER THE SEA.

Neoclassicism (1750–1800). Reaction from ROCOCO towards ancient-Roman (not Greek) models, exemplified in the LOUIS SEIZE and ADAM STYLES; leading figures included the painter David and the sculptors Canova and Flaxman.

Néo-Destour (1933). A radical splinter group of DESTOUR.

Neolithic Age (New Stone Age) Age of polished stone implements which began about 6000 BC in Asia, and during which man learnt to harvest crops, domesticate animals, weave, and make painted pottery – the 'Neolithic revolution' which spread slowly via Anatolia and the Mediterranean to Europe, and also to China. Megalithic monuments (Carnac, Avebury, Stonehenge) were built from the eastern Mediterranean to the Shetlands. In Western Europe the age ended about 1700 BC.

Neoplatonism Last of the Greek philosophies, founded by the Greek Plotinus (3rd century

AD), who was born in Egypt and settled in Rome. It was derived from Platonic idealism, Stoic ethics and oriental religions, and laid stress on religious ecstasy attained through asceticism. It opposed, but greatly influenced, Christianity, teaching that the soul is enmeshed in the life of the flesh but can free itself and turn to God.

Nepeta Genus that includes the catmints.

Neptune Roman god equivalent to the Greek POSEIDON.

Neptune's Bodyguard Nickname of the Royal Marines.

Nereids In Greek legend, sea-nymphs, the 50 daughters of NEREUS, including AMPHITRITE and THETIS, who escorted POSEIDON. (Pronounced neer'i-idz.)

Nereus Greek god of the Aegean Sea, father of the NEREIDS. (Pronounced neer'ews.)

Neroni, Signora Madeline Exotic creature in Trollope's BARCHESTER NOVELS. The daughter of Prebendary Stanhope, she claims to be the mother of the last of the Neros by a husband she mysteriously left behind in Italy after 6 months of marriage.

Nesselrode Ice pudding with *marrons glacés* (candied chestnuts).

Nessie Loch Ness Monster.

Nessus In Greek legend, a Centaur shot by Heracles with a poisoned arrow for trying to abduct his wife Deianira. Later she gave Heracles a shirt stained with the blood of Nessus, who had told her that it would act as a love charm; instead it killed Heracles.

Nestlé Swiss firm with headquarters at Cham and Vevey, which carries on an international trade in tinned milk, chocolates, frozen foods, ice-cream and instant drinks.

Nestor In Greek mythology, a King of Pylos who lived to a great age and whose advice, whether because it was wordy or because it was usually wrong, was esteemed equal to that of the gods.

Nestorian heresy That Christ had 2 distinct natures, and that Mary was not the mother of God but only of the human Jesus; condemned by the Council of EPHESUS. The Nestorian Church still exists in Syria, Persia, Iraq and southern India. (Nestorius, partriach of Constantinople, 428–31.)

Netherlands (1) Historically, the region of the Rhine, Meuse and Scheldt deltas (equivalent to modern Holland, Belgium, Luxembourg and adjacent areas of France and Germany); see AUSTRIAN NETHERLANDS; SPANISH NETHERLANDS. (2) Kingdom more usually called in Britain (and often by Dutchmen) by the name of its 2 richest provinces – Holland.

Neuilly, Treaty of (1919). Post-war treaty with Bulgaria, which came off lightly, but lost access to the Aegean by having to cede Western Thrace to Greece.

Neuve Chapelle (1915). In World War I the scene of heavy indecisive fighting in which British and Indian troops suffered severe casualties. (Village south-west of Armentières, France.)

Nevsky Prospekt Avenue which radiates from the Admiralty in Leningrad and stretches for $2\frac{1}{2}$ miles to the Alexander Nevsky monastery. Following the revolution it was renamed 'Avenue of the 25th of October' but reverted to Nevsky Prospekt.

Newbery Medal US equivalent to the Library Association's CARNEGIE MEDAL.

Newcastle disease Virus disease of chickens which reduces egg production and paralyses chicks; preventible by vaccination.

Newcomen engine (1705). Early form of steam engine, used for pumping water in mines; it was while repairing one of them 60 years later that James Watt obtained the idea for his improved model.

Newcomes, The (1855). Thackeray's family saga. The patient, honest, Col. Newcome loses his fortune and retires to the CHARTERHOUSE; his artist son, Clive, first marries the vulgarian Widow Mackenzie and, when she dies, at last wins his cousin Ethel, destined by her family for a richer marriage.

New Deal (1933–9). (USA) Series of measures to deal with the DEPRESSION, introduced by F. D. Roosevelt on first taking office, and much hampered by an obscurantist Supreme Court which ruled that the AGRICULTURAL ADJUSTMENT ADMINISTRATION and the NATIONAL RECOVERY ADMINISTRATION were unconstitutional. Other measures included the WAGNER ACT, TVA and a Social Security Act. ('A new deal for the American people ', a phrase from a pledge made by Roosevelt in 1932 before his election as President.)

Newdigate prize (1806). Annual prize for English verse, open to Oxford undergraduates.

New Economic Policy (1921–8). Temporary compromise policy instituted by Lenin in the face of urban and rural rioting in Russia. It halted the forced levy of food for the cities, and permitted trading for private profit, sale of some farm produce on the free market, and small-scale private industry.

New England (USA) Name given to the area now comprising the states of Massachusetts, Connecticut, Vermont, New Hampshire, Maine and Rhode Island, where the first settlers were of English Puritan stock; for long a centre of stability and culture in American life.

New English Art Club (1886). Movement founded by British artists who under French influences became dissatisfied with the standards of the Royal Academy. Steer and Sickert were among the leading founder-members of the group, which became closely associated with the Slade School. In 1911 some members founded the CAMDEN TOWN GROUP and later the LONDON GROUP.

New English Bible Translation of the Bible by a British interdenominational committee; the New Testament was published in 1961 and the Old in 1970.

New English Dictionary Earlier name of the Oxford English Dictionary.

Newgate Old London prison, outside which public hangings took place until the 1860s; the site is now occupied by the OLD BAILEY.

New Granada Pre-Liberation name of Colombia. (Pronounced gran-ahd'a.)

New Grange Megalithic chambered round barrow of unusual size, in a circle of tall monoliths, near Drogheda, Ireland.

New Hall (1954). College of Cambridge University.

New Hall (1781–1825). One of the 3 English hard-paste porcelain factories, at Shelton, Staffordshire, the patent having been bought from Bristol (see BRISTOL PORCELAIN). Most of it imitated Chinese decoration, pink and orange mandarins being typical. The firm also made inferior bone china from 1810.

Newham (1965). London borough consisting of the former county boroughs of East Ham and West Ham, with the part of the former metropolitan borough of Greenwich that lies north of the Thames.

New Kingdom (c. 1550–712 BC) Last great period in Egyptian history, when the pharaohs of the 18th–24th Dynasties ruled at THEBES; the 'Second Empire' was extended southwards and as far as the Euphrates to the east. Thereafter, Egypt suffered successive invasions by Assyrians, Persians and Greeks. See 18TH DYNASTY.

Newlands Cape Town cricket ground where Test matches were played.

Newlands Corner Famous beauty spot near Guildford, overlooking the Dorking–Guildford valley.

New Learning English form of the REVIVAL OF LEARNING, inspired by Erasmus, Colet and More and influencing the English Reformation movement.

New Left, The (1956). Neo-Marxist movement in the UK, USA, France and elsewhere, mainly of young people disillusioned with the leadership of Communist and Socialist parties, and inspired by such writers as Georg Lukács.

New Look (1947). Reaction in fashion introduced by Dior, with long billowing skirts as a welcome change from the austerities of wartime and post-war clothes rationing; the term has since been applied *ad nauseam* to any change or new development.

New Model Army (1645). ROUNDHEAD army as reorganized under Sir Thomas Fairfax after the SELF-DENYING ORDINANCE, with Oliver Cromwell in command of the cavalry; it won its first victory at NASEBY.

Newnham (1871). Second oldest college for women at Cambridge.

New Order in Europe Hitler's plan to consolidate the whole of Europe under German leadership; see TRIPARTITE PACT.

New Party (1931). Short-lived political party formed by Oswald Mosley when he left the Labour Party, which had rejected his plan to remedy unemployment and economic depression; it was joined briefly by John Strachey.

Newsom report (1) Report (1963) entitled *Half Our Future*, which recommended that school-leaving age should be raised to 16 in 1970, and that state schools should offer a choice of programmes, including courses related to future careers, in the last 2 years. (2) First report (1968) of the Public Schools Commission, which recommended that some boarding public schools should reserve at least half their places for assisted pupils.

Newstead Abbey Byron's home at Linby, Nottinghamshire, now owned by the Nottingham Corporation.

New Stone Age See NEOLITHIC AGE.

New Style Present or Gregorian calendar; see OLD STYLE.

Newton Aycliffe (1947). NEW TOWN in Co. Durham, 6 miles north-west of Darlington, designed to take 45,000 inhabitants.

Newton's laws of motion (1) A body remains in a state of rest or of uniform motion in a straight line unless acted on by an external force. (2) Rate of change of momentum is proportional to the force causing it and is in the same direction. (3) To every action there is always an equal and opposite reaction.

New Towns Overspill towns to take surplus population from conurbations, built in most cases by development corporations under various New Towns Acts (1946 onwards).

New Wave, The Movement in French novels (the New Novel), drama (the New Theatre) and films which began in the late 1950s and appears to be the reverse of the interior-monologue approach, concentrating on objective description, or cryptic, laconic dialogue, from which character and motive have to be deduced. LAST YEAR AT MARIENBAD and GODOT are examples. (Translation of French *La Nouvelle Vague*.)

New World Symphony (1893). Dvořák's fifth and last symphony, written after a sojourn in New York, and in part inspired by Negro tunes; there are for example echoes of 'Swing Low, Sweet Chariot' in the 2nd movement.

New Yorker (1925). Internationally famous weekly which combines political satire, cartoons, humorous verse and outstanding short stories.

NGC number In astronomy, the number given to star clusters, galaxies and clouds of gas, in the New General Catalogue, a 19th-century revision of Herschel's list. See M-NUMBER.

Nibelungenlied (Lay of the NIBELUNGS) Thirteenth-century German epic poem based on stories in the Scandinavian VOLSUNGA SAGA and the EDDA, combined with legends of Germanic westward migrations under pressure from the Huns. It tells the story of SIEGFRIED, HAGEN and KRIEMHILD. See next entry.

Nibelungs (1) In Scandinavian mythology a race of dwarfs who possess a hoard of gold. (2) In the NIBELUNGENLIED the name passed to successive owners of the gold, i.e. SIEGFRIED's men and the Burgundians.

Nicaea, Council of (325). First Oecumenical Council, summoned by the Emperor Constantine the Great to crush the ARIAN HERESY; it issued the NICENE CREED defining the mystery of the TRINITY and affirming the consubstantiality of the Son of God; it also fixed the date of Easter. (Nicaea in Bithynia, Asia Minor; now Iznik, Turkey; pronounced ny-see′a.)

Nicene Creed One creed that unites the Roman Catholic, Anglican and Eastern Orthodox Churches (the last introducing modifications), drawn up by the Council of NICAEA to combat the ARIAN HERESY, and enlarged by the Council of CONSTANTINOPLE. Used at Mass and Holy Communion.

Nicholas Nickleby (1839). Dickens's novel in which the hero goes around rescuing the victims of improbable cruelty; redeemed in part by the picture of Wackford SQUEERS at DOTHEBOYS HALL and other minor characters.

Nicol prism Optical device for producing plane-polarized light.

Nicotiana Genus of 66 tobacco plants, named after the French ambassador to Portugal who introduced tobacco to both France and Portugal. (Pronounced nik-o-te-a-na, but popularly neko-she-a-na.)

Nicotine Poisonous alkaloid forming the essential principle of tobacco, from which it is obtained; the word comes from Jacques Nicot, who introduced tobacco into France in 1560.

Nietzschean Connected with Nietzsche's view, deduced from nature, that the force behind life is not desire for happiness and well-being but a drive towards transformation, strength and growth, which he called 'the will to power'. See SUPERMAN. (Friedrich Nietzsche, German philosopher (1844–1900); pronounced neech'e-an.)

Nigella Genus name of love-in-the-mist.

Nigger of the 'Narcissus', The (1897). Joseph Conrad's sea story of James Wait, a Negro dying of tuberculosis, and of Donkin, the mean-spirited offspring of the slums who nearly starts a mutiny.

Night and Day (1929). Epstein's stone carvings on the outside walls of the headquarters of London Transport, in Broadway, Westminster.

Nightmare Abbey (1818). Thomas Love Peacock's plotless novel, characteristically replete with delightful satire on the current absurdities of his day, and especially on Coleridge, Byron and Shelley.

Night of the Long Knives (1) Name given to the massacre in June 1934, on Hitler's orders, of Röhm and other Storm Troopers (see SA). (2) Name given to the dropping of 6 of his Cabinet by Harold Macmillan in July 1962.

Night Thoughts, Young's (1742–5). In full, Edward Young's *The Complaint: Night-Thoughts on Life, Death, and Immortality*, verse of portentous solemnity and deep melancholy, tailored to suit the contemporary taste.

Night Watch, The (1642). Rembrandt's painting of a militia company of musketeers about to set out; it was commissioned by the officers, who were not at all pleased with it. Now in the Rijksmuseum, Amsterdam.

Nike (1953). US surface-to-air interceptor missile, which became the chief anti-aircraft weapon guarding American cities and strategic points.

Nike Apteros Wingless Victory, or Athene-Nike, to whom the small but lovely temple at the entrance to the Acropolis is dedicated. ATHENE is called 'wingless' in distinction from the goddess Nike (Victory) herself, who was represented as winged. (Greek name; pronounced ny'kee apt'er-os.)

Nile, Battle of the (1798). Nelson's victory off Aboukir, which cut off Napoleon's forces in Egypt.

Nimbus Weather satellite which supplements the TIROS series by sending back infra-red pictures of the night side of the earth.

Nimrod (1) Described in Genesis 10:9–11, as ruler of Shinar (Sumeria) and a mighty hunter (i.e. of men) before the Lord; he has not been identified from local records. (2) Pen-name of C. J. Apperley (1779–1843), the sporting writer who wrote, in particular, about the prodigious John Mytton. His books were illustrated with ALKEN PRINTS.

Nimrod aircraft World's first all-jet sea-reconnaissance aircraft, a Hawker Siddeley version of the Comet III which replaced the SHACKLETON.

Nimrud Earliest capital of the Assyrian empire, near NINEVEH, during a period of expansion in the 9th century BC under Assurbanipal II and his successors.

Nine Tailors Method of change-ringing church bells which became known outside the world of bell-ringers through Dorothy L. Sayers's murder story of that name, the plot of which (elucidated, as usual, by Lord Peter WIMSEY) is interwoven with a study of the subject. (Tailor for 'teller', a stroke on the bell at a funeral; 6 for a woman, 9 for a man.)

1984 (1949). George Orwell's terrifying novel of a future totalitarian state where citizens are watched through a TV system installed in every home ('Big Brother is watching you'); words are twisted to mean their opposite ('newspeak'); the Party line is continually changed, creating mutually contradictory dogmas which nevertheless have to be accepted (by a process he calls 'double-think'); and those who fall from grace become 'unpersons', all mention of whom is systematically expunged from the records.

1914 Star (Mons Medal). Medal given to members of the British Expeditionary Force who served in France before 23 November 1914.

Nineteen Propositions (1642). LONG PARLIAMENT's demand for control of government, the immediate cause of the ENGLISH CIVIL WAR.

19th Amendment (1920). Amendment to the American Constitution which introduced women's suffrage.

1922 Committee Sounding-board for the opinions of the Conservative Members of Parliament and a bridge between the front and back benches in Parliament. It is not authorized to formulate policy.

Nineveh Assyrian capital in succession to NIMRUD, from the 8th century until it was destroyed by the Medes in 612 BC. Its site is on the Tigris near Mosul, at a place now called Kuyunjik.

Ninian Park Home of the Cardiff City football club.

Ninth Commandment 'Thou shalt not bear false witness' (Exod. 10:16). To Roman Catholics this is the Eighth Commandment.

Niobe In Greek legend, wife of AMPHION; because she boasted that she had more children than their mother, Apollo and Artemis killed all 12 of them. Niobe returned to her country, Lydia, and asked Zeus to turn her to stone; this he did, and her tears ran eternally down the rock face. (Pronounced ny'o-bi.)

Nipponese Japanese; *Nipponism*, the spirit of self-sacrificial patriotism. (Japanese *nipun*, 'sunrise'.)

Nirvana Buddhist concept, not clearly defined by Buddha, which to some means complete annihilation of the individual self, and to others the absorption of self in 'the All', a state of perfect serenity attained by the eradication of all desire for the things of the senses through following Buddhist precepts.

Nisei Person of Japanese descent born in USA. (Pronounced nee'say; no change in the plural.)

Nissen hut (1916). Tunnel-shaped hut of corrugated iron on a cement foundation, invented by Col. Nissen (RE), and first used on the Western Front in World War I.

Nivelle offensive (April–May 1917). Ambitiously planned all-out attack on the line of the River Aisne (including the CHEMIN DES DAMES) in World War I by the over-confident French General Nivelle. French losses were enormous, and 54 divisions mutinied; Pétain replaced Nivelle and succeeded in restoring discipline. Sometimes called Second Aisne.

Nivernaise (Cooking) With carrots. (French, 'of Nevers', Nièvre *département* prefecture.)

NKVD (1935–45). Soviet People's Commissariat for Internal Affairs, which absorbed the OGPU and included the Administration for State Security. It was responsible under the 3 successive leaders, Yagoda, Yezhov and Beria, for waves of mass purges and the running of the slave-labour camps. It was renamed the MVD.

Nobel prizes Founded by the Swedish inventor of dynamite, Alfred Nobel (died 1896), and awarded for the year's most outstanding work in literature, physics, chemistry, medicine, economics, or physiology, and the promotion of peace.

Nod, Land of A name from Genesis 4:16: 'Cain ... dwelt in the land of Nod, on the east of Eden.' Swift first used it in the sense 'sleep', since when it has become standard usage in the nursery.

'Noddy' 'Kind little fellow' who lives in Toyland. A character in the books by Enid Blyton. Loved by thousands but the antis found him odious, unwholesome and wet.

Noh-play Highly stylized 14th-century Japanese form of historical drama; the 2 main actors wear masks and elaborate costume, and are assisted by dancers, singers and a narrator; the performance lasts some 7 hours. (Noh = accomplishment.)

Nok culture (5th century BC-2nd century AD). Culture of a region of Northern Nigeria, south-west of Jos, where numerous remarkable terracotta heads were found in the 1940s.

Noli me tangere Name given to paintings of Christ appearing to Mary Magdalene at the Sepulchre. (Latin for 'touch me not', the phrase used by Jesus in John 20:17; pronounced noh'li mee tang'ėr-e.)

Noll A nickname for Oliver Cromwell, also called Old Noll; see next entry.

Nolly Now obsolete abbreviation for Oliver; applied particularly to Goldsmith, of whom David Garrick wrote unkindly: 'Here lies Nolly Goldsmith, for shortness called Noll, / Who wrote like an angel but talk'd like poor Poll.'

Nomanhan incident (May 1939). First of a series of little publicized Japanese attempts to invade Siberia from the Mongolia–Manchukuo border, decisively repulsed by Zhukov.

Nonconformist conscience, The Moral rectitude of NONCONFORMISTS, especially as manifested in politics during the period (up to the time of Lloyd George) when they were a main source of Liberal Party strength.

Nonconformists Protestants who would not conform with the principles of the Established Anglican Church, in particular rejecting the rule of bishops. They include the Baptists, Independents, (English) Presbyterians (see EPISCOPALIANS), and Methodists. Up to the Restoration, they were called Puritans or Dissenters.

Nonsense verse The two masters of nonsense Edward Lear (1812–83) and Lewis Carroll (Charles Lutwidge Dodgson) (1832–98) wrote inspired examples of the genre. Lear has 'The Akond of Swat', thought to be a rendering of an Indian title, 'The DONG WITH A LUMINOUS NOSE', and 'The Yonghy-Bonghy-Bo'. Lewis Carroll gave us JABBERWOCKY, 'The Walrus and the Carpenter' and 'The Hunting of the Snark'.

Nonsuch (1539). Huge palace built for Henry VIII in Nonsuch Park, on the Epsom road near Ewell, Surrey; only the foundations remain.

No Orchids for Miss Blandish (1939). Novel by J. Hadley Chase for the tough sex market; it is an admitted English plagiarism of William Faulkner's pot-boiler, *Sanctuary* (1931).

'No Popery' riots Another name for the GORDON RIOTS.

Nordic Term sometimes applied to the tall fair-haired racial type of Scandinavia. There is a small Nordic element in Germany (as there is in Britain), and Nazi theorists were able to persuade themselves that the Germans were, under the leadership of the dark and undersized Hitler and Goebbels, essentially Nordic. See ARYAN MYTH.

Nordic Council Body formed by the governments of Scandinavia, Finland and Iceland which has achieved a certain degree of economic co-ordination between these countries.

Nordic events (Skiing). Cross-country skiing races, and ski-jumping; see ALPINE EVENTS.

Nore Mutiny (1797). Mutiny in the British North Sea Fleet following a mutiny a month earlier in the Channel Fleet at Spithead, which had won pay increases. At the Nore, however, some of the mutineers, inspired by the French Revolution, demanded not only improved conditions but political reforms. Their leaders were hanged, and the fleet put to sea the same year to win CAMPERDOWN. (Anchorage near Sheerness in the Thames Estuary.)

Norfolk (USA). Naval base in south-east Virginia, headquarters of the Supreme Allied Commander, Atlantic, a Nato command.

Norfolk jacket Single-breasted belted jacket with box pleat at the back worn for duck shooting in Norfolk.

Norland nurse (1892). Nurse trained at the Norland Nursery Training College at Hungerford, Berkshire.

N or M Answer to the first question (What is your name?) in the Anglican catechism. (Stands for 'state your name or names'; M is a corruption of NN; N stands for Latin *nomen*, 'name', and its duplication is the medieval copyists' shorthand method of indicating the plural.)

Norman architecture (11th–12th centuries). English form of ROMANESQUE ARCHITECTURE, exemplified in Winchester, Durham and St Albans cathedrals, and the Abbey Church of Tewkesbury.

Normande (Cooking) With shellfish or fish sauce; or with apples.

Normandy, Duke of Title of the Queen of England in the Channel Islands.

Norns Three Fates of Scandinavian mythology who water YGGDRASIL.

Norris, Aunt In Jane Austen's MANSFIELD PARK, the selfish, poisonous aunt of the Bertrams, who bullies the heroine, Fanny Price.

Norroy and Ulster One of the Kings of Arms at the COLLEGE OF ARMS, responsible for England north of the Trent and for Ireland.

Norsemen See VIKINGS.

North and Hillard Names of co-authors used as short title of a standard school textbook on Latin prose.

Northanger Abbey (1818). Jane Austen's novel; see MORLAND, CATHERINE.

North Atlantic Treaty (1949). See ATLANTIC PACT.

Northcliffe Lectures in Literature Annual lectures on English and foreign literature, given under the auspices of the University College, London University. (Named after Lord Northcliffe, newspaper proprietor.)

North-East Passage Sea-route north of Russia, the search for which began with Chancellor's voyage to the White Sea (1553) but was not successful until 1879.

Northern Earls, Rising of the (1569). One of several Roman Catholic plots to dethrone Elizabeth I.

Northern Lights Another name for the AURORA BOREALIS.

North German Confederation (1866–71). Grouping of the German states north of the Main (i.e. excluding Baden, Württemberg and Bavaria) under the King of Prussia as President, with Bismarck as Chancellor; incorporated in the German Empire in 1871.

North Sea oil (and **gas**) Discoveries of oil and gas in the North sea since the mid-1960s have made the UK and several other European countries almost self-sufficient in their energy needs. Reserves should last into the 21st century.

North Star Polaris, the Pole Star, a bright star in the LITTLE BEAR to which the Pointers of the GREAT BEAR point.

North Star State Nickname of Minnesota.

Northstead, Manor of Stewardship of this manor (in Yorkshire) is a fictitious office serving the same purpose as the CHILTERN HUNDREDS.

Northumberland Plate Flat-race run at Newcastle in June/July, known as the Pitman's Derby and immensely popular locally.

North-West Frontier Province Indian province created (1901) for the better administration of the troublesome Pathans on the Afghan border; now part of Pakistan.

North-West Passage Sea-route north of Canada, sought from Tudor times as a possibly shorter route to the East; discovered by Franklin (1847) but not traversed till 1905.

Norvic Abbreviation for the Bishop of Norwich.

Norwich School (1803). School of English landscape painters founded by J. S. Cotman and John Crome, who both lived at Norwich. They had many followers, including their sons.

Norwood report (1943). Report on secondary education and examinations which sharply criticized the restrictive effect on the curriculum of the School Certificate examinations. Its recommendations prepared the way for their replacement by the GCE and for the introduction of comprehensive schools. (Sir Cyril Norwood.)

Nosey Parker Colloquialism for 'inquisitive busybody'.

Nostromo (1904). Joseph Conrad's best novel, about the demoralizing effect of the greed for riches (represented by the local silver mines) on a closed community in a small South American republic. (For Italian *nostr'uomo*, 'our man', i.e. the mining firm's chief stevedore, a central character.)

Notes and Queries (1846). Monthly, formerly weekly, paper devoted to oddments of information likely to be of interest to antiquaries and literary men; it also provides a forum in which they can answer one another's questions.

Notre-Dame Name in French-speaking countries of many churches dedicated to Our Lady, but used specifically of the cathedral in Paris.

Notre Dame de Paris (1831). Victor Hugo's novel, set in the 15th century, about Quasimodo, the hunchback bell-ringer of Notre-Dame, who saves the gypsy dancer Esmeralda from the lustful Archdeacon Frollo, whom he hurls to his death from the top of the cathedral.

Nottingham Club Calling system at Bridge in which an opening bid of 1 Club indicates great strength.

Nottingham Goose Fair (1284). Fair held on the first Thursday of October, in olden times lasting 3 weeks and selling huge quantities of geese; the only survivor of several goose fairs held at Michaelmas, now chiefly of historical interest and not selling geese.

Nottingham ware (1690–1800). Fine lustrous salt-glaze stoneware, also called brownware, variously decorated. Jugs and mugs were the commonest form. The name is also given to the inferior products of numerous factories in the Nottingham district.

Notting Hill Scene of racial disturbances in August 1958.

Nouvelle Vague, La See NEW WAVE.

Novum Organum Francis Bacon's revolutionary work (1620) stressing the superiority of inductive reasoning, from particular instances to general laws, over the prevailing ARISTOTELIAN METHOD. (Latin, 'new instrument', i.e. for scientific and philosophical investigations.)

NQU Initials used in some families for 'not quite us', i.e. deemed slightly lower in the social pecking order. There are numerous variants.

NSMAPMAWOL Initials of *Not So Much a Programme, More a Way of Life*, the BBC's successor to TW3.

Nuffield College, Oxford (1937). Postgraduate college to encourage research, especially in social studies, founded by Viscount Nuffield.

Nuffield Foundation (1943). Endowed by Viscount Nuffield (William MORRIS, the car manufacturer) with £10 million of shares in his companies, it promotes, primarily, medical and sociological research; it represents only part of the money he gave away during his lifetime, estimated to total about £30 million.

Nuffield Professor Holder of one of 5 chairs at Oxford: Obstetrics and Gynaecology, Anaesthetics, Clinical Medicine, Orthopaedic Surgery, Surgery.

Nuits-Saint-Georges See CÔTE DE NUITS.

Number One, London Old postal address of Apsley House in Piccadilly, the first Duke of Wellington's home.

Numbers Fourth book of the PENTATEUCH, recounting the wanderings of the Israelites in the desert and their invasion of Canaan. (The title refers to the census of the people, Numbers 1:2.)

'Number 2, The Pines' (1920). Max Beerbohm's miniature masterpiece, a biographical sketch of Swinburne and Watts-Dunton, named after the Putney house where they lived together (1879–1909). It appears in a volume of essays, *And Even Now*.

Numidians See BERBERS.

Nunc Dimittis First words, used as the title, of the canticle taken from Luke 2:29: 'Lord, now lettest thou thy servant depart in peace'; used as a noun-phrase meaning 'readiness to die'. (Latin, 'now dismiss thou'.)

Nunn May spy case (1946). Trial of Alan Nunn May, sentenced to 10 years' imprisonment for passing information to Russia regarding the atomic bomb, 'as a contribution to the safety of mankind'; released 1952. See OTTAWA SPY RING.

Nun's Priest's Tale, The In the CANTERBURY TALES, the story of how CHANTICLEER AND PERTELOTF outwit a fox.

Nunthorpe Stakes Five-furlong flat-race run at York in August.

Nürburgring Grand Prix motor racing circuit in the Eifel mountains, south of Bonn, West Germany.

Nuremberg Laws (1935). German National-Socialist (Nazi) legislation which deprived the Jews of all civic rights, and prohibited their inter-marriage with 'Aryan' Germans. See ARYAN MYTH.

Nuremberg rallies (1933). Annual mass rallies of the Nazis, which Hitler made the occasion of some of his major speeches. (Ancient Bavarian city, north of Munich.)

Nuremberg trials (1945–6). Trials of German war criminals; Ribbentrop and Streicher, among others, were executed; Goering committed suicide before execution; Hess was sentenced to life imprisonment and died in SPANDAU in 1987.

Nutcracker Man See ZINJANTHROPUS.

Nutcracker Suite, The See CASSE-NOISETTE.

Nutmeg State Nickname of Connecticut. (The early inhabitants were traditionally the sort of people who would sell wooden nutmegs as real.)

Nye Familiar name for Aneurin (pronounced a-*nyr'*in) Bevan, the Labour Minister of Health who introduced the National Health Service.

Nymphenburg porcelain (1753). Products of a factory near Munich, perhaps second in prestige to MEISSEN, and especially famous for figures modelled by Anton Bustelli in 1754–63. The factory still operates today.

O

Oak-apple Day 29th May, Charles II's birthday, named after the oak-apples (or oak-leaves) worn by Royalists in memory of his escapade at BOS-COBEL. (Oak-apples, the small round galls found on oak leaves attacked by the gall-fly.)

Oaks, Boysie Anti-hero of John Gardner's tongue-in-cheek thrillers, a James Bond with all the aggressiveness of FERDINAND THE BULL.

Oaks, The Classic flat-race for 3-year-old fillies, run over 1½ miles at Epsom.

OBAFGKM Classification of stars in descending order of surface temperature and absolute magnitude (intrinsic brightness), and ranging in colour from blue to red. Most stars (the MAIN SEQUENCE STARS) fit into this classification. Examples are: Algol (B), Sirius (A), Pole Star (F), Sun (G), Aldebaran (K), Betelgeuse (M). In an older (Ptolemaic) classification the brightest are called 1st-magnitude, the faintest 6th-magnitude stars.

Oberammergau Bavarian village in the Alps south of Munich, famous for its PASSION PLAY performed since 1633 by a huge cast (1,250) of the villagers, normally every tenth year, as an act of gratitude for escape from a plague epidemic.

Oberon (1) King of the Fairies, husband of TITANIA or Queen Mab. The name is derived from the German ALBERICH through the French form, Auberon. (2) Title of Weber's opera (1826).

Oblomov (1858) Goncharov's best novel. Oblomov is a typical Russian whose gifts and virtues are shrouded by innate lethargy. His name has passed into the Russian language as a symbol of Russian passivity and inertia. (Pronounced ob-lom'of.)

O'Brien, Flann Pen-name of the Irish writer Brian O'Nolan (1911–66); see AT SWIM-TWO-BIRDS.

Occam's razor Principle that the guiding rule in philosophical speculation should be simplicity; the number of assumptions made should be kept to the minimum, all inessential concepts being cut out as with a razor. (Advanced by William of Ockham, or Occam, 14th-century English theologian.)

Occasionals Oxford University hockey club of the 60 best players in residence.

Ockenden Venture, The (1951). Charitable organization which provides homes and education for stateless or refugee children and students, mainly from Eastern Europe, Tibet and Africa. It has houses in various parts of England and schools for Tibetans in India. (Ockenden is the name of the first house and present headquarters, at Woking, Surrey.)

O'Connell Street Principal street of Dublin, better known under its old name, Sackville Street. (Named after 'The Liberator', Daniel O'Connell (died 1847), who founded a movement for Irish independence.)

Octagon Code name of the second Quebec Conference (September 1944), a meeting at which

Churchill and Roosevelt discussed strategic policies and the MORGENTHAU PLAN.

Octavian Gaius Octavius, who was renamed Gaius Julius Caesar Octavianus when adopted by Julius Caesar, and in 27 BC given the title of Augustus when he became the first Roman Emperor (in all but name).

October Manifesto (1905). Tsar Nicholas II's promise to permit an elected DUMA, extracted from him after Trotsky had set up a workers' soviet at St Petersburg and called a general strike.

October Revolution (1917). Bolshevik revolution of 7 November 1917 (25 October Old Style), led by Lenin and Trotsky; to be distinguished from the February Revolution (March New Style) which established a republic under a provisional government led by Prince Lvov and later by Kerensky.

Oddfellows, Independent Order of (Manchester Unity) (1810). Large friendly society, a revival of earlier Oddfellow societies, with central headquarters at Manchester and lodges in the UK, USA, the Dominions, and various European countries. It has a Masonic-type ritual. (Explained as derived from the fact that the earliest founders were regarded as odd fellows.)

Oddjob Impassive Korean who guards GOLDFINGER, his main weapon of offence a steel bowler-hat.

Oder–Neisse line Current boundary between them formally recognized by East Germany and Poland under the Görlitz agreement (1950). It is formed by the River Oder (Odra) and its tributary the western Neisse (Nisa), and gives a fifth of pre-war Germany to Poland, including East Prussia and German Silesia, and notably the cities of Stettin and Breslau.

ODESSA German National-Socialist (Nazi) organization for helping senior members of their party to escape from Germany at the end of the Second World War and to evade arrest thereafter. (Initials of German for Organization of ss Members.)

Ode to a Nightingale (1819). Keats's poem pensively contrasting his own mortality with the immortality of the bird's song – the same, he surmises, as may have been heard by Ruth 'amid the alien corn' and have often 'charm'd magic casements, opening on the foam / Of perilous seas, in faery lands forlorn'.

Odette de Crécy In Proust's REMEMBRANCE OF THINGS PAST, a cocotte who becomes SWANN's mistress and later his wife, and the mother of GILBERTE. Widowed twice, she eventually becomes the mistress of the Duc de GUERMANTES.

Odin, Woden, Wotan Chief god of Scandinavian mythology, god of wisdom and of war. Wednesday is named after him.

Odium theologicum Bitter hatred of rival religionists. 'No wars so sanguinary as holy wars; no persecutions so relentless as religious persecutions; no hatred so strong as theological hatred.'

Odtaa (1926). Novel by John Masefield; the title is made up of the initials of 'One damn thing after another'.

Odysseus (Ulysses) In Greek legend, King of Ithaca and one of the Greek leaders in the TROJAN WAR. After the adventures described in the ODYSSEY, he returned in disguise to Ithaca, slew PENELOPE's suitors and was reunited to his wife. In Homer he is wise and resourceful, in later authors crafty and treacherous. Tennyson's splendid poem 'Ulysses' represents him as still restless for adventure in his old age: 'How dull . . . to rest unburnish'd, not to shine in use.' (Pronounced od-is'ews.)

Odyssey, The Homer's epic poem recounting the adventures of ODYSSEUS on his return voyage from Troy, e.g. those involving CALYPSO, NAUSICAA, the LOTUS-EATERS, POLYPHEMUS, CIRCE, and SCYLLA AND CHARYBDIS. (Pronounced od'is-i.)

Oecumenical Council See VATICAN COUNCIL.

Oecumenical Patriarch The head of the EASTERN ORTHODOX CHURCH, the Bishop of Constantinople.

OED Initials used for the *Oxford English*

Dictionary, completed in 10 volumes (1928); 2nd edn, 1989.

Oedipus Greek legendary hero who, after solving the riddle of the Sphinx which plagued Thebes, was made King of Thebes. Unknowingly, he killed his father and married his own mother, JOCASTA. When TIRESIAS revealed his true identity, Oedipus blinded himself, cursed his sons (see SEVEN AGAINST THEBES), and was led by his only faithful child, ANTIGONE, to Colonus. He appears in Sophocles' plays *Oedipus Rex* and *Oedipus at Colonus*.

Oedipus complex Freud's term for the psychological results of a boy's excessive attachment to his mother and consequent (often unconscious) jealousy of and hostility to his father. See ELECTRA COMPLEX. (See OEDIPUS.)

Oenothera The genus name of the evening primrose.

Oerlikon Swiss light quick-firing 20-mm anti-aircraft gun, used by both sides in World War II. (Name of town where made; pronounced or'likon.)

Offa's Dyke Earth and stone rampart from the mouth of the Wye at Beachley to the mouth of the Dee in Flint, traditionally built by Offa, 8th-century king of Mercia, to keep out the Welsh, but probably earlier.

Off-Broadway theatre Small New York theatres where, from the 1950s, experimental plays and revivals of classics have been staged which were of too limited an appeal to pay their way on Broadway.

Officer in the Tower Name given to Lt N. Baillie-Stewart, imprisoned in the Tower of London (1933) for passing secret information to Germany, and again sentenced in 1946 for his wartime broadcasts from Germany.

Officers' Plot (July 1944) Attempt on Hitler's life by Col. von Stauffenberg and other officers. He left a bomb in a briefcase near Hitler at the Wolf's Lair; it caused extensive damage, but Hitler was only slightly injured.

Of Human Bondage (1915). Somerset Maugham's most ambitious novel, a forthright semi-autobiographical story about Whitstable, where he was brought up, Canterbury, where he went to school, and London, where he qualified in medicine.

Oflag German prisoner-of-war camp for officers. (Abbreviation of *Offizier* and *Lager*, 'camp'.)

Ogam (Ogham) Celtic alphabet consisting of groups of lines, used in inscriptions on memorial stones dating from about the 5th century AD, found mainly in south-west Ireland but also elsewhere in the British Isles.

Ogpu (1924–34). The name given to the GPU when it was given all-Union status; replaced by the NKVD. (Initials of the Russian for 'All-Union State Political Organization'.)

O'Hara, Scarlett Hot-tempered heroine of GONE WITH THE WIND.

Oh Dad! (1961). Short title of *Oh Dad, Poor Dad, Mama's Hung You in the Closet and I'm Feeling So Sad*, Arthur Kopit's undergraduate fantasy play about a phenomenally possessive mother, who carries her dead husband about with her in a coffin, and her son who has not the courage to escape her thrall.

Ohm's law At a given temperature, the ratio of the potential difference between 2 points of a conductor and the current flowing between them is a constant. For a potential difference of E volts and a current of I amps, the resistance (R) in ohms is E/I. The result of research by a German physicist, Georg Simon Ohm.

Oh, What a Lovely War! (1963). Musical revue produced by the THEATRE WORKSHOP, satirizing attitudes towards the First World War, and made into a film in 1969.

OK Originates from an American Indian expression meaning, 'It is so, and in no other way.' It is to be found in Byington's *Grammar of the Choctaw Language*, edited by D. G. Brinton (1870). President Wilson always insisted that 'Okeh' was the proper spelling, but popular use is 'OK'.

Okhrana (1881–1917). Russian Imperial secret police, originally formed to check terrorism.

Okinawa landing (April–June 1945). A successful US assault against fanatical Japanese opposition, including KAMIKAZE (suicide bombers) and one-man rockets. (Name of the largest of the Ryukyu Islands.)

Oklahoma! (1943). Record-breaking musical, the first Rodgers and Hammerstein smash hit, and the first in which a ballet was successfully integrated into the plot, by Agnes de Mille. Among its hit songs were 'The Surrey with the Fringe on Top' and 'Oh, What a Beautiful Mornin'!' It was based on a folk drama, *Green Grow the Lilacs* (1931) by Lynn Riggs.

Old Adam, The Original sin inherent in man.

Old Alleynian Old Boy of Dulwich College. (From the name of the founder, Alleyn; pronounced a-layn'yen.)

Old Bailey Central Criminal Court of Greater London, formerly an Assize, now a CROWN COURT. The Lord Mayor and City Aldermen retain the ancient privilege of sitting in it as judges. (Name of the street it is in.)

Old Believers See RASKOLNIKI.

Old Berkeley Hunt Eighteenth-century fox-hunting pack with kennels near Aylesbury.

Old Bill Walrus-moustached veteran of the Flanders mud, the creation of the cartoonist Capt. Bruce Bairnsfather in World War I; his most famous cartoon showed Bill and another Tommy under fire in a waterlogged shell-hole in no man's land, with the caption: 'Well, if you knows of a better 'ole, go to it!'

Old Boy net Means of getting what one wants through the freemasonry of public school Old Boys; or (by extension) through knowing the right people in the right places.

Oldbury-on-Severn (1969). One of the MAGNOX type of nuclear power-stations. (Coastal village, opposite Chepstow, in Gloucestershire.)

Old Contemptibles British Expeditionary Force which fought at Mons (1914). (From the phrase, doubtfully attributed to the Kaiser, 'the con-temptible little British army'. However, the Kaiser appears to have said 'ridiculously small army' and the expression was thought to have been invented by Sir Frederick Maurice to encourage the troops during the Mons retreat. See MAURICE CASE.)

Old Crome Name given to the painter John Crome to distinguish him from his son J. B. Crome, also a member of the NORWICH SCHOOL.

Old Curiosity Shop, The (1841). Dickens's sentimental novel about Little Nell and her grandfather, whose London curiosity shop is seized by QUILP for debt, and who flee together to wander through the countryside until after many adventures they settle in a quiet village.

Old Deer Park Rugby home, at Richmond, Surrey, of the London Welsh RUFC, and formerly of Rosslyn Park.

Old Dominion, The Nickname of Virginia.

Old English Also called Anglo-Saxon, the language of the ANGLES and SAXONS from their arrival in England in the 5th century AD until it was modified into MIDDLE ENGLISH in the 11th century. The Saxon dialect of Wessex predominated in this period.

Old Faithful Most famous, though not the largest, geyser in the YELLOWSTONE NATIONAL PARK. It spouts a 150-ft column of hot water and steam for a few minutes at near-regular intervals of about an hour, year in and year out.

'Old Folks at Home' Stephen Foster's Negro song about the 'SWANEE Ribber'.

Old Ghana (8th–11th centuries AD). Kingdom of the Sudan, west of Timbuktu, conquered by the ALMORAVIDS. Modern Ghana has no connection with it, racially or geographically.

Old Glory Stars and Stripes, the US flag.

Old Grog Admiral Vernon, who ordered (1740) that the rum ration should be diluted, in which form it became known as grog, in his memory. (From his coat of grogram, a coarse cloth of wool and mohair.)

Old Hickory Nickname of Andrew Jackson; see JACKSONIAN DEMOCRACY.

Old Hundred Tune, of uncertain origin, now attached to the metrical version of the hundredth psalm, 'All People That on Earth Do Dwell'.

Old Kent Road Road in South London made famous through Albert Chevalier's music-hall song 'Knocked 'em in the Ol' Kent Road'. ('Knocked' for 'astonished'.)

Old King Cole Merry old soul of the nursery rhyme, variously identified with a 3rd-century prince who built Colchester, a rich Reading clothier named Colebrook, and others.

Old Kingdom (Ancient Egypt) Period of some 500 years from about 2800 BC, when the 3rd–6th Dynasties ruled at MEMPHIS; the Age of the Pyramids.

Old Lady of Threadneedle Street Bank of England, which is in that street.

Old Man and the Sea, The (1952). Novel in which Ernest Hemingway, in the guise of a Cuban fisherman battling alone with the elements, turned his back on the world which had spurned his previous work, ACROSS THE RIVER AND INTO THE TREES (1950).

Old Man of the Mountain Name given to the founder of the ASSASSINS sect in Persia (around AD 1100) after he had moved his secret headquarters to Mount Lebanon.

Old Man of the Sea Troublesome character in the *Arabian Nights* who climbed on the back of Sindbad the Sailor; a person one cannot shake off, an incubus.

Old Man's Beard Wild clematis, so named from its winter appearance.

Old Marshal, The Chang Tso-lin, governor of Manchuria, which he declared independent of China in 1921 and ruled ruthlessly but efficiently until he died of wounds received in a Japanese air-raid in 1928.

Old Masters Great European painters from Giotto to the 18th century; extended to include the acknowledged great of the 19th century; the works of these.

Old Moore's Almanac Name given to at least 4 modern imitations of a 17th-century publication by Francis Moore, quack and astrologer.

Old Mortality (1816). Walter Scott's novel, and the nickname of the old man in it who tries to keep green the memory of the COVENANTERS who fell victims to BLUIDIE CLAVERS by tending their graves all over Scotland.

Old Parr Thomas Parr, a Shropshire man, on slender evidence said to have died aged 152 in 1635, living under 10 reigns, marrying first at 80 and then at 120, with children by both wives. Buried in Poet's Corner in Westminster Abbey through some royal whim.

Old Possum Name taken by T. S. Eliot in writing his whimsical *Old Possum's Book of Practical Cats* (1939). See MACAVITY.

Old Pretender James Stuart, 'James III', son of James II by his second wife. He died in Rome, 1766. See FIFTEEN.

Old Q Fourth Duke of Queensberry, a notorious old rake of the 18th century.

Old Red Sandstone Freshwater deposits of the DEVONIAN PERIOD, in which red sandstone predominates; rich in fossil fishes and marsh plants.

Old Rowley Nickname of Charles II, from one of his racehorses; hence the Rowley Mile at Newmarket. (Not connected with Anthony Rowley, of the nursery rhyme 'A frog he would a-wooing go'.)

Old Sarum Original site of Salisbury, 2 miles north of the present town; famous as a 'rotten borough'. (Corruption of the Latin name *Sarisburia*.)

Oldsmobile (1902). First US mass-produced car, made by R. E. Olds.

Old Stone Age See PALAEOLITHIC AGE.

Old Style Julian calendar, abandoned in Britain in 1752, when 3 September became by law 14 September (NEW STYLE); and in Russia in 1918.

Old Time dances Name given to such dances as the lancers, two-step and polka.

Old Trafford Park 2 miles south-west of Manchester in Stretford; the first cricket ground outside London to be used for Test matches, and the football home of Manchester United.

Olduvai Gorge Site in the Serengeti plains, north Tanzania, where remains were found of ZINJ-ANTHROPUS and 'HOMO HABILIS'.

Old Vic London theatre in the Waterloo Road which from 1914 under Lilian Baylis staged Shakespeare's plays and later, until SADLER'S WELLS was reopened, opera. After World War II, it became an unofficial national theatre with an all-round classical repertoire.

Old Wives' Tale, The (1908). Best of Arnold Bennett's FIVE TOWNS novels, telling the life story of Constance Baines, draper's daughter, who stays in, and marries into, the business; and of her sister Sophia, who elopes with a rascally commercial traveller, runs a *pension* in Paris during the Franco-Prussian War, and returns to spend her last years with the now widowed Constance.

Old World Eastern hemisphere, specifically Europe.

Oleaceae Olive family of trees and shrubs, which includes the olive, ash, jasmine, privet and lilac.

O-level Examination taken at age 16 or earlier, requiring a higher standard than the old School Certificate; now replaced by GCSE. (O for Ordinary.)

Oligocene Epoch Second subdivision of the TERTIARY PERIOD, lasting from about 50 to 25 million years ago. Present-day mammals began to appear, e.g. cats and dogs, and primitive apes, as well as the sabre-toothed tiger. (Greek, 'few of the modern', i.e. few modern forms of life found.)

Oliver See ROLAND.

Oliver Twist (1838). Dickens's novel about the foundling Oliver's persecution by BUMBLE in a workhouse, his subsequent adventures with FAGIN and Bill SIKES, further persecution by his half-brother out to deprive him of his inheritance, and his final adoption by the kindly Dr Brownlow.

Olivia Character in Shakespeare's *Twelfth Night* who falls in love with Viola who is disguised as a page.

Olney hymns (1779). Those written, in collaboration with John Newton, by William Cowper when he was living at Olney, Buckinghamshire.

Olney Pancake Race (1445). Run on Shrove Tuesday at Olney, Buckinghamshire, by housewives carrying and tossing a pancake in a frying-pan.

Oloroso One of the 2 main types of sherry (see FINO), full-bodied, deep gold or brown; in its natural state, dry; but for export blended with sweet wine to form, in order of increasing sweetness, Amoroso, Cream, Golden and Brown dessert sherries.

Olympia (1) See OLYMPIC GAMES; (2) exhibition buildings in Hammersmith, London, opened in 1886. The Ideal Home Exhibition and Dairy Show are staged there.

Olympiad Four-year period between OLYMPIC GAMES.

Olympian (Person who is) awe-inspiring, stately, condescending, aloof.

Olympic Games (1) Ancient Greek celebration in honour of Olympian Zeus at Olympia in the Peloponnese, at which there were contests in drama, music and athletics; (2) modern revival of the athletics section of these, begun in Athens in 1896.

Olympus Home of the Greek gods, identified with the 10,000-ft mountain at the eastern end of the range that separates Greece and Macedonia.

OM Initials placed after the name of a recipient of the Order of Merit, a British Order limited to 24 members, for men and women of especial distinction; instituted in 1902.

Omaha Beach Code name of a beach north-west of Bayeux, one of the US landing sites on D-Day.

Omar, Mosque of Mosque on the site of SOL-OMON'S TEMPLE at Jerusalem; originally a Byzantine church.

Omayyads Dynasty of Caliphs who ruled at Damascus (661–750) and in Spain (756–1031).

Ombudsman Official appointed by government to investigate complaints by individuals against oppressive bureaucratic action; appointed in Sweden in 1809, New Zealand 1962 and Britain 1966. There are also ombudsmen in the UK for local government, banking, building societies and insurance. See PARLIAMENTARY COM-MISSIONER FOR ADMINISTRATION.

Omnium, Dukes of The first Duke appears in Trollope's *Framley Parsonage* as a very rich, self-assured and scandalously unscrupulous character. His nephew, Plantagenet Palliser ('Planty Pall'), married to the admirable Lady Glencora, inherits the title and becomes Prime Minister in the PHINEAS FINN series of novels. In contrast to the first Duke, he is a sensitive, honourable man.

Oneida Community (1847–79). Small communistic society which formed and successfully managed a farm settlement at Oneida Creek, New York State; at first polygamy and polyandry were permitted. They were also called Perfectionists. (Pronounced oh-ny'da.)

One Thousand Guineas Classic flat-race for 3-year-old fillies run over the Rowley Mile at the first spring meeting, Newmarket.

One-Ton Cup (1898). International ocean-sailing team race, originally for yachts in the 1-ton class, but now for those not exceeding 22 ft (RORC RATING); held in July.

One Upmanship (1952). Stephen Potter's sequel to LIFEMANSHIP, a study of the art of discon-certing one's fellows. For example, if a man has just bought a large country house, the Lifeman will ask him patronizingly: 'Well, how's the cottage?' If the proud householder is also a Lifeman, he will reply: 'What with those National Trust fellows and the Society for the Preservation of Ancient Buildings nosing round, I'm beginning to regret I ever bought it.'

One-Way Pendulum (1959). N. F. Simpson's contrived fantasy play satirizing suburban distortions of values and proneness to obsessions. Upstairs, Kirby has taught all but one of a battery of 'speak-your-weight' machines to sing the Hallelujah Chorus (the one sticks grimly to '15 stone 10 lb'); below, his father has constructed a model of the Old Bailey, where he puts his son on trial for multiple murder.

Onion Patch Trophy US equivalent of the AD-MIRAL'S CUP.

Only Way, The (1899). Dramatized version by Freeman Wills of Dickens's TALE OF TWO CITIES, in which Sir John Martin Harvey acted the part of Sydney CARTON.

On the Beach (1957). Nevil Shute's novel about the last survivors of the complete destruction of the inhabited globe after an atomic war.

On the Road (1957). Best-known of the beatnik novels, by the American Jack Kerouac.

On the Spot (1931). Edgar Wallace thriller inspired by the career of SCARFACE AL CAPONE.

Oom Paul Nickname of Paul Kruger, President of the Transvaal and Boer leader in the Boer War. (Afrikaans *oom*, 'uncle'.)

007 Secret Service designation of James BOND; the 00 signifies a licence to kill when necessary.

Op art (1965). Designs on fabrics, tableware etc., and to a less important extent paintings, usually in black and white, which exploit the effects of after-images and various types of optical illusion, so that the whole or part of the design appears to move. ('Op' for 'optical'; no connection with Pop art.)

OPEC (1960). Initials used for the Organization of Petroleum Exporting Countries, formed by oil-producing states to protect themselves from unfair exploitation by the large Western oil companies. Membership consists of Algeria, Ecuador, Gabon, Indonesia, Iran, Iraq, Kuwait, Libya, Nigeria, Qatar, Saudi Arabia, United Arab Emirates and Venezuela.

Open-door policy Trade access on equal terms to all nations without discrimination. When foreign powers were carving out spheres of influence in a weakened China, the British suggested that this policy should guide them; it was adopted and enunciated by the US Secretary of State John Hay (1899). Later it was applied elsewhere in the Far East.

Open Skies policy (1955). Policy suggested by Eisenhower at the GENEVA SUMMIT of permitting unrestricted air reconnaissance and the exchange of complete blueprints of military establishments in order to convince the world that the two Powers were guarding against surprise nuclear attacks, thus lessening danger and tension. The Russians said *nyet*; hence U2 and COSMOS.

Open University (1971). Integrated TV–radio-correspondence courses organized by an autonomous body which awards its own degrees in the normal university subjects and also provides refresher and research courses. Suggested by Harold Wilson and Jennie Lee in 1963, it was intended mainly for technologists and technicians who had left school early and for clerks and housewives, but the initial response was overwhelmingly middle-class (especially teachers) and for non-technical subjects. HQ at MILTON KEYNES, with regional study centres.

Ophelia In Shakespeare's *Hamlet*, the daughter of Polonius; driven mad by Hamlet's treatment and her father's death, she drowns herself.

Ophir, Land of According to 1 Kings 10:11, the source of the gold and precious stones brought to King Solomon; probably somewhere in Arabia.

Opium War (1839–42). Extraordinary war in which the British fought for the right to import opium from India into China, bombarding Canton and occupying Hong Kong. It was considered that Chinese confiscation of opium belonging to British merchants justified this.

Oppenheimer case (1954). (USA) Suspension of Dr Robert Oppenheimer, chairman of the advisory committee to the Atomic Energy Commission, because he had failed to disclose Communist interests in earlier years. Although he had supervised the making of the first atomic bomb, he opposed the development of the hydrogen bomb, and so fell a victim to MCCARTHYISM, and was not rehabilitated until 1963.

Oppidans All boys at Eton other than KING'S SCHOLARS. (Latin *oppidum*, 'town'; they live in boarding houses in the town, the scholars live in college.)

Opus Dei (1928). International Roman Catholic organization, mostly of laymen, dedicated to the inconspicuous dissemination of the ideals of Christian living by the example of their own lives. It was founded in Spain. (Latin, 'work of God'.)

Oracle, Sir Reference to Gratiano's lines in Shakespeare's *Merchant of Venice*, in which he rebukes his friend Antonio: 'As who should say, "I am Sir Oracle, / And when I ope my lips let no dog bark".'

Oradour massacre (1944). Massacre by German soldiers of nearly all the inhabitants of Oradour-sur-Glane, near Limoges, France, on the grounds that arms had been found hidden there. The Germans had apparently confused it with another Oradour, where Resistance forces had been active.

Orange A town north of Avignon in France; formerly an independent principality governed (1530–1673) by the Dutch House of ORANGE-NASSAU.

Orange Bowl Sports stadium at Miami, Florida.

Orangemen Members of the Orange Society, formed by Irish Protestants (1795) to protect the ASCENDANCY and the Protestant religion against Wolfe Tone's Society of United Irishmen, by then turned republican and seeking aid from the French DIRECTORY; now used generally of Ulster Protestants. (Named after William III of England, Prince of Orange.)

Orange-Nassau, House of Dynasty founded by

William the Silent, to which William III of England belonged; it is still the Royal House of the Netherlands.

Orange Pekoe (1) Originally, a high-quality China tea manufactured from the youngest leaves and scented with orange blossom. (2) Now a trade term merely indicating a grade of tea rather better than Pekoe. (Chinese, 'white hair' referring to the down on the young leaf.)

Orc In William Blake's private mythology, the spirit of rebellion, violence and passion, which continually strives to loosen the shackles of URIZEN.

Orcadian (Native) of the Orkney Islands. (From Latin name, *Orcades*.)

Ordeal of Gilbert Pinfold, The (1957). Evelyn Waugh's novel of a man plagued by hallucinations; it is based on a personal experience.

Ordeal of Richard Feverel, The (1859). George Meredith's partly autobiographical novel of a father who tries to give his son the perfect upbringing; the latter, however, marries a girl his father refuses to receive, and the consequences are disastrous to all.

Ordovician Period Second earliest period of the PALAEOZOIC ERA, lasting from about 500 to 450 million years ago. Fossils are found of the earliest vertebrates (primitive fishes) and land plants (algae). (Latin *Ordovices*, tribe of North Wales; pronounced ord-o-vish'i-an.)

Oregon Trail Route from Independence (Missouri) to Fort Laramie (Wyoming) and Portland (Oregon), used by American pioneers going West and especially by those taking part in the Californian Gold Rush. Francis Parkman's autobiographical narrative (1847) is an account of his journey across the eastern end of the trail.

Oresteia, The (458 BC) Only complete trilogy of Greek drama to survive, comprising *Agamemnon*, *Choephoroi* ('Libation-pourers') and *Eumenides* ('The Furies'), written by Aeschylus. It records the murder of AGAMEMNON, his son ORESTES' revenge on Clytemnestra, and his acquittal. (Pronounced oh-res-ty'-a.)

Orestes In Greek legend, the son of AGAMEMNON and brother of ELECTRA; they avenge their father's murder by killing Aegisthus and CLYTEMNESTRA and are acquitted of matricide by the intervention of Apollo and Athene. Orestes appears in the ORESTEIA and in 4 plays of Euripides.

Organization of African Unity (1963). Organization of African states to promote unity and to stamp out colonialism; headquarters at Addis Ababa.

Organization of American States (1948). Organization of the USA and all the independent states of Central and South America (Cuba, though suspended from OAS activities in 1962, is still a member, and Bolivia, which seceded in 1963, rejoined in 1990). It tries to ensure the peaceful settlement of internal disputes and to co-ordinate external policies. Canada is not a member.

Oriana See AMADIS DE GAUL.

Orient Express Train which formerly travelled from Calais via Paris, Lausanne, Milan, Venice and Trieste to Yugoslavia, Greece and Turkey but now a luxury train travelling London–Venice.

Original sin Adam and Eve, parents of the race, defied God and so transmitted to their descendants the original sin that stains everyone, irrespective of their own actions of redemption. The doctrine is based on Genesis 2 and 3 and elaborated by St Paul, especially in Romans 5. The theory of evolution destroyed this tradition.

Origin of Species, The (1859). Short title of Darwin's *On the Origin of Species by means of* NATURAL SELECTION, *or the Preservation of Favoured Races in the Struggle for Life*. In contrast to the then prevailing view that each species was separately created, this was the first clear formulation of the theory that the entire animal kingdom has in the course of time evolved from one primitive form of life. See DARWIN'S FINCHES.

Orion In Greek legend, a mighty hunter, son of Poseidon, who is blinded but has his sight restored. His death is engineered by Apollo, who fears that Artemis may fall in love with him; with his belt and sword, he then takes his place among the constellations (see next entry).

Orion The Hunter, the most conspicuous northern constellation; the Belt consists of 3 second magnitude stars across the centre; below the Belt is the Great Galactic Nebula, visible to the naked eye. BETELGEUSE and RIGEL are the brightest stars in Orion. (See last entry.)

Orlando Italian form of ROLAND, the medieval hero.

Orlando (1928). Virginia Woolf's unclassifiable fantasy in which Orlando starts as a young Elizabethan male poet and grows into a modern woman poet. This race through the centuries affords opportunities for satirical digressions on literary and social themes.

Orlando Furioso (1532). Ariosto's epic poem, with stories of monsters, a trip to the moon in Elijah's chariot, and other such fantasies, having in fact little to do with Orlando (ROLAND). (Italian, 'Orlando mad'.)

Orleanist Monarchy (1830–48). In French history the reign of Louis-Philippe, KING OF THE FRENCH; also called the July Monarchy. (Louis was the son of PHILIPPE ÉGALITÉ, Duke of Orleans.)

Orleans, Duke of Fourteenth-century title which became extinct but was revived in 1661 by Louis XIV, who bestowed it on his brother. Philippe Égalité was one of the line; see previous entry.

Orlon Man-made acrylic fibre manufactured by DU PONT and used as a wool-substitute in knitwear.

Orly International airport south of Paris, comprising Orly-Sud and Orly-Ouest, used by Air France among others. See LE BOURGET.

Ormuzd, Ormazd See AHURA MAZDA.

Ornithogalum Genus that includes the South African chincherinchees.

Orphée (1946). Jean Cocteau's film about a poet who had lost his inspiration, and a princess who represents his own personal death. He also wrote a play with this title in 1926. (French spelling of ORPHEUS.)

Orpheus Legendary Greek musician, the son of a king of Thrace and one of the Muses, who was given a lyre by Apollo with which he charmed even the trees and stones (and see EURYDICE). His grief over his loss of Eurydice was so prolonged that the women of Thrace took it as an insult, and the Maenads (BACCHANTS) tore him to pieces as having offended Dionysus. (Pronounced or'fews.)

Orpheus and Eurydice (1762). Gluck's first opera, which broke completely with the traditions of Italian opera.

Orpheus in the Underworld (1858). Offenbach's comic operetta in which Orpheus, a popular violinist, reluctantly rescues his wife from the Underworld at the insistent demand of his public.

Orphic Mysteries Greek cult of the 6th century BC associated with the name of ORPHEUS. Devotees preached purity, asceticism and atonement for sin, believed in an afterlife, and worshipped the man–god Orpheus, who had suffered torment on earth. The cult influenced Pythagoras and Plato, and foreshadowed Christian beliefs.

Orpington Large and hardy dual-purpose breed of domestic fowl, typically buff coloured ('Buff Orpington'). (Orpington, Kent.)

Orpington by-election (March 1962). Gain of a hitherto safe 'new' Conservative seat by the Liberal Party, thought at the time (mistakenly) to herald a revival of Liberal fortunes. (At that time a west Kent urban district, now part of Bromley borough, London.)

Orrery Astronomical device to show the movements of the planets about the sun, invented by George Graham; one of these instruments was made for Charles Boyle, Earl of Orrery.

Orthodox Church Another name for the EASTERN ORTHODOX CHURCH.

Orthoptera Order of insects with mouths equipped to bite, and which run and jump but do not always fly; the cockroaches, locusts, crickets, grasshoppers, etc.

Orwellian Resembling the world created by George Orwell in *1984* and ANIMAL FARM.

Osagyefo Title assumed by Kwame Nkrumah when President of Ghana. ('Redeemer.')

Osbaldistone, Frank Hero of Scott's ROB ROY who marries Diana Vernon. His cousin Rashleigh Osbaldistone is his bitterest enemy and, after betraying his fellow Jacobites, is killed by Rob Roy. (Pronounced oz-bèl-dis'tèn.)

Osborne House Originally a royal residence, near Cowes in the Isle of Wight, where Queen Victoria died; it then became a Royal Naval college (1903–21) and later a hospital for officers. Now open to the public.

Osborne judgement (1909). House of Lords ruling which made the trade union political levy illegal; reversed in 1913. (*Osborne* v. *Amalgamated Society of Railway Servants*.)

Oscar Gold-plated figurine annually awarded by the Academy of Motion Picture Arts and Sciences, Hollywood, for the highest achievement in film production; (loosely) a similar award for acting or scenario-writing. (Name chosen arbitrarily.)

Oscar Slater case Outstanding example of wrongful imprisonment; Slater was found guilty of murder in 1909; the sentence was quashed 19 years later, and he was released and paid £6,000 compensation.

Osiris Ancient Egyptian ox-god, sometimes regarded as a sun-god but also as a god of the dead, represented in art as a crowned mummy. ISIS was his sister and wife, and he was killed by his brother SET, but was resurrected. His worship developed into a fertility cult resembling that of Tammuz and Dionysus.

Osprey (1952). A national class dinghy designed by Ian Proctor and raced, mainly in the south-west, by a crew of 2 or 3; overall length 17 feet 6 inches.

Ossewabrandwag South African right-wing pro-German organization, disowned by D. F. Malan, the National Party leader (1933–54), when it became clear that it was sabotaging the war effort.

Ossian In Irish legend, the son of FINN, also spelt Oisin; he lived to tell, aged about 150, the old Irish legends to St Patrick.

Ossianic poems (1760–63). Spurious poems by a Scottish MP, James Macpherson, partly translated from Gaelic and Erse originals, but mostly cleverly invented by him and passed off as authentic. (See previous entry.)

Osterley Park House Robert Adam house near the Great West Road, Osterley, now administered by the Victoria and Albert Museum.

Ostrogoths Eastern GOTHS, who ruled Italy from 493 until the Emperor Justinian drove them out in 534.

OTC (1908). Initials used for Officers' Training Corps, the cadet force at public schools and universities. At the outset of World War II it was divided into a junior (schools) branch which was later merged with the COMBINED CADET FORCE, and a senior branch which remains the University OTC.

Otello (1887). Verdi's opera, based on Shakespeare's OTHELLO.

Otéro, La Belle (1868–1965). Spanish grande cocotte of the BELLE ÉPOQUE, loved by kings and grand dukes.

Othello Moor who in Shakespeare's play (1604) of that name is led by IAGO to suspect DESDEMONA's fidelity.

Other Club, The (1911). London political and private dining club founded by Winston Churchill and F. E. Smith (Lord Birkenhead) as a rival to The CLUB. It has no premises and its members, Conservative, Liberal and a few Labour politicians, meet at the Savoy on alternate Thursdays when Parliament is sitting.

Ottawa agreements (1932). These established IMPERIAL PREFERENCE between Britain and the Dominions and (1933) the Colonies, marking Britain's final abandonment of FREE TRADE in the face of the World DEPRESSION. In practice Britain had to tax vital foreign foodstuffs (e.g. US wheat and Argentine meat) to assist the Dominions, who gave little compensation by granting preference, but by no means free entry, for British manufactures.

Ottawa spy ring (1945). Network uncovered by the defection of a Soviet diplomat, Igor Gouzenko, at Ottawa; it led to the arrest of FUCHS, NUNN MAY and the ROSENBERGS.

Otterburn (1388). Border battle between the Douglases and the Percys, the subject of an old ballad.

Ottoman Turks (1300–1920). Second wave of Turks, who displaced the SELJUK TURKS and ruled until Turkey became a republic; also called Osmanlis. In the 15th century they destroyed what was left of the Byzantine Empire, and reunified the Islamic world from the Balkans to Tunis. (Named after the founder, Othman, also spelt Osman or Usman.)

Oudenarde, Battle of (1708). Third victory over the French in the War of the SPANISH SUCCESSION, won by Marlborough and Prince Eugène of Savoy. (Town near Ghent in east Flanders, Belgium; pronounced oo'den-ard.)

Ouida Pen-name of Louise de la Ramée, English-born half-French author of UNDER TWO FLAGS (1867) and many other melodramatic novels; she is remembered with delight for her gorgeous young Guards officers, with their moustaches drenched in scent, and the remark (to be fair, wrongly attributed to her and coming from Desmond Coke's parody, *Sandford of Merton*): 'All rowed fast, but none so fast as stroke.' (Nursery pronunciation of Louise.)

Our Dumb Friends See BLUE CROSS.

Our Mutual Friend (1864). Charles Dickens's last complete novel. John Harmon is left a fortune on condition that he marries Bella Wilfer, whom he has never met. He therefore arrives under an assumed name to see how the land lies, and eventually marries her. The story is heavy with symbolism and brooding melancholy.

Our Town (1938). Thornton Wilder's play sympathetically depicting everyday life in a small New Hampshire town at the turn of the century, remarkable for the device of a voluble stage manager commenting to the audience on the progress of the play. In the last act, set in a cemetery, the dead proclaim their faith in the age-old values and in the essential harmony of the universe. The play was made into a movie (1940) with music by Aaron Copland.

Outer Mongolia Northern part of Mongolia, formerly Chinese, which proclaimed itself the Mongolian People's Republic (1924) and was recognized by Chiang Kai-shek in 1946; capital, Ulan Bator.

Outline of History, The (1920). H. G. Wells's remarkable and original history of mankind from prehistoric times down to his own day.

Outsider, The (1956). Book of essays by Colin Wilson analysing the pessimism of contemporary culture and discussing 'social misfits' such as Van Gogh, Nijinsky and Col. Lawrence. It became, without due cause, associated with the ANGRY YOUNG MEN image.

Outward Bound (1923). Sutton Vane's play in which a small group of passengers find themselves in a liner bound for heaven or hell, and come to realize gradually that they are dead.

Outward Bound Schools (1941). Schools run by a Trust, in Wales, the Lake District and overseas, where boys and girls are taught to face hazards and hardships on mountain and sea, and trained in rescue work. Inspired by Kurt Hahn, of GORDONSTOUN and the ATLANTIC COLLEGE Council.

Oval, The Surrey County cricket ground at Kennington, south of the Thames, traditionally the scene of the final match of most Test series; also the name of the test-match ground at Adelaide, Australia. There is a Kensington Oval ground in Barbados. Scene of the first Test match in England (1880).

Oval office, The US President's office in the White House, Washington DC.

Overloaded Ark, The (1953). First of several delightful accounts by the zoologist, Gerald Durrell, of his travels in various parts of the world in search of animals for the Jersey zoo.

Overlord

Overlord Code name of the final plan for the landings in Normandy in 1944.

Ovra Italian Fascist secret police. (Initials of Italian for 'Security organization for the repression of anti-Fascism'.)

'Owl and the Pussy-Cat, The' One of Edward Lear's *Nonsense Songs*.

Owls, The Nickname of the Sheffield Wednesday football team.

Ox-Bow Incident, The (1943). Sombre film based on an American novel, on the subject of lynching. It was released in Britain as *Strange Incident*, but is now better known in cinema history under its American title.

Oxbridge Portmanteau word for Oxford and Cambridge Universities.

Oxfam (1942). Voluntary organization with headquarters at Oxford which helps to relieve poverty and suffering in all parts of the world by providing food, clothing, medical attention, shelter, training and education. (For Oxford Committee for Famine Relief.)

Oxford and Cambridge University Club See UNITED OXFORD AND CAMBRIDGE UNIVERSITY CLUB.

Oxford Group, The Early nickname for BUCHMANISM. (Dr Buchman formed a group, one of many, when he visited Oxford in 1921; there was no special association of the movement with Oxford.)

Oxford Movement (1833). Movement towards ANGLO-CATHOLICISM started by J. H. (later Cardinal) Newman and John Keble. They tried to revive pre-Reformation religion in the Church of England, with emphasis on ritual, sacraments, the confessional, etc.

Oxford shoe Ordinary laced shoe.

Oxford University English university, a centre of learning since *c.* 1167, consisting of 40 separately administered residential colleges (including 2 for women only), the oldest being University College (1249), Balliol (1263) and Merton (1264). A HEBDOMADAL COUNCIL administers the university's affairs. There are some 10,000 students.

Oxford University Press Ancient, world-famous, most respected of presses, ceased its printing activities in 1989. Printing has been a feature of Oxford since 1517, but publishing had proceeded since 1478. One of the presses privileged to print the Bible, the OUP was noted for fine, accurate and scholarly books. In 1671 Dr Fell (the subject of the well-known rhyme) took part in the management; his name is also perpetuated by being given to the beautifully cut lettering of a fount of printing type. Perhaps the OUP's most famous work was the series of Oxford English Dictionaries.

Oxon. Abbreviation for (1) (Bishop) of Oxford, (2) of Oxford University. (For Latinized name *Oxoniensis*, from older name Oxenford.)

Oxus Ancient name of the Amu Darya river, USSR.

Oxyrhynchus papyri See SAYINGS OF CHRIST. (Oxyrhynchus, a city of Middle Egypt, where early Christians settled, about 120 miles south of Cairo.)

Oz Australia (Australian slang).

Oz, The Wizard of Character in a series of children's stories about the Kingdom of Oz written by L. F. Baum, beginning with *The Wonderful Wizard of Oz* (1900), which was made into a musical comedy and a film.

Ozone layer Region of ozone concentration in the stratosphere that absorbs high-energy solar ultraviolet rays.

'Ozymandias' (1818). Shelley's sonnet on the ruins of a mighty statue set up in the desert by some ancient tyrant, with the inscription; 'My name is Ozymandias, King of Kings: / Look on my works, ye Mighty, and despair.' On which Shelley commented: 'Nothing beside remains . . . / The lone and level sands stretch far away.' (Ozymandias may be Rameses II.)

P

Pace Egging Easter Monday celebration in Lancashire, Yorkshire and Cheshire, marked by a children's performance of a 16th-century play with traditional characters (St George, Bold Hector, Bold Slasher, etc.); the Toss Pot, wearing a top hat, goes round with a basket collecting eggs (money is now an acceptable substitute) from the spectators. (Presumably from Paschal or Pâques.)

Pacem in terris (1963). Pope John XXIII's encyclical on the role of the Church in the nuclear age and on the supreme need for world peace. (Latin, 'peace on earth'.)

Pacific Ocean So called by Magellan, the Portuguese navigator, because he experienced calm weather and a calm sea when he sailed across it.

Pacific Security Pact See ANZUS.

Pacific Standard Time (USA) Time in the western states, 8 hours earlier than GMT.

Pact of Steel (May 1939). Full military and political alliance between Italy and Germany which developed from the ROME–BERLIN AXIS.

Paddington Former London metropolitan borough, since 1965 part of the borough of WESTMINSTER (City of).

Pádraigh Irish spelling of Patrick.

Paeonia Flowering plant, named after Paeon, a physician of ancient Greece, who used the plant for medical purposes.

Page 3 girl Photographs of scantily clad females on this page of popular newspapers are supposed to increase sales.

Paget's Irregular Horse Nickname, won in India, of the 4th (Queen's Own) Hussars.

Pagliacci, I (1892). Leoncavallo's opera in which Canio, the clown, stabs his faithless wife to death in the course of a 'play within a play', a production of Columbine and Harlequin. See CAV. AND PAG. (Italian, 'the strolling players'; pronounced ee pah-lyaht'-chi.)

Painterly Abstraction Alternative name for ABSTRACT EXPRESSIONISM. (Painterly, translation of German malerisch, in the sense that the emphasis is not on line but on form and colour.)

Painter-Stainers, Worshipful Company of (1581). LIVERY COMPANY, originally a guild of painters on wood, metal and stone, and stainers of cloth and hangings.

Paisleyism (1966). Extremist Ulster Protestant movement led by the Rev. I. R. K. Paisley, who describes himself as a fundamentalist Calvinist.

Paisley pattern Characteristic peacock-feather design, originally used in the imitation cashmere shawls first made at Paisley. (Town near Glasgow, Scotland.)

Pakeha Maori name for Europeans. (Pronounced pah-kee-hah.)

Pakhtunistan Afghan government's name for a

border region of Pakistan which they claim. Also called Pashtunistan, Pathanistan. ('PATHAN-land'; see also PUSHTU.)

Pakistan Name coined in 1933 from the initials of Punjab, Afghan (i.e. the Pathans of the North-West Frontier Province) and Kashmir, and the termination of Baluchistan; the case for its adoption was strengthened by the fact that it could well come from Persian *pak*, 'pure', 'holy' + *stan*, 'land'.

Pal West German Telefunken system of 625-line colour TV adopted by Britain for use in 1967. (Stands for Phase Alternation Line.)

Palaeolithic Age (Old Stone Age) Period of perhaps a million years, covering the Ice Age and ending about 8000 BC, during which early forms of Man learnt to walk upright, speak, make fire and make tools, and the first types of *Homo sapiens* produced remarkable cave paintings, such as those of ALTAMIRA.

Palaeologus Name borne by the last dynasty of Byzantine emperors, who ruled from 1261 until the fall of Constantinople (1453).

Palaeozoic Era Geological era lasting from about 600 to 240 million years ago, divided into the CAMBRIAN, ORDOVICIAN, SILURIAN, DEVONIAN, CARBONIFEROUS and PERMIAN PERIODS. During this era fossils become abundant and include fishes, amphibians, reptiles, insects and primitive plants. The climate was at first mild, but there was a long spell of cold at the end. (Greek, 'ancient life'.)

Palais-Bourbon (1728). In Paris, the seat of the National Assembly, on the Left Bank.

Palamon and Arcite Two Theban knights captured by Duke Theseus of Athens, who fall in love with their captor's daughter; a tale told by Boccaccio and by Chaucer in *The Knight's Tale*. (Pronounced pal'a-mon, ar'syt.)

Palatinate Specifically, the Rhine Palatinate, formerly ruled by the Count Palatine of the Rhine (an ELECTOR); divided into the Rhenish (Lower) Palatinate, capital Heidelberg, since 1946 merged in the *Land* Rhineland-Palatinate, and the Upper Palatinate, capital Amberg, now in Bavaria. (See next entry.)

Palatine German count (Count Palatine) or English earl (Earl Palatine; see COUNTY PALATINE) having supreme, almost royal, jurisdiction within his fief in medieval times. See previous entry. (Derived ultimately from Latin *Palatium*, 'PALATINE HILL'.)

Palatine Hill One of the 7 hills of Rome, where the first Roman settlements were made, and the site of the palaces (so named after it) of the early Roman Emperors.

Palestine Liberation Organization (1964). Co-ordinating council for Palestine refugee organizations. Consists of many guerrilla groups and is dominated by EL FATAH. It has the status of government-in-exile and in 1974 received UN recognition as well as being considered the government of a future Palestinian state.

Pale, The (1) Area around Dublin where from the 12th century to Tudor times England imposed direct rule and banned Irish law and custom. (2) In the Tsarist times Russian Jews were required to live in a defined area called the Pale of Settlement, and it was only in exceptional circumstances that a Jew could move out of the Pale. (Pale meaning a fenced area.)

Paley's Evidences Short title of *View of the Evidences of Christianity* (1794) by William Paley, the study of which was prescribed for entrants to Cambridge University until 1920.

Palgrave See GOLDEN TREASURY.

Pali Aryan dead language of northern India in which the Buddhist scriptures are preserved in Ceylon and Burma.

Palinurus Pilot in Virgil's *Aeneid* who fell asleep at the helm and was swept overboard; he reached the shore, but was there murdered.

'Palinurus' Pen-name under which the English critic Cyril Connolly wrote *The Unquiet Grave* (1945), a handbook for pessimists.

Palladian architecture Style developed for town and country houses in northern Italy by Andrea Palladio (1508–80), who had made a close study of classical Roman architecture. It was introduced to England by Inigo Jones in the

17th century, and revived there by William Kent in the 18th. Symmetrical façades with classical columns were the main characteristics.

Pallas Epithet frequently applied to ATHENE; its meaning is disputed, the most usual translations being 'virgin' or 'brandisher of the spear'.

Pall Mall London street linking Trafalgar Square to St James's Palace, and with St James's Street the home of the more prestigious social clubs ('clubland'). (Named from Charles II's favourite *pallamaglio* – 'ball and mallet' – probably the earliest form of croquet played in St James's Park near by.)

Pall Mall Gazette (1865). Distinguished Liberal, later Conservative, paper, absorbed by the London *Evening Standard* in 1925.

Palmetto State Nickname of South Carolina.

Palm Sunday Sunday before Easter commemorating Jesus' entrance into Jerusalem, when the people welcomed him with branches of palm trees strewn in his way (John 12:13); palm fronds figure in processions and ceremonies on that day.

Palm-wine Drinkard, The (1952). First novel of the Nigerian Amos Tutuola, and the first novel from Black Africa to receive general acclaim from British critics. As the title indicates, it moulds English to African uses in telling a traditional spook-ridden story of West Africa.

Palmyra Former capital of the state of Palmyra, where Queen Zenobia reigned in the 3rd century AD; its ruins are in the desert north-east of Damascus.

Palomares bombs (1966). Hydrogen bombs from a US bomber which crashed near a Spanish Mediterranean village. A large task force was sent to find them, 3 on land, the fourth – most difficult to trace – eventually recovered from the sea. Some plutonium was released and, despite extensive decontamination, the possibility of long-term harmful effects has not been dismissed.

Paludrin Synthetic quinine-substitute discovered in 1944. (Trade name; from 'paludism', old name for malaria.)

Pamela (1740–41). Sometimes regarded as the first novel, written by Samuel Richardson in the form of letters from a virtuous maidservant who is at last persuaded by her amorous 'young master' to marry her.

Pan Greek god of shepherds and flocks, with goat's feet, horns and prick ears. He invented the 7-reed syrinx or Pan's pipe, and liked to startle travellers in lonely places (hence 'panic fear').

Pan-Africanist Congress (1959). Formed by the more militant members of the AFRICAN NATIONAL CONGRESS, led by Robert Subukwe.

Panama Hat made of the plaited leaves of the *Carludovica palmata* plant which grows wild in Central and South America. The industry is based in Ecuador.

Panama scandal (1888–92). French political scandal arising from a project to build a canal in Panama. Ferdinand de Lesseps, who had built the Suez Canal, was put in charge, though already in his 70s. He misjudged the difficulties of the terrain and the company formed to build the canal went bankrupt. It then transpired that several leading politicians who supported a last-minute scheme to save it had sold their votes. Lesseps was, unjustly, one of those accused of bribery and corruption. Many Jews were involved, and French anti-Semitism increased.

Pan-American Highway All-season road from Texas via Mexico City, Panamá and Valparaiso to Buenos Aires.

Pan American Union (1910). Successor to the International Union of the American Republics (1890) and the predecessor of the ORGANIZATION OF AMERICAN STATES.

Panay **incident** (1937). International crisis which arose when Japanese aircraft sank the US gunboat *Panay* in the Yangtze river.

Panchen Lama Tibetan priest who ranks second only to the DALAI LAMA, and was formerly the abbot of a monastery in western Tibet; also called the Tashi Lama.

Panda cars Police cars used in patrolling urban

areas, thus permitting a reduction in the number of men on beat duty on foot.

Pandarus (1) Trojan leader in the Trojan War. (2) In Chaucer and Shakespeare, the uncle of Cressida, from whose name the word 'pander' is derived. See TROILUS AND CRESSIDA.

Pandit Title of esteem in India, bestowed e.g. on Jawaharlal Nehru. (Hindu spelling of 'pundit'.)

Pandora's box In Greek legend, a box containing all the evils, which Zeus gives to Epimetheus ('afterthought') on his marriage to the Greek Eve, Pandora ('all-gifted'). She opens the box and the evils escape to plague the world, leaving only Hope (which also escapes, in some versions). This was Zeus' revenge on man for having obtained the gift of fire from PROMETH-EUS.

Pan-Germanism Advocacy of the integration of all German-speaking people into one state, i.e. German claims to absorb Austria, Alsace–Lorraine, Luxembourg, and parts of Czechoslovakia, Switzerland, Poland and Flanders. The names Mitteleuropa and Grossdeutschland were used of such a projected state. See NEW ORDER IN EUROPE.

Pangloss, Dr Tutor in Voltaire's *Candide* who, in the teeth of all evidence, persists in his assertion that 'all is for the best in the best of possible worlds' – a caricature of Leibniz's views.

Panhandle State Nickname of West Virginia. (Has panhandle-shaped projections into neighbouring states.)

Panhard–Levassor (1892). French firm of car manufacturers who at first used DAIMLER engines mounted in front of the chassis, and introduced the front radiator, a transmission shaft to the rear wheels, and a clutch. The Panhard 70 (1902) was their most famous car, and an earlier type in 1899 won a 354-mile race at 34 m.p.h.

Panjandrum, The Grand Mock title for a pompous busybody. (Coined by the 18th-century actor Samuel Foote when composing a nonsense-speech to test the memory of a fellow-actor. This piece, beginning 'So she went into

the garden to cut a cabbage-leaf to make an apple-pie' became surprisingly well known.)

Panmunjom Scene in Korea from 1951 of protracted negotiations for a settlement of the Korean War. An armistice was signed in 1953.

Pantagruel Son of Gargantua. See GARGANTUA AND PANTAGRUEL. (Pronounced pan-tag'ru-el.)

Pantaloon Stock character of the COMMEDIA DELL'ARTE, a foolish old merchant of Venice, wearing spectacles, slippers and pantaloons, the butt of the Clown. (Venetian patron saint, Pantaleone.)

Panthéon (1789) Building in the Latin Quarter of Paris; originally conceived as a church, it became on completion at the Revolution a Hall of Fame, where the remains of Mirabeau, Voltaire and Rousseau were buried. Thereafter, now church, now Hall of Fame, according to the regime in power, it assumed the latter (and present) function in 1885, on the burial there of Victor Hugo. (Greek, 'temple of all the gods'.)

Panther (1942). German tank of the Second World War: 44 tons, 700 h.p., 30 m.p.h. It had a short mechanical life.

Pantiles, The Traffic-free promenade leading to the chalybeate springs at Royal Tunbridge Wells, Kent, paved since Queen Anne's day with Dutch tiles; down one side the ground floors of the old buildings are set back to form a covered way. The name is a mistake; pantiles are ogee-curved roof tiles.

Panurge Character in Rabelais's GARGANTUA AND PANTAGRUEL; unable to decide whether to marry, he accompanies Pantagruel to Cathay to consult the oracle of the Holy Bottle, which answers his question with the one word: Drink. (Greek, 'all-doer'.)

Paolo and Francesca Two lovers put to death for adultery in 1289 in Ravenna, he being the handsome young brother of the unattractive man she had been forced by her parents to marry. Their story is told by Dante and many other writers, in poems, plays and opera.

Papa Doc François Duvalier, dictator of Haiti

1957–71 who managed to retain power through his TONTONS MACOUTE. He was succeeded by his son Jean-Claude, who fled the country in 1986.

Papal Infallibility (1870). Dogma announced by Pope Pius IX that the Pope cannot err when he speaks *ex cathedra*, i.e. when solemnly enunciating, as binding on all Catholics, a decision on a question of faith or morals.

Papal States Territory of central Italy, stretching across the peninsula and from Tuscany to the Kingdom of Naples, over which the Pope was nominally temporal sovereign from the 8th century until 1870, when it was incorporated into Italy. See VATICAN CITY.

Papaveraceae Poppy family, characterized by the narcotic milky juice; it includes mecanopsis and eschscholtzia.

Paphos Ancient city of Cyprus associated with Aphrodite; hence Paphian, of illicit love.

Papilionaceae Pea-flower subfamily which includes all the British specimens of LEGUMINOSAE. It is characterized by a butterfly-shaped flower; typical examples are the sweet pea, bean, clover, vetch, groundnut, lupin, gorse, laburnum, wistaria. (Latin *papilio*, 'butterfly'.)

Papworth Village Settlement (1917). Imaginatively planned settlement for tuberculosis patients near Godmanchester, Cambridge, founded by a group of philanthropists and financed by private donations, except for the hospital which has now been absorbed into the NHS. In addition to housing and hostels, there are several factories affording employment to patients during rehabilitation.

Paracelsus Name adopted by a Swiss physician, alchemist and astrologer, Theophrastus von Hohenheim (1493–1541).

Paraclete The Holy Ghost; literally, the Advocate; the Comforter of John 14:26.

Paradise Term used in the Greek Septuagint to translate 'Garden of Eden'; since life there was perfect it came to be used of the perfect life after death. (Persian word.)

Paradise Lost (1667). Milton's great epic on the Old Testament theme of 'Man's first disobedience' in the Garden of Eden, of which Satan is the dominant character throughout.

Paradise Regained (1671). Milton's lesser epic on the New Testament theme of Christ's triumph over temptation.

Paraguay tea Maté.

Paranthropus See ZINJANTHROPUS.

Parazoa See PORIFERA.

Parcae Latin name for the FATES.

Parc Monceau Park in north-west Paris, once famous as a playground for the children of the aristocracy.

Parent–Teacher Association Association to promote co-operation between parents and teachers in the interests of the children at a particular school.

Parian marble Fine-textured marble from the Aegean island of Paros.

Parian ware Form of porcelain which can be moulded in liquid state but looks like marble when set; used in the mass production of classical busts for the cottager, first by COPELAND AND GARRETTS (1840). Early examples were good but later work deteriorated into sentimentality. This ware was used by Minton and others, and for some kinds of domestic china.

Paris (Greek legend) Son of PRIAM, who carried off HELEN OF TROY, thus starting the Trojan War in which, though a coward, he killed Achilles but was himself killed by Philoctetes. See JUDGEMENT OF PARIS.

Paris Commune (1) (1792–4). Revolutionary municipal government of Paris, which played a large part in the Reign of TERROR. (2) (March–May 1871) Socialist government of Paris set up when the Germans withdrew after the Franco-Prussian War; besieged by French government troops ('Versaillists'), its overthrow was followed by a 'Week of Blood'.

Paris green Insecticide derived from arsenic.

Parish Clerks, Worshipful Company of (1441). Now a guild of parish clerks, churchwardens, etc., not strictly a LIVERY COMPANY.

Paris-Match (1949). Leading French illustrated weekly with an international reputation for its brilliant articles and illustrations.

Paris Peace Conference (1) Conference (1919–20) of allied powers after the First World War which, with great difficulty, framed the treaties of Versailles, Saint-Germain, Trianon, Neuilly and Sèvres. (2) Conference (1946) after the Second World War which framed treaties with Italy, Romania, Hungary, Bulgaria and Finland.

Paris Summit Conference (1960). Projected meeting of 4 heads of state (Eisenhower, Khrushchev, Harold Macmillan and de Gaulle), cancelled at the eleventh hour because of the U-2 INCIDENT.

Park Avenue New York street running north from Fourth Avenue, once the site of the luxury apartments of the FOUR HUNDRED set, now largely taken over by new office blocks.

Parker Tribunal (1958). See BANK RATE TRIBUNAL.

Parkhurst prison Prison in a suburb of Newport, Isle of Wight, used for long-sentence prisoners and noted for strict discipline; a special security block for men serving very long sentences was added in 1966.

Parkinsonism Condition very like PARKINSON'S DISEASE, found as a sequel to sleeping sickness.

Parkinson's disease Paralysis agitans or shaking palsy; a condition characterized by trembling hands, expressionless face and a shuffling gait. (James Parkinson, 1755–1824, British neurologist.)

Parkinson's law (1958). 'Work expands so as to fill the time available for its completion' and 'subordinates multiply at a fixed rate regardless of the amount of work produced'. (Discovered by C. Northcote Parkinson, historian and wit.)

Parkman (Francis) prize US literary prize for a

work of history; it carries great prestige. (US historian, died 1893.)

Parliamentary Commissioner for Administration Colourless title for the British OMBUDSMAN.

Parliamentary Private Secretary An MP appointed by a Minister to assist him in maintaining contact with back-benchers and in assessing the feeling of the House generally. The post is unpaid. See PARLIAMENTARY SECRETARY.

Parliamentary Secretary Junior Minister appointed as a Minister's deputy; he also acts as his chief liaison official with MPs of his party. The post is paid; the head of a large department may have more than one Parliamentary Secretary. Parliamentary Under-Secretary of State is the corresponding title when the Minister is a Secretary of State. See PARLIAMENTARY PRIVATE SECRETARY.

Parliament of Saints Another name for the BAREBONES PARLIAMENT.

Parmentier (Cooking) With potatoes. (Name of man said to have introduced the potato to France.)

Parmesan Very hard dry granular cheese, used in grated form in soups and with macaroni. There are 2 distinct kinds, made in the North Italian provinces of Emilia (where Parma is) and Lombardy. (Originally made in the Duchy of Parma; pronounced par-mè-zan'.)

Parnassians Group of 19th-century French poets led by Leconte de Lisle who, reacting against the excessive emotionalism of their predecessors, turned to cold and pessimistic objectivity and an obsession with form. Some of them later transferred their loyalties to the SYMBOLISTS. (From *Le Parnasse contemporain*, 1866–76, an anthology of their work.)

Parnassus Mountain in Greece north of Delphi, one of the traditional homes of the Muses; also sacred to Apollo and Dionysus.

Parnell divorce, The (1889). C. S. Parnell, leader of the Irish Nationalist Party holding the balance of power at Westminster, persuaded Gladstone to offer Home Rule but, on being involved in a divorce, lost the support both of Gladstone's Nonconformist followers and of the Irish Catholics.

Parsifal (1) German spelling of PERCIVAL. (2) Title of Wagner's opera on the story of the HOLY GRAIL.

Parsis Small Indian community settled around Bombay, descendants of Persians who fled from Muslim persecution in the 8th century. They retain some beliefs of ZOROASTRIANISM but have been influenced by Hinduism. (Also spelt Parsees; pronounced par-seez'.)

Parsons' Pleasure Oxford University open-air swimming pool on the Cherwell.

Parthenon, The (438 BC) Temple of Athene on the ACROPOLIS at Athens, built by Pericles to house a famous chryselephantine (i.e. gold and ivory) statue of her. It became in turn a church, a mosque, and an ammunition store which blew up, but much of it still stands, a noble monument to the Golden Age of Greece. Some of the ELGIN MARBLES came from this source. (Greek, 'temple of the maiden goddess'.)

Parthians Scythian people of the Caspian region, famous as mounted archers who closed on their enemies (notably the Romans) shooting off their arrows, and continued to shoot, backwards, as they fled again; hence a 'Parthian shot' for a parting shot, repartee or invective uttered on departure and affording no opportunity for reply.

Partington, Dame According to the Rev. Sydney Smith, king of wits, in a political speech at Taunton, a lady with a house on the beach at Sidmouth, Devon, who during a great storm in 1824 was seen with her mop vigorously sweeping back what Smith calls the 'Atlantic Ocean'. He compared her action to the efforts of the House of Lords to obstruct the Reform Bill of 1832.

Partisans In World War II a name given specifically to the Communist-led guerrilla forces built up by Tito in Axis-occupied Yugoslavia.

Partition (1) Of Poland by Russia, Austria and Prussia in 1772, 1793 and 1795, and in 1939 by Germany and Russia; (2) of Ireland (1921) into the Irish Free State and Northern Ireland; (3) of India (1947), into India and Pakistan; (4) of Palestine (1948), into Israel and Jordan.

Partridge Shorthand title for Eric Partridge's *A Dictionary of Slang and Unconventional English*, first published in 1937 and several times revised and enlarged; also, to a lesser extent, for any of his other lexicographical works.

Pascal's *Pensées* Collection of random notes by Blaise Pascal, the French mathematician and JANSENIST, on religion, philosophy and morals. He died in 1662, since when numerous editions of the *Pensées*, the first in 1670, have appeared.

Pascendi (1907). Pope Pius X's encyclical, which took a conservative stand against the growing modernist movement in the Church.

Pasht Egyptian goddess; see BUBASTIS.

Pashtunistan Alternative name for PAKHTUNISTAN; see PUSHTU.

Pasionaria, La *Nom de guerre* of the Joan of Arc of the Spanish Civil War; a miner's daughter and a dedicated Communist, whose real name was Dolores Gómez Ibarruri. After Franco's victory she went into exile in Moscow, returning to Spain in 1977, dying there in 1989. (Spanish, 'passion-flower'.)

Pasiphaë In Greek legend, the wife of Minos, changed into a cow by Poseidon; she gave birth to the MINOTAUR. (Pronounced pas-if'a-ee.)

Passage to India, A (1924). E. M. Forster's novel on the barriers to mutual understanding between individuals and races, demonstrated in the reactions of the Indian and British communities in a small township to an Englishwoman's hysterical accusation against an Indian, Dr Aziz.

Passchendaele Belgian village near Ypres, scene of one of the bitterest and costliest struggles of World War I from July to November 1917, in which the Canadians captured the ridge overlooking it but suffered very severe casualties. The Battle of Passchendaele is properly a part of the 3rd Battle of Ypres, but is sometimes used as a synonym for it. (Pronounced pash-'en-dayl.)

Passing bell Bell which is tolled to announce the death of someone of the parish.

Passion, The Sufferings of Jesus Christ on the Cross. (Latin *passio*, 'suffering'.)

Passion Play Miracle play on the PASSION; see OBERAMMERGAU.

Passion Sunday Second Sunday before Easter; see PASSION, The.

Passion Week (1) Week following PASSION SUNDAY. (2) In the Anglican Church, the week after (1) i.e. HOLY WEEK.

Pass Laws South African laws which required all Africans to carry passes (identity cards); organized opposition to them was first demonstrated by a resolution of the AFRICAN NATIONAL CONGRESS in 1919.

Passover Jewish feast, celebrated in April or May, commemorating the sparing ('passing over') of the Jewish first born described in Exodus 12.

Pasteur, Louis French chemist (1822–95). On his findings the modern study of bacteriology was based. In 1888 the Institut Pasteur was founded. Pasteurization, to sterilize, is a process invented by him; and he also worked in the field of vaccines.

Paston Letters (1434–1509). Family letters of the Pastons of Norfolk, not meant for publication, written in the time of the Wars of the Roses, and published in the 18th century.

***Pastoral* Symphony, The** (1808). Beethoven's Sixth Symphony, on themes of the kind indicated by its title. e.g. bird-song, a storm, a shepherd's hymn.

Pathans Muslim PUSHTU-speaking people of Afghanistan, fierce warriors who used to give much trouble on the north-west frontier of British India. See also PAKHTUNISTAN. (Pronounced pa-tahnz'.)

Pathétique (1) Beethoven's piano sonata (1798), so named by its publisher on account of its depiction of passionate feeling and suffering. (2) Tchaikovsky's last symphony, No. 6, first performed a few days before his death (1893), instinct with prophetic foreboding.

Pathet Lao Nationalist party in Laos which, supported by the VIETMINH, was prominent in the fight for independence from 1953 onwards.

Pathfinder force Specially selected and trained RAF pilots and navigators of bombers which dropped flares over a target area to guide the main attack force, first used in raids on Germany in the autumn of 1942.

Path to Rome, The (1902). Hilaire Belloc's discursive description of his walk from France across the Alps to Rome.

Patience (1881). Gilbert and Sullivan opera satirizing the aesthetic movement of the day in the person of Bunthorne, the fleshly poet. Patience, a milkmaid, dithers between him and a rival poet. Grosvenor, who describes himself as the apostle of simplicity. There is a chorus of Rapturous Maidens and Officers of the Dragoon Guards.

Patmos Aegean island where, according to Revelation 1:9, St John had his vision of the APOCALYPSE.

Patna rice Trade term for high-quality long-grain rice of the kind served with curries. (A district of Bihar, India.)

Patriarchs, The In New York City, a club of the extremely rich founded by one of the Astor family and Ward McAllister (see FOUR HUNDRED); it holds an annual Patriarch's Ball.

Patroclus Cousin and bosom companion of ACHILLES. (Pronounced pat-rok'lus.)

Pattenmakers, Worshipful Company of (1670). LIVERY COMPANY, now associated with the manufacture and sale of rubber footwear.

Patterne, Sir Willoughby Conceited and humourless man whose character gives its name to George Meredith's *The Egoist* (1879); his egoism loses him 2 fiancées.

Paul et Virginie (1787). Pastoral romance of Bernardin de Saint-Pierre about 2 orphans brought up in idyllic surroundings in Mauritius.

Paul Jones Dance which, under the direction of a 'caller', affords opportunity to change partners at intervals.

Paul Revere (*The Midnight Ride of*) Longfellow's ballad on the American hero who rode from Boston to LEXINGTON in 1775 to give a warning of British troop movements that ensured victory in the first engagement of the War of Independence.

Paviors, Worshipful Company of LIVERY COMPANY, originally a guild of road-makers, with a membership now recruited from road engineering and allied trades. It was never granted a charter of incorporation.

Pavlovian reflex Phrase in popular use for a reflex action such as a dog's salivation at the sight of food or, more accurately, for salivation at a signal which he has learnt to associate with food (i.e. a conditioned reflex). (I. B. Pavlov, Russian physiologist died 1936.)

Peabody's buildings Blocks of flats built for the London poor by an Amerian expatriate philanthropist, George Peabody (died 1869).

Peace (1942). Hybrid tea rose which produces very pale yellow flowers with pink edges.

Peace Ballot (1935). British national ballot organized by the LEAGUE OF NATIONS UNION; 10 millon people voted in favour of reducing armaments; the result was said to have encouraged Hitler.

Peace Corps Body of American volunteers recruited (1961) by President Kennedy to provide teachers, doctors, agriculturists and other trained staff to work in underdeveloped countries at subsistence rates of pay; similar corps were formed in other Western countries.

Peaceful Co-existence Soviet policy announced by Khrushchev; he defined it as 'A form of intensive struggle, economic, political, ideological, between the proletariat and the aggressive forces of imperialism', which seems to make it an ORWELLIAN phrase, meaning its opposite.

Peace Pledge Union (1934). Pacifist organization founded by the Rev. Dick Sheppard of ST MARTIN-IN-THE-FIELDS.

Peach Melba Peach slices with ice cream, and cream; in hotel French, Pêche Melba. (Named after Dame Nellie Melba, Australian soprano.)

Peachum, Polly In the BEGGAR'S OPERA, the daughter of a receiver of stolen goods who marries Capt. Macheath.

Peacocks, The Nickname of the Leeds United football team.

Peake's *Commentary* (1919). Short title of a commentary on the Bible by A. S. Peake. A revised edition was published in the 1950s.

Peanuts (1950). Charles Schulz's comic strip in which tiny children with yapping mouths act out adult foibles at a new pitch of intensity. CHARLIE BROWN is the leader, plagued by the bullying Lucy, and accompanied by his dog SNOOPY.

Pearl Harbor (7 December 1941). Surprise attack by Japanese naval aircraft on the US fleet at the naval base on the island of Oahu, Hawaii, which brought the USA into World War II.

Pearly King and Queen Winners of competitions held from time to time (e.g. at the International Horse Show) for the best examples of the cockney costermongers' traditional ceremonial dress ('Pearlies'), covered with mother-of-pearl buttons from top to toe.

Pears Cyclopaedia (1897). Book of background information and reference for everyday use. Published annually and originally owned by the manufacturers of Pears Soap, but now by PENGUIN.

Peasant Brueghel Nickname of Pieter Brueghel I (1525–69), the greatest of a family of Flemish painters, father of VELVET BRUEGHEL and HELL BRUEGHEL. He was so called because his favourite subject was peasant life; he himself was far from being a peasant. See 'MASSACRE OF THE INNOCENTS'. (Pronounced broog'l; also spelt Breughel or Breugel, and pronounced brèrg'l.)

Peasants' Revolt, The (1381). Rising in Kent and Essex led by John Ball, Wat Tyler and Jack Straw, who captured London and compelled Richard II to abolish serfdom. After Tyler's murder the rising was put down and all concessions cancelled.

Pebble Mill Television studios in Birmingham.

Pecksniff Arch-hypocrite of Dickens's MARTIN CHUZZLEWIT, a relative of Martin's, with 2 famous daughters, Charity and Mercy.

Peculiar People, The (1838). Sect founded in London, without creed or clergy, who in illness rely on prayer, rejecting medical aid. (From Titus 2:14, 'and purify unto himself a peculiar people'.)

Peeler Old name for a policeman. (After Sir Robert Peel, who founded the London Metropolitan Police in 1829; the alternative nickname, 'bobby', comes from his Christian name.)

Peelites Those who supported Sir Robert Peel when he repealed the CORN LAWS (1846) in the teeth of opposition, led by Disraeli, from his own Conservative Party. They then formed a third party which in 1859 was mainly absorbed into the Liberal Party. Gladstone was a leading Peelite.

Peel Report (1937). Report of a Royal Commission which recommended the partition of Palestine.

Peenemünde Research station on the north-east coast of Germany where the Germans developed (1937–45) liquid-fuel rockets (including the v-2) and guided missiles; bombed by the RAF in August 1943.

Peeping Tom In a late addition to the Lady GODIVA legend, the tailor who peeped at her as she rode naked through Coventry, and was struck blind.

Peer Gynt (1867). Ibsen's verse fantasy in many episodes of a warm-hearted but irresponsible peasant lad who, feeling unworthy of the virtuous Solveig, sets out to taste all experience. His character deteriorates during his adventures in many lands, which include successful slave-trading. He comes back to find a mysterious

Button Moulder waiting to melt him down as useless dross, but is redeemed by Solveig's continuing love for him. (Pronounced peer, in Norwegian pair, gint.)

Peer Gynt **Suite** (1876). Grieg's incidental music for Ibsen's drama (see preceding entry), commissioned by Ibsen.

Pegasus In Greek legend a winged horse caught by BELLEROPHON.

Pegasus Amateur football club recruited from Oxford and Cambridge Universities.

Peggotty, Clara In Dickens's DAVID COPPERFIELD, David's nurse, member of a Yarmouth fisherman's family which plays a prominent part in the story.

Peking incident, The See MARCO POLO BRIDGE INCIDENT.

Peking Legations, Siege of (1900). Culmination of the BOXER MOVEMENT, when the Boxers besieged the foreign communities in Peking for 2 months, with the secret support of the Dowager Empress. They were relieved by an international force, including British, US, Japanese and Russian troops.

Peking Man A specimen of PITHECANTHROPINE found 1927–9 near Peking.

Pekoe See ORANGE PEKOE.

Pelagianism Christian doctrine of those who denied original sin and the eternal damnation of unbaptised infants; they believed in free will and that the first steps towards salvation could be taken by the human will ('justification by works') unaided by God's mercy ('grace'), a view contrary to that of St Augustine but to which the Jesuits tended. (Pelagius, Latin name of 5th-century British monk called Morgan, who taught in Rome and was condemned by the Pope.)

Pelargonium See GERANIUM.

Pelican State Nickname of Louisiana.

Pelion and Ossa Two mountains of Greece; according to legend giants, variously named, piled Pelion on Ossa in order to reach the abode of the immortals and rape Hera and Artemis. They were defeated and imprisoned under the earth, where they cause earthquakes and volcanic eruptions.

Pelléas et Mélisande Title of Maeterlinck's play (1892) and Debussy's opera (1902) based on it. Mélisande falls in love with Pelléas, the brother of her husband, who kills him; she dies after giving birth to Pelléas's child.

Pelmanism (1) System of memory training introduced about the time of World War I. (2) Memory-testing card game. (Proprietary name.)

Peloponnesian War (431–404 BC). War between Athens and Sparta caused by dislike of Athenian imperialism. It destroyed for ever Athenian political dominance of Greece. The great *locus classicus* of the War is the incomparable *History* by Thucydides.

Pelops (Greek legend) Son of Tantalus and founder of the dynasty which ruled the Peloponnesus. He won his wife by bribing a charioteer to lose a race to him, but murdered him when he claimed his reward. This was the origin of the curse of Pelops inherited by the House of ATREUS, who was his son.

Pelton wheel One of the 3 main types of wheel used in hydroelectric plant; the rim is fitted with cup-shaped paddles which are struck by high-pressure jets of water.

PEN, International (1921). International association of writers. (Initials stand for: Poets, Playwrights, Editors, Essayists, Novelists.)

Pendennis (1850). Thackeray's novel about Arthur Pendennis, who gets himself involved with various women, including the daughter of a blackmailing escaped convict about whom his uncle, Major Pendennis, misadvises him. In the end he marries the girl with whom he was brought up, Laura Bell.

Penelope (Greek legend) Faithful wife of ODYSSEUS. She spent his 20-year absence bringing up their son Telemachus and fending off her suitors (Odysseus was presumed dead) by promising to marry one of them when she had finished weaving a shroud for her father-in-law; this she wove all day and unravelled each night, so that she was still busy on it when Odysseus returned.

Penguin Island (1908). Anatole France's amusing novel of a blind monk who blesses a colony of penguins thinking they are human, which they miraculously become. The account of their subsequent development affords the author opportunity to satirize French history, with special reference to the DREYFUS CASE. (French title, *L'Île des pingouins*.)

Penguin (1935). Earliest of the British paperback editions, originally of reprints sold at 6d (2½p) each; to these other series were later added, such as Pelicans (1937; cultural and scientific, including newly commissioned books), Puffins (for children), etc. (Firm founded by Sir Allen Lane.)

Penguins Oxford University lawn tennis club of the 30 best players not in the university team.

Peninsular War (1808–14). Begun by a Portuguese appeal for help after invasion by France, and the placing of Napoleon's brother Joseph on the Spanish throne. Wellesley (the future Duke of Wellington) defeated the French in Portugal; Sir John Moore went to Spain (see CORUNNA); Wellington returned and drove the French out of Spain, after victories at Salamanca and Vittoria.

Peninsula State Nickname of Florida.

Penitential Psalms Seven psalms which are used as penitential devotions; they are numbers 6, 32, 38, 51, 102, 130 and 143.

Penkovsky spy case (1962). Case of the Soviet Colonel, Oleg Penkovsky, who for a year leaked important information to the West through Greville WYNNE. He may have disclosed Russian intentions in the CUBAN CRISIS.

Pennsylvania Dutch Name given to 18th-century ANABAPTIST refugees from the Rhineland; their descendants; their dialect. (From Deutsch, German; no connection with Dutch.)

Penny Black (1840). First adhesive postage stamp, but by no means the rarest; it bears the head of Queen Victoria.

Pen Ponds Ponds in the middle of Richmond Park, Surrey, famous for open-air ice-skating.

Penseroso, Il See ALLEGRO, L'.

Penseur, Le Rodin's sculpture of a seated figure, originally intended to represent Dante in a larger work. (French, 'the thinker'.)

Penshurst Place Country house near Tunbridge Wells, Kent, dating back to the 14th century; the birthplace of Sir Philip Sidney and still the home of the Sidney family (Viscount De L'Isle).

Pensioners, The Nickname of the Chelsea football team.

Pentagon, The US Defense Department, a huge complex of 5 concentric pentagons of buildings, completed in 1942 at Arlington, Virginia, across the Potomac from Washington DC.

Pentateuch First 5 books of the Old Testament, traditionally written by Moses, actually in the 4th century BC. (Greek, 'five books'; pronounced pent'a-tewk.)

Pentathlon Olympic contest for women in which individuals compete in all of 5 events: high and long jump, putting the weight, hurdle race, 200 metres. Also a similar men's contest (dropped from the Olympic Games) in long jump, discus, javelin, 200- and 1,500-metre events. (Greek, '5 contests'; see MODERN PENTATHLON.)

Pentecost (1) Jewish harvest festival, held on the 50th day after the 2nd day of the PASSOVER (Lev. 23); this came to be associated also with the celebration of the giving of the Law to Moses on Mount Sinai. (2) Earlier name of the Christian celebration on WHIT SUNDAY. (Greek, '50th'.)

Pentonville (1842). Built as a 'model' prison in London to embody Howard's (see HOWARD LEAGUE FOR PENAL REFORM) reform of combining solitary confinement (at night) with hard work and religious instruction.

People's Budget, The (1909). Name for Lloyd George's Liberal Budget, which introduced supertax, children's allowances, car and petrol tax and (the biggest blow of all for Conservatives) land taxes. It was thrown out by the Lords, thus starting the great battle between the 2 Houses which led to the 'VETO' BILL.

People's Commissars Early designation, abolished by Stalin in 1946, of Ministers of the USSR.

PEP (1987). Personal Equity Plan, a method of investment which allows the interest or dividends and the capital gains to be tax-free.

Pepys's *Diary* Uninhibited diary of Samuel Pepys (1633–1703), a highly efficient Secretary to the Admiralty for many years and a President of the Royal Society. Written in his own private shorthand, which was not deciphered until 1825, it covers the 9 years of his life from 1660. Almost the whole of it was published in 1893–9. A new and unexpurgated transcription was published 1970–83. (Pronounced peeps.)

Percival (Perceval, Parsifal) Pure knight of Arthurian legend to whom the HOLY GRAIL was revealed.

Percy's Reliques Collection of traditional ballads rescued from oblivion by Bishop Percy in his *Reliques of Ancient English Poetry* (1765).

Perdita and Florizel (1) Characters in Shakespeare's *A Winter Tale*; Perdita is marooned on what Shakespeare calls 'the sea-coast of Bohemia', and at the end of the play marries the King of Bohemia's son, Florizel. (2) Nicknames of Mrs Robinson, mistress of the Prince Regent (George IV), an actress who made her name playing the part of Perdita, and of the Prince. (Latin, 'lost (i.e. marooned) woman'; pronounced pèr'di-ta, flor'i-zel.)

Père Goriot (1834). One of the novels of Balzac's COMÉDIE HUMAINE, in which a foolishly fond father squanders his last sou on a pair of preternaturally cold, ungrateful daughters, both of whom have made rich marriages.

Perestroika Russian for restructuring, and reform, advocated by President Mikhail Gorbachev, also the title of a book by him *Perestroika: Our Hopes for the Country and the World*, published in 1987.

Perfidious Albion Phrase attributed to Napoleon (but he was not the first to call England 'perfidious').

Pergamum Important city of Asia Minor (north of modern Izmir) in the 3rd–2nd centuries BC, where parchment, named after it, was made; famous for its library and sculptures.

Pericles, Prince of Tyre (1608). Shakespeare's play in which Pericles is parted from his wife and then his daughter in circumstances which lead him to presume them dead, but is reunited to both in the end. (Pronounced per'i-kleez.)

Périgord (Périgueuse) Cooking term for dishes served with truffles.

Perissodactyla Order of hoofed mammals with an uneven number of toes (see ARTIODACTYLA), including the horse, rhinoceros and tapir.

Permian Period Most recent of the periods of the PALAEOZOIC ERA, lasting from about 275 to 240 million years ago. (Permia, an ancient kingdom east of the Volga.)

Permissive Society Allowing freedom and tolerance in matters of sex, made easier by the PILL.

Permutit process Proprietary name of a standard method of softening water by the use of a group of minerals called zeolites.

Perpendicular (1375–1575). Final stage of English GOTHIC ARCHITECTURE, most easily recognized by the vertical lines running right through the windows from bottom to top. The effect of loftiness was often enhanced by elaborate fan vaulting, of which one of the finest examples is King's College Chapel, Cambridge.

Perseid meteors Shoal of meteors which orbit the sun and through which the earth passes each August, producing a display of shooting-stars emanating from the direction of PERSEUS. (Pronounced per'si-id.)

Persephone Greek goddess of spring (Roman Proserpina), daughter of Zeus and DEMETER, abducted to the Underworld by Hades. Zeus arranged that she should spend 8 months of the year with her mother on earth (compare ADONIS; TAMMUZ). See ELEUSINIAN MYSTERIES. (Pronounced per-sef'on-ee.)

Persepolis ACHAEMENID capital of Persia begun by Darius I, today an impressive ruin north-east of Shiraz.

Perseus Major hero of Greek legend, son of Zeus by DANAË. He cut off MEDUSA's head, with which he turned Atlas into a mountain, and other enemies into stone. He rescued ANDROMEDA, and their son was the traditional ancestor of the Persians. (Pronounced per'sews.)

Perseus Northern constellation between CASSIOPEIA and TAURUS, representing Perseus holding Medusa's head in his left hand. In the head of Medusa are ALGOL (beta-Persei) and the nova observed in 1901. (See previous entry.).

Perseus (1554). Cellini's bronze sculpture of Perseus holding up the severed head of the Gorgon; now standing in the Loggia dei Lanzi, Florence.

Pershing US tactical ground-to-ground ballistic missile, with a range of 400 miles.

Persian carpets Typically large, fine-textured and expensive, with stylized designs of flowers, animals, birds, medallions. See ARDABIL, BAKHTIARI, HAMADAN, HERAT, ISFAHAN, KASHAN, KIRMAN, SHIRAZ, TABRIZ, TEHERAN CARPETS; also the next entry.

Persian knot The carpet-weaving knot in which one tuft of yarn surfaces between each warp thread, in contrast to the Turkish (or GHIORDES) knot, in which 2 tufts emerge between alternate pairs of warps. Both knots are used in Persia; the Turkish is used also in ANATOLIAN and CAUCASIAN CARPETS, the Persian in Central Asia and the Far East. The *jufti* (or 'fraudulent') knot is a fairly modern device in which 4 warps are knotted together, making for greater speed but poorer quality. (Also called the Senneh or Senna knot, from the town of origin in Persian Kurdistan, now called Sanandaj.)

Persimmon Horse that won the 1896 Derby for the Prince of Wales (later Edward VII). It was the full brother of DIAMOND JUBILEE.

Perspex Proprietary name of a lightweight transparent plastic sheet used for safety as a glass substitute in car windscreens, etc.

Persuasion (1818). Jane Austen's last novel, published posthumously. Anne Elliot is overpersuaded by a friend into rejection of her suitor Frederick Wentworth, a naval officer, but after many vicissitudes and misunderstandings accepts him.

Pestalozzi Children's Village Trust Formed to provide care and education for deprived children from the less-developed countries; runs a children's village at Sedlescombe, Sussex. See next entry.

Pestalozzi system Earliest of a series of schemes for reforming infant education, based on learning by doing, nature study and other forms of accurate observation to promote accurate thinking; aimed at the full development of the potentialities of each individual. (Johann Pestalozzi, Swiss educationist, 1746–1827.)

Peter and the Wolf (1940). Prokofiev's orchestral piece in which a narrator tells a fairy-tale against the musical background. The characters are each represented by a particular instrument, e.g. Peter by the violins.

Peter Bell (1819). Poem by William Wordsworth of how a thief about to steal a donkey is converted to a new life by observing the donkey's devotion to its master; in it critics, including Shelley, felt that the poet had strayed too far along his chosen path of sublime simplicity.

Peterborough Column in the *Daily Telegraph*, compiled by various hands and named after the paper's former office address in Peterborough Court.

Peterborough Show (1878). Royal Hound Show at Peterborough, the chief foxhound show in Britain.

Peter Grimes (1945). Benjamin Britten's opera based on a poem by Crabbe (1810), who was born in Aldeburgh where Britten settled. Grimes is a fisherman suspected of having brought about the death at sea of his apprentice. He is too proud and stubborn to accept the help offered him in establishing his innocence.

Peterlee (1948). NEW TOWN 11 miles east of Durham.

Peterloo (1819). Incident at St Peter's Fields (now the site of the Free Trade Hall), Manchester, when a large but orderly working-class crowd listening to a speech on political reform was broken up by cavalry; in the confusion, some were killed and many were injured (the figures were never established), but the Manchester magistrates were congratulated by the Home Secretary for ordering out the troops. (Coined derisively on the analogy of Waterloo.)

Peter Pan (1904). J. M. Barrie's evergreen play for children, in which Peter Pan, the boy who wouldn't grow up, and the fairy Tinker Bell, whisk off Wendy and her brothers to Never-Never Land, full of pirates and Indians, not to mention a crocodile which has swallowed an alarm clock. There is a statue to Peter in Kensington Gardens.

Peter Principle, The (1969). Book subtitled 'Why Things Always Go Wrong' which states that 'in a Hierarchy, every employee tends to rise to his level of incompetence', i.e. a man who does his job well is promoted until he reaches one he cannot cope with, and there he sticks. He can be removed by pseudo-promotion, e.g. Percussive Sublimation (i.e. kicked upstairs) or Lateral Arabesque (i.e. given a larger desk and thicker carpet in some remote part of the building out of harm's way). (By Canadian-born U S professor, L. J. Peter.)

Peter Rabbit (1901). Children's book written and illustrated by Beatrix Potter.

Petersham Ribbed or corded stiffener used for strengthening skirt waistline, etc.

Peter Simple (1834). (1) Best of Capt. Marryat's vigorous naval stories, notable for its lively characterizations. (2) Column in the *Daily Telegraph*.

Peter's Pence (1) Tax of a penny per householder collected from Anglo-Saxon times until the Reformation as a gift to the Pope. (2) Now used of voluntary contributions to the papal treasury.

Petit Caporal, Le Napoleon I's nickname among his soldiers.

Petition of Right (1628). Request by Parliament for the abolition of illegal taxation, imprisonment and billeting, accepted by Charles I.

Petit Trianon Château in the park at Versailles, a few hundred yards from the GRAND TRIANON; built by Louis XV for Mme de Pompadour, given by Louis XVI to Marie Antoinette and by Napoleon to Marie-Louise. See TRIANON ADVENTURE.

Pet Marjorie Margaret Fleming, who died aged 8, but not before she had penned the immortal lines (of a pug dog): 'His noses cast is of the roman / He is a very pretty weoman / I could not get a rhyme for roman / And was oblidged to call it weoman.'

Petra John Burgon's 'rose-red city half as old as Time'; its ruins can still be seen south of the Dead Sea in the Jordanian desert. It was first the Edomite, then the NABATAEAN capital. (Pronounced pee'tra.)

Petriburg: Abbreviation for (Bishop) of Peterborough.

Petrofina (1920). Belgian petroleum firm which refines and (as Fina) distributes petrol in many parts of the world.

Petrov spy case (1954). Vladimir Petrov, a Soviet spy in the Soviet embassy in Australia, defected and disclosed the existence of a Russian spy ring in that country.

Petruchio See KATHARINA.

Petrushka (1911). Popular Fokine ballet to Stravinsky score; about puppets which come to life; the setting is a fair at St Petersburg.

Petticoat Lane London street market, in Middlesex Street E1, between Liverpool Street and Aldgate Stations, where on Sundays a wide range of second-hand goods is sold.

Petty Cury Short narrow street in the centre of Cambridge, leading to the market-place. ('Little street of the cooks', from Latin *curare*, 'to preserve meat'.)

Petty Sessions Lowest courts, with summary jurisdiction (i.e. without jury) in minor offences and powers of up to 6 months' imprisonment for any one offence. In small towns they comprise not less than 2 JUSTICES OF THE PEACE assisted by a magistrate's clerk, usually a solicitor; in bigger towns, a stipendiary (paid) magistrate, who is a barrister and sits alone; in London, a metropolitan police magistrate. All these also hold preliminary inquiries into more serious cases which may have to go to CROWN COURTS; and they deal with various civil matters (e.g. maintenance orders, licences).

Petulengro Gypsy in George Borrow's LAVENGRO and *The Romany Rye*. (Gypsy, 'shoe-smith'.)

Petworth House Country house at Petworth, Sussex, dating mainly from the 17th century, which has one of the finest art collections in Britain, and notable Grinling Gibbons carving.

Peulhs See FULANI.

Pevsner Shorthand for a series of volumes on the 'Buildings of England' compiled and edited by Sir Nikolaus Pevsner and published by PENGUIN. The series is now extended to Ireland, Scotland and Wales; revised editions are with co-editors.

Pewterers, Worshipful Company of (1473). LIVERY COMPANY.

Peyton Place (1956). Seamy story of a decayed textile town in New Hampshire, USA, written by Grace Metalious, who was born there.

PG Parental Guidance (British Board of Film Classification); some scenes may be unsuitable for young children.

Phaedra (Greek legend) Daughter of Minos and wife of Theseus. Aphrodite made her fall in love with her stepson, HIPPOLYTUS, who rejected her. She then accused him of trying to seduce her. The story is told in Racine's *Phèdre* (1677). (Pronounced fee'dra.)

Phaedra complex Psychoanalytic term for the emotional reactions between step-parents and stepchildren, especially (since the mother usually has the custody of her children) between a teenage girl and her stepfather. By appealing to him, she tends to win any dispute with her mother; *per contra*, he is jealous of her boyfriends.

Phaethon (Greek legend) Son of Helios who, allowed to drive his father's chariot of the sun, was unable to control the horses. Zeus struck him dead with a thunderbolt lest he should burn up the earth. (Pronounced fay'e-thon; but the 4-wheeler named after him is spelt *phaeton* and pronounced fay'tn.)

Phantom of the Opera (1925). Films and stage musical about a disfigured composer who haunts the sewers under the Opera House in Paris and takes a beautiful young singer as his protegée. There have been three films: 1925, with Lon Chaney and Mary Philbin; 1943, with Claude Rains and Susanna Foster; and 1962, with Herbert Lom and Heather Sears. The stage musical with Michael Crawford and Sarah Brightman opened in 1986 with Andrew Lloyd-Webber as composer. In 1977 there was a rock version, *Phantom of the Paradise*.

Pharisees Jewish sect which arose in the 2nd century BC, strict observers of the Law, in conflict with the SADDUCEES; certain Pharisees were sharply attacked in the Gospels. The Jews of modern times regard themselves as descendants in this sect. (Hebrew, 'the separated ones'.)

Pharos Lighthouse at Alexandria built during the reign of the Ptolemies and numbered among the SEVEN WONDERS OF THE WORLD. The light was provided by torches or fires.

Phèdre (1677). Racine's play about the PHAEDRA legend.

Phi Beta Kappa (1776). US fraternity or 'honor society' for those distinguished in the field of general scholarship, founded at WILLIAM AND MARY COLLEGE; the first fraternity to use Greek letters.

Phi Kappa Phi (1897). US fraternity or 'honor society' for those distinguished in general scholarship.

Philadelphus Genus name of the mock orange, incorrectly called SYRINGA.

Philby spy case (1963). Defection of H. A. R. ('Kim') Philby to Russia in 1963. He was recruited by the Russians as a Communist sympathizer on coming down from Cambridge in 1933, rose high in MI-6 during the Second World War, acted as liaison with the US CIA, tipped off BURGESS AND MACLEAN in 1951, and was still in British government pay when he fled from Beirut, where he was an *Observer* correspondent.

Philemon and Baucis In Greek legend a poor Darby and Joan couple whose wish that they should remain together even in death is granted when Zeus turns them into 2 trees with intertwining branches, as a reward for the hospitality they had offered him. (Pronounced fil-eem'on, baw'sis.)

Philip Drunk and Philip Sober According to tradition, a woman condemned by Philip of Macedon (father of Alexander the Great) when he was drunk told him she would appeal when he was sober; hence 'an appeal from Philip drunk to Philip sober'.

Philippe Égalité Duke of Orleans who at the French Revolution adopted the name Égalité and voted for the execution of his own cousin, Louis XVI; he was himself guillotined later. His son was Louis-Philippe, KING OF THE FRENCH.

Philippi (42 BC). Battle in which Mark Antony and Octavian (the future Augustus) defeated Brutus and Cassius who, 2 years earlier, had assassinated Julius Caesar. (City of Macedonia; pronounced fil-ip'y.)

Philippine Sea, Battle of the (June 1944). Decisive US naval victory over the Japanese in the Marianas.

Philippopolis Greek name for Plovdiv, a town in Bulgaria. (Founded by Philip of Macedon in the 4th century BC.)

Philips (1891). Dutch firm with headquarters at Eindhoven, manufacturing electrical and electronic equipment (including radio and TV), chemicals and engineering products.

Phillips curve Mathematical method applied by

the London economist, A. W. Phillips, to an attempt to establish the relationship between the level of unemployment and the rate of change of money wages. As it appeared to show that wage stability entails a high rate of unemployment (17% in the USA), economists have been busy since trying to prove that 'it ain't necessarily so'.

Phillips (Sarah Tryphen) lectures (1961). Lectures given on American history and literature, under the auspices of the British Academy.

Philoctetes Hero of Greek legend abandoned on the island of Lemnos suffering from a terrible wound. He has Heracles' bow and arrows, without which Troy cannot be taken; in Sophocles' play *Philoctetes* he is persuaded to come to Troy, where he kills Paris. (Pronounced fil-ok-tee'teez.)

Philomela In Greek legend, a princess of Athens raped by her brother-in-law Tereus, and changed into a nightingale. Her sister Procne becomes a swallow. (Pronounced fil-o-mee'la.)

Phineas Finn (1869–80). Title of Trollope's 'parliamentary' novels, consisting of *Phineas Finn*, *Phineas Redux*, *The Prime Minister* and *The Duke's Children*. Phineas is a penurious Irishman of great charm who comes to London and eventually becomes Under-Secretary of State for the Colonies. See OMNIUM, DUKES OF.

Phiz The pseudonym of Hablot K. Browne (1815–82), who illustrated Dickens's novels and the first Jorrocks novel of Surtees.

Phlegethon In Greek legend the river of flames, one of the rivers of the Underworld. (Pronounced fleg'e-thon.)

Phoebus See APOLLO.

Phoenicians Greek name for the Semitic people of the coastal cities (Tyre, Sidon, Byblos, Megiddo) of what is now Lebanon; the Canaanites of the Bible. Confined by mountains to their coastal strip, they turned to seafaring, and founded Carthage. They were excellent goldsmiths and jewellers, and famous for their Tyrian purple dye.

Phoenix Park Large Dublin park containing a zoo, racecourse, polo ground and the official residence of the President of Ireland.

Phoenix Park murders (1882). Assassination by FENIANS of the British Chief and Under Secretaries for Ireland, in Dublin. (See previous entry.)

Physalis Genus that includes Chinese lantern and the Cape gooseberry.

Physicists, The (1962). Friedrich Dürrenmatt's play in which 3 of the world's leading scientists take refuge in an asylum in order to keep their latest discoveries from mankind.

Physiocrats Group of 18th-century French economists led by Quesnay, who held that agriculture was the sole source of wealth, deprecated commerce, and advocated a single land tax paid by all.

Picardy Former province of France, capital Amiens. It corresponds to the modern *département* of Somme and neighbouring parts of Artois, Oise and Aisne.

Pickfords Old-established cartage firm.

Pickwick Papers, The (1837). Dickens's best-known novel, a series of episodes in the lives of members of the Pickwick Club. See BARDELL V. PICKWICK; DINGLEY DELL; EATANSWILL; JINGLE; WARDLE; the WELLERS.

Picts Probably pre-Celtic race in central Scotland, absorbed by the Scots.

Picture Post (1938–57). London weekly illustrated magazine on the lines of the American *Life*.

Pictures at an Exhibition (1874). Mussorgsky's piano suite describing 10 pictures in an exhibition held after the death of his artist friend Hartmann.

Piedmont Region of northern Italy between the Alps and the Apennines, capital Turin; it was under the House of SAVOY from the 11th century. (Pronounced peed'mont.)

Pied Piper of Hamelin In German legend a

stranger who rid Hamelin Town in Brunswick of rats by playing his pipe; when the townsfolk refused to reward him, he piped their children away. The best-known version is Robert Browning's poem (1842).

Pieds Noirs, Les Algerians' name for, and adopted by, the French *colons* in Algeria and still applied to the 800,000 or so repatriated to the French Midi since 1962 (see ALGÉRIE FRANÇAISE). (Name derived from the early settlers' black boots, which much impressed the sandalled Algerians.)

Pierrot Late addition to the stock characters of pantomime, created in Paris in the early 19th century; a white-faced melancholy figure in loose white fancy clothes.

Piers Plowman, Vision Concerning (14th century). William Langland's alliterative poem, a religious allegory castigating the evils of Church and society, and painting a vivid picture of his times.

Pietà In art, a representation of the Madonna mourning the dead Christ. Among the most famous are Michelangelo's versions in Florence Cathedral, Milan and St Peter's, Rome; and a Tintoretto (1571) at Milan. (Italian, 'pity'.)

Pig and Whistle Inn sign, corruption of Piggin and Wassail. (*Piggin*, a small wooden drinking vessel.)

Pike's Peak or bust! The motto of those who took part in the Gold Rush (1859) around what is now Denver City. (A Rocky Mountain peak in Colorado.)

Piledriver Mixed drink of vodka, bitters and an orange liqueur.

Pilgrimage of Grace (1536–7). Revolt in the north of England, after the DISSOLUTION OF THE MONASTERIES, of nobles, clergy and peasants. Under Robert Aske they took York and Doncaster, but withdrew on a promise of pardon which was not honoured.

Pilgrim Fathers (1620). Puritans who fled from England to Leyden in Holland in the early years of James I's reign and, led by John Bradford,

sailed thence, called at Plymouth where they joined others, and crossed the Atlantic in the *Mayflower* to found the first of the New England (and second of the American) settlements, at (New) Plymouth, now in Massachusetts.

Pilgrims, The (1902). Club founded in memory of the PILGRIM FATHERS, with premises in London (Pilgrims of Great Britain) and New York (Pilgrims of the US; 1903).

Pilgrim's Progress (1678). John Bunyan's description of Christian's allegorical journey from the City of Destruction to the Celestial City. See DOUBTING CASTLE; SLOUGH OF DESPOND; VANITY FAIR.

Pilgrim Trust (1930). Founded by the US railway magnate, banker and philanthropist, Edward S. Harkness, who left £2 million to be spent for the benefit of Britain. It is used for the preservation of ancient buildings, grants to learned societies, the NATIONAL TRUST and social welfare schemes, and for the purchase of works of art.

Pilkington Report (1962). Report on broadcasting which severely criticized the low moral and intellectual standards of commercial TV and recommended that the planning of its programmes should be handed over to the ITA, who would sell advertising time to the TV companies. No significant action was taken on this, but a recommendation that the next new TV service should be allotted to the BBC, not to ITV, was implemented by the establishment of BBC-2.

Pilkington Bros. (1826). Large family firm of glass-makers, with headquarters at St Helens; it absorbed Chance Brothers, and makes Fibreglass.

Pill, The (1960). Oral contraceptive of which there are 26 different kinds.

Pillars of Hercules Greek name for the Straits of Gibraltar.

Pillars of Society (1877). Ibsen's play about a corrupt and hypocritical industrialist.

Pillnitz, Declaration of (August 1791). Announcement by the Emperor of Austria and the King of Prussia that the cause of Louis XVI was the cause of monarchies everywhere; the chief reason for the French Revolutionary Wars, see VALMY.

Pilsen German name of the Czech city, Plzen. See next entry.

Pilsener Originally beer brewed at PILSEN; now a generic term for pale beer strongly flavoured with hops.

Piltdown Man Type of early Man deduced from the faked fossil of a skull constructed of ape jaw and human cranium by Charles Dawson. He announced its discovery in 1912, and fooled most of the anthropological world until 1953, when it was proved to be a hoax. (Piltdown, a Sussex village where he claimed to have found it.)

Pimms Proprietary name of a series of alcoholic long drinks, more potent than they taste, of which the formula is secret. The most popular is Pimms No. 1, with a gin base, but there are varieties numbered 2 and 3. They should be served with cucumber-tasting borage and other embellishments.

Pimpernel See SCARLET PIMPERNEL.

PIN Personal Identification Number issued to bank customers to obtain currency from cash dispensers.

Pinafore, HMS (1878). Gilbert and Sullivan opera. Able Seaman Ralph Rackstraw falls in love with his Captain's daughter, to whom the First Lord of the Admiralty is paying court. His case seems hopeless until Little Buttercup, a Portsmouth bumboat woman, reveals that she switched Ralph and the Captain when they were babies. Not only does Ralph get his girl, but the Captain is happy to marry Little Buttercup.

Pinakothek (Munich) See HAUS DER KUNST. (German from Greek for 'picture depository'.)

Pinchbeck Alloy, a mixture of copper and zinc, invented by Christopher Pinchbeck (1670–1732) a London clock-maker.

Pincherle Catalogue of Vivaldi's concertos and symphonies compiled by Marc Pincherle. (Abbreviation 'P'.)

Pindaric odes (5th century BC). Odes written by the Greek poet Pindar, commissioned by the victors in the Olympic, Pythian and other similar Games, whose praises he sang.

Pine Tree State Nickname of Maine.

Pinewood Studios Rank's film studios at Iver, near Slough, Buckinghamshire.

Pinfold, Gilbert See ORDEAL OF GILBERT PINFOLD.

Pinkerton, Lt See MADAME BUTTERFLY.

Pinkerton, The Misses In Thackeray's VANITY FAIR, the dignified sisters who ran an academy for young ladies in Chiswick Mall, where Becky SHARP was educated and taught French.

Pinkerton's American private detective agency founded by Allan Pinkerton (1819–84), head of the American secret services, who in 1861 was a guard to Abraham Lincoln.

Pink Gin Gin with a few drops of ANGOSTURA, and Perrier (or other mineral water, or soda-water), and ice.

Pink Lady Mixed drink of gin, cider, grenadine and egg white.

Pink Pills for Pale People, Dr Williams's A US competitor for BEECHAM'S PILLS, on much the same level of efficacy.

Pink 'Un, The Sporting Times, now defunct, printed on pink paper and regarded by its Edwardian addicts as very 'naughty'.

Pinocchio (1939). Walt Disney's feature-length cartoon, based on a 19th-century Italian tale of a puppet who comes to life, and whose nose grows bigger whenever he lies.

Pinyin Chinese phonetic alphabet devised in 1958 and officially adopted in 1979 by China. The previous transcription scheme, WADE GILES, was abandoned, but is still used in TAIWAN. Beijing is Pinyin and Peking, Wade Giles.

Piozzi, Hester Name, after her second marriage, of

Mrs Thrale, friend of Dr Johnson, about whom she published her *Anecdotes* 2 years after his death.

Pippa Passes (1841). Robert Browning's dramatic poem of a girl who goes singing through the streets songs by which, unknowingly, she changes the lives of 4 people who overhear her, and, incidentally, her own. The most famous of her songs ends: 'God's in His heaven – All's right with the world!', expressing Pippa's (not Browning's) innocent optimism.

Pip, Squeak and Wilfred (1919–55). Characters of a strip cartoon in the *Daily Mirror* by A. B. Payne. (2) Nickname for the 3 medals awarded to those who served throughout World War I (1914–15 Star, General Service Medal and Victory Medal).

Pirates of Penzance, The (1879). Gilbert and Sullivan opera. Frederic, indentured by mistake to a very gentle and unsuccessful band of pirates, has completed his apprenticeship and feels bound to denounce them. They quite understand, and when the police order them to yield in the Queen's name they kneel in homage to their Sovereign. It is then revealed that they are in fact delinquent noblemen, and are at once released to take their rightful places in the House of Lords.

Pisces Fishes, 12th of the constellations of the Zodiac, between Aquarius and Aries; the sun enters it about 21 February. Astrologers claim that those born under this sign may be weak, unpractical, restless, affectionate. (Pronounced pis'eez, pisk'eez, py'seez.)

Pisgah Mount Pisgah, north-east of the Dead Sea, from which at Jehovah's command Moses gazed upon the Promised Land that he himself would never enter (Deut. 3:27). (Pronounced piz'gė.)

Pistol Cowardly braggart who, with BARDOLPH, follows FALSTAFF in the *Merry Wives* and *Henry IV*, and reappears in *Henry V*; he marries Mistress QUICKLY.

Pithecanthropines ('ape-men') Middle Pleistocene creatures living some 400,000 years ago, with brains twice as large as AUSTRALOPITH-

ECINES; they made stone tools, used fire and hunted. Some regard them as probably true men but of a different species from ours, and group them under the specific name *Homo erectus*. They include JAVA MAN and the later PEKING MAN.

Pitman Form of shorthand. Sir Isaac Pitman (1813–97) was a schoolteacher who in 1837 published his *Stenographic Sound Hand*, a manual of the principles of his shorthand system. Pitman's career was largely devoted to the development of shorthand and spelling reform.

Pitt, The Elder William Pitt, the Great Commoner (1708–78), Prime Minister under George II and under George III until 1767, and Earl of Chatham from 1766. He was the father of the Younger Pitt (1759–1806), twice Prime Minister under George III.

Pitt Club (1835). Cambridge University equivalent to the Oxford BULLINGDON CLUB. Membership is limited to 220 students.

Pitti One of the 2 great art galleries in Florence (the other is the UFFIZI).

Pitt Professor Holder of the chair of American History and Institutions at Cambridge.

Pitt-Rivers Museum (1883). Ethnological museum at Oxford University.

Plague, The (1947). Albert Camus's novel about an outbreak of plague at Oran. The hero is a doctor who does what he can, knowing (like the author) that most of what he does will be unavailing but hoping that a little of it may prove of value. (French title, *La Peste*.)

Plaid Cymru (1925). Welsh nationalist party, first represented in the House of Commons in 1966. (Welsh, 'Welsh party'.)

Plain, The In the French Revolution, the moderate, but ineffective, middle-class Girondist majority of the CONVENTION. (So called in contrast to the MOUNTAIN; in French, *Le Marais*.)

Plain Bob One of the principal methods of change-ringing church bells.

Plain Tales from the Hills (1887). Kipling's collection of early stories of life in India, including the first appearance of the heroes of SOLDIERS THREE.

Plaisterers, Worshipful Company of (1500). LIVERY COMPANY, originally a guild of plasterers.

Planck's constant (1900). In quantum theory a constant which, multiplied by the frequency of a radiation, gives its quantum of energy; its symbol is *h*. (Max Planck, German physicist.)

Planetarium, London (1958). Hall adjoining Madame Tussaud's, Baker Street, which houses the only English planetarium. The movements of the stars and planets are demonstrated by a lecturer with the aid of moving images projected on to the domed ceiling.

Plantagenets (1154–1399). Kings of England from Henry II to Richard II; also called the Angevins ('of Anjou'). (Nickname of Geoffrey, Count of Anjou and father of Henry II, from the Latin *planta genista*, 'broom', which he wore in his hat.)

Plantation Colonies Virginia (1607); Maryland (1632), a Catholic settlement founded by Lord Baltimore; North and South Carolina (1663), founded by Lord Clarendon; Georgia (1732), by General Oglethorpe.

Plantations, The Settlement in the 1550s of Englishmen and 'loyal' Irish in King's County (Offaly) and Queen's County (Laoighis) in Mary's reign after the suppression of the revolt of the O'Mores and O'Connors, a policy continued in later reigns in other parts of Ireland, e.g. Ulster in 1608 (see ULSTER, PLANTATION OF). See also CROMWELLIAN SETTLEMENT.

Plassey (1757). Clive's defeat of Suraj ud Dowlah after the BLACK HOLE OF CALCUTTA.

Plastic Credit cards.

Plataea (479 BC). Final defeat of the Persians by the Greeks after SALAMIS. (City of Boeotia; pronounced plat-ee′a.)

Platyhelminthes Flatworms, a phylum which includes the Trematodes (liver flukes parasitic on sheep) and Cestodes (tapeworms, parasitic on man and other animals).

Play (1963). Beckett's play in which the 3 characters speak their lines buried to the neck in urns. The whole play lasts 10 minutes, and is then repeated *in toto*, verbatim, which must, critics feel, be the *reductio ad* something or other.

Playboy of the Western World, The (1907). J. M. Synge's play of the timid boy, Christie Mahon, who thinks he has 'destroyed his da'' and finds himself regarded as a hero on that account; this goes to his head – until the old man turns up in pursuit of him.

Playing Cards, Worshipful Company of Makers of (1628). LIVERY COMPANY still closely associated with the trade.

Plays: Pleasant and Unpleasant (1898). Two volumes of Bernard Shaw's plays. The Pleasant comprise *Arms and the Man, Candida, The Man of Destiny* and *You Never Can Tell*; the Unpleasant, *The Philanderer, Mrs Warren's Profession* and *Widowers' Houses*.

Plaza-Toro, Duke of Spanish grandee in Gilbert and Sullivan's *Gondoliers*; when there was any fighting 'he led his regiment from behind – he found it less exciting'.

Pléiade (16th century). Group of 7 French poets, including Ronsard and du Bellay, who set out to reform the vocabulary of French poetry, drawing extensively on classical models. (See next entry.)

Pleiades (Greek legend). Seven daughters of Atlas, who give their name to a constellation (see next entry). (Pronounced ply′a-deez.)

Pleiades Best-known open (or galactic) star cluster, containing several nebulae: eta-Tauri (Alcyone) is the brightest. It is mentioned in Job 38:31. (See previous entry.)

Pleistocene Epoch Earlier subdivision of the QUATERNARY PERIOD, lasting from about one million to 25,000 years ago. It coincided with most of the Great ICE AGE and of the PALAEOLITHIC AGE; PITHECANTHROPINES and early Man (NEANDERTAL MAN, HOMO SAPIENS) developed.

Plimsoll mark Ship's maximum summer load-line, a circle intersected by a horizontal line, painted amidships; also used of similar markings for winter, tropical seas, freshwater etc. load-lines. (Named from 19th-century English campaigner for shipping safety.)

Pliocene Epoch Most recent subdivision of the TERTIARY PERIOD, lasting from about 5·5 to 1·8 million years ago. The earliest fossil remains of AUSTRALOPITHECINES and of HOMO HABILIS date from this epoch.

Plonk Poor wine; but also used to mean good cheap wine for everyday casual drinking.

Plon-Plon Nickname of Prince Napoleon Joseph Charles Bonaparte, son of Napoleon's youngest brother, gained in the Crimean War. (Corruption of *Craint-plon*, 'fear-bullet'.)

Plough, The English name of the 7 bright stars conspicuous in the constellation of the GREAT BEAR; also used incorrectly for the whole constellation.

Plowden report (1965). Report on the reorganization of the aircraft industry which recommended state control of the 2 main aircraft companies (BAC and Hawker-Siddeley), and European co-operation in future development. (Baron Plowden, former chairman of the Atomic Energy Authority.)

Plowden report (1967). On primary education, a report by the Central Advisory Council on Education. It recommended that a 3-year 'first school' period should replace the 2-year infant school, so that the child can master reading before passing on to a 4-year middle-school education (8–12); transfer to secondary school to be at 12 + instead of 11 +. (Lady Plowden, Chairman.)

Plumbers, Worshipful Company of (1611). LIVERY COMPANY which finances technical instruction in the trade and keeps a register of plumbers qualified by proficiency in examinations.

Plumed Serpent, The (1926). D. H. Lawrence's novel of Mexico, full of highly evocative nature descriptions combined with all but incoherent philosophizing based on a revival of the blood-stained Aztec religion by a Nietzschean SUPER-MAN type. (The title is a translation of Quetzalcoatl, the Aztec god.)

Plumian Professor Holder of the chair of Astronomy and Experimental Philosophy at Cambridge.

Plummer (John Humphrey) Professor Holder of one of 3 chairs at Cambridge: Colloid Science, Physics, Theoretical Chemistry.

Pluto (Roman god) See HADES.

Pluto Code name for the submarine pipelines conveying petrol across the English Channel for the Normandy landings, 1944. (Initials of 'pipe line under the ocean'.)

Plymouth Brethren (1828). Calvinistic sect founded by an Irish curate, J. N. Darby, and established in 1831 at Plymouth. They have no clergy and meet in a 'room' each Sunday for the 'Breaking of the Bread'. Many splinter-groups have seceded from the main body, e.g. the EX-CLUSIVE BRETHREN.

Plymouth gin Generic term for a gin with a distinctive flavour said to be due to the addition of sulphuric acid before distillation; originally made in the West Country.

Plymouth porcelain (1768–70). Earliest hard-paste wares made in England. The secret of their manufacture was discovered by William Cookworthy, who moved to Bristol after only 2 years. See BRISTOL PORCELAIN.

Plymouth Rock (1) Rock at Plymouth, Massachusetts, on which the Pilgrim Fathers are said to have first stepped ashore. (2) US breed of poultry. (3) Derogatory term for a Plymouth Brother.

PNEU (1888). Initials used for the Parents' National Educational Union, a society formed to propagate the views of Charlotte Mason on education, including character-forming, through various schools in the UK and overseas, and to provide guidance in home tuition for individual parents and small communities serving abroad where no suitable schools are available.

Pobble Who Has No Toes, The Nonsense poem by Edward Lear; see RUNCIBLE CAT.

Podsnap Character in Dickens's *Our Mutual Friend* who had the courage of all his convictions; anyone or anything that interfered with them was swept on one side.

Poet and Peasant Popular overture to an otherwise unremembered operetta by the 19th-century Austrian composer Suppé.

Poet Laureate Office that evolved, perhaps from Chaucer's time, with the duty of writing verse on royal occasions; a recalcitrant Muse sometimes withheld the requisite instant inspiration, though it is apparently untrue that Alfred Austin wrote (of the future Edward VII): 'Across the wires the electric message came/ "He is no better, he is much the same".' The Poet Laureate in Ordinary ranks in the Royal Household next above the Bargemaster and the Keeper of Swans; the pay varies, Tennyson got £72 p.a. + £27 in lieu of a butt of sack. The last 8 Laureates have been: Wordsworth, Tennyson, Austin, Bridges, Masefield, Day Lewis, Betjeman and Hughes.

Poetry Bookshop, The (1912). Founded in Bloomsbury by the poet Harold Monro, as a place where poets could meet, hold poetry readings and, if they wished, lodge for a minute rent. See GEORGIAN POETRY.

Poets' Corner Area of the south transept of Westminster Abbey filled with tombs or other memorials to the great British poets and writers, from Chaucer onwards.

Poets' Poet, The Name given to Edmund Spenser, as a poet to be fully appreciated only by fellow poets.

Poil de Carotte Story by Jules Renard, turned into an outstanding French film by Julien Duvivier, using a non-professional cast in a village setting. (French, 'carroty-head'.)

Poinsettia Tropical perennials, named after a Mexican traveller, de Poinci.

Point Counter Point (1928). Aldous Huxley's novel of hate in which few features of contemporary society go unscathed. Many characters are based on leading figures of the day and of the past, while the author himself appears as Philip Quarles.

Poirot, Hercule Belgian detective who first appeared in Agatha Christie's *Mysterious Affair at Styles* (1920), when he had already drawn a police pension for 16 years, making him about 130 today. Splendidly conceited and glorying in his preposterous moustache, age has not withered him nor custom staled his infinite variety.

Polack (US, derogatory) Person of Polish descent. (A survival from Shakespearian times; pronounced poh'lak.)

Polaris (Astronomy) Latin name for the Pole star.

Polaris An ICBM designed for firing from a submerged POLARIS SUBMARINE; it was so fired in 1960, and is the only ICBM to be tested with a nuclear warhead. A1 has a range of 1,200 miles, A2 1,400 miles (with an 800-kiloton warhead), and A3 a range of some 2,500 miles. See POSEIDON.

Polaris submarines (1960). Nuclear submarines each armed with 16 POLARIS A3 missiles. The Royal Navy has 4 (see RESOLUTION), built in the UK but with the complete weapon system supplied by the USA; the missiles are kept in the USA. Their role is to take over the British deterrent from the RAF's V-bombers. The US completed their 41st and last Polaris submarine in 1966.

Polaroid Proprietary name for a thin transparent plastic sheet which plane-polarizes light; used in spectacles and car windscreens to prevent glare.

Poldhu Site in south-west Cornwall from which the first transatlantic radio signal was transmitted, in 1901. (North of Mullion Cove; pronounced pol'dew.)

Polesden Lacey Regency villa near Dorking, Surrey, owned by the NATIONAL TRUST and housing the Greville art collection.

Pole Star See NORTH STAR.

Polish Corridor (1919–39). Strip of territory dividing East Prussia from the rest of Germany, given under the VERSAILLES TREATY to an otherwise landlocked Poland to permit access to

387

the free port of Danzig and to Gdynia on the Baltic. Hitler took the first opportunity to recapture it for Germany. It is now part of Poland again.

Polish October (1956). Uprising against Russian dominance in Poland, which led to the return of Gomulka (who had been in disgrace for supporting Tito) and the dismissal of the Russian-born Polish Minister of Defence, Marshal Rokossovsky.

Politburo Supreme policy-making body of the Soviet Communist Party, renamed in 1952 the Praesidium of the CENTRAL COMMITTEE, but reverting to the old title in 1966. (Abbreviation of Russian for Political Bureau.)

Poll tax See COMMUNITY CHARGE.

Pollux Less bright of the 2 stars in the heads of the GEMINI 'twins' (the first being CASTOR).

Polly, Alfred Small tradesman of H. G. Wells's *The History of Mr Polly* (1910), who escapes from his dreary home (which he burns down) and from his horrible wife, to taste the joys of freedom; together with his Uncles Pentstemon and Jim forming a trio of Wells's most memorable creations.

Pollyanna Absurdly optimistic person, from the heroine of Eleanor Porter's novel *Pollyanna* (1913), who was given to playing 'the glad game', i.e. looking on the bright side no matter what.

Polonaise (Cooking) With beetroot and sour cream.

Polonius In Shakespeare's *Hamlet* the aged Lord Chamberlain, father of Ophelia and Laertes, killed accidentally by Hamlet when lurking behind the arras; in playing his part his worldly wisdom used to be stressed, but now his sententious wordiness gets more attention.

Polycentrism Freedom for national Communist parties to adapt their methods to local conditions, provided the ideological unity of the movement is not thereby weakened. (Idea and name proposed by the Italian Communist leader Togliatti, 1956.)

Polycrates, Ring of According to a story in Herodotus, Polycrates, a tyrant of Samos in the 6th century BC waxed rich on piracy and was advised to throw away his most treasured possession to avert NEMESIS. He threw a ring into the sea, but it reappeared in a fish served up to him. So Nemesis overtook Polycrates, who died a violent death.

Polydeuces See CASTOR AND POLLUX. (Pronounced pol-i-dews'eez.)

Polyeucte Hero of Corneille's play of that name, a Christian convert executed by Félix his father-in-law and Roman governor of Armenia; his martyrdom results in the repentant conversion of both Félix and his own widow.

Polynesians Group of Pacific races, including the Maori and the peoples of Hawaii, Tonga, Samoa, Tahiti and the Marquesas. (Greek, 'many-island people'.)

Polyphemus In Greek legend a Cyclops, a one-eyed giant, who shut up ODYSSEUS and his men in a cave. Odysseus blinded him and they escaped by clinging underneath the giant's flock of sheep, but only after Polyphemus had eaten 6 of their companions.

Polytechnic, The (1882). First of many polytechnics, in Upper Regent Street, London, founded by Quintin Hogg and now officially called the Royal Polytechnic Institute. It was a pioneer experiment in providing part-time education for the young and for adults, and holds day and evening classes in a very wide range of subjects.

Pomerania Former German Baltic province, now divided between Eastern Germany and Poland. (German, Pommern; Polish Pomorze.)

Pomerol Claret similar to, but not generally so good as, that from nearby SAINT ÉMILION.

Pommard See CÔTE DE BEAUNE.

Pommy (or **Pom**) Word used by Australians and New Zealanders for an Englishman. Various explanations have been given for its origin of which POME (Prisoner of Mother England, i.e. a convict) is best known and least convincing.

Pomona Roman goddess of fruit-trees; she has no Greek equivalent.

Pompadour Name usually linked with the ROCOCO style, although Mme de Pompadour, Louis XV's mistress was a leading advocate of a return to classical models (neoclassicism); also used of a rolled-back hair style she affected, and of a claret-purple colour she liked.

Pompeii Ancient Roman port and pleasure resort, buried beneath lava from Vesuvius (see LAST DAYS OF POMPEII). Excavations begun in 1763 and now near completion have revealed much of the city as it was on the day of the disaster.

Pompey (1) Naval nickname for Portsmouth. (2) Nickname of the Portsmouth football team. (Origin unknown.)

Ponderevo, Uncle See TONO-BUNGAY.

Pondo One of the African races of the TRANSKEI.

Pons Asinorum Old nickname for the fifth theorem in Euclid's geometry, a stumbling-block for beginners. It states that 2 equal sides of any triangle make equal angles with the third side. (Latin, 'asses' bridge'.)

Pontecorvo spy case (1950). Dr Bruno Pontecorvo, employed in Canada on atomic research, defected to Russia.

Ponte Vecchio Old Bridge at Florence, forming a street across the River Arno for pedestrians only, lined on both sides with quaint old shops clinging on to it precariously. It survived World War II but was damaged in the floods of 1966.

Pontine Marshes Marshes of the CAMPAGNA around Rome, Mussolini was aptly nicknamed the Bullfrog of the Pontine Marshes, although it has to be said for him that he did drain them.

Pont-l'Évêque Semi-hard cheese of Normandy.

Pont Street Dutch One of Osbert Lancaster's wittily named categories of modern 'architecture'. (Pont Street, Knightsbridge, London.)

Pony Club (1929). Club formed to encourage the young to ride, open to all under 17.

Pony Express (1860–61). (USA) Fast mail service from St Joseph, Missouri, to Sacramento, California. Mail was carried at the gallop, horses being changed at 190 relay stations spaced at 12-mile intervals. With the establishment of a telegraph line, the service closed down after only 18 months' operation. Among the riders were BUFFALO BILL and WILD BILL HICKOK.

Pooh-Bah In Gilbert and Sullivan's MIKADO, the Lord High Everything Else; hence applied to a Jack-of-many-offices.

Pool of London The Thames immediately below London Bridge, the highest point for vessels of medium size.

Poor Bitos (1956). Anouilh's play in which aristocrats torment poor Bitos, a self-made man who, however, deserves little sympathy.

Poor Richard's Almanack (1732–57). Annual almanac compiled by Benjamin Franklin under the name Richard Saunders and famous for its pawky aphorisms, many of them borrowed from the Old World and Americanized. Among them were: 'God helps those who help themselves'; 'Three may keep a secret, if two of them are dead'; and 'Some are weather-wise, some are otherwise'.

Pooter, Mr Kind, dim, highly respectable London clerk invented by the brothers George and Weedon Grossmith in *The Diary of a Nobody* (1894), which sympathetically describes the very minor crises of life at The Laurels, Brickfield Terrace, Holloway, in the 1880s.

POP Initials standing for Post Office Preferred and referring to standardized sizes of envelopes which facilitate mechanical sorting.

Pop Properly the Eton Society, an elected club of some 20 Etonians who maintain school discipline and have certain privileges of dress (e.g. damask waistcoats), etc. (From Latin *popina*, 'cookshop', as early meetings were held over a confectioner's.)

Pop Art (1950s). Term which can have no settled meaning as the essence of POP CULTURE is its ephemerality. It is however used of semi-abstract paintings and collages full of allusion to modern urban life, e.g. its advertisements, fashions in dress, industrial design etc.

Pop culture (early 1950s). Product among the younger generation of urban life, mass production, ample spending money and a general revolt against the standards of older people. It is characterized by ephemerality (e.g. last week's eagerly sought top of the pops record will be forgotten next week), living for the moment, overriding horror of being thought out of date, a superficial approach to problems of the day and, a redeeming feature, absence of class or race consciousness.

Pope Joan (1) Legendary female pope of the 9th century, an Englishwoman who died in childbirth during a papal procession. The story was widely believed in the Middle Ages. (2) Card game; the name is said to have no connection with (1).

Popeye Internationally famous one-eyed sailor-man with a corncob pipe, created by Elzie Segar in 1929 and continued by others in strip, movie and radio form. A tin of spinach would suffice to give him superman strength and Crystal City, Texas, the spinach centre, gratefully put up a monument to him. His stringy wife Olive Oyl and his friend Wimpy are no less well known.

Popish plot (1678). Plot invented by Titus Oates, a renegade Anglican clergyman; he alleged that the Jesuits planned with French assistance to kill Charles II and put James II on the throne; many innocent Catholics were hanged on his evidence.

Poplar Former London metropolitan borough, since 1965 part of the borough of TOWER HAMLETS.

Pop music Music meant for the teenage masses but not, like folk-song, originating among the masses (here lies the difference between pop and popular). After warnings from Bing Crosby's crooning (1930s) and Frank Sinatra's heart-throbs (1940s), it took shape (1953) in the USA with ROCK 'N' ROLL and in Britain with Tommy Steele (1956), the earliest to receive the distinguishing accolade of hysterically screaming girls (see BEATLEMANIA). The BEATLES then added BEAT MUSIC to Rock and, with the ROLLING STONES, put Britain in the lead until Bob Dylan redressed the balance.

Popolo d'Italia (1914). Italian newspaper founded by Mussolini and edited by him until 1922; it became the chief Fascist daily.

Poppy Day (1921). Traditional collection for EARL HAIG'S FUND on REMEMBRANCE SUNDAY. The poppies, made by disabled ex-servicemen, represent the characteristic flower of the fields of Flanders where so many British soldiers of World War I lie buried.

Popski's Private Army Nickname of a unit of the LONG-RANGE DESERT PATROL formed (October 1942) by Vladimir Peniakov, a Russian-born Belgian subject serving with the British army.

Popular Front (1935). Communist device recommended to non-Communist countries by the Comintern for strengthening opposition to Fascism by sinking differences between Socialist parties and the Communists to form a (temporary) common front. (For 'popular', see PEOPLE'S.)

Porgy and Bess (1935). George Gershwin's Negro opera set in Charleston, South Carolina.

Porifera Sponges, the only phylum of the sub-kingdom Parazoa.

Port Arthur Chinese naval base (renamed Lüshun), now grouped with Dairen as the conurbation of LÜ-TA.

Portcullis Pursuivant of the COLLEGE OF ARMS.

Porter, Jimmy Original ANGRY YOUNG MAN, the chief character of LOOK BACK IN ANGER.

Porterhouse steak Large steak cut from the thick end of the short loin, containing a T-shaped bone and a large piece of tenderloin. (A porterhouse served steaks, chops and the dark beer called porter.)

Portia (1) Ingenious heiress of Shakespeare's *Merchant of Venice* who, disguised as a lawyer, resists SHYLOCK's claim, and marries BASSANIO. (2) In Shakespeare's *Julius Caesar* the wife of Brutus.

Portland cement Cement named after the Isle of Portland because it is similar in colour to the stone quarried there.

Portland Club (1816). London club in Half Moon Street, the recognized authority on Bridge which drew up the first authoritative rules of the game.

Portland Club Cup British Bridge competition for mixed pairs.

Portland secrets case (1961). Trial of LONS-DALE, HOUGHTON AND GEE, and the KROGERS for espionage on behalf of Russia in connection with work at the Underwater Weapons Establishment, Portland, where equipment for the nuclear submarine *Dreadnought* was being developed.

Portland Vase Greek urn of dark-blue glass ornamented with figures in white, found in the 17th century near Rome in a grave of the 3rd century AD. The Duke of Portland lent it to the British Museum, where it was smashed to pieces in 1845 by a madman, but skilfully put together again.

Portmeirion (1925). Unique private hillside village overlooking Tremadog Bay near Porthmadog, Gwynedd; designed and built by Sir Clough Williams-Ellis, architect, town-planner and conservationist. Resembling a well-designed set for an Italian operetta, it has towers, arches, columns, exotic trees and miles of sand; there is a waterfront hotel but guests can also rent rooms in a wide variety of colourful buildings. Many famous writers and artists have worked there.

Portobello Road London street market for antiques, at Notting Hill, frequented by tourists as well as dealers.

Port of London Thames from Teddington Lock to the Nore.

Porto Rico Name until 1932 of Puerto Rico, a group of West Indian islands ceded to USA in 1898.

Portrait of the Artist as a Young Man (1916). James Joyce's autobiography of his childhood and early manhood, in which he appears as Stephen DEDALUS. Using the 'interior monologue' technique of *Ulysses*, he describes how he came to reject family, religious and patriotic ties to achieve freedom as an artist.

Port-Royal Abbey near Versailles, headquarters of JANSENISM; it was razed by Louis XIV.

Port Salut Soft pale yellow cheese of France with a very mild, mellow flavour.

Portsmouth, Treaty of (1905). Treaty that ended the Russo-Japanese War. (Portsmouth, New Hampshire. USA.)

Portugaise (Cooking) With tomatoes and onion or garlic.

Poseidon Bigger version of POLARIS, carrying twice the payload. It is a 'doomsday weapon', i.e. for use in a 'second strike' retaliation, and has penetration devices, such as multiple warheads, to defeat enemy defence measures, thus giving it what is called 'assured destruction capability'.

Positivism 'Religion' of Auguste Comte (1798–1857). Mankind had tried unsuccessfully to explain the universe in terms first of theology and then of philosophy. Comte advocated a scientific approach, seeking objective 'positive' truth. He tried, and failed, to found a church, the god of which was Humanity, with his own liturgy and a calendar of saints (i.e. those who had most benefited mankind).

Possessed, The Dostoyevsky's novel; see STAV-ROGIN.

Post-Impressionism (1910). Movement of reaction against IMPRESSIONISM, associated with Van Gogh, Gauguin and Cézanne. Dissatisfied with impressionistic sketches, they tried to stress the permanent element in their subjects. (Name given by Roger Fry.)

Post Office Tower (1965). A high tower in London built to house the main link in a country-wide network of microwave towers to provide telephone circuits and TV channels supplementing those already in existence.

Postumus Friend of Horace to whom he addressed one of his most famous odes: *Eheu fugaces, Postume, Postume, / Anni labuntur.* This was freely translated in one of the INGOLDSBY LEGENDS: 'Years glide away, and are lost to me, lost to me!'

Potato Famine (Irish) In 1845–7 blight caused a total failure of Ireland's staple crop, the death from hunger and typhus of perhaps a third of the population, and mass emigration to America.

Potemkin, Battleship, see BATTLESHIP POTEMKIN.

Pothouse Colloquial abbreviation for Peterhouse, Cambridge.

Potiphar's wife Wife of Pharaoh's captain of the guard who, having failed to seduce JOSEPH, accused him of having tried to seduce her; he was put in prison (Gen. 39:17–20).

Potsdam Conference (July–August 1945). Conference attended by Truman, Stalin, Churchill and Attlee (who had just become Prime Minister), which discussed post-war settlements and issued a demand for unconditional surrender by Japan. As the conference began, Truman heard of the test explosion of the first atomic bomb.

Potteries, The The FIVE TOWNS of Stoke-on-Trent, north Staffordshire, where the potteries of Wedgwood, Minton, Doulton, Longton and many others were established.

Potterism (1920). Dame Rose Macaulay's novel about Mr Potter, a successful newspaper proprietor, and his best-selling novelist wife. They represent the prostitution of talents in a philistine pursuit of commercial success, a policy opposed by their children who form an Anti-Potter League. The author attacks both sides alike.

Pott's fracture Combined dislocation and fracture of the ankle, caused by twisting the foot.

Poughkeepsie regatta Premier US rowing event. (On the Hudson, in south-east New York; pronounced pé-kip'si.)

Pouilly-Fuissé See BURGUNDY.

Poujadists (1955–8). Members of a French petit-bourgeois political party whose programme, against parliamentary government, taxes and any concessions to nationalism in North Africa, won them $2\frac{1}{2}$ million votes in 1956; by 1958 they had disappeared. (Founded by Pierre Poujade.)

Poulters, Worshipful Company of (1503). LIVERY COMPANY, originally a guild of sellers of poultry, rabbits, eggs and butter. Members include leaders of the industry.

Pour le Mérite (1740). Prussian, later German, order of merit awarded either for military valour or for distinction in science or art.

Powderham Castle Home near Exeter of the Earls of Devon, dating back to the 14th century.

Powellism Policies put forward in the late 1960s by the Conservative MP, Enoch Powell; they include the stricter control of immigration, sharp reductions in taxation offset by reductions in public investment and government subsidies, withdrawal of the British 'presence' east of Suez, and increased attention to winning the workers' votes.

Poynings' Law (1495). Act applying all English laws to Ireland and severely restricting the Irish Parliament powers; repealed 1782.

Poyser, Mrs Character in ADAM BEDE who looks after her husband's niece, Hetty Sorrel. Garrulous, kind-hearted but sharp-tongued, she is said to be a portrait of George Eliot's mother.

Poznań riots (June 1956). Agitation in the city against Soviet domination which preceded POLISH OCTOBER.

PPE (Oxford University) Initials standing for Philosophy, Politics and Economics; see MODERN GREATS.

PPP (Oxford University) Initials standing for Psychology, Philosophy and Physiology, a course for the final BA examination of exceptionally difficulty.

PPS (Parliament) Initials used for PARLIAMENTARY PRIVATE SECRETARY.

Prado (1819). Spanish national art gallery at Madrid, containing the treasures collected by the Spanish Habsburgs.

Praesidium (of the Supreme Soviet) (USSR) Elected body to which the SUPREME SOVIET delegates its powers; its chairman is the President of the USSR. The POLITBURO directs its actions through Party members on the Praesidium.

Pragmatic Sanction (1) Imperial decree; (2) specifically, the Emperor Charles VI's decree (1713) setting aside the Salic Law so that his daughter Maria Theresa could inherit the Hapsburg dominions of Austria. (Translation of an old Latin legal term.)

Pragmatism (1896). School of philosophy founded by the American, William James. If an idea (e.g. the idea of God) 'works', it is expedient to believe it; whether it is objectively true is a minor consideration.

Prairial In the French Revolution calendar, the month from 20 May to 18 June. ('Meadow-month'.)

Prairie Oyster Raw egg swallowed whole in sherry and Worcester sauce, a means of conveying sustenance to a queasy stomach on the morning after.

Praise-God Barebones Name of a fanatical Puritan member, also spelt Barbon, who gave its name to the BAREBONES PARLIAMENT.

Prater Large park in Vienna, in which is situated a kind of permanent fairground; the chief feature of this is a large Ferris wheel, from the cars of which one has a fine view of the city.

Pratt's Club (1841). London club in a Park Place basement off St James's Street, named after the Duke of Beaufort's steward who started it; its distinguished members excel in *éminence grise*-manship.

Prattware (1) Generic term for primitive Staffordshire earthenware figures, jugs, teapots, etc. (1790–1830) decorated with a distinctive range of underglaze colours which could withstand the heat of the glazing kiln – ochre, blue, green, brown, purple – made by Felix Pratt of Fenton and many others. (2) Plates, etc. decorated with transfer prints of the potlid type made (1840–80) by Felix Pratt's son at the Fenton factory.

Pravda (1912). Soviet Russia's chief daily newspaper, representing the party viewpoint (see IZVESTIA). (Russian, 'truth'.)

Preakness, The (1873). One of the 3 US classic flat-races for 3-year-olds, run in May over a distance of 1 mile $1\frac{1}{2}$ furlongs at the Pimlico racecourse, Baltimore. Maryland.

Pre-Cambrian Era Geological era earlier than the CAMBRIAN PERIOD, i.e. earlier than about 600 million years ago. Fossils are rare, but traces of sponges, seaweeds, molluscs and other marine life have been found. Rocks rich in metallic ores were formed.

Précieuses ridicules, Les (1659). Molière's one-act comedy of the 2 snobbish daughters whose rejected suitors avenge themselves by introducing their 2 valets as noblemen; the girls mistake their extravagant manners for the height of fashion. (French, 'the ridiculous BLUE-STOCKINGS'.)

Precious Bane (1924). Mary Webb's novel about the gloomy rustics of the Worcester–Shropshire border. It leapt into fame when praised by the Prime Minister, Stanley Baldwin (a Worcestershire man). It may well have been the chief inspiration of COLD COMFORT FARM.

Preedy, George R. One of the many pen-names used by Marjorie BOWEN.

Prelude, The (1799–1805, published 1850). Wordsworth's autobiographical poem about the 'growth of the poet's mind', his passionate attachment to Lakeland, and 'the self-sufficing power of Solitude'. The original (1805) version was published in 1926.

Premium Bonds (1956). Premium Savings

Bonds, a semi-lottery device for raising capital introduced by Harold Macmillan; numbered bonds in units of £1, redeemable at par and bearing no interest, but eligible for prizes for the numbers selected each month by ERNIE. There are over 200,000 prizes each month from £50 to £250,000, and 3 weekly prizes of £25,000, £50,000 and £100,000. Minimum purchase £100 of bonds (£10 for bonds bought for children under 16).

Prensa, La (1869). Argentine daily newspaper with an international reputation; suppressed during the Peronista Party's regime.

Prentice Cup Lawn tennis match between teams of 6 from Oxford and Cambridge and from Yale and Harvard, played in alternate years and in Britain and USA alternately.

Pre-Raphaelite Brotherhood (1848–53). Misleading nickname of a group of English painters, notably Rossetti, Holman Hunt, Millais and Burne-Jones, who, inspired by what little they knew of the Italian painters before Raphael (i.e. before the 16th century), depicted serious biblical and literary themes in bright colours and meticulous detail. The name clung to them after they had broken up and gone their separate ways, and especially to those who, like Burne-Jones, turned to romantic medieval subjects.

Presbyterianism Form of Church governance adopted by the Church of Scotland and various Churches in England, Ireland and USA. It comprises the kirk sessions of the individual churches; presbyteries; synods; and a General Assembly presided over by an annually elected Moderator. Ministers (presbyters) are all of equal rank and are elected by their congregations, as are the lay elders who watch over the spiritual and moral welfare of church members. See COVENANTERS; WESTMINSTER CONFESSION.

President's Cup (show-jumping). World championship based on points awarded for wins in various international events.

Press Association, The British news agency for home news, run by the newspapers as a co-operative.

Press Barons Name for the newspaper proprietors raised to the peerage during this century: e.g. Lords Northcliffe, Rothermere, Beaverbrook, Kemsley, Thomson.

Press Council (1963). Council with chairman and some members unconnected with the press, the rest representing proprietors, editors and journalists. It aims to discourage encroachments on the freedom of the press, monopolistic mergers, and unwarranted intrusions into the private lives of individuals.

Prester John Legendary 12th-century Christian king in the East or, in later versions, in Abyssinia. (John the Priest or Presbyter.)

Preston, Battle of (1648). Engagement in which Cromwell defeated the northern Royalists and their Scottish allies, ending the second phase of the ENGLISH CIVIL WAR.

Prestonpans See FORTY-FIVE.

Prestwick International airport 3 miles north of Ayr on the Scottish coast; also the site of a famous golf-course.

Previous (examination) Another name for RESPONSIONS; also the official name at Cambridge of the LITTLE-GO.

Previous Question, The Parliamentary device, the question being whether a vote should be taken on the subject under debate; used when the House cannot come to a decision, it takes the form of a motion such as: That the Question be not now put.

Priam In Greek legend, King of Troy, husband of Hecuba, father of 50 sons, including Paris and Hector, and several daughters, including Cassandra. He was killed when Troy fell.

Priapus Greek god of fertility and eroticism, the son of Aphrodite and Dionysus. (Pronounced pry-ayp'us.)

Price, Fanny See MANSFIELD PARK.

Pride and Prejudice (1813). Most famous of Jane Austen's novels of '3 or 4 families in a country village'; see the BENNET FAMILY.

Pride's Purge (1648). Occasion when Cromwell sent Col. Pride with a regiment to purge the LONG PARLIAMENT of those who opposed the trial of Charles I; the remainder became known as the RUMP PARLIAMENT.

Primate, The Archbishop of Canterbury, strictly the Primate of All England, to be distinguished (if logically possible) from the Primate of England, who is the Archbishop of York.

Primates Highest order of mammals, ranging from lemurs and monkeys to Man. (Pronounced pry-may'teez, but more usually written 'primates' with a small *p*, and pronounced as spelt.)

Primavera (1477). Botticelli's painting in which Mercury heralds the approach of Spring, who is ushered by Flora (goddess of flowers) and Zephyrus (the west wind) into the presence of Venus, while Cupid aims his arrow at the Three Graces. Now in the Uffizi, Florence. (Italian, 'spring'.)

Prime of Miss Jean Brodie, The (1961). Novel by the Scottish Catholic convert Muriel Spark about an unorthodox Edinburgh schoolmistress with Fascist leanings who has advanced views on introducing her girls to the problems of adult life. It is the basis of a play by Jay Allen and was also made into a film.

Primrose, Dr See VICAR OF WAKEFIELD.

Primrose League (1883). Political association founded in memory of Disraeli by Lord Randolph Churchill to propagate the principles of TORY DEMOCRACY.

Prince, The (1513). Florentine philosopher Machiavelli's handbook for princes on how to retain power by exploiting the greed and other weaknesses of mankind, by hypocrisy, bad faith, terror and any other methods that may seem expedient. See MACHIAVELLIANISM.

Prince Albert US name for a frock-coat, as worn by Queen Victoria's consort.

Prince and the Pauper, The (1880). Mark Twain's historical novel which became a children's favourite. The little pauper briefly changes places with the 10-year-old Prince Edward just before he succeeds his father, Henry VIII, as Edward VI.

Prince Charming The prince in the CINDERELLA story.

Prince Igor (1889). Borodin's unfinished opera based on a contemporary poem about a historical event. In 1185 the Prince of Novgorod, Igor, raided the nomadic Polovtsy and was taken prisoner, but escaped. The opera was completed by Rimsky-Korsakov and Glazunov. (Pronounced ee'gor.)

Prince Monolulu Racing tipster seen until his death in the 1960s on most racecourses, dressed in Red Indian garb. Punters, but not horses, responded to his slogan 'White man for pluck; black man for luck'.

Prince of Peace Christ. (From Isa 9:6: 'For unto us a child is born . . . The Prince of Peace.')

Prince of Wales Cup (1927). Sailing championship for INTERNATIONAL FOURTEENS, raced at Cowes in July.

Prince of Wales Cup (show-jumping; 1909). Competition at the Royal INTERNATIONAL HORSE SHOW for teams of 4 amateurs of the same nationality. (Formerly, the King Edward VII Cup.)

Prince Philip Cup Coxed fours rowing event at Henley Regatta.

Prince Regent Prince who acts as regent; applied specifically to the Prince of Wales who acted (1811–20) for his father George III during his mental illness, until he succeeded to the throne as George IV.

Princes in the Tower Edward V (who reigned for 3 months) and his brother Richard, murdered in the Tower of London (1483), according to Tudor tradition by their uncle the Duke of Gloucester, who seized the throne as Richard III.

Princess, The (1847). 'Medley' by Lord Tennyson, chiefly remembered for the exquisite lyrics inserted in a later edition. See IDA, PRINCESS.

Princesse (Cooking) With asparagus.

Princess Elizabeth Cup Henley Regatta rowing event for school eights.

Princess Ida See IDA, PRINCESS.

Princess Victoria British Rail ferry-boat which sank off Ireland in 1953 with passengers and crew.

Princeton (1746). One of the IVY LEAGUE universities, at Princeton, NJ, USA.

Principalities An order of angels according to a 4th-century work, grouped with arch-angels and angels. See DOMINIONS AND POWERS.

Principles of Human Knowledge (1710). Bishop Berkeley's main work. He held that all we know, all our ideas, come through the senses; apart from what goes on in our own minds there is nothing of which we have knowledge. Thus there is no reason to suppose that matter exists at all. A critic has commented: '. . . God / Must think it exceedingly odd / If he finds that this tree / Just ceases to be / When there's no one about in the Quad.' To which an anonymous wit replied: 'Dear Sir, Your astonishment's odd: / *I* am always about in the Quad. / And that's why the tree / Will continue to be, / Since observed by Yours faithfully, God.'

Prinny Nickname of the PRINCE REGENT (later George IV).

Printanière (Cooking) With early spring vegetables.

Printemps, Au Large Paris department store near the Opéra.

Printing House Square The original site of the offices of, and used in allusion to, the London *Times*.

Prisoner of Zenda, The (1894). Anthony Hope's novel of RURITANIA.

Private Angelo (1946). Eric Linklater's amusing novel of the reluctant Italian warrior who finds little difficulty in dodging war service in a land where unthinking patriotic self-sacrifice is not very highly esteemed.

Private Eye (1961). Satirical London fortnightly which combines serious investigations into fraud with scurrilous attacks on public figures and ranges from the best traditions of undergraduate debunking wit down to heavy-footed lavatorial humour. Its accusations have involved it in legal expense.

Private Life of Henry VIII, The (1933). Famous film directed by Alexander Korda, which launched Charles Laughton into world fame in the title role.

Private Lives (1930). One of the most typical of the early Noël Coward comedies; a divorced couple find themselves on honeymoon in adjacent rooms of a hotel in the South of France, each having in desperation married an extremely dull partner.

Privy Council Developed from the Norman King's Council and powerful in Tudor and Stuart times; it now has only formal powers, and consists of holders of certain offices, Cabinet ministers, and distinguished persons nominated to it.

Prix de L'Arc de Triomphe International flat-race over $1\frac{1}{2}$ miles, run at LONGCHAMP in October.

Prix des Nations International jumping event held at recognized International Horse Shows. Teams of 4 from each competing country jump over the same course twice in a day; each competitor rides one horse only.

Prix Goncourt (1903). Annual prize awarded to a novelist, preferably young, by the Académie Goncourt founded by Edmond Goncourt in 1896.

Proconsul MIOCENE fossil ape living some 20 million years ago, the first fragments of which were found in Kenya in 1926; thought to belong to the common ancestry of Man and modern anthropoid apes.

Procrustes In Greek legend, a bandit who tied his victims to a bed. If they were too long for it, he lopped off their feet; if too short, he stretched them until they fitted it. (Pronounced pro-krus'-teez.)

Prof., The Familiar name for Professor Lindemann (Lord CHERWELL).

Profumo case (1963). Resignation of the Secretary of State for War, John Profumo, when it was found that he had been associating with the mistress of a Russian naval attaché; see DENNING REPORT.

Program Computer-speak for a sequence of instructions that when converted into machine code (i.e. the binary signals used in a machine language) directs a computer to perform specific operations.

Progress, Reporting Parliamentary device used when a committee of the whole House, which cannot adjourn itself, moves 'That the Chairman report Progress'; this brings the Speaker back, and he can then adjourn the sitting.

Prohibition (USA) Period 1920–33 during which the sale of intoxicating liquor was made illegal, leading to bootlegging and gangster warfare; ended by the 21st Amendment. See 18TH AMENDMENT.

Proinsias Irish name equivalent to Frank.

Promenade des Anglais Sea-front at Nice, built at the expense of English visitors as a token of gratitude for hospitality received.

Prometheus In Greek legend, a Titan who at Zeus' command fashions men out of mud. He becomes their benefactor, stealing fire from heaven to improve their miserable lot. Zeus punishes him by chaining him to a Caucasus mountain, where an eagle pecks his liver all day, the liver being renewed each night; he punishes man by PANDORA'S BOX. The idea that the gods begrudge mankind any knowledge that will increase their independence is found in Genesis 3:22, where Jehovah complains that 'man is become as one of us' and casts Adam and Eve out of Eden. See TREE OF KNOWLEDGE. See next 2 entries. (Greek 'forethought'; pronounced pro-meeth'ews.)

Prometheus Bound Aeschylus' tragedy which portrays the sufferings of PROMETHEUS chained to the mountain. He prophesies that Zeus will be overthrown by his own son, the identity of whose mother (Thetis) is known to Prometheus alone; when he refuses to reveal this secret, Zeus hurls him into Tartarus. In the sequel, *Prometheus Unbound* (now lost), he reveals it and is released. See next entry.

Prometheus Unbound (1820). Shelley's dramatic allegorical poem in which PROMETHEUS symbolizes those who fight for freedom against tyranny.

Promised Land, The (1) CANAAN, as promised to Abraham and his descendants (Gen. 12:7; 13:15 etc.). (2) Heaven.

Proms, The (1895). Colloquial abbreviation for the Henry Wood Promenade Concerts at Queen's Hall, and later Albert Hall; no seats are provided on the ground floor so as to accommodate as many musical enthusiasts as possible at a minimum entrance charge. ('Promenade' because it is possible to walk about during the performance.)

Propylaea Entrance to the ACROPOLIS at Athens. (Greek, 'before the gates'; pronounced prop-i-lee'a.)

Proserpina See PERSEPHONE. (Pronounced pros-erp'in-a.)

Prospero In Shakespeare's *The Tempest*, the rightful Duke of Milan and the father of Miranda, blessed with magic powers which enable him to call on the services of ARIEL, control CALIBAN, engineer his usurping brother's repentance and his own rescue from the island on which he is marooned with Miranda.

Protection Economic doctrine, opposed to FREE TRADE, that home industry should be protected from foreign competition by the imposition of import duties or quotas. It was not adopted by the British government until 1932, when Neville Chamberlain introduced the Protective Tariff Act. See IMPERIAL PREFERENCE.

Protectorate, Cromwell's (1653–9). Name given to the later period of Oliver Cromwell's rule under a written constitution which he had to abandon for lack of a competent or co-operative Parliament; and to a brief period under his son Richard.

Protector Somerset Edward Seymour, Duke of Somerset, Protestant leader, who ruled England as LORD PROTECTOR (1547–9) during the first years of the minority of his nephew, Edward VI, until displaced by John Dudley, Earl of Warwick (later Duke of Northumberland).

Proterozoic Period Term sometimes used for the later stages of the PRE-CAMBRIAN ERA. (Greek *proteros*, 'earlier', *zoé*, 'life'.)

Protestantism Generic term for the religion of the Lutheran, Reformed, Anglican and Nonconformist Churches.

Proteus In Greek legend, a prophet who tended Poseidon's seals. He could assume any shape he chose, and the only way to force him to prophesy the truth was to catch him and hold him fast. (Pronounced proh'tews.)

Proteus Character in Bernard Shaw's *The* APPLE CART, said to represent Ramsay MacDonald. See previous entry.

Protocols of Zion (of the learned elders of Zion) Forgery purporting to be a report of Zionist meetings at Basle in 1897, at which plans were laid for Jews and Freemasons to overwhelm Christendom. They were concocted by the Russian secret police from a French satire covertly attacking Napoleon III, and were published in 1903.

Protozoa A phylum of one-celled microscopic animals, including amoebas and the Sporozoa (e.g. malaria, sleeping sickness and other parasites).

Proudie, Mrs Forceful wife of the Bishop of Barchester (who first appears in *Barchester Towers*, see BARCHESTER NOVELS), who dominates not only her husband but the whole diocese, vanquishing her only rival, Mr SLOPE.

Proustian Resembling the world created by Proust in REMEMBRANCE OF THINGS PAST, or his literary style.

Provençale (Cooking) Rich in garlic and olive oil.

Provence Old province of south-east France now divided between the *départements* of Var, Bouches-du-Rhône, Basses-Alpes and part of Vaucluse. The old capital was Aix. (Latin, *Provincia*.)

Provisionals (1970). Unofficial wing of the Irish Republican Army (IRA). More militaristic than the official IRA, who tend to prefer pamphlets to gelignite.

Provos (1965–8). Nickname of youngsters of Amsterdam ('the Provotariat') who, dissatisfied with life as they find it, indulge publicly in practical jokes and whimsies such as leaving white-painted bicycles about the city for use by any who want them. After a surfeit of publicity they sank progressively to demonstrations, riots and molesting the public. They have no leader or programme. (Abbreviation of Dutch for 'provokers'.)

Prune, Pilot Officer (1935). (1) RAF nickname for an over-reckless pilot. (2) Wartime cartoon figure.

Pru, The Abbreviation commonly used for the Prudential (1848), largest of the life-insurance firms, originally an industrial life firm. Much of its business is in small policies, premiums being collected on the doorstep; hence the expression 'The Man from the Pru'.

Prufrock, J. Alfred Character who appears in T. S. Eliot's *The Love Song of J. Alfred Prufrock* (1915). He is a very ordinary man but, vaguely aware that his life is meaningless and empty, he struggles to rise above it, too half-heartedly to succeed.

Prunier A Paris restaurant near the Opéra specializing in sea-food.

Prunus Very large genus that includes almonds, apricots, peaches, plums, flowering cherries, etc.

Prussia Former German kingdom, capital Berlin, consisting of the land of the Teutonic Knights (Prussia proper) and Brandenburg, which later established domination over a unified Germany. It ceased to be a political entity under the National-Socialists (Nazis), and its territories are now divided between Germany and (East Prussia, former capital, Königsberg) between Poland and USSR.

Psmith The hero of the pre-WOOSTER novels of P. G. Wodehouse, such as *Psmith in New York* and *Leave it to Psmith* (1923).

Psyche In later Greek legend, a beautiful girl who personifies the soul purified by suffering to become worthy of true love; see CUPID AND PSYCHE. (Greek, 'breath', 'soul'; pronounced sy'kee.)

Pteridophyta Obsolescent term for the seedless plants, most of them extinct, but including ferns, horsetails and club-mosses.

Ptolemaic system System of astronomy in which the earth was regarded as the centre of the universe, around which the sun revolved. It is named after Ptolemy, an astronomer of Alexandria in the 2nd century AD. See COPERNICAN THEORY.

Ptolemies (332–30 BC). Dynasty of Macedonian rulers of Egypt founded by one of Alexander the Great's generals; the last to rule was Cleopatra (see ACTIUM).

Public Enemy No. 1 (USA) Phrase used when the FBI first started a genuine campaign to stamp out thuggery in Chicago, giving this title to the chief surviving thug, against whom they concentrated their attention; applied specifically to J. H. Dillinger, shot dead in 1934, after he had terrorized Chicago for 14 months.

Public Record Office Official repository of the national records, which date back to the Conquest and include Domesday Book; the office is in Kew.

Public Trustee Office (1908). Government office which acts as executor and trustee if so appointed by a court order or under the terms of a will.

Pucelle, La Name for Joan of Arc, used by Shakespeare and Voltaire among others. (French, 'the maid'.)

Puck (1) Generic name for all kinds of elf. (2) By Shakespeare in MIDSUMMER NIGHT'S DREAM converted into a proper name for ROBIN GOODFELLOW; his Puck is a mischievous spirit who can 'put a girdle round about the earth / In forty minutes'. (Connected with the West Country word pixie, with similar forms in other languages.)

Puck of Pook's Hill (1906). Rudyard Kipling's book of short stories in which the fairy PUCK appears and takes 2 children on a conducted tour down through English history.

Pueblo Indians American Indians of various tribes who from 500 BC settled in the semi-desert regions of New Mexico and Arizona, and adjacent areas of Texas and Mexico, building communal homes of adobe and stone on cliff tops. Some 30,000 survive, speaking Spanish. (Spanish pueblo, 'town'.)

Puff 'Practitioner in panegyric' in Sheridan's comedy The Critic (1779).

Pugwash movement (1957). Movement inspired by Einstein and Bertrand Russell, which brings together scientists of all nations to discuss the diversion of scientific effort from destructive to constructive purposes; it promotes international co-operation in space and other forms of research, gives help to developing countries, fosters exchanges of scientists and information, etc. See also VIENNA DECLARATION. (Pugwash, Canadian town where the first conference was held.)

Pulcinella Stock character of the COMMEDIA DELL'ARTE, with a hooked nose, from which the hump-backed hero of the Punch and Judy show is derived. (Neapolitan, 'little turkey-cock'; French spelling, Polichinelle; older English form, Punchinello.)

Pulitzer prizes Awarded annually by the trustees of Columbia University, New York City, for American works of fiction, history, biography, poetry, journalism, etc. (Endowed by Joseph Pulitzer, newspaper proprietor; pronounced pew'lit-sėr.)

Pullman George M. Pullman, first to establish a comfortable railway service, particularly for night travel, in the 1880s.

Pulsatilla Genus that includes P. vulgaris, the pasque flower, also classified as Anemone pulsatilla.

Pulteney Bridge (1771). Florentine bridge at Bath, Avon, designed by Robert Adam, with shops on either side.

Pumpernickel Malted wholemeal rye bread, originally from Westphalia.

Punch See PULCINELLA.

Punch (1841). Satirical weekly, permanently 'not as good as it was', i.e. faithfully reflecting the interests and social mores of the day and thus unpopular with the more die-hard of successive older generations. Its editors have included Henry Mayhew and Mark Lemon (the first), Owen Seaman, EVOE, FOUGASSE; its illustrators Tenniel (DROPPING THE PILOT), Phil May, Du Maurier, PONT, ANTON; its writers APH. The subtitle *The London Charivari* came from a similar Paris publication, *charivari* being French for 'disapproving uproar'. 'Mr Punch's advice to those about to marry', a joke current for generations, was 'Don't'.

Punchestown Races Famous point-to-point meeting at Kildare, Ireland, held in April.

Punic faith Treachery, the Carthaginians (see next entry) having a reputation for this among the Romans.

Punic Wars Three wars between Rome and the Phoenician colony of Carthage. *First* (265–242 BC): the Romans defeated Hamilcar at sea, became the strongest naval power in the Mediterranean, and won Sicily. *Second*, or Hannibalic War (218–201): Hannibal crossed the Alps and crushed the Romans at Lake Trasimene (217) and Cannae (216), but was defeated in Africa near Zama. *Third* (149–146): the Romans utterly destroyed Carthage itself. (Punic, from Latin *Punicus* from Greek *Phoenix*, 'Phoenician'; Carthage was about 10 miles north of modern Tunis.)

Punjab Former Indian province, now divided between West Punjab (in Pakistan), Haryana and Punjabi Suba. (Persian, '5 rivers', i.e. the Indus and its 4 main tributaries; pronounced pun-jahb'.)

Purbeck marble Hard limestone quarried in the Isle of Purbeck, the Dorset peninsula near Swanage; it was used particularly in medieval churches.

Purchas his Pilgrimes With his earlier works under similar titles, a continuation (1625) by another clergyman, Samuel Purchas, of HAKLUYT'S VOYAGES.

Purdy Name associated with excellence in shotguns. (US 19th-century gunsmith.)

Purgatory Place where the souls of the departed undergo purification and preparation for life in Heaven; a medieval addition to Christian beliefs still accepted by Roman Catholics, who hold that the duration of stay can be shortened by the prayers of the living.

Purim Jewish festival held in March a month before the Passover, in celebration of the deliverance of the Jews in Persia; see ESTHER. (Pronounced pewr'im.)

Puritans Dissenters; earlier name for NONCONFORMISTS; also used generally of the strictly religious and/or moral.

Purple Heart (1) US army medal awarded to those wounded on active service. (Silver heart with a purple ribbon.) (2) Stimulant tablet, a mixture of amphetamine ('pep pill') and barbiturate (sleeping pill). (Heart-shaped.)

Pursuivants Four officials of the COLLEGE OF ARMS bearing the titles: Bluemantle, Portcullis, Rouge Croix, Rouge Dragon. (Norman-French, 'followers'; pronounced pèr'si-vants.)

Puseyites Name for members of the OXFORD MOVEMENT. (E. B. Pusey, one of its leaders.)

Pushtu Official language of Afghanistan, spoken by the PATHANS. It is related to Persian. Also spelt Pashtu.

'Puss in Boots' Fairy-tale of some antiquity about a youngest son who inherits only a cat from his father. This cat, however, turns out to be an ingenious and unscrupulous ally who by various ruses secures for his master a princess and a fortune.

Pussy foot Johnson Chief architect of PROHIBITION, so nicknamed from his stealthy methods of catching criminals when an officer of the US Indian Service.

Putain respectueuse, La (1946). Sartre's play set in the southern states of USA on a racial theme about a trumped-up charge against a Negro. (French, 'the respectful prostitute'.)

Putonghua The form of Chinese spoken by the educated classes, based on the Peking dialect; called by foreigners 'Mandarin'.

Pygmalion (1913). Bernard Shaw's play in which the phonetician, Professor Higgins, as a Pygmalion (see next entry) creates an elegant lady out of the Covent Garden flower-seller, Eliza Doolittle; she breaks away from his tyranny. The basis of the record-breaking musical, *My Fair Lady* (1956).

Pygmalion and Galatea In Greek legend Pygmalion is a sculptor of Cyprus who makes an ivory statue of a woman; he finds it so beautiful that he gets Aphrodite to bring it to life. He then marries his own creation, calling her Galatea. See previous entry. (Pronounced pig-mayl'i-on, gal-a-tee'a.)

Pyramids, Battle of the (1798). Napoleon's defeat of the MAMELUKES outside Cairo.

Pyramus and Thisbe Two lovers of Babylon who arrange a secret tryst, from which Thisbe flees, frightened by a lion which bespatters with blood a garment she had dropped. Seeing it, Pyramus assumes she has been killed and commits suicide; Thisbe, returning to find her lover dead, does likewise. The story is told by Ovid and Chaucer, and a parody of it is played by Bottom and company in Shakespeare's MIDSUMMER NIGHT'S DREAM.

Pyrex Proprietary name of a heat-resistant glass.

Pytchley Fox-hunting pack with kennels near Northampton, which hunts country in Northamptonshire and Leicestershire. (Pronounced pytsh'li.)

Pythagoras' theorem That in a right-angled triangle the square on the hypotenuse (the side opposite the right angle) is equal to the sum of the squares on the other 2 sides. (Greek philosopher of the 6th century BC.)

Pyx, Trial of the Test of samples of all coins from the Mint, held each March at the Goldsmiths Hall by the Goldsmiths' Company. (*Pyx*, the box in which the coins are put.)

Q

Q Pen-name of Sir Arthur Quiller-Couch, Professor of English Literature at Cambridge from 1912.

Qantas Initials of the Queensland and Northern Territory Air Service which served the outback regions of Australia, and later developed into the Australian international airline.

Q-boats (1915). Armed ships disguised as trading vessels, used by the British in World War I as decoys for German submarines.

Q-cars Patrol cars used by the CRIMINAL INVESTIGATION DEPARTMENT of the London Metropolitan Police.

Q-fever (1937). Potentially fatal disease, similar to viral pneumonia, with symptoms including rapid weight loss, high fever and hepatitis.

QSGs (1965). Initials used for Quasi-Stellar Galaxies, objects in far distant parts of space discovered by Mount Palomar observatory; they are powerful emitters of ultra-violet and blue light, but their nature has yet to be explained.

Quadragesimo anno (1931). Pope Pius XI's encyclical on politics and the working classes and, issued after the LATERAN TREATY, supporting a Christian CORPORATIVE STATE. (Latin, 'in the 40th year'.)

Quadrant (August 1943). Code name of the wartime conference at Quebec at which Churchill and Roosevelt discussed the relative priority of OVERLORD and the Italian campaign, and agreed on ANVIL.

Quadruple Alliance (1815). See CONCERT OF EUROPE.

Quai d'Orsay Site of, and used for, the French Foreign Office in Paris. (Name of a Seineside street; *quai* = quay; pronounced kay-dor-say.)

Quaker Cousinhood, The Name given to the group of Quaker families who since the 17th century have exercised much influence in the UK in many fields: the Lloyds of Lloyds Bank and Stewart & Lloyds, the Barclays of Barclays Bank and the brewery, the Frys and Cadburys of the chocolate firms, together with the Hoares, Buxtons, Butlers, etc.

Quakers Common name for the Society of Friends, a Protestant sect which follows the teaching of George Fox (1624–91), rejects priesthood, sacraments and all dogma, eschews oaths and violence, and believes that each individual is guided by the inner light of the Holy Ghost. Quakers hold 'meetings' addressed by any member moved to do so. Although pacifist, they have a fine record of service in ambulance corps in time of war. (Name derives from Fox's bidding a magistrate to 'quake at the word of the Lord'.)

Quality Street (1901). J. M. Barrie's play set in Napoleonic times when spinsters were 'put on the shelf' at an absurdly early age. The heroine, Phoebe Throssel, jumps off the shelf, with satisfactory results.

Quango *Quasi*-autonomous *non*-governmental organization.

Quare Fellow (1956). Play set in a prison just before an execution, produced by THEATRE WORKSHOP from a script by Brendan Behan.

Quarterly Review (1809). London publication which began life as the Tory rival to the Whig EDINBURGH REVIEW; it was founded by John Murray with the support of Sir Walter Scott.

Quarter Sessions (1388). Criminal courts which, until 1972 (see COURTS ACT), were held quarterly (or oftener), intermediate in jurisdiction between PETTY SESSIONS and ASSIZES. The operations of each court were confined to a county (where it comprised 2 or more JPs presided over by a lawyer-chairman) or a borough (a RECORDER, sitting alone); within these inappropriate boundaries they were almost autonomous and thus differed widely in policy, standards and pressure of work. Trial was by jury.

Quartier Latin See LATIN QUARTER.

Quasars Astronomers' abbreviation for 'quasi-stellar radio source', first observed in 1963. Although in an optical telescope they look like individual stars, they emit far more energy than most galaxies. The initial theory was that they must be the most distant objects in the universe, but this was soon challenged, and their contradictory properties have generated many contradictory theories. Over 100 have been identified, but their nature is still an unsolved problem.

Quasimodo The hunchback of Notre Dame; see NOTRE DAME DE PARIS.

Quatermain, Allan Principal figure in several of Rider Haggard's adventure stories, including one named after him.

Quaternary Period Later period of the CENOZOIC ERA, lasting from about one million years ago down to the present; subdivided into the PLEISTOCENE and RECENT EPOCHS.

Quattrocento Italian for '15th century', the period of Renaissance art (excluding the HIGH RENAISSANCE) and of the REVIVAL OF LEARNING. See CINQUECENTO. (Italian, '400' for '1400', i.e. the 1400s; pronounced kwaht'tro-chen'to.)

Quebec Conferences (1943–4). See QUADRANT; OCTAGON.

Quechuan American Indian language; see KECHUAN.

Queen, Ellery Pseudonym of the joint authors of, and also the name of the detective in, *The Roman Hat Mystery* (1929) and many subsequent stories; the authors also published *Ellery Queen's Mystery Magazine* from 1941.

Queen Anne period (1702–14). Period when a distinctively English style of furniture was developed, characterized by elegance, comfort and simplicity. Walnut veneer and the cabriole leg were the hallmarks, and the bureau the typical product. Marquetry and lacquer were used.

Queen Anne's Bounty (1704). Small fund, now administered by the CHURCH COMMISSIONERS, formed by Queen Anne to improve the houses and stipends of the clergy. (In origin the proceeds of a tax collected from the clergy and paid to the Pope until the Reformation.)

Queen Charlotte's Ball Occasion in May when débutantes officially 'come out' at the beginning of the London SEASON, now that they are no longer (since 1958) presented at Court; dressed in white, they curtsy to a huge ceremonial birthday cake.

Queen Elizabeth II (1969). Cunard liner, third of the QUEENS. Because of airline competition on the Atlantic run, she was designed for cruises as well as the transatlantic service. (Popularly called the *QEII*.)

Queen Elizabeth II Cup (show-jumping) Competition at the Royal INTERNATIONAL HORSE SHOW for individual ladies, virtually constituting a world championship.

Queen Mab Wife of Oberon, called by Shakespeare TITANIA.

Queen Mary's College Unit of London University, in the Mile End Road.

Queen of Hearts, The Formidable lady in ALICE IN WONDERLAND whose cry 'Off with his/her head' rings through the latter half of the book;

the rest of her conversation is equally trenchant.

Queens Borough of New York City at the west end of Long Island.

Queens, The The Cunard liners *Queen Mary, Queen Elizabeth* and *Queen Elizabeth II.*

Queen's Awards to Industry (1966). Annual awards for outstanding achievement either in the export drive or in technological innovation. They may be made to firms, research associations or to bodies with industrial functions established by central or a local government. Awarded to about 100 firms a year and is held for 5 years. The logo can be used on goods and a special flag can be flown.

Queen's Beasts, The Supporters of the Royal Arms, of which replicas were made for Queen Elizabeth II's coronation. They comprise the Lion of England, Unicorn of Scotland, White Horse of Hanover, Greyhound and Red Dragon of the Tudors, Black Bull of Clarence (son of Edward III), White Lion of the Mortimers, Yale of the Beauforts, Falcon of the Plantagenets, and the Griffin of Edward III.

Queen's Bench Division Division of the High Court of Justice. It deals with Common Law cases such as debt, breach of contract, damages for injury, defamation. The Court of Criminal Appeal has the same panel of judges, 3 forming a quorum.

Queensberry Rules (1867). Boxing rules compiled by John Chambers, laying down the 3-minute round with 1-minute rest, etc., still used, with modifications. (Named after their sponsor, the 8th Marquess.)

Queen's Club (1886). London club at Baron's Court with facilities for lawn tennis and squash, but also known as the centre for real tennis and rackets.

Queen's College, The Oxford College. (Named after Edward III's Queen.)

Queens' College Cambridge college. (Founded by Henry VI's Queen and refounded by Edward IV's.)

Queen's Counsel Senior barrister (a 'silk') appointed by the Lord Chancellor, nominally as Counsel to the Crown; any barrister of 10 years' standing may apply 'to take silk', as it is called. A QC wears a silk gown and in court must be accompanied by a junior barrister.

Queen's County Former English name for LAOIGHIS, Irish Republic.

Queen's Flight Queen's fleet of aircraft (including helicopters), serviced by the RAF. The King's Flight was first established by Edward VIII (1936).

Queen's Guide Equivalent in the Girl Guides to the QUEEN'S SCOUT.

Queen's House, The Inigo Jones's Palladian masterpiece at Greenwich Park, London, built for Charles I's Queen; now the central part of the National Maritime Museum.

Queen's Lawn Most exclusive part of the ROYAL ASCOT ENCLOSURE, where the old rule banning divorcees still obtains.

Queen's lecture (1965). Annual lecture, delivered in West Germany by a distinguished British figure, instituted after the Queen's German state visit in 1965.

Queen's Medal for Poetry Gold medal awarded to a British subject for a book of verse selected by a committee under the chairmanship of the Poet Laureate.

Queen's Messenger Member of the Corps of Queen's Diplomatic Messengers, mainly staffed by retired officers of the 3 services, who deliver secret documents to overseas embassies. Except in thrillers, it is apparently a humdrum airport-to-airport existence.

Queen's Park Only amateur football team in the Scottish League; it plays at HAMPDEN PARK, Glasgow.

Queen's Park Rangers Professional football team playing at Ellerslie Road, Shepherd's Bush, London. The address is often referred to as Loftus Road.

Queen's Plate (1860). Canada's oldest and chief

flat-race, for Canadian-bred 3-year-olds over a course of 1¼ miles. (Prize augmented by a purse given by the Queen.)

Queen's Prize (1860). Premier award for rifle shooting at Bisley, open to all subjects of the Queen; consists of a gold medal and badge, £250 and a signed portrait of the Queen. (Known as the King's Prize when a king reigns.)

Queen's Proctor Official of the Treasury Solicitor's department who represents the Crown in divorce cases. Should he learn of any irregularity in an application for divorce he must intervene to stop a decree nisi being made absolute.

Queen's Remembrancer Officer of the Supreme Court who represents the Exchequer in the collection of debts due to the Crown. See QUIT RENTS CEREMONY.

Queen's Scout Scout rank attained only by the highest efficiency.

Queen's Speech Government's programme of parliamentary business for the forthcoming session read, normally by the Queen, at the state opening in the House of Lords, where both Houses are assembled for the occasion; it is drafted in Cabinet.

Queenstown (Ireland) Former name of CÓBH.

Queen's University (1908). University at Belfast, founded (1849) as a college of the Queen's University of Ireland. Magee University College, Londonderry, until 1950 a college of the University of Dublin, is now a college of Queen's.

Queen Victoria (1921). Lytton Strachey's second essay in debunking biography; but he fell under the spell of his subject, who emerges as almost a heroine.

Quentin Durward (1823). Scott's novel in which Quentin is an archer in the Scottish Guard of King Louis XI of France, of whom the novel gives a vivid presentation.

Quest for Corvo, The (1933). A. J. A. Symons's biography of the self-styled Baron CORVO, which started a vogue for that eccentric man's works, notably *Hadrian the Seventh*.

Question Time (Parliament) Daily period (2.45–3.30 p.m.), while the Commons is in session, at which members may put questions, of which they have given previous notice, to the member of government concerned; questions may also be put down for written reply. The prime minister answers questions on Tuesdays and Thursdays.

Quetzalcoatl Toltec god who was adopted by the AZTECS as their chief god. ('Plumed serpent'; pronounced ket-sahl-ko-aht'l.)

Quiche Lorraine Bacon and egg flan.

Quickly, Mistress Gullible hostess of FALSTAFF's favourite Boar's Head Tavern, who marries PISTOL.

Quick Professor Holder of the chair of Biology at Cambridge.

Quicunque vult Alternative name for the ATHANASIAN CREED. (First words in Latin, 'Whoever wishes (to be saved)'.)

Quiet Flows the Don, And (1928). Novel by the Russian Mikhail Sholokov about the mixed reception given to the Communist Revolution by the Don Cossack villages in the Kuban, where he was born. A sequel, *The Don Flows Home to the Sea*, was completed in 1940.

Quilp Repulsive dwarf who relentlessly pursues Little Nell and her grandfather in *The* OLD CURIOSITY SHOP.

Quins Common abbreviation for the HARLEQUINS rugby club.

Quirinal One of the hills of Rome, site of the royal palace (1870–1947), now the President's official residence. (From Latin *Quirinus*, name given to Romulus after he was deified; pronounced kwir'in-al.)

Quisling Traitor who collaborates with the enemy. (From Major Quisling, who ruled German-occupied Norway from 1940 until he was executed in 1945.)

Quito Pre-Liberation name of Ecuador, and still the name of its capital.

Quit Rents ceremony (October) Quaint ceremony at the Law Courts, of medieval origin, at which the Corporation of London presents the QUEEN'S REMEMBRANCER with horse-shoes, billhooks, etc. as rent for 2 pieces of land which can no longer be identified.

Quondams Name for former Fellows of ALL SOULS, Oxford. (Latin, 'formerly'.)

Quorn Fox-hunting pack, with kennels founded by Hugo Meynell in the 1750s at Quornden Hall, near Loughborough, which hunts country mainly in Leicestershire.

Quo Vadis? (1895). Historical novel by Henry Sienkiewicz, a Polish writer, set in Nero's Rome. The hero is the pagan Petronius Arbiter. The Christian heroine is thrown to the lions in the arena but escapes to marry a man converted by Peter and Paul. (Latin, 'whither goest thou?')

R

Ra Egyptian hawk-headed sun-god whose cult was introduced at HELIOPOLIS at the beginning of the OLD KINGDOM, worshipped as their family god by the Pharaohs, while their subjects worshipped the Pharaohs as the incarnations of HORUS, later of OSIRIS. His cult was associated with the introduction of mumification, royal tombs and pyramids.

Rab Nickname, based on his initials, of R. A. Butler (Lord Butler of Saffron Walden).

Rabbi Term of respect meaning 'my master', given by the Jews to a doctor of the law. Nowadays applied only to one authorized by ordination to deal with law and ritual.

Race for the Sea, The (September–November. 1914). In World War I, the name give to the northward extension of the battle line by both sides on the Western Front until it reached the Channel ports.

Race Relations Board (1966). Body set up by Parliament with power to intervene in any instance of racial discrimination which a local conciliation committee has been unable to settle; if necessary it reports the matter to the Law Officers of the Crown.

Rachmanism (1963). Term comprehending extortionate rents extracted by terroristic methods, and in particular the brutal exploitation of the housing needs of prostitutes and coloured immigrants, symbolized by the operations in Paddington, London, of a Polish property owner named Peter Rachman, whose misdeeds came to light through the PROFUMO CASE, some of the women in which had been his mistresses. The revelations, a year after his death, were put to political use by opponents of the Conservative government's rent policies.

RADA (1904). Initials normally used for the Royal Academy of Dramatic Art, Gower Street, London, a leading school of acting. (Pronounced rah'da.)

Radames See AIDA.

Radar *Ra*dio *d*etection *a*nd *r*anging. A system for detecting aircraft, ships, coasts and other objects by sending out short radio waves which they reflect.

Radcliffe Camera General library at Oxford University. (Founded by Dr Radcliffe, 1650–1714.)

Radcliffe Reports (1) In 1956 on Cyprus; (2) in 1959 on the working of the monetary and credit system, recommending changes in the relationship between the Bank of England and the Treasury; (3) in 1962 on the extent of Communist infiltration into the British civil service and trade unions. (Lord Radcliffe.)

Radcliffe Tribunal (1963). Investigation into the circumstances which led to the VASSALL CASE; in the course of it 3 journalists were committed to prison for refusing to reveal sources of information. (Lord Radcliffe.)

Radical In British politics, a vague term for one who supported radical reform (e.g. the REFORM BILLS), applied e.g. to Cobden, Joseph Chamberlain (in his earlier days), Lloyd George (pre-1914). In France the Radical Party (under Clemenceau, Herriot, Daladier) was anti-clerical, and opposed nationalization, capitalist combines and anything detrimental to the freedom of the individual.

Radio Caroline First (1964) of the programmes broadcast from ships anchored outside British territorial waters to evade the ban on commercial radio, and consisting almost exclusively of pop music and advertising. Closed down in 1967.

Radio City (USA) Complex of buildings in the ROCKEFELLER CENTER, New York, used by RCA and NBC.

Radio Doctor, The Role in which the future Lord Hill, Chairman of ITA and from 1967 of the BBC, first appeared before the public, as the deep-voiced reassuring adviser on medical matters in a wartime radio programme.

RAF Commemoration Day (September 15). Day in the 1940 BATTLE OF BRITAIN when an exceptional number of German planes were shot down.

Raffles Gentleman burglar and cricketer of E. W. Hornung's *The Amateur Cracksman* (1899).

Raffles Hotel Hotel in Singapore, named after Sir Thomas Stamford Raffles (1781–1826), who governed Java and Sumatra and advised the annexation of Singapore.

Rag, The Old nickname of the Army and Navy Club (1837), in Pall Mall. (Origin disputed.)

Ragged Trousered Philanthropists, The (1914). Proletarian novel by Robert Tressell, pen-name of a house decorator named Noonan. It is a semi-autobiographical study of contemporary working conditions, notable for authentic dialogue.

Raglan Coat or cardigan with sleeves that are not joined to the garment on the shoulder, but continue sloping from the bottom of the armhole up to the neck. A coat so designed was first worn by Lord Raglan (1788–1855), the British commander-in-chief in the Crimean War.

Ragnarok GÖTTERDÄMMERUNG of Scandinavian mythology.

Ragtime (1890s). Original name of JAZZ, typically a piano form featuring syncopation. See ALEXANDER'S RAGTIME BAND.

Ragusa Italian name of the Yugoslav port of Dubrovnik.

Rahat Lakhoum Turkish Delight, a sweet made of flavoured jelly covered with icing-sugar. (Pronounced rah'hat lak-oom'.)

Rail Splitter Nickname for Abraham Lincoln who, when the family moved to Illinois (1830), helped his father clear and fence his new farm. (One who splits logs into fence rails.)

Railway Children, The (1906). Children's book by Edith Nesbit which was also a successful film (1970).

Railway King, The Nickname of George Hudson (1800–71), who made and lost a fortune in speculative railway promotion in Yorkshire and was then accused of fraud.

Rain (1922). Somerset Maugham's play, based on his short story 'Miss Thompson', about a missionary in the South Seas who first converts and then seduces a prostitute, Sadie Thompson. Filled with remorse, he kills himself.

Rainbow, The (1915). D. H. Lawrence's novel introducing the BRANGWEN family, some of whom reappear in WOMEN IN LOVE. It displays the usual Laurentian characteristics: powerful, moving descriptions of nature, and tortuous nonsense about dark fecund forces.

Rainbow Corner, London Resort of US forces during World War II, previously Lyon's Corner House, Shaftesbury Avenue. (Named after the US 42nd or Rainbow Division, prominent in World War I, and so named because they were recruited from all sections of the community.)

Rainbow Room Restaurant in the ROCKE-FELLER CENTER, New York.

Rajah Brooke (1841–1946) Name given to 3 white rulers of Sarawak, which was ceded to Sir James Brooke (the White Rajah) by the Sultan of Brunei as a reward for his help in a DAYAK revolt. After Japanese occupation in World War II, Sarawak became a Crown Colony.

Rajputs Hindu landowner–warrior caste of north-west India which founded the states of Jodhpur, Jaipur, Bikaner and Udaipur, now grouped in the state of Rajasthan. (Pronounced rahj′put.)

Rake's Progress, The (1735). (1) Hogarth's series of satirical oil-paintings, in the style of MARRIAGE À LA MODE. (2) Stravinsky's opera (1951) inspired by (1). (3) Ballet on theme of (1) choreographed by Ninette de Valois.

Raleigh lectures (1919). Annual lectures on history, sponsored by the British Academy.

Ralph Roister Doister (1533). Earliest English comedy, written by a headmaster of Eton, Nicholas Udall; a naïve, robust play in doggerel verse about Ralph's unsuccessful wooing of the Widow Custance.

Rama Incarnation of Vishnu; see RAMAYANA.

Ramadan Muslim month during which the faithful fast from sunrise to sunset, and ending with the Lesser BAIRAM feast when the new moon is seen. It is traditionally the month when Allah sent down the Koran to earth. (Pronounced ram′a-dan.)

Ramayana (500 BC). One of the 2 great Hindu epic poems (see also MAHABHARATA), recounting the wars of Rama, an incarnation of VISHNU; representing perhaps Aryan incursions into south India. (Sanskrit, 'deeds of Rama'; pronounced rah-my′ė-na.)

Rambler, The (1750–52). Periodical in 208 numbers, the contents of which are essays of all kinds of subjects, character studies, allegories, criticism, and so on; with the exception of 5 all were written by Dr Johnson, and were meant to convey wisdom and piety, and the refinement of the English language.

Rambo (1982). Extremely violent and un-

pleasant character in the films *First Blood* and *First Blood Part Two* playing the part of a Vietnam war veteran. He became a national comic-strip hero in the USA.

Rambouillet Fourteenth-century royal château, used by Catherine de Medici and the place where Napoleon spent his last night of freedom; now the official summer residence of the French President, but usually open to the public. It lies in the forests half-way between Versailles and Chartres.

Ramillies, Battle of (1706). Marlborough's second victory over the French in the War of the SPANISH SUCCESSION, which resulted in the expulsion of the French from the Netherlands. (Village in Brabant, north of Namur, Belgium.)

Rand See WITWATERSRAND.

Rand Corporation (1946). A US non-profit research organization or 'think-factory' largely financed by the Air Force, with headquarters at Santa Monica, California. It does research on military planning through 'war games' (i.e. working out the relative advantages of all possible combinations of strategic moves and countermoves, e.g. in controlled escalation), a mechanistic approach later extended to politico-military problems e.g. the biological and environmental effects of nuclear war on populations. See HUDSON INSTITUTE.

Ranelagh Once a famous polo ground, adjoining HURLINGHAM, but now a derelict waste. (Pronounced ran′il-a.)

Rangers, The (1) Glasgow professional football team that plays at Ibrox Park; see CELTIC. (2) Nickname of the QUEEN'S PARK RANGERS.

Rangers, US In World War II, American commandos, who first saw action in the 1942 DIEPPE RAID. (Name borrowed from units of various kinds in earlier US history.)

Ranji Short for K. S. Ranjitsinhji, Maharajah of Nawanagar, famous Cambridge, Sussex and England cricketer, uncle of DULEEP.

Ranunculaceae Buttercup family, characterized by indented leaf patterns and conspicuous flowers; it includes meadow rue, monkshood, larkspur, columbine, clematis.

Ra I and *II* The papyrus-reed rafts in which Heyerdahl (see KON-TIKI) tried to prove that the Ancient Egyptians could have discovered America. *Ra I* (1969) was abandoned waterlogged 600 miles from Barbados, 56 days out from Safi (Morocco). She was built with reeds from Ethiopia by Lake Chad boatmen near the Pyramids, using 3,000-year-old Egyptian wall-paintings as guide. *Ra II* (1970) was built by Peruvian Indians in Morocco, again with Ethiopian reeds, and with a crew of 8 crossed from Safi to Barbados in 57 days in May/July.

Rapacki plan (1958). Proposal to create a neutral zone in Central Europe (Germany, Czechoslovakia and Poland) where nuclear arms would be prohibited. It was supported by USSR and rejected by the West. (Named after its sponsor, the Polish Foreign Minister; pronounced rapatsk'i.)

Rapallo Treaty (1) Treaty between Italy and Yugoslavia (1920) allotting Dalmatia to Yugoslavia and Triestino to Italy, declaring Fiume independent, and pledging joint opposition to a Habsburg restoration (then much mooted). (2) Treaty 1922 by which Germany became the first state to recognize Soviet Russia, a huddling together of 2 nations who felt slighted by the Great Powers. (Italian coastal resort near Genoa.)

Rape of Lucrece See LUCRECE.

Rape of the Lock, The (1714). Pope's burlesque poem on a contemporary family feud caused by Lord Petre's cutting off a lock of a girl's hair.

Rape of the Sabines. The ROMULUS' method of providing wives for the settlers in the new Rome. At his invitation the neighbouring Sabines attended a feast, leaving their womenfolk behind; the Roman youths took advantage of this to kidnap the younger women.

Raphael One of the chief angels in Jewish tradition, who appears in TOBIT and *Paradise Lost*. In paintings he is often shown carrying a pilgrim's staff or the fish that restored Tobit's sight.

Ras Ethiopian title of a royal prince; e.g. the Emperor Haile Selassie was Ras Tafari before he succeeded to the throne.

Rashomon (1951). First post-war Japanese film to make a major impact in the West, directed by Akira Kurosawa (who also directed *The Seven Samurai*); it won the Venice Festival prize.

Raskolniki Old Believers of Russian dissenters who in the 17th century refused to accept the patriarch Nikon's reform of the services of the Russian Orthodox Church.

Raskolnikov Atheist hero of Dostoyevsky's *Crime and Punishment* (1866), who committed murder to prove to himself that he was 'beyond good and evil', yet was driven by his 'irrational' subconscious to a voluntary confession of the deed.

Rasselas Prince of Abyssinia who, in Dr Johnson's philosophical romance, escapes from his father and the paradise of Happy Valley and goes to Cairo, where he finds that the usual recipes for happiness prove worthless; chastened, he returns to his father.

Rastafarians Black sect which flourishes in Jamaica founded when Ras Tafari (see RAS) became Emperor of Ethiopia in 1930. They adopted the idea of a return to Africa, first propagated by Marcus Garvey, and grew beards in imitation of Ras Tafari, whom they chose as their future patron in Africa.

Rastignac, Eugène de Character whose career is traced in several novels of Balzac's COMÉDIE HUMAINE, from penurious law student to rich statesman. Like the equally detestable Sorel in LE ROUGE ET LE NOIR, he makes ruthless use of women to advance the only cause dear to him – his own success.

Rasumovsky Quartets (1806). Beethoven's 3 string quartets (Op. 59) dedicated to the Russian Count Rasumovsky (himself a musician).

'Raven, The' (1845). E. A. Poe's poem with the refrain: 'Quoth the Raven, "Nevermore".' The poet is lamenting the death of 'the rare and radiant maiden whom the angels name Lenore', and hears the raven give this one dread answer to all his desperate hopes of reunion with her in some future life.

Reader's Digest (1922). US and international monthly pocket-size magazine, containing condensed versions of material from world periodicals; it carried no advertisements until 1955.

Reagan doctrine Active support for democratic elements around the world to counter the spread of international Communism, first stated in a speech to the British Parliament in 1982.

Real Presence Presence of the body and blood of Christ at the Eucharist either by TRANSUBSTANTIATION, Consubstantiation (a slightly different, Lutheran, doctrine) or 'after an heavenly and spiritual manner' (Anglican definition).

Réaumur scale Temperature scale in which 0° is the freezing-point of water, 80° its boiling-point.

Rebecca Isaac's wife, selected by Abraham's servant at a well in Mesopotamia (Gen. 24:12–15). Of their children, she preferred Jacob above Esau.

Récamier, Mme (1800). J. L. David's portrait of a lady reclining on a neoclassical couch; the sitter went off in a pet before he had finished it. She was a famous beauty whose salon was much frequented under the Directory and First Empire. Now in the Louvre. See DIRECTOIRE.

Recessional Music, or words to which it is set, played when the clergy and choir leave at the end of a service. See next entry.

'Recessional' (1897). Kipling's poem published in *The Times* on the occasion of Queen Victoria's Diamond Jubilee; it begins: 'God of our fathers, known of old, / Lord of our far-flung battle-line.'

Rechabites, Independent Order of (1835). Large friendly society for total abstainers founded at Salford, Lancashire; its lodges are called 'tents'. (From the Biblical Rechabites, a nomadic tribe who abstained from wine, Jer. 35:6–8.)

Recherche du temps perdu, A la See REMEMBRANCE OF THINGS PAST.

Reckitt (Albert) lectures (1951). Lectures on archaeology, given under the auspices of the British Academy.

Reconstruction Period (1865–77) after the AMERICAN CIVIL WAR when the Confederate states were rehabilitated under military rule and northern 'carpet-baggers' exploited the defenceless inhabitants for personal gain; called the Black Reconstruction in the South.

Rectory Field Rugby home of the Blackheath RUFC, at Blackheath.

Recusants Roman Catholics and others who refused to attend Church of England services in the 16th–17th centuries. (Pronounced rek'ewzants.)

Red Arrows, The Leading aerobatic squadron of the RAF.

Red Badge of Courage, The (1895). Psychological novel which brought Stephen Crane lasting literary fame and was remarkable for graphic descriptions of battle in the Civil War, of which the author had no firsthand knowledge. The hero enters the war with romantic illusions about his courage, quickly learns fear, runs away and, after an unmerited decoration, progresses through humility to real courage.

Red Baron Nickname of Baron von Richthofen, see RICHTHOFEN CIRCUS. (His plane was painted red.)

Red Biddy Glasgow Irish name for cheap red wine laced with methylated spirits, a favourite in the city's slums at one time; the name and the drink spread elsewhere, and is now applied to other nauseous concoctions of the kind.

Red Branch Knights Army of CONCHOBAR, King of Ulster, so named from their emblem, a rowan branch with red berries.

Redbrick Name applied to any modern British university, in contrast to Oxford and Cambridge and other ancient foundations.

Redbridge (1965). New London borough consisting of the former boroughs of Wanstead–Woodford, Ilford and part of Dagenham, together with the urban district of Chigwell; headquarters at Ilford, Essex.

Red Brigades, The Groups of urban guerrillas in Italy, with the German Red Army faction, Japanese Red Army, and Palestinian extreme groups. They were responsible for the kidnapping of many captains of industry and for the murder of Aldo Moro in 1978.

Red Caps Nickname for the provost branch of the Royal Military Police, a radio-equipped mobile force which watches discipline outside barracks, and in wartime controls prisoners of war, refugees, looters, etc.

Redcoat (1) British soldier in the days when red uniforms were worn. (2) An entertainment organizer at BUTLIN'S, whose uniform is a red blazer.

Red Crescent Emblem of the Red Cross Society in a Muslim country.

Red Dean, The Dr Hewlett Johnson, Dean of Canterbury (1931–63), who wrote the best-selling *The Socialist Sixth of the World* (1939), and persuaded himself that there was much good even in Stalinist Russia, which he often visited.

Red Devils Nickname of the SPECIAL AIR SERVICE Regiment of the British Army.

Red Douglas Nickname given to the Earls of Angus, in distinction from the Earls of Douglas, called BLACK DOUGLAS. The 2 branches of the family were united in the Dukedom of Hamilton.

Red Duster Sailors' name for the Red Ensign.

Rede lecture (1524). Annual lecture at Cambridge University given by a leading scientist or writer. (Endowed by Sir Robert Rede.)

Red Ellen Nickname for Ellen Wilkinson, Labour MP for Jarrow (1935–47), appointed Minister of Education in 1945.

Red Flag, Order of the Soviet order awarded for services to international revolution.

'Red Flag, The' British Labour Party's 'school song', written by an Irishman, sung at the annual conference – with less than universal enthusiasm since it contains such antiquated gems as 'Come dungeon dark or gallows grim, / This song shall be our parting hymn' and 'Though cowards flinch, and traitors jeer, / We'll keep the Red Flag flying here'.

Red Giant Type of star formed when most of the hydrogen in a MAIN SEQUENCE STAR has been used up. The interior contracts and heats up, the exterior expands, cools and glows red. BETELGEUSE is a typical example, with very low density and a huge diameter of some 200 million miles. The next stage of development is the WHITE DWARF.

Red Guards Mobs of undisciplined young Chinese who were set to enforce Mao's CULTURAL REVOLUTION from 1966 onwards, each carrying the LITTLE RED BOOK of Mao.

Red Hand of Ulster Badge of Ulster, originally of the O'Neills; also called the Bloody Hand.

Redouté roses Perhaps the most famous rose paintings ever made, published in *Les Roses* (1817–24) by Pierre Redouté, who also produced numerous volumes of equally skilful paintings of other flowers. There are cheap modern reproductions to trap the unwary.

Red Poll Breed of red dual-purpose cattle developed in East Anglia.

Red Queen, The Character in THROUGH THE LOOKING GLASS intended by Lewis Carroll to be 'the concentrated essence of all governesses'.

Redshirts, Garibaldi's See GARIBALDI'S THOUSAND REDSHIRTS.

Red Square Square in Moscow lying along the north-east wall and moat of the Kremlin. It has existed since the 15th century as a market, and many main roads converged there. Much of the square was destroyed in 1812. Osip Buvet replanned it and his buildings include the present state department store GUM; it is the site of military parades and displays on public holidays. Lenin's mausoleum lies in front of the east walls.

Red Star Soviet Defence Ministry's newspaper.

Red tape Unnecessary bureaucracy; from the pink/red tape still used by lawyers to secure documents.

Redwing National class of one-design clinker-built 14-foot dinghy, designed by Uffa Fox especially for use in the West Country; the sails are always red.

Reeder, J. G. Elderly detective who appears in many of Edgar Wallace's crime stories.

Reeve's Tale, The In the CANTERBURY TALES, a ribald story of how 2 students seduce a miller's wife and daughter.

Reformation, The Protestant revolt, part religious, part nationalist, against the supremacy of the Pope, brought to a head in 1517 by Luther in Germany, followed by Zwingli and Calvin in Switzerland and John Knox in Scotland. They wanted reform of the priesthood, an end to the sale of indulgences (i.e. buying salvation from priests), and the translation of the Bible and prayer book into languages that could be understood; they repudiated transubstantiation and the worship of the Virgin Mary, but believed in salvation through faith alone as opposed to 'justification by works' (salvation through doing good deeds or buying indulgences). In England Henry VIII took the middle way, retaining Catholic doctrine but severing all ties with the Pope.

Reformation Parliament (1529–36). Summoned by Henry VIII when the Pope refused to sanction his divorce from Catherine of Aragon, it passed the legislation which carried through the English Reformation.

Reform Bills Bills extending the franchise, particularly (1) the Whig measure (1832) which gave the vote to the middle classes and abolished rotten boroughs; (2) Disraeli's Bill (1867) which extended the vote to the urban working-class.

Reform club (1832). London club in Pall Mall founded in the year of the great Reform Bill, to which members must still make a token obeisance, although the membership is no longer Radical; it is frequented by Treasury officials, economists and judges with a propensity for writing letters to *The Times*, and wields considerable political influence.

Reformed Church CALVINIST Church, which separated from the main Lutheran movement after Calvin and Luther disagreed on the significance of the Last Supper. It became particularly strong in Switzerland, Holland (the DUTCH REFORMED CHURCH) and France (the HUGUENOTS).

Regan One of the 2 evil daughters of KING LEAR; see GONERIL.

Regency period In the English decorative arts, a term applied to the period (about 1790–1830) overlapping the Regency (1811–20) of the future George IV. It corresponded with and was influenced by the French EMPIRE STYLE and was characterized in furniture by rosewood, brass inlay, and copies of ancient Roman and Egyptian models.

Regicides, The (1649). Men who condemned Charles I to death, including Cromwell and Ireton.

Regulation 18b Clause of a British Emergency Powers Act under which, at the beginning of World War II, persons such as Sir Oswald Mosley who were considered to be security risks were interned in a concentration camp in the Isle of Man.

Reichenbach Falls Waterfall near Interlaken, Switzerland, perhaps most famous in Britain as the scene of Sherlock HOLMES's first death in 1891.

Reichsführer Title taken by Hitler in his dual capacity of head of state and supreme commander of the armed forces. (German, 'state leader'.)

Reichstag fire (February 1933). Burning down of the German Parliament house, which gave Hitler the excuse to establish a one-party regime, declaring that the state was threatened by a Communist conspiracy. The fire seems to have been the work of a Dutch half-wit, Van der Lubbe, who was executed.

Reichswehr Old name for the German Army, now called BUNDESWEHR. (German, 'state defence'.)

Reid Professor Holder of the chair of Music at Edinburgh University.

R18 certificate (1982). Granted by British Board of Film Classification to films for restricted distribution only (through segregated premises to which no one under the age of 18 is admitted).

Reign of Terror See under TERROR.

Reilly 'To lead the life of Reilly' is to live in luxury. From Pat Rooney's song (USA, 1882) which has the lines: 'Is that Mr Reilly that owns the hotel? / Well, if that's Mr Reilly, they speak of so highly, / Upon me soul, Reilly, you're doin' quite well.'

Reith lectures (1947). Annual series of radio broadcasts given by outstanding leaders of contemporary thought. (Named in honour of Lord Reith, first Director-General of the BBC.)

Relate New name for the former Marriage Guidance Council.

Religio Medici (1643). Sir Thomas Browne's learned meditations on a wide range of subjects, such as religious belief, nature, superstition, life and death. Although a devout Anglican, he had had, as a physician, scientific training, and therefore tempered reverence with scepticism.

Religious Wars, French (1562–98). Series of civil wars fought on religious issues, ended by the EDICT OF NANTES. See HOLY LEAGUE; HUGUENOTS; ST BARTHOLOMEW MASSACRE.

Remagen Bridge over the Rhine between Cologne and Koblenz, where an armoured division of the US 1st Army made the first Allied crossing of that river, March 1945.

Remembrance of Things Past (1913–27). Marcel Proust's immensely long masterpiece, a study of Parisian society as seen by the narrator, Marcel, like the author a hypersensitive introspective young man. He traces the lowering of barriers by the aristocratic GUERMANTES family, who eventually accept, even in marriage, the VERDURINS, SWANN'S daughter GILBERTE and his widow, ODETTE DE CRÉCY. (The French title is *À la recherche du temps perdu*, published in 7 parts.)

Remembrance Sunday Sunday before, on, or on the morrow of, 11 November (ARMISTICE DAY), when the dead of 2 world wars are remembered.

Remenham Club Clubhouse used by various Thames rowing clubs during Henley Regatta.

Remploy (1945). Company established to provide jobs for the severely disabled (physically or mentally). They manufacture such things as kitchen furniture and bedding.

Renaissance (Renascence) Primarily the rebirth of classical learning and art, which began in North Italian city-states in the 14th century and spread to England, France and Spain; extended to cover the transition from the feudal, monastic Middle Ages to the secular urban civilization of the modern West, which coincided with the discovery of America, printing and the Copernican system.

Renaissance architecture (15th–17th centuries). European revival of the classical orders and the rounded Roman arch which, pioneered by the buildings of Brunelleschi in Italy, gradually replaced Gothic. It did not reach England until a century later, coming to full development in the work of Inigo Jones, Wren and the Adam brothers.

Renishaw Country house near Sheffield on the Yorkshire–Derbyshire border, the home of the Sitwell family, well known through Osbert Sitwell's autobiographies. See LEFT HAND! RIGHT HAND!

Reno divorce Easy divorce obtainable under the state laws of Nevada, USA, which accept many trivial grounds and only 6 weeks' residence; associated particularly with Reno, as the state's largest city, situated on the Californian border and thus convenient for Hollywood film stars, etc.

Renown, HMS British POLARIS SUBMARINE.

Rentacrowd Term coined by Peter Simple in the *Daily Telegraph* in satirical reference to student protest demonstrations; speedily transferred to other spheres, e.g. Rentabishop, Rentaguest, etc. (From Rentaset, TV hire firm, and similar trade names.)

Rentenmark (1923). Temporary German currency introduced to stabilize money during the inflationary period that followed World War I.

Representative, The (1963). Hochhuth's Theatre of Fact play attacking Pope Pius XII for, according to the German playwright, not having condemned Hitler's anti-Semitism.

Republican calendar Revolutionary fervour produced at the time of the French Revolution a break with the Gregorian calendar and the Christian tradition; the republican year began usually on 22 or 23 September (as determined by the date of the autumn equinox) and consisted of 12 months of 30 days each, and these were divided into three *décades* of 10 days each instead of 7-day weeks.

Republican Party (1828). (USA) Party (at first called Whigs) which seceded from the old Republican Democratic Party to campaign for high tariffs. Strengthened by a further secession of Northern Democrats who stood for the abolition of slavery, they became the party of big business and economic imperialism, and after Woodrow Wilson's presidency (see DEMOCRATIC PARTY), brought the country back to isolationism. Their influence was crippled by failure to deal with the Great DEPRESSION in the 1930s and they remained out of power until 1969, except under Eisenhower whose election was on personal rather than party grounds. Ronald Reagan was elected in 1980 and the Republicans were still in power with the election of George Bush in 1988.

Requiem (1) First word of a prayer used in the Roman Catholic requiem mass, a service for the souls of the dead. (2) Musical setting for this, e.g. Mozart's, Verdi's. (3) Similar setting for a special occasion, e.g. Brahms's *German Requiem*, written after his mother's death. (*Requiem aeternam dona*, 'grant them eternal rest'; pronounced rek'wi-em.)

Rerum novarum (1891). Pope Leo XIII's encyclical on social questions, specifically approving legislation which improved the lot of the working-class, but attacking Socialism.

Rescue, The (1920). Joseph Conrad's novel in which Capt. LINGARD reappears, faced with a choice between duty and love.

Resistance movement Name given, especially in France, to the underground movement of resistance and sabotage in German-occupied territory during World War II.

Responsions First of the 3 examinations for the degree of BA at Oxford University; candidates with good academic qualifications are exempted from taking it.

Restoration, The (1660). Restoration of the monarchy, in the person of Charles II, after the ENGLISH CIVIL WAR.

Restoration period (1660–89). In English decorative arts, a period of reaction from Cromwellian austerities typified by walnut furniture with elaborate carving and barley-sugar turning. Veneering, marquetry, lacquer, gilding, glued joints, cane-seated chairs, glass-fronted bookcases, and day-beds all came into vogue. Grinling Gibbons's carvings were much in demand.

Restoration plays Comedies produced during the Stuart Restoration period (1660–1714), notably those by Dryden, Wycherley, Vanbrugh, Congreve and Farquhar, characterized in general by polished wit, licentiousness, artificiality and heartlessness – in natural reaction from a surfeit of Puritan austerity.

Restrictive Practices Court (1956). A court of judges and laymen sitting at the Law Courts in London, which decides the legality of firms' agreements to fix prices and markets.

Resurrection (1) Rising of Christ from the tomb on the third day, commemorated on Easter Sunday. (2) General resurrection of the dead.

Resurrection Men Term first applied to BURKE AND HARE, and then used generally of graverobbers.

Retreat, The One of the world's leading hospitals for mental disorders, at York.

Return of the Native, The (1878). Thomas Hardy's Wessex novel of Clym Yeobright who, to escape city life, opens a school on EGDON HEATH; he loses his sight, becomes first a furzecutter and then an itinerant preacher, his fickle wife having drowned.

Reuter (1849). Leading news and information organization. It compiles and distributes computer-based information for the world's financial and business communities and for news agencies, newspapers, radio and television stations in 137 countries. It has over 10,000 employees and was founded by Paul Julius Reuter.

Revenge, The (1880). Tennyson's poem of Sir Richard Grenville's fight (1591) with the Spanish fleet at Flores in the Azores. It contains the following: 'Sink me the ship, Master Gunner – / Sink her, split her in twain!'

Revere, Paul See PAUL REVERE.

Revised Version Revision of the AUTHORIZED VERSION made by English and American scholars, completed in 1885 (Apocrypha, 1895).

Revival of Learning (or **Letters**) Literary aspect of the Renaissance, the study of the literature, language and antiquities of Greece and Rome; Humanism. See NEW LEARNING.

Revolutionary War US name for the AMERICAN WAR OF INDEPENDENCE.

Revolutions of 1848 Uncoordinated series of European revolutions, in Paris, Vienna, Prague, Budapest, the Italian and German states and elsewhere, mainly led by middle-class intellectuals inspired by the French Revolution; their occurrence in one year was due to an economic slump and bad harvests. The English manifestation of this unrest was Chartism (see CHARTISTS).

Revue des deux mondes (1829). Leading French literary and political review, published fortnightly in Paris.

Rexists (1936). Belgian party formed by Léon Degrelle, inspired by the example of National-Socialism, and collaborationist during the war. (From *Christus Rex*, 'Christ is King', slogan of a Roman Catholic Young People's Society.)

Reynard the Fox Cycle of medieval tales of Reynard's stratagems to ensure survival in the animal world, a vehicle for satire on human affairs used in many languages and styles. (Pronounced ren'ĕd.)

Reynard the Fox (1919). John Masefield's poem of a fox-hunt, as seen by the hunters and the hunted.

Rhadamanthus In Greek legend, a brother of Minos; wise and just on earth, he was appointed one of the judges of the underworld.

Rhaetia Ancient Roman province extending over the modern Grisons canton of east Switzerland and part of Tirol. It gave its name to the Rhaetic Alps (which run parallel with the ENGADINE) and the Rhaeto-Romanic dialects of that region (Swiss Romonsch and Tirolese Ladin); see ROMANCE LANGUAGES. (Pronounced reesh'a.)

Rhea Greek equivalent to CYBELE.

Rhea Silvia in Roman legend, a Vestal Virgin, the mother of Romulus and Remus by Mars.

Rheingold, Das (1869). Prologue to Wagner's RING OF THE NIBELUNGS cycle. The Rhine Gold is the hoard of the Nibelungs, guarded by the RHINE MAIDENS.

Rh factor An agglutinating agent in the blood; its presence or absence is an inherited characteristic, of importance in certain rare conditions and in blood transfusions. (Rh for *Rhesus* monkey, in which it was first observed.)

Rhine Maidens In Wagner's RING OF THE NIBELUNGS cycle, the guardians of the Nibelungs' hoard of gold buried in the bed of the Rhine. ALBERICH steals this and makes a magic ring from it, which at the end of the cycle returns to the eternal possession of the Rhine Maidens.

Rhine Province Former Prussian province, capital Cologne, including Saarland and part of the Ruhr. The northern districts are now in North Rhine-Westphalia, the southern in the RHINELAND-PALATINATE.

Rhinoceros (1958). Ionesco's Theatre of the ABSURD play on the theme of the urge to conform with mass fanaticism. One by one a town's inhabitants opt to become rhinoceroses, until one is left with the courage of his convictions, listening to the herd stampeding up and down the main street.

Rhodesia and Nyasaland, Federation of (1953–63). Short-lived federation of what were then the colonies of Northern and Southern Rhodesia and Nyasaland. After it broke up it resolved itself into its component parts, which were renamed Zambia, Zimbabwe and Malawi respectively.

Rhodes Professor Holder of the chair of Race Relations at Oxford.

Rhodes scholarships Endowed by Cecil Rhodes (died 1902) for students at Oxford from USA, the Commonwealth, South Africa and Germany.

Rhus Genus name of the sumachs.

Rhys (Sir John) Memorial lectures (1925). Lectures on the Celtic world, given under the auspices of the British Academy.

Rhys (John Llewellyn) Memorial Prize Annual prize of £500 for a memorable work by a citizen of the Commonwealth under 30. (In memory of an RAF pilot killed in 1940 and awarded a Hawthornden Prize posthumously.)

Rialto (1591). Bridge over the Grand Canal at Venice; the neighbouring district, which has many markets.

Ribbentrop–Molotov Pact (1939). See HITLER-STALIN PACT.

Ribes Genus that includes the gooseberry, currants and the flowering currant.

Ribston Pippin One of the best dessert apples, with yellow and red fruit ripening in November. (Ribston, Yorkshire, where first introduced from Normandy in the 18th century.)

Ricardo's theory of rent Population increases with the increase of capital; demand for land from which to feed the increased population becomes more insistent, forcing up rents to the benefit of landowners, who become the blameless and passive recipients of ever-increasing wealth in accordance with an economic law over which they have no control and for which there is no remedy. (David Ricardo, British economist, 1772–1823.)

Rice, Archie Third-rate music-hall comic of John Osborne's disenchanted play *The Entertainer* (1957).

Riceyman Steps (1923). Arnold Bennett's drab novel of a miserly second-hand bookseller in Clerkenwell who starves himself to death.

Richard of Bordeaux See DAVIOT, GORDON.

Richardson, Henry Handel Pen-name of Henrietta Richardson; see FORTUNES OF RICHARD MAHONEY.

Richmond Herald Officer of the COLLEGE OF ARMS.

Richmond Palace (14th century). Royal palace by the Thames at Richmond, Surrey, of which only a gateway now remains. Originally called Sheen, it was renamed Richmond by Henry VII. Queen Elizabeth died there.

Richmond upon Thames London borough since 1965 consisting of the former boroughs of Richmond, Barnes and Twickenham, with headquarters at Twickenham.

Richter scale Scale used in measuring the severity of earthquakes. It was invented by Charles Francis Richter, professor of seismology at the California Institute of Technology, in association with Dr Bruno Gutenberg, and sometimes called the Gutenberg–Richter scale.

Richthofen Circus German fighter squadron in World War I, which introduced new team tactics to replace the individual 'dog-fights' hitherto prevailing. (Led by Baron von Richthofen, shot down in 1918; 'circus' because their planes were painted in vivid colours. His No. 2 was Goering.)

Rickettsiae Minute organisms intermediate in size between bacteria and viruses. Introduced into the blood by lice, they cause typhus.

Riddle of the Sands, The (1903). Spy story in which the future Irish rebel, Erskine Childers, did much to alert Britain to the possibilities of a German invasion.

Rideau Hall Residence of the Governor-General

of Canada, in the Ottawa suburb of New Edinburgh.

Riders of the Purple Sage (1912). Most famous and successful of Zane Grey's Westerns; film versions were made in 1931 and 1941.

Riders to the Sea (1904). J. M. Synge's grim one-act tragedy of old Maurya, who one by one loses all her menfolk.

Ridgemanites See MELUNGEONS.

Ridley Hall Theological training college at Cambridge.

Ridolfi plot (1571). Roman Catholic plot to dethrone Elizabeth I and, with Spanish help, to replace her by Mary Queen of Scots, who was to marry the Duke of Norfolk. (Italian banker, one of the conspirators.)

Riemannian geometry (1854). Non-Euclidean geometry which, not being confined to a 3-dimensional space, was invaluable to Einstein in formulating his Relativity theories. (G. F. B. Riemann, German mathematician, 1826–66.)

Rienzi (1835). Lord Bulwer-Lytton's historical novel about the LAST OF THE ROMANS; see ROMAN REPUBLIC (2).

Riesling Best of the types of grape used in making hock and similar wines.

Rievaulx Abbey (1131). Abbey near Helmsley, Yorkshire, formerly the best example of Cistercian architecture in England, now in ruins. (Pronounced ree'vo.)

Riffs Berber tribe of the Rif Mountains in Morocco who in 1909 first rebelled against the Spanish, whom they defeated at ANUAL, and later against the French, who under Pétain ended the rebellion in 1926, capturing its leader Abd-el-Krim.

Rifle Brigade, The (1816). Now the 3rd Battn The ROYAL GREEN JACKETS. It was formed from 2 battalions of the 95th Foot (and a new regiment of 95th Foot, the Derbyshire Regiment, later the 2nd Sherwood Foresters, replaced it), and was itself never a numbered regiment of the line.

RI Galleries (1881). Art gallery in Piccadilly, London, built for the Royal Institute of Painters in Water Colour; now also the home of the Pastel Society, the National Society of Painters, Sculptors and Engravers, and similar societies, which all exhibit there.

Rigel Beta-Orionis, 7th brightest star, in the foot of ORION; an 'energetic' star for which a relatively short life is predicted. (Pronounced ry'gl.)

Rights of Man, The (1) Thomas Paine's defence (1791–2) of the French and American revolutions and his suggestion for social reform, which included many of the features now found in a welfare state; he also suggested the limitation of armaments, and graduated income tax. (2) See DECLARATION OF THE RIGHTS OF MAN.

Rigoletto Duke of Mantua's hunchbacked jester whose daughter Gilda the Duke seduces, in Verdi's opera of that name (1851). Rigoletto plots to murder him, but Gilda sacrifices her own life to spare his; it is not until Rigoletto hears the Duke he thought dead singing the famous aria 'La donna è mobile' that he begins to realize that he has brought about his own daughter's death. The plot is derived from Victor Hugo's *Le Roi s'amuse*.

Rig-Veda Chief of the VEDAS, containing 1,000 hymns of varying antiquity. (Sanskrit *rik*, 'praise'; pronounced rig-vay'da.)

Rijeka A Yugoslav city and port, formerly known by its Italian name of Fiume. (Pronounced ri-yayk'a.)

Rikki-Tikki-Tavi Mongoose adopted as a pet, in one of the stories of Kipling's JUNGLE BOOKS.

Riksdag Swedish Diet, or Parliament.

Rillington Place murders (1953). Murder in Notting Hill, London, of at least 6 women by J. R. H. Christie, who was hanged. In 1966 a judicial inquiry found that he also probably murdered the baby daughter of Timothy Evans, living at the same address. Evans, who had been hanged for this, was given a posthumous free pardon, but the same inquiry found that he probably strangled his wife, a crime of which he had not been convicted.

Rima (1) Indian 'bird-girl' in W. H. Hudson's *Green Mansions*, a romantic tale of the South American jungle. (2) W. H. Hudson Memorial by Epstein (1925) in the bird sanctuary of Kensington Gardens, London.

Rimmon Babylonian god of storms; in 2 Kings 5:18, the Syrian general Naaman, who had been cured of leprosy through the agency of Elisha and thus converted to the religion of Israel, asks Elisha's permission to 'bow down in the house of Rimmon' when he goes there with his king. Hence this phrase is used of doing what is wrong but expedient.

Rinaldo Hero of medieval romance, paladin of Charlemagne, cousin of ROLAND, owner of the horse BAYARD (Baiardo), bold, unscrupulous, rapacious. (Also spelt Renault, Reynold.)

Ring and the Book, The (1869). Robert Browning's long poem giving differing versions of a famous 17th-century crime, as told by 12 people involved (the criminal, the victims, the Pope, etc.). A bankrupt Florentine count, Guido, marries for money and then murders his wife and her putative parents.

Ring of the Nibelungs (1869–76). Wagner's Ring Cycle of 4 operas: *Das Rheingold, Die Walküre, Siegfried* and *Götterdämmerung*, first performed at Bayreuth in 1876. The story is based on the NIBELUNGENLIED and earlier Scandinavian sagas.

Ring Round the Moon (1947). Christopher Fry's translation of Anouilh's frivolity about twin brothers, one good, one wicked. (French title, *L'Invitation au château*.)

Ringstrasse (1860). Two-mile tree-lined boulevard which encircles inner Vienna.

Rintelen spy ring Organization for espionage and sabotage formed (1915) in the USA by the German naval captain, Franz von Rintelen, during World War I; he was arrested in 1917.

Rin-Tin-Tin First animal to become a film star, making a fortune for Warner Brothers just after World War I. The dog was found in a German dug-out near Metz, France, by a Capt. Duncan, who took him home to Los Angeles. Rin-Tin-Tin died in 1932.

Rio Grande River which forms the Texas–Mexico boundary, properly the Rio Grande del Norte, to distinguish it from other rivers of the name. (Pronounced, in USA, ree'o grand.)

Rioja Best known wine-producing region of Spain, situated in the north-east of the country.

Riom trials (1942). Vichy government's attempt to pin the blame for the fall of France on to their leading opponents, e.g. Blum, Paul Reynaud and Daladier. The trial was suspended by Laval, but the defendants remained in prison. (Town of central France; also spelt Riyom.)

Rio Treaty (1947). Reaffirmation of the LIMA DECLARATION, whereby the American republics (except Ecuador and Nicaragua) agreed that an attack on one of them was to be considered as an attack on all.

Ripon Hall Theological training college at Oxford.

Rip Van Winkle Character in a story of Washington Irving's (1819) who sleeps for 20 years and wakes as an old man to find that America, formerly a colony, has become independent and his nagging wife is dead; applied to a person who is impossibly old-fashioned.

Rip Van Winkle gas A gas, for use in warfare, that deprives the enemy of aggressive instincts but inflicts no permanent injury. (See previous entry.)

Risaldar-Major Rank in the old (British) Indian Army nominally equivalent to Regimental Sergeant-Major but in practice carrying much greater responsibilities.

Rising Tide of Color (against White World-Supremacy) (1920). Once widely read book by an American, Lothrop Stoddard. It gave added encouragement to NORDIC racial theories.

Risorgimento Nineteenth-century Italian nationalist movement which, under Mazzini, Cavour and Garibaldi, drove the Austrians from the north and the Bourbon BOMBA from the south (the Kingdom of the TWO SICILIES), created the Kingdom of Italy (1861) under Victor Emmanuel II of Sardinia, and completed the unification of Italy by occupying Rome (1870) and ending the temporal power of the Pope, who was confined to the Vatican. (Italian, 'resurgence'.)

Rite of Spring, The (1913). Nijinsky's ballet to Stravinsky's score, considered revolutionary and discordant when first produced in Paris. It depicts a solemn pagan rite, a circle of seated elders watching a girl dance herself to death in propitiation of the god of spring. (French title, *Le Sacre du printemps*.)

'Ritual Fire Dance' Gypsy dance in Falla's LOVE THE MAGICIAN and included in the orchestral suite made from it.

Ritz, The (1906). London hotel in Piccadilly over-looking Green Park, opened by the Swiss hotelier César Ritz, whom D'Oyley Carte brought to England and installed at his Savoy. There is also a Ritz in the Place Vendôme, Paris (see ESPADON GRILL), and a Ritz-Carlton in New York and other North American cities.

Rivals, The (1775). Sheridan's comedy; see Lydia LANGUISH; Sir Anthony ABSOLUTE; Mrs MALAPROP.

River Plate, Battle of the (December 1939). Naval engagement in which British cruisers attacked the German battleship GRAF SPEE, and forced her to take refuge in Montevideo harbour.

RLS Initials standing for Robert Louis Stevenson.

R-month Months September–April when oysters are in season in the northern hemisphere, i.e. are safe to eat. (All these months, and none of the others, are spelt with an *r*.)

RNAS (1914). Initials used for the Royal Naval Air Service. In a long struggle over unification of air forces, it was merged with the RAF in 1918, separated again in 1937 as the Fleet Air Arm, and is now named the Naval Air Command. During World War II the RAF Coastal Command was under Admiralty control.

RNLI Initials of the Royal National Lifeboat Institution which, in liaison with the Coastguard Service, maintains and operates lifeboats. It relies on voluntary subscriptions and on the voluntary services of crews.

Road to Wigan Pier, The (1937). George Orwell's documentary novel about working-class conditions in the Great Depression.

Roanoke adventure (1585–7). First and unsuccessful American colony, of mostly unsuitable men, sent out by Sir Walter Ralegh; they settled on Roanoke Island off the north-east coast of North Carolina, but soon disappeared without trace, leaving a vague Indian tradition of dispersal among them. See MELUNGEONS. (Pronounced roh-è-nohk'.)

Roaring Forties. The Belt of southern ocean around and south of the 40th parallel where, unobstructed by land-masses, west winds blow strongly all the year round, making eastward circumnavigation preferable for sailing ships, although the early explorers, e.g. Magellan and Drake, went the hard way – westwards round Cape Horn.

Robbins report (1963). Report on higher education which recommended that CATS should be given university status and enlarged to take 3,000–4,000 students each; and that teacher-training colleges should also be enlarged and renamed Colleges of Education.

Roberts (Earl) Cup British long-range championship held under the auspices of the National Small-bore Rifle Association.

Robert sauce *Espagnole*-type sauce spiced with mustard, vinegar, etc. and served with pork.

Robert the Devil (1831). Meyerbeer's opera on Robert le Diable, father of William the Conqueror, a bold and cruel Duke of Normandy. (Italian title, *Roberto il diavolo*.)

Robin Goodfellow Mischievous spirit who can also be friendly and do odd chores about the house during the night; the equivalent of the German Knecht Ruprecht ('Servant Robin'); also called Hobgoblin, and by Shakespeare PUCK.

Robin Hood Legendary outlaw and crack shot with the bow and arrow, who lived in Sherwood Forest, Nottinghamshire, where he robbed the rich to help the poor; he was supposed to have lived in the 12th–13th centuries, and many attempts were made to identify him with historical characters, e.g. an Earl of Huntingdon.

Robinia Shrubs and trees, named after Jean Robin, botanist and herbalist to Henry IV of France.

Robinson Crusoe (1719). Daniel Defoe's classic desert-island story, based on Alexander Selkirk's experiences when Dampier landed him on the island of Juan Fernández, off Chile, from which he was rescued by Woodes Rogers 4½ years later in 1709. Defoe later claimed that the novel was an allegory of his own struggles with his conscience and with the external world.

Rob Roy (1817). Walter Scott's novel based on the history of Rob Roy Macgregor, the Scottish Robin Hood who died in 1734. He is responsible for the final triumph of Frank OSBALDISTONE, whose cousin Rashleigh he kills. ('Robert the Red'.)

Robsart, Amy See KENILWORTH.

Rochdale Pioneers (1844). First co-operative society, founded by weavers at Rochdale, near Manchester, Lancashire.

Rochester, Mr (Edward) Moody hero of JANE EYRE. Jane learns only on the day they are to marry that he has a mad wife locked away

Rockall sea area That lying north-west of Ireland, west of the Malin and Hebrides, and south of the Bailey sea areas. (Name of an isolated rock 200 miles west of the Outer Hebrides.)

Rockefeller Center (1947). New York City's 13-acre privately owned business and amusement centre (including RADIO CITY), housed in 15 buildings between Fifth and Sixth Avenues.

Rockefeller Foundation (1913). Established by John D. Rockefeller Sr 'to promote the welfare of mankind throughout the world'.

'Rocket, The' (1829). George Stephenson's locomotive which attained 29 m.p.h. on the Manchester–Liverpool line, drawing one coach. A greatly improved version of his earlier inventions of 1814 onwards, it finally tipped the balance in favour of the development of rail transport.

Rockingham Term more indiscriminately used than most in the antique trade. True Rockingham, which is very rare, consists of (1) earthenware (1778–1820), a typical product being brown-glazed CADOGAN TEAPOTS; and (2) bone china (1820–43) tea-services, etc. with buff, grey or pale blue grounds and gilding. Contrary to popular beliefs, decoration was not usually over-elaborate, there is probably no such thing as a Rockingham cottage, and genuine Rockingham is usually marked. (Made on the estate of the Marquis of Rockingham at Swinton, near Rotherham.)

Rock 'n' Roll (1953). Essentially, the white musicians' version of black RHYTHM AND BLUES, the violent beginning of guitar-based POP MUSIC combined with JIVE, with great emphasis on rhythm and repetitive phrase, popularized in the USA by Bill Haley and Elvis Presley; favoured in Britain by TEDDY BOYS and Rockers. 'Rock Around the Clock' was a characteristic example.

Rocky Mountains Rockies extend 3,200 miles from Alaska to New Mexico, with the highest peaks in Canada (Mt Logan) and Alaska (Mt McKinley). They form North America's main watershed, the GREAT DIVIDE. At the heart of the range is the Rocky Mountain National Park (1915) in north-central Colorado, containing 65 peaks over 10,000 ft.

Rococo (1700–60). Frivolous final stage of BAROQUE, which flourished particularly in Vienna, Prague, Munich, Dresden and the Paris of Louis XV; the characteristics were shell-motifs, scrolls, arabesques and curves in general, used in architecture (notably in Bavarian churches), art (Watteau, Boucher, Fragonard), silver, porcelain, furniture etc. It was succeeded by a NEO-CLASSICAL reaction. (French *rocaille*, 'shell-work'.)

Roderick Hudson (1876). Henry James's first novel, on what was to become his favourite theme, the impact of Europe on the sensitive American. Roderick is a sculptor who comes from New England to Rome and fails to adapt himself to his new life.

Roderick Random (1748). Tobias Smollett's picaresque novel in which the hero seeks adventure at sea, in France and finally in South America, where he finds his long-lost father and returns enriched to marry the girl of his choice.

Rodgersia Hardy perennials, named after John Rodgers, a US admiral.

Roedean Girls' public school near Brighton, Sussex.

Roehampton Club (1901). London club in Roehampton Lane, with facilities for golf, tennis, squash, swimming and croquet. There is a polo fortnight each year, when the Roehampton Cup and County Cup are decided.

Roffen: Abbreviation for (Bishop) of Rochester.

Rogation Days Three days before ASCENSION DAY when, in the Roman Catholic Church, the litany is chanted in public procession. (From Latin for 'supplication', 'litany'.)

Roger Code word used in radiotelephony for 'understood', for the morse letter 'R' used similarly in telegraphy, called Roger in a now obsolete phonetic alphabet.

Roget's *Thesaurus* (1852). Short title of a *Thesaurus of English Words and Phrases*, a dictionary of synonyms and antonyms for the use of writers, often revised and published in various modern forms. (British physician and a founder of London University.)

Rois fainéants Later MEROVINGIAN Kings of the Franks, who allowed their powers to be usurped by the Mayors of the Palace, the greatest of whom was Pepin, father of Charlemagne and founder of the CAROLINGIAN dynasty which ousted them. (French, 'do-nothing kings'.)

Roi Soleil Name given to Louis XIV, during whose reign (1643–1715) the arts and literature flourished but France was bankrupted by extravagance and wars. (French, 'the Sun King'.)

Rokeby Venus Common name of Velázquez's only painting of a female nude, properly called *The Toilet of Venus*. It is in the London National Gallery where, in 1914, it was slashed by a suffragette. (Named after Rokeby, Yorkshire, where its former owners, the Morritt family, lived; pronounced rohk'bi.)

Roker Park Football home of the Sunderland club.

Roland (Italian, Orlando) In troubadour songs, the nephew and chief paladin of Charlemagne, who through treachery is ambushed and slain with his friend Oliver at RONCESVALLES. See next entry.

Roland for an Oliver Tit for tat; an effective retort. ROLAND and Oliver were close friends, who emulated each other's exploits; once they fought each other for 5 days.

Rolling Stones Rock group that at one time rivalled the BEATLES and helped to popularize RHYTHM AND BLUES (1964). Led by Mick Jagger they concentrated on outraging the squares (as the general citizenry were then called) by their shaggy hair, scruffy clothes, sexuality, obscenity and general anti-social behaviour. This proved highly remunerative.

Rollright Stones Stone circle, perhaps Druidic, between Great and Little Rollright, Oxfordshire.

Romance languages Modern languages derived from Latin, e.g. French, Spanish, Italian and Romanian, together with older languages such as Provençal. They stem from the 'vulgar Latin' used by the Roman legionaries and the common folk under Roman rule.

Roman Club Complicated Italian calling system at Bridge, with numerous artificial bids. The opening bid indicates distribution rather than strength, in contrast to the NEAPOLITAN CLUB system.

Roman de la Rose Thirteenth-century romantic poem by 2 authors; part 1 is an allegory distantly based on Ovid's *Ars Amatoria*, part 2 consists of vigorous satire and, for its time, daring philosophical speculation. It was imitated by Chaucer (*Romaunt of the Rose*) and others, and greatly influenced European literature.

Romanée-Conti See CÔTE DE NUITS.

Roman Empire (31 BC to AD 395). Empire ruled from Rome from the time of Augustus until it was divided in two (see BYZANTINE EMPIRE); at its height it extended from Britain to the Persian Gulf and the Caspian, bounded on the north by the Rhine and Danube, and on the south by the North African littoral. The Western Empire (AD 395–476) continued in nominal existence until the deposition of its last Emperor, Romulus Augustulus, and then came under Byzantine rule.

Romanes lecture (1891). Annual lecture at Oxford University on a literary or scientific theme, given by an eminent authority. (G. J. Romanes. 1848–94; pronounced ro-mahn'iz.)

Romanesque architecture (10th–13th centuries). The West European style which preceded GOTHIC ARCHITECTURE and is characterized by the round arch and massive construction. In England it is called NORMAN ARCHITECTURE.

Roman holiday Phrase 'Butchered to make a Roman holiday' comes from Byron's CHILDE HAROLD, and refers to gladiators made to fight to the death in Roman arenas to entertain the mob.

Romanovs (1613–1917). Name given to the dynasty that ruled Russia until the Revolution, though from the 18th century the Tsars were mainly of German blood, connected with the Romanovs only in the female line. See EKATERINBURG. (Pronounced roh-mahn'ofs.)

Roman Question, The Problems raised by the opposition of the Italian people to the Pope's position as temporal ruler of the city of Rome. It came to a head in 1848 when Pope Pius IX was temporarily ejected, and Mazzini and Garibaldi proclaimed a ROMAN REPUBLIC; it was not finally settled until 1929, by the LATERAN TREATY.

Roman Republic (1) Period in ancient Roman history (509–31 BC) from the final ejection of the TARQUINS to the beginning of the ROMAN EMPIRE. (2) Republic of the city of Rome proclaimed by RIENZI (1347) during the AVIGNONESE CAPTIVITY; it lasted only a few months. (3) Republic declared by Mazzini in 1849 (see ROMAN QUESTION) which also lasted only a few months.

Romantic composers Weber, Schumann,

Chopin, Wagner, Berlioz, among many others. See ROMANTICISM.

Romanticism Reaction from Classicism, emphasizing individualism and revolt, emotion, imagination, humour and pathos rather than wit; creativeness rather than criticism; content rather than form. The 2 attitudes to art existed side by side, and sometimes in the same person at different periods. In Europe Romanticism was inspired by Rousseau and the French Revolution, and its founders are generally regarded as Weber in music, Delacroix in art and Goethe in literature. See following and previous entries.

Romantic poets Leading figures include (1) *English:* Wordsworth, Coleridge, Scott, Byron, Shelley, Keats; (2) *French:* Lamartine, Hugo, Musset, Vigny; (3) *German:* Goethe, Schiller, Heine. See ROMANTICISM.

Romantic Revival Name sometimes given to the period of the full flowering of ROMANTICISM in literature. Apart from the work of the ROMANTIC POETS, typical examples include the novels of Goethe, Scott and Hugo, as well as the GOTHIC NOVELS.

Romany Gypsies' own name for Gypsy and for their language. (Gypsy *rom* = a Gypsy, adjective *romany*; pronounced rom'an-i.)

Romany rye (1) One who identifies himself with the gypsies. (2) Title of George Borrow's sequel (1857) to LAVENGRO. (*Rye,* 'gentleman'.)

Rome, Sack of (1527). During the interminable struggle for power between France, the Habsburgs and the Papacy, a mutinous, starving army of Spanish, German and other mercenaries (for whose action the Emperor Charles V disclaimed responsibility while reaping its benefits) in 8 days destroyed two-thirds of Rome (including all its churches), imprisoned the Medici Pope Clement VIII, beheaded priests, raped nuns, stabled horses in St Peter's, and in general exceeded even the contemporary norm for barbarity. The event made a deep impression on Europe, though its historical significance was small.

Rome, Treaty of (1957). Treaty establishing the

European Economic Community, which came into being on 1 January 1958.

Rome–Berlin Axis (1936). Name coined by Mussolini for the alliance formed by Italy and Germany when the League of Nations imposed sanctions on Italy, which had invaded Abyssinia; extended to Japan in 1940 (the Rome–Berlin–Tokyo Axis) by the TRIPARTITE PACT. See also PACT OF STEEL.

Romeo and Juliet (1595). Shakespeare's play of the feud between Montagues and Capulets at Verona. The Montague Romeo is secretly married to the Capulet Juliet by Friar Laurence, kills her cousin to avenge his friend Mercutio's death, and is banished. Their joint suicide leads to a reconciliation between the families. Gounod wrote an opera (1867) based on this play.

Rome Protocols (1934). Agreements that embodied plans for a Danubian bloc of Italy, Austria and Hungary, directed against France and the LITTLE ENTENTE, and also against Hitler's ambition to unite Austria with Germany.

Romer report (1961). Report on the breaches of security disclosed by the PORTLAND SECRETS CASE, which severely criticized the Admiralty.

Romford, Facey Hero of Surtees' *Mr Facey Romford's Hounds* (1865).

Romneya Genus name of the Californian tree poppy.

Romney Marsh (sheep) See KENT.

Romola (1863). George Eliot's novel set in Florence in the time of Savonarola, under whose influence Romola comes. (Pronounced rom'ė-lė.)

Romulus and Remus Legendary founders of Rome, who were exposed in accordance with custom because they were born to a vestal virgin, but were rescued and suckled by a wolf. They lived to restore their grandfather, Numitor, as ruler of Alba. Romulus killed Remus, and was responsible for the RAPE OF THE SABINES.

Ronan Point (1968). Site of a 22-storey block of flats in London's East End dockland, part of which collapsed, killing 5 and causing bitter controversy about safety standards in such buildings; it is the real though disguised subject of Joan Littlewood's play, *The Projector* (1970).

Roncesvalles (778). Scene of the defeat by Basques of the rearguard of Charlemagne's army returning from Spain. The troubadours turned this into a story of treachery and ambush by a huge Saracen army; see ROLAND. (A pass in the Pyrenees.)

Ronchamp chapel (1955). Notre-Dame du Haut on a hill in the Haute-Sâone, a remarkable building designed by Le Corbusier; the hill is an ancient place of pilgrimage.

Ronde, La (1950). Max Ophüls's film version of a play (1902) by the Austrian Arthur Schnitzler, in which in successive scenes 10 couples make love, one of each pair appearing in the next scene; the last scene is linked to the first by the prostitute who appears in both. A cynical observer with a merry-go-round comments on the proceedings.

R-101 British airship which crashed in flames at Beauvais on a flight to India (1930); the disaster ended the development of airships in Britain.

Röntgen rays Another name for what Professor Röntgen himself, who discovered them, called X-rays. (Pronounced ront'yen.)

Roodee Local name for the Chester race-course. (Situated on Roodee Common.)

Roof of the World Translation of the local name of the Pamirs, a mountainous region, mostly in Tadzhikistan SSR, partly in Afghanistan and China.

Rooinek (Roinek) Afrikaans name for the British in the Boer War; now extended generally to include new immigrants from Europe. (Afrikaans, 'red-neck'; pronounced roh'in-ek.)

Rookes v. *Barnard* (1961). Court ruling that, in a case where a trade union had forced the dismissal of one of their number whom they had designated a 'blackleg', the union officials were liable to damages for conspiracy to terminate his contract of service.

Room, The Underwriting room at Lloyd's, where the LUTINE BELL hangs.

Room at the Top (1957). John Braine's success story of a ruthless young man with business and social ambitions, set in Bradford.

Room of One's Own, A (1929). Virginia Woolf's plea for women's economic independence.

Room with a View, A (1908). E. M. Forster's novel of central Italy, on the themes of the clash of Latin passion and Anglo-Saxon puritanism, and of upper-class prejudice with less shallow emotions.

Root and Branch Bill (1641). Bill for the abolition of bishops, which led to sharp and continuing dissension in the LONG PARLIAMENT.

Roquefort Semi-hard blue cheese made of ewes' milk and ripened in limestone caves at Roquefort; the name is officially restricted to cheeses so made, but there are imitations. Genuine Roquefort at the right stage of maturity has a pungent flavour much admired by the connoisseur. (Roquefort-sur-Soulzon, a village in the Aveyron *département* of south-central France; there is another village of Roquefort in south-west France.)

RORC rating A yacht handicapping formula which superseded the TM; it is based on waterline length and sail area (which increase speed) as well as beam and draught (which decrease it). The Cruising Club of America has a different formula. (Introduced by the Royal Ocean Racing Club.)

Rorke's Drift (1879). Battle in the Zulu War in which a horde of Zulus under Cetewayo fanatically charged a handful of British troops and were mown down by machine-guns. This avenged an earlier disaster, and a record number of VCs were awarded. (Site in Natal, South Africa.)

Rorschach ink-blot test Psychoanalytical test in which patients are asked to describe what a series of complex ink-blots suggest to them; their answers are said to reveal character, intelligence and emotional state. (H. Rorschach, Swiss psychoanalyst, 1884–1922.)

Rosaceae Rose family, which includes the genus PRUNUS, various berry-bearing plants (strawberry, raspberry, blackberry), fruit trees such as the apple and pear, as well as hawthorn, rowan, spiraea, japonica, etc.

Rosa eglanteria Species name of the sweet briar.

Rosalind Daughter of the Duke in Shakespeare's AS YOU LIKE IT who falls in love with Orlando.

Rosamunde overture Well-known overture composed by Schubert, originally for a play called *The Magic Harp*, but then substituted for one he had written, together with a ballet and incidental music, for an otherwise unimportant play about a Princess Rosamunde.

Roscius Name applied to various great actors, including Garrick. (Quintus Roscius, a Roman actor of the 1st century BC.)

Rose Bowl Sports stadium at Pasadena, California, where the first BOWL GAME was played. (Named after the tournament of Roses celebrated there annually on New Year's Day from 1890, inspired by the BATTLE OF FLOWERS at Nice.)

Rosemoor Gardens owned by the Royal Horticultural Society at Great Torrington, Devon, England, given by Lady Anne Palmer in 1988.

Rosenberg spy case (1950). The FBI's arrest, arising from the FUCHS case, of Julius and Ethel Rosenberg, executed (1953) for passing H-bomb secrets to Russia. The KROGERS were involved but escaped.

Rosencrantz and Guildenstern Two obsequious hypocritical courtiers in Shakespeare's *Hamlet*.

Rosencrantz and Guildenstern are Dead (1967). Play by Tom Stoppard, in which these 2 characters from *Hamlet* (see previous entry) meditate on their role in the Elsinore dynastic struggle and on human affairs in general.

Rosenkavalier, Der (1911). Richard Strauss's half sentimental, half ironic opera of the bluff and hearty Baron Ochs who loses his girl to a younger rival, in an 18th-century Vienna setting.

Rosetta stone (2nd century BC). Slab of black basalt, now in the British Museum, discovered by a Frenchman in 1799, which first supplied the key to the deciphering of Egyptian hieroglyphics, being inscribed in 3 languages including Greek. (Found near Alexandria at the Rosetta mouth of the Nile.)

Rosh Hashanah Jewish New Year, falling in September or October.

Rosicrucians Originally a medieval society of alchemists and magicians, about which almost nothing is known. The name was subsequently borrowed by Freemasons and others, including an American correspondence course in mysticism which confers supernatural powers (and riches) for a few dollars. (Variously derived from Latin *rosa crucis*, 'rose of the Cross', the old society's emblem, or the Latinized name of the alleged German founder, Christian Rosencreuz.)

Rosinante DON QUIXOTE's scraggy old horse. (Pronounced rohz-in-an'te; Spanish Rocinante.)

Ross, J. H. Name T. E. Lawrence assumed when he first joined the RAF as an aircraftman (1922) to escape publicity; later he changed his name to T. E. SHAW.

Ross, Martin Pen-name of Violet Florence Martin (1862–1915), one of the co-authors of EXPERIENCES OF AN IRISH RM.

Rossini (Cooking) With foie gras and truffles. (Named after the composer.)

Rosslyn Park (1879). Rugby club which used to play at the OLD DEER PARK, now at Roehampton.

Rotary Club (1905). Club started in Chicago, consisting of one representative of each profession and trade of the city, to encourage a spirit of service to others and promote the city's trade and other interests. The movement spread all over the world. Members are called Rotarians.

(So named because the original club met at each member's house in rotation.)

Rothschild, N. M. (1804). London merchant bank and acceptance house, founded by Nathan Rothschild, a Manchester cotton merchant; it once financed Wellington's army in Spain.

Rothschild dynasty Financial family dynasty founded by M. A. Rothschild of Frankfurt am Main (died 1812). Of his 10 sons, 4 scattered in Napoleonic times to Paris, Vienna, Naples and London (see previous entry), and a fifth remained in Frankfurt. These subdynasties are symbolized in the family sign of 5 arrows.

Rôtisserie de la Reine Pédauque (1893). Anatole France's novel which introduces his mouthpiece, the Abbé Coignard, a modern Rabelais. (The title is the name of a restaurant.)

Rotten Row Riding track running along the south side of Hyde Park from Hyde Park Corner to Kensington Gardens; also called The Row. (Traditionally a corruption of *route de roi*, 'king's way'.)

Rotterdam blitz (May 1940). Purposeless German destruction of the centre of Rotterdam by systematic air attack.

Rouge Croix Pursuivant of the COLLEGE OF ARMS.

Rouge Dragon Pursuivant of the COLLEGE OF ARMS.

Rouge et le noir, Le (1830). Stendhal's novel of a repellent young man, Julien Sorel, who uses women to win advancement in the Church, the only career which he thinks likely to provide him with the power he seeks. (*Rouge* represents the military career, *noir* the clerical.)

Rougemont, Louis de Assumed name of a Swiss-born rogue who achieved fame by addressing the British Association in 1898 on his experiences among the Australian aborigines, later shown to be entirely imaginary. He also wrote an equally bogus account of Eskimo life.

Roundheads In the ENGLISH CIVIL WAR the name given to the Parliamentary Party, mostly

Puritans, who fought against Charles I, or for parliamentary rights, for the abolition of bishops or against Charles's Catholic supporters; strong in the south and east, controlling London and the ports. (From their close-cropped hair, a reaction against Royalist curls.)

Round Table In 12th-century additions to Arthurian legend, the table made for UTHER PENDRAGON by MERLIN; also a feature of other medieval romances.

Round-table Conference Conference seated at a round table, so that no problems of precedence arise (an idea borrowed from King Arthur's Round Table); specifically applied to a series of conferences (1930–32) on Indian constitutional reform.

Round the World in Eighty Days (1873). Jules Verne's novel about the feat of Phileas FOGG and his valet, Passepartout.

Rouse Ball Professor Holder of the chair of Mathematics at Oxford or Cambridge, or of English Law at Cambridge.

Route 66 (USA) Highway running 2,200 miles from Chicago to Los Angeles, through 6 states.

Rover Solihull (Warwicks) firm, makers of the Rover cars, the LAND-ROVER and the 4-wheel-drive all-purpose Range Rover (1970).

Rowlandson cartoons Ferocious political caricatures (many aimed at Napoleonic France) and scenes of low life by Thomas Rowlandson (1756–1827), who also illustrated the books of various novelists and produced a celebrated series on DR SYNTAX.

Rowland Ward (1892). Abbreviated title used for *Records of Big Game* published by Rowland Wards, the London taxidermists; it gives detailed measurements of outstanding specimens of big game shot by sportsmen.

Rowley Mile Mile course at Newmarket, named after OLD ROWLEY. The Thousand Guineas and Two Thousand Guineas are run over this.

Rowley poems, The See BRISTOL BOY.

Rowton Houses 'Poor man's hotels', the first of which was opened in London (1892) and was so successful that a company was formed to build others, to provide decent accommodation for the poor at no higher price than was charged for the dormitory accommodation then available in the common lodging-house. (Lord Rowton, 1838–1903, who financed the scheme.)

Roxana, Roxane (1) Bactrian wife of Alexander the Great. (2) Sultana of Turkey. See BAJAZET. (3) Heroine of Rostand's CYRANO DE BERGERAC. (4) 'Heroine' of Defoe's *Roxana* (1724).

Roxburghe Club (1812). Exclusive club for bibliophiles, named after one of their number, the 3rd Duke of Roxburghe, who died in 1804.

Royal, The (1839). Common abbreviation for the Royal Agricultural Society's show, until 1967 held in a different part of the country each year, and now having a permanent home at the National Agricultural Centre, Kenilworth, Warwickshire. It provides a shop-window for British agriculture and agricultural machinery.

Royal Academy (1768). Shortened title of the Royal Academy of Arts, which holds an annual summer exhibition of contemporary painting and sculpture, and occasional exhibitions of the art of a particular country or period. There are 40 Royal Academicians (RAs), who become Senior Academicians at 75 to create vacancies for younger candidates. See BURLINGTON HOUSE.

Royal Academy of Music (1822). Senior college of music, in Marylebone, London; admission is by examination. See ROYAL COLLEGE OF MUSIC.

Royal and Ancient, The (1754). St Andrews Golf Club, recognized outside the USA as the world headquarters of golf.

Royal Ascot (1711). Four-day race meeting at Ascot in June, a fortnight after the Derby, a social event marked by considerable ceremonial, e.g. the royal party's ride in state from nearby Windsor and down the course.

Royal Ascot enclosure Formerly the Royal Enclosure, a part of the stands at ROYAL ASCOT

427

closed to all who have not obtained entry badges through the Earl Marshal's office.

Royal Assent After a Bill has passed all stages in both Houses of Parliament it is remitted to the Queen for the Royal Assent, which has not been withheld since the reign of Queen Anne. The Bill then becomes an Act of Parliament.

Royal Automobile Club (1897). London Club in Pall Mall, founded in the early days of motoring; it has a swimming pool and squash courts, and a country club outside London. It also acts as the national motoring authority which controls motor racing.

Royal Ballet, The (1957). Title under which the SADLER'S WELLS Ballet (Covent Garden), the Sadler's Wells Theatre Ballet (the junior company at Sadler's Wells Theatre, from 1989 the BIRMINGHAM ROYAL BALLET), and the Sadler's Wells ballet school (see next entry) were merged.

Royal Ballet School (1957). Originally the SADLER'S WELLS ballet training school (1931), which teaches ballet to children from the age of 9 at the WHITE LODGE and elsewhere. See previous entry.

Royal Birkdale Golf club and links at Waterloo Road, Birkdale, on the outskirts of Southport, Lancashire.

Royal Botanic Gardens Official name of Kew Gardens (London) and of the garden at Edinburgh.

Royal College of Art London college at Kensington Gore, given university status in 1967. It has a faculty of Fashion-designing.

Royal College of Music (1883). College in Kensington, London, which combines with the ROYAL ACADEMY OF MUSIC and colleges in Manchester and Glasgow in holding local examinations.

Royal Commonwealth Society (1868). Club, originally the Royal Colonial Institute, later the Royal Empire Society, with a specialist library for those interested in Commonwealth affairs.

Royal Courts of Justice See LAW COURTS.

Royal Court Theatre See ENGLISH STAGE COMPANY.

Royal Dutch/Shell (1906). Full title of the company generally known as Shell; a merger by Henri Deterding of Holland and Marcus Samuel, now the second largest petroleum group, with headquarters in London and The Hague. There are several hundred subsidiaries established in most countries of the world and given very considerable independence. British shareholders are in the majority, followed by American and Dutch. See SHELL-MEX; SHELL-MEX AND BP.

Royal Enclosure (Ascot) See ROYAL ASCOT ENCLOSURE.

Royal Festival Hall (1951). London concert hall built on the South Bank of the Thames for the Festival of Britain, and later extended. Particular attention was paid to the acoustics.

Royal Fine Art Commission (1924). Government-appointed body which has powers (not apparently used to any great effect) to draw attention to any planning which appears likely to affect public amenities adversely, and to call for information regarding such planning. There is a separate commission for Scotland.

Royal George, The Admiral Kempenfelt's ship, which capsized at Spithead and sank with all hands (1782); celebrated in William Cowper's poem of that name; see SCIPIO MARCH.

Royal Green Jackets, The (1966). A 'large' infantry regiment comprising: 1st Battn The Royal GREEN JACKETS (43rd and 52nd); 2nd Battn The Royal Green Jackets (The KING'S ROYAL RIFLE CORPS); 3rd Battn The Royal Green Jackets (The RIFLE BRIGADE). In 1968, it became part of the LIGHT DIVISION and the Rifle Brigade was disbanded.

Royal Horse Guards (The Blues), The (1661). One of the 2 regiments of the HOUSEHOLD CAVALRY, in origin a ROUNDHEAD regiment; they wear blue tunics and red plumes.

Royal Hospital, Chelsea See CHELSEA HOSPITAL.

Royal Humane Society (1774). Society which makes awards of which the Stanhope Gold Medal is the highest) for exceptional bravery in saving people from drowning, mining disasters, etc. It also promotes training in life-saving.

Royal Hunt Cup Flat-race run at Ascot in June over a distance of 7 furlongs, 155 yd.

Royal Institute of British Architects (1834). Professional body which supervises the training of architects, lays down scales of fees, etc. Its headquarters building in Portland Place, London, is a surprising example of non-functional architecture.

Royal Institute of International Affairs, The (1920). CHATHAM HOUSE, a London association for the study and discussion of international affairs, with a library of books and world press cuttings on the subject. Its US counterpart is the Council of Foreign Relations.

Royal Institution (1790). London association for the Diffusion of Science and Useful Knowledge, which has endowed 4 professorships (of natural philosophy, astronomy, chemistry and physiology) and sponsors public lectures, including Christmas lectures for schoolchildren.

Royal Lytham and St Annes Golf club at St Annes-on-the-Sea, Lancashire.

Royal Mail case (1931). See KYLSANT CASE.

Royal Mile, The Comprehensive name for the principal street in the Old Town, Edinburgh, leading from the Castle to Holyrood, each section having its specific name, e.g. Canongate.

Royal Military Academy (1) Until 1946 the WOOLWICH ROYAL MILITARY ACADEMY. (2) From 1946, SANDHURST.

Royal Oak Name of warships and inns, derived from Charles II's oak at BOSCOBEL.

Royal Observatory Established at Greenwich in 1675 by Charles II to improve methods of navigation. Latterly the telescopes have been removed

to HERSTMONCEUX Castle, Sussex, because of superior visibility there; the meridian of zero longitude of course still passes through the old site. The Royal Observatory is responsible for the time service of the UK, and the time zones of the world were based on Greenwich Mean Time. However, the Royal Observatory is now to be based at La Palma, Canary Is. The buildings at Greenwich are now occupied by the National Maritime Museum.

Royal Opera House See COVENT GARDEN.

Royal Over-Seas League (1910). Club founded by Sir Evelyn Wrench, with headquarters off St James's Street, London, and branches elsewhere. It provides hospitality for overseas visitors and has a large membership, chiefly of those who have served overseas.

Royal Parks (London) Term includes Hyde, St James's, Regent's, Greenwich, Richmond, Hampton Court and Bushy Parks, and Kensington Gardens.

Royal Pavilion, Brighton Prince Regent's fantasy palace in Mogul style with Chinese decor, built by Holland and Nash. The original furniture has been put back in the State Apartments.

Royal Road (500 BC). Strategic road built by Darius I to link Susa (then the Persian capital) and Sardis, capital of Lydia in western Anatolia and the entrepôt for trade between Persia and Europe.

Royal Sailors' Rests See AGGIE WESTON.

Royal St George's Championship golf course at Sandwich, Kent.

Royal Scots (The Royal Regiment), The (1633). Oldest regiment in the British Army, and therefore the 1st Foot. Now a regiment of the LOWLAND BRIGADE.

Royal Scot See LMS.

Royal Shakespeare Company (1960). Company which sprang from the Shakespeare Memorial Theatre at Stratford and also took over the Aldwych Theatre (1961) in London while new theatres in the Barbican were constructed.

Royal Society, The (1645). Oldest and leading

scientific society in Britain; full title: The Royal Society for Improving Natural Knowledge. The Fellowship (FRS) is a high distinction, and the Copley and other medals it awards also carry great prestige. The papers read at BURLINGTON HOUSE are published in the *Proceedings* or *Philosophical Transactions* of the Society.

Royal Society Medal Award instituted by George IV; 2 medals annually for the most important contributions to science published in the British Commonwealth.

Royal Society of Arts (1754). London learned society formed to foster the application of scientific knowledge to the arts, manufacture and commerce, which now deals mainly with industrial design, exercising influence through lectures, exhibitions and awards. It is housed in an Adam building in the Adelphi, near Charing Cross.

Royal Society of Literature award See HEINEMANN BEQUEST.

Royal Society Research Professorships Eight professorships in the grant of the Royal Society for research scientists for whom no university chair is available; see also FOULERTON, Henry DALE and WOLFSON PROFESSORSHIP.

Royal Sovereign General favourite among strawberries, producing fruit of excellent flavour and flourishing everywhere except in very light soils.

Royal Tournament Display given by the 3 services each June at Earls Court, London; regular features include a musical ride and a team competition in dismantling, transporting over obstacles and reassembling field guns. The Tournament is preceded by a parade in Battersea Park of all those taking part.

Royal Variety Show Annual command performance by the pick of the music-hall artists, given in aid of the Variety Artists' Benevolent Fund and attended by Royalty.

Royal Victorian Order (1896). Sovereign's personal award. Instituted by Queen Victoria because she thought that politicians had too much patronage. GCVO, Knight or Dame Grand Cross; KCVO, Knight Commander; DCVO, Dame Commander; CVO, Commander; LVO, Lieutenant; MVO, Member.

Royal Worcester Porcelain Co. Name of the chief WORCESTER PORCELAIN factory from 1788 to 1793, and again from 1862 until today.

Ruanda–Urundi Former Belgian Trust Territory in Central Africa, now divided between the 2 states of Burundi and Rwanda.

Rubáiyát of Omar Khayyam, The Twelfth-century Persian poem on the general theme of 'carpe diem' (make merry while you may) rendered familiar through Edward Fitzgerald's memorable translation (1859). Some stanzas have been set to music (e.g. 'Myself when young did eagerly frequent/Doctor and Saint and heard great argument'). See JAMSHID.

Rubicon, The Small river forming the boundary between Julius Caesar's province, Cisalpine Gaul, and Italy. In 49 BC Caesar crossed it, declaring 'the die is cast', and this decisive step started the civil war in which he triumphed over his rival, Pompey.

Rubik's cube Complicated puzzle invented by Erno Rubik.

Ruby Blended port of rich ruby colour, younger, lighter and cheaper than TAWNY.

Rudbeckia Herbaceous perennials, named after Olaf Rudbeck (1630–1702), a Swedish botanist.

Ruddigore (1887). Gilbert and Sullivan opera about the Baronets Murgatroyd who under the old curse must commit a crime a day or die in agony; they find the obligation increasingly tiresome, and the latest of the line is rebuked by his ancestors, who step out of their frames in the Picture Gallery to point out that his crimes do not come up to the required standard. Thus pressed, he finds an ingenious solution to his dilemma.

Rüdesheimer HOCK from Rhinegau vineyards at Rüdesheim, darker and with a fruitier flavour than other hocks. (Pronounced rood'es-hy-mèr.)

Rudolph Valentino Association Still-active

society dedicated to the remembrance of the handsome young film star of THE FOUR HORSE-MEN OF THE APOCALYPSE, who died in 1926.

Ruff's Guide (1842). Short title for *Ruff's Guide to the Turf*, a racegoers' annual combined since 1959 with the *Sporting Life Annual*.

Rugby fives A game which differs from ETON FIVES in having no 'pepper'; singles and doubles are played.

Rugby League (1893). Breakaway professional league formed when the RUGBY UNION banned professionalism. The game is played mainly in Lancashire, Yorkshire and Cumberland, between teams of 13 (instead of 15).

Rugby Union (1871). Formed after the Football Association had banned handling the ball. The game is played exclusively by amateurs (see RUGBY LEAGUE) and mainly in Britain, Ireland, New Zealand, Australia, South Africa and France. There are 15 a side (though a fast game with 7 a side has more recently been developed), and the ball is oval.

Ruhr, The Centre of German heavy industry, the Dortmund–Essen–Duisburg area along the River Ruhr, a tributary of the Rhine.

RUKBA Initials fused for the Royal United Kingdom Beneficent Association, a charity which helps gentlefolk in need.

Rumford Medal (1796). Royal Society biennial award for the most important discoveries in heat or light.

Rum Jungle Site south of Darwin, Northern Territory, Australia, where an important source of uranium was discovered in 1949.

Rumpelmeyers Paris tea-shop in the Rue de Rivoli long famous for its magnificent confectionery; it now carries on under a new name. There used also to be a Rumpelmeyers in London and there still is one in New York.

Rumpelstiltskin In German folklore a dwarf who taught a girl to spin gold from straw in return for her first-born, but then promised to release her from the bargain if she could find out his

name. He inadvertently gave it away himself, and killed himself in a rage.

Rump Parliament (1649–59). What was left of the LONG PARLIAMENT after PRIDE'S PURGE; it voted for a republic and abolished the House of Lords, was dissolved by Oliver Cromwell (1653) but recalled by Richard Cromwell to abolish the PROTECTORATE.

Runcible Cat, The Mentioned in Edward Lear's *The Pobble Who Has No Toes*: 'He has gone to fish for his Aunt Jobiska's Runcible Cat with crimson whiskers.'

Runcorn (1964). NEW TOWN in Cheshire situated near the existing town, designed to take 70,000 new inhabitants.

Runnymede Meadow on the Surrey side of the Thames near Egham, the site (1) where King John signed Magna Carta (1215); and (2) of Sir Edward Maufe's memorial, on a hill above it, to those members of the Air Forces of the Commonwealth who have no known grave.

Rupert Bear (1920). Cartoon character created by Mary Tourtel, taken over by Albert Bestall, RA, in 1935 and by a panel of artists in 1965. The innocent Rupert lives in Nutwood Cottage and has many friends, e.g. Bill Badger, Algy Pug, Edward Trunk.

Rupert of Debate Phrase taken from the line 'Frank, haughty, rash – the Rupert of Debate' in a poem of Lord Lytton's, who was referring to the Tory prime minister, Lord Derby, in his clashes with the Irish politician Daniel O'Connell. (Prince Rupert, a dashing Royalist leader in the English Civil War.)

Rupert of Hentzau (1898). Anthony Hope's novel of RURITANIA.

RUR (1921). Karel Čapek's play about Rossum's Universal Robots, half-human automatons which threaten world destruction while the managing director of the firm who manufactured them gloats over his profits from their sale. (*Robot*, an old Slav word for serf labour.)

Rural Rides (1830). Vigorous commentary on English rural life by William Cobbett, journalist and radical politician.

Ruritania Central European country invented by Anthony Hope as a setting for his romances of adventure and court intrigue, *The Prisoner of Zenda* and *Rupert of Hentzau*; hence any state where the intrigues of a reactionary court dominate politics, as in the old Balkan kingdoms.

Ruskin College (1899). First residential college for working men (and later, women), founded at Oxford by an American and supported by trade unions, etc. (Named in honour of John Ruskin, British radical writer and art critic.)

Russelites Name for JEHOVAH'S WITNESSES.

Russell's paradox Is a man who says 'I'm a liar' to be believed? If he is telling the truth, the statement may be a lie; if he is lying . . .? (Quoted by Bertrand Russell, but actually going back to at least the 4th century BC.)

Russian Revolutions (1) Workers' revolt in 1905 resulting from the Russo-Japanese War, quickly suppressed; see BLOODY SUNDAY. (2) The Menshevik revolution of February 1917. (3) The Bolshevik revolution of November 1917; see OCTOBER REVOLUTION.

Russian roulette Suicidal gamble in which a six-shooter is loaded with one bullet, the cylinder spun round, the revolver placed to the temple and fired, thus giving a 5–1 chance of survival.

Russo-Japanese War (1904–5). War which arose from rival claims to Korea and Manchuria, and ended in Russia's crushing defeat at TSUSHIMA.

Rutgers (1766). US university at New Brunswick, New Jersey.

Ruth Brief book of the Old Testament telling how Naomi lost her husband and sons in Moab, whither they had migrated from Bethlehem. One of her daughters-in-law, Ruth, a Moabitess, refused to desert her and went back with her to Bethlehem, where she became a gleaner 'amid the alien corn' (in the words of Keats) in the fields of Boaz, whom she later married. Their son was the grandfather of David.

Ruth, Babe Greatest name in US baseball; he played (1914–35) successively for Boston Red Sox, New York Yankees and Boston Braves.

Ruth Draper garden One which was a mass of colour last month and will be so next month, but right now appears to be a dying wilderness; the product of the fertile imagination of the American *diseuse* Ruth Draper (1884–1956) in one of her best-known sketches.

Ruth Ellis case (1955). Trial of the last woman to be hanged in Britain, found guilty of murdering her lover, David Blakely.

Ruthenia Former region of Austria-Hungary dominated by the Carpathians; it was divided in 1918 between Czechoslovakia, Poland and Romania. After World War II Soviet Russia seized all 3 parts and incorporated them in the Ukraine.

Rutherford, Mark Pen-name of William Hale White (1831–1913), a British novelist and lapsed Congregationalist who in *The Autobiography of Mark Rutherford* (1881) and other novels gives a sincere portrait of a Dissenter in revolt against provincial narrow-mindedness.

Rutherford Laboratory Government laboratory for research in high-energy nuclear physics, with a powerful proton accelerator, Nimrod, at Chilton, a village near Didcot, Berkshire.

Rutherford lecture (1952). Royal Society lecture in honour of Lord Rutherford, delivered in New Zealand or elsewhere in the overseas Commonwealth. (Lord Rutherford, the physicist, was born in New Zealand.)

Ruthless Rhymes for Heartless Homes (1899). Illustrated book by Harry Graham (1874–1936) of light-heartedly cold-blooded little verses, typified by: 'Philip, foozling with his cleek, / Drove the ball through Helen's cheek; / Sad they bore her corpse away, / Seven up and six to play.'

Ruy Blas (1) Play by Victor Hugo (1838), chiefly remembered through (2) Mendelssohn's overture (1839) written for it. (Pronounced roo'i blahs.)

Ruy López Conventional opening in chess. (Pronounced roo'i lohp'ez.)

RV *Verzeichnis* of Vivaldi's work compiled by Peter Ryom.

RWS (1804). Initials used for the Royal Society of Painters in Water Colour, which has galleries in Conduit Street, London, where spring and autumn exhibitions are held.

Ryder Cup (1927). Professional golf contest between Europe and USA, held in alternate years, with 4 foursomes and 8 singles.

Ryecroft, Henry Hero of *The Private Papers of Henry Ryecroft* (1903) by George Gissing, a semi-autobiographical account in diary form of escape from poverty and city life.

Rye House Plot (1683). Alleged Whig plot, for which there is little evidence, to kill Charles II and the future James II. (Rye House Farm, Hertfordshire, where the conspirators are said to have met.)

Ryswick, Treaty of (1697). See AUGSBURG, WAR OF THE LEAGUE OF.

S

SA (1922). Initials of the German name of the mass organization of Hitler's followers. Its leaders were massacred in 1934 (see NIGHT OF THE LONG KNIVES) at Hitler's command, and the ss then became supreme. Also called Brownshirts. (German *Sturmabteilung*, 'Storm troops'.)

SAAB Swedish aircraft firm which also makes cars, missiles and electrical equipment.

Sabah Formerly British North Borneo, now a federal unit of Malaysia.

Sabbath chain Chain across a road in Israel to prevent its use for vehicles on the Sabbath.

Sabbath Day's journey Distance, equivalent to less than $\frac{3}{4}$ mile, prescribed by Jewish tradition based on Exodus 16:29, as the maximum to be travelled on the Sabbath.

Sabbatical Year (1) Seventh year, when under Mosaic law land must be left fallow (Exod. 23:11) and a moratorium on debts declared (Deut. 15:1–2). (2) At certain universities, a year's vacation from teaching, to be devoted to travel or research, granted to professors and other teaching members of the university, originally every 7th year.

Sabena (1923). Chief Belgian airline. Initials of Société Anonyme Belge d'Exploitation de la Navigation Aérienne.

Sabin vaccine Poliomyelitis vaccine made of living viruses, which can be taken orally and is effective over a long period. (Dr Albert Sabin, US scientist.)

Sabine Women, The (1799). J. L. David's painting of the RAPE OF THE SABINES in which he emphasizes the courage of the women, in gratitude to his estranged wife who had pleaded for his release from prison, where he had been sent for revolutionary activities; now in the Louvre.

Sabrina Roman name for the River Severn, mentioned in Milton's *Comus*, about whom an English legend was told to account for the Latin name of the river.

Sacco and Vanzetti Two Italian anarchist immigrants found guilty of murder by a Massachusetts court (1921) but not executed till 1927, after many appeals and accusations of judicial prejudice.

SACEUR Supreme Allied Commander, Europe, the general in command of Nato land forces.

Sacher's Vienna hotel once frequented by the aristocracy of Imperial Austria.

Sachertorte Rich chocolate sponge with jam filling, named after SACHER'S.

Sachsenhausen Nazi concentration camp.

Sackville Street Principal street of Dublin, now renamed O'CONNELL STREET.

Sacré-Cœur (1914). White church on top of Montmartre in Paris, work on which began in 1876 as an expression of contrition and hope after the disastrous Franco-Prussian War of 1870.

Sacred and Profane Love (1510). Titian's painting now in the Borghese Gallery, Rome, with one clothed and one nude female figure, variously interpreted as representing Earthly and Heavenly Love or Grace and Truth (or Beauty).

Sacred College College of Cardinals, whose duty it is to elect one of their number as Pope when the throne falls vacant.

Sacre du printemps, Le See RITE OF SPRING.

Saddleback Hardy breed of black baconer pig (Essex and Wessex) with a white 'saddle' over the shoulders and forelegs; mainly used for crossing purposes.

Saddlers, Worshipful Company of (1363). LIVERY COMPANY.

Saddleworth, The Pack of foxhounds which hunt country just east of Manchester. Its motto is 'We never cop owt', and it once got lost in a fog.

Sadducees Ancient Jewish sect, the priestly caste, opposed to the PHARISEES, not accepting the oral traditional law, denying the existence of angels and immortality of the dead. (Said to be named after Zadok the Priest.)

Sadhu Indian title for an ascetic or holy man. (Sanskrit, 'good'; pronounced sah'doo.)

Sadleirian Professor The holder of the chair of Pure Mathematics at Cambridge.

Sadler's Wells (1931). Theatre in Rosebery Avenue, Finsbury, opened by Lilian Baylis to do for North London what the OLD VIC had done for South London, i.e. provide good plays at cheap prices. It then concentrated on opera in English (absorbing the CARL ROSA OPERA COMPANY) and (Dame) Ninette de Valois's ballet companies (see ROYAL BALLET). In 1968 the Sadler's Wells Opera was rehoused at the London Coliseum, and renamed the English National Opera. The Sadler's Wells Theatre is now used for visiting opera and ballet companies. (Site of a well, named after its owner, which was developed into a spa, where a theatre was built in 1756.)

Sadowa (1866). Battle that ended the SEVEN WEEKS WAR, in which the Prussians under Moltke, using a new breech-loading rifle, defeated the Austrians; it marked the decline of Austria and the rise of Prussia as dominant power in Central Europe. (Village near König-gratz, by which name the battle is also known; the latter is now called Hradec Králové and is 63 miles east of Prague.)

Safavids (1502–1736). Dynasty which presided over a renaissance of Persian art, building a magnificent new capital at Isfahan in the reign of Shah Abbas the Great.

'Safety First' The slogan with which Baldwin lost the 1929 general election to Labour.

Sagebrush State Nickname of Nevada.

Sagittarius The Archer, 9th of the constellations of the Zodiac, between Scorpio and Capricornus, representing a centaur drawing a bow; the sun enters it about 21 November. It contains many novae and planetary nebulae and may be the centre of our galaxy. Astrologers claim that those born under this sign may be adventurous, extravagant and unreliable. (Pronounced saj-i-tair'i-us.)

Saguenay Legendary kingdom up the Ottawa River sought by the French 16th-century navigator Jacques Cartier; name subsequently given to a river in Quebec.

Saint, The Gentleman-burglar, Simon Templar, created by Leslie Charteris in 1928. His symbol, on the dust-covers of some 40 novels, is a haloed pin-man.

St Agnes's Eve See EVE OF ST AGNES.

St Andrews Royal burgh on the east coast of Scotland, famous for its ancient university and as the home of the ROYAL AND ANCIENT.

St Antony's (1948). Postgraduate college of Oxford University.

St Bartholomew Massacre (1572). Massacre of French Huguenots begun in Paris on St Bartholomew's Day, ordered by Catherine de Medici, mother of the young King Charles IX. See GUISE, HOUSE OF.

St Benet's (1897). Private hall at Oxford University for members of the Benedictine Order.

St Brendan's Isle In medieval Irish legend, an island paradise discovered in mid-Atlantic by the 6th-century Irish saint of that name (also spelt Brandan).

St Catharine's (1473). College of Cambridge University.

St Catherine's (1962). College of Oxford University.

St Clement Danes (17th century). One of the island churches in the Strand, London, restored after World War II as the church of the RAF; it is the church of the nursery rhyme 'Oranges and Lemons'. (Thought to have been built on the site of a Danish settlement.)

St Cross (1) College (1965) of Oxford University. (2) A religious and charitable foundation near Winchester, founded by Henry de Blois (1133).

Saint-Cyr (1806). French Sandhurst, founded on the site of Mme de Maintenon's convent near Versailles, destroyed in World War II, and now at Coëtquidan near Rennes, the capital of Brittany.

St Dunstan's (1915). Organization for the care of members of the armed forces blinded in World War I and subsequent wars. (First founded at his home – St Dunstan's Lodge, Regent's Park, London – by Sir Arthur Pearson, the newspaper proprietor, who became blind in 1910.)

Saint-Émilion Dark claret; Château Cheval Blanc and Château Ausone are among the best.

St George and the Dragon Legend of obscure origin. Nothing is known for certain about St George, the patron saint of England; the dragon is simply the embodiment of evil. Gibbon's identification of him with St George of Cappadocia, fraudulent supplier to the Roman forces, is highly dubious.

St George (Royal Society of) Cup English long-range championship held under the auspices of the National Small-bore Rifle Assocation.

St George's Chapel (15th century). Perpendicular chapel at Windsor Castle, famous for its fan vaulting. The GARTER CEREMONY is held here.

St George's, Hanover Square Eighteenth-century London church, famous throughout its history for fashionable weddings.

St George's Vase (1862). Individual rifle-shooting competition held at Bisley in July, second in importance only to the Queen's Prize. The range at the final stage is 900 yd.

Saint-Germain (Cooking) With peas.

St Germain, Treaty of (1919). Post-war treaty with Austria (a separate, TRIANON, treaty was made with Hungary) which broke up the Austro-Hungarian Empire. Austria ceded huge areas to the new states of Czechoslovakia, Yugoslavia and Poland; lost South Tirol to Italy; and was left a scarcely viable state cut off from access to the sea, with only a quarter of its pre-war population.

St Giles's Fair Ancient Midlands market, held at Oxford after St Giles's Day (1 September), which survives as a pleasure fair.

St-Gobain Largest European firm to specialize in glass manufactures, much bigger than PILKINGTONS, at Saint-Gobain near Saint-Quentin, France. The group's other interests include chemicals, oil, paper and machinery.

St Helena Island in the South Atlantic where Napoleon lived in exile from 1815 until his death in 1821.

Saint-Hubert (Cooking) With game.

St James's Palace Building, facing St James's Street, which succeeded Whitehall in the Hanoverian period as the principal royal palace in London until Queen Victoria moved to Buckingham Palace. It was then used as a residence for royal princes and for levees. Ambassadors are still officially accredited to 'the Court of St James's'.

Saint Joan (1923). Bernard Shaw's play which characteristically portrays the newly canonized

Joan of Arc as an early nationalist and Protestant whose views are a menace to contemporary Church and society, and therefore meet to be burnt.

St John Ambulance Voluntary organization which provides first aid, nursing and welfare services in hospitals, homes, at public and sporting events where first aid may be required, and in times of emergency. See KNIGHTS OF ST JOHN.

St John of Jerusalem, Order of See KNIGHTS OF ST JOHN.

St Lawrence Seaway Improved system of canals and locks, completed 1959, which opened up the Great Lakes to seagoing vessels.

St Leger (1776). Last classic of the flat-racing season for 3-year-olds over a course of more than 1¾ miles at Doncaster.

Saint-Loup, Marquis de In Proust's REMEMBRANCE OF THINGS PAST, a member of the GUERMANTES family; at first infatuated with a prostitute, Rachel, he turns homosexual and wins Morel from CHARLUS. He then marries GILBERTE.

St Luke's Summer Period of mild sunny weather in October, equivalent to the US Indian Summer. (St Luke's Day, 18 October.)

St Margaret's, Westminster (1523). London church in Parliament Square, since 1614 the official church of the House of Commons.

St Mark's Part-Byzantine cathedral which is the focal point of Venice.

St Martin-in-the-Fields (1726). London church in Trafalgar Square, famous as the church whose vaults were thrown open to the poor and homeless, and for the Rev. Dick Sheppard's sermons broadcast from it when he was vicar.

St Martin's Summer Period of mild sunny weather in November; compare ST LUKE'S SUMMER. (MARTINMAS, 11 November.)

St Marylebone See MARYLEBONE.

Saint-Nazaire raid (March 1942). Small British commando raid on the repair docks at Saint-Nazaire, at the mouth of the Loire, carried out successfully but with heavy loss.

St Pancras Former London metropolitan borough, since 1965 part of the borough of CAMDEN.

Saintpaulia Genus name of the African Violet, named after Baron Walter von St Paul who discovered it.

St Pauls (1980). District of Bristol and scene of anti-police riot.

St Paul's School (1509). Public school for boys in Hammersmith, London; founded by the Dean of St Paul's Cathedral, John Colet.

St Peter's (1929). College of Oxford University.

St Peter's, Rome (1506). Chief cathedral of the Roman Catholic Church, situated in the Vatican.

St Petersburg The capital of Imperial Russia; renamed during the World War I Petrograd, and later Leningrad.

Saints, The Nickname for (1) the CLAPHAM SECT; (2) Southampton and St Johnstone football teams.

St Stephen's Entrance to the House of Commons, originally a chapel and later the place where the House sat.

St Trinian's, The Belles of (1954). Film and book by Ronald Searle. Alastair Sim played the double role of headmistress and bookie and others in the cast were Hermione Baddeley, George Cole, Joyce Grenfell, Beryl Reid and Joan Sims.

St Valentine Day massacre (1929). Murder of leaders of Bugs Moran's gang, which left SCARFACE AL CAPONE supreme in the Chicago underworld.

Saki Pen-name of H. H. Monro (1870–1916), writer of numerous satirical sketches.

Sakkara, Saqqara Necropolis of MEMPHIS, south of Cairo, it is the site of the Step Pyramid of Zoser (3rd Dynasty), earliest known pyramid of the Pharaohs.

Salamis (480 BC). Greek naval victory over the Persians (following THERMOPYLAE). (An island in the Gulf of Aegina, near Athens; pronounced sal'a-mis.)

Salchow Ice-skating jump, of which there are various types.

Salcombe Week Chief West Country regatta, held in South Devon.

Salem witch-hunt (1692). Hysterical outburst at Salem, Massachusetts, started by a maid, dismissed by her master and ex-lover, denouncing her mistress as a witch. As a result 19 people were hanged for witchcraft.

Salerno (September 1943). Allied landing in Italy south of Naples, at a point north of the British 8th Army, which had crossed from Sicily a few days earlier; made just after the Italian surrender, it met with stiff German opposition.

Salic Law Ancient law of the Franks, later interpreted to include a prohibition against a woman's accession to the French throne; this prohibition was adopted by other states of Europe. See PRAGMATIC SANCTION. (From name of tribe of Franks from which the MEROVINGIANS descended.)

Salk vaccine (1954). First effective vaccine against poliomyelitis; prepared from dead viruses, it has to be administered in repeated injections; see SABIN VACCINE. (Dr Jonas Salk, USA.)

Sally Army Colloquial abbreviation for the SALVATION ARMY.

'Sally in Our Alley' Eighteenth-century ballad of which the words were written by Henry Carey but set to an older traditional air.

Sally Lunn Kind of teacake, named after the woman who made them at Bath in the 18th century.

Salmanazar Measure the equivalent of 12 bottles of champagne.

Salmonella Genus of bacteria found in meat or vegetables when they become contaminated. The disease can be fatal to the old or weak. The bacteria was identified by Daniel Elmer Salmon (1850–1914), an American veterinary surgeon.

Salmon Report (1966). Report on tribunals of inquiry which recommended that inquiries in camera of the type that led to the DENNING REPORT should never again be held. (Lord Justice Salmon.)

Salome In the New Testament story, Salome asked her stepfather Herod Antipas for the head of John the Baptist, who had denounced her mother for her incestuous second marriage (Matt. 14:8). See next entry.

Salome Title of a play by Oscar Wilde and an opera based on it by Richard Strauss, which add to the biblical story (see previous entry) the suggestion that Salome was in love with John, and Herod with Salome.

Salon des Refusés (1863). Exhibition of works refused by the Salon, the French equivalent of the Royal Academy; organized by Manet and his friends, with the approval of Napoleon III, it was a protest against the conservatism of the Salon jury.

Salonika Usual English name for the Greek port of Thessaloniki.

Salopian (1) Of Shropshire. (2) Of Shrewsbury School. (From Anglo-Norman name of Shrewsbury.)

Salopian porcelain See CAUGHLEY.

Salteena, Mr Butcher's son with social ambitions in *The* YOUNG VISITERS, who said of himself: 'I am not quite a gentleman but you would hardly notice it.'

Salters, Worshipful Company of (1558). One of the Great Twelve LIVERY COMPANIES, originally a guild of producers and sellers of sea-salt and those who preserved food with it. It gives financial support to education and research in chemistry, particularly through the Salters' Institute.

Salvation Army (1877). Organization for the relief of the destitute, originally called the East End Revival Society; it was founded by William Booth, a Methodist, who reorganized it as an 'army', with uniforms, brass bands and military ranks. The movement spread from London to most countries of the world.

Salzburg Festival Annual festival of Mozart's music held in July and August at the composer's birthplace.

Salzkammergut Austrian mountain Lake District east of Salzburg. (German, 'salt domain'.)

Sam Under-disciplined private of Stanley Holloway's monologue who refused to pick up the musket knocked out of his hand by Sergeant, until the Duke of Wellington rode up (on a lovely white 'orse) to plead with him to do so 'just to please me'.

Samara Old name of Kuibyshev, a city of the RSFSR.

Samaritaine Large Paris department store near the Louvre.

Samaritans, The (1953). Voluntary organization founded by Rev. Chad Varah, which gives help and advice to people in distress, particularly to those who appear to be contemplating suicide. (See GOOD SAMARITAN.)

Sam Browne Military belt originally designed to carry an officer's sword, the wearing of which was made optional in the British Army at the beginning of World War II. (Named after Gen. Sir Sam Browne, VC, died 1901.)

Samian ware Red-clay domestic crockery of ancient Rome; examples of it have been found all over the Empire, normally in fragments as it broke very readily.

Samian wine One of the favourite wines of ancient Rome. (Made in Samos.)

Samizdat Term coined by Soviet dissenters for the system of preparing and circulating writings privately so as to avoid official censorship; the word, which dates from the mid-1960s, is a parody of the official acronym Gosizdat (State Publishing House) and means 'self-publishing' or 'do-it-yourself publishing'.

Sam McGredy (1937). Hybrid tea rose with very large perfectly formed cream or buff flowers.

Samsoe Semi-hard Danish cheese, pale yellow, with a mild nutty flavour.

Samson Hercules of the Israelites; rendered powerless when DELILAH cut off his hair, he was captured by the Philistines who blinded him and took him to Gaza (EYELESS IN GAZA). There he pulled down the pillars of a temple, which collapsed on him and all the lords of the Philistines (Judg. 16:21–31). See next entry.

Samson Agonistes (1671). Milton's dramatic poem on the blind SAMSON's defiant act of self-destruction. (Greek *agonistes*, 'struggler'.)

Samson reproductions (1845). Brilliantly accurate copies of Meissen, Chelsea, Derby, etc. porcelain, made in Paris by the firm of Samson. Many of these bore an honest 'S' (sometimes erased by the unscrupulous) in addition to the copied factory mark, and fetch high prices on their own merits.

Samuel Prophet whose life story is told in 1 Samuel. As a child he heard Jehovah's voice one night, and was sent to become a priest under Eli at SHILOH. He rallied the Israelites after their defeat by the Philistines, and became their 'judge' or ruler; but they demanded a king, and he reluctantly anointed SAUL as the first King of Israel (1 Sam. 10:1). See next entry.

Samuel (mostly 7th century BC). Name of 2 books of the Old Testament. 1 Samuel opens with the defeat of the Israelites by the Philistines, who captured the Ark, and tells the stories of SAMUEL, Saul and the early years of David. 1 Samuel deals with the later years of David's reign.

Samuel Coal Commission (1926). Commission set up when government decided to withdraw subsidies to the coal industry. Its report recommended the reorganization of the industry and was published at the time of the GENERAL STRIKE. (Sir Herbert, later 1st Viscount, Samuel.)

Samuelites Remnant of the Liberal Party, after the defection of the SIMONITES (1931), led by Herbert (later Viscount) Samuel.

Samurai Military caste which dominated Japan during the TOKUGAWA SHOGUNATE; replaced after the MEIJI RESTORATION by a conscript army. See BUSHIDO. (Pronounced sam'oor-y.)

San Andreas faultline One of the major fractures of the earth's crust. It runs for about 970 km (600 miles) from Point Arena in north-west California, USA, to the Colorado desert. The rocks do not move at a uniform rate; they stick and jerk and cause disastrous earthquakes such as the one in San Francisco in 1906.

Sancho Panza DON QUIXOTE'S rustic squire who accompanies him on his donkey, Dapple; he is chiefly interested in food, drink and sleep, but indulgent to his master's whims. (Spanish *panza*, 'paunch'; pronounced sang-ko-pan'za.)

'Sanctus' Hymn beginning 'Holy, Holy, Holy' which marks the end of the Preface to the Eucharist service, and during which the Sanctus bell is tolled. (Latin, 'holy'.)

Sand, George French novelist (1804–76), pen-name of Lucile-Aurore Dupin, baronne Dudevant. Over forty years she wrote novels, critical and biographical essays and dramatic works. She had many liaisons, notably with Chopin and Alfred de Musset.

Sanders of the River (1911). Edgar Wallace's story of an intrepid empire-builder in West Africa.

Sandhurst (1759). ROYAL MILITARY ACADEMY (formerly College) at Camberley, Surrey, where army officer cadets are trained for commissions, originally in the cavalry and infantry only but, after amalgamation with the RMA Woolwich (1946), in all army units.

Sandringham House (1861). Royal residence in Norfolk.

Sands Cox Professor Holder of the chair of Anatomy at Birmingham University.

Sandwich Snack meal invented by Lord Sandwich (1718–92); a gambler who was reluctant to leave the gambling table. It meant that food need not interrupt play.

SANE Committee for a Sane Nuclear Policy, the US equivalent of the CND, under the chairmanship of Dr Spock (see SPOCK BOOK).

San Francisco Conference (1945). International conference that adopted the UNITED NATIONS CHARTER.

San Francisco earthquake (1906). Earthquake which almost completely destroyed the city, though with comparatively small loss of life.

Sanger's Circus English circus developed from Astley's Circus (1768) by 'Lord' George Sanger, who took it over in 1871.

Sanhedrim Priests and elders of the Israelites sitting together as the highest court of law from about the 3rd century BC until AD 70; after that their jurisdiction was restricted to religious matters only. (Hebrew from Greek, 'sitting together'; pronounced san'i-drim.)

Sankey and Moody hymns Those written or collected by Sankey and used by Moody in his evangelical campaigns in USA and later in Britain.

Sankey report (1919). Report of a commission of inquiry into the coal-mining industry; its 12 members disagreed widely but there was a majority minimum recommendation for the nationalization of coal (not of the industry). This was not implemented.

San Michele, The Story of (1929). Dr Axel Münthe's anecdotal autobiography, which includes his account of how he built himself the villa of San Michele on Capri.

Sans Culottes Radical republicans who, to signify that they were manual workers, wore trousers rather than the knee-breeches of the pre-revolutionary aristocrats. Originally a term of reproach, but the revolutionaries assumed the name with pride and applied it to themselves as 'patriots'. In 1792–4 it was applied to a specific group that was pressuring the Convention by mobilizing local clubs and assemblies. (French, 'without breeches'.)

Sanskrit Oldest known INDO-EUROPEAN LAN-GUAGE, still the scriptural language of Hinduism. It is the parent of HINDUSTANI.

Sans Souci (1747). Name given by Frederick the Great to the palace he built at Potsdam. (French, 'without a care'.)

Santa Fe Trail Eight-hundred-mile wagon route which linked Santa Fe, New Mexico, via Fort Dodge (near Dodge City) and Kansas City almost in a straight line to Independence on the Missouri; of great importance from 1821 until the Santa Fe railroad was completed in 1880.

Santa Maria **incident** (1961). Seizure at sea of the Portuguese liner, *Santa Maria*, by a body of Portuguese passengers led by Capt. Galvão, as a propagandist gesture against the Portuguese dictatorship.

Santa Sophia (AD 537). One of the most famous and characteristic of Byzantine churches, at Istanbul; long since converted into the Great Mosque.

Santo Domingo (1) Old name of the Dominican Republic, in eastern Hispaniola. (2) Name of its capital, except for the period 1936–61 when it was called Ciudad Trujillo.

Sapper Pen-name of Cyril McNeile, a colonel in the Royal Engineers, author of BULLDOG DRUMMOND.

Sappers, The Nickname for The Royal Engineers.

Sapphira Wife of ANANIAS. (Pronounced saf-yr'a.)

Sappho Greek poetess of the 7th century BC, born on the Aegean island of Lesbos, said to have indulged in homosexuality, hence the terms Sapphism and Lesbianism.

Saracens Name, of obscure origin, for: (1) Bedouins; (2) Muslims; (3) the Seljuk Turks against whom the Crusaders fought; (4) the Muslim pirates who in the 9th and 10th centuries terrorized Mediterranean shipping.

Sarah Abraham's wife, mother of Isaac.

Sarajevo assassination (28 June 1914). Assassination of the Archduke Franz Ferdinand, heir to the Austro-Hungarian throne, by a Bosnian Serb, Gavrilo Princip; the proximate cause of World War I. (Town in Bosnia, Yugoslavia; pronounced sar'e-ye-vo.)

Saratoga, Battle of (1777). Battle in the American War of Independence which frustrated British attempts to isolate the New England colonies; Gen. Burgoyne's force moved down from Canada to join up with Gen. Howe, but was cut off and forced to surrender. (A town in New York state, now called Schuylerville, near Saratoga Springs.)

Sardanapalus (1) Greek name of the last King of Assyria. According to Greek stories he was effete and pleasure-loving, but capable of vigorous action when required. Defeated by rebels, he set fire to his palace and was burnt to death together with his women and servants. This scene inspired Delacroix's great canvas in the Louvre. Sardanapalus is usually identified with the historical Assurbanipal (7th century BC). (2) Byron's tragedy (1821) on this theme. (Pronounced sar-dan-ap'a-lus.)

Sarin US lethal nerve gas (also called GB), causing death in from 2 minutes to 2 hours. Made at NEWPORT, INDIANA.

Sarsten stones Sandstone boulders, quarried locally, which were used for the largest features (trilithons) of Stonehenge. (Saxon corruption of Saracen, as popularly supposed to be Druidic and thus heathen.)

Sartor Resartus (1836). Thomas Carlyle's work of which the first part consists of the views of the imaginary German Professor Teufelsdröckh on the philosophy of clothes; the second purports to be the professor's autobiography, actually an account of Carlyle's own spiritual crisis. (Latin, 'the tailor repatched'.)

Sarum Ecclesiastical name of Salisbury, used in the Bishop of Salisbury's signature.

Sarum lecture Lecture at Oxford University given every other year, alternating with the

BAMPTON LECTURE, 'in support of the Christian faith'.

Sasanids (AD 226–641). Persian dynasty, capital Ctesiphon, who conquered the Parthians and Medes and carried on continual warfare with Rome until they succumbed to Muslim invasions. The founder was Ardashir (Artaxerxes), the son of Sasan.

Sassenach Scottish name for an Englishman. (Gaelic *Sasunnach*, 'Saxon'.)

Satchmo Nickname of Louis Armstrong, the American black jazz trumpet virtuoso, born in New Orleans in 1900. (Satchel mouth).

Satellites World's first artificial satellite was launched on 4 October 1957; *Sputnik* I was designed by S. P. Korolev and V. P. Glushko; *Sputnik* II carried a dog; and *Sputnik* III housed a geophysical laboratory and sent back television pictures, the first of the far side of the moon.

Satsuma ware (1) 18th-century Japanese cream-coloured crackleware tastefully decorated in enamel colours and gilt; not exported. (2) Japanese ware made specially for Western markets in the 1870s and 1880s, smothered with gaudy decoration and worthless.

Saturday Evening Post (1728). Popular US illustrated magazine, carrying general articles and short stories dealing with American life; published in Philadelphia, Pennsylvania; ceased publication 1969, but revived as a quarterly in 1971.

Saturn Roman god equivalent to the Greek CRONOS.

Saturn Name given to a series of US rockets, of which Saturn V was the base of the 3-stage rocket designed to land 3 men on the moon under the APOLLO SPACE PROGRAM. It is claimed that it could put 36 men into orbit, and was first tested in 1967.

Saturnalia Major festival held in late December in ancient Rome, possibly to celebrate the end of the vintage. Slaves were treated as equals during this period, which was marked by considerable licence. It was adopted by the early Christians

and transformed into the Christmas festivities; the custom of exchanging presents was common to both celebrations.

Satyagraha Passive resistance, advocated by Gandhi. (An Indian word.)

Satyr Woodland god of the Greeks and Romans, being half man, half goat.

Satyricon Satirical novel written by Petronius. Nero's director of entertainments, in prose and verse. Parts of it have survived, including a description of the banquet given by the upstart Syrian, Trimalchio.

Sauchiehall Street One of the main shopping streets of Glasgow. (Pronounced sok-i-hol'.)

Saudi Arabia Name given by Ibn Saud in 1932 to the kingdoms of Hejaz and Nejd which he had united in 1927.

Saughton goal Edinburgh gaol.

Saul First King of Israel, anointed by SAMUEL. He was jealous of his son Jonathan's love for his harpist David. The phrase 'Is Saul also among the prophets?' (1 Sam. 10:11–12) is used of one who unexpectedly supports what he had previously attacked.

Saul of Tarsus St Paul's name before he was converted to Christianity. See Acts 9:11; 13:9.

Saulte Sainte Marie Canals Two ship canals, one in Canada, one in the USA, north and south of rapids between Lakes Huron and Superior; they are claimed to be the world's largest and busiest. (Name of twin towns, one in Michigan, the other in Ontario. Pronounced Soo' San Ma'ree.)

Sauternes Sweet white Bordeaux wine from grapes left to shrivel on the vine; includes the highly regarded Château-d'Yquem, and Château-Guiraud.

Savage Club (1857). London club, markedly bohemian in tone; the members, who call themselves Brother Savages, are mostly artists, actors, comedians or broadcasting personalities.

Savannah (1) First steamer to cross the Atlantic

(1819), a voyage which, aided by sail, took 25 days. (Built at Savannah, Georgia, USA). (2) First nuclear-powered merchant vessel, launched in 1959.

Save the Children Fund (1919). Voluntary organization to help sick, deprived and hungry children.

Savidge Inquiry (1928). Investigation which followed the acquittal of Sir Leo Chiozza Money on a charge of indecent behaviour with Irene Savidge in Hyde Park. It was alleged that 2 police had perjured themselves and that in a subsequent police inquiry third-degree methods had been used against Miss Savidge. The police were criticized but not prosecuted. Shortly afterwards Money was convicted of assaulting a woman on a train.

Savile Club (1868). London club in Brook Street, with a membership including authors, publishers, actors and broadcasters, less staid than the GARRICK, more so than the SAVAGE.

Savile Row London centre for men's tailoring.

Savilian Professor Holder of one of 2 chairs at Oxford: Astronomy, Geometry.

Savill Gardens (1930). Gardens in Windsor Great Park world-famous for outstanding rhododendrons, azaleas and herbaceous borders, laid out by Sir Eric Savill, deputy ranger and director of gardens, 1930–70.

Savoy Ancient duchy south of Lake Geneva, the major part of which was ceded to France by the King of Sardinia (1860); the Italian Royal family belonged to the House of Savoy.

Savoyard Member of the cast of a SAVOY OPERA.

Savoy Chapel Queen's Chapel of the Savoy, Savoy Street, Strand, the private property of the British monarchy, inherited from John of Gaunt; headquarters of the Royal Victorian Order.

Savoy Hill British Broadcasting Company's London station (1923–32) in the Strand. Its call-sign was 2LO.

Savoy operas Another name for GILBERT AND SULLIVAN OPERAS, as produced at the Savoy theatre; see D'OYLY CARTE OPERA CO.

Savundra crash (1968). Collapse of the Fire, Auto and Marine Insurance Co., for his part in which Emil Savundra was given an 8-year prison sentence.

Sawyer, Bob Happy-go-lucky medical student who with his fellow medico Ben Allen figures in the final episodes of Dickens's *Pickwick Papers*.

Saxifraga Large genus that includes many kinds of rock plant; the best known is *S. umbrosa*, London Pride.

Saxophone Musical instrument invented by Adolph Sax.

Saxons Teutonic invaders from north-west Germany who, from the 5th century AD, settled in Essex, Middlesex, Sussex and Wessex.

Saxony Former kingdom and province of Germany, capital Dresden. Half the kingdom was given to Prussia in 1815 and, with the Duchy of Anhalt, became the *Land* of Saxony-Anhalt, now in Eastern Germany. Lower Saxony, capital Hannover, is a *Land*, and was formed from Hannover, Brunswick and Oldenburg.

Sayings of Christ Brief statements attributed to Christ in some fragments of papyrus found at OXYRHYNCHUS in Egypt in 1897 and 1903. The manuscripts date to the 3rd century, but the sayings themselves may have been first written down in the 1st or 2nd centuries.

Scala, La (1778). Milan opera-house, one of the largest in the world.

'Scandal in Bohemia, A' (1891). First of many Sherlock HOLMES short stories to be published in the *Strand Magazine*.

Scanderbeg Turkish name of a 15th-century Albanian patriot who successfully rebelled against the Ottoman Turks and held out against them until his death. (Corruption of Iskander Beg, i.e. Lord Alexander.)

Scapa Flow Britain's chief naval base in the Orkney Islands, until it was closed in 1957, and the scene of the scuttling of the German fleet in 1919. (Pronounced skap'a.)

Scapin Ingenious and unscrupulous valet in Molière's comedy, *Les Fourberies* ('trickeries') *de Scapin* (1671).

Scaramouche Spanish 'don' dressed in black, the cowardly braggart of the COMMEDIA DELL'ARTE, constantly belaboured by Harlequin. (Italian *scaramuccia*, 'skirmish'.)

Scarface Al Capone Most notorious of the Chicago gang-leaders in the Prohibition days; he was not brought to justice until 1931 when BIG BILL THOMPSON's reign ended, and then only on an income-tax charge, for which he was given a 10-year prison sentence.

Scarlet Letter, The (1850). Novel by Nathaniel Hawthorne about 17th-century Boston. The title refers to the red letter A which the heroine, Hester Prynne, is condemned to wear because of her adultery. Her husband devotes himself to mercilessly tracking down the clergyman who had seduced her, and is shown in the process to be the greater sinner of the two.

Scarlet Pimpernel, The (1905). Novel by the Hungarian-born English writer, Baroness Orczy, in which Sir Percy Blakeney, to outward appearance a brainless fop, is the intrepid and 'demned elusive' Scarlet Pimpernel, who rescues victims of the French Revolution and smuggles them to England. There were many sequels.

Scarlet Woman Term of abuse for the Roman Catholic Church, still used by some extreme Protestants (e.g. in Ulster); derived from the 'Mother of Harlots' described in Revelation 17:1–6, who probably symbolized Imperial Rome.

Scarpia, Baron Villain of TOSCA.

Scarteen Black and Tans, The An Irish foxhunting pack with kennels at Scarteen near Knocklong, Tipperary, which hunts country on the Limerick–Tipperary border. It has been in the hands of the Ryan family for over 200 years, with the same strain of hounds, which have a characteristic bay.

Schadenfreude Malicious enjoyment of the discomfiture of others. (German.)

Scheduled Castes See UNTOUCHABLES.

Scheherazade Daughter of the Vizier of the Indies who marries the Shah of an unspecified country. He, after discovering his first wife's infidelity, has sworn to marry a new wife each day and strangle her next morning. Scheherazade, by telling her stories (the ARABIAN NIGHTS) by instalments, always breaking off each night before the denouement, retains the Shah's interest for 1,001 nights, after which he cancels his threat. (Pronounced shi-heer-é-zahd'é.)

Scheherazade (1) Orchestral suite by Rimsky-Korsakov. (2) Ballet set to this by Fokine. (See previous entry.)

Schicklgruber Name borne by Adolf Hitler's illegitimate father, until he proved that his real name was Hitler; used in derision of Adolf by early political opponents.

Schick test Skin test to determine whether a patient is immune to diphtheria.

Schipperke Small tailless dog with smooth black coat, originally developed in Flanders as a barge watch-dog. (From Dutch *schipper*, 'boatman'; pronounced skip'er-ke or ship'er-ke.)

Schizostylis Genus name of the kaffir lily.

Schlegel-Tieck prize (1964). Award of £2,000 for the best translation into English of a 20th-century German work; administered by the Society of Authors and the Translators' Association.

Schneider Trophy (1913). International race for seaplanes. In 1931 Britain, after setting up several world speed records in it, won the trophy outright by 3 successive victories with Supermarines. (Founded by a Frenchman, Jacques Schneider.)

Scholar-Gypsy, The (1853). Matthew Arnold's poem of a legendary Oxford student who joined the gypsies.

Scholasticism (1) Doctrines of the SCHOOLMEN.

(2) Unimaginative emphasis on the trivial in teaching theological dogma and tradition.

Schönbrunn (1696). Rococo royal palace in a park on the outskirts of Vienna.

Schöne Müllerin, Die (1823). Schubert's cycle of songs about a miller's love for a girl who has been spirited away by a mysterious huntsman; the 20 songs are held together by the sound of the mill stream heard in the accompaniment. Also known as the *Müllerliede* (miller songs), especially as they were written by a Wilhelm Müller. (German, 'the fair maid of the mill'.)

School for Scandal, The (1777). R. B. Sheridan's comedy in which, amid various love intrigues and backbiting gossip, the rich Sir Oliver Surface discovers that, of his 2 nephews, Joseph is only after his money and the reckless Charles has at least some good points.

Schoolmen (1100–1500). Philosophers and theologians of Western Europe who tried to reconcile Aristotle with the Bible, reason with faith. Of these the greatest were Abélard (see HÉLOÏSE), Albertus Magnus, Aquinas (see THOMISM), Duns Scotus and Ockham (see OCCAM'S RAZOR). In the 14th century the Schoolmen descended to trivial disputation (see SCHOLAS-TICISM), and disappeared with the coming of the Renaissance.

School of Oriental and African Studies (1917). Constituent college of London University, opened as a central language school for officers of the civil and military services posted to Asia or Africa; now an institution covering all major aspects in the study of Asia and Africa, particularly languages.

Schröder Professor Holder of the chair of German at Cambridge.

Schuhplattler Tirolean and Bavarian traditional courtship dance, in which the dancer slaps thigh, buttock and knee to LÄNDLER-style music.

Schuman plan (1950). Plan which led to the formation of the EUROPEAN COAL AND STEEL COMMUNITY in 1952, and so to the Common Market. (Robert Schuman, French Foreign Minister.)

Schweich lectures (1908). Lectures on biblical archaeology, given under the auspices of the British Academy.

Schweik in the Second World War (1943). Brecht's play using the hero of Hašek's novel, the GOOD SOLDIER SCHWEIK.

Science and Health with Key to the Scriptures (1875). Scripture of the Christian Scientists, frequently revised by its author, Mrs Eddy, the founder of the sect.

Science Research Council (1965). A body which took over from the Department of Scientific and Industrial Research the Royal Greenwich Observatory, space research and the National Institute for Research in Nuclear Science.

Scientology (1955). Business (later 'church') founded in East Grinstead (but registered in California) by L. Ron Hubbard, an American science-fiction writer, who is said to have visited Heaven and to believe in a world conspiracy of psychiatrists, who torture patients in mental homes; in 1970 he claimed to have severed connections with the organization. Scientologists pay high fees, increasing at each stage, for instruction and treatment which 'transforms their lives'; they have to cut themselves off from their families and are forbidden to criticize their authoritarian instructions under pain of dire penalties.

Scilla Genus of squills or wild hyacinths, including the common English bluebell; see CAMPANULA.

Scipio march, The March from Handel's opera *Scipione*, to which the words of William Cowper's 'The loss of the ROYAL GEORGE' were later set.

Scone Stone Ancient Scottish coronation stone taken by Edward I from Scone Castle (near Perth) and placed beneath Edward the Confessor's Chair in Westminster Abbey; removed by a Scottish nationalist in 1950 but returned a few months later. (Pronounced skoon.)

Scopes trial (1925). Deliberately sought test case in which a schoolmaster, J. T. Scopes of Dayton, Tennessee, was accused of teaching Darwinism contrary to Tennessee law, and fined $100 (later remitted).

Scorpio Scorpion, 8th of the constellations of the Zodiac, between Libra and Sagittarius; the sun enters it about 21 October. Astrologers claim that those born under this sign may be masterful, possessive and intuitive.

Scorton Arrow (1673). Silver arrow, the trophy in an archery contest held in Yorkshire, presented to the first to hit a 3-inch bull at 100 yd. He becomes Captain and chooses next year's venue. (Traditionally first presented by Queen Elizabeth I, lost, and found later at Scorton, near Richmond, Yorkshire.)

Scotch Cup (1959). International curling championship.

Scotch porridge case (1969). RACE RELATIONS BOARD's ruling that an offence had been committed by an Eastbourne citizen advertising for a Scotch cook who could make porridge in the traditional Scotch way.

Scotch woodcock Scrambled eggs on toast, with anchovy paste.

Scotland Yard Whitehall headquarters from 1890 of the London Metropolitan Police, and later also of the CRIMINAL INVESTIGATION DEPARTMENT; name retained to cover New Scotland Yard (opposite the House of Commons) and new buildings (1966) in Broadway near by.

Scots Guards (1660). Third regiment of the GUARDS DIVISION; they wear their buttons in threes, and have no plume.

Scots-Irish US name for Ulstermen.

'Scots, wha hae' (1793). Scotsman's national anthem, composed by Robert Burns, beginning: 'Scots, wha hae wi' Wallace bled,/ Scots wham Bruce has aften led, / Welcome to your gory bed, / Or to victorie.'

Scott expedition (1910–12). Antarctic expedition which reached the South Pole (shortly after Amundsen) and in which Captain Scott and his 4 companions lost their lives.

Scott Holland lecture Lecture delivered at King's College, London, on a religious subject.

Scottish Blackface Widely distributed long-wool breed of hill sheep.

Scottish Division, The (1968). One of the 6 infantry divisions, formed from the HIGHLAND and LOWLAND BRIGADES.

Scottish Nationalist Party (1928). Movement for Scottish Home Rule, which has had the support of Scottish writers such as Hugh MacDiarmid, Compton Mackenzie, etc.

Scottish TV Commercial programme-contracting company for Scotland.

Scott-Moncrieff prize (1964). An award of £1,500 for the best translation into English of a 20th-century French work; administered by the Society of Authors and the Translators' Association.

Scottsboro trials (1931–2). (USA) Trials of a group of young blacks found in a railway truck with some poor-white prostitutes. To save what there was of their reputation the women accused them of rape; the men were given death sentences commuted on appeal to long terms of imprisonment, but in the face of public outcry were eventually released. (Town in Alabama.)

Scourge of God, The Name for Attila, King of the Huns, who swept through the Roman Empire in the 5th century.

Scouse Liverpudlian, originally a nautical nickname of long standing. (From *lobscouse*, some kind of Lancashire hotpot.)

SCR Initials used for (1) Senior Common Room, a room set aside as an after-dinner meeting place for teachers at a school or for Fellows at Oxford University; (2) Senior Combination Room, the Cambridge term for (1).

Scrabble Spelling game in which words are built up on a squared board with lettered counters having scoring values graded according to frequency of occurrence.

Scrap of Paper, The Bethmann-Hollweg's description (1914) of the Treaty of London (1839) by which Prussia, Austria, Britain and France guaranteed the neutrality of Belgium; he was protesting against Britain's declaration of war when Germany invaded Belgium.

Screwtape Letters, The (1941). Serio-comic book by C. S. Lewis in which Screwtape, a devil, teaches a subordinate how to lead human beings to damnation.

Scriblerus Club (1713). Group of writers, led by Pope, John Arbuthnot, Swift, Gay and Congreve, who met to discuss the pedantry and poor literary taste of their day. One by-product was the memoirs of the fictious Martinus Scriblerus, who had read not wisely but too much, and who embodied all they deplored.

Scripps–Howard press First chain of US newspapers, started by the Scripps family with the *Cleveland Press* (1878) and joined by R. W. Howard of UP (also founded by Scripps) in 1920. One of its chief acquisitions was the *New York World Telegram*.

Scriveners, Worshipful Company of (1617). LIVERY COMPANY, originally a guild of clerks who prepared legal documents. Membership is confined to the legal profession, and all notaries practising in or near the City are Freemen of it.

Scrooge, Ebenezer Supreme miser and misanthrope who in Dickens's *A Christmas Carol* (1843) becomes a reformed character after the ghost of his deceased partner visits him on Christmas Eve and he has visions of his past and his probable future if he does not change his ways.

Scrophulariaceae Snapdragon (antirrhinum) family, which includes many common wildflowers and garden plants, e.g. foxglove, speedwell (veronica), mullein (verbascum), toadflax. (Named after a plant once used as a remedy for scrofula.)

Scrubs, The Old lags' name for Wormwood Scrubs prison, in Acton, West London.

Scrutiny (1932–53). Literary review, the sounding-board of the F. R. Leavis or Cambridge school of critics which handed down ukases on what one should read and how. Their oddly assorted twin idols were George Eliot and D. H. Lawrence.

Scuba US name for the aqualung. (Initials of Self-Contained Underwater Breathing Apparatus.)

Scutari Former Italian name of (1) Turkish city of Usküdar; (2) Albanian town of Shkodër.

Scylla and Charybdis In Greek legend, the 2 monsters who sat on either side of the Straits of Messina between Italy and Sicily, and destroyed any ships that came too close. Hence 'between Scylla and Charybdis' means 'between the Devil and the deep blue sea'.

Sea-Beggars, The Sixteenth-century Protestant Dutch sailors who raided Spanish shipping and plundered Roman Catholic churches, putting new heart into the struggle to throw off Spanish domination of the Netherlands. (French *Les Gueux*, 'beggars', a name given to the Dutch Calvinists who in 1566 signed a 'Compromise', a pledge to drive out the Spaniards.)

Seaby Standard catalogue of coins and medals, issued by the London firm, B. A. Seaby Ltd.

Sea Cadet Corps (1942). Royal Navy's voluntary youth organization for boys aged 14–18 likely to be interested in a career at sea.

Sea-green Incorruptible, The Carlyle's name for Robespierre, who in the French Revolution kept to his own democratic principles, refusing to compromise with the more moderate Girondins or the terrorists, and thus making so many enemies that he ended on the scaffold.

Seagull, The (1896). Chekhov's play of the young writer Trepliov's jealousy of the successful Trigorin who walks off with, but then abandons, Nina, the girl he loves. She returns and compares herself with the seagull Trepliov had shot earlier in the play and given to her as a token of his ruined ambitions after the humiliating failure of his first play.

Sea-island cotton Fine quality long-staple cotton, originally cultivated on islands off the coast of South Carolina and Georgia, USA.

Sea King Royal Navy Westland helicopter equipped with anti-submarine weapons and sonar.

Sea Lion German code name for the proposed invasion of southern England in 1940.

Séamas Irish name equivalent to James. (Pronounced shay'mas.)

Seán Irish form of the name John. (Pronounced shawn.)

Sea of Tranquillity Area where the first two men landed on the moon, from APOLLO II.

Searchlight Tattoo Spectacular pageant by the British armed forces, with massed military bands, now held each August at the White City, London, in aid of Service charities. It developed from the Aldershot Tattoo of the 1920s at Rushmore Arena, at which searchlights played a prominent part.

Sears Roebuck The largest mail-order firm in the world, with headquarters at Chicago; since the 1920s it has also owned a chain of retail stores.

Season, The London season which begins in May with the Royal Academy's Private View Day and QUEEN CHARLOTTE'S BALL, and ends with COWES WEEK in August.

Seasons, The (1726–30). James Thomson's long poem in blank verse, chiefly notable as the first example of nature description 'on location' instead of through the study window, based on intimate knowledge of his native Teviotdale in Roxburghshire, Scotland.

Seaton Delaval Hall Last country house to be designed by Sir John Vanbrugh, near Whitley Bay on the Northumberland coast.

Seawanhaka Cup (1895). International race for 6-metre yachts. (Cup presented by the Seawanhaka-Corinthian Yacht Club of Oyster Bay, Long Island, New York.)

Sebring (1952). US 5-mile car-racing circuit, 160 miles from Miami, Florida, where a 12-hour international endurance race is held each year, one of the events comprising the Sports-GT championship.

Secam The French system of colour TV.

Second Coalition (1799). Alliance of Britain, Austria and Russia which drove the French out of Italy, Switzerland and the German states but disintegrated when Russia and Austria quarrelled and was ended by Moreau's victory over Austria in 1800 at HOHENLINDEN.

Second Coming The return of Christ to earth; see ADVENTISTS.

Second Commandment 'Thou shalt not make . . . any graven image' (Exod. 20:4–6). Regarded as part of the First Commandment by Roman Catholics.

Second Empire (1852–70). In French history the reign of Emperor Napoleon III which intervened between the Second and Third Republics, and ended with the French defeat in the FRANCO-PRUSSIAN WAR.

Second Front Name given to the concept of an attack on Europe by the Western Allies after the fall of France in 1940; Stalin never ceased to press for this, regarding the North African campaign as a minor operation, and suspecting that the West was content to watch the Germans and Russians destroy each other.

Second International (1) Workingmen's Association formed in Paris (1889); it lost influence when it failed to unite Socialist parties to prevent World War I. (2) Federation of non-revolutionary Socialist political parties formed after that war (Socialist International).

Second Mrs Tanqueray, The (1893). Pinero's immensely popular play about a woman whose husband, despite his love for her, cannot overcome his suspicions about her past, leading to revelation, recrimination and Mrs Tanqueray's suicide.

Second Reading (Parliament) Main stage in the the passing of an Act. The House debates the principles of the Bill which, if the majority so decides, is referred to a committee of the whole House for detailed consideration, clause by clause, and amendment (the Committee stage). See THIRD READING.

Second Republic (1848–52). In French history, the republic set up after the revolution which deposed Louis Philippe, KING OF THE FRENCH; it ended when President Louis Napoleon became the Emperor Napoleon III (see SECOND EMPIRE).

Second Sea Lord A post combined with that of Chief of Naval Personnel, under the Secretary of State for Defence.

Secret Agent, The (1907). Joseph Conrad's story of East End anarchists; Stevie, who is somewhat simple, is persuaded by his brother-in-law Verloc, an agent provocateur, to blow up Greenwich Observatory, but succeeds only in blowing himself up. Verloc's wife kills her husband and then commits suicide.

Secret Doctrine, The (1888). Bible of the theosophists, written by Mme Blavatsky; see THEOSOPHICAL SOCIETY.

Securicor British private security corps, dating from the 1930s, reorganized 1956, and since 1960 undertaking the transport of cash. It is now by far the largest of these organizations. The men are armed only with night sticks and protected by goggles. Among their services is the supply of women to watch for shoplifters.

Security Council Supreme body of the United Nations, comprising 5 permanent members (USA, USSR, UK, France and China, any of which can veto a decision of the rest of the council) and 10 members elected for 2-year terms.

Sedan (1870). Defeat of the French in the FRANCO-PRUSSIAN WAR; Napoleon III was taken prisoner. (French frontier fortress in the Ardennes; the Germans again broke through there in 1940.)

Seddon murder case (1912). Trial of Frederick Seddon and his wife, charged with murdering their aged lodger, Miss Barrow, by poison. Seddon was executed but his wife, defended by Marshall Hall, was acquitted.

Sedgemoor, Battle of (1685). Engagement which ended MONMOUTH'S REBELLION. (Marsh near Bridgwater, Somerset.)

Sedleian Professor Holder of the chair of Natural Philosophy at Oxford.

Sedley, Jos In Thackeray's VANITY FAIR a spineless retired Collector from India, whom Becky SHARP cheats out of his money.

Sedum Genus name of the stonecrops.

Seebohm report (1968). Report which recommended that major local authorities should establish unified departments combining children's and welfare services with some of the social services of the health, education and housing departments; also a new central government department to oversee them. It commented on the relative neglect of the very old, the under-fives, the physically and mentally handicapped, disturbed adolescents, and 'the flotsam and jetsam of society'.

Segrave Trophy Award made annually by the Royal Automobile Club to the British subject who had done most to demonstrate the possibilities of transport by air, land or water. (In memory of Sir Henry Segrave, who put up car and motor-boat speed records; died 1930.)

Sejm The Polish legislative assembly. (Polish, 'assembly'; pronounced saym.)

Selborne See NATURAL HISTORY AND ANTIQUITIES OF SELBORNE.

Select Committee (Parliament) Committee appointed for a specific purpose laid down in terms of reference.

Selene Greek moon-goddess, sister of Helios and Eos; the Roman Luna. Later she became identified with Artemis. (Pronounced sel-ee'nee.)

Seleucids (312–64 BC). Dynasty of kings of Syria founded by Seleucus I, one of Alexander the Great's generals; at times they ruled over Mesopotamia, but lost it after transferring their capital to Antioch.

Self-Denying Ordinance (1645). The measure under which the ROUNDHEAD members of both Houses of Parliament resigned their military commissions to permit the formation of the NEW MODEL ARMY under competent leadership.

Self-Help (1864). Book written by Samuel

Smiles (1812–1904) which was successful at home and sold well abroad. It promotes the belief that self-help is the root of mental and moral well-being. Smiles was an advocate of political and social reform. The opening sentence of this work is: 'Heaven helps those who help themselves.'

Seljuk Turks First wave of Turks to move west from Turkestan, in the 11th century conquering Persia and Anatolia, and taking over the temporal powers of the ABBASID Caliphs of Baghdad; they are the 'infidel' Saracens in Palestine against whom the crusades were sent. At the end of the 13th century they were displaced by the OTTOMAN TURKS. (Named after the first ruler; pronounced sel-jook'.)

Sellotape Proprietary name for an adhesive tape. One of the great inventions of the 20th century.

Semele (1) In Greek mythology, the mother of Dionysus by Zeus, who was resurrected from the Underworld each spring. (2) Dramatic cantata by Handel, containing the beautiful aria 'Where'er you walk'. (Pronounced sem'é-lee.)

Semiramis (1) Historical Queen of Assyria of whom little is known except that she wielded great influence. (2) A legendary version of (1), later identified with ISHTAR, to whom was attributed the building of Babylon and other cities. She is the heroine of several plays and of Rossini's opera *Semiramide*. (Pronounced se-mir'a-mis.)

Semites (1) Peoples, traditionally descended from SHEM, who speak SEMITIC LANGUAGES. (2) Used (incorrectly) as a synonym for the Jews, as in 'anti-Semitism'.

Semitic languages Group of languages spoken in the Middle East and adjacent countries; they include Akkadian (Assyrian, Babylonian), Hebrew, Aramaic, Phoenician, and Amharic (in Abyssinia). They share a neat system whereby basic ideas are expressed by 3-consonant roots which, modified by vowel changes and prefixes, express all shades of derivative meanings, e.g. k-t-b ('writing') forms, in Arabic, *kitab*, 'book'; *kataba*, 'he wrote'; *maktub*, 'letter' *maktab*, 'office', etc.

Semon lecture (1913). Annual lecture on a medical subject, given at London University.

Sempervivum Genus name of the house leek.

Senior, The Familiar name for the United Service Club.

Senior Common (Combination) Room See SCR.

Senior Service tournament (1962). Stroke-play open golf tournament with prize fund totalling £13,000. (Sponsored by Gallahers, makers of Senior Service cigarettes.)

Senior Wrangler Until 1909 the title at Cambridge University of the man who came out top in the Mathematical Tripos. The other Wranglers were ranged in order of merit, instead of in classes as today, and the Wooden Spoon was presented to the unfortunate man who came last.

Sense and Sensibility Jane Austen's novel; see DASHWOOD FAMILY.

Sentimental Journey through France and Italy, A (1768). Sterne's unfinished account of his travels (he died before he reached the description of his experiences in Italy). He wrote it under the name of YORICK. See also SMELFUNGUS.

Senussi Muslim puritan sect in Libya, founded in the 19th century by Muhammad es-Senussi; they led several revolts against Italian rule before and after World War I. Their leader became the first king of Libya in 1951.

Seoirse Irish name equivalent to George.

Seosamh Irish name equivalent to Joseph.

Sephardim Jews of southern European, North African and Middle Eastern (excluding Israel) descent, especially of Spanish and Portuguese descent, who, up until this century, spoke Ladino, a form of 15th-century Spanish, as their lingua franca. See ASHKENAZIM. (Sepharad in Obad 20; pronounced séfard'im.)

Sepoy Mutiny Name (chiefly US) for the INDIAN MUTINY.

September Massacres (2–5 September 1792). In the French Revolution, the wholesale butchering of a large number of political prisoners, in Paris and some provincial towns, suspected of disloyalty to the republic; the result of panic after the Prussians had reached Verdun.

Septuagint Greek translation of the Old Testament and Apocrypha, traditionally begun by Palestinian Jews working at Alexandria in the 3rd century BC, but not completed until early Christian times. (Latin *septuaginta*, 70; according to legend, the Pentateuch was translated by 72 men in 72 days.)

Sequoia Coniferous trees, the redwoods of California, named after Sequoiah, inventor of the Cherokee alphabet.

Seraphim First mentioned in Isaiah 6:2, as having 6 wings; later regarded as the highest order of angels, grouped with CHERUBIM and Thrones. (Plural of *seraph*, perhaps 'fiery serpent'.)

Serapis Egyptian god; see APIS. (Pronounced ser'a-pis.)

Serbo-Croat South Slavonic languages spoken in Yugoslavia (in Serbia, Bosnia, Dalmatia, Croatia), closely akin to SLOVENIAN. (Pronounced sėr'bo-kroh'at.)

Serbonian bog Place mentioned in Milton's PARADISE LOST: 'A gulf profound as that Serbonian bog / ... Where armies whole have sunk.' It was, historically, a bituminous lake on the Egyptian coast in which part of a Persian army was swallowed up in 350 BC.

Serena Professor Holder of the chair of Italian at Oxford.

Serendip Old name for Sri Lanka. *The Three Princes of Serendip* is a fairy-story in which the princes were always finding delightful things by sheer chance; from it Horace Walpole coined the useful word 'serendipity', the faculty of doing this.

Seretse Khama case (1948). Seretse Khama, then a Bamangwato chief in Bechuanaland, having married an English wife against the wishes of his uncle and Regent, Tshekedi Khama, was exiled but allowed to return in

1956. (Subsequently he became the first President of the Republic of Botswana.)

Serialism Theory of time advanced by J. W. Dunne, aircraft designer, mathematician and philosopher, in his *An Experiment with Time* (1927) and later books. By inducing friends to keep bedside notebooks for instant record of dreams, he showed that many people dream of future events. This he attributed to the contents of time being as real as those of space, and built round this hypothesis a mathematical theory of a 4-dimensional space–time which individuals observe in sleep and could, but for habit, observe when awake.

Serjeant Musgrave's Dance (1959). A play by John Arden in which 19th-century army deserters react to the horrors of war.

Sermon on the Mount, The Summary of the core of Christ's teachings, given at length in Matthew 5–7, more briefly in Luke 6:20–49. It includes the BEATITUDES, the Lord's Prayer and many of the most familiar phrases from the New Testament: turn the other cheek; let not thy right hand know . . .; lay not up for yourselves treasure upon earth; God and Mammon; consider the lilies of the field; sufficient unto the day . . .; judge not, that ye be not judged; motes and beams; pearls before swine; bread and stone; and many more.

Serpentine, The Lake in Hyde Park, London, which provides boating, skating, fishing and, for the hardy few, year-round bathing.

Sesame and Lilies (1865). Popular work by John Ruskin consisting of lectures on reading, education and the role of educated women in society.

Sesostris Greek name for the Pharaoh Rameses II, and for 3 kings of a much earlier Egyptian dynasty.

Sestos and Abydos Towns on opposite shores of the Hellespont; see HERO AND LEANDER.

Set Aboriginal God of Egypt who became god of night and evil and killed OSIRIS; portrayed in art with a snout and donkey's ears. The peasantry of Upper Egypt remained faithful to him despite the introduction of the HORUS and RA cults. The Greek equivalent was Typhon.

Settebello, The Italian luxury train running daily Milan–Bologna–Florence–Rome–Naples; first-class only, all seats reserved.

Settlement Day (Stock Exchange) See ACCOUNT DAY.

Seuss, Dr Pen-name of Theodor Seuss Geisel (born 1904), author and illustrator of amusing and popular children's books.

Seven against Thebes, The (467 BC). Aeschylus' play about a legendary war in which 7 Argive heroes fight to restore the rightful King of Thebes. The rival claimants to the throne are the sons of OEDIPUS and, under the influence of his curse on them, fight in single combat in which both are killed.

Seven Bishops, Trial of the (1688). Acquittal of the Archbishop of Canterbury and 6 others, charged with seditious libel for opposing James II's DECLARATION OF INDULGENCE to Roman Catholics; a prime cause of the GLORIOUS REVOLUTION.

Seven Deadly Sins Classified by early Christians as pride, covetousness, lust, anger, gluttony, envy and sloth.

Seven Lamps of Architecture, The (1849). John Ruskin's discussion of the 7 principles of architecture and his defence of the Gothic style.

Seven Pillars of Wisdom, The (1926). T. E. Lawrence's description of his desert campaign against the Turks in World War I; he also wrote an abridged version, *Revolt in the Desert* (1927).

Seven Sages, The Name given in ancient times to Thales of Miletus (the founder of Greek philosophy), Solon (the lawgiver of Athens) and other wise men of Greece, to whom some of the traditional Greek mottoes (such as 'know thyself', 'nothing in excess') were attributed, in most cases erroneously.

Seven Seas, The The North and South Atlantic, North and South Pacific, Indian, Arctic and Antarctic Oceans.

Seven Sisters, The Translation of an ancient Greek name for the PLEIADES.

Seven Sleepers, The Seven legendary Christians of Ephesus who, mewed up in a cave at a Roman Emperor's command in the 3rd century, fell into a miraculous sleep which lasted until the 5th century. Discovered by chance, they awoke, told their tale, and fell dead. The story, apparently of Syrian origin, is also found in the Koran.

17th Amendment (1913). Amendment to the US Constitution which enacted that Senators should be elected by popular vote.

17th Congress (USSR) Congress held in 1934, in the USSR, at which Stalin admitted that the peasantry had slaughtered half the country's livestock in protest against collectivization.

17th Parallel (of latitude) Boundary fixed between North and South Vietnam (1954).

Seventh Avenue Heart of the fashion and garment district in mid-Manhattan, New York.

Seventh Commandment 'Thou shalt not commit adultery' (Exod 20:14). To Roman Catholics this is the Sixth Commandment.

Seventh Day Adventists (1863). Largest of the American ADVENTIST sects, founded by William Miller after Christ had failed to appear in 1843 as he had prophesied. They still believe that the Second Coming is imminent, and keep Saturday very strictly as their Sabbath.

Seven Types of Ambiguity (1930). Book written by William Empson, aged 21, giving a detailed analysis of the rich store of verbal nuances, allusions, double meanings, etc. to be found in English poetry.

Seven Weeks War (1866). Prussian attack on Austria to secure leadership of the NORTH GERMAN CONFEDERATION. The Austrians were defeated at SADOWA but were more successful against Prussia's Italian allies.

Seven Wonders of the World Various lists were given in ancient times, which usually included the Hanging Gardens of Babylon, the Colossus of Rhodes, the Mausoleum, the Pharos (lighthouse) at Alexandria, the Pyramids, the Statue of Jupiter by Phidias, and the Temple of Diana at Ephesus.

Seven Years War (1756–63). War precipitated by the King of Prussia, Frederick the Great, in which he triumphed, against all expectation, over France, Austria and Russia, England, which had subsidized him, took the opportunity while France was thus engaged to strengthen the foundations of its dominion in Canada and India through Wolfe and Clive.

Severn bore Tidal bore producing a wave of up to 5 ft in height in the lower reaches of the River Severn at the spring tides.

Severn Wildfowl Trust See SLIMBRIDGE.

Sèvres Products of a French porcelain factory founded at VINCENNES and moved (1756) under royal patronage to Sèvres, south-west Paris, where it still operates today. The characteristic wares were decorated with panels of landscapes, flowers, exotic birds, etc. on the famous coloured grounds of green, *bleu du roi*, *rose Pompadour*, etc. At first soft, and from 1769 hard, paste porcelain was made. Their styles were imitated by many English factories, and extensively faked.

Sèvres Treaty (1920). Post-war treaty with Turkey which Mustapha Kemal (Atatürk) refused to ratify and was replaced by the LAUS-ANNE TREATY.

Seward's Folly Alaska, the seemingly valueless territory which Secretary of State William Henry Seward succeeded in buying from Russia (1867) for 2 cents an acre only 30 years before the Klondike gold rush.

's Gravenhage Dutch name of The Hague.

Shackleton British long-range maritime-reconnaisance aircraft, later fitted with an auxiliary jet engine to increase range; succeeded by NIMROD AIRCRAFT.

Shadrach, Meshach and Abed-nego Three Jews who refused to worship the golden image set up by Nebuchadnezzar, and emerged unscathed from the fiery furnace to which he consigned them (Dan 3:12–30). (Pronounced shay'drak, mee'shak, a-bed-nee'go.)

SHAEF Initials used for Supreme Headquarters, Allied Expeditionary Force, established in London early in 1944 under General Eisenhower to prepare for D-Day.

Shaftesbury Society (1844). Charitable society, with London headquarters, which provides residential schools for physically handicapped children, hostels for young victims of muscular dystrophy, and other such institutions. Formerly called the Ragged School Union. (Founded by the 7th Earl of Shaftesbury.)

Shaggy Dog Stories (1925). Series of surrealist stories of English origin, in vogue in the 1950s. Characteristic is that of 2 elephants facing away from each other, feet together, motionless. A passing big-game hunter asked them what they were at and was told: 'Ssh! We're playing bookends.' A cricketing horse who batted well but when asked to bowl protested, 'Who ever heard of a horse bowling?'; a horse which claimed to have won the Derby (but lied, he was second); and the plutonium atom who said to a uranium atom 'Have the next neutron on me', which he did, and blew up, are typical. (Named from a long and rather pointless story about a lost dog.)

Shakers, The (1747). Sect which seceded from the Quakers and formed a communistic, celibate settlement near Albany, New York State. They believed in a male and a female Christ, the latter being 'Mother Anne' who joined them from Manchester in 1758. By the 1860s the movement had lost popularity, although the last Eldress died only in 1990. (So called because they trembled in religious ecstasy.)

Shallow, Justice Fool of a JP. always boasting of his imaginary exploits, who appears in Shakespeare's *Merry Wives* with his cousin Slender, a country bumpkin. He also figures in *Henry IV Part II* with his fellow justice Silence.

Shamanism Belief that the world is governed by good and evil spirits which can be propitiated through a *Shaman* (witch-doctor). The name was first applied to the beliefs prevailing among the Ural-Altaic peoples of Siberia, and then to the Indians of north-west America and to others.

(Word of Slavonic origin; pronounced sham'anizm.)

Shambles, The Medieval street in the centre of York which has been associated with butchers for a thousand years.

Shamrock Name of the 5 yachts with which Sir Thomas Lipton made successive attempts to win the AMERICA'S CUP (1899–1930).

Shang dynasty (16th–11th centuries BC). Earliest Chinese dynasty of which we have any record; ritual bronze vessels and jade work had already reached a high standard of artistry. See ANYANG.

Shangri La The name given by James Hilton in his novel *Lost Horizon* (1933) to a mythical Himalayan Utopia.

Shannon Airport Transatlantic airport, west of Limerick, on the Shannon estuary, Co. Clare, Ireland.

Shans Mongoloid people of Burma, akin to the Siamese, who live in the Shan States bordering on China, Laos and Siam. (Pronounced shahnz.)

Shape of Things to Come, The (1933). H. G. Wells's novel giving a glimpse of a science-dominated, aseptic space age of the future.

Sharp, Becky Adventuress of Thackeray's VANITY FAIR. A governess, she secretly marries her employer's son, Rawdon CRAWLEY, who is disinherited; she, however, is kept by Lord Steyne until forced abroad to live by her wits. There she meets again the man she first set her cap at, Joseph SEDLEY, her school friend's rich brother, and ruins him.

Sharpeville shootings (March 1960). Shooting by Transvaal police of 72 Pan-Africanist demonstrators against the pass-laws. The banning of the AFRICAN NATIONAL CONGRESS followed this incident.

Shaston Town in Thomas Hardy's Wessex novels, meant to represent Shaftesbury.

Shavian Adjective used in reference to George Bernard Shaw.

Shaw, T. E. Name T. E. Lawrence assumed when he joined the Tank Corps (1923), and subsequently adopted by deed poll. See J. H. ROSS.

Shaw's Corner G. B. Shaw's home at Ayot St Lawrence, Hertfordshire, from 1906 till his death, preserved by the NATIONAL TRUST.

Shaymen, The Nickname of the Halifax Town football team, which plays at Shay Ground.

She Rider Haggard's novel; see AYESHA.

Sheba, Queen of Queen of Sabaea (the Yemen), who visited Solomon to see for herself whether the stories of his wisdom and riches were true (1 Kgs 10:1–13); according to Ethiopian tradition she bore him a son, David or Menelek, ancestor of the Abyssinians.

Sheffield plate (1743). Wares made in silver-plated copper (i.e. with sheets of sterling silver fused to a copper base), an English invention intended to provide a 'poor man's silver' but now highly prized. Many marks (e.g. 'Sheffield plated') on imitations were designed to mislead.

Sheila (Shelagh) Australian name for women from a very common name of many Irish women who were transported.

Sheldonian Sheldonian Theatre, the Oxford University Senate House, designed by Wren. (Named after a 17th-century archbishop).

Shell See ROYAL DUTCH/SHELL.

Shell Chemicals (1959). Company now entirely independent from ROYAL DUTCH/SHELL.

Shell-Mex A merger formed by ROYAL DUTCH/SHELL and the Mexican Eagle company founded by Weetman Pearson.

Shell-Mex and BP A purely marketing subsidiary owned by ROYAL DUTCH/SHELL and BP jointly, and formed to sell petrol in Britain.

Shell Professor Holder of the chair of Chemical Engineering at Cambridge.

Shell Transport and Trading British parent company of ROYAL DUTCH/SHELL; there is a second, Dutch, parent.

Shelter (1966). Organization founded to enable people to get decent housing at fair rents, operating all over Britain. It raises funds, makes grants to housing associations and helps in slum-clearance projects.

Shem Eldest of Noah's sons, and traditional ancestor of the SEMITES.

'Shenandoah' Old capstan and windlass shanty with the words: 'Oh Shenandoah, I love your daughter; / Away, you rolling river.' The name is that of a famous Red Indian chief and of several rivers and a town called after him; but 'Shenandoah' and, later in the song, 'Missouri' were names arbitrarily chosen merely because they sounded well.

Shenyang Modern name of Mukden, former capital of Manchuria, now of the Liaoning Province of China.

Sheol Babylonian and Hebrew name signifying both Death personified and the abode of the dead, regarded as a dark hollow ('pit') under the earth. The word was often mistranslated as 'Hell' in the Authorized Version of the Old Testament. (Pronounced shee'ohl.)

Shepheard Hotel Famous hotel in Cairo which, as an exclusive rendezvous frequented by British imperialists, was burnt down in the Black Saturday riots of 1952.

Sheppard Cup (1929). British open rackets championship.

Shepperton Studios British Lion film studios near Staines, one of which was the largest in Europe.

Sherardian Professor Holder of the chair of Botany at Oxford.

Sheraton Name given to furniture resembling designs published by Thomas Sheraton (1751–1806), who did not himself make furniture. Characteristic are satinwood, designs inspired by NEOCLASSICISM, slender elegance, tapering legs, and a preference for straight lines.

Sherman Anti-Trust Act (1890). (USA) First trust-busting Act, which forbade every monopolist combination in restraint of trade. Courts, presidents and state legislation saw to it that it became and remained inoperative. (John Sherman, Republican politician.)

Sherpas Mongoloid mountain race of Nepal, who have provided guides and carriers for many Himalayan expeditions. Tensing Norkey, a Sherpa, was the first man to reach the summit of Everest (with Hillary), in 1953.

Sherry Familiar name of Richard Brinsley Sheridan (1751–1816), Irish playwright and politician.

Sherry Cobbler Name given to a variety of drinks based on sweet sherry, with added port, spirit or liqueur, and decorated with fruit.

Sherston's Progress (1928–36). Trilogy of fictionalized autobiography by Siegfried Sassoon: *Memoirs of a Fox-hunting Man, Memoirs of an Infantry Officer* and *Sherston's Progress*; they depict the life of an English country gentleman in war and peace.

Sherwood Forest Ancient royal forest, mainly in Nottinghamshire and associated with Robin Hood, of which patches still survive between Worksop and Nottingham.

She Stoops to Conquer (1773). Goldsmith's comedy in which the plot turns on 2 young men, Marlow and Hastings, misdirected by Tony LUMPKIN, mistaking Squire Hardcastle's house for an inn. See LIBERTY HALL.

Shetland pony Breed of small stocky hardy ponies, with long mane, tail and rough coat; also called Sheltie. (Originated in the Shetland Isles.)

Shi'ites (Shiahs) Members of one of the 2 major Muslim sects. They seceded from the orthodox SUNNITES because they do not recognize the authority of the Sunna or the first 3 Caliphs, regarding MOHAMMED'S son-in-law Ali (fourth Caliph) as the first. They are found mainly in Persia. (Arabic shi'ah, 'sect'.)

Shiloh (1) Town in Palestine, near Jerusalem, where the Ark of the Covenant was kept; Shiloh was destroyed by the Philistines. (2) Name for the Messiah. (Pronounced shy'lo.)

Shinar, Plain of Biblical name for Babylonia or Mesopotamia.

Shinto Chinese name for the Japanese religion of ancestor and nature worship, to which were later added Buddhism and reverence for the Mikado as the descendant of the sun-goddess. After the MEIJI RESTORATION Shinto became state-sponsored, nationalistic and militaristic, but it was deflated after World War II by the Emperor Hirohito's public renunciation of his divinity. ('Way of the gods'.)

Shipwrights, Worshipful Company of (1605). LIVERY COMPANY; it encourages technical education in the industry.

Shiraz rugs Rugs, similar to CAUCASIAN RUGS, made by the Kashkai nomads north-west of Shiraz, Persia. Diamond medallions are characteristic, and the red or blue grounds are rather garish. (Pronounced sheer-ahz'.)

Shire Midland breed of farm and cart horse, similar in colour to the Clydesdale but coarser in build.

Shire, The Peaceful, pleasant HOBBIT country, based on the author's recollections of an unspoilt country district in the West Midlands where he was brought up.

Shires, The Leicestershire and Northamptonshire, the leading fox-hunting counties, where the Quorn, Pytchley, Belvoir, Cottesmore and Fernie packs hunt.

Shirley (1849). Charlotte Brontë's novel set in Yorkshire at the time of the LUDDITE RIOTS, in which the heroine, Shirley Keeldar, is based on the author's sister Emily.

Shirley poppy Cultivated variety of wild poppy. (Named after Shirley Rectory, Croydon, where first evolved.)

Shkodër Albanian town, formerly known by its Italian name, Scutari.

Shock-Headed Peter See STRUWWELPETER.

Shogun Former title of the hereditary commander-in-chief of the Japanese army; see TOKUGAWA SHOGUNATE.

Sholem Aleichem Pen-name of Solomon J. Rabinowitz (1859–1916), Russian-born author of highly praised humorous Jewish stories. See FIDDLER ON THE ROOF. (Yiddish for 'Peace be with you', traditional greeting.)

Shop, The Former Royal Military Academy, Woolwich.

Shoreditch Former London metropolitan borough, since 1965 part of the borough of HACKNEY.

Shorthorn Most popular breed of beef cattle, from which Polled Shorthorns and Dairy Shorthorns have also been developed; red and white in varying proportions, or roan.

Short Parliament (1640). Four-week Parliament, the first convened by Charles I for 11 years, dismissed for being as stubborn as the ADDLED PARLIAMENT.

Shotover, Capt. See HEARTBREAK HOUSE.

Shoulder Arms (1918). Early Charlie Chaplin comedy about life in the trenches in World War I.

Show Boat (1) Edna Ferber's novel (1926) about a theatrical family founded by the owner of a Mississippi showboat. (2) Highly successful musical (1927) based on it by Oscar Hammerstein and Jerome Kern. (A river steamboat equipped as a travelling theatre to stage shows at stopping-places.)

Show Me State Nickname of Missouri. See 'MISSOURI, I'M FROM'.

Shrapnel (1793). Shrapnel shell was invented by Henry Shrapnel.

Shrewsbury cake Rich sweet biscuit, a speciality of Shrewsbury, Shropshire.

Shrine, The (1870). (USA) Short title of The Ancient Arabic Order of Nobles of the Mystic Shrine of North America, a group of Freemasons of high degree who in various parts of the USA parade in red fezzes and jewelled fancy dress to collect funds for its hospitals for crippled children of all races and creeds. (Originally it claimed descent from an ancient Arab secret society, as a gimmick in a worthy cause.)

Shrivenham Royal Military College of Science, transferred from Woolwich in 1946, where officers of the Home and Overseas Services take courses in engineering and science. (Village near Swindon, Wiltshire.)

Shropshire Lad, A (1896). A. E. Housman's book of pastoral verse, noted for its brooding pessimism.

Shrovetide Three days before Lent, when Christians were shriven (i.e. made their confessions); it was marked by a final bout of festivities on Shrove Tuesday (the day before Ash Wednesday), now represented only by the eating of pancakes in England; but see BATTLE OF FLOWERS; FASCHING.

Shuttle, Space Reusable rocket which 8 minutes after lift-off reaches the earth's orbit 200 km above ground. It carries a crew of between 2 and 8 and the average length of missions has been 7 days and the maximum 30. Once the shuttle is in space the main task has been to launch satellites. The first mission was in 1981. One flight in *Challenger* exploded in mid-flight in January 1986 killing the crew. The shuttle returns to earth as if it were an ordinary aircraft, and is returned to the launch site on an adapted jumbo-jet 'piggy back'.

Shylock Jewish moneylender of Shakespeare's *Merchant of Venice* who demands a pound of Antonio's flesh in default of repayment of a debt, and is foiled by PORTIA.

Sial (Geology) Relatively light rocks (e.g. granite) forming the continents; see SIMA. (Coined from their characteristic elements, *si*licon and *al*uminium.)

Sian incident (1936). Chiang Kai-shek was kidnapped by his own deputy in a (successful) attempt to persuade him to form a common front with the Chinese Communists against Japan; this coup is said to have been suggested by Stalin.

Sibylline Books (1) Books of prophecies bought from the Cumaean Sibyl (priestess of Apollo's temple near Naples) by King Tarquin of Rome. Accidentally burnt, they were replaced by a new version compiled from other sources, itself burnt in Nero's reign. The Romans consulted them in times of crisis. (2) Collection of Jewish and Christian prophecies compiled in the 2nd century AD and much consulted in the Middle Ages.

Sicilian Vespers, The (1282). Revolt against the harsh rule of Charles I of Anjou, King of the Two Sicilies, in which the Sicilians massacred the French troops as the bells tolled for vespers on Easter Monday. They then summoned the help of the Aragonese of Spain, who took the place of the Angevin rulers.

Sick Man of Europe Name for Turkey in its 19th–20th century decline. See EASTERN QUESTION.

Side car Cocktail made of 8 parts brandy, 1 Cointreau, 2 lemon juice or, less satisfactorily, of equal proportions of these.

Sidcott A fire- and waterproof overall flying suit. (From name of designer, Sid Cotton.)

Sidewinder US Navy's solid-fuel air-to-air missile, mounted in Starfighters; it was used by the Chinese Nationalists against China in 1958.

Sidhe Irish name for fairies. ('People of the hills'; pronounced shee.)

Sidney Street siege (1911). 'Siege' by a handful of troops of a house in Sidney Street, Whitechapel, London, where some foreign anarchists were resisting arrest. Winston Churchill, then Home Secretary, watched the proceedings, and was accused by political opponents of courting publicity by doing so.

Sidonia Enormously rich Spanish Jew who appears in Disraeli's CONINGSBY and *Tancred*. A banker and philosopher, cold and aloof, he is said to be based partly on one of the Rothschild family and partly on the author himself.

Siegfried Idyll (1870). Wagner's exquisite serenade for small orchestra, on themes from the finale of his RING OF THE NIBELUNGS opera *Siegfried*; written as a surprise birthday present for

457

Siegfried (Sigurd)

Cosima (whom he had married that year) and also to celebrate the birth of their son Siegfried, it was not intended for publication.

Siegfried (Sigurd) Hero of Scandinavian myth who seized the Nibelungs' gold from Fafnir. In the *Nibelungenlied* he is a prince of the lower Rhine who, aided by a cloak of invisibility, wins Brunhild for Gunther, who gives him his sister KRIEMHILD in marriage. He is killed by HAGEN.

Siegfried Line (1) In World War I, another name for the HINDENBURG LINE. (2) In World War II the British name for the WESTWALL.

Siegfried's Journey (1938–45). Three-volume autobiography by Siegfried Sassoon, covering the same period as SHERSTON'S PROGRESS.

Siemens, House of (1822). German firm engaged in all branches of electrical engineering, from microminiature devices to power-stations.

Sigma Xi (1886). US fraternity or 'honor society' for those distinguished in the field of scientific research.

Sikes, Bill Generic term for a burglar, from the associate of FAGIN in OLIVER TWIST, who murders his mistress, Nancy.

Sikhs Indian religious sect of the Punjab founded by Nanak at the end of the 15th century. He tried, unsuccessfully, to bring Hindu and Muslim together under one monotheistic religion which rejected the Hindu caste system. In the 17th century the Sikhs developed into a military race fighting against MOGUL rule. They have since provided the British Army with soldiers as renowned as the Gurkhas, identifiable by their distinctive turban, beard and comb. See GRANTH. (Hindu, 'disciple'; pronounced seekz.)

Silas Lapham, The Rise of (1885). Dean Howells's best novel, in which Silas, who has made his pile in the sawmills, tries to move into Boston society; he finds the going very hard, and learns more about ethics than etiquette; meanwhile his daughter finds her own way to happiness.

Silas Marner (1861). George Eliot's novel in which Silas, a village weaver embittered by a false accusation of theft, turns recluse and miser. His faith in God is restored through chancing upon and bringing up a foundling girl, Eppie, who remains true to him even when her father comes to claim her many years later.

Silbury Hill Largest prehistoric mound in Europe, adjoining AVEBURY and on the A4 between Marlborough and Chippenham. It dates from *c.* 2200 BC (500 years before Stonehenge, 15 miles away); it is estimated that it would have taken 500 men 10 years to complete this impressive work which, according to legend, has solid gold buried in it.

Silent Majority, The Term used in 1969 by US Vice-President Spiro Agnew for students, trade unionists, etc. who oppose left-wing agitation, but only silently, thus leaving the field clear for small but vociferous minorities of troublemakers to claim majority backing.

'Silent Night' (1818). Carol composed by an Austrian village schoolmaster, which became world famous. (Original title, 'Heilige Nacht', 'holy night'.)

Silent Spring (1963). Rachel Carson's book which first awakened the lay world to the destruction of wildlife and the danger to human life resulting from man's vastly increased use of chemical pesticides and weedkillers.

Silenus In Greek mythology, a drunken old coward who accompanies Dionysus.

Silesia Former region of Prussia (and to a less extent of Austria), fertile and rich in minerals, divided into Upper (eastern) Silesia, capital Katowice, and Lower (western) Silesia, capital Breslau (Wrocław). In 1919 part was ceded to Poland and Czechoslovakia; in 1945 the rest of it east of the ODER–NEISSE LINE was ceded to Poland. Both countries expelled the German inhabitants. (Polish, Śląsk; Czech, Slezsko.)

Silhouette Profiles cut from black paper, by Étienne de Silhouette, a French minister of finance.

Silk Road Ancient trade route linking China and Europe via Bokhara, Samarkand and a series of oases across the deserts north of Tibet

(Xizang) to Beijing. Chinese merchants carried silk to the West and brought back amber.

Silly Season Traditionally August, when daily papers, short of news in the holiday season, would blow up any trivial incident to make a headline. The years 1914 and 1939 have rather dented the tradition.

Silurian Period Third period of the PALAEOZOIC ERA, lasting from about 450 to 410 million years ago. Fossils for the first time become abundant. (Latin *Silures*, Welsh tribe of the Ludlow border area, where the rocks of this period were first studied; pronounced sil-ewr'i-an.)

Silver Box, The (1907). Galsworthy's first play, about a charwoman, Mrs Jones, at the house of a Liberal MP whose son, when drunk, unknowingly brings the char's husband into the house one night. Jones steals the silver cigarette box of the title.

Silver Ghost (1907–27). Early Rolls-Royce car, an exceptionally silent 6-cylinder 40/50 model made for 20 years almost without change.

Silver Goblets and Nickalls Challenge Cup The international amateur championship for pair-oars, rowed at Henley.

Silver Ring Cheaper enclosure at a race-meeting; so named because its patrons would normally bet in silver coins rather than in the golden guineas of TATTERSALL'S.

Silverstone (1948). Motor-racing circuit near Towcester, Northamptonshire, which became the chief circuit after Brooklands and Donington were closed; often the venue for the British Grand Prix.

Silver Vaults, The Underground arcade of small shops beneath Chancery Lane, London, where antique silver is sold.

Sima (Geology) Dense, heavy rocks (e.g. basalt) under the oceans and under SIAL. (Coined from their characteristic elements, silicon and *magnesium*.)

Simnel Rebellion (1487). Yorkist attempt to place a rogue named Lambert Simnel on the English throne as Edward VI. A force of Irishmen and Flemish mercenaries was defeated at Stoke-on-Trent by Henry VII.

Simon Artz's Once-famous department store, founded at Port Said by a Hungarian-born Englishman.

Simon Boccanegra (1857). Verdi's sombre opera, full of sinister plotting but not without lighter touches.

Simon Fraser University (SFU) Canadian university built on top of Burnaby Mountain near Vancouver, British Columbia; sometimes called the 'instant university' as it is open all the year round, with 3 long terms, to expedite the production of graduates.

Simonites Twenty-five Liberals led by Sir John (later Viscount) Simon who broke with the party on the Free Trade issue and formed the Liberal National (later National Liberal) Party which joined MacDonald's coalition in 1931. See SAMUELITES.

Simon Magus Sorcerer of Samaria mentioned in Acts 8:18–21, as having offered Peter and John money for the power of laying on hands (hence 'simony', trafficking in ecclesiastical offices). Many legends were later added to this story.

Simon report (1930). A report on India which recommended the replacement of DYARCHY by responsible provincial government and the retention of separate ('communal') electorates for the various religious and racial communities. (Sir John Simon.)

Simonstown Naval base near Cape Town, handed over by Britain to the South African government in 1957.

Simplicissimus (1896). Satirical German periodical famous for its savage cartoons of Queen Victoria during the Boer War period, and of the German military caste.

Simplon express An evening train from Paris via the Simplon Tunnel, Milan and Rome (reached at lunch-time) to Naples (afternoon).

Sinai, Mount Mountain, usually identified with

Jebel Musa in southern Sinai, where Moses received the Law (Exod. 19–20); symbolically the starting-point of Jewish history, where the Israelites and others (Exod. 12:38), after crossing the Red Sea in the 13th century BC, evolved into a single community worshipping one God. In a monastery there Tischendorff discovered (1844–59) one of the 2 earliest Greek manuscripts of all the New Testament and much of the Old (the *Codex Sinaiticus*), most of it now in the British Museum.

Sindbad the Sailor Merchant mariner in the *Arabian Nights* who recounts a series of tall stories of magical adventures on his voyages. In one, he kills the OLD MAN OF THE SEA, in others he encounters the roc, a bird with a wing-span which enables him to carry off elephants to his nest.

Singh SIKH name, meaning 'lion', used ever since the time of Govind Singh, the last Sikh Guru (1675–1708).

Singhalese Indo-European language of southern Sri Lanka, closely related to PALI but with many borrowings from DRAVIDIAN LANGUAGES. Attempts to impose it on the TAMIL population as the only official language have led to much unrest. Also spelt Sinhalese.

Sing Sing (1825). US state prison at Ossining, New York.

Single European Act (1985). European Community aim of Europe (meaning the EC countries) without frontiers by 1992 so that goods, people and capital can flow freely between member countries. This only fulfils the promises in the TREATY OF ROME.

Sinister Street (1913–14). Compton Mackenzie's 2-volume autobiographical novel of childhood, school and Oxford, giving an insight into the minds of the young people who were shortly to be plunged into World War I.

Sinistrality Estimates of left-handedness among the UK population vary widely (from 2% to 30%). The left has long been thought of as clumsy or maladroit, a sign of inferiority. However, Judges 20:16 gives a different view, and there are a great number of distinguished left-

handers, e.g. Leonardo da Vinci, Benjamin Franklin. In the Muslim world food is eaten only with the right, or clean, hand. In boxing, baseball, etc. the left-hander is known as a 'southpaw'. The ancient Greeks thought that all signs seen by them over the left shoulder were unlucky, the given reason being that the west (or left) side was towards the setting sun.

Sinn Féin (1902). Irish nationalist organization (see IRA) founded by Arthur Griffith; in the 1918 election most Irish seats were won by its candidates, who declined to go to Westminster and formed an unofficial DÁIL; in 1921 they accepted Partition and Dominion status. (Erse, 'ourselves alone'; pronounced shin fayn'.)

Sino-Tibetan languages Family of languages with 2 main divisions: (1) Siamese and Chinese; (2) Burmese, Tibetan and Nepalese.

Sioux Dakota tribe of American Indians, once found from Saskatchewan to southern USA. (Pronounced soo; plural, sooz.)

Sioux State Nickname of North Dakota.

Sioux Wars (1) War of 1862–8, when SITTING BULL led attacks on whites in Iowa and Minnesota during the Civil War and was finally forced to accept Sioux reservation in Dakota Territory. (2) War of 1875–6, caused by threatened encroachments on their new reserves. Allied with the Cheyenne, Sitting Bull and Crazy Horse won the Battle of Little Big Horn (CUSTER'S LAST STAND) in 1876, but were eventually defeated.

Sirdar Title of the British governor and commander-in-chief of Egypt (1882–1936). (Urdu-Persian, 'chief commander'; pronounced sèr'dar.)

Sirens In Greek legend, 2 sea nymphs who lure sailors to destruction by the beauty of their singing. Odysseus got by through tying himself to the mast and filling the ears of his crew with wax. This so upset the Sirens that they drowned themselves. In *Urn Burial* Sir Thomas Browne rashly says: 'What song the Syrens sang . . . is not beyond all conjecture.'

Sir Garnet, All Obsolete colloquialism for 'all correct'. (Field Marshal Sir Garnet Wolseley, Commander-in-Chief, 1895–1900.)

Sirius Dog Star, the brightest star in the heavens, in CANIS MAJOR; it has a companion star, a WHITE DWARF. (Greek, 'scorching'; pronounced sir'i-us.)

Sir John Soane's Museum Situated on the north side of Lincoln's Inn Fields, this was the residence of Sir John Soane, RA (1753–1837), architect. In about 1832 the house was established as a museum, which is now a unique collection of antiquities and pictures; Hogarth, Canaletto and Piranesi are represented, among others.

'Sir Patrick Spens' Fifteenth century historical ballad beginning: 'The king sits in Dunfermline town / Drinking the blude-red wine.' The king sends Sir Patrick ('the best sailor that ever sail'd the seas') to fetch the King of Norway's daughter, but the ship sinks with all hands.

Sisera Captain of the Canaanite army who was defeated by Barak. Jael offered him asylum in her tent and then killed him by nailing his head to the ground while he slept (Judg. 4:21). See DEBORAH.

Sister Anne Phrase 'Sister Anne, Sister Anne, do you see no one coming?' was uttered by BLUE-BEARD's last wife when anxiously awaiting rescue by her brothers.

Sistine Chapel Pope's private chapel adjoining St Peter's, Rome, decorated with Michelangelo's ceiling fresco of the Creation, and his 'LAST JUDGEMENT'. (Named after Pope Sixtus IV.)

Sistine *Madonna* Raphael's *Madonna* (1511), formerly at Dresden, now in Russian possession. (Named after the Church of St Sixtus, Piacenza, where it once was.)

Sisyphus In Greek legend, a man who for his crimes on earth is condemned to roll up a hill a huge stone which always rolls back before he gets to the top. Hence a Sisyphean task, an unending task on which immense energy is expended with little to show for it. (Pronounced sis'i-fus.)

Sitcom Situation comedy.

Sittang River disaster (February 1942). Incident during the Japanese invasion of Burma. Orders were prematurely given to blow up the only bridge across the river before the main body of British and Indian troops had reached it in their retreat.

Sitting Bull Sioux (Dakota) chief who after CUSTER'S LAST STAND fled to Canada, returned in 1881, and was killed 9 years later by police who were trying to arrest him. (More accurately, his name was 'The Bull in Possession'.)

Siva, Shiva One of the 2 main gods of modern Hinduism, and one of the Trinity formed with VISHNU and BRAHMA. He is the ruthless destructive principle in life, and also the regenerative force that follows destruction; often represented with 4 arms, 3 eyes or several faces. He also appears as the consort of KALI, worshipped as a phallic god, especially at Benares. (Pronounced s(h)iv'a, s(h)ee'va.)

Six Characters in Search of an Author (1921). Pirandello's play in which actors rehearsing an earlier play of his are interrupted by 6 people claiming to be the characters in it; they want to add to the play parts left out by the author. Unfortunately, their versions of the same events differ widely, and all ends in a tangle of illusions and illusion of illusions, which take some sorting out.

Six Counties, The Northern Ireland, which consists of 6 of the counties of ULSTER.

Six-Day War (1967). Between Israel and Egypt (supported by Jordan, Syria, Lebanon and Iraq). In May Egypt had secured the withdrawal of the UN force on the Israeli border and closed the Gulf of Aqaba to Israel. On 5 June Israel opened a pre-emptive blitzkrieg by destroying first the air forces (in a matter of hours) and then the armies of Egypt, Jordan and Syria. Nasser accepted a cease-fire on the 8th, but Israel, alleging breaches of it, continued to attack Syria until the 10th. Israel conquered the West Bank of Jordan (with 650,000 inhabitants), the Gaza Strip and Sinai peninsula (to the Suez Canal), the old city of Jerusalem and the Golan Heights in Syria. Some 200,000–300,000 Arabs became refugees; Israel lost 803 dead. The Arabs, because of an apparently genuine misunderstanding, falsely accused the USA and UK of providing air cover for the Israeli attack. The Soviet Union supported the Arabs.

Six Nations Contest Swimming competition between teams from Britain, Italy, Sweden, the Netherlands, Germany and France.

16th Amendment (1913). Amendment to the US Constitution which introduced Federal income tax.

Sixth Commandment 'Thou shalt not kill' (Exod. 20:13). To Roman Catholics this is the Fifth Commandment.

$64,000 question The crucial question.

Sizewell (1968). Site of a MAGNOX nuclear power-station ('A') and of the projected pressurized water reactor 'B' station. (Coastal village north of Aldeburgh, Suffolk.)

Skerryvore (1844). Lighthouse and rock south-west of Tiree Island in the Inner Hebrides off the coast of Mull. The light is 158 ft above sea-level.

Skid Row (US slang) District or community of people 'on the skids', i.e. at or near the bottom of the downward path. (From the 'Skid Road' in Seattle, made of greased logs, over which lumbermen skidded timber; 'road' corrupted to 'row'.)

Skiffle (1956). Short-lived British form of POP MUSIC based on black folk-song, popularized by Lonnie Donegan. Youngsters armed with guitars and cheap substitutes for conventional instruments such as the washboard and broom-handle bass fiddle appeared all over the country.

Skimpole, Harold Character in Dickens's BLEAK HOUSE, supposed to represent Leigh Hunt. An artist of charm but completely self-centred, he assumes that his friends will always be happy to help him out of his perennial financial difficulties and will not expect to be thanked for it.

Skin Game, The (1920). Galsworthy's play about the efforts of the *nouveau riche* industrialist, Hornblower, to gain social recognition by the aristocratic Hillcrists. Failing, he threatens to build a factory to ruin the view from the Hillcrists's mansion; a by-product of the struggle is the attempted suicide of a girl used as a pawn in it.

Skinheads (1960s) working-class heirs to the MODS (but scooterless) with cropped hair, heavy steel-shod bovver (i.e. 'bother') boots and oversize LEVIS held at half-mast by thin red braces. Originating as northern city street gangs, they got their fun from provoking 'agro' (aggravation) by disturbing soccer and pop-concert crowds, wrecking football trains, attacking anyone 'flash' and Paki-bashing (beating up Pakistanis). They now have links to the NATIONAL FRONT and other right-wing extremist groups.

Skinners, Worshipful Company of (1327). One of the oldest of the Great Twelve LIVERY COMPANIES, originally a guild of fur merchants. It governs Tonbridge School, founded by a Skinner in the 16th century.

Skopje (Skoplje) Capital of Macedonia, Yugoslavia. Almost completely destroyed by an earthquake in 1963, it was rebuilt on an adjacent site. Formerly known by its Turkish name, Üsküb. (Pronounced skop'yay.)

'Skye Boat Song' Song about Bonnie Prince Charlie; the air is based on an old sea shanty, the words by Sir Harold Boulter (1859–1935): 'Speed, bonny boat, like a bird on the wing . . . / Over the sea to Skye.' R. L. Stevenson wrote another version.

Slade Name formed from the initials of the Society of Lithographic Artists, Designers, Engravers and Process Workers.

Slade Professor Holder of the chair of Fine Art at Oxford, Cambridge, or University College, London University. (See next entry.)

Slade School (1871). School of art, now attached to University College, London University. (Named after Felix Slade, art collector, died

1868, who endowed the Slade professorships, see previous entry.)

Slavonic languages Group of Indo-European languages including Russian, Polish, Ukrainian, Bulgarian, and the languages of Czechoslovakia and Yugoslavia.

Slavs People of Asian origin who, by settling round the inaccessible Pripet marshes in Russia managed to keep out of the way of successive invasions of Europe for hundreds of years. About the 5th century AD they began to migrate to south Russia, to the Balkans, and via Hungary to the Baltic coast. They were the ancestors of the numerous peoples who speak SLAVONIC LANGUAGES.

Slazenger Championship (1946). Professional lawn tennis championship played at Devonshire Park, Eastbourne.

Slazenger Trophy Golf contest between Britain and a team representing the Commonwealth and Empire; it comprises foursomes and singles.

'Sleeping Beauty, The' Fairy-tale of a princess put into an enchanted sleep in her father's castle, round which a dense forest springs up to protect her. A good fairy arranges that after 100 years she shall be woken by a kiss from a handsome prince brave enough to penetrate the forest. The earliest printed version is in Perrault's collection and is entitled 'La Belle au bois dormant'.

Sleeping Beauty, The (1889). Petipa's ballet to Tchaikovsky's score follows the traditional fairy-tale (see previous entry) and also introduces various figures from other nursery tales, e.g. Red Riding Hood, Puss-in-Boots.

Sleeping policeman Ramp built across roads to cause a jolt and prevent vehicles from travelling at high speed.

Sleep of Prisoners, A (1951). Religious verse drama by Christopher Fry, designed to be produced in a church.

Slimbridge Site on the Severn, west of Stroud, Gloucestershire, of Sir Peter Scott's Wildfowl Trust bird sanctuary.

Slivovitz Plum brandy made in Yugoslavia and Hungary. (Pronounced sliv'o-vits.)

Sloane Ranger Special kind of upper-class young ladies, who take the name from Sloane Square and its surroundings. Their taste in fashion may be seen in London, Paris and Amsterdam, but it does not slavishly follow the trend of the day, quality is an essential.

Slope, Mr In the BARCHESTER NOVELS, Bishop Proudie's scheming hypocrite of a chaplain who dares to dispute the hegemony established by Mrs PROUDIE over her husband and the diocese – a forlorn enterprise.

Slough of Despond Quagmire in PILGRIM'S PROGRESS into which Christian flounders, unable to escape unaided because of the burden of sin on his back. (Pronounced slow, des-pond'.)

Slovak SLAVONIC LANGUAGE spoken in eastern Czechoslovakia (in Slovakia and south Moravia, a region formerly under Hungary), closely allied to Czech.

Slovenian SLAVONIC LANGUAGE spoken in northwest Yugoslavia (a region formerly under Austria), akin to SERBOCROAT but more archaic.

Slump, The (1930s). Colloquial term for the world-wide effects of the WALL STREET CRASH. Also called the (Great) Depression.

Small Back Room, The (1943). Nigel Balchin's novel about the back-room boys or boffins, i.e. men engaged on secret scientific research in wartime.

Smelfungus Sterne's name in his SENTIMENTAL JOURNEY for Smollett, whom he represents as an ill-tempered traveller.

Smerdyakov See *The* BROTHERS KARAMAZOV.

Smersh According to Ian Fleming's *From Russia with Love* (a James BOND novel), the nickname among its personnel for the 'Soviet murder organization, operating at home and abroad'. (Said to be from Russian *smert' shpionam*, 'death to spies'.)

Smitane (Cooking). With sour cream and onions.

Smith-Connally Act (1943). (USA) A wartime anti-strike Act making the instigation of strikes in government factories or in mines a criminal offence.

Smithfield Market London market, specializing in meat and poultry.

Smithfield Show, Royal Held each December at Earls Court, London, the premier exhibition of British agricultural machinery and of livestock.

Smith's Lawn Polo ground in Windsor Park.

Smithsonian Institution (1846). Institution at Washington DC which comprises a national museum (mainly of ethnology and zoology), zoo, art gallery and an astrophysical observatory. (Endowed by James Smithson, mineralogist, illegitimate son of a Duke of Northumberland.)

Smith's prizes Prizes at Cambridge University for mathematics and natural philosophy. (Endowed by Robert Smith, died 1768.)

Smith Square, Westminster The London square where the headquarters of the Conservative and Unionist Party is situated.

Smith (W. H.) & Son Award An annual literary prize of £10,000 for the most outstanding contribution to literature by a British or Commonwealth author.

Smoke, The Name for London, also called the Great (or Big) Smoke.

Smuts Professor Holder of the chair of the History of British Commonwealth at Cambridge.

Smyrna Ancient Greek port in Asia Minor, now Turkish and known as Izmir.

Snake, The (1971). Early attempt by the European Economic Community to obtain exchange-rate parity. It was looked on with suspicion by those opposed to economic and political union. France left the snake in 1976 and it was replaced by the European Monetary System in 1979.

Snark, The Creature sought by the BELLMAN'S crew in Lewis Carroll's poem *The Hunting of the Snark*. Some Snarks have feathers and bite,

others have whiskers and scratch, but the only kind to dread is the BOOJUM.

SNCF Initials used for the French State Railways, Société Nationale des Chemins-de-fer Français.

Sno-cat Treaded vehicle used to draw sled-trains in the Antarctic.

Snodgrass, Augustus Poetical young companion of Pickwick, in Dickens's novel.

Snoopy Widely read (but unfortunately voiceless) canine philosopher of PEANUTS, subject to wild fantasies in which he is a World War I air ace scouring the skies for the RED BARON, the subject of songs and a musical.

Snowball Character in Orwell's ANIMAL FARM who represents Trotsky.

Snowball Mixture of Advocaat and a lemon drink.

Snowdonia (1951). National Park surrounding Snowdon in North Wales.

'Snows of Kilimanjaro, The' (1936). Hemingway's outstanding short story about a writer on safari in Africa with his rich wife; he contracts gangrene and as he lies dying he dreams of a huge frozen leopard on Mt Kilimanjaro, a symbol of his own destruction through failure to match his achievements to his ideals and talents.

Snow White and the Seven Dwarfs (1938). First feature-length animated cartoon in colour, made by Walt Disney.

Snowy Mountains scheme (1949). Ambitious Australian hydroelectric and irrigation project in the south-east of New South Wales, near Canberra. The waters of the Snowy River and its tributaries have been directed by a system of dams and miles of tunnels bored through the Snowy Mountains to fall into the Murrumbidgee and Murray rivers. Thus water which used to flow south where it was not required can now be put to good use in the dry areas to the north.

Soane Museum See SIR JOHN SOANE'S MUSEUM.

Soap opera Radio or TV serial with stock domestic situations, often melodramatic or sentimental.

Soapy Sam Nickname of Samuel Wilberforce, Bishop of Oxford and son of William Wilberforce; he was a noted 19th-century opponent of Darwinism and the Tractarians.

Sobranje Bulgarian elective national assembly. (Bulgarian, 'assembly'; pronounced so-brahn'-yè.)

Social and Liberal Democrats (1988). British political party (SLD) formed from the Liberal party and sections of the Social Democratic party.

Social Contract, The (1762). Jean-Jacques Rousseau's plea for government by the whole sovereign people, in whose natural goodness he believed. It contains the phrase: 'Man is born free and is everywhere in chains'.

Social Credit Economic theory advanced by a Canadian, Major C. H. Douglas, suggesting that universal prosperity could be based on the payment to all of an annual 'national dividend' varying with a country's wealth. See next entry.

Social Credit Party (1920). Canadian political party at first advocating SOCIAL CREDIT, now abandoned.

Social Democrats Name adopted in 1869 by a German party which accepted Marxist theory but rejected Marxist revolutionary strategy. It has been used since by parties in many countries which are prepared to work for Marxist ends by democratic means through parliament, i.e. by patiently undermining, rather than violently overthrowing, capitalism.

'Socialism in one country' Doctrine of Lenin and Stalin, vigorously opposed by Trotsky; see TROTSKYISM.

'Socialism in our time' Slogan with which Ramsay MacDonald won the 1929 general election.

Socialist Realism Form of art and literature officially approved by the Soviet government, typified by pictures of muscle-bound workmen wielding axes, and stories of muscle-bound workmen sacrificing all to reach a productivity norm.

Socialist Sixth of the World, The See RED DEAN.

Social Realism Movement in the art and literature of Western countries, unconnected with SOCIALIST REALISM. The American name 'Ashcan school' and the English, 'Kitchen Sink school', indicate its content; its aim is emphatic criticism of modern Western urban society.

Society for Psychical Research (SPR) A body set up in 1882 to investigate all paranormal phenomena, including hypnotism, in a scientific spirit.

Socratic irony Pretence of ignorance by a teacher, designed to encourage pupils to air their own views and thus display their own real ignorance; a major feature of the SOCRATIC METHOD.

Socratic method Method of instruction peculiar to Socrates; he would put a series of questions so chosen as to force his pupils step by step to the one logical solution of the problem posed, a process Plato called 'midwifery'. See previous entry.

Sodom, Apple of See DEAD SEA FRUIT.

Sodom and Gomorrah (1) Cities of the Plain destroyed by fire and brimstone for their wickedness, and now lying beneath the Dead Sea. (Gen. 18:20 to 19:25.) (2) In French (Sodome et Gomorrhe) the title of Part iv of Proust's *Remembrance of Things Past* (*Cities of the Plain* in English).

Sod's law Law expressing the general cursedness of things. In a controlled experiment reprinted in the TLS in 1960, 735 out of 1,000 slices of bread fell butter-side down on an office carpet, but 938 did so on a valuable Bokhara rug. Sod thought to be a fictitious person.

Soho Section of London between Oxford Street, Shaftesbury Avenue and Regent Street, famous for foreign-cuisine restaurants, delicatessens, street markets, traffic jams, call-girls and crime. The first foreigners were 17-century French Huguenot refugees. Soho Square was laid out in 1681. (Anglo-French hunting cry, *cq ho!*, uttered on sighting the quarry.)

Sohrab and Rusum (1853). Matthew Arnold's epic fragment based on the legend of how Rustum, the Persian Hercules, unwittingly killed his son Sohrab.

Soissonaise (Cooking) With French white beans (haricots blancs).

Soka Gakkai Militant mass Buddhist movement in Japan, of which the political arm is the Komeito (Clean Government Party) which campaigns against corruption in politics.

Sol Roman sun-god, equivalent to the Greek HELIOS.

Solanaceae Nightshade family, many members of which contain alkaloids, e.g. belladonna or atropine in deadly nightshade, hyoscine in henbane. Other members are the potato, tomato, capsicum, cape gooseberry, tobacco plant, petunia, salpiglossis.

'Soldier, The' Rupert Brooke's poem beginning: 'If I should die, think only this of me: / That there's some corner of a foreign field / That is for ever England.'

Soldier Field (1926). Large sports stadium at Chicago.

Soldiers, The Hochhuth's Theatre of FACT (or rather in this case 'fact') play about the guilt of those who ordered the mass bombing of Germany; in it Churchill is accused of planning the air crash in which the Polish statesman Gen. Sikorsky was killed in 1943. The National Theatre thought this a suitable play to stage; the Lord Chamberlain disagreed.

Soldiers Three (1888–9). Kipling's collection of early short stories about Ortheris, Learoyd and Mulvaney, serving in the Indian Army; they had already appeared in PLAIN TALES FROM THE HILLS.

Solemn League and Covenant See COVENANTERS.

Solera System of blending sherry from wines of many vintage years; as a term on a bottle label it has no significance.

Sole sea area That lying south-west from Land's End, and south of the Shannon and Fastnet sea areas. It includes the Sole banks.

Solferino (1859). Second French victory over the Austrians in Italy (after MAGENTA); the casualties in both battles were so high on both sides that Napoleon III offered an armistice, which was accepted. The Red Cross owes its origin to the battle.

Solicitor-General See LAW OFFICERS OF THE CROWN.

Solicitors, Worshipful Company of (1944). LIVERY COMPANY with membership restricted to solicitors practising within one mile of the Bank of England.

Solidago Genus name of the golden rods.

Solidarity Polish trade union founded in the Gdańsk shipyards and led by Lech Wałęsa. Following free elections, after years of repression (it was proscribed and its leaders detained in 1981) and difficulties, Solidarity were asked to form a government in 1989.

Solid South, The (USA) Southern states which until recent years could be relied on to vote solidly for the Democratic Party.

Solomon Son of David and BATHSHEBA, a King of Israel of the 10th century BC who gained a legendary reputation for wisdom and wealth, not apparently justified by historical fact. See next 2 entries and SHEBA, QUEEN OF.

Solomon, Judgement of In a dispute between 2 harlots about the ownership of a child, King SOLOMON proposed to divide the child and give half to each. One woman agreed; the other begged the king to give it to her adversary rather than slay it, and was adjudged the true mother. (1 Kgs 3:16–28.)

Solomon's Temple (1006 BC). Israelites' chief temple, built by King Solomon (2 Chronicles 3) on Mount Zion, Jerusalem. Destroyed by Nebuchadnezzar (6th century BC), it was restored by Herod the Great (20 BC) and finally destroyed by Titus (AD 70). The site is now occupied by a mosque and the only remaining portion is the WAILING WALL.

Solutrean culture Period of the PALAEOLITHIC AGE, perhaps lasting from 18,000 to 15,000 BC, during which the making of flint tools and spearheads was perfected. (La Solutré, near Mâcon, France.)

Solveig Peasant girl who loves PEER GYNT; her song was set to music by Grieg.

Somali Cushite race (see HAMITES), originally and still mainly a nomadic cattle people of SOMALIA; the Somali of northern Kenya and of Ethiopia occasionally agitate for union with Somalia.

Somalia (Somali Republic) Formed (1960) from the union of former British and Italian Somaliland.

Somerset and Cornwall Light Infantry, The (1959). Regiment of the LIGHT INFANTRY BRIGADE, an amalgamation of The Somerset Light Infantry (Prince Albert's) and The Duke of Cornwall's Light Infantry.

Somerset Club Exclusive men's club in Boston, Massachusetts.

Somerset Herald Officer of the COLLEGE OF ARMS.

Somerset House Thames-side building which now houses the COURTAULD INSTITUTE OF ART and King's College, London University. (Duke of Somerset, the Protector.)

Somerset Maugham Award Literary prize of £4,000 awarded annually to young British authors who have published a literary work of outstanding promise; the money is intended to be used for travel.

Somerville and Ross See EXPERIENCES OF AN IRISH RM.

Somme Battle (July–November 1916). One of the costliest battles in terms of human life of World War I. The British used tanks for the first time, but in too few numbers and with too little faith in them. Co-operation between the RFC (the future RAF) and the army was another new feature. The battle achieved nothing.

Somnus God of sleep; he was a son of Night and a brother of Death.

Son et Lumière (1950s). Tourist attraction consisting of selective flood-lighting of a famous building (such as the Parthenon at Athens) synchronized with features of its history broadcast over loudspeakers to an outdoor audience. (French, 'sound and light'; first used by the French at the Loire châteaux.)

Song of Songs, The (3rd century BC). Collection of love-songs which strayed into the Bible inadvertently. Early Christians expended much ingenuity on trying to assign allegorical meanings to them. Also called *The Song of Solomon*, but not the work of Solomon.

Song of the Earth, The (1908). Mahler's song-cycle for solo voices and orchestra, with words translated from the Chinese. (German title, *Das Lied von der Erde*.)

'Song of the Shirt, The' (1843). Thomas Hood's poem about a poor drudge of a seamstress, 'Sewing at once with a double thread, / A shroud as well as a shirt.' The poem called attention to sweated labour in early 19th-century cottage industries, and helped to improve conditions.

Sons, The Nickname of the Dumbarton football team.

Sons and Lovers (1913). D. H. Lawrence's largely autobiographical novel of the Nottinghamshire coalfields where he was born, and of Paul Morel's (i.e. his own) emotional attachment to his mother.

Sooner State Nickname of Oklahoma. (Sooners, those who evaded regulations and occupied the best land before the law-abiding arrived.)

Sopwith Camel (1916). Later development of the SOPWITH PUP, faster and with longer range.

Sopwith Pup Best-known of the British fighter aircraft of World War I. (Made by the firm founded by T. O. M. Sopwith, later chairman of the Hawker Siddeley Group.)

Sorbonne, The (1253). Leading French university, in Paris. (Founded as a theological college by Richard de Sorbon.)

Sorcerer's Apprentice, The (1897). Dukas's symphonic scherzo, based on a ballad by Goethe. To save himself trouble, the Apprentice misuses his master's magic and finds himself overwhelmed by a flood of water which he is powerless to stop. (Translation of *L'Apprenti sorcier*.)

Sorel, Julien See *Le* ROUGE ET LE NOIR.

Soroptimist clubs Women's clubs consisting of one member only from each profession or business. Members must be over 25 years old and of high standing in their calling. They engage in work for handicapped children, the aged and others in need of help. There is a Soroptimist International Association.

Sorrel, Hetty See ADAM BEDE.

Sorrows of Satan, The (1895). One of Marie Corelli's best-selling novels.

Sorrows of Young Werther, The (1774). Goethe's short sentimental novel, in the form of letters, about a maundering German student who shoots himself because he cannot win his neighbour's wife.

Sotheby's London auction rooms for antiques, paintings, first editions, etc., situated in New Bond Street. (Pronounced sudh'ė-biz.)

Soubise (Cooking) With onions.

Souchong Once a name associated with high-quality China tea; now a trade term for a grade of tea poorer than ORANGE PEKOE or Pekoe.

Soul American primitive, emotional form of revived Negro BLUES based on recollections of church music and originating from Memphis and Detroit; from 1965 it became the most popular form of black music, claiming that 'little bit extra' of emotional depth exemplified by 'In the Midnight Hour' (1965). Aretha Franklin (Queen of Soul), Thelonius Monk and Roland Kirk were leading exponents.

Sound of Music, The (1960). Last of the Rodgers and Hammerstein musicals (and films), in which Maria, during a not very promising novitiate at the local nunnery, becomes governess to Captain Trapp's 7 children and with them escapes from the Austrian Nazis. Among many charming songs were 'My Favourite Things', 'Do-Re-Mi' and 'Edelweiss'.

Sourdough (Originally, in western USA) a prospector, pioneer; (Canada and Alaska) one who has spent more than one winter in the Arctic; an oldtimer. (From their use of sour dough kept from one batch of baking to the next.)

Sousa marches Famous military marches composed by the bandmaster of the US Marines, J. P. Sousa (died 1932); among the best-known are 'Liberty Bell', 'Stars and Stripes Forever' and 'The Washington Post'.

Sous les toits de Paris (1930). One of the earliest sound films of merit, made by René Clair, with a well-known accordion theme-tune.

South African Wars (1) *First* (1881), caused by British vacillation over withdrawing from the Transvaal after helping to quell Zulu risings. The Boers inflicted a sharp defeat on a small British force at Majuba Hill and regained independence for the 2 Boer republics. (2) *Second*, see BOER WAR.

Southall Former municipal borough of Middlesex, since 1965 part of the borough of EALING. (Pronounced sow'thal.)

Southcottians Those who believed the claims of a Devonshire farm servant, Joanna Southcott (died 1814), to prophetic powers. She left a box, to be opened only in time of national crisis and in the presence of all the bishops. There was some public demand for this during World War I, but it was not till 1927 that a bishop could be found to assist in the ceremony. Inside were some odds and ends, including a pistol; but even this did not kill the legend.

South Devon (South Ham) cattle Large red dual-purpose breed, producing excellent beef, and milk from which Devonshire cream is made.

Southdown Breed of short-wool sheep noted for its meat and for its close fine wool which covers face and ears. It has been much used in producing the DOWN BREEDS. (Originally local to the Sussex Downs.)

Southern Christian Leadership (1954). Black civil rights movement led by Martin Luther King; it supported the NAACP and organized such demonstrations as the MONTGOMERY BUS BOYCOTT.

Southern Comfort New Orleans liqueur made of BOURBON flavoured with oranges and peaches, 87° proof.

Southern Cross (Crux Australis) Most conspicuous constellation of the southern hemisphere, within the Antarctic Circle, with 4 bright stars forming a cross. It contains the Coal-sack, a dark nebula.

Southern Cross The name of the Fokker monoplane used in the first trans-Pacific flight, made by the pioneer Australian airman Sir Charles Kingsford-Smith.

Southgate Former municipal borough of Middlesex, since 1965 part of the borough of ENFIELD.

South Pacific (1949). Rodgers and Hammerstein musical (made into a film in 1958), with a love story in a Pacific island setting peopled by US sailors during World War II and adapted from James A. Michener's Pulitzer-prize-winning *Tales of the South Pacific*. Among the many endearing songs were 'Bali Ha'i', 'Some Enchanted Evening', 'I'm Gonna Wash That Man Right Outa My Hair' and 'A Wonderful Guy'.

South Riding (1936). Winifred Holtby's best-selling novel about her native Yorkshire; also a film made from it.

South Sea Bubble (1720). Collapse of the South Sea Co., formed in 1711 to trade with Spanish America on the favourable terms expected to result from the ASIENTO and the Treaty of UTRECHT. Speculation in its shares reached frenzied heights and created the atmosphere for the floating of numerous hare-brained schemes in other spheres. The inevitable crash involved the government, the royal family and thousands of small investors, and brought Sir Robert Walpole to power.

South Tirol Austrian name for ALTO ADIGE.

Southwark Inner London borough since 1965 consisting of the former metropolitan boroughs of Southwark, Bermondsey and Camberwell.

South Wind (1917). Norman Douglas's witty novel depicting the losing battle fought by a pre-war English colony against the assimilation of their standards to those of the natives of a Capri-type island.

Sovereign's Parade Passing-out ceremony for Sandhurst Cadets, at which the Sword of Honour is presented to the Cadet adjudged the most meritorious of his year.

Soviet Term derived from the Russian word meaning council, the function of Soviets is summed up by Stalin – 'transmission belts from the Party to the masses'.

Soviet Academy of Sciences Body which until 1961 had executive power over all activities in the fields of pure and applied science in USSR, and managed all research institutions; it is now restricted to theoretical research.

Soviet–German Non-aggression Pact (August 1939). Pact signed by Ribbentrop and Molotov to ensure that Germany should be free to attack Poland (which they later agreed to divide) and France without fear of attack from Stalinist Russia. Talks had gone on secretly while Britain and France were negotiating an alliance with Russia against Hitler.

Soviet Russia Term for the USSR (the Union of Soviet Socialist Republics), a country administered at all levels, from the village to the constituent republics and the Union itself, by soviets ('councils'), since 1936 elected directly by the whole electorate concerned. (Originally 'soviet' was used of the councils of workers, peasants and soldiers formed during the 1905 Revolution; pronounced soh'vi-et, sov'i-et or sov'yet.)

Sower, The Millet's painting of a peasant scattering seed, personifying the dignity of labour and also the Present sowing the Future.

Soweto Black African township in the Transvaal, Republic of South Africa, the largest in southern Africa. Scene of riots in 1976 when over 100 were killed and 1,200 injured. (Acronym for *South-West townships*.)

Soyuz Series of Russian spacecraft. *Soyuz 1* crash-landed on return to earth (1967) as the parachute failed; it killed the cosmonaut, the first to die on a space mission.

Space travel First manned space flight, in which Yury A. Gagarin orbited the earth, occurred on 12 April 1961; and on 18 March 1965 A. A. Leonov was the first man to walk in space from the *Voskhod 2*.

Spaghetti Junction (1972). Three-level interchange at Gravelly Hill, Birmingham, connecting the M6, M5 and, via the Aston Expressway, M1; thus an important link in routes between Scotland, London and the South-West, and when built the largest of its kind in Europe.

Spalato Italian name of Split, now a Yugoslav port.

Spalding Tulip Time Tourist attraction in April and May in Kesteven and Holland, the bulb-farming Fenland districts of Lincolnshire, of which Spalding is the centre.

Spam Proprietary name for canned pork luncheon meat. (*Sp*iced h*am*.)

Spandau Quarter of Berlin which gives its name to the gaol where German war criminals were imprisoned. The prison was demolished after the death of Rudolf Hess, the last prisoner.

Spanish Civil War (1936–9). A war to overthrow the Spanish government. Gen. Franco invaded Spain with Moroccan troops but failed to take Madrid, despite support from the Church, the upper classes, German planes and Italian troops. In 1938 he gradually drove a wedge between Republican forces (sparingly aided by Russia) around Madrid and those around Barcelona, and moved in for the kill in March 1939. See BURGOS; GUERNICA; INTERNATIONAL BRIGADE; NON-INTERVENTION COMMITTEE.

Spanish Farm, The (1924–7). Trilogy of novels by R. H. Mottram about World War I.

Spanish flu (April–November 1918). Influenza world epidemic which killed perhaps 20 million people all over the world, and seriously weakened the fighting forces on both sides in the last phases of World War I.

Spanish fly The metallic-green CANTHARIDES beetle (*Lytta–* formerly *Cantharis–vesicatoria*) which forms blisters on the skin that break, forming several more blisters. The blistering agent, called cantharidin, is used as a diuretic, and once had a (spurious) reputation as an aphrodisiac.

Spanish Main (1) South American mainland between Panama and the Orinoco; (2) the adjoining Caribbean Sea, where 16th–17th century English pirates harried Spanish shipping. (*Main* in the old sense 'wide expanse of land or sea'.)

Spanish Netherlands The NETHERLANDS countries (modern Belgium, Holland and Luxemburg) under the Spanish Hapsburgs from the time of Emperor Charles V (1516) until the revolt of the northern Protestant Dutch as the UNITED PROVINCES (1581); thereafter the Belgian Catholic region in the south until the treaty of UTRECHT (1713), when it became the AUSTRIAN NETHERLANDS.

Spanish omelette Omelette with the addition of tomato, onions and green peppers.

Spanish Riding School Sixteenth-century Viennese school, for which the Riding Hall was built in 1735, and which used and still uses only LIPIZZANER horses; it continues to be the chief school for classical or *haute école* riding. (So named after the horses, of Spanish origin.)

Spanish Steps (18th century). Mecca for British and American tourists in the artists' quarter of Rome, a wide flight of 137 steps ascending to a church. At the foot are the house where Keats died (with the Keats–Shelley Memorial Museum), a fountain by Bernini and an English tea-shop.

Spanish Succession, War of the (1701–13). War fought by the GRAND ALLIANCE to prevent the union of France and the Spanish Empire (Spain, Netherlands, Spanish America, Naples and Milan) under one crown after the succession of Louis XIV's grandson as Philip V of Spain. The main battles were fought by Marlborough, who won BLENHEIM, RAMILLIES, OUDENARDE and MALPLAQUET before he lost favour with Queen Anne and was dismissed (1711). The war ended with the Treaty of UTRECHT. Philip remained King of Spain on condition that he did not inherit the French throne.

Spanish Tragedy, The (1594). Thomas Kyd's tragedy in blank verse, an early example of the 'revenge' plays popular at the time. The hero exacts an elaborate and spectacular revenge on the murderers of his son and then takes his own life.

Spartacists (1919). German Communist Party founded by Karl Liebknecht and Rosa Luxemburg which tried to seize Berlin. The rising was suppressed by the FREIKORPS, who murdered the 2 leaders. (See next entry.)

Spartacus rising (73–71 BC). Revolt of Roman gladiators and slaves led by Spartacus. They held several Roman armies at bay while they ravaged most regions of Italy, but finally Spartacus was killed and his followers crucified.

Spartans DORIC people of the ancient Greek state of Laconia (capital, Sparta) in the southern Peloponnesus, noted for bravery, frugality, stern self-discipline, 'laconic' terseness, and dependence of their economy on conquered alien serfs (helots). Also called Lacedaemonians.

Spartium junceum Species name of the Spanish broom, taller than the CYTISUS which it resembles, and flowering later and longer.

Speaker, The President of the House of Commons who is responsible for order and discipline, selects members to speak to the motion in such a way as to give a fair hearing to all parties (they are said to 'catch the Speaker's eye'), and himself neither speaks nor votes (except when a casting vote is needed). He is elected by agreement between the parties at the beginning of each Parliament.

Speakers' Corner Site in Hyde Park, near Marble Arch, where street orators of all persuasions unburden themselves of their pet obsessions to crowds of amiable hecklers. The name is also given to similar rendezvous on Tower Hill and at Whitestone Pond, Hampstead Heath.

Special Air Service (1940). British uniformed paratroops used on sabotage missions in enemy territory in World War II, and later e.g. in Malaya against Communist rebels. In 1950 they became a permanent regiment of the regular army.

Special Branch (Scotland Yard). Nearest equivalent in Britain to secret police, which deals, in co-operation with MI-5, with offences against the state (e.g. treason, sabotage, subversive activities), investigates aliens, and guards foreign VIPs visiting Britain; first founded in 1886 to deal with the IRA; its strength is an offical secret.

Specialist, The Charles Sale's classic of lavatory humour.

Special Operations Executive (1940). British secret organization set up on the fall of France, originally to train men to act as a fifth column in enemy-occupied territory, and later to co-ordinate or initiate subversion and sabotage against the enemy.

Spectacle Makers, Worshipful Company of (1629). LIVERY COMPANY which holds examinations for, and grants diplomas to, opticians.

Spectator, The (1711–14). Successor to THE TATLER, edited by Steele and Addison, reporting their views through the mouths of members of the fictional Spectator club, one of whom was Sir Roger de COVERLEY. The modern *Spectator* was started in 1828.

Speech Day School's family gathering at the end of the academic year, when, traditionally, a distinguished Old Boy/Girl makes a speech saying 'I was always bottom of the class and look at me now' / and the headmaster/headmistress tactfully but firmly dispels this vision of *per pigritiem ad astra*. Prize-giving follows and possibly a play which is literally all Greek to the audience. See also FOURTH OF JUNE.

Speenhamland system (1795). Method of poor relief which used the rates to pay a cost-of-living allowance to supplement unduly low wages, which were thereby perpetuated; superseded by a new Poor Law (1834). (A place on the outskirts of Newbury, Berkshire, where started.)

Speke Hall Elizabethan black-and-white manor-house, near Liverpool Airport, leased from the NATIONAL TRUST by Liverpool Corporation.

Spencerianism (1) View that everything must, or should, be left to natural laws of evolution; see SURVIVAL OF THE FITTEST. (2) Optimistic view that progress is not an accident but a natural law, at work everywhere through an evolution from the simple to the complex. (Herbert Spencer, English philosopher, 1820–1903.)

Spengler's *Decline of the West* (1918). Book in which the German philosopher Oswald Spengler developed a theory of the inevitable eclipse, already begun, of the Western world, after a period of 'Caesarism'.

Spenlow and Jorkins The partners in a legal firm in DAVID COPPERFIELD. Spenlow was, he said, the most generous of men but was unfortunately always restrained by the stern, unbending (and invisible) Jorkins.

Sphinx, The (1) In Greek legend, a winged lion with the head and breast of a woman, which plagued Thebes and ate those who could not solve her riddles. Oedipus was the first to solve one, whereupon she destroyed herself. (2) In Egyptian legend, a lion with a man's head, origin of the Greek legend. Of the many Sphinx statues in Egypt, the most famous is that at GIZA.

Spiegel **affair** (1962). Arrest, on the orders of the Defence Minister, Franz-Josef Strauss, of the editor of *Der* SPIEGEL allegedly for publishing secret information about technical faults revealed by combined manoeuvres. Five West German ministers resigned in protest and Chancellor Adenauer reluctantly dropped Strauss. The editor had for years accused Strauss of incompetence, inebriety, high-handedness and corruption.

Spiegel, *Der* (1947). Popular West German weekly magazine, published in Hamburg; it has a reputation for fearless exposure of matters embarrassing to the government. (German, 'the mirror'.)

Spinet Small harpsichord made by Giovanni Spinetti in about 1500.

Spinoza's God Pantheistic conception, a God who reveals himself in the harmony of all being but is without personality or consciousness and does not concern himself with the actions of men. (Spinoza, 17th-century Dutch Jewish philosopher.)

Spion Kop (1) Hill for which a battle was fought (1900) during the siege of Ladysmith in the Boer War. (Near Ladysmith, in Natal.) (2) Name of the Derby winner in 1920.

Spiraea Genus name of the meadowsweet.

Spirit of St Louis Name of the aircraft in which Lindbergh made his solo flight across the Atlantic (1927).

Spitfire Supermarine fighter which made its name in the Battle of Britain, and by the end of the war had attained altitudes of 45,000 ft.

Spithead Mutiny (1797). See NORE MUTINY.

Spithead Review An annual assembly of the Grand Fleet in the Solent off Portsmouth. The last, held just before World War I, is famous because Churchill, as First Lord, on his own initiative ordered the ships not to disperse. The Fleet was thus in a state of covert mobilization long before the Cabinet decided to declare war on Germany.

Split A Yugoslav port, formerly known by its Italian name, Spalato.

Spock baby book, The (1946). *The Common-sense Book of Baby and Child Care* by Dr Benjamin Spock (USA), which sold 26 million copies in its first 9 years.

Spode (1770–1847). Firm founded by Josiah Spode I, at first making domestic earthenware, later decorated with underglaze transfer printing. In 1794 he introduced bone china, which soon became and still is the standard form of porcelain. Under Josiah II (1797–1827) the firm excelled in accurate reproductions of Meissen, French, Chinese and leading English styles in the new material. See COPELAND & GARRETT.

Sponge, Mr Hero of *Mr Sponge's Sporting Tour* (1853) by R. S. Surtees. He is a horse-coper who clings like a leech to any hospitality he can grab, impervious to all hints and snubs, driving his unwilling hosts to distraction.

Spoonerism Inadvertent transposition of sounds from one word to another, e.g. '. . . three cheers for the queer old dean' this kind of slip was made by the Rev. W. A. Spooner (1844–1930), dean (1876–89) and warden (1903–24) of New College, Oxford.

Sporozoa See PROTOZOA.

Sport of Kings, The Horse-racing, as owing much to the early support of the Stuarts from James I onwards.

Sportsman of the Year Selected by the new NATIONAL SPORTING CLUB as the man with the best all-round achievement in sport, and the guest of honour at the club's annual Celebrity Banquet.

Spread Eagle, The Inn sign, once denoting that German wines were on sale. (Taken from the Arms of Germany.)

Spring Awakening (1891). German Wedekind's play on problems of adolescent sex, amazingly outspoken for 1891 and originally banned in England.

Springboks (1) South Africans; (2) the South African rugby football team. (An antelope, the national emblem.)

Spring Double Bet on the Lincolnshire and the Grand National, both run in March.

Springer empire German newspaper and periodical group built up by Axel Springer. The chief units are the mass-circulation *Bild Zeitung* (1952) and the influential quality daily *Die Welt* (bought 1953), together with their Sunday counterparts.

Springfield rifle (1855). Repeating rifle made at Springfield, Massachusetts, by SMITH AND WESSON.

Spurs, The See HOTSPURS.

Sputnik Russian name for their first series of earth satellites. *Sputnik I*, launched 4 October 1957, was the first man-made satellite to orbit the earth, and *Sputnik II*, a month later, the first to carry a living creature (a dog). (Russian, 'travelling companion'.)

Spy Pseudonym of the caricaturist Sir Leslie Ward (1851–1922), whose work was published in *Vanity Fair*.

Spycatcher This was the title of a book written by Peter Wright, a one-time senior intelligence officer of the British service. The book caused a sensation not on its (debatable) merits but because the British government, in the courts of Australia and Great Britain, tried to suppress it. The various hearings caused enormous legal expense and achieved more notoriety for the book than it would otherwise have achieved. Perhaps the most outstanding *mot* uttered in the course of one action was the admission by a senior British civil servant that he had been been, in evidence, 'economical with the truth'.

Spy Who Came in from the Cold, The (1963). John Le Carré's disillusioned novel about the seamy side of spying, set in Berlin; it was made into a successful film.

Square Mile, The Name for the City of London.

Squarson A man who doubled the parts of squire and parson, typically paying more attention to the former; a result of the rise in status of the clergy during Hanoverian times. (Portmanteau word, squire + parson.)

Squeers, Wackford Illiterate rogue in Dickens's *Nicholas Nickleby* who runs DOTHEBOYS HALL.

Squiffites Contemporary nickname for the followers of the former Liberal Prime Minister, H. H. Asquith, after he had been displaced by Lloyd George in December 1916. (Abbreviation and corruption of 'Asquithites'.)

Squire Toby Rarer form of Toby jug in which a handsome squire, sitting in a corner chair and holding a churchwarden pipe, replaces the TOBY FILLPOT of the standard jug.

Squirrel Nutkin (1903). Children's book written and illustrated by Beatrix Potter.

SR-N Designations of a series of HOVERCRAFT. SR-N1 was the first to cross the English Channel (1953); -N3 a large version designed for anti-submarine use; -N4 (Mountbatten Class), over 100 tons, built for cross-Channel service (1968); -N6 a smaller version built for the same purpose, and in operation from 1966. (SR for Saunders-Roe, the original manufacturers.)

SS Hitler's personal army, originally a small and highly disciplined section of the SA. In 1936 they were merged with the GESTAPO. They kept close watch on Army officers and officials of the National-Socialist (Nazi) Party and government; organized the FINAL SOLUTION; staffed the concentration camps; and terrorized occupied countries. See also WAFFEN-SS. (Schutzstaffeln, 'security units'; also called Blackshirts.)

SSAFA Initials of the Soldiers', Sailors' and Airmen's Families Association, a voluntary body which assists ex-servicemen and their families in distress. (Pronounced saf'a.)

Stabat Mater (*dolorosa*) Thirteenth-century hymn on the 7 sorrows of Mary at the Cross, of which there are musical settings by Palestrina and many other composers. (Latin, 'The Mother stands mourning', the first words; pronounced stah'bat mah'ter or stay'bat may'tèer or sta'bat may'tèr dol-or-oh'a.)

Stade Roland Garros French and international clay-court tennis equivalent of Wimbledon, at Auteuil, south-west Paris; the stadium is also used for other sports. (French aviator.)

Staff College, Camberley College where selected army officers are given training for the holding of staff appointments; after graduation the letters psc (passed Staff College) are added after their names in service lists.

Staffordshire Regiment (The Prince of Wales's), The (1959). A regiment of the MERCIAN BRIGADE, an amalgamation of The South Staffordshire Regiment and The North Staffordshire (The Prince of Wales's) Regiment.

Stag at Bay, The One of the most popular of Landseer's paintings; see MONARCH OF THE GLEN.

Stahlhelm German monarchist ex-servicemen's organization, taken over by Hitler and dissolved in 1935. (German, 'steel helmet'.)

Stakhanovite Title of honour in Soviet Russia for a worker whose output greatly exceeded the norm. (Alexei Stakhanov, a coalminer who in 1935, by a combination of hard work and intelligent time and motion study, produced phenomenal outputs.)

Stalag German prisoner-of-war camp for NCOs and men. (Abbreviation of *Stamm*, 'main body', and *Lager*, 'camp'.)

Stalingrad City of RSFSR, now renamed Volgograd. See next entry.

Stalingrad, Battle of (August 1942 to February 1943). The successful Russian defence of the city now known as Volgograd against German assault, the turning-point in Hitler's Russian campaign.

Stalinist purges (1934–40). Series of mass purges of leading Russian Communists during Stalin's regime, under successive heads of the secret police: under Yagoda (1934–6), started by the LAW OF DECEMBER 1; under Yezhov (1936–8; see YEZHOVSHCHINA); and under Beria (1939–40). A peculiar feature was the extraction of public 'confessions' of treason for some of the victims, who were shot whether or not they confessed.

Stalin Prize Name given to the LENIN PRIZE, 1940–54.

Stalky and Co. (1899). Kipling's fictionalized account of his schooldays at the United Services College, Westward Ho!, Devon. Of the main characters, Stalky is the future commander of DUNSTER FORCE, Beetle is the author and M'Turk is George Charles Beresford.

Stamboul An earlier form, used by Europeans, of the name ISTANBUL (Constantinople).

Stamford Bridge Fulham home of the Chelsea soccer team and (1909–31) of the AAA championships.

Stamp Act (1765). British government's measure

imposing stamp duty on newspapers, legal documents, etc., on the American colonies, the most resented of the Acts of 1764–7 (Sugar, Customs Collecting, Revenue, Tea) and the least wise, since it upset those ever-vocal elements, the lawyers, editors and land speculators. Opposition centred on James Otis's slogan 'No taxation without representation'; the Act was repealed the next year, but the damage was done and events moved inexorably on to the BOSTON TEA PARTY.

Stampa, La (1867). One of the 2 most influential newspapers in Italy, the other being the COR-RIERE DELLA SERA of Milan; published in Turin, controlled by the Fiat group. (There is no correspondingly influential Rome daily.)

Stamp Memorial lecture (1945). An annual lecture on an economics subject, given at London University.

Standard Oil of New Jersey (1882). J. D. Rockefeller's oil giant which controls Exxon, Cleveland Petroleum, Imperial Oil, etc., and operates in most parts of the world.

Standfast, Mr Character in Part II of PILGRIM'S PROGRESS who formerly lived by hearsay and faith 'but now I go where I shall live by sight'.

Stanford (1885). US university near Palo Alto, California.

Stanhope Gold Medal See ROYAL HUMANE SOCIETY.

Stanislavsky system Rigorous system of training, introduced at the Moscow Art Theatre by which an actor is taught to sink his personality completely into his role; the US/ source of the American METHOD ACTING.

Stanley Cup Playoffs (North America) Annual ice hockey series in the National Hockey League, a major event in the US/Canadian sporting calendar.

Stanley Gibbons (1856). London firm of stamp dealers, one of the largest in the world.

Stannaries (1305). Tin-mining districts of Devon and Cornwall with special courts. The jurisdiction of the courts was abolished in 1897.

Stansgate, Baron See WEDGWOOD BENN CASE.

Stansted Airfield near Bishop's Stortford, Essex. Its selection in 1967 for expansion as the second subsidiary of London Airport (the first being GATWICK) aroused vociferous opposition, and further consideration was given to alternatives.

Star and Garter Home (1916). Home for permanently disabled ex-servicemen, on Richmond Hill, Surrey.

Star Chamber Court manned by royal councillors, first effectively used by the Tudors to try cases affecting Crown interests; abused by Charles I to persecute opponents, and abolished in 1641. (Met in room with ceiling decorated with stars.)

Starfighter The US Lockheed F-104, a single-seat multi-purpose supersonic fighter; very many of those in service with the Luftwaffe crashed.

Starkers Slang phrase for 'stark naked' or 'stark mad'.

Star of David A 6-pointed star, emblem of Judaism; also the yellow cloth badge (German, *Schandeband*, 'shame-band') in this shape which National-Socialists (Nazis) forced Jews to wear.

Stars and Stripes, The (1) Flag of the United States, with 13 red and white horizontal stripes representing the original seceding colonies (Mass., RI, Conn., NH, NY, NJ, Penn., Del., Md, Va, NC, SC, Ga) and, on a blue union, one white star for each state. (2) The chief (GI) US Armed Forces daily, which first appeared in France in 1918 and was reborn in London (1942), eventually with special editions for the various war fronts.

'Stars and Stripes Forever, The' (1897). One of the SOUSA MARCHES.

'Star-Spangled Banner, The' Officially proclaimed the US national anthem in 1931, with words written in 1814 by Francis Scott Key to the 18th-century English melody (attributed to John Stafford Smith) of an academic *jeu d'esprit* entitled 'To Anacreon in Heaven'. Towards the end of the War of 1812, Key bearded an English admiral aboard his flagship to plead for a friend's release, and thus became an involuntary spectator of the Royal Navy's unsuccessful night bombardment of Fort McHenry (Baltimore). As dawn broke he was overjoyed to see the Stars and Stripes still flying from the fort and, inspired by its defenders' refusal to capitulate, began then and there to scribble down the words of his poem on the back of an old letter. Under the title 'The Defense of Fort McHenry' it was published in a Baltimore paper a few days later; the modest author 'believed it to have been favourably received'.

Star Wars Popular name for the Strategic Defense Initiative (SDI), a space-based anti-missile system being researched in the USA. Since the initial announcement in 1983 the budget for this project has been drastically reduced. (After a 1977 science-fiction film.)

State Department US equivalent of the British Foreign Office, under the Secretary of State.

State Enrolled Nurse Qualification obtainable after a simpler course of training than for SRN (State Registered Nurse).

Stately Homes Great English country houses. (From the opening line of a poem by Mrs Hemans resuscitated in a Noël Coward parody.)

State of the Union message (USA) Equivalent to the Queen's Speech; at the beginning of each session of Congress the President outlines the programme of legislation that has been prepared for its consideration.

State Opening Ceremonial opening of Parliament by the Queen at the beginning of the new session in late October or early November, and when a new Parliament assembles after a general election. It is the occasion of the QUEEN'S SPEECH.

States-General French assembly of the 3 Estates: Nobility, Clergy and Commons (THIRD ESTATE); Louis XVI was forced to summon it in 1789, for the first time since 1614, to pass measures necessitated by the country's bankruptcy.

Statesman's Year-Book, The Standard book of reference giving statistical and other information about the countries of the world, published annually since 1864.

States' Rights Party (USA) See DIXIECRATS.

Stationers and Newspaper Makers, Worshipful Company of (1557). LIVERY COMPANY, originally a guild of dealers in and producers of books. Membership is restricted to those in the printing, publishing and allied trades, who meet at Stationers' Hall, where a register of copyrights is kept.

Stations of the Cross Series of 14 pictures or frescoes on the walls of Roman Catholic churches, representing scenes from the last hours of Christ, from the condemnation to death to the placing of the body in the tomb; prayers are offered at each station. Also called the Via Crucis (Way of the Cross).

Stavisky scandal (1933–4). Revelation of large-scale frauds by a French financier, Alexandre Stavisky, which led to his suicide, the fall of the government (a minister being involved) and right-wing riots in Paris.

Stavrogin Chief character of Dostoyevsky's *The Possessed* (1872), a member of the upper class who gets involved with Nihilists and who, after confessing to being the cause of a young girl's suicide, hangs himself.

STD Abbreviation for Subscriber Trunk Dialling, the telephone system which enables calls to be made without the intervention of an operator.

Steady State theory (1948). A cosmological hypothesis that continuous creation of matter produces new galaxies which force older galaxies ever outwards; put forward by Bondi and Gold and supported for a time by Fred Hoyle. It postulates a universe that has always existed and will always exist, in contrast to the BIG BANG THEORY, and was suggested by the EXPANDING UNIVERSE THEORY.

Stedman One of the principal methods of change-ringing church bells. (Fabian Stedman of Cambridge, its 17th-century inventor.)

Steerforth In Dickens's *David Copperfield*, a rich young cad who leads Little Em'ly Peggotty astray and is drowned at sea. His rival, Ham Peggotty, is drowned trying to save him.

Stella Jonathan Swift's name for his friend Esther Johnson (whom he may later have married). His letters to her, written 1710–13 and not meant for publication, were posthumously published in 1766–8 as the *Journal to Stella*.

Stellenbosch South African town near Cape Town, in the Boer War a military base of minor importance; hence 'to Stellenbosch' became an army term for moving out of harm's way a senior officer who had failed in the field.

'Stem van Suid-Afrika, Die' ('Die Stem') South African national anthem, introduced 1936 and replaced the British in 1957. (Afrikaans, 'the voice of South Africa'.)

Stentor Greek herald in the Trojan War whom Homer credited with the voice of 50 men; hence stentorian, 'loud-voiced'.

Stepney Former London metropolitan borough, since 1965 part of the borough of TOWER HAMLETS.

Steptoe and Son BBC TV series, script by Alan Simpson and Ray Galton, about the love–hate relationship of 2 Cockney 'totters' (junk merchants), father and son, and also featuring, until his lamented death, their horse Hercules.

Stern (1948). Hamburg weekly glossy aimed at the younger generation and improved East–West relations; lively coverage of serious issues mingles with crime, sex and fashion. (German, 'star'.)

Stern gang Anti-British terrorist organization active in Palestine in the 1940s; they assassinated the UN mediator, Count Bernadotte (1948). (Led by Abraham Stern, fighting under the *nom de guerre* Yair; killed by the CID in 1942.)

Stetson Ten-gallon cowboy hat. (John B. Stetson hat company.)

Stettin German name of the city of Szczecin, now in Polish Pomerania.

Stevenage (1946). One of the earliest NEW TOWNS, adjoining the existing town in Hertfordshire.

Stevenson Committee (1922). Committee which recommended restrictions in the production of

rubber, the price of which had fallen disastrously after World War I; a principle later applied to world tin production.

Stewards' Cup (1840). Six-furlong flat-race run at Goodwood in July.

Stewards' Cup (1841). Second senior challenge cup at Henley Regatta, for coxless fours.

Stewards' Enclosure At Henley Regatta, a small lawn by the finishing post.

Steyne, Lord See Becky SHARP.

Stiffkey, Rector of (1932). The Rev. Harold Davidson, who was unfrocked for immoral conduct and then went round the fairs exhibiting himself in a barrel, etc., until killed by a circus lion.

Stilton Semi-hard blue British cheese made in Leicestershire which gets its name from the original mainroad selling-point, Stilton, in Huntingdonshire. The belief that it is improved by pouring port or beer into it is baseless.

Stirling (1941). Heavy 4-engined Short bomber used by the RAF in World War II.

Stockbroker Belt Outer ring of suburbs round London (or other cities) with prosperous-looking houses standing well back from the road, of the kind that imagination peoples with stockbrokers and their 'income-bracket' like.

Stockholm Appeal (1950). Appeal to ban the atomic bomb, allegedly signed by 500 million people, not all of them Communists.

Stockholm Treaty (1959). Treaty under which EFTA was established.

Stock prize (1919). Annual literary prize of £40 presented by the French magazines *Fémina* and *Vie heureuse* for an imaginative work by a young British author, or by one who has not been adequately recognized. See FÉMINA-VIE HEUREUSE PRIZE.

Stockwell Ghost (1772). Hoax perpetrated in Stockwell, London, by a servant girl, similar to the COCK LANE GHOST.

Stoicism Mainly ethical philosophy that counsels acceptance of a fate decreed by divine wisdom, the primacy of virtue, the need to subdue passion and to endure hardship with courage. Founded in the 4th century BC by the Greek, Zeno, it made a special appeal in the 1st and 2nd centuries AD in Rome, where it was propagated by Seneca, Epictetus and Marcus Aurelius. (From the *Stoa Poikilē*, 'painted porch', in Athens, where Zeno taught.)

Stoke Mandeville Leading hospital for spinal diseases and injuries, near Aylesbury, Buckinghamshire.

Stoke Newington Former London metropolitan borough, since 1965 part of the borough of HACKNEY.

Stokes-Adams syndrome Condition resembling epilepsy in which the ventricles of the heart stop beating long enough to produce loss of consciousness. It is a possible sequel to myocarditis (disease of the heart muscle).

Stokes mortar (1915). British trench mortar, used in both world wars to lob small HE (high-explosive), gas, smoke or incendiary bombs into enemy positions. (Sir Frederick Stokes.)

Stonehenge Stone circle on Salisbury Plain by the A303 west of Amesbury, constructed and rearranged over a period of 1,000 years. It comprises a horsehoe of 5 sets of SARSEN trilithons (*c.* 1750 BC), 16–22 ft high, with an 'altar' stone; a surrounding circle of 30 Sarsen stones, 14 ft high, all originally supporting mortised lintels; a horseshoe and circle of Bluestones, first brought from the Prescelly Hills, Pembroke, *c.* 2150; and an outer ditch (2700 BC), inside which is a circle of ritual pits (Aubrey holes). Stonehenge, like WOODHENGE, is oriented on the midsummer sunrise, but the Hele stone outside the ditch is not, and never was, on this line. Bronze Age weapons are carved on some Sarsens, one resembling a Mycenaean dagger. AVEBURY and SILBURY HILL are near by. (From Old English *hengen*, 'hanging', referring to the lintels.)

Stonehouse affair (1974). In 1976 John Stonehouse, a Member of Parliament and ex-Postmaster-General was given 7 years' imprisonment having been found guilty of multiple frauds and false pretences in obtaining passports. He disappeared from Miami, USA, in November 1974 leaving a pile of clothes on the beach but was detained in Melbourne, Australia, in December 1974 and extradited to UK in July 1975. His downfall began when he founded the British Bangladesh Trust in 1972.

Stone Mountain World's largest granite monolith, near Atlanta, Ga, it covers 583 acres and rises to 1,680 ft above sea-level.

Stones, The Expression used by travelling people in the 1980s, in the early summer as they travel towards STONEHENGE.

'Stonewall' Jackson Southern general in the American Civil War, so named from his stubborn resistance in the first Battle of BULL RUN (1861).

Stonyhurst College Roman Catholic public school for boys, near Clitheroe, Blackburn, Lancashire.

Stormont Castle in Belfast, Northern Ireland, and the government administrative centre for the province. Also used as an expression meaning the Parliament or Assembly of Northern Ireland when this existed.

Storm over Shanghai See CONDITION HUMAINE.

Storm Troops Name for the National-Socialist (Nazi) SA.

Storting Norwegian Parliament.

Stowe Eighteenth-century Palladian country house near Buckingham, since 1923 housing the public school of that name.

Strabismus, Dr Leading BEACHCOMBER character, usually referred to as Dr Strabismus (Whom God Preserve) of Utrecht. (Strabismus = squint.)

Strachan and Chatham See WALCHEREN EXPEDITION.

Stradivarius Name given to violins made at Cremona, Italy, by Antonio Stradivari (1644–1737), reputed to be the best ever made. (Pronounced strad-i-vahr'i-us.)

Straffen murder case (1951). Trail of John Thomas Straffen, market gardener, found unfit to plead to the charge of strangling 2 small girls at Bath and sent to Broadmoor, from which he escaped. Charged with strangling another small girl, he was found fit to plead, sentenced to death but reprieved, and imprisoned.

Straits Convention (1841). International agreement that, as long as Turkey was at peace, the Dardanelles were to be closed to the warships of all nations. This effectually bottled up the Russian Black Sea fleet, and the agreement was modified in subsequent years.

Straits Settlements (1826–1946). British Crown Colony consisting of Singapore, Penang, Malacca, Labuan and various small islands; capital Singapore.

Straker, Henry Chauffeur in Shaw's MAN AND SUPERMAN. Writing in 1903, Shaw chose him as the representative of a new class whose imminent rise to importance he foresaw – the skilled mechanic.

Strangers and Brothers C. P. (Lord) Snow's series of novels begun in 1940, some partly autobiographical, narrated by Lewis Eliot, treating in general the theme of conflict between conscience and ambition in the struggle for power in a Cambridge college, the world of scientific research, the civil service, etc.; his *Corridors of Power* (1964) was a continuation of this theme in the political field.

Strangers' Galleries Galleries in the Houses of Parliament from which members of the public can listen to debates. Certain sections are reserved for 'distinguished strangers' (ambassadors, etc.) and for those with special interest in a particular debate.

Strangeways Prison Manchester prison.

Strasbourgeoise (Cooking) With foie gras or sauerkraut.

Strathcona Cup (1903). Curling contest between Scotland and Canada.

Strathspey Cup Skiing competition held in the Cairngorms, Scotland, in April.

Strawberry Hill House at Twickenham, rebuilt by Horace Walpole (1717–97) in a style generally held to herald the Gothic Revival, and called at the time 'Gothick'.

Street, The (1) Fleet Street, London, formerly the world of newspapers and journalists. (2) (US) WALL STREET, New York City.

Streetcar (1947). Common abbreviated title of Tennessee Williams's play of New Orleans, *A Streetcar Named Desire*. Blanche, Williams's usual faded Southern belle, is staying with her sister. Her brother-in-law Stanley, angry at her airs and graces, warns off a possible suitor. Blanche is raped by Stanley, and is carried off to an asylum. (The French title is *Tramway*.)

Street Which is Called Straight, The Covered (once colonnaded) street which runs east and west through Damascus, the scene of St Paul's conversion (Acts 9:11).

Strelitzia Bird-of-paradise flower, named after Charlotte, Queen of George III, of the House of Mecklenburg-Strelitz.

Strength Through Joy National-Socialist (Nazi) organization providing regimented leisure for German workers, including theatres, sport and, especially, foreign travel and cruises at cheap prices. (German, *Kraft durch Freude*.)

Strephon (1) Shepherd in Sir Philip Sidney's *Arcadia*. (2) Conventional name for any rustic swain. (3) Half fairy, half mortal son of IO-LANTHE in the Gilbert and Sullivan opera, who becomes a Member of Parliament.

Strife (1909). Galsworthy's play, giving a balanced presentation of both points of view in an industrial struggle between John Anthony ('No compromise') for the owners, and David Roberts ('No surrender'), the strike leader. Roberts's wife dies, both sides throw over their leaders and agree on the terms offered before the strike began.

Strine Australian for Australian.

Stroganoff Used adjectivally of beef, etc. sliced thin and cooked in a sauce of consommé, sour cream, mustard, onion and condiments. (Count

Paul Stroganoff, 19th-century Russian diplomat and gourmet.)

Strongbow Nickname of Richard de Clare, Earl of Pembroke, one of the first Anglo-Norman adventurers to start the English conquest of Ireland in 1170. His tomb is supposed to be in Dublin.

Strong country, The Area, marked by signs 'You are entering the Strong country', served by the Strong brewery of Romsey and its public houses in Hampshire, Dorset and Wiltshire. (Now part of Whitbreads.)

Structuralism System of analysis of culture and society. It seeks to uncover underlying patterns and structures, and basic elements from which such patterns are constructed. The leading figure in the structuralist movement is the French social anthropologist Claude Lévi-Strauss.

Struwwelpeter (1847). Heinrich Hoffman's illustrated book of cautionary verse for children, introducing such characters as Fidgety Phil (who would not keep still) and Little Johnny Head-in-air. It was written in German and translated into many languages. (German, 'shock-headed Peter'.)

Stuart period (1603–1714). Blanket term in the decorative arts sometimes used to cover the JACOBEAN, RESTORATION, WILLIAM AND MARY and QUEEN ANNE periods.

Stuarts Dynasty that ruled Scotland 1371–1603 (Robert II to James VI), and England and Scotland 1603–1714 (James I to Queen Anne). (Originally Stewart or Steuart, a family founded by an 11th-century Breton immigrant who became Steward of Scotland to King David I; Robert II was son of Robert the Bruce's daughter; James VI and I was son of Mary Queen of Scots, James V's daughter, who adopted the spelling 'Stuart'.)

Stubbs Author's name used for his standard work. *The Constitutional History of England* (1874–8).

Student Prince, The (1924). Light opera, music by Sigmund Romberg, libretto by Dorothy Donnelly. Among its highlights were the 'Drinking Song' and the waltz 'Deep in My Heart, Dear'.

Study in Scarlet, A (1887). Conan Doyle's first Sherlock HOLMES story.

Study of History, A (1935–61). Arnold Toynbee's 12-volume philosophical study of the pattern of rise, growth and fall of world civilizations. He believed that they rise always in, and spurred by, adverse conditions, and decay after creating a 'universal' religion. A 2-volume abridgement was later published.

Stukas (1937). German Junkers-87 dive-bombers, first tried out in the Spanish Civil War and then used in the early stages of World War II.

Stupor Mundi Name given to the 13th-century Holy Roman Emperor Frederick II on account of his vast erudition combined with statesmanship and military competence. (Latin, 'wonder of the world'.)

Sturm and Drang (18th century). German literary movement, of which the principal figures were Goethe and Schiller, in their early work, and which reacted against the rationalism and formalism of contemporary writers. (German, 'storm and stress', in the title of a play which initiated the movement.)

Stylites Christians who practised a form of extreme asceticism started in the 5th century by the Syrian, Simeon Stylites, who spent some 40 years sitting on top of pillars; this extreme practice continued until the 16th century. (From Greek for 'pillar'; pronounced sty'lyts; as a name, sty-ly'teez.)

Styx, Stygian Lake Hated river or lake which, in Greek legend, guarded the passage to the Underworld and over which CHARON ferried the dead. (Pronounced stiks, stij'i-an.)

Sublime Porte (1) Ottoman court at Constantinople. (2) Used as a synonym for the Turkish (Imperial) government. (French translation of Turkish for 'lordly gate'.)

Subtopia Name coined from 'suburban Utopia' for the fringe suburbs of large cities which have invaded the countryside, undistinguished and indistinguishable.

Suchow, Battle of (November 1948). Decisive battle in which the Chinese Red Army defeated the Kuomintang forces; the Communist regime was established the following year. (Former Treaty Port, on the Grand Canal, west of Shanghai; also spelt Soochow, Hsüchow.)

Sucker State Nickname of Illinois.

Sudeten crisis (1938). Hitler's claim to Czech SUDETENLAND on the grounds that the inhabitants were mainly German; contested by Czechoslovakia because it formed a natural frontier and provided skilled labour for Czech industry. The area was given to Hitler by the MUNICH AGREEMENT but restored after World War II to the Czechs, who expelled the German population.

Sudetenland Mountainous region formerly in Austria–Hungary and populated mainly by Germans. Strictly, it is the Sudeten range from the Oder to the Neisse on the border between Bohemia and Moravia (in Czechoslovakia) and Silesia (Poland); but in common usage includes the Erz Gebirge (Ore Mountains) range between Bohemia and Saxony (Germany). See preceding entry.

Sudra Lowest Hindu caste (except for the Untouchables), of peasants, artisans and labourers.

Sue Ryder Homes Homes for the chronic sick and homeless of all ages, especially those who suffer as a result of Nazi persecution.

Suez Canal Canal linking the Mediterranean with the Red Sea. Opened in 1869 and built by Ferdinand de Lesseps. Except in time of war the canal is open to vessels of all nations. It was blocked by Egypt in 1967 and reopened in 1975.

Suez crisis (29 October to 6 November 1956). Situation which arose from Egyptian hostility to Israel; USA's consequent denial of finance for the ASWAN HIGH DAM; Nasser's nationalization of the Suez Canal as a substitute source of revenue, arousing British fears for freedom of passage through it; and Egyptian aid to Algerian rebels against France. Israel, Britain and France concerted attacks on Egypt which had to be called off within a week when Eisenhower and Dulles unexpectedly threatened financial retaliation.

Suez rebels Name given (1954) to Tory MPs who, headed by Capt. Waterhouse, defied their leaders by voting against the ratification of an agreement with Egypt for the withdrawal of British troops from the Suez Canal, 2 years before the Suez crisis.

Suffolk (sheep) Widely distributed breed of short-wool sheep, with black face, ears and legs; it produces good meat and a thick fleece.

Suffolk Punch Short-legged powerful farm horse, chestnut in colour with flaxen mane and tail.

Sufism Muslim form of GNOSTICISM; the Sufis were organized in orders of dervishes (fakirs), some of whom induced trance-like states by religious dances. (Arabic *suf*, 'wool', from the rough woollen garments worn.)

Sugar Bowl Sports stadium at New Orleans, Louisiana.

Sulawesi Group of Indonesian islands, formerly known as the Celebes.

Sulgrave Manor Small Elizabethan manor house near Banbury, Northamptonshire, built by George Washington's ancestor.

Sullom Voe Europe's largest oil and liquefied gas terminal situated on a deep coastal inlet in the Shetland Islands, Scotland.

Sumer Earlier name of Babylonia, which from about 3,000 BC was a country of city-states (including Ur of the Chaldees), united only in religion.

Sumerians Non-Semitic race of unknown origin, possibly related to the aboriginal peoples of southern India, who settled in SUMER (southern Mesopotamia) about 4000 BC. Deeply religious, they founded a civilization which, with their religion and cuneiform writing, was adopted by their successors, the Akkadians, Babylonians and Assyrians.

'Sumer is icumen in' Earliest known English lyric, dating to the mid 13th century; the second line is 'Lhude sing cuccu!', from which it gets its name 'Cuckoo song'.

Summerhill (1924). Coeducational boarding school at Leiston, Suffolk, founded and run by A. S. Neill, a Scottish schoolmaster who began to propagate his views in 1915 (*A Dominie's Log*, etc.). The children run the school, work when they feel like it and at what they choose. Staff stand by to help if asked.

Summit Conference See GENEVA SUMMIT CONFERENCE; PARIS SUMMIT CONFERENCE.

Sun (1964). Successor to the Labour *Daily Herald*, rescued from bankruptcy in 1969 by an Australian, Rupert Murdoch, and transformed into an independent paper of more popular appeal.

Sunday In spite of attempts by some diary printers, Sunday is historically the first day of the week, and the provenance of this is in the actions of the Church father Justin Martyr (*c.* 100 to *c.* 165); he said the Christians chose their particular day for Gospel reading and to celebrate the Eucharist. 'It is on what is called the Sun's day . . .'

Sunderland (1937). Short flying boat used in World War II; from it was developed the Empire class airliner which pioneered many overseas routes.

Sunderland ware (1740–1897). Earthenware made at several Sunderland (Durham) factories; notably the blotchy-pink lustre jugs decorated with transfer prints of the Wearmouth Bridge, opened 14 miles from Sunderland in 1796. Also noted for Sunderland lion ornaments and frog mugs.

Sunflower State Nickname of Kansas.

Sunflowers Vivid painting, one of a series on the same subject, by Van Gogh during the ARLES period; it was intended for Gauguin's bedroom and has become one of the most widely reproduced of French Impressionist paintings.

Sung dynasty (Song dynasty) (960–1279). Dynasty which ruled central China from Hangchow as capital, Genghis Khan having established Mongol rule in the north. It was an age of literary and artistic brilliance, famous for celadon ware and paintings of landscapes, animals, birds and flowers. The YÜAN DYNASTY followed.

Sunnites (Sunni) Orthodox Muslims who accept Abu Bakr as having been rightfully chosen to succeed MOHAMMED as the first Caliph. (*Sunna*, book of sayings attributed to Mohammed, not recognized by the SHI'ITES.)

'Sunny Jim' (1902). Character illustrated on the first breakfast cereal of wheat flakes, 'Force'. By the 1930s everybody knew 'High o'er the fence leapt Sunny Jim / Force is the food that raises him'. A rag doll of Sunny Jim is still available.

Sunset Boulevard (1) Street that winds down to the Pacific from downtown Los Angeles. Part of it has large houses built by Hollywood stars; another part is the SUNSET STRIP. (2) Film directed by Billy Wilder in which Gloria Swanson made her comeback in 1950.

Sunset Strip One-mile section of Sunset Boulevard, LA, the psychedelic haunt of hippies, with blue movies, homosexual dance-halls, topless waitresses and bottomless pop-groups. It thus has claims to be the Sodom of some latter-day Genesis, where Lot's wife might be expected to turn into a pillar of rock candy.

Sunshine State Nickname of New Mexico.

Supercalifragilisticexpialidocious Invented by MARY POPPINS for her charges, meaning 'super'.

Superfortress Boeing B-29, a US high-altitude, heavily armed giant bomber used (1944) in raids on Japan from bases in China, India and later the Marianas. It also made the first nonstop, flight-refuelled circumnavigation of the world (1949).

'Supermac' Harold Macmillan. See VICKY.

Superman Concept developed by Nietzsche in THUS SPAKE ZARATHUSTRA. It is man at the utmost limits of his possible development, the objective towards which man should bend the whole of his will-power, not shrinking from trampling on the weak if necessary, in the hope that in some future generation it will be achieved. The National-Socialists (Nazis) adapted this idea to fit their theory of German racial superiority.

'Superman' (1938). The hero of US comic strips and TV films, seemingly immortal; a shy bespectacled man who, when occasion arises, is transmogrified into a magnificent hero whose powers of flight and feats of strength (e.g. pushing planets back into their orbit) made Hercules look very small beer – and his creator very rich.

Super Tuesday Day in March during Presidential election year in USA on which primary elections and caucuses take place in a large number of states which generally give an indication of who will be the candidates for the presidency.

Supply Bills Finance Bill which imposes taxation and the CONSOLIDATED FUND Bill which authorizes government expenditure.

Supreme Court See LAW COURTS.

Supreme Soviet Highest legislative organ of the USSR. It consists of two chambers with equal legislative rights, elected for a term of 5 years, the Soviet of the Union, and the Soviet of Nationalities.

Supremo Unofficial wartime title for Lord Louis Mountbatten, Supreme Commander, South-East Asia (1943–5). (Possibly suggested by El Supremo, a character in the first of the HORN-BLOWER series.)

Surbiton Former municipal borough of Surrey, since 1965 part of the borough of KINGSTON UPON THAMES.

Surface, Joseph and Charles See SCHOOL FOR SCANDAL.

Suriname A state in South America, formerly called Netherlands Guiana. (Pronounced soor-i-nam'.)

Surrealism (1924). Successor to DADAISM, inspired by Freudian theories, and chiefly associated with Chirico and Spanish artists such as Dali and Miró. They depicted, with meticulous attention to detail, a dream world in which miscellaneous objects of startling incongruity are brought together. The movement spread to writers, who attempted to dredge up the contents of the subconscious mind.

Surrender of Breda (1635). Velázquez's painting (in the Prado, Madrid) depicting the Dutch surrendering the keys of Breda to the Spanish in 1625. Sometimes called *The Lances*.

Surrey University (1967). Formerly Battersea CAT, moved to a new site near Guildford Cathedral.

Surtsey Island created off the coast of Iceland by volcanic activity, 1963–5.

Survival of the Fittest Phrase first used by Herbert Spencer (see SPENCERIANISM) in regard to economic man. He opposed any state interference such as poor relief or free education, holding that it tended to perpetuate the survival of the unfit. Darwin borrowed the phrase in connection with NATURAL SELECTION.

Susanna and the Elders (1st century BC). Story told in the Apocryphal book The History of Susanna, set in Babylon. Susanna repels the advances of 2 Jewish Elders who revenge themselves by accusing her of adultery. The prophet Daniel interviews them separately, proves they are lying, and has them put to death. Hence the expression 'a Daniel come to judgement' used in Shakespeare's *Merchant of Venice*.

Sutter's fever (1848). Excitement generated by the discovery of gold at Sutter's Mill in the Sacramento Valley 40 miles north-east of Sacramento, Calif., which precipitated the gold rush.

Sutton London borough since 1965 consisting of the former boroughs of Sutton–Cheam and Beddington–Wallington and the urban district of Carshalton.

Sutton Hoo Site near Woodbridge, Suffolk, of a 7th-century AD Saxon royal ship-burial, discovered in 1939. The varied treasures of silver and gold are in the British Museum.

Suvarov (Cooking) With foie gras, truffles and Madeira.

Suvla Bay landing (1915). See DARDANELLES CAMPAIGN.

Svengali Character in George Du Maurier's novel *Trilby* (1894). A Hungarian musician and hypnotist, Svengali mesmerizes an artists' model, Trilby, into becoming a famous singer. When he dies the spell is broken, she loses her voice, and herself dies broken-hearted.

Sverdlovsk City of the RSFSR, formerly EKATERINBURG.

Swabia Region corresponding to the medieval German duchy of that name, the home of the HOHENZOLLERNS, ruled by the HOHENSTAUFENS in the 12th–13th centuries and then by the Counts of Württemberg; chief town, Stuttgart. It now lies in Baden-Württemberg and Bavaria. The Swabian dialect is still spoken in Württemberg; Swabians have been regarded as the best German soldiers from Roman times, and as notably industrious.

Swahili (1) Bantu people, originally of Zanzibar and the neighbouring African coast. (2) Their language, which became the lingua franca of central Africa, taught in the schools of Kenya, Tanzania and part of the Congo. (Arabic, 'of the coasts'.)

Swallow National class of keel-boat, once but no longer an Olympic class.

Swanee River Corruption of Suwannee River, which flows through Florida to the Mexican Gulf; it is the river of Stephen Foster's 'Old Folks at Home' and many subsequent songs. (Suwannee is itself probably a Negro corruption of San Juanee, 'little St John'.)

Swanhild In Norse legend, the daughter of Sigurd (Siegfried), wooed by a king who sends his son as his emissary. The son, falsely accused of seducing her, is sentenced to be hanged, and Swanhild, the innocent cause of the trouble, to be trampled to death by horses.

Swan Lake (1876). Petipa's and Ivanov's ballet to Tchaikovsky's score based on a German legend about a princess turned by a magician into a creature half swan, half woman. Siegfried falls in love with her but, cheated of happiness, by the magician they drown themselves in an enchanted lake.

Swann, Charles In Proust's REMEMBRANCE OF THINGS PAST, a man of Jewish blood accepted in high society, unlike his mistress (and later wife) ODETTE DE CRÉCY. He is the father of GILBERTE.

Swan of Avon, The Ben Jonson's name for Shakespeare, born at Stratford-upon-Avon.

Swanscombe skull Fossil 150,000 years old, found in Thames gravels together with well-made flint tools; thicker than, but otherwise resembling, a modern human skull.

Swansea porcelain (1814–17). Porcelain factory which during its brief existence, like the NANTGARW firm with which it was connected, imitated the fine French wares. Billingsley (see BILLINGSLEY FLOWERS) worked at both factories.

Swedenborgianism (1788). Religion, founded in England, of those who accepted the claim of Emanuel Swedenborg (died 1772) of Sweden, made in his sixties after a distinguished career as scientist and philosopher, to be the prophet of the New Jerusalem that came into being after the Last Judgement, which he said had taken place in 1757.

Swedish Nightingale, The Jenny Lind, a Swedish coloratura soprano who became a popular idol in England when she sang Alice in Meyerbeer's *Robert le Diable* (1847), and who then settled in England.

Sweeney Character appearing in several of T. S. Eliot's poems, representing modern man at his most earthy and unattractive level.

Sweeney Todd (1847). Lurid and highly popular melodrama concocted by Dibdin Pitt from a novelette about a 'demon barber' of Fleet Street; there were other versions by various hands which were merged to form the definitive text of this hardy perennial.

'Sweet Adeline!' BARBER-SHOP classic, the tune composed by a Boston boy, Harry Armstrong, in 1896; with words by Richard Gerard Husch it was first published in 1903. The full title is 'You're the Flower of My Heart, Sweet Adeline!' Jerome Kern composed the operetta *Sweet Adeline!* in 1929.

Swing (1924). JAZZ that retained characteristically Negro features of energy and an intricate pattern of melodic rhythm woven round the steady 4–4 beat (or 'swing') of the percussion. It almost died out in the Depression but was rescued (1934) by Benny Goodman, King of Swing. Swing then came to mean highly commercialized jazz popularized (1935–46) by large, mainly white bands featuring exhibitionist solo playing. Finally Swing became a synonym for jazz.

Swinging London (1964–7). London of discothèques, mini-skirted dolly-girls and easy abortion for au pair girls, which succeeded the CHELSEA SET period and the golden era of expense-account entertaining in murky nightclubs. Success and/or beauty gave the entrée to a classless society of photographers and their models, admen, the rag trade, pop groups, etc., i.e. gossip-column fodder.

Swiss Admiral Nickname for a commissionaire, referring to his uniform, which is often such as might have been designed for the admiral of a non-existent navy.

Swiss Family Robinson, The (1813). Children's story, on the lines of *Robinson Crusoe*, about a clergyman and his family cast on a desert island; written by Prof. Wyss, a Swiss.

Swiss Guards (1506). Regiment of Swiss mercenaries; they formed the French royal bodyguard from 1616. Guard and police duties are undertaken by them in the Vatican.

Swiveller, Dick Eloquent clerk in *The* OLD CURIOSITY SHOP who marries the 'Marchioness', the overworked maid in his employer's household.

Sword of Honour, The See SOVEREIGN'S PARADE, Sandhurst.

Sword of Honour, The (1952–61). Evelyn Waugh's trilogy of novels of World War II, consisting of *Men at Arms, Officers and Gentlemen* and *Unconditional Surrender*.

Sybaris Ancient Greek colony in southern Italy; the word 'sybarite' derives from legends of the luxury and self-indulgence of its people.

Sybil See TWO NATIONS.

Sydney–Hobart race (1945). Chief Australian offshore yacht race, held annually.

Syllabus errorum (1864). Pope Pius IX's encyclical condemning liberalism and nationalism; it greatly inflamed the anti-clerical parties in France and Italy.

Sylphides, Les (1909). One-act ballet choreographed by Fokine. It is a purely romantic ballet without plot, to music written by Chopin. In the USSR it is known as Chopiniana

Sylvaner Type of grape used in hocks, etc.

Sylvester Medal (1901). Royal Society medal awarded every 3 years for mathematical research.

Symbolists Group of 19th-century French poets who, in reaction against the PARNASSIANS with whom they had earlier associated, aimed at individuality and freedom from classical forms, and in particular made great use of esoteric symbols of their own devising, and of oblique suggestion in preference to direct statement. They exercised a wide influence on future generations not only of poets but of prose writers of the world. Led by Verlaine and Mallarmé, they acknowledged Gérard de Nerval as the source of their inspiration.

Symphonie fantastique (1830). Berlioz' romantic programme music on 'episodes in the life of an artist'.

Symposium, The Plato's dialogue in which Socrates, Alcibiades, Aristophanes and others discuss the nature of love. (Greek, 'drinking together'.)

Syndicalism (1907). Form of revolutionary socialism which substitutes workers' for state ownership and control of industry, and advocates the abolition of the state. It achieved fame by violent 'direct action' strikes just before World War I, especially in France, but then faded into the background. See INDUSTRIAL WORKERS OF THE WORLD.

Synoptic problem, The Problem of the

relationship of the Synoptic Gospels – Matthew, Mark and Luke – which, in contrast to John, give similar accounts of Christ's mission. The orthodox view is that Mark is the earliest, and the main source for the other 2 books. (From Greek for 'seeing together'.)

Syon House Historic Thames-side home at Brentford, Middlesex, of the Dukes of Northumberland, with a fine Adam interior.

Syr Darya Kazakhstan river known in ancient times as the Jaxartes.

Syringa Genus name of lilac; the name is incorrectly given to the mock orange (*Philadelphus*).

Syrinx Nymph who, being pursued by Pan, was metamorphosed into a reed, of which Pan then made his shepherd's pipe, usually called Pan's pipe.

Système-D, Le Sardonic French name for methods of cutting through the red tape and side-stepping regulations; cunning in this ensures survival in a country where *paperasserie* (form-filling) has reached insane proportions. (*D* for *débrouillardise*, 'skill in disentangling'; *débrouillard*, a troubleshooter.)

Szczecin City of Pomerania, Poland, formerly known by its German name, Stettin. (Pronounced schech'in.)

T

TAB Standard vaccine used in immunization against typhoid and paratyphoid.

Tabard, The Southwark tavern from which Chaucer's Canterbury pilgrims set out. It was near London Bridge in what is now the Borough High Street.

Tabernacles, Feast of the Jewish feast commemorating the wanderings of the Israelites in the desert, celebrated in October. (*Tabernacle*, the portable tent they used as a sanctuary for the ARK OF THE COVENANT.)

Table Talk (1821–2). William Hazlitt's astringent essays on life and letters.

Tabriz carpets Fine-textured carpets with an exceptionally wide range of colour and elaborate design, including 16th-century hunting scenes (copied in the 19th) as well as the more traditional medallion and floral patterns, typically on cream, red or blue grounds; also some silk prayer rugs. (Third city of Iran; pronounced ta-breez'.)

Tabs Name for undergraduates of Cambridge University, short for Cantabs or Cantabrigians, the Latinized form of the name.

Tachisme See ABSTRACT EXPRESSIONISM.

Tacitean In the style of the Roman historian Tacitus (AD 55–117), famous for his incomparably terse and pregnant comments on characters, such as *capax imperii, nisi imperasset*, '(he would have been taken for) an able ruler, had he not ruled' (of the Emperor Servius Galba).

Tacna–Arica dispute Dispute between Chile and Peru over possession of 2 provinces occupied by Chile after a war in 1880. In 1929 it was agreed that Chile should keep Arica and restore Tacna to Peru.

Tadpole and Taper Twin political 'operators' (in the modern American sense) of Disraeli's *Coningsby* and *Sybil*.

Taffrail Pen-name of Capt. H. T. Dorling (born 1883), who served in the Royal Navy during both World Wars, and wrote numerous books and stories about naval life.

Taff Vale judgement (1901). Court ruling that a trade union could be sued for damages arising out of its agents' actions during a strike; reversed by the Trade Disputes Act, 1906. (Taff Vale, a Welsh mining area.)

Taffs, The Nickname of the WELSH GUARDS.

Taft-Hartley Act (1947). (USA) Republican labour legislation cancelling concessions gained under the NEW DEAL. It prohibited the closed shop and the use of union funds at Federal elections, and imposed 80-day 'cooling-off' periods in trade disputes.

Tagalog Name of the Malayan language and people dominant in the Philippines. (From *taga*, 'native'; *ilog*, 'river'.)

Tagetes Genus name of the African, French and many other marigolds; see CALENDULA.

Taiping Rebellion (1851–64). Peasant revolt in China which aimed to establish a 'Heavenly Kingdom of Great Peace'; the rebels were able to dominate several provinces from their capital, Nanking, as the rest of the country was in chaos. The revolt was finally suppressed only with help from foreign officers, including General Gordon.

Tait Professor Holder of a chair of Natural Philosophy at Edinburgh University.

Taiwan FORMOSA, or 'Republic of China', but considered by People's Republic of China to be an integral part of China.

Taizé Community founded in Burgundy during the Second World War by Roger Schutz. It is a Protestant order dedicated to the destruction of all Christian sects and revival of a united Church. The home of about 70 men who have renounced the possibility of marriage and have abandoned all private possessions. A place of pilgrimage and retreat.

Taj Mahal (1630–50). White marble mausoleum, with pool and gardens, at Agra (Uttar Pradesh) built by the Mogul Shah Jahan to the memory of his favourite wife. (Corruption of his wife's title, Mumtaz Mahal, 'distinguished abode'; pronounced tahj ma-hahl'.)

Tale of a Tub, A (1704). Swift's satire in which a man leaves a shirt each to his sons Peter (the Roman Catholic Church), Martin (Luther; the Anglicans) and Jack (John Calvin; extreme Protestants), on condition that they do not alter them. As time goes by, they all alter them, adding an ornament here, removing a button there. (Title based on sailors' custom of throwing an old tub to a whale – in this case Hobbes's *Leviathan* – to divert him from attacking the ship.)

Tale of Two Cities, A (1859). Dickens's story of London and Paris during the French Revolution; a French émigré returns to France to rescue a servant and is himself rescued by Sydney CARTON.

Tales of Hoffmann (1881). Offenbach's light opera inspired by stories written by E. T. A. Hoffmann (died 1822). Hoffmann, seated in a Nuremberg tavern, tells the story of his 3 love affairs and of how they were thwarted by his evil genius, who appears in various guises.

Talien Chinese name of Dairen.

Talisman, The (1825). Walter Scott's story of the Crusade led by Richard I, in which Saladin, in disguise, cures the ailing Richard with a talisman.

Tallinn Capital of the Estonian SSR, formerly known by its Russian name, Revel.

Tallow Chandlers, Worshipful Company of (1461). LIVERY COMPANY, originally a guild of makers of cheap candles (i.e. made of animal fats instead of wax).

Tall Ships race (1956). International sailing race held in July/August every 2 years over different courses, e.g. Plymouth–Tenerife, Norway–Fair Isle–Norway, Lisbon–Bermuda, Falmouth–Copenhagen. The ships may be square-riggers or fore-and-afters and have ranged from 12 to 2,350 tons; half the crew must be trainees, to prevent domination by semi-professional racing crews; most of the crews are young, at least 2 have been all-female; entrants include navies, governments, cadet-training schools, etc. There is also a small-craft race over a much shorter course. The sponsors are the Sail Training Association.

Talmud Jewish civil and religious law not contained in, though mainly derived from, the PENTATEUCH, and including the MISHNAH. The Babylonian version carries more authority, and dates from the 5th–6th centuries AD; the shorter Jerusalem or Palestinian version was about a century earlier. (Hebrew, 'instruction'.)

Tamburlaine, Tamerlane, Timur-i-Leng Mongol conqueror, descendant of Genghis Khan, who from his capital at Samarkand conquered the Caucasus region, Persia and north India, and died while preparing to attack China. In Marlowe's play *Tamburlaine the Great* (1590) he is presented as corrupted by power and success. See BAJAZET. (The name means Timur the Lame.)

Tamerlane See TAMBURLAINE.

Tamil DRAVIDIAN LANGUAGE of southern Madras and north-east Ceylon.

Taming of the Shrew, The See KATHARINA.

Tammany Hall (1789). USA) Originally a benevolent society, later an anti-British and then anti-aristocratic political club which, from the early 19th century, developed into the official organization of the Democratic Party in Manhattan (New York) and, through corruption and terror, came to dominate the Party system throughout New York State; synonymous with political graft and gangsterism. (Name of a 17th-century Delaware Indian chief.)

Tammuz Babylonian vegetation god (derived from a Sumerian god), beloved by ISHTAR who brought him back from the Underworld each spring. He is the Phoenician Adon, and the Greek ADONIS; compare also the PERSEPHONE myth.

'Tam o' Shanter' (1791). Robert Burns's poem of a drunk farmer who interrupts a witches' sabbath in the kirkyard of ALLOWAY and, pursued by CUTTY SARK to the Doon River, barely escapes with his life.

TAM-ratings Assessments of the numbers and composition of the audience for TV programmes, obtained from meters attached to sample TV sets. (Initials of Television Audience Measurement, a service provided for advertisers and TV organizations, film companies, etc. by the Attwood group in Britain (until 1968) and by Neilsens in USA. See AGB.)

Tanagra figures (350–250 BC). Terracotta statuettes found in thousands in Ancient Greek graves, of exceptional charm even though their colours have flaked off. They depicted everyday scenes (e.g. a boy on a donkey, a dancing girl, 2 gossips). Similar figures were found in MAGNA GRAECIA and Asia Minor. (Tanagra, village in Boeotia where originally made; pronounced tan'a-gra.)

Tanaka Memorial (1927). Japanese plan for world conquest, followed closely in subsequent aggression in China and in World War II; Japan denied its authenticity. (General Tanaka, prime minister, died 1929.)

Tananarive French spelling of Antananarivo, capital of Madagascar.

Tancred (1) In Tasso's *Gerusalemme liberata*, a Crusader who unwittingly kills Clorinda, the Persian girl he loves; Rossini wrote an opera about him (1813). (2) Father in the DECAMERON who sends his daughter her murdered lover's heart; she commits suicide. (3) Nineteenth-century hero of Disraeli's novel of that name, who has a revelation in the Holy Land where he has gone on a 'new crusade'.

T & G Common abbreviation for TGWU ('Transport and General').

Tanganyika Former British Trust Territory now, with Zanzibar, called Tanzania.

T'ang dynasty (AD 618–906). Most brilliant period of Chinese history and art. True porcelain was invented, and the tomb figures of animals (particularly horses) and people are famous. Naturalistic figure painting reached a high peak. The capital was Ch'ang-an near Sian (Shensi Province). The T'angs were succeeded after an interregnum by the SUNG DYNASTY.

Tanglewood Tales (1853). Children's stories, based on Greek myths, written by Nathaniel Hawthorne.

Tango Originally the Tangana, an erotic North African dance brought by the Moors to Spain and by black slaves to Cuba (where it became the Habanera). It reached the world's ballrooms from Argentina, where it had been tamed and civilized.

Tannenberg Site of 2 battles. (1) Defeat of the TEUTONIC KNIGHTS (1410) by the Poles and Lithuanians; (2) Overwhelming defeat (August 1914) by Hindenburg of Russian armies which had invaded East Prussia. (Village in Poland, formerly in East Prussia.)

Tanner, John Passionate rationalist to whom is attributed *The Revolutionist's Handbook* appended to Shaw's play MAN AND SUPERMAN. In the main body of the play he falls rather reluctantly into the arms of the charming Ann Whitefield but, since the 'Don Juan in Hell' scene in Act 3 is rarely staged, his exposition of Shaw's LIFE FORCE theme usually goes unheard.

Tannhäuser (1845). Wagner's opera giving his own version of a medieval legend about a fairy land (Venusberg) beneath a Thuringian mountain, where Venus lures Tannhäuser, a German troubadour. He eventually breaks away from the spell of Venus and returns to find the loving Elizabeth still faithful to him. He unsuccessfully seeks the Pope's forgiveness, returns from Rome to find Elizabeth has died of despair, and himself dies. (Pronounced tan-hoiz'ér.)

Tannochbrae Fictitious Scottish town made famous in the BBC TV series, *Dr Finlay's Casebook*.

Tannoy Proprietary name of a public loudspeaker system, used at railway stations, etc.

Tantalus In Greek mythology, a favourite of Zeus who gets into trouble through stealing the gods' ambrosia for his friends, and serving up his son PELOPS as a dish for the gods. He is punished in Hades by having to stand in water which retreats when he tries to quench his thirst, and under a bough of fruit which moves away when he reaches for it. Hence to 'tantalise' and the 'tantalus', a stand for decanters, lockable so that the contents can be seen but not drunk.

TanZam Railway (1970). Railway 892 km long from a station north of Broken Hill in Zambia on the existing north–south railway, running north-east along the line of the Great North Road to Dar-es-Salaam. Financed and built as a political exercise by the Chinese.

Taoiseach Irish name for 'prime minister'. (Erse, 'leader'; pronounced thee'shek.)

Taoism (Daoism) (1) Chinese mystical religion regarding which nothing is certain except the existence of its brief bible, *The Way of Life*, which preaches non-violence and complete passivity in the face of evil. This is attributed to Lao-tse ('Old Philosopher'), who may never have existed, and it was possibly compiled about the 3rd century BC. (2) Unrelated and degenerate system of magic which usurped its name, gathering deities by the hundred from all quarters. (Chinese *dao*, 'way'; pronounced tow'izm.)

Tapley, Mark Humble but indomitably cheerful companion who visits America with Martin in Dickens's MARTIN CHUZZLEWIT.

Tara Hill Hill in Co. Meath, Ireland, the traditional capital of the FIR BOLG and their successors, where the FEIS OF TARA was held. Abandoned in the 6th century, only earthworks remain.

Taranto raid (1940). British Fleet Air Arm's attack on the Italian fleet in Taranto harbour, which inflicted severe damage by air torpedo.

Taras Bulba (1835). Gogol's novel of a 17th-century Cossack, Taras Bulba; he kills his son who, for the sake of a girl, has deserted to the Polish enemy. He and his other son are tortured to death by the Poles.

Tara's halls See TARA HILL. 'The harp that once through Tara's halls/ The soul of music shed' are the opening lines of one of Thomas Moore's *Irish Melodies* (1807–35).

Tar Baby, The In UNCLE REMUS, a tar doll made by Brer Fox, to which Brer Rabbit gets himself stuck fast.

Targa Florio Road race for sports cars held in Sicily.

Tar Heel State Nickname of North Carolina. (Various fanciful derivations have been suggested.)

Tariff Reform Movement to end FREE TRADE and introduce protective tariffs for British industry, to meet in particular the growing threat of German competition; advocated by Joseph Chamberlain and his TARIFF REFORM LEAGUE, and linked with IMPERIAL PREFERENCE, it split the Conservatives and led to the Liberal landslide victory in the 1906 Election.

Tariff Reform League (1903). Founded to support Joseph Chamberlain's campaigns for TARIFF REFORM and IMPERIAL PREFERENCE.

Tarka the Otter (1927). Most popular of Henry Williamson's animal stories.

Tarot Fortune-teller's card pack, adapted by 14th-century Italians from the standard pack recently introduced from the East, with 22 added cards bearing symbols of virtues, vices, death, etc.

Tarpeian rock Rock of ancient Rome on the Capitoline Hill, from which traitors were cast to their death.

Tarquins, The Dynasty of ETRUSCAN kings who reigned in Rome down to the 6th century BC, when the 7th of the line, Tarquinius Superbus, was expelled and the Republic was founded. See LARS PORSENA; LUCRECE.

Tarr (1918). Percy Wyndham Lewis's novel of a cosmopolitan group of art students in Paris, led by an Englishman, Frederick Tarr.

Tarsus Birthplace of Saul (St Paul), 'a citizen of no mean city' (Acts 21:39), an ancient city of Cilicia (now in Turkey).

Tartare, Sauce Egg-mayonnaise flavoured with mustard, capers, etc.

Tartarin de Tarascon Typical Provençal braggart who tells of his astonishing exploits in 3 of Alphonse Daudet's books (1872–85).

Tartars (1) Mongolian nomadic tribe, speaking a Turkish language, of obscure origin, probably from east Mongolia. The MANCHUS were a Tartar people. (2) Name applied by Europeans in the 13th century to all MONGOLS; they did not use the latter name until later. (3) Muslim inhabitants of the USSR, in the Tatar ASSR (capital, Kazan), Crimea (Krim Tartars) and south-west Siberia. They speak a Turkish language but have little Mongol blood in them. (Tartar is a long-established mis-spelling of Tatar.)

Tartarus Greek name for the Underworld; in Homer, for the lowest depths of it, where the Titans and other evil-doers suffer eternal punishment.

Tartary European name used in the 14th century for a vast area of Central Asia and south Russia inhabited by 'TARTARS', i.e. Mongols.

Tartuffe Religious hypocrite of Molière's comedy (1664) of that name who is foiled in his attempts to swindle the credulous Orgon out of his money.

Tarzan Athletic scion of English nobility aban-doned in infancy by his careless parents in the African jungle, where he was brought up by apes. The hero of Edgar Rice Burroughs's *Tarzan of the Apes* (1914), he has since appeared in countless sequels, films, comic strips and TV serials. Now a grandfather, he still goes on, though his creator died in 1950.

Tashkent Declaration (1966). Treaty renouncing the use of force in the Kashmir dispute between India and Pakistan, signed by the Russian premier Kosygin, who convened the meeting, President Ayub Khan and (just before his death) the Indian prime minister, Lal Bahadur Shastri. (Capital of Uzbek SSR.)

Tass (1925). Official Soviet Russian news agency. (Initials of Russian for Soviet Telegraph Agency.)

Tassili Plateau in the Sahara where Henri Lhote discovered (1956) thousands of neolithic rock paintings of people and animals.

Taste of Honey, A (1958). Play by Shelagh Delaney and the THEATRE WORKSHOP, about a young girl who is told by her mother to ruin her life in her own way, and does that.

Tatars See TARTARS.

Tate, The (1897). Abbreviated name for the Tate Gallery, Millbank, London, an important collection of British art from the 16th century (including the Turner Bequest), and of 19th- and 20th-century foreign paintings, particularly Impressionists and Post-Impressionists. (Sir Henry Tate, the sugar merchant, founder.)

Tatler, The (1709–11). Thrice-weekly periodical, consisting mainly of essays by Sir Richard Steele (under the name Isaac Bickerstaff), Addison and Swift. It was succeeded by *The* SPECTATOR.

Tattenham Corner Crucial corner of the Epsom racecourse, a sharp turn at the foot of a slope into the final straight.

Tattersall's (1) London auction room for bloodstock, established near Hyde Park Corner (1766), and still functioning at Brompton near by. (2) Tattersall's Committee, an unofficial body which supervises betting on horse-races. (3) Tattersall's ring, the principal betting enclosure on a race-course. (Richard Tattersall, stud-groom to the Duke of Kingston.)

Tau Beta Kappa (1885). US fraternity or 'honor society' for those distinguished in the field of engineering. (*Tau* pronounced taw.)

Tauchnitz editions (1841). Cheap German paper-back editions of English and American novels, once popular with Continental travellers. (Pro-nounced towk'nits.)

Taurus The Bull, 2nd of the constellations of the Zodiac, between Aries and Gemini; the sun enters it about 21 April. It contains the PLEIADES, HYADES, CRAB NEBULA and ALDE-BARAN. Astrologers claim that those born under this sign may be unimaginative, slow, staunch.

Tavistock Clinic London psychiatric institution founded by H. Crichton-Miller. Attached to it is the Tavistock Institute of Human Relations, which studies the social implications of psy-chiatry, e.g. in industry. Psychotherapists and social workers are trained, group therapy taught, and the psychiatric treatment of marital problems studied.

Taylorian, The (1845). Abbreviated name of the Taylorian Institute, Oxford, where modern lan-guages are taught; it has an important library. (Endowed by Sir Robert Taylor, died 1788.)

Taylorism 'Scientific' factory management, based on the works of F. W. Taylor (1856–1915), US engineer, who introduced the idea of time-and-motion study.

Taz Russian car designed by Fiat and made in a factory built by Fiat under a 1966 agreement, at Stavropol (renamed Togliatti). (Togliatti Auto-mobile Zavod.)

Tbilisi Capital of Georgian SSR, formerly known as Tiflis. (Pronounced tbil-yee'si.)

T-bone steak Choice steak, with a T-shaped bone, cut from the sirloin of beef.

TCD (1591). Initials commonly used for Trinity College, Dublin, Ireland's oldest university.

Teamsters Union (USA) International Brother-hood of Teamsters, a large union of truck-drivers, renowed for its violent anarchy and corruption. The AFL/CIO expelled it in 1957, and in 1967 its leader, James Hoffa, was at last consigned to gaol for trying to bribe a jury.

Teapot Dome scandal (1929). Discovery that the US Secretary of the Interior, Albert B. Fall, had leased to a private company government oilfields in the Teapot Dome reserve, Wyoming. He was convicted of receiving a large bribe and sent to prison.

Teazle, Lady In Sheridan's SCHOOL FOR SCAN-DAL, an attractive young girl from the country married to an old man, who finds her hiding behind a screen in Joseph Surface's rooms in circumstances not quite so compromising as they seem.

Teddy boys (1955). Working-class teenagers who celebrated their post-war economic em-ancipation by spending (collectively) vast sums on a caricature of Edwardian fashions (long velvet-collared jackets, tight trousers, bootlace ties), expensive hair-styles (with 'side-burns') and gramophone records. Frenzied by ROCK 'N' ROLL, they wrecked dance-halls and cinemas, and used flick-knives and bicycle chains in local-ized gang warfare. A sullen expression was *de rigueur*. Their successors were the Mods and Rockers. (Teddy for 'Edwardian'; also called Teds.)

Teddy Hall Abbreviation for St Edmund's Hall, Oxford.

Teddy Tail (1915). Hero of the first English strip-cartoon for adults, drawn by various artists and published in Northcliffe's *Daily Mail*.

Te Deum Opening words used as the name of a 4th-century hymn to the Trinity attributed to St Ambrose. It is sung at church services and par-ticularly at services of public thanksgiving. It has been set to music by Purcell, Handel, Haydn, Verdi, Bruckner and others. (Latin, *Te Deum laudamus*, 'we praise thee, O God'.)

Tedworth Drummer, The (1661). First docu-mented report of poltergeist phenomena. A vagrant drummer was arrested at Tedworth,

Wiltshire, and his drum confiscated. Sounds of drumming, which could not be traced to any source, were intermittently heard over a long period in the house of the magistrate responsible.

TEE (1957). Trans-Europe Expresses, a network of 35 named daytime first-class-only trains linking 150 cities at speeds up to more than 130 m.p.h. The coaches, painted red and cream, are sound-proofed and air-conditioned; secretaries and radio-telephones may be provided.

Teflon President Said of Ronald Reagan, on whom 'nothing would stick'.

Teheran Conference (November–December 1943). Meeting of Churchill, Roosevelt and Stalin immediately after the CAIRO CONFERENCE, at which Stalin agreed to co-ordinate a new Soviet offensive with OVERLORD.

Teilhardism (1940). Mystical philosophical attempt to reconcile supernatural Christianity and modern science, appealing to French agnostics and Catholics alike as offering an optimistic alternative to the gloom of EXISTENTIALISM and STRUCTURALISM. It postulates a progressive purposeful unification of all things in the universe, guided by 'love' (the affinity of being with being, even atom with atom) through stages of increasing complexity: matter (in every corpuscle there is psychical as well as physical energy, manifested as rudimentary self-consciousness); 'hominization' (everything becomes brainier, as a hostile critic put it); 'socialization' (a growing together of human minds in a 'noosphere' until they act as one, and become one); the ultimate 'Omega-point' to which all things converge – a suprapersonal universe united with God. (Teilhard de Chardin, 1881–1955, French Jesuit palaeontologist exiled by his Order to China.)

Tel Aviv Founded as a Jewish garden city near Jaffa (1909), and now part of Tel Aviv-Jaffa, Israel.

Telefís Éireann TV service in the Republic of Ireland.

Telemachus Son of ODYSSEUS, who grew up while his father was at Troy and helped him outwit the suitors on his return. (Pronounced tel-em'a-kus.)

Telex Post Office service which hires out teleprinters to subscribers, enabling them to send printed messages over telephone lines to subscribers similarly equipped, at home or abroad.

Telford (1968). Industrial NEW TOWN between Shrewsbury, Stafford and Wolverhampton, enveloping the largest urban area of Shropshire and including Wellington; it borders on COALPORT, COALBROOKDALE and IRONBRIDGE (the Severn Gorge).

Tell el-Amarna See AMARNA. (*Tell*, 'mound'.)

Tell, William Legendary hero of 14th-century Switzerland. Forced by an Austrian tyrant to shoot through an apple placed on the head of his small son, he used a second arrow to kill his tormentor and then raised a rebellion. The story has no historical basis; it was used by Schiller in his play *Wilhelm Tell* (1804) and by Rossini in his opera (1829) of the same name.

Telstar 1 First communications satellite to amplify the signals it relayed, launched from USA in 1962.

Telugu The DRAVIDIAN LANGUAGE spoken in ANDHRA PRADESH. (Pronounced tel'u-goo.)

Tempest International class of 2-man keel-boat designed by Ian Proctor, for which there is a world championship raced at Weymouth in August.

Tempest, The (1611). Shakespeare's last play; see PROSPERO.

Templars (1) See KNIGHTS TEMPLARS. (2) Members of the Good Templars, a temperance society. (3) Lawyers and law students with chambers in the TEMPLE (London).

Temple, The (London) Site between Fleet Street and the Thames originally occupied by the KNIGHTS TEMPLARS. Edward III gave it to the law students, for whom the INNER TEMPLE and MIDDLE TEMPLE were established.

Temple Bar (1673). Originally a City of London gateway, rebuilt by Wren to mark the City boundary at the junction of Fleet Street and the Strand, close to the entrance to the TEMPLE. In

1878 it was moved to a private park at Cheshunt and replaced by a Victorian memorial.

Temple Church (1185). Church in the TEMPLE which incorporates the Knights Templars' 'round' church (a copy of the Church of the Holy Sepulchre at Jerusalem), now shared by the INNER TEMPLE and the MIDDLE TEMPLE. Badly damaged during World War II, it was restored in the 1950s.

Templewood, Viscount Sir Samuel Hoare; see HOARE–LAVAL PACT.

Temps modernes, Les (1946). Sartre's Existentialist magazine, the forum for his quarrel (1948) with Camus, who was quicker than Sartre to reject Communism.

Ten Commandments Laws were given orally by God to Moses in Sinai, according to tradition. Moses engraved them on two stones which, when accidentally broken, were reinscribed. Later the stones were placed in the Ark of the Covenant and were lost when the Ark was lost. Jesus used the short, simple form of the Commandments. See Exodus 20, Mark 10:19.

10 Downing Street The address of the British Prime Minister's official residence off Whitehall, known as Number 10.

Tennant Trophy Skiing competition held at Glenshee, near Devil's Elbow, Scotland, in March.

Tennessee Valley Authority See TVA.

Tennis Court Oath (1789). Resolution by the French NATIONAL ASSEMBLY not to dissolve until Louis XVI accepted a new constitution. (The assembly adjourned to a near by real-tennis court.)

1066 and All That (1931). A résumé of British history by R. J. Yeatman and W. C. Sellar, written as if by one of the less-gifted schoolboys. Kings and queens are tersely dismissed as 'good' or 'bad', their acts as 'Good things' or 'Bad things'. Genealogical trees of startling simplicity (and inaccuracy) and the richest of howlers combined to make the book a wonderful tonic during the Great Depression. A stage version was also very popular.

Tenth Commandment 'Thou shalt not covet thy neighbour's house . . .' (Exod. 20:17). Split by Roman Catholics into 2 Commandments, the Ninth and Tenth.

Teocalli Aztec terraced pyramid with a flat top, on which a temple was built. (Literally, 'god-house'; pronounced, in English, tee-ė-kal'i.)

Terpsichore Greek muse of dancing. (Pronounced tėrp-sik'or-i.)

Terrans Name used by science-fiction writers for the backward inhabitants of the speck in the universe commonly called the Earth. (Latin *terra*, 'earth'.)

Terra Nova, **HMS** Ship in which Capt. Scott sailed on his last Antarctic expedition (1910).

Terriers Nickname for the TERRITORIAL ARMY.

Territorial Army Territorial Army role is to provide a national reserve for employment on specific tasks at home and overseas and to meet the unexpected when required; and, in particular, to complete the Army order of battle of Nato-committed forces and to provide certain units for the support of Nato headquarters, to assist in maintaining a secure UK base in support of forces deployed on the Continent of Europe and to provide a framework for any future expansion of the Reserves. In addition, men who have completed service in the regular Army normally have some liability to serve in the regular Reserve. All members of the TA and regular Reserve may be called out by a Queen's Order in time of emergency or imminent national danger and most of the TA and a large proportion of the regular Reserve may be called out by a Queen's Order when warlike operations are in preparation or in progress. There is a special Reserve force in Northern Ireland, the Ulster Defence Regiment, which gives support to the regular Army.

Territorials, The (1) Old shortened name of the TERRITORIAL ARMY. (2) Name officially given (1967) to the Territorial and Army Volunteer Reserves. (3) The home service force.

Terror, Reign of (1793–4). Period of the French Revolution during the regime of the COMMIT-

TEE OF PUBLIC SAFETY from the overthrow of the GIRONDINS to the execution of Robespierre (THERMIDOR).

Tertiary Period Earlier part of the CENOZOIC ERA, lasting for about 70 to 1 million years ago, divided into the EOCENE, OLIGOCENE, MIOCENE and PLIOCENE EPOCHS. During this period modern types of mammals and flowering plants gradually evolved and, towards the end, the AUSTRALOPITHECINES appeared. (Tertiary because the 2 earlier eras were originally called Primary and Secondary.)

Terylene (1941). Trade name of a polyester synthetic fibre made from 1955 by ICI; it has less elasticity than nylon, but much greater resistance to acids and to deterioration in sunlight. Called Dacron in USA.

Tess Ill-used heroine of Thomas Hardy's *Tess of the d'Urbervilles* (1891). Seduced by Alec, a local man of means, she marries the rector's son Angel Clare who, on her disclosing that she is 'a maiden no more' (in the words of the novel), deserts her. She returns to Alec, where she is found by the repentant Angel; she kills Alec and is sentenced to death. In the words of the pessimistic Hardy: 'The President of the Immortals had ended his sport with Tess.'

Test, Test-match One of a series of matches (usually 5, originally of cricket) between fully representative teams of 2 countries. (So named as being a test of superiority.)

Test Act (1673). Enacted that all office holders must be members of the Church of England and take oaths of allegiance; passed by Parliament after James, Duke of York (James II), had declared himself a Roman Catholic.

Testament of Beauty (1929). Long philosophical poem by Robert Bridges written in loose alexandrines and idiosyncratic spelling, a distillation of what he had learnt from life offered as guidance to a despairing generation.

Testament of Friendship (1940). Vera Brittain's biography of her friend Winifred Holtby, the novelist.

Test-ban Treaty (1963). Treaty banning tests in the atmosphere (but not underground) of nuclear weapons; signed by Britain, USA, USSR, later joined by a hundred other countries, but not by France.

Teufelsdröckh, Professor See SARTOR RESARTUS.

Teutonic Knights (1190). German order founded at Acre to tend wounded Crusaders. In the 13th–14th centuries it campaigned against the pagan Prussians and Lithuanians, and massacred the Slavs. TANNENBERG (1410) began its decline, and it was dissolved by Napoleon, but revived in Austria in 1840 as a semi-religious order which carries out ambulance work.

Teutonic languages Germanic branch of the Indo-European language group, of which the modern representatives include German, English, Dutch, and the Scandinavian languages. (From *Teutones*, Latin name for the German tribes.)

Texaco (1926). US oil company which operates throughout the Americas and in Saudi Arabia, etc.; see BAHREIN PETROLEUM CO.

Tey, Josephine Pen-name assumed by Elizabeth Mackintosh when writing detective stories, of which the best was *The Franchise Affair* (1948). She was also the GORDON DAVIOT who wrote *Richard of Bordeaux*.

TGV French *train à grande vitesse*, capable of speeds in excess of 186 mph.

TGWU (1922). Initials of the Transport and General Workers' Union, the biggest British, or European, trade union, with a membership of bus-drivers, quarrymen, dockworkers, etc. Founded by Ernest Bevin, and later associated with the name of Frank Cousins, its headquarters are at TRANSPORT HOUSE in Smith Square, Westminster.

Thaïs (1) Athenian courtesan, mistress of Alexander the Great and later wife to Ptolemy I, King of Egypt; she is said to have persuaded Alexander to destroy the Persian capital, Persepolis in 331 BC. (Pronounced thay'is.) (2) Courtesan of 1st-century Alexandria who became a nun and resisted seduction by her

495

converter; the subject of a novel by Anatole France (1890) and an opera by Massenet (1894). (Pronounced tah-ees'.)

Thakin Burmese equivalent to the Indian word *sahib*, meaning 'master', adopted by individual nationalists as a gesture of mild defiance against the British regime; used in the name of the nationalist Thakin Society, which led the Burmese forces fighting with Japan against Britain (1942); and retained by individuals after the war as a title indicating a revolutionary past.

Thalia (1) The Greek muse of comedy and pastoral verse. (2) One of the GRACES. (Pronounced thal-*y*'a.)

Thalictrum Genus name of the meadow rues.

Thames Cup (1868). Open event at Henley Regatta for eights not in the GRAND CHALLENGE CUP class.

Thammuz See TAMMUZ.

Thanksgiving Day (USA) National holiday on the fourth Thursday in November, commemorating the first harvest festival held by the Pilgrim Fathers at New Plymouth in 1621. Turkey with cranberry sauce is the traditional dish on this day.

Thatcherism Policy advanced by Margaret Thatcher during her prime ministership which advocated self-help, MONETARISM and privatization.

THC Synthetic form of hashish (cannabis).

Theatre of the Absurd, Cruelty, Fact See under those words.

Theatre Royal (London) The official name of the theatres better known as Drury Lane and the Haymarket.

Theatre Workshop Repertory theatre started by Joan Littlewood in the East End of London during the 1950s, where the plays such as *Fings Ain't Wot They Used t'be* and *Sparrers Can't Sing* were built up by copious improvisation during rehearsals.

Thebes (Egypt) Ancient capital of Upper Egypt during the MIDDLE KINGDOM, and a religious and cultural centre under the NEW KINGDOM, situated at the bend of the Nile, on both sides of the river. The modern villages of KARNAK and LUXOR lie to the north and south of the site on the right bank, and the VALLEY OF THE KINGS on the left bank.

Thebes (Greece) Ancient capital of Boeotia; see OEDIPUS. (Named after the nymph Thebe; no connection with Egyptian Thebes.)

Theory of the Leisure Class, The (1899). Sociological study by the American left-wing economist, Thorstein Veblen, in which he popularized the term 'conspicuous consumption', a vice he attributed to the idle rich or leisure class, in the days before it became the vice also of the non-idle non-rich.

Theosophical Society (1875). Founded in New York by the Russian Mme Blavatsky, who claimed to be inspired by a White Brotherhood of adepts living in the Himalayas. It propagates a mixture of Hindu and Buddhist mysticism.

Thérèse Desqueyroux (1927). François Mauriac's novel of a woman who tires of her bourgeois husband, tries to murder him, and is acquitted at the subsequent trial.

Thermidor In the French Revolution calendar, the month from 19 July to 17 August; 9 Thermidor (1794) is the date of Robespierre's assassination, marking the end of the Reign of TERROR and of the Revolution. 'Thermidor' is consequently used of a victory of the bourgeoisie over revolutionaries. ('Gift of Warmth.')

Thermopylae (480 BC). Narrow pass on the Greek coast opposite Euboea, where the King of Sparta, Leonidas, and 1,000 Spartans and Thespians fought to the last man to delay the invading Persian host under Xerxes. Simonides wrote their epitaph: 'Go, tell the Spartans, thou who passest by, / That here obedient to their laws we lie.' (Pronounced ther-mop'i-lee.)

Thermos flask Flask or bottle kept hot or cold by surrounding an interior vessel with a vacuum jacket to prevent the conduction of heat; this device was invented by Sir James Dewar, FRS (1842–1923), a Cambridge professor.

Thersites In Homer's *Iliad* an ugly and scurrilous Greek with a gift for invective; Achilles killed him for jeering at him. (Pronounced thėr-sy′teez.)

Theseus Major hero of Greek legend, the King of Athens who overcame the Centaurs, slew Procrustes and the Minotaur, deserted ARIADNE, married first Hippolyta, the Queen of the Amazons against whom he was fighting, and after her death Phaedra. He appears in Chaucer and the *Midsummer Night's Dream* as Duke of Athens. (Pronounced thee′sews.)

Thespian Actor or actress. (From *Thespis*, a Greek playwright or actor of the 6th century BC of whom little is known.)

Thessaloniki Greek name of Salonika.

Thetis (1) (Greek legend) A NEREID, mother of Achilles. (Pronounced thet′is.) (2) Name of a British submarine that sank shortly before World War II. (Pronounced thee′tis.)

Thieves' Kitchen, The FAGIN'S nest of pickpockets in *Oliver Twist*.

Things Fall Apart (1958). Remarkable first novel by a Nigerian writer, Chinua Achebe.

Thinker, The Rodin's sculpture; see *Le* PENSEUR.

Thin Man, The (1934). Dashiell Hammett's last novel. Nick Charles, a retired detective, discovers that the thin man of the title, suspected of a murder, had himself been killed months before the crime was committed, by the real culprit. More notable for comedy than detective ingenuity, it gave birth to a series of extremely popular films starring William Powell and Myrna Loy.

Thin Red Line, The (1) Nickname of the Sutherland Highlanders, won at Balaclava. (2) Applied in general to British infantry in action.

Thira Greek island in the Aegean where an American-Greek team found the remains of a large Minoan city, buried under volcanic ash about 1500 BC; it is regarded as possible evidence that the legend of ATLANTIS was based on memories of this disaster.

Third Coalition (1805–7). Final alliance against France, formed by Pitt and including Britain, Austria, Russia, and later Prussia. After the initial victory of TRAFALGAR it met with a series of defeats at ULM, AUSTERLITZ, JENA, Eylau and Friedland, and was ended by the Treaty of TILSIT. See NAPOLEONIC WARS.

Third Commandment 'Thou shalt not take the name of . . . God in vain' (Exod. 20:7.) To Roman Catholics this is the Second Commandment.

Third Estate (*Tiers État*) The Commons of the French STATES-GENERAL. When Louis XVI insisted that the 3 Estates should have one vote each, so ensuring that the Commons would be outvoted, the latter broke away and formed the NATIONAL ASSEMBLY (June 1789).

Third Force (1945). General de Gaulle's conception of a European coalition, including West Germany, to form an economic and military unit big enough to compete with, stand up to and mediate between the 2 superpowers, USA and USSR. See also 'KEEP LEFT' GROUP.

Third International Alternative name of the COMINTERN.

Third Man, The (1950). Graham Greene's thriller set in post-war Vienna; written specifically for a film by Carol Reed with a popular Harry Lime theme-tune played on a zither.

Third of May, 1808, The (1814). Goya's horrific picture of a firing squad, summing up the terror of the French occupation of Spain, which was also portrayed in his series of etchings entitled *The Disasters of War*. Now in the Prado, Madrid.

Third Programme (1946). Original name of the BBC's third radio programme, designed to appeal to a higher level of artistic and intellectual taste than the other programmes. From 1957 its wavelength was shared with Network 3, which gave detailed coverage of major sporting events etc.

Third Reading (Parliament) Generally the final stage in the treatment of a bill in each House of Parliament; the House considers the bill as a whole and can make only minor amendments. If approved, it then goes to the Lords, and if they pass it, becomes law on receiving the ROYAL ASSENT.

Third Reich (1933–45). Hitler's own name for the National-Socialist regime, which he said would last 1,000 years. ('Third' because he regarded the Holy Roman Empire and the German Empire as the first 2 great periods of German dominance in Europe.)

Third Republic (1875–1940). Period of French history from the Franco-Prussian War to the capitulation of France and the institution of the Vichy government; notorious in the 1920s and 1930s for the fratricidal strife of factionalized chameleon parties under leaders all striving for office and most of them achieving it, if only for a few weeks.

Third World Countries of Africa, Asia and Latin America which are neutral in East–West political alignment and are the poorer and underdeveloped areas of the world. (The First and Second Worlds are the West and the Communist bloc, respectively.)

Third World War Favourite journalistic theme, almost rivalling the Return of the Ice Age.

'Thirteen Plots of 13 May' (1958). Political turmoil in France which led, not without his connivance, to General de Gaulle's return to power.

13th Amendment (1865). Amendment to the US Constitution which abolished slavery throughout the Union.

38th Parallel (of latitude) Boundary between North and South Korea fixed in 1945 when they were occupied by Russian and US troops respectively; unaltered by the subsequent Korean War of 1950–53.

Thirty-Nine Articles (1571). Restatement of the Protestant doctrines of Cranmer's 42 Articles (1553), authorized by Elizabeth I, to which Anglican clergy are obliged to subscribe.

Thirty-Nine Steps (1915). John Buchan's thriller in which Richard Hannay pursues German spies round Britain.

Thirty Years War (1618–48). Religious war between Protestants and Catholics which the Habsburgs used as a pretext for an unsuccessful attempt to gain control of the German states. Fought mainly by mercenaries, it devastated Germany which, however, retained its freedom. It started with a Bohemian Protestant revolt; Gustavus Adolphus of Sweden joined in on the Protestant side, as did France, which emerged the dominant European power. The Treaty of WESTPHALIA ended the war.

'This is Your Life' Originally an American TV tearjerker series, introduced to Britain by Eamonn Andrews, in which a personality whose life has been secretly researched in depth is lured unsuspecting to the studio and, before an audience, suddenly confronted with a résumé of his or her life backed up by people who figured in it, some possibly flown from the far corners of the earth and not seen by the victim for many a long year.

Thistle, Order of the (1687). The Scottish equivalent of the GARTER; Knights-Companions are limited to 16.

Thomas Cup (1948). Men's international badminton championship. (Sir George Thomas.)

Thomas's (1213). Short title of St Thomas's Hospital, originally at Southwark, moved (1868) to the South Bank opposite the Houses of Parliament. (Named after St Thomas à Becket.)

Thomism Religious and philosophical doctrines of St Thomas Aquinas, since 1879 the official basis of Roman Catholic theology. Aquinas, striving to reconcile new learning with old belief, held that reason and faith could never conflict, since both derived from God and revealed him; and that there was no salvation outside the true Church. Thus, the unbaptised and those who died, unabsolved, in mortal sin were condemned to eternal torment. (Thomas of Aquino, a 13th-century Dominican; pronounced tohm'izm.)

Thompson, Sadie See RAIN.

Thor Son of Odin in Scandinavian mythology, god of thunder and war, after whom Thursday is named.

Thorndon Park Golf club at Brentwood, Essex.

Thorndyke, Dr Character created by R. Austin Freeman (1907); he is at once a leading criminal lawyer and a doctor of medicine who specializes in poisoning cases.

Thoroughbred English racehorse, bred for speed by crossing domestic and Middle Eastern strains. The world's Thoroughbreds can, without exception, be traced through the male line to Matchem (1748), grandson of the Godolphin Arabian, Herod (1758), great-grandson of the BYERLY TURK, or ECLIPSE (1764), great-grandson of the Darley Arabian. The average height is 16 hands.

Thoth The Ancient Egyptian god of learning, wisdom and magic, represented in art as having the head of an ibis. Equivalent to the Greek Hermes. See HERMES TRISMEGISTUS.

Thousand and One Nights, The See: ARABIAN NIGHTS; SCHEHERAZADE.

Thousand Days, A (1965). Account of the presidency of J. F. Kennedy written by one of his aides, Prof. Arthur Schlesinger.

Thrale, Mrs See PIOZZI, HESTER.

Threadneedle Street Site of the Bank of England in the City of London.

Three Choirs Festival (1724). Festival of sacred music held in September at Worcester, given by the choirs of Gloucester, Worcester and Hereford cathedrals.

Three-Cornered Hat, The (1919). Massine's ballet choreographed for Diaghilev, with a score by Falla and Picasso as designer.

Three Kings, The Traditionally Gaspar, Melchior and Balthazar, who came to worship the infant Jesus. They are not mentioned in the New Testament, but are suggested by Isaiah 60:3–6. See MAGI.

Three Musketeers, The (1844). Alexandre Dumas's popular novel, based on the semi-fictitious *Mémoires de M. d'Artagnan* by Courtilz de Sandras (1709), set in the 17th-century France of Cardinal Richelieu. The Musketeers, Athos, Porthos and Aramis, are members of Louis XIII's bodyguard, and are joined by the penniless Gascon, d'Artagnan. These characters reappear in various sequels.

Three Peaks race Toughest British cross-country race, over a 22-mile course across 3 mountain-tops to finish near Chapel-le-Dale, Yorkshire.

Threepenny Opera (1928). Brecht's opera giving a modern sociological slant to Gay's BEGGAR'S OPERA. (German title, *Die Dreigroschenoper*.)

Three Plays for Puritans (1901). Volume of Bernard Shaw's plays, comprising *The Devil's Disciple*, *Caesar and Cleopatra* and *Captain Brassbound's Conversion*.

Three Rs, The Phrase for reading, writing and 'rithmetic, dating back to the early 19th century.

Three Sisters, The (1901). Chekhov's play of sisters in a provincial garrison town who hope officers of the regiment stationed there will rescue them from their drab lives and take them off to Moscow. Their schemes go awry, the regiment departs, and they are left still dreaming of Moscow.

Three Star (☆☆☆) **Cognac** Trade term for standard-quality brandy, probably 3–4 years old.

Three Weeks (1907). Elinor Glyn's Edwardian *succès de scandale*, memorable for its passionate heroine posturing about on leopard-skins in a fantasy-*affaire* of the kind that the author seems to have acted out in real life with such an unlikely partner as Nathaniel Lord Curzon.

Throckmorton's plot (1584). One of several Roman Catholic plots against Elizabeth I.

Throgmorton Street The site of, and used for, the London Stock Exchange.

Thrones Order of angels; see CHERUBIM.

Throstles, The Nickname of the West Bromwich Albion football team.

Through the Looking Glass (1872). Sequel to ALICE IN WONDERLAND, in much the same vein; Alice climbs through a looking-glass into a country set out like a chessboard, with walking, talking chessmen.

Thrums J. M. Barrie's imaginary town, representing his birthplace, Kirriemuir (Angus); the setting of his novel, *A Window in Thrums* (1889) and his novel and play, *The Little Minister* (1891).

Thruxton Centre for motor-cycle racing near Andover, Hampshire.

Thunbergia Greenhouse climbers, clock vines, named after Carl Peter Thunberg (1743–1828), a Swedish botanist and student of Linnaeus.

Thunderer, HMS The Royal Naval Engineering College, Manadon, Plymouth.

Thunderer, The Nickname of *The Times*, which dates back to a paragraph in the *Morning Herald* of 1830.

Thundering Herd, The (USA) Nickname of the largest stockbroking firm, Merrill Lynch, Pierce, Fenner & Smith Inc.

Thunder over Mexico (1932). One of 3 versions of Eisenstein's *Que viva Mexico!*, a vivid reconstruction of the Mexican Revolution, filmed in Mexico.

Thurston's London's principal billiards hall and rendezvous for sportsmen in Edwardian times; it was in Leicester Square, and was closed in 1955.

Thus Spake Zarathustra (1892). Work in which Nietzsche developed his theory of SUPERMAN, using Zarathustra (ZOROASTER) as his mouthpiece.

Thynne Family name of the Marquesses of Bath.

Thyssens German iron, steel and engineering firm, with headquarters at Duisburg; it also manufactures cement and chemicals. (The full name is August Thyssen-Hütte.)

Tia Maria Jamaican liqueur made of spirit distilled from sugar-cane and flavoured with Blue Mountain coffee.

Tiananmen Square In 1949 Mao proclaimed the founding of the People's Republic of China from Tiananmen Square (Gate of the Heavenly Peace) in Beijing. In April–May 1989 thousands of students demonstrated for democracy and over 3,000 went on hunger strike. A first attempt by the Army to regain the square failed but on 3 June a further attempt was made and up to 5,000 were killed and as many as 10,000 injured.

Tichborne claimant (1866). Arthur Orton, a Wapping butcher who claimed to be Roger Tichborne, heir to an ancient baronetcy, presumed drowned in a shipwreck. Although Lady Tichborne 'recognized' her son, he was unmasked after the longest trial in English history, and sentenced to 14 years' imprisonment.

Tichborne dole Lady Day ceremony at Alresford, Hampshire; in the 12th century Lady Tichborne as she lay dying made her skinflint husband promise to give to the poor all the farmland she could crawl round before a torch she carried burnt out. She managed to get round no less than 23 acres, which still provide a dole of flour for the poor.

Ticker-tape parade US speciality, in which streamers (including ticker-tape) and confetti are thrown from upper storeys over a passing parade for a celebrity.

Tien Shan observatory (Tyan Shan) Chinese observatory in Sinkiang at a height of 6,500 feet in the Tien Shan Mountains, where work began in 1958 on a 236-inch telescope, i.e. larger than that at MOUNT PALOMAR OBSERVATORY.

Tiergarten Berlin park made by Frederick the Great.

Tietjens tetralogy (1924–8). Ford Madox Ford's novels: *Some Do Not*, *No More Parades*, *A Man Could Stand Up* and *The Last Post*. They portray, impressionistically, the decline of the Edwardian upper classes, as exemplified by the hero, Christopher Tietjens. (Also known as *Parade's End*.)

Tiffany glass Beautiful opalesque glass made by

a process patented (*c.* 1880) by Louis Tiffany (1848–1933), son of the famous New York jeweller, and himself a painter, stained-glass artist and leader of the Art Nouveau movement in the USA. Many vases were in the shape of flowers or plants; some pieces are marked 'Favrile', the name he invented for this type of glass.

Tiffany's Fashionable New York jewellers.

Tiger, The Nickname of Georges Clemenceau, formidable French premier (1906–9, 1917–20).

Tiger at the Gates (1955). Christopher Fry's translation of Jean Giraudoux's *La Guerre de Troie n'aura pas lieu* (1935). HECTOR persuades the Trojan leaders to avoid war with the Greeks, but the people, aroused by a lying rumour, precipitate one nevertheless.

Tiger Bay Area of Cardiff's dockland.

Tiger Moth See MOTH.

Tiger stadium Sports stadium at Baton Rouge, Louisiana.

Tikopia Small Pacific island in the Solomons, known through intensive studies carried out there by the anthropologist Raymond Firth.

Tilbury Review (1588). Occasion when Queen Elizabeth addressed her troops on the approach of the Spanish Armada.

Till Eulenspiegel (German folklore) A practical joker who represents the despised peasant triumphing over the slick townsman; Richard Strauss used the legend in his tone-poem. *Till Eulenspiegel's Merry Pranks* (1894). (German, literally 'owl-glass', 'mischief-maker'; pronounced oil'enshpee-gèl.)

Tilsit, Treaty of (1807). After Prussia's defeat at JENA, Napoleon met Tsar Alexander I on a raft at Tilsit and agreed to an alliance against Britain; Prussia was divided up between a kingdom of Westphalia under Jerome Bonaparte, a new duchy of Warsaw under the King of Saxony, and Russia. See THIRD COALITION.

Tilsit cheese Exceptionally evil-smelling cheese,

highly prized by connoisseurs and still made at Tilsit.

Time (1923). Weekly tabloid news-magazine founded by Henry R. Luce and another; in 1936 its publishers launched *Life*, a weekly which specializes in high-quality and often sensational pictures. See also LIFE INTERNATIONAL.

Time and the Conways (1937). First of J. B. Priestley's plays to show his preoccupation with theories of time (see SERIALISM). The Conway family experience a future event in the present.

Time Machine, The (1895). H. G. Wells's remarkable first novel, a science-fiction tale of a man who was able to travel backward to the beginning of time and forward to an era when the sun is cooling down. He passes through an era when the Morlocks, descended from today's proletariat, live underground, herding aristocrats for meat.

Times New Roman Creation of this beautiful typeface took three years of work by Stanley Morison, in the 1930s. He was at that time typographic adviser to *The Times*. Times New Roman first appeared in *The Times* on 3 October 1932, in the redesigned newspaper. A year later it was released for general use, becoming the most successful and universally used original type-design of this century. But in 1972 it was abandoned in favour of Times Europa, which was thought to be more readable in the smaller sizes and better suited to the poorer quality of paper then in use.

Times Square Once the New York theatre and restaurant area adjoining Broadway at 42nd Street but now fairly sordid and a centre for muggers and junkies. (Named after *The New York Times*, which has now moved out of it.)

Timon of Athens (1607). Shakespeare's play in which Timon discovers when he loses his riches that he has only fair-weather friends; he turns misanthrope and retires to a cave, with one faithful servant.

Timur See TAMBURLAINE.

Tin Drum, The (1959). Strange novel by a

Danziger, Günter Grass. (German title, *Die Blechtrommel*.)

Tin Lizzie Contemporary nickname for the MODEL T Ford Car.

Tin-pan Alley (USA) Nickname for the district of New York where publishers of popular music congregated, originally in 14th Street, later in the Times Square area; also applied to the composers of such music.

Tin Plate Workers, Worshipful Company of (1670). LIVERY COMPANY, the membership of which now includes representatives of the tin-plate and electrical industries.

Tinsley Green Sussex village near Crawley where on Good Friday there is an international marbles contest for a silver cup; the village's association with the game goes back to 1600.

Tintagel Site of a castle on the north coast of Cornwall which figures in ARTHURIAN legend as the home of King MARK; the ruins which can still be seen are of a later date. See CAMELOT. (Headland near Camelford.)

Tintern Abbey (1131). A Cistercian abbey, now in ruins, on the Wye near Chepstow, Monmouthshire; the setting inspired Wordsworth's 'Lines Composed a Few Miles above Tintern Abbey' (1798), in which the poet communes with nature.

Tintin (1929). Cartoon character and the hero of many books, created by the Belgian Hergé.

'Tipperary' (1912). A music-hall song, which became popular just before World War I, and was then adopted as the chief marching song of the British Expeditionary Force in France.

Tiresias In Greek legend, a blind seer of Thebes who plays a prominent part in the OEDIPUS cycle of legends. (Pronounced ty-rees'i-as.)

Tirol Austrian alpine province of which the capital is Innsbruck; it formerly included the ALTO ADIGE, now in Italy.

Titania Name given by Shakespeare to the Queen of the Fairies in MIDSUMMER NIGHT'S DREAM;

the wife of Oberon. By other writers she is called Queen Mab. Ovid gives Titania as a name of the goddess Diana. (Pronounced ti-tahn'i-a or, in Shakespeare ty-tayn'i-a.)

***Titanic* disaster** (1912). Sinking of a White Star liner after striking an iceberg in the North Atlantic, with the loss of over 1,500 lives.

Titans Giant children of URANUS and Ge (sky and earth) who appear in a bloodthirsty series of early Greek legends. CRONOS led them in revolt against their father, and they in turn were vanquished by a new generation of gods led by ZEUS, who consigned them to Tartarus.

Tithonus (Greek legend) A Trojan youth of great beauty with whom Eos, goddess of the dawn, fell in love. Zeus conferred on him the gift of immortality but not of perpetual youth, and after a period of shrivelled old age he turned into a cicada.

Titograd Modern name of the capital of Montenegro, Yugoslavia, formerly known as Podgorica.

Titoism The heresy, in Stalinist eyes, of believing that there are different roads to Socialism (see POLYCENTRISM) and of acting on that belief. Tito, knowing that Yugoslavia's problems differed fundamentally from Russia's, refused to impose collectivization or to victimize the *kulak* (rich peasant) class; in foreign affairs he took a neutral stand between the Soviet bloc and the West. For these crimes he was condemned by the Cominform (i.e. Stalin) in 1948 and, to the world's surprise, survived unscathed until normal relations were resumed in 1955.

Titus Andronicus (1594). Tragedy attributed to Shakespeare, a revenge play of the type of *The* SPANISH TRAGEDY, full of corpses and atrocities. Titus is a Roman general. (Pronounced in this play andron'i-kus; otherwise an-dro-ny'kus.)

Tiw, Tiu Scandinavian god of wisdom, after whom Tuesday is named.

Tizard mission Mission under Sir Henry Tizard sent to USA in September 1940 to communicate the findings of the MAUD COMMITTEE.

TLS (1902). Initials used for the *Times Literary*

Supplement. London's leading literary weekly, famed for its correspondence columns, where potent words such as 'sic', 'so-called' and 'simplistic' are freely used in furious, often transatlantic, slanging matches which demonstrate that the spirit of the WASP OF TWICKENHAM lives on.

'Toad, Mr' 'Bad, low animal' in *The* WIND IN THE WILLOWS, an egotistical reprobate who steals cars, drives recklessly and goes to gaol. His love for speechifying and loud clothes, and his sticky end, are said to have been suggested by Horatio Bottomley and Oscar Wilde. A. A. Milne borrowed him for his children's play, *Toad of Toad Hall* (1929).

Tobacco Road (1932). Erskine Caldwell's novel of rural squalor in Georgia, USA, which, like GOD'S LITTLE ACRE, sold in immense quantities, especially after it had been made into a successful play.

Tobit Book of the Apocrypha, telling the story of Tobit, a Jew in Nineveh during the Babylonian captivity, who sends his son Tobias to fetch 10 talents of silver he had deposited in Media. The angel Raphael, in disguise, accompanies him, helps him get the money, cures Tobit's blindness, and then reveals himself.

Tobruk Important harbour in Cyrenaica in the North African campaign of 1941–2. Captured by Australians (Jan. 1941), it was left as an invested enclave from April–December (during which period the Australians were evacuated at their government's request); in June 1942 it was again surrounded and the garrison surrendered.

Toby (1) Dog in the Punch and Judy show. (2) See UNCLE TOBY.

Toby Fillpot Person depicted in the standard toby jug, said to be based on an 18th-century Yorkshireman, Harry Elwes, who once drank 2,000 gallons of beer without taking food.

Toc-H (1915). Christian voluntary organization which helps old and young, those in hospital, and refugees; it also forms social groups throughout the UK. (*Toc*, old army signallers' designation for letter T; for Talbot House, name of the first chapel and club founded by the Rev. 'Tubby' Clayton at Poperinghe, Belgium, in memory of Gilbert Talbot, killed in World War I.)

Todt Organization German organization which conscripted labour for construction work, notably on the WEST WALL (1938) and the ATLANTIC WALL (1940). (Directed by an engineer named Todt.)

Tokay, Imperial Hungarian sweet wine, one of a family of Tokays, from the Austrian Emperor's own vineyards; much drunk in the best RURITANIAN circles. (Pronounced, in English, to-ky'.)

Tokugawa Shogunate (1614–1868). Period during which Japan was ruled nominally by the Emperor at Kyoto, but actually by a military dictatorship in Tokyo of SHOGUNS of the Tokugawa family. The last Shogun resigned after failing to eject foreigners, and this led to the Imperial MEIJI RESTORATION.

Tokyo Round Ministerial meeting of the General Agreement on Tariffs and Trade (GATT), held in Tokyo in 1973 and attended by over 100 contracting parties to initiate the process of obtaining an agreement on a new set of cuts in tariffs and other barriers to world trade. Negotiations were completed in 1979. It was subsequently called the 'Tokyo Round'. Other 'rounds' have included the Dillon Round, the Kennedy Round and the URUGUAY ROUND.

Told by an Idiot (1923). One of Rose Macaulay's early attacks on the illusions of mankind.

Tolkien Society of America Devoted to the study of the works of Professor J. R. R. Tolkien, author of *The* LORD OF THE RINGS.

Tollund Man One of the BOG PEOPLE, exceptionally well preserved; the tranquillity of expression is remarkable, especially as he died by hanging.

Tolpuddle martyrs (1834). Six farm-labourers who, for forming a trade union, were sentenced to 7 years' transportation to Australia by a local bench of landowners secure in the knowledge of the Whig government's antipathy to trade unionism. There was such a public outcry that the men were brought back 2 years later. (Tolpuddle, a Dorset village near Dorchester.)

Toltecs Early inhabitants of Mexico of whom little is known. In the 12th century AD some of them moved to Yucatán and merged with the MAYAN CIVILIZATION. Their legendary leader or god was QUETZALCOATL.

Tom and Jerry Cartoon characters appearing in many films. They first appeared in a Tom and Jerry broadsheet of 1822.

'Tom Bowling' Charles Dibdin's 18th-century sea-song in which Tom, 'the darling of our crew', represents the poet's brother: 'Faithful, below, he did his duty; / But now he's gone aloft.' (Name taken from that of the seafaring uncle of Smollett's RODERICK RANDOM.)

Tom Brown's Schooldays (1857). Thomas Hughes's novel of life at Rugby in the days when Thomas Arnold was headmaster; there was a sequel, *Tom Brown at Oxford* (1861).

Tom Collins A COLLINS made with OLD TOM GIN.

Tom, Dick and Harry Just anybody, the common herd; often used disparagingly.

Tom-Gallon Trust Fund administered by the Society of Authors from which an award is made biennially to a fiction writer of limited means. (Founded by Miss Nellie Tom-Gallon.)

Tom Jones (1749). Fielding's masterpiece, the long rambling story of the adventures of the likeable rascal, Tom Jones, interspersed with the author's comments, addressed to the reader, on various social and moral issues. See Squire ALLWORTHY; BLIFIL.

Tomnoddy, My Lord Character in one of the INGOLDSBY LEGENDS.

Tom o' Bedlam Old name for a wandering beggar; many were, or pretended to be, mad (see BEDLAM); also called Abraham-men, after the name of a ward at Bedlam.

Tompion Name associated with the finest old English clocks and barometers. (Thomas Tompion, 1639–1715.)

Tom Sawyer (1876). Mark Twain's novel about Tom, who runs away from his respectable Aunt Sally in Missouri and camps out on an island with his friend Huck Finn. They are presumed dead, and return in time to hear their praises sung at their funeral service. They have further adventures finding treasure buried by Injun Joe. The 2 friends reappear in HUCKLEBERRY FINN.

Tom Thumb, General (1844). A midget exhibited in BARNUM & BAILEY SHOWS. (Name taken from a 16th-century nursery story.)

Tom Tiddler's ground Place where money can be easily made. (From the children's game in which one side chants 'We're on Tom Tiddler's ground / Picking up gold and silver', and tries to keep the others out.)

Tom Tower Wren's clock tower at the entrance to Tom Quad, Christ Church (College), Oxford. (Contains the bell called Great Tom.)

Tongking, Tonkin Former French protectorate, now part of North Vietnam.

Tono-Bungay (1909). Novel by H. G. Wells, it tells of George Ponderevo, son of the housekeeper of Bladesover (representing the house where the novelist's mother was lady's maid), apprenticed to his uncle Ponderevo, the village chemist who moves to London and makes a fortune out of a quack remedy he calls Tono-Bungay. The book depicts the passing of the old landed aristocracy, yielding place to brash get-rich-quick charlatans.

Tontons Macoutes Haitian secret police and personal bodyguard of one-time President Duvalier; they have won an unenviable reputation for utter lawlessness.

Tony award The Broadway (i.e. US theatre) equivalent of the Hollywood OSCAR.

Tonypandy Village in the Rhondda Valley, Glamorgan, where a miners' strike in 1910 led to serious riots and false rumours that troops had fired on the strikers.

Top-Hat schemes Tax-avoidance schemes for top executives whereby a proportion of salary can be set aside as pension premiums (which may bring considerable tax relief); on retirement these can be converted (in part) into tax-free capital and thence into valuable annuities.

Tophet (1) Mentioned in 2 Kings 23:10 and Jeremiah 19:6 and the place, near Gehenna, where children were sacrificed to MOLOCH; later used as a refuse pit. (2) Hell. (Probably means 'fire place'; also spelt Topheth; pronounced toh'fet.)

Topsy Slave girl in UNCLE TOM'S CABIN who said she 'never was born . . . I 'spect I grow'd'.

Torah (1) Jewish name for the PENTATEUCH; (2) the whole body of Jewish religious literature. (Hebrew, 'instruction'.)

Torch Code-name for the Allied invasion of north-west Africa, 1942 (earlier named Super-Gymnast).

Tordesillas, Treaty of (1494). Agreement to share newly discovered territories: Spain was to have those west of a line drawn from pole to pole 370 leagues west of the Cape Verde Islands, and Portugal those to the east (in effect, Brazil).

Tories Name given in the 1670s to the Court party which supported Charles II and the Anglican Church against the Country Party (WHIGS), drawing its strength from country squires and clergy; the forerunner of the Conservative Party. Now used of right-wing Conservatives, or as a mildly hostile name for any Conservatives. (Originally the name of Irish outlaws who harried the English settlers.)

Torpids Oxford University spring college boat-races. (Torpid, originally a club's second, slower, boat.)

Torrey Canyon disaster (1967). Grounding of a US oil-tanker off the Scillies, discharging vast quantities of oil to foul British and French coasts; she had to be destroyed by bombing.

Torricellian tube Early name for a mercury barometer. (In 1643 the Italian, Torricelli, demonstrated that changes in atmospheric pressure are shown by movements of a column of mercury in a tube closed at one end and inverted in a bowl of mercury; the space in the tube above this column, which contains mercury vapour, is called a Torricellian vacuum. Pronounced tor-i-chel'i-an.)

Tory Democracy New concept of British Conservatism introduced by Disraeli and propagated by Lord Randolph Churchill (see PRIMROSE LEAGUE), based on an appeal to the people to recognize that the interests of all classes of the nation are identical, and on government measures for the steady improvement of working-class conditions (see TWO NATIONS).

Tosca, La (1900). Puccini's opera, based on a French melodrama, in which the young painter Cavaradossi is sent to his death by the chief of police, Scarpia, who is murdered by the jealous singer Tosca, the young man's lover.

Tosti's 'Goodbye' Once extremely popular song composed by Sir F. P. Tosti, Italian-born composer who settled in England where he died in 1916.

Tote (1872). Abbreviation for totalizator, set up on racecourses for recording bets and payment of winnings on the principle that all stake money is pooled and shared by those who have backed winners, subject to a percentage reduction. It was introduced to the UK and USA in 1930.

Totentanz Dance of Death, an allegorical representation of Death leading all conditions of humankind to the grave. Among others Holbein produced a series of woodcuts illustrating the Danse Macabre.

To the Lighthouse (1927). Virginia Woolf's novel, a moving evocation of the changes wrought in a group of people by the passage of time. The lighthouse is the objective of a boating trip, postponed in the early section but made many years later at the end of the book.

Tottenham Former municipal borough of Middlesex, since 1965 part of the borough of HARINGEY.

Touchstone Cynical jester of the Duke's court in AS YOU LIKE IT.

Tour d'Argent Roof-top restaurant in Paris on the South Bank with a marvellous view of Notre Dame opposite.

Tour de France (1903). Major cycling race of the year in France, over a route of nearly 2,800 miles of road (including mountainous stretches), taking over 3 weeks to complete.

Tours, Battle of (732). Decisive battle in which the Franks under Charles Martel (grandfather of Charlemagne) finally checked the Arab conquest of Europe.

Tower Hamlets (1965). New inner London borough consisting of the former metropolitan boroughs of Bethnal Green, Poplar and Stepney.

Tower of London (11th century). Thames-side fortress which has been a royal palace, prison, Mint, Treasury, and observatory. It is now an armoury and a museum containing the Crown jewels, garrisoned by the Yeoman Warders.

Town Like Alice, A (1950). Nevil Shute's novel partly about Alice Springs, a township in the Northern Territory of Australia.

Townswomen's Guilds Self-governing clubs formed for self-education in civics, crafts, amateur dramatics, music, etc. They are the urban equivalent of the WOMEN'S INSTITUTES.

Toxteth District of Liverpool; the scene of rioting in July 1981.

Toynbee Hall (1884). Universities' Settlement in East London, a house of residence for men from Oxford and Cambridge who want to do social work in the East End; the first of many such social settlements.

Toy **Symphony** (1788). Cheerful little symphony, formerly attributed to Haydn, but perhaps by Mozart's father.

Toyota Large Japanese car-manufacturing firm.

Trabzon Modern Turkish name of Trebizond, a Black Sea port, formerly the ancient Greek colony of Trapezus.

Tractarians See OXFORD MOVEMENT. (So called from Newman's *Tracts for the Times*.)

Tractatus Logico-philosophicus (1922). The forbidding title of Wittgenstein's major treatise

which inspired LOGICAL POSITIVISM. He held that the solution of philosophical problems was mainly a matter of accurate definition of the terms used, an aspect neglected in all previous philosophical systems.

Trad (1944). Revival of New Orleans JAZZ in reaction against the commercialized SWING bands; associated in the UK with Ken Colyer, Chris Barber and, with Mr Acker Bilk, a West Country clarinettist dressed like an ageing Edwardian music-hall comic. (For 'traditional'.)

Trade Disputes Acts Various Acts, of which the most important are: (1) A 1906 (Liberal) Act which annulled the TAFF VALE JUDGEMENT, and also legalized peaceful picketing; (2) a (Conservative) 1927 Act, following the 1926 General Strike, which prohibited certain kinds of strike and substituted 'contracting in' for 'contracting out' (i.e. no union member need contribute to political funds unless he specifically contracted to do so); (3) a (Labour) 1946 Act repealing this; (4) the (Conservative) Industrial Relations Act 1971 laid down new laws for the regulation of industrial relations and the curbing of strikes but was repealed by Labour in 1974; (5) in 1980 the (Conservative) Employment Act moderated the closed shop, provided for secret ballots and limited picketing, and this was further strengthened in 1982; (6) the Trade Union Act 1984 strengthened union democracy.

Trader Horn (1927). The pawky reminiscences of an illiterate English tramp, Aloysius Horn, as recorded by Mrs Lewis in South Africa. She read each chapter back to him and then appended his comments on it. Horn had been an ivory trader in West Africa in what he called 'the earlies', and tells of gorilla and elephant hunting, cannibalism and the local slave trade.

Tradescantia Greenhouse and hardy herbaceous perennials, named after John Tradescant (*c.* 1570–1638), gardener to Charles I.

Trafalgar (21 October 1805). Nelson's victory over a Franco-Spanish fleet which removed the danger of a French invasion of England; Nelson was fatally wounded. See THIRD COALITION. (Cape in south-west Spain, near Gibraltar.)

Trafalgar Square London square laid out in 1829–41 to commemorate Nelson, whose statue stands atop a 184-ft column in the centre, guarded by LANDSEER'S LIONS and surrounded by fountains. Facing it are the National Gallery, St Martin-in-the-Fields, South Africa House, Canada House and the CAVELL MEMORIAL. It is a favourite venue for mob orators on Sundays and pigeons on weekdays.

Traminer Type of grape used in hocks, etc.

Tranby Croft scandal (1891). Case arising from an accusation of cheating at cards made at a country house party in Yorkshire; King Edward VII (then Prince of Wales), who was a member of the party, had to give evidence in court.

Tranmere Rovers Birkenhead football team, which plays at Prenton Park.

Transbay Bridge (1936). (USA) Double-tiered bridge across the San Francisco Bay, joining Oakland to San Francisco in 2 main spans of 2,310 ft each.

Trans-Canada Highway (1962). All-season 5,000-mile road from St John's, Newfoundland, to Victoria, British Columbia.

Transcendentalism (1840s). Mystical philosophical and literary movement associated particularly with the New England writers Emerson and Thoreau. They disregarded dogma and relied on their own intuitions as the only guide to the comprehension of reality.

Transcendental Meditation Therapeutic technique (the Science of Creative Intelligence) stressing the need to minimize activity in order to release energy, creativity and intelligence in everyday affairs; a gospel of love and FLOWER POWER is inculcated and the need to meditate for 20 minutes twice daily under instruction from qualified teachers. Introduced to the West by Maharishi Mahesh Yogi, who won fame by getting the BEATLES to meditate on the banks of the Ganges (1968), the movement now has an international HQ in Switzerland, a Maharishi International University (1974) at Fairfield, Iowa, and hotels in Majorca for disciples.

Transfiguration, The Scene described in Mark 9:2–8, when Peter, James and John saw Jesus transfigured on a mountain with Elijah and Moses, and heard a voice coming out of a cloud, saying: 'This is my beloved Son: hear him.' The scene is portrayed by Raphael in a painting (1520) now in the Vatican.

Transit Name given to US navigation satellites, first launched in 1961; they are orbiting radio beacons which permit very exact position-fixing by ships and submerged submarines.

Transjordan Older name of the kingdom of Jordan before it took over Palestine territory west of the Jordan.

Transkei (1963). First BANTUSTAN, formed for the XHOSA. It has its own parliament (whites in the territory have no vote) and is given a large measure of self-government. Formerly in Cape Province, it lies south-east of LESOTHO. It is not recognized as independent by the rest of the world. (Pronounced trans-ky'.)

Transport House (1928). Building in SMITH SQUARE, Westminster, shared as headquarters by the TGWU and the Labour Party.

Trans-Siberian Railway (1904). At first a single-track line linking Chelyabinsk in the Urals via Omsk, Irkutsk, Chita and the CHINESE EASTERN RAILWAY to Vladivostok. In 1916 an all-Russian line was opened via Khabarovsk. The track was not doubled until the 1930s.

Transubstantiation Conversion of bread and wine at the Eucharist into the body and blood of Christ; i.e. the doctrine of the REAL PRESENCE, first put forward in the 9th century and finally defined and accepted by the Roman Catholic Church at the COUNCIL OF TRENT.

Trappists (1664). Order of monks and nuns who revived the CISTERCIAN rule in a most rigorous form, including a vow of silence. They have monasteries at Coalville (Leicestershire), Caldy Island (off Tenby, South Wales) and elsewhere. (La Trappe, Normandy, France, where founded.)

Traquair One of the oldest inhabited houses in Scotland, at Innerleithen, near Peebles, associated with Scottish royalty since the 12th century. (Pronounced trė-kwair'.)

Trastevere Region in Rome west of the Tiber, with narrow streets peopled by the most typically Roman of the populace: small shopkeepers, artisans, etc. (Italian, 'across the Tiber'; pronounced trastay'vèr-e.)

Travellers' Club (1819). London club in Pall Mall founded under the aegis of the first Duke of Wellington; members, under an outdated rule, must have travelled 500 miles from London. It is frequented by diplomats and Foreign Office officials.

Traveller's Joy Wild clematis, whose winter name is old man's beard.

Travels with a Donkey (1879). R. L. Stevenson's account of his travels in the Cévennes, the hills north-west of Avignon in France.

Traven, B. Pen-name of the mysterious author of books sold by the million. Variously stated to be an American born of Scandinavian parents in 1890 and living in Mexico, a son of Kaiser William II, etc., his well-written novels (*The Death Ship*, published in Germany 1926) and short stories (*The Night Visitor*, published in England 1967) carry an anarchist message. Some of his work has been filmed, e.g. *The Treasure of the Sierra Madre* (John Huston, 1947).

Traviata, La (1853). Verdi's opera, based on LA DAME AUX CAMÉLIAS, with the names of the characters changed (Marguerite becomes Violetta, Armand Alfredo). (Italian, 'the courtesan'.)

Trawsfynydd (1968). One of the Magnox series of nuclear power-stations. (Village on the Dolgellau–Ffestiniog road in Snowdonia, Merionethshire.)

Treason Trial, The (1956–61). (South Africa) The prolonged trial of (initially) 140 people charged with plotting against the state, i.e. with opposing apartheid. All had been acquitted by 1961.

Treasure Island (1883). Archetypal boy's story of buried treasure marked on an old map, written by R. L. Stevenson.

Treasure State Nickname of Montana.

Treasury bench In the House of Commons, the front bench on the Speaker's right, where ministers sit.

Treasury Knights Senior civil servants at the Treasury.

Treaty Ports (1842–1947). Chief ports of China, some 40 in number, which came by treaty under the ownership or control of various Western Powers, whose nationals enjoyed extraterritorial rights. This arrangement, a major irritation to the Chinese, was cancelled from 1943 onwards.

Trebizond See TRABZON.

Treble Bob One of the principal methods of change-ringing church bells.

Treblinka (1942–3). Nazi extermination camp in Poland where some 800,000 Jews, mostly Polish, were killed in the gas chambers. In 1943 the Jews rose in revolt, burnt down the camp and killed some of the staff. Some 500 escaped, but only 52 survived.

Tree of Knowledge, The Tree of the knowledge of good and evil whose fruit Jehovah told Adam he must not eat (Gen. 2:17). By eating it (Gen. 3:6) Adam and Eve (i.e. mankind) lost their innocence, i.e. became able to distinguish right from wrong, and thus incurred moral responsibility. See The FALL; PROMETHEUS.

'Trees' (1913). Poem which brought fame to Joyce Kilmer and also to Oscar Rasbach when he made a popular song of it (1922). It begins 'I think that I shall never see / A poem lovely as a tree' and ends 'Poems are made by fools like me, / But only God can make a tree'.

Treetops Hotel Kenya hotel literally built in a tree, from which visitors could watch wild game. It was destroyed by Mau Mau in 1954, but has since been rebuilt.

Trelawny of the 'Wells' (1898). Pinero's comedy of the actress, Rose Trelawny, who jilts an aristocrat to return to the stage, whither he follows her.

Trematodes See PLATYHELMINTHES.

Trent Bridge (1840). Nottinghamshire county cricket ground, at Nottingham, since 1899 one of the Test match grounds.

Trent's Last Case (1912). Highly regarded detective story by E. C. Bentley in which Philip Trent, the artistic dilettante and amateur detective, solves the murder of an American millionaire.

Tre, Pol and Pen Cornish name prefixes. Tre ('farm') is commoner in the east of the county, Pol ('pool') in the west, Pen ('peak') in the middle. There is an old saying: 'By Tre, Pol and Pen, / You shall know the Cornish men.'

Trial, The (1925). Kafka's allegorical novel about 'Jozef K', arrested and tried on a charge that is never specified; it has been described as the *Pilgrim's Progress* of the subconscious, and represents a search for divine justice. (German title, *Das Prozess*.)

Trial by Jury (1875). Gilbert and Sullivan one-act opera in which Angelina sues Edwin for breach of promise before a susceptible judge who tries to resolve a legal impasse by offering to marry the plaintiff himself.

Trianon See GRAND TRIANON; PETIT TRIANON.

Trianon, Treaty of (1920). Post-war treaty with Hungary, which had to cede two-thirds of its territory, including Transylvania, Slovakia and Croatia, to neighbouring states.

Trianon Adventure (1901). Extraordinary experience recounted by Miss Moberly, Principal of St Hugh's College, Oxford, and Miss Jourdain, its Vice-Principal, in *An Adventure* (1911). When visiting the gardens of the Petit Trianon, Versailles, they found themselves apparently back in the year 1789, and thought they saw Marie Antoinette.

Triassic Period Earliest period of the MESOZOIC ERA, lasting from about 240 to 200 million years ago. Fossils of small warm-blooded mammals appear, together with dinosaurs, icthyosaurus and turtles. (Greek *trias*, 'triad', from a threefold subdivision of rocks of this period in Germany.)

Triboro' Bridge (1936). (New York City) A system of bridges and viaducts spanning the East River, with 3 arms linking the boroughs of Manhattan, Queens and the Bronx.

Tricel (1954). Man-made fibre used particularly for pleated garments.

Tricoteuses Name given to Parisian women during the TERROR, politically zealous, attending executions, also known as Les Tricoteuses de Robespierre and Les Furies de la Guillotine. (French, 'knitters'.)

Trident (1964). Medium-range airliner developed by De Havilland and Hawker-Siddeley. Trident-3 has 3 rear-mounted engines and is the equivalent of the US BOEING 727. Trident-1 has twin engines.

Trident Code-name for the Washington Conference (May 1943) of Churchill and Roosevelt, at which the former pressed for a landing in Italy. It was decided to step up the bombing of Germany and to open the Second Front in May 1944.

Triffids See DAY OF THE TRIFFIDS.

Trigorin See *The* SEAGULL.

Trilby Du Maurier's novel; see SVENGALI.

Trim, Corporal UNCLE TOBY'S servant in TRISTRAM SHANDY, honest, ignorant but, unlike his master, voluble.

Trimalchio's Feast See SATYRICON.

Trinity, The God the Father, God the Son and God the Holy Ghost. The dogma was laid down in the NICENE CREED that God is one but exists in these 3 Persons, which are co-eternal and co-equal; the Son is begotten of the Father, of one substance with the Father; the Holy Ghost 'proceeds' from Father and Son (from the Father only for the Eastern Orthodox Church; the word *filioque*, 'and from the Son', was added by the Council of Toledo in 589).

Trinity House, The Corporation of (1514).

Principal lighthouse and pilotage authority in the UK. It licenses pilots and maintains the lighthouses, lightships and buoys of England and Wales, and some elsewhere. See ELDER BRETHREN. (Name of headquarters at Tower Hill, London.)

Trinity Sunday Sunday after Whit Sunday.

Trinity term Legal term after Easter, and at Oxford the last term of the academic year (called Easter term at Cambridge).

Tripartite Pact (September 1940). Alliance which extended the ROME-BERLIN AXIS to include Japan; Germany and Japan were to unite to oppose any US interference with the development of their respective plans: the NEW ORDER IN EUROPE and the GREATER EAST ASIA CO-PROSPERITY SPHERE. The alliance was joined later by Hungary, Romania, Bulgaria and others (called the Axis powers).

Triple Alliance (1882). Italy's accession, arranged by Bismarck, to the DUAL ALLIANCE (1879) of Austria–Hungary and Germany, which was directed against Russia and France. Italy broke away when World War I came (see LONDON, SECRET TREATY OF).

Triple Crown (1) Mythical award to the English, Scottish, Welsh or Irish international rugby team that in one season defeats all 3 of its opponents. (2) Also applied to a horse that wins the Two Thousand Guineas, Derby and St Leger or (USA) the Kentucky Derby, Preakness and Belmont Stakes.

Triple Entente Informal understanding (developing from the ENTENTE CORDIALE) between Britain, France and Russia, which took shape in 1907–8 in reaction to the TRIPLE ALLIANCE.

Tripolitan War (1911–12). War waged by Italy against Turkey, forcing the latter to acknowledge the Italian conquest of LIBYA (Turkish Tripoli).

Tripos Final examination for an honours degree at Cambridge University. (Variously explained; pronounced try'pos.)

Trip to Jerusalem, The (1189). England's oldest pub, in an ancient cave, one of many hollowed out of the sandstone of Castle Rock, Nottingham.

Tristram In Arthurian legend, a nephew of King Mark of Cornwall who fell in love with his uncle's bride, ISEULT (Isolde), and was killed either by Mark or by his own wife. (Also spelt Tristam, Tristan.)

Tristram Shandy, The Life and Opinions of (1759–67). Magnificently incoherent novel by Laurence Sterne, in which Tristram tries hard to tell the story of his life but does not get very far, being unable to resist any irrelevancy that may occur to him. See UNCLE TOBY; Corporal TRIM.

Tritoma See KNIPHOFIA.

Triton In Greek mythology, a sea-god, son of Poseidon and Amphitryon; he is depicted in art as part man, part fish, and blowing his 'wreathed horn' (a conch, or shell) to soothe the oceans. 'Triton of (or among) the minnows', a phrase used by Shakespeare, signifies a person who appears great only because his followers or rivals are so insignificant.

Trobriand Islanders Inhabitants of islands off New Guinea, whose way of life is known to the world through the intensive studies of the Polish-born British anthropologist Malinowski.

Trocadero (1) Fortress at Cádiz captured by the French in 1823. (2) The name of the gardens in Paris now occupied by the Palais de Chaillot, across the Seine from the Eiffel Tower. (3) Name adopted by various hotels and restaurants. (Pronounced, in England, trok-a-deer'o; in French the *è* is accented.)

Troika plan (1962). Plan put forward by Khrushchev for replacing the UN Secretary-General by a committee of 3. (Russian, a vehicle drawn by 3 horses abreast.)

Troilus and Cressida Troubadour's tale, with no classical basis, used by Boccaccio, Chaucer and Shakespeare among others; the Trojan hero Troilus falls in love with the faithless Cressida, whom Pandarus persuades to yield to him; later she deserts Troilus for Diomede.

Trois Quartiers, Aux Large Paris department store near the Louvre.

Trojan Horse, The In Greek legend, the huge and hollow wooden horse, full of armed Greeks, which the Trojans, persuaded that it was an offering to the gods that might bring them luck, dragged into Troy. The Greeks emerged at night and took the city, which had withstood a 10-year siege. Hence the expression 'I fear the Greeks even when they bring gifts' (*timeo Danaos et dona ferentes*).

Trojan War (12th century BC). Legendary siege of Troy by the Greeks under Agamemnon (see previous entry). The end of the story is told in the ILIAD and the AENEID. The *casus belli* was HELEN OF TROY, but the legend probably had its origin in a struggle to control a main trade route between East and West; the strategic importance of Troy is evidenced by the remains of 9 successive cities built on the same site, near modern Hissarlik at the entrance to the Dardanelles.

Trollius The genus name of the globe flower.

Troon Resort in Kyle and Carrick district of Strathclyde, Scotland, where Open golf championships are held.

Trooping the Colour (1755). (London) Ceremony performed by the Guards regiments on or about the Sovereign's official birthday in June at Horse Guards Parade, Whitehall. (Particular instance of a traditional military ceremony.)

Tropaeolum Genus name of the nasturtium and the canary creeper.

Trotskyism Advocacy of world Communist revolution instead of the 'Socialism in one country' preached by Lenin and Stalin, which Trotsky regarded as a manifestation of undesirable Russian nationalism. (Leon Trotsky, opponent of Stalin, exiled 1924 and assassinated 1940.)

Trotters, The Nickname of the Bolton Wanderers football team.

Trotwood, Betsey DAVID COPPERFIELD'S aunt who had disowned him at birth because he was not a girl, but later champions his cause. Sharp-

tongued but kind-hearted, she also looks after Mr DICK.

Troubles, The (January 1919 to August 1923). Period of civil war in southern Ireland between the FREE STATERS and those members of the IRA who rejected PARTITION. It ended when the IRA leader, De Valera, was captured, called for a cease-fire, and founded FIANNA FÁIL.

Trout Quintet, The Schubert's quintet for piano and strings, in which the fourth movement consists of variations on the tune of his song 'The Trout'.

Trovatore, Il (1853). Verdi's opera of violent passion, witchcraft and villainy among the Biscayan gypsies. (Italian, 'the troubadour'.)

Troy See TROJAN WAR.

Trucial States (Trucial Oman) Former name for seven small independent sheikhdoms on the Persian Gulf; they are separate from the Sultanate of Muscat and Oman, which lies to the east and south. (Named from the truce made with Britain in 1820 which was combined with a promise to suppress piracy and the slave trade.) In 1971 the United Arab Emirates was established.

Trud Soviet Russian newspaper for the workers, published by the central council of trade unions.

Truman Doctrine, The (1947). That whenever aggression, direct or indirect, threatened US security, action would be taken to stop it; pronounced when Congress authorized military aid to Greece and Turkey to counter and contain Communist activities.

Trumpet Voluntary, The Familiar in Sir Henry Wood's arrangement and once attributed to Purcell, but composed by Jeremiah Clarke (c. 1673–1707) as 'The Prince of Denmark's March' for harpsichord, in the natural scale of the trumpet.

Trundle Hill Hill at Goodwood which gives a bird's-eye view of the whole racecourse and countryside.

Trusteeship Council (1946). UN successor to the League of Nations MANDATES COMMISSION; it comprises member countries that administer

trust territories and those members of the SECU-
RITY COUNCIL who do not administer trust
territories. Only the Pacific Islands formerly
mandated to Japan (USA) are still under trusteeship.

Tsaritsyn City of RSFSR now known as Volgograd (and formerly as Stalingrad).

Tsarskoe Seloe One of the chief palaces of Imperial Russia, now a museum in the Leningrad
suburb of Pushkin. (Russian, 'Tsar's village'.)

Tschiffeley's Ride (1925–7). Journey of 13,350
miles from Buenos Aires to Washington DC,
ridden by the Swiss-born Argentinian, A. F.
Tschiffeley, using 2 horses only. His purpose was
to demonstrate the stamina of a certain Argentinian breed. The journey took $2\frac{1}{2}$ years.

T-shirt (Originally US) Casual cotton shirt, short-
sleeved and collarless. (So called from its shape.)

TSSA Initials standing for the Transport
Salaried Staffs Association, one of the 3 railway
unions.

Tsushima (May 1905). Scene of the crushing
defeat inflicted by the Japanese Admiral Togo, in
the straits between Japan and Korea, on the
Russian fleet sent from the Baltic. (Pronounced
tsoo'shi-ma.)

Tu Abbreviated name for a series of Russian
aircraft, including: the first Russian pure jet, Tu-
104 (1956); the world's biggest airliner, Tu-114
(1961), a swept-wing turboprop carrying up to
220 passengers; and Tu-144, which came into
service about the same time as Concorde, of
which it is the slightly smaller equivalent, i.e.
the first Russian supersonic airliner. (Abbreviated from the designer's name, Andrei
Tupolev.)

Tuaregs Nomadic BERBER race of the Sahara,
who wear veils as a protection from driving
sand.

Tuatha Dé Danann In Irish legend, the successors to the FIR BOLG; they were driven into
the hills by the 'Milesians' and returned as
fairies. ('Tribes of Danu', the mother of the
gods.)

Tube Alloys British wartime code name for
atomic bomb research. See MAUD COMMITTEE;
MANHATTAN PROJECT.

Tucker report (1957). Report of a commission
which recommended the exclusion of the press
from committal proceedings before examining
magistrates; it arose from the trial of Dr Bodkin
Adams for murder, in which it was thought that
press reports prejudiced a fair trial.

Tudor period (1485–1603). Period in the decorative arts typified by heavy oak furniture with
bulbous legs, the elaborate 4-poster bed, linen-
fold panelling decorated with varied carved
motifs, e.g. the Tudor rose.

Tudors Dynasty of English kings (1485–1603)
begun by Henry VII (see BOSWORTH FIELD)
and continued by Henry VIII, Edward VI, Mary
and Elizabeth. (Henry VII was a grandson of
Owen Tudor.)

Tuileries Paris gardens made in the 16th century
and redesigned by the 17th-century landscape
gardener Le Nôtre. They lie between the Louvre
and the Place de la Concorde, and contained
the Jeu de Paume gallery which formerly
contained Impressionist paintings and the
Orangerie, now in the Musée d'Orsay. (French
tuile, 'tile'; the site was once a pottery clay-
pit.)

Tulane (1834). US university at New Orleans,
Louisiana.

Tulip Mania (1630s). Wild outburst of speculation in tulip bulbs, which spread from Holland
over Europe. Some varieties fetched £500
apiece, and thousands of people went bankrupt
when the market collapsed.

Tulliver aunts, The Strong-and narrow-minded
Mrs Glegg and the self-centred hypochondriac
Mrs Pullet who with Mrs Tulliver, Maggie's
mother, form the trio of Dodson sisters in George
Eliot's *The Mill on the Floss*. Poor Maggie was
constantly reminded that 'no Dodson ever did'
the things she did.

Tully Old-fashioned name for the Roman orator
Cicero (Marcus Tullius), Cicero being merely a
nickname ('warty').

Tum-Tum Nickname of King Edward VII.

Tunbridge ware Form of pictorial wood marquetry developed at Tunbridge Wells, Kent, from the 17th century, and particularly popular in the 19th century. Designs depicting old castles, landscapes, etc. were made by assembling countless narrow strips of different woods, stained to varying shades by steeping in the local mineral waters. These were then sawn through lengthwise, producing many copies of the same design, which were then applied to boxes, trays etc.

Tupamaros (1964). Urban guerrillas of Uruguay who fight injustice and Yanqui imperialism, killing without compunction and financing operations by robbing banks and casinos. Their leaders come from prominent Catholic families. (From Túpac Amaru, Inca chief who rebelled against Spanish rule in Bolivia and was executed by being torn apart, 1783.)

Tupí-Guaraní American Indian group of languages spoken over a wide area of Brazil and Paraguay.

Turandot (1926). Puccini's unfinished opera (completed by another hand). Turandot, Princess of China, will marry any suitor who can answer her 3 riddles; those who fail will be beheaded. An Unknown Prince solves them and then reveals himself as the son of Timur, King of Tartary. See LIU. (Pronounced toor'an-doh, more correctly toor'an-dot, according to Eva Turner, one of the greatest interpreters of the part.)

Turanian languages Old term for Asian languages which are neither Semitic or Indo-European, i.e. the URAL-ALTAIC LANGUAGES. (Turan, ancient name of the land east of Iran – Persia – beyond the Oxus.)

Turf Club (1868). London club where the social élite can keep in touch with racing results.

Turfites, The Nickname of the Burnley football team, which plays at Turf Moor.

Turkish Blood Drink concocted of beer and red Burgundy.

Turkomans Trade name for the red carpets and rugs of Central Asian steppes, comprising the BOKHARA, AFGHAN and BALUCHI; mostly made by nomads and semi-nomads, from the 13th century onwards, often to hang in tent doorways, as prayer rugs or as saddle-bags. (Persian name for Turk-like tribes of Turkestan, Afghanistan, northern Iran and east of the Caspian.)

Turksib (1931). Short title of the Turkestan–Siberian Railway, which runs south from the Trans-Siberian Railway at Novosibirsk to Alma-Ata and Tashkent.

Turl, The Oxford street across which Jesus and Exeter colleges face one another.

Turners, Worshipful Company of (1604). LIVERY COMPANY, originally a guild of makers of lathe-turned wooden domestic articles; it still encourages craftsmanship through exhibitions and prizes.

'Turnip' Townshend Nickname of Charles, 2nd Viscount Townshend (1674–1738), who changed British agriculture by adopting on his Norfolk estate at Raynham new crop rotations and the winter feeding of turnips to cattle.

Turn of the Screw, The (1898). Henry James's long short story about a governess whose 2 charges are under the influence of evil ghosts. It is the basis of a play and an opera, the latter by Benjamin Britten.

Turpin, Dick Eighteenth-century highwayman who appears in several ballads and stories; see BLACK BESS. He was hanged for horse-stealing.

Turveydrop Minor character in Dickens's BLEAK HOUSE, a dancing-master, 'a very gentlemanly man', intensely selfish and vain.

Tuscany, The ranks of Etruscan army, the enemy; phrase from Macaulay's *Horatius* (see LARS PORSENA): 'And even the ranks of Tuscany / Could scarce forbear to cheer.'

Tusitala Name given to R. L. Stevenson in Samoa. ('Teller of tales'; pronounced too-si-tah la.)

Tuskegee Institute (1881). Black coeducational college in eastern Alabama, founded by Booker T. Washington, black American educationist. (Pronounced tus-kee'gi.)

Tutankhamen's Tomb (14th century BC) First intact royal sepulchre of ancient Egypt to be discovered, by Howard Carter (1922) in the VALLEY OF THE KINGS. Tutankhamen was AKENATEN'S successor.

Tutsi A Nilotic cattle people who once ruled Burundi and Rwanda in Central Africa. In 1964 the HUTU massacred the Tutsi of Rwanda, many of whom fled to the kingdom of Burundi. Inexplicably, the feudal Tutsi were supported by the Chinese Communists. Also called Watutsi, Batutsi.

TVA (1933). Initials commonly used for the Tennessee Valley Authority, set up as a NEW DEAL measure in the backward, impoverished region along the Tennessee River, in Kentucky, Mississippi, Tennessee, Alabama, Georgia, North Carolina and Virginia. It constructed 21 dams for power generation, flood control and irrigation; taught anti-erosion and improved agricultural techniques; reafforested the area; and stamped out malaria. This vast and successful venture was widely copied abroad, but at home was denounced as Socialism and Federal interference in local affairs.

Tver Russian city of the RSFSR, previously renamed Kalinin, now reverted back to Tver.

Twain, Mark Pen-name of Samuel Langhorne Clemens. (From the leadsman's call 'By the mark, twain', indicating a depth of 2 fathoms; used on Mississippi steamboats and elsewhere.)

Tweedledum and Tweedledee Names invented by an 18th-century poet for 2 people whose opinions or looks are alike; adopted by Lewis Carroll in *Through the Looking Glass* for 2 pugnacious little fat men.

Tweedsmuir, 1st Baron John Buchan, the novelist, Governor-General of Canada, 1935–40.

Twelfth, The The 12th of August, the first day of the grouse-shooting season.

Twelfth Night The 6th of January, Christmas Day OLD STYLE, the feast of Epiphany, and once the culmination of Christmas festivities. (Twelve days after Christmas Day.)

Twelfth Night (1600) Shakespeare's comedy with a complicated plot centring round the confusion caused by the resemblence of twin brother and sister, the latter (VIOLA) disguised as a boy. The scene is Illyria, and the characters include AGUECHEEK, BELCH, FESTE, and MALVOLIO.

Twelfth of July 'The Glorious Twelfth', inaccurately celebrated as the anniversary of the Battle of the BOYNE, which took place on 1 July OLD STYLE (11 July New Style); still an important date to Ulster Protestants.

Twelve, The Member-states of the European Communities. The original membership consisted of Belgium, France, the Federal Republic of Germany, Italy, Luxembourg and The Netherlands, and were joined in 1973 by Denmark, Ireland and the UK, in 1981 by Greece, in 1986 by Spain and Portugal.

'12' certificate (1989). Granted by British Board of Film Classification to films suitable for children aged between 12 and 15.

'Twelve Days of Christmas' English 'cumulative' carol enumerating the gifts made to a lover on each day from Christmas to Twelfth Night: 'The first day of Christmas / My true love sent to me / A partridge in a pear tree', followed by turtle doves, French hens, colly birds, gold rings, geese, swans, maids, drummers, pipers, ladies and lords.

Twelve Pound Look, The (1913). J. M. Barrie's one-act comedy, like *What Every Woman Knows* an attack on male egoism, personified in the pompous, ridiculous Harry Sims.

Twelve-tone music System of atonal music introduced by Schoenberg which replaced the orthodox system of keys by a series ('tone-row') of 12 notes of the chromatic scale, all treated as of equal importance, with no hierarchy of dominant or key notes.

20th Congress (USSR) Crucial meeting in February 1956 when Khrushchev denounced Stalin in his 'secret speech', and in a public speech announced a reversal of policy; peaceful coexistence; different paths to Socialism; revolution without violence; abandonment of the doctrine of the inevitability of war with the West.

21st Amendment (1933). Amendment to the US Constitution which repealed PROHIBITION.

Twenty-One Demands (1915). Made by Japan on China for increased rights in Shantung, Mongolia and Manchuria.

22nd Amendment (1951). Amendment to the US Constitution which limited tenure of the Presidency to 2 terms.

Twenty Thousand Leagues under the Sea (1869). Jules Verne's novel, written before submarines were invented, in which a party of scientists are captured by the mysterious Capt. Nemo and kept prisoners in his pirate submarine.

Twickenham Former municipal borough of Middlesex, since 1965 part of the borough of RICHMOND UPON THAMES.

Twickenham London home of English rugby and of the HARLEQUINS RUFC; the Oxford and Cambridge University match and the Service Championship matches are also played there.

Twiggy Nickname of a 1960s London fashion model, referring to her emaciated frame (hence the lapel button: Forget Oxfam–Feed Twiggy).

Twilight of the Gods See GÖTTERDÄMMERUNG.

Twist, The (1960). Dance in which the dancers energetically twist their hips in time to rhythmic music.

Two Cheers for Democracy (1952). E. M. Forster's sequel to ABINGER HARVEST.

Two Cultures The scientific and the classical and literary; C. P. (later Lord) Snow suggested (1959) that the conservative upper middle class, reared in the latter culture, underrated the vital importance to the nation of the former, which was lower middle class in origin.

Two Gentlemen of Verona (1595). Shakespeare's comedy about the changing loves and fortunes of Valentine and Proteus, 2 friends and

rivals for the hand of the Duke of Milan's daughter.

2LO Call-sign of the SAVOY HILL broadcasting station in London.

Two Nations Rich and poor in Britain at the time of the Chartists; a phrase used as the secondary title of Disraeli's influential novel *Sybil* (1845), depicting the appalling condition of the working class.

Two plus Four (1990). German unification talks between the Federal Republic of Germany, the German Democratic Republic and the four victorious World War II Allied powers, USSR, France, UK and USA.

Two Sicilies, Kingdom of the (1734–1860). Spanish Bourbon kingdom of Naples (i.e. southern Italy) and Sicily.

Two Thousand Guineas Classic flat-race for 3-year-olds run over the Rowley Mile at the first Spring meeting, Newmarket.

TW3 (1962). Abbreviation for TWTWTW, the initials of *That was the Week, That was*, the earliest of the BBC's late-night satirical TV programmes.

Tyburn Tree Triangular gallows near where the Marble Arch now stands in London; until 1783 public executions took place there.

Tycho's star One of the 3 supernovae observed in the Milky Way, discovered in CASSIOPEIA by Tycho Brahe, the Danish astronomer, in 1751–2. (Pronounced ty'koh.)

Tylers and Bricklayers, Worshipful Company of (1568). LIVERY COMPANY.

Tyler's Rebellion See PEASANTS' REVOLT.

Tyndale's Bible (1526–30). First printed English Bible; William Tyndale's translation, into the plain English we know today, of the New Testament and some of the Old; the main source for subsequent English versions. (Pronounced tind'l.)

Tyne-Tees The commercial TV company serving the Newcastle area.

Tynwald

Tynwald Legislative assembly of the Isle of Man, consisting of the Lieutenant-Governor, the Legislative Council of 12 ex-officio and nominated members, as an Upper House, together with the HOUSE OF KEYS. (Old Norse, 'field assembly'; pronounced tin'wold, tyn'wold.)

Tynwald ceremony Annual open-air meeting of the TYNWALD on Tynwald Hill on 5 July (Old Midsummer Day, called Tynwald Day), at which laws passed in England during the preceding year are formally declared applicable to the Isle of Man.

Typefaces Most of the classic or standard typefaces have been named after famous printers or type-founders; they include Baskerville, John (1706–75); Bodoni, Giambattista (1740–1813); Caxton, William (1692–1766); Fournier, Pierre Simon le Jeune (1712–68); Garamond, Claude (d. 1561); Gill, Eric (1882–1940); Granjon, Robert (*c.* 1500); Plantin, Christopher (1520–80). See GILL SANS; TIMES NEW ROMAN.

Typhoon (1903). Joseph Conrad's short novel, with a vivid description of a storm at sea, through which the unimaginative Capt. Mac-Whirr calmly brings his ship to safety.

Tyrian purple See PHOENICIANS.

Tyrol See TIROL.

Tyrone rebellion (1597–1601). Rebellion in Ulster led by Hugh O'Neill, Earl of Tyrone. It was suppressed by Lord Mountjoy, the successor to the Earl of Essex (see ESSEX REBELLION). See ULSTER, PLANTATION OF.

Tzigane Hungarian gypsy; applied adjectivally to Hungarian gypsy music. See ATHINGANOI. (French form of the Hungarian name.)

U Burmese equivalent of 'Mr'. (Pronounced oo.)

U and non-U Class stratification of English people by speech habits, based on upper-class shibboleths, in a game popularized by Nancy Mitford (1955) from an idea suggested in a lecture by Professor Ross; thus e.g. 'lunch' is held to be non-U for 'luncheon'. (U = upper class.)

Ubangi-Shari Former French colony, now the Central African Republic.

Uber Cup (1956). Ladies' international badminton championship.

U-boat German submarine. (For German Unterseeboot.)

Ubu Roi (1896). Alfred Jarry's burlesque of Oedipus Rex, in which a coarse and cowardly bourgeois makes himself King of Poland and, drunk with power, invades Russia, where he is soundly beaten.

UCCA Initials used for the Universities Central Council on Admissions, set up to co-ordinate the previously rather haphazard arrangements for directing students to the universities where places are available for them.

Uc certificate British classification of video tapes suitable for all and particularly of interest to children.

'U' certificate (1982). Granted by British Board of Film Classification to films suitable for all age groups.

UDI Unilateral Declaration of Independence, made by the Smith regime in Southern Rhodesia (now Zimbabwe), 11 November 1965.

Uffington White Horse See VALE OF THE WHITE HORSE.

Uffizi One of the 2 great art galleries in Florence (the other is the PITTI). (Pronounced oof-fits'i.)

UFO Abbreviation for Unidentified Flying Object, the official name for a FLYING SAUCER or other phenomenon of that type.

'Ugly Duckling, The' Original fairy-tale by Hans Andersen about a cygnet hatched out by a duck. He is brought up to regard himself merely as an ugly duckling until one day he runs away and is adopted by swans who restore his self-respect. Andersen's moral is: it matters not to have been born in a duck-yard if one has been hatched from a swan's egg.

Uhlans German cavalry (originally lancers) who played a prominent part in the early months of World War I. (Originally a Tartar word.)

Uhuru! The slogan used in the campaign for Kenya's independence. (Swahili, 'freedom'.)

Uitlander Afrikaans name for the British in the old Boer Republics of Transvaal and the Orange Free State. (Literally, 'outlander'; pronounced ayt'land-er.)

Ulema Those learned in Muslim law and theology; a term used in the Turkish Empire and revived (1931) when a league of Ulema was formed in Algeria as part of an Arab Muslim renaissance. (Arabic (plural) word, 'learned'; pronounced oo'lem-a.)

Ulex Genus name of gorse, the strong-scented shrub which flowers all the year round; also called whin or furze, but these names are sometimes given to species of GENISTA and CYTISUS.

Ulm, Battle of (October 1805). Napoleon marched 500 miles across Europe in 21 days and at Ulm overwhelmed Austria; he then occupied Vienna. See THIRD COALITION. (Town on the Danube, now in Baden-Württemberg.)

Ulster (1) (Loosely) Northern Ireland. (2) The Celtic kingdom and former northern province of Ireland; now divided between the Six Counties forming Northern Ireland (Antrim, Armagh, Down, Fermanagh, Londonderry and Tyrone) and 3 counties in the Irish Republic (Cavan, Donegal and Monaghan).

Ulster, Plantation of (1608–12). Colonization of Ulster by Scottish Presbyterians and a few English after the TYRONE REBELLION had led to the forfeit of Ulster to the English Crown. See PLANTATIONS.

Ulster Covenant (September 1912). Pledge to resist Home Rule for Ireland, signed at Belfast by the followers of Sir Edward Carson and leading to the formation of the ULSTER VOLUNTEERS.

Ulster Volunteer Force Paramilitary force raised by Protestant extremists and quickly declared illegal (1966).

Ulster Volunteers (1912). Sir Edward Carson's 'private army' formed to resist Home Rule.

Ultima Thule (1) Most northerly part of the world known to the Greeks and Romans. (2) Distant unknown land; the furthest limit attainable. (Latin *ultima*, 'farthest'; *Thule*, an island north of Britain, perhaps the Shetlands, Iceland or Norway; pronounced ult'i-ma thoo'lee.)

Ultra In April 1940 for the first time German signals in cipher were intercepted and the cipher broken at Bletchley Park, Buckinghamshire, England. This operation was code-named Ultra – ultra secret. (See also ENIGMA.)

Ultramontanists Roman Catholics who believe in the absolute authority of the Pope even outside Italy. ('Beyond the mountains', i.e. the Alps.)

Ulysses Latin name of ODYSSEUS. (Pronounced ew-lis'eez.)

Ulysses (1922). James Joyce's plotless account of one day in the lives of Leopold BLOOM, his wife Molly, and Stephen DEDALUS, in which stream-of-consciousness or interior monologue reveals their inmost thoughts in language replete with symbolism, allusion and portmanteau-puns which demand a knowledge of several languages and all folklore to unravel.

Ulysses deriding Polyphemus (1829). One of J. M. W. Turner's masterpieces, now in the London National Gallery. See POLYPHEMUS.

Umbellifers Carrot family, characterized by umbrella-shaped flowers; it includes parsley, ground elder, hemlock, etc.

Umkonto we Sizwe Military wing of the AFRICAN NATIONAL CONGRESS in South Africa. ('Spear of the Nation'.)

Uncle Remus (1880). Joel Chandler Harris's book of American Negro folk tales, as told by Uncle Remus to a white boy, with characters such as Brer Fox and Brer Rabbit.

Uncle Sam (1) US government personified; (2) US nation or people. (Possibly through the letters 'US' stamped on kegs of meat for the Army during the war of 1812 being jokingly identified with Uncle Sam, i.e. Samuel Wilson, a meat packer.)

Uncle Toby Chief, though inarticulate, character in TRISTRAM SHANDY. An ex-officer, wounded in Flanders, who occupies himself by reconstructing Marlborough's campaigns in his garden, and, by dint of his complete guilelessness, eludes the advances of the buxom Widow Wadman. Tristram is his nephew.

Uncle Tom Chief character in UNCLE TOM'S CABIN, who is persecuted by Simon LEGREE and beaten to death. The term is used by US blacks of a fellow black who is subservient to white Americans.

Uncle Tom Cobbleigh Best known of the various people who wanted to go to WIDDICOMBE FAIR; from the chorus 'Old Uncle Tom Cobbleigh and all'.

Uncle Tom's Cabin (1852). Harriet Beecher Stowe's novel about slavery in Louisiana and Kentucky, which greatly influenced opinion on the subject in the Northern states. See UNCLE TOM.

UNCTAD (1964). UN Conference on Trade and Development, held at Geneva. It showed that the dominant interest of the underdeveloped countries was in getting aid for economic development, and that political alignment with East or West was a matter of indifference to most of them.

Underground, The In World War II, a synonym for the RESISTANCE MOVEMENT.

Under Milk Wood (1954). Dylan Thomas's radio play in which the inhabitants of the Welsh village of Llareggub, which lies under Milk Wood, muse aloud and betray their fears and desires and other inmost thoughts.

Under-Secretary of State See PARLIAMENTARY SECRETARY.

Undershaft, Andrew Father of MAJOR BARBARA in Shaw's play, an armaments tycoon with enlightened views. He observes that the world scraps obsolete machinery but not obsolete religion, morality, or political constitutions. It is poverty, not sin, that breeds crime (a novel idea in those days).

Under the Greenwood Tree (1872). Hardy's rustic idyll of the love of a young couple whose path runs unusually smooth for a Hardy novel.

Under the Volcano (1947). Malcolm Lowry's

Joyce-inspired novel of European expatriates in Mexico.

Undertones of War (1928). Poet Edmund Blunden's classic novel of World War I, giving a restrained presentation of the soldier's view of the war, in which he himself served.

Under Two Flags (1867). Ouida's masterpiece of romantic fatuity. The hero is the Hon. Bertie Cecil, 1st Life Guards, who breakfasts exclusively off a glass of curaçao. Falsely accused of forgery, to save a woman's name he seeks anonymity in the ranks of the French Chasseurs in Algeria. After heroic deeds, this dedicated fall guy faces a firing squad but Cigarette, playmate of the regiment, clutching his reprieve shields him with her body and receives the fusillade intended for him.

Under Western Eyes (1911). Joseph Conrad's novel about Russian revolutionaries in Geneva at the turn of the century.

Undine Water-sprite who falls in love with a mortal in a German tale (1811) which was turned into an opera by E. T. A. Hoffmann (1816). (Pronounced un'deen.)

Unesco (1946). UN Educational, Scientific and Cultural organization. Has three main functions: to encourage international intellectual cooperation; to assist member states in its fields of activity, including communication; and to promote peace, human rights and human understanding; headquarters in Paris.

Unfinished **Symphony, The** (1822). Schubert's 8th Symphony of which he wrote the first 2 movements and part of the third. It is not known why he never finished it, and the manuscript was not discovered until 1865.

Ungulates Obsolescent term for the order of hoofed mammals, divided into the ARTIODACTYLA and the PERISSODACTYLA.

UNHCR See UNITED NATIONS HIGH COMMISSIONER FOR REFUGEES.

Unicef See UNITED NATIONS CHILDREN'S FUND. (Initials of original title: UN International Children's Emergency Fund.)

Unilever (1929). Anglo-Dutch group, sixth largest in the world, with headquarters at London and Rotterdam, formed by merging Lever Bros (Sunlight, Pears, Lifebuoy, Lux soaps) and the Dutch Margarine Unie. Its largest, semi-autonomous unit, the United Africa Co., has oilseed, timber, shipping, cement, beer and plastics interests in West Africa, mainly Nigeria and Ghana.

Union, The (1) Old name for the workhouse (short for union workhouse, i.e. one which was administered by a union of parishes formed to administer the Poor Law). (2) A university debating society and club.

Unionists In Ulster an alternative name for Conservatives; after the Liberal split (1886) over Gladstone's Irish HOME RULE policy, Joseph Chamberlain formed the Liberal Unionist Party, which joined (1895) a coalition government with the Conservative Party; this became the Conservative and Unionist Party. ('Union' here = union of all Ireland and Great Britain, i.e. opposition to Home Rule.)

Union Jack National flag of Great Britain which amalgamates the crosses of St George, St Andrew and St Patrick (also known as the Union flag).

Union Jack Club (1907). Hostel and club for men of the regular forces, in Waterloo Road, London; there are adjoining clubs for the women's services and for forces' families.

Union Movement British Union of Fascists in new guise, refounded by Sir Oswald Mosley in 1948; now long defunct.

Union of Democratic Control (September 1914). Party formed by those, led by Ramsay MacDonald, E. D. Morel and Bertrand Russell, who opposed British entry into World War I; they advocated early peace negotiations, and open diplomacy to minimize the danger of stumbling into further world wars through secret diplomatic moves such as preceded the first.

Unisex Term deriving from the increasing difficulty in telling long-haired boy from girl, turned to commercial account in selling boyish clothes to girls and girlish to boys.

Unitarians Christians who believe in the single personality of God and do not accept the TRINITY. The term covers various shades of belief, from a Jesus who had divine powers delegated to him to a Jesus who was merely a good man; Unitarians also reject original sin, atonement, eternal punishment and all creeds. Their Church flourishes in New England.

United Arab Republic (February 1958). Formed by Egypt and Syria; President Nasser retained the name for Egypt, until 1971, despite Syria's secession in 1961.

United Arab States Short-lived union of the United Arab Republic (Egypt and Syria) and Yemen.

United Empire Party Political party founded by Lord Beaverbrook and another press baron, Lord Rothermere, to get candidates into Parliament who would support EMPIRE FREE TRADE.

United Free Church of Scotland (1900). Formed by the Free Church of Scotland and the United Presbyterian Church; reunited with the Church of Scotland in 1929. See WEE FREES.

United Kingdom See ACTS OF UNION.

United Methodist Church Formed 1907, rejoined the Methodist Church in 1932.

United Nations Building (1952). Headquarters of the United Nations, in Manhattan, New York City, overlooking the East River.

United Nations Charter (June 1945). Agreement signed at San Francisco which set up the United Nations Organization, with the chief aim of ensuring international peace.

United Nations Children's Fund or Unicef (1946). Organization set up to promote child health, nutrition and welfare programmes.

United Nations Day The 24th October, the day on which the UN Organization came into existence in 1945.

United Nations High Commissioner for Refugees (UNHCR: 1951). Appointed to continue the work of the INTERNATIONAL REFUGEE ORGANIZATION, with the headquarters at Geneva.

United Nations Pact (Declaration) Signed at Washington on 1 January 1942 by 26 Allied states (including Russia and China), by which they subscribed to the principles of the ATLANTIC CHARTER and promised not to make a separate peace with the Axis powers. (The first official use of the phrase 'United Nations'.)

United Nations Relief and Rehabilitation Administration Better known as UNRRA.

United Nations Special Fund (1957). Organization which assists developing countries to finance major projects expected to produce early large-scale improvements in their economies.

United Oxford and Cambridge University Club Large club in Pall Mall, London. Originally founded in 1830 as the Oxford and Cambridge University Club but amalgamated with the United University Club (founded in 1821) in 1972.

United Provinces Name taken by the northern NETHERLANDS (Holland) when they declared their independence of Spanish rule (1581) as a Protestant republic.

United Provinces (India) Now renamed Uttar Pradesh.

United Reformed Church (1972). Union of Presbyterian and Congregational Protestant churches in England.

Unités d'habitation Housing units designed by LE CORBUSIER, of which the most famous is the Cité Radieuse at Marseille (1952); virtually self-contained towns incorporating shopping streets, schools, etc.

Universal Aunts (1921). London organization, designed primarily to render services to non-Londoners by finding accommodation, doing their shopping, escorting their young children across London, etc.

University College London (UCL; 1826) The largest unit of London University, to which are attached the Slade School, Bartlett School of Architecture and the UC Hospital medical school.

University Funding Council (1989). Body set up to advise government on the allocation of grants to universities and on the development of university education facilities in general. Successor to the University Grants Committee.

University of Buckingham Opened in 1976 as the University College of Buckingham, receiving its royal charter in 1983. It offers two-year honours-degree courses and the academic year consists of 4 10-week terms. In 1988 it had 710 full-time students.

Unknown Political Prisoner (1953). Reg Butler's sculpture which won an international competition for a work on this theme.

Unknown Warrior, Tomb of the (1920). Tomb of an unidentified soldier who was buried in Westminster Abbey as a representative of all who fell in World War I; there are similar memorials in other countries. Also called the Unknown Soldier.

Unleaded Petrol containing no lead, introduced into the UK in June 1986. The permitted amount of lead in petrol was reduced from 0·4 to 0·15 grams per litre from 1 January 1986.

Unofficial Rose, An (1962). Iris Murdoch's novel about a circle of people who have reached the restless stage in their married lives; they have various schemes and ambitions but find in the end that they are largely creatures of circumstance or other people's interests, and that even if they attain an objective it disappoints expectation.

UNR In France, initials of the Union pour la Nouvelle République, the party of right-wing Gaullists which was victorious in the 1958 elections, and later formed a coalition with the UDT.

UNRRA (1943–9). UN Relief and Rehabilitation Administration. An organization to provide emergency, mainly US, aid to liberated territories of eastern Europe, China and, later, Austria, Italy, etc.

UNRWA (1949). Initials of the UN Relief and Works Agency, established to resettle Arab refugees after the Republic of Israel had been formed.

Unsocial hours Hours of work for certain jobs falling outside the normal working day and therefore being socially inconvenient.

Unter den Linden A mile-long street in Berlin running from the BRANDENBURGER TOR past the Marx-Engels Platz (site of the Imperial Palace razed to the ground by the Russians) to the Alexander Platz. Once the centre of Berlin life, with an avenue in the middle lined with lime trees until Hitler cut them down. (German, 'under the limes'.)

Untouchables Those in India who belong to none of the main castes. 'Untouchability' was officially abolished in 1947, and their name altered to 'Scheduled Castes' or 'Depressed Classes'.

Upanishads (600 BC). Final stage of ancient Hindu literature, some 250 books of hymns and philosophical or mystical speculation, pantheistic in tenor, and a reaction from the earlier BRAHAMANAS. (Sanskrit, 'sitting close to the instructor', i.e. 'esoteric'; pronounced *u*-pun'i-shèdz.)

Up Helly A Fire festival held in Lerwick, Shetland, on the last Tuesday in January. Villagers in costume throw torches into a Viking war galley. The custom dates back to the days of Norse rule (9th–15th centuries).

Upholders, Worshipful Company of (1626). LIVERY COMPANY, originally a guild of upholsterers.

Upper Volta Former French West African colony, now Burkina Faso.

Up the Junction See CATHY COME HOME.

Upton Park Home of West Ham United football club, in London.

Ur- Prefix borrowed from German, meaning 'primitive', 'earliest', 'original', 'source of', as in 'Ur-*Hamlet*', a (lost) early version of Shakespeare's play. (Pronounced oor.)

Ural-Altaic languages Language family of north-

ern Europe and Asia, of which the FINNO-UGRIAN and ALTAIC LANGUAGES are divisions. (Named after the Ural and Altai mountain ranges.)

Uranus Chief of the earliest generation of Greek deities, god of the heavens, father of CRONOS who deposed him. (Pronounced ewr'an-us.)

Urartu Powerful neighbour state to Assyria in the 9th–7th centuries BC, centred on Lake Van and ruling over what is now Soviet Armenia and Iranian Azerbaijan.

Urdu Form of HINDUSTANI spoken by educated Muslims in Pakistan and India, written from right to left in an Arabic–Persian script; the official language of West Pakistan. Although its grammar and everyday vocabulary closely resembles HINDI, it has borrowed much more from Persian and, through religious sources, from Arabic.

Urga Older name of Ulan Bator, capital of the Mongolian People's Republic.

Uriah Hittite husband of BATHSHEBA.

Urizen In William Blake's private mythology, the forces restricting man's full development, such as authority, repressive morality and dry rationalism; opposed by ORC, regenerated by LOS.

Urn Burial (1658). Sir Thomas Browne's essay which begins with a report on some Roman burial urns but grows into a general meditation on mortality and the vanity of human monuments; also known by its Greek name, *Hydriotaphia*.

Ur of the Chaldees City of SUMER, and the birthplace of Abraham (Gen. 11:31); it was then at the head of the Persian Gulf, but the site is now more than 100 miles inland. Splendid treasures have been excavated there, including a famous gold statuette of a ram caught in a thicket, now in the British Museum.

Ursa Latin for 'bear'; hence *Ursa Major*, the GREAT BEAR, and *Ursa Minor*, the LITTLE BEAR.

URT infection Doctors' shorthand for Upper Respiratory Tract infection, i.e. of the nose–throat–larynx–windpipe area; the term includes all the various forms of the common cold but excludes influenza.

Uruguay Round, The (1986–). Continuing multilateral trade negotiations under the auspices of GATT aiming at bringing about further liberalization and expansion of world trade for the benefit of all countries, especially less-developed countries.

US Play staged against the Vietnam war by the Royal Shakespeare Theatre Co. at the Aldwych, London. (US stands both for 'USA' and 'us'.)

USA (1938). Trilogy of novels by John Dos Passos, comprising *The 42nd Parallel, 1919* and *The Big Money*, in which he gives a panoramic and cinematic survey of all facets of US life.

Uses of Literacy, The (1957). Richard Hoggart's honest, almost anthropological, analysis of the working class. Written by a highly educated member of that class from Leeds, it deals despondently with the attitudes of working-men to art, books, religion, domesticity, etc.; he wonders whether the 'tamed helots of a machine-minding class' are 'exchanging their birthright for a mess of pin-ups'.

Üsküb Turkish name for Skop(l)je, capital of Macedonia, Yugoslavia.

Üsküdar Turkish city, formerly known by its Italian name, Scutari.

Ussher's Notation (1654). Book responsible for the calculation that the world was created in 4004 BC, a date which used to appear as a marginal note to Genesis 1; also adopted by Freemasons as the Annus Lucis (referring to Genesis 1:3, 'let there be light') from which they date official documents. (James Ussher, Archbishop of Armagh.)

Usumbura Former name of the capital of Burundi; see BUJUMBURA.

Uther Pendragon Father of King Arthur. (*Pendragon*, a Welsh title given to a paramount chief in times of crisis.)

Utilitarianism View that actions are morally right if they are useful in promoting the greatest happiness of the greatest number; associated with J. S. Mill and Jeremy Bentham (18th–19th centuries).

Utopia Imaginary land described by St Thomas More (1516) where man and his institutions are perfect. (Greek, *ou topos*, representing 'Nowhere' – compare EREWHON – and *eu topos*, representing 'good place'.)

Utrecht, Peace of (1713). Treaty that ended the War of the SPANISH SUCCESSION. From France England gained Nova Scotia, Newfoundland and control of the St Lawrence (threatening French Canada); from Spain, Gibraltar and Minorca. Austria received the Spanish Netherlands (Belgium), Milan, Naples and Sardinia; the grandson of Louis XIV, Philip V, remained on the Spanish throne.

U-2 aircraft High-altitude photo-reconnaissance plane used by the CIA (1956–60) to photograph Russia. It was exceptionally light in weight, had a range of 3,000 miles, a speed of 500 m.p.h. and a ceiling of 90,000 ft. See next entry.

U-2 incident (1960). Shooting down by the Russians of an American U-2 reconnaissance aircraft over the Urals, which caused the cancellation of the PARIS SUMMIT CONFERENCE a few days later. See previous entry.

U-235 Natural isotope of uranium used by Frisch and Peierls in the first demonstration of nuclear fission, at Birmingham.

Uxbridge Former municipal borough of Middlesex, since 1965 part of the borough of HILLINGDON.

V

Vaccinium Genus that includes the cranberry, bilberry (blaeberry) and whortleberry.

VAD (1909). Initials used for the Voluntary Aid Detachments of men and women trained in first aid and nursing, formed by the British Red Cross Society and liable for war service with the forces.

Vailima Letters (1895). The letters of R. L. Stevenson published the year after his death. (Vailima, the house in Samoa where he spent the last 6 years of his life.)

Vaisya Hindu caste of farmers and traders. (Sanskrit, 'peasant'; pronounced vy'si-a.)

Valentine's Brook One of the major hazards of the GRAND NATIONAL.

Vale of the White Horse The valley which runs from near Swindon to Abingdon north of the Marlborough and Berkshire Downs, named after the white horse carved in the chalk hills near Uffington. See VWH.

Valhalla In Norse mythology, the hall in Odin's palace reserved for heroes selected by the VALKYRIES.

Valiant-for-Truth, Mr Character in Part II of PILGRIM'S PROGRESS whose last words are often quoted: 'My sword, I give to him that shall succeed me in my pilgrimage, and my courage and skill to him that can get it.'

Valjean See *Les* MISÉRABLES.

Valkyries Daughters of Odin who charged into battles, selected those marked for death, and conducted them to Valhalla. (Old Norse, 'choosers of the slain'; pronounced valky'er-iz or val'kir-iz.)

Valley Forge Village in south-east Pennsylvania, famous as the winter quarters of Washington in 1777–8 during the American War of Independence.

Valley of the Kings Area, once part of ancient THEBES, facing KARNAK and LUXOR across the Nile; the burial place of pharaohs of the 18th–20th Dynasties, the most famous being TUTANKHAMEN'S TOMB.

Valley of the Shadow of Death Place in PILGRIM'S PROGRESS full of Hobgoblins, Satyrs and Dragons of the Pit, through which Christian has to pass. (Phrase taken from Psalms 23.)

Vallombrosa Valley near Florence, familiar through Milton's lines in *Paradise Lost*: 'Thick as autumnal leaves that strow the brooks / In Vallombrosa.'

Valmouth Fictional English village where Ronald Firbank, in the novel of that name (1918), gathers a weird group of cranks and perverts. The book was turned into a musical comedy by Sandy Wilson in 1958.

Valmy, Cannonade of (1792). Occasion of the first appearance in Europe of a disciplined national democratic army, the French revolutionary army under Kellermann, whose victory after a heavy artillery duel over the best dynastic army of Europe (the Prussians) caused Goethe, who was present, to foretell the advent of a new era in human history. After their victory the French occupied the Austrian Netherlands (Belgium). (Village between Verdun and Paris.)

Valois, House of CAPETIAN dynasty which ruled France 1328–1589, and was succeeded by the Bourbon dynasty in the person of Henry IV of Navarre (who had married a Valois).

'Valse Triste' Waltz by Sibelius taken from his symphonic poem *Kuolema.*

Value-added tax (VAT) Indirect tax applied at each point of exchange of goods or services from production to consumption but ending up paid by the final consumer. Used in the European Communities as the method of computing the Community's budget.

Van Allen belts Belts of particles emanating from the sun and trapped by the earth's magnetic field; indications of their existence were first given by the satellite EXPLORER I. Their altitude varies, the outer belt, of electrons, being about 10,000 miles from the earth; the inner, of protons, about 2,000 miles up.

Vance, Philo American amateur detective who first appeared in *The Benson Murder Case* (1926), created in his own image by the learned art-lover who took the pen-name of S. S. Van Dine.

V & A Abbreviation in common use for Victoria and Albert Museum.

Vandals East German people allied to the Wends, many of them Arian Christians, who invaded Gaul and Spain about AD 400 and then crossed to North Africa, where they were vanquished by the Roman Belisarius in 533. In 455 they sacked Rome. Vandalism became a synonym for wanton destruction.

Vandenberg missile base US Air Force base at Lompoc, north of Los Angeles, California, used as a training ground for IRBMs and ICBMs, and as a launching site for the Pacific Missile Range, and for some satellites.

Vanderbilt (1872). US university at Nashville, Tennessee.

Vanderbilts American millionaire family which made its fortune in shipping lines and railways; founded by Cornelius, died 1877.

Van der Hum South African Cape brandy with tangerine and a little rum. (Afrikaans, 'What's-his-name'.)

Vanitas In art, a still-life painting of objects symbolic of man's mortality, e.g. a skull, hour-glass, guttering candle.

Vanity Fair (1848). Thackeray's novel depicting the vanities and snobberies of London society in Hanoverian times, mainly through the adventures of Becky SHARP.

Vanity-Fair In PILGRIM'S PROGRESS a perpetual fair at the town of Vanity, where Beelzebub and his like sell honours, preferments, kingdoms and other vanities; when Christian and Faithful refuse to buy anything they are arrested, but escape.

Ven Meegeren forgeries Remarkably skilful paintings in the style of various Old Masters, the work of a Dutch artist, Hans van Meegeren, who made some £500,000 out of them; he was sent to prison in 1947 but died the same year. His motive was resentment at the critics' neglect of his own original work. (Pronounced van may'gèr-en.)

Van Riebeeck Day (South Africa) 6 April, the day in 1652 on which Jan van Riebeeck landed at the Cape and founded the first settlement there.

Varanasi (India) Formerly BENARES.

Vardon, Dolly Heroine of Dickens's *Barnaby Rudge,* daughter of a locksmith. She wore a straw hat trimmed with ribbons, 'worn the merest trifle on one side – just enough to make it the wickedest and most provoking head-dress that ever malicious milliner devised'. This started a fashion in hats which lasted for decades.

Varieties of Religious Experience (1902). US philosopher William James's widely read study of the psychology of religion, from which he drew the pragmatic conclusion that any religion is true in so far as it provides emotional satisfaction. See PRAGMATISM.

Variety Club of Great Britain Theatrical organization formed to raise money for children's charities; see CHIEF BARKER.

Varroasis Disease of bees which has invaded most of the world, but which has not yet reached the UK. The disease is caused by a mite, *Varroa jacobsonii*, named after the Roman author Marcus Terentius Varro, called 'the most learned of Romans', who wrote about bees.

Vasa, **The** Seventeenth-century Swedish man-of-war at Stockholm, which sank in the harbour as soon as built and, found to be well preserved, was raised in 1964. She now lies in a dry dock, open to the public, and furnished with appropriate museum exhibits.

Vassall case (1962). Trial of John Vassall, sentenced to 18 years' imprisonment for passing secret information to Russia; see RADCLIFFE TRIBUNAL.

Vassar (1861). Leading US women's college, now coeducational, at Poughkeepsie, New York state.

Vathek (1786). 'FONTHILL' BECKFORD'S tale, a mixture of *Arabian Nights* and GOTHIC NOVEL, in which a young Caliph sells his soul to the Devil and finds himself in the Hall of Eblis (see IBLIS).

Vatican, The (1) Pope's palace on Vatican Hill, west of the Tiber adjoining St Peter's. (2) Papal government; see next entry. (Latin, *mons vaticanus*, 'hill of the soothsayers'.)

Vatican City Independent Papal State (109 acres, about 1,000 residents) established in Rome under the LATERAN TREATY. It includes the VATICAN, St Peter's and, outside Rome, CASTEL GANDOLFO. The Vatican Palace buildings include the SISTINE CHAPEL, 3 museums of antiquities and an impressive collection of Old Masters in the Pinacoteca.

Vatican Council, Second (1962–6). Council of some 3,000 prelates from all over the world summoned to the Vatican by Pope John XXIII and continued under Paul VI. It condemned anti-Semitism, acknowledged that there were elements of truth in Buddhism, Hinduism and Islam, declared that religious freedom was a fundamental human right, and dealt with various new problems of the modern world.

Vaudois See WALDENSIANS.

Vautrin Major character in Balzac's COMÉDIE HUMAINE, an ex-convict whose 'real' name was Jacques Collin. He turns up in several novels in the guise of a chief of police, a Spanish priest and philosopher, etc.

Vauxhall Gardens (1660–1859). London pleasure gardens in Lambeth, where concerts and firework displays were held and balloon ascents were made; in later years they acquired an unsavoury reputation. (Named after Fulkes, a medieval lord of the manor; pronounced voks-hawl, voks'awl.)

Vedanta The mystical system of philosophy based on the UPANISHADS and the older VEDAS. (Sanskrit, 'end of the Veda'; pronounced ve-dahn'ta.)

Vedas (1500 BC). Oldest layer of Hindu religious writings, consisting of 4 main books (including the RIG-VEDA) of hymns, prayers and charms. The gods are represented as on the whole benevolent, and doctrines of asceticism and pessimism have not yet appeared. They are the works of the Aryan conquerors of the Dravidian aborigines. (Sanskrit, 'knowledge'; pronounced vay'daz.)

V-E Day 8 May, Victory in Europe Day, commemorating the ending of the war in Europe after the German surrender on 7 May 1945.

Vedomosti First Russian newspaper, published irregularly from 1703. The first edition was edited by Peter the Great. (Russian, 'news'.)

Vega Brightest star in the northern sky, and 4th brightest of all stars; a white star in LYRA. (From Arabic name for the constellation Lyra; pronounced vee'ga.)

Velcro (1948). Invention of Georges de Mestral, who was inspired to create this fastener after wondering why burrs stuck to his trousers. It consists of two strips, one having tiny loops and the other tiny hooks so that this may be fastened and unfastened simply by pressing together or pulling apart. (Combination of 'velvet' and 'crochet', French for hook.)

Velvet Brueghel Nickname of Jan (1568–1625), son of PEASANT BRUEGHEL; so called because of his smoothly painted detailed studies of flowers and other still-life subjects.

Velvet-collar crime Criminal acts made in the world of high finance and generally involved in takeover bids.

Vendée, La Province of western France, the scene (1793–5) of a peasant counter-revolutionary insurrection, occasioned by a conscription decree and fomented by the clergy.

Vendémiaire First month of the French Revolution calendar, from 22 September to 21 October; 13 Vendémiaire (1795) is the date when Napoleon ended a Royalist insurrection in Paris with a 'whiff of grapeshot', one brief cannonade – the first step in his ascent to the throne as Emperor. See DIRECTORY. ('Vintage time'.)

Venerable Bede, The English historian and scholar (died AD 735) who spent most of his life in a monastery at Jarrow, where he earned his posthumous title of 'Venerable' by writing commentaries on the Bible and a history of the English.

Venlo incident (Nov. 1939). Capture by a German counter-espionage unit of 2 British officers in command of an MI-6 network operating in Europe; it led to the arrest of many other British agents. (Dutch town.)

Venta Belgarum Roman name of Winchester.

Venus Roman goddess equivalent to the Greek APHRODITE.

Venus Name given to Russian space probes directed at Venus.

Venus and Adonis (1593). Shakespeare's first published work, a long poem in which Adonis rejects Venus' advances and is killed by a boar.

Venus and Cupid Titian painting now in the Uffizi, Florence.

Venusberg See TANNHÄUSER.

Venus de Milo (2nd century BC). Best-known Greek sculpture, artist unknown, now in the Louvre. (French form of the name; Milo = Melos, the island where it was found in 1820.)

Venus Observed (1950). Christopher Fry's verse tragi-comedy about the problems of growing up.

Verbascum Genus name of the mulleins, including aaron's rod.

Verdant Green, Adventures of Mr (1857). Once popular novel about a much put-upon undergraduate in his first year at Oxford, by 'Cuthbert Bede' (the Rev. E. Bradley).

Verdun (Feb.–June 1916). Exceptionally heavily fortified key-point on the Western Front, very nearly taken by the Germans in a 5-month siege of the French garrison, finally abandoned.

Verdurins, The Nouveau riche couple in Proust's REMEMBRANCE OF THINGS PAST who occupy themselves by launching artists at their innumerable soirées. After Verdurin's death, his widow marries the Prince de GUERMANTES.

Vereeniging Treaty (31 May 1902). Treaty which ended the Boer War.

Vernon, Dorothy See HADDON HALL.

Veronica Genus name of the speedwells.

Versailles, Palace of Palace built by Louis XIV, and the permanent home of Louis XV from 1738; Louis XVI was the last king to live there. Built to house 5,000 people, with huge gardens in which stand the PETIT TRIANON and the GRAND TRIANON, its most famous feature is the Hall of Mirrors, where the 1919 treaty (see next entry) was signed. (The town, built at the same time, is 13 miles south-west of Paris.)

Versailles Treaty (June 1919). Treaty made with Germany after World War I (there were separate treaties for each ex-enemy country), which like the others incorporated the LEAGUE COVENANT. Germany lost Alsace-Lorraine and other territory, including all its colonies; military occupation of the Rhineland and payment of reparations were also imposed.

Verulamium Roman name of St Albans.

Vesta Roman goddess of the hearth (the Greek Hestia); in her temple in the Forum VESTAL VIRGINS tended the sacred fire.

Vestal Virgins In Rome, patrician priestesses of VESTA, selected at the age of 6–10. They took a vow of 30 years' celibacy and were buried alive if they broke it.

Veteran Car Run (1896). London to Brighton run held annually on a Sunday in early November to commemorate the repeal of the regulation that a car had to be preceded by a man with a red flag.

Veterans of Foreign Wars US ex-servicemen's organization, founded before the First World War.

'Veto' Bill, The (1911). Liberal bill to reduce the powers of the House of Lords, a major political issue in the years before the First World War. When passed after a long struggle and a threat to pack the Lords with newly created peers, the Act abolished the House's power to veto money bills and reduced its delaying powers over other measures.

VG Initials used for 'variable geometry', i.e. swing-wing or movable-wing aircraft. The purpose of the design is to combine fast flight with short take-off and landing.

VHF Initials used for Very High Frequency radio, which has short range and consequent freedom from interference from Continental stations. The first BBC VHF service was broadcast from Wrotham, Kent, in 1955.

Via Crucis See STATIONS OF THE CROSS.

Via Dolorosa Route along which Jesus had to carry his cross to Calvary. (Latin, 'way of sorrow'.)

VIBGYOR Initials used as a mnemonic for the colours of the spectrum: violet, indigo, blue, green, yellow, orange, red; red having the longest wavelength.

Viborg (1) Danish town in Jutland. (2) Swedish name for VYBORG.

Viburnum Genus that includes the guelder rose (*V. opulus*), snowball bush (*V. opulus sterile*), laurustinus (*V. tinus*) and wayfaring tree (*V. lantana*).

Vicar and Moses Famous Staffordshire pottery group, perhaps made by Aaron Wood (see WOOD FAMILY), representing a vicar asleep in his pulpit while his clerk reads the sermon.

Vicar of Bray Turncoat, of a 17th-century song about a historical character who clung to his benefice by changing his creed 3 times under the last 3 Tudors. In the song he is transferred to 'good King Charles's golden days', and maintains: 'That whatsoever King shall reign, / I'll be the Vicar of Bray, Sir!' (Village near Maidenhead, Berkshire.)

Vicar of Christ Title of the Pope since the 12th century.

Vicar of Wakefield, The (1766). Oliver Goldsmith's story of the massive misfortunes that descend upon the gentle vicar, Dr Primrose, and his family; it appealed to the rapidly growing reading public of its time.

Vice Versa (1882). F. Anstey's fantasy about a father and son who, under an Indian magician's spell, exchange bodies but not minds. Mr Bultitude has to go to school, while his son lords it at home. (Pronounced *vy'si ver'sa*.)

Vichy government French government formed (June 1940) by Marshal Pétain on the fall of France, which made Vichy, in the unoccupied zone, its headquarters; it was forced into increasing collaboration with the Germans, who occupied northern (and from 1942 all) France. Laval and Darlan dominated the by then senile Pétain.

Vichy water Bottled mineral water from the springs of Vichy, France, said to be good for gout, digestive troubles, etc.

Vickers Group (1862). Armaments and engineering group which has built all kinds of warships and liners; the Maxim gun; Spitfire, Wellington, Viscount and VC-10 aircraft; Valentine tanks. It has a 75% interest in the English Steel Corporation, and in recent years has branched out into office equipment (Roneo), chemical engineering, surgical instruments, etc.

Vicksburg, Capitulation of (July 1863). First major Confederate defeat in the American Civil War, at the hands of Gen. Ulysses Grant. (Town on the Mississippi.)

Vicky Pseudonym of Victor Weisz (died 1966), a left-wing political cartoonist of Hungarian parentage who came to England in 1935. From 1958 he became famous for his cartoons in the *Evening Standard*, especially for his creation of 'Supermac' (Harold Macmillan in the guise of the US strip cartoon character 'Superman').

Victoria, **The** First ship to sail round the world (1519–22); her crew of 18 were the only survivors of an expedition of 265 men in 5 ships under Magellan, who was killed en route in the Philippines.

Victoria Club London bookmakers' club where periodical call-overs are held before the big races which furnish a guide to ante-post betting prices.

Victoria Cross British award for conspicuous bravery; this medal, which takes precedence over all other decorations, was instituted in 1856 (awarded retrospectively to 1854). The first 62 crosses were presented by Queen Victoria in Hyde Park, London on 26 June 1857.

Victoria History of the Counties of England (1900). County-by-county history from earliest to modern times.

Victoria League Society to promote Commonwealth friendship by encouraging people in Britain to invite Commonwealth visitors to their homes; it also runs hostels for students.

Victoriana Furniture, silver, ceramics, etc. of the age of Victoria (reigned 1837–1901), the earlier specimens of which are coming to be accepted as antiques as time moves on and the supply of real antiques begins to dry up; quaintness rather than artistic merit marks the later products.

Victory (1915). Joseph Conrad's novel of exiles in the East Indies and of the mutual fidelity of Heyst and Lena, the girl he befriends. Their island home is invaded by thugs and she sacrifices her life to save his.

Victory, **HMS** Nelson's flagship, now lying in Portsmouth dockyard and open to the public.

Victory Bonds Bogus bonds by the issue of which Horatio Bottomley, editor of *John Bull* and Liberal MP, deprived thousands of poor people of their savings. In 1922 he was sentenced to 7 years' penal servitude for fraud.

Vieille Cure Golden liqueur made in the monastery of Cenon, near Bordeaux, from Cognac, Armagnac and aromatic herbs.

Vienna Award (1940). Hitler's decree that Romania should restore half Transylvania to Hungary.

Vienna Declaration (1958). Made by the PUGWASH MOVEMENT, a warning of the dangers of radioactive fall-out whether from 'clean' (fusion) or 'dirty' (fission) bombs.

Vienna porcelain (1719–1864). Wares made at a factory which owed its early high reputation to having been the first to steal the secret MEISSEN recipe for hard-paste porcelain. The figures made in 1750–84 were of high quality; later work had little merit.

Vienna School (1929). Philosophical school inspired by Ernst Mach which founded LOGICAL POSITIVISM. Wittgenstein (who went to Cambridge – see TRACTATUS LOGICO-PHILOSOPHICUS) and Carnap (who went to USA) were among their number.

Vietcong (1958). The nationalist movement in South VIETNAM which came under VIETMINH direction (1960) in opposing successive US-sponsored South Vietnamese governments by undeclared civil war which led to the VIETNAMESE WAR.

Vietminh (1941). Originally the resistance movement against Japanese occupation founded in Annam by Ho Chi Minh. After the war, in collaboration with Chiang Kai-shek's occupying forces, it gained control of North VIETNAM and strong support in the south (then under French occupation); see VIETCONG. After DIEN BIEN PHU (1954), by then renamed the Fatherland Front, it installed the LAO DONG Communist government in North Vietnam. Despite the change of name, Vietminh is still used as a synonym for Ho Chi Minh's regime in the north. ('League for the Independence of Vietnam'.)

Vietnam A country of South-East Asia formed (1945) from the former French colonies of Annam, Tongking and Cochin China, but divided at the 17th parallel of latitude between Communist North and non-Communist South Vietnam. (Chinese, 'farther south'; pronounced vi-et-nam'.)

Vietnamese War (1964). The war between North Vietnam (see VIETMINH) and the US-sponsored government of South VIETNAM, and also the civil war against the VIETCONG who had gained control of much of the south. The US government was forced by events to step up its aid to the south from the supply of arms, military instruction and guidance, to full-scale military and especially air support against the Vietcong, which had been greatly assisted in its guerrilla tactics by terrain and by passive or active support from the local inhabitants. Later, massive air attacks on supply routes from the north, and on North Vietnam itself, became necessary.

Viipuri Finnish name for VYBORG (Viborg).

Vikings (8th–11th centuries). Scandinavian pirates who scoured the seas as far as the Mediterranean, Russia, Iceland and VINLAND, establishing colonies at Kiev, Dublin and the Isle of Man, among many others, and finally settling the DANELAW in England and Normandy in France; also called Norsemen or Normans. The typical Viking ship, with high prow and stern, was propelled by 20 oarsmen and a large square sail.

Viking sea area Water lying between the FAIR ISLE SEA AREA and the south-west coast of Norway.

Vilikins and his Dinah Characters of a Cockney mock-heroic ballad dating back at least to the early 19th century. (Vilikins for Wilkins.)

Villa Borghese Traditional name of a park in

Rome and of a museum and art gallery in it. Officially it has been renamed the Villa Umberto I. (Former summer residence of the Borghese family.)

'Village Blacksmith, The' (1841). Longfellow's poem, among the best-known in the English language, beginning 'Under the spreading chestnut tree / The village smithy stands', and ending 'Something attempted, something done, / Has earned a night's repose'.

Villa Mauresque Famous as Somerset Maugham's home for many years, at Cap Ferrat on the French Riviera.

Villa Park Football home of Aston Villa, at Birmingham.

Villa Umberto I See VILLA BORGHESE.

Ville, The Old lags' name for PENTONVILLE.

Ville radieuse See UNITÉS D'HABITATION.

Villette (1853). Charlotte Brontë's largely autobiographical novel, in which Lucy Snowe goes to Villette (Brussels) as a schoolteacher and falls in love with Professor Paul (who is the Constantine Heger of Charlotte's own life).

Villains, The Nickname of the Aston Villa football team.

Vilna, Vilno, Wilno Alternative spellings of Vilnius, capital of the Lithuanian SSR.

Vimy Vickers biplane used in World I War, and by Alcock and Brown on the first non-stop transatlantic flight (1919).

Vimy Ridge Scene of heavy fighting on the Western Front during much of the World War I. It was held by the French from September 1915 to May 1916, and recaptured by the Canadians in April 1917, with heavy loss of life. (Ridge 5 miles north-east of Arras.)

Vinca Species name of the periwinkles.

Vincennes porcelain (1738–51). Wares produced by the factory south-east of Paris which became world-famous when it moved to SÈVRES.

Vincent's Oxford University Social club for leading athletes.

Vinegar Joe Nickname of the American General Joseph Stilwell, who commanded Chiang Kai-shek's troops in Burma during World War II.

Vinerian Professor Holder of the chair of Law at Oxford.

Vinho verde Portuguese wine, very dry and slightly effervescent, with a flavour of the green grape. ('Green wine.')

Vinland Part of North America discovered by the VIKINGS; usually identified with the island of Martha's Vineyard, Massachusetts, USA.

Vintage port Bottle-matured wine of a specific year declared a 'vintage year' (i.e. exceptionally good) by an individual shipper; declarations range from nil to over 30 in the finest years (1927, 1934, 1935). It is bottled after 2 years, either in Portugal or by the importer, and left to mature, preferably for 15–20 years, but will keep for 50.

Vintners, Worshipful Company of (1437). One of the Great Twelve LIVERY COMPANIES, with a fine hall rebuilt after the Great Fire. It shares with the DYERS' COMPANY the right to keep swans on the Thames.

Viola Heroine of Shakespeare's *Twelfth Night*; she disguises herself as a boy and becomes page to the Duke Orsino with whom she falls in love, while Olivia falls in love with her. Viola is the niece of Sir Toby BELCH. (Pronounced vy'o-lē.)

Violetta See TRAVIATA.

VIP Abbreviation for Very Important Person, which came into use in World War II to designate air passengers to be accorded special facilities and red-carpet treatment on arrival. This ensures that the only people who could put things right are never aware of the appalling conditions at some airports.

Virginia ham Flat lean hickory-smoked ham with dark red meat from a peanut-fed razorback pig such as is bred in the south-eastern states of the USA.

Virginian, The (1902). First 'Western', written by Owen Wister, about cowboys in Wyoming, complete with bad men, poker games and pistol-duels.

Virginians, The (1857). Thackeray's sequel to *Henry Esmond*, about the twin nephews of Beatrix Esmond (now Baroness Bernstein), who fight on opposite sides in the American War of Independence. George Washington and Gen. Wolfe appear in the book.

Virginia reel US name for the Sir Roger de Coverley country dance, which begins with 2 lines of partners facing each other.

Virgin Lands scheme (1954). In the USSR, Khrushchev's ambitious scheme which brought approximately a million new acres into cultivation, mainly under spring wheat, in south-west Siberia and northern Kazakhstan.

Virgin of the Rocks Famous painting by Leonardo da Vinci, in the National Gallery, London; another version is in the Louvre.

Virgin Queen, The Name for Elizabeth I of England.

Virgo The Virgin, 6th of the constellations of the Zodiac, between Leo and Libra, representing a woman holding an ear of corn, identified with ISHTAR; the sun enters it about 21 August. It contains a galaxy cluster. Astrologers claim that those born under this sign may be industrious, sensible and loyal.

Vishnu One of the 2 main gods of modern Hinduism, and one of the Trinity formed with SIVA and BRAHMA; a benevolent saviour of mankind who reappears on earth in successive incarnations, the eighth being as KRISHNA, the ninth as Buddha.

Visigoths Western GOTHS who, under Alaric, sacked Rome (410) and ruled Spain from Toledo until the Moorish conquest (711).

Vision and Design (1920). Roger Fry's collection of essays on the essential qualities and relations of form in art.

Visitors' Cup (1847). Coxless fours event at Henley Regatta for colleges and schools.

Vita Nuova, La (1291). Dante's collection of poems linked by an autobiographical prose account of his love for BEATRICE. (Italian, 'new life'.)

V-J Day (UK) 15 August, the day Japanese surrender became effective; (USA) 2 September, the day the Japanese signed a formal surrender (1945).

Vlachs Another name for Romanians, especially those of Wallachia. (Slavonic form of Teutonic name for all peoples of Roman provinces.)

Vlissingen Dutch name of the seaport called Flushing in English.

Vogue (1892). Condé Nast's glossy women's magazine which in 1936 absorbed *Vanity Fair*; there is an allied British magazine (1916). It covers fashion, house decoration, travel and general topics.

Voice & Vision See COLMAN, PRENTIS & VARLEY.

Voice of America Propaganda organization run by the US Information Agency; it broadcasts in over 40 languages all over the world.

Voiceprint Pictorial representation of the human voice, the pattern of which is as unique to each individual as are his fingerprints. Voiceprints thus have potentialities in identifying criminals. (Devised by Lawrence Kersta at the American Bell Telephone laboratories.)

Volapük (1880). Artificial language invented by an Austrian priest, it was too complicated to have the success of Esperanto, invented a few years later. ('English-speech'; pronounced vol'a-puk.)

'Volga Boatmen, Song of the' Russian folk-song sung by the men who towed barges along the Volga. It was first popularized by the Russian bass singer Chaliapin.

Volgograd Current name of the city of Stalingrad, RSFSR.

Völkische Beobachter German daily newspaper which during the National-Socialist (Nazi) regime was Hitler's chosen mouthpiece. ('People's Observer'.)

Volkswagen German car firm with headquarters at Wolfsburg, near Brunswick. It produced the ubiquitous 'Beetle', a post-war development of Hitler's 'People's Car' (1938).

Volpone (1605). Ben Jonson's satirical play on human greed and self-deluding folly. When a rich and childless Venetian, Volpone (the Fox), pretends to be dying, he is showered with gifts by those who hope to benefit under his will; when he pretends to be dead, he is blackmailed by his servant-accomplice. In the end the plot is revealed and all are punished. (Pronounced vol-poh'ni.)

Volstead Act (1919). US Act defining 'intoxicating liquor', an essential preliminary to the enforcement of PROHIBITION.

Volsunga Saga Icelandic saga from which the NIBELUNGENLIED is derived.

Volta Primary unit of measure of electromotive force, named after Alessandro Volta (1745–1827), Italian physicist who developed the theory of current electricity.

Volta River project (1961). Hydroelectric and irrigation scheme in eastern Ghana, based on the damming of the River Volta at Akosambo 50 miles north of the new harbour of Tema. One of the chief purposes is to provide power for an aluminium smelter to process the bauxite in which the country is rich.

Voluntary Service Overseas (1958). Scheme under which young people volunteer for a year or so's service in developing countries, mostly teaching posts. They are paid little more than their keep.

Volunteer State Nickname of Tennessee. (Furnished a large number of volunteers in the Civil War.)

V-1 German flying bomb, first launched against London in June 1944 and later (Oct. 1944 to Mar. 1945) against Antwerp, Brussels and Liège; the attacks ended when the launching sites were overrun in the Allied advance. The

V-1 was a winged, pilotless plane with engines pre-set to cut out over the target. (V for *Vergeltung*, 'retaliation'.)

Voortrekkers (1835–7). Ten thousand Boers who took part in the Great Trek away from British Liberal rule in Cape Colony, north-east over the Vaal River to found the Transvaal Republic, and over the Drakensberg Mountains into Zululand and Natal.

Voronoff monkey-gland grafts Method of rejuvenating old men by the transplantation of apes' testes. Great claims were made, but the method is now discredited. (Serge Voronoff, Russian working in Paris; died 1951.)

Voroshilovgrad Now renamed Lugansk, see DONBAS.

Vortex, The (1924). Noël Coward's play and first big success, which shocked contemporary audiences by dwelling on drug addiction.

Vorticism (1912–15). English school of abstract painting derived from FUTURISM and CUBISM, created by Wyndham Lewis (see BLAST) and largely incomprehensible except perhaps as a way of coming to terms with an ugly mechanical age. The term was sometimes extended to analogous literary experiments of Ezra Pound (see CANTOS).

Voshkod Russian name for earth satellites manned by more than one person. *Voshkod I* (1964) carried 3 men; *Voshkod II* carried the first man to walk in space (1965).

Vostok Russian name for the first series of manned satellites. *Vostok I*, launched 12 April 1961, carried the first man into space.

Vougeot See CÔTE DE NUITS.

Voyager 2 US space probe for which planning began in 1972 and launched in 1977. In 1979 it observed Jupiter and discovered 3 new moons; 1981 Saturn with 7 new moons; 1986 Uranus with 10 moons, and finally in August 1989 observed Neptune with 4 new moons and 2 new rings. Voyager then left the solar system and will not come within one light-year of any star for 958,000 years.

Voyage of the Beagle, The (1840). Darwin's journal of his trip (1831–6) to South America and Australia as naturalist aboard the survey ship *Beagle*. See DARWIN'S FINCHES.

Vronsky See ANNA KARENINA.

VSOP Initials standing for Very Special Old Pale. They can be legally tacked on to the name of any brandy, good or bad, and thus have no meaning.

V/STOL Abbreviation for Vertical or Short Take-Off and Landing, a term which includes aircraft needing a short runway and true VTOLs.

VT fuses Variable-time or proximity fuses, which cause shells to burst on coming within range of the target.

VTOL Abbreviation for Vertical Take-Off and Landing, a term theoretically applicable to helicopters but reserved in practice for military aircraft needing no runway. They either have 2 sets of jets, one for vertical lift and the other for horizontal flight, or one movable set for both purposes. See FLYING BEDSTEAD; KESTREL; V/STOL. (Pronounced vee'tol.)

V-2 The first missile, a liquid-fuel rocket developed at PEENEMÜNDE by von Braun, and first tested in 1942. V-2s were used against London (Sept. 1944 to Mar. 1945), and from November 1944 against Antwerp. (V for *Vergeltung*, 'retaliation'.)

Vulcan Roman god equivalent to the Greek HEPHAESTUS.

Vulgate Latin translation of the Bible made by St Jerome (end of 4th century), and still the basic text for the Roman Catholic Church.

VWH (1831). Fox-hunting pack based on Cirencester which hunts country in Wiltshire, Gloucestershire and south-west Oxfordshire. (Initials of VALE OF THE WHITE HORSE.)

Vyborg Russian name for the Baltic naval port founded by the Swedes as Viborg, which became Finnish as Viipuri, and was annexed by the USSR in 1940. (Pronounced vee'borg.)

W

WAAC See ATS.

WAAF Initials of the Women's Auxiliary Air Force; see WRAF.

'Wacht am Rhein, Die' (1840). German patriotic song beginning: 'Es braust ein Ruf wie Donnerschall' (A shout rings out like a thunderclap).

Wade-Giles Phonetic alphabet, widely used system of romanization of the Chinese language until PINYIN was adopted in China. It was developed by Sir Thomas Wade and H. A. Giles.

Wade's roads First metalled roads to be built in the Scottish Highlands, straight strategic roads built by Gen. Wade after the FIFTEEN; hence the old rhyme: 'Had you seen these roads before they were made, / You would lift up your hands and bless General Wade.' ('Made' here means 'properly surfaced'.)

Wafd (1918). Egyptian nationalist party. (Arabic, 'delegation'; so named because Zaghlul Pasha led a delegation to the British High Commissioner in Cairo demanding Egyptian representation at the Paris Peace Conference.)

Waffen-SS More fanatical members of the SS, who fought with the German army in World War II as an independent elite corps. ('Armed SS'.)

Wagner Act (1935). (USA) Labor Relations Act which legalized collective bargaining and set up a National Labor Relations Board, one of the NEW DEAL measures.

Wagon, The (Astronomy) See AURIGA; BOÖTES.

Wagram (1809). Napoleon's costly victory over the Austrians. (Village near Vienna.)

Wahabis Followers of the 18th-century Muslim puritan reformer Abd al-Wahabi, who advocated a very strict and ascetic form of the religion, and converted an ancestor of Ibn Saud, King of Saudi Arabia from 1932. (Pronounced wa-hah′bi.)

Waikiki Beach Lido of Hawaii, in Honolulu harbour. (Pronounced wy′kee-kee.)

Wailing Wall, The Wall in Jerusalem, traditionally part of Solomon's Temple, where Jews gather to bewail the Temple's destruction. It adjoins a mosque, and Muslim–Jewish riots have been frequent there down the ages, and especially violent in 1929. Now known as the Western Wall.

Wait and See Favourite slogan of H. H. Asquith (later Lord Oxford and Asquith), Prime Minister (1908–16), during the period of the controversies over Home Rule, the VETO BILL, etc.

Waiting for Godot See GODOT.

Waiting for Lefty (1935). Clifford Odets's short play about a strike of US taxi-drivers enraged by the murder of their leader, Lefty.

Walcheren expedition (1809). British expedition to gain a foothold in Napoleonic Europe by a landing at the mouth of the Scheldt. It suffered heavy loss from fever and achieved nothing. The leaders, Lord Chatham on land and Strachan at sea, are remembered through an epigram: 'Great Chatham with his sabre drawn / Stood waiting for Sir Richard Strachan; / Sir Richard, longing to be at 'em, / Stood waiting for the Earl of Chatham.' (Pronounced vahl′kėr-ėn.)

Waldensians (1170). Early Protestant sect which rejected papal authority; it survived persecution to join in the Reformation and still exists. The French name is Vaudois. (Founded by Peter Waldo of Lyons.)

Wales, University of Federation of the Colleges at Aberystwyth, Bangor, Cardiff, Lampeter, and Swansea, together with a medical school and (the latest addition) the former Welsh CAT at Cathays Park, Cardiff.

Walker Art Gallery (1877). Collection, mainly of English paintings, at Liverpool.

Walker Cup (1922). Amateur golf contest between Britain and USA, held in alternate years, with 4 foursomes and 8 singles.

Wallace Collection (1900). Art collection, particularly of French furniture, pictures and porcelain, at Hertford House, Manchester Square, London. (Sir Richard Wallace, died 1890.)

Wallenberg, Raoul Wallenberg, a Swedish diplomat who saved thousands of Jews, disappeared in Hungary in 1945. Some believe that he was still alive in 1990.

Wallenstein (1799). Schiller's historical tragedy about the Austrian General Wallenstein who, after serving his country well in the THIRTY YEARS WAR, was murdered (1634) by his officers at the instigation of the Emperor, who had reason to suspect his loyalty.

Wall Game, The Eton's most famous and odd football game (they play other kinds), played each St Andrew's Day (30 November) on a strip of ground under a wall built in 1717, 11 a side, 5 from each scrumming down against the wall whenever the ball goes out of play. The ball is worked along the wall to one of the goals (a tree and a doorway respectively). On average a goal is scored only once in a generation, and the main objectives seem to be mud and mayhem.

Walloon Language or inhabitant of Belgium south of a line drawn approximately from Courtrai through Brussels to Liège. In contrast to the FLEMINGS, they are anti-clerical, republican and culturally closer to the French than to Holland; relations between the 2 communities are bitter. The language is a dialect of French with Flemish borrowings.

Wall Street (New York City) Chief financial centre of USA, at the southern tip of Manhattan Island.

Wall Street crash (October 1929). Sudden collapse of the New York Stock Exchange, caused by mass gambling in shares pushed to excessive prices at a time when the economy was threatened by over-production. The realization of this led to panic selling, the closing of banks and factories, mass unemployment, and an economic depression which spread to the rest of the world, especially Europe.

Walmer Castle Official residence at Walmer, Kent, of the Lord Warden of the Cinque Ports.

Walpole Society (1911). Society which encourages the study of the history of British art. (Named after Horace Walpole.)

Walpurgis Night Eve of May Day, when the witches made revel, especially (in German legend) on the BROCKEN, the setting of a famous scene in FAUST. (Feast day of St Walpurgis, an English abbess who introduced Christianity to the Germans in the 8th century; pronounced val-poor′gis.)

Walrus and the Carpenter, The Characters in a ballad recited by Tweedledee in THROUGH THE LOOKING GLASS, containing the lines: '"The time has come", the Walrus said, / "To talk of many things: / Of shoes – and ships – and sealing-wax / Of cabbages and kings!".'

Walsingham Abbey Abbey between Wells and Fakenham, Norfolk, built on the site of the 11th-century Shrine of Our Lady of Walsingham, once visited by pilgrims from all over Europe.

Waltham Forest (1965). New London borough consisting of the former boroughs of Walthamstow, Chingford and Leyton; headquarters at Forest Road E17.

Walthamstow Former municipal borough of Essex, since 1965 part of the borough of WALTHAM FOREST.

Walton figures (1806–35). Staffordshire pottery figures which copied Chelsea and Derby groups for the cottage mantelpiece, complete with simplified bocages, made by John Walton of Burslem or his imitators. He also depicted biblical and rural themes. All were gaily printed in overglaze enamels, and sometimes marked with the title of the subject.

Walton gaol Liverpool gaol.

Walton Heath Golf Club near Tadworth, Surrey.

'Waltzing Matilda' Australian national song, written by Andrew Paterson (1864–1941), beginning: 'Once a jolly swagman camped by a billy-bong.' (*Waltz*, 'carry'; *matilda*, 'swag, 'hobo's roll'.)

Walwal incident (December 1934). Minor skirmish on the Italian Somaliland and Ethiopia border, used as a pretext for Mussolini's invasion.

Wanderers HARLEQUIN rugby club's second team.

Wandering Jew, The Jew of medieval legend who insulted Jesus on his way to the Crucifixion and was condemned to walk the earth until the Day of Judgement. Ahasuerus (= Xerxes) is one of the many names under which he appears. The best-known fictional treatments of this theme are *Melmoth the Wanderer* (1820) by C. R. Maturin, and *The Wandering Jew* (1845–7) by Eugène Sue.

Wandering Willie (1) Blind fiddler in Walter Scott's novel *Redgauntlet*, set in the period of the FORTY-FIVE. (2) Title of a poem by Robert Burns.

Wandervögel Hordes of hikers who used to wander through the German countryside in the 1930s singing patriotic songs and meditating

on the greatness of the HERRENVOLK. (German, 'birds of passage'.)

Wandsworth Inner London borough since 1965 consisting of the former metropolitan boroughs of Wandsworth and Battersea.

Wandsworth Prison Largest of British prisons: it takes only recidivists mostly from south London where it is situated.

Wankel (1950s). Four-stroke internal combustion engine in which the rotor replaced the pistons. It is less fuel-efficient than conventional petrol engines. Invented by a German engineer, Felix Wankel.

Wanstead and Woodford Former municipal borough of Essex, since 1965 part of the borough of REDBRIDGE.

Wantage Research Laboratory Headquarters of the Atomic Energy Authority's Research Group, with an Isotope School (1951) where new uses for isotopes are investigated. (Town in Berkshire.)

Warag Abbreviation for the War Agricultural Committee, a major feature of British rural life during and after World War II; one was set up for each county, and through them the Ministry of Agriculture directed local agricultural policy and practice.

War and Peace (1869). One of Leo Tolstoy's 2 greatest novels. The vast canvas includes a study of the utter fortuitousness of war (Napoleon's defeat of Kutuzov at Borodino in 1812); Pierre's capture by the French after his scruples had caused him to spare Napoleon's life at Moscow; his escape and marriage to the delightful Natasha; and his conversion by a peasant to the wisdom of a simple life (echoing a theme in ANNA KARENINA).

Warbeck Rebellion (1497). Yorkist attempt to place Perkin Warbeck on the English throne. He was a native of Tournai masquerading as the younger of the PRINCES IN THE TOWER. With support from Burgundy, Scotland and Ireland, he landed in the south-west but deserted his forces at Taunton and was eventually executed.

Warburg, S. G. (1946). A London, formerly Hamburg, merchant bank and acceptance house.

Warburg Institute (1905). Originally a private research library founded at Hamburg, moved to London 1933 and since 1944 part of London University; devoted to the history of the classical tradition.

Ward Artemus Pen-name of the American humorist Charles Farrar Browne (1834–67), who wrote numerous sketches purporting to be the work of an illiterate travelling show-man.

Warden, The (1855). One of Trollope's BAR-CHESTER NOVELS; the conscientious Rev. Septimus Harding accepts with great reluctance the well-paid sinecure post of warden of a hospital for 12 bedesmen, only to be hounded out of it by a press campaign.

Wardle, Mr The amiable host at DINGLEY DELL to the Pickwick Club in Dickens's novel. His daughters marry Snodgrass and Trundle and one elopes with Alfred JINGLE.

Wardour Street A street in Soho, London. (1) Formerly associated with fake antique furniture; hence *Wardour Street English*, fake antique English of the 'quotha, methinks, anent, perchance' school. (2) Now associated with the cinema industry.

Ware, The Great Bed of An oak four-poster bed, nearly 11 ft square, thought to have been moved from Ware House to an inn in Ware, near Hertford, in the 16th century, and now in the Victoria and Albert Museum. It is mentioned in Shakespeare's *Twelfth Night*.

'Waring' (1842). Robert Browning's poem beginning: 'What's become of Waring / Since he gave us all the slip?' It refers to a friend of his who had emigrated to New Zealand.

War of 1812 War between Britain and USA during the Napoleonic Wars, arising from the Royal Navy's restrictions on the freedom of the seas which hurt American interests. US forces made unsuccessful attempts to invade Canada, but set fire to Toronto (1813); the British failed to take Baltimore (see STAR-SPANGLED BANNER) but burnt Washington (1814). See GHENT, TREATY OF.

War of the Worlds, The (1898). H. G. Wells's story of the invasion of England by creatures from Mars (see MARTIAN INVASION SCARE); armed with poison gas and a heat ray, they proved a formidable enemy until they were vanquished by our native diseases.

War on Want London organization (closed 1990) which seeks to educate the British public on the urgent need for a campaign against world poverty, and collects funds to use for this purpose in India and elsewhere.

Warren Commission (1964). Inquiry into the circumstances of President Kennedy's assassination, subsequently criticized for not examining more rigorously suggestions that there was a conspiracy involving more than one assassin. (Earl Warren, Chief Justice of the Supreme Court.)

War Requiem (1962). Benjamin Britten's musical setting of a poem by Wilfred Owen, composed for the new Coventry Cathedral.

Warsaw Ghetto Rising (April–June 1943). A pathetic revolt by the Jews against their German tormentors.

Warsaw Pact (1955). Communist bloc's equivalent, and answer, to NATO.

Warsaw Rising (August–October 1944). Abortive attempt to seize Warsaw from the Germans, made by the Polish underground movement in the expectation of help from the approaching Russian armies, which was perhaps deliberately withheld as the revolt was led by non-Communists.

Wars of the Roses (1455–85). Civil war between the LANCASTRIANS and the YORKISTS, rival claimants to the throne descended from Edward III; ended by BOSWORTH FIELD. (Red and white roses were the badges respectively of Lancaster and York.)

Warton lectures (1910). Annual lectures on English poetry, sponsored by the British Academy.

Warwick the Kingmaker Richard Neville, Earl of Warwick and Salisbury, who fought on both sides in the WARS OF THE ROSES, first putting the Yorkist Edward IV on the throne and then briefly restoring the Lancastrian Henry VI.

Washington (1963). NEW TOWN in Co. Durham, adjoining the existing town 5 miles from Gateshead, designed to take 70,000 inhabitants.

Washington and the Cherry-tree Story of the young George Washington's ruining his father's tree with a hatchet and owning up instantly with the words 'I can't tell a lie, Pa', which first appeared in a biography published a year after his death, but was publicized more widely, and in more decorous English, by Mark Twain ('Father, I cannot tell a lie'). There is no reason to believe it.

Washington Conference (1) Post-War meeting (1921–2) of the major powers which tried to ensure a lasting peace. It guaranteed Chinese independence, cancelled the Anglo-Japanese alliance, and in general relieved tension arising from international rivalries in the Pacific area. Its chief success was the WASHINGTON NAVAL AGREEMENT. (2) For conferences during World War II, see ARCADIA and TRIDENT, their code-names.

Washington Naval Agreement (1922). Chief achievement of the WASHINGTON CONFERENCE (1921–2). It fixed a 10-year holiday from building capital ships, which were put on a 5:5:3 tonnage ratio as between Britain, USA and Japan and limited in size. This and the agreement reached at the LONDON NAVAL CONFERENCE (1930) were denounced by Japan in 1934.

Washington Square (1) Once an exclusive residential district of New York City, at the southern end of Fifth Avenue on the edge of Greenwich Village. (2) Title of a novel by Henry James, made into a play, *The Heiress*.

Washkansky case (1967). Attempt to save the life of Louis Washkansky (aged 55) in South Africa by transplanting into him the heart of a mortally injured girl. His death 18 days later was attributed to lung failure following double pneumonia, and not to heart failure. The case started a many-faceted controversy remarkable for the absence of dispassionate scientific assessment.

WASP (USA) Abbreviation for White Anglo-Saxon Protestant.

Wasp of Twickenham, The Well-earned nickname of Alexander Pope who, during the latter half of his life, lived at Twickenham (now part of Greater London).

Wasps (1) Middlesex rugby club founded in 1867 before the Rugby Union was formed; its headquarters are at Sudbury and it fields 13 teams. (2) Nickname of the Alloa football team.

Wasps, The (422 BC). Aristophanes' comedy, like *The* KNIGHTS an attack on Cleon, and on the Athenian weakness for litigation.

Wassermann test (1906). Blood test for syphilis.

Waste Land, The (1922). T. S. Eliot's first major poem, contrasting the sterility of modern civilization with the fertility of ancient beliefs. It is important for its complete break with poetic tradition, parallel with that of Joyce's *Ulysses*. As with Joyce, his settings are taken from everyday life but his allusive comments of inspissated erudition demand from the reader a knowledge of several languages and of the books that have been important to the author, only partially supplied by enigmatic footnotes. It set a fashion by which many a modern poet is held incommunicado.

'**Watch on the Rhine'** See WACHT AM RHEIN.

Watch Tower Bible and Tract Society Name for JEHOVAH'S WITNESSES.

Water-babies, The (1863). Charles Kingsley's fairy-tale of a chimney-sweep boy who falls in the river and is welcomed by the water-babies

Waterford glass (1784–1851). Glass made by an English firm established in Waterford, Ireland, to evade tax. It is indistinguishable from Stourbridge and other English glass, although the myth that it has a distinctive blue tinge has been perpetuated by modern fakes purposely so coloured.

Watergate (1970s). US political scandal. Five men were arrested while burgling the Democrats' headquarters at the Watergate Hotel, Washington, DC. They were attempting to remove bugging apparatus which had earlier been placed there. At their trial the *Washington Post* accused the White House of hiding facts. President Nixon denied all knowledge of the affair but after many delays taped conversations were produced although many were missing and some erased. President Nixon was impeached, charged with obstructing justice. Nixon resigned but was given a free pardon by his successor President Gerald Ford.

Waterloo (18 June 1815). Final battle of the Napoleonic Wars, in which Wellington held the French until Blücher arrived with his Prussians. After this defeat Napoleon abdicated and was sent to St Helena. (Village 8 miles south of Brussels.)

Waterloo Cup Chief coursing prize, contested at Altcar, near Southport each February; also called the Courser's Derby and the Blue Riband of the Leash. (Founded by the proprietor of the Waterloo Hotel, Liverpool.)

Watermen and Lightermen, Worshipful Company of (1827). Body, not strictly a LIVERY COMPANY, which still has the power of binding apprentices.

Watermen's Derby See DOGGETT'S COAT AND BADGE.

Water Music (1717). Handel's suite composed for a royal picnic on the Thames, originally in 41 movements but now generally heard in Sir Hamilton Harty's version of 7 movements.

Water Rats, Order of (1890). Society, originally of music-hall artists, recruited by invitation, whose motto is Philanthropy, Conviviality and Social Intercourse. It holds a banquet with an impromptu, unorthodox cabaret on the last Sunday in November, before the pantomime season begins. The Order has collected vast sums for charity and helped to found the Variety Artistes' Benevolent Fund. Its officers have titles such as King Rat, Scribe Rat. (Origin of name uncertain.)

Watkin's Glen Motor-racing circuit in Finger Lakes Park. New York State, where the US Grand Prix is held.

Watling Street Roman road from Dover via St Albans to Wroxeter; it was at one time the boundary between the Anglo-Saxons and the DANELAW.

Watson Dr Slow-witted foil to Sherlock HOLMES, said to be a self-mocking portrait of his creator, Conan Doyle.

Watts Black ghetto in Los Angeles, the scene in August 1965 of a 6-day race riot marked by arson, looting and the death of 34 people. It was the worst of its kind in US history and shocked the whole nation.

Watt steam-engine (1769). Engine developed by James Watt from the NEWCOMEN ENGINE by adding a separate condenser and an air-pump. A few years later he joined Boulton at the Soho Ironworks, Birmingham, where his engine was further developed.

Wavell's offensives First (December 1940 to February 1941) drove the Italians out of Egypt into Libya; the second (June 1941), known by the code-name Battleaxe, failed, and Gen. Wavell was replaced by Gen. Auchinleck.

Waverley (1814). First of Scott's WAVERLEY NOVELS, about a Capt. Waverley who fights for the YOUNG PRETENDER; it portrays the clash of the old feudal Highlands and the rising bourgeois Lowlands.

Waverley novels Novels of Sir Walter Scott, named after the first of them which was published anonymously, while subsequent books were described as being by 'the author of WAVERLEY'.

Waves, The (1931). Virginia Woolf's novel of the relationship of 6 sharply contrasted characters who were brought up together as children, as revealed through their inner thoughts. At the end, one of them sums up all their lives and sees that they fit together as if they had been one person.

Wavy Navy, The Nickname of the former Royal

Navy Volunteer Reserve. (From the wavy rank stripes worn on the cuffs.)

Wax Chandlers, Worshipful Company of (1483). LIVERY COMPANY, see TALLOW CHANDLERS.

Wayland the Smith English name of a figure in Scandinavian mythology. The English Wayland was an invisible smith who lived in a cromlech on the RIDGEWAY near Lambourne, Berkshire; if you left a fee there he would shoe your horse for you while you slept.

Waynflete Professor Holder of one of 4 chairs at Oxford: Chemistry, Metaphysical Philosophy, Physiology, Pure Mathematics.

Way of All Flesh, The (1903). Samuel Butler's vitriolic novel reflecting his own revolt against his family and the Victorian Church.

Way of the World, The (1700). William Congreve's comedy of Mirabell's efforts to marry the captivating Millamant, a play of scintillating if unfeeling wit.

Ways and Means, Committee of Committee of the whole House of Commons which, on the basis of the Budget, gave detailed consideration to the means of raising the money voted by the Committee of SUPPLY; its decisions were embodied in the Finance Act. Now abolished.

Wayzgoose Annual outing or entertainment given by a master-printer to his men, or a similar festive occasion organized by the men.

Wealth of Nations, The (1776). Adam Smith's *Inquiry into the Nature and Cause of the Wealth of Nations*, the first major analysis of economic theory; he emphasized self-interest and advocated free trade, which he was convinced would be adequately regulated by natural laws of universal application.

'We are not amused' Phrase frequently attributed to Queen Victoria as a supporter to her alleged status as the foundation and origin of all that is implied by the term 'Victorian' – sometimes it has a pejorative tone. However, no less an authority than Princess Alice, Countess of Athlone, said, in a television broadcast, that Queen Victoria '. . . never said it'.

'Wearin' o' the Green, The' (18th century). Self-pitying Irish street ballad: 'O Paddy dear, an' did ye hear the news that's goin' round? / The shamrock is by law forbid to grow on Irish ground! . . . / She's the most disthressful country that iver yet was seen, / For they're hangin' men an' women for the wearing' o' the Green.'

Weavers, Worshipful Company of (1155). LIVERY COMPANY with the longest documented history of any City guild; it still plays a part in the craft and industry of weaving.

Webley Revolver (0·455) usually chosen by British Army officers (who had to buy their own) from the 1880s to 1915. Thereafter they were issued with Enfields. There was also a Webley 0·455 automatic, used by the Royal Navy.

Webster (1828). Chief American dictionary, bought up by G. & C. Merriam Co. in 1844. In 1961 they published *Webster's Third New International Dictionary of the English Language* (2,662 pages); also known as the Merriam-Webster, as the name Webster has been used by other firms. (First produced by Noah Webster.)

Wedgwood Benn case Anthony Wedgwood Benn renounced (1960) the right to succeed to his father's title as Viscount Stansgate, was elected to the House of Commons but refused permission to take his seat until 1963, when the Peerage Act came into force legitimizing such disclaimers.

Wedgwood blue Cold pale blue, lighter than powder blue, used by WEDGWOOD as ground colour for JASPER WARES.

Wedgwoods (1759). Family firm of Staffordshire potters founded by Josiah Wedgwood at Burslem and moved to the Etruria factory in 1769. It produces JASPER WARE, black stoneware ('basaltes', from 1766), Queen's ware (a soberly decorated creamware) and, from 1788, bone china.

Wee Frees Members of the Free Church of Scotland who refused to join the United Free Church of Scotland in 1900.

Wehrmacht German armed forces. (German, 'defensive force'.)

Weigela See DIERVILLA.

Weil's disease Epidemic jaundice, spread by sewer rats, affecting liver and kidneys; severe but not fatal, and now rare in the West.

Weimar German town which, when capital of the Duchy of Saxe-Weimar, was associated with Goethe, who lived there from 1775, holding a court post and directing the theatre. Schiller also spent the last years of his life there, working with Goethe. (See next entry.)

Weimar Republic (1919–33). German Republic formed after the Kaiser's abdication, and suspended by Hitler. (Constitution formulated by the National Assembly sitting at Weimar, which at first was the new capital; later in the German Democratic Republic, near Leipzig; pronounced vy'mahr.)

Weir of Hermiston (1896). R. L. Stevenson's last and unfinished novel, by many thought to contain his best writing. Archie Weir is banished by his father to live in the village of Hermiston, where he falls in love with a girl. The novel ends at this point, but the outline of the rest of the plot is known.

Welbeck College Army's own 6th-form public school, at Worksop, Nottinghamshire, preparing boys for Sandhurst as an alternative to direct entry.

Welfare State System, introduced in Britain in 1948 and based on the National Insurance and National Health Service Acts, whereby the social services of the country cease to be a form of poor relief. The main features are free medical services available to all, and the joint financing by employee and employer of insurance against old age, unemployment, etc. (Phrase said to have been coined by William Temple, Archbishop of Canterbury.)

Wellers, The In Dickens's novel, Sam Weller is Pickwick's loyal Cockney servant, full of wise saws and modern instances; his father, Tony, is a fat coachman with strong views on the place of women in a man's world.

Wellington Vickers twin-engined bomber used by the RAF in the early years of World War II.

Wellington An ex-Admiralty sloop moored to the Thames Embankment, and serving as the floating livery hall of the Honourable Company of MASTER MARINERS.

Wellington Museum See APSLEY HOUSE.

Well of Loneliness, The (1928). First novel to deal sympathetically with the theme of lesbian relationships, written by (Margaret) Radclyffe Hall.

Wells, John Wellington 'Dealer in magic and spells' in Gilbert and Sullivan's *The Sorcerer*.

Wells Fargo (1850). (USA) Pioneer mail, courier and banking service in the developing west, which ran a stage-coach service between Sacramento (California), Portland (Oregon) and Salt Lake City. Its founders also developed the AMERICAN EXPRESS CO. in the eastern states, and the 2 companies joined forces in 1925. (W. G. Fargo, died 1881, and Henry Wells, died 1878.)

Wellsian Resembling the world created by H. G. Wells in his novels of the future, from WAR OF THE WORLDS and *The* FIRST MEN IN THE MOON to *The* SHAPE OF THINGS TO COME.

'Well-tempered Clavier, The' Title of J. S. Bach's 48 preludes and fugues, written to demonstrate the advantages of 'equal temperament' (i.e. tuning the instrument so as to distribute inequalities of interval over all keys), then an innovation, now normal.

Welsh Black Docile breed of longhorn dual-purpose cattle, bred in North Wales.

Welsh Brigade Infantry brigade comprising: The Royal Welch Fusiliers; The South Wales Borderers; the Welch Regiment. Since 1968, part of the PRINCE OF WALES'S DIVISION.

Welsh corgi Short-legged long-backed breed of dog with a foxy head. There are 2 varieties: (1) the Cardigan, with rounded ears, bow-legs and long tail; (2) the Pembroke, with pointed ears, straight legs and short tail. As Queen Elizabeth II's favourite breed, they have become very popular, despite their alleged bad temper.

Welsh Disestablishment Political issue in the years before World War I, since the disestablishment and disendowment of the Church in Wales, in deference to the great growth of Noncomformity there, was opposed by the House of Lords. An act was passed in 1914 but because of the war remained inoperative until 1920.

Welsh dresser Heavy oak kitchen sideboard comprising a lower section of drawers and cupboards surmounted by open shelves for displaying plates and dishes.

Welsh Guards (1915). Junior regiment of the GUARDS DIVISION; they wear their buttons in fives, and a white and green plume.

Welsh rabbit Toasted cheese; grated cheese, often seasoned, placed on toast, browned under the grill. (The variant 'rarebit' is an English genteelism without etymological basis.)

Welsh Wizard, The Nickname for David Lloyd George (1863–1945). Prime Minister, 1916–22, created Earl 1945.

Welt, Die (1946). Hamburg daily newspaper, originally started by the British-occupation authorities.

Wembley Former municipal borough of Middlesex, since 1965 part of the borough of BRENT.

Wembley Stadium (1923). Built as the centrepiece of the British Empire Exhibition (1924–5) but opened in April 1923, amid scenes of wild disorder, for the FA Cup Final. It seats 100,000 and, with its Empire Pool and Sports Arena, has been used for athletics (until 1948), covered-court tennis championships, greyhound and speedway racing, swimming, boxing, horse shows and for some of the Olympic Games events in 1948.

Wenceslas The Good King Wenceslas of the carol was a 10th-century Duke of Bohemia converted to Christianity, who was assassinated by his brother for trying to convert his subjects.

Wends Slavs of eastern Germany, once numerous and widespread, who now survive only in parts of Saxony.

Wendy house House built for Wendy in PETER PAN; small play-house for children.

Wensleydale cheese Once a gourmet's delight, made in the North Riding of Yorkshire; the name, like that of double Gloucester, is now applied to cheeses which appear to lack character.

Wentworth Club Golf club at Virginia Water, Surrey. See 'BURMA ROAD'.

Wernher Collection Collection of Old Masters, tapestries, Fabergé jewels and other *objets d'art*, on view at LUTON HOO.

Werther See SORROWS OF YOUNG WERTHER.

'We Shall Overcome' Civil rights movement's song, heard wherever 2 or 3 protesters are gathered together.

Wesker trilogy (1958–60). The plays *Chicken Soup with Barley, Roots* and *I'm Talking about Jerusalem*, in which Arnold Wesker examines capitalism and socialism through the eyes of an East End Jewish family.

Wesleyans See METHODISM.

Wessex (1) Kingdom of the West Saxons founded by Cerdic (Cedric) in the 6th century, which dominated all England from the time of Egbert and Alfred in the 9th century, but disappeared as a political unit under William I. It corresponded to Hampshire, Dorset, Wiltshire, Berkshire, Somerset and Devon. (2) Name given by Thomas Hardy to the setting of his Wessex novels, corresponding to Dorset and neighbouring counties.

Wessex Brigade Infantry brigade comprising: The Devonshire and Dorset Regiment; The Gloucestershire Regiment; The Royal Hampshire Regiment; The Duke of Edinburgh's Royal Regiment (Berkshire and Wiltshire). Since 1968, part of the PRINCE OF WALES'S DIVISION.

West Bank Israeli-occupied area following the SIX-DAY WAR, containing 97% Palestinian

Arabs. Administered as a district of Judea-Samaria. In 1988 King Hussein assumed that Jordan had abandoned its efforts to administer the West Bank and surrendered its claim to the PALESTINE LIBERATION ORGANIZATION.

Westchester Cup (1886). International polo match between Britain and USA.

Westcott House Theological training college at Cambridge.

Western, Squire In Fielding's novel, the semi-literate irascible father of Sophia, whom TOM JONES marries.

Western Empire, The See ROMAN EMPIRE.

Western European Union (1955). Name given to the BRUSSELS TREATY ORGANIZATION when it was expanded to include West Germany and Italy on their regaining full independent sovereign status.

Western Wall See WAILING WALL.

West Galloway Alternative name for Wigtownshire, itself now part of Dumfries & Galloway Region.

West Germany See GERMAN FEDERAL REPUBLIC.

West Ham Former Essex country borough, since 1965 part of the London borough of NEWHAM.

West Indies, University of (1962). University at Mona, Jamaica, with branches in Trinidad and Barbados.

West Indies Federation (1958–62). Group of British West Indies territories which broke up when Jamaica and Trinidad became Dominions. Most of the remainder agreed in 1962 to form a new federation (the Eastern Caribbean Federation or 'Little Seven'), consisting of Barbados, the Leeward Islands and the Windward Islands, with a capital in Barbados.

West Irian See IRIAN BARAT.

Westminster, City of Inner London borough which in 1965 absorbed the former metropolitan boroughs of Paddington and St Marylebone.

Westminster, Palace of Official name of the Houses of Parliament, built on the site of the palace where the Kings of England lived from Edward I until Henry VIII moved to Whitehall Palace. The original building was burnt down in 1834, only WESTMINSTER HALL surviving.

Westminster, Statute of (1931). Final definition of DOMINION STATUS.

Westminster Confession (1647). Declaration of Calvinist beliefs accepted as the basis of PRESBYTERIANISM.

Westminster Gazette (1893). Distinguished Liberal evening, later morning, paper, absorbed by the *Daily News* in 1928.

Westminster Hall Only surviving part of the old Palace of Westminster (see WESTMINSTER, PALACE OF); it was incorporated on the west side of the new Houses of Parliament. Built by William II and rebuilt by Richard II, it was used by early Parliaments, and until 1882 as the Courts of Justice.

Westphalia Former German duchy, capital Münster, incorporated in Prussia and now part of North Rhine-Westphalia.

Westphalia, Treaty of (1648). Treaty which ended the THIRTY YEARS WAR. France gained Alsace; Sweden Pomerania; the United Netherlands and Switzerland were declared independent of the Empire; and the German states remained free from Hapsburg rule. The Bohemian Protestants who started the war gained nothing.

West Point US Military Academy at West Point, New York State, on the Hudson River; the equivalent of the British Sandhurst.

West Side Story (1957). Leonard Bernstein's extremely successful musical, devised and directed by Jerome Robbins who integrated fantastically energetic dances into a Romeo and Juliet plot set against a background of teenage gang warfare in New York.

West Wall (or **Siegfried Line**) Line of German fortifications opposite the Maginot Line and protecting the Rhineland; breached by the Allies in September 1944.

Westward Ho! (1855). Charles Kingsley's romance of gallant Elizabethan sea-dogs, Spanish Dons and the Inquisition.

West Wind, Ode to the (1820). Shelley's prayer to the wild West Wind, 'thou breath of Autumn's being', to scatter his 'dead thoughts over the universe / Like withered leaves to quicken a new birth'.

Wet, A One who lacks intellectual or political toughness but treated as a compliment by those who wish to be more pragmatic on political and economic issues.

Wettin Name of a family going back to the 10th century, from which many European dynasties were descended. The Dukes of Saxe-Coburg-Gotha, and thus Albert, Prince Consort and his son, Edward VII, were Wettins. The name of the Royal family was changed to WINDSOR in 1917, although according to some authorities the correct name should be GUELPH or Wipper.

WEU See WESTERN EUROPEAN UNION.

Wexford, Massacre at (1649). See CROMWELLIAN SETTLEMENT.

WFTU (1945). Initials used for the World Federation of Trade Unions, founded by the union organizations of 54 countries, including USSR. In 1949 the British TUC, the American CIO and many others seceded to form the non-Communist ICFTU.

WG Initials standing for W. G. Grace, the cricketer (1848–1915).

W. H., Mr 'Onlie begetter' to whom Shakespeare dedicated his *Sonnets*. His identity is an unsolved mystery, the strongest candidates being the Earl of Southampton (Henry Wriothesley) and the Earl of Pembroke (William Herbert).

What Every Woman Knows (1908). J. M. Barrie's play about the egotist John Shand, in which male pretensions to superiority are deflated.

'What's My Line' First of the US TV panel games, introduced to Britain in the 1950s. A panel (of which Gilbert Harding was a member and Eamonn Andrews the chairman) cross-questioned challengers and tried to guess their jobs.

Wheatstone Professor Holder of the chair of Physics at King's College, London University.

Wheelwrights, Worshipful Company of (1669). LIVERY COMPANY.

When We Were Very Young (1924). Collection of A. A. Milne's verse written for, and often about, his son CHRISTOPHER ROBIN; it includes the poems about young DUPREE and the king who plaintively asked for 'some butter for the Royal slice of bread'.

Whewell Professor Holder of the chair of International Law at Cambridge. (Pronounced hew'ĕl.)

Which? See CONSUMERS' ASSOCIATION.

Whieldon ware (1) Varied types of earthenware made (1745–95) by Thomas Whieldon, who invented his own beautiful and distinctive brown, yellow, green and blue glazes and a tortoiseshell glaze, as well as using 2-coloured clays under coloured glazes. His work included toby jugs and charmingly naïve musicians, horsemen, women seated in chairs, etc. (2) Similar wares made by others. See ASTBURY WARE.

Whig Ascendancy Period from the accession of George I to that of George III, during which the chief offices of state were given to the Whigs, who supported the Hanoverian succession. See JACOBITES.

Whig interpretation of history View of English history as a steady progress, from the time of the Whig Revolution of 1688 and particularly in the period of Whig domination from 1714, towards parliamentary democracy, religious toleration, social betterment, wealth, liberty and order. It was prominent in the works of Lord Macaulay, which reflected the general complacency of the Victorian era. Later historians paid greater attention to the horrors of the Industrial Revolution.

Whigs (1673). Originally the Country Party, formed by the Earl of Shaftesbury to exclude the Catholic James, Duke of York, from the succession. It opposed the Court (Tory) Party, stood for parliamentary supremacy and religious toleration, drew its strength from Nonconformists and 'trade' and was the nucleus of the 19th-century Liberal Party. (Possibly from Scottish nickname for COVENANTERS, of unknown significance.)

Whipsnade (1931). Zoo-park of the Zoological Society, on Dunstable Downs, Bedfordshire, in which animals and birds enjoy the maximum possible freedom.

Whiskey Rebellion, The (1794). First test of Federal strength, when impoverished mountain farmers of western Pennsylvania reacted violently to an excise tax on alcohol. Troops were called out and Washington rode to the scene with his Secretary of the Treasury, Alexander Hamilton. Republicans attacked the latter for his high-handedness; he replied, 'I have (long) learned to hold popular opinion of no value.'

Whisky Galore (1947). Compton Mackenzie's rampageous story of a cargo of whisky which come ashore on one of the Western Isles of Scotland.

Whisky Mac Equal parts of whisky and green-ginger wine plus a slice of lemon.

'Whistler's Mother' Popular name of the painting which Whistler titled *Arrangement in Black and Grey – The Artist's Mother*.

Whitaker (1868). Abbreviated title of *Whitaker's Almanack*, an annual reference book containing 'an account of astronomical phenomena' together with a vast amount of information and statistics on every kind of subject, all excellently indexed.

White Australia policy Policy of prohibiting the immigration of Asians, particularly Japanese and Chinese, into Australia. It is still in force though rarely acknowledged officially; known to Asians as the WAP.

'White Christmas' (1942). Ever-popular song, 'I'm Dreaming of a White Christmas' written by Irving Berlin for the movie *Holiday Inn*, and now an inescapable feature of the Christmas festival, being an easily sung non-denominational secular carol. In its original context it was in part an expression of homesick disillusion among troops then serving overseas. Heifetz made a violin solo of it.

White Dwarfs Smallest of stars, extremely dense and glowing feebly. They are formed when the helium nuclei in a RED GIANT fuse; the outer mantle is flung into space, leaving only the white-hot core, mainly of helium. White Dwarfs are common; they eventually evolve into supernovae.

White Friars See CARMELITES.

White goods Retailers' expression for household appliances such as cookers and refrigerators that earlier meant sheets, towels and tablecloths.

Whitehall (1) Originally a palace built by Cardinal Wolsey, seized by Henry VIII. The only surviving part, the BANQUETING HALL, was added later. (2) Street running through this site, from Trafalgar Square to the Houses of Parliament, lined with government departmental offices. (3) Hence, the British government, British bureaucracy.

Whitehall farce One of various farces staged at the Whitehall Theatre, London, by the actor-manager Brian Rix, notable for their bedrock humour. The most famous were the first two: *Reluctant Heroes* and *Dry Rot* (1950–58).

White Hart Lane Football home of Tottenham Hotspur, at Tottenham.

Whitehead, Cmdr David Ogilvy's creation for a Schweppes advertisement in USA; under the hypnotic gaze of this splendid specimen of high-ranking British naval officer, Americans first learnt to drink tonic water with their gin, having previously only known it as quinine water, with both *i*'s pronounced long and the accent on the wrong syllable, at that.

White Highlands In Kenya, old name for the highlands around Nairobi, where settlement by white farmers began in 1902. Legends of the displacement of Kikuyu population are untrue; the area was almost uninhabited and belonged to the nomadic Masai.

White Horse Inn Austrian lakeside inn at St Wolfgang, made famous by a popular musical comedy of that name. (Translation of Austrian *Weisser Rössel*, literally 'white little horse'.)

White House, The (1799). Official residence and offices of the US President, at Washington. Hence used as a synonym for US Presidential policy or office; the US executive.

White Knight (1) In Lewis Carroll's *Through the Looking Glass* the incompetent horseman and obsessional inventor who sang to Alice the inconsequent song about an 'aged aged man / A-sitting on a gate'. (2) Financial terms for a person or company buying controlling interest in a firm in order to avoid that firm being taken over by an unwelcome purchaser.

Whitelaw Cup British Bridge tournament for teams of 4 women.

White Lodge, The House in Richmond Park, Surrey, built by George II; birthplace of the Duke of Windsor, it is now the home of the ROYAL BALLET SCHOOL.

White Man's Burden, The Name for the task of administering tropical countries in the days before independence; it was the title of one of Kipling's poems.

White Man's Grave, The Name for West Africa, well earned in the 19th and early 20th centuries when the mortality among Europeans was extremely high.

Whiteoak family See JALNA.

White Queen, The Character in THROUGH THE LOOKING GLASS, a gentle, vague, stupid creature, a foil for the RED QUEEN. It was she who claimed that she could believe 'as many as 6 impossible things before breakfast', and who laid down the rule: jam tomorrow, and jam yesterday – but never jam today.

White Rabbit First character met by ALICE IN WONDERLAND; he reappears throughout the book, always in a pother.

White Rajah See RAJAH BROOKE.

White Russia English name of Byelorussian SSR.

White Russians (1) People of Byelorussia or White Russia. (2) Anti-Bolshevists of the civil war period in Russia (1918–21).

White's Club (1693). Oldest of London's clubs, in St James's Street, proudly aristocratic, philistine and Tory, with a name for late nights, gambling and eccentricity. It has no political importance.

White Staves Name given to the ladies, dressed in white, who at Buckingham Palace garden parties present guests to the Queen.

Whit Monday Monday following WHIT SUNDAY, until 1967 a Bank Holiday, which was then moved to the last Monday in May or the first in June and called the Spring Holiday.

Whitstable oysters Best English oysters, from Whitstable Bay, Kent.

Whit Sunday Day appointed in the Christian Church to commemorate the descent of the Holy Spirit on the Disciples, which occurred on the day of PENTECOST (Acts 2:1–4). It falls on the seventh Sunday after Easter, between 10 May and 13 June.

Whittaker Chambers case See HISS CASE.

Whittington, Dick Legend which has not been traced back further than the 17th century. In fact, Whittington was the son of a Gloucestershire knight, became fabulously rich as a mercer in London and was 3 times Mayor (1397–1419). A stone on Highgate Hill traditionally marks the spot where Dick Whittington, a poor orphan who was running away from his master, heard Bow Bells intoning: 'Turn again, Whittington, thrice Mayor of London.' He returned, to find that his cat, apparently a highly accomplished mouser, had been sold to the King of Barbary at a great price, the basis of his future fortune.

Whittle jet engine World's first jet engine, designed in Britain by Sir Frank Whittle and tested in 1937. It was used in the first British jet plane, the Gloster E 28/39 of 1941 (see METEOR).

Whodunnit Colloquial term for a detective story.

Whore of Babylon, The Phrase used in the same way as SCARLET WOMAN, and from the same source.

Who's Afraid of Virginia Woolf? (1962). Edward Albee's melodrama set in a US university, where a history professor and the daughter of the college president whom he has married tear each other to shreds.

Who's Who (1849). Annual biographical dictionary, mainly of British subjects who have received honours or decorations, but also including distinguished foreigners.

Who Was Who Series of selected biographies from past editions of WHO'S WHO of people who have died since 1897, each volume covering a period of approximately 10 years.

Wicked Uncles, The Queen Victoria's uncles, the sons of George III, who included George IV, William IV, and the Dukes of Cumberland (later King of Hanover), Cambridge, York and Sussex.

Wickham, Mr Jane Austen character; see BENNET FAMILY.

'Widdicombe Fair' Old Dartmoor ballad about a party who want to borrow Tom Pearse's grey mare to go to the fair; they are Bill Brewer, Jan Stewer, Peter Gurney, Peter Davey, Dan'l Whiddon, 'arry 'awk and Uncle Tom Cobbleigh. (A village on Dartmoor, now spelt Widecombe.)

Widmerpool See MUSIC OF TIME.

Widow, The (1) Victorian nickname for champagne, from Veuve Clicquot, a favourite in England. (2) Obsolete slang for the gallows, from the older French nickname (*la veuve*) for the guillotine. (3) Widow of Windsor, Queen Victoria.

Widowers' Houses (1892). Bernard Shaw's first play, dealing with the iniquities of slum landlordism.

Widow Twankey Stock pantomime character, played by a man. (Obsolete slang for 'gin'; from Chinese *Tun-ki*, a kind of green tea.)

Widow Wadman See UNCLE TOBY.

'Wiegenlied' German for 'Cradle Song', the title of various songs by Brahms, Schubert, Mozart, etc.

Wiener schnitzel Veal cutlet dipped in egg and crumbs and fried in deep fat; the Austrian name for the French *escalope de veau*. ('Vienna cutlet'; pronounced veen'ér shnit'zl.)

Wife of Bath Rumbustious and much-married pilgrim in Chaucer's CANTERBURY TALES, who favours obedience and generosity in husbands. See next entry.

Wife of Bath's Tale, The In the CANTERBURY TALES, the story of one of King Arthur's knights who, to save his life, has to find out what women love most. The answer (sovereignty over their husbands) is revealed to him, on condition he marries her, by an old witch who then turns into a beautiful girl.

Wigan Pier Allusions to this became a standard music-hall joke (Wigan itself being regarded as a joke, and being far from the sea); the phrase was adopted by George Orwell in his ROAD TO WIGAN PIER (1937), essays on social problems.

Wightman Cup Anglo-US women's international tennis team competition, last played 1990.

Wild Bill Donovan See OSS.

Wild Bill Hickok US marshal who after an adventurous career, the theme of many westerns, was killed while playing poker in a saloon at Deadwood, South Dakota, in 1876. (See DEADWOOD DICK.)

Wild Duck, The (1884). Ibsen's play on the theme that for some people only self-deception makes life bearable.

Wilde (Oscar) case (1895). Trial for homosexual offences of the writer Oscar Wilde; he was found guilty and given a 2-year sentence. He had himself precipitated the case by bringing a libel action against the 8th Marquess of Queensberry whose son, Lord Alfred Douglas, was the *casus belli*.

Wild Macraes, The Nickname of the 72nd Foot (The Seaforth Highlanders); see QUEEN'S OWN HIGHLANDERS.

Wilhelmine Germany Reich under the last two German emperors, Wilhelm I and II (1871–1918) and the IRON CHANCELLOR (1871–90), when the economy (and cultural values) were subordinated to a disastrous militaristic imperialism. See MAN OF STRAW.

Wilhelmstrasse Once used as a synonym for the German Foreign Office, which was situated in the Berlin street of that name.

Wilkins lecture (1947). Royal Society lecture on the history of science.

Willesden Former municipal borough of Middlesex, since 1965 part of the borough of BRENT.

William and Mary College (1693). Ancient foundation at Williamsburg, Virginia.

William and Mary period (1689–1702). Transitional period in the decorative arts from that of the Restoration to that of Queen Anne. The characteristic innovation was the curved stretcher for tables and chairs, an idea brought from Holland by Dutch William's cabinet-makers. The tallboy came into vogue.

William Hickey Name given to a gossip column in the *Daily Express* created by Tom Driberg, subsequently a Labour MP. (Name of a 19th-century writer of racy memoirs.)

William of Orange William III of England, Prince of Orange, James II's nephew and son-in-law, invited by Whigs and some Tories to England at the GLORIOUS REVOLUTION.

Williamsburg, Colonial Restoration of 18th-century buildings and living conditions in historical areas of Williamsburg, Va, between Yorktown and Jamestown, which was founded as a palisaded outpost in 1663 and became capital of Virginia from 1699. It includes a reproduction of the old Capitol, the governor's palace, Raleigh Tavern and some 500 colonial buildings, with craft shops, gardens, slave quarters etc. Restoration began in 1926, financed by John D. Rockefeller Jr.

William the Silent Sobriquet of the Prince of Orange, who was the Dutch nationalist leader against Spanish rule in the 16th century; so called because he knew when to keep his own counsel.

William Wyse Professor Holder of the chair of Social Anthropology at Cambridge.

Willing's Press Guide An annual index and handbook of the world's newspapers and periodicals, started nearly a century ago.

Willink report (1961). Report of a Royal Commission on the police which recommended the retention of independent police forces.

Willow Pattern (1780). Traditional English design on blue-and-white china invented by Thomas Turner of CAUGHLEY. The story of the mandarin chasing his daughter and her lover was invented to account for the design, of which there are many versions. Approximately, the fewer people on the bridge the earlier the china; the number of apples on the tree also helps in assigning date and maker.

Willy One of the pen-names of COLETTE's first husband, Henri Gauthier-Villars, music critic and journalist. Colette for a time wrote under the name of Colette Willy. (Pronounced, by him, as in English.)

Wilmington, Long Man of Ancient figure of a man 230 ft high, with a staff in each hand, cut in the chalk downs of Windover Hill above the Sussex village of Wilmington, near Eastbourne. He may represent the war-god Woden (Odin).

Wilson cloud chamber (1912). Apparatus invented by C. T. R. Wilson which through being saturated with water vapour, makes visible the tracks of ionizing radiations, e.g. alpha, beta, gamma and X-rays.

Wilton carpets Generic term for a type which differs from AXMINSTER CARPETS by having most of the pile yarn woven into the backing, which is smoother.

Wilton House Seventeenth-century home at Wilton, near Salisbury, of the Earl of Pembroke, particularly famous for the perfect proportions of Inigo Jones's 'double-cube' room.

Wimbledon Former municipal borough of Surrey, since 1965 part of the borough of MERTON.

Wimbledon (1877). Short name of the lawn tennis championships (men's and women's singles, doubles and mixed doubles), played at the end of June at the ALL ENGLAND LAWN TENNIS AND CROQUET CLUB, Wimbledon Park, London. They were thrown open to professionals in 1968.

Wimbledon Cup Rifle-shooting competition for individuals, held at Bisley in July; the range is 600 yds.

Wimpy Trade name for a beef hamburger sold at 'Wimpy Bars'; invented in Chicago.

Wimsey, Lord Peter Benevolent amateur detective created by Dorothy Sayers, who first appeared in *Whose Body?* (1923).

Wincarnis (1890). One of the best-known of tonic or 'invalid' wines, advertised as 'the surest way to health ...' and containing malt and meat extract. (Presumably *wine* + Latin *caro*, *carnis*, 'flesh', 'meat'.)

Winchester rifle (1866). US magazine rifle; the 0·44 model (1873) is famous as a sporting rifle. (O. F. Winchester, manufacturer.)

Wind in the Willows, The (1908). Kenneth Grahame's children's story of Mole, Water Rat and Mr Toad, which contains the immortal phrase: 'There is *nothing* ... half so much worth doing as simply messing about in boats.'

Windmill, The London vaudeville theatre which became famous during World War II for its proud slogan 'We Never Closed', having kept going throughout the air-raids, giving its almost non-stop (6 performances a day) production of the *Revudeville* show.

Windmill Hill people Neolithic farmers of southern England (2500–1800 BC). (Named after an ancient camp-site near Avebury, Wiltshire.)

Wind of Change speech (1960). Speech at Cape Town by the British Prime Minister, Harold Macmillan, who referred to the wind of change blowing through Africa, i.e. the upsurge of nationalism which rendered the policy of apartheid both untimely and dangerous.

Window Wartime code-name for tinfoil strips dropped to confuse German radar during air-raids (the Germans had a similar device). First used in 1943.

Windscale Site of the Atomic Energy Authority's experimental AGR reactor, which began feeding the grid in 1963. Now renamed Sellafield, Cumbria.

Windsor, House of Official designation of the Royal Family since 1917. In 1960 the Queen decided that certain of her descendants should bear the family name of Mountbatten-Windsor. See WETTIN; GUELPH.

Windsor Castle Official royal residence since the 11th century.

Windsor chair Traditional English style of plain wooden chair, with a back consisting mainly of straight rods, and with straight legs slanting outwards.

Windsor Greys Royal horses used in ceremonial processions, formerly kept at Windsor, now at the Buckingham Palace mews. The original Hanoverian breed was dispersed during World War I and later replaced from various sources; they do not, therefore, represent any specific breed.

Windsor Herald Officer of the COLLEGE OF ARMS.

Windy City, The Nickname for Chicago, earned by its exposed position on the south-west shore of Lake Michigan.

Winfrith Site of the Atomic Energy Research Establishment, where a reactor has been tested as part of the international DRAGON PROJECT. A high-temperature steam generating heavy-water reactor (SGHWR) has been developed to produce power at a more competitive price than the AGR reactor. It began to feed the national grid in 1968, but closed in

1990. (A heath north of Lulworth Cove, Dorset.)

Winged Victory of Samothrace (200 BC). Sculpture in the form of a ship's figurehead, commemorating a victory of the people of Rhodes; the original is now in the Louvre.

Wingfield Sculls Since 1952 regarded as the British amateur sculling championship, rowed on the Thames from Putney to Mortlake since 1832. Also known as 'The Wingfields'.

Wingless Victory See NIKE APTEROS.

Winkle, Nathaniel In Dickens's *Pickwick Papers*, a great sportsman, according to all accounts (which happened to be false), and the son of a Birmingham wharfinger.

Winnie Nickname of Winston Churchill.

Winnie-the-Pooh (1926). A. A. Milne's story for children of all ages about the teddy-bear Pooh and his friends Piglet (whose ancestor was Trespassers W), Wol the Owl, and EEYORE.

Winslow Boy, The (1946). Terence Rattigan's play, based on the historical Archer-Shee case, about a naval cadet falsely charged with theft and his father's struggle against Admiralty indifference to clear his name.

Winston Chestnut police horse ridden for many years by the Queen at the Trooping of the Colour; he was killed in an accident in 1957.

Winterhilfe Major National-Socialist (Nazi) charity to which all Germans had to contribute, set up under the slogan 'War against Hunger and Cold'. (German, 'winter aid'.)

Winter Palace (1762). Tsars' Baroque palace at Leningrad, now a major art gallery and museum.

Winterreise (1827). Second of Schubert's song-cycles; 24 songs with words by Wilhelm Müller on the theme of a journey that revives memories of an unhappy love affair. (German, 'winter journey'.)

Winter's Tale, The (1611). Shakespeare's play

about King Leontes of Sicily who is morbidly suspicious of his faithful wife Hermione, and puts her in prison; see also AUTOLYCUS; PERDITA AND FLORIZEL.

Winter War, The (1939–40). Name for the Russian campaign against Finland.

Winton: Abbreviation for (Bishop) of Winchester.

Wipers See YPRES.

Wisden (1864) Standard reference book on cricket, started by a Sussex player, John Wisden, and published annually.

Wisdom of Jesus Alternative name of ECCLESIASTICUS.

Wisdom of Solomon Book of the Apocrypha traditionally attributed to Solomon but probably compiled in Alexandria about the 1st century BC. The first part exhorts orthodox Jews to remain true to their religion and discusses wisdom in human affairs. The second part is a fanciful history of the Jews.

Wise forgeries Forgeries of rare Victorian first editions, by T. J. Wise, an outstanding and respected authority on books; discovered a few years before he died in 1937.

Wise Men of the East See MAGI.

Wisley Gardens Showplace of the Royal Horticultural Society, near Ripley, Surrey.

Wisteria Climbing flowering shrubs named after Caspar Wistar, a University of Pennsylvania professor. Also called Wistaria.

Witan (Witenagemot) Council which advised Anglo-Saxon kings. (Old English, 'meeting of wise men'.)

Witches' Sabbath Gathering of townspeople or villagers who, in the Middle Ages, once a quarter (on CANDLEMAS, the eve of May Day, LAMMAS, and HALLOWE'EN) celebrated ancient pagan rites through the night, led by a coven of 12 initiates under a 'devil' (i.e. a priest). See WALPURGIS NIGHT.

Witt Collection The COURTAULD INSTITUTE OF ART's unique collection of photographs of all noteworthy paintings and other works of art; there is also a library of reference books on art.

Wittelsbachs Dynasty which ruled Bavaria from 1180 to 1918, when King Ludwig III abdicated.

Witwatersrand Full name of the Rand, the Transvaal goldfields. (Afrikaans, 'white waters ridge'; usually pronounced as spelt, properly vit-vaht'ers-rahnt.)

Wizard of Oz, The Character in Frank Baum's classic fairy-tale *The Wonderful Wizard of Oz* (1900), its many sequels, a musical extravaganza (1903), silent (1925) and Technicolor musical movies (1939), the latter with a song-hit, 'Over the Rainbow', added, and in countless versions continued by other hands after Baum's death. Oz is a happy land to which Dorothy and her dog Toto are whirled by a cyclone from her drab Kansas home; there she encounters the Wizard, a talking Scarecrow, Cowardly Lion, Tin Woodman and many others.

Woburn Abbey Georgian home of the Dukes of Bedford near Bletchley, Bedfordshire, with 14 richly decorated state apartments, and a park containing bison and deer. (Pronounced woo'b-ern.)

Woden English form of ODIN.

Wolfenden report (1957). Report of a committee on homosexual offences and prostitution. (Lord Wolfenden, former headmaster of Shrewsbury, chairman.)

Wolfe-Noel Cup Squash rackets contest between British and US women's teams.

Wolf Rock (1870). Lighthouse and rock halfway between Land's End and the Scilly Isles.

Wolfson College (1966). Graduate college at Linton Road, Oxford, financed by Sir Isaac Wolfson and the Ford Foundation; it specializes in the natural sciences.

Wolfson Foundation (1955). Fund which finances scientific and technological education,

medical research and the provision of medical services. (Sir Isaac Wolfson.)

Wolfson Professorships (1) Chair of criminology at Cambridge University (1959). (2) Oxford University chair of Metallurgy. (3) A research professorship in the gift of the Royal Society. (Sir Isaac Wolfson.)

Wolverine State Nickname of Michigan.

Wolves, The Nickname of the Wolverhampton football team.

Woman in White Early Picasso, copies of which sold in immense numbers in the USA.

Woman in White, The (1860). Mystery story by Wilkie Collins, in which the villain, Count Fosco, attempts to substitute a bogus heiress for the Woman in White, who is in a lunatic asylum.

Woman Who Did, The (1895). Grant Allen's novel about a woman who preached and practised the doctrine that marriage is incompatible with the emancipation of women. Although a serious novel, the title inevitably became a catch-phrase for what in those days was called a 'fallen woman'.

Wombles Imaginary animals, in a television series for children, who live on Wimbledon Common.

Women in Love (1920). D. H. Lawrence's novel in which he analyses the unexpressed instinctive feelings that mould human relationships. See BRANGWEN, GUDRUN.

Women's Institutes Self-governing organizations created to improve and develop conditions of rural life. Originally founded in Canada they were established in the UK in 1915 and by 1989 had over 9,000 institutes. See TOWNSWOMEN'S GUILDS.

Women's Land Army (1917). Corps of Land Girls formed to release agricultural workers for military service in the First World War; it was re-formed in 1939.

Women's Lib Movement, originating in the USA, which aims at the removal of attitudes and practices based on sexism, i.e. the assumption that men are superior to women. (Abbreviated from Women's Liberation.)

Women's Social and Political Union (1903). Original suffragette organization formed by Mrs Emmeline Pankhurst.

Women's Transport Service (FANY) See FIRST AID NURSING YEOMANRY.

Wonder State Nickname of Arkansas.

Woodbine Willie Nickname of a famous padre of World War I, the Rev. Studdart Kennedy.

Wooden Spoon, The See SENIOR WRANGLER.

Wood family (potters) Burslem (Staffordshire) family of Ralph Wood (1715–72) who worked in the ASTBURY–Whieldon tradition and may have made the first toby jug; his brother and modeller, Aaron (1717–85), to whom is attributed the VICAR AND MOSES group; his son Ralph II (1748–95), who used a wider range of colours in the PRATTWARE style; and his nephew Enoch (1760–1840) who introduced bright enamel colours and made accurate portrait busts, e.g. of Wesley.

Woodforde diary Diary for the years 1758–1802 kept by James Woodforde, giving a picture of rural life in Somerset and Norfolk, where he was a parson.

Wood Green Former municipal borough of Middlesex, since 1965 part of the borough of HARINGEY.

Woodhenge Archaeological site near Stonehenge where traces of 6 concentric circles of timber posts were discovered by aerial photography. They date back to late neolithic times.

Woodhouse, Mr See EMMA.

Woods of Bath, The John Wood the Elder (1705–54), the chief architect of the Upper Town, Bath; and his son John (1728–81), who completed his father's work and designed the Royal Crescent at Bath.

Woodstock (1826). Walter Scott's novel of the Civil War, in which Oliver Cromwell and the fugitive Charles II figure prominently. Woodstock was a royal lodge (later to be replaced by Blenheim Palace) looked after by a fiery Cavalier, Sir Henry Lee, to whose daughter Lee's Roundhead nephew and, Charles II both pay court.

Woodstock Festival (1969). Three-day rock festival ('Music and Arts Fair'), attended by a reputed 400,000, on a farm in upstate New York. The event is enshrined in a film and an album.

Woodward Corporation Schools High Church boarding schools founded from 1848 onwards by Nathaniel Woodward, who had a gift for fund-raising. The schools include King's (Taunton), Denstone, and Ardingly.

Woodwardian Professor Holder of the chair of Geology at Cambridge.

Wookey Hole Series of caves near Wells, Somerset, with multicoloured stalactites, where remains of palaeolithic man have been found.

Woolmen, Worshipful Company of LIVERY COMPANY, originally a guild, probably of middlemen between grower and exporter of wool; there is no record of its charter.

Woolsack, The (1) Large square cushion stuffed with wool on which Lord Chancellors have sat since Edward III's time, originally as heads of the Court of Chancery, now as Speakers of the House of Lords. (2) Used as a synonym for 'Lord Chancellorship'. (Introduced when the wool trade was of prime importance to England.)

Woolwich Former London metropolitan borough, since 1965 divided between the boroughs of GREENWICH and NEWHAM.

Woolwich Royal Arsenal Government arsenal developed on the south bank of the Thames near London from an early Tudor Powder House, supplemented by a foundry in 1716. The WOOLWICH ROYAL MILITARY ACADEMY was built inside its walls. By 1966, when it was closed down, the Arsenal covered 1,200 acres.

Woolwich Royal Military Academy (1741). Until 1946 the training college for future officers of the Royal Artillery, Royal Engineers and Royal Signals; now moved to and merged with SANDHURST. (Also known as 'the Shop'.)

Woolworths (1879). International group of chain stores, which started in Utica, New York State, as a '5-cent store' (i.e. all articles were sold at that price), later a 5 and 10 cent store. Branches were established in England after World War I as 3d and 6d stores, and the organization has continued to expand in various countries ever since. The holding company is Kingfisher plc.

Woomera (1946). British rocket range in South Australia, 100 miles north-west of Port Augusta, where the first British atomic missile was exploded in 1953.

Wooster, The Hon. Bertie Amiable nitwit of innumerable P. G. Wodehouse stories who has constantly to be rescued from disaster by his valet JEEVES.

Worcester, Battle of (1751). Engagement in which Cromwell almost annihilated the forces of Charles, Prince of Wales, who escaped to France, thus ending the final phase of the ENGLISH CIVIL WAR.

Worcester Pearmain Fine-flavoured red dessert apple, ripening in September. (Possibly from Latin *Parmanus*, 'of Parma'; pronounced pair'-mayn or pair-mayn'.)

Worcester porcelain (1751). Wares produced by a factory at Worcester which frequently changed its name; see (in chronological order) DR WALL PERIOD; ROYAL WORCESTER PORCELAIN CO.; FLIGHT & BARR; CHAMBERLAIN WORCESTER.

Worcester sauce Proprietary bottled piquant sauce made from a secret recipe 'obtained from a Worcestershire gentleman' in 1845. The original manufacturers were Lea & Perrins at Worcester.

Workers' Educational Association (1903). Association which promotes the formation of groups of men and women over 18 to study under a teacher of their own choice a subject they want to learn about for its own

sake, not to pass an examination or gain a qualification.

Work in Progress Provisional name given by James Joyce to FINNEGANS WAKE during the 17 years he spent writing it.

World Bank (1946). International Bank for Reconstruction and Development, set up after Bretton Woods to provide long-term loans for reconstruction in war-devastated countries, and for the exploitation of natural resources and the provision of public utilities in developing countries; half the capital was supplied by USA and Britain.

World Council of Churches (1948). Body representing the oecumenical movement towards cooperation between the Churches; Anglican, Protestant and Orthodox Churches are members, but not the Catholics.

World Cup (1930). Solid gold cup (the JULES RIMET TROPHY) presented to the national team winning the football championship of the world, held every 4 years under the auspices of FIFA.

World Disarmament Conference (1932–4). Geneva meeting of 60 nations (including USA and Soviet Russia – not members of the League of Nations) defeated of its ambitions by French demands for prior guarantees of security (against Germany) in the form of an international army; Hitler's advent to power and Germany's withdrawal from the League; and Russian insistence on complete world disarmament combined with a rejection of its international supervision. The complete failure of the conference led to a massive increase in world armaments.

World Food Council Executive body of the FAO.

Worldly-Wiseman, Mr Character in PILGRIM'S PROGRESS who tries to persuade Christian to give up his pilgrimage for ease and plenty.

World Refugee Year (1959–60). Year in which a concerted international effort was made to solve outstanding problems regarding refugees.

World Series (US baseball) Best-of-seven-games competition played each autumn between the winning teams of the 2 major leagues (the National and American) to determine the professional champions of USA.

Worms, Diet of (1521). Imperial assembly before which Luther was called and outlawed by the Emperor Charles V after he had refused to recant. (Pronounced vormz.)

Wormwood Scrubs Prison in West London.

Worth, Patience Spirit who, as it is claimed, from 1913 dictated to Mrs Curran (born in the US Middle West), mainly through an ouija board, about 3 million words of fiction, poetry, proverbs and prayers, some in 17th-century English dialect. These works displayed a knowledge of history quite outside Mrs Curran's range. Patience said she was a 17th-century Dorset farm-girl who migrated to America and was murdered by Indians. The case was exhaustively investigated, without any logical explanation forthcoming.

Wotan German form of ODIN.

Wozzeck (1912). Alban Berg's opera based on a grim 19th-century play about a half-witted army private who murdered his wife.

WRAC See ATS.

WRAF (1918). Women's Royal Air Force; disbanded after World War I and re-formed as the WAAF (Women's Auxiliary Air Force) from units of the ATS. It retained this name from 1939 to 1948, then reverting to its original title and becoming a permanent unit.

'Wreck of the Hesperus, The' (1841). Longfellow's ballad, based on a contemporary event, beginning with perhaps at one time the most widely known lines of English verse: 'It was the schooner *Hesperus*, / That sailed the wintry sea; / And the skipper had taken his little daughter, / To bear him company.'

Wren Colloquial name for a member of the WRNS (Women's Royal Naval Service) formed in 1917, re-formed in 1939, and now a permanent unit.

Writer to the Signet (WS) Member of society of legal practitioners in Edinburgh, Scotland. So named because they were originally clerks to the office of the King's secretary, whose task was to prepare documents ready for sealing with the King's signet, one of the three legally recognized British seals for authenticating documents.

Wrocław A city of Polish Silesia, once known by its German name, Breslau. (Pronounced vrawts'-wahf.)

WRVS (1938). The Women's Royal Voluntary Service (until 1966 the Women's Voluntary Services) formed for ARP (Air Raid Precautions) duties. In peacetime it performs a wide range of social services, e.g. MEALS ON WHEELS, helping in flood disasters, etc.

Wurlitzer organ (1) Cinema organ, an electric contraption which produces a rich variety of sounds, although its chief glory is when it sinks into the bowels of the auditorium, bathed in coloured light. (2) Jukebox that played 78 and 45 r.p.m. records.

Württemberg Former German kingdom, capital Stuttgart, now part of BADEN-WÜRTTEMBERG.

Wuthering Heights (1847). Emily Brontë's grim masterpiece recounting the disruption of the EARNSHAW FAMILY by HEATHCLIFF. (*Wuthering*, Yorkshire dialect for 'stormy'.)

WVS See WRVS.

Wyatt's rebellion (1554). Uprising in Kent led by Sir Thomas Wyatt in protest at Queen Mary's alliance with Spain. It led to the execution of Lady Jane Grey (who was not implicated) and the imprisonment of the future Queen Elizabeth in the tower.

Wycliffe's Bible Fruit of Wycliffe's demand (see LOLLARDS) that the Bible should be available to Englishmen in their own language; the first complete English translation, in 2 versions, neither printed, made *c.* 1382–8.

Wye College Part of London University, at Ashford, Kent, specializing in agriculture.

Wyfold Cup Coxless fours event at Henley Regatta for those not in the Stewards' class.

Wykehamist Schoolboy or ('Old Wykehamist') Old Boy of Winchester College, the school founded by William of Wykeham. (Pronounced wik'e:m-ist.)

Wykeham Professor Holder of one of 3 chairs at Oxford University. Ancient History, Logic, Physics. (Pronounced wik'ém.)

'Wynken, Blynken and Nod' 'Dutch lullaby' by Eugene Field (1850–95), later set to music. It begins: 'Wynken, Blynken and Nod one night / Sailed off in a wooden shoe / Sailed on a river of crystal light / Into a sea of dew.'

Wynne (Greville) case (1963). Moscow trial of the English businessman who acted as courier in the PENKOVSKY SPY CASE. He was given an 8-year sentence, but exchanged for Gordon Lonsdale in 1964.

X

X, Les (France) Students and Old Boys of the École Polytechnique (1794) founded by Napoleon as a school for military engineering, science and mathematics. It now has enormous prestige, providing technical officers for the Army, Navy and Air Force as well as the élite of the higher civil servants. In Old Boy networkmanship Les X yield to no man. (Pronounced layz-iks'.)

Xanadu Place where Coleridge's KUBLA KHAN 'did . . . a stately pleasure-dome decree' and where 'ALPH, the sacred river, ran'. *The Road to Xanadu* (1927) by J. L. Lowes is a thorough and fascinating piece of detective work on the sources of the names and allusions in this poem and in *The Rime of the Ancient Mariner*.

Xanthippe Bad-tempered wife. (Name of Socrates' wife; pronounced zan-thip'i.)

Xerox Proprietary name of a system for photocopying documents of all kinds. (From Greek word for 'dry'; pronounced zeer'oks.)

Xhosa Most numerous Black race of TRANSKEI and CISKEI in South Africa. (Pronounced kaw'sa.)

XJ Range of Jaguar saloon cars introduced in 1968.

Y

Y, The Ultimate abbreviation for YMCA.

Yahoos Bestial creatures in human form whom the HOUYHNHNMS keep in subjection, in GULLIVER'S TRAVELS; they represent Swift's conception of mankind at its worst.

Yak Series of Soviet military and civil aircraft named after Aleksandr Yakovlev (b. 1906), the designer.

Yale (1701). US university at New Haven, Conn.

Yale Bowl (1914). Yale University's sports stadium.

Yalta Conference (February 1945). Meeting at which Churchill, Roosevelt and Stalin discussed post-war problems, the defeat and occupation of Germany, setting up of the United Nations and the entry of Russia into the war against Japan. (Crimean holiday resort.)

Yalu River River forming the boundary between Korea and China, prominent in the Russo-Japanese and Korean wars.

Yang di-Pertuan Malayan name from 1957 for the Head of State of Malaysia, who is elected for a term of 5 years.

Yankee Term originally applied by the New York Dutch to the New Englanders. In the South, it is a term of abuse for a Northerner. (Possibly from Dutch *Janke*, 'Johnny', but many other derivations have been suggested.)

Yankee (bet) Complex bet on 4 selections, comprising 6 doubles, 4 trebles and an accumulator.

Yankee Doodle Tune of unknown origin, the words to which were possibly added by a British soldier just before the War of Independence and adopted by their American opponents. (YANKEE + doodle = ?tootle, i.e. a tune for the flute or fife.)

Yankees, The One of two New York baseball teams.

Yankee stadium Sports stadium at New York City, primarily for baseball, home of the above.

Yaoundé Conventions Agreements between a number of independent African states, which were formerly French, Belgian and Italian colonies, to improve trade between them and the European Economic Community. The first was signed in 1963 and the second in 1969. The second Convention was replaced by the LOMÉ CONVENTION in 1975.

Yapp Style of bookbinding with limp leather cover projecting over edges of leaves, named after William Yapp, a London bookseller.

Yarborough Hand at Bridge with no card higher than a 9. (Earl of Yarborough, who laid 1,000–1 against its occurring, about half the mathematical odds.)

Yard, The Abbreviation for New Scotland Yard.

Yarrow, The River in Selkirkshire (in Borders Region), Scotland, which has inspired many poems, notably some by Wordsworth and Walter Scott.

Yasnaya Polyana Tolstoy family estate south of Moscow, where Count Tolstoy, the novelist, was born and lived until shortly before his death. The house is now a Tolstoy museum. (Russian, 'clear glade'.)

Yassiada trial (1960–61). Trial of the Turkish premier, Menderes (who was executed), and of some 400 of his supporters, held on Yassiada island.

Year One of Liberty In the French Revolution calendar this began on 1 VENDÉMIAIRE (22 Sept.) 1792.

Yekaterinoslav, Ekaterinoslav City of the Ukrainian SSR, now renamed Dnepropetrovsk. (Named after Catherine the Great.)

Yellow Book, The (1894–7). Illustrated quarterly made famous by the contributions of Aubrey Beardsley, Max Beerbohm and others.

Yellow Jack Old name for yellow fever.

Yellow Kid, The (1895). First coloured comic-strip cartoon, an early experiment in colour printing, in a New York newspaper, from which the YELLOW PRESS gets its name

Yellow Peril, The Threat that over-population in China and Japan would imperil the Western world; a phrase used by the German Kaiser at the turn of the century, and strengthened by the publication of *The* RISING TIDE OF COLOR.

Yellowplush Correspondence, The (1838). Thackeray's book of sketches purporting to have been written by a London footman, Mr C. J. Yellowplush. It has dated in the same way as 19th-century *Punch* jokes about flunkeys, and no longer amuses.

Yellow Press (1895). Cheap sensational newspapers. (See YELLOW KID.)

Yellow River The Hwang-ho, China.

Yellowstone National Park (1872). First of the world's national parks, in north-west Wyoming (USA) and adjacent areas of Montana and Idaho, on a volcanic plateau averaging 8,000 ft in height and almost encircled by mountains. It contains the Yellowstone River canyon, spectacular falls, more geysers than in all the rest of the world, and one of the finest wildlife sanctuaries, with moose, grizzlies, etc.

Yenan period (1935–45). In China, the nostalgically regarded era of pristine revolutionary fervour in the days when Mao Tse-tung directed the struggle in North China from a cave near Yenan (see LONG MARCH); thereafter the Revolution was moved from the countryside to the cities.

Yeomen of the Guard (1485). The BEEFEATERS proper, who together with the Gentlemen at Arms form the Queen's dismounted bodyguard. One of their duties is to search the vaults under the Houses of Parliament before the State Opening – an echo of the Gunpowder Plot. They wear the same uniform as the YEOMEN WARDERS, plus a cross-belt. Their Captain is the Assistant Chief Whip in the House of Lords.

Yeomen Warders Guards of the TOWER OF LONDON; see BEEFEATERS.

Yerkes Observatory (1897). University of Chicago's observatory at Williams Bay, Wisconsin.

Yeshiva University (1886). Oldest Jewish university in the USA, in New York City.

Yes man Acquiescent person, a sycophant or toady.

Yeti See ABOMINABLE SNOWMAN.

Yezhovshchina Russian name for the period of the particularly barbarous purges presided over by N. I. Yezhov as head of the NKVD (1936–8).

Yggdrasil, Igdrasil In Scandinavian myth the tree of the world, an ash with roots in the underworld which rises up to heaven and embraces the universe.

YHA (1930). Initials used for the Youth Hostels Association, a self-governing organization to provide hostels for young hikers (also available to the not so young). Simple accommodation and fare at minimum prices are provided in return for co-operation in such minor tasks as washing up. At some hostels there is provision for joint study of natural history.

Yiddish Until the mid-20th century the common language of Jews in Europe and America, compounded of medieval German, Hebrew, Polish, Russian and other languages, and written in the Hebrew alphabet. (From German *jüdisch*, 'Jewish'.)

Yoga (300 BC). Name given to various forms of Hindu mystic practice which aim at union with God through asceticism, meditation and a complicated series of difficult breathing exercises and postures (such as the 'lotus position' often depicted in Hindu art). (Sanskrit 'union'.)

Yogi Practitioner of YOGA.

Yoknapatawpha County Setting of most of William Faulkner's novels, an imaginary county of the state of Mississippi.

Yom Haatzmaut Jewish festival, held in May, celebrating the establishment of the modern state of Israel.

Yom Kippur Jewish fast-day, the Day of Atonement, which falls in October (Lev. 16). (Pronounced yohm kípur.)

Yorick (1) In Shakespeare's play, the murdered king's jester, whose skull HAMLET apostrophizes in a famous speech beginning 'Alas! poor Yorick' in the graveyard scene. (2) Parson in Sterne's TRISTRAM SHANDY, who claims descent from (1). (3) The name under which Sterne wrote his SENTIMENTAL JOURNEY.

York Herald Officer of the COLLEGE OF ARMS.

Yorkists Descendants of Edmund, Duke of York: Edward IV and V, Richard III (1461–85). See WARS OF THE ROSES.

York round In archery, a match in which 6 dozen arrows are shot at distances ranging from 60 to 100 yards.

Yorkshire Brigade Infantry brigade comprising: The Prince of Wales's Own Regiment of Yorkshire; The Green Howards (Alexandra, Princess of Wales's Own Yorkshire Regiment); The Duke of Wellington's Regiment (West Riding); The York and Lancaster Regiment. Since 1968, part of the KING'S DIVISION.

Yorkshire Post Book of the Year Awards of 2 prizes totalling £1,400 annually for the best works of fiction and non-fiction published during the year.

Yorkshire TV (1968). Commercial programme-contracting company which took over Yorkshire from Granada and ABC-TV. It has headquarters in Leeds and is financed by the *Yorkshire Post* and other local papers, local trade unions and Baird TV.

Yorktown, Siege of (1781). Last major event of the American War of Independence; Lord Cornwallis, finding himself cut off by the Americans on land and blockaded by the French fleet, surrendered to Washington. (Town in south-east Virginia.)

Yoruba Semi-Bantu race of Western Nigeria. (Pronounced yor'oo-ba.)

Youll Cup Public schools lawn-tennis competition played at Wimbledon in July.

You Never Can Tell (1897). G. B. Shaw's comedy of a wife who unwittingly invites her ex-husband to lunch while staying at a Torbay hotel with her daughter, who has fallen in love with a local dentist. The hotel's head waiter, William, sagely smooths out various difficulties that arise, the title being one of his favourite aphorisms.

Young England (1840s). Group of young Tory critics of Peel, led by Disraeli, which had for its testament his novels CONINGSBY and SYBIL and the doctrines of TORY DEMOCRACY.

Young England (1934). Serious patriotic play which seized the imagination of London's younger generation, who turned up night after night to chant the 'strong' lines just before the cast could get to them, so that the entertainment was transferred from the stage to the audience, greatly prolonging the run of what had been turned into a boisterous farce.

Young Farmers' Club (1932). Rural clubs for people of both sexes aged 10–25, which aim to produce 'good farmers, good countrymen and good citizens'. Amateur dramatics, sport, training in public speaking and home crafts are among their many activities.

Younghusband Mission (1904). British mission which went to Lhasa and signed a treaty with the Dalai Lama, as a measure against a supposed Russian threat to India. (Sir Francis Younghusband.)

Young Jolyon Non-conforming Forsyte of *A* MODERN COMEDY, who married Irene, divorced wife of Soames Forsyte.

Young Lords (USA) Puerto Rican movement modelled on the BLACK PANTHERS.

Young Plan (1929). Scheme for German payments of reparations which superseded the DAWES PLAN and was equally unsuccessful.

Young Pretender Charles Edward Stuart, 'Bonnie Prince Charlie', son of the OLD PRETENDER; died 1788. See FORTY-FIVE.

Young Turks (1) Militant nationalist movement which forced the Sultan Abdul Hamid to restore the 1876 Constitution in 1908 and deposed him in 1909; (2) hence applied to the militantly radical or reformist group of a political party.

Young Visiters, The (1919). Story written by Daisy Ashford at the age of 9; the hero is Mr SALTEENA.

Young Woodley (1928). Van Druten's play of a schoolboy who falls in love with his housemaster's wife.

Ypres Name of 3 long, bloody and inconclusive battles (including PASSCHENDAELE) of World War I fought around the Belgian town of Ypres, south of Ostend, in 1914, 1915 and 1917. (Belgian pronunciation, eepr; British Army pronunciation and spelling, Wipers.)

Ysolde, Yseult Alternative spellings of ISEULT.

Yüan dynasty (1279–1368). Dynasty established by Kublai Khan, the first Mongol Emperor of China; it lasted until the MING DYNASTY restored Chinese rule. In art, this period saw the first blue-and-white and copper-red underglaze porcelain; the painting of landscapes in ink was developed. The capital, Peking, was visited by Marco Polo.

Yugoslavia (1929). Name given to the state which from its establishment in 1918 had been called the Triune Kingdom of the Serbs, Croats and Slovenes; it was first used when King Alexander established a military dictatorship. (Meaning 'country of the southern Slavs'.)

Yuppie Abbreviation from US for Young Urban Professional or Young Upwardly Mobile Professional. Generally high-earning and high-spending and many employed in the finance industry (also known as Yups).

Yuzovska Original name of Donetsk, a city in the Ukraine. (John Hughes, the Welshman who founded it.)

Yvetot, Le Roi d' (1) French expression for a good easygoing king. (From a town in Normandy, the lord of which was given the honorary title of king.) (2) Title of a French anti-Napoleonic song (1813) beginning: 'Il était un roi d'Yvetot / Peu connu dans l'histoire.'

YY Pen-name of Robert Lynd, British essayist (1879–1949).

Z

Zabern incident (1913). Climax of numerous German sabre-rattling incidents in Alsace, which created great scandal in France and led to rioting. (Garrison town near Strasbourg, now known by its French name, Saverne.)

Zadig Virtuous young Babylonian philosopher, in Voltaire's novel of that name (1748), who learns from his own successive disasters that evil is a necessary concomitant of good.

Zadok the Priest (1) Priest appointed by King Solomon in place of the last of the house of Eli (1 Kgs 2:35); he was regarded as the ancestor of the SADDUCEES. (2) Title of Handel's Coronation Anthem.

Zaharoff (Sir Basil) lecture (1918). Annual lecture at Oxford University on French art, archaeology, history, literature, science or sociology.

Zantedeschia aethiopica Species name of the florists' white ARUM LILY.

ZANU (1963). (Rhodesia) Initials used for the ZIMBABWE African National Union, which under the Rev. N. Sithole broke with ZAPU. Both parties were declared unlawful by the Rhodesian government.

ZAPU Initials used for the ZIMBABWE African People's Union, the chief nationalist party of Rhodesia, led by Joshua Nkomo, and banned by the government. See ZANU.

Zarathustra Spelling of ZOROASTER used by Nietzsche in THUS SPAKE ZARATHUSTRA.

Zauner, Café Austrian *pâtisserie* shop at Bad Ischl, made famous through its patronage by the Emperor Franz Josef.

Z cars (1962). Long-running television series. Character study of cops and robbers rather than cops against robbers. Two leading characters were Inspector Barlow and Sergeant Watt.

Zealots Members of an extreme Jewish political party that resisted Roman rule in Palestine in the 1st century AD.

Zebu Humped Indian cattle, grey or black, used in India for working and for milk.

Zeeman effect (1896). Difference in light emitted by atoms when they pass through a magnetic field; its discovery made it possible to plot the distribution of the magnetic field of the sun and in interstellar space.

Zeitgeist General outlook of a specific period of time especially as it is reflected in the taste and outlook of art, literature and philosophy. (German, 'time spirit.')

Zen Peculiarly Japanese form of Buddhism, which inspired the SAMURAI to do whatever seemed good to them ('acting on intuition'). By destroying the habit of rational thought it seeks to produce sudden intuitive flashes of enlightenment.

Zend-Avesta Zoroastrian and Parsee scriptures (*avesta*) with interpretations (*zend*). The earliest manuscript is 13th century, but the scriptures are attributed to Zoroaster (6th century BC).

(Zend was at first incorrectly assumed to be the name of the language – which is allied to Old Persian – in which the *Avesta* were written.)

Zenith Town where BABBITT lived.

Zenocrate Wife of TAMBURLAINE. (Pronounced zen-ok′ra-ti.)

Zéphirine Drouhin (1868). Thornless climbing rose which produces quantities of fragrant rich clear pink semi-double flowers and repeats the performance in the autumn.

Zeppelin, Count Ferdinand von German army officer (1838–1917); in the years 1897–1900 he built his first airship or dirigible balloon.

Zero-zero Proposed withdrawal of long and short-range intermediate nuclear missiles from Europe. Also known as double zero.

Zetland Scottish county comprising the Shetland Islands, and an alternative name for the islands.

Zeus Chief Greek god, son of CRONOS. He spent much of his time hiding his amours from his formidable sister–wife Hera by consummating them in a series of extraordinary disguises, e.g. a shower of gold or a swan. He was quick to hurl thunderbolts at those who displeased him. He might fairly be described as a cowardly bully, unworthy of high office. His Roman counterpart is Jupiter. (Pronounced zews.)

Zhdanov City of Ukranian SSR, formerly Mariupol.

Ziegfeld Follies Series of lavishly spectacular revues staged in New York by Florenz Ziegfeld in most years from 1907 to the year before his death in 1932. It was the proving ground for countless song-writers, comedians and others who later became famous on stage and screen, and particularly remembered for its glamorous chorus.

Zigeuner German word for Gypsies, see ATHINGANOI. (Pronounced tsig-érn′ér.)

Zimbabwe Ruins of extensive dry-stone buildings in south-east Zimbabwe, east of Bulawayo, probably built in the 17th–18th centuries, although some timber found there has been carbon-dated back to the 6th century. There were fragments of Ming and other oriental pottery, presumably brought by Arab traders, but the buildings themselves are now thought to be the work of an African tribe. ('Stone houses', in the language of the Shona of Mashonaland.)

Zimmer Type of walking frame used for orthopaedic purposes.

Zimmermann telegram (1917). Telegram which revealed German proposals to persuade Mexico to attack the USA, offering as bribe the restoration of the 'lost territories' of New Mexico, Texas and Arizona; and also to induce Japan to change sides. Intercepted, deciphered and published, it precipitated US entry into the war. (Zimmermann was the German Foreign Secretary, who sent it to his ambassador in Mexico.)

Zimri (1) Captain of chariots of 1 Kings 16:9–20, who usurped the throne of Israel and, when himself overthrown, committed suicide. (2) Dryden's name in ABSALOM AND ACHITOPHEL for George Villiers, 2nd Duke of Buckingham.

Zingari Italian word for Gypsies, see ATHINGANOI. (Pronounced zing′gar-i.)

Zinjanthropus (Nutcracker Man) At first taken to be the earliest specimen of AUSTRALOPITHECINE, found in OLDUVAI GORGE in 1959; now generally classified as Paranthropus, a form of ape which branched off quite early from the main Australopithecine line leading to modern man, and became extinct.

Zinnia Half-hardy annual flower named after Johann Gottfried Zinn, a German professor of botany.

Zinoviev letter (1924). Letter supposed to have been addressed by the COMINTERN secretary, Zinoviev, to the British Communist Party, advocating red revolution. Forged in Germany, it was published in the *Daily Mail* by some Conservatives a few days before the Conservative electoral victory which deposed the first Labour government. There was a loud Labour outcry at the time over these tactics, but it is now thought to have had very little impact on the phlegmatic electorate.

Zion (1) Hill in Jerusalem on which SOLOMON'S TEMPLE stood. (2) Hence a synonym for Jerusalem, Israel, or Christianity.

Zionism (1896). Movement for the establishment of a Jewish state in Palestine (then Turkish). Originally a non-religious movement, frowned on by the orthodox. See ZION; PROTOCOLS OF ZION.

Zip code US equivalent of British post-code, from Zone Improvement Plan.

Zollverein German for *customs union*, applied specifically to that formed in 1834 by most of the German-speaking states (except Austria) under Prussian leadership. (Pronounced tsol'fer-yn.)

Zorba the Greek (1964). Film, from the 1946 novel by Nikos Kazantzakis, with Anthony Quinn and Alan Bates. Exciting music and excellent camera work.

Zoroaster (6th century BC). Traditional founder of ZOROASTRIANISM. (Greek form of Persian Zarathustra.)

Zoroastrianism Ancient Persian religion, tradi-tionally founded by ZOROASTER, based on the conflict between AHURA MAZDA and AHRIMAN. See THUS SPAKE ZARATHUSTRA; ZEND-AVESTA.

Zuider Zee See IJSSELMEER.

Zuleika Dobson (1911). Satirical fantasy by Max Beerbohm about the lovely Zuleika, an ex-conjuror of outstanding inability, with whom all the men of Oxford University fall desperately in love, to the point of mass-suicide. So she leaves for fresh woods and pastures new – by train to Cambridge. (Pronounced zu-lee'ke.)

Zulu Numerous Black tribe of South Africa, chiefly found in north-east Natal.

Zurich, Faceless Gnomes of A phrase attributed to George Brown when British Minister of Economic Affairs in 1964, referring to the anonymous but powerful international bankers of Switzerland.

Zurich agreements (1959). Agreements reached by Britain, Greece and Turkey, under which the British colony of Cyprus became an independent republic.